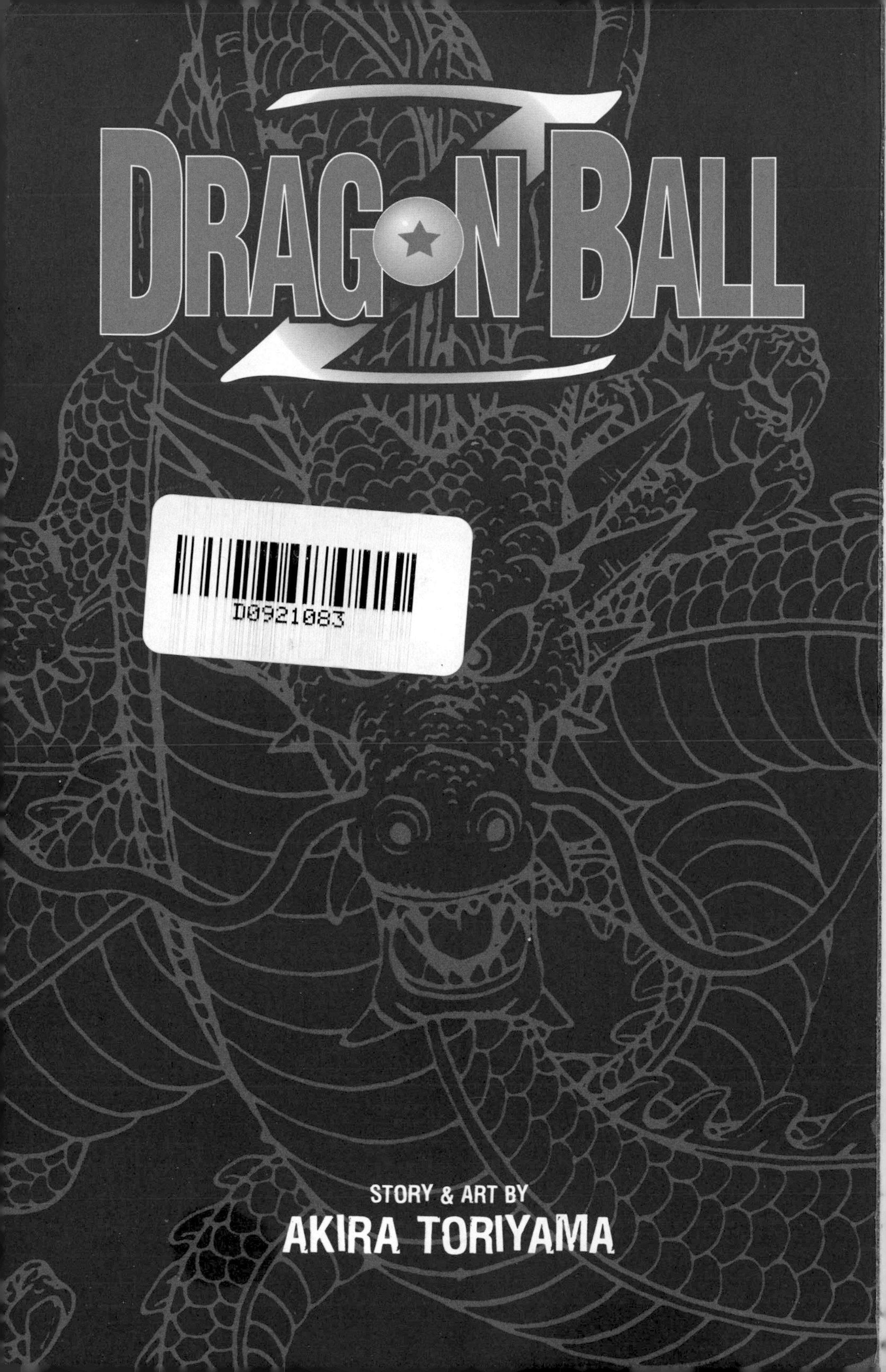

DRAGON BALL Z

STORY & ART BY
AKIRA TORIYAMA

Dragon Ball Z
Volume 4
VIZBIG Edition

STORY AND ART BY
AKIRA TORIYAMA

Translation **Lillian Olsen**
Touch-up Art & Lettering **Wayne Truman, Eric Erbes & HudsonYards**
Shonen Jump Series Design **Sean Lee**
VIZBIG Edition Design **Frances O. Liddell**
Shonen Jump Series Editor **Jason Thompson**
VIZBIG Edition Editor **Daniel Gillespie**

Printed in China

Published by VIZ Media, LLC
P.O. Box 77010
San Francisco, CA 94107

11
First printing, April 2009
Eleventh printing, September 2021

VIZ MEDIA
www.viz.com

VIZBIG EDITION

DRAGON BALL Z

VOLUME 10
GOKU VS. FREEZA

VOLUME 11
THE SUPER SAIYAN

VOLUME 12
ENTER TRUNKS

STORY & ART BY
AKIRA TORIYAMA

SHONEN JUMP MANGA . VIZBIG EDITION

CONTENTS

VOLUME 11
THE SUPER SAIYAN

VOLUME 12
ENTER TRUNKS

CAST OF CHARACTERS

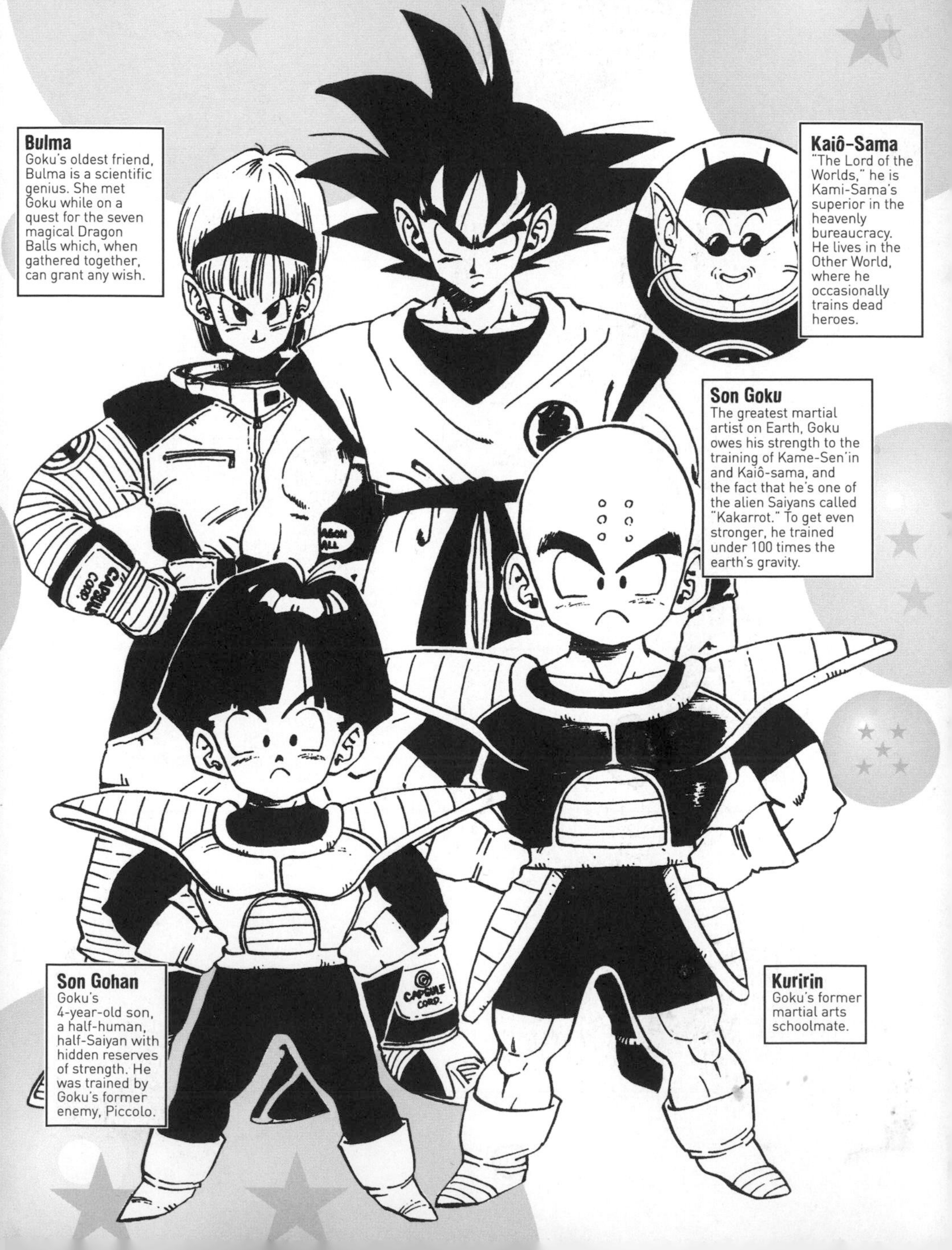
CAPSULE CORP.

Bulma
Goku's oldest friend, Bulma is a scientific genius. She met Goku while on a quest for the seven magical Dragon Balls which, when gathered together, can grant any wish.

Kaiô-Sama
"The Lord of the Worlds," he is Kami-Sama's superior in the heavenly bureaucracy. He lives in the Other World, where he occasionally trains dead heroes.

Son Goku
The greatest martial artist on Earth, Goku owes his strength to the training of Kame-Sen'in and Kaiô-sama, and the fact that he's one of the alien Saiyans called "Kakarrot." To get even stronger, he trained under 100 times the earth's gravity.

Son Gohan
Goku's 4-year-old son, a half-human, half-Saiyan with hidden reserves of strength. He was trained by Goku's former enemy, Piccolo.

Kuririn
Goku's former martial arts schoolmate.

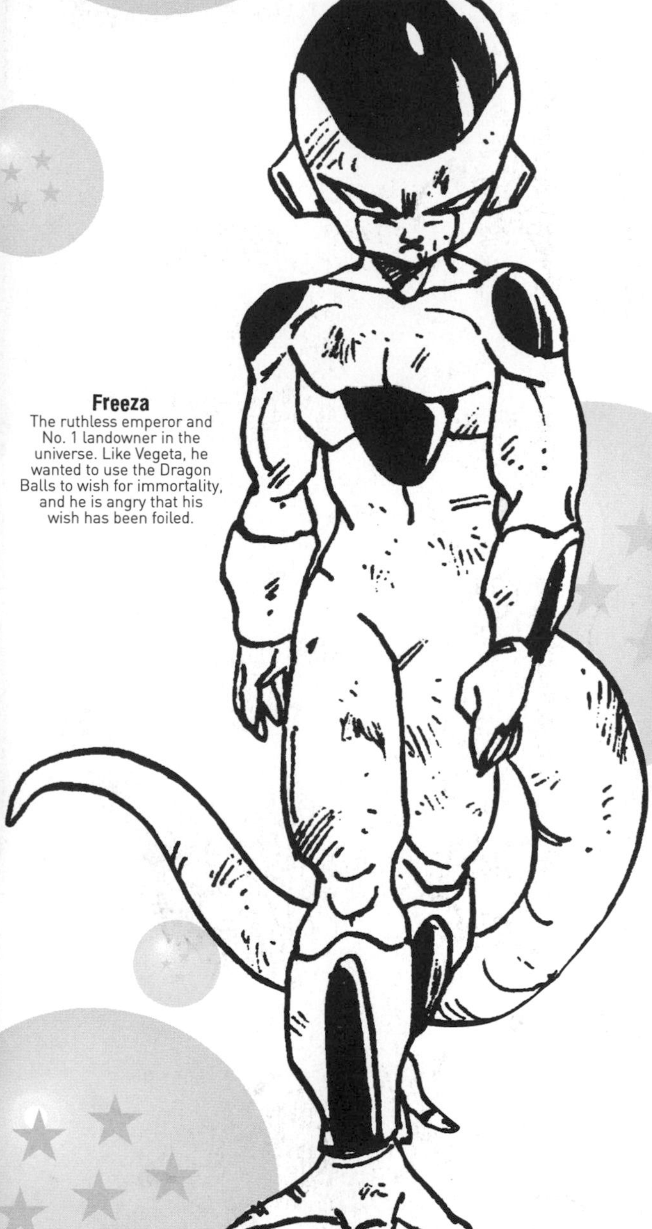

Freeza
The ruthless emperor and No. 1 landowner in the universe. Like Vegeta, he wanted to use the Dragon Balls to wish for immortality, and he is angry that his wish has been foiled.

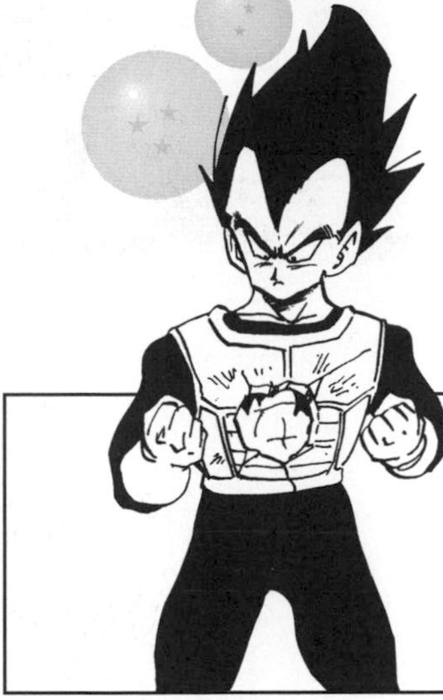

Vegeta
The evil Prince of the Saiyans. While on Earth, he inadvertently caused Earth's Dragon Balls to be destroyed. Now that Namek's Dragon Balls are gone as well, his last hope is to become a "Super Saiyan"—the legendary strongest fighter in the universe.

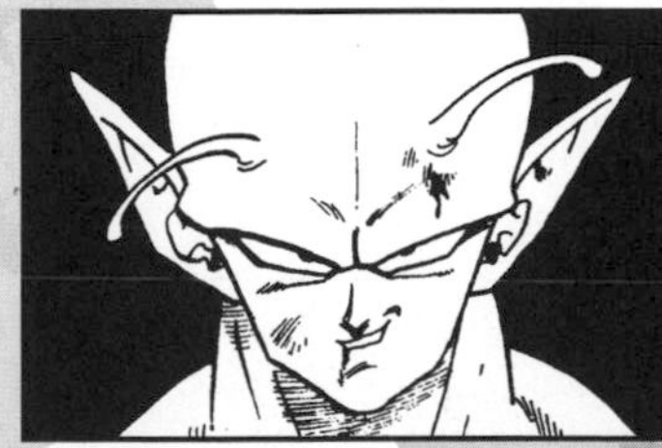

Piccolo
Goku's former archenemy, the Namekian Piccolo is the darker half of Kami-sama, the deity who created Earth's Dragon Balls (and whose existence maintains them). After training under Kaiô-sama and fusing with the fallen warrior Nail, he has become incredibly strong. If Piccolo dies, Kami-sama dies too, and vice-versa.

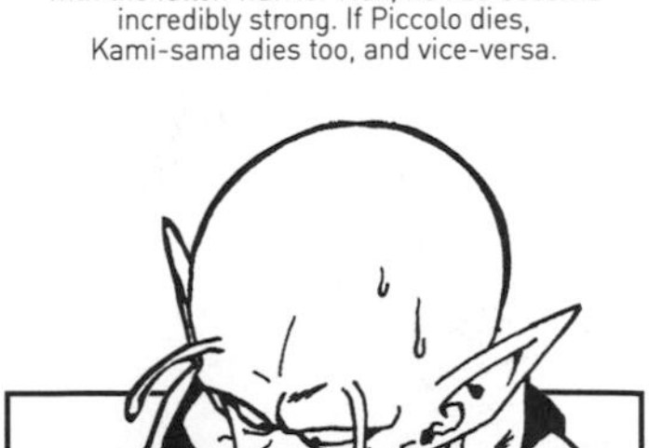

Dende
A Namekian child who was saved by Gohan and Kuririn. He possesses healing powers.

DragonBallZ

VOLUME 10

GOKU VS. FREEZA

DBZ:107 • Freeza vs. Piccolo, Part 2

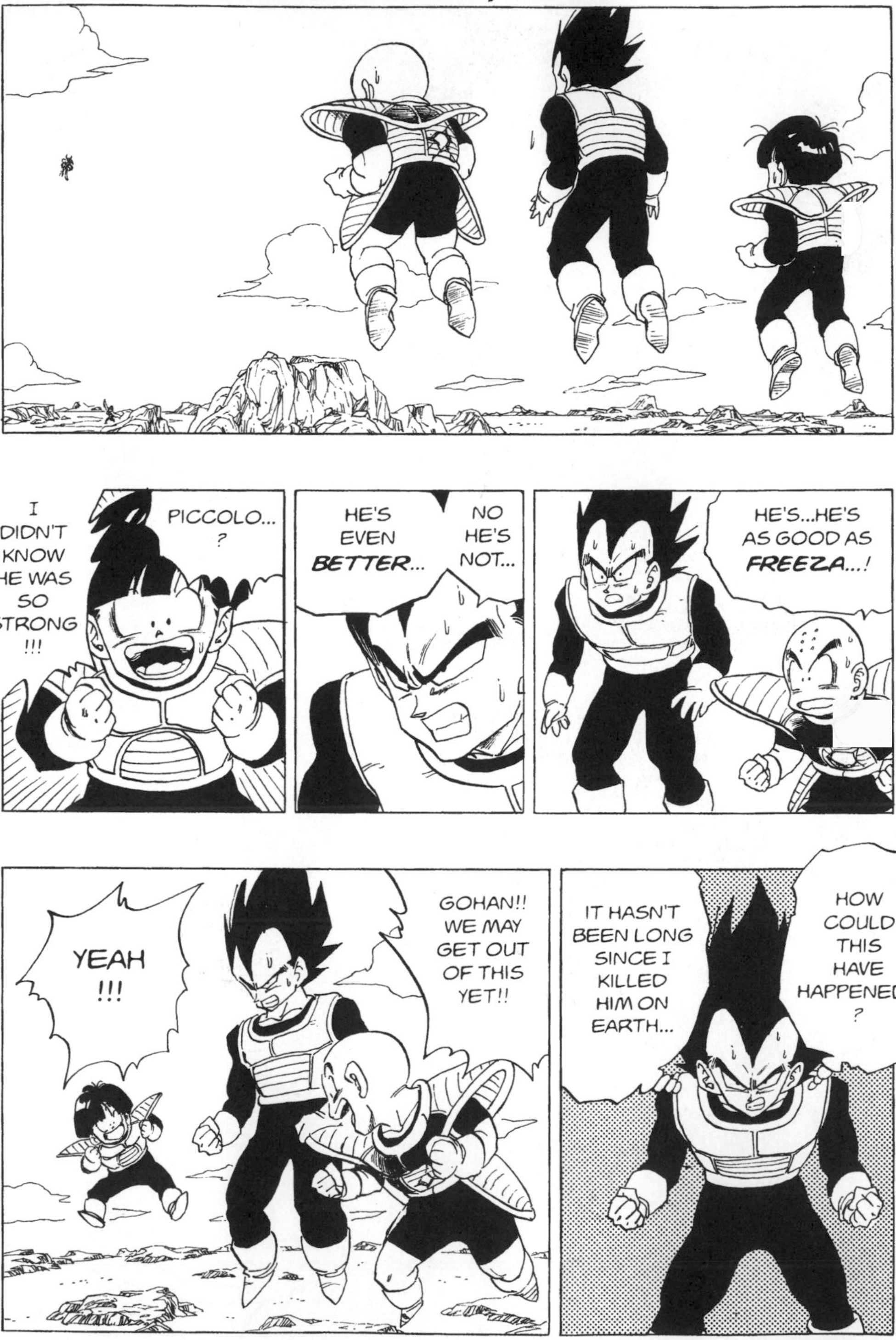
PICCOLO... ?
I DIDN'T KNOW HE WAS SO STRONG !!!
NO HE'S NOT...
HE'S EVEN BETTER...
HE'S...HE'S AS GOOD AS FREEZA...!
GOHAN!! WE MAY GET OUT OF THIS YET!!
YEAH !!!
HOW COULD THIS HAVE HAPPENED... ?
IT HASN'T BEEN LONG SINCE I KILLED HIM ON EARTH...

SSS...
TMP
HENH

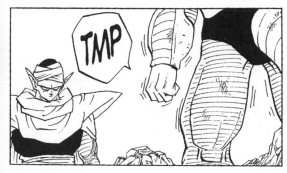

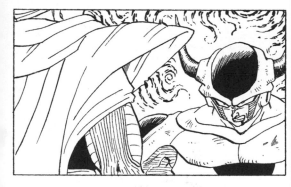

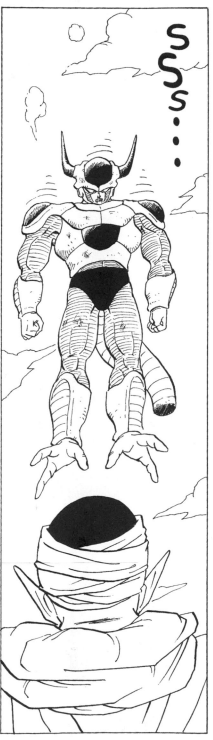

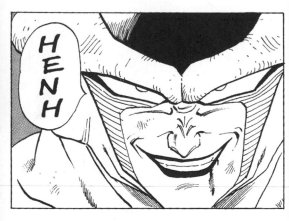

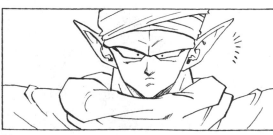

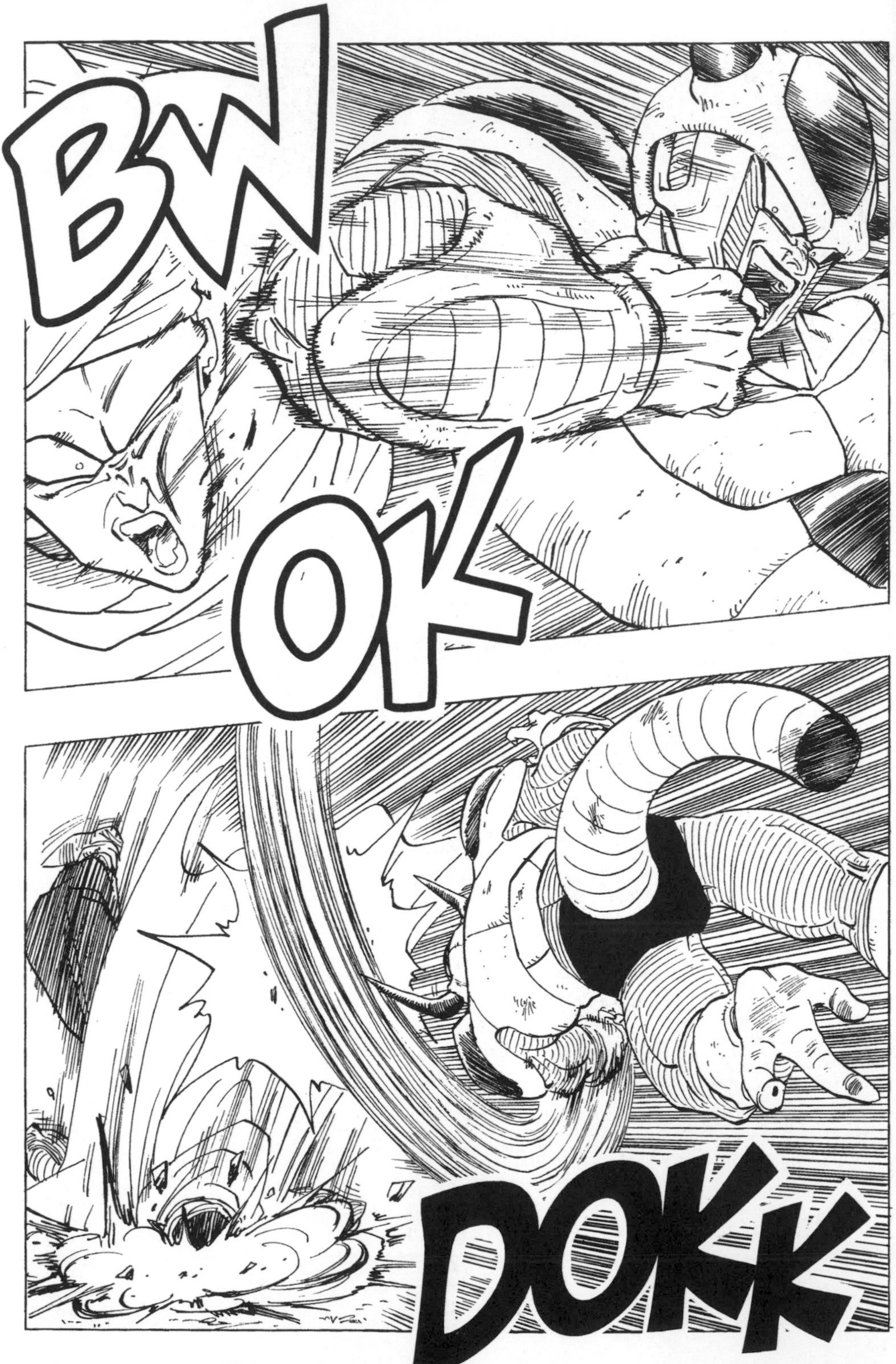
BWOK
DOKK

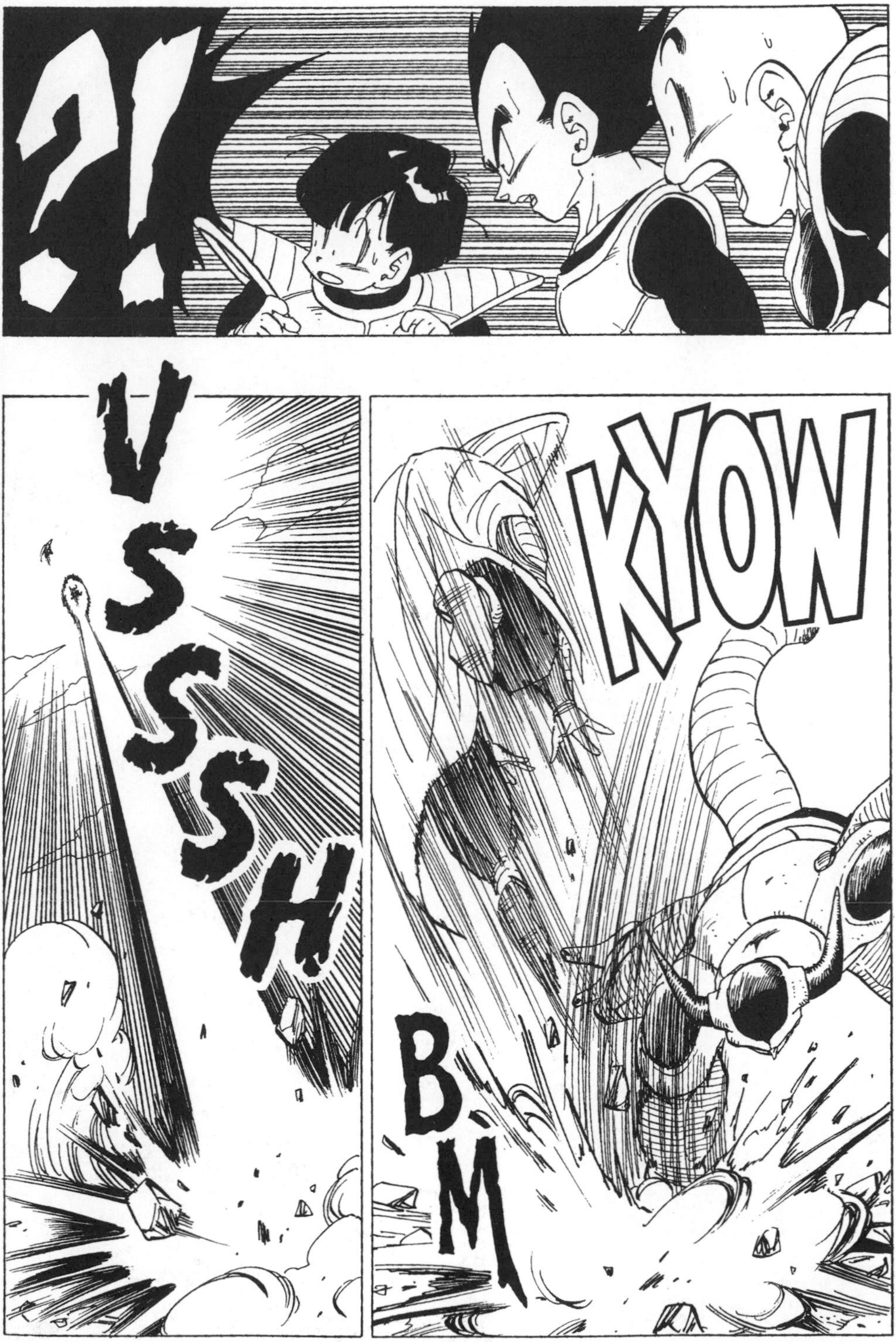
?!
VSSSH
KYOW
BM

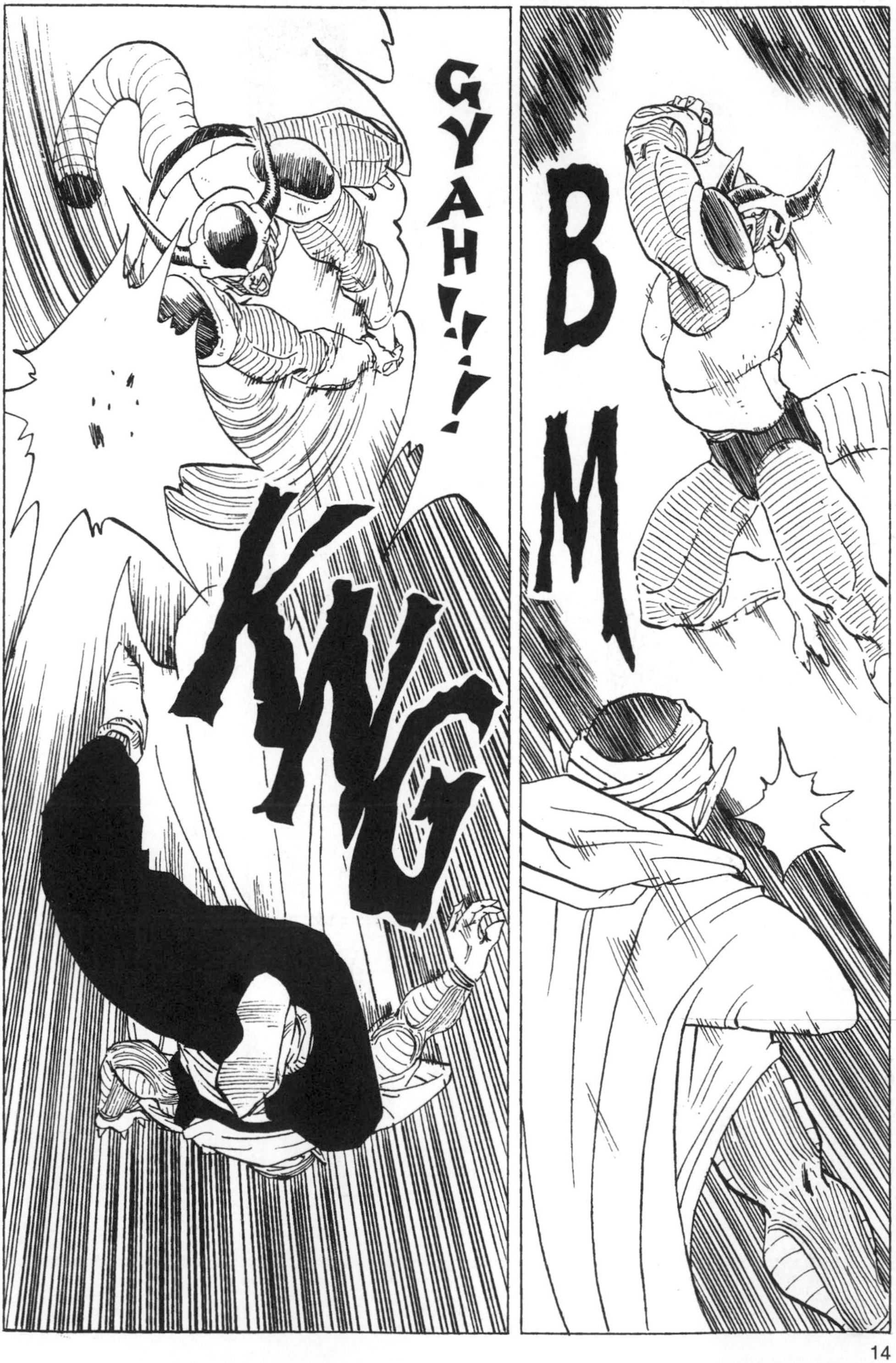
B
M
GYAH!!!!
KNG

RRRMMMM

D·KOOOM

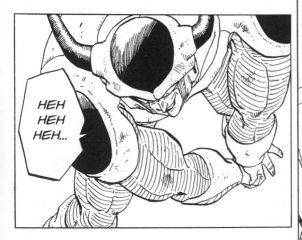

HEH
HEH
HEH...

OH NO...
HE WAS...
JUST FAKING
IT...

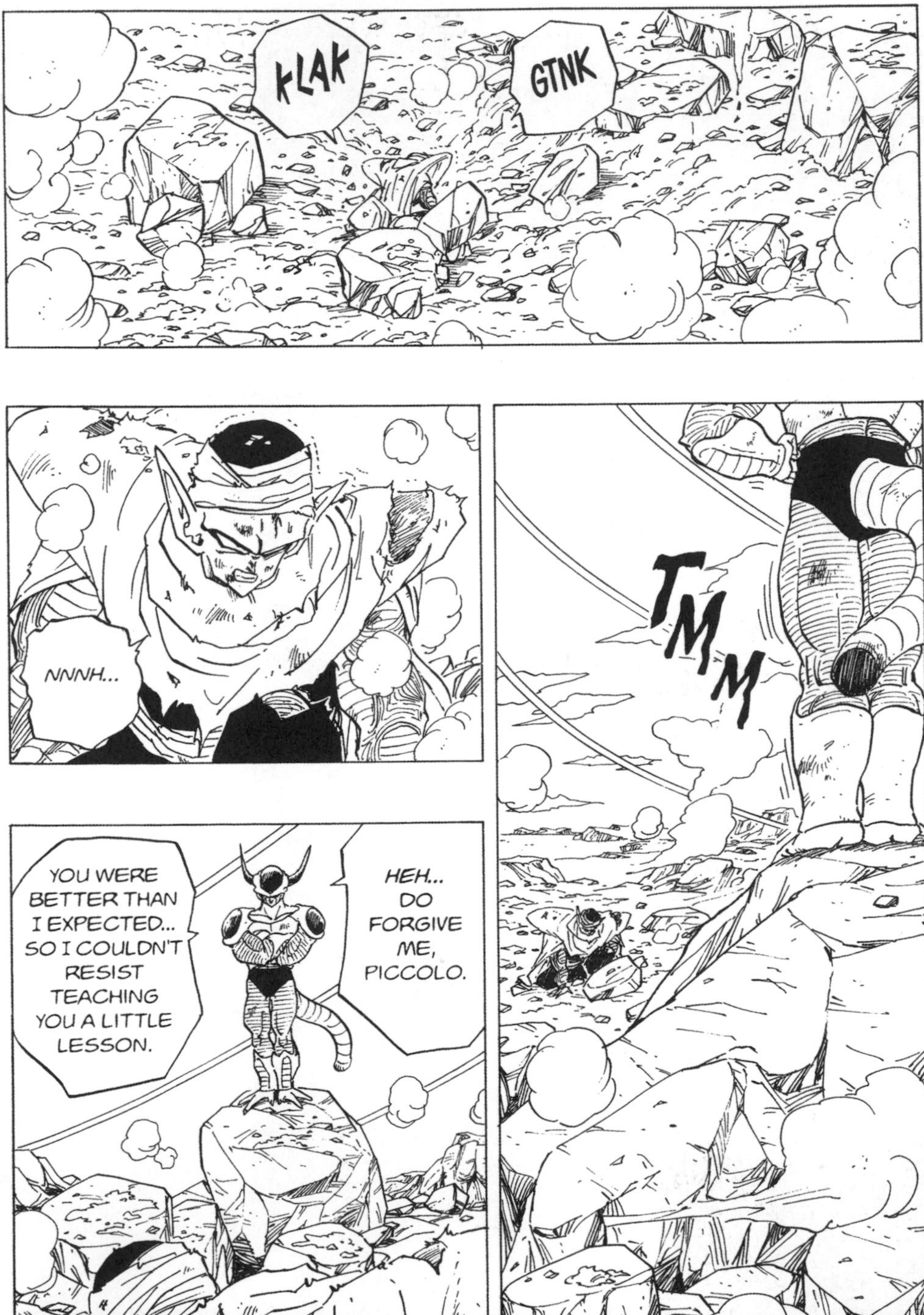
GTNK
KLAK
TMM
NNNH...
HEH... DO FORGIVE ME, PICCOLO.
YOU WERE BETTER THAN I EXPECTED... SO I COULDN'T RESIST TEACHING YOU A LITTLE LESSON.

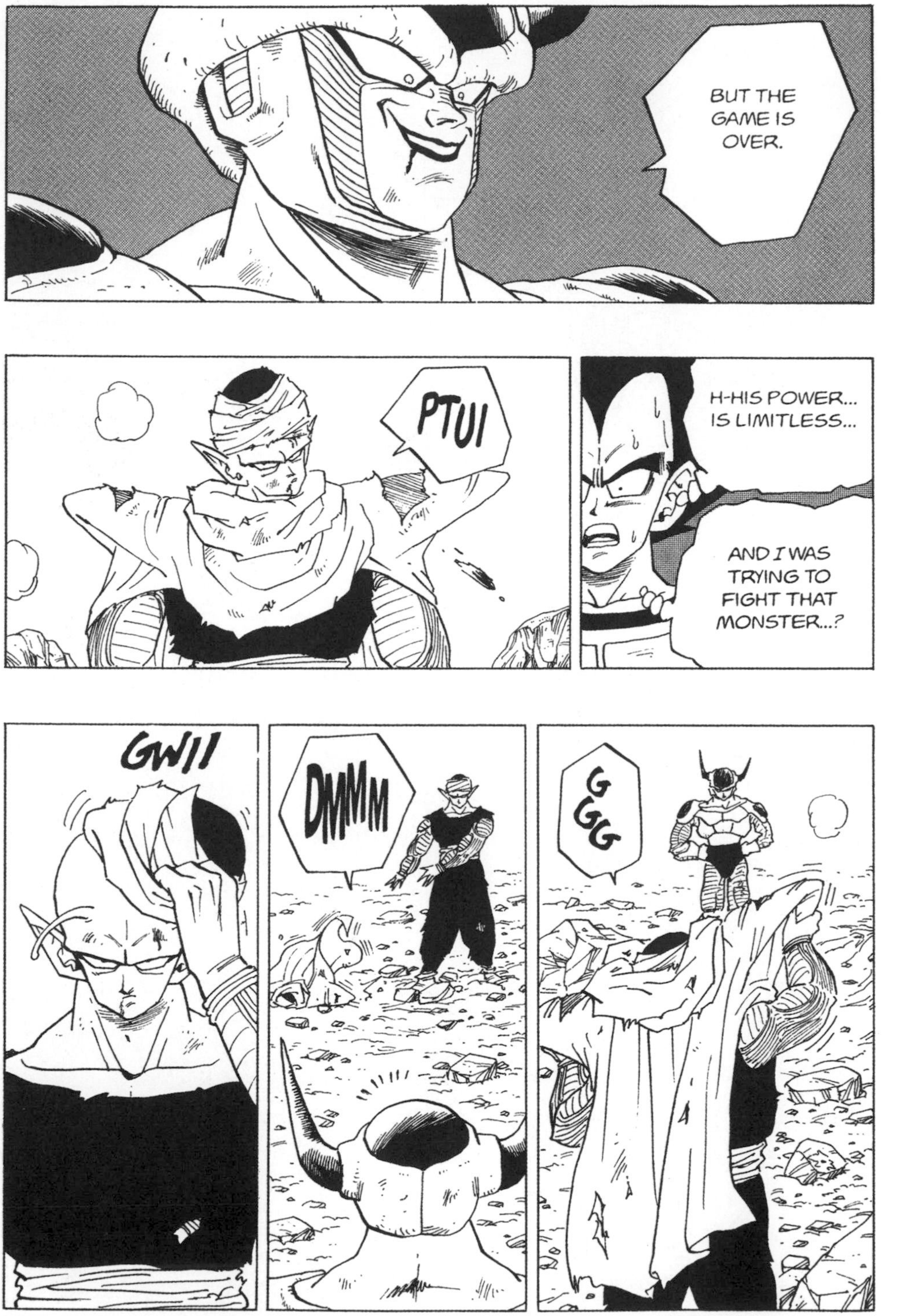
BUT THE GAME IS OVER.
PTUI
H-HIS POWER... IS LIMITLESS...
AND I WAS TRYING TO FIGHT THAT MONSTER...?
GWII
DMMM
G GG

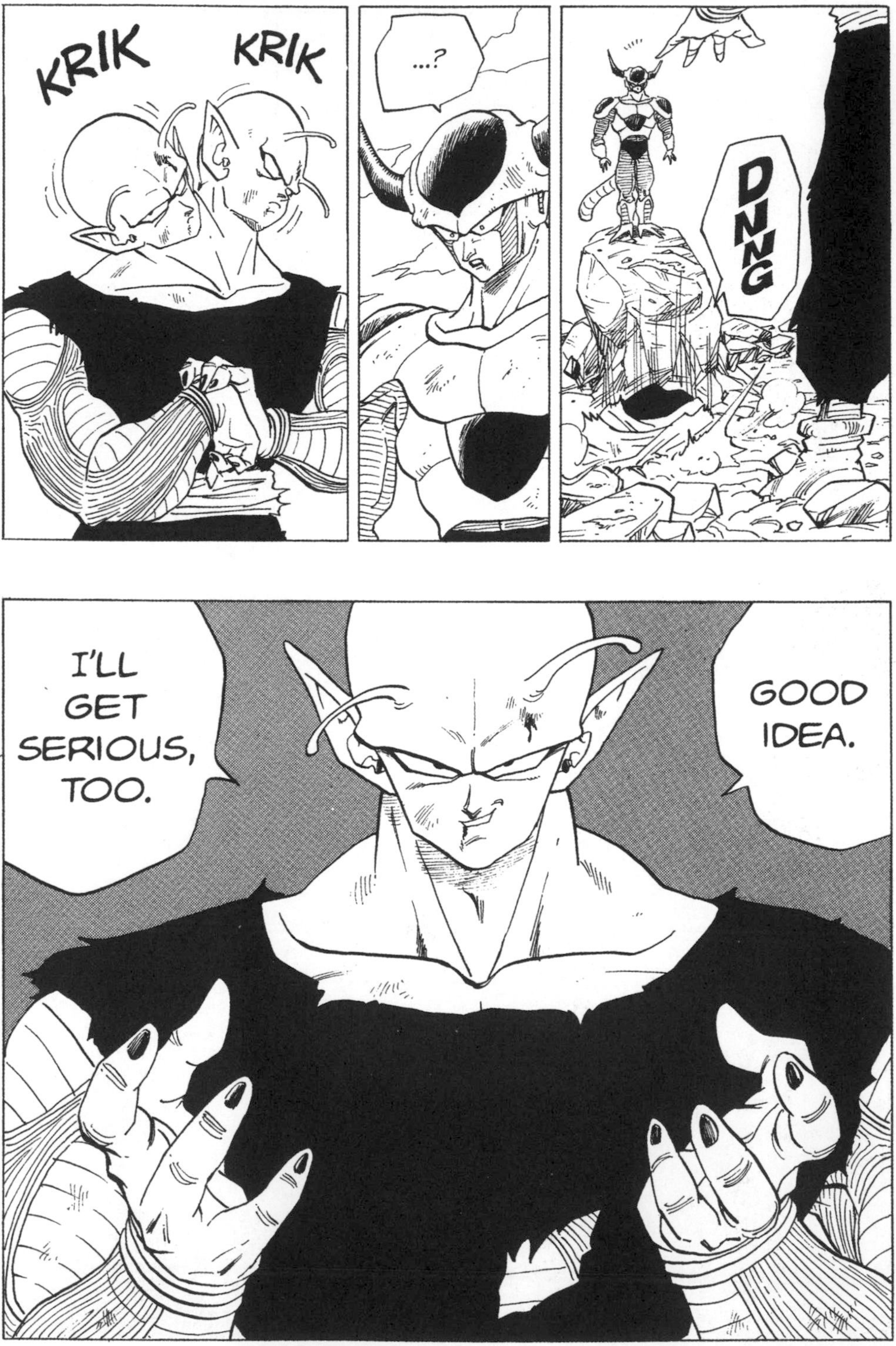
KRIK
KRIK
...?
DNNG
I'LL GET SERIOUS, TOO.
GOOD IDEA.

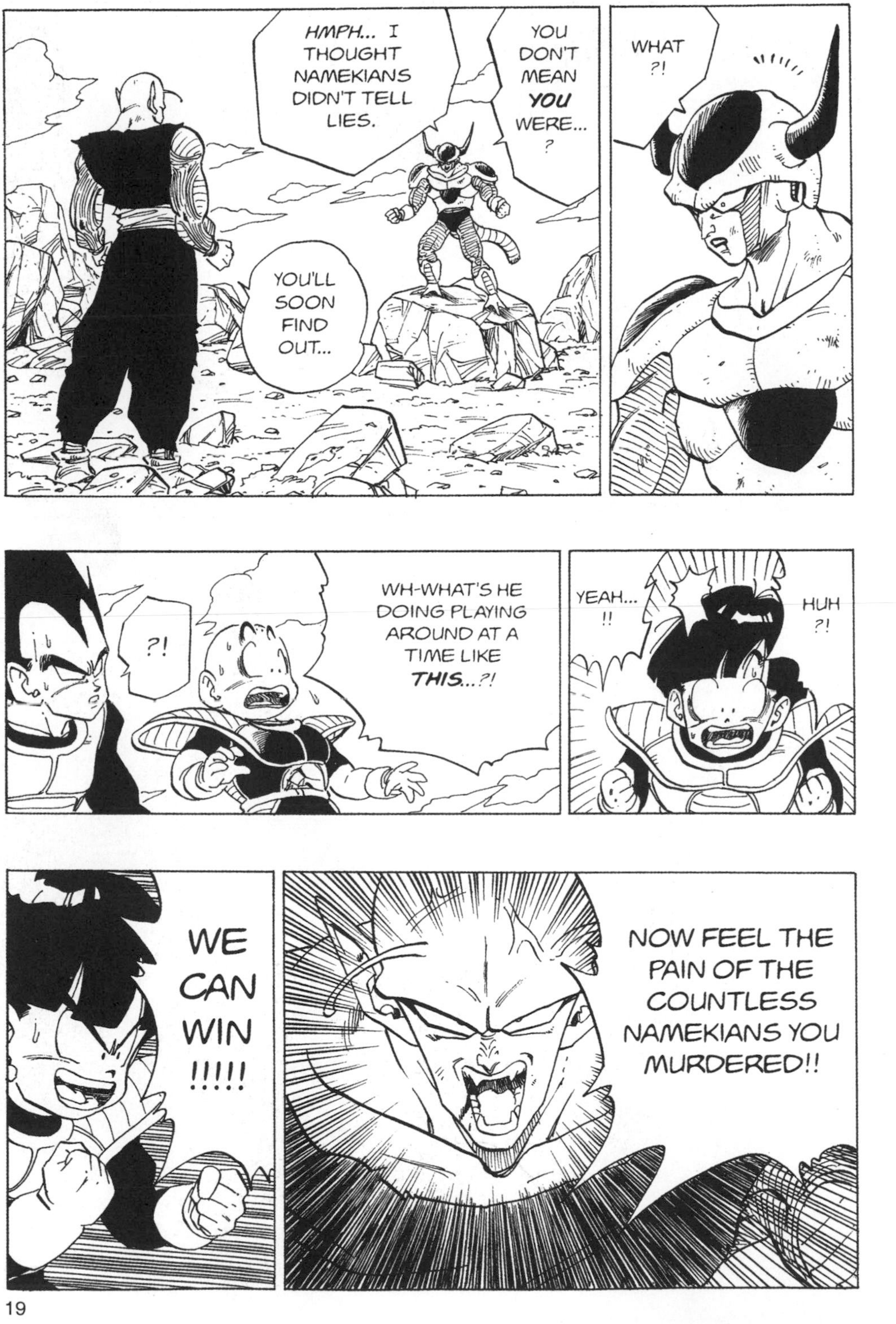
HMPH... I THOUGHT NAMEKIANS DIDN'T TELL LIES.
YOU DON'T MEAN YOU WERE...?
YOU'LL SOON FIND OUT...
WHAT ?!
?!
WH-WHAT'S HE DOING PLAYING AROUND AT A TIME LIKE THIS...?!
YEAH... !!
HUH ?!
WE CAN WIN !!!!!
NOW FEEL THE PAIN OF THE COUNTLESS NAMEKIANS YOU MURDERED!!

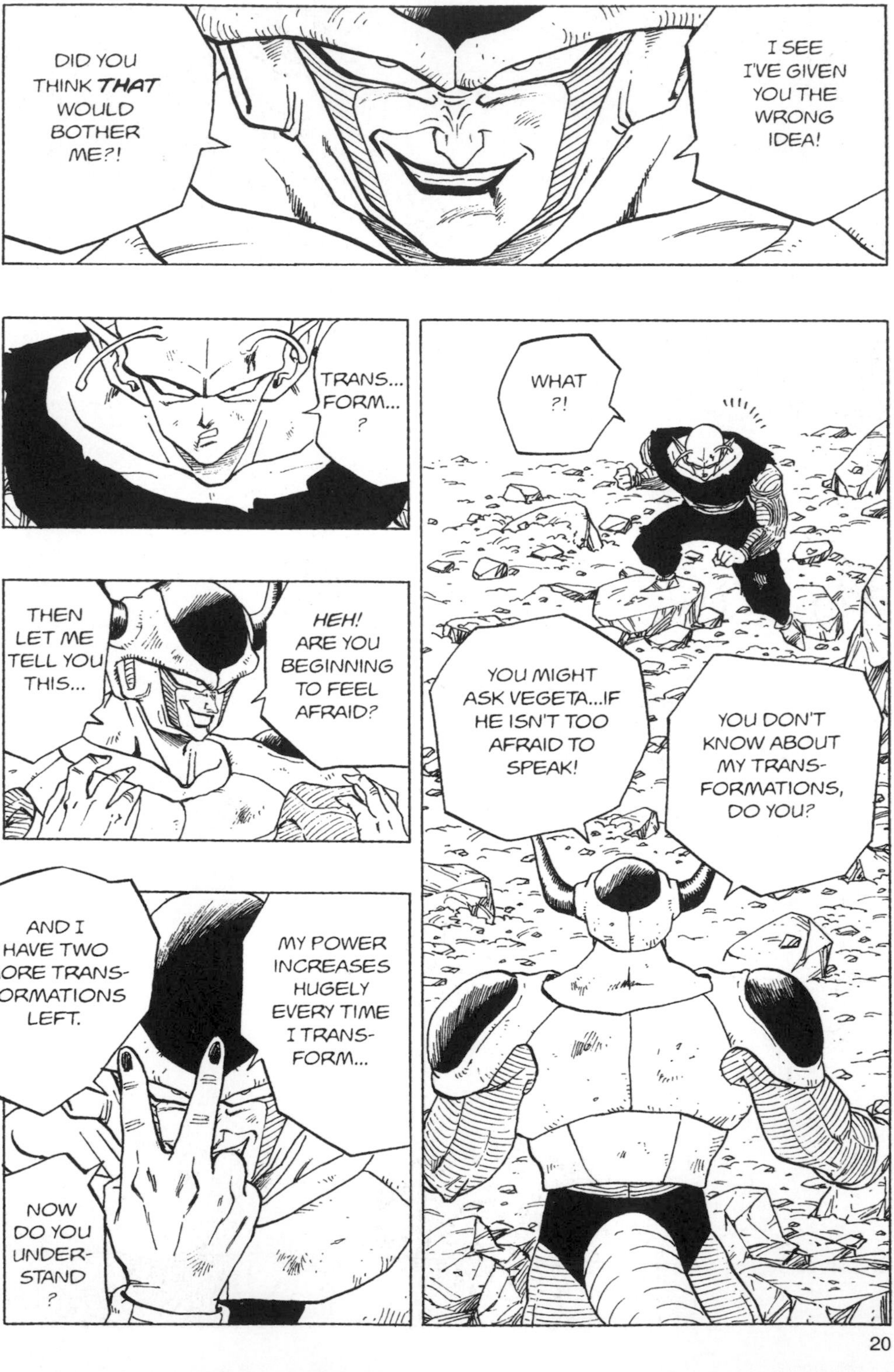
I SEE I'VE GIVEN YOU THE WRONG IDEA!
DID YOU THINK **THAT** WOULD BOTHER ME?!
WHAT ?!
YOU DON'T KNOW ABOUT MY TRANS-FORMATIONS, DO YOU?
YOU MIGHT ASK VEGETA...IF HE ISN'T TOO AFRAID TO SPEAK!
TRANS... FORM... ?
HEH! ARE YOU BEGINNING TO FEEL AFRAID?
THEN LET ME TELL YOU THIS...
MY POWER INCREASES HUGELY EVERY TIME I TRANS-FORM...
AND I HAVE TWO MORE TRANS-FORMATIONS LEFT.
NOW DO YOU UNDER-STAND ?

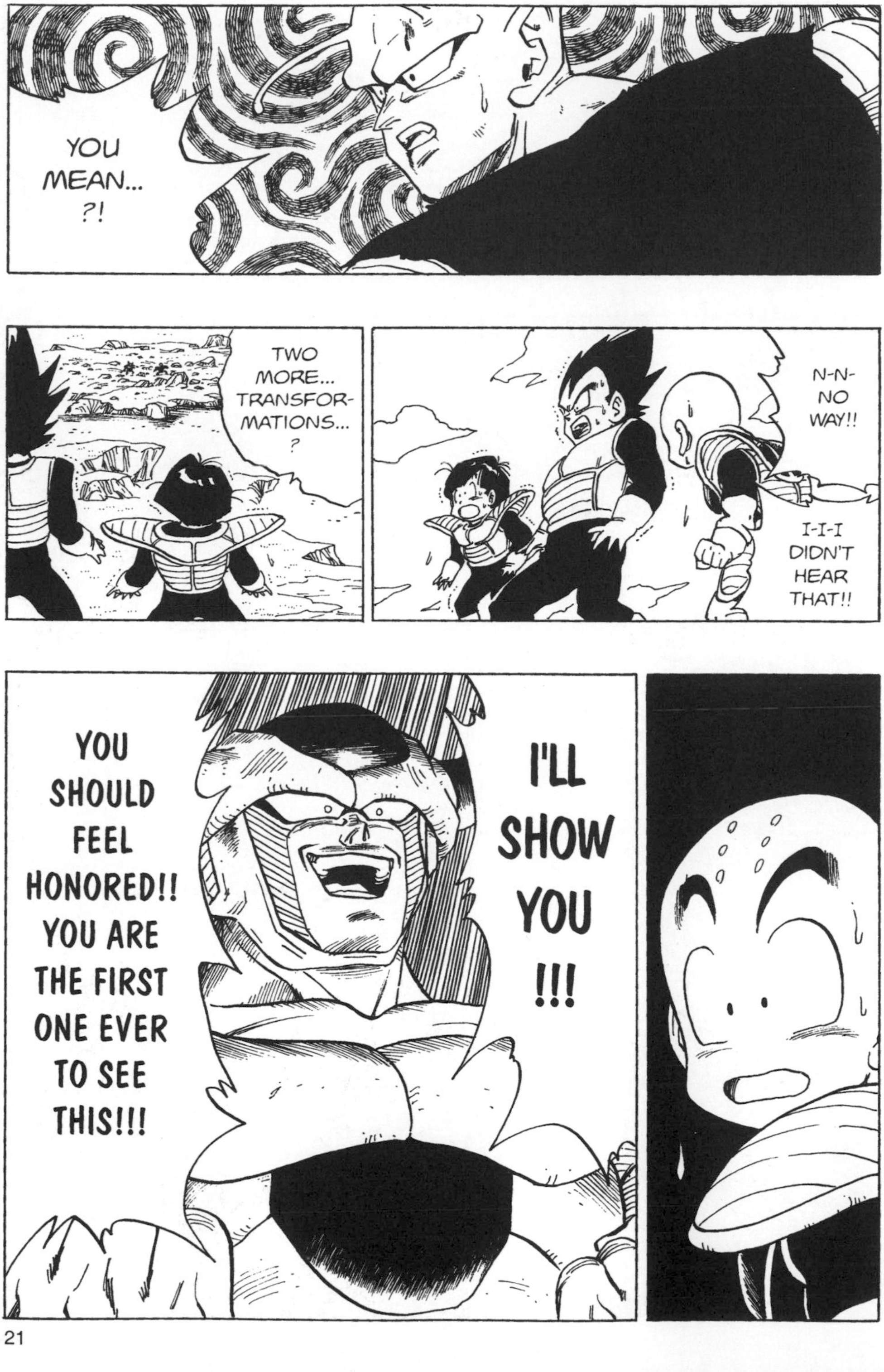

YOU MEAN... ?!
TWO MORE... TRANSFORMATIONS... ?
N-N-NO WAY!!
I-I-I DIDN'T HEAR THAT!!
I'LL SHOW YOU !!!
YOU SHOULD FEEL HONORED!! YOU ARE THE FIRST ONE EVER TO SEE THIS!!!

DBZ:108 • Freeza's Third Form

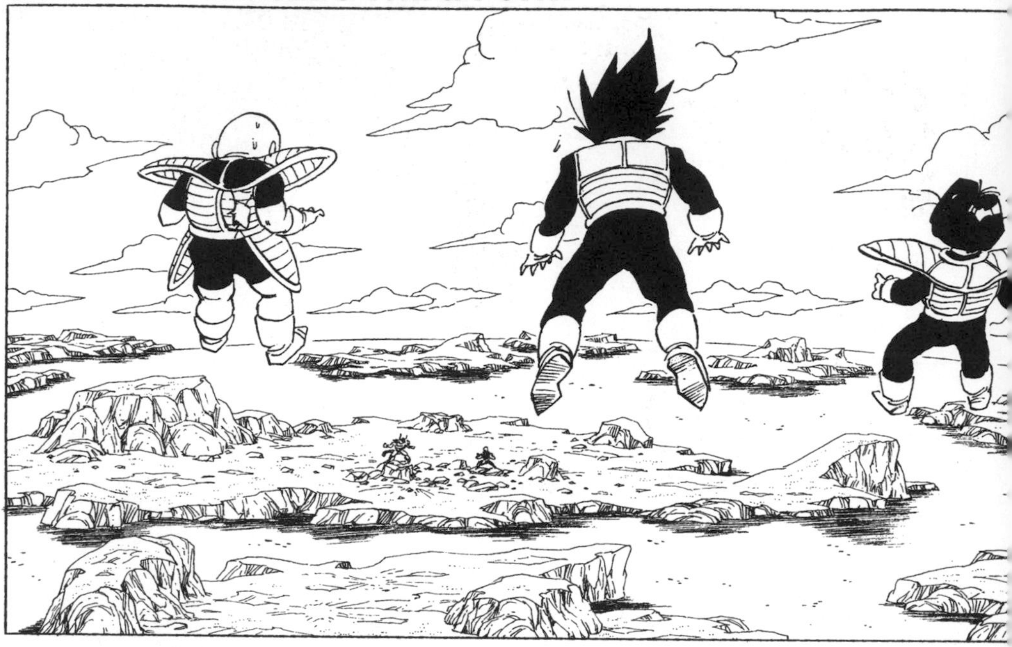

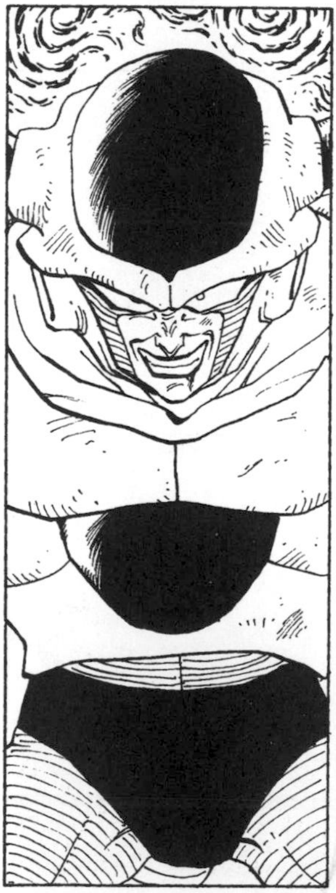

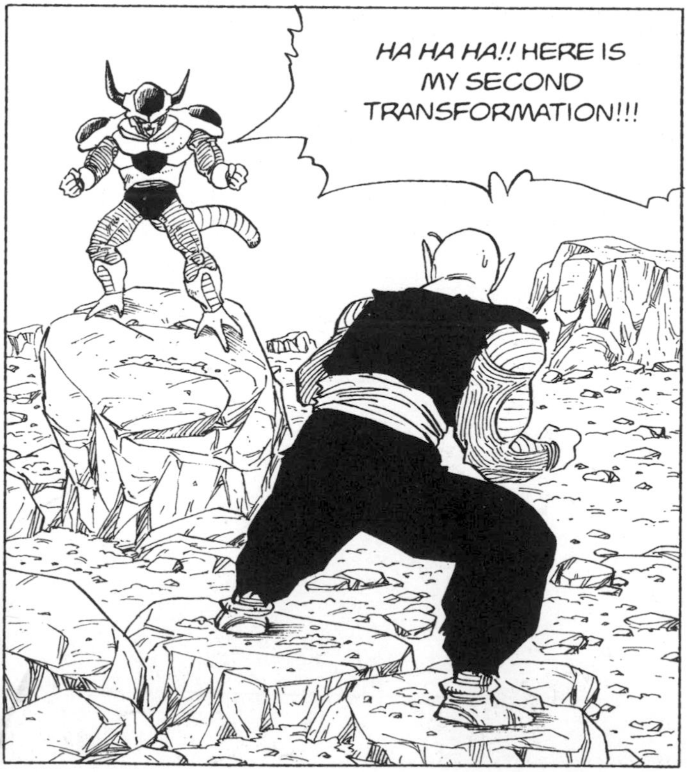
HA HA HA!! HERE IS MY SECOND TRANSFORMATION!!!

GHHH !!!!
!!
BLUK BLUK
NRR RH... !!!!

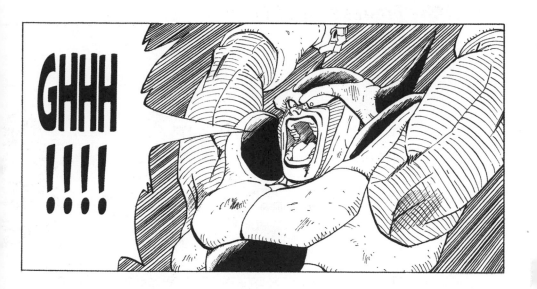

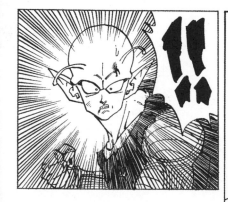

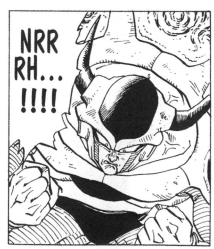

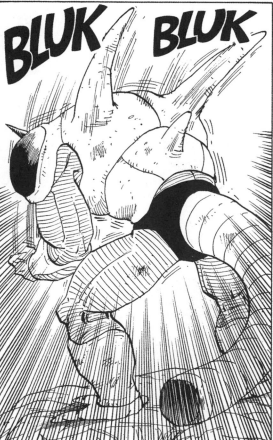

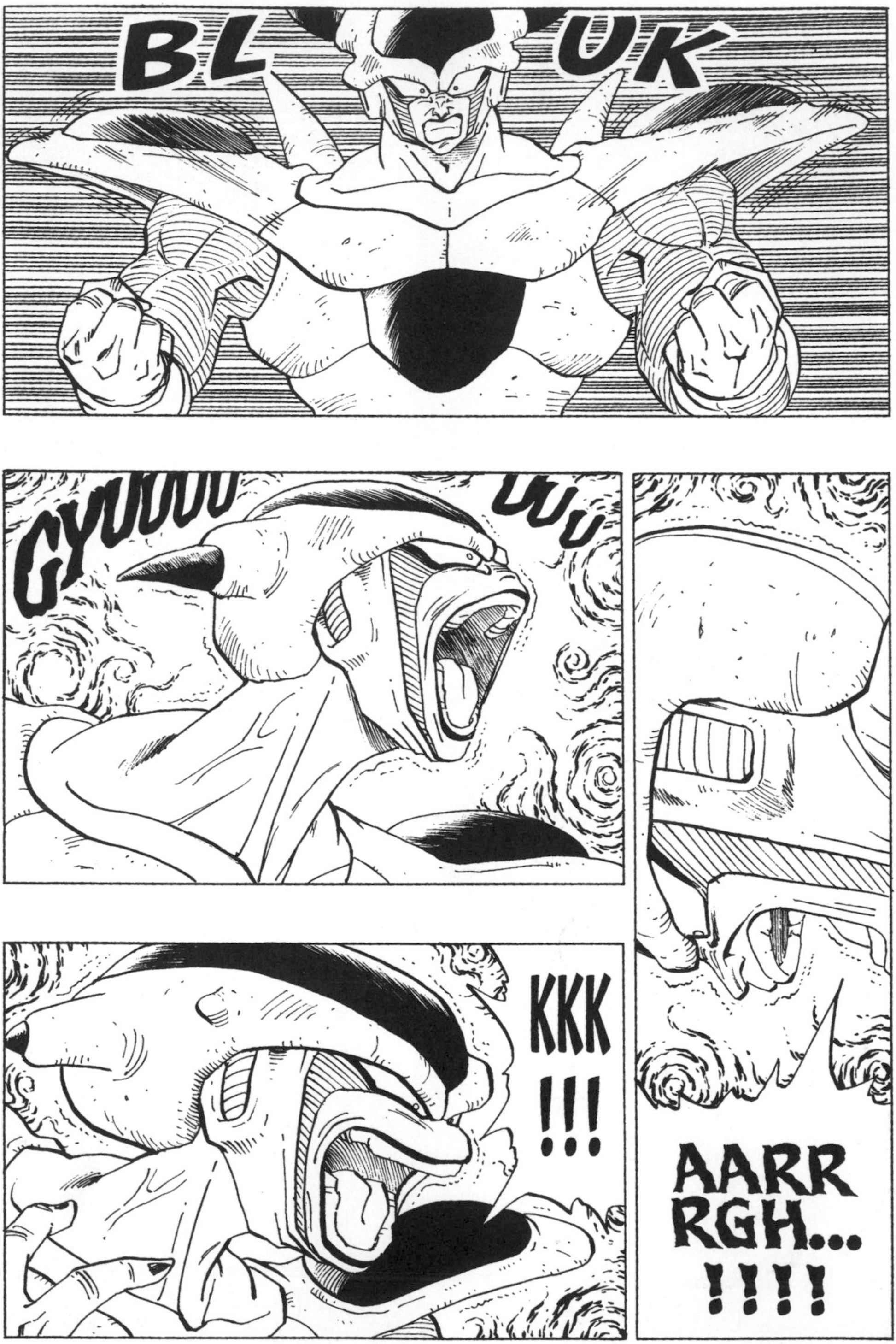
BL UK
GYUUUU UUU
AARR RGH... !!!!
KKK !!!

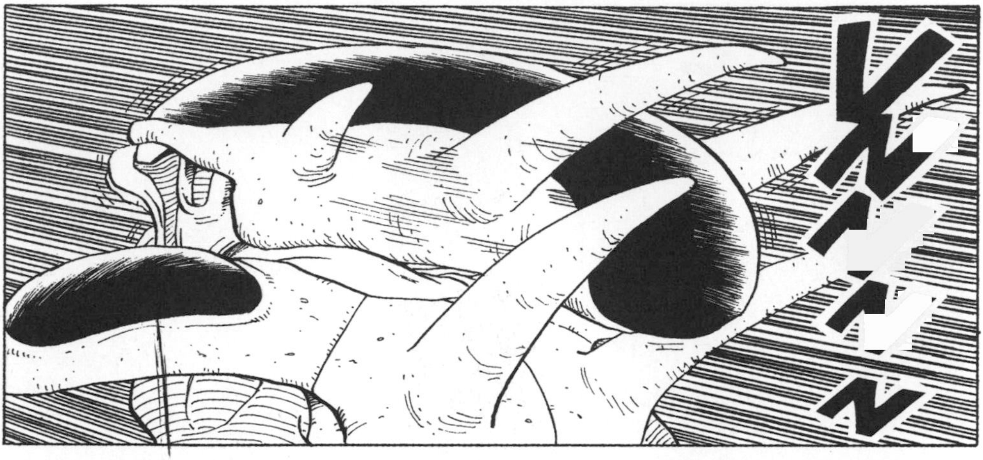

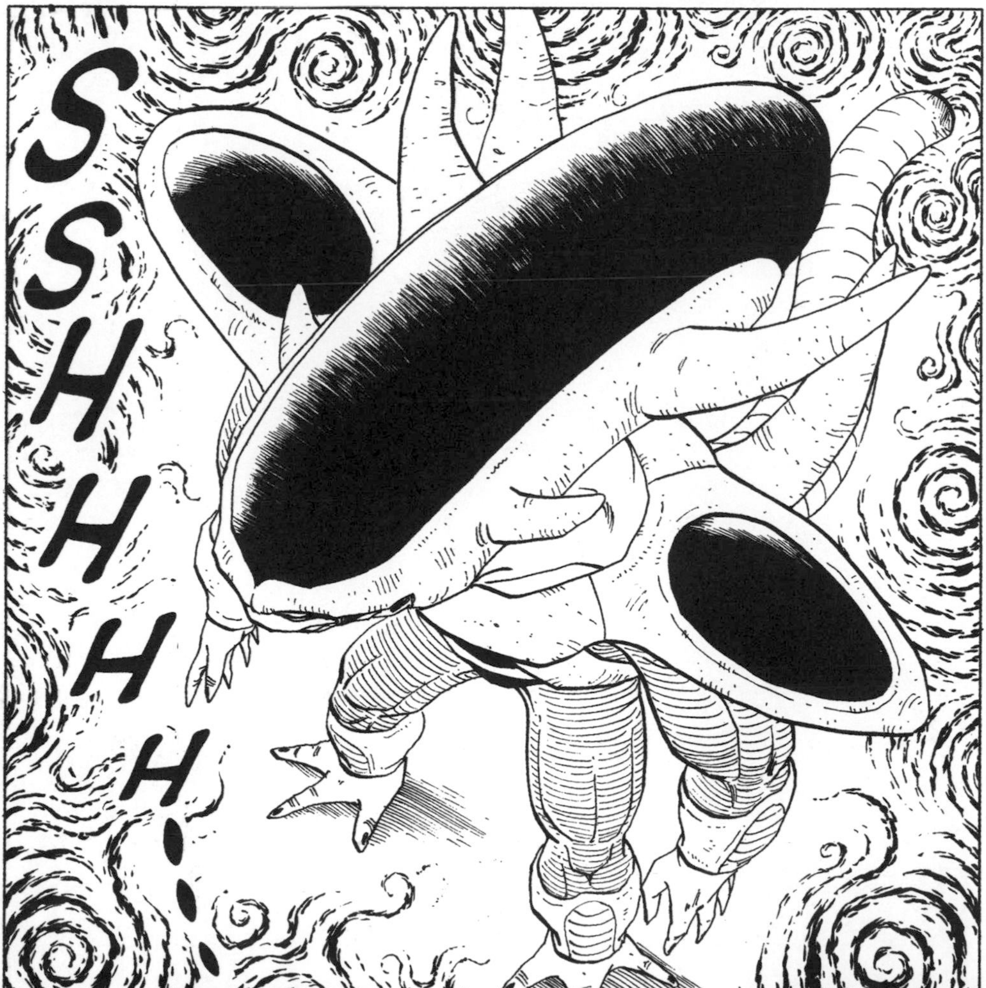
SSHHHH...

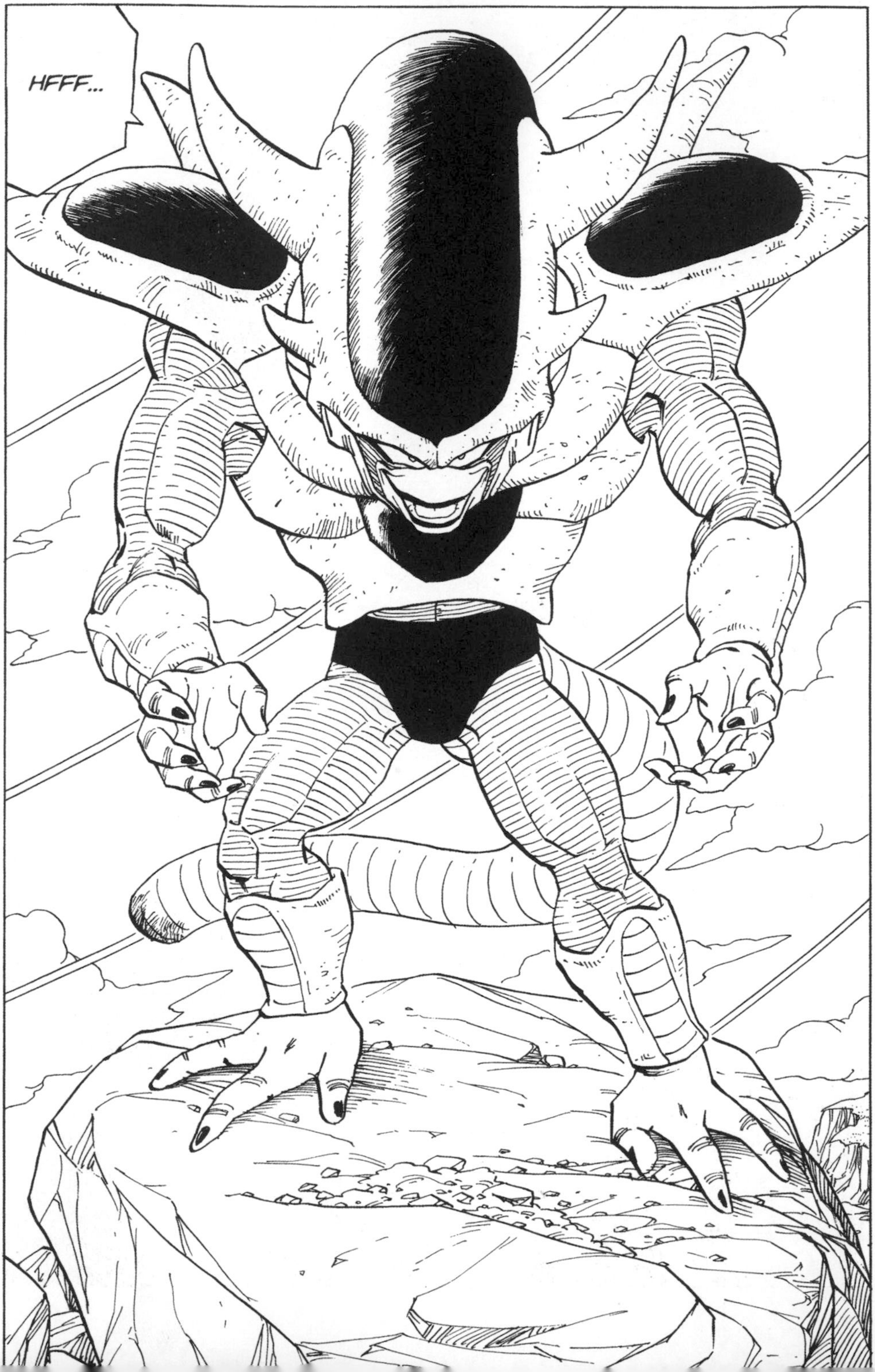
HFFF...

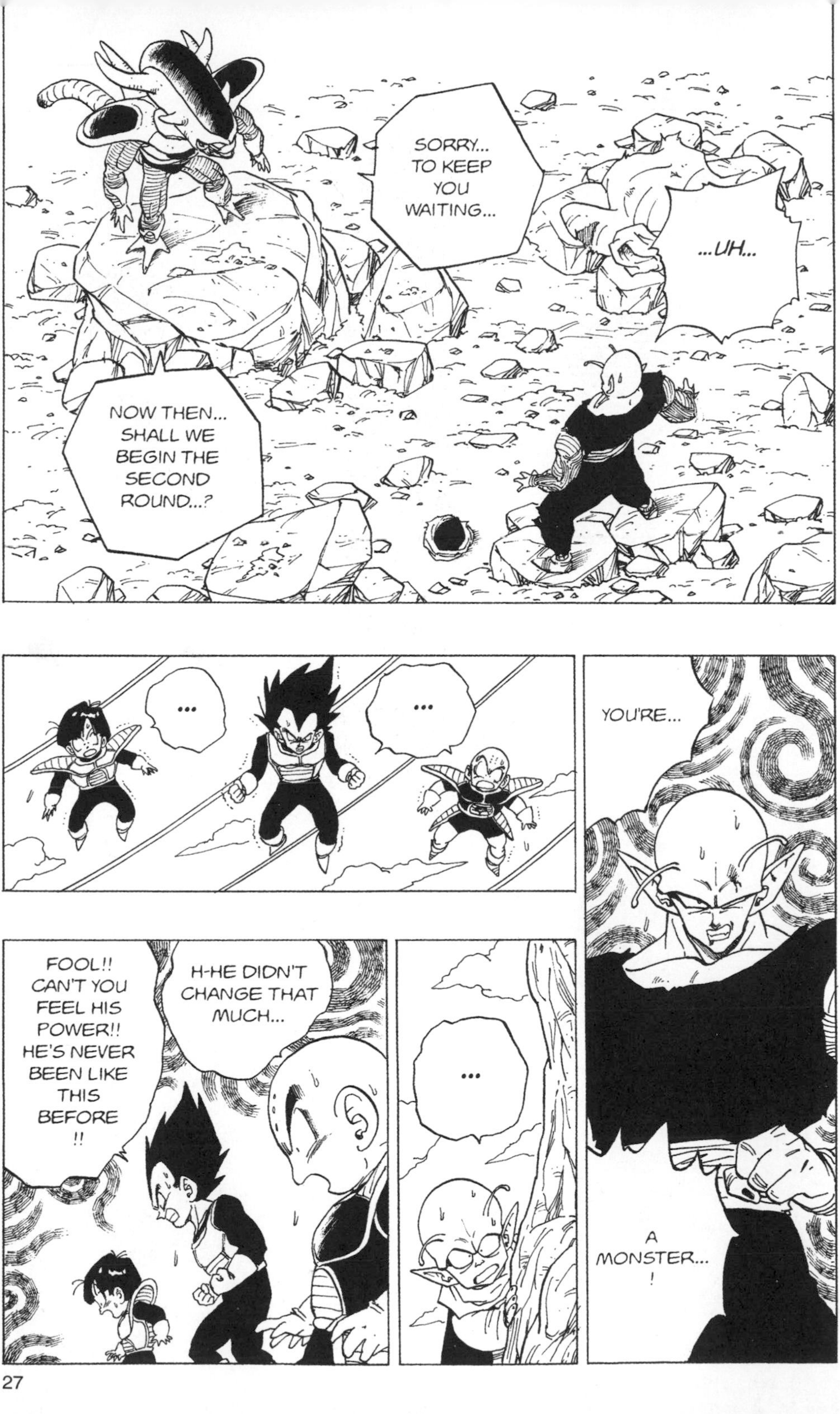
SORRY... TO KEEP YOU WAITING...
...UH...
NOW THEN... SHALL WE BEGIN THE SECOND ROUND...?
...
...
H-HE DIDN'T CHANGE THAT MUCH...
FOOL!! CAN'T YOU FEEL HIS POWER!! HE'S NEVER BEEN LIKE THIS BEFORE!!
...
YOU'RE...
A MONSTER...!

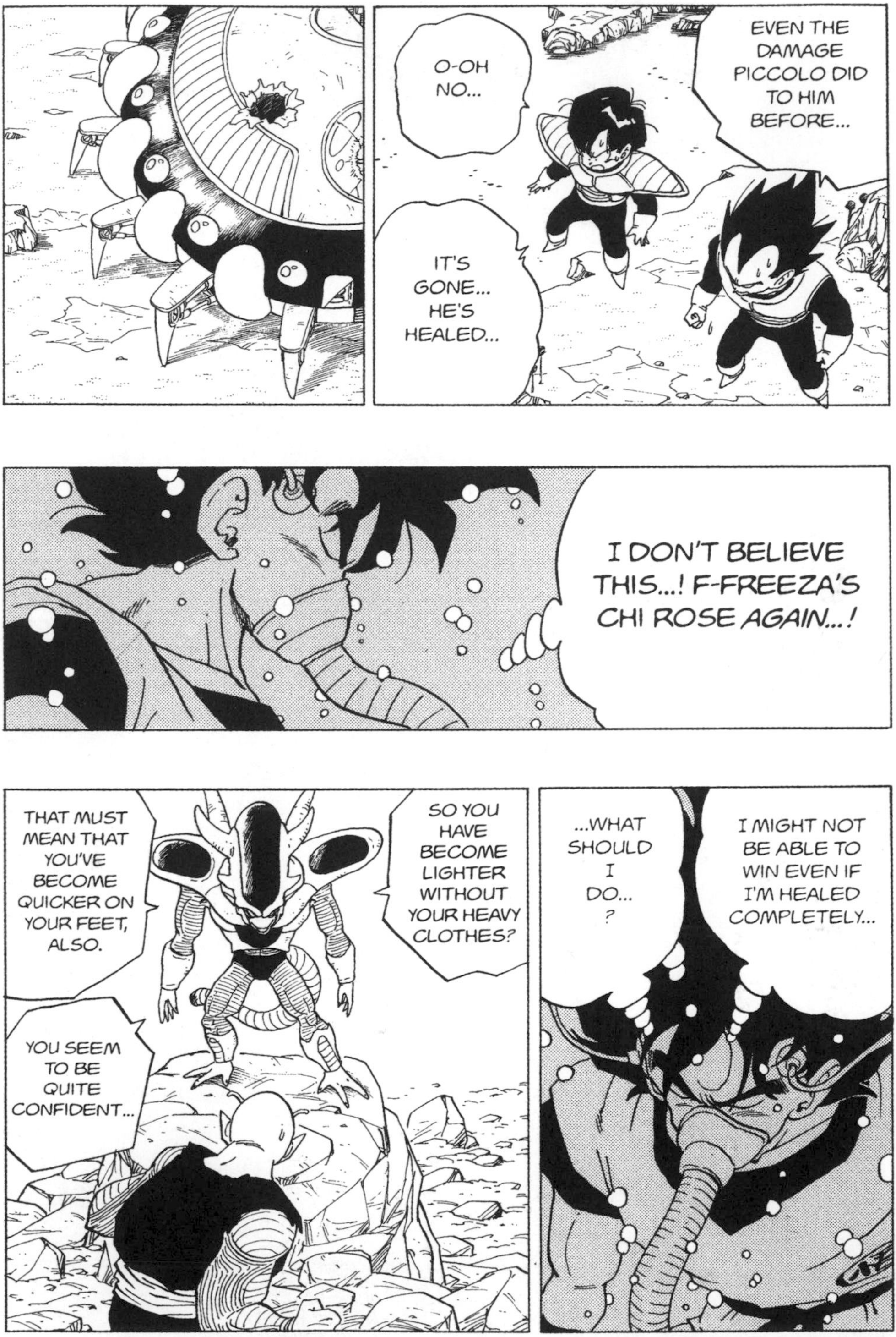
EVEN THE DAMAGE PICCOLO DID TO HIM BEFORE...
O-OH NO...
IT'S GONE... HE'S HEALED...
I DON'T BELIEVE THIS...! F-FREEZA'S CHI ROSE *AGAIN*...!
I MIGHT NOT BE ABLE TO WIN EVEN IF I'M HEALED COMPLETELY...
...WHAT SHOULD I DO...?
SO YOU HAVE BECOME LIGHTER WITHOUT YOUR HEAVY CLOTHES?
THAT MUST MEAN THAT YOU'VE BECOME QUICKER ON YOUR FEET, ALSO.
YOU SEEM TO BE QUITE CONFIDENT...

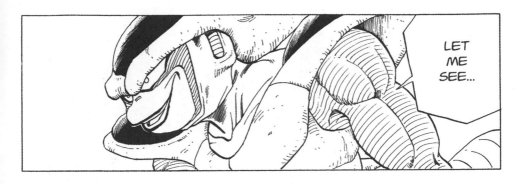

LET ME SEE...

WOOOSH

FWA

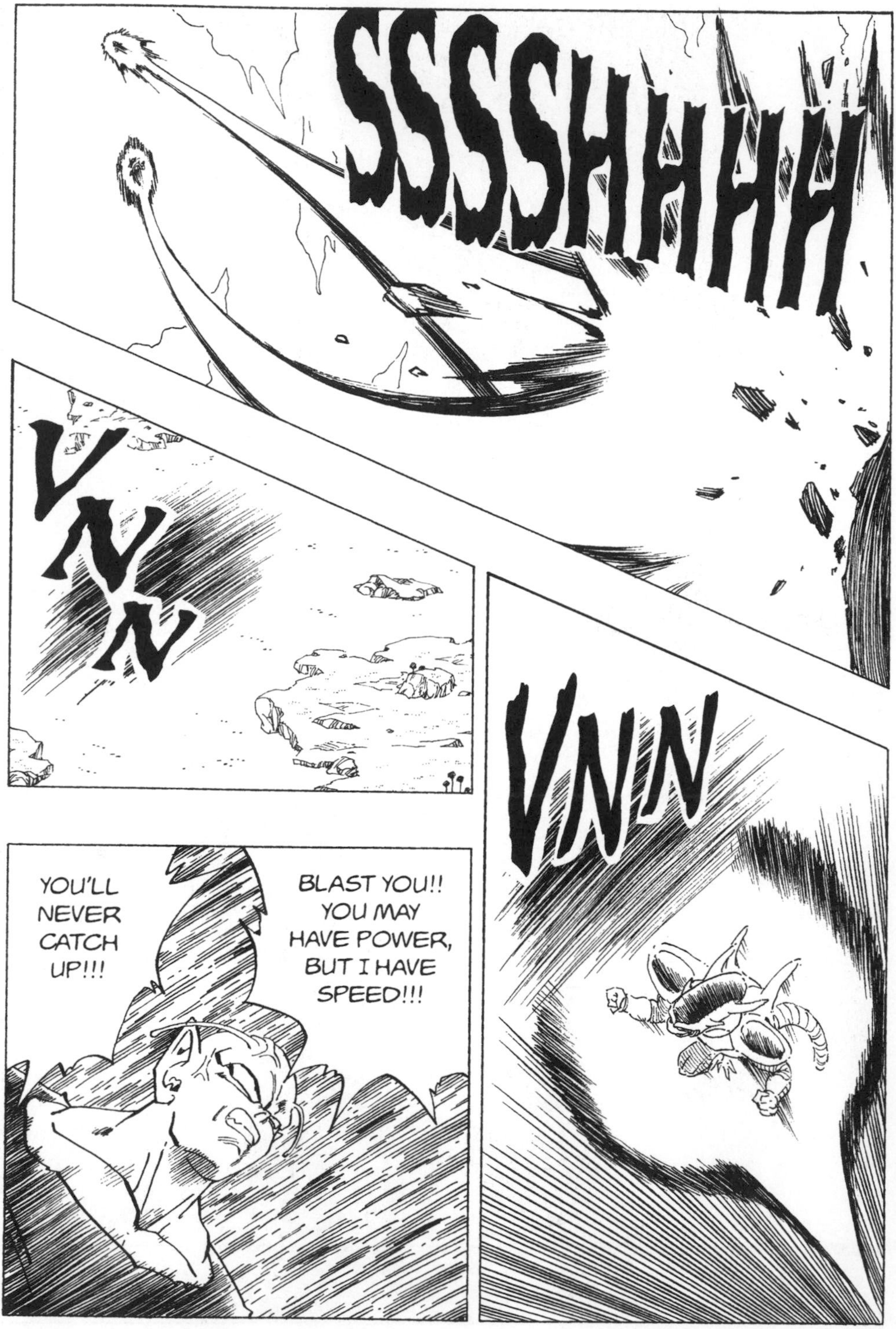
SSSSHHHH
VNN
VNN
BLAST YOU!! YOU MAY HAVE POWER, BUT I HAVE SPEED!!!
YOU'LL NEVER CATCH UP!!!

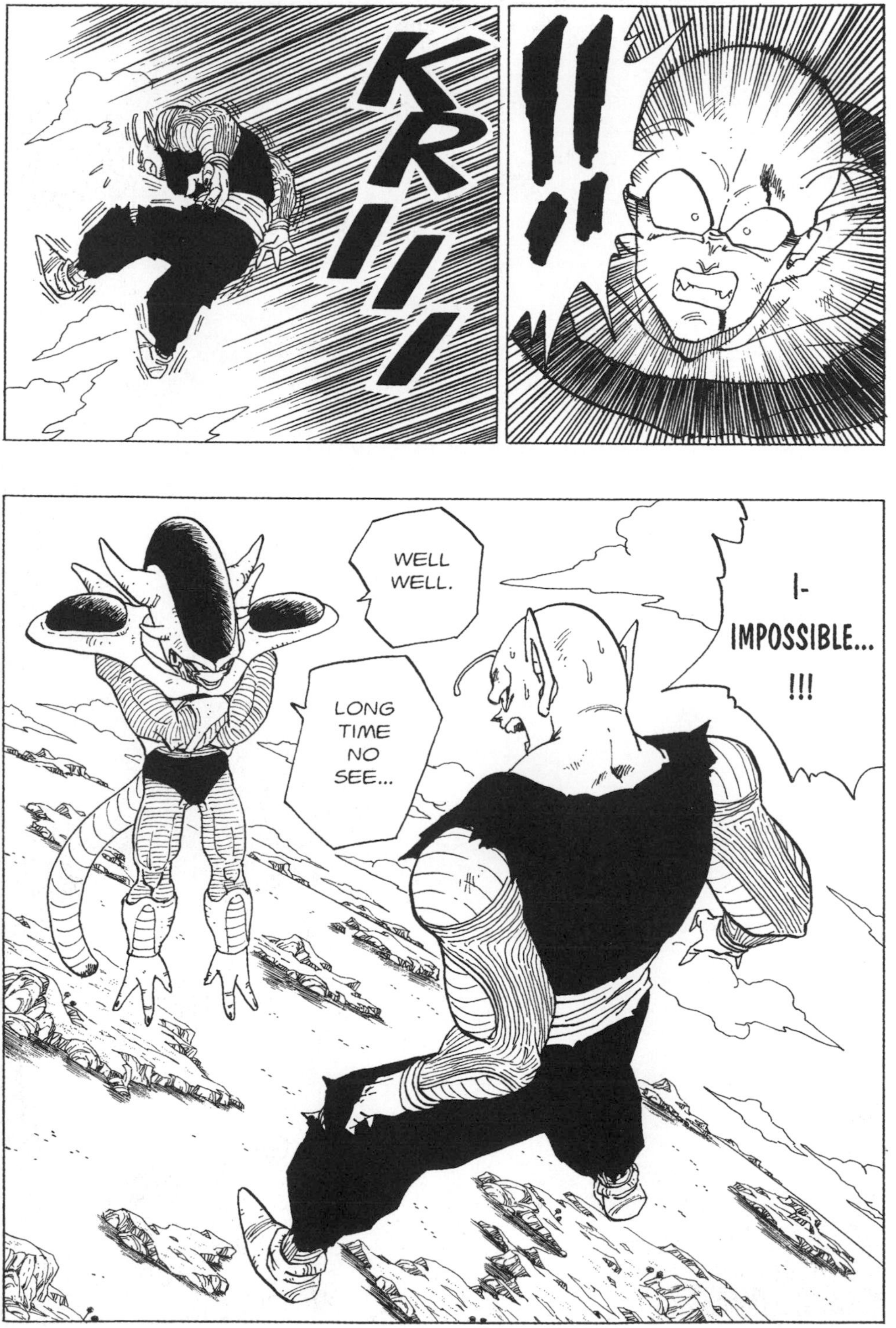
!!
KRIII
I- IMPOSSIBLE... !!!
WELL WELL.
LONG TIME NO SEE...

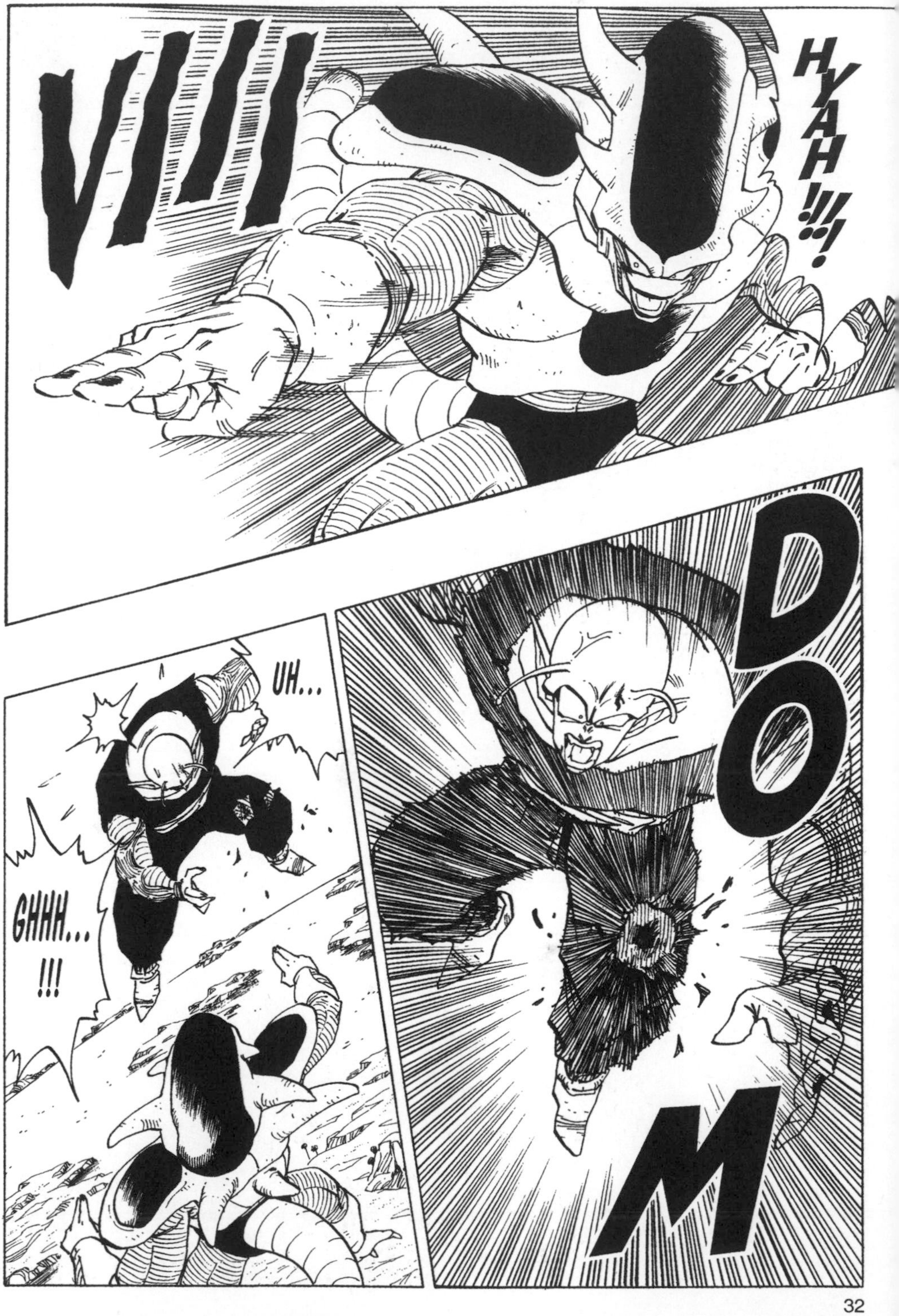
HYAH!!!!
VIIII
DOM
UH...
GHHH... !!!

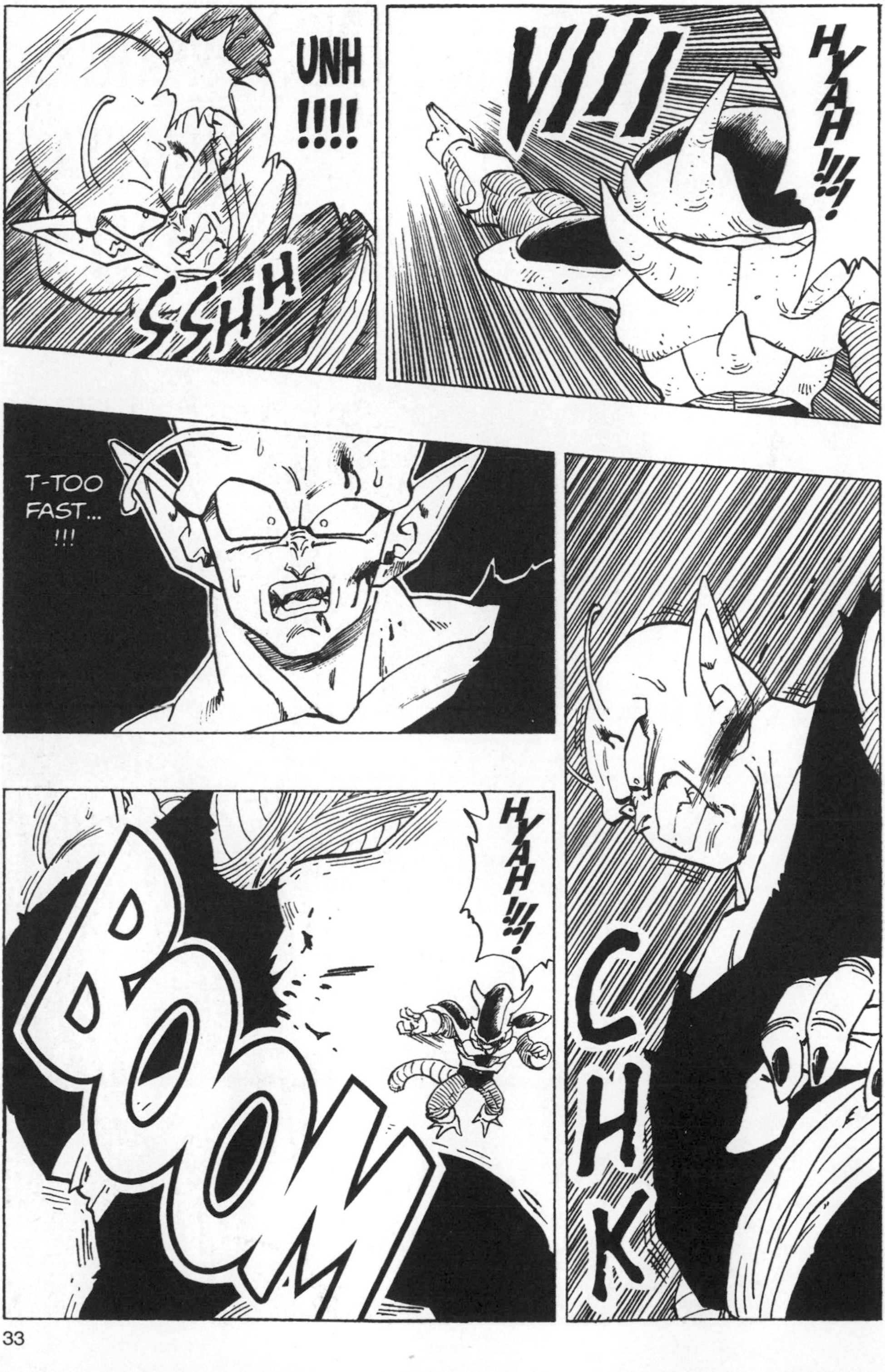
HYAH!!!
VIII
UNH!!!!
SSHH
T-TOO FAST... !!!
CHK
HYAH!!!
BOOM

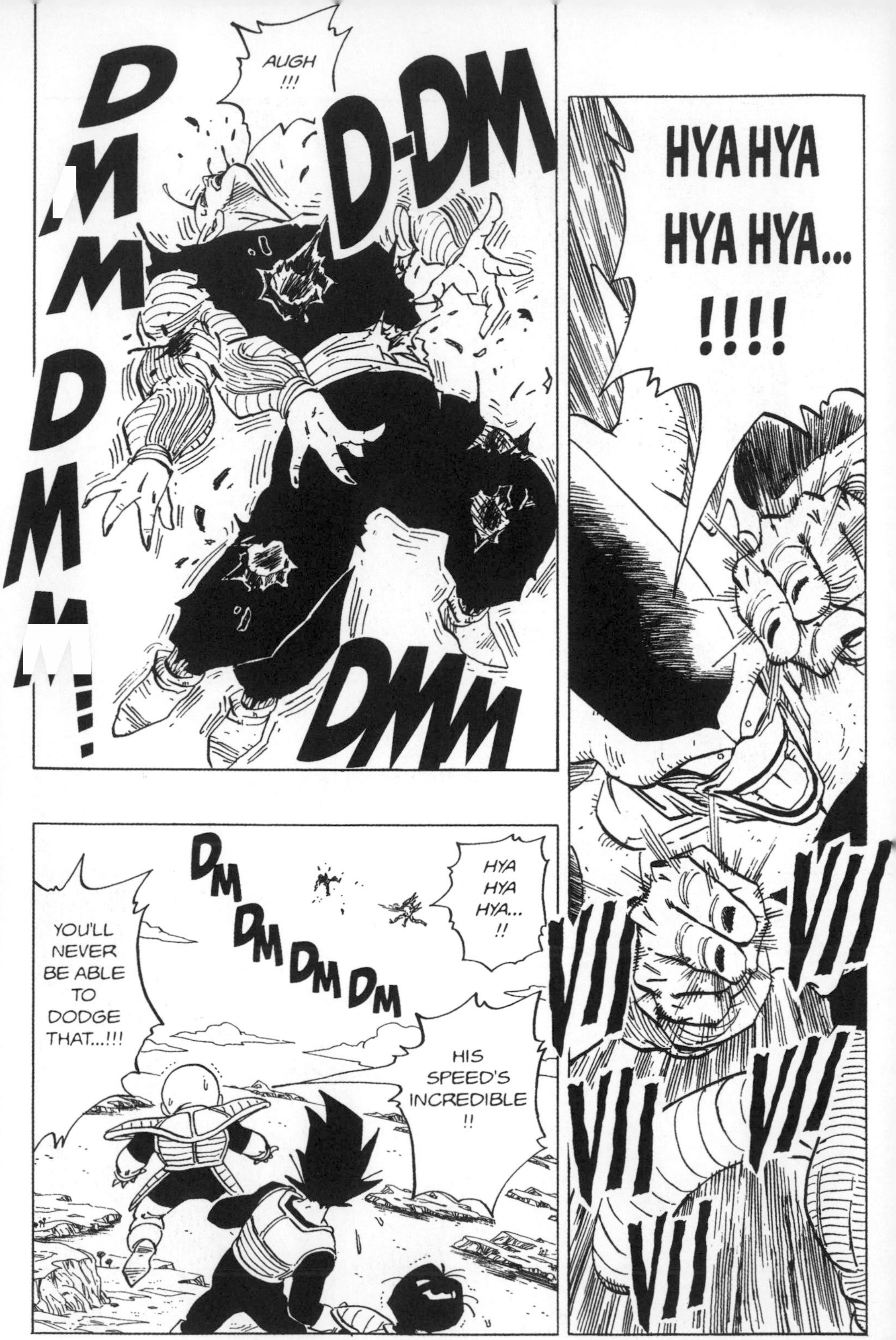
HYA HYA HYA HYA... !!!!
VII VII VII VII VII VII
D-DM
AUGH !!!
DMMM DMMMM!!!
DMM
DM DM DM DM DM
HYA HYA HYA... !!
HIS SPEED'S INCREDIBLE !!
YOU'LL NEVER BE ABLE TO DODGE THAT...!!!

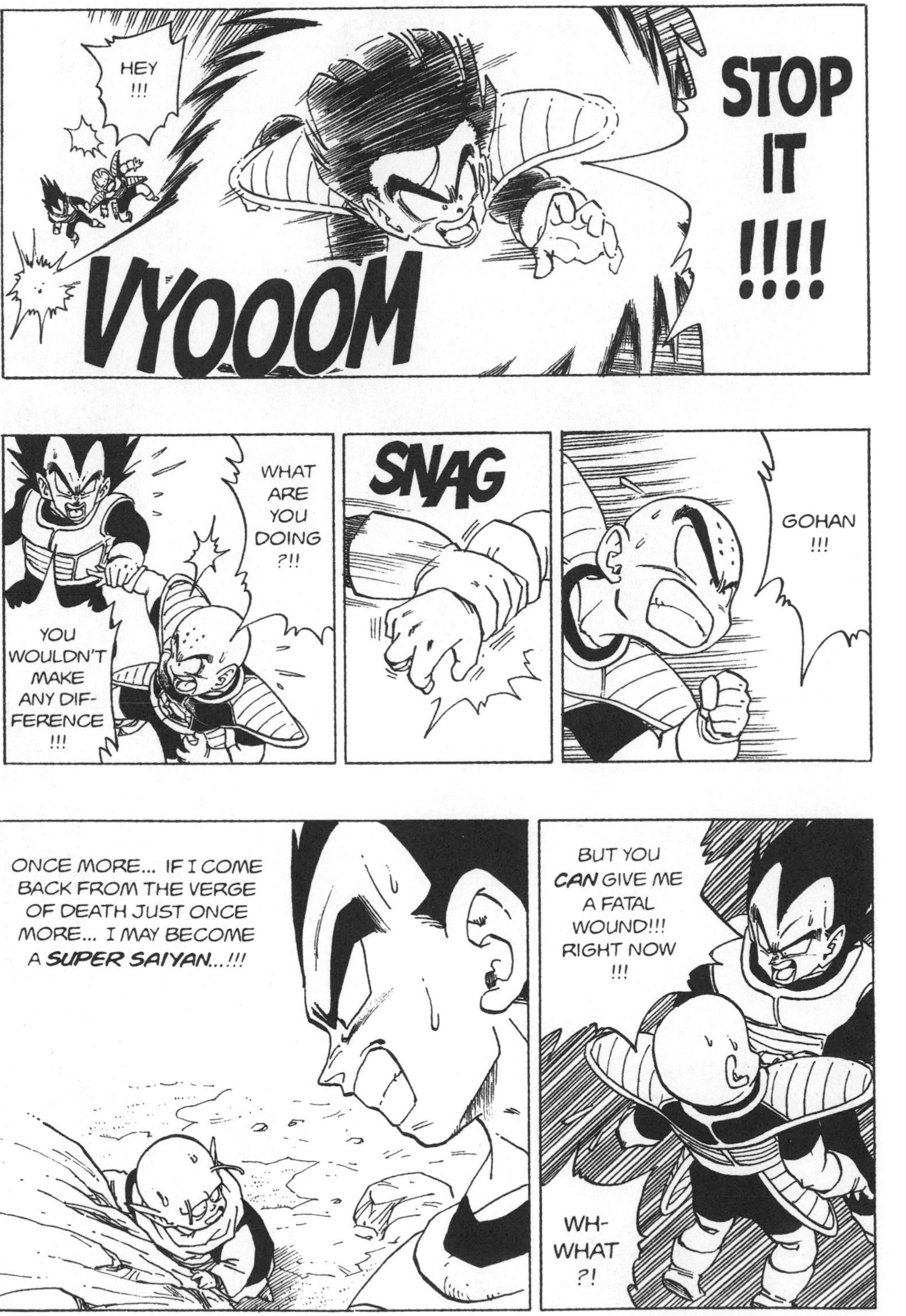
HEY !!!
STOP IT !!!!
VYOOOM
WHAT ARE YOU DOING ?!!
YOU WOULDN'T MAKE ANY DIF- FERENCE !!!
SNAG
GOHAN !!!
ONCE MORE... IF I COME BACK FROM THE VERGE OF DEATH JUST ONCE MORE... I MAY BECOME A SUPER SAIYAN...!!!
BUT YOU CAN GIVE ME A FATAL WOUND!!! RIGHT NOW !!!
WH- WHAT ?!

DBZ:109 • Vegeta's Ploy

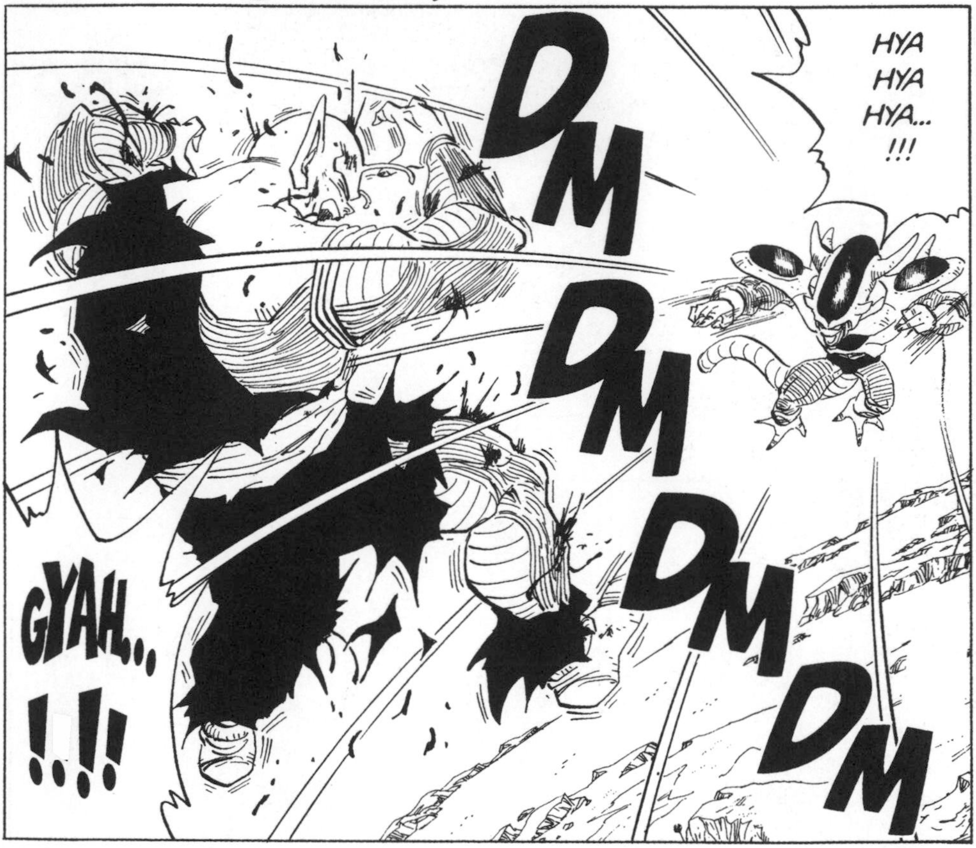
HYA HYA HYA... !!!
DM DM DM DM
GYAH... !..!!

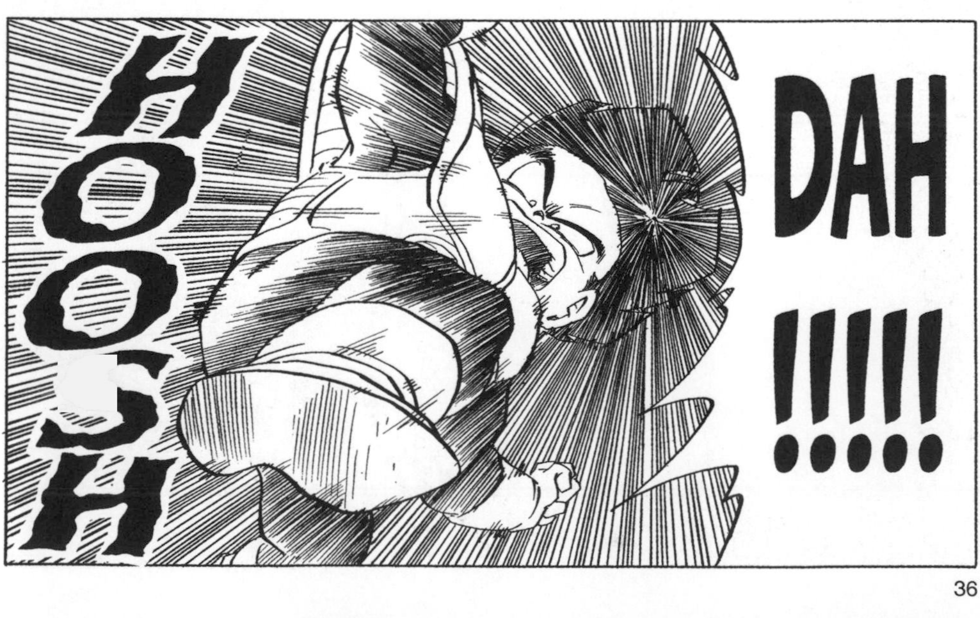
DAH !!!!!
HOOOSH

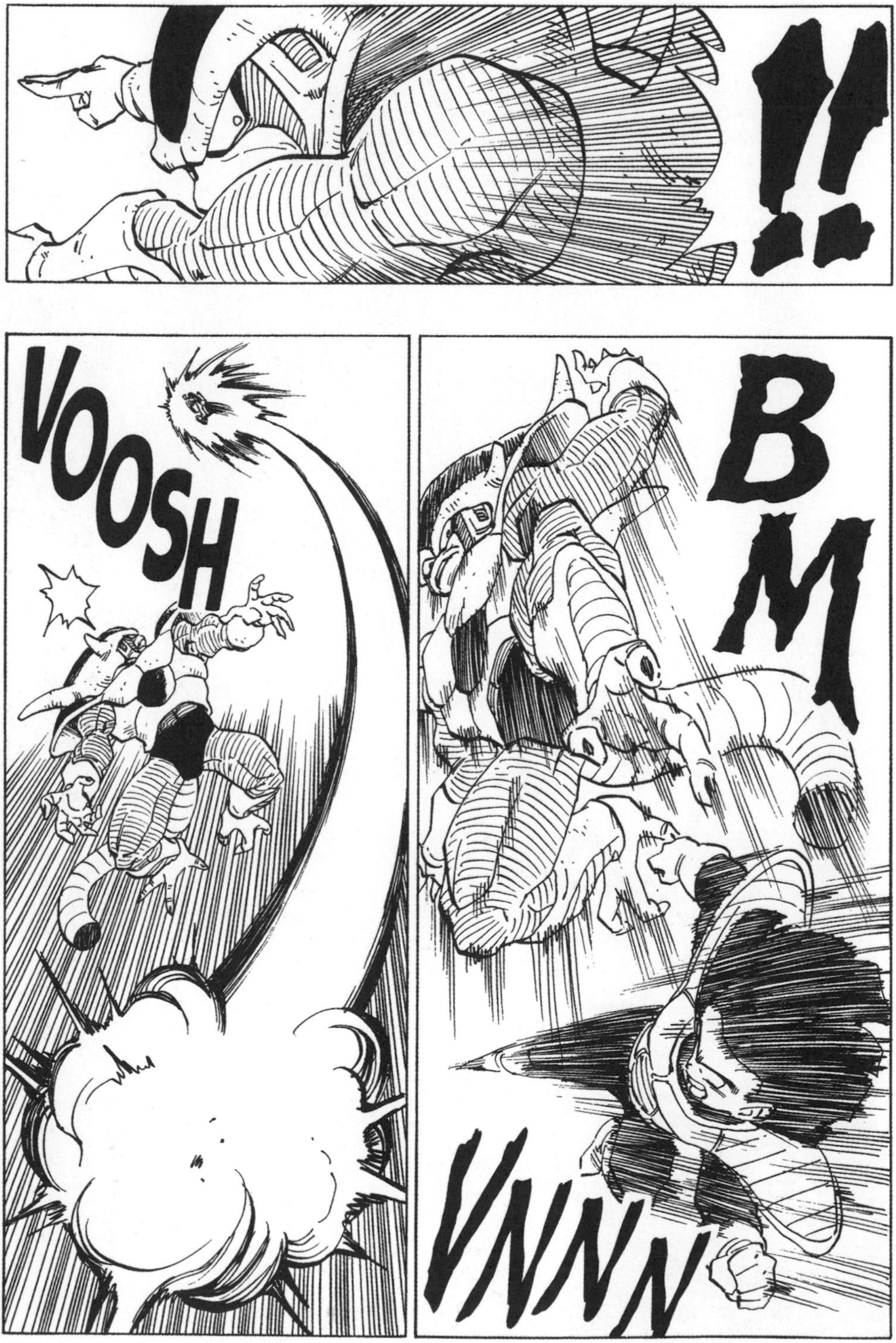
!!
BM
VOOSH
VNNN

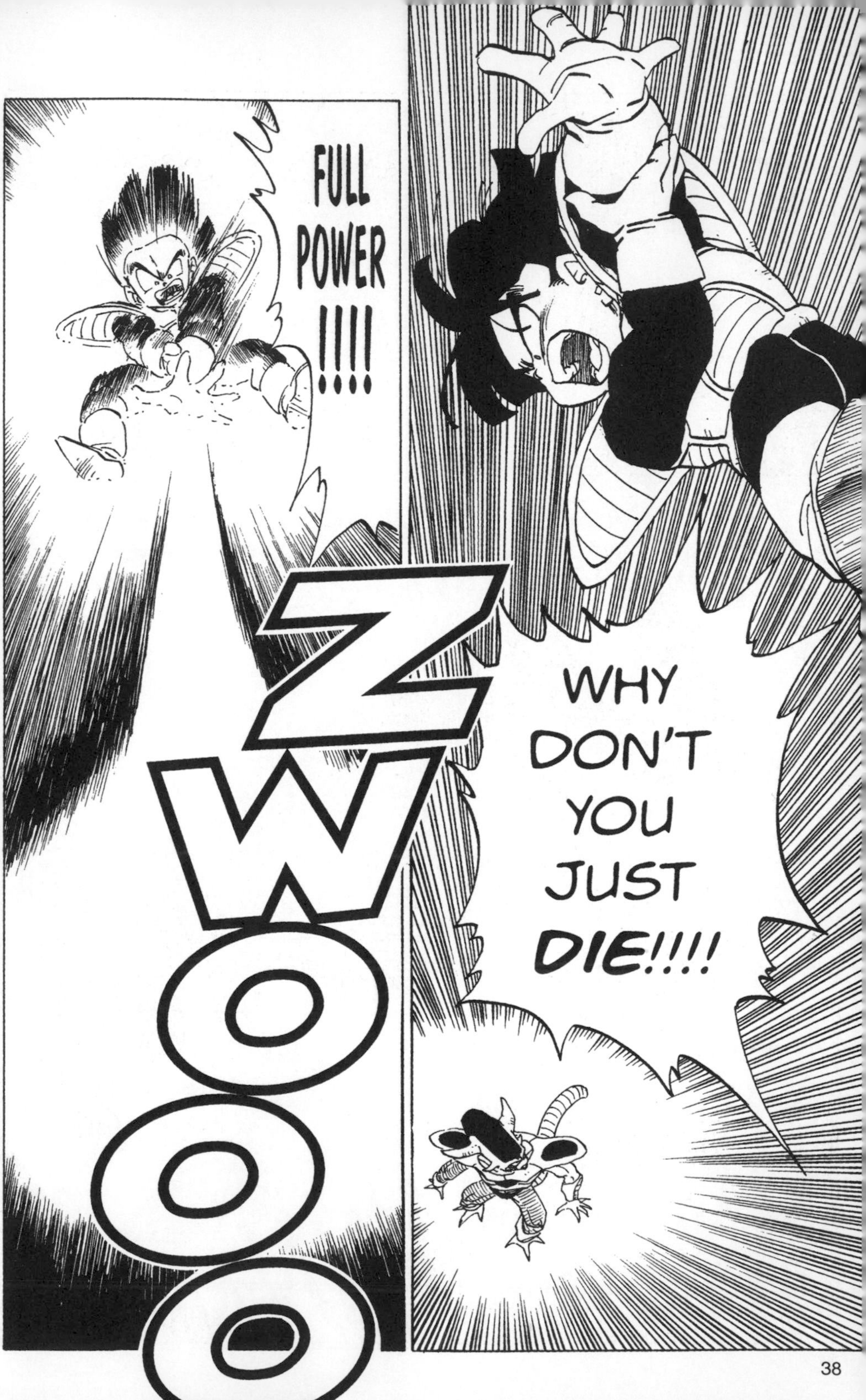

WHY DON'T YOU JUST DIE!!!!
FULL POWER !!!!
ZWOOOO

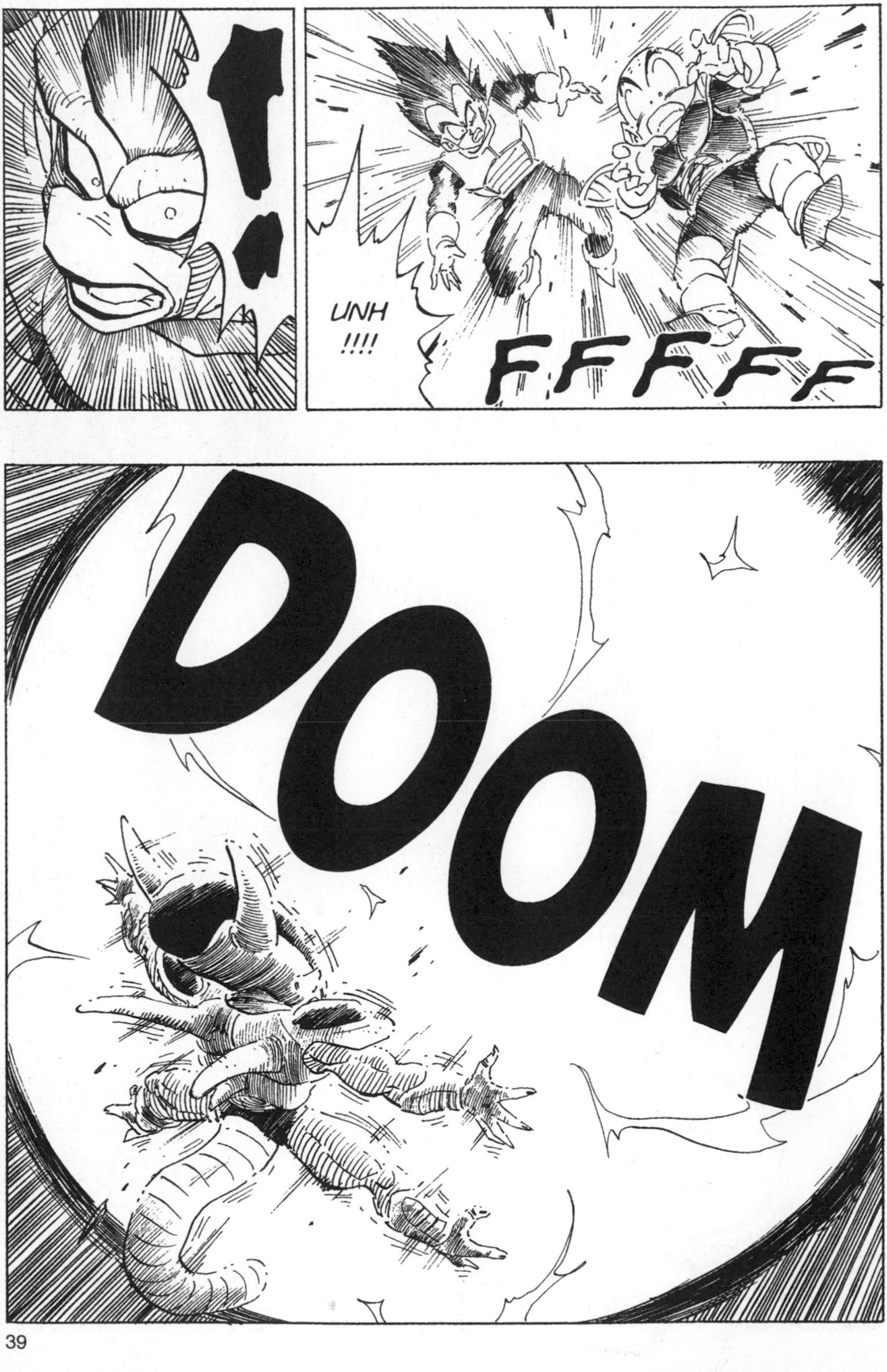
!!
UNH !!!!
FFFFFF
DOOM

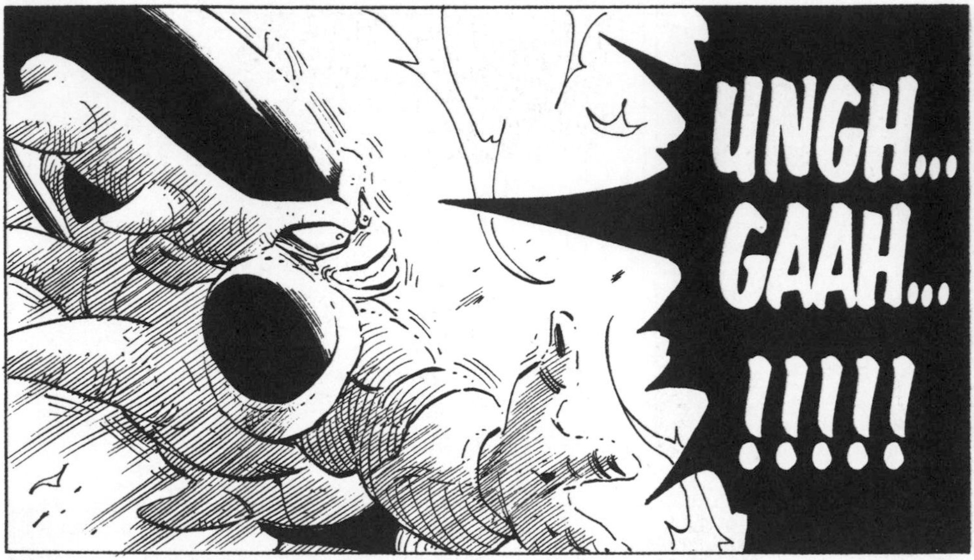
UNGH... GAAH... !!!!!!

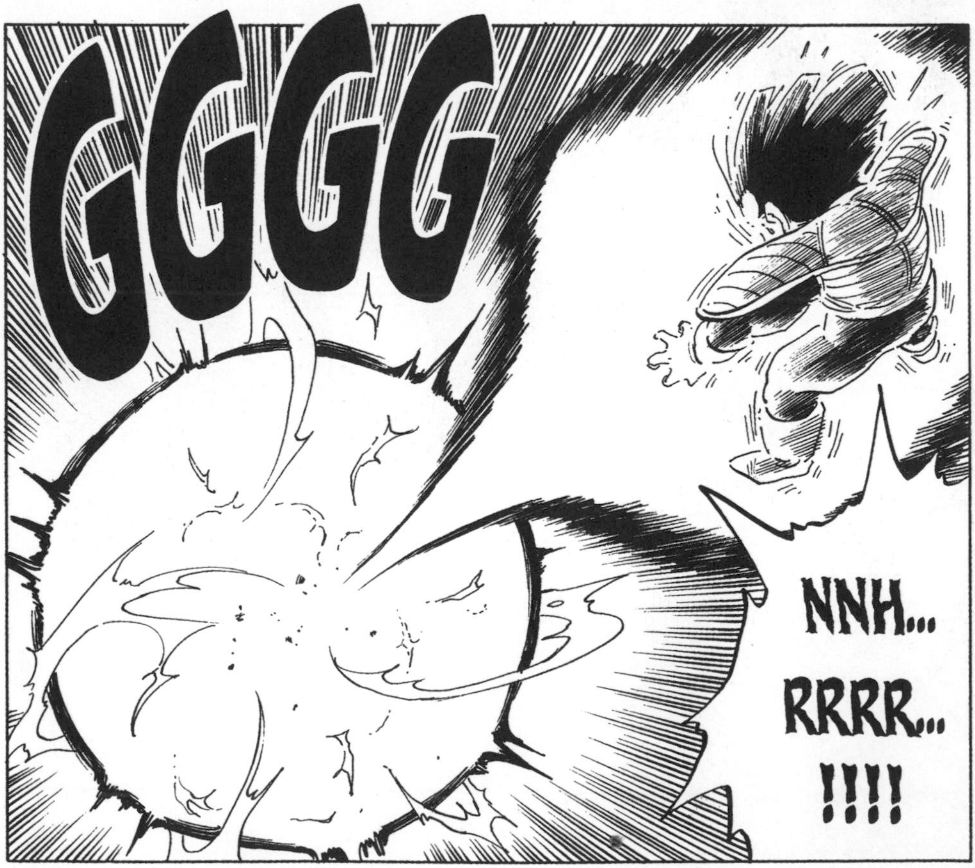
GGGG
NNH... RRRR... !!!!

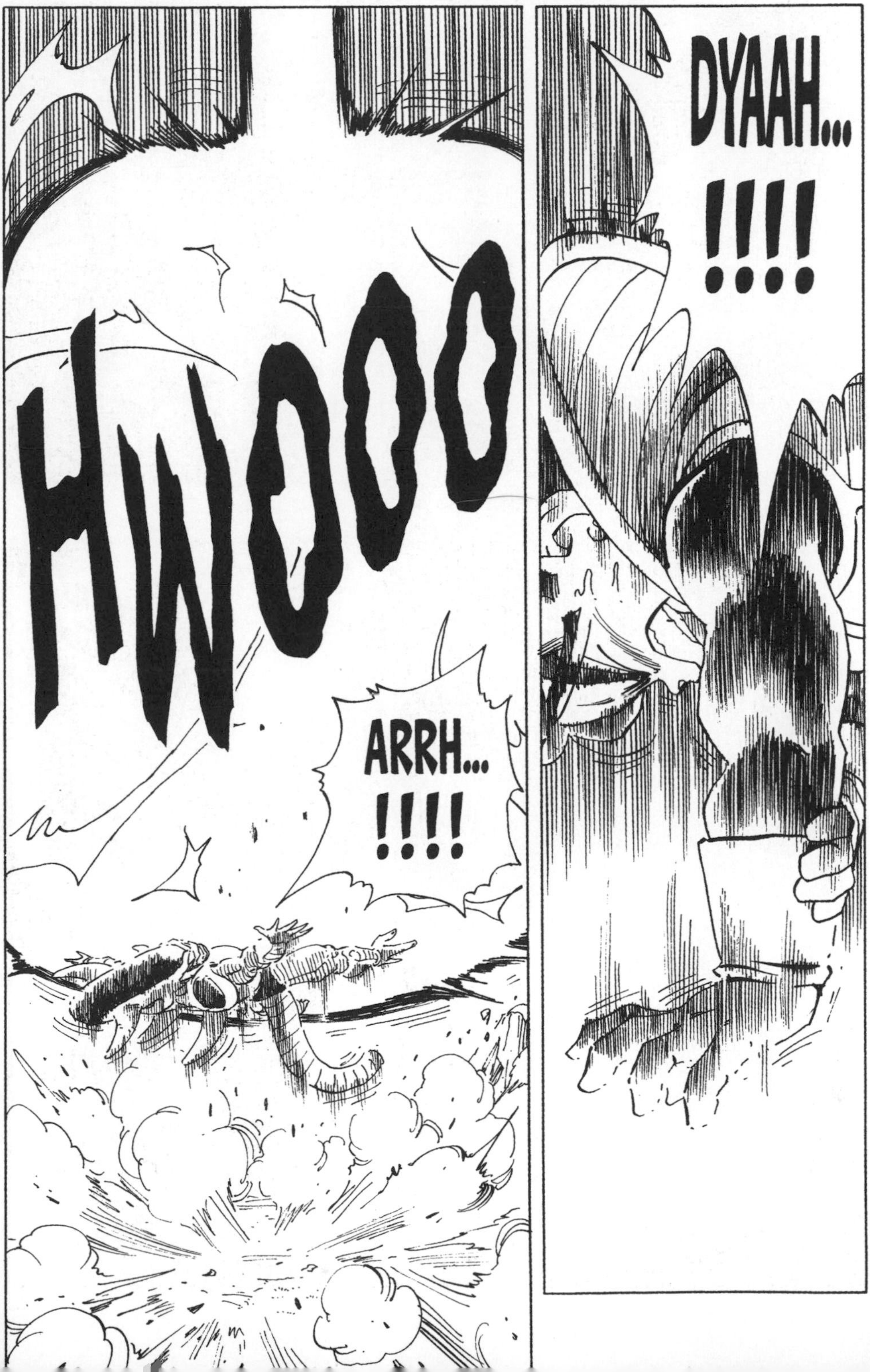
DYAAH...!!!!
HWOOO
ARRH...!!!!

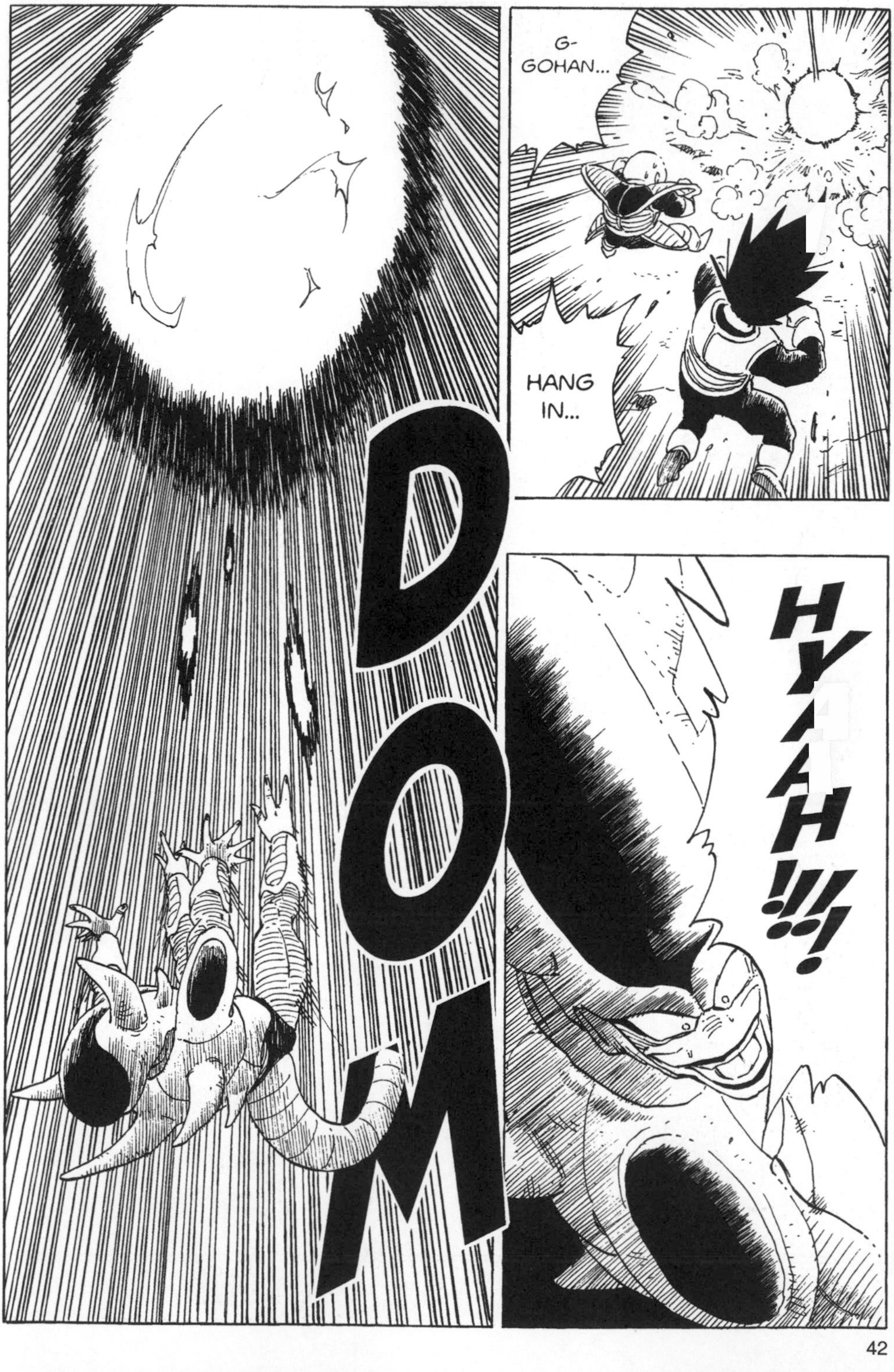
DOM
G-
GOHAN...
HANG
IN...
HYAAH!!!!

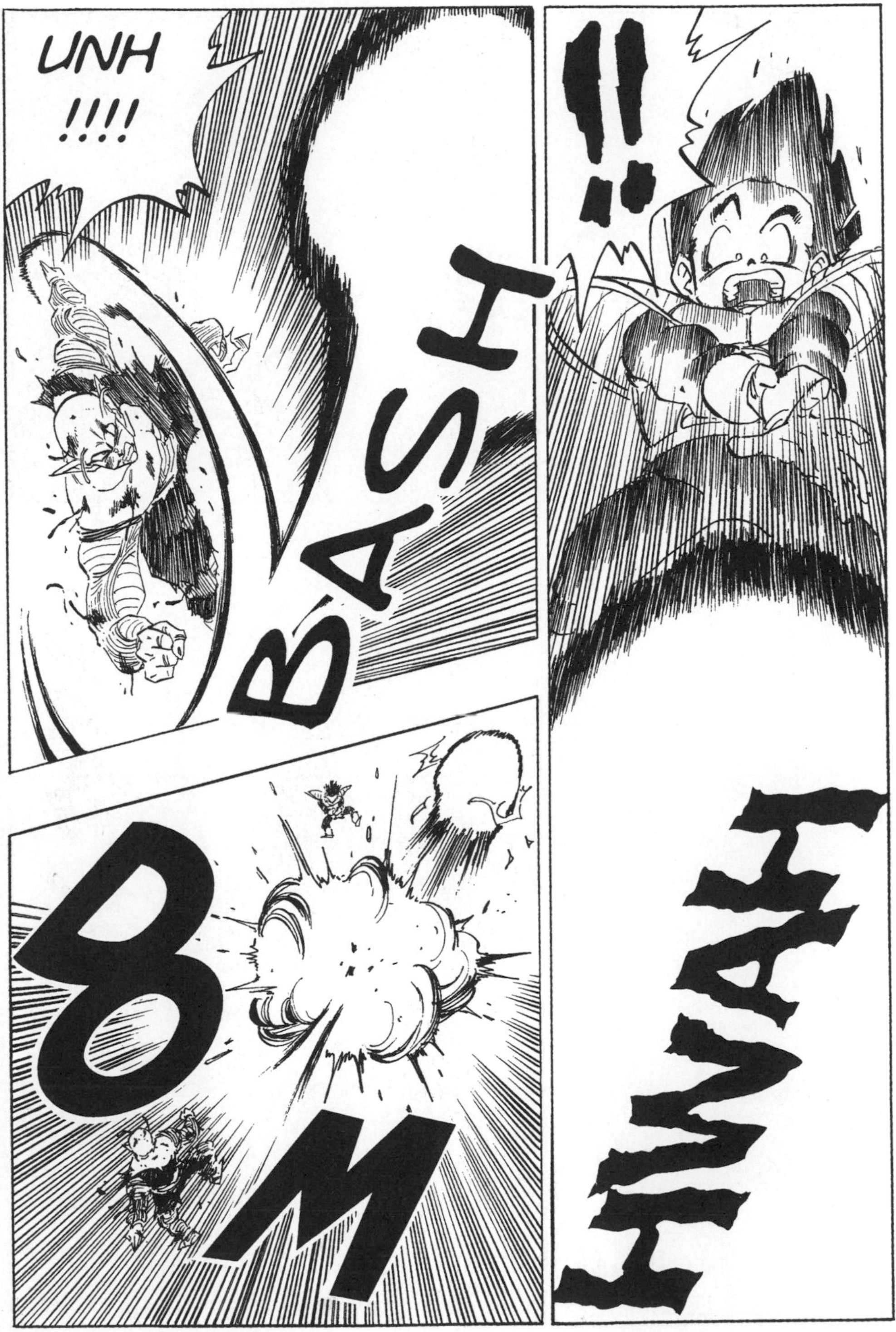
!!
HWAH
UNH !!!!
BASH
BOM

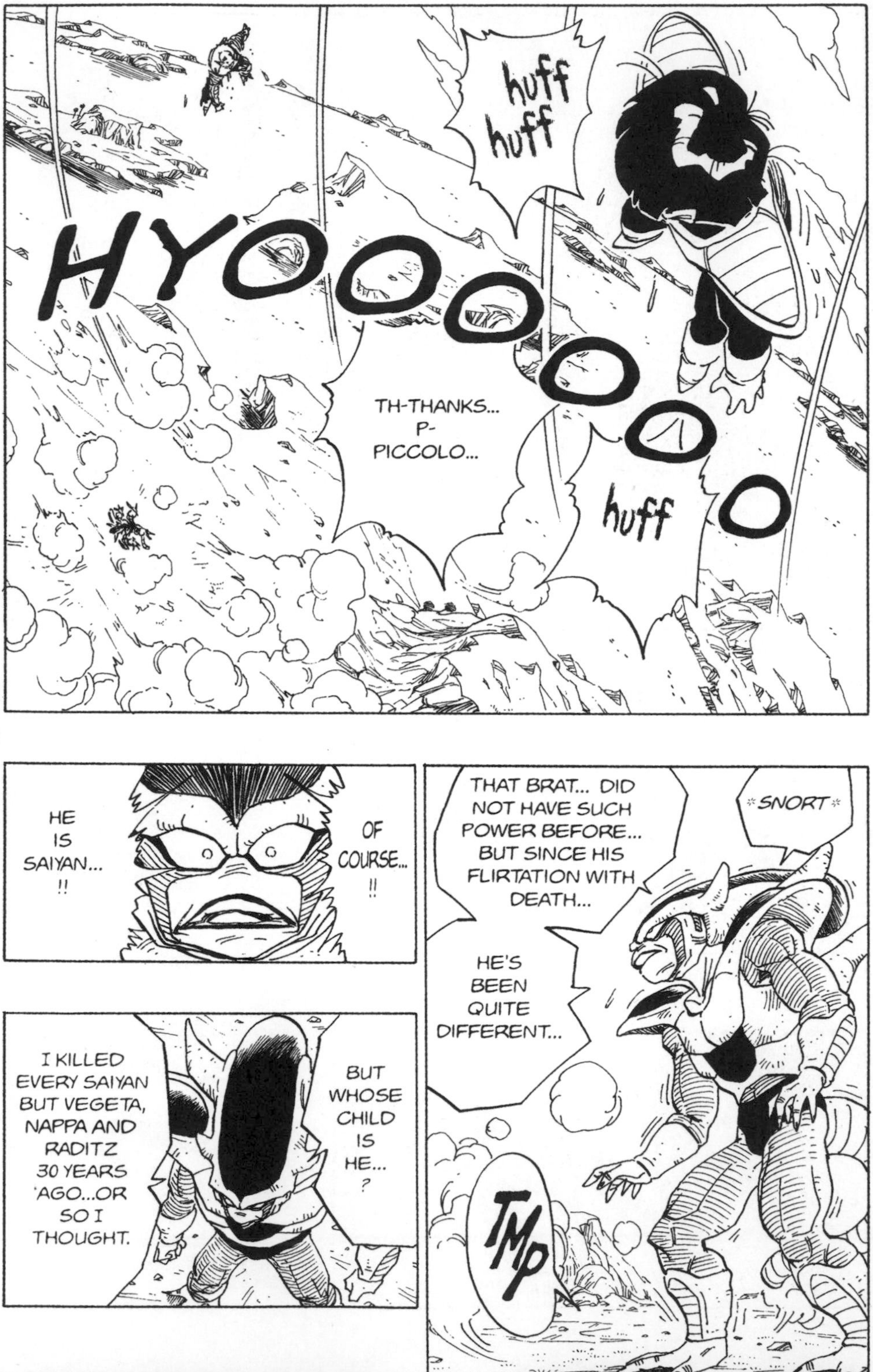
huff huff
HYOOOOOOOO
TH-THANKS... P-PICCOLO...
huff
HE IS SAIYAN... !!
OF COURSE... !!
I KILLED EVERY SAIYAN BUT VEGETA, NAPPA AND RADITZ 30 YEARS 'AGO...OR SO I THOUGHT.
BUT WHOSE CHILD IS HE... ?
THAT BRAT... DID NOT HAVE SUCH POWER BEFORE... BUT SINCE HIS FLIRTATION WITH DEATH...
HE'S BEEN QUITE DIFFERENT...
SNORT
TMP

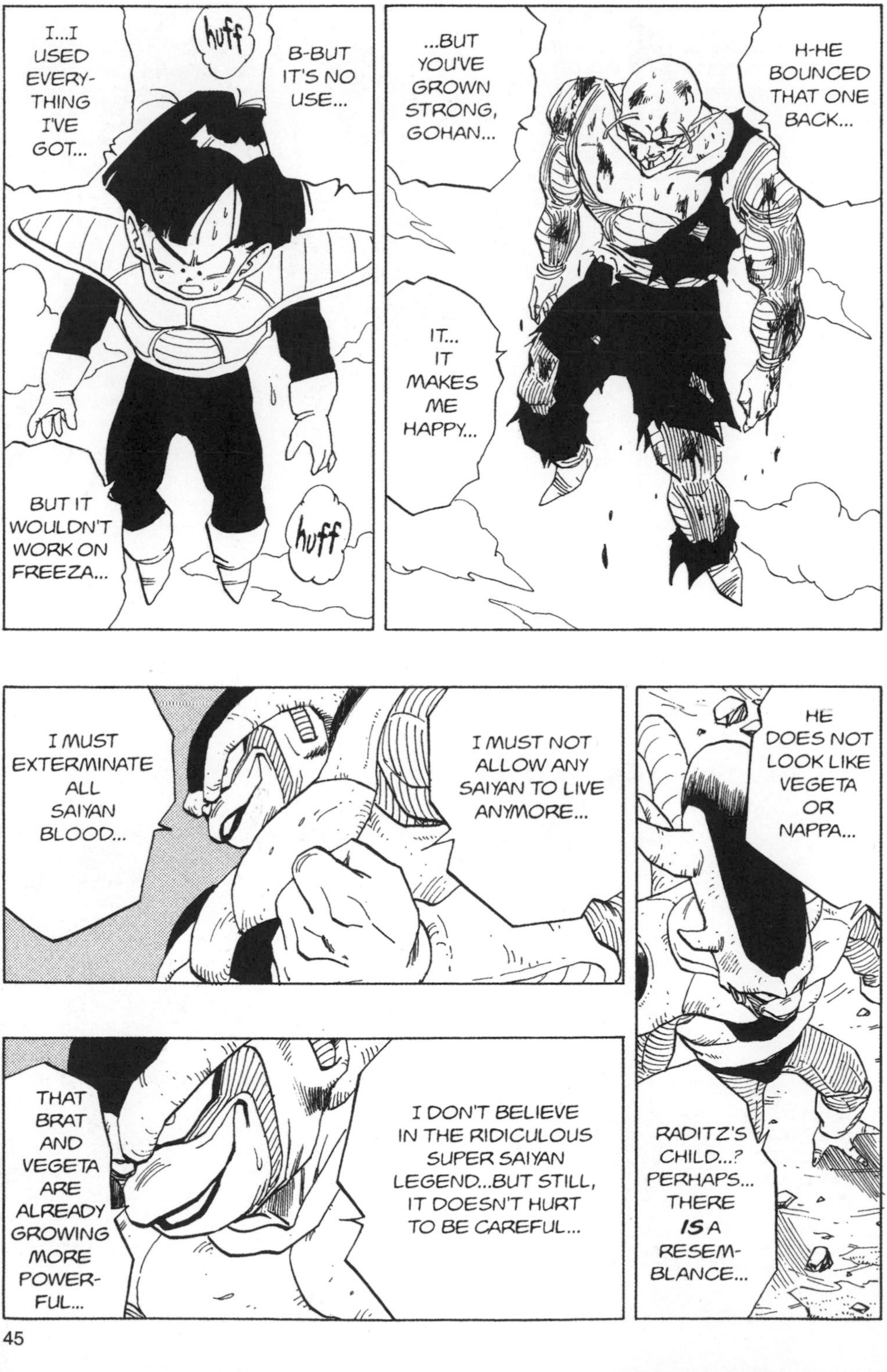

I...I USED EVERY-THING I'VE GOT...
huff
B-BUT IT'S NO USE...
BUT IT WOULDN'T WORK ON FREEZA...
huff
...BUT YOU'VE GROWN STRONG, GOHAN...
H-HE BOUNCED THAT ONE BACK...
IT... IT MAKES ME HAPPY...
I MUST EXTERMINATE ALL SAIYAN BLOOD...
I MUST NOT ALLOW ANY SAIYAN TO LIVE ANYMORE...
HE DOES NOT LOOK LIKE VEGETA OR NAPPA...
RADITZ'S CHILD...? PERHAPS... THERE *IS* A RESEM-BLANCE...
THAT BRAT AND VEGETA ARE ALREADY GROWING MORE POWER-FUL...
I DON'T BELIEVE IN THE RIDICULOUS SUPER SAIYAN LEGEND...BUT STILL, IT DOESN'T HURT TO BE CAREFUL...

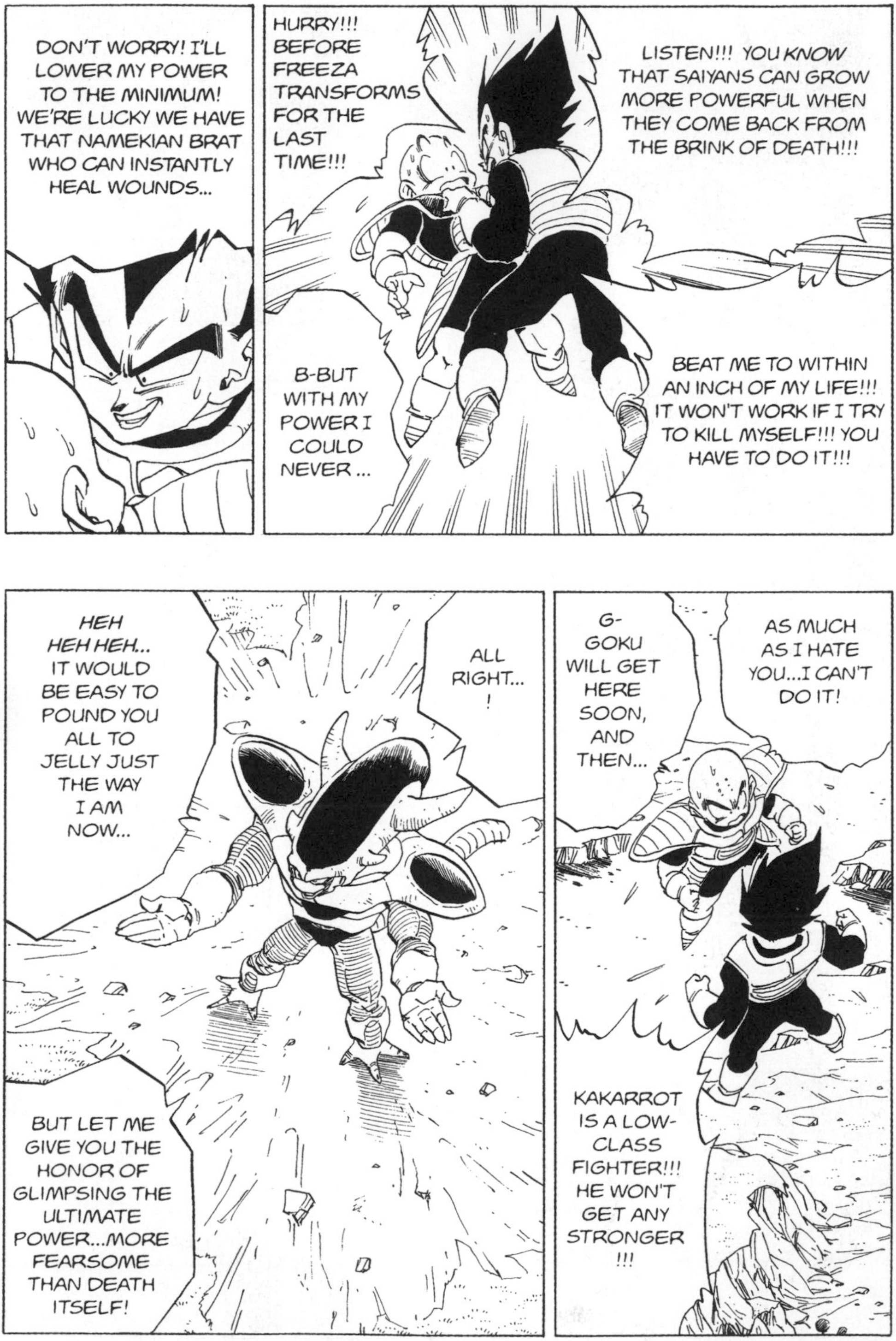
DON'T WORRY! I'LL LOWER MY POWER TO THE MINIMUM! WE'RE LUCKY WE HAVE THAT NAMEKIAN BRAT WHO CAN INSTANTLY HEAL WOUNDS...
HURRY!!! BEFORE FREEZA TRANSFORMS FOR THE LAST TIME!!!
LISTEN!!! YOU KNOW THAT SAIYANS CAN GROW MORE POWERFUL WHEN THEY COME BACK FROM THE BRINK OF DEATH!!!
B-BUT WITH MY POWER I COULD NEVER...
BEAT ME TO WITHIN AN INCH OF MY LIFE!!! IT WON'T WORK IF I TRY TO KILL MYSELF!!! YOU HAVE TO DO IT!!!
HEH HEH HEH... IT WOULD BE EASY TO POUND YOU ALL TO JELLY JUST THE WAY I AM NOW...
ALL RIGHT... !
BUT LET ME GIVE YOU THE HONOR OF GLIMPSING THE ULTIMATE POWER...MORE FEARSOME THAN DEATH ITSELF!
AS MUCH AS I HATE YOU...I CAN'T DO IT!
G-GOKU WILL GET HERE SOON, AND THEN...
KAKARROT IS A LOW-CLASS FIGHTER!!! HE WON'T GET ANY STRONGER !!!

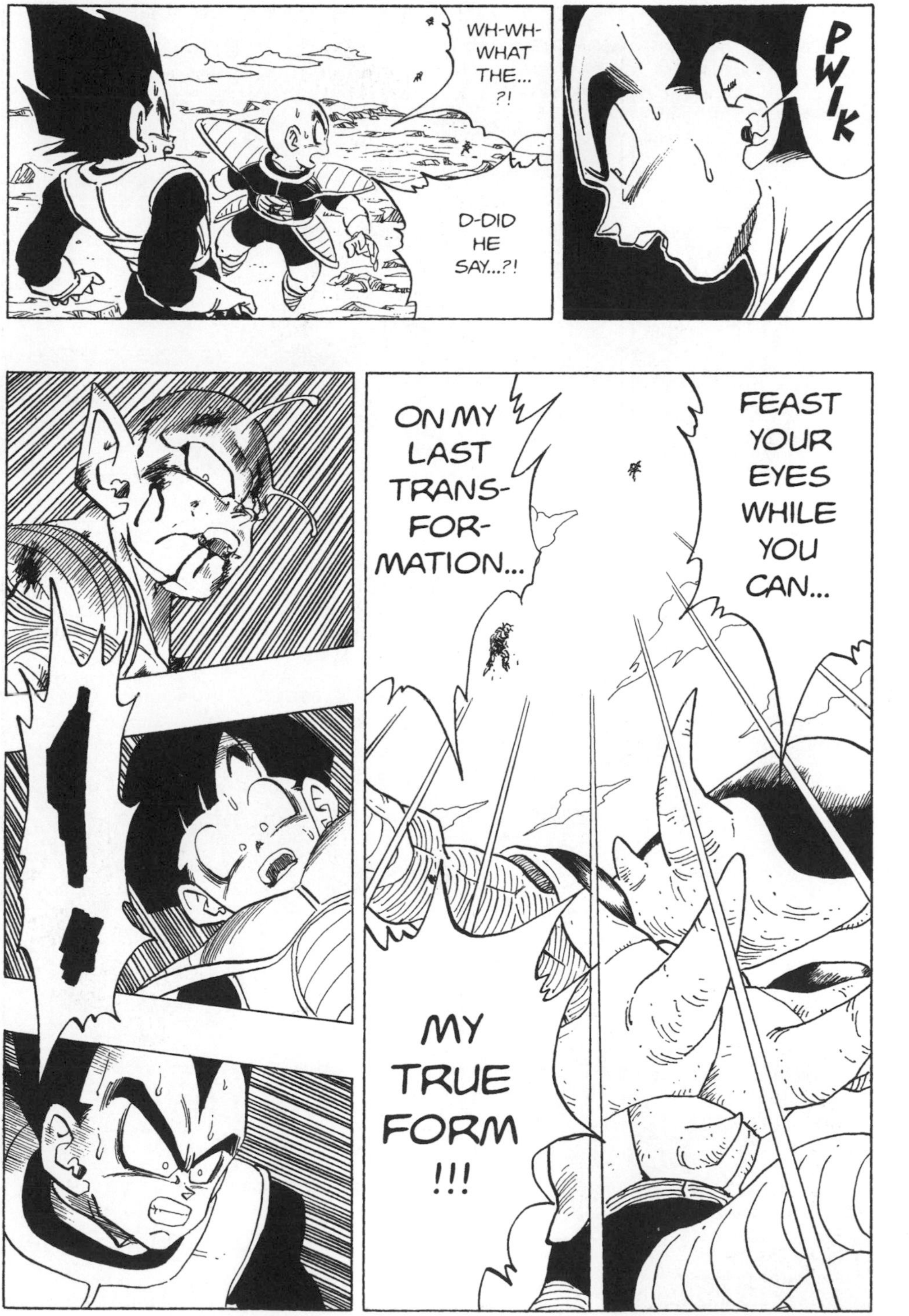
WH-WH-WHAT THE... ?!
D-DID HE SAY...?!
PWIK
FEAST YOUR EYES WHILE YOU CAN...
ON MY LAST TRANS-FOR-MATION...
MY TRUE FORM !!!

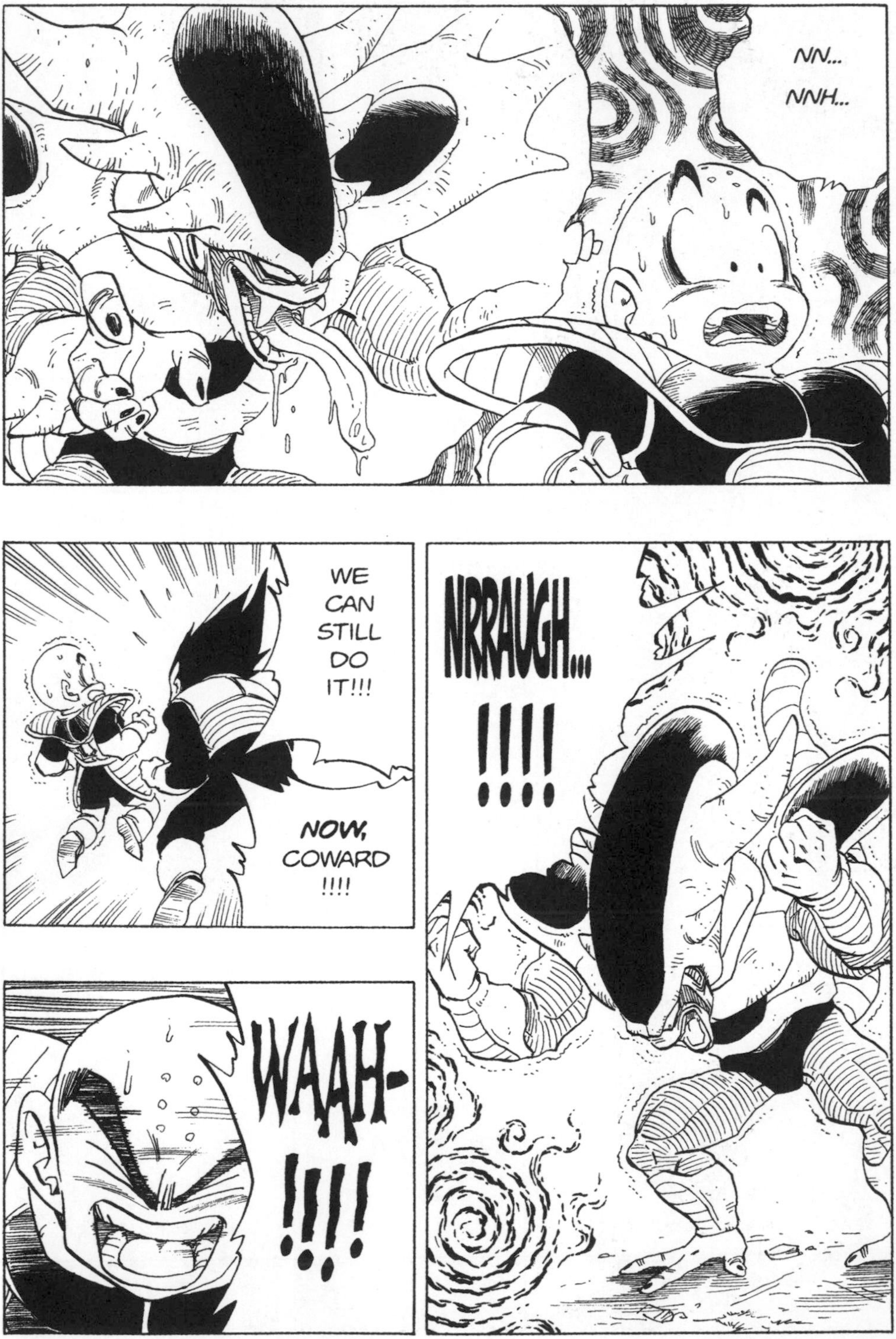
NN...
NNH...
NRRAUGH...!!!!
WE CAN STILL DO IT!!!
NOW, COWARD!!!!
WAAH-!!!!

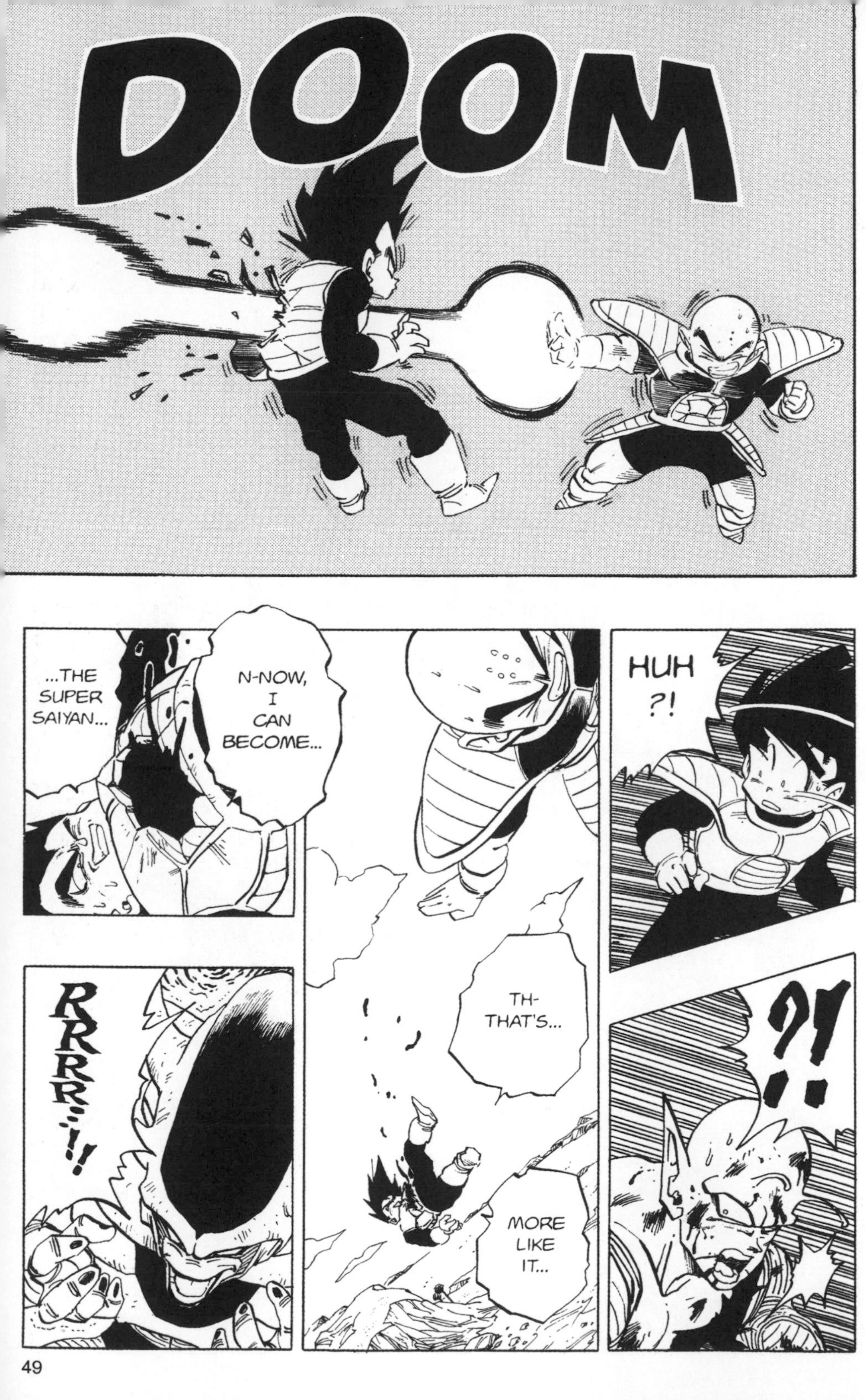
DOOM
N-NOW, I CAN BECOME...
...THE SUPER SAIYAN...
HUH ?!
RRRR...!!
TH- THAT'S...
MORE LIKE IT...
?!!

DBZ:110 • The Final Transformation

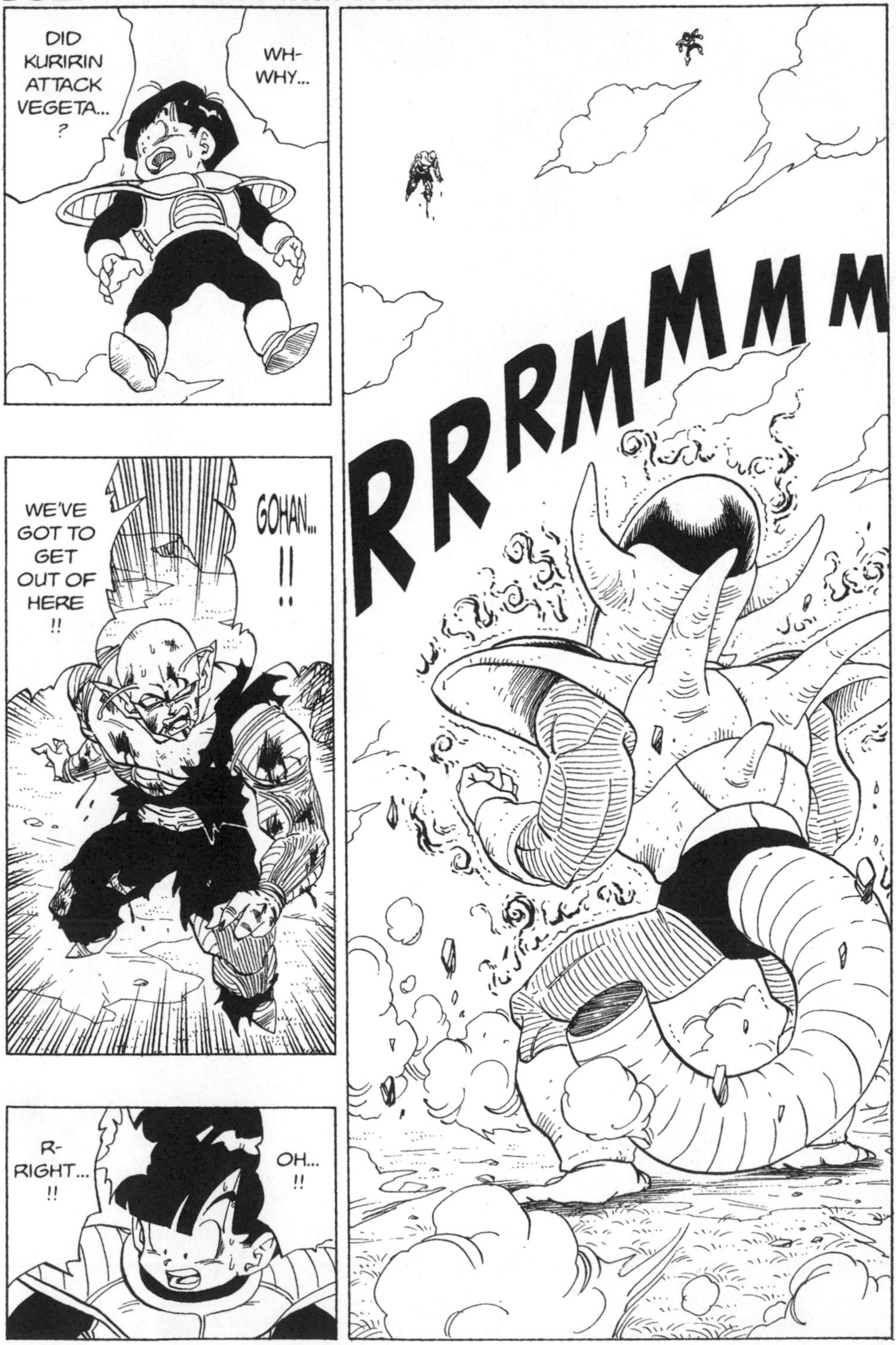
DID KURIRIN ATTACK VEGETA... ?
WH- WHY...
RRRMMMMM
WE'VE GOT TO GET OUT OF HERE !!
GOHAN... !!
R- RIGHT... !!
OH... !!

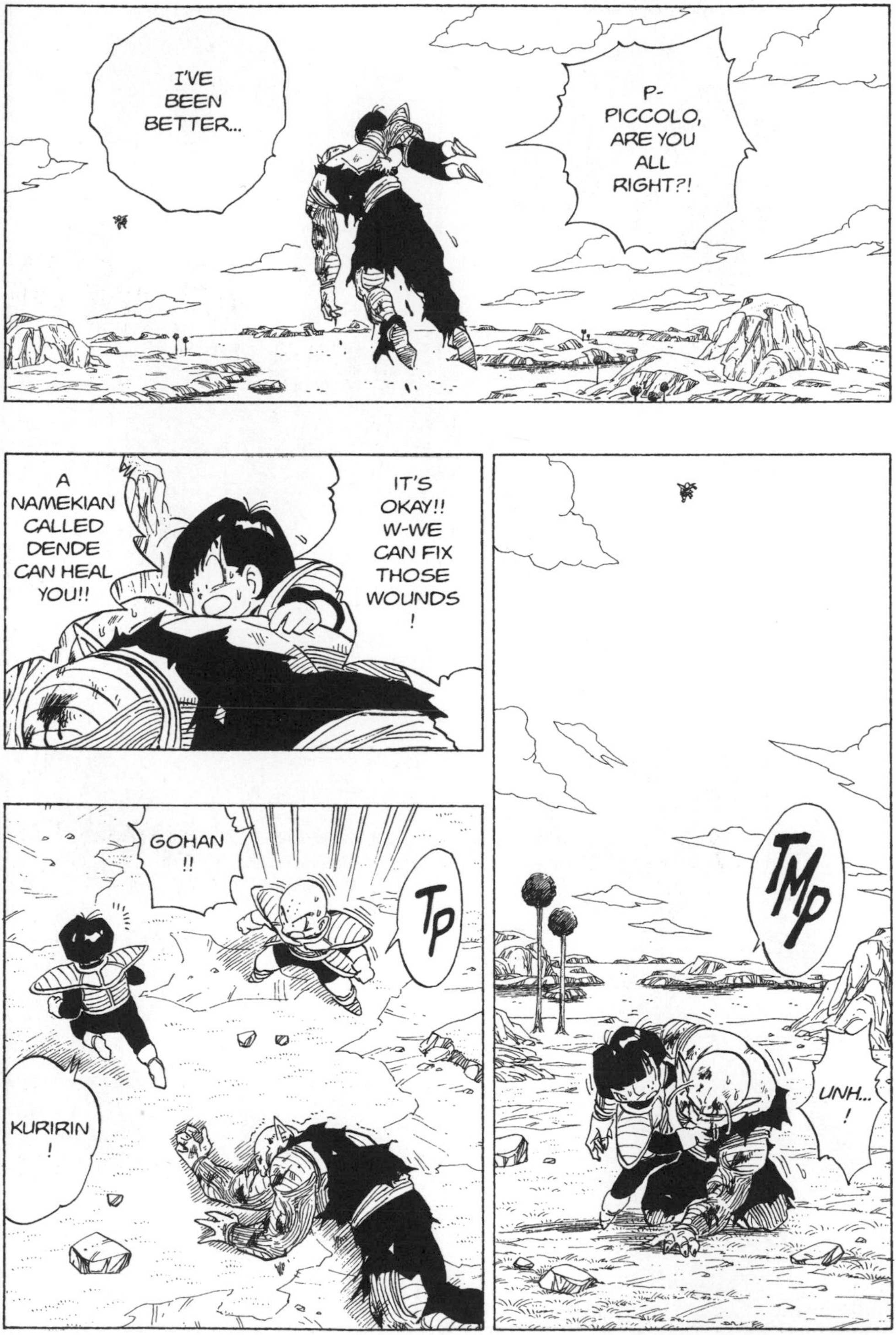
P-PICCOLO, ARE YOU ALL RIGHT?!
I'VE BEEN BETTER...
TMP
UNH...!
IT'S OKAY!! W-WE CAN FIX THOSE WOUNDS!
A NAMEKIAN CALLED DENDE CAN HEAL YOU!!
TP
GOHAN!!
KURIRIN!

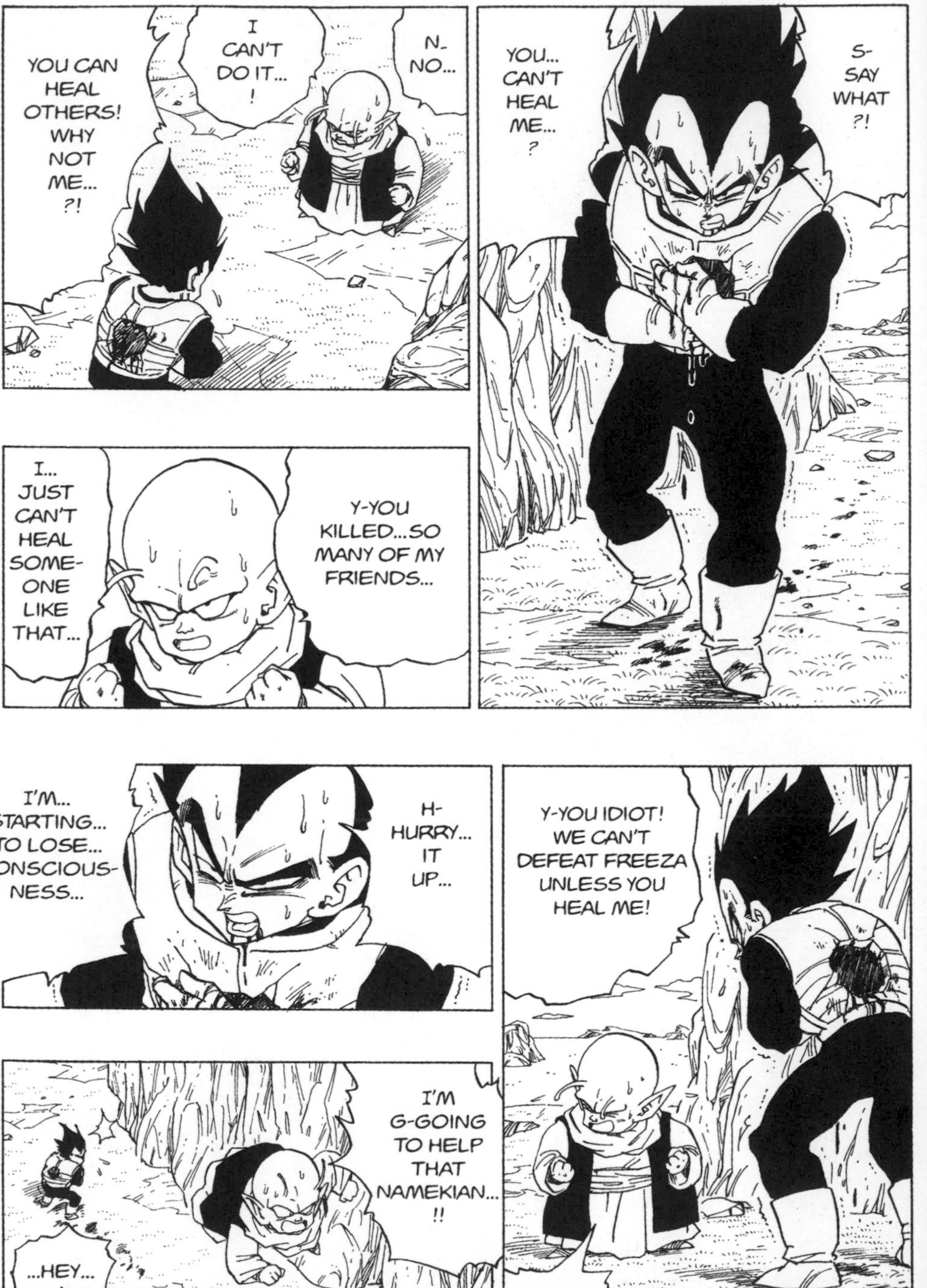
YOU CAN HEAL OTHERS! WHY NOT ME...?!
I CAN'T DO IT...!
N-NO...
YOU... CAN'T HEAL ME...?
S-SAY WHAT?!
I... JUST CAN'T HEAL SOME-ONE LIKE THAT...
Y-YOU KILLED...SO MANY OF MY FRIENDS...
I'M... STARTING... TO LOSE... CONSCIOUS-NESS...
H-HURRY... IT UP...
Y-YOU IDIOT! WE CAN'T DEFEAT FREEZA UNLESS YOU HEAL ME!
I CAN'T! I WON'T!!
I'M G-GOING TO HELP THAT NAMEKIAN...!!
...HEY...!

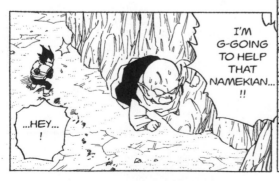

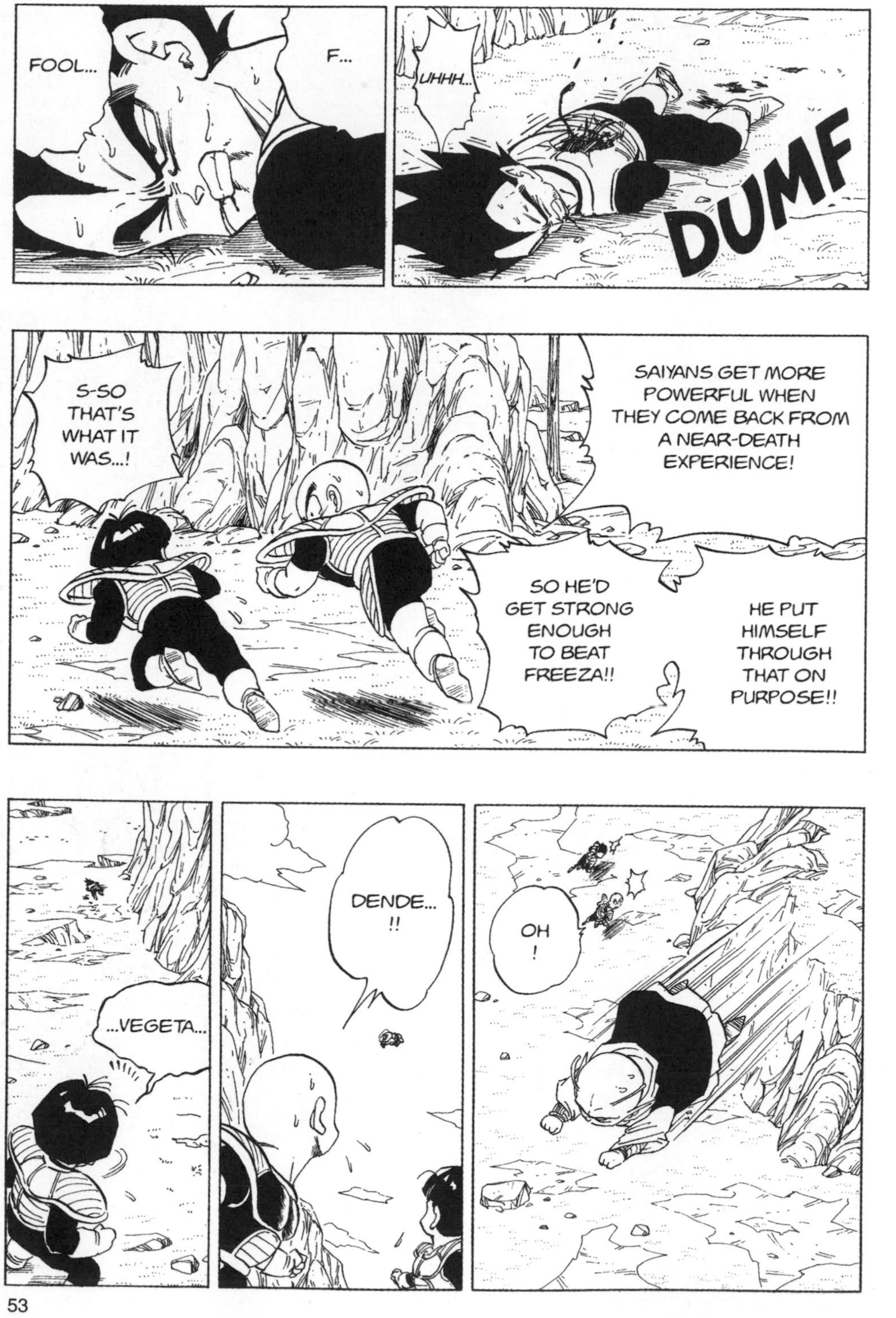
FOOL...
F...
UHHH...
DUMF
S-SO THAT'S WHAT IT WAS...!
SAIYANS GET MORE POWERFUL WHEN THEY COME BACK FROM A NEAR-DEATH EXPERIENCE!
SO HE'D GET STRONG ENOUGH TO BEAT FREEZA!!
HE PUT HIMSELF THROUGH THAT ON PURPOSE!!
...VEGETA...
DENDE... !!
OH !

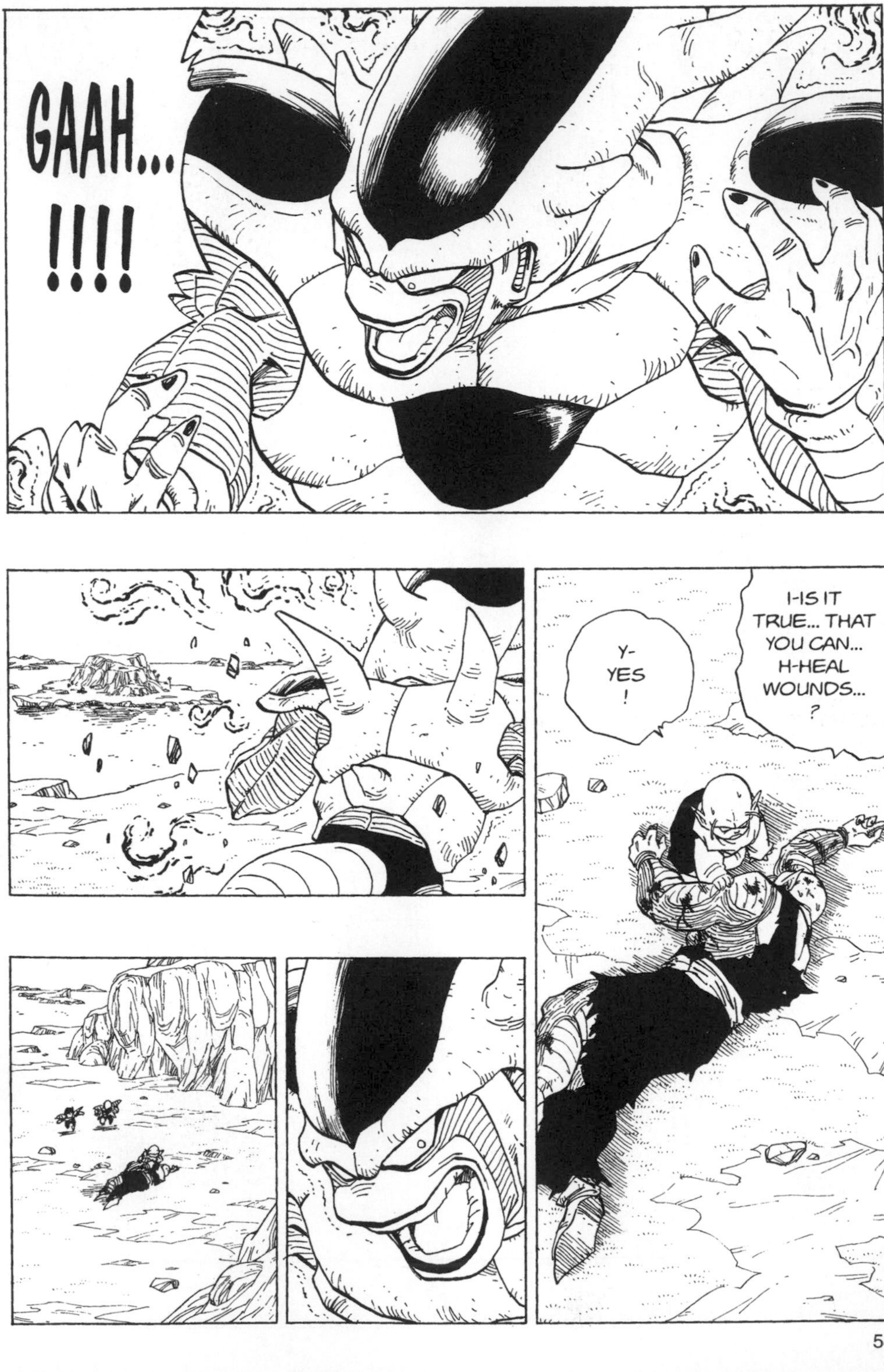
GAAH... !!!!
I-IS IT TRUE... THAT YOU CAN... H-HEAL WOUNDS...?
Y-YES!

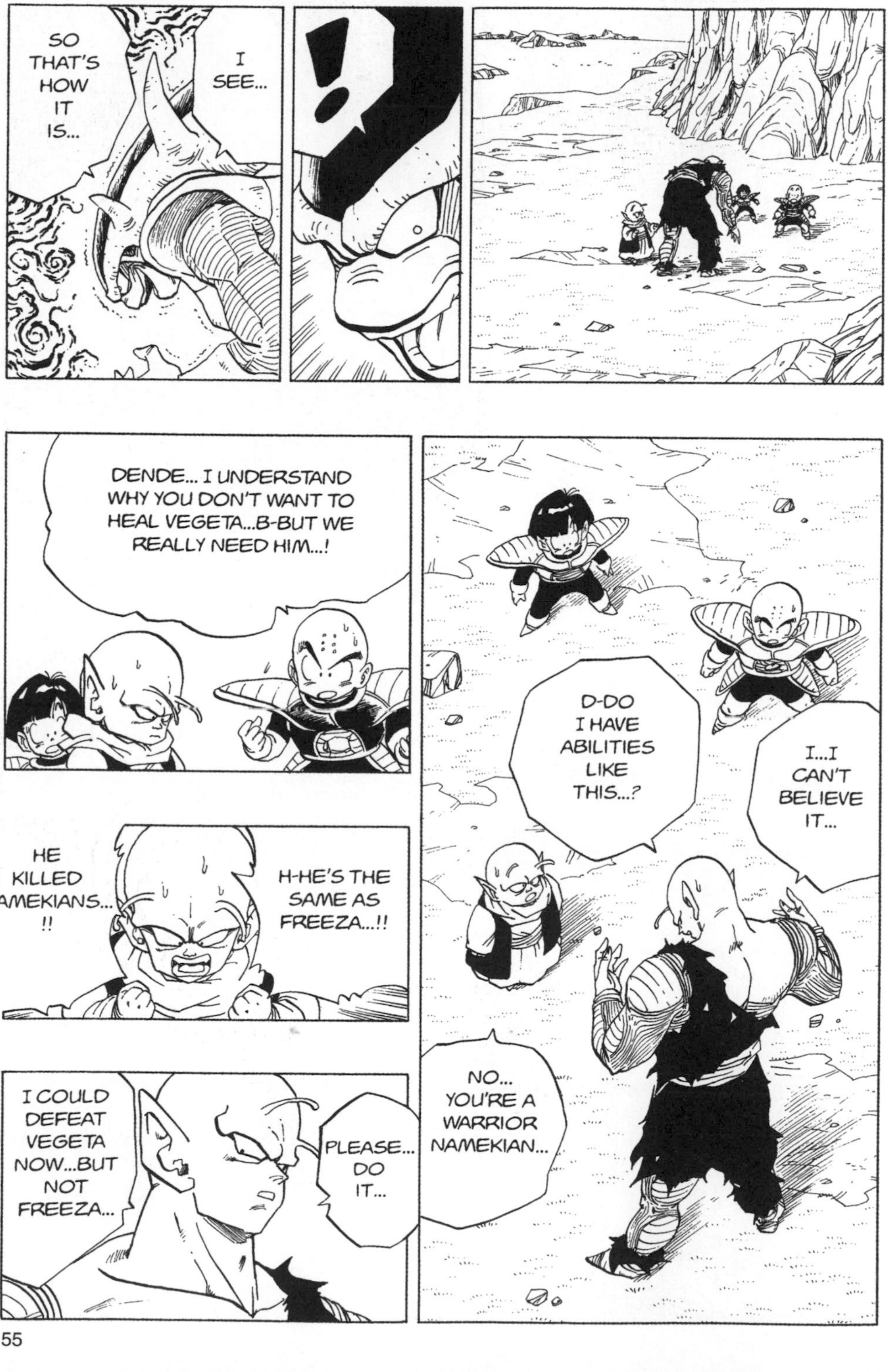
I SEE...
SO THAT'S HOW IT IS...
I...I CAN'T BELIEVE IT...
D-DO I HAVE ABILITIES LIKE THIS...?
NO... YOU'RE A WARRIOR NAMEKIAN...
DENDE... I UNDERSTAND WHY YOU DON'T WANT TO HEAL VEGETA...B-BUT WE REALLY NEED HIM...!
H-HE'S THE SAME AS FREEZA...!!
HE KILLED NAMEKIANS...!!
PLEASE... DO IT...
I COULD DEFEAT VEGETA NOW...BUT NOT FREEZA...

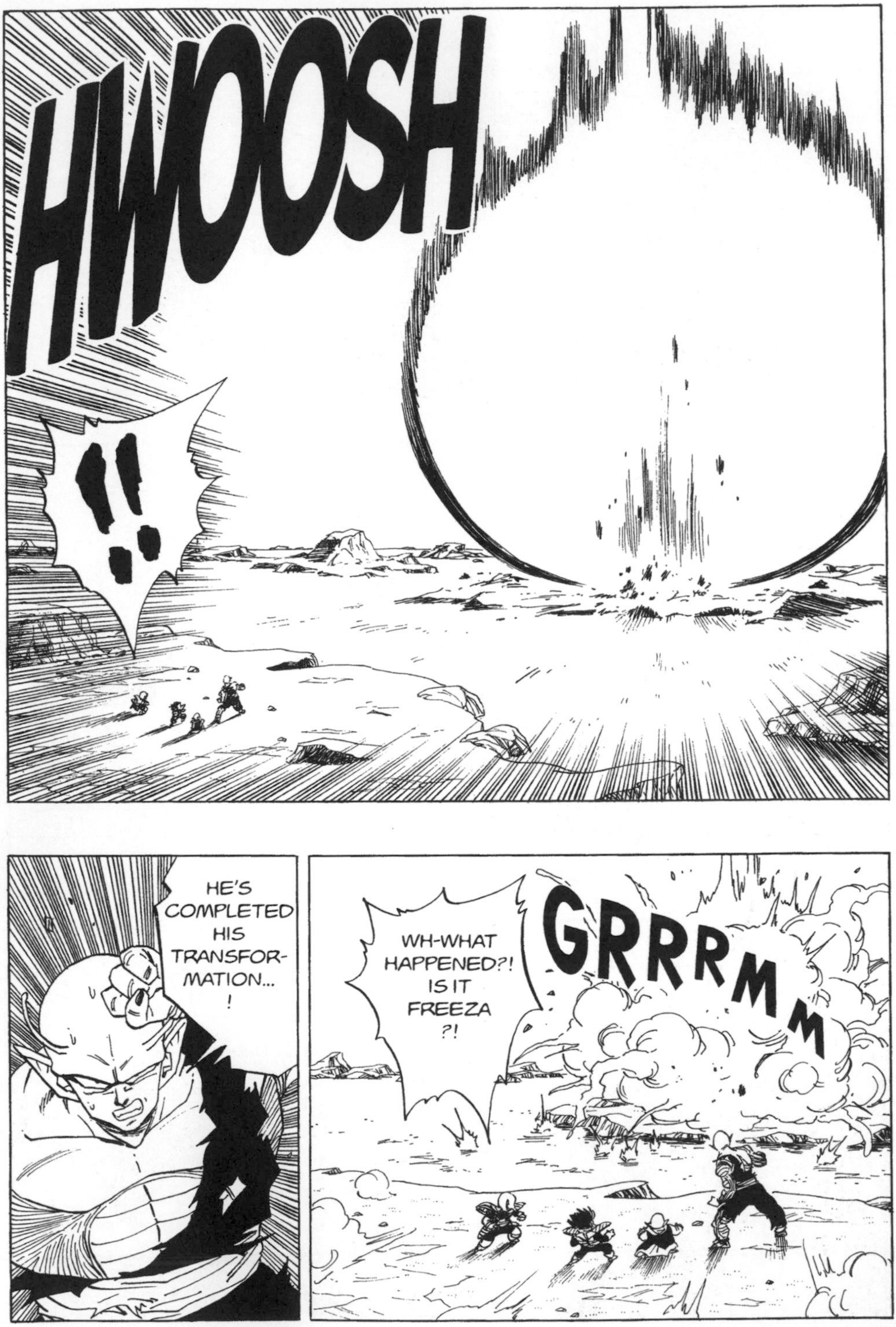
HWOOSH
!!
HE'S COMPLETED HIS TRANSFORMATION... !
WH-WHAT HAPPENED?! IS IT FREEZA ?!
GRRRMMM

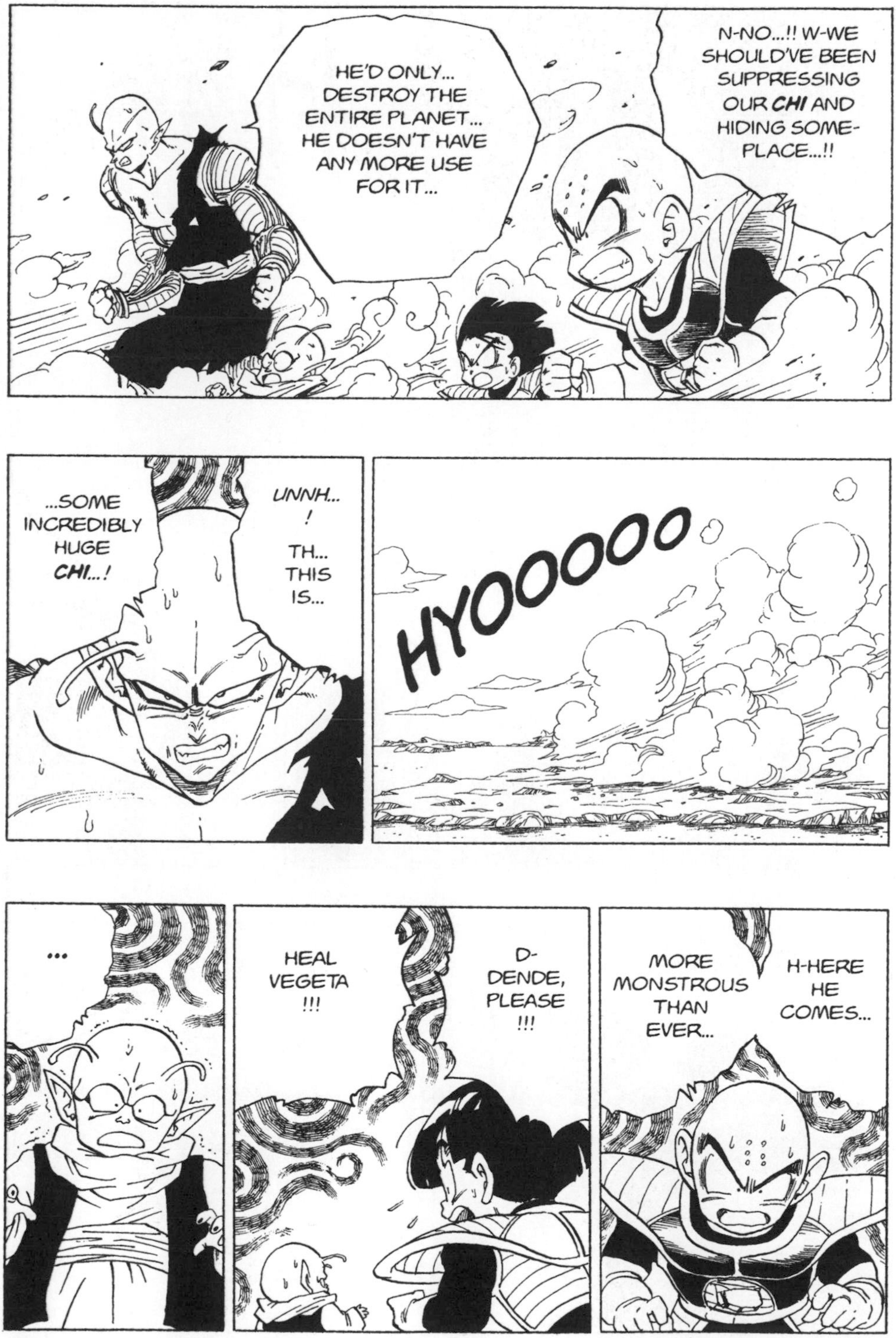

N-NO...!! W-WE SHOULD'VE BEEN SUPPRESSING OUR **CHI** AND HIDING SOME-PLACE...!!
HE'D ONLY... DESTROY THE ENTIRE PLANET... HE DOESN'T HAVE ANY MORE USE FOR IT...
HYOOOOOO
UNNH... !
TH... THIS IS...
...SOME INCREDIBLY HUGE **CHI**...!
H-HERE HE COMES...
MORE MONSTROUS THAN EVER...
D-DENDE, PLEASE !!!
HEAL VEGETA !!!
...

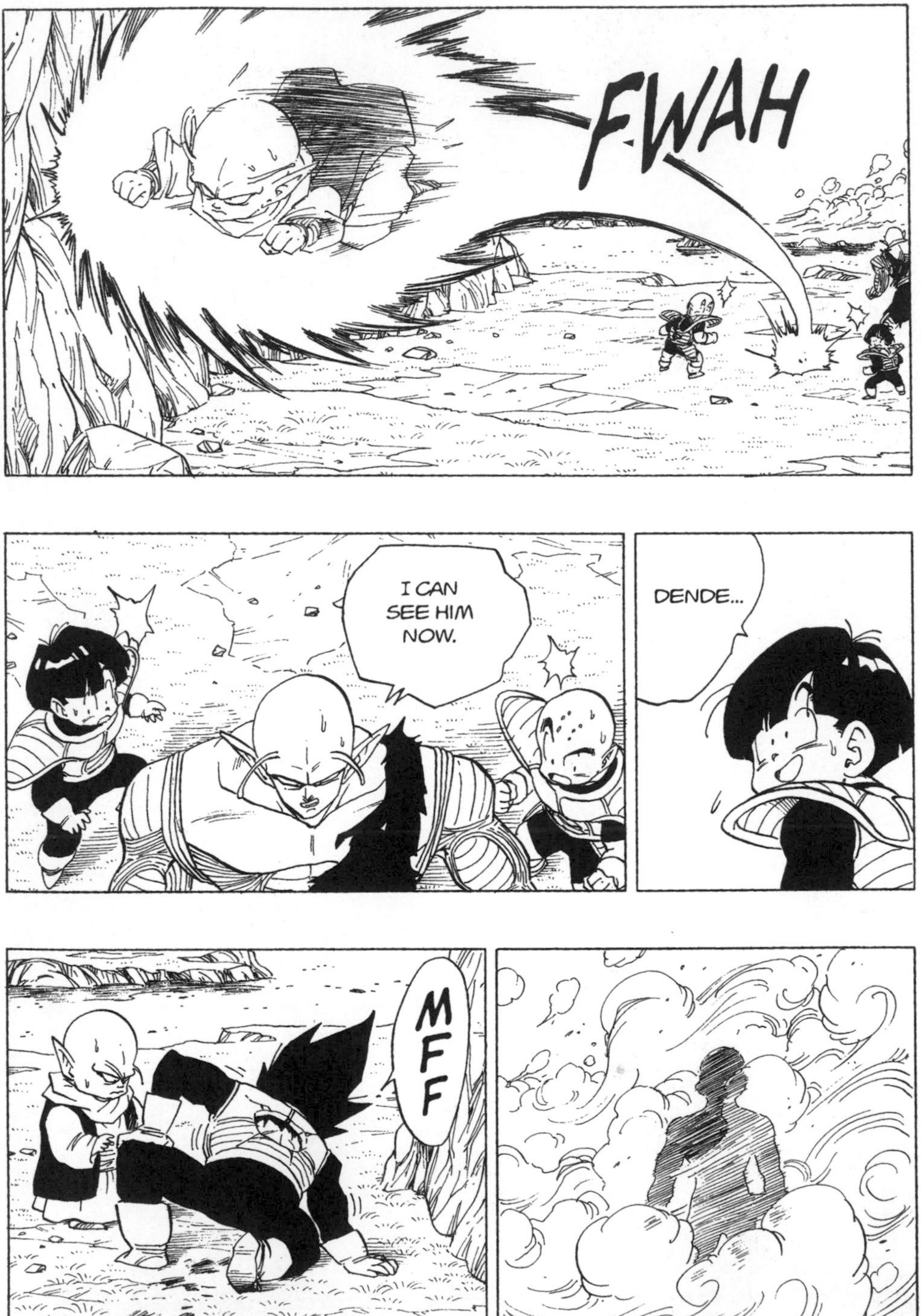
FWAH
I CAN SEE HIM NOW.
DENDE...
MFF

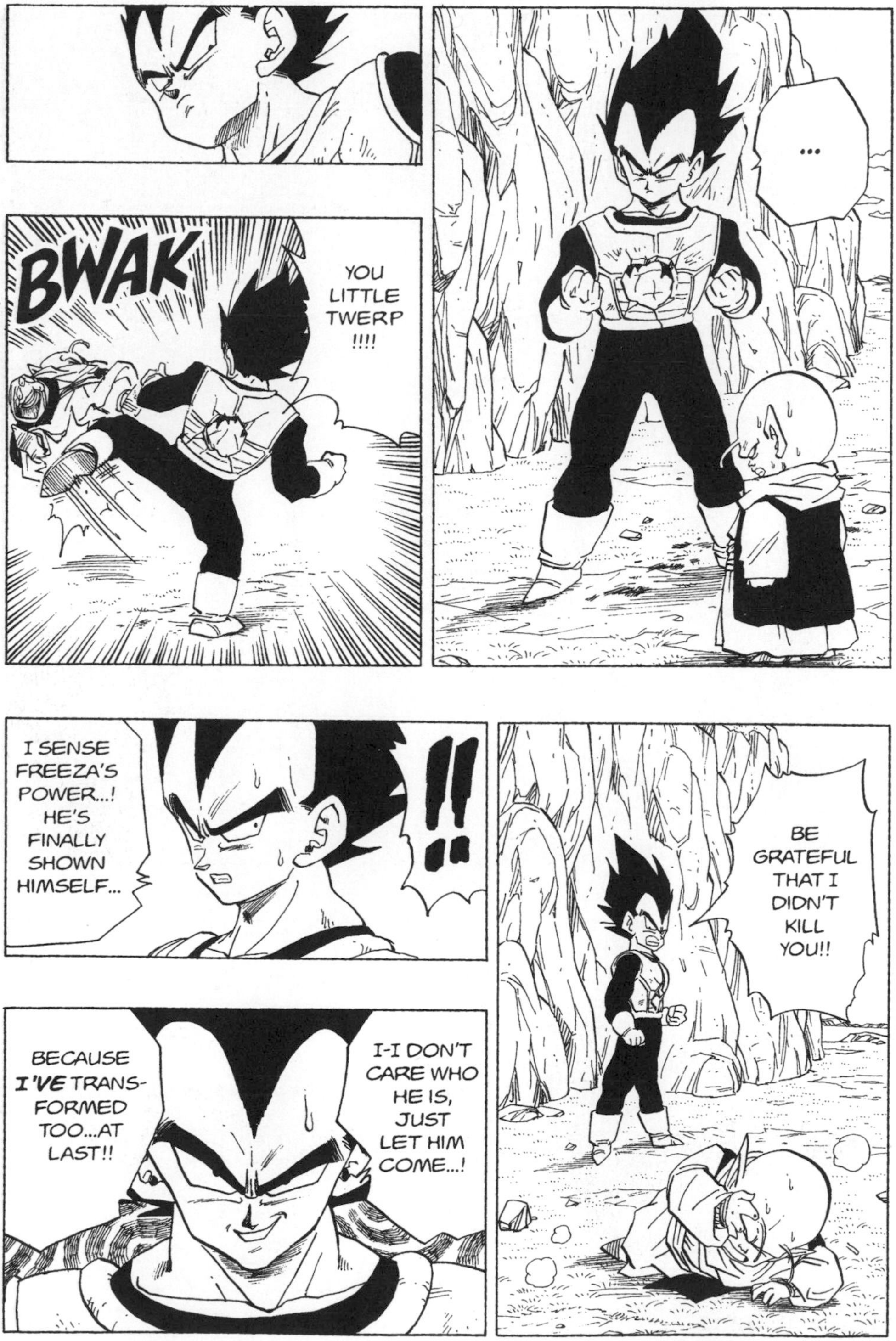
...
BWAK
YOU LITTLE TWERP !!!!
BE GRATEFUL THAT I DIDN'T KILL YOU!!
I SENSE FREEZA'S POWER...! HE'S FINALLY SHOWN HIMSELF...
!!
I-I DON'T CARE WHO HE IS, JUST LET HIM COME...!
BECAUSE ***I'VE*** TRANS-FORMED TOO...AT LAST!!

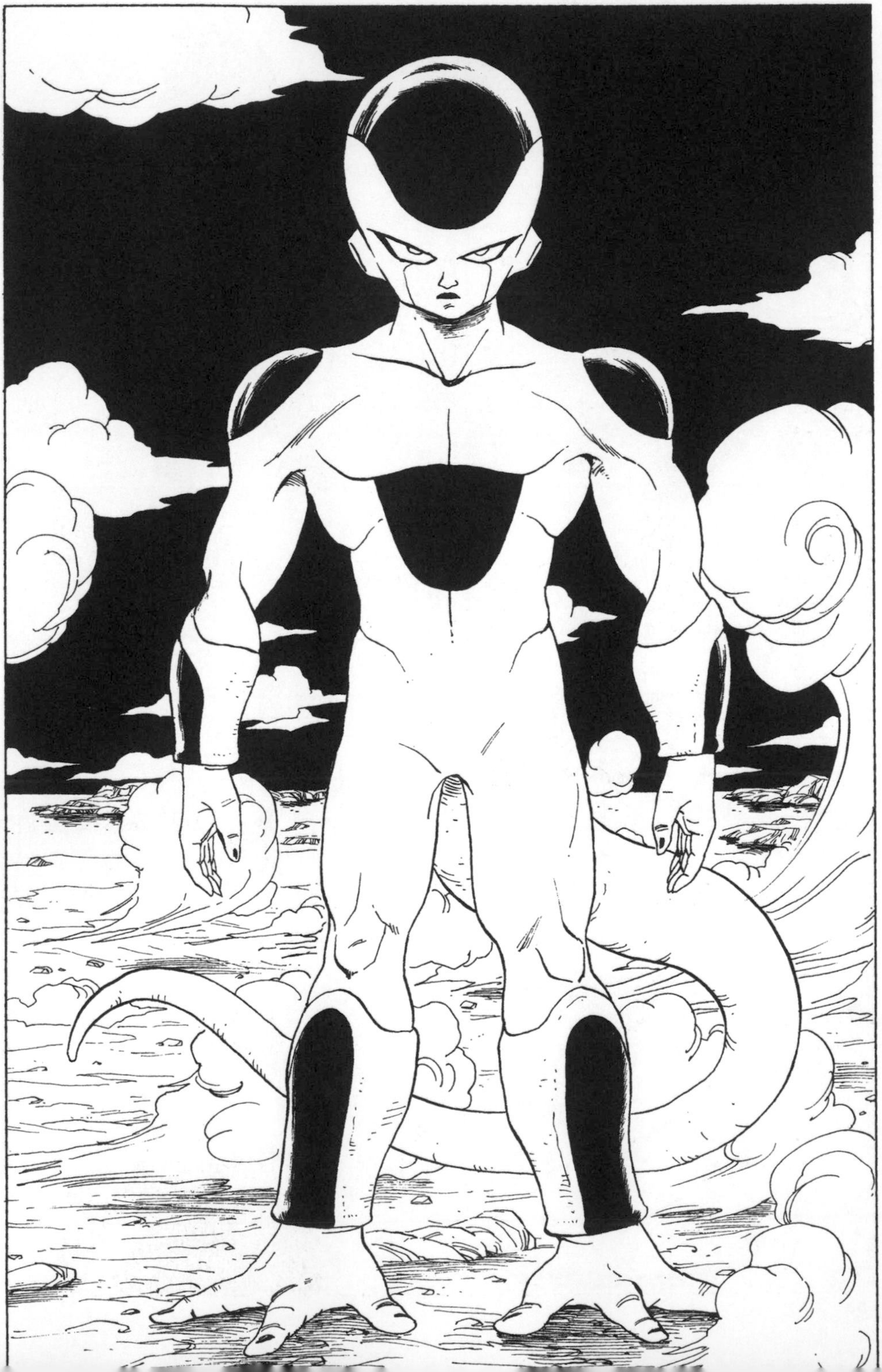

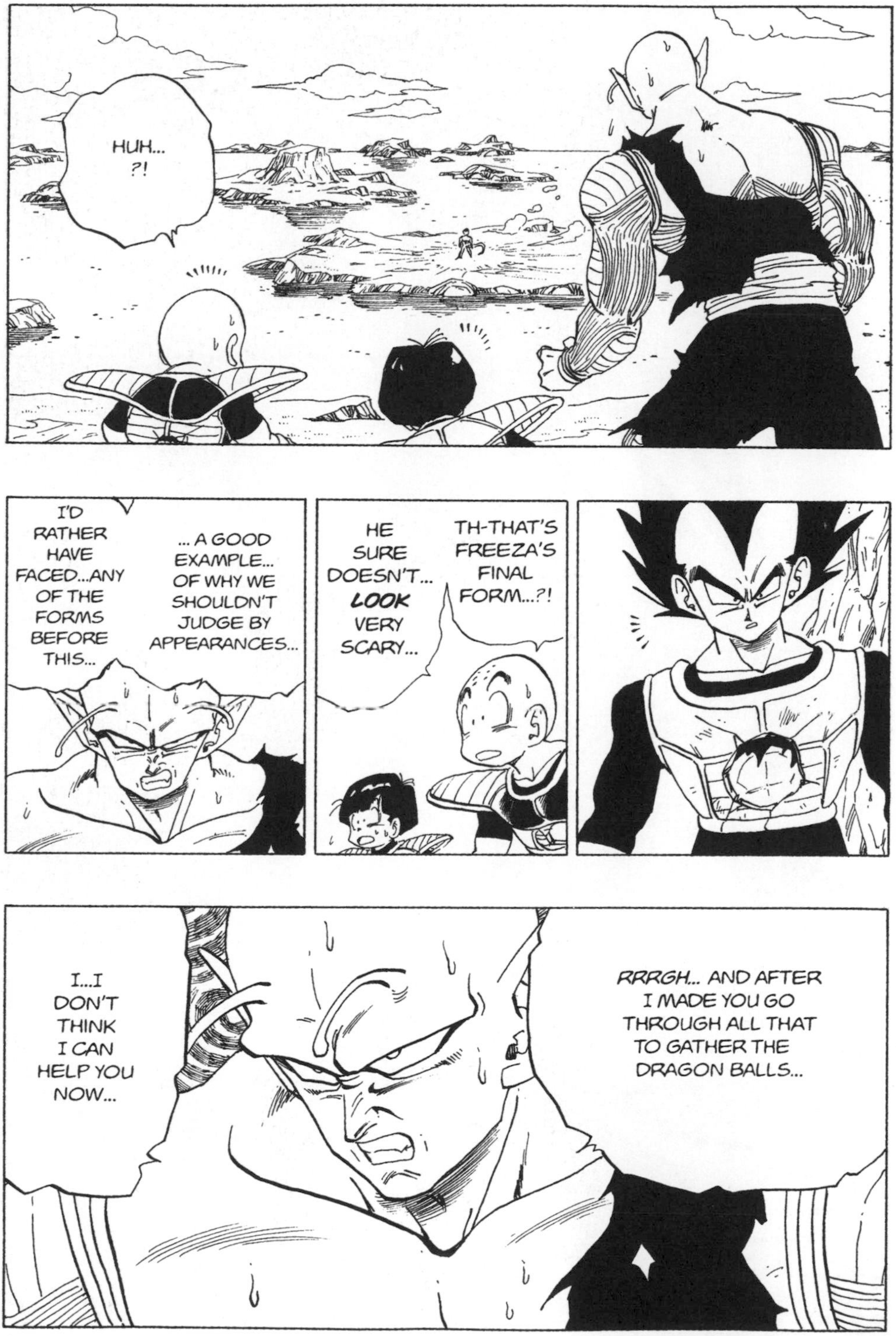
HUH... ?!
TH-THAT'S FREEZA'S FINAL FORM...?!
HE SURE DOESN'T... LOOK VERY SCARY...
... A GOOD EXAMPLE... OF WHY WE SHOULDN'T JUDGE BY APPEARANCES...
I'D RATHER HAVE FACED...ANY OF THE FORMS BEFORE THIS...
RRRGH... AND AFTER I MADE YOU GO THROUGH ALL THAT TO GATHER THE DRAGON BALLS...
I...I DON'T THINK I CAN HELP YOU NOW...

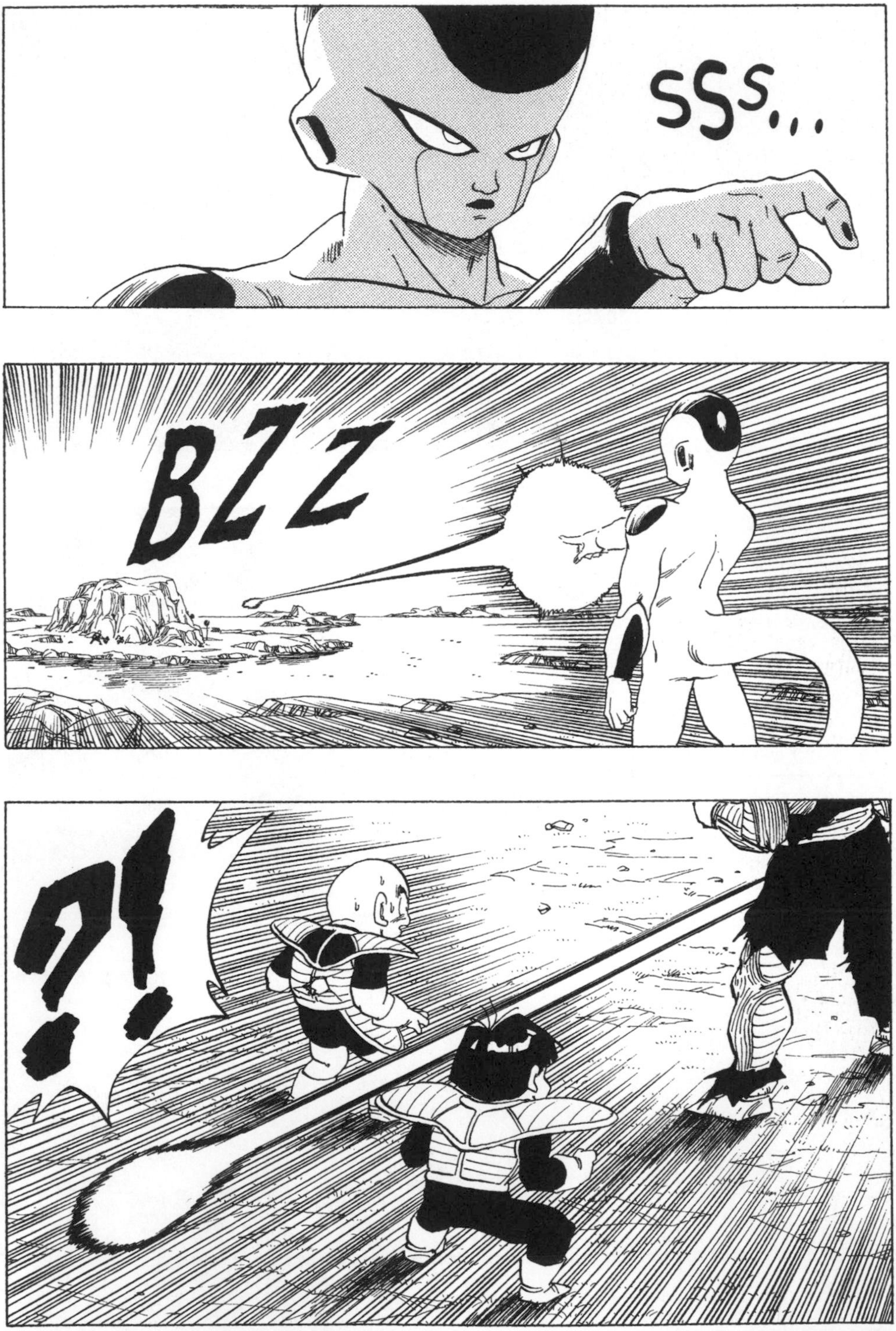
SSS...
BZZ
?!

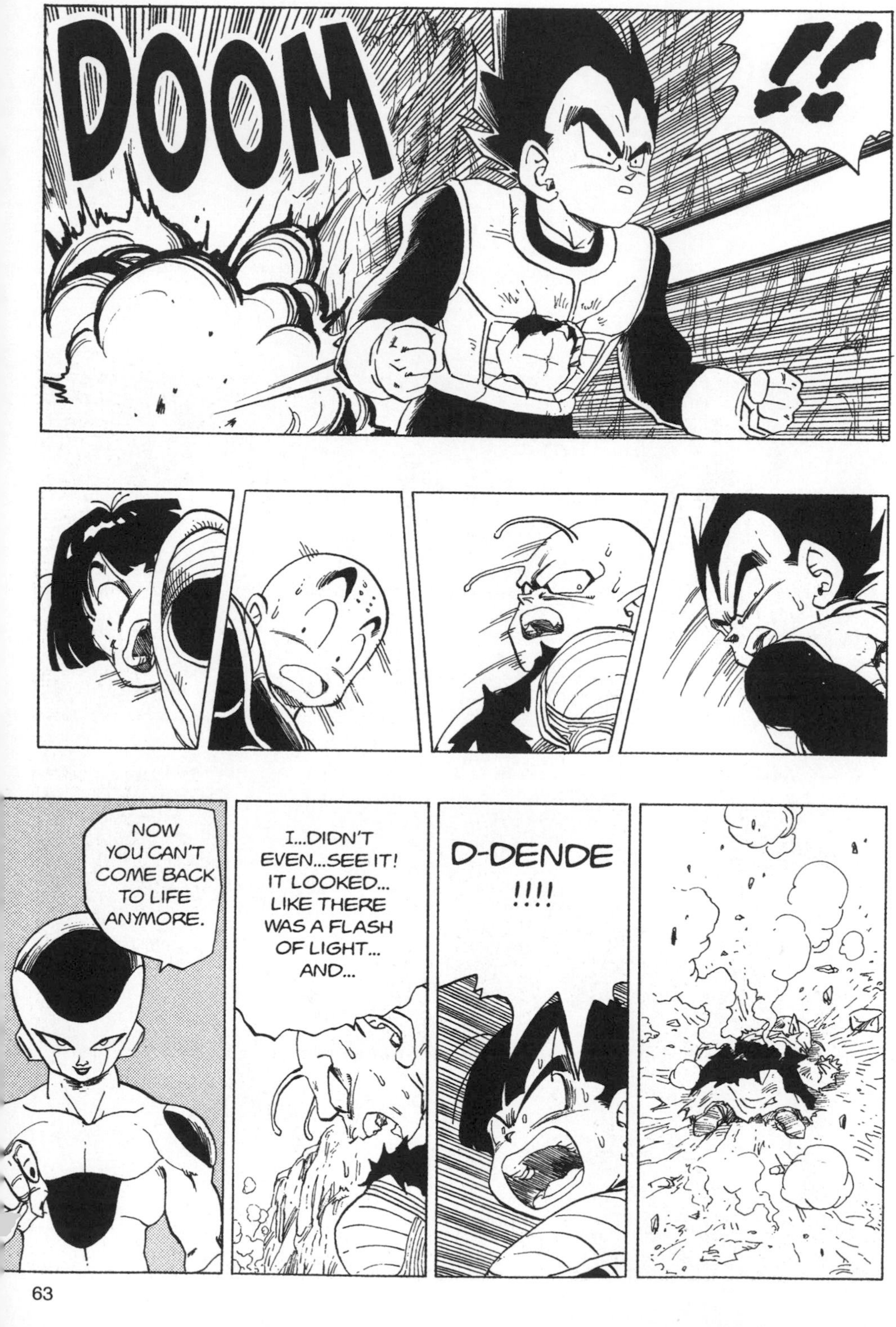
DOOM!!
NOW YOU CAN'T COME BACK TO LIFE ANYMORE.
I...DIDN'T EVEN...SEE IT! IT LOOKED... LIKE THERE WAS A FLASH OF LIGHT... AND...
D-DENDE !!!!

DBZ:111 •
Will It Be Freeza? Or Vegeta?

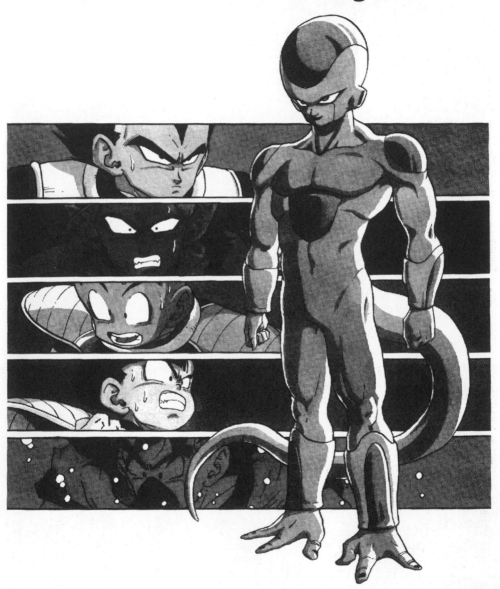

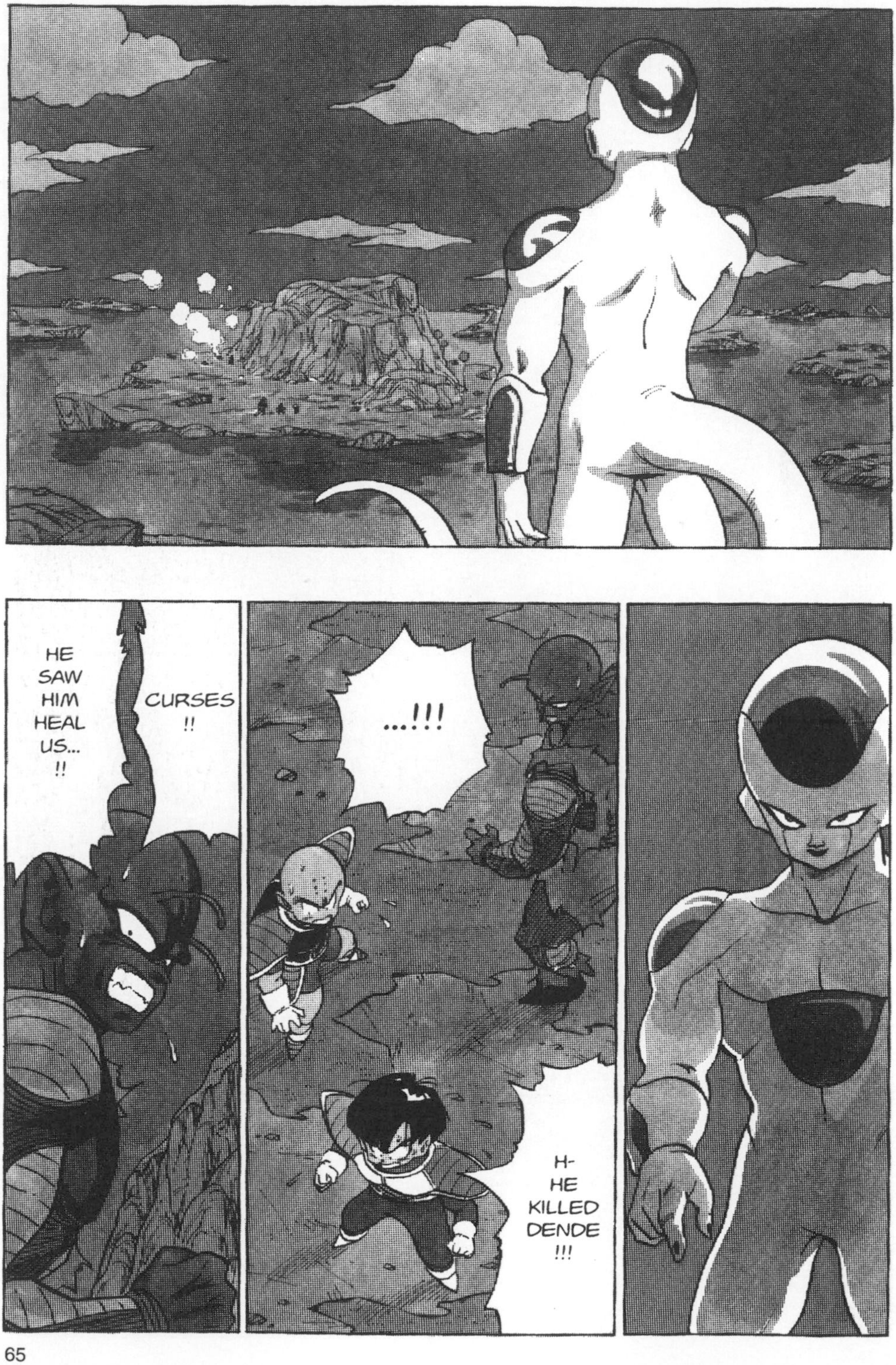
...!!!
H-HE KILLED DENDE!!!
CURSES!!
HE SAW HIM HEAL US...!!

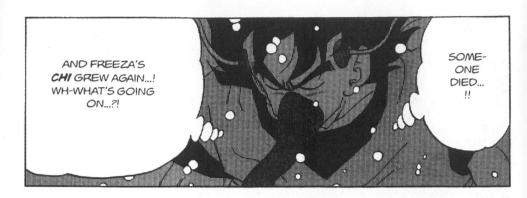

AND FREEZA'S *CHI* GREW AGAIN...! WH-WHAT'S GOING ON...?!

SOME-ONE DIED...!!

H-HE DISAP-PEARED!!!

PFF

I PROMISED THAT I'D SHOW YOU A FEAR WORSE THAN DEATH...

PFF

UNH!!!!

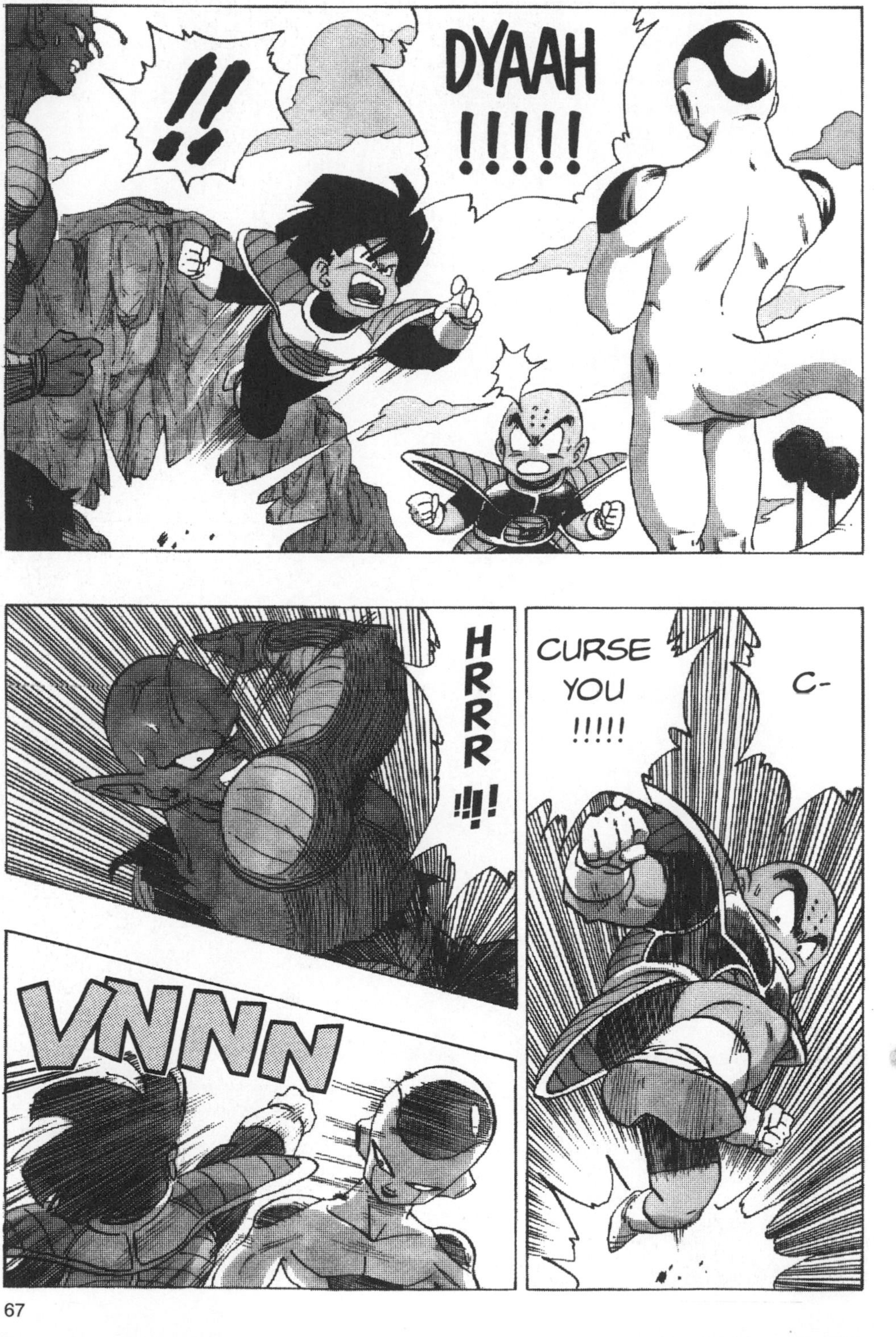
DYAAH !!!!!
!!
C-
CURSE YOU !!!!!
HRRR !!!!
VNNN

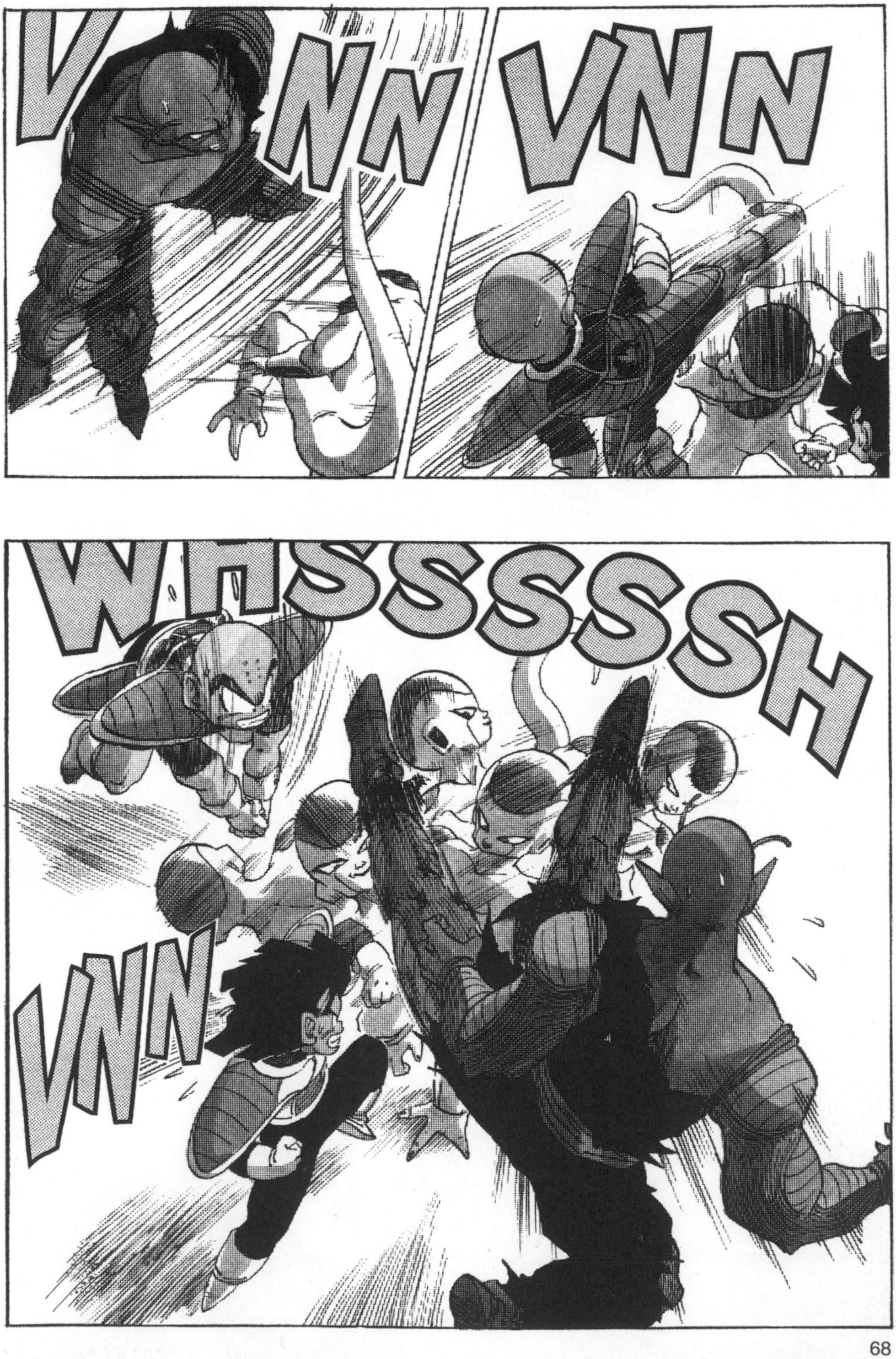
VNN
VNN
WHSSSSSH
VNN

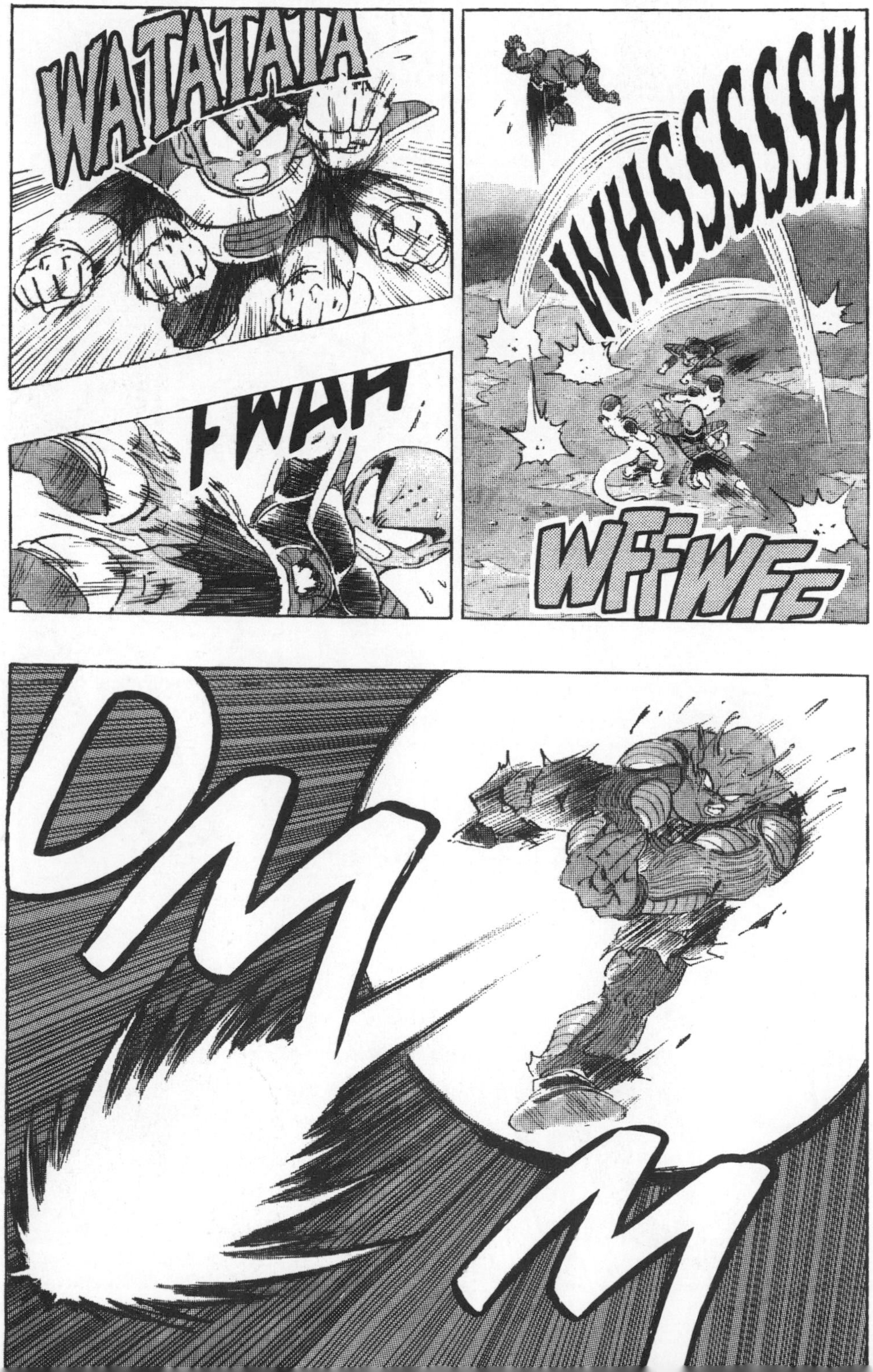
WHSSSSSH
WFFWFF
WATATATA
FWAH
DMMM

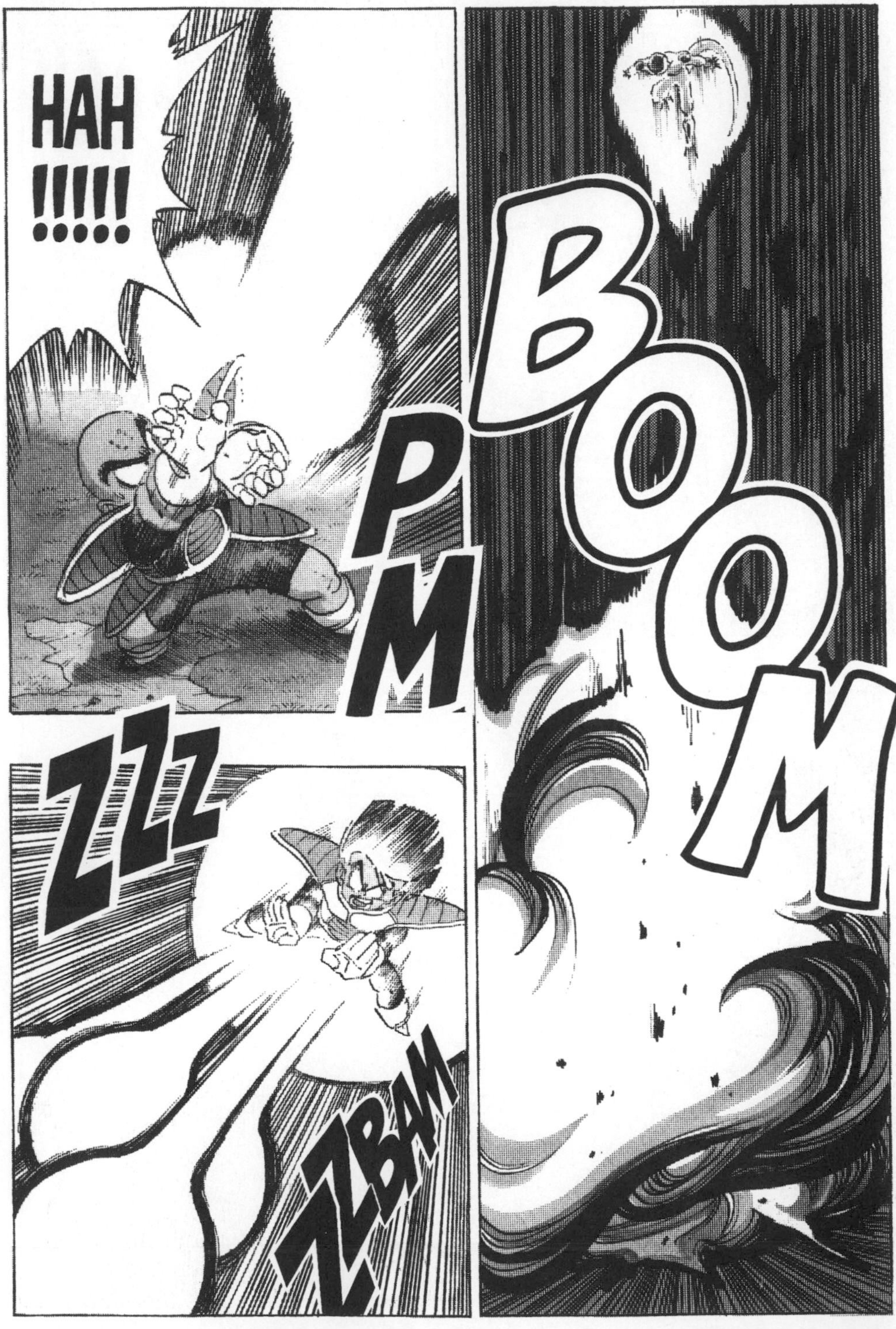

BOOOM
HAH !!!!!
PM
ZZZ
ZZBAM

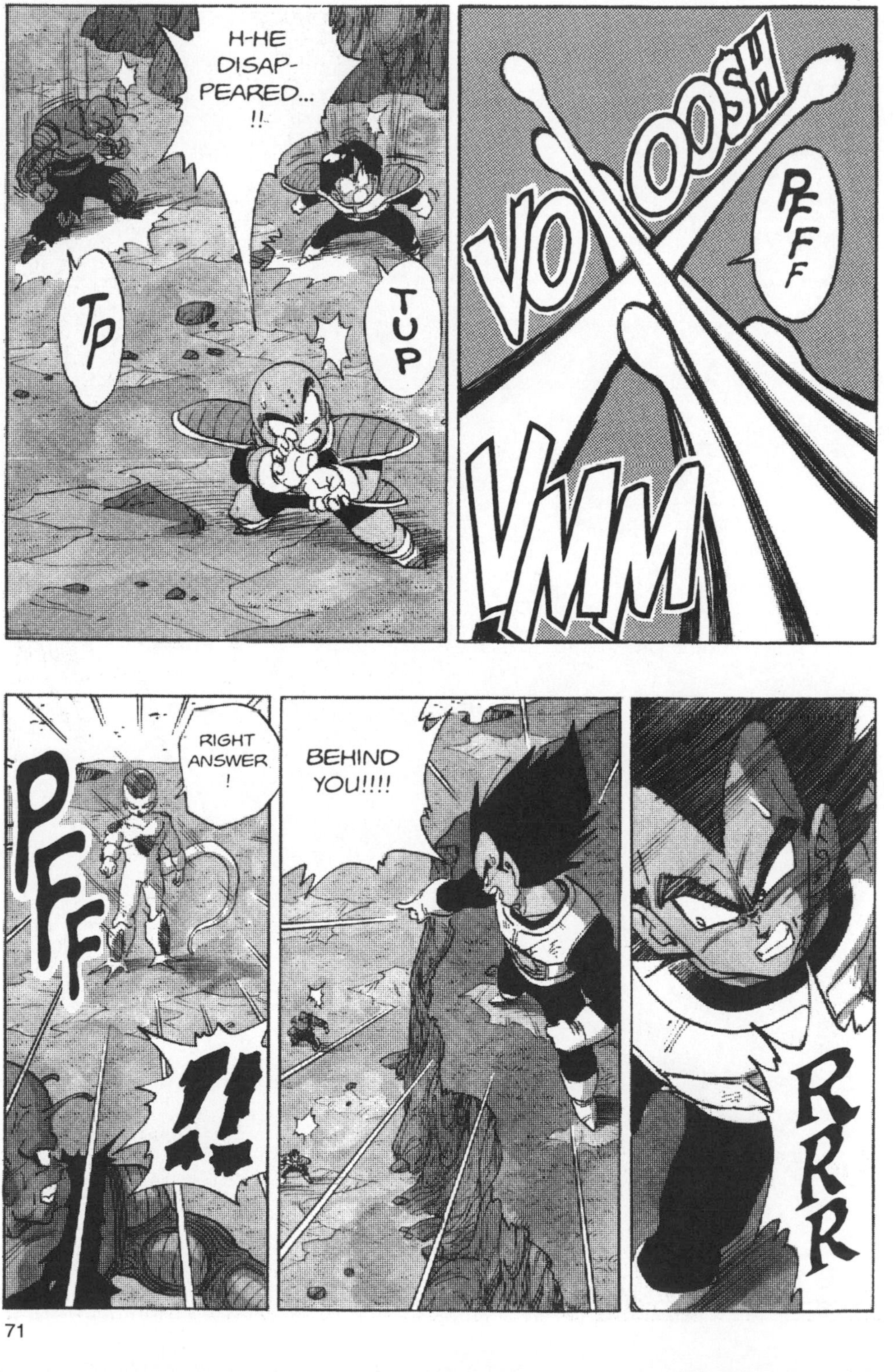

H-HE DISAP-PEARED... !!
TP
TUP
VOOOSH
RFFF
VMM
PFF
RIGHT ANSWER !
!!
BEHIND YOU!!!!
RRR

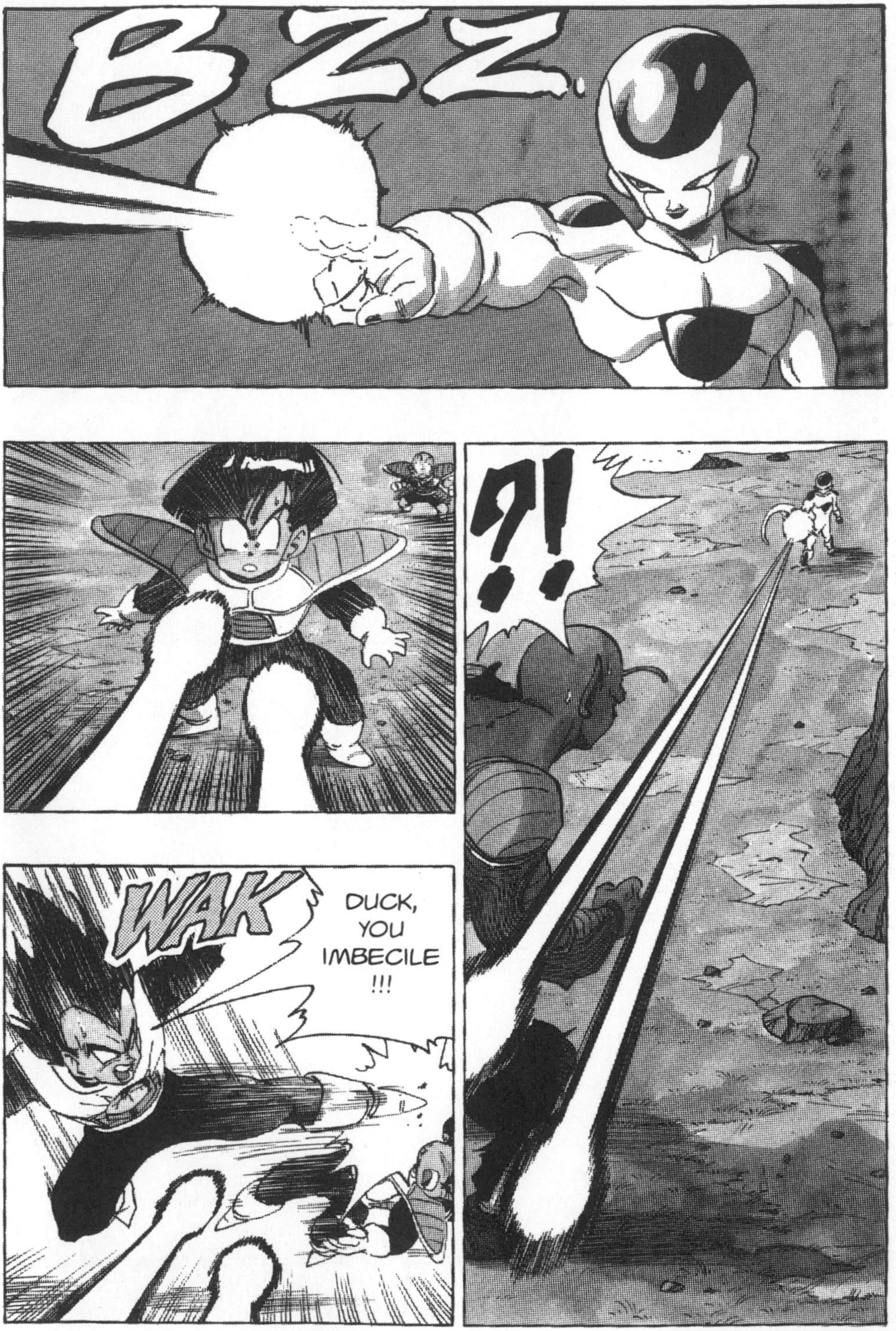

BZZ
?!!
WAK
DUCK, YOU IMBECILE !!!

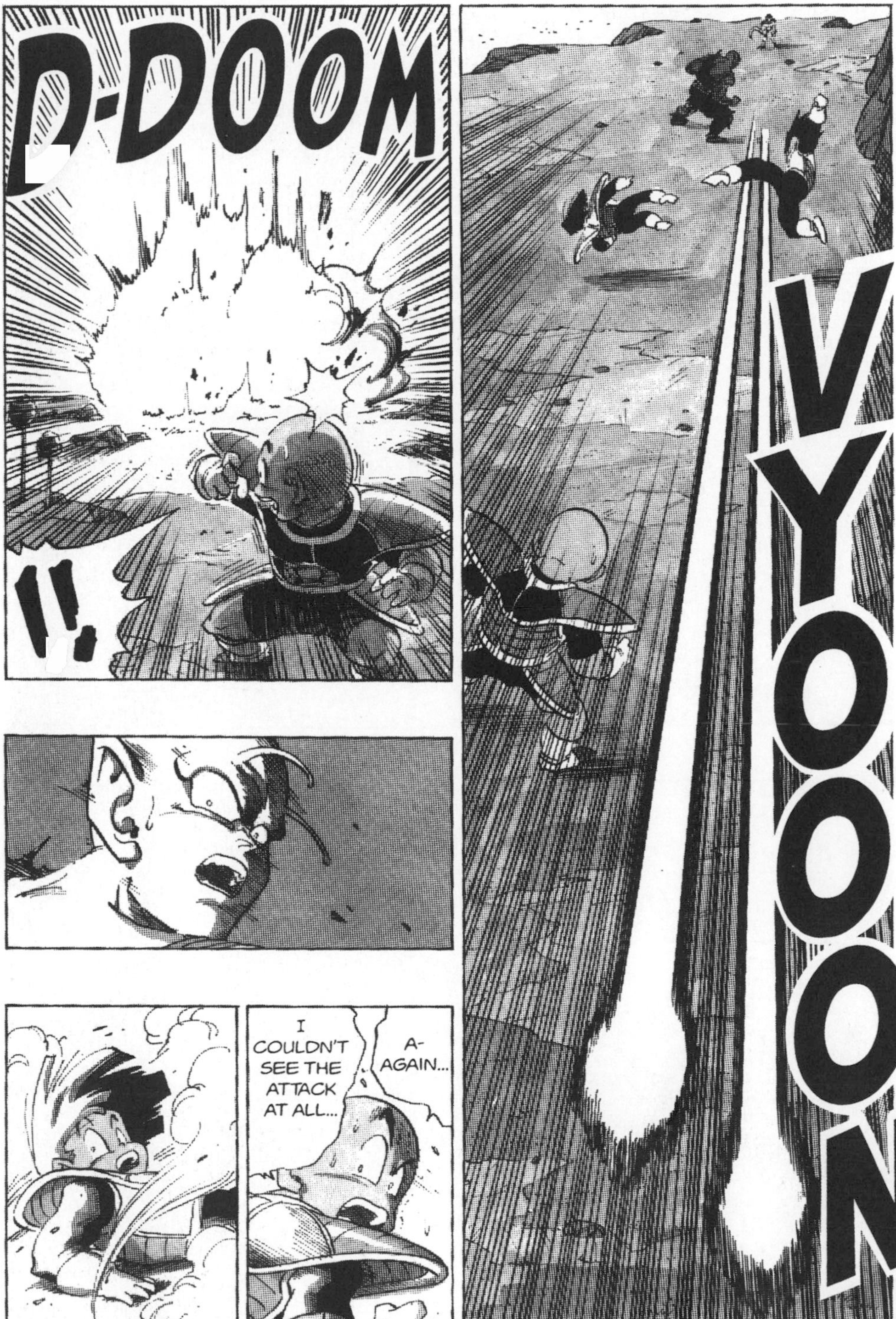
D-DOOM
!!
VYOOON
I COULDN'T SEE THE ATTACK AT ALL...
A- AGAIN...

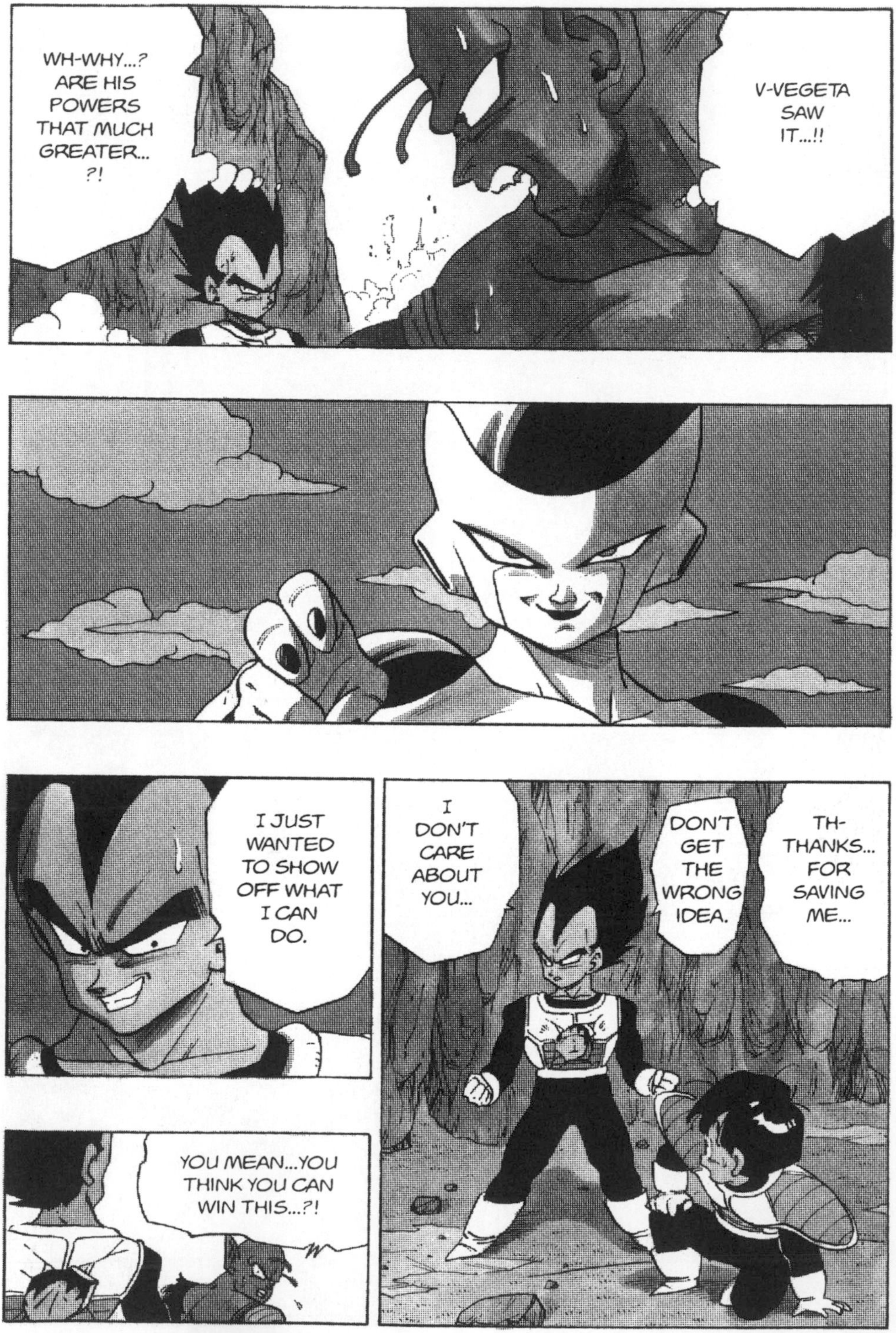
V-VEGETA SAW IT...!!
WH-WHY...? ARE HIS POWERS THAT MUCH GREATER...?!
TH-THANKS... FOR SAVING ME...
DON'T GET THE WRONG IDEA.
I DON'T CARE ABOUT YOU...
I JUST WANTED TO SHOW OFF WHAT I CAN DO.
YOU MEAN...YOU THINK YOU CAN WIN THIS...?!

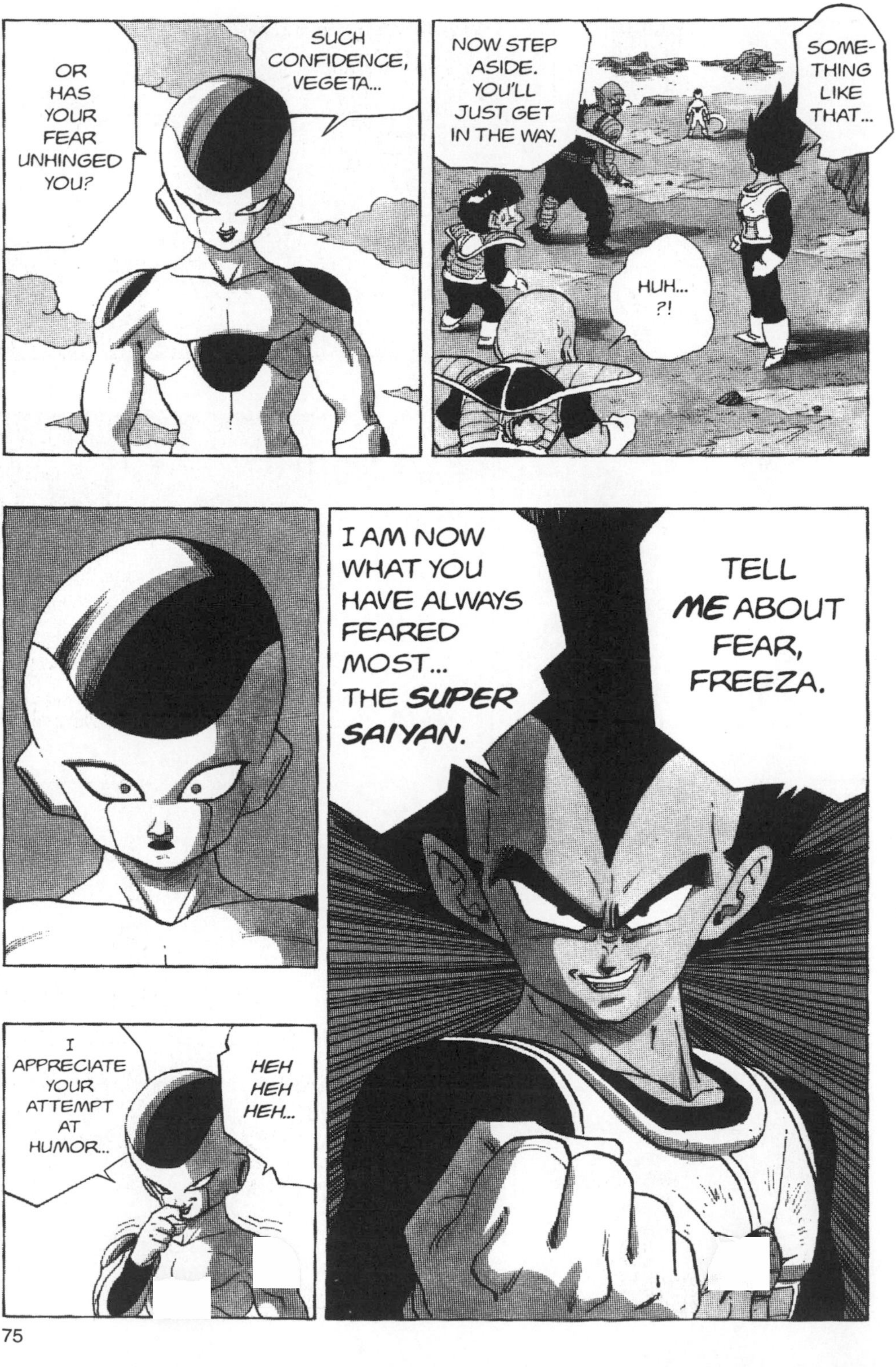
SUCH CONFIDENCE, VEGETA...
OR HAS YOUR FEAR UNHINGED YOU?
SOME-THING LIKE THAT...
NOW STEP ASIDE. YOU'LL JUST GET IN THE WAY.
HUH... ?!
TELL ME ABOUT FEAR, FREEZA.
I AM NOW WHAT YOU HAVE ALWAYS FEARED MOST... THE SUPER SAIYAN.
HEH HEH HEH...
I APPRECIATE YOUR ATTEMPT AT HUMOR...

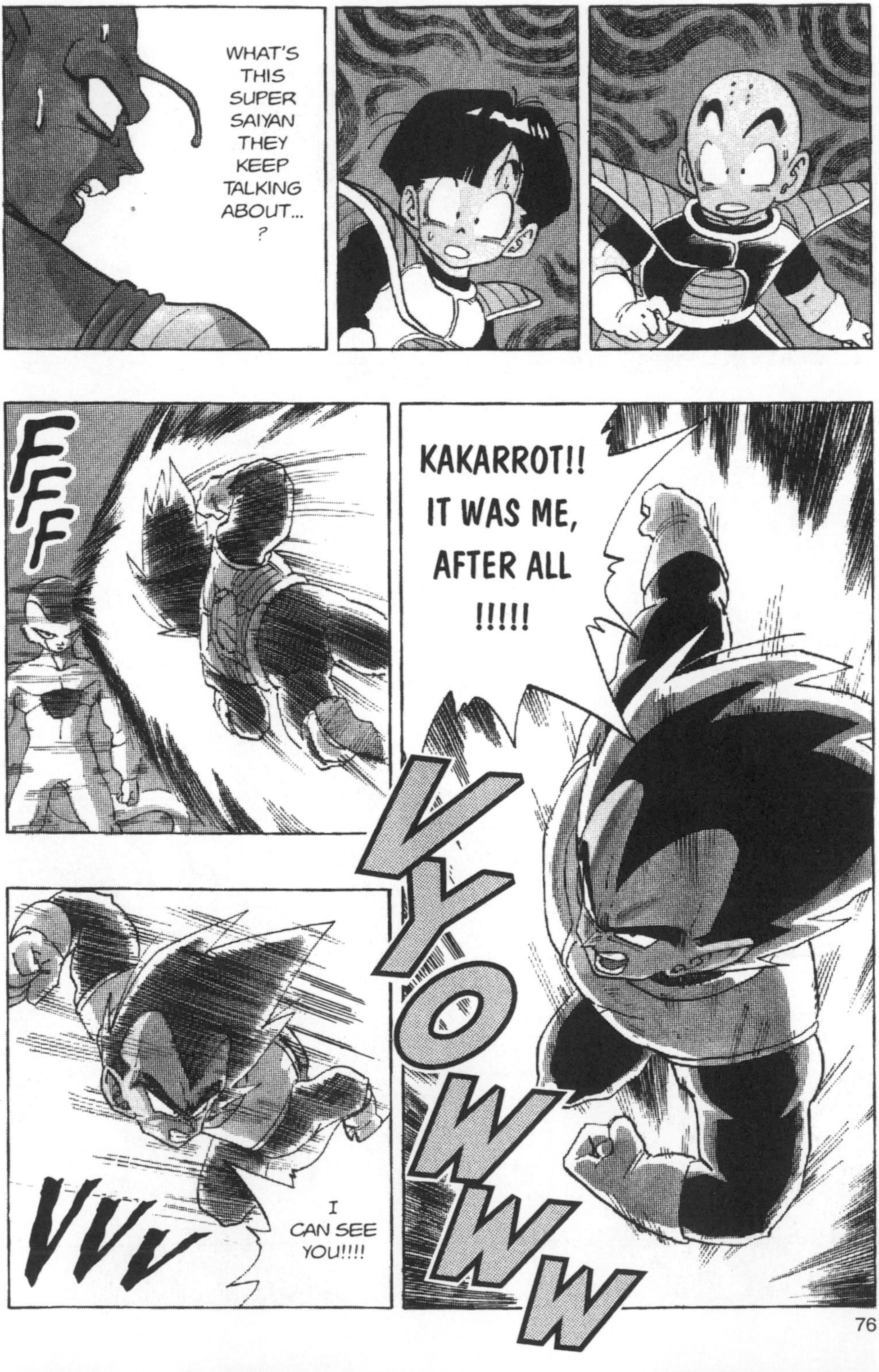
WHAT'S THIS SUPER SAIYAN THEY KEEP TALKING ABOUT...?
FFF
KAKARROT!! IT WAS ME, AFTER ALL !!!!!
VYOWWWW
VVV
I CAN SEE YOU!!!!

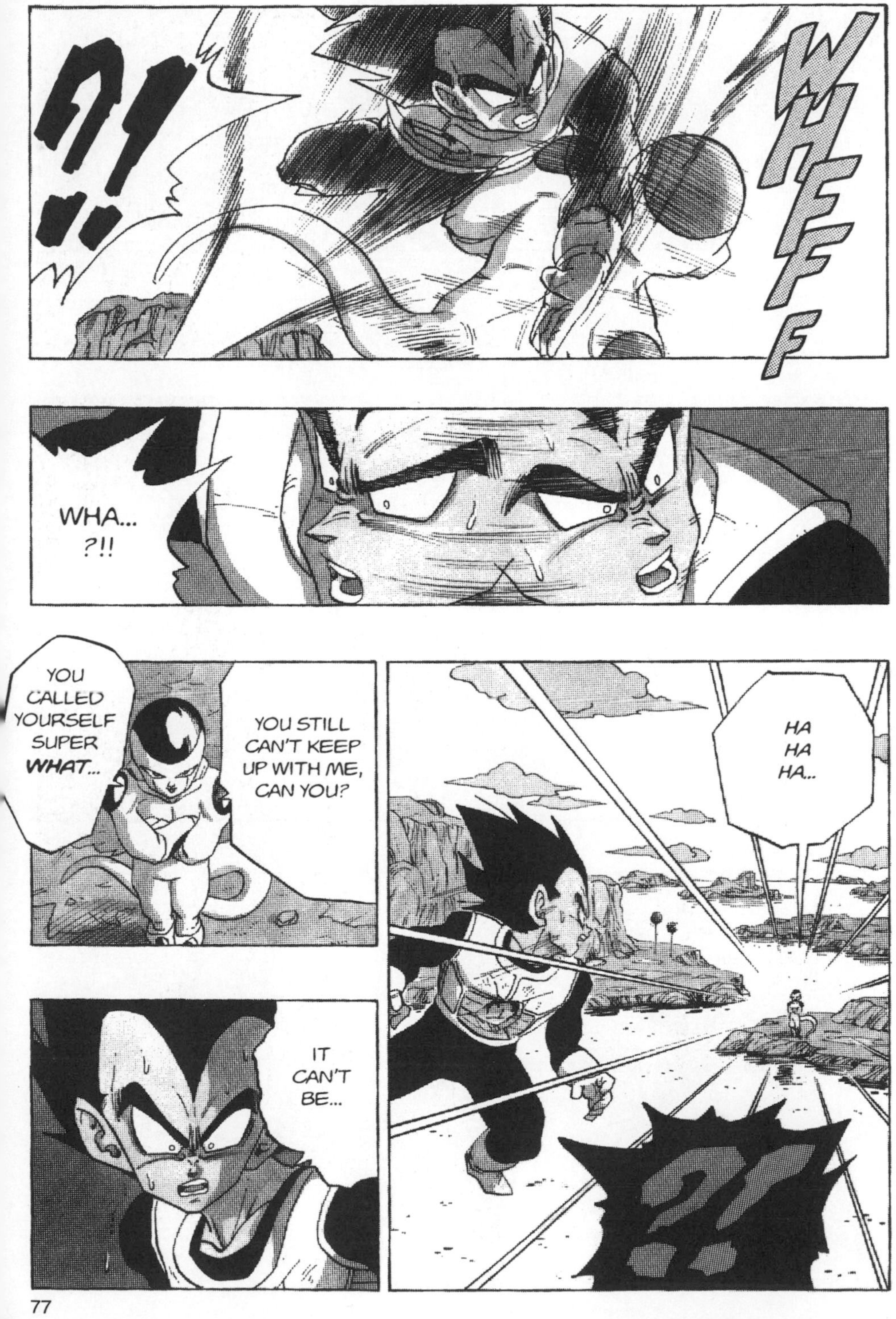
WHFFF
WHA... ?!!
HA HA HA...
YOU STILL CAN'T KEEP UP WITH ME, CAN YOU?
YOU CALLED YOURSELF SUPER **WHAT**...
IT CAN'T BE...

DBZ:112 • Son Goku... Resurrected!!

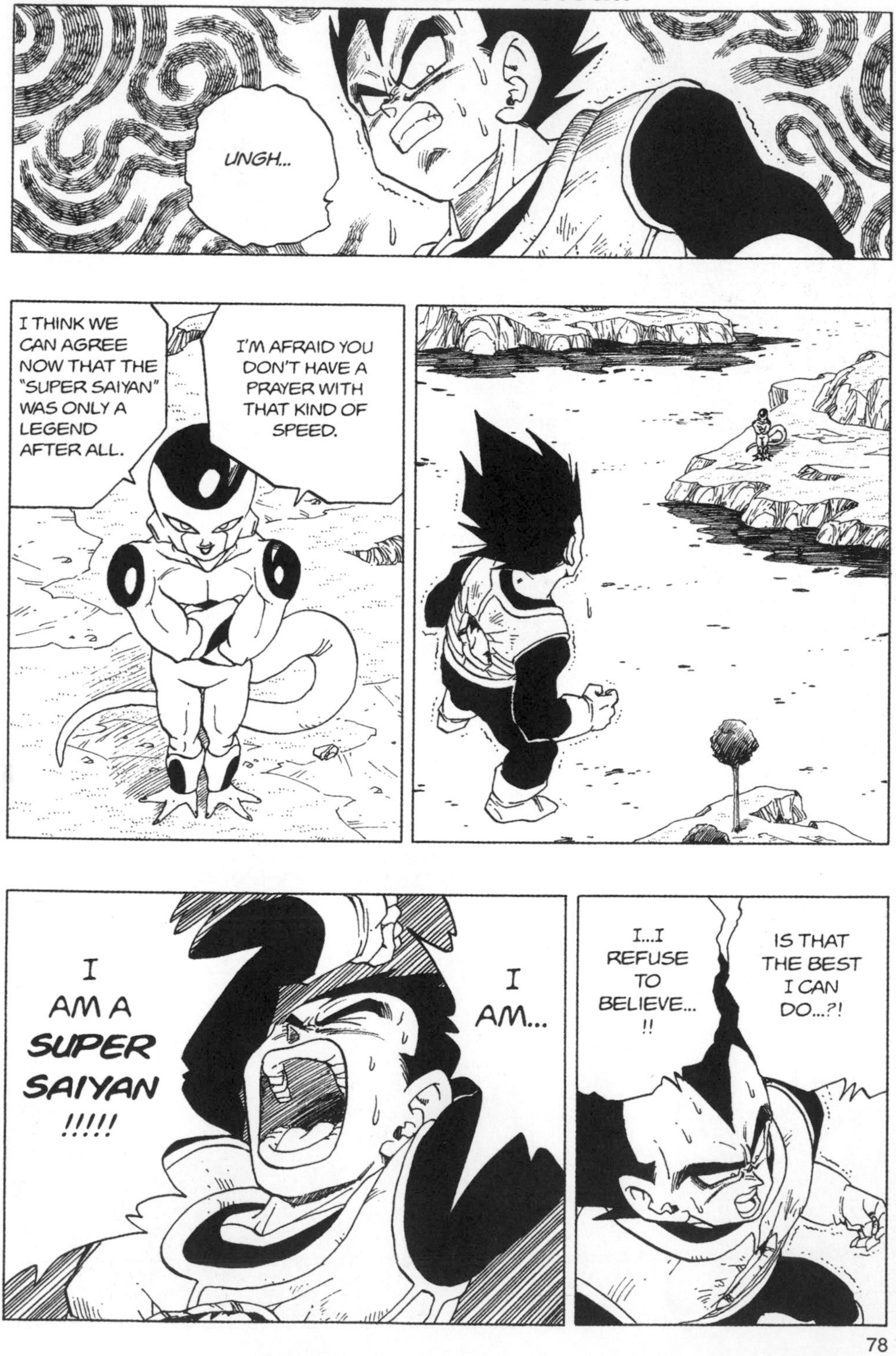
UNGH...
I'M AFRAID YOU DON'T HAVE A PRAYER WITH THAT KIND OF SPEED.
I THINK WE CAN AGREE NOW THAT THE "SUPER SAIYAN" WAS ONLY A LEGEND AFTER ALL.
IS THAT THE BEST I CAN DO...?!
I...I REFUSE TO BELIEVE... !!
I AM...
I AM A SUPER SAIYAN !!!!!

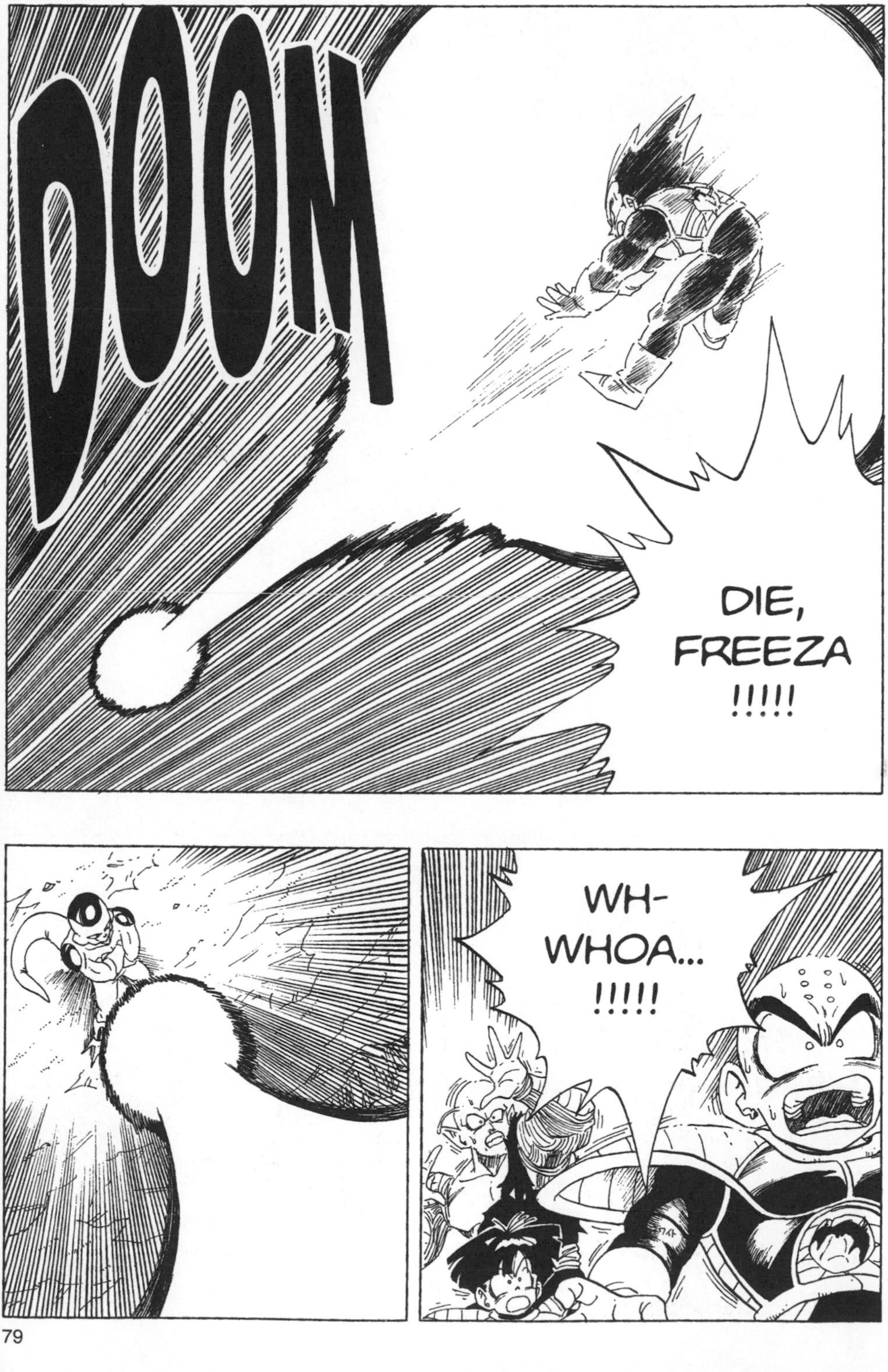
DOOM
DIE, FREEZA !!!!!
WH- WHOA... !!!!!

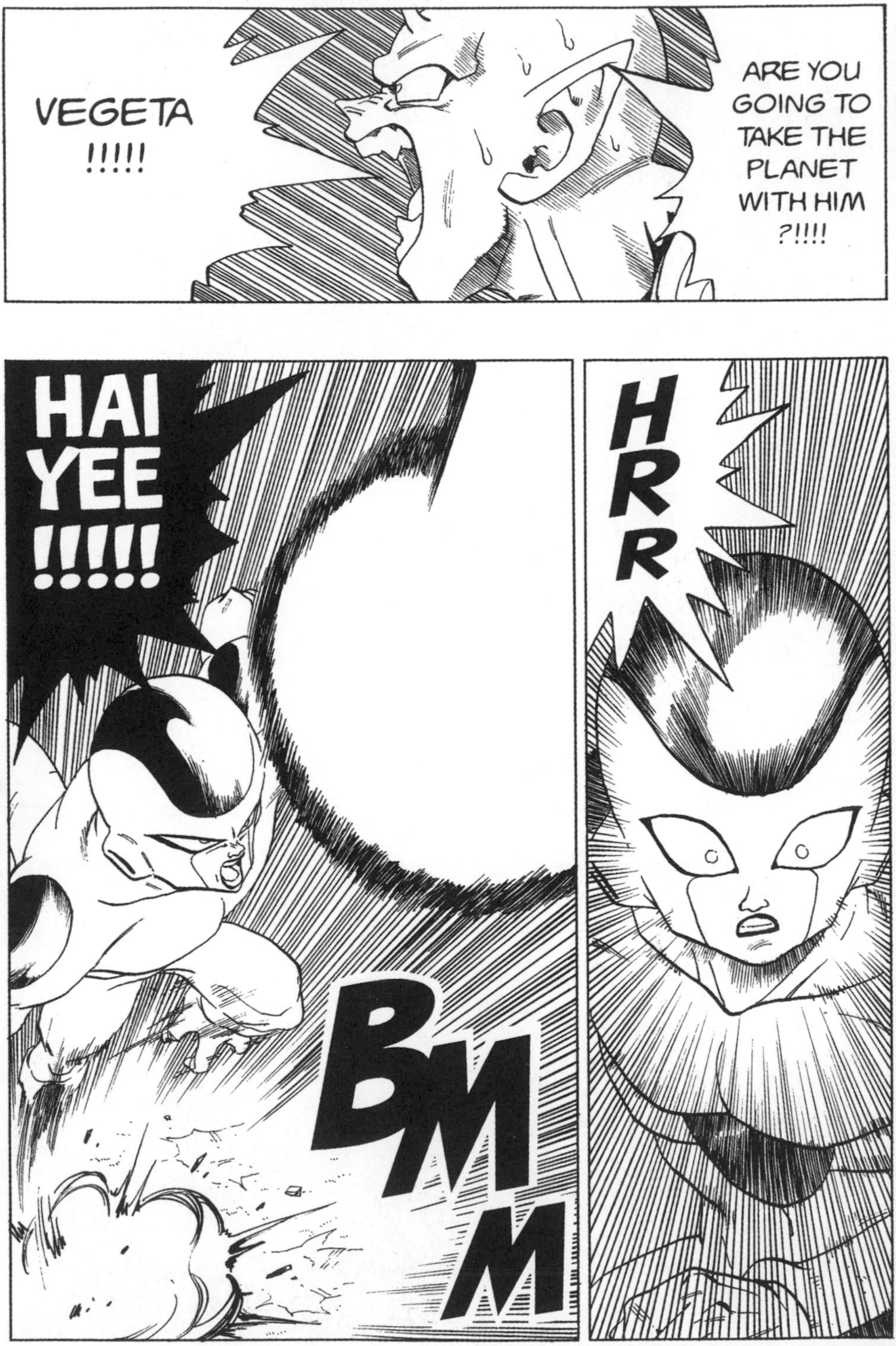
ARE YOU GOING TO TAKE THE PLANET WITH HIM ?!!!!
VEGETA !!!!!
HRR
HAI YEE !!!!!
BMM

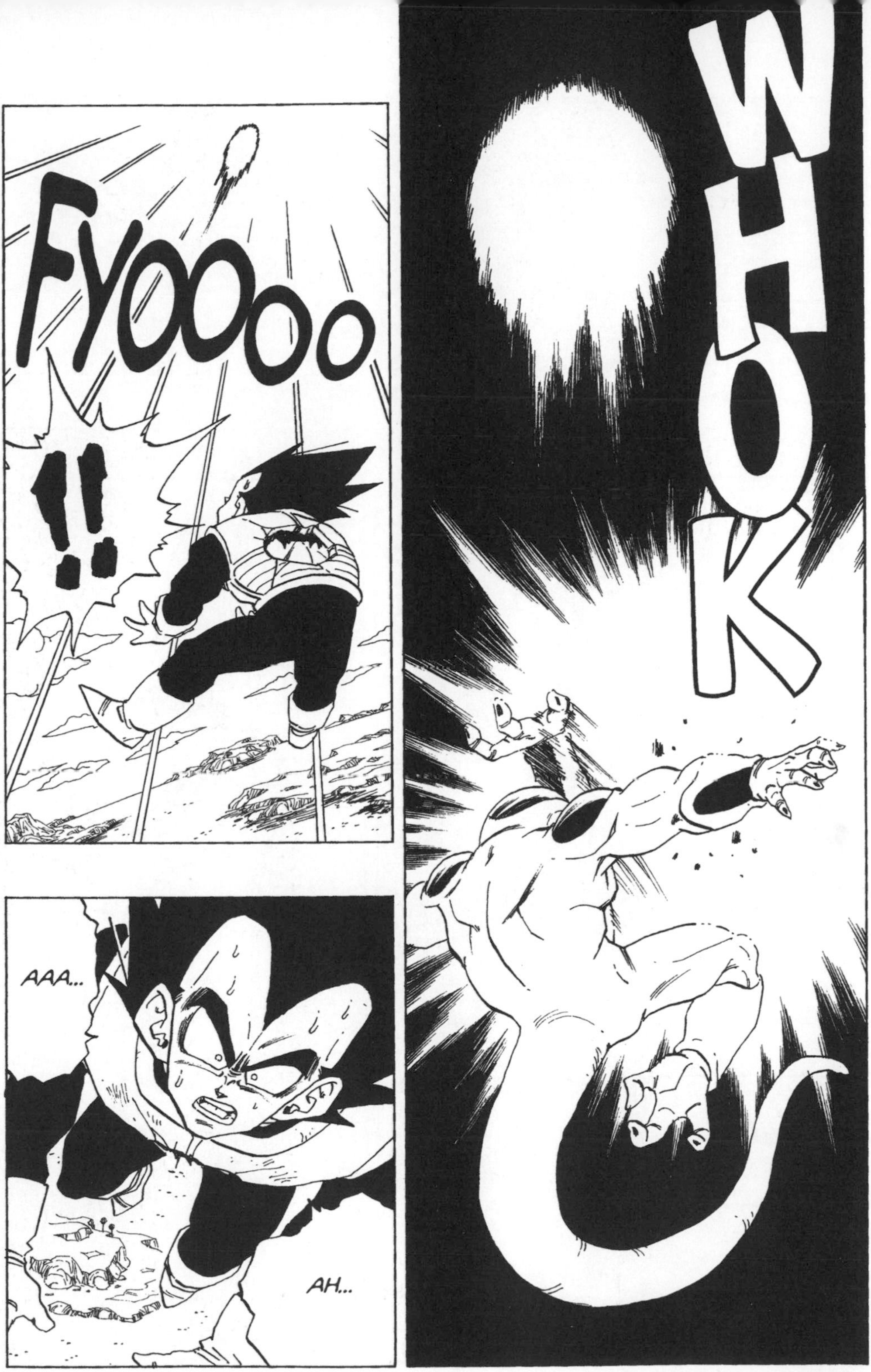
WHOK
FYOOOO
!!
AAA...
AH...

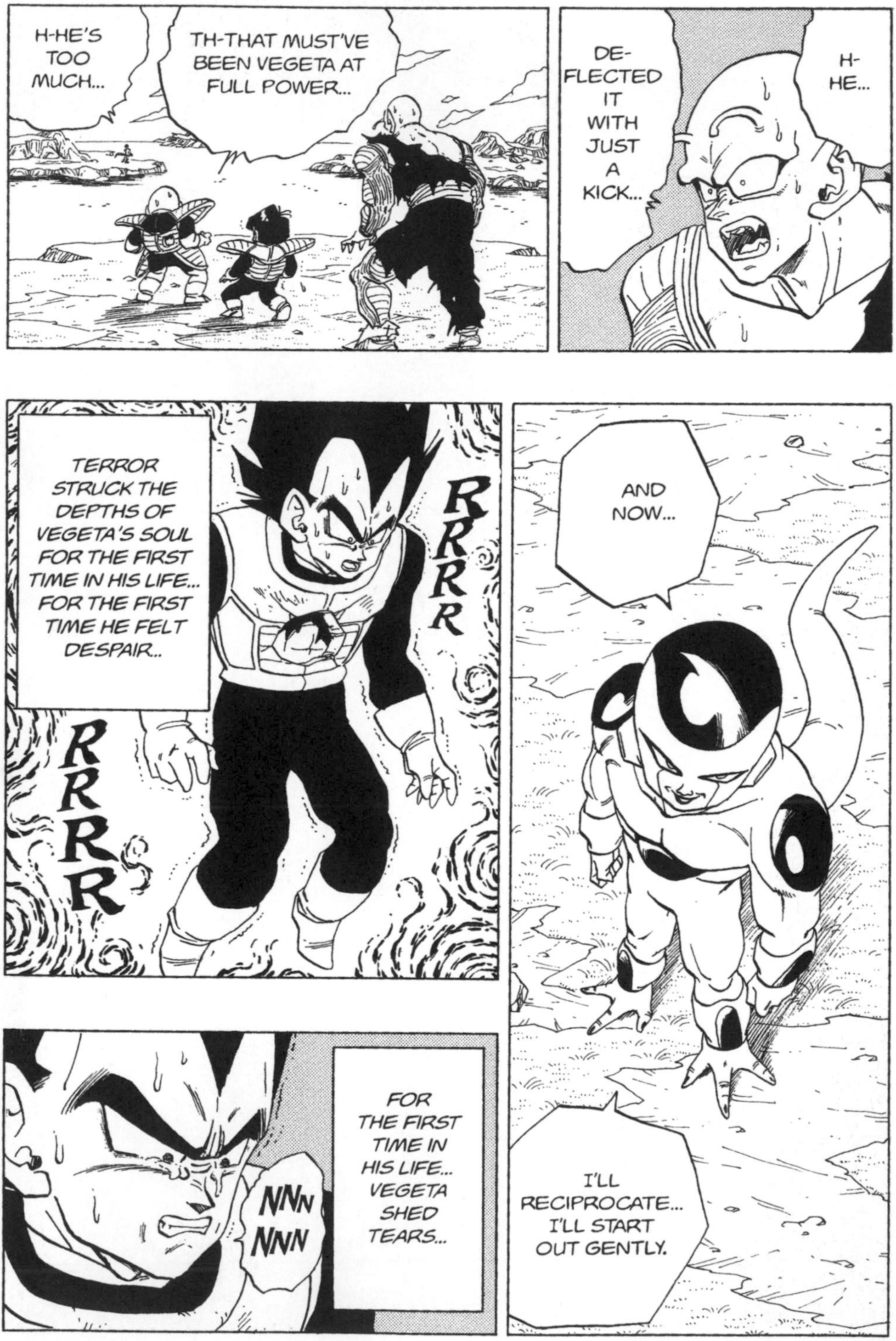
H-
HE...
DE-
FLECTED
IT
WITH
JUST
A
KICK...
TH-THAT MUST'VE BEEN VEGETA AT FULL POWER...
H-HE'S TOO MUCH...
AND NOW...
I'LL RECIPROCATE... I'LL START OUT GENTLY.
TERROR STRUCK THE DEPTHS OF VEGETA'S SOUL FOR THE FIRST TIME IN HIS LIFE... FOR THE FIRST TIME HE FELT DESPAIR...
RRRR
RRRR
FOR THE FIRST TIME IN HIS LIFE... VEGETA SHED TEARS...
NNN NNN

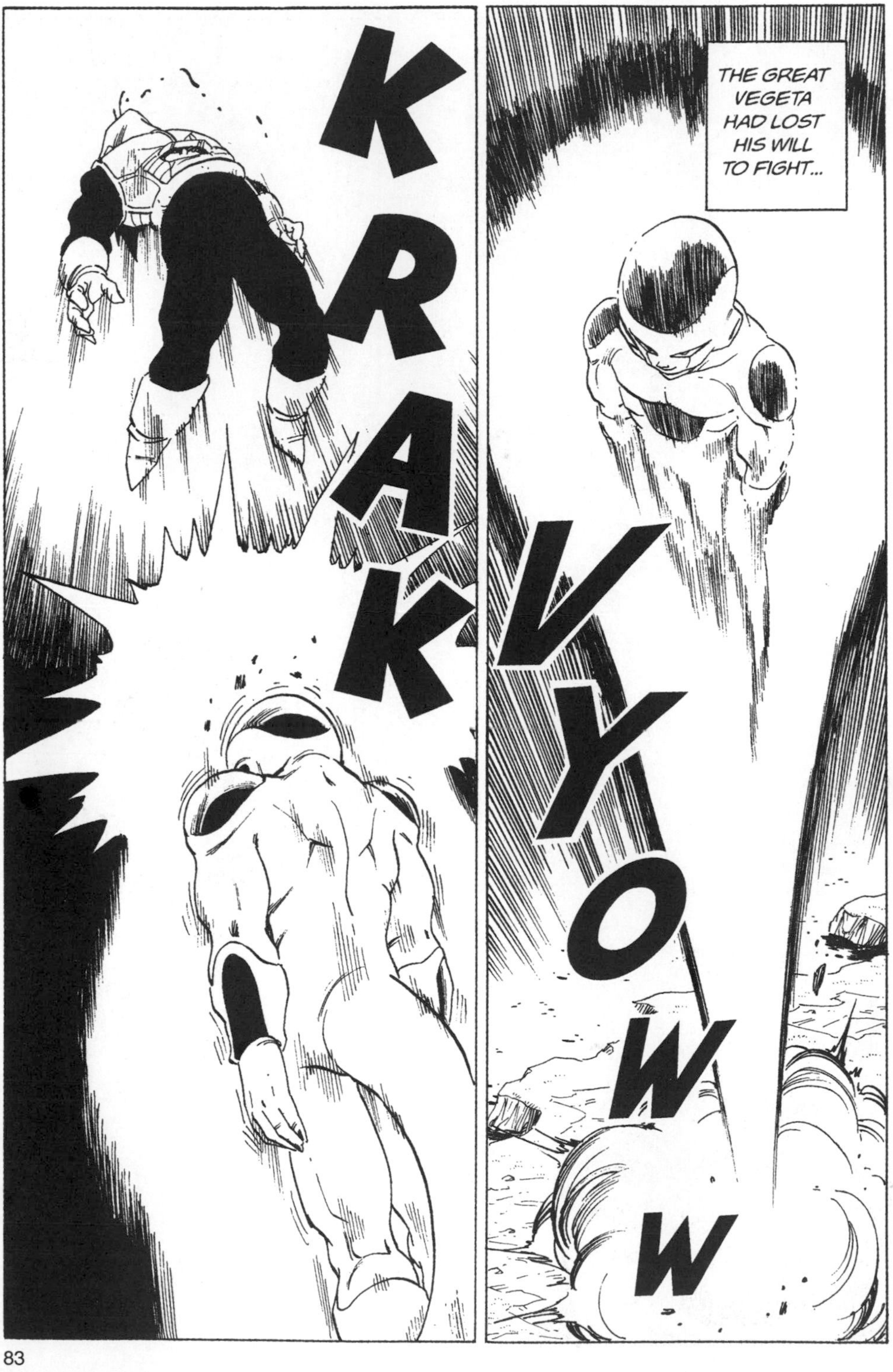
KRAK
THE GREAT VEGETA HAD LOST HIS WILL TO FIGHT...
VYOWW

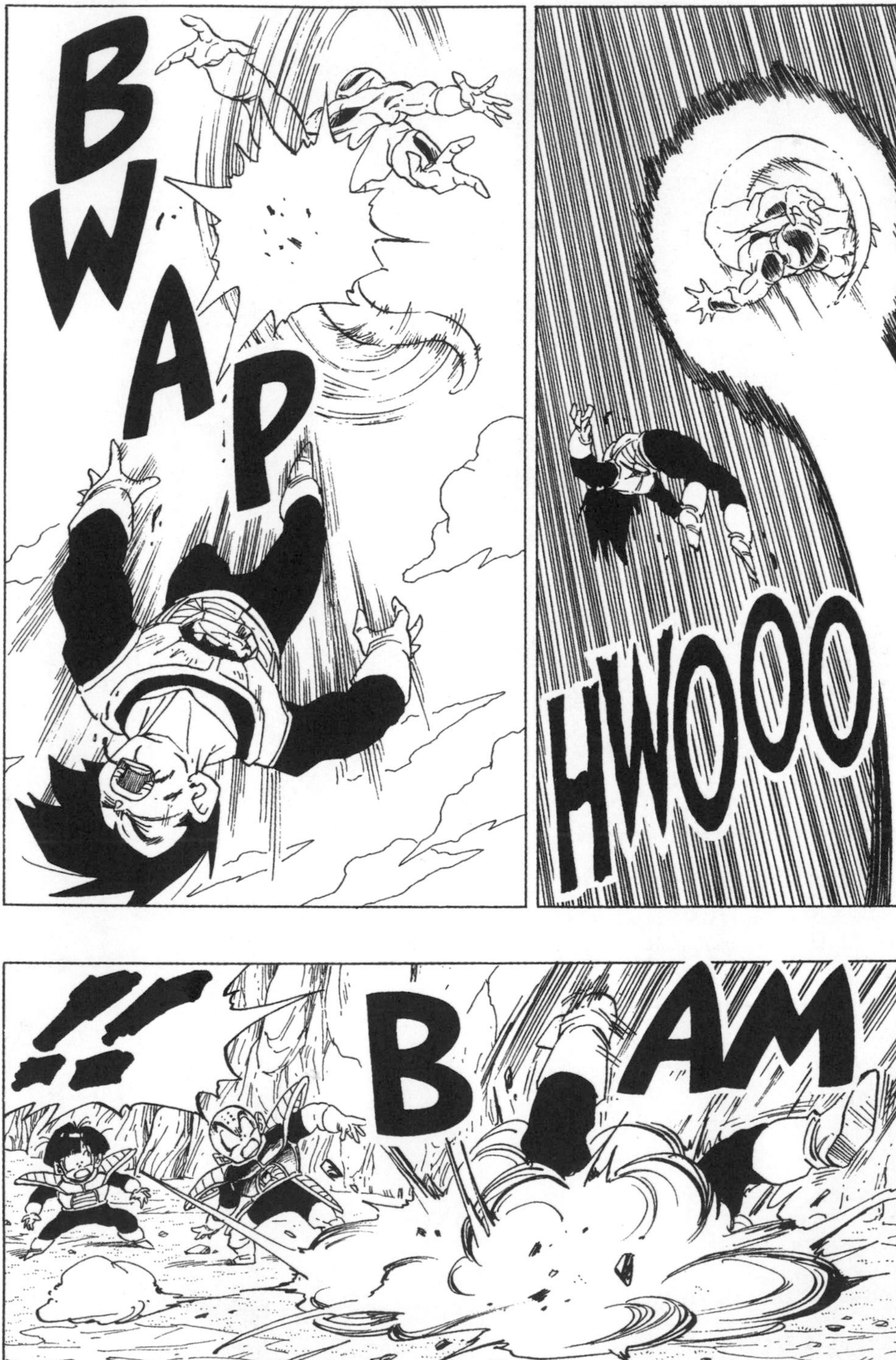

HWOOO
BWAP
!!
!!
BAM

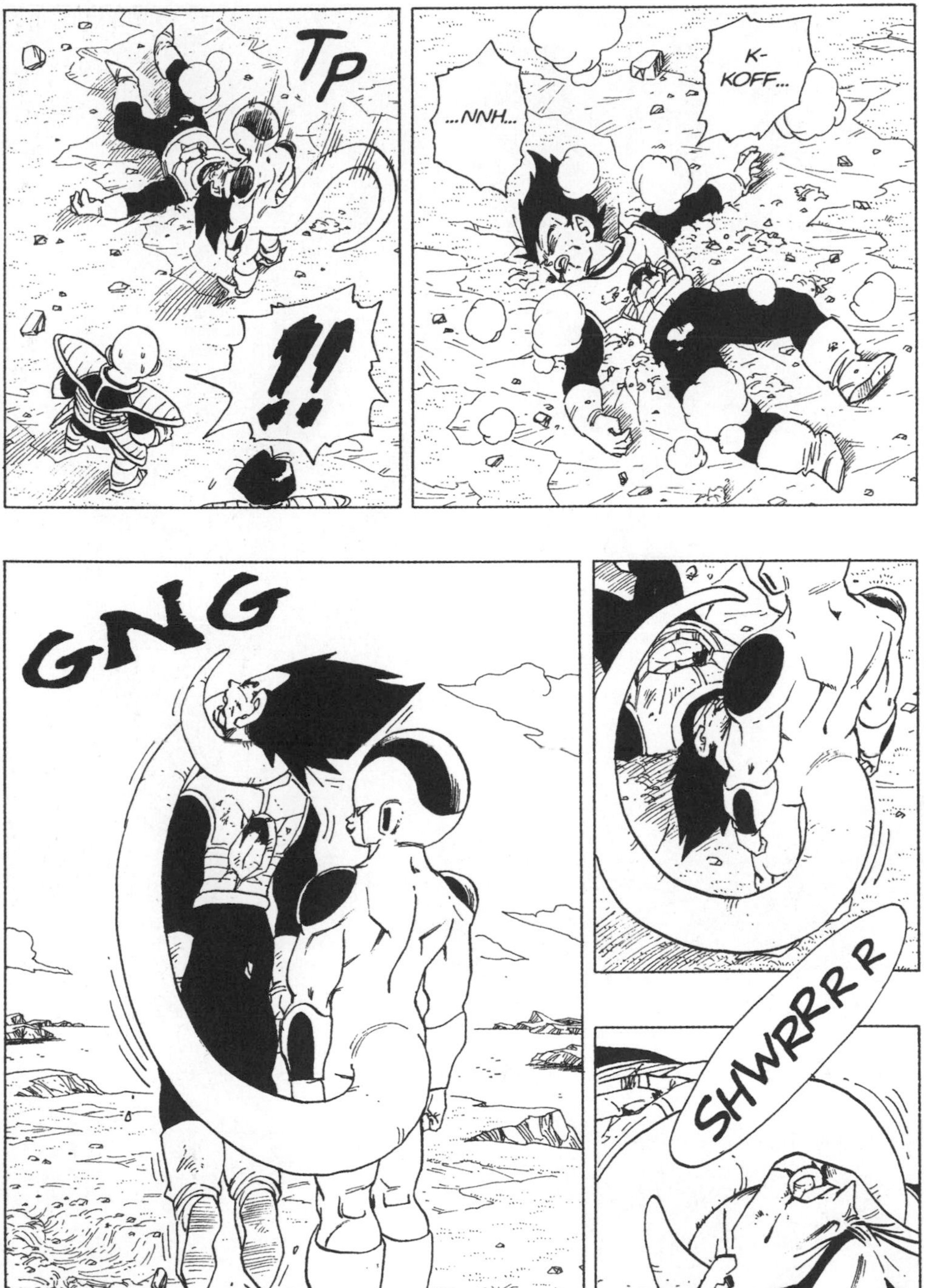
TP
!!
...NNH...
K-
KOFF...
GNG
SHWRRR R

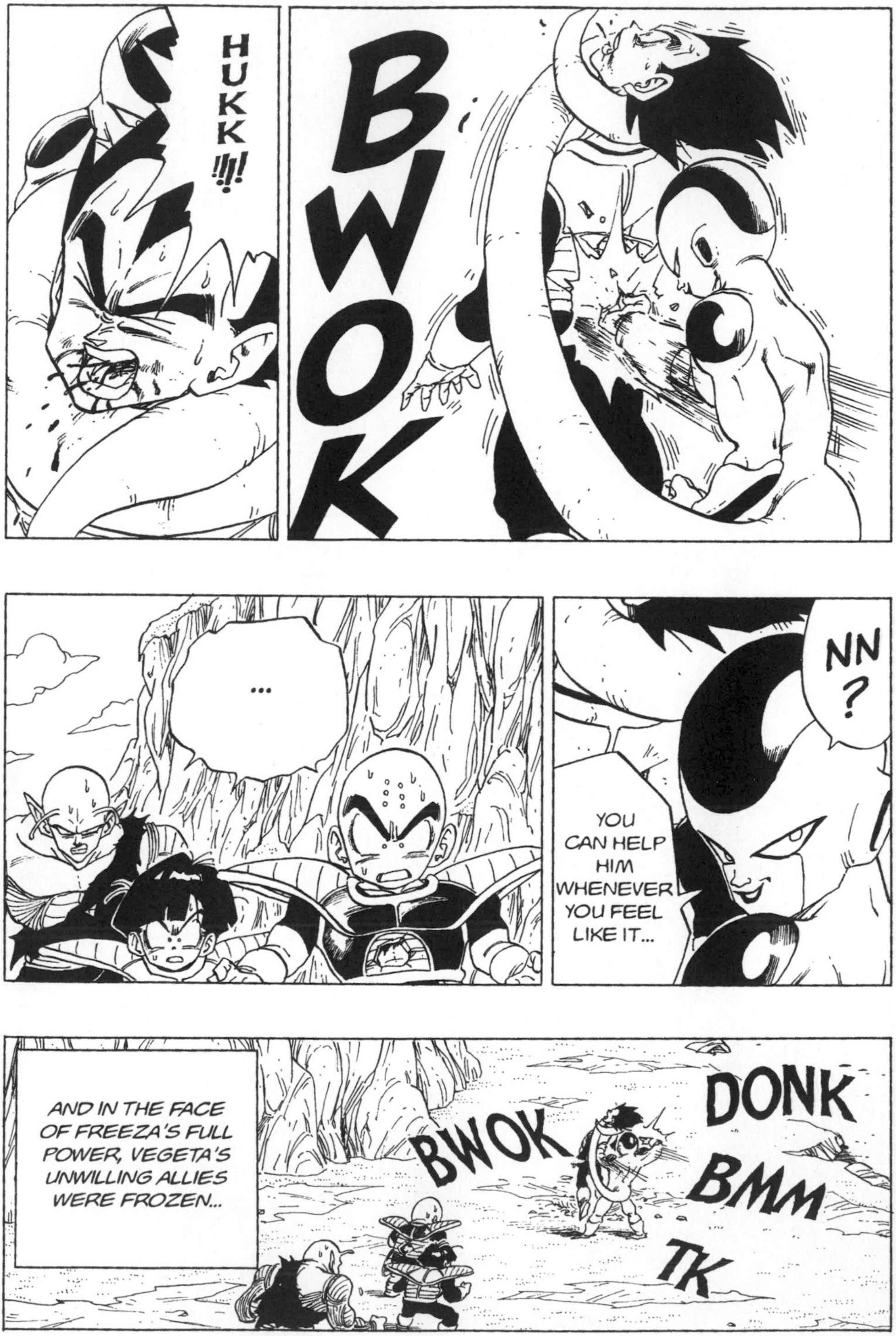
BWOK
HUKK !!!!
...
NN ?
YOU CAN HELP HIM WHENEVER YOU FEEL LIKE IT...
AND IN THE FACE OF FREEZA'S FULL POWER, VEGETA'S UNWILLING ALLIES WERE FROZEN...
DONK
BWOK
BMM
TK

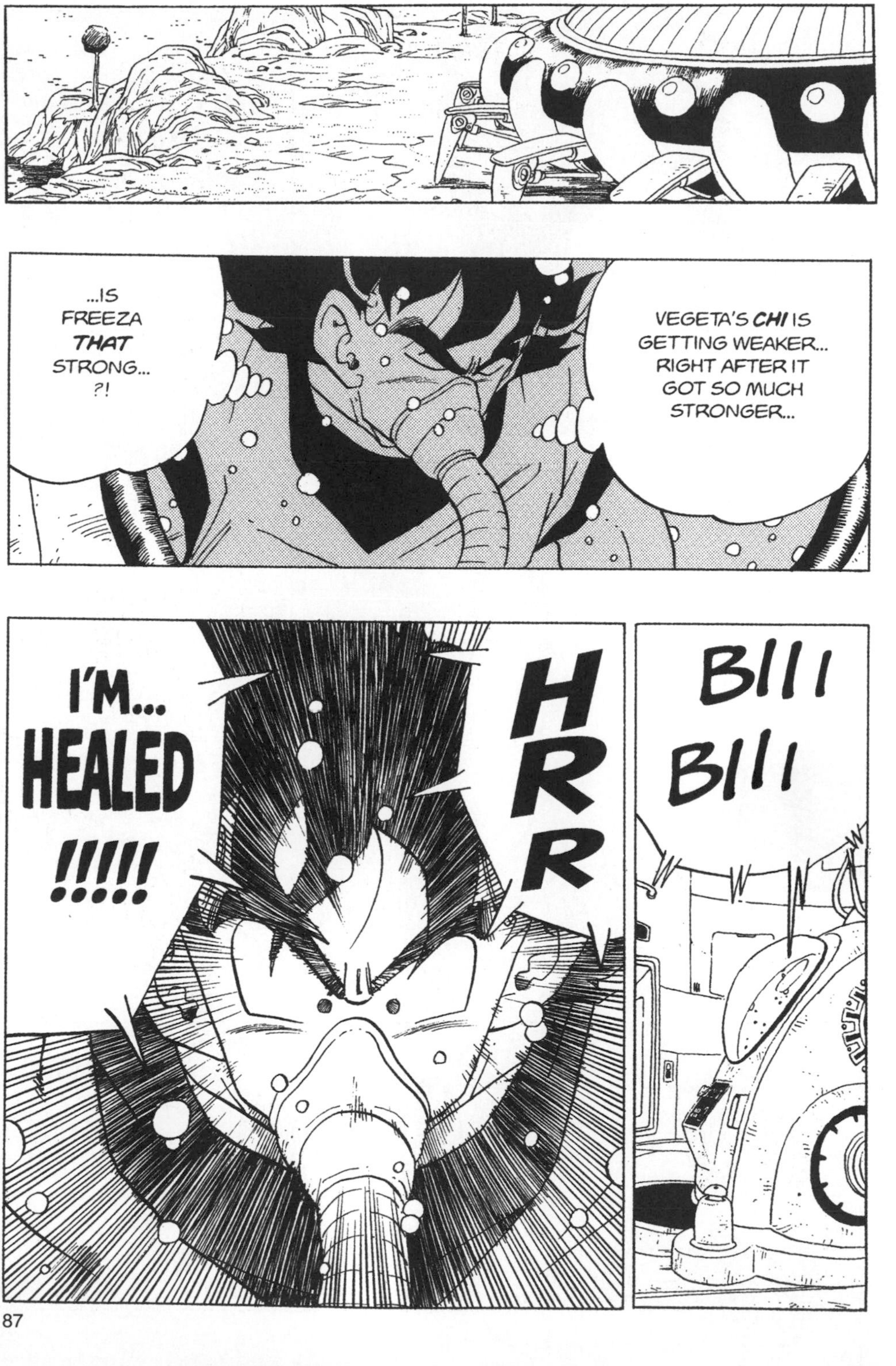
VEGETA'S CHI IS GETTING WEAKER... RIGHT AFTER IT GOT SO MUCH STRONGER...
...IS FREEZA THAT STRONG...?!
BIII BIII
HRR
I'M... HEALED !!!!!

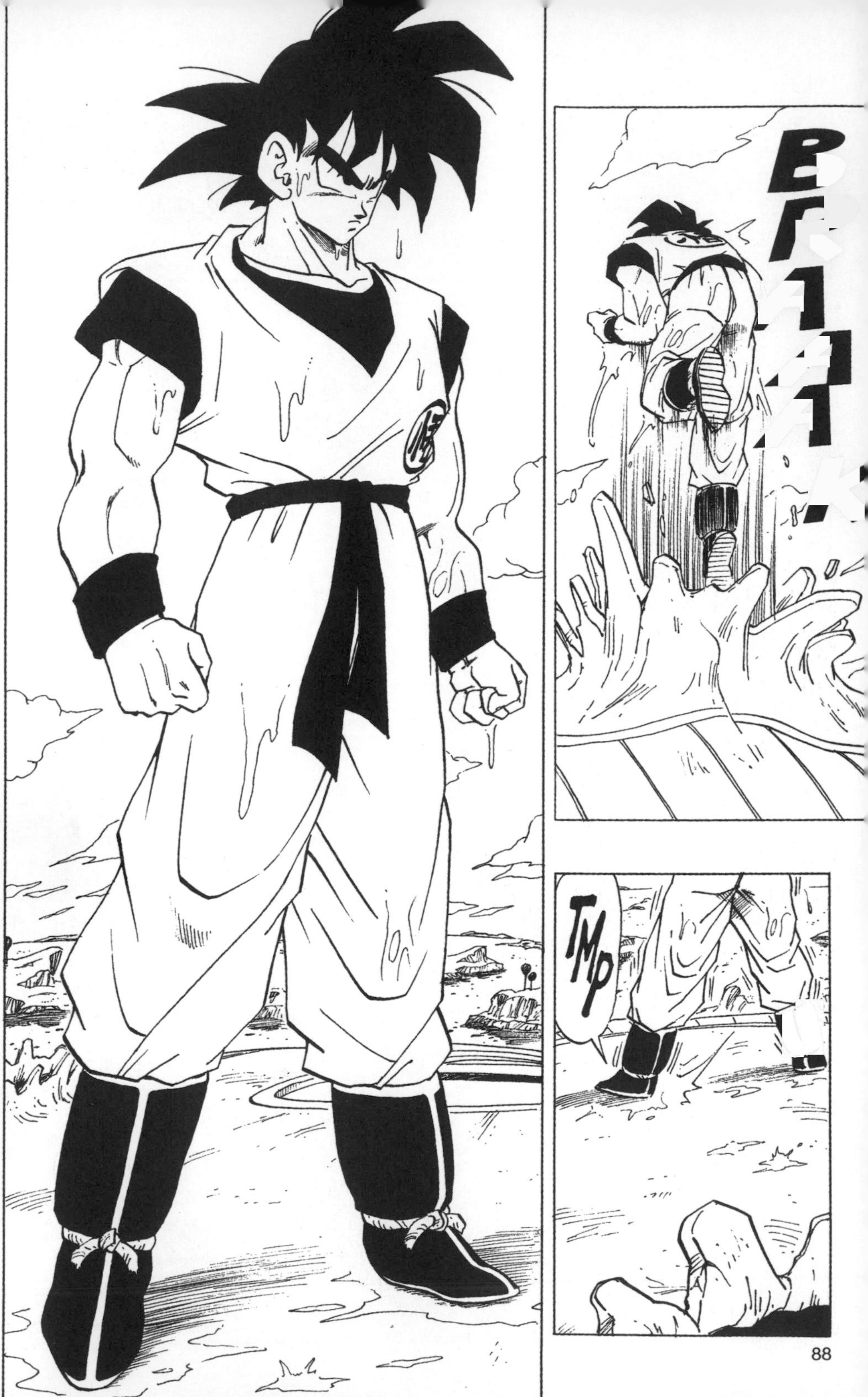
BRAAAK
TMP

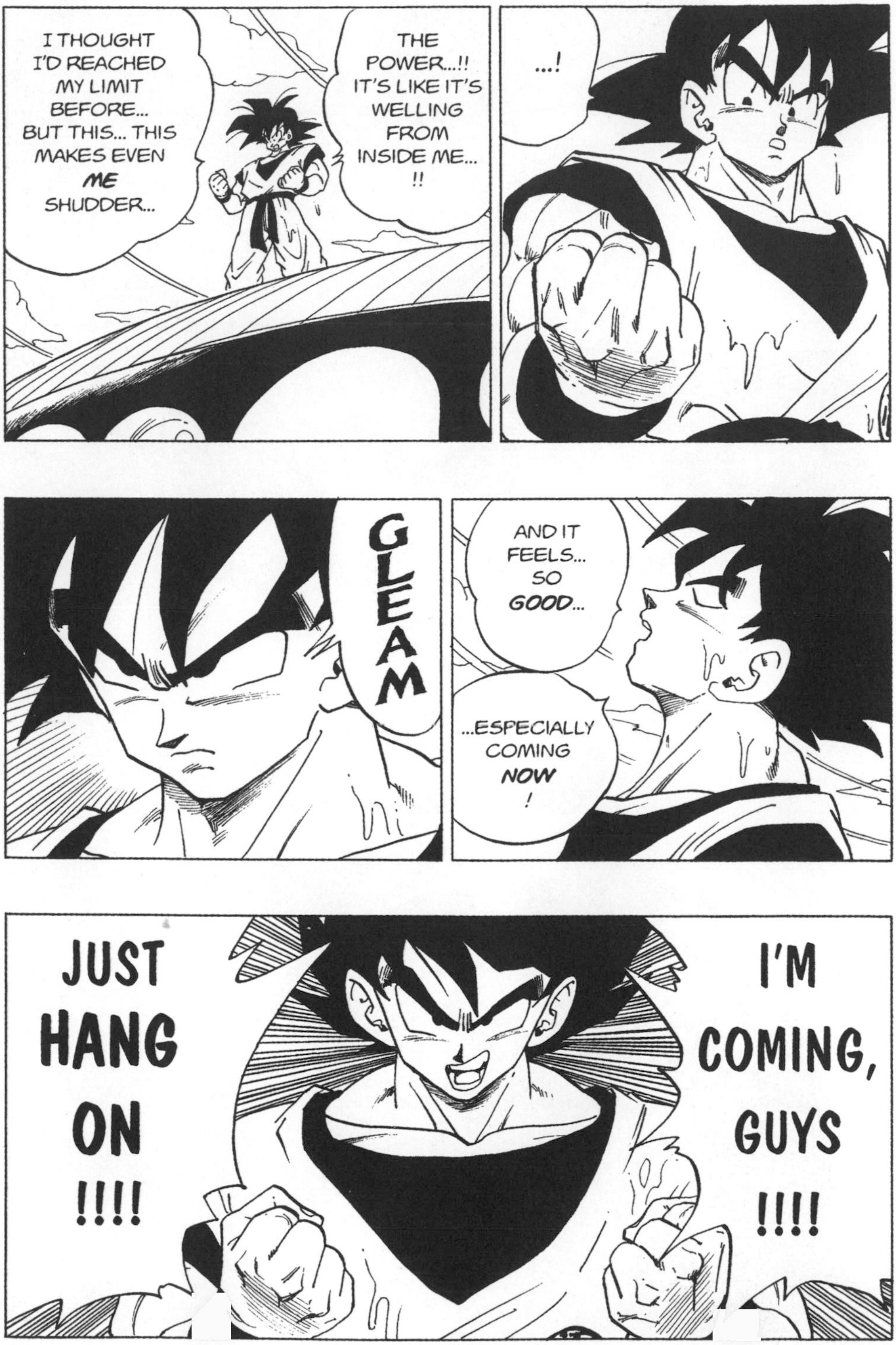
I THOUGHT I'D REACHED MY LIMIT BEFORE... BUT THIS... THIS MAKES EVEN *ME* SHUDDER...
THE POWER...!! IT'S LIKE IT'S WELLING FROM INSIDE ME... !!
...!
GLEAM
AND IT FEELS... SO *GOOD*...
...ESPECIALLY COMING *NOW* !
JUST HANG ON !!!!
I'M COMING, GUYS !!!!

DBZ:113 • The Ultimate Battle Begins!

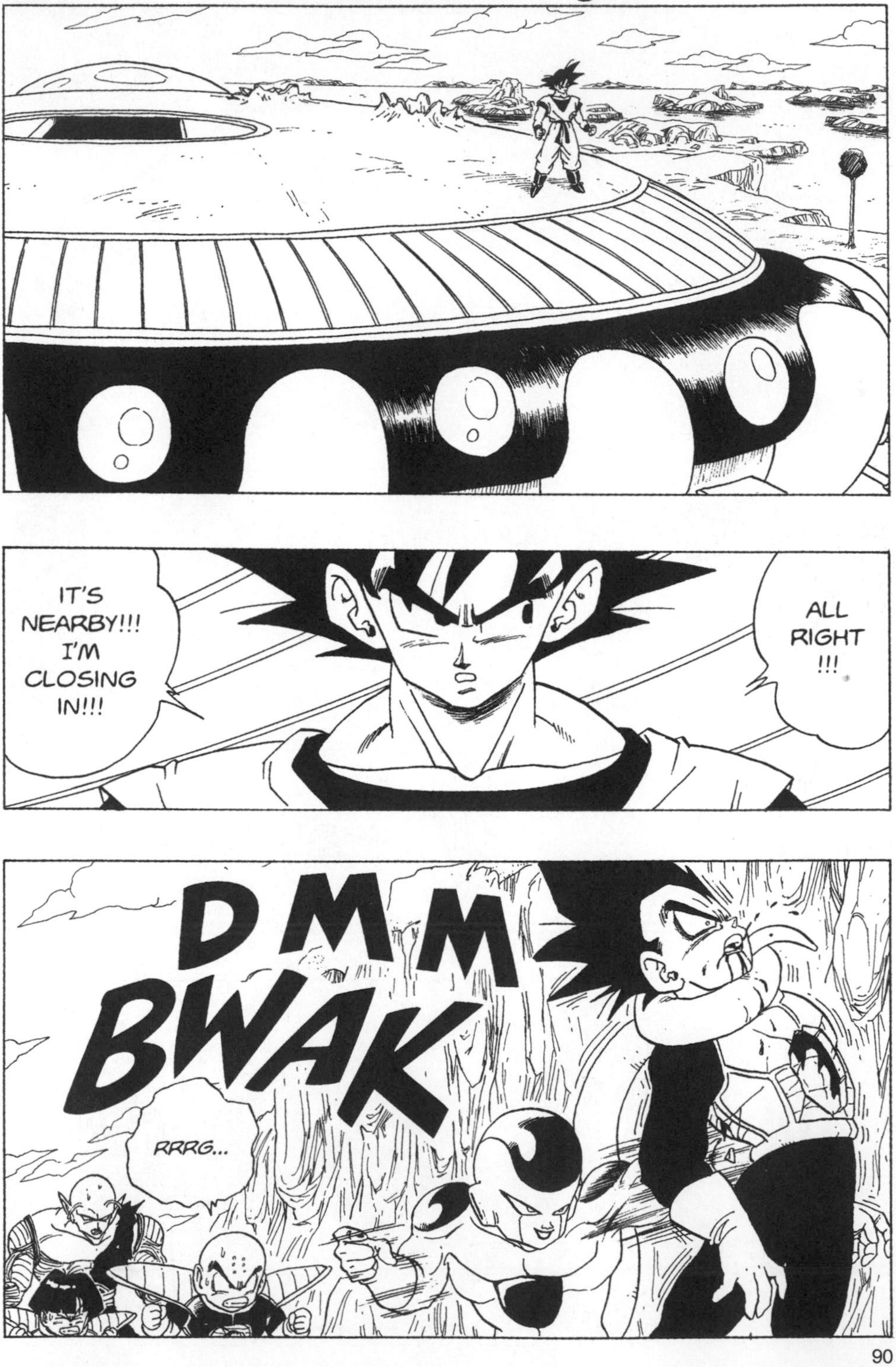
ALL RIGHT !!!
IT'S NEARBY!!! I'M CLOSING IN!!!
DMM
BWAK
RRRG...

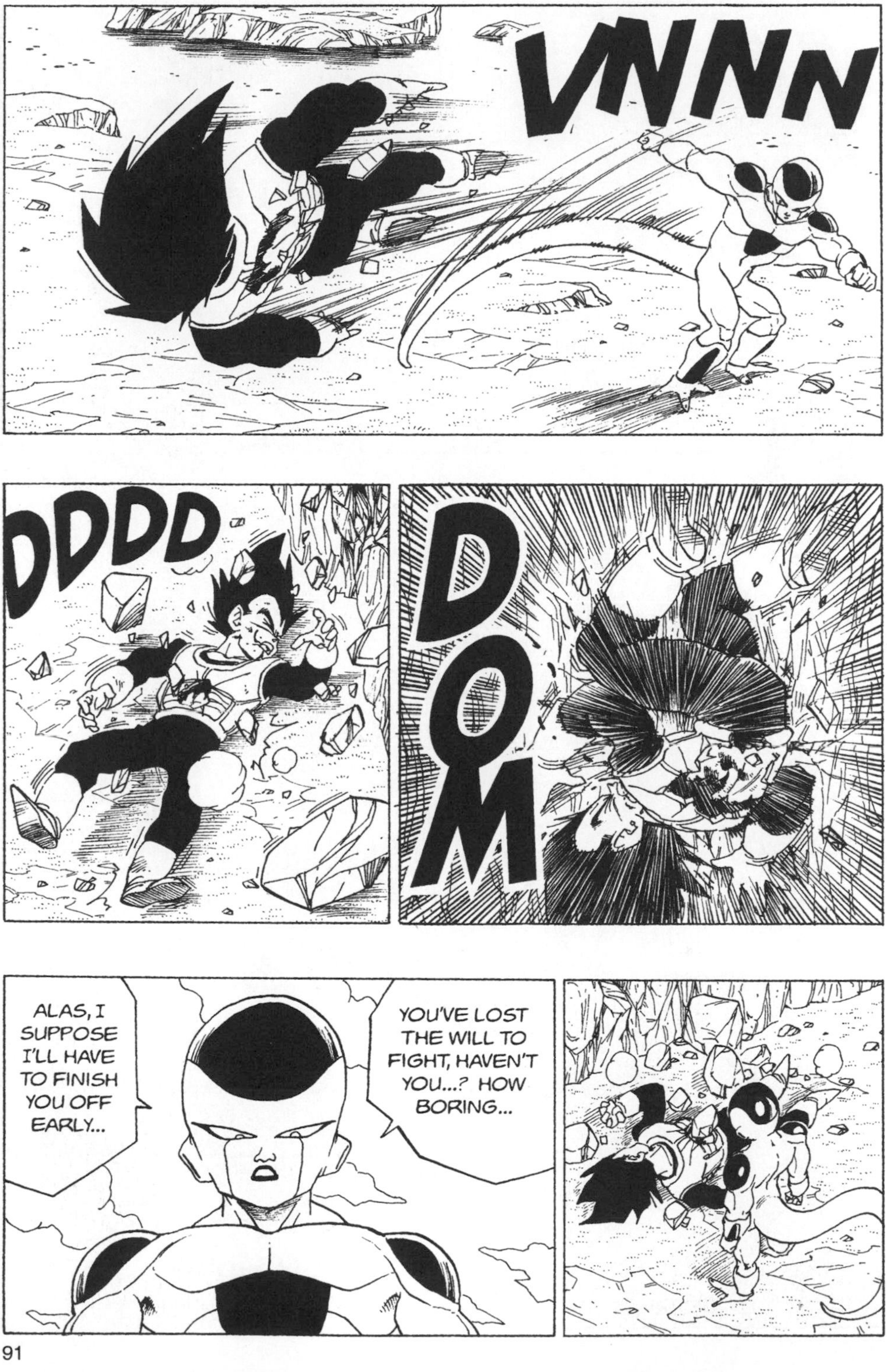
VNNN
DDDD
DOM
YOU'VE LOST THE WILL TO FIGHT, HAVEN'T YOU...? HOW BORING...
ALAS, I SUPPOSE I'LL HAVE TO FINISH YOU OFF EARLY...

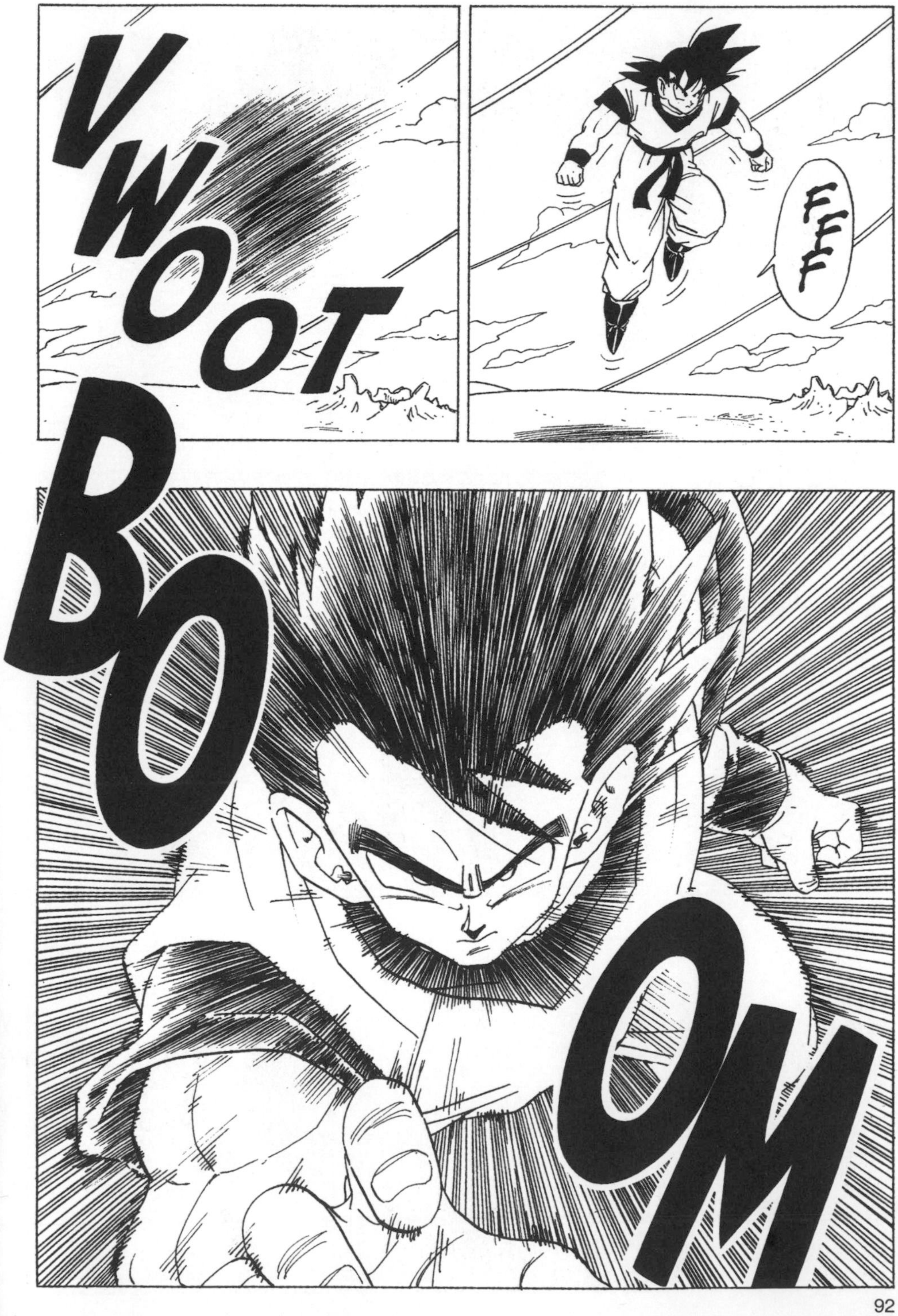
VWOOT
FFF
BOOOM

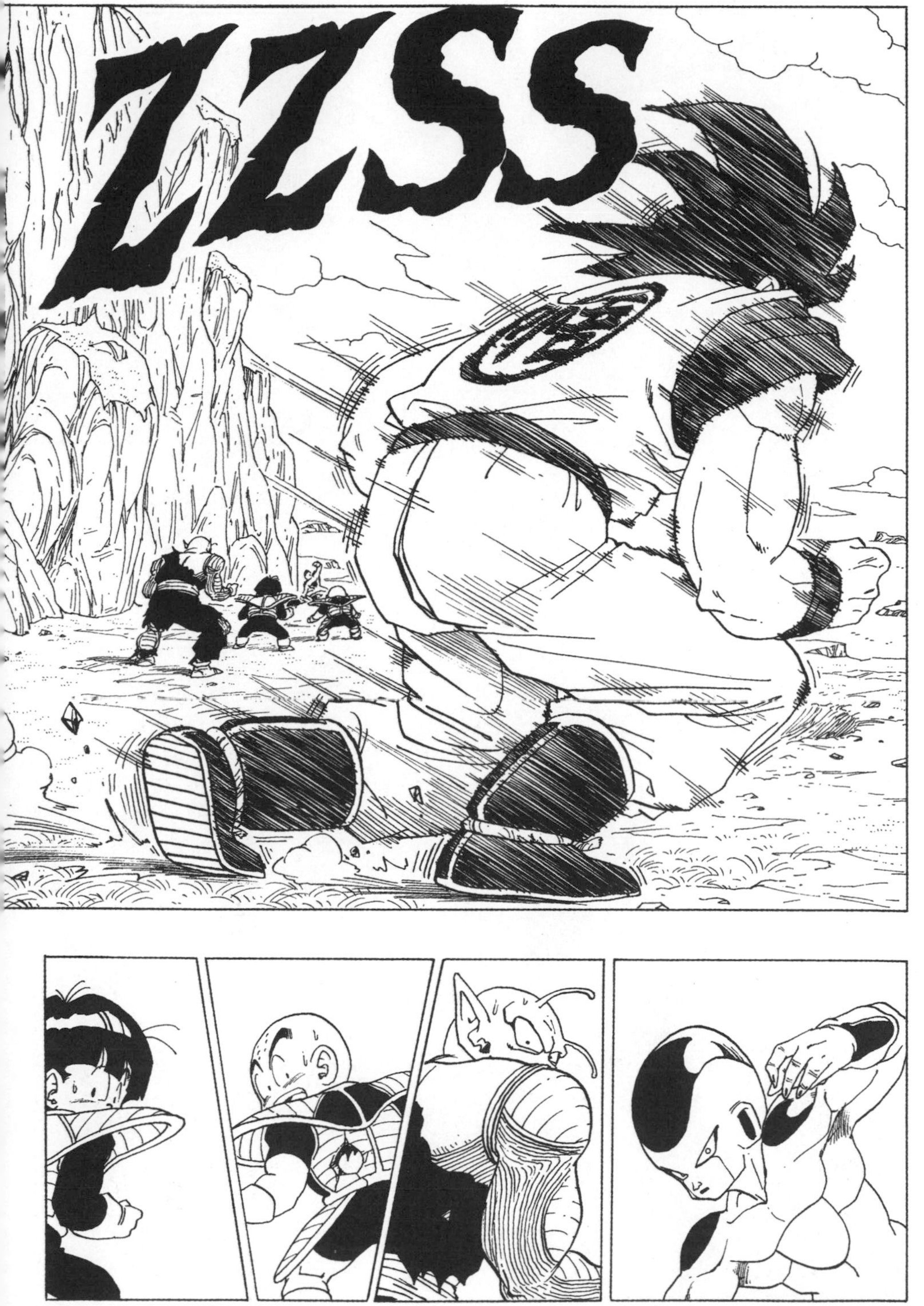
ZZSS

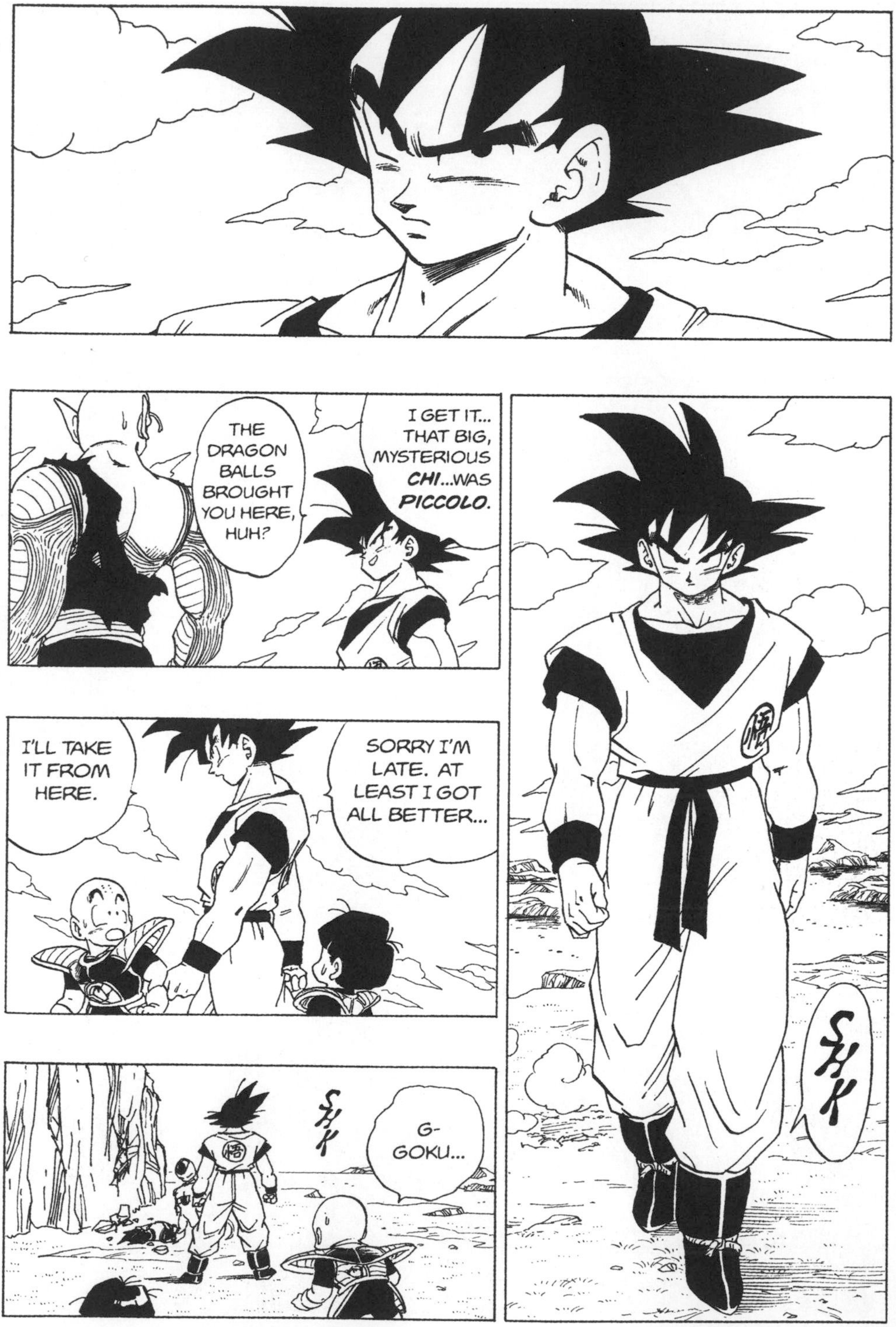
SHK
I GET IT... THAT BIG, MYSTERIOUS CHI...WAS PICCOLO.
THE DRAGON BALLS BROUGHT YOU HERE, HUH?
SORRY I'M LATE. AT LEAST I GOT ALL BETTER...
I'LL TAKE IT FROM HERE.
SHK
G-GOKU...

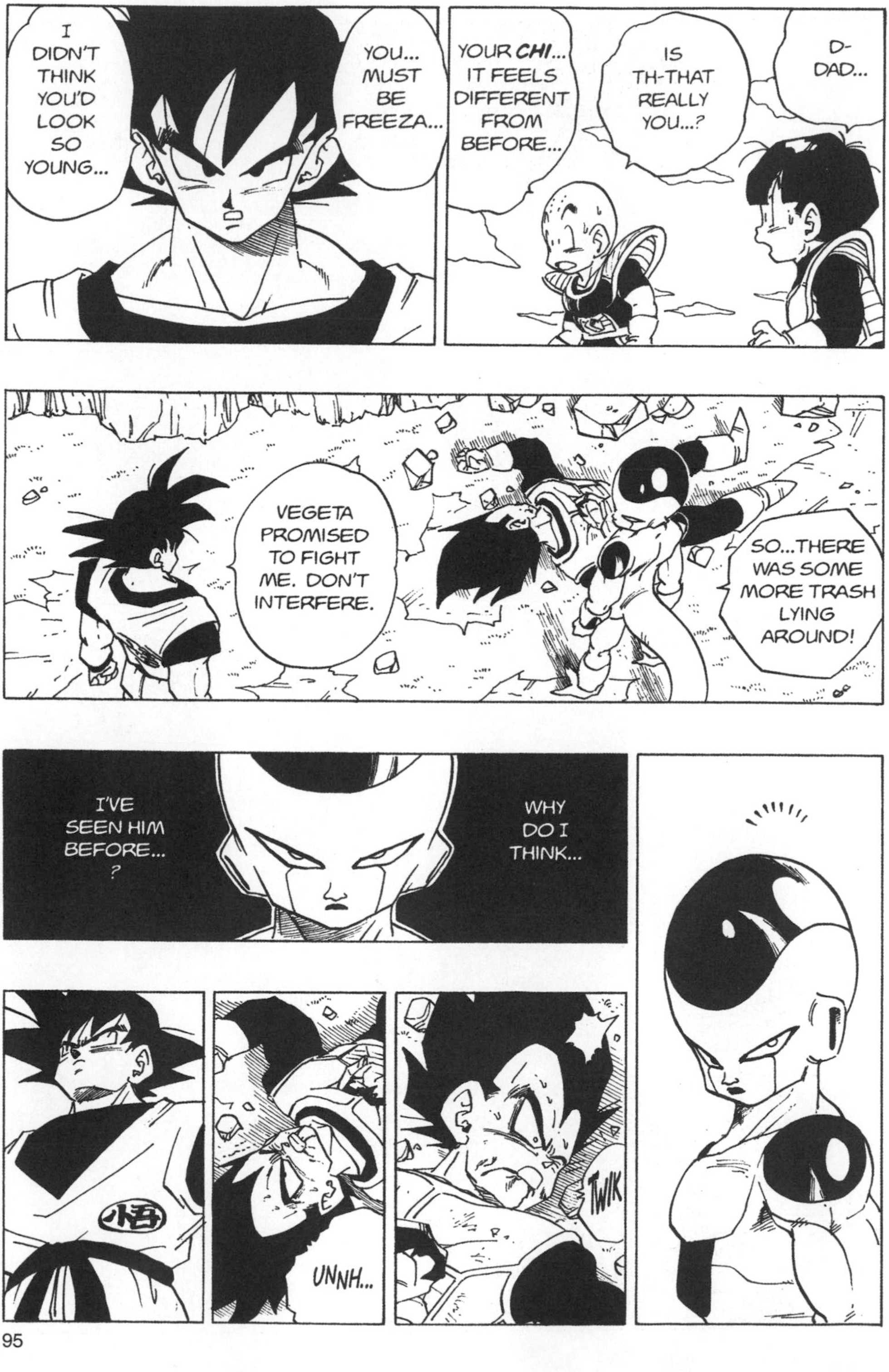
I DIDN'T THINK YOU'D LOOK SO YOUNG...
YOU... MUST BE FREEZA...
YOUR *CHI*... IT FEELS DIFFERENT FROM BEFORE...
IS TH-THAT REALLY YOU...?
D-DAD...
VEGETA PROMISED TO FIGHT ME. DON'T INTERFERE.
SO...THERE WAS SOME MORE TRASH LYING AROUND!
I'VE SEEN HIM BEFORE... ?
WHY DO I THINK...
UNNH...
TWIK

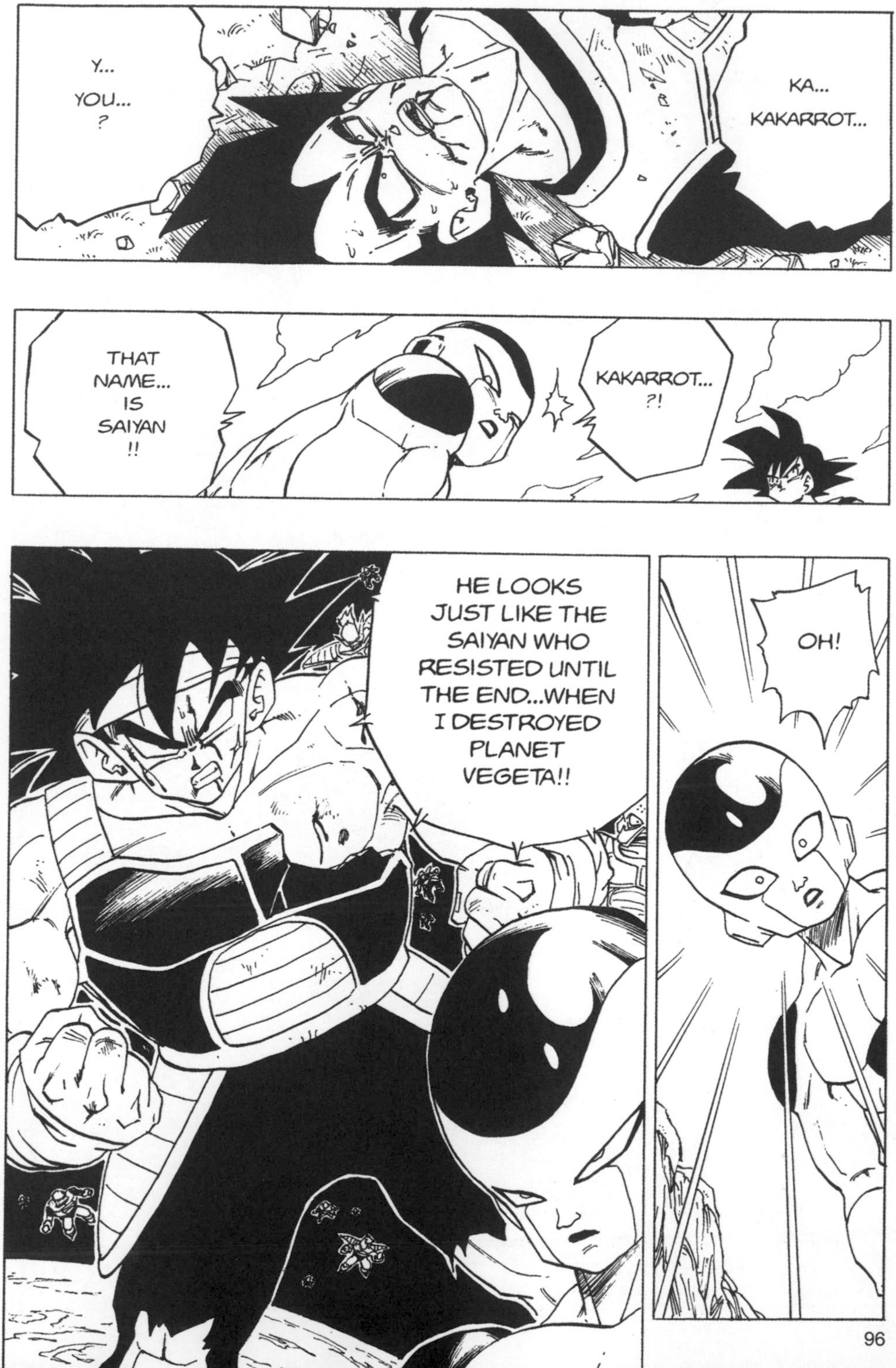
Y...
YOU...
?
KA...
KAKARROT...
THAT NAME... IS SAIYAN !!
KAKARROT... ?!
HE LOOKS JUST LIKE THE SAIYAN WHO RESISTED UNTIL THE END...WHEN I DESTROYED PLANET VEGETA!!
OH!

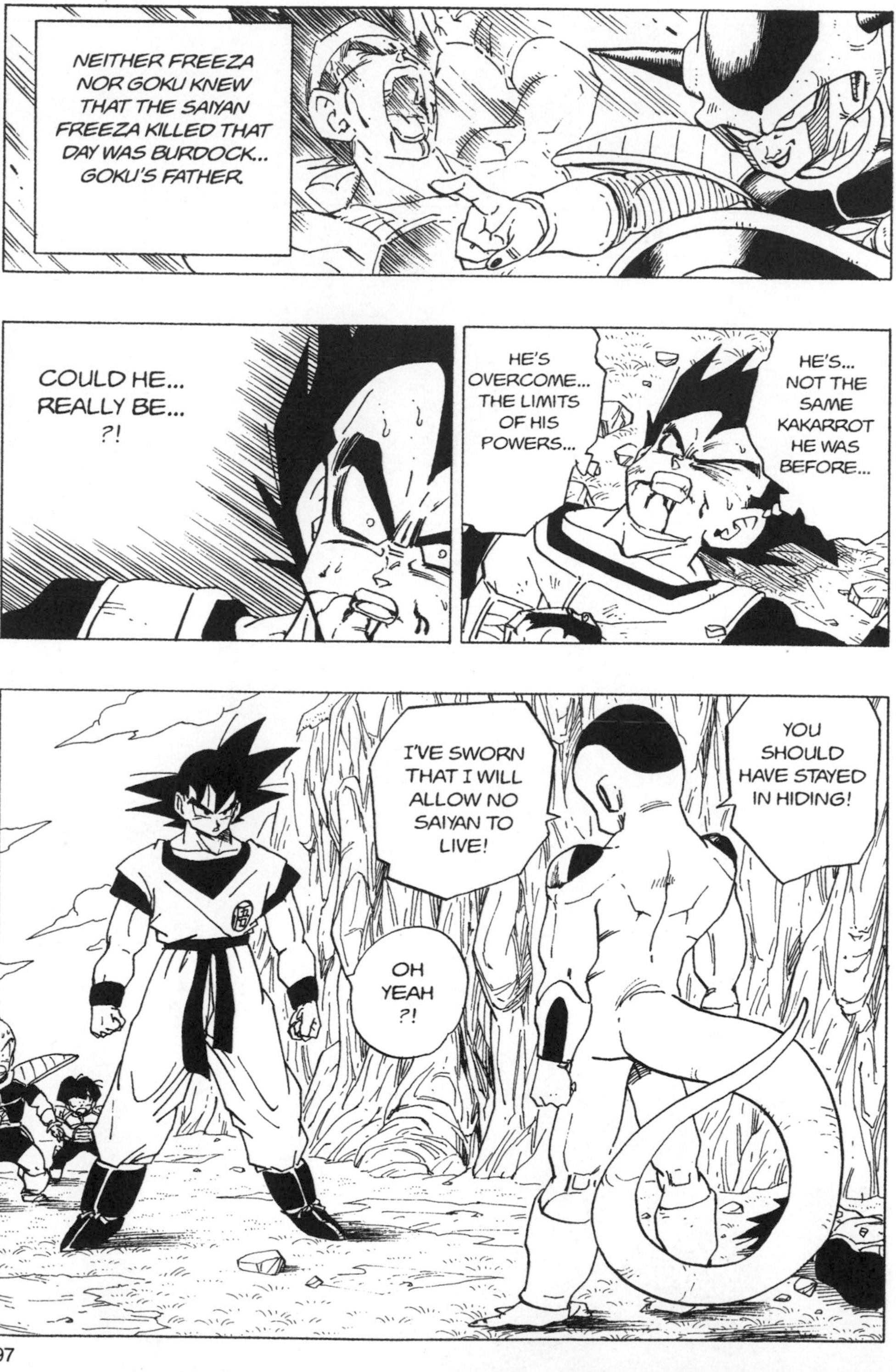
NEITHER FREEZA NOR GOKU KNEW THAT THE SAIYAN FREEZA KILLED THAT DAY WAS BURDOCK... GOKU'S FATHER.
COULD HE... REALLY BE... ?!
HE'S OVERCOME... THE LIMITS OF HIS POWERS...
HE'S... NOT THE SAME KAKARROT HE WAS BEFORE...
YOU SHOULD HAVE STAYED IN HIDING!
I'VE SWORN THAT I WILL ALLOW NO SAIYAN TO LIVE!
OH YEAH ?!

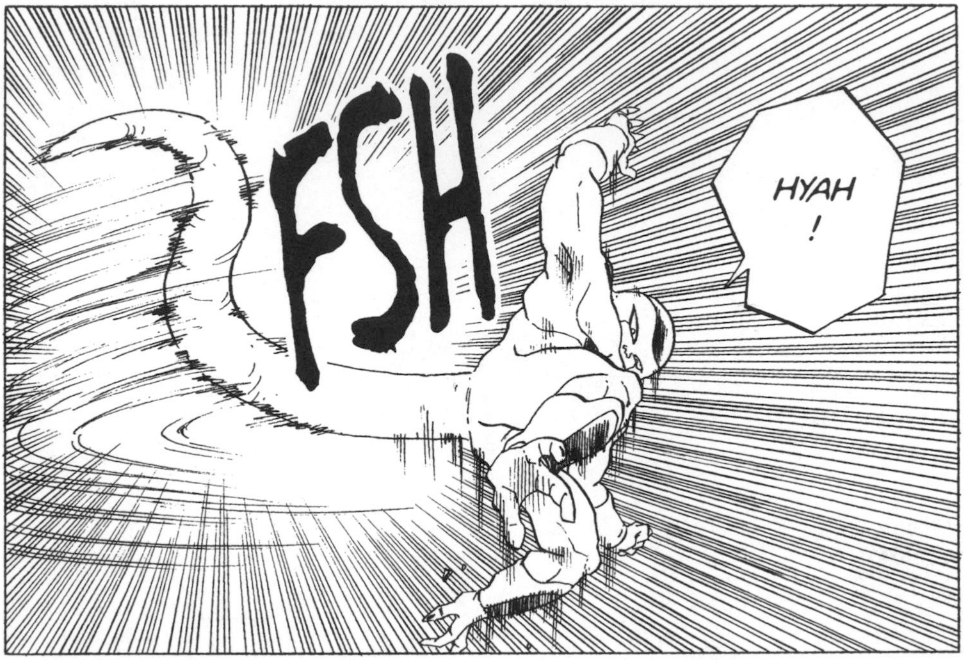
HYAH
!
FSH

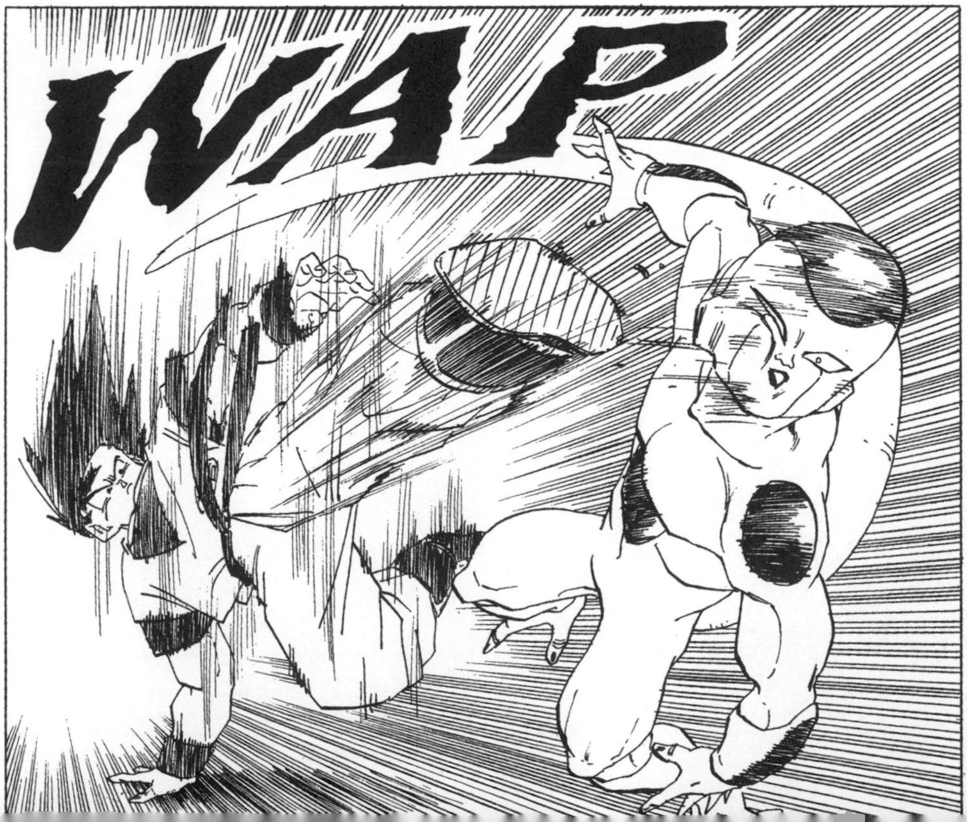
WAP

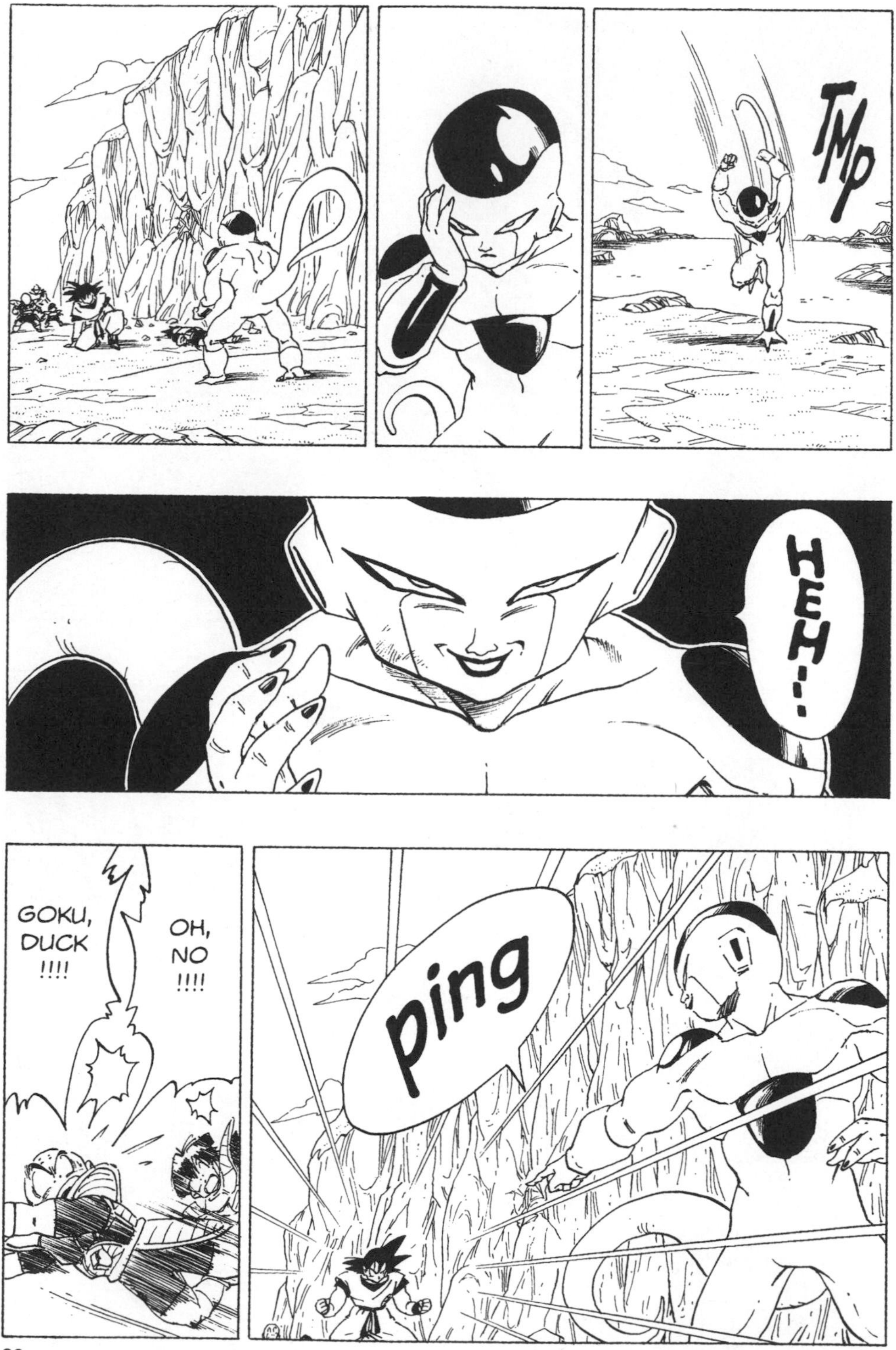
TMP
HEH...
GOKU, DUCK !!!!
OH, NO !!!!
ping
!

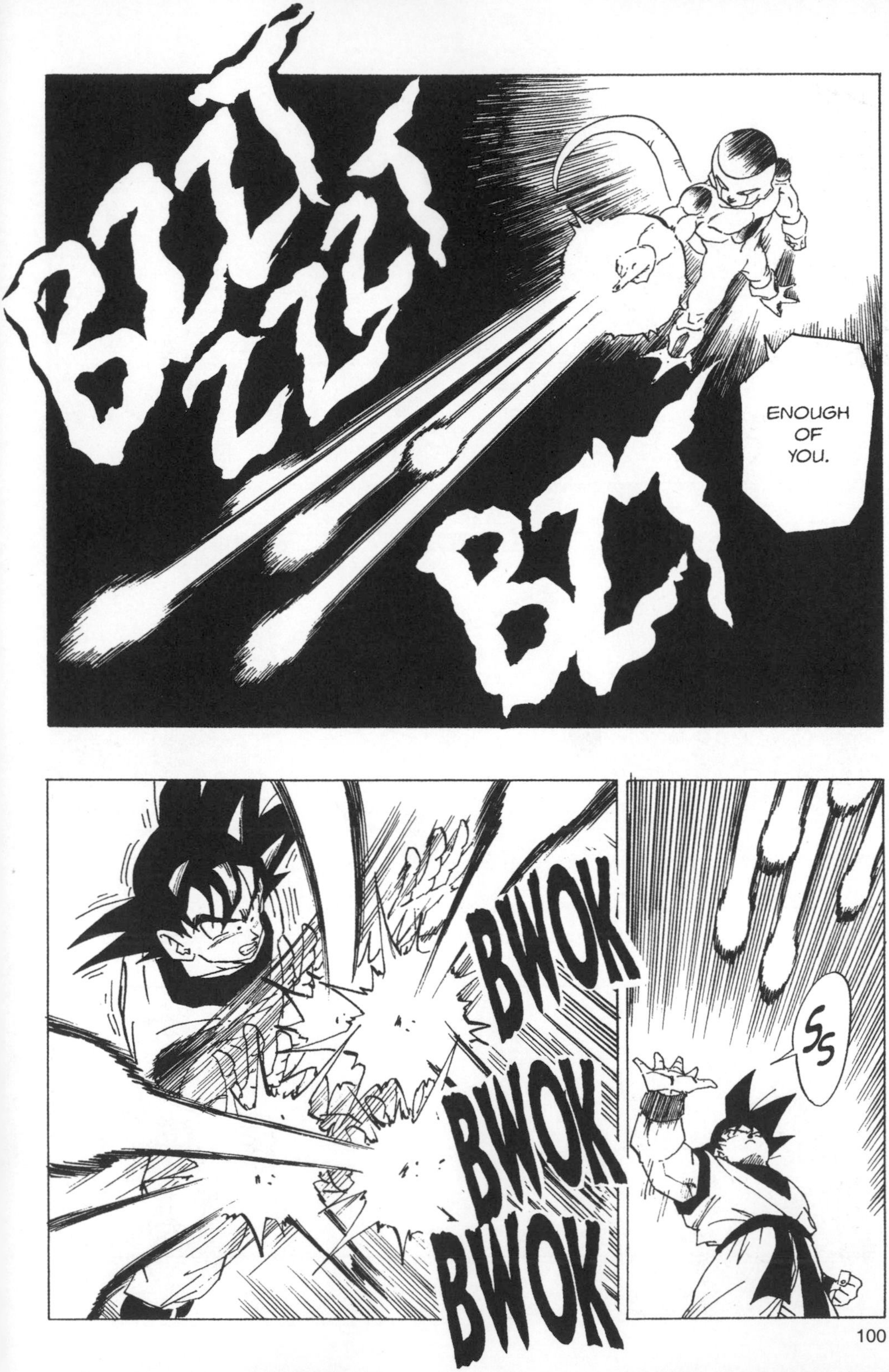
ENOUGH OF YOU.
BZZZZZT
BZT
SS
BWOK
BWOK
BWOK

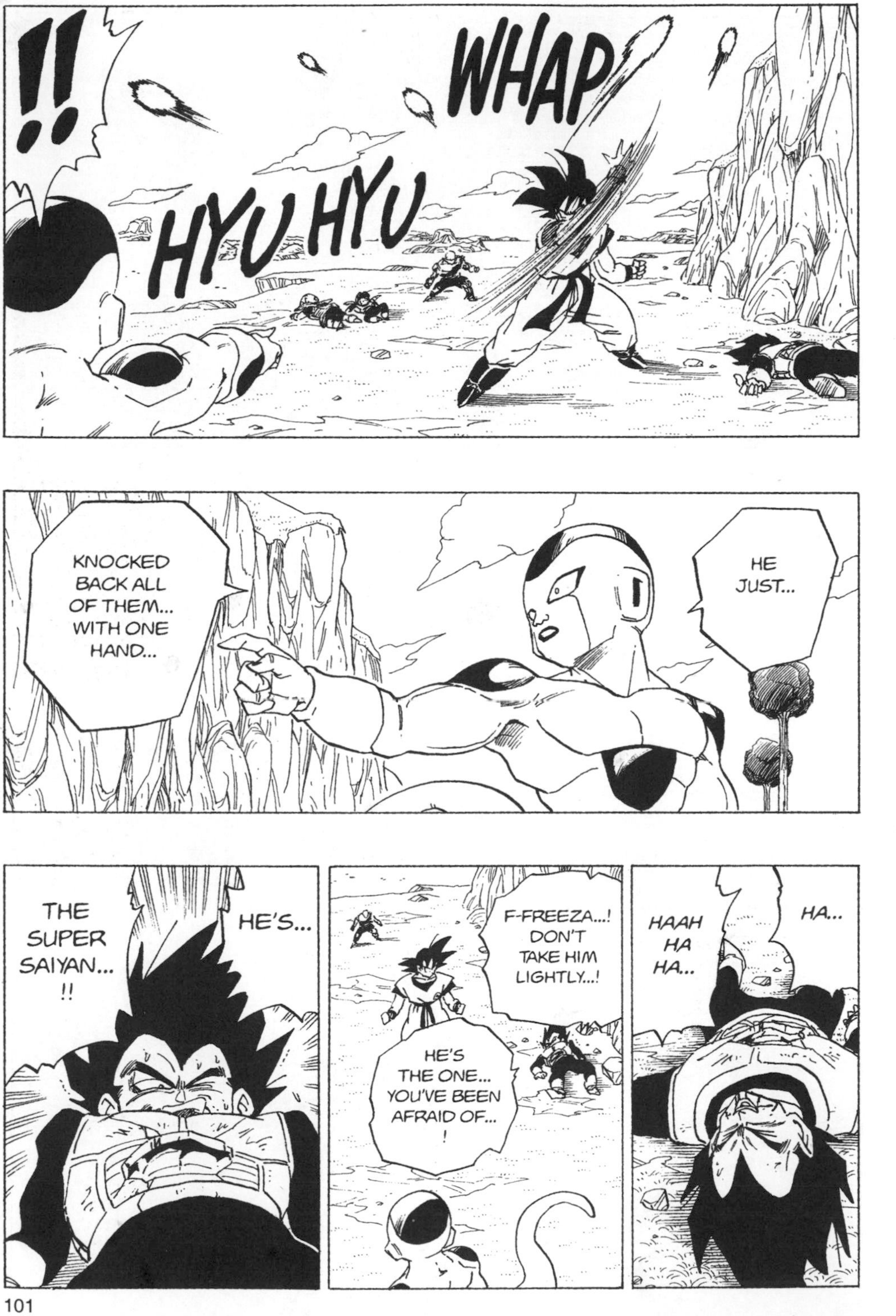
WHAP
HYU HYU
!!
HE JUST...
KNOCKED BACK ALL OF THEM... WITH ONE HAND...
HA...
HAAH HA HA...
F-FREEZA...! DON'T TAKE HIM LIGHTLY...!
HE'S THE ONE... YOU'VE BEEN AFRAID OF...!
HE'S...
THE SUPER SAIYAN...!!

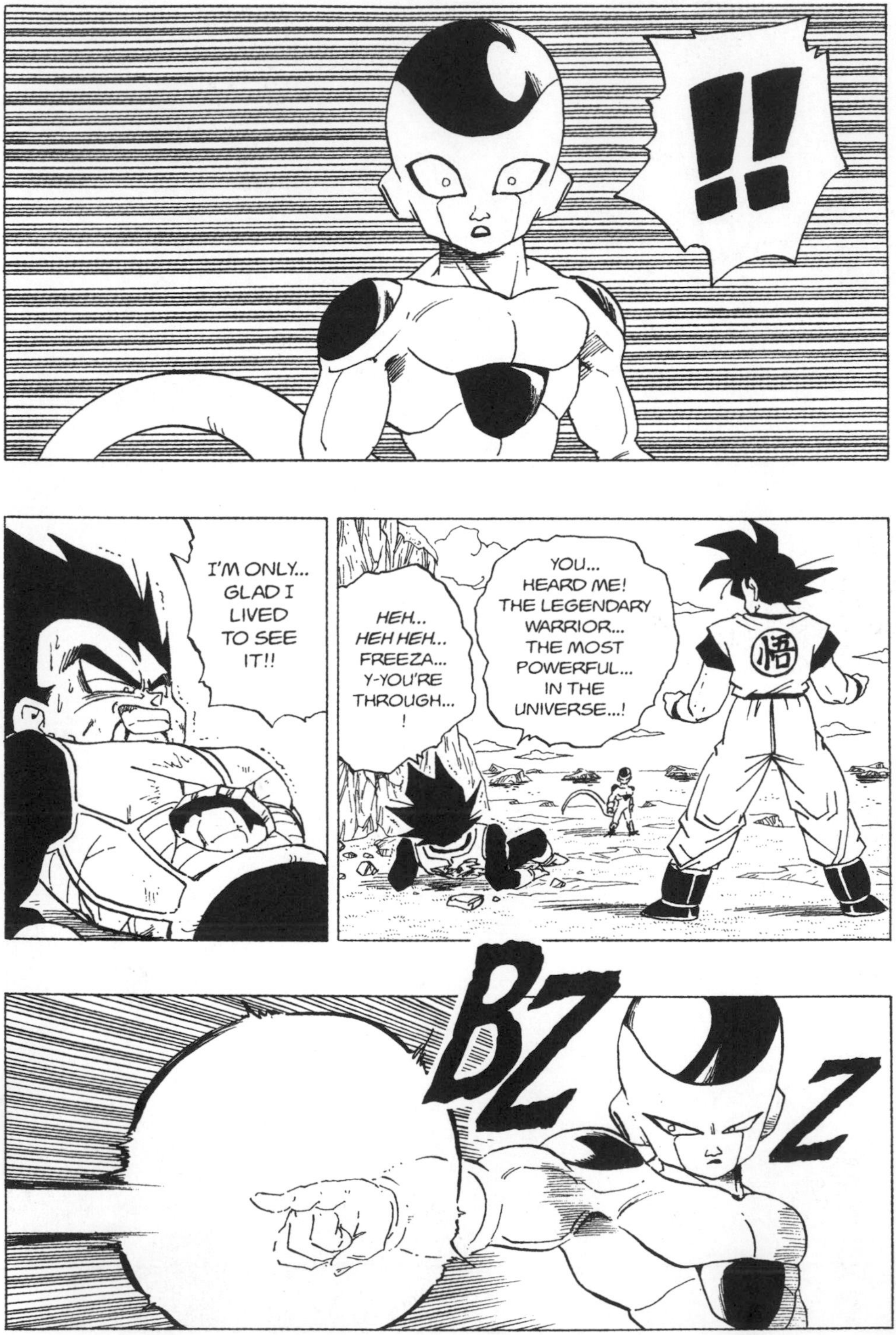
!!
I'M ONLY... GLAD I LIVED TO SEE IT!!
HEH... HEH HEH... FREEZA... Y-YOU'RE THROUGH... !
YOU... HEARD ME! THE LEGENDARY WARRIOR... THE MOST POWERFUL... IN THE UNIVERSE...!
BZZ

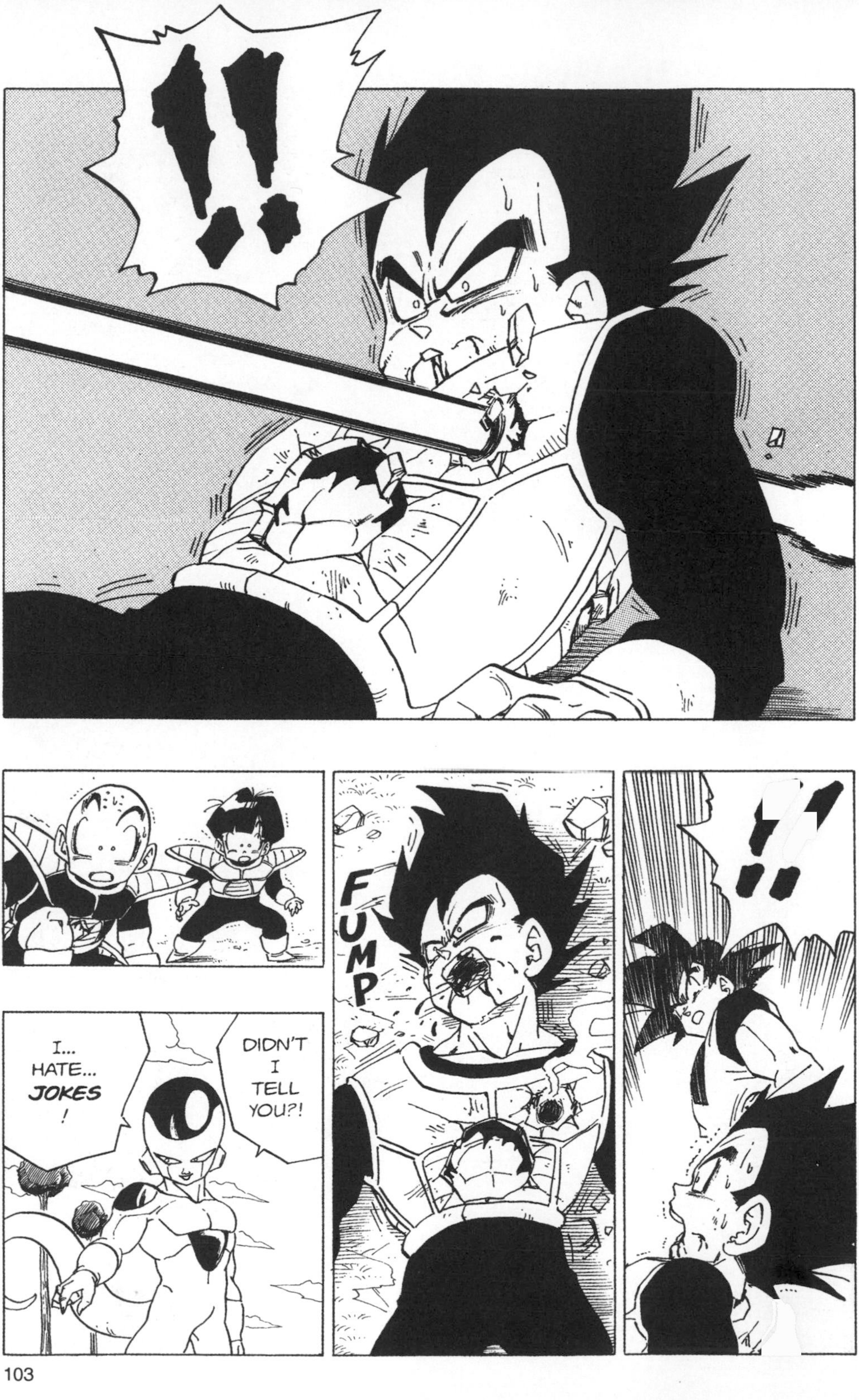
!!
FUMP
!!
DIDN'T I TELL YOU?!
I... HATE... JOKES!

DBZ:114 • The Death of Vegeta

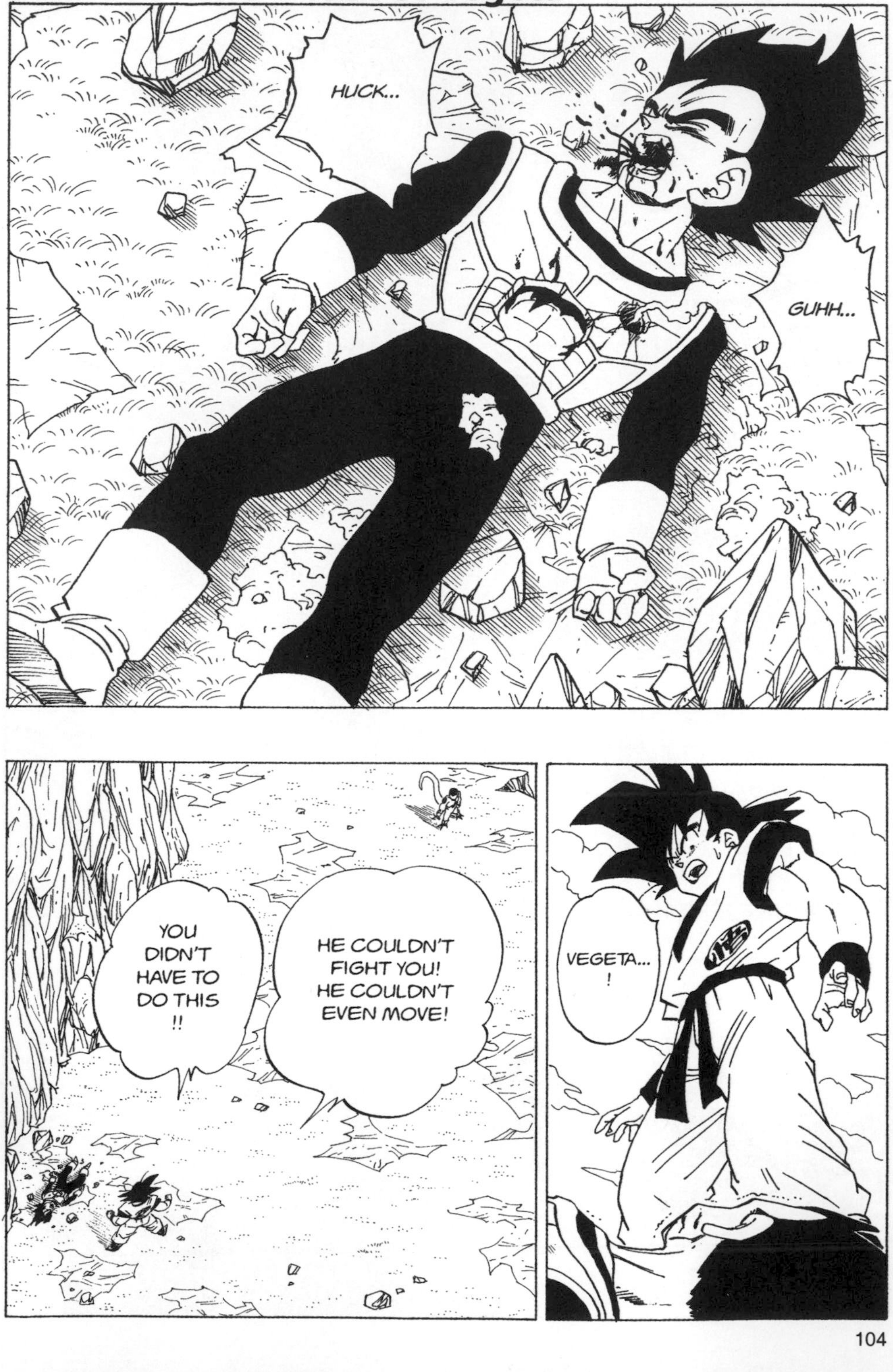
HUCK...
GUHH...
YOU DIDN'T HAVE TO DO THIS !!
HE COULDN'T FIGHT YOU! HE COULDN'T EVEN MOVE!
VEGETA... !

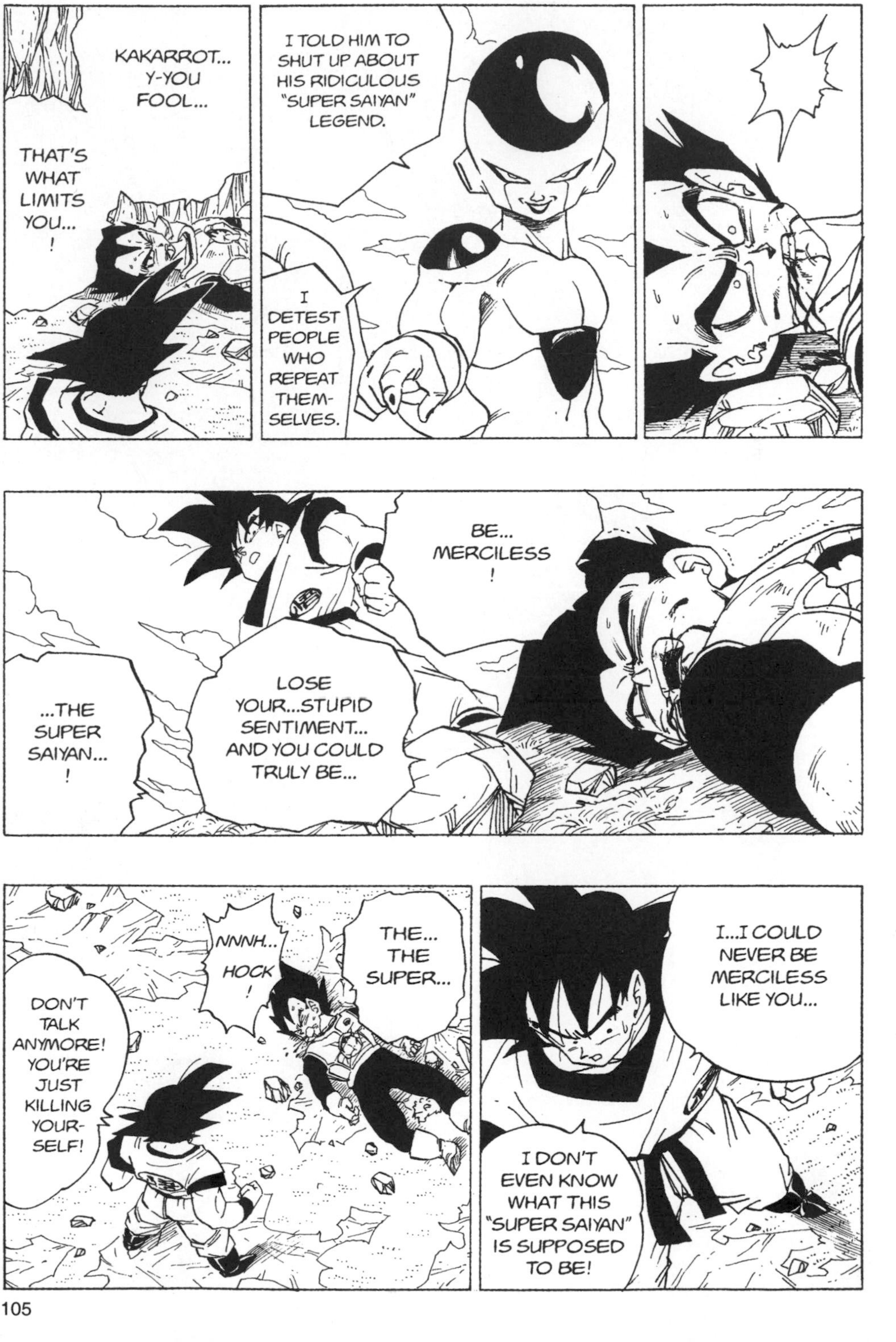
KAKARROT... Y-YOU FOOL...
THAT'S WHAT LIMITS YOU...!
I TOLD HIM TO SHUT UP ABOUT HIS RIDICULOUS "SUPER SAIYAN" LEGEND.
I DETEST PEOPLE WHO REPEAT THEM-SELVES.
BE... MERCILESS!
LOSE YOUR...STUPID SENTIMENT... AND YOU COULD TRULY BE...
...THE SUPER SAIYAN...!
NNNH... HOCK!
THE... THE SUPER...
DON'T TALK ANYMORE! YOU'RE JUST KILLING YOUR-SELF!
I...I COULD NEVER BE MERCILESS LIKE YOU...
I DON'T EVEN KNOW WHAT THIS "SUPER SAIYAN" IS SUPPOSED TO BE!

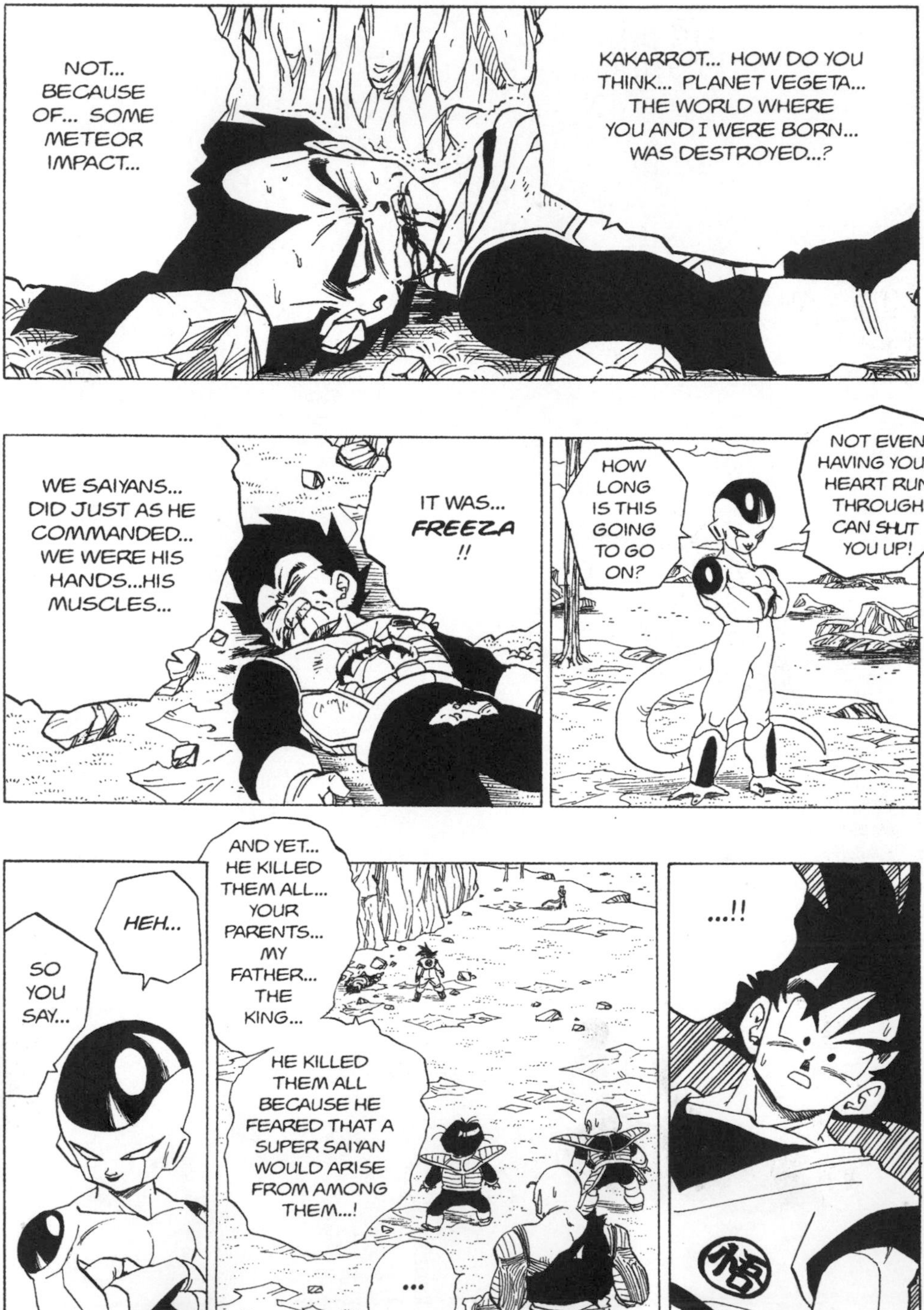
KAKARROT... HOW DO YOU THINK... PLANET VEGETA... THE WORLD WHERE YOU AND I WERE BORN... WAS DESTROYED...?
NOT... BECAUSE OF... SOME METEOR IMPACT...
IT WAS... *FREEZA* !!
WE SAIYANS... DID JUST AS HE COMMANDED... WE WERE HIS HANDS...HIS MUSCLES...
HOW LONG IS THIS GOING TO GO ON?
NOT EVEN HAVING YOUR HEART RUN THROUGH CAN SHUT YOU UP!
AND YET... HE KILLED THEM ALL... YOUR PARENTS... MY FATHER... THE KING...
HE KILLED THEM ALL BECAUSE HE FEARED THAT A SUPER SAIYAN WOULD ARISE FROM AMONG THEM...!
...
HEH...
SO YOU SAY...
...!!

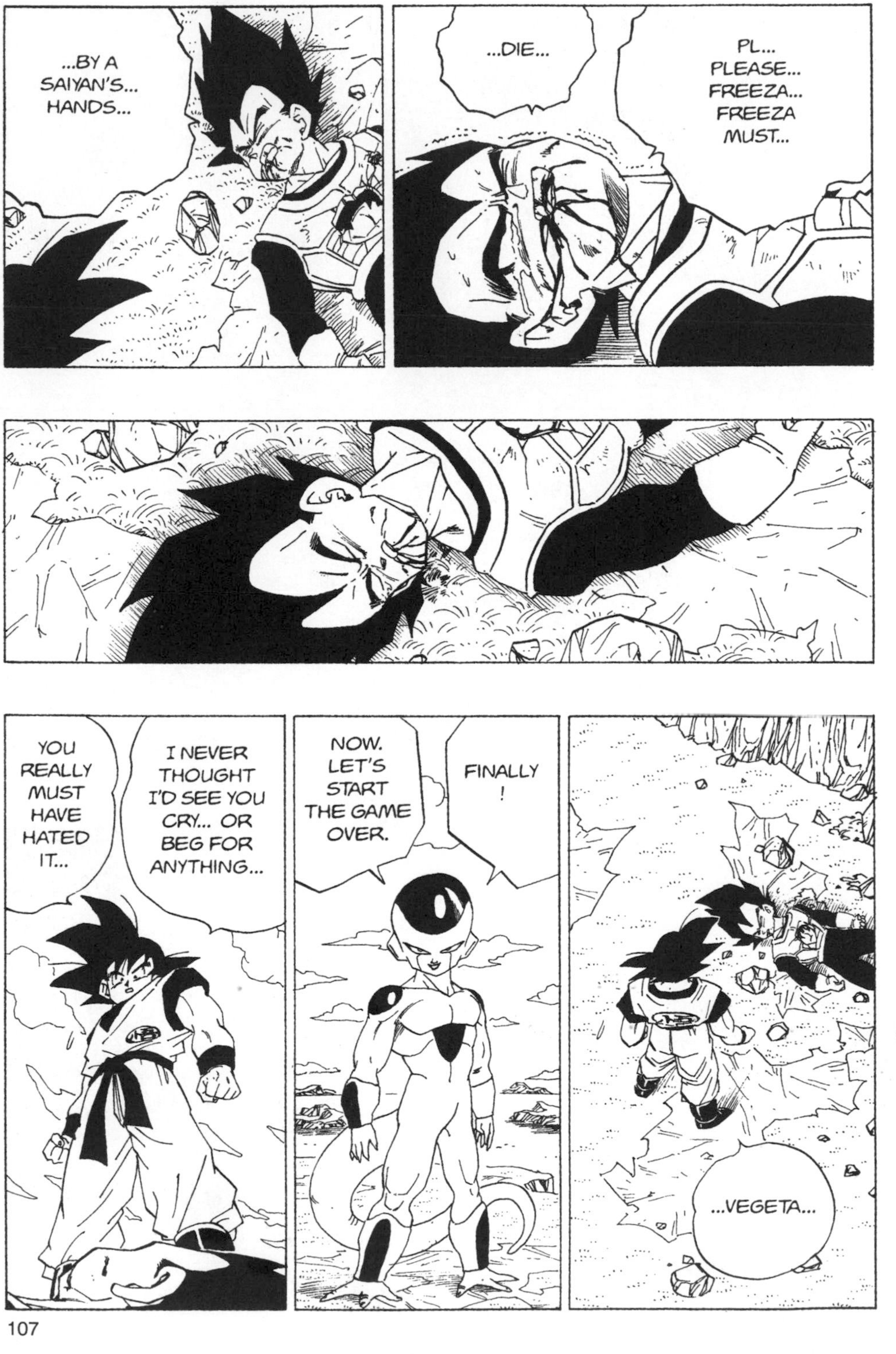
PL... PLEASE... FREEZA... FREEZA MUST...
...DIE...
...BY A SAIYAN'S... HANDS...
...VEGETA...
FINALLY !
NOW. LET'S START THE GAME OVER.
I NEVER THOUGHT I'D SEE YOU CRY... OR BEG FOR ANYTHING...
YOU REALLY MUST HAVE HATED IT...

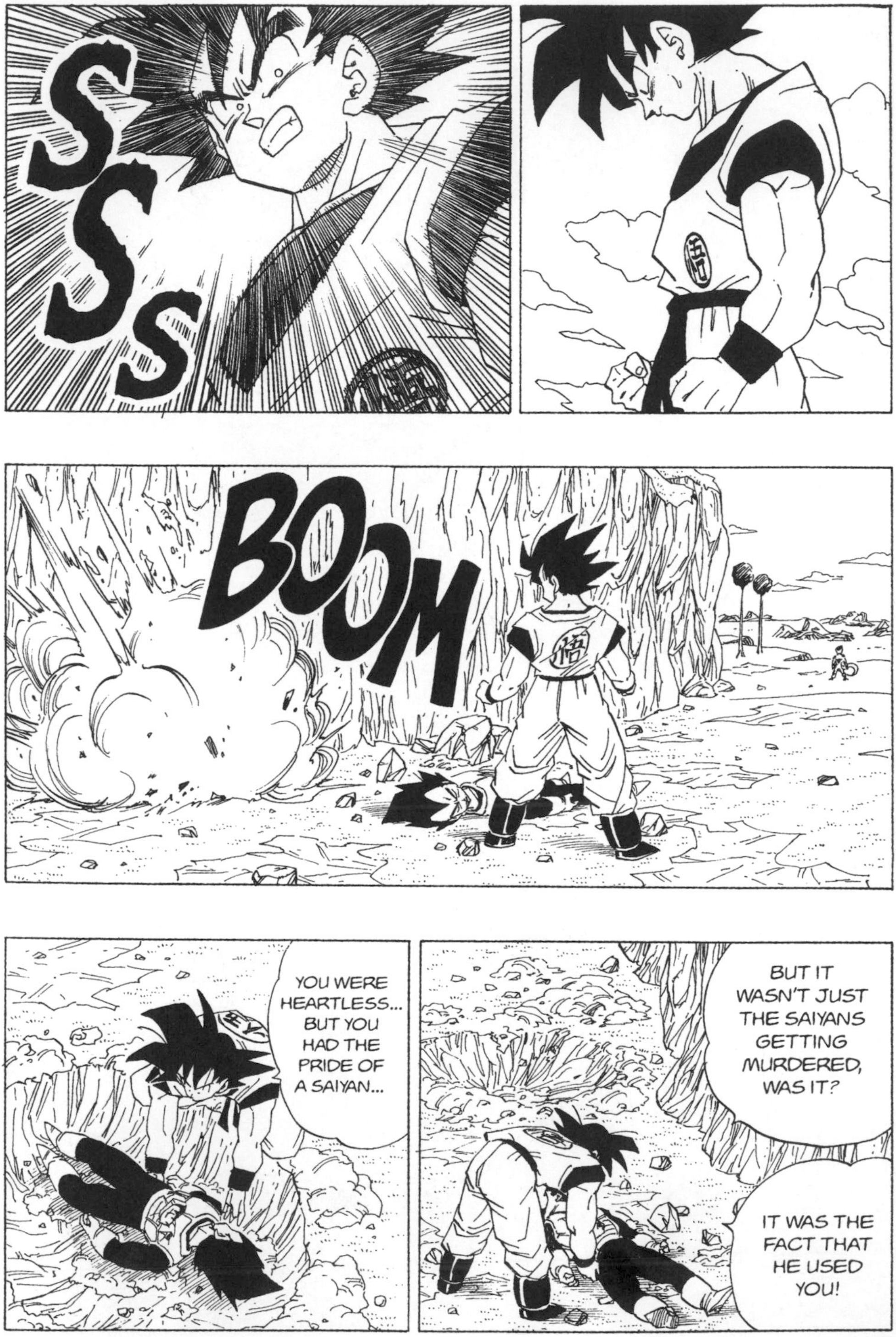
SSS
BOOM
YOU WERE HEARTLESS... BUT YOU HAD THE PRIDE OF A SAIYAN...
BUT IT WASN'T JUST THE SAIYANS GETTING MURDERED, WAS IT?
IT WAS THE FACT THAT HE USED YOU!

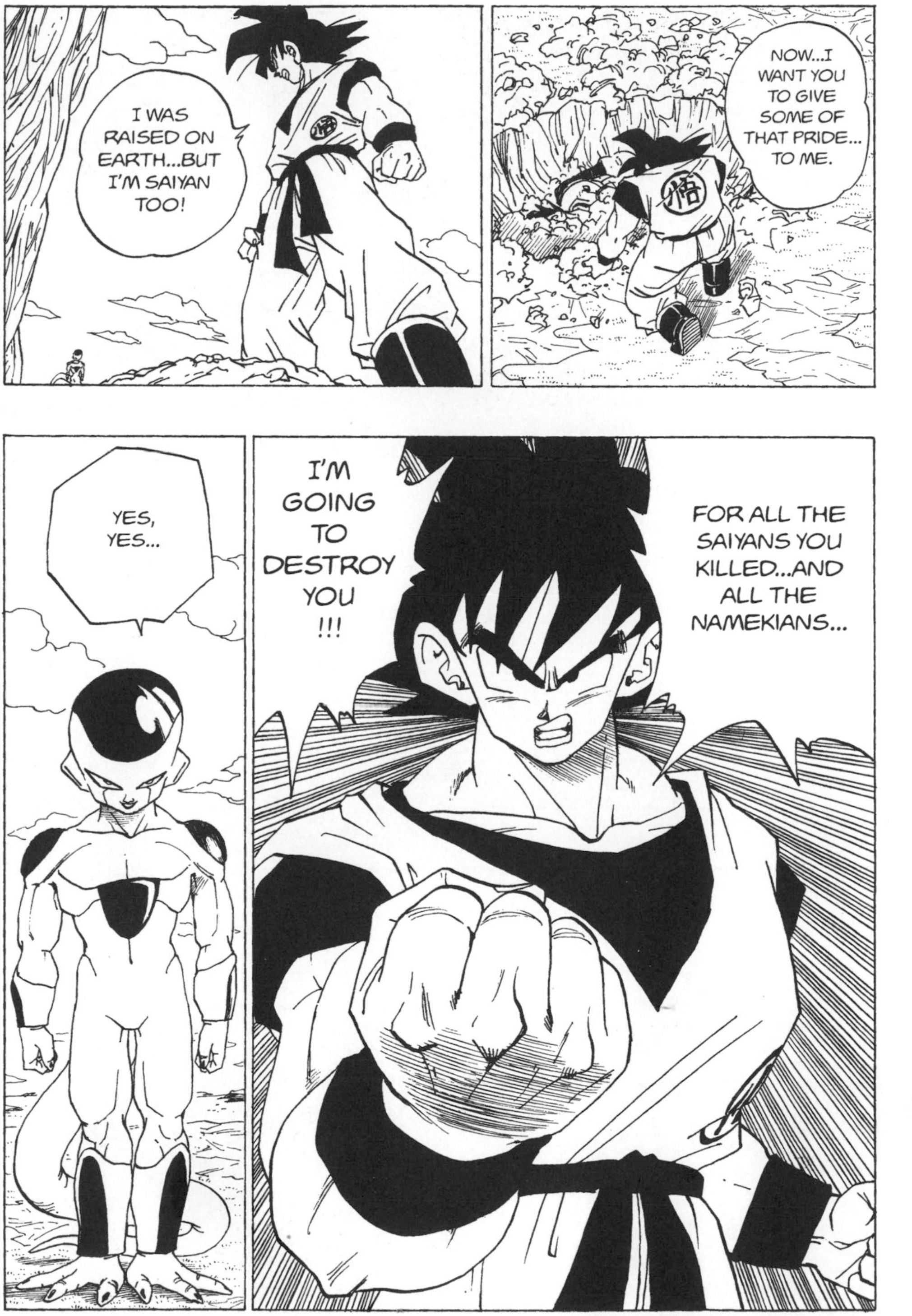

I WAS RAISED ON EARTH...BUT I'M SAIYAN TOO!
NOW...I WANT YOU TO GIVE SOME OF THAT PRIDE... TO ME.
FOR ALL THE SAIYANS YOU KILLED...AND ALL THE NAMEKIANS...
I'M GOING TO DESTROY YOU!!!
YES, YES...

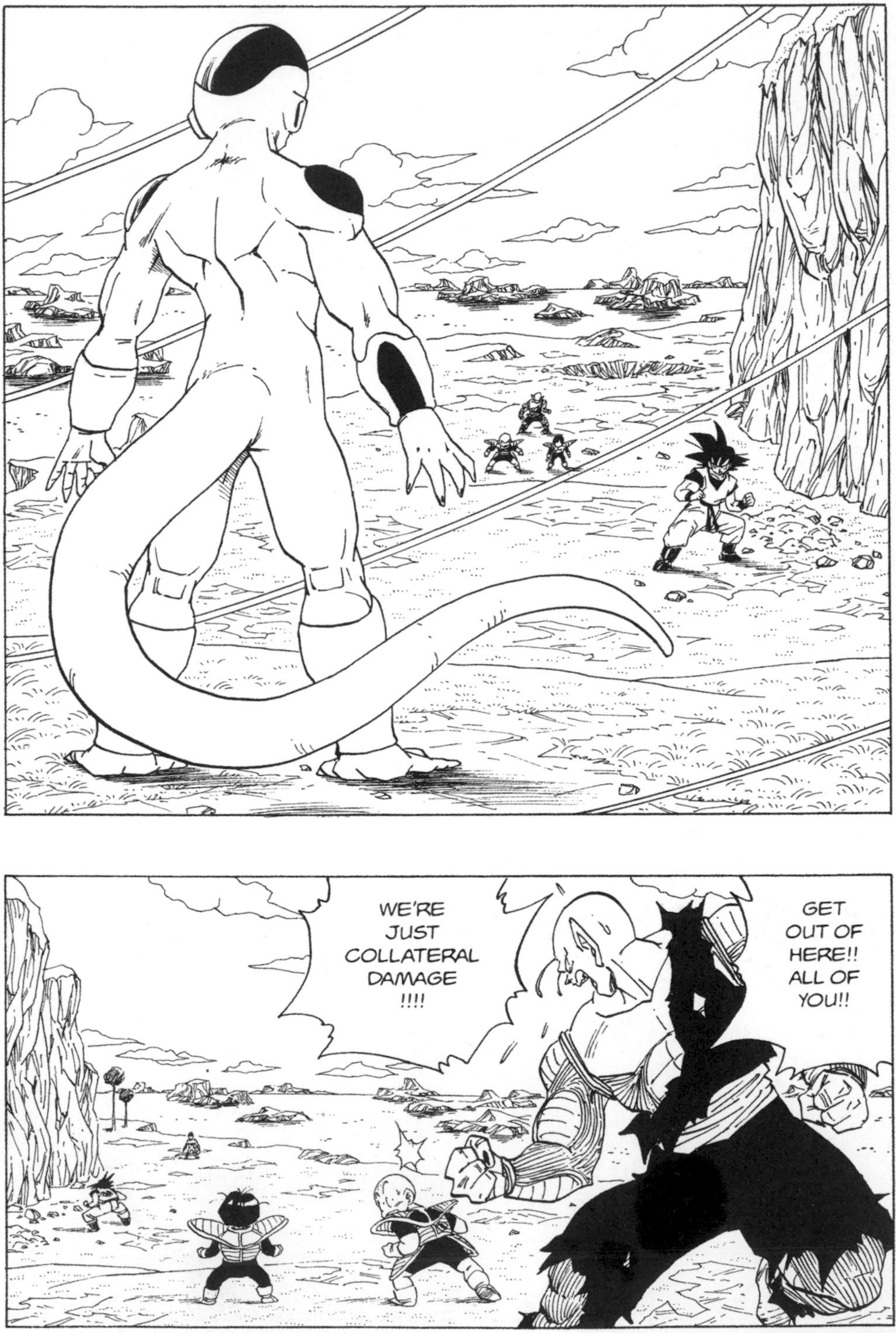
GET OUT OF HERE!! ALL OF YOU!!
WE'RE JUST COLLATERAL DAMAGE !!!!

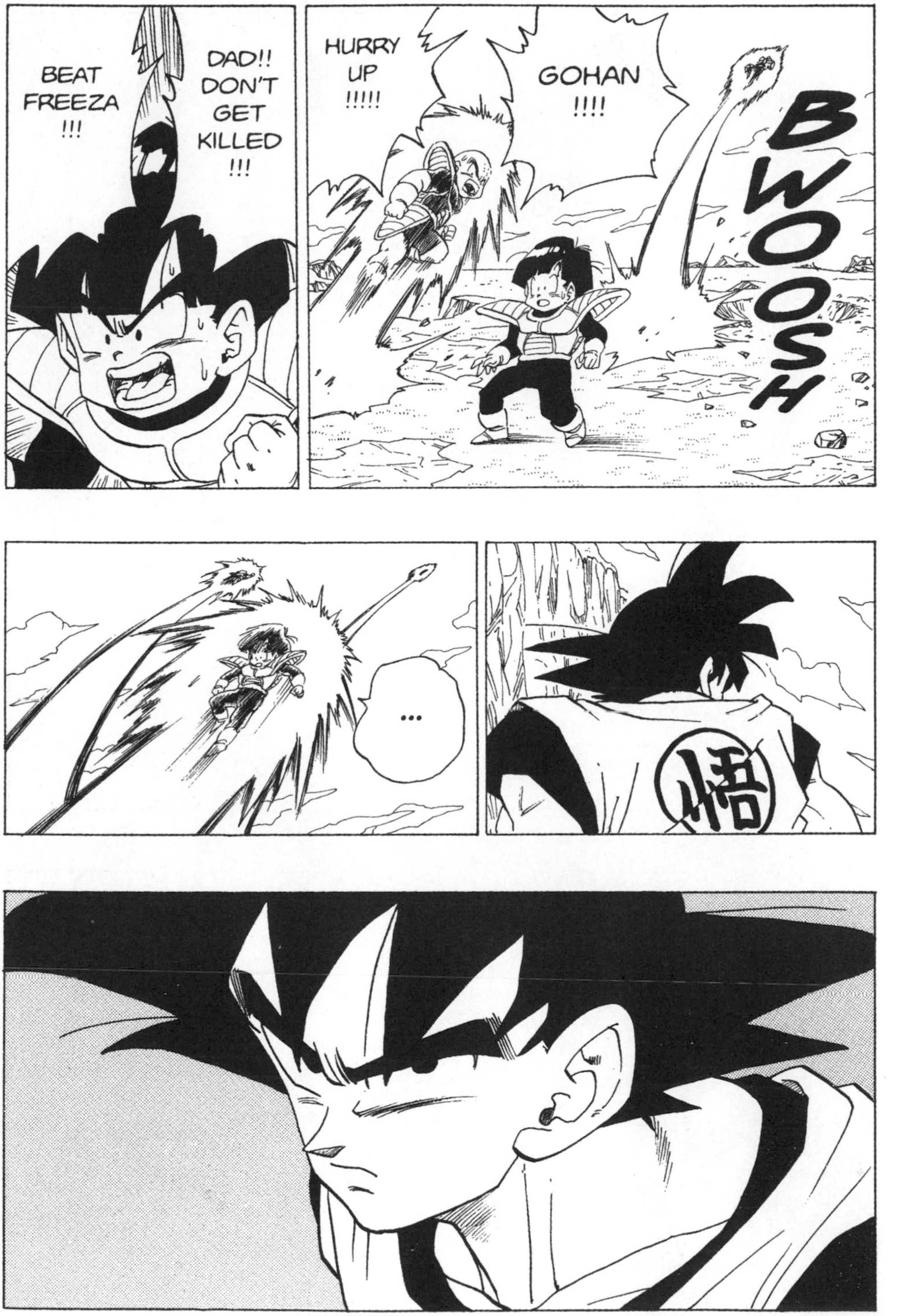
GOHAN !!!!
HURRY UP !!!!!
BWOOSH
DAD!! DON'T GET KILLED !!!
BEAT FREEZA !!!
...

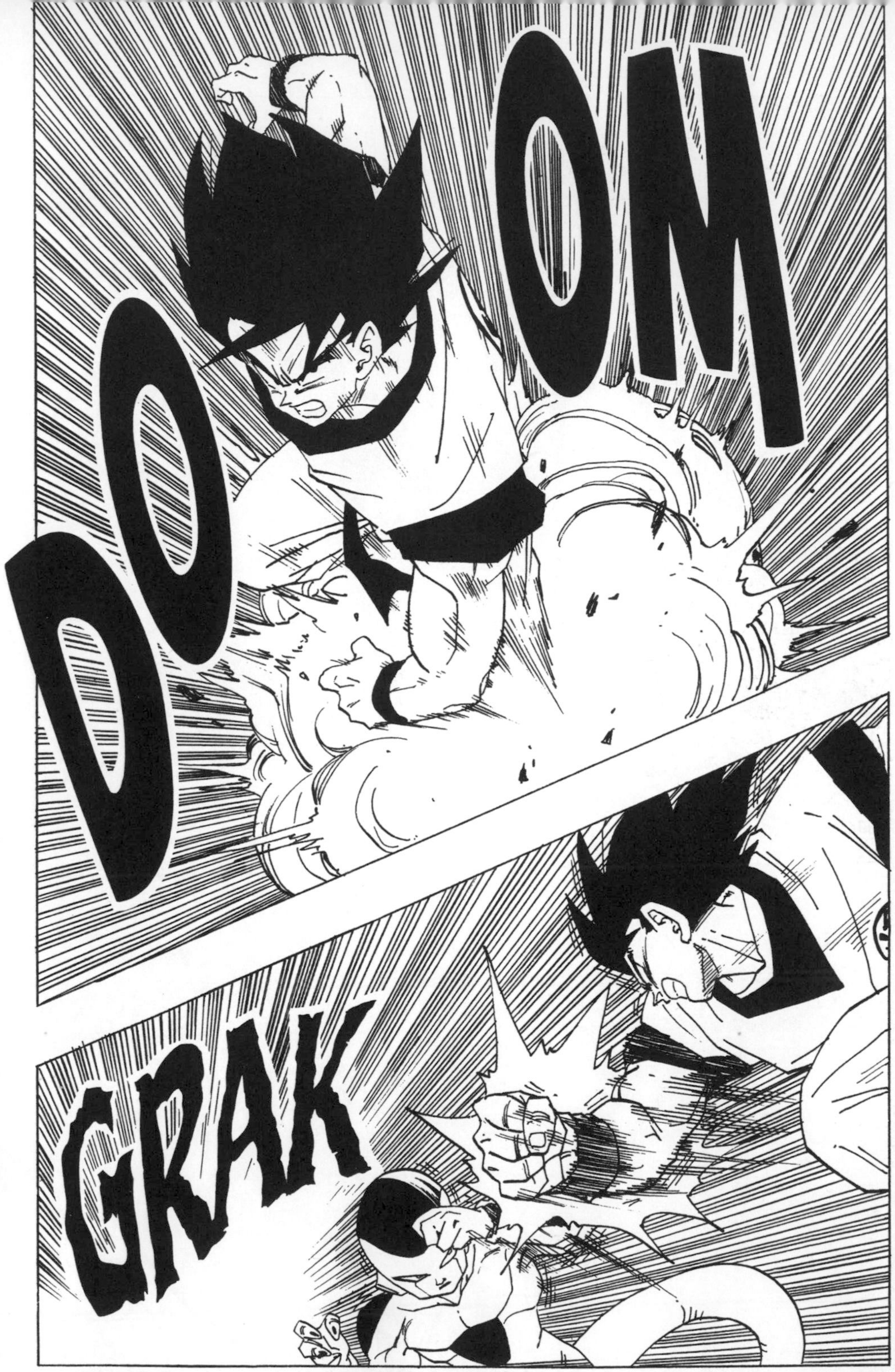
DOOOM
GRAK

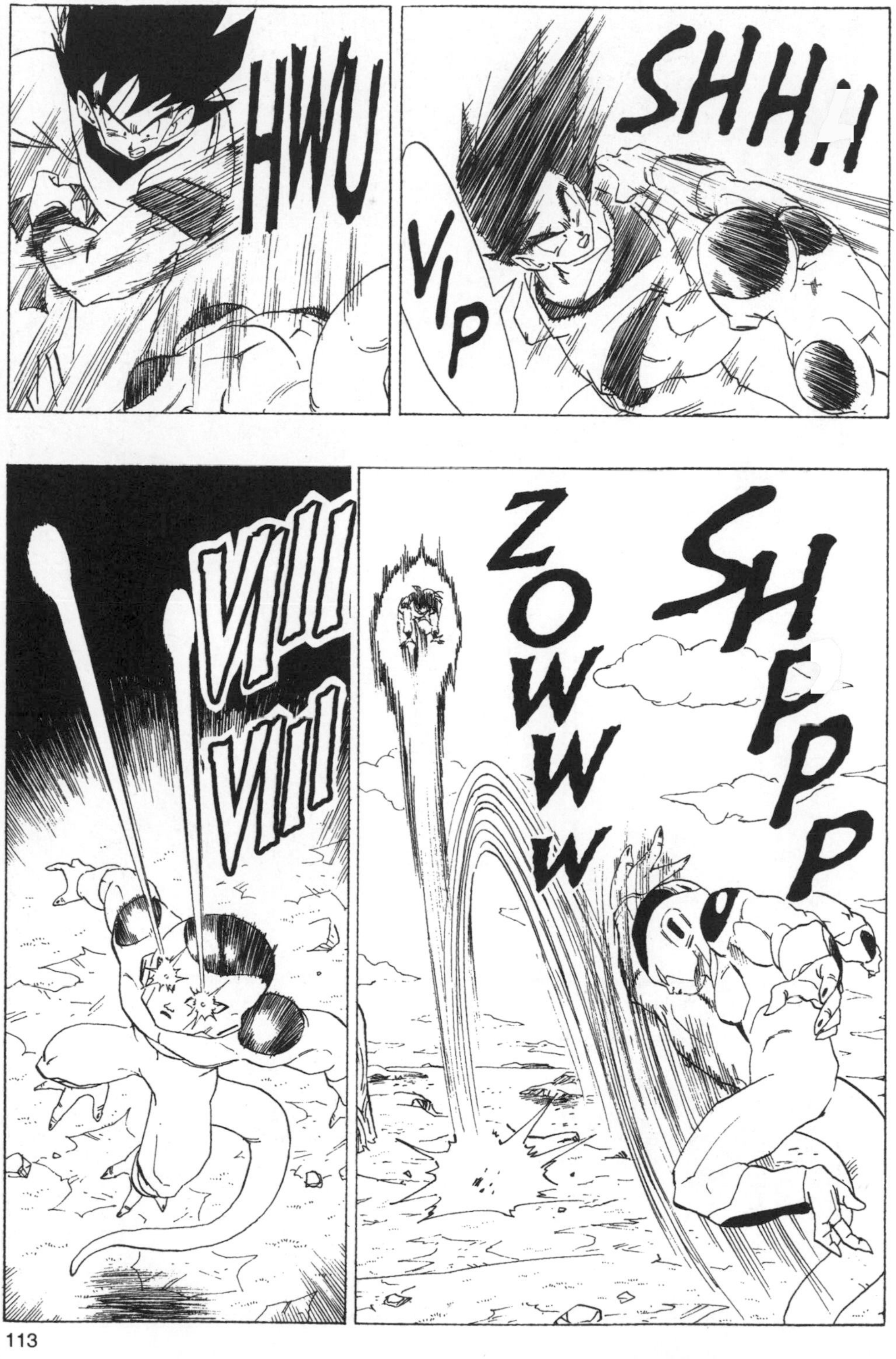
HWU
VIP
SHH
VIII
VIII
ZOWWW
SHFPP

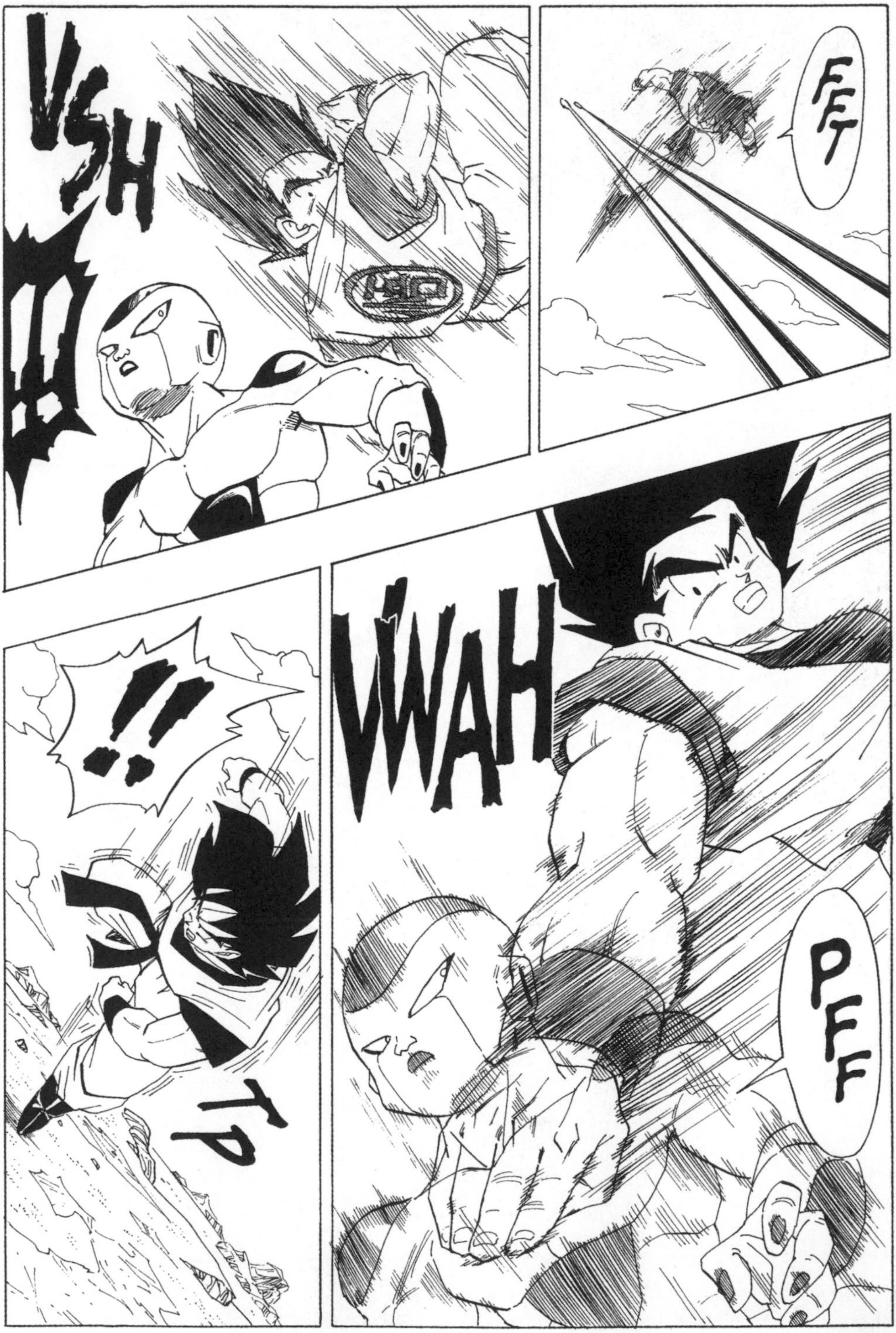
FFT
VSH!!
VWAH
PFF
!!
TP

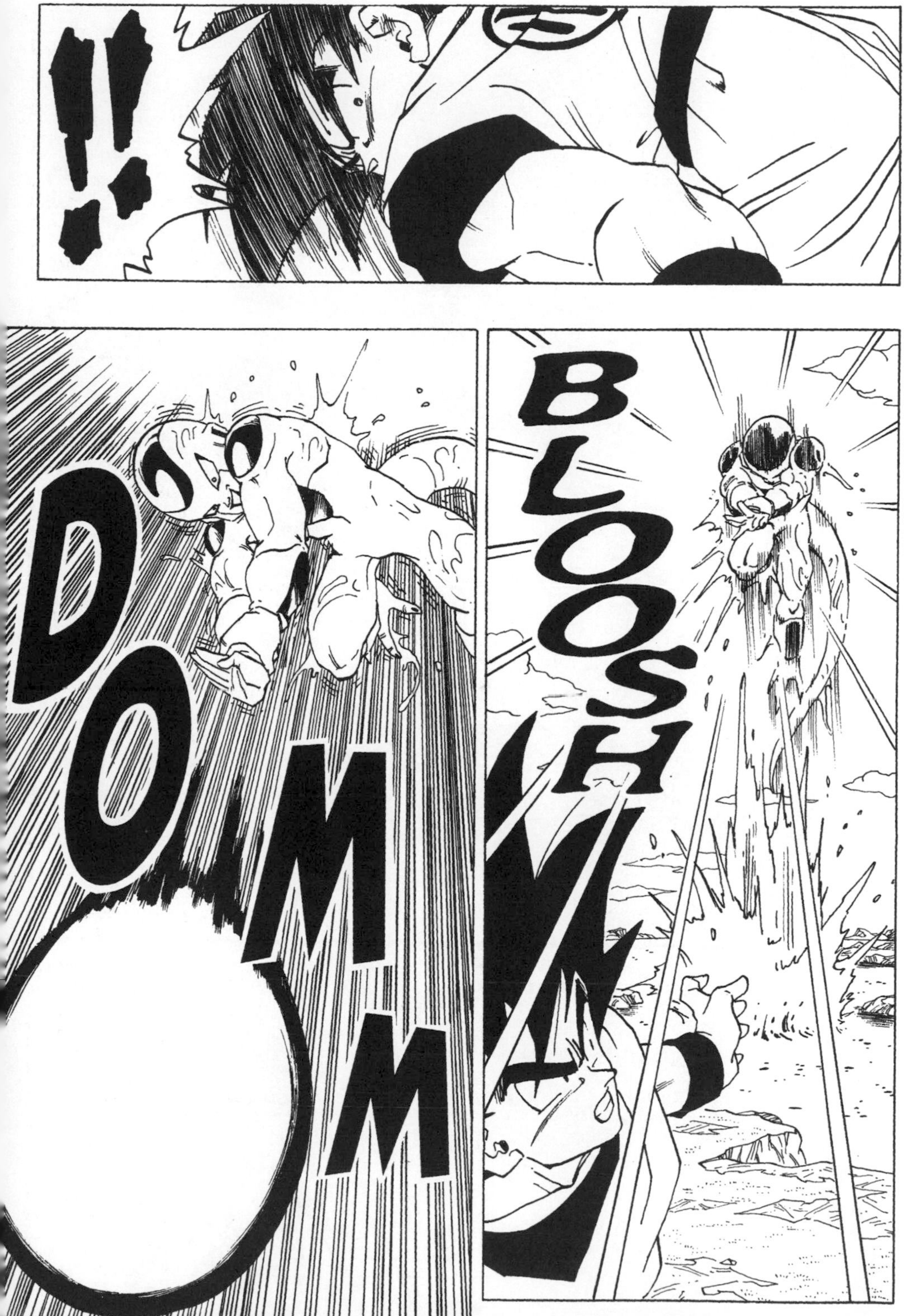
!!
BLOOSH
DOOMMM

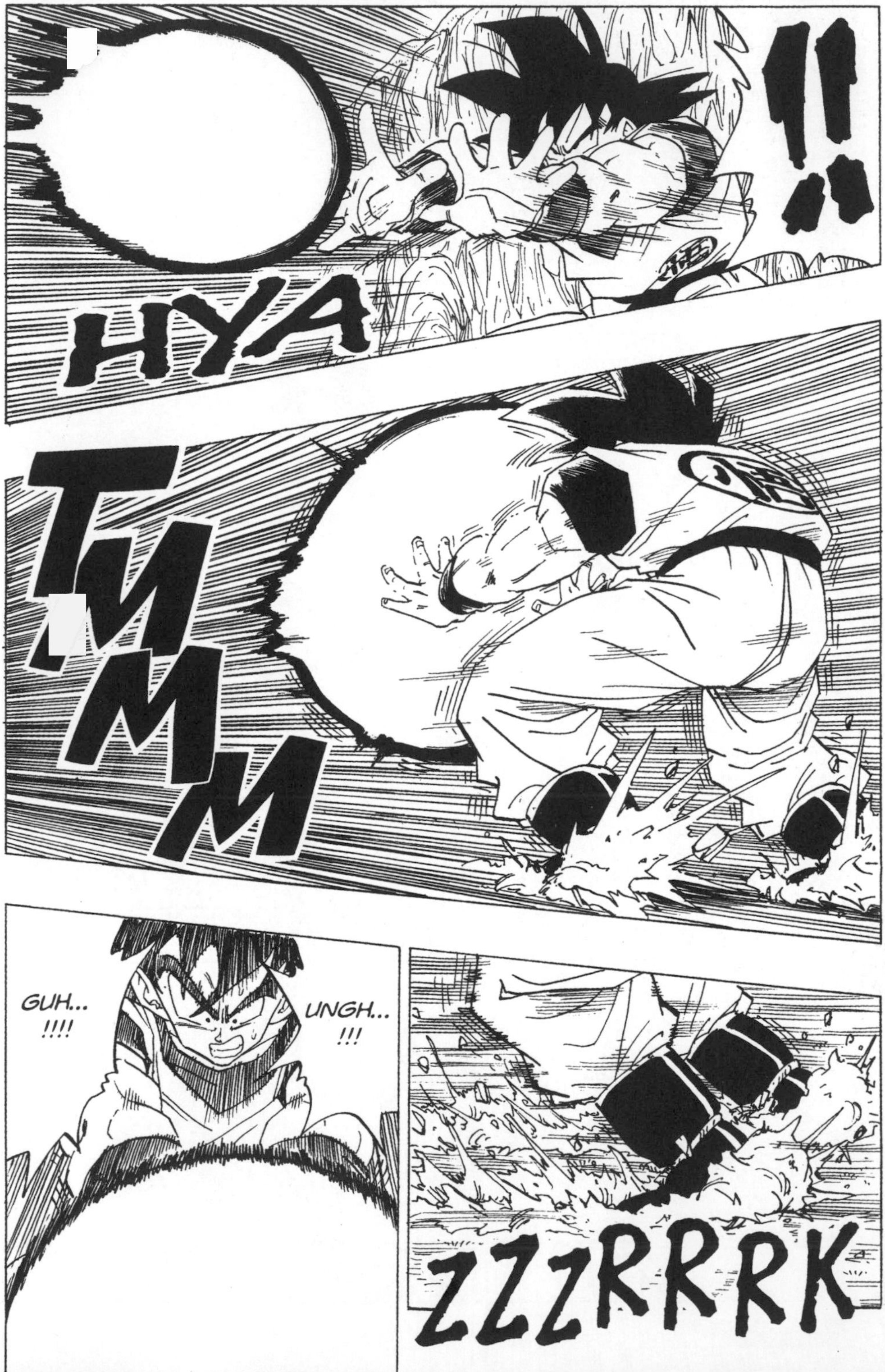
!!
HYA
TMMM
UNGH... !!!
GUH... !!!!
ZZZRRRK

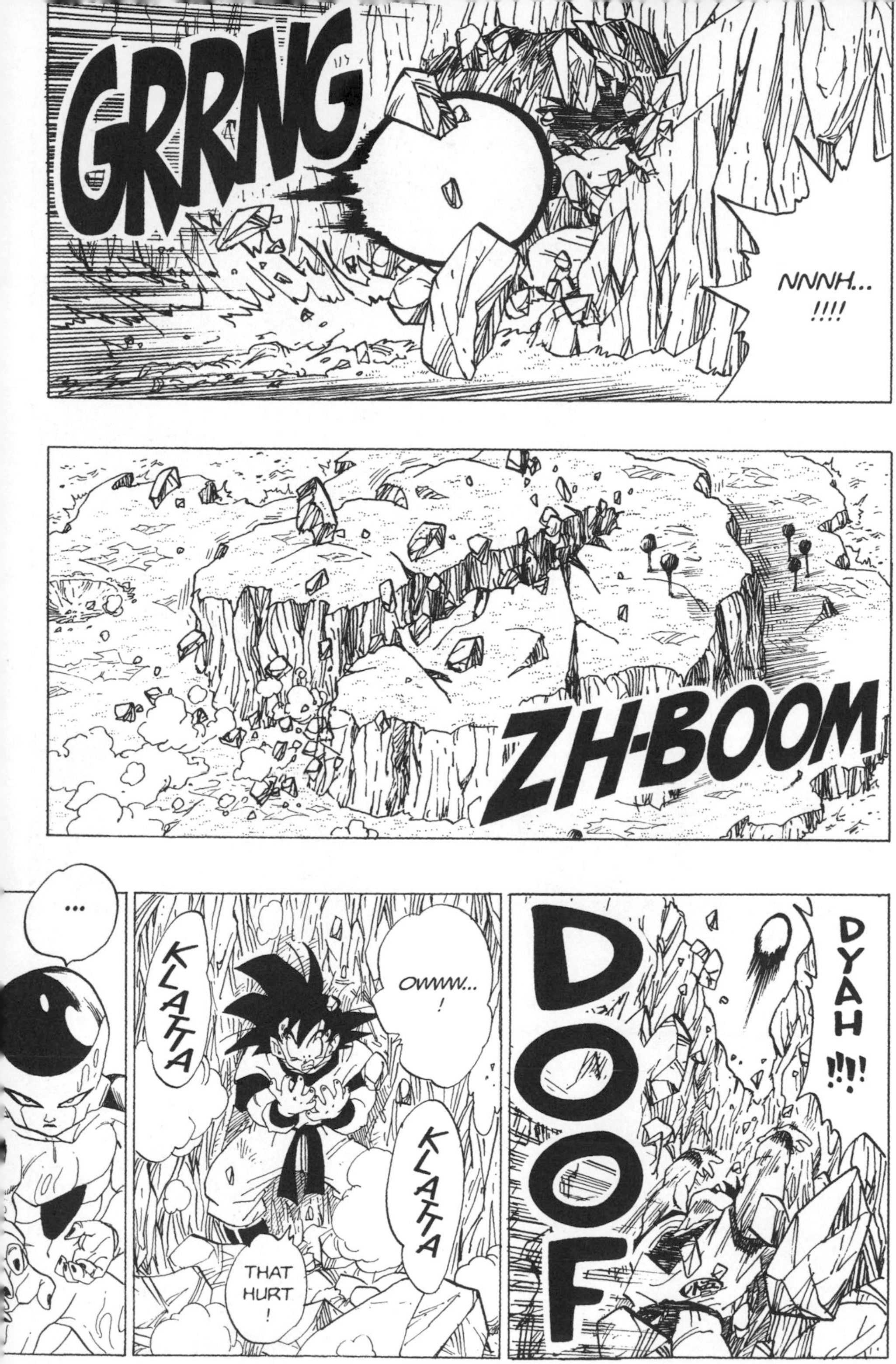
GRRNG
NNNH... !!!!
ZH-BOOM
...
KLATTA
OWWW... !
KLATTA
THAT HURT !
DOOF
DYAH !!!!

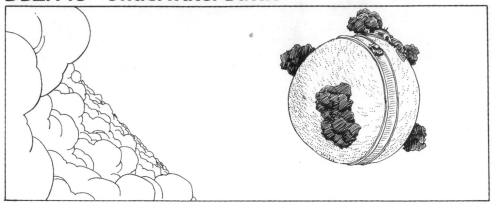

VEGETA HAS DIED...

WHAT'S HAPPENING ON PLANET NAMEK...?

A-AND WHAT ABOUT SON GOKU...?!

HE'S THAT *POWERFUL*...?

THEY'VE BEGUN TO FIGHT...

V- VEGETA...?! *HE* DIED ?!

MMM... FREEZA KILLED HIM... EASILY.

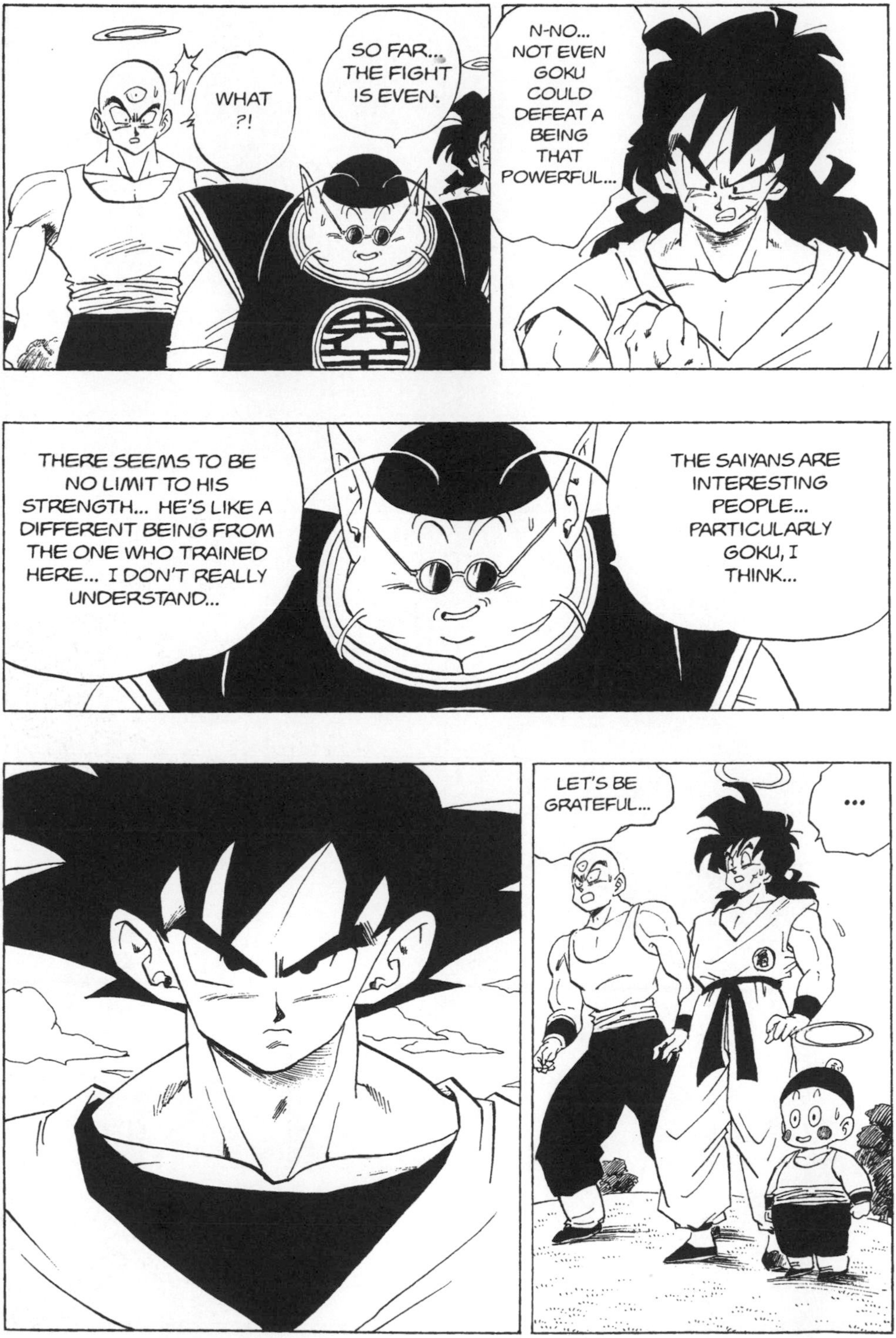
N-NO... NOT EVEN GOKU COULD DEFEAT A BEING THAT POWERFUL...
SO FAR... THE FIGHT IS EVEN.
WHAT ?!
THE SAIYANS ARE INTERESTING PEOPLE... PARTICULARLY GOKU, I THINK...
THERE SEEMS TO BE NO LIMIT TO HIS STRENGTH... HE'S LIKE A DIFFERENT BEING FROM THE ONE WHO TRAINED HERE... I DON'T REALLY UNDERSTAND...
...
LET'S BE GRATEFUL...

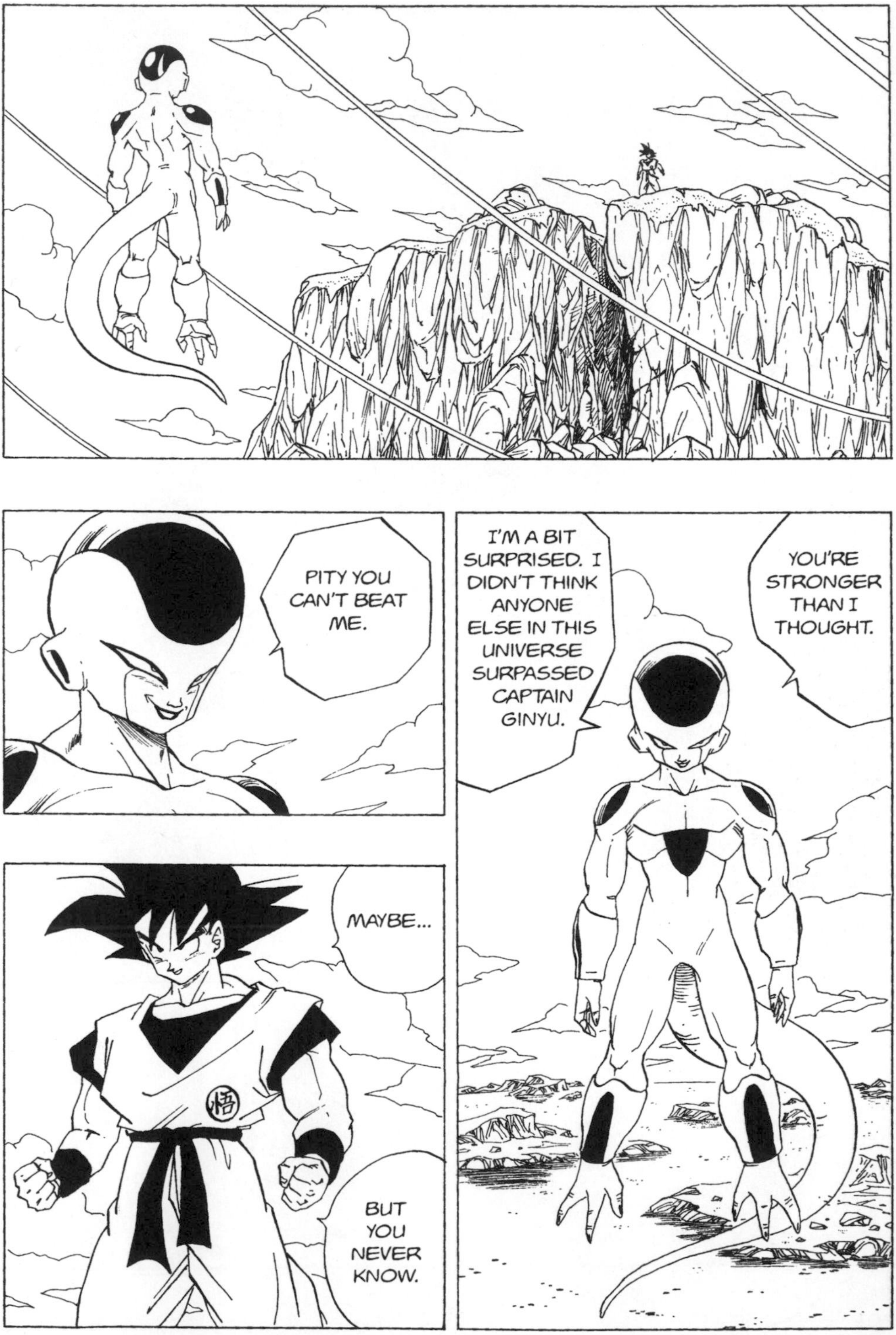
I'M A BIT SURPRISED. I DIDN'T THINK ANYONE ELSE IN THIS UNIVERSE SURPASSED CAPTAIN GINYU.
YOU'RE STRONGER THAN I THOUGHT.
PITY YOU CAN'T BEAT ME.
MAYBE...
BUT YOU NEVER KNOW.

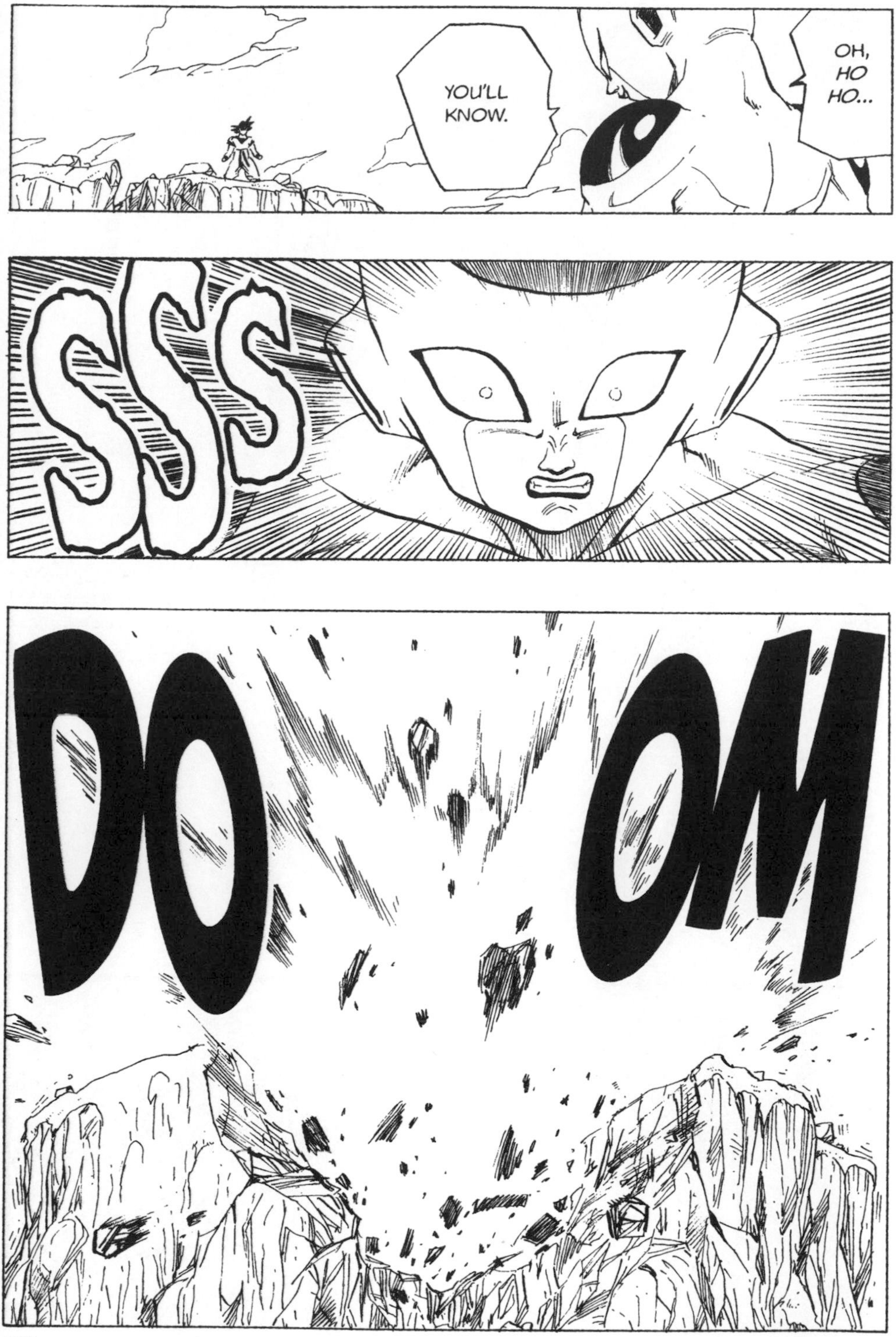
OH, HO HO...
YOU'LL KNOW.
SSS
DO OM

RIGHT BACK AT YOU!!

VIT

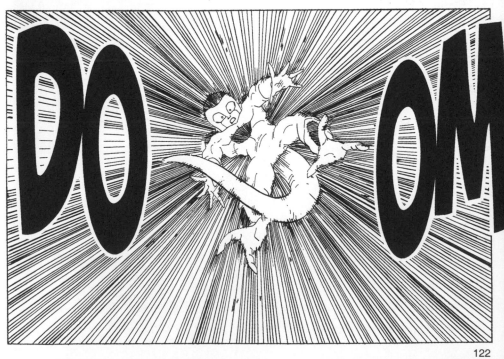

DOOM

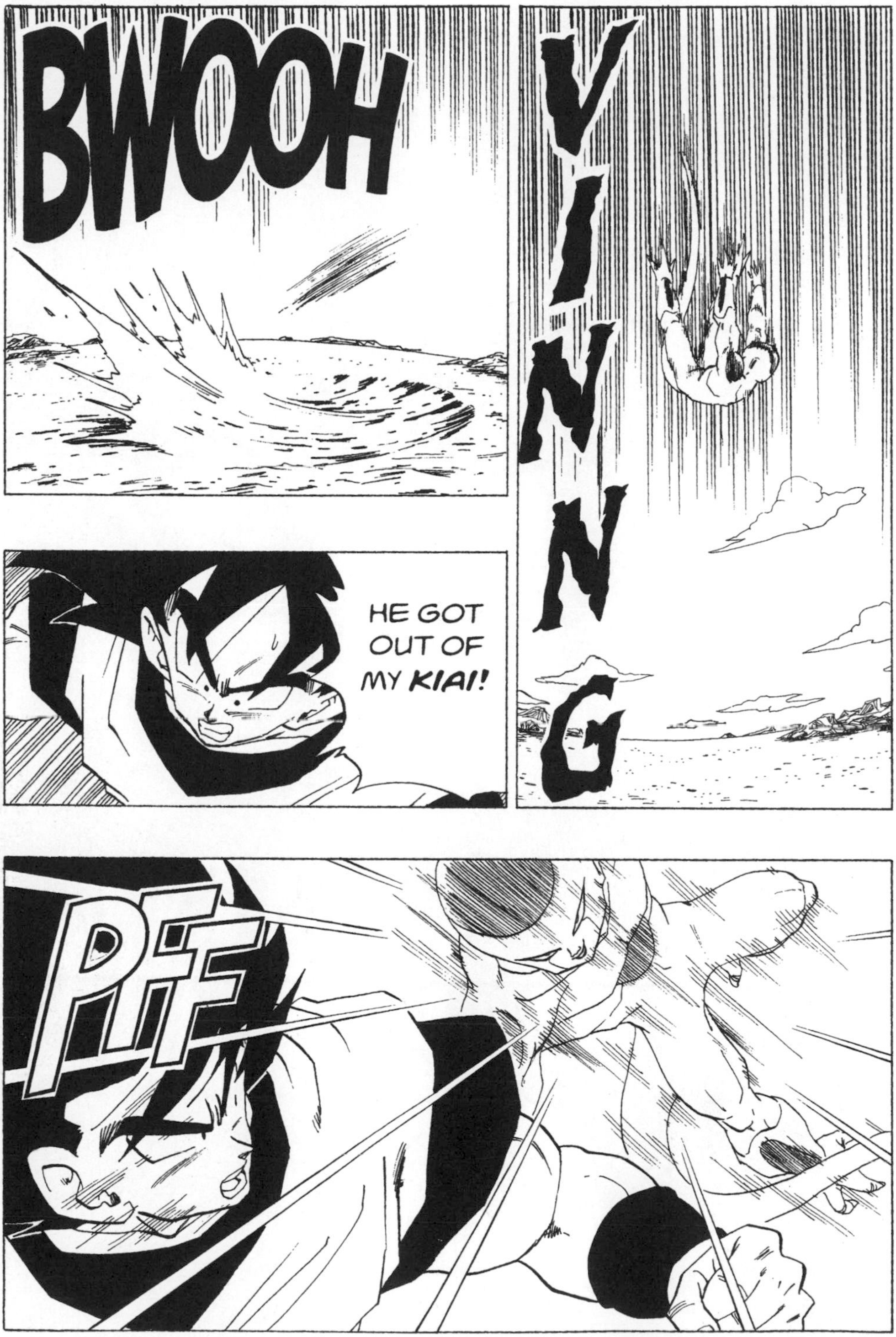
VINNG
BWOOH
HE GOT OUT OF MY *KIAI*!
PIF

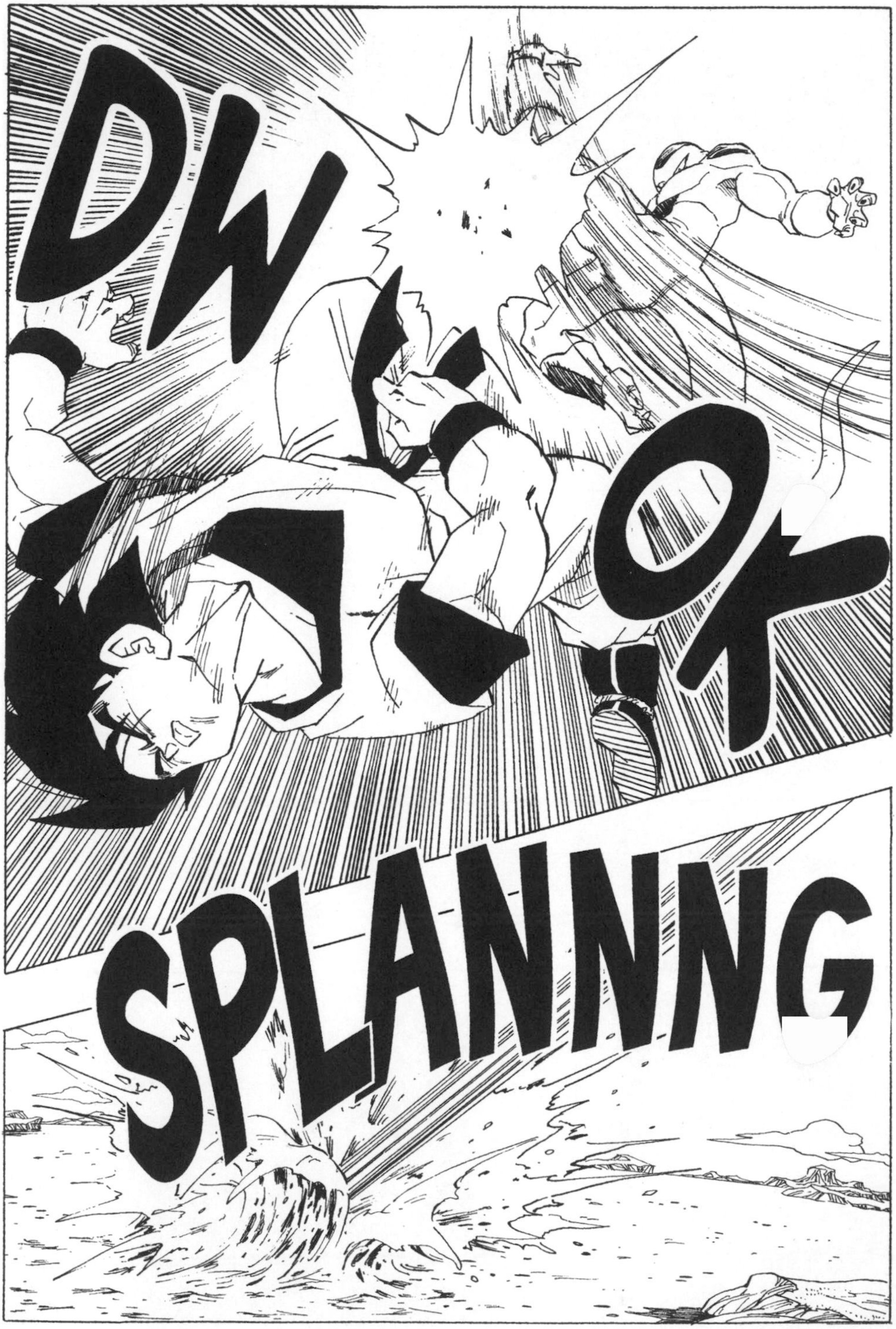
DWOK
SPLANNG

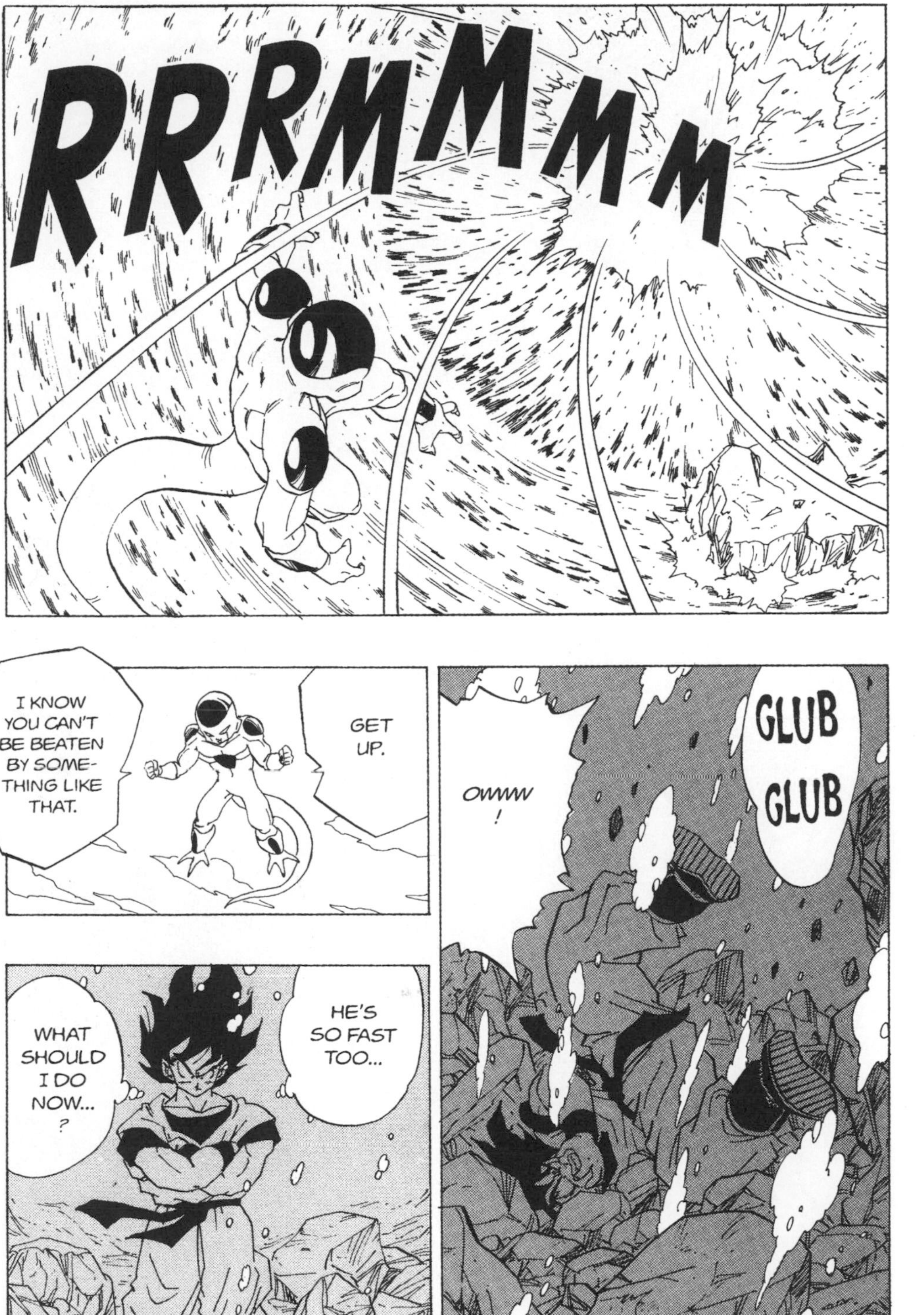
RRRMMMM
I KNOW YOU CAN'T BE BEATEN BY SOME-THING LIKE THAT.
GET UP.
HE'S SO FAST TOO...
WHAT SHOULD I DO NOW... ?
OWWW!
GLUB GLUB

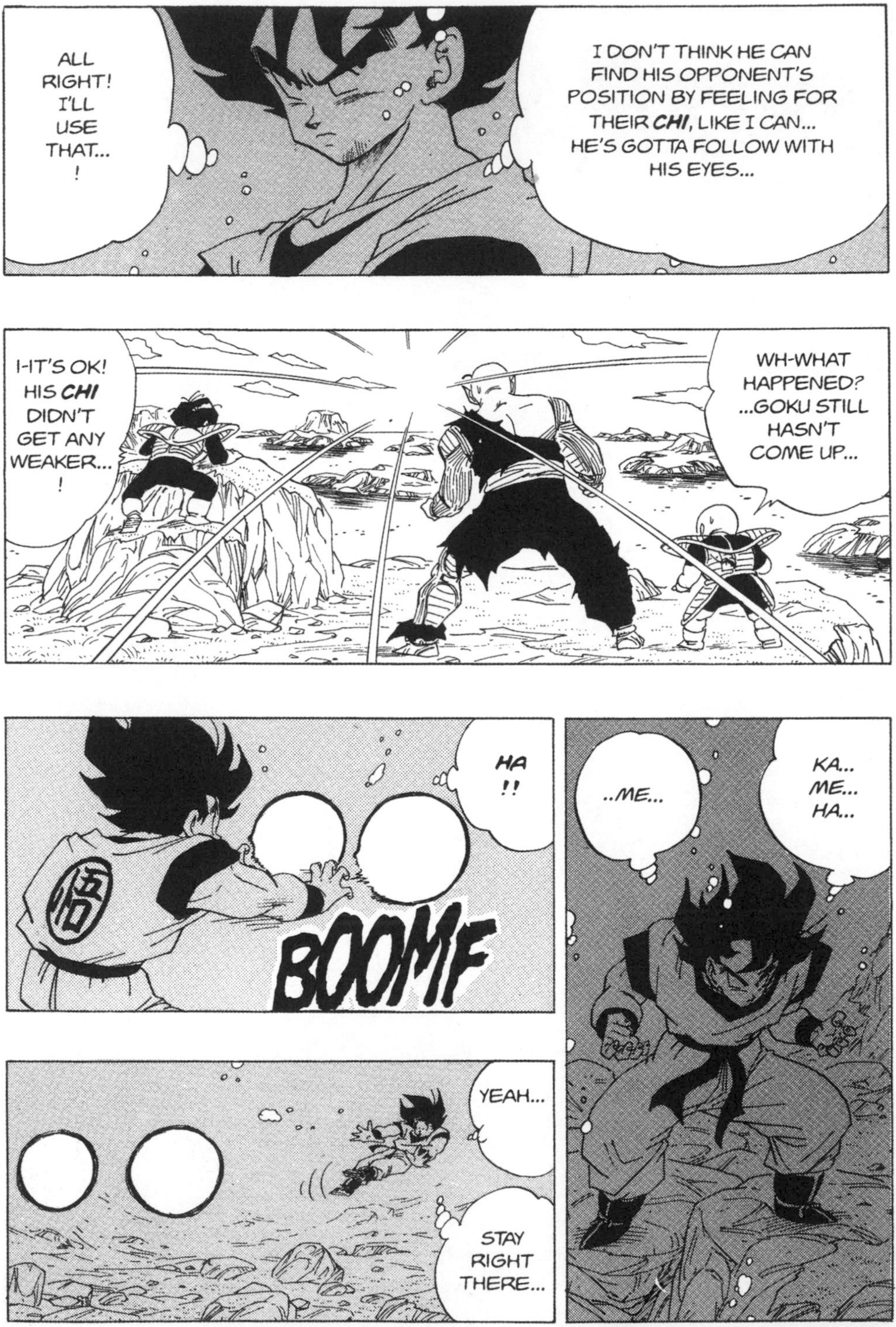

I DON'T THINK HE CAN FIND HIS OPPONENT'S POSITION BY FEELING FOR THEIR ***CHI***, LIKE I CAN... HE'S GOTTA FOLLOW WITH HIS EYES...
ALL RIGHT! I'LL USE THAT...!
WH-WHAT HAPPENED? ...GOKU STILL HASN'T COME UP...
I-IT'S OK! HIS ***CHI*** DIDN'T GET ANY WEAKER...!
KA... ME... HA...
..ME...
HA!!
BOOMF
YEAH...
STAY RIGHT THERE...

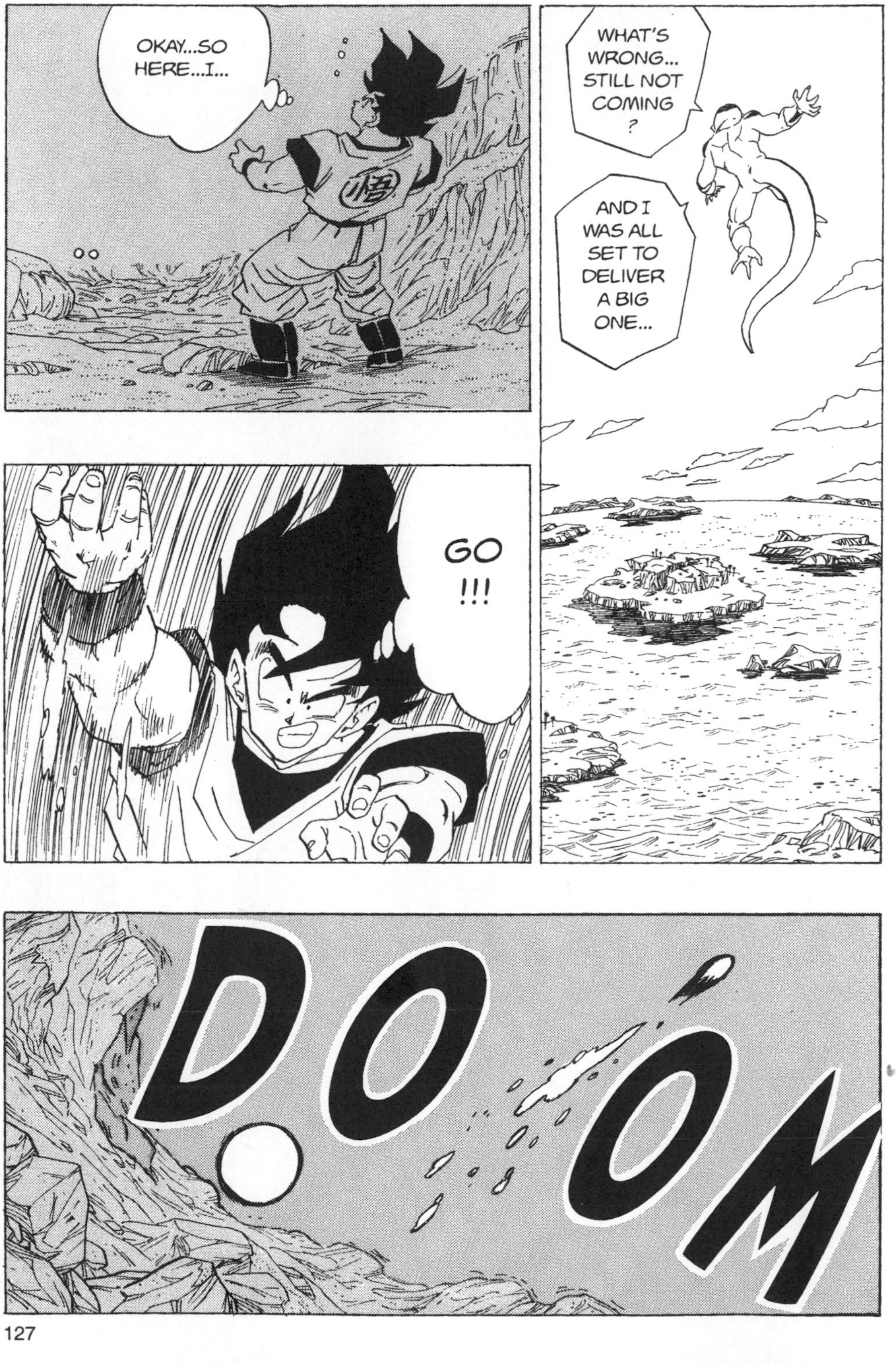
OKAY...SO HERE...I...
WHAT'S WRONG... STILL NOT COMING ?
AND I WAS ALL SET TO DELIVER A BIG ONE...
GO !!!
DOOM

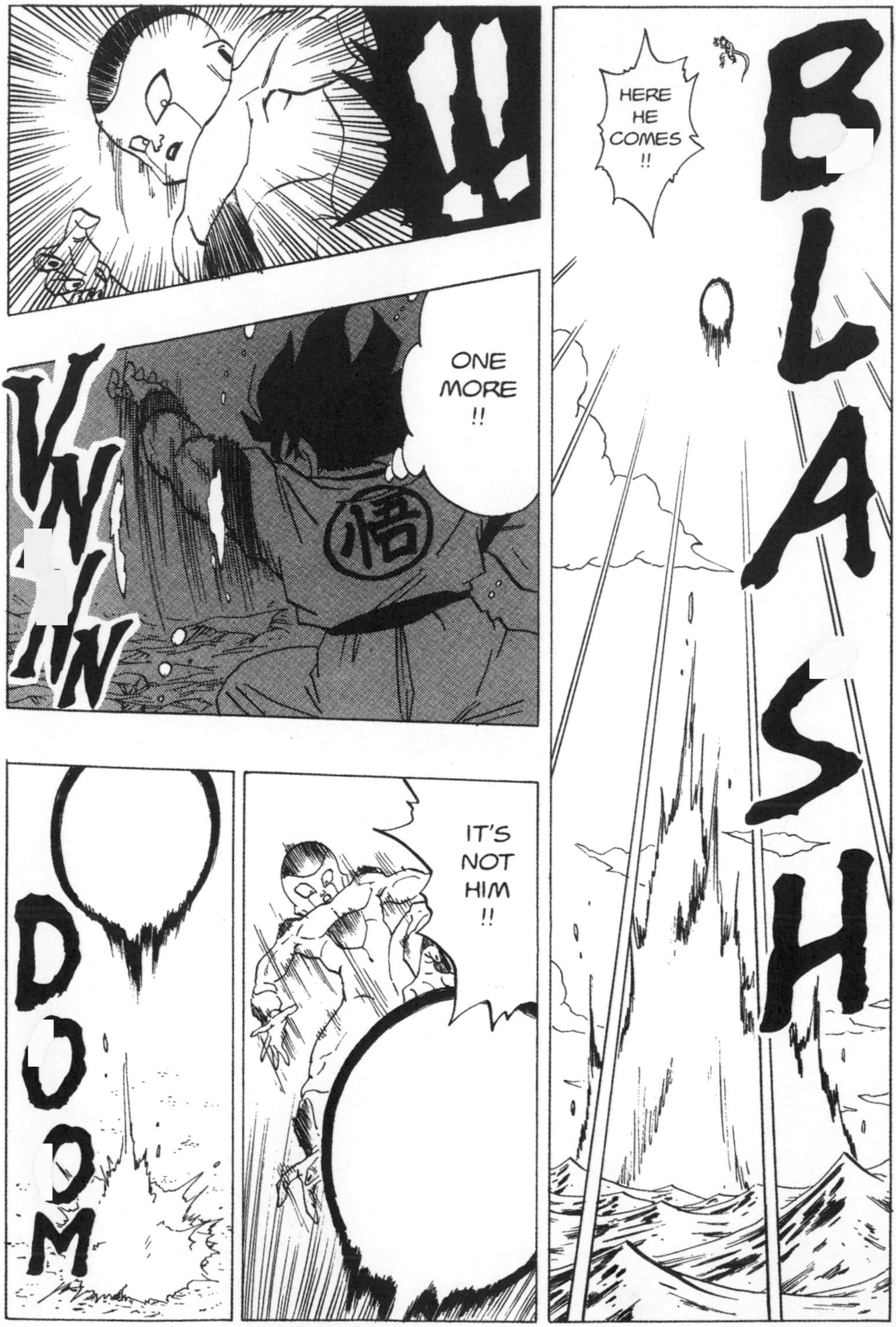
BLASH
HERE HE COMES!!
!!
ONE MORE!!
IT'S NOT HIM!!
DOOM

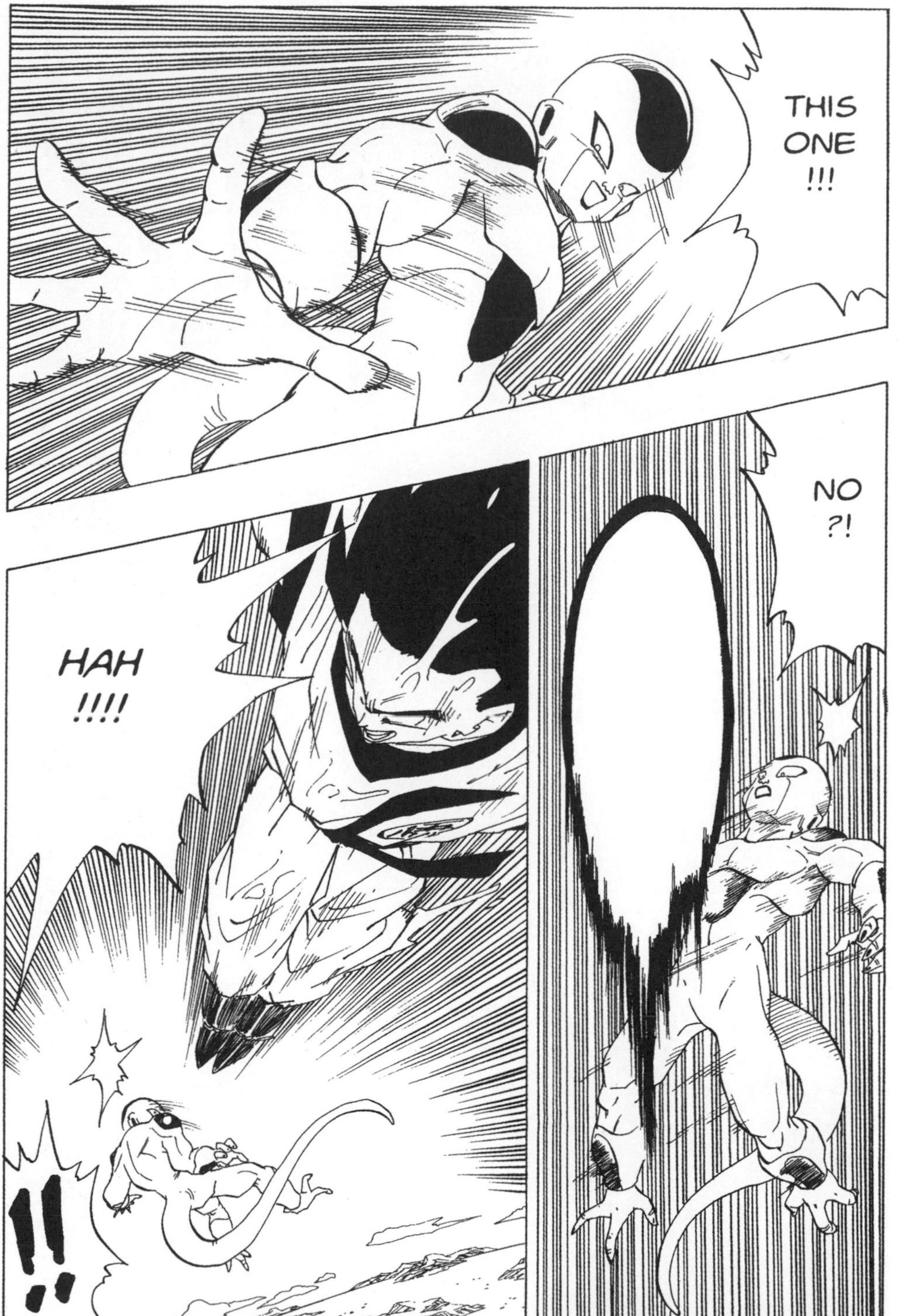
THIS ONE !!!
NO ?!
HAH !!!!
!!

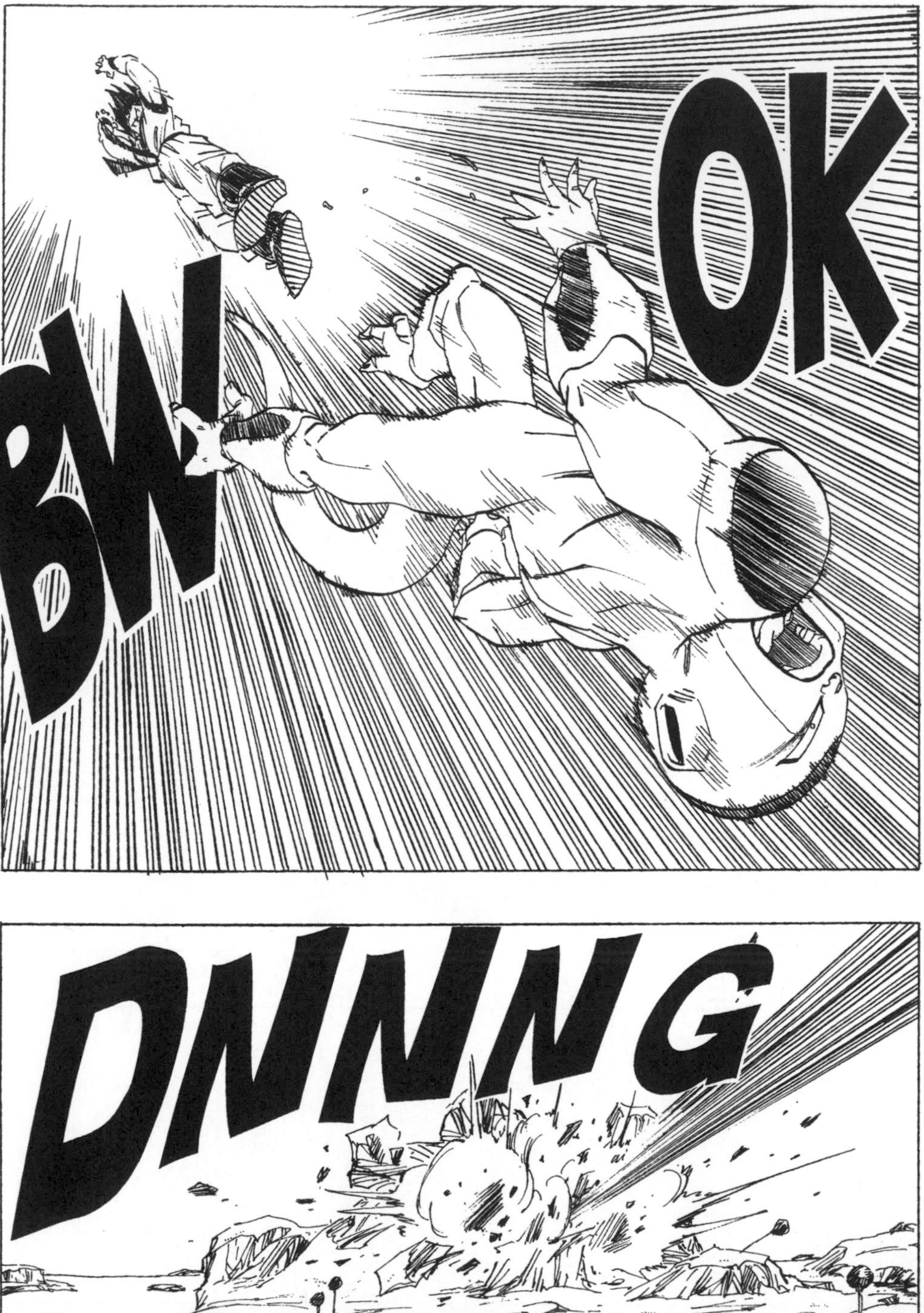
BWOK
DNNNG

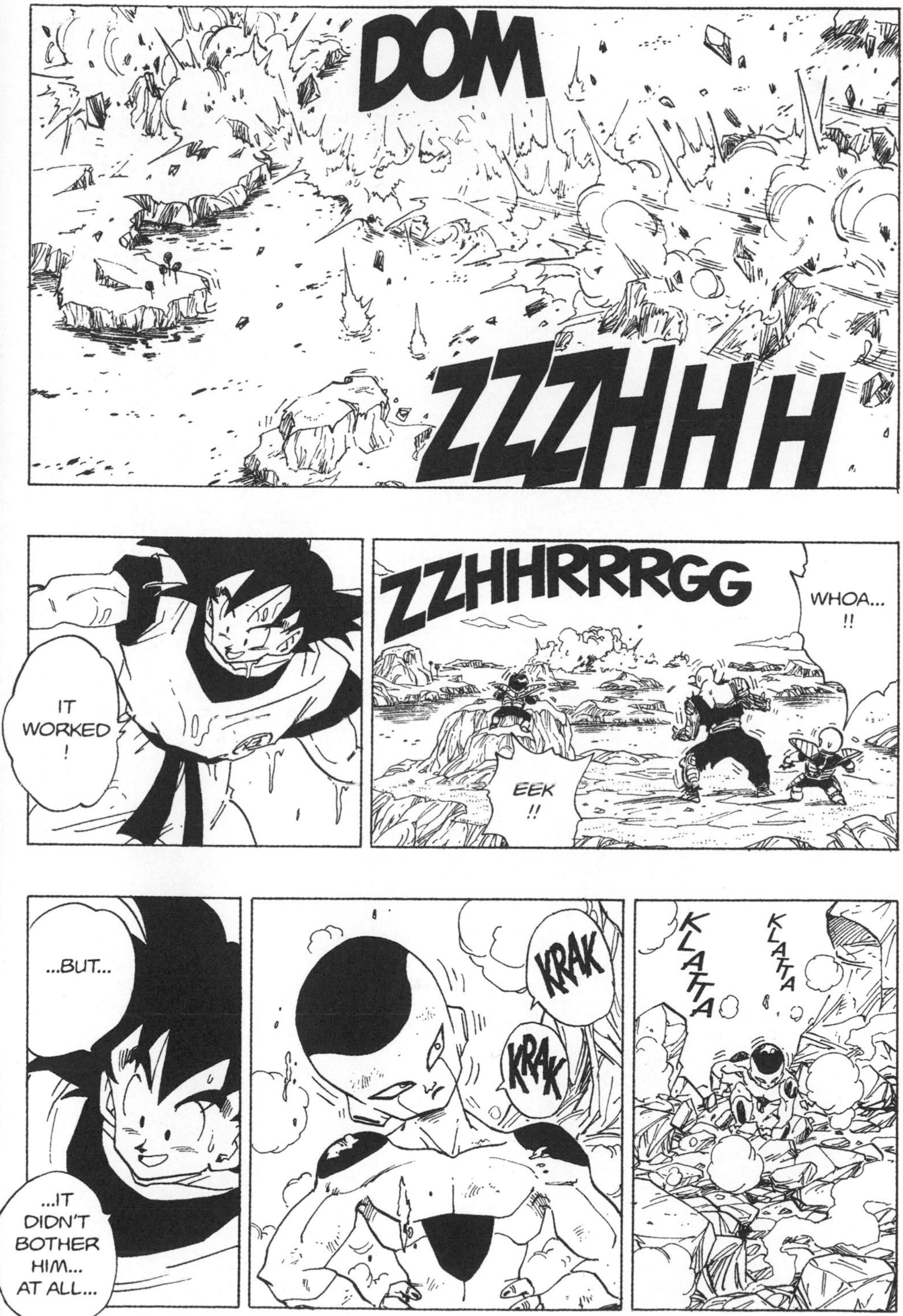
DOM
ZZZHHH
IT WORKED!
ZZHHRRRGG
WHOA...!!
EEK!!
...BUT...
...IT DIDN'T BOTHER HIM... AT ALL...
KRAK
KRAK
KLATTA
KLATTA

DBZ:116 • Aerial Battle

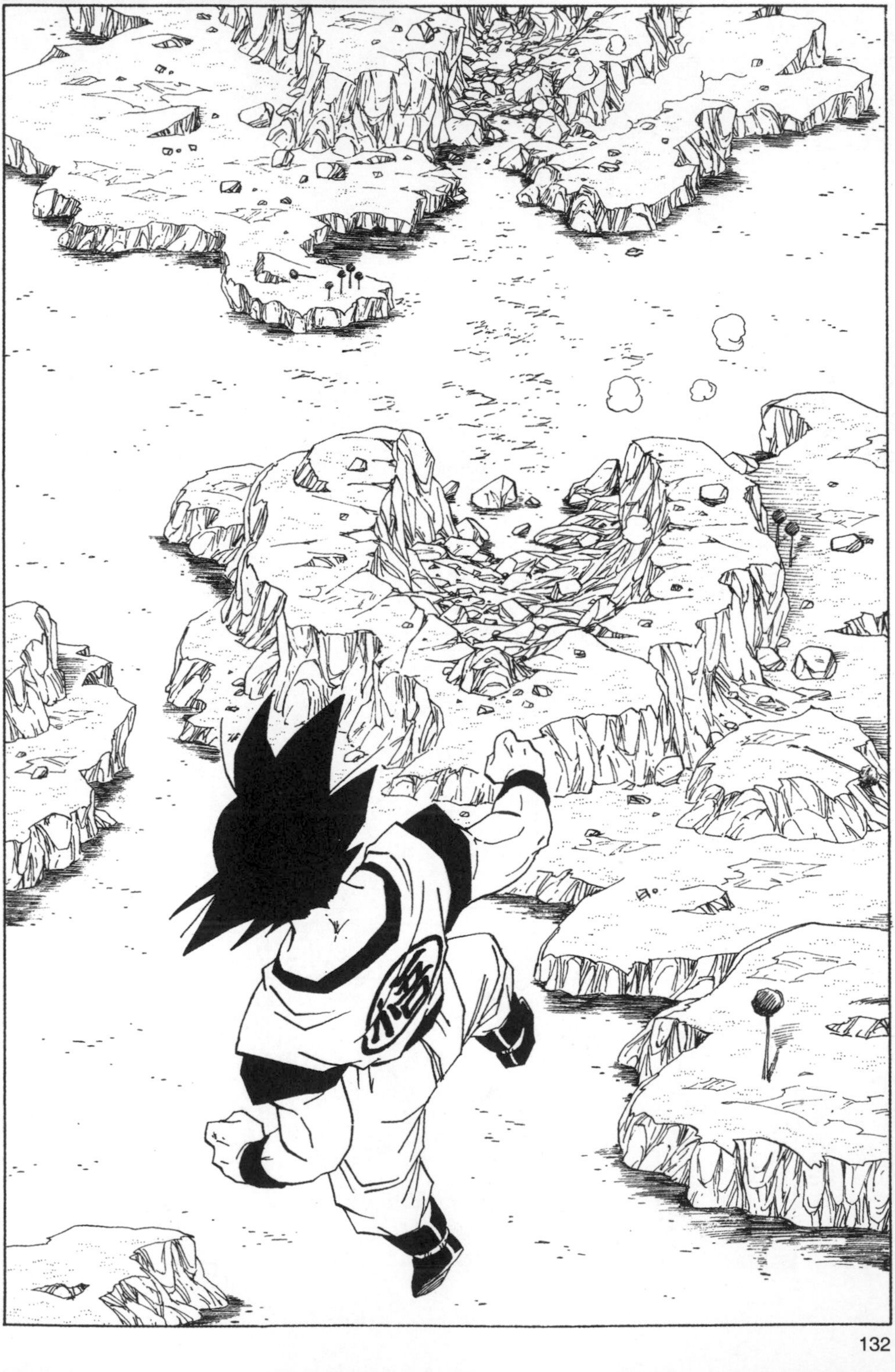

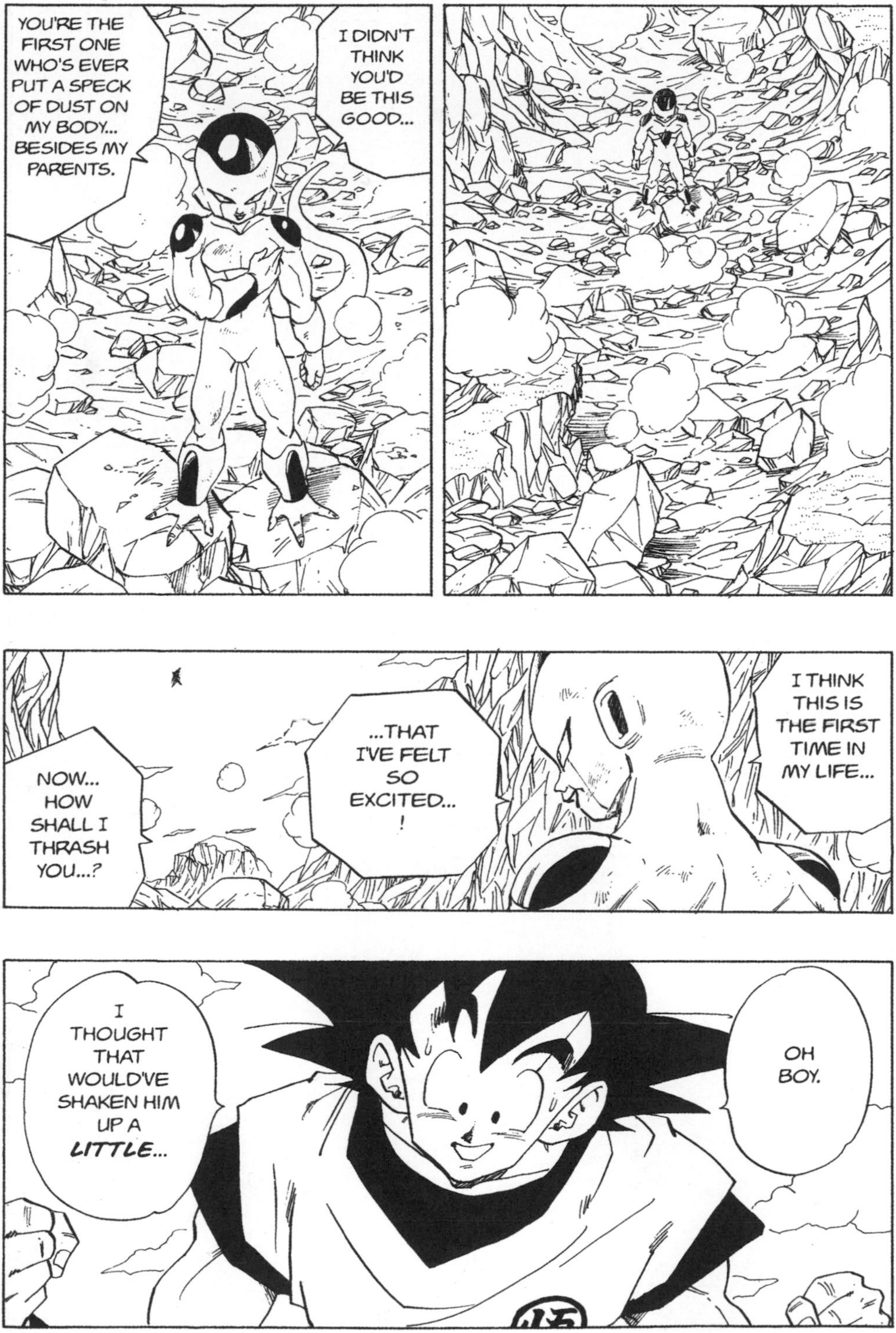
I DIDN'T THINK YOU'D BE THIS GOOD...
YOU'RE THE FIRST ONE WHO'S EVER PUT A SPECK OF DUST ON MY BODY... BESIDES MY PARENTS.
I THINK THIS IS THE FIRST TIME IN MY LIFE...
...THAT I'VE FELT SO EXCITED... !
NOW... HOW SHALL I THRASH YOU...?
OH BOY.
I THOUGHT THAT WOULD'VE SHAKEN HIM UP A *LITTLE*...

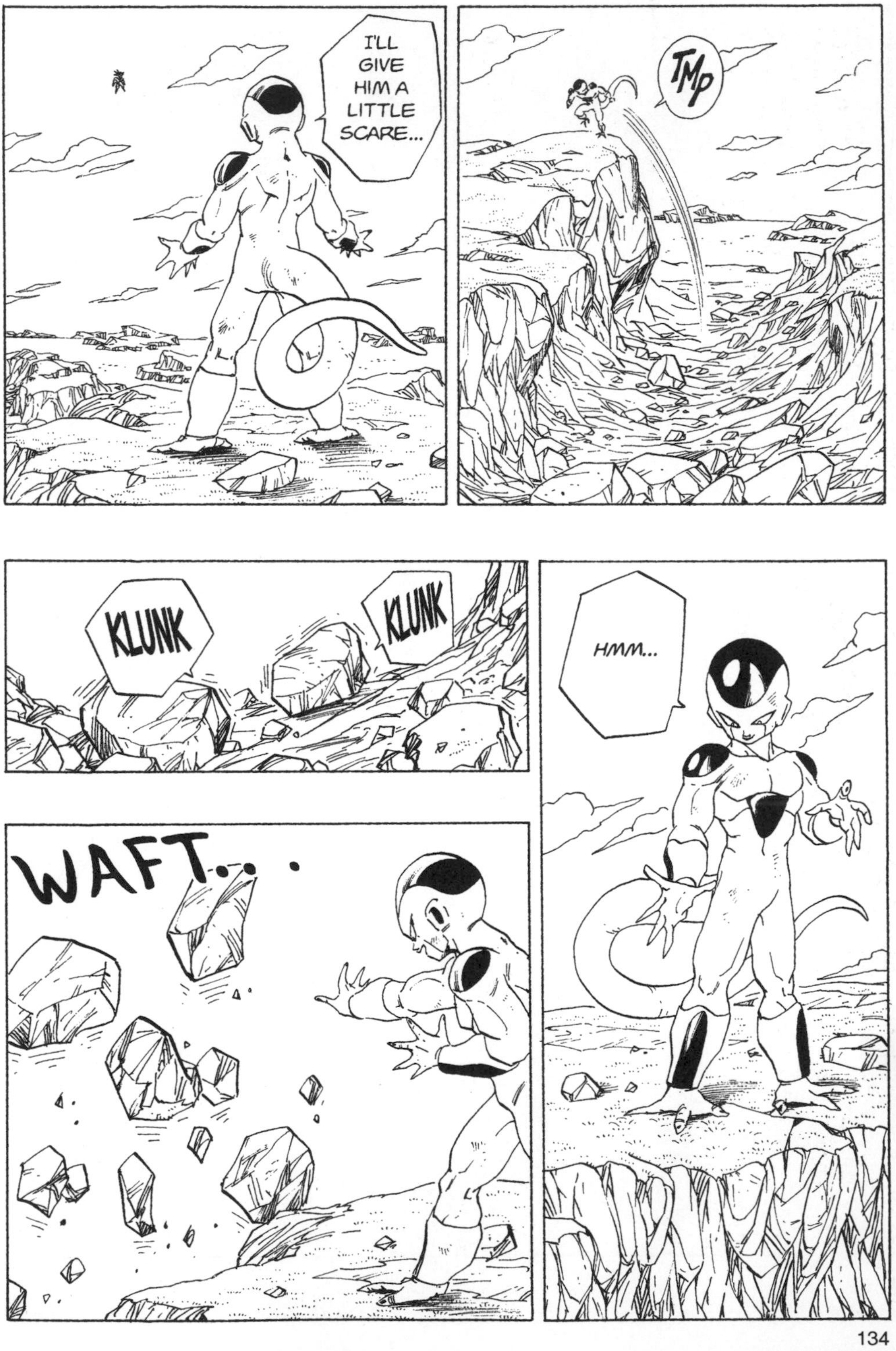

I'LL GIVE HIM A LITTLE SCARE...
TMP
KLUNK
KLUNK
WAFT...
HMM...

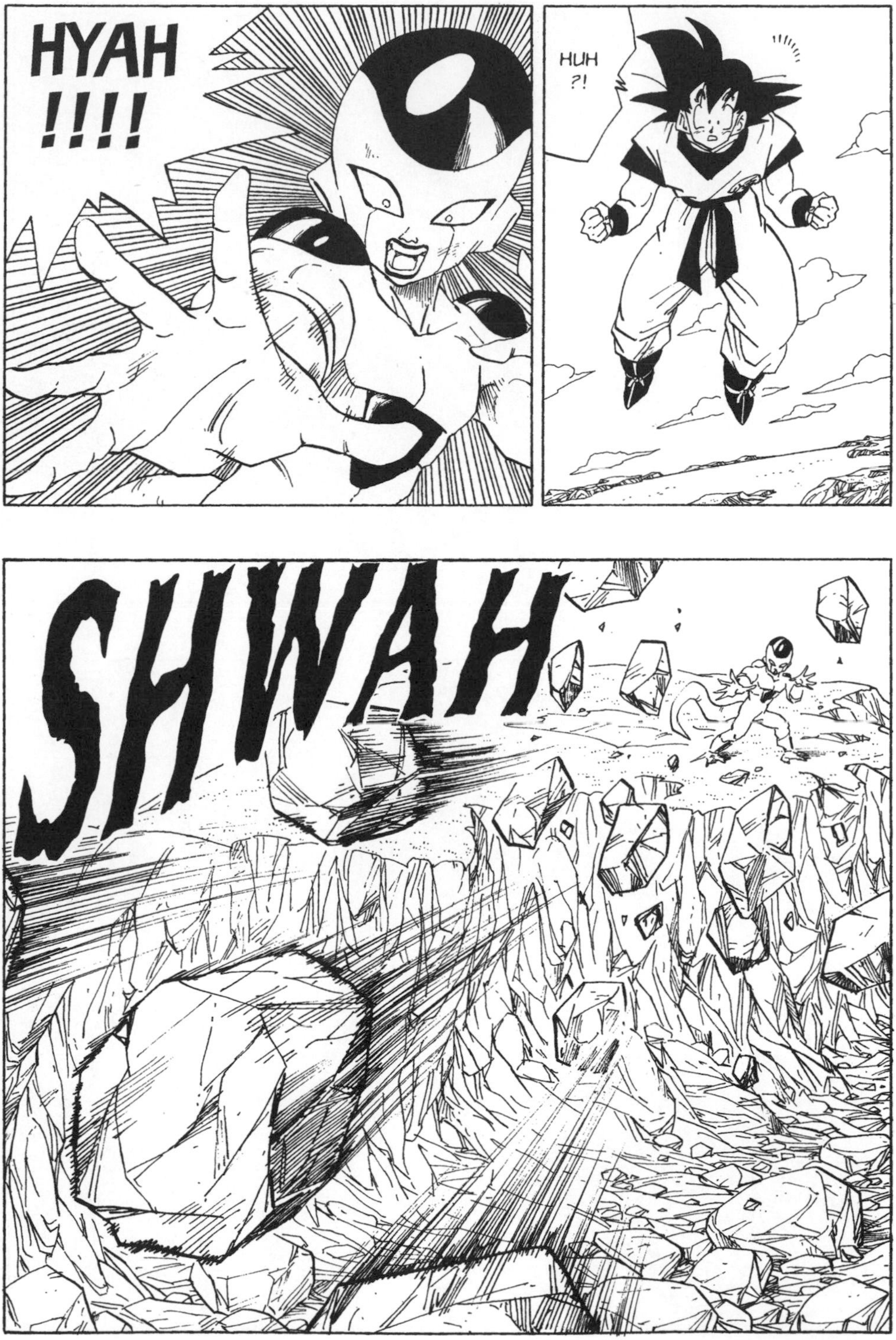
HYAH
!!!!
HUH
?!
SHWAH

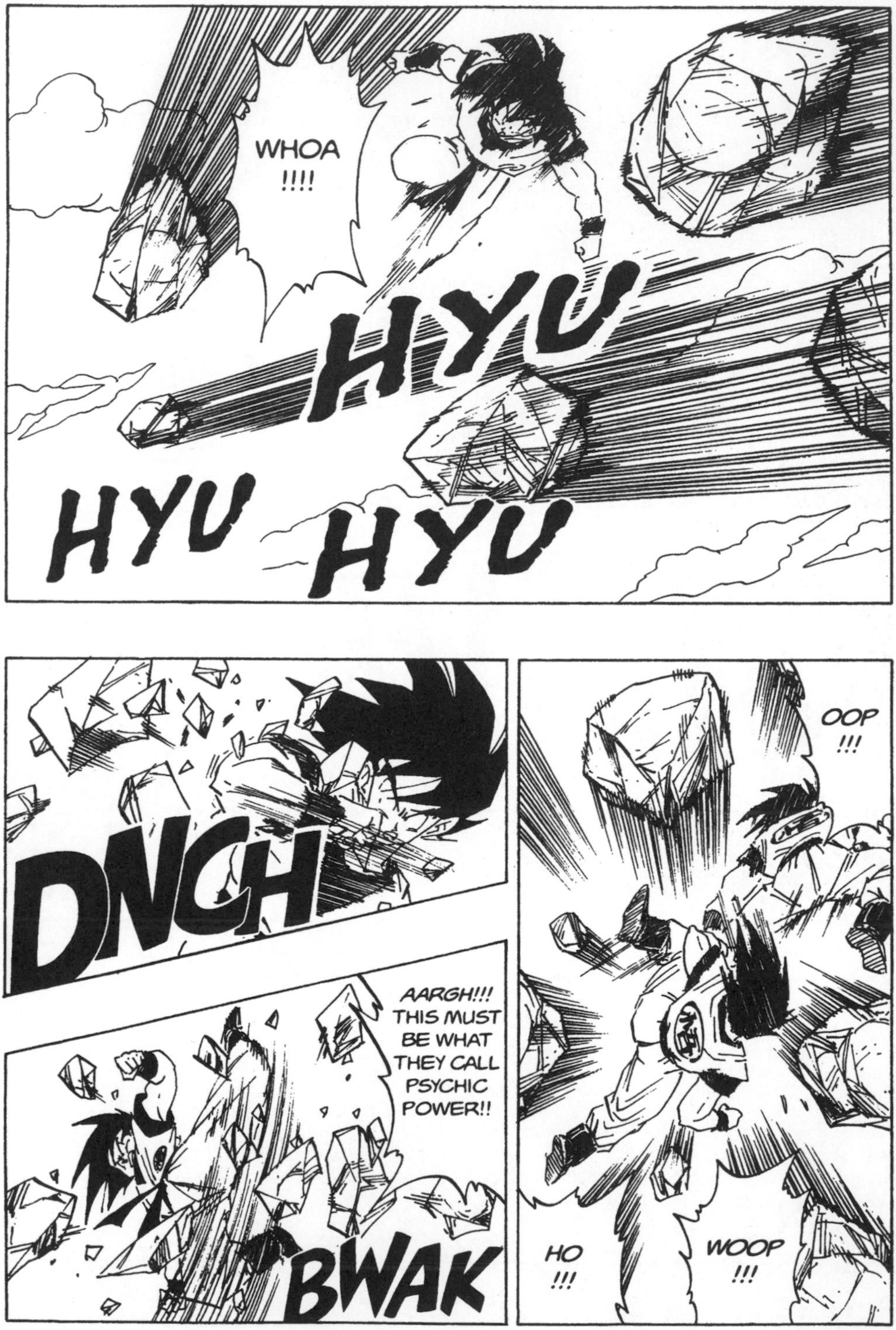
WHOA !!!!
HYU
HYU
HYU
OOP !!!
HO !!!
WOOP !!!
DNCH
AARGH!!! THIS MUST BE WHAT THEY CALL PSYCHIC POWER!!
BWAK

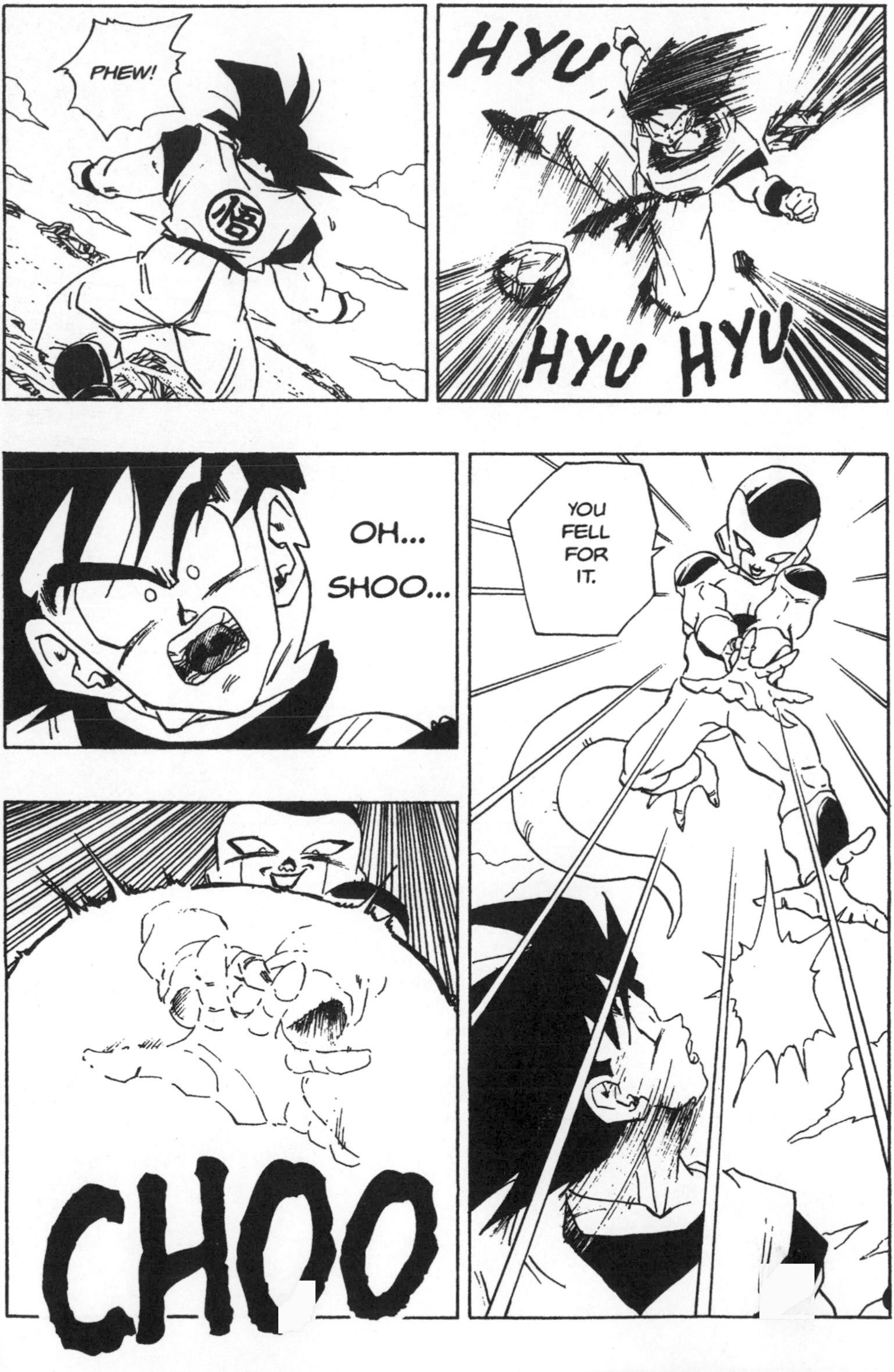
HYU
HYU HYU
PHEW!
YOU FELL FOR IT.
OH... SHOO...
CHOO

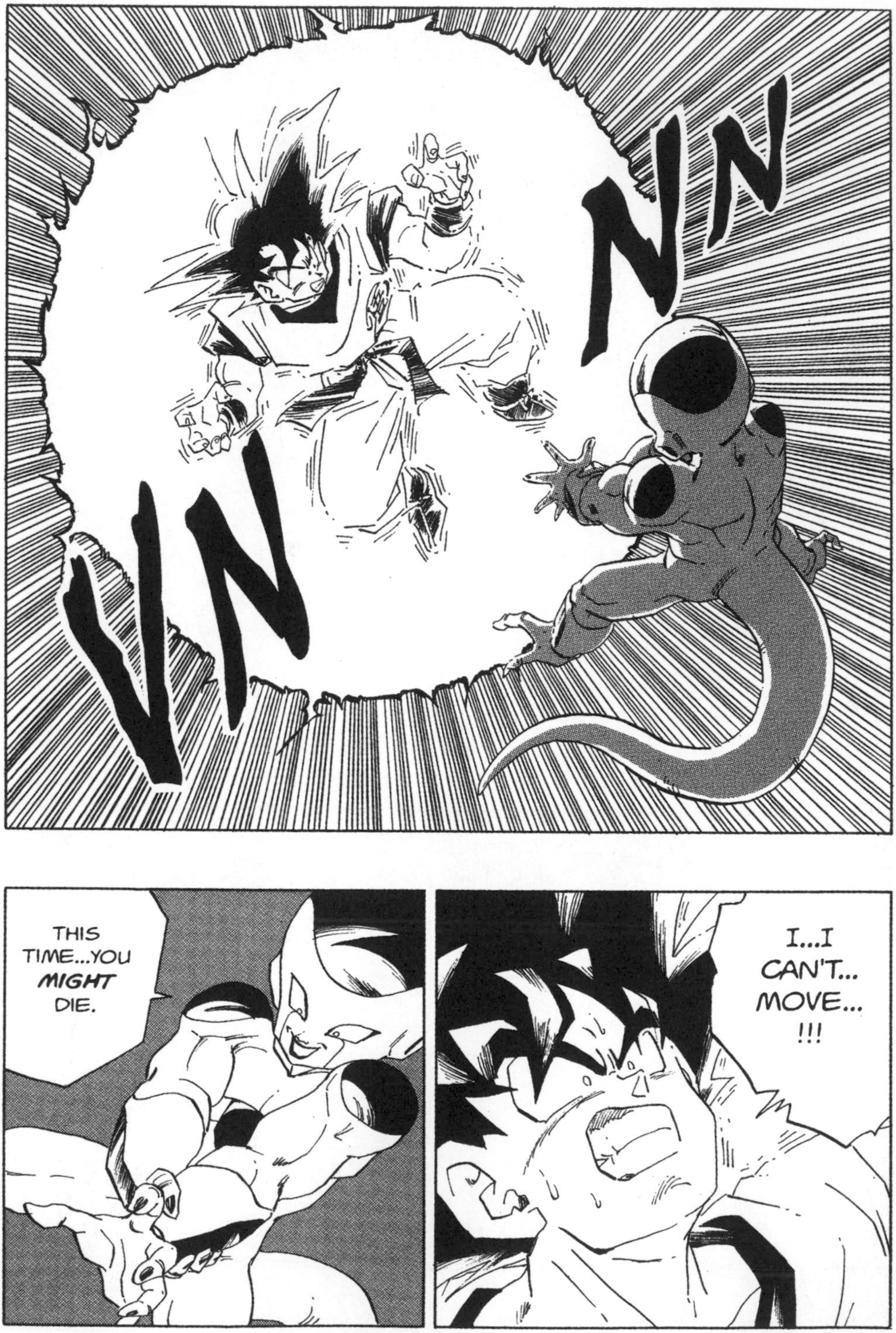
NN
NN
I...I CAN'T... MOVE... !!!
THIS TIME...YOU *MIGHT* DIE.

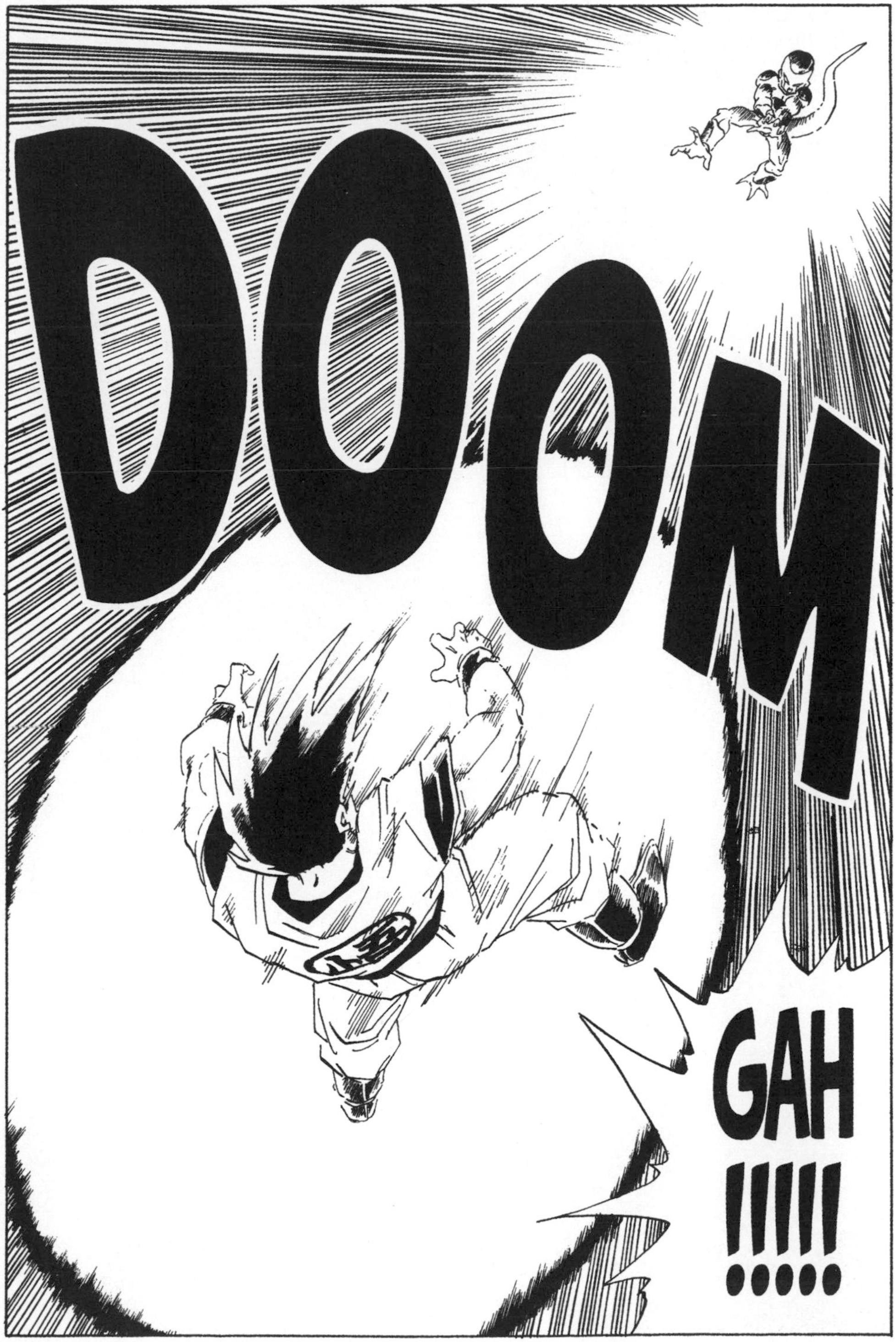
DOOM
GAH!!!!!!

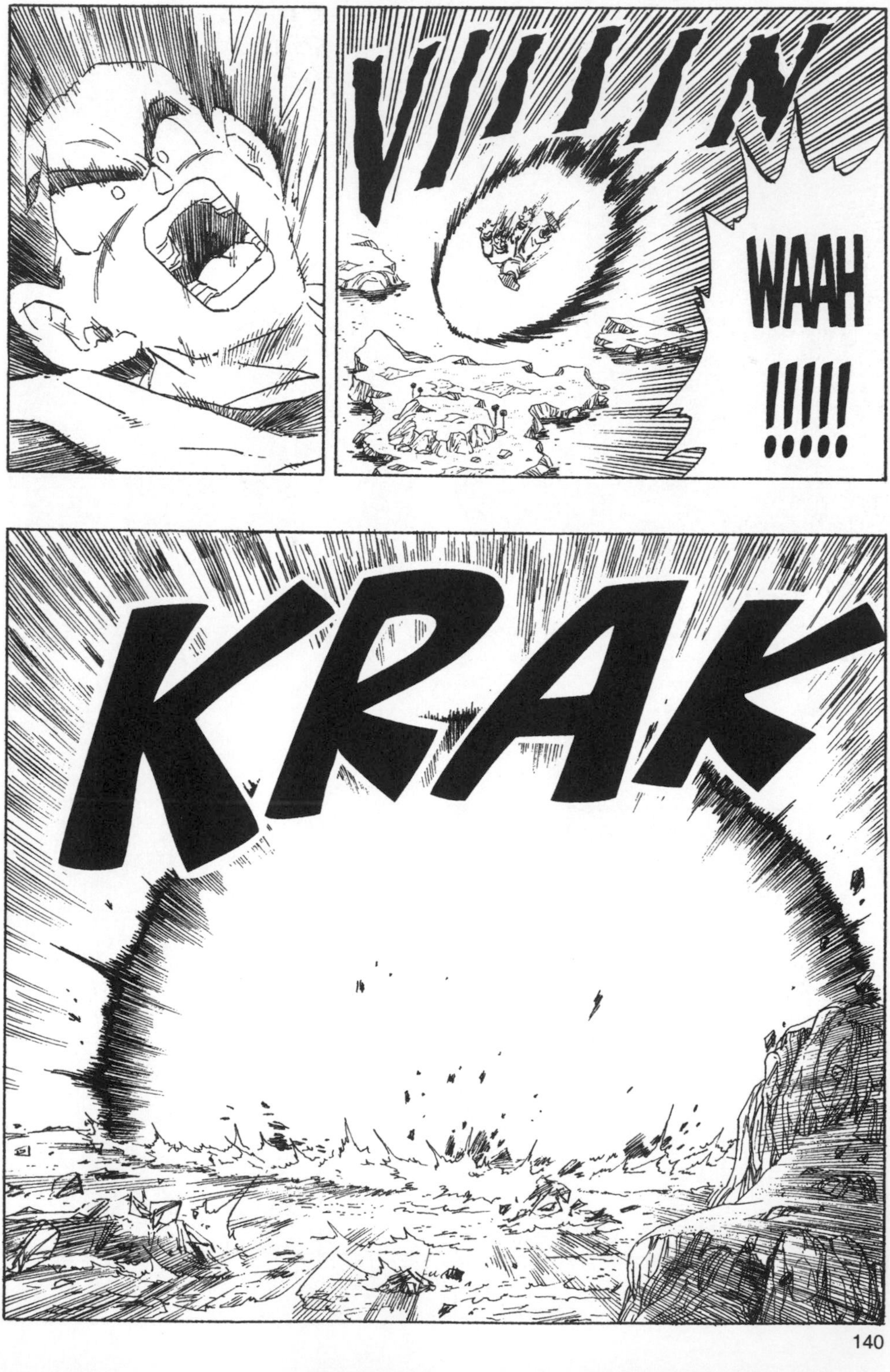
VIIIIN
WAAH
!!!!!!
KRAK

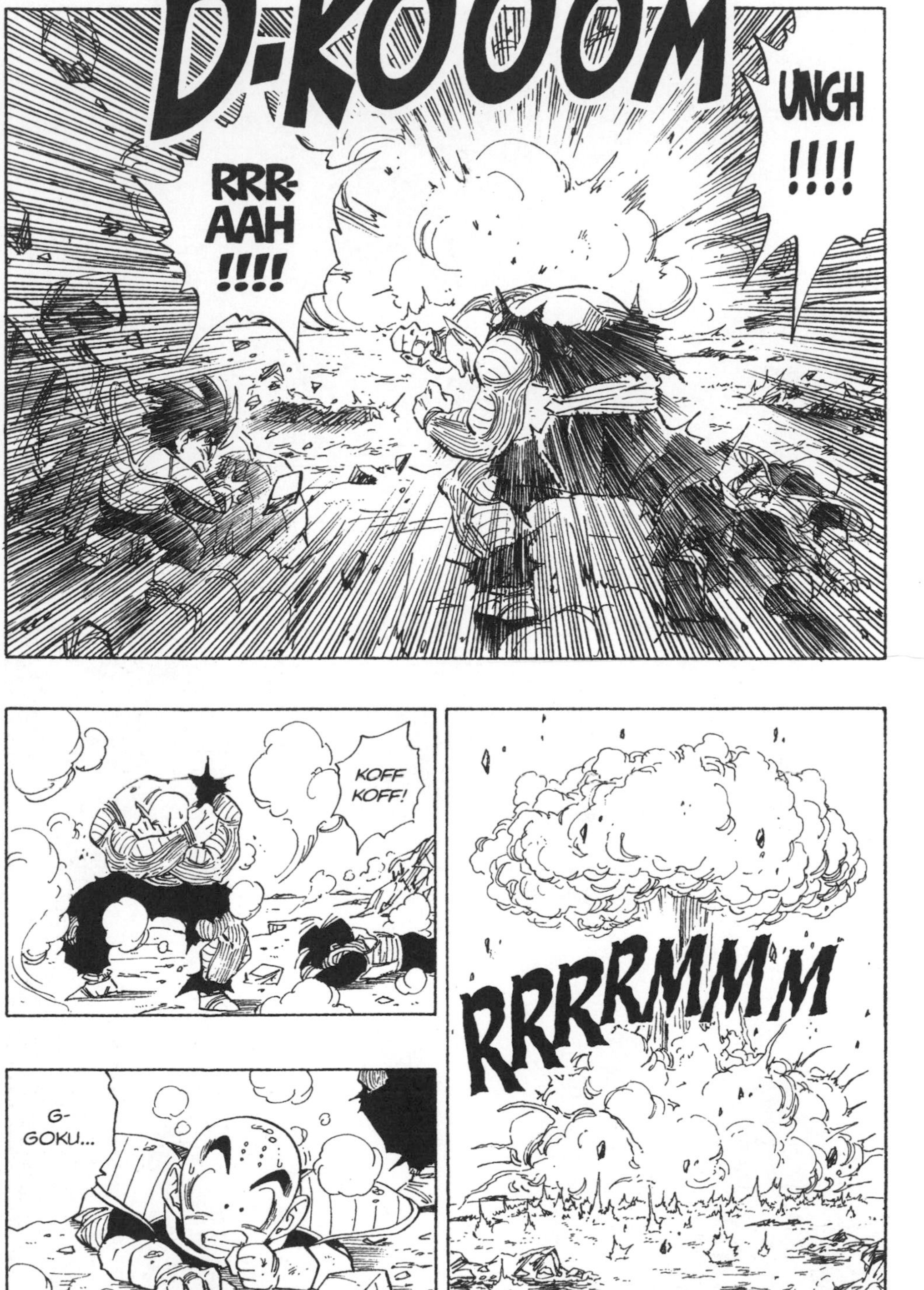
D-KOOOM
UNGH !!!!
RRR-AAH !!!!
RRRRMMMM
KOFF KOFF!
G-GOKU...

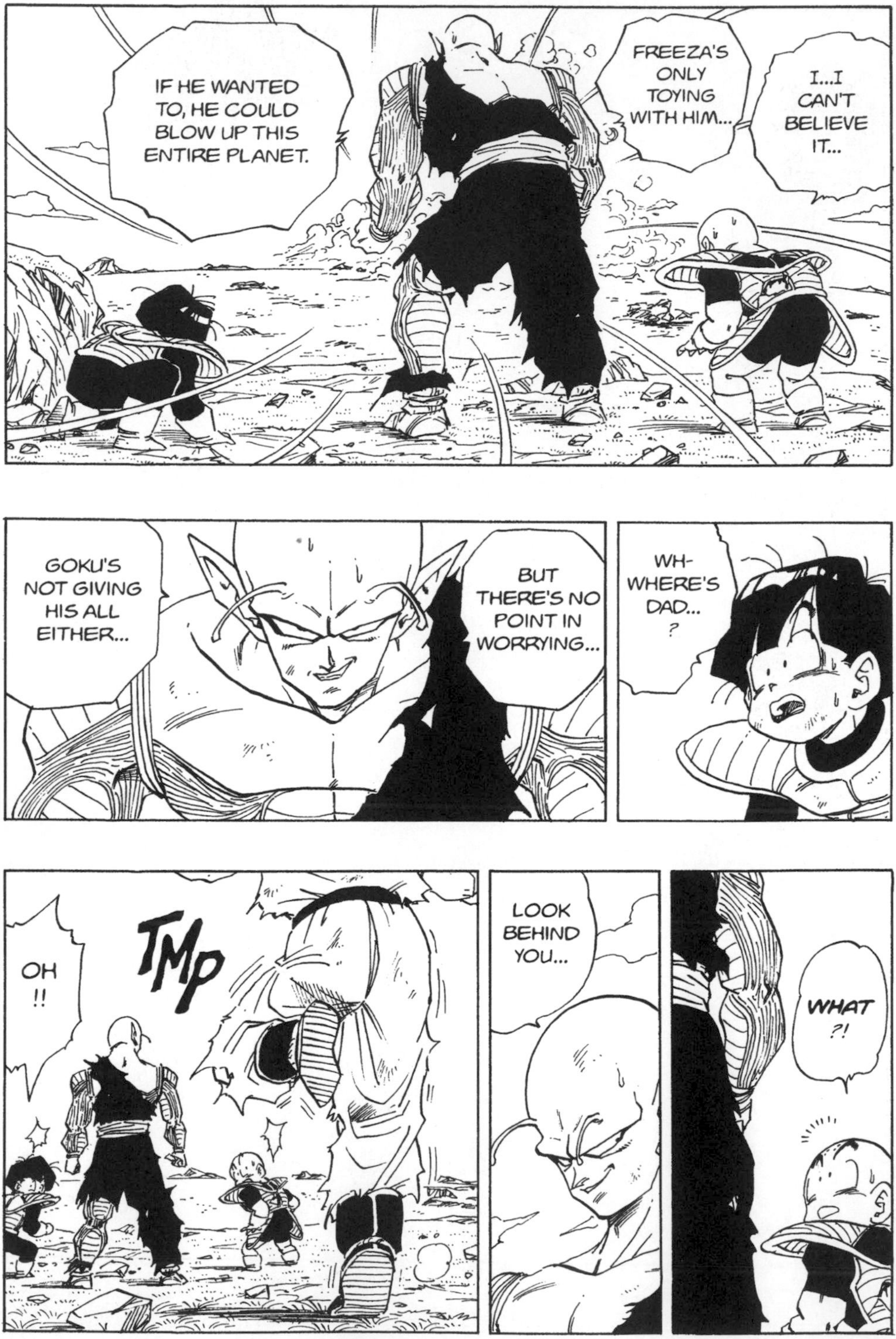
IF HE WANTED TO, HE COULD BLOW UP THIS ENTIRE PLANET.
FREEZA'S ONLY TOYING WITH HIM...
I...I CAN'T BELIEVE IT...
GOKU'S NOT GIVING HIS ALL EITHER...
BUT THERE'S NO POINT IN WORRYING...
WH- WHERE'S DAD...?
OH !!
TMP
LOOK BEHIND YOU...
WHAT ?!

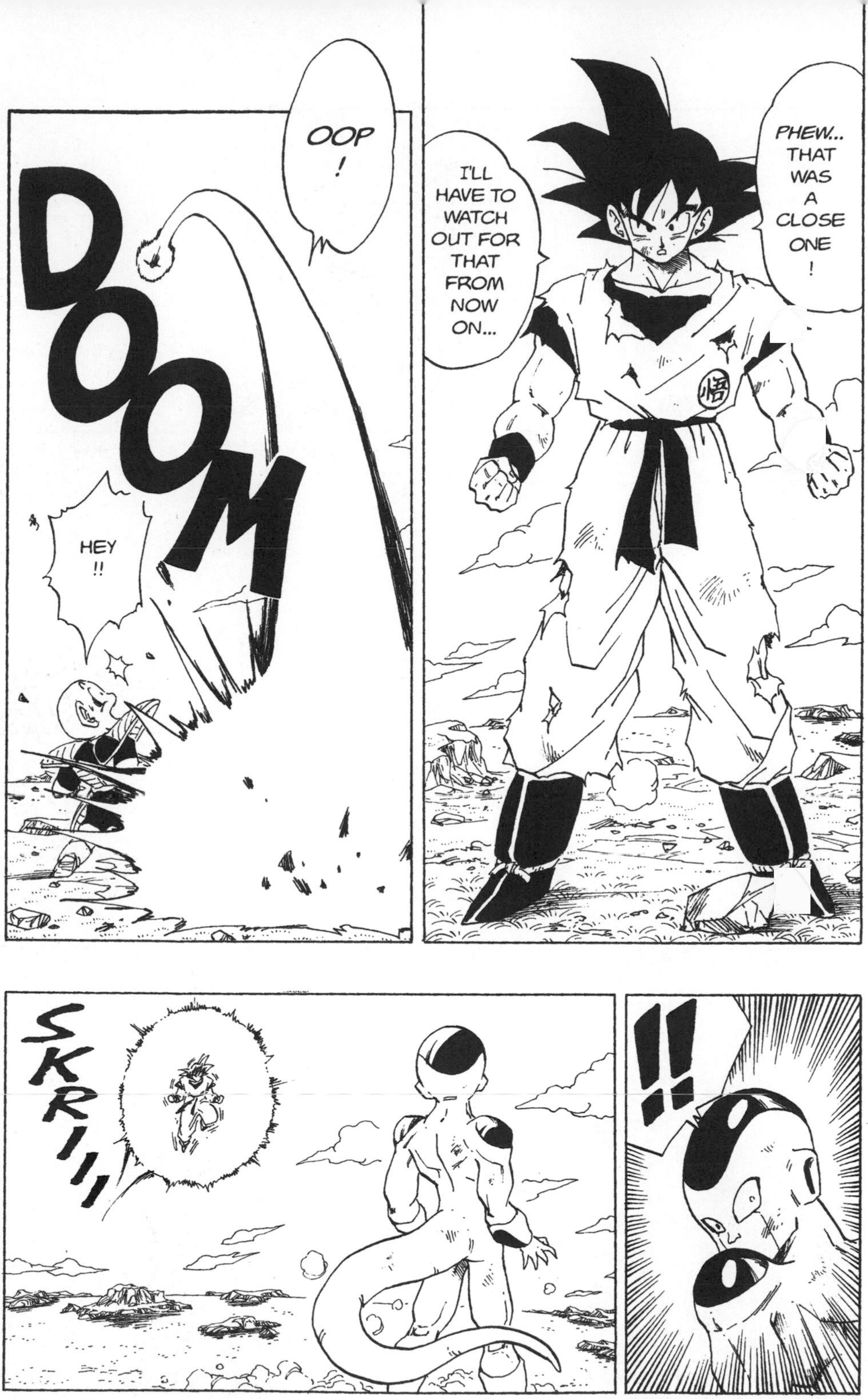
PHEW... THAT WAS A CLOSE ONE!
I'LL HAVE TO WATCH OUT FOR THAT FROM NOW ON...
OOP!
DOOM
HEY!!
!!
SKRIIII

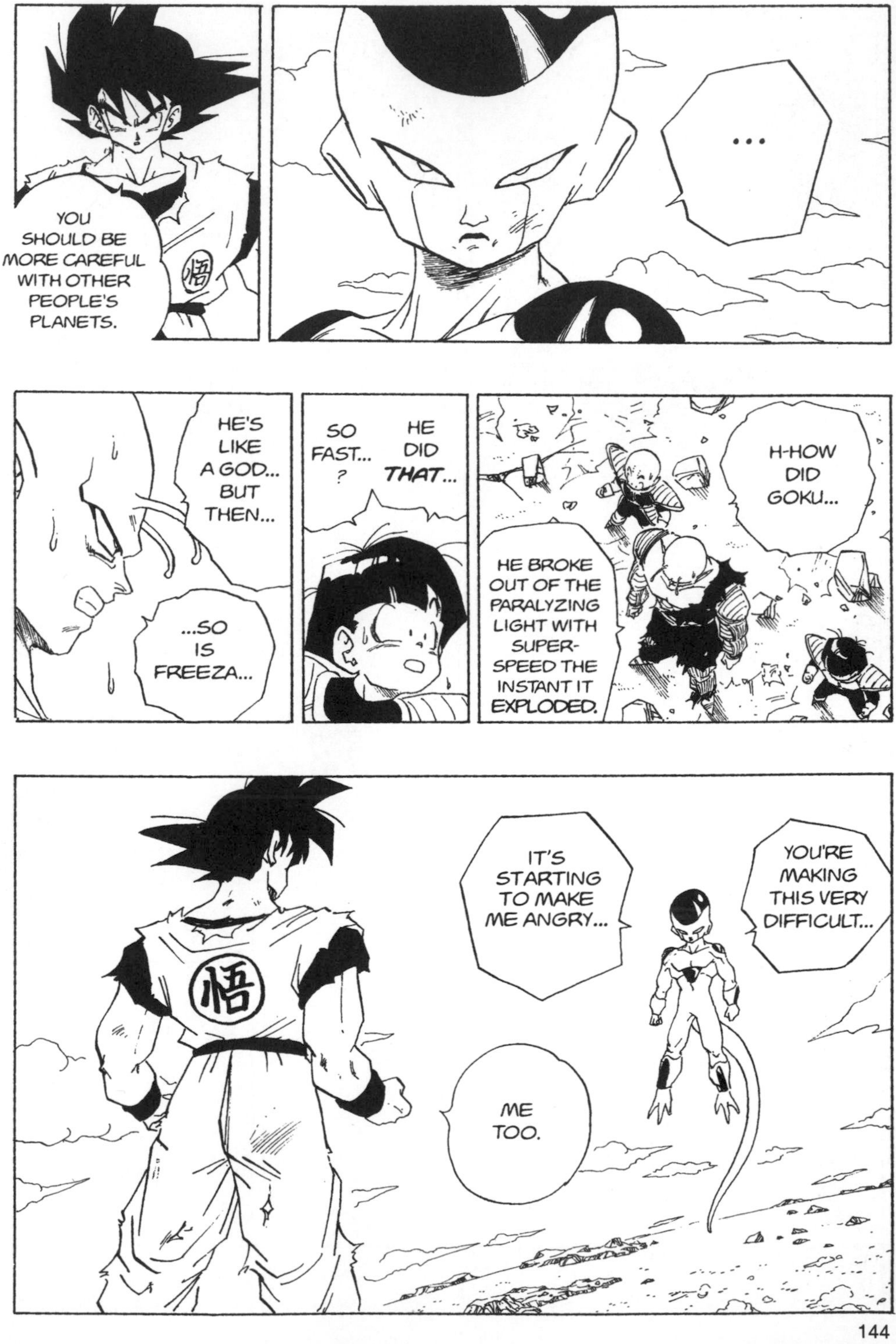
YOU SHOULD BE MORE CAREFUL WITH OTHER PEOPLE'S PLANETS.
...
HE'S LIKE A GOD... BUT THEN...
...SO IS FREEZA...
SO FAST... ?
HE DID *THAT*...
H-HOW DID GOKU...
HE BROKE OUT OF THE PARALYZING LIGHT WITH SUPER-SPEED THE INSTANT IT EXPLODED.
IT'S STARTING TO MAKE ME ANGRY...
YOU'RE MAKING THIS VERY DIFFICULT...
ME TOO.

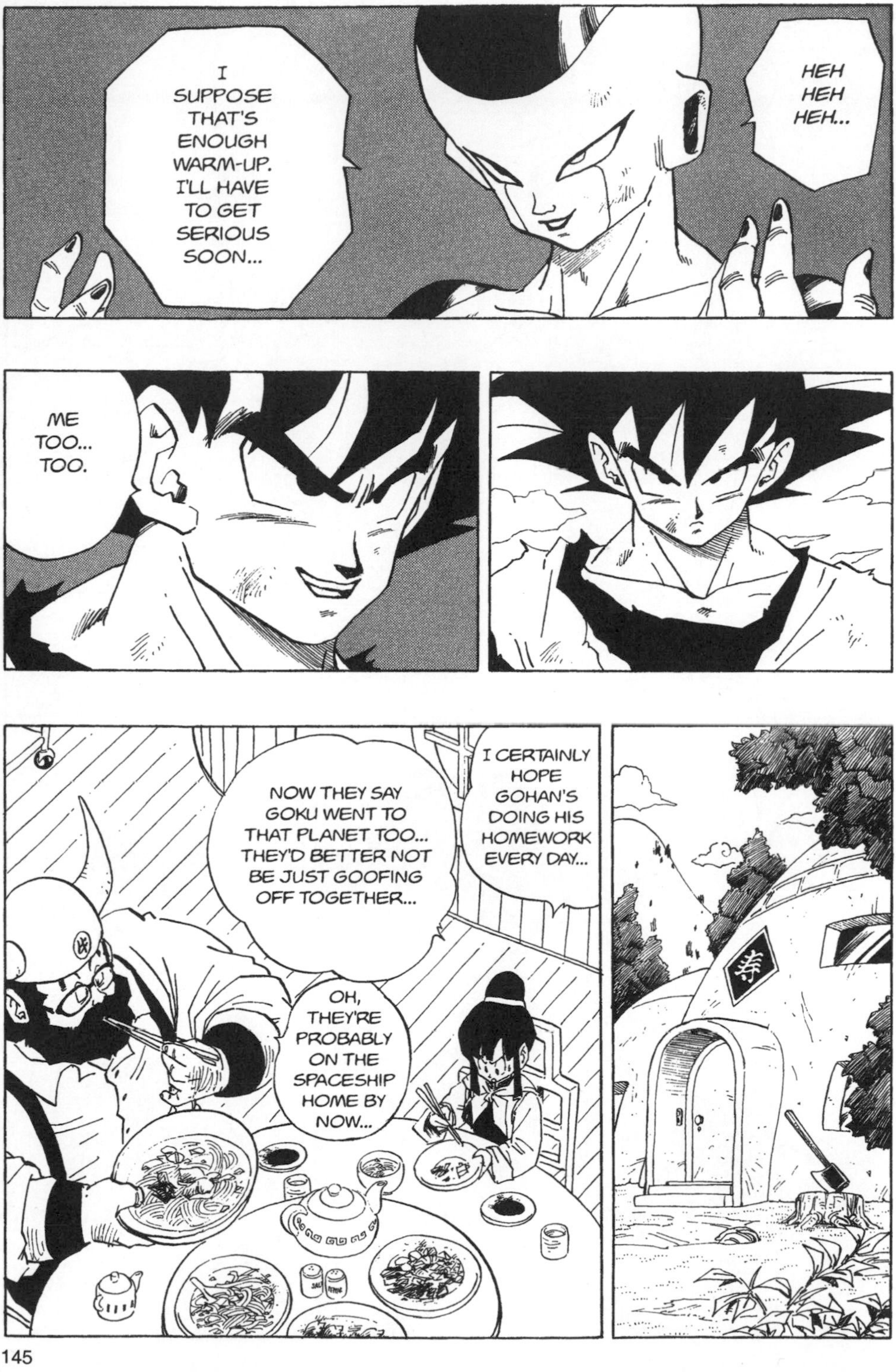
I SUPPOSE THAT'S ENOUGH WARM-UP. I'LL HAVE TO GET SERIOUS SOON...
HEH HEH HEH...
ME TOO... TOO.
I CERTAINLY HOPE GOHAN'S DOING HIS HOMEWORK EVERY DAY...
NOW THEY SAY GOKU WENT TO THAT PLANET TOO... THEY'D BETTER NOT BE JUST GOOFING OFF TOGETHER...
OH, THEY'RE PROBABLY ON THE SPACESHIP HOME BY NOW...

DBZ:117 • Hand to Foot

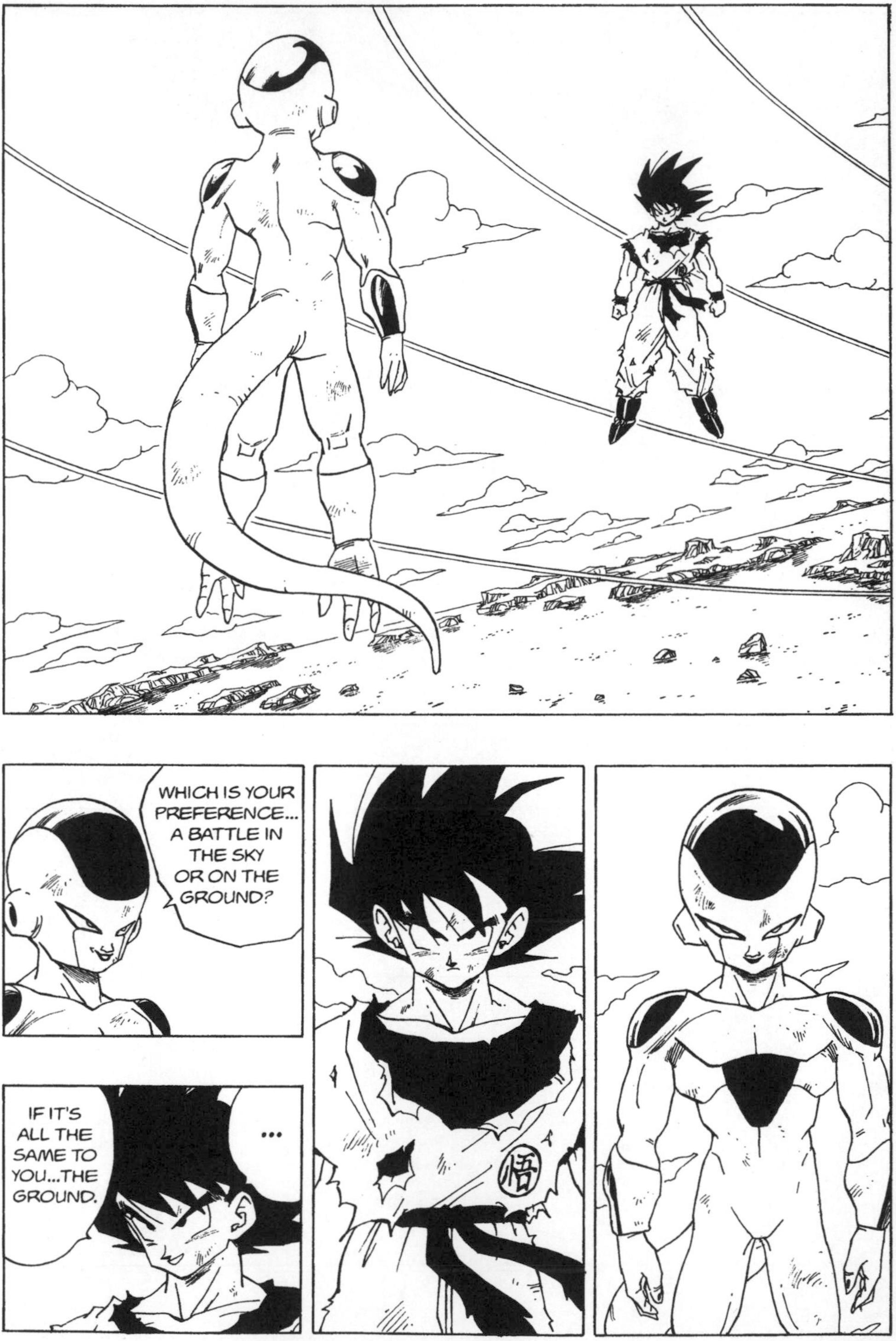
WHICH IS YOUR PREFERENCE... A BATTLE IN THE SKY OR ON THE GROUND?
...
IF IT'S ALL THE SAME TO YOU...THE GROUND.

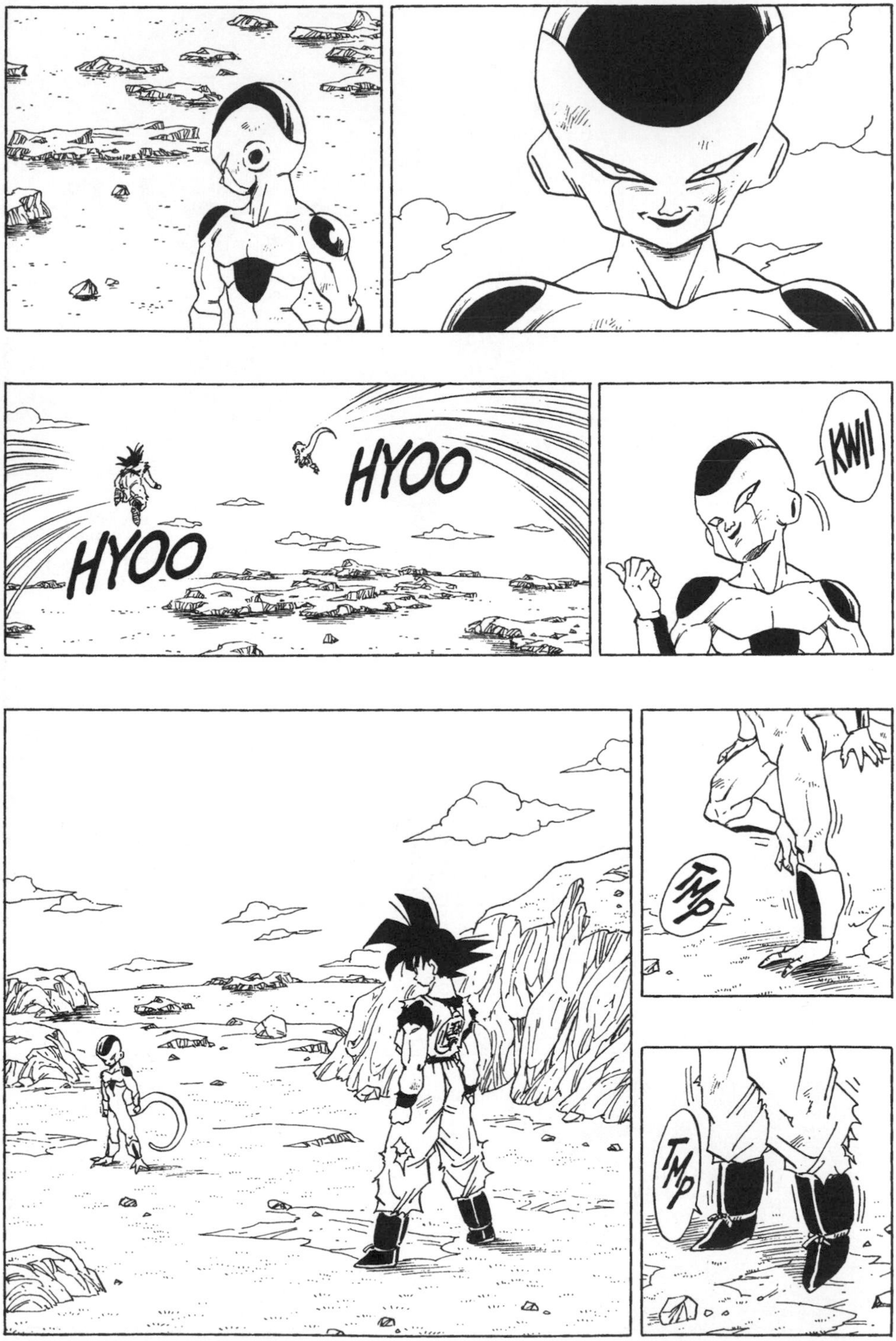
HYOO
HYOO
KWII
TMP
TMP

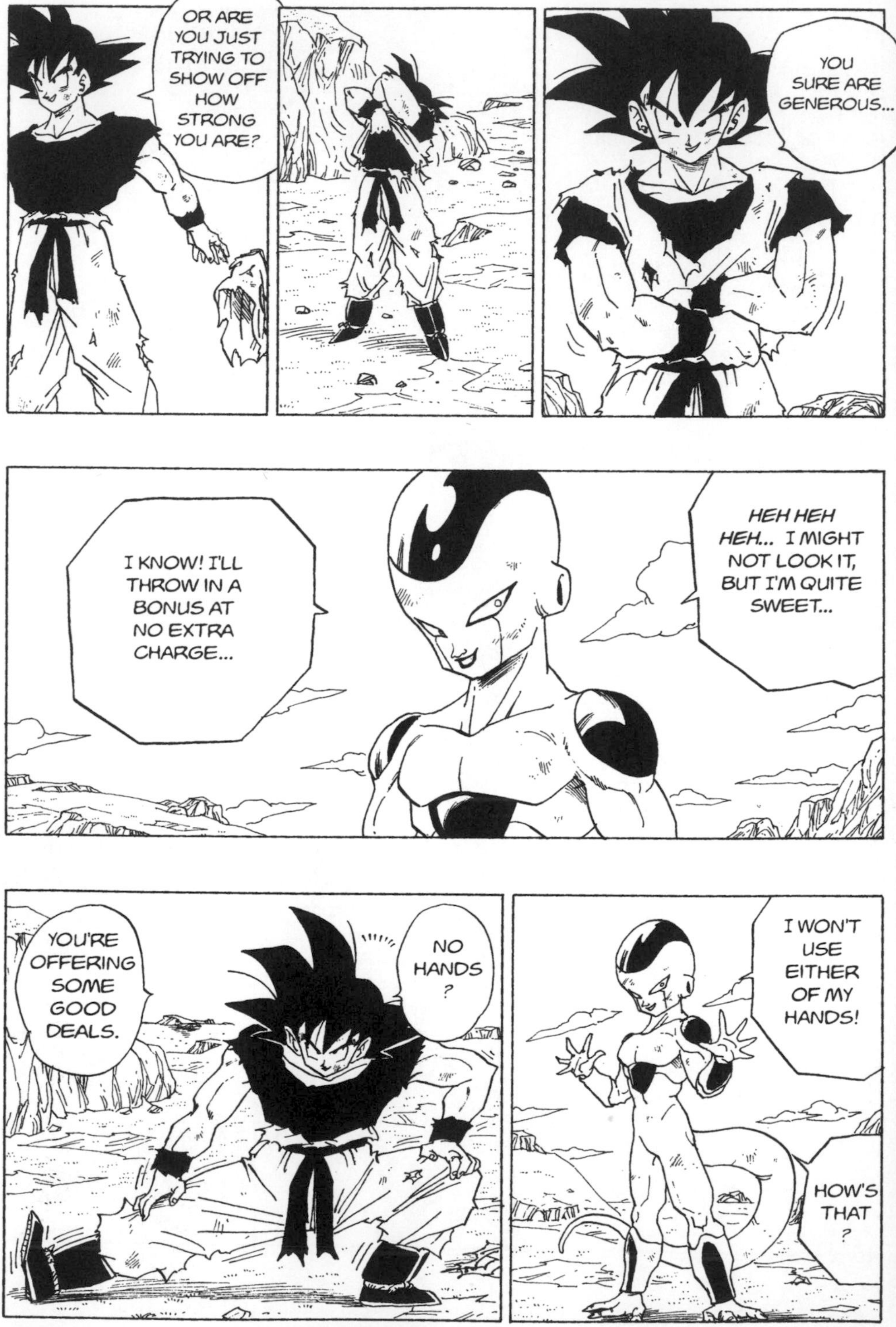
YOU SURE ARE GENEROUS...
OR ARE YOU JUST TRYING TO SHOW OFF HOW STRONG YOU ARE?
HEH HEH HEH... I MIGHT NOT LOOK IT, BUT I'M QUITE SWEET...
I KNOW! I'LL THROW IN A BONUS AT NO EXTRA CHARGE...
I WON'T USE EITHER OF MY HANDS!
HOW'S THAT?
NO HANDS?
YOU'RE OFFERING SOME GOOD DEALS.

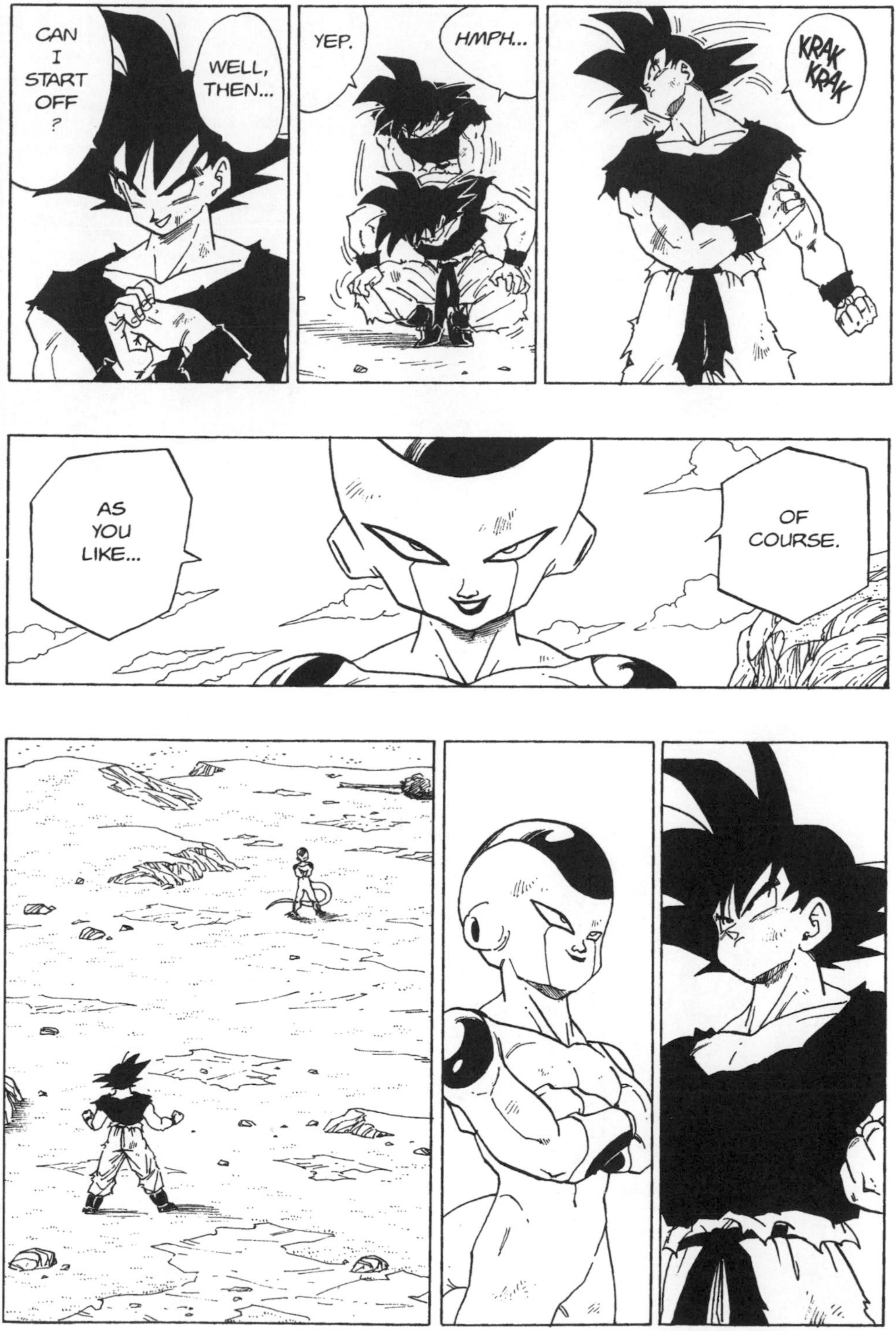
CAN I START OFF ?
WELL, THEN...
YEP.
HMPH...
KRAK KRAK
AS YOU LIKE...
OF COURSE.

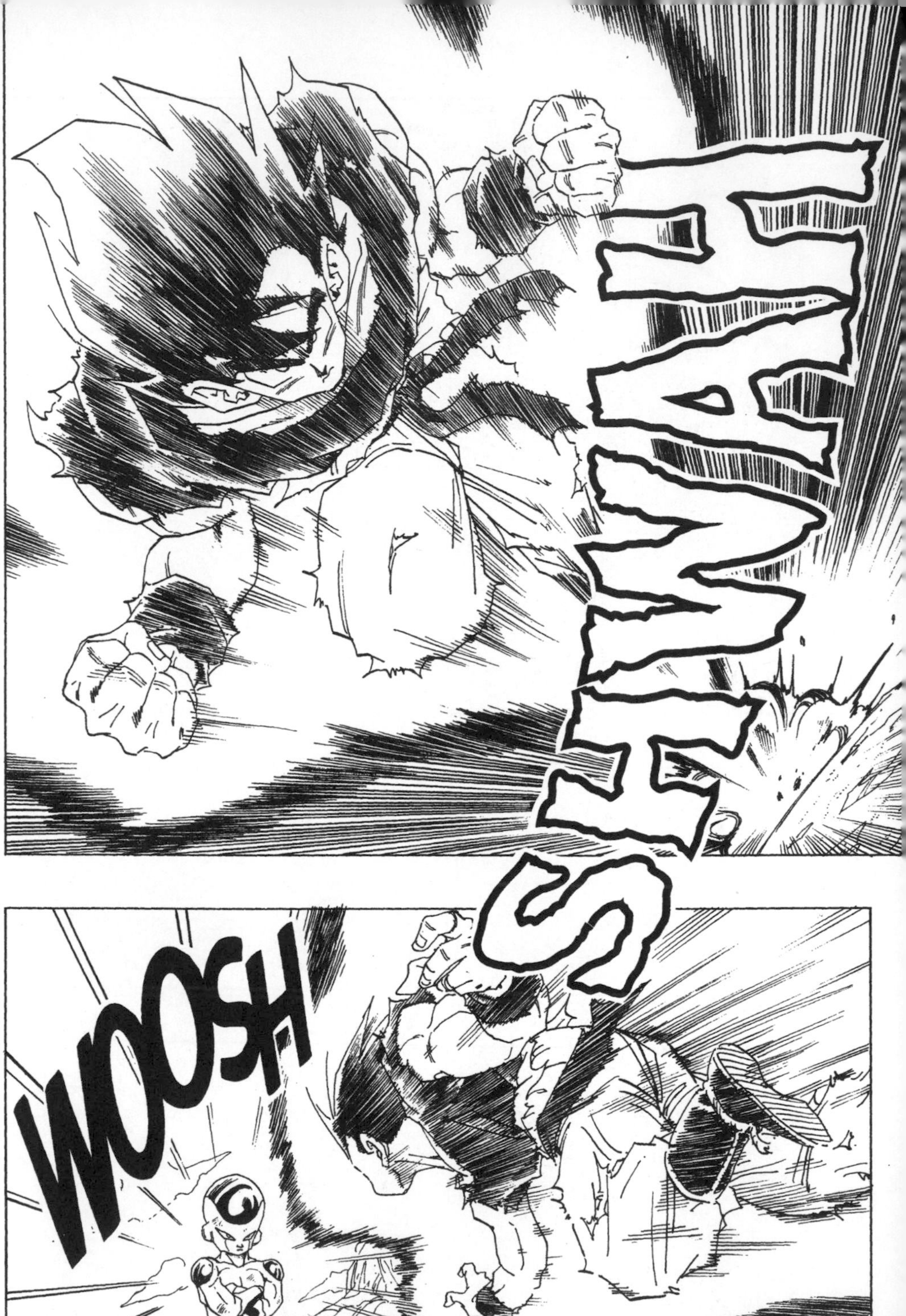
SHWAH
WOOSH

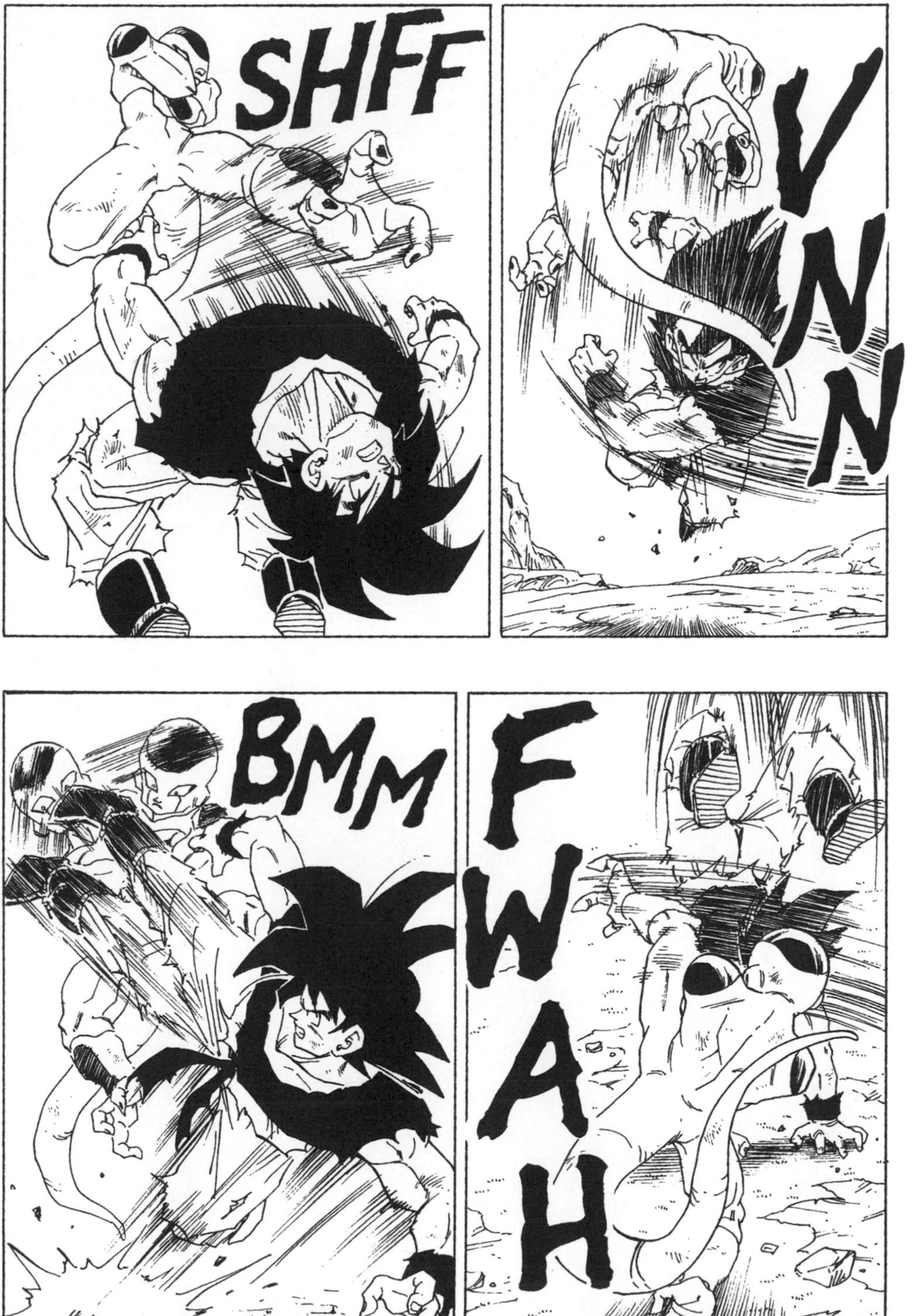
VNN
SHFF
FWAH
BMM

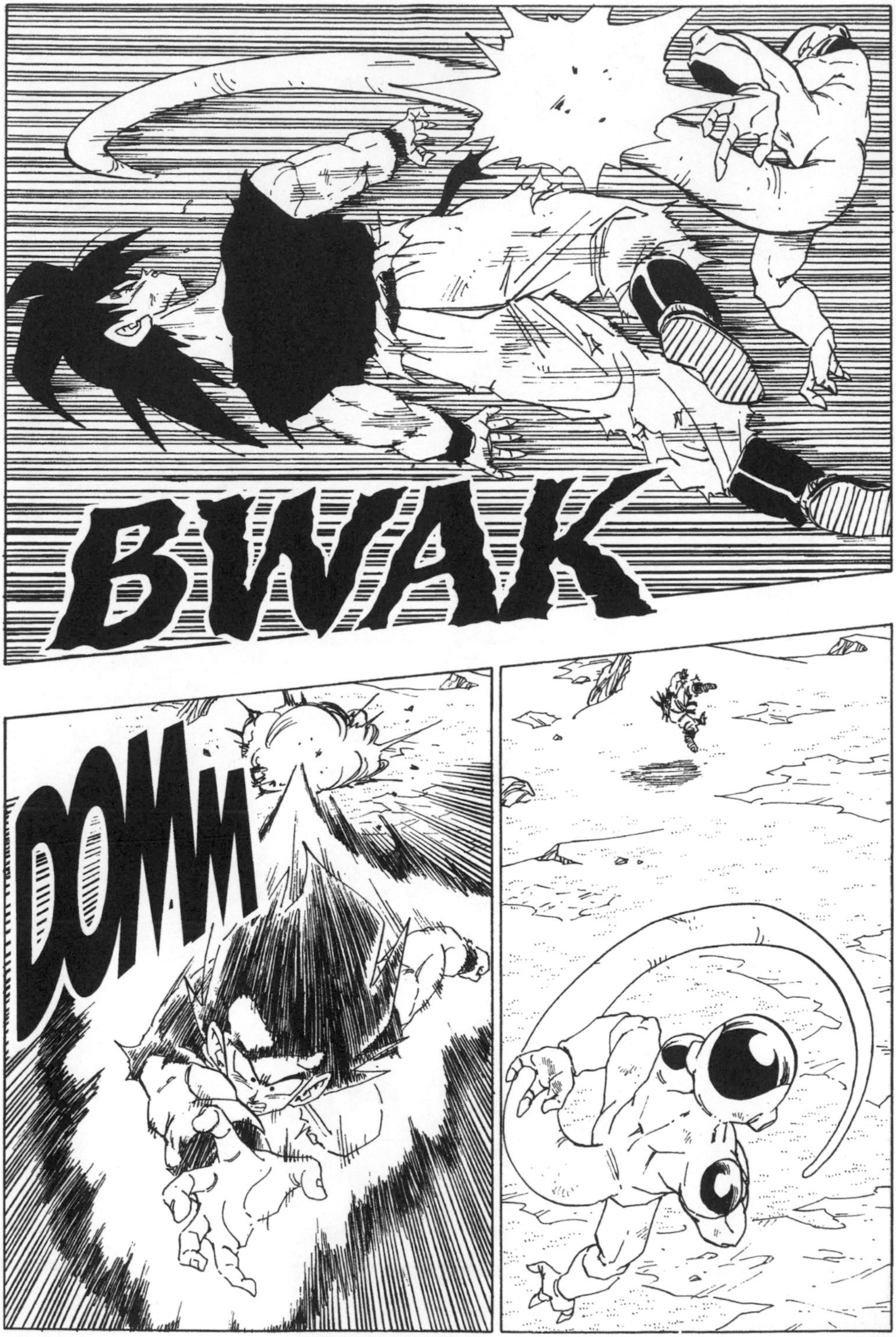
BWAK
DOMM

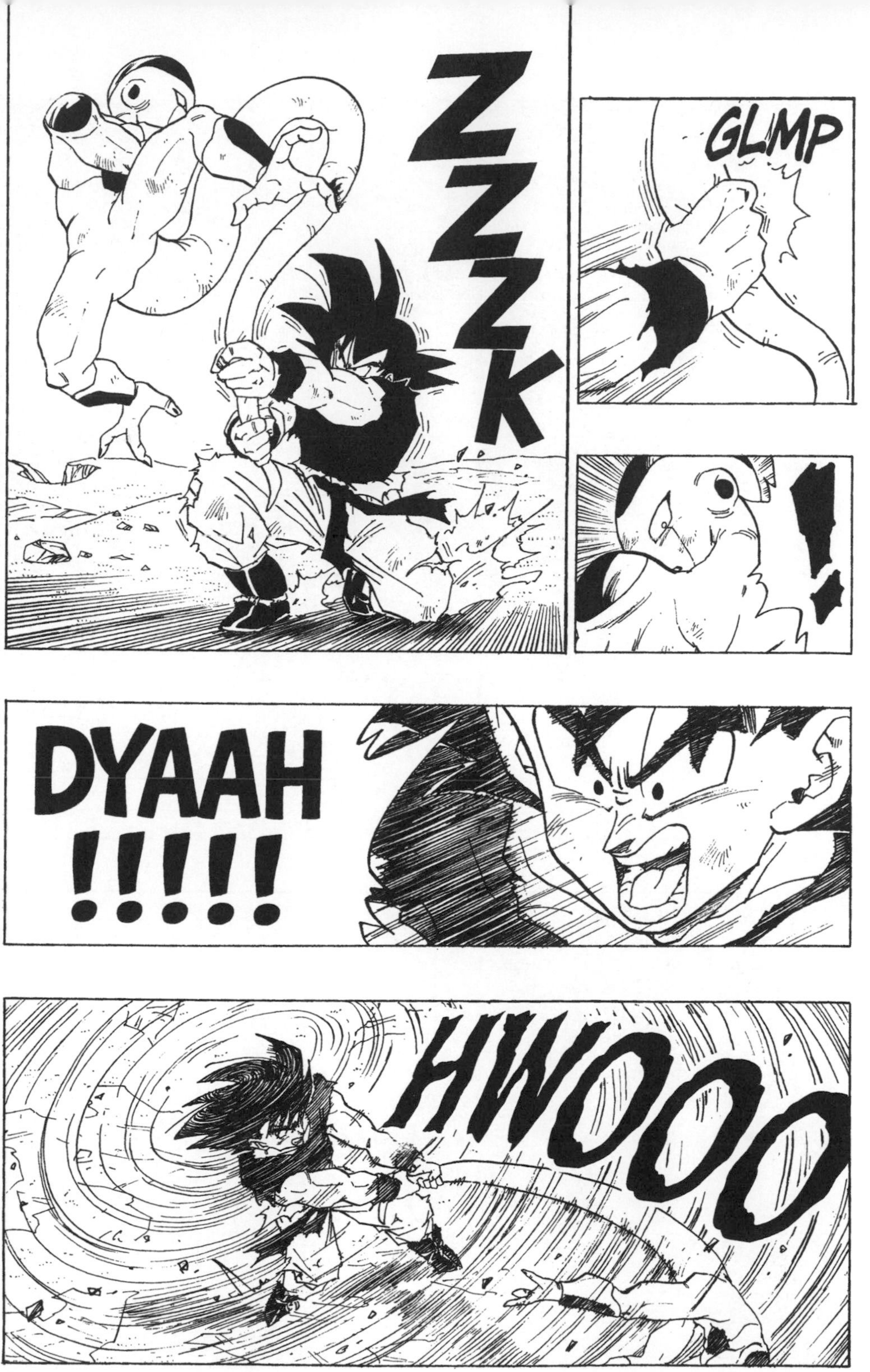
ZZZK
GLMP
!!
DYAAH !!!!!
HWOOO

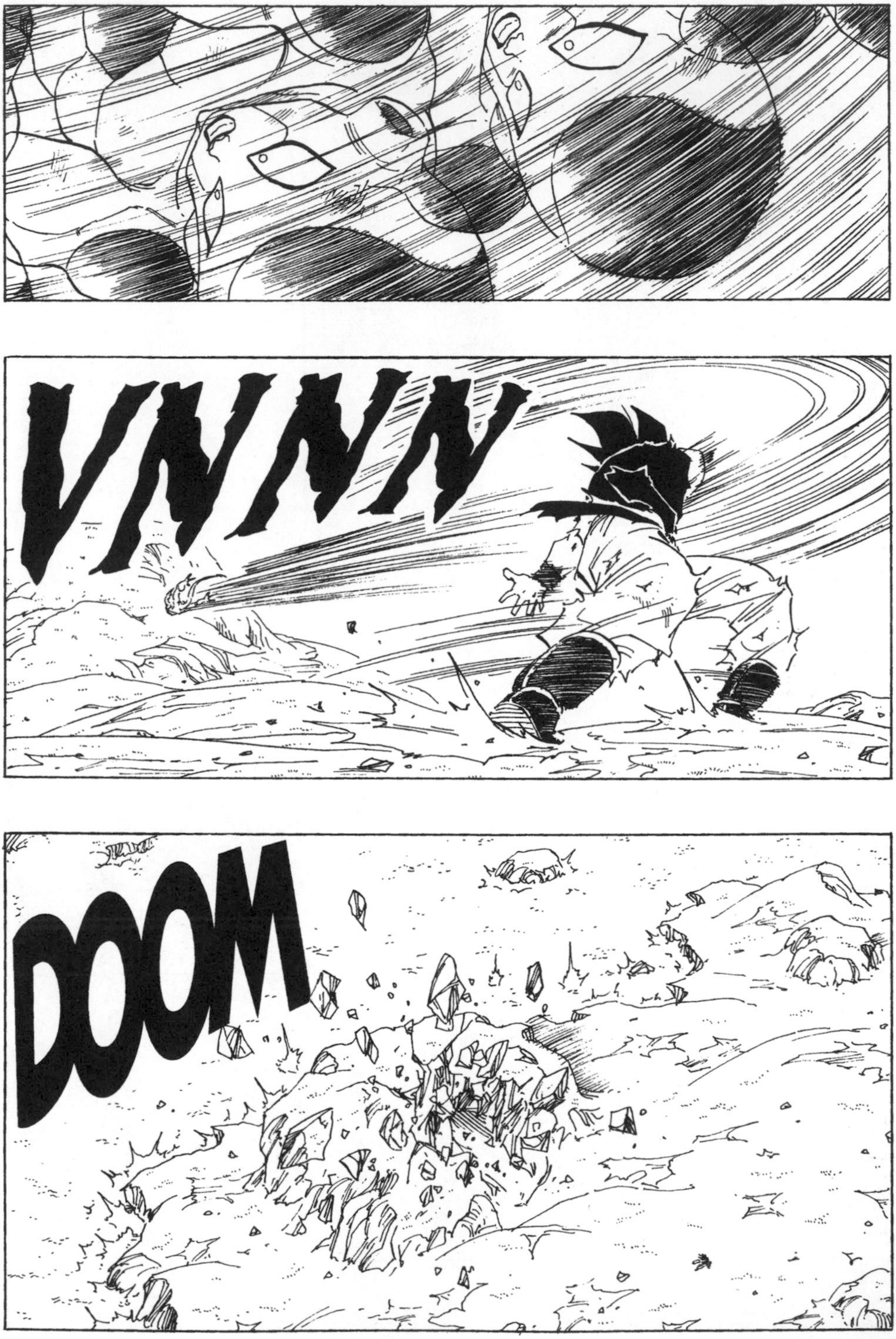
VNNN
DOOM

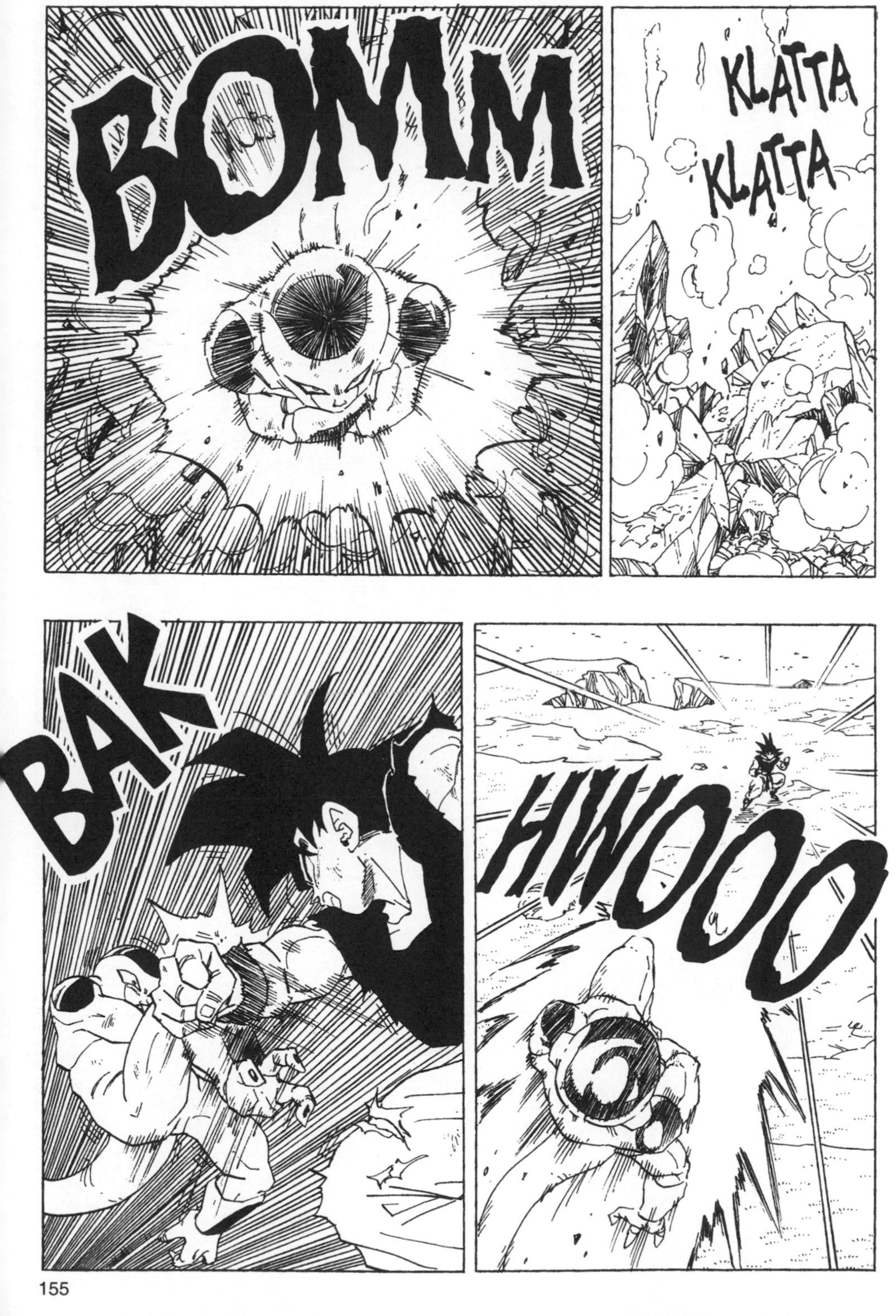
BOMM
KLATTA
KLATTA
BAK
HWOOO

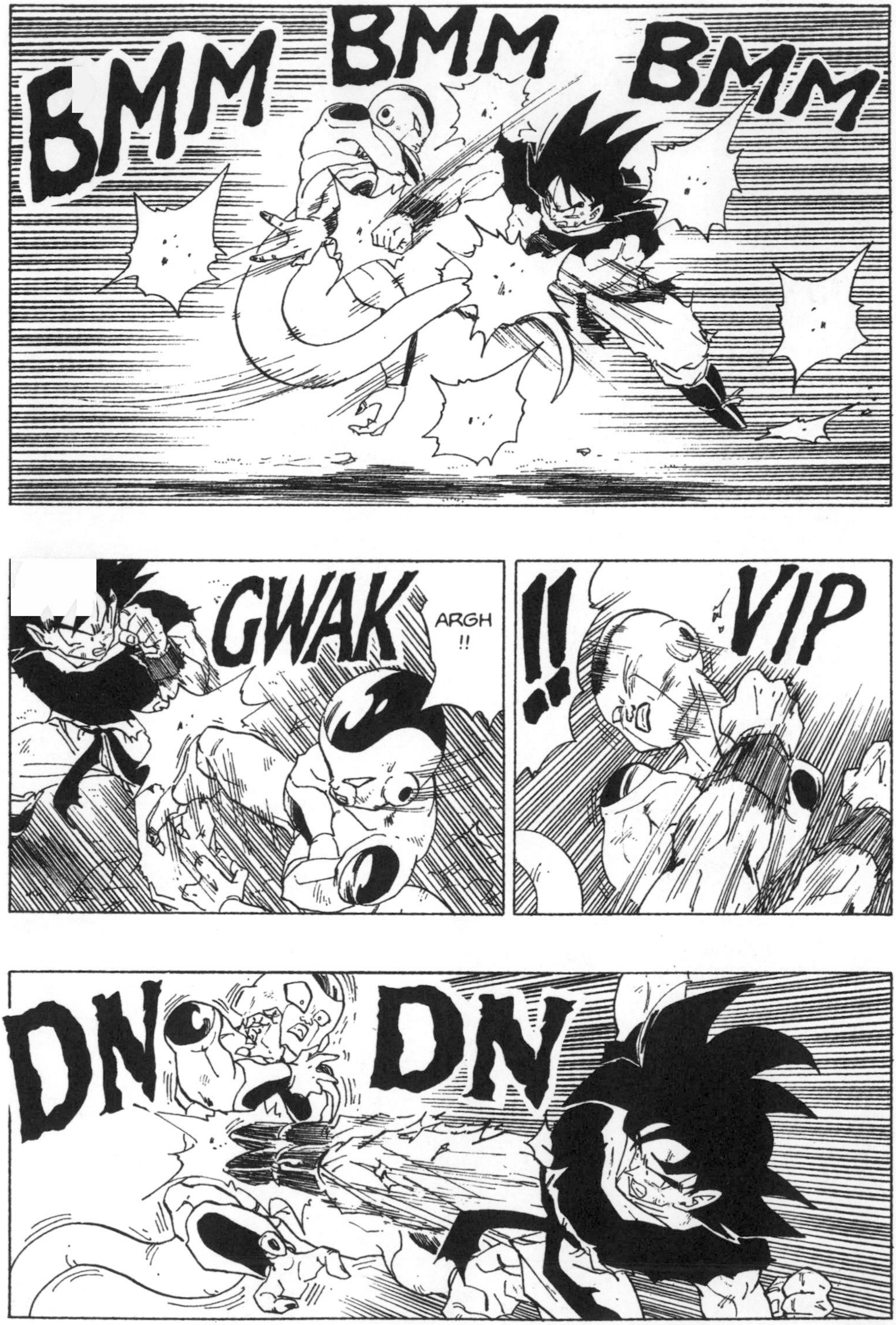
BMM BMM BMM
GWAK
ARGH !!
!!
VIP
DN DN

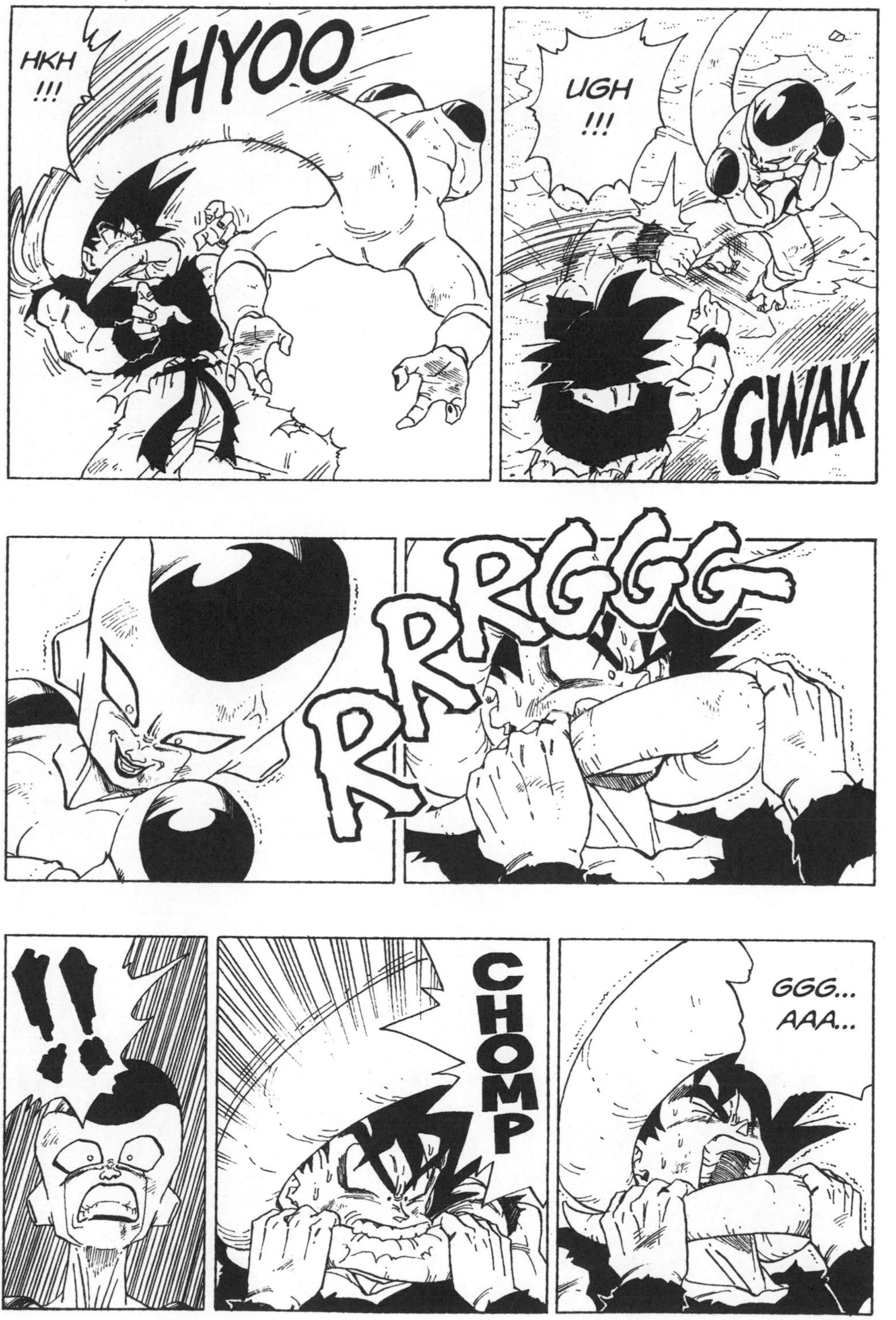

UGH
!!!
GWAK
HKH
!!!
HYOO
RRRGGG-
GGG...
AAA...
CHOMP
!!

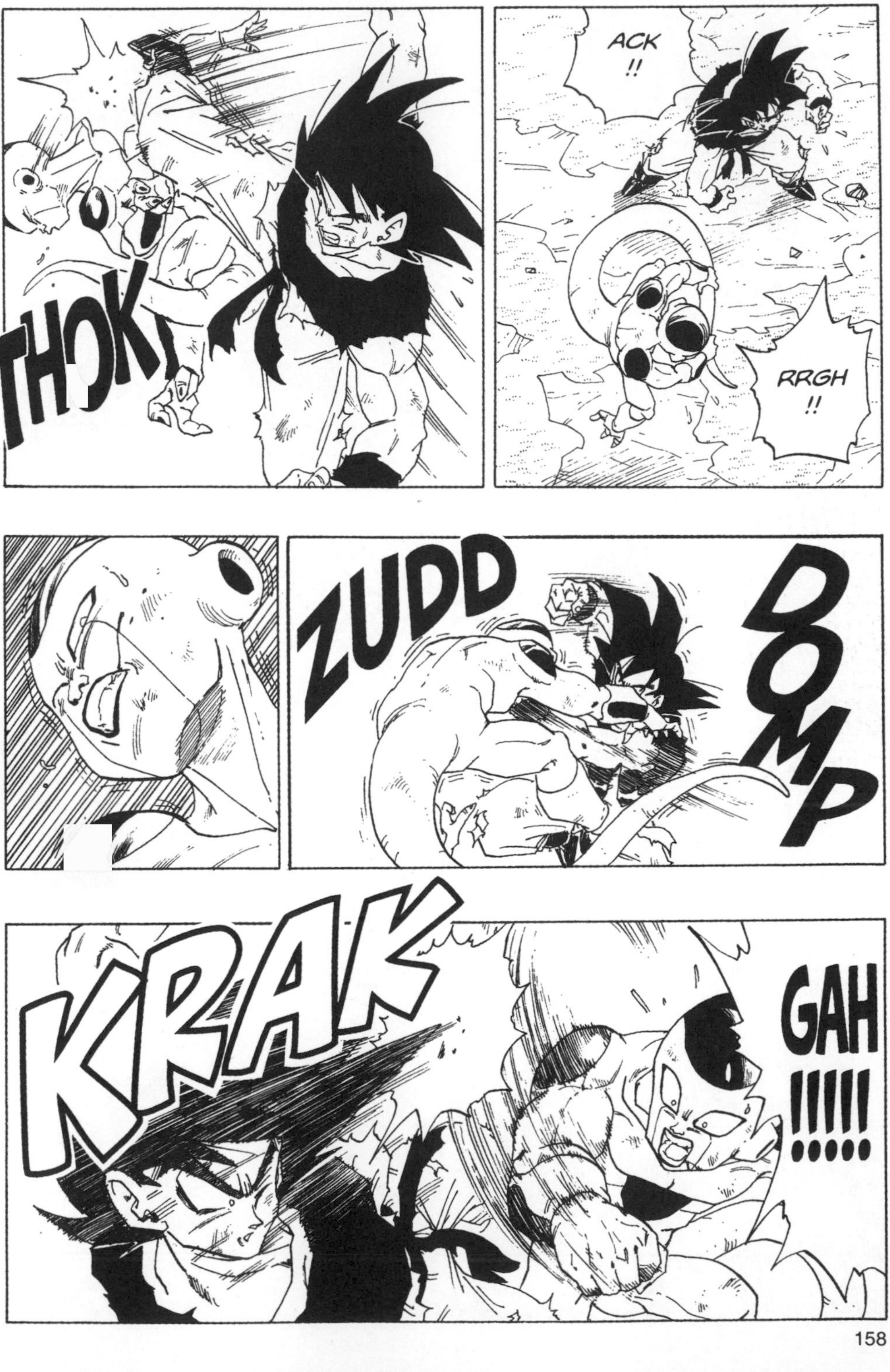
ACK
!!
RRGH
!!
THOK
DOMP
ZUDD
KRAK
GAH
!!!!!!

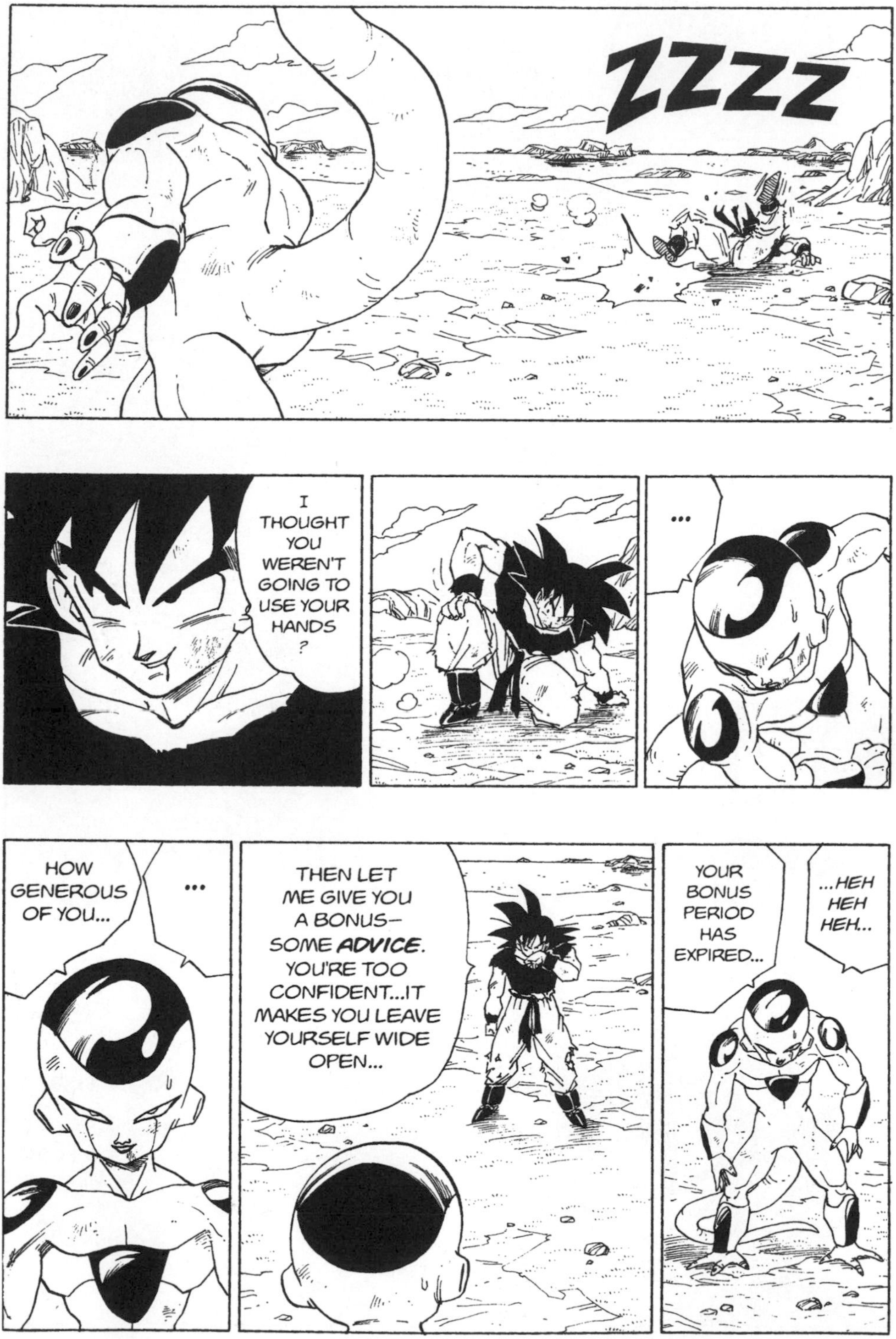
ZZZZ
I THOUGHT YOU WEREN'T GOING TO USE YOUR HANDS ?
...
HOW GENEROUS OF YOU...
...
THEN LET ME GIVE YOU A BONUS— SOME ADVICE. YOU'RE TOO CONFIDENT...IT MAKES YOU LEAVE YOURSELF WIDE OPEN...
YOUR BONUS PERIOD HAS EXPIRED...
...HEH HEH HEH...

DBZ:118 • 50% Maximum Power

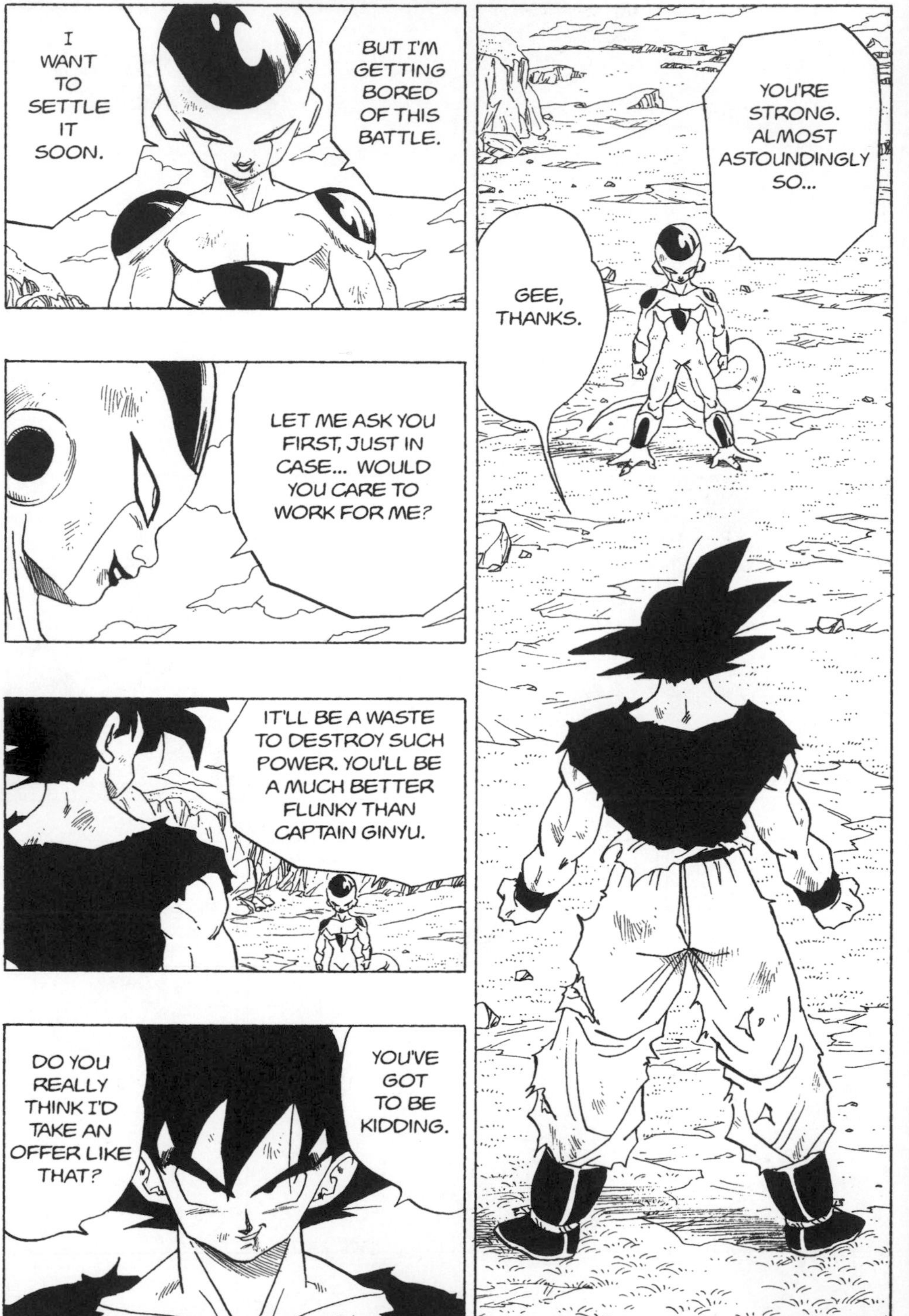

YOU'RE STRONG. ALMOST ASTOUNDINGLY SO...
GEE, THANKS.
BUT I'M GETTING BORED OF THIS BATTLE.
I WANT TO SETTLE IT SOON.
LET ME ASK YOU FIRST, JUST IN CASE... WOULD YOU CARE TO WORK FOR ME?
IT'LL BE A WASTE TO DESTROY SUCH POWER. YOU'LL BE A MUCH BETTER FLUNKY THAN CAPTAIN GINYU.
YOU'VE GOT TO BE KIDDING.
DO YOU REALLY THINK I'D TAKE AN OFFER LIKE THAT?

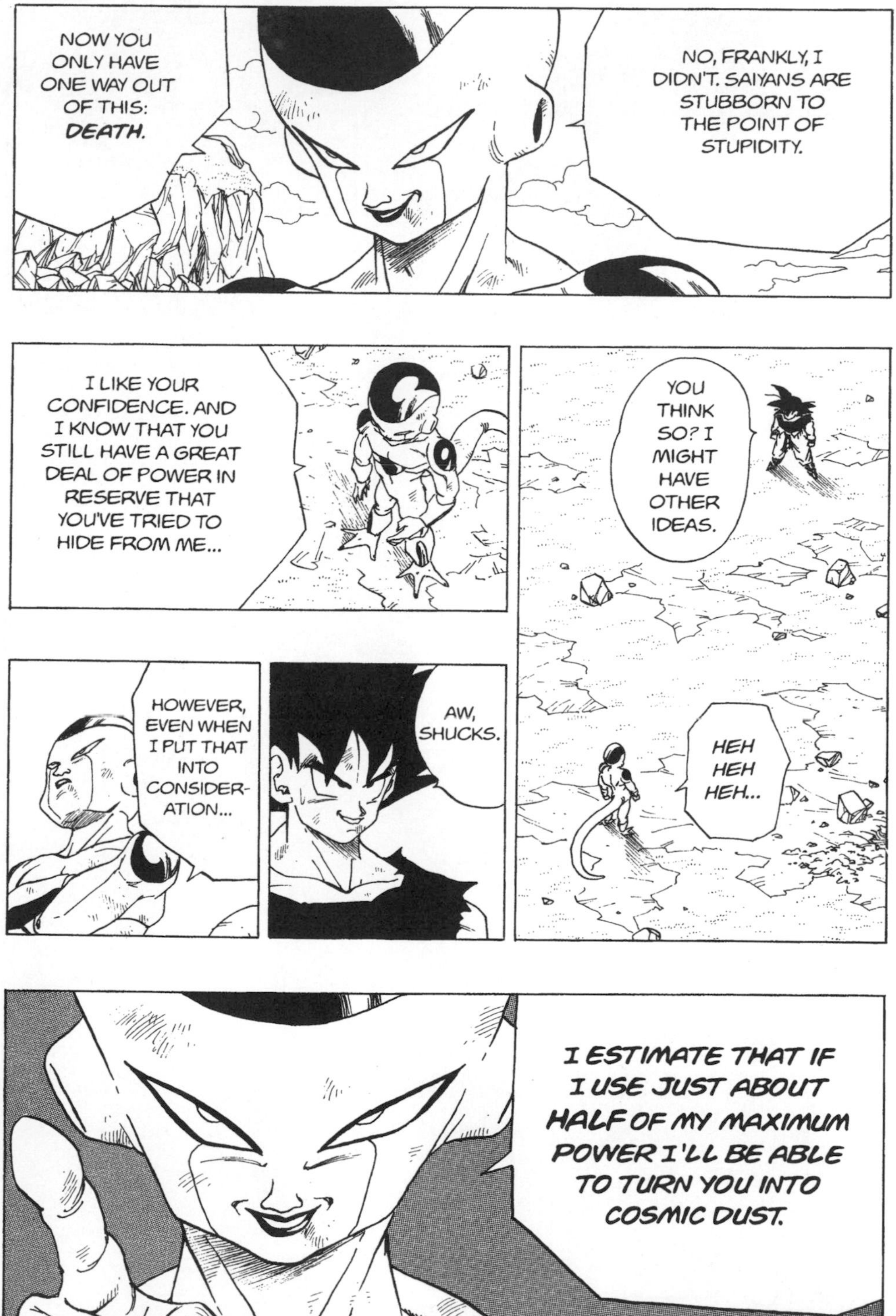
NO, FRANKLY, I DIDN'T. SAIYANS ARE STUBBORN TO THE POINT OF STUPIDITY.
NOW YOU ONLY HAVE ONE WAY OUT OF THIS: DEATH.
YOU THINK SO? I MIGHT HAVE OTHER IDEAS.
I LIKE YOUR CONFIDENCE. AND I KNOW THAT YOU STILL HAVE A GREAT DEAL OF POWER IN RESERVE THAT YOU'VE TRIED TO HIDE FROM ME...
HEH HEH HEH...
AW, SHUCKS.
HOWEVER, EVEN WHEN I PUT THAT INTO CONSIDER-ATION...
I ESTIMATE THAT IF I USE JUST ABOUT HALF OF MY MAXIMUM POWER I'LL BE ABLE TO TURN YOU INTO COSMIC DUST.

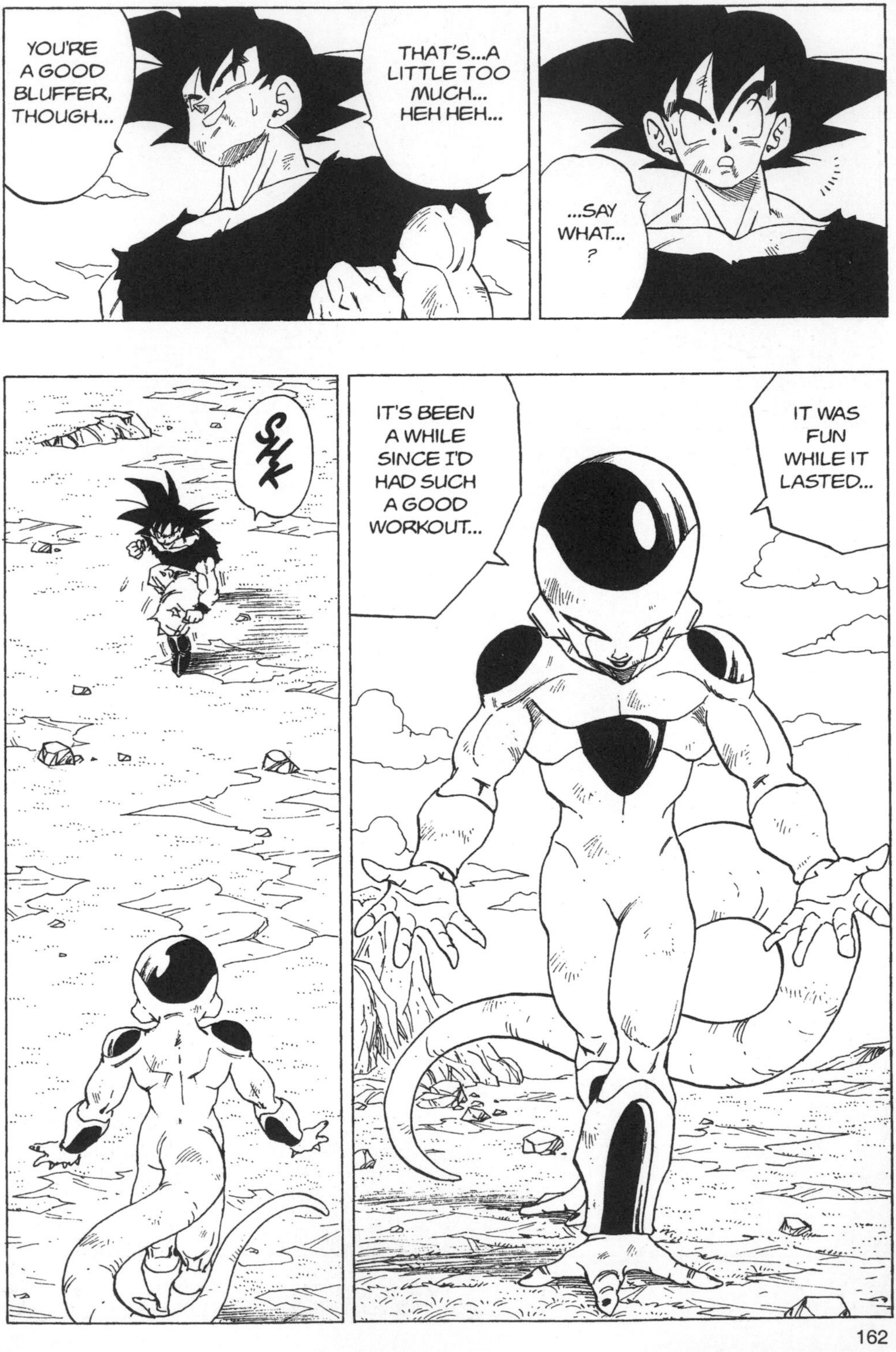
YOU'RE A GOOD BLUFFER, THOUGH...
THAT'S...A LITTLE TOO MUCH... HEH HEH...
...SAY WHAT... ?
SHK
IT WAS FUN WHILE IT LASTED...
IT'S BEEN A WHILE SINCE I'D HAD SUCH A GOOD WORKOUT...

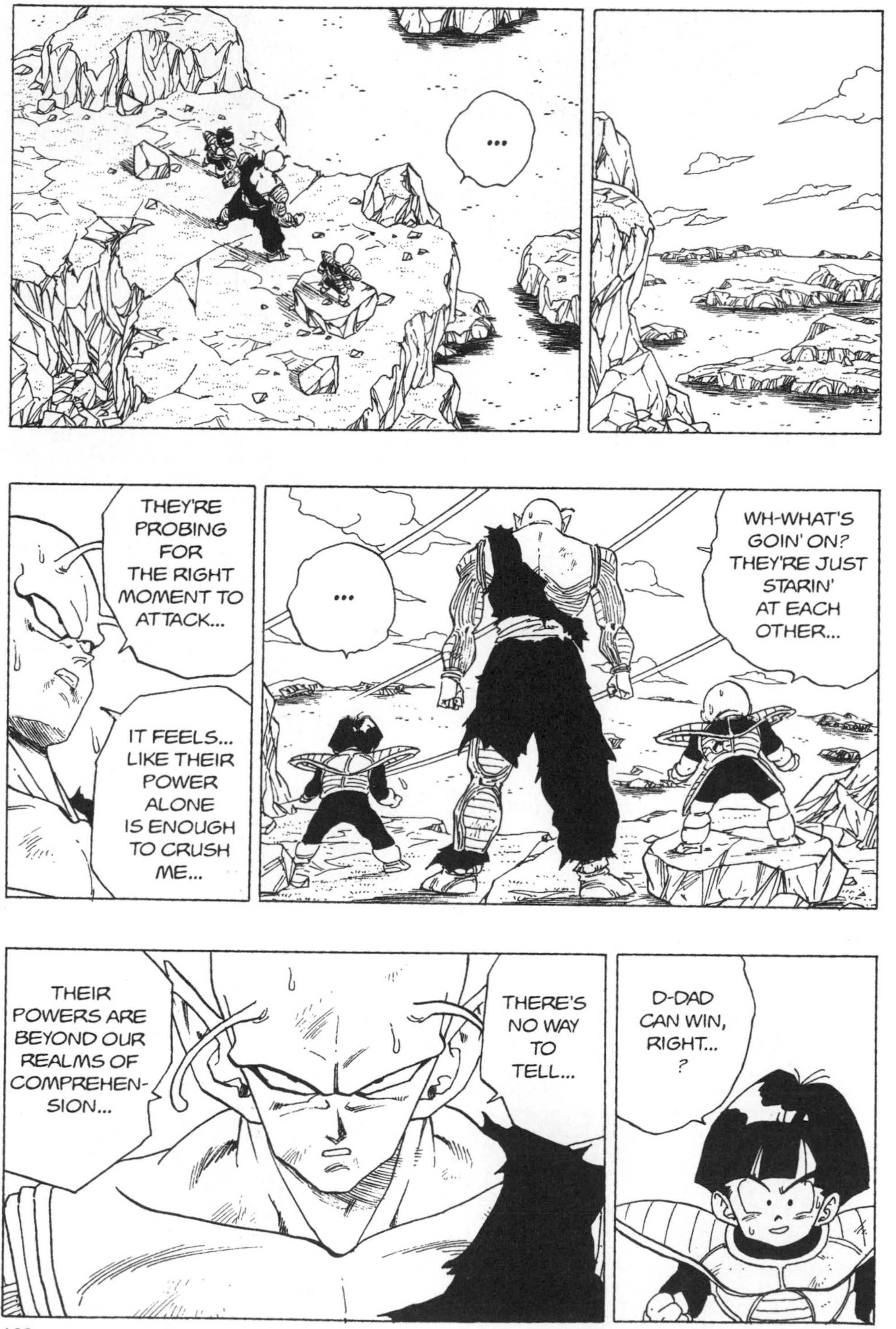
...
WH-WHAT'S GOIN' ON? THEY'RE JUST STARIN' AT EACH OTHER...
...
THEY'RE PROBING FOR THE RIGHT MOMENT TO ATTACK...
IT FEELS... LIKE THEIR POWER ALONE IS ENOUGH TO CRUSH ME...
D-DAD CAN WIN, RIGHT...?
THERE'S NO WAY TO TELL...
THEIR POWERS ARE BEYOND OUR REALMS OF COMPREHEN-SION...

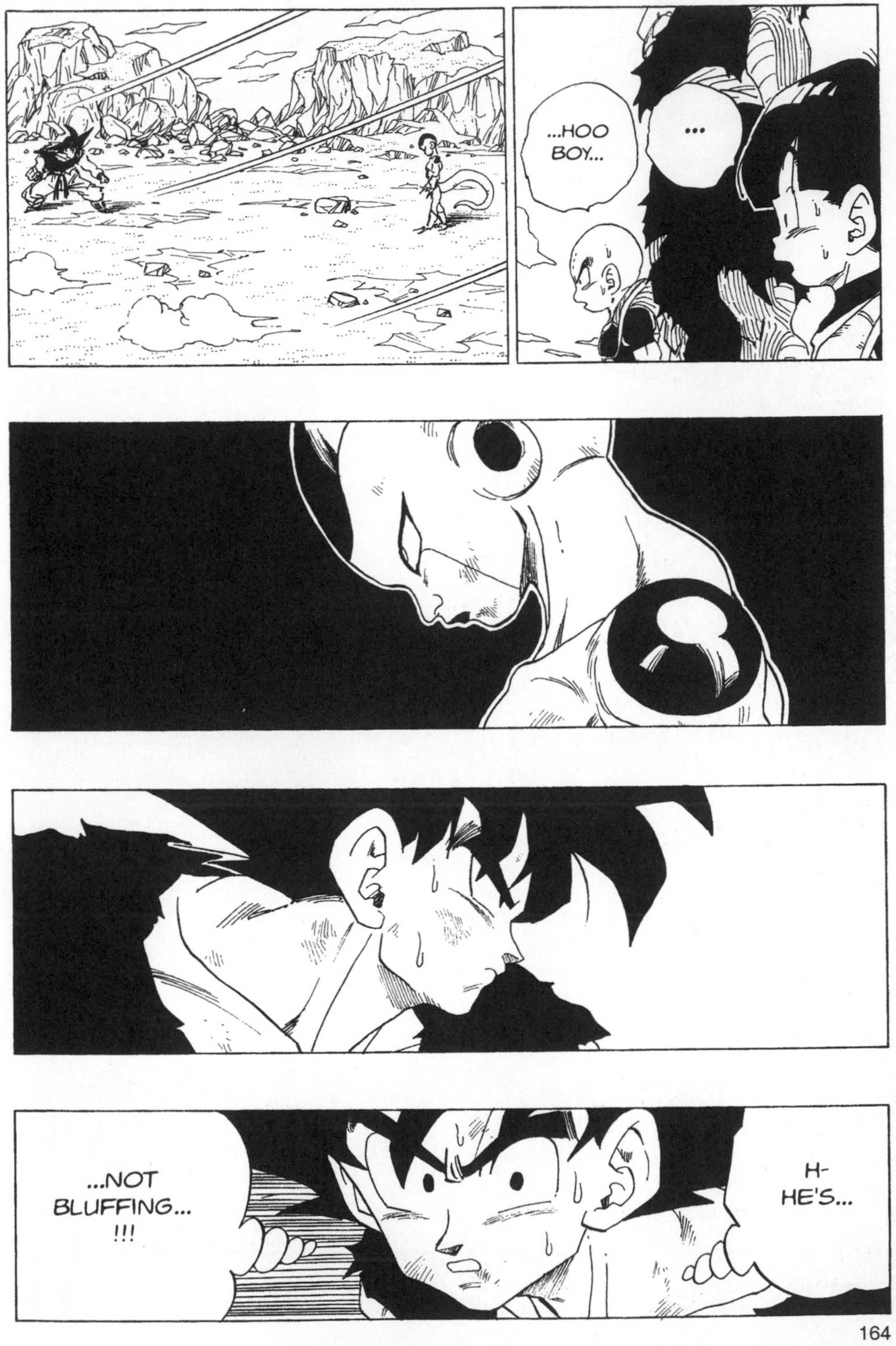
...
...HOO BOY...
H- HE'S...
...NOT BLUFFING... !!!

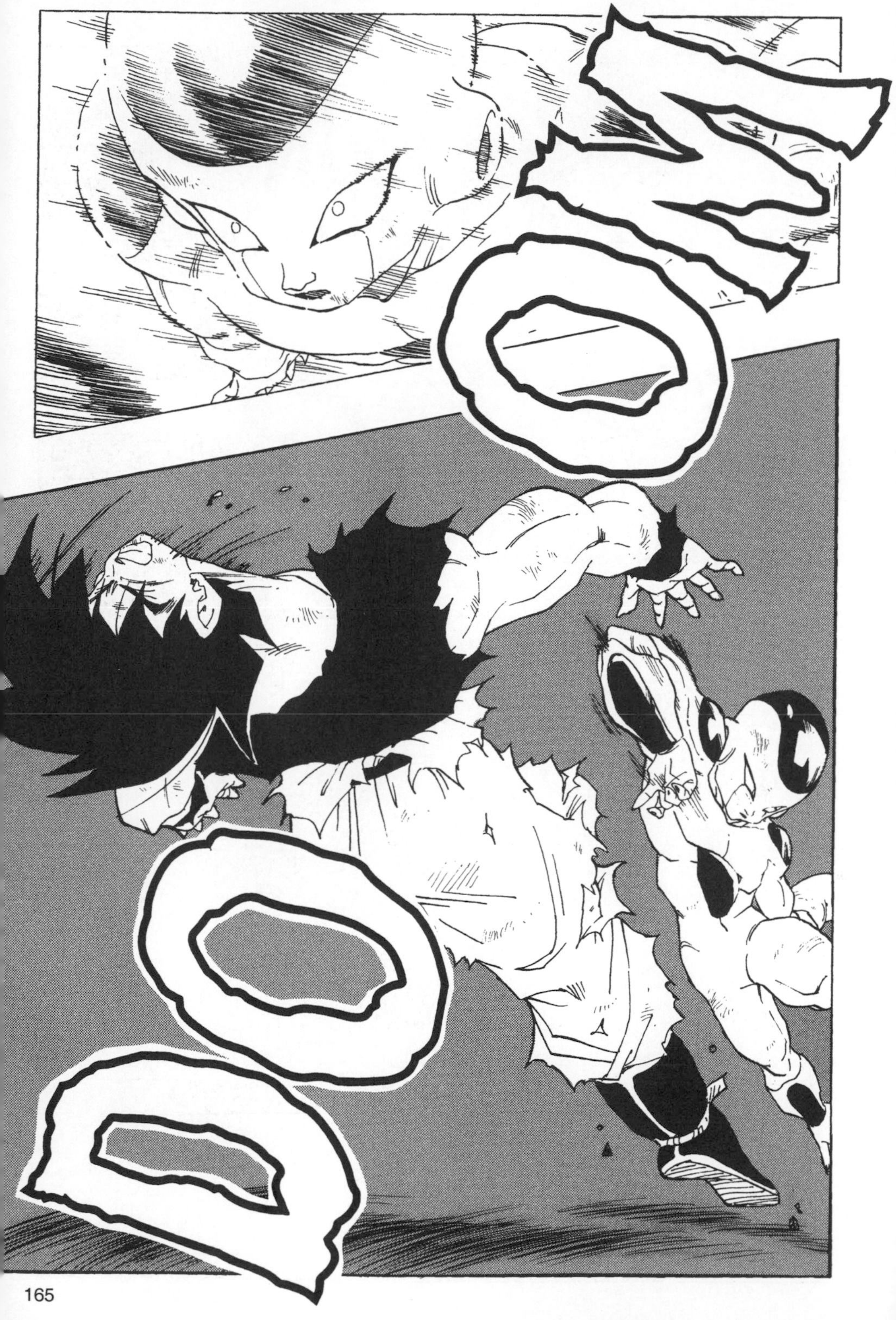
DOOM

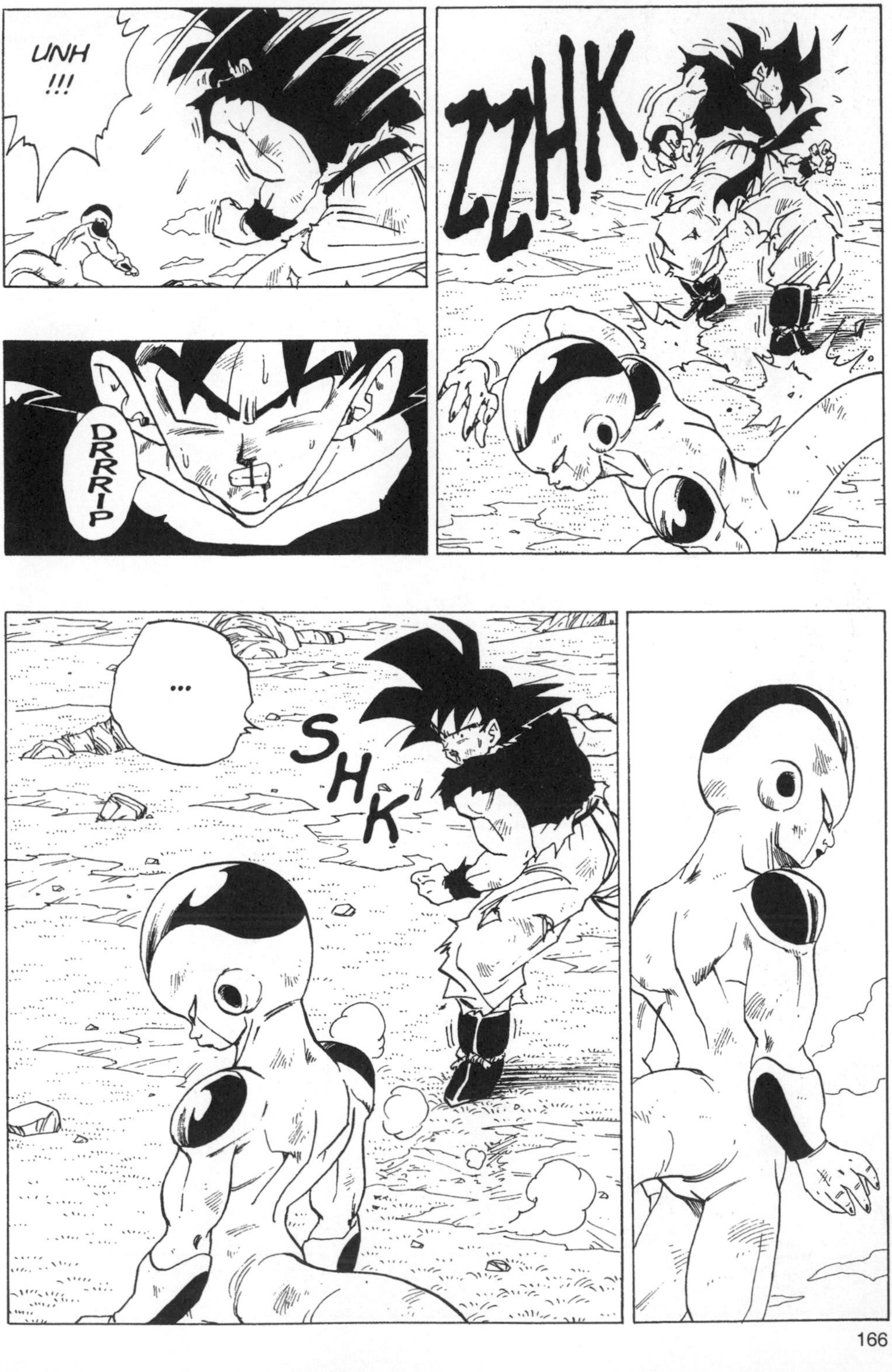
ZZHK
UNH !!!
DRRRIP
...
SHK

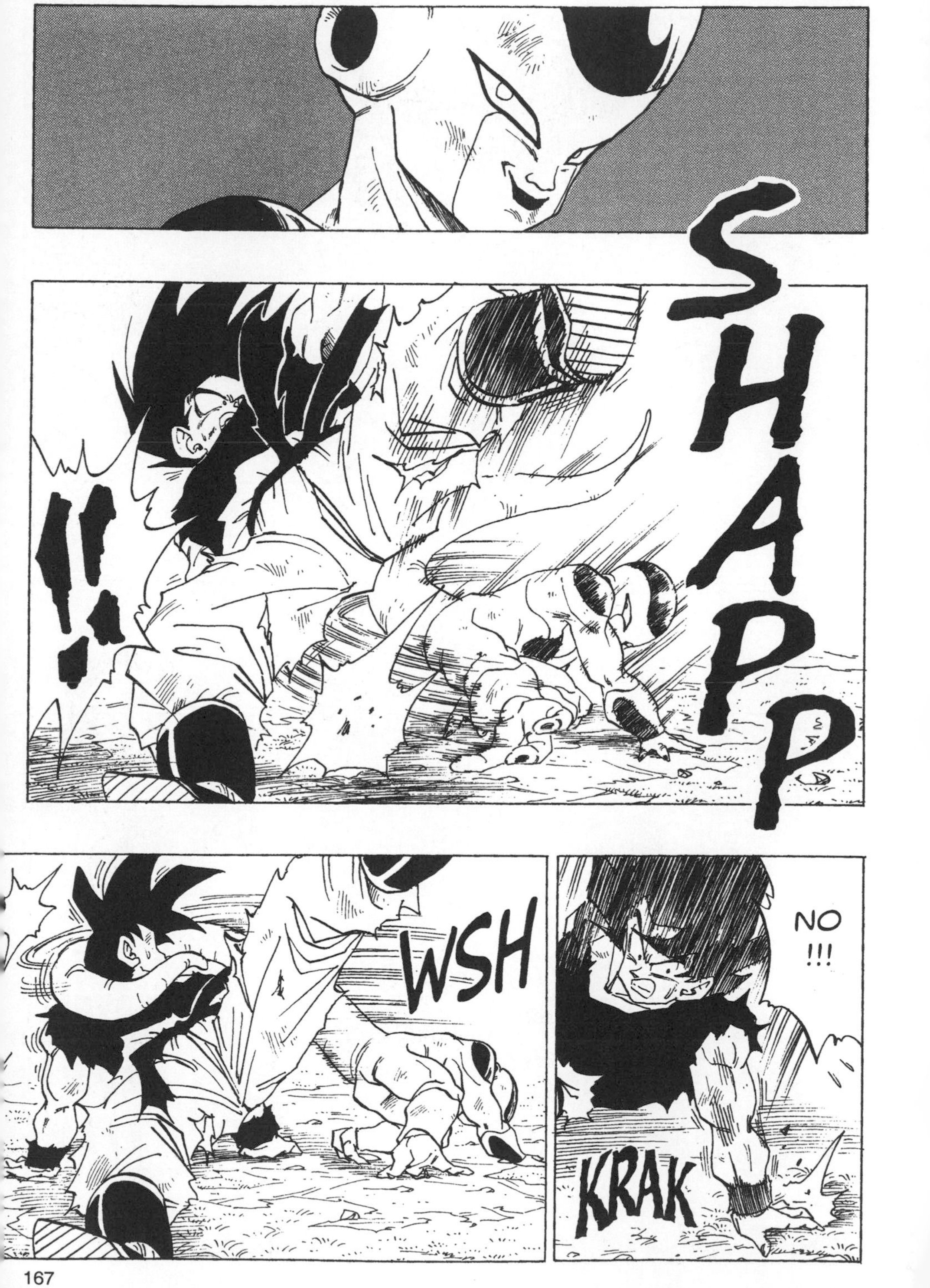
SHAPP
!!
WSH
NO !!!
KRAK

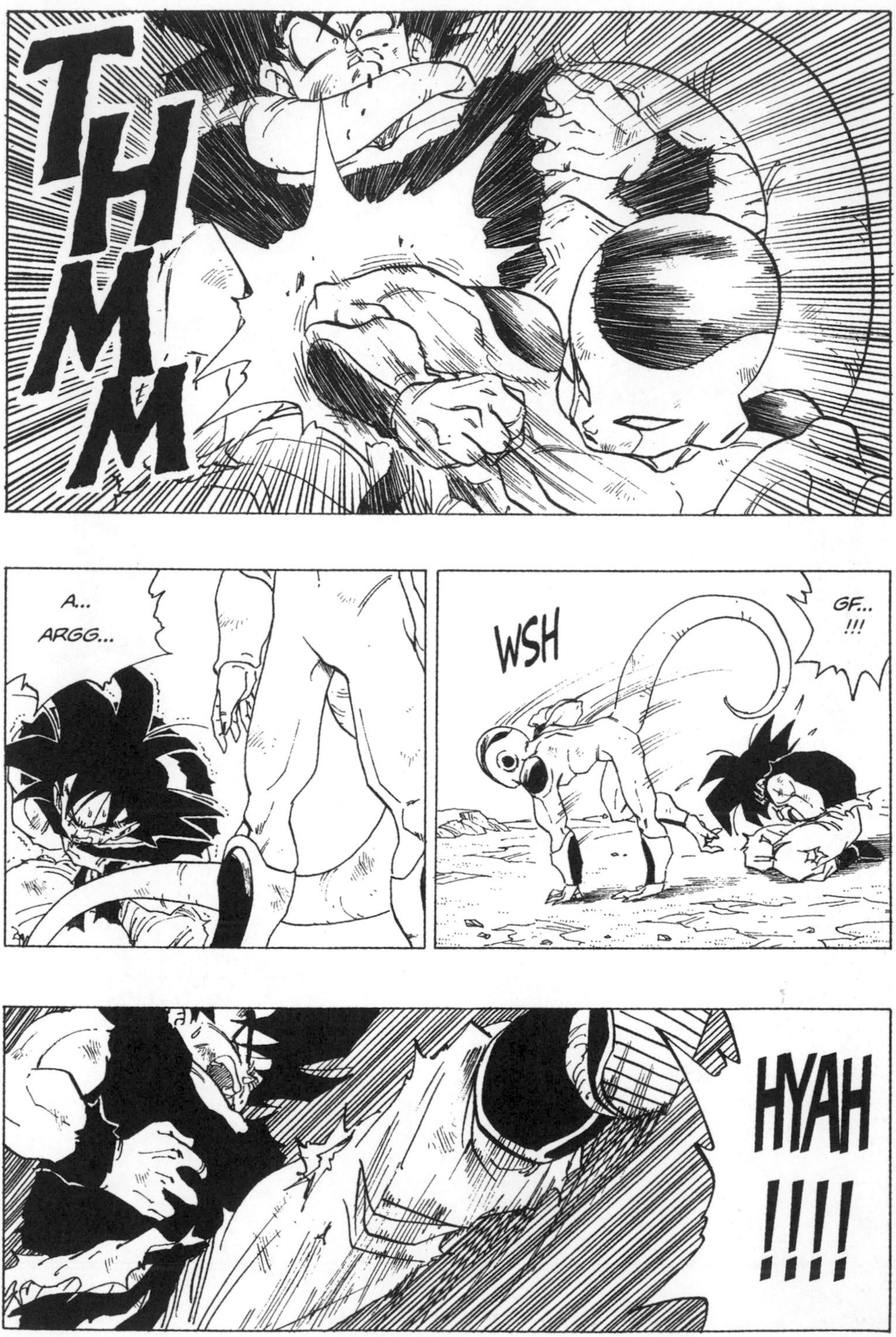
THMM
A...
ARGG...
WSH
GF...
!!!
HYAH
!!!!

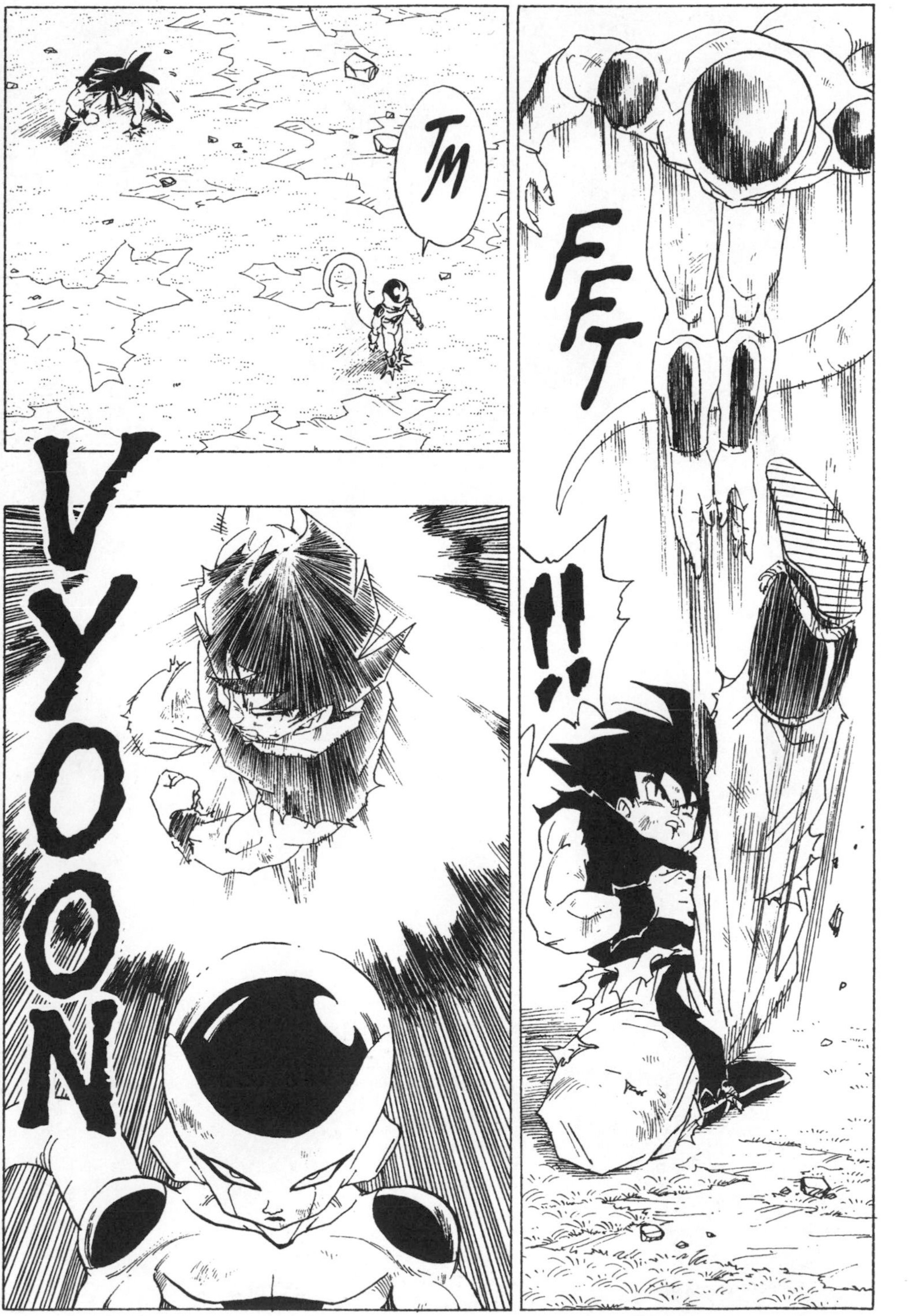
FFT
!!
TM
VYOON

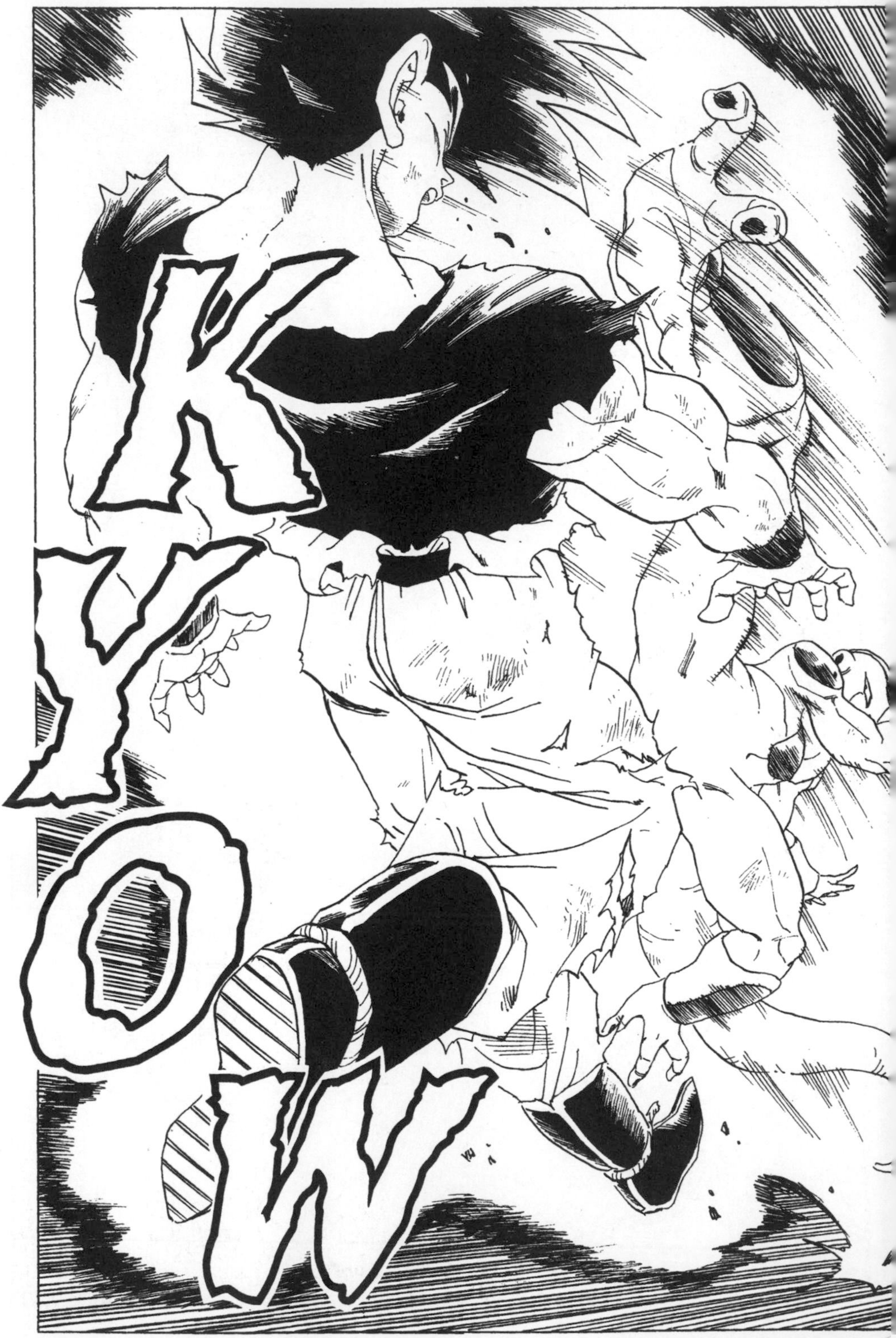
KYOW

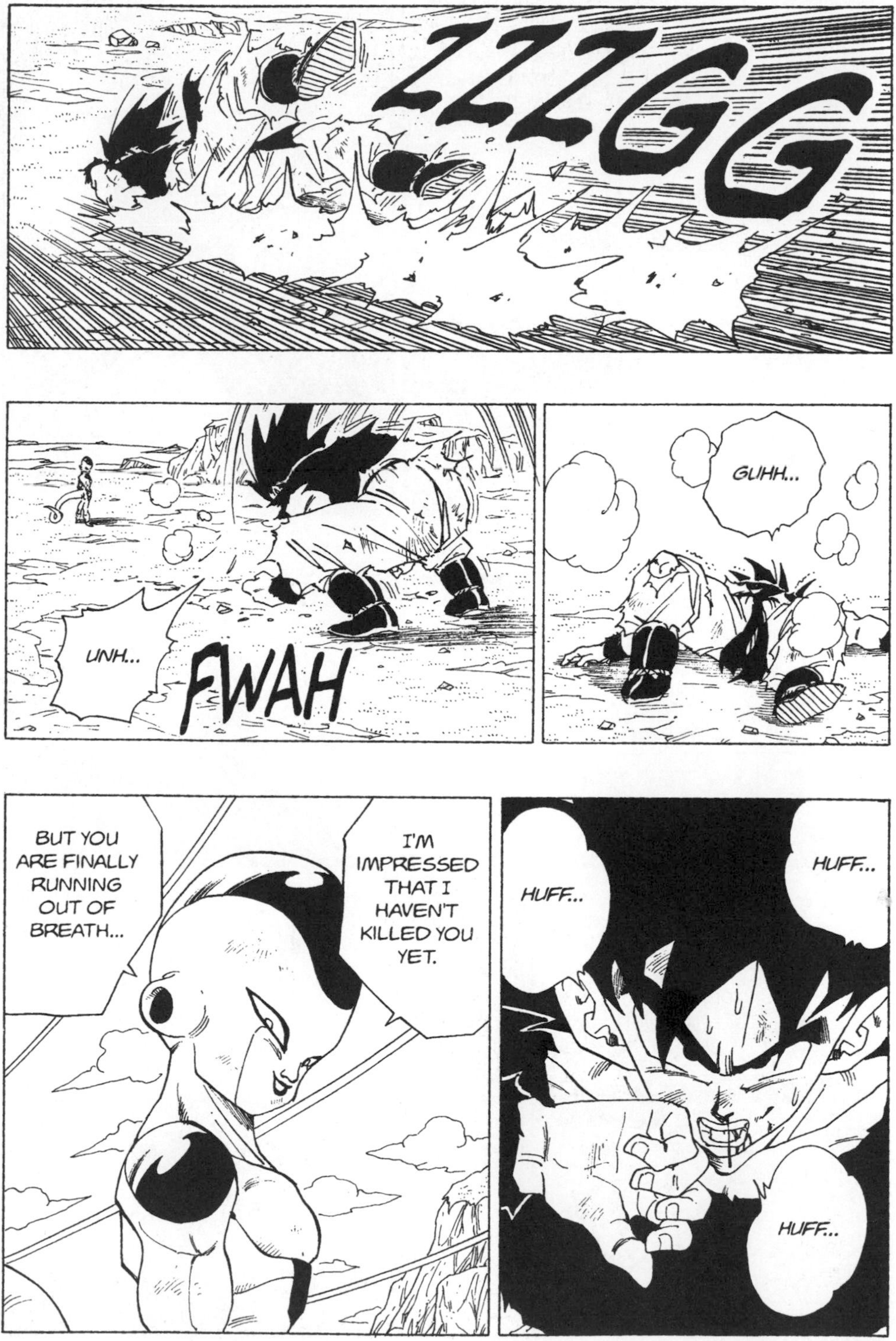

ZZZGG
UNH...
FWAH
GUHH...
I'M IMPRESSED THAT I HAVEN'T KILLED YOU YET.
BUT YOU ARE FINALLY RUNNING OUT OF BREATH...
HUFF...
HUFF...
HUFF...

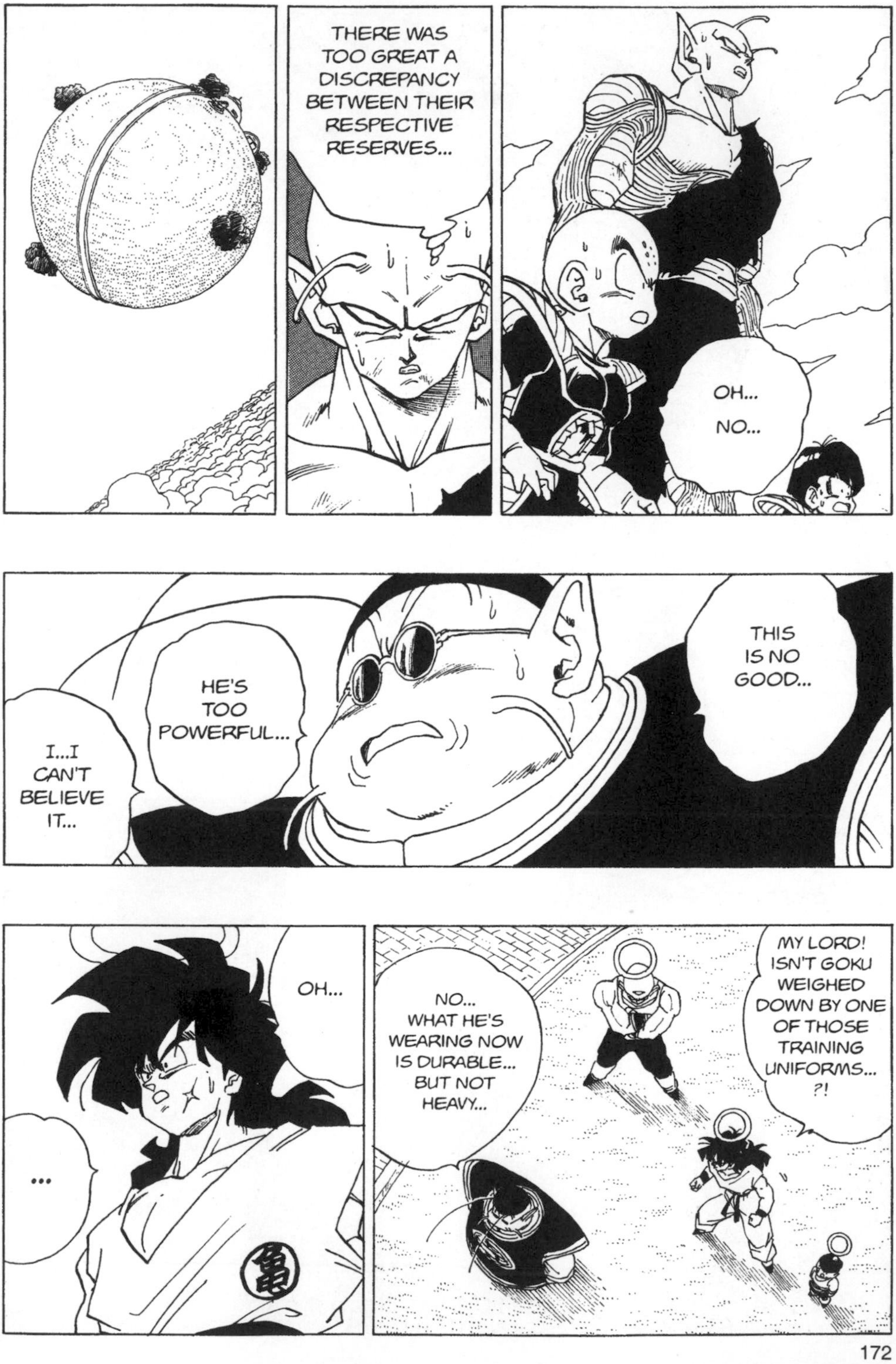
THERE WAS TOO GREAT A DISCREPANCY BETWEEN THEIR RESPECTIVE RESERVES...
OH... NO...
I...I CAN'T BELIEVE IT...
HE'S TOO POWERFUL...
THIS IS NO GOOD...
OH...
...
MY LORD! ISN'T GOKU WEIGHED DOWN BY ONE OF THOSE TRAINING UNIFORMS...?!
NO... WHAT HE'S WEARING NOW IS DURABLE... BUT NOT HEAVY...

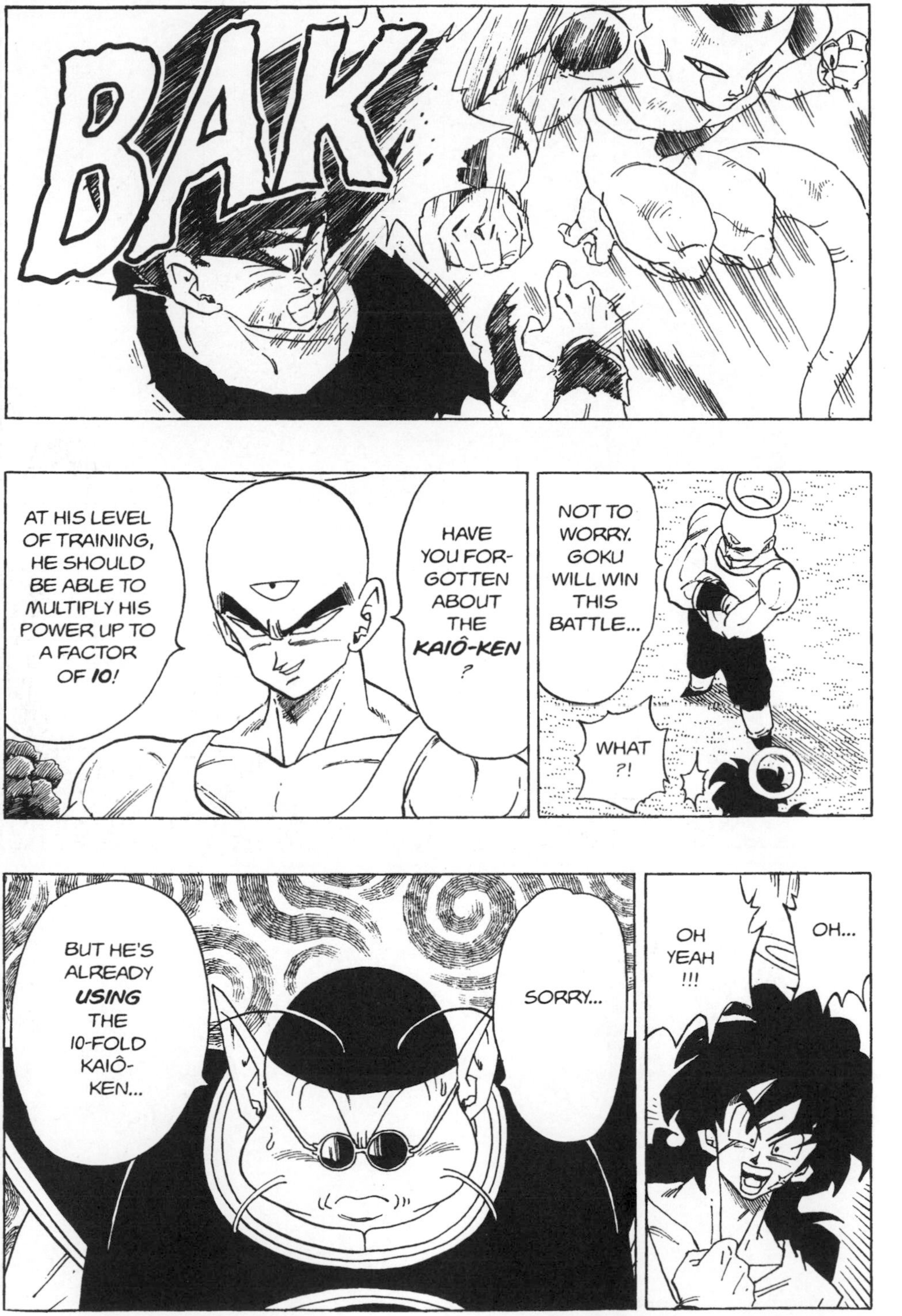
BAK
NOT TO WORRY. GOKU WILL WIN THIS BATTLE...
WHAT ?!
HAVE YOU FOR-GOTTEN ABOUT THE KAIÔ-KEN ?
AT HIS LEVEL OF TRAINING, HE SHOULD BE ABLE TO MULTIPLY HIS POWER UP TO A FACTOR OF 10!
OH...
OH YEAH !!!
SORRY...
BUT HE'S ALREADY USING THE 10-FOLD KAIÔ-KEN...

DBZ:119 • Kaiô-ken times 20!!!

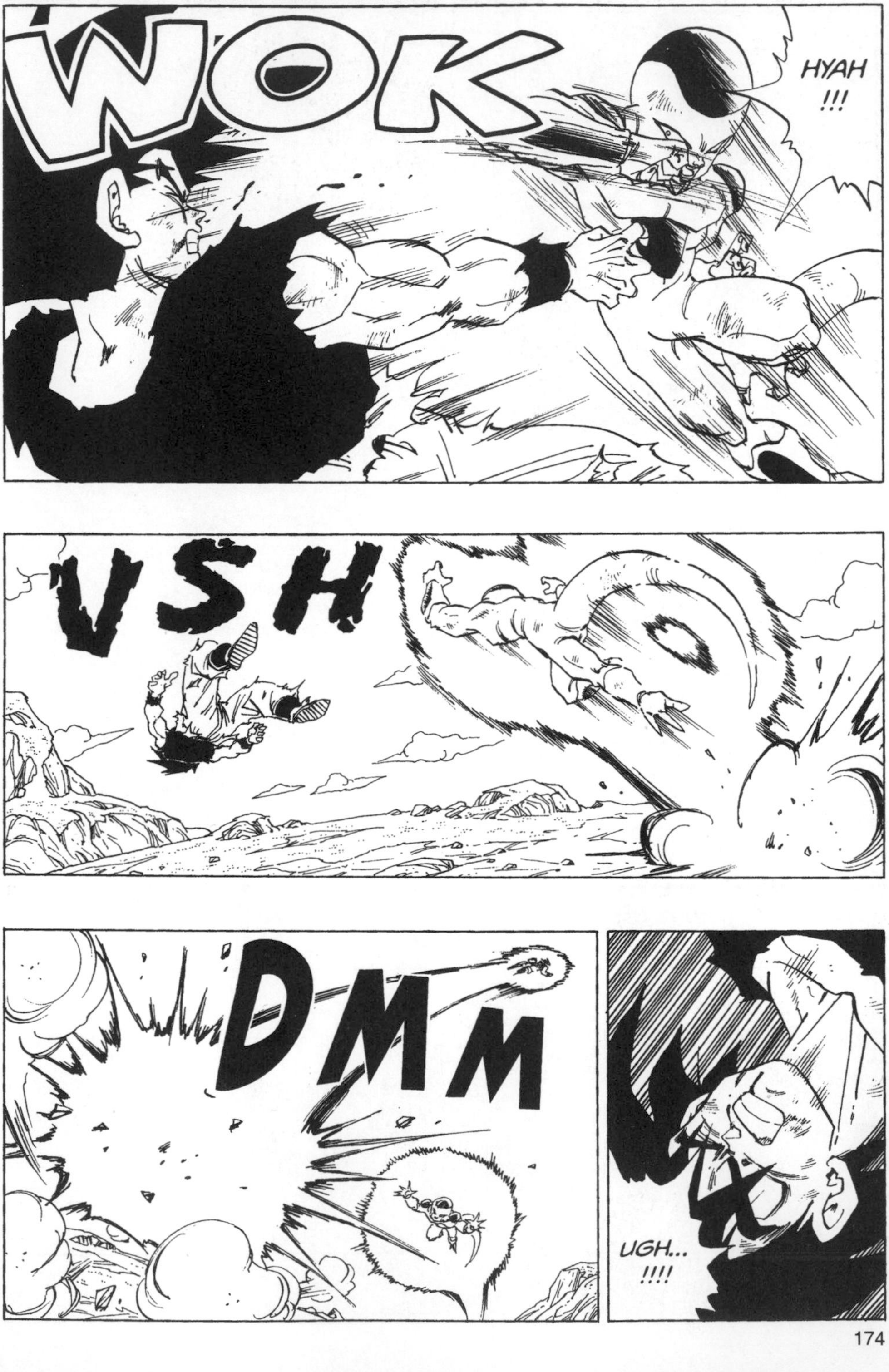
WOK
HYAH !!!
VSH
UGH... !!!!
DMM

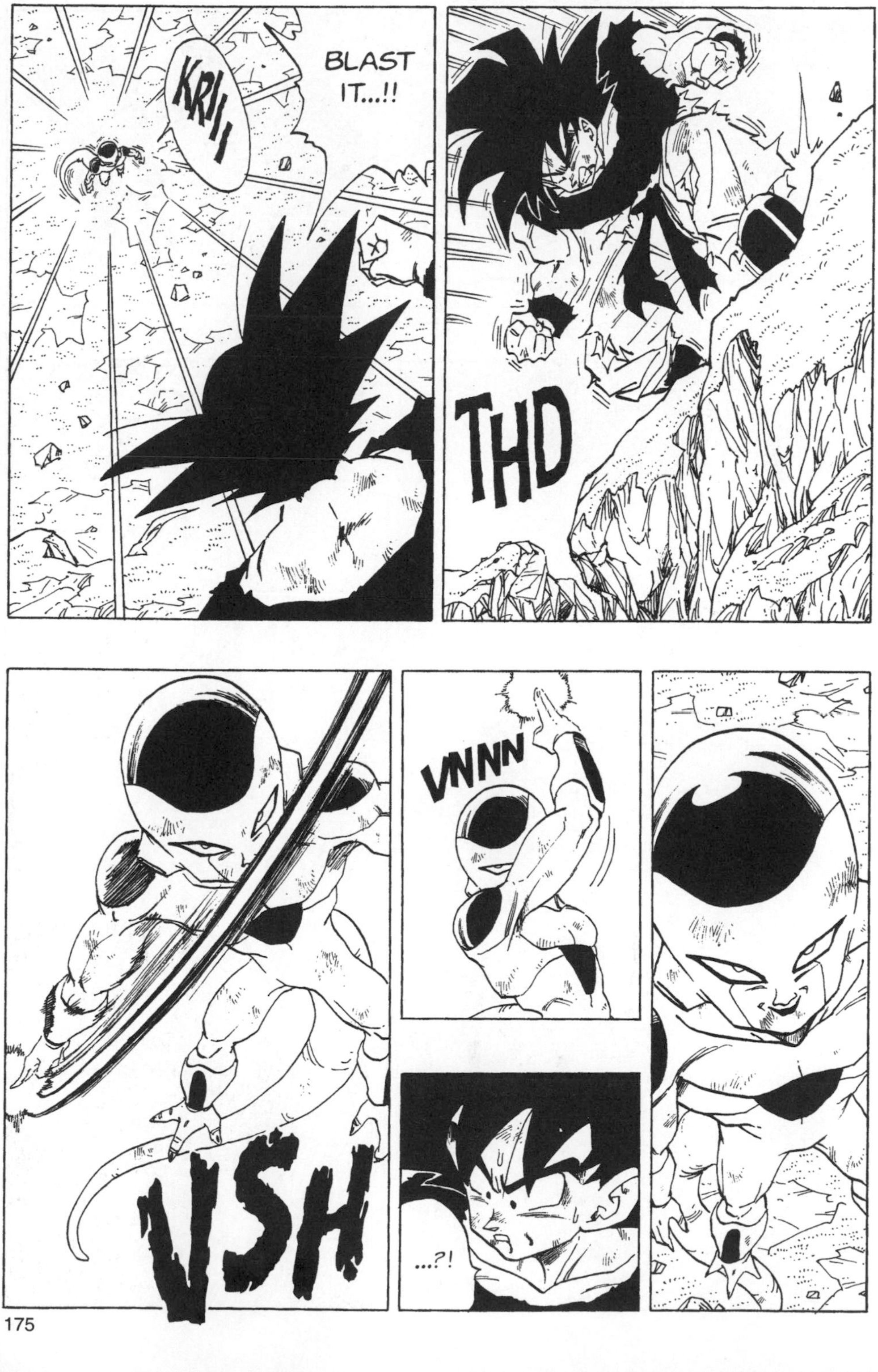
KRIII
BLAST IT...!!
THD
VSH
VNNN
...?!

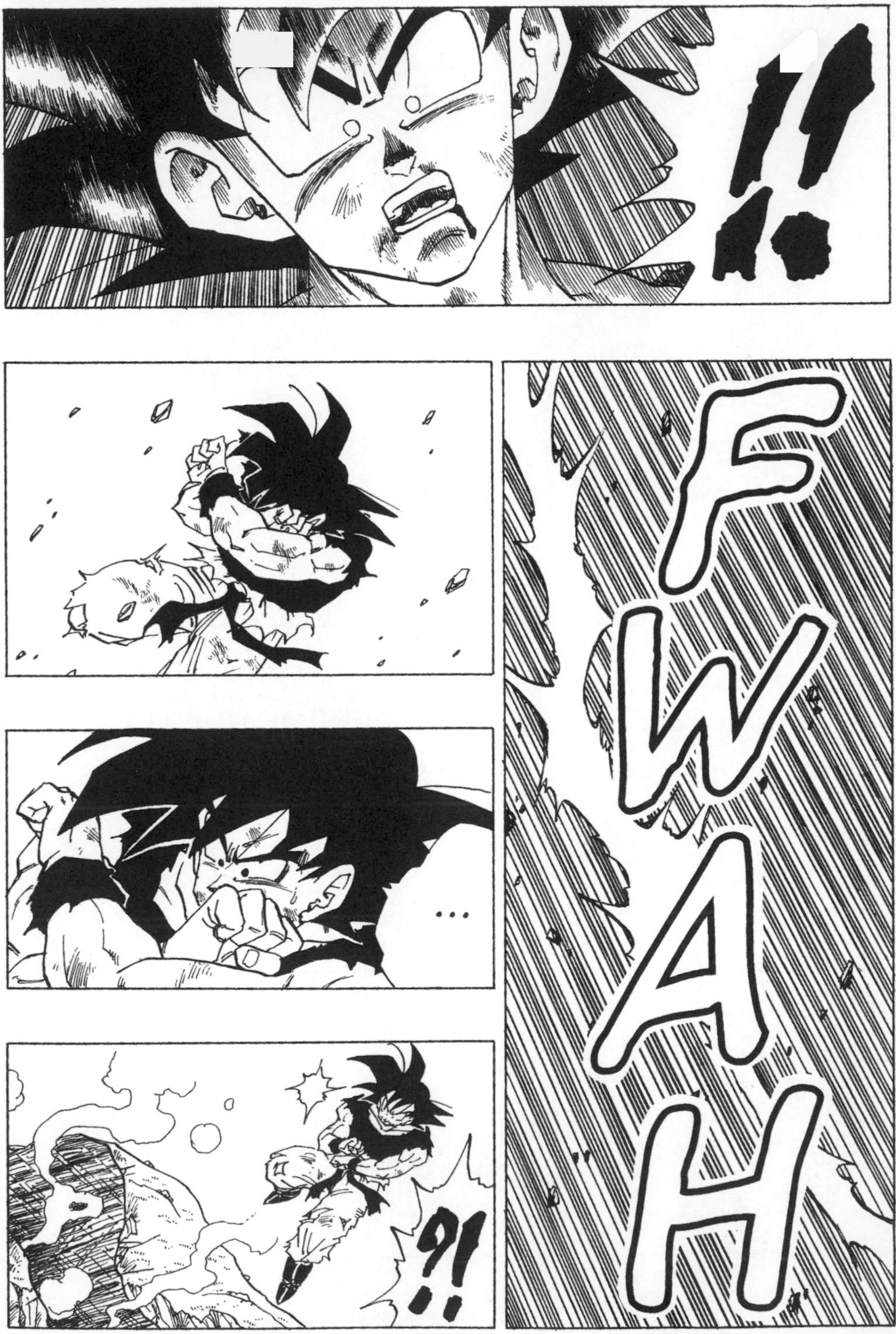
!!
FWAH
...
?!!

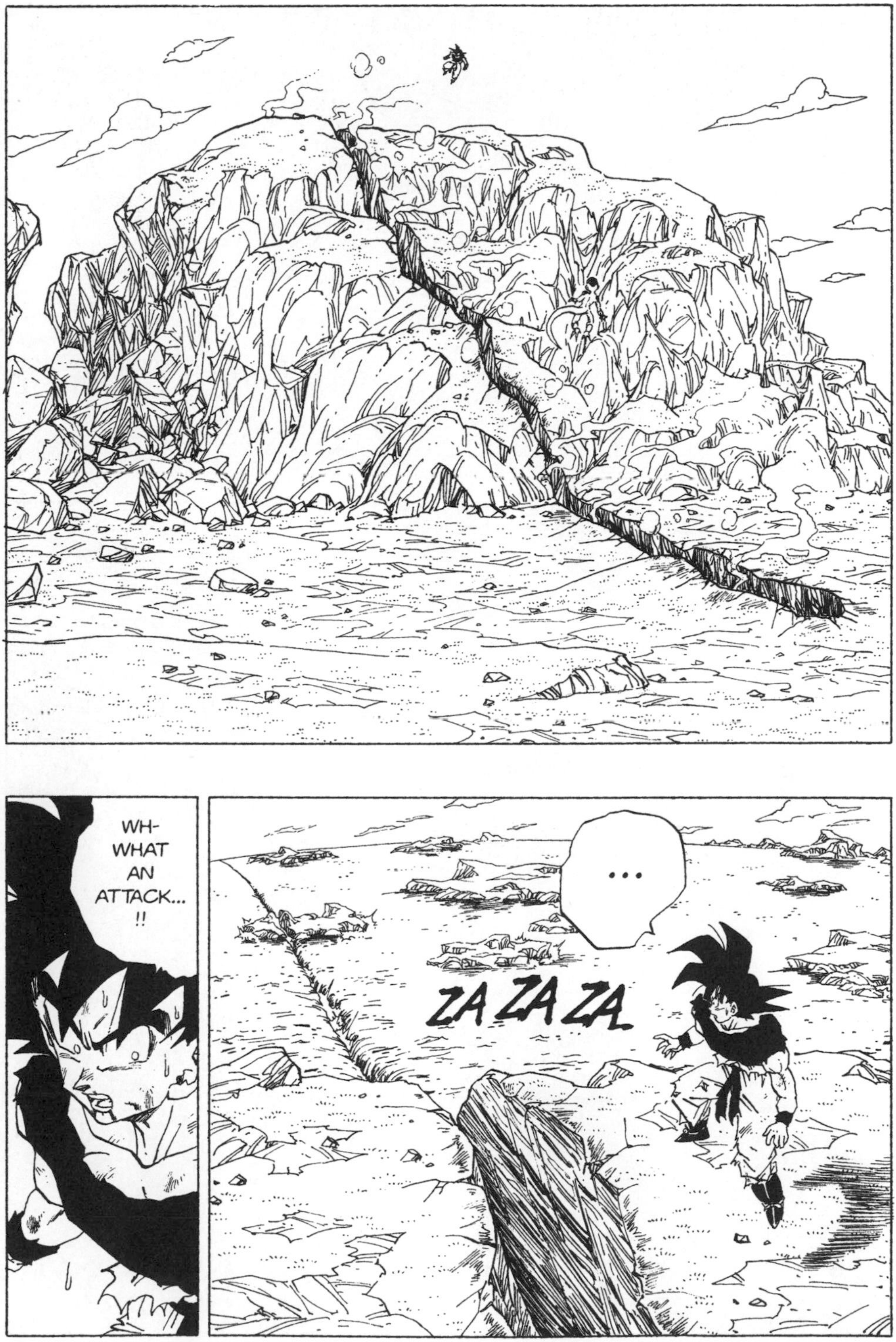
...
ZA ZA ZA
WH-WHAT AN ATTACK...!!

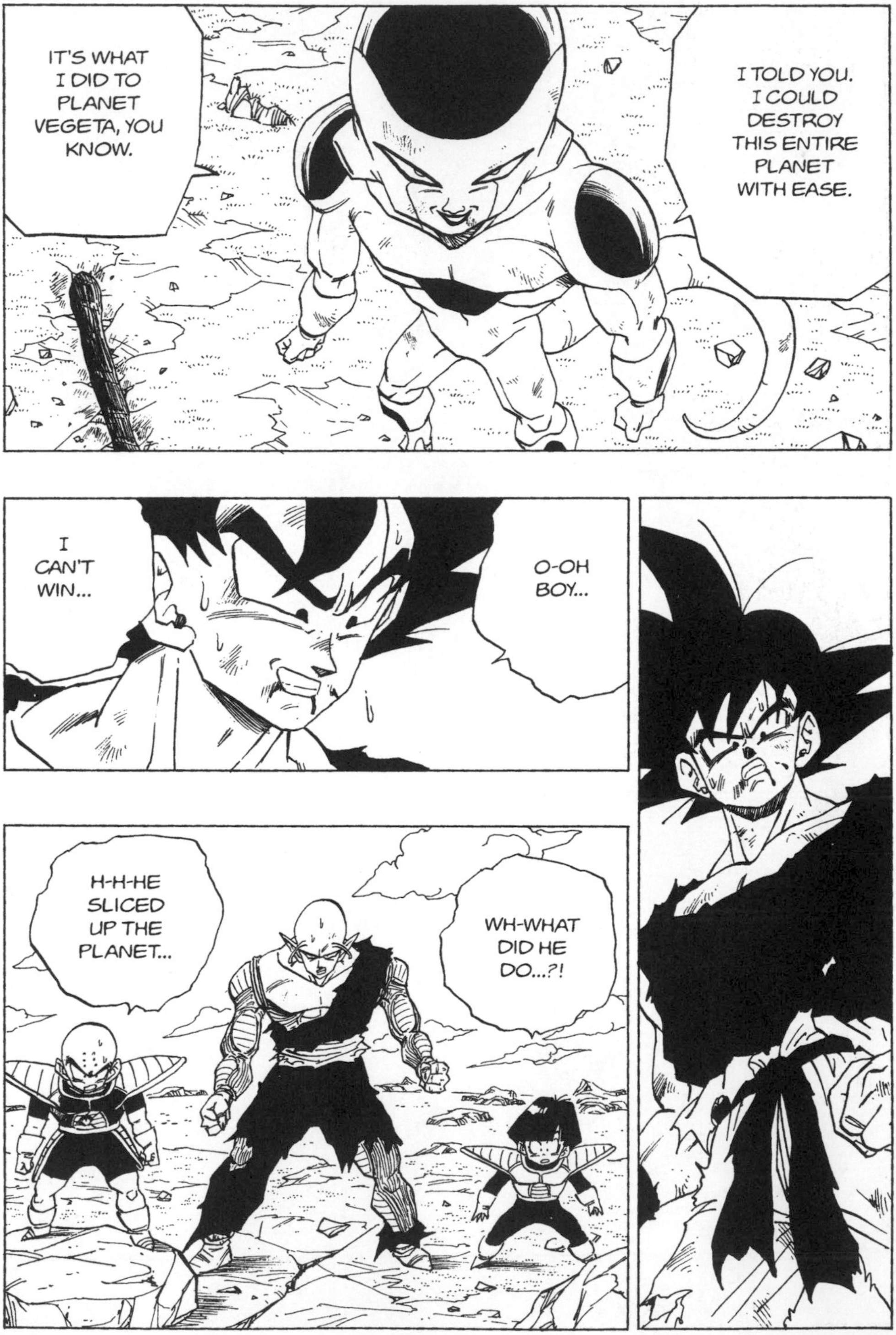
I TOLD YOU. I COULD DESTROY THIS ENTIRE PLANET WITH EASE.
IT'S WHAT I DID TO PLANET VEGETA, YOU KNOW.
O-OH BOY...
I CAN'T WIN...
WH-WHAT DID HE DO...?!
H-H-HE SLICED UP THE PLANET...

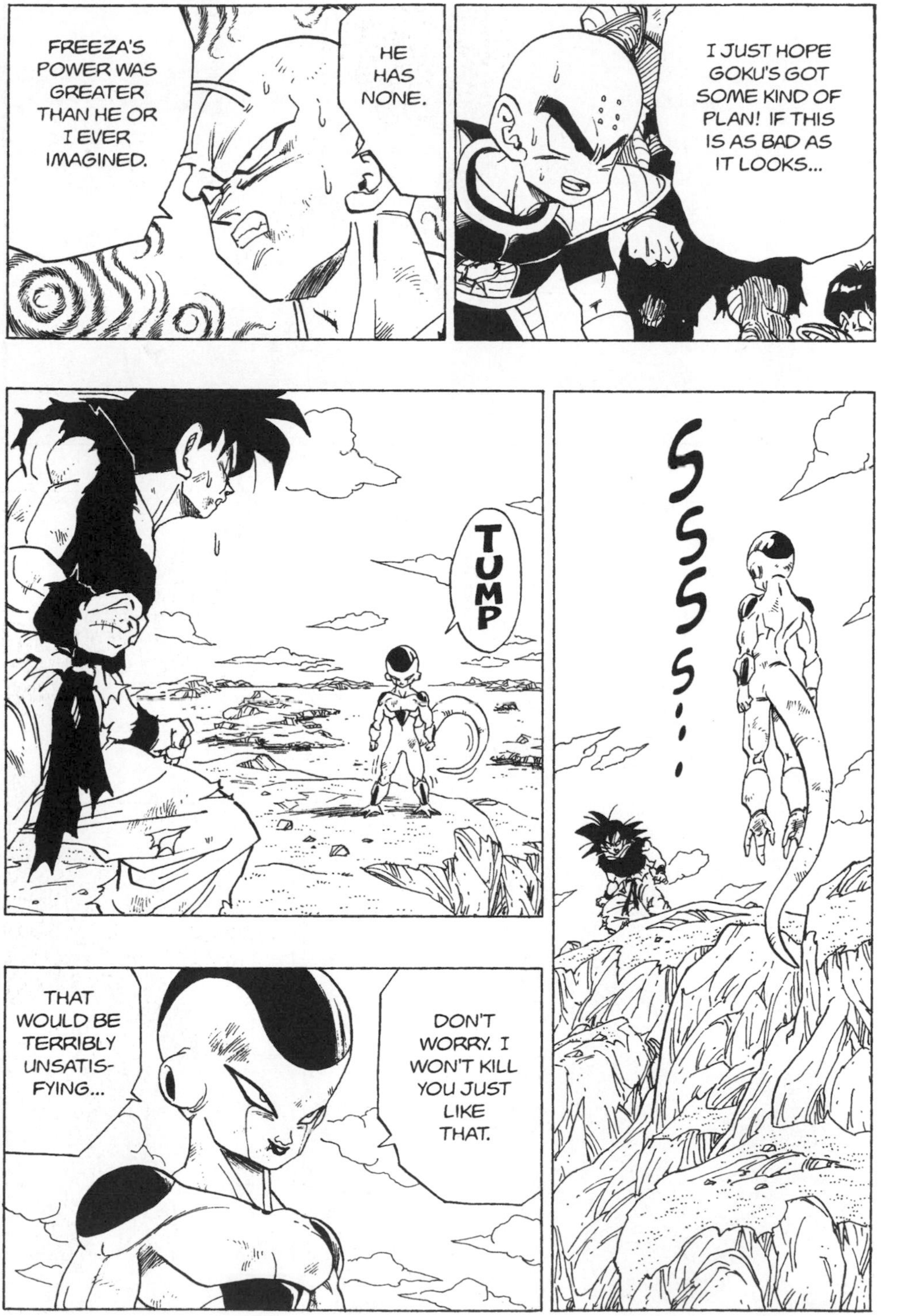
FREEZA'S POWER WAS GREATER THAN HE OR I EVER IMAGINED.
HE HAS NONE.
I JUST HOPE GOKU'S GOT SOME KIND OF PLAN! IF THIS IS AS BAD AS IT LOOKS...
TUMP
SSSS...
THAT WOULD BE TERRIBLY UNSATIS-FYING...
DON'T WORRY. I WON'T KILL YOU JUST LIKE THAT.

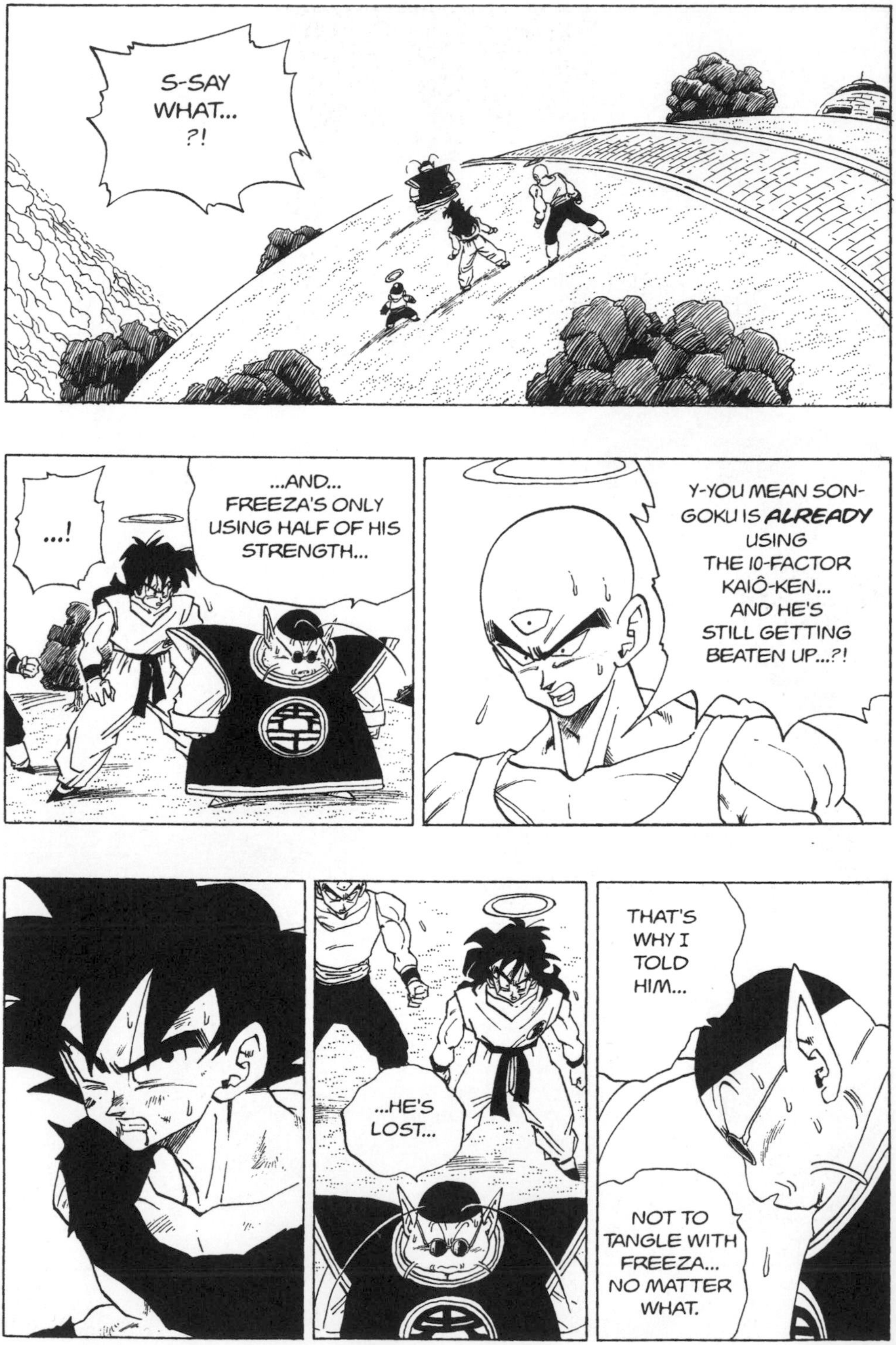
S-SAY WHAT... ?!
...!
...AND... FREEZA'S ONLY USING HALF OF HIS STRENGTH...
Y-YOU MEAN SON-GOKU IS **ALREADY** USING THE 10-FACTOR KAIÔ-KEN... AND HE'S STILL GETTING BEATEN UP...?!
...HE'S LOST...
THAT'S WHY I TOLD HIM...
NOT TO TANGLE WITH FREEZA... NO MATTER WHAT.

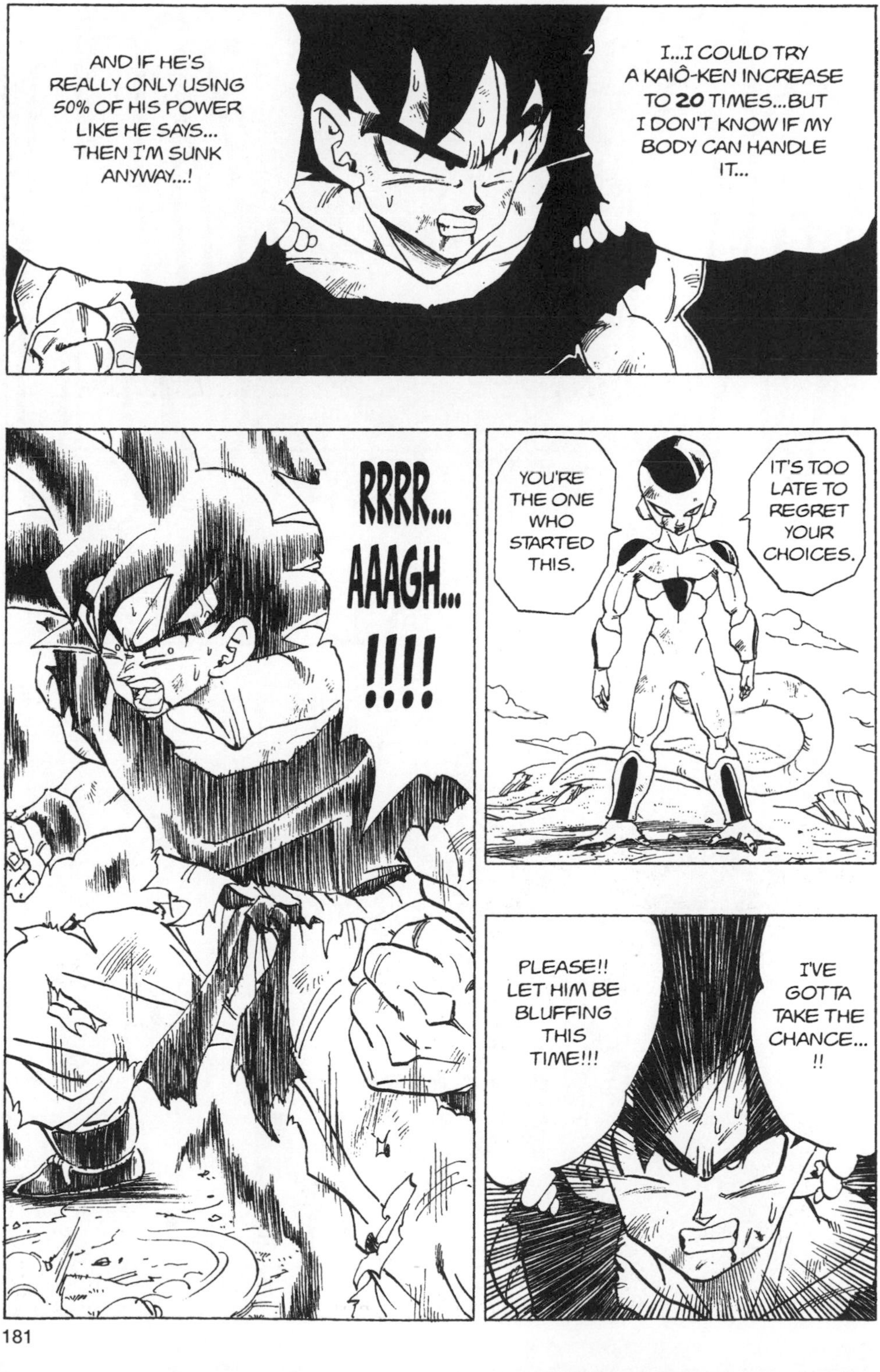
I...I COULD TRY A KAIÔ-KEN INCREASE TO 20 TIMES...BUT I DON'T KNOW IF MY BODY CAN HANDLE IT...
AND IF HE'S REALLY ONLY USING 50% OF HIS POWER LIKE HE SAYS... THEN I'M SUNK ANYWAY...!
IT'S TOO LATE TO REGRET YOUR CHOICES.
YOU'RE THE ONE WHO STARTED THIS.
I'VE GOTTA TAKE THE CHANCE... !!
PLEASE!! LET HIM BE BLUFFING THIS TIME!!!
RRRR... AAAGH... !!!!

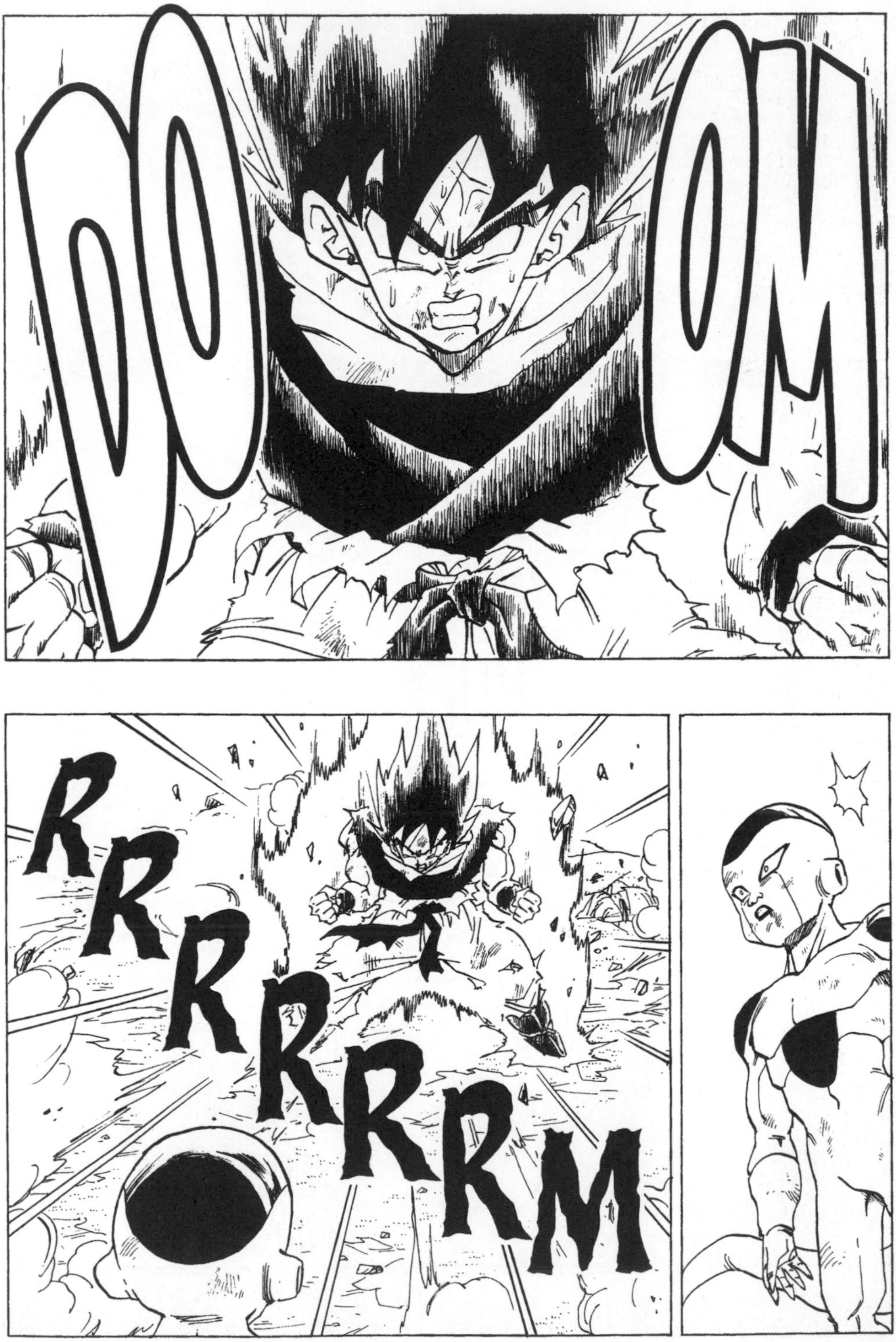
DOOM
RRRRRRM

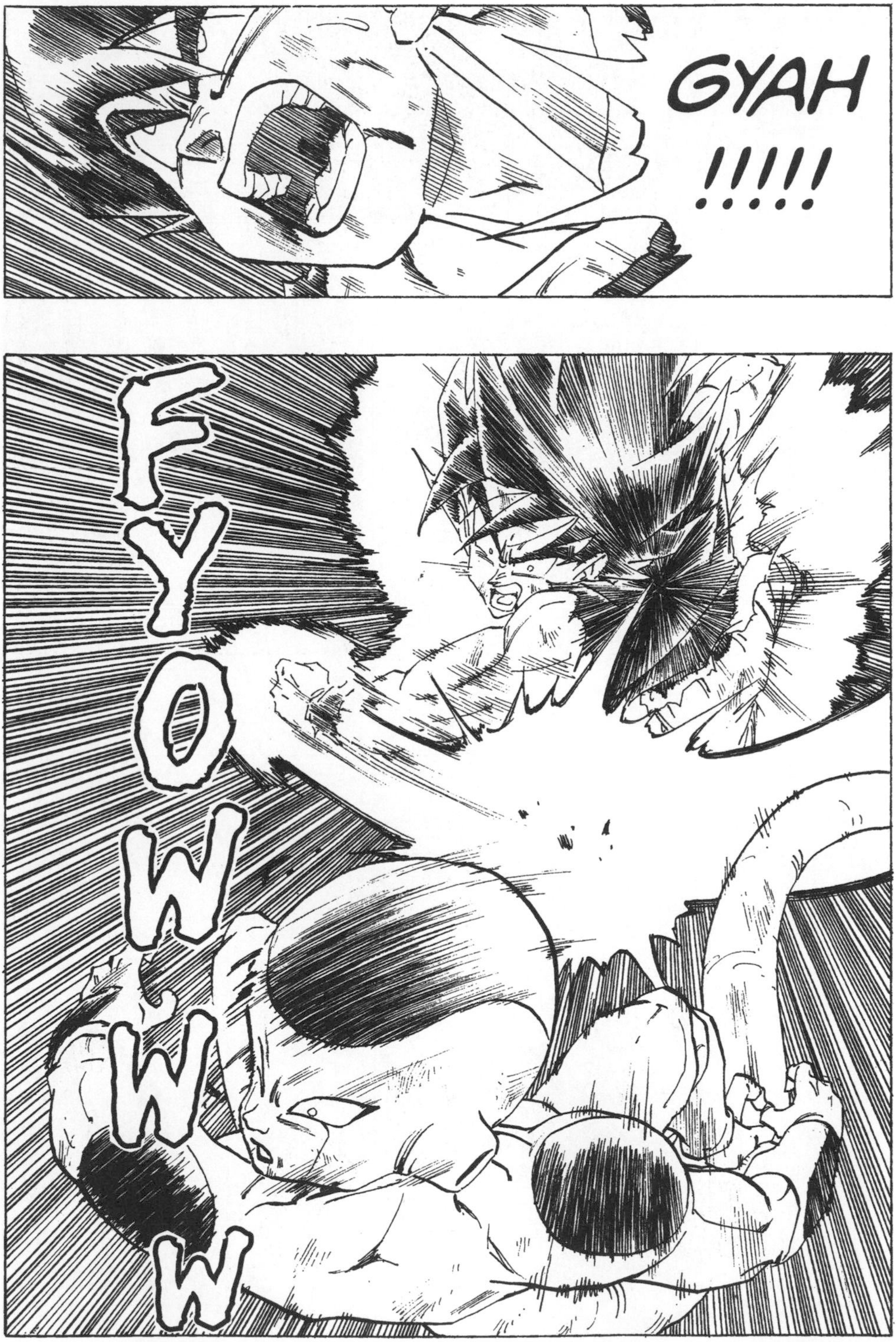
GYAH
!!!!!
FYOWWW

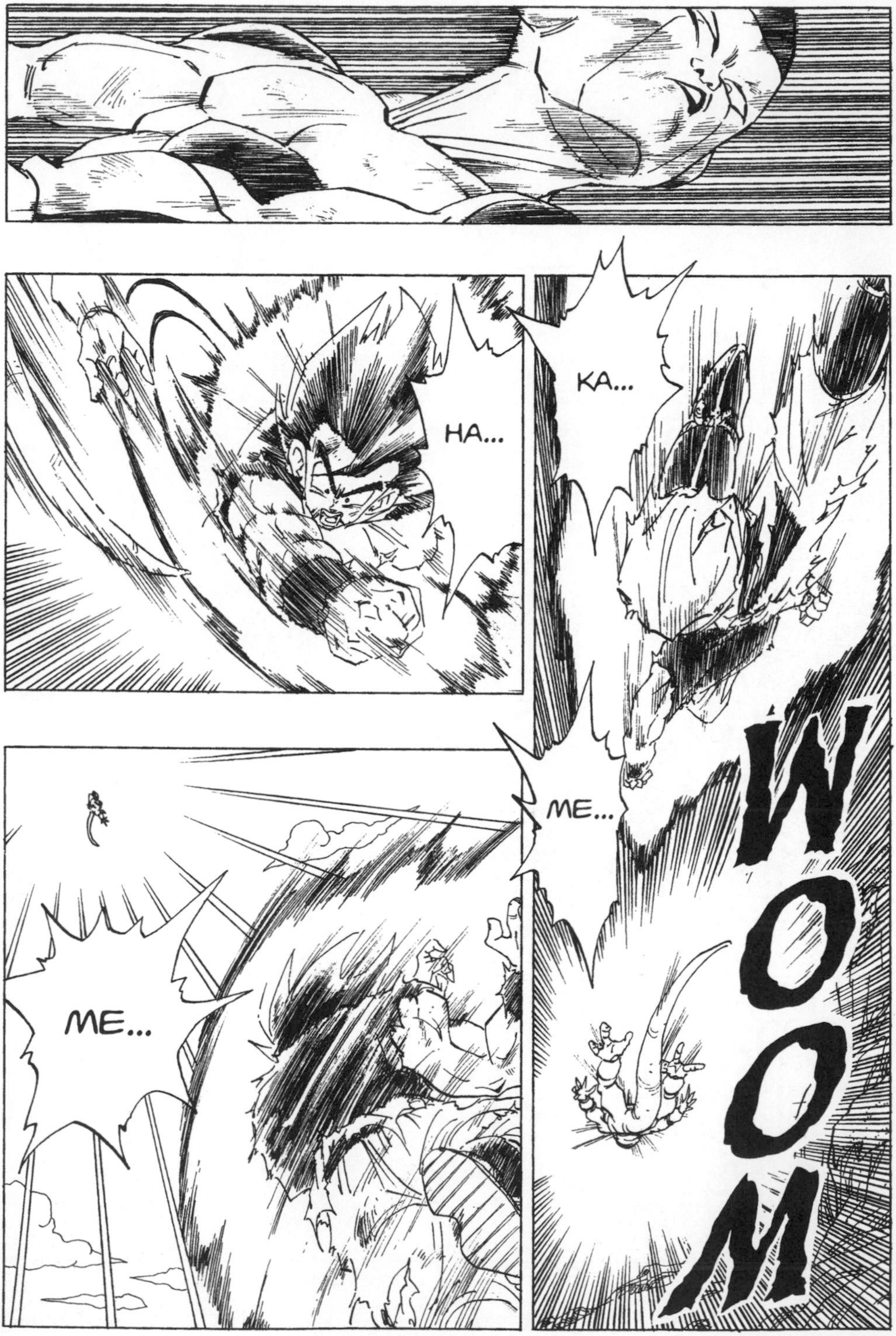
HA...
KA...
ME...
ME...
WOOM

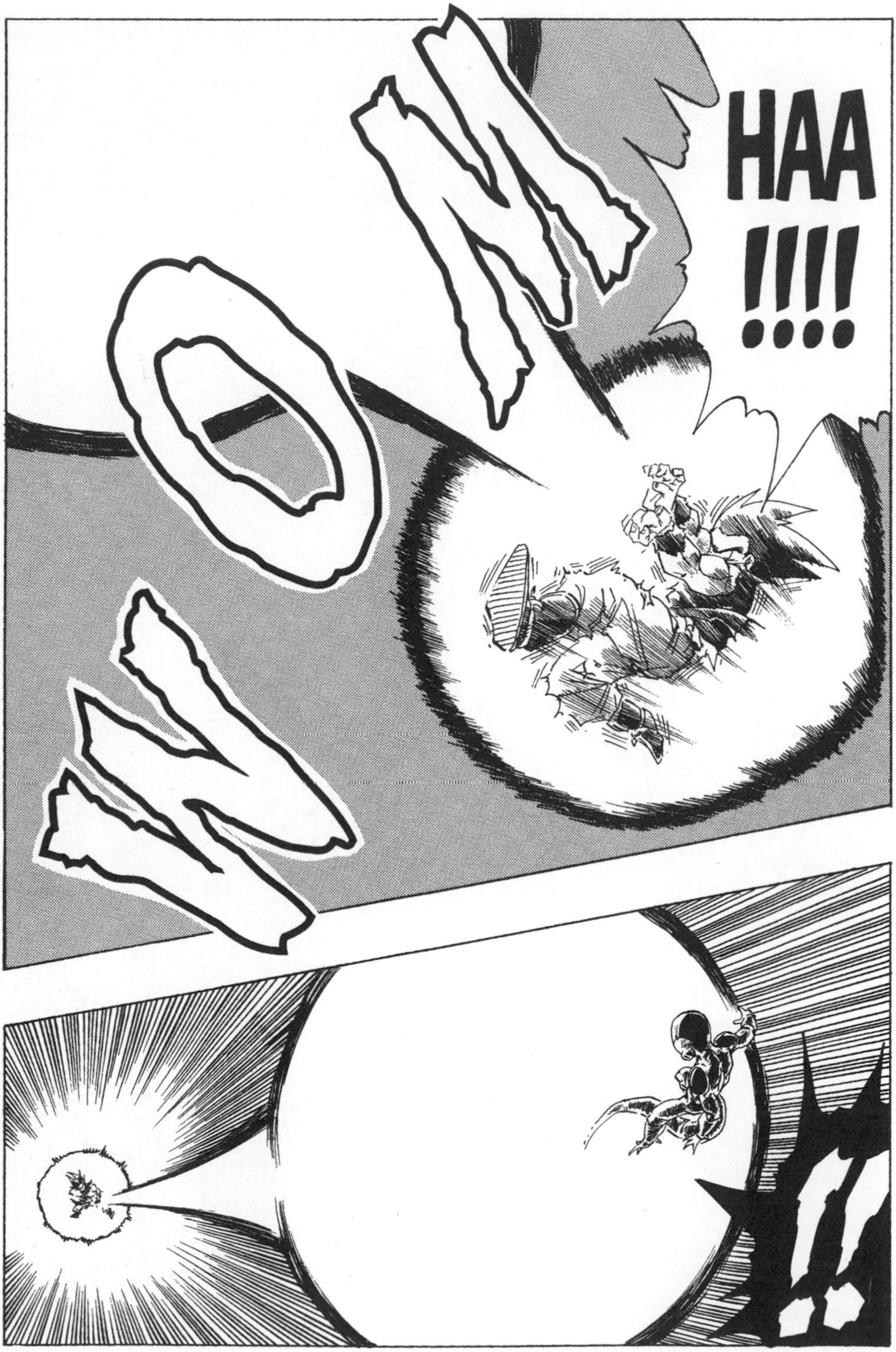
HAA !!!!
!!

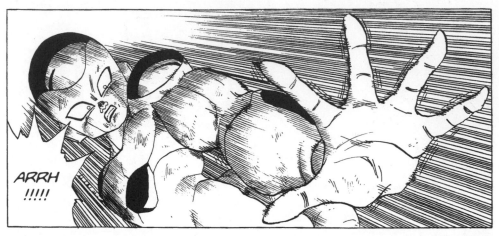

ARRH
!!!!!

VOOH

RRR-
AUGH
!!!!!

NNN...
NNH...
!!!

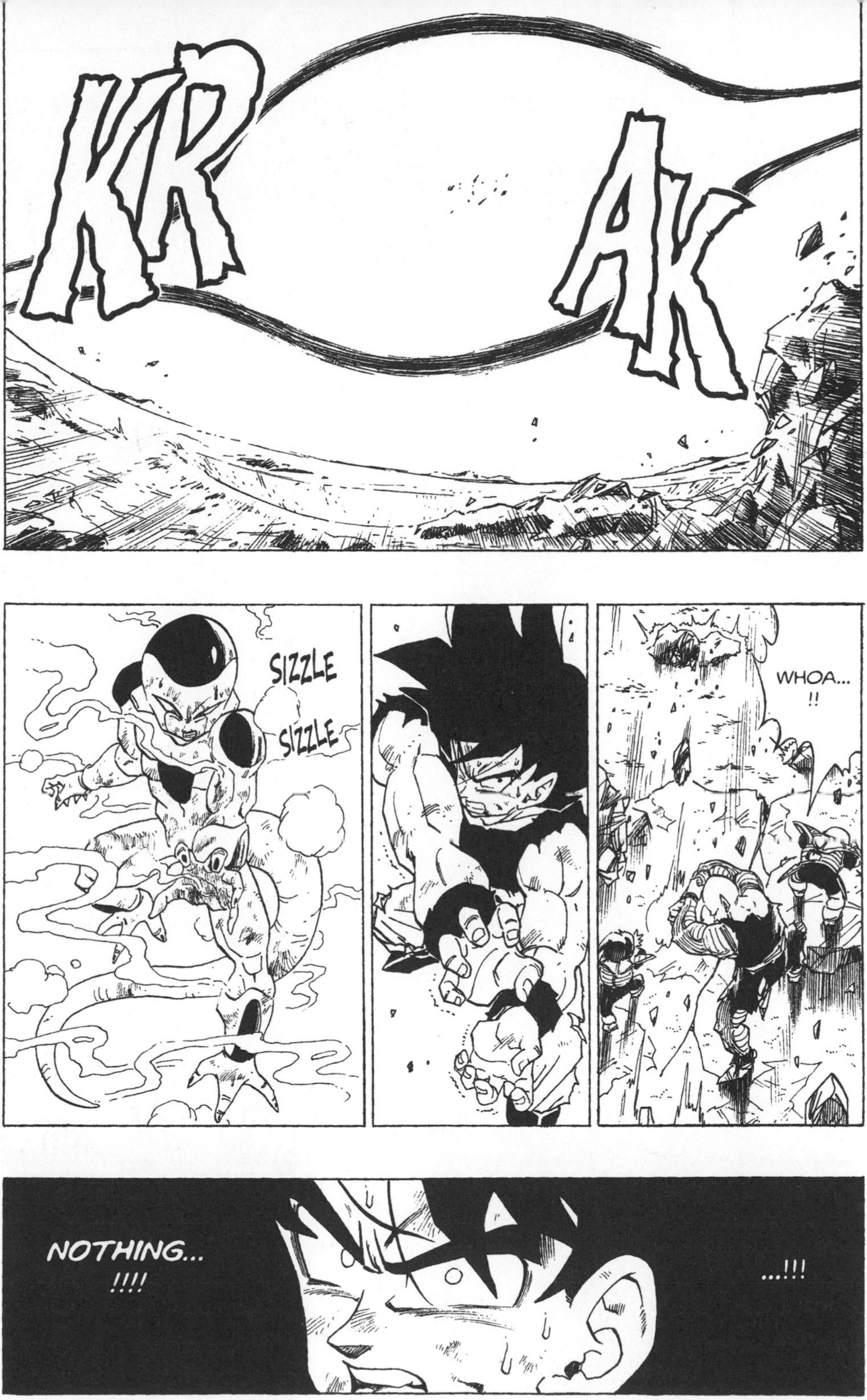
KRAK
SIZZLE
SIZZLE
WHOA...
!!
NOTHING...
!!!!
...!!!

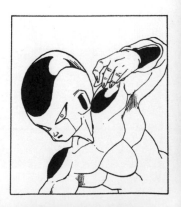

DragonBallZ

VOLUME 11

THE SUPER SAIYAN

DBZ:120 · The Great Genki-Dama

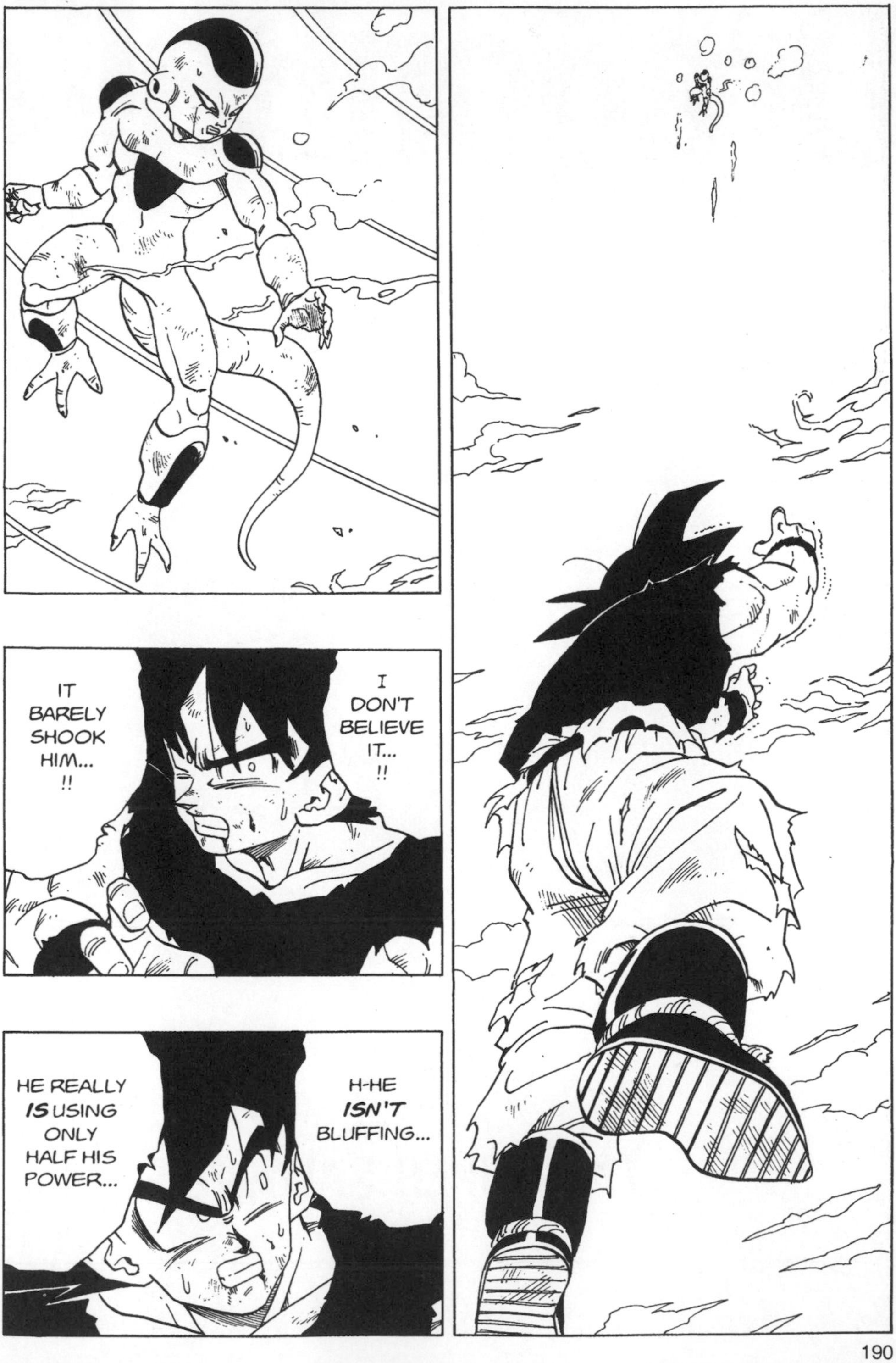
I DON'T BELIEVE IT... !!
IT BARELY SHOOK HIM... !!
H-HE *ISN'T* BLUFFING...
HE REALLY *IS* USING ONLY HALF HIS POWER...

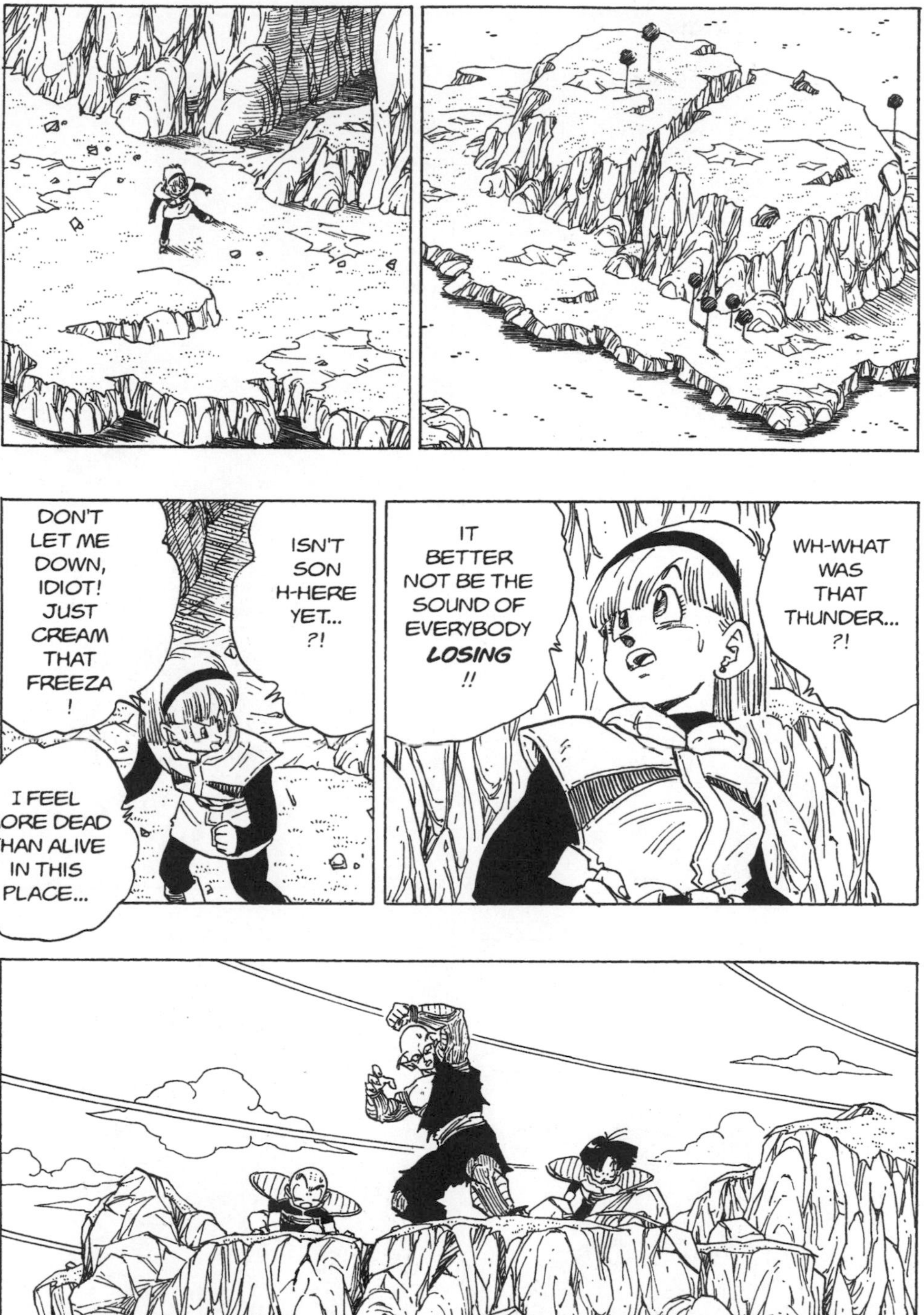
WH-WHAT WAS THAT THUNDER... ?!
IT BETTER NOT BE THE SOUND OF EVERYBODY ***LOSING*** !!
ISN'T SON H-HERE YET... ?!
DON'T LET ME DOWN, IDIOT! JUST CREAM THAT FREEZA !
I FEEL MORE DEAD THAN ALIVE IN THIS PLACE...

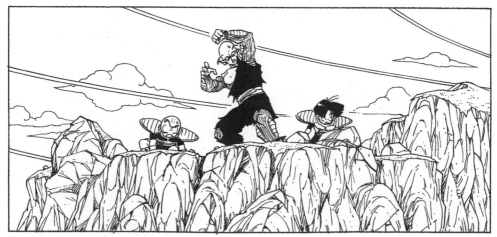

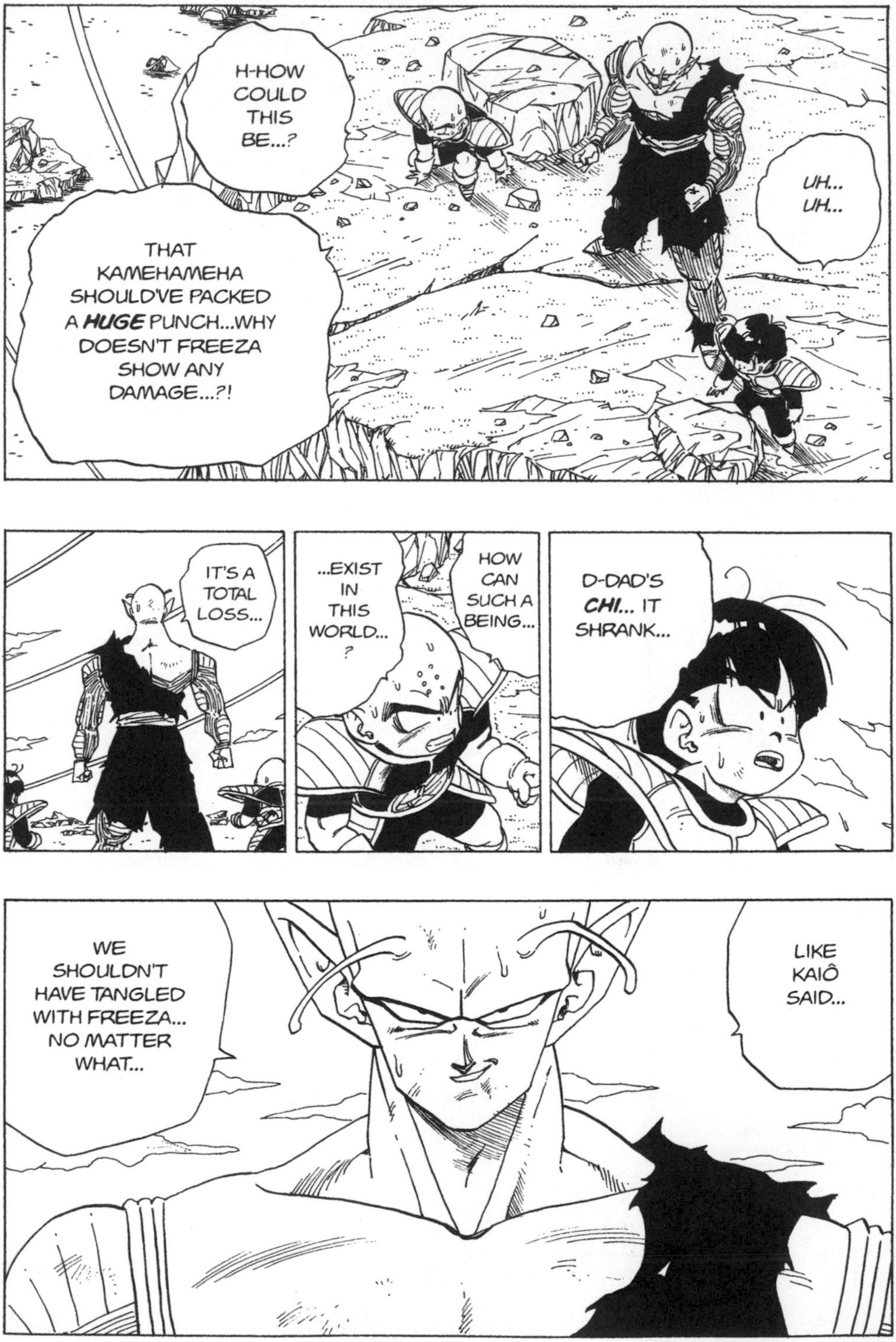
H-HOW COULD THIS BE...?
UH... UH...
THAT KAMEHAMEHA SHOULD'VE PACKED A **HUGE** PUNCH...WHY DOESN'T FREEZA SHOW ANY DAMAGE...?!
IT'S A TOTAL LOSS...
HOW CAN SUCH A BEING...
...EXIST IN THIS WORLD...?
D-DAD'S **CHI**... IT SHRANK...
LIKE KAIÔ SAID...
WE SHOULDN'T HAVE TANGLED WITH FREEZA... NO MATTER WHAT...

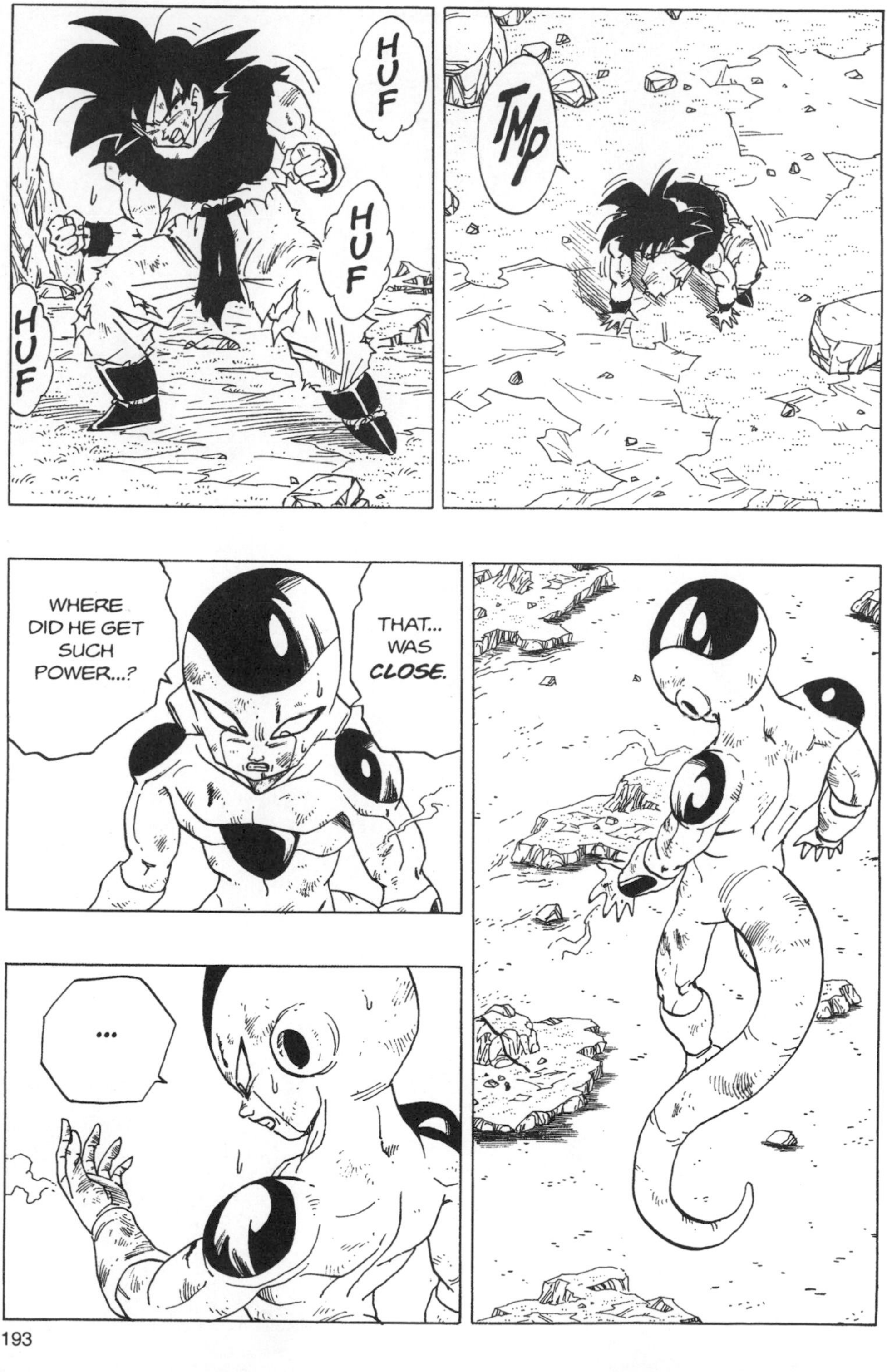
HUF
HUF
HUF
HUF
HUF
HUF
TMP
WHERE DID HE GET SUCH POWER...?
THAT... WAS CLOSE.
...

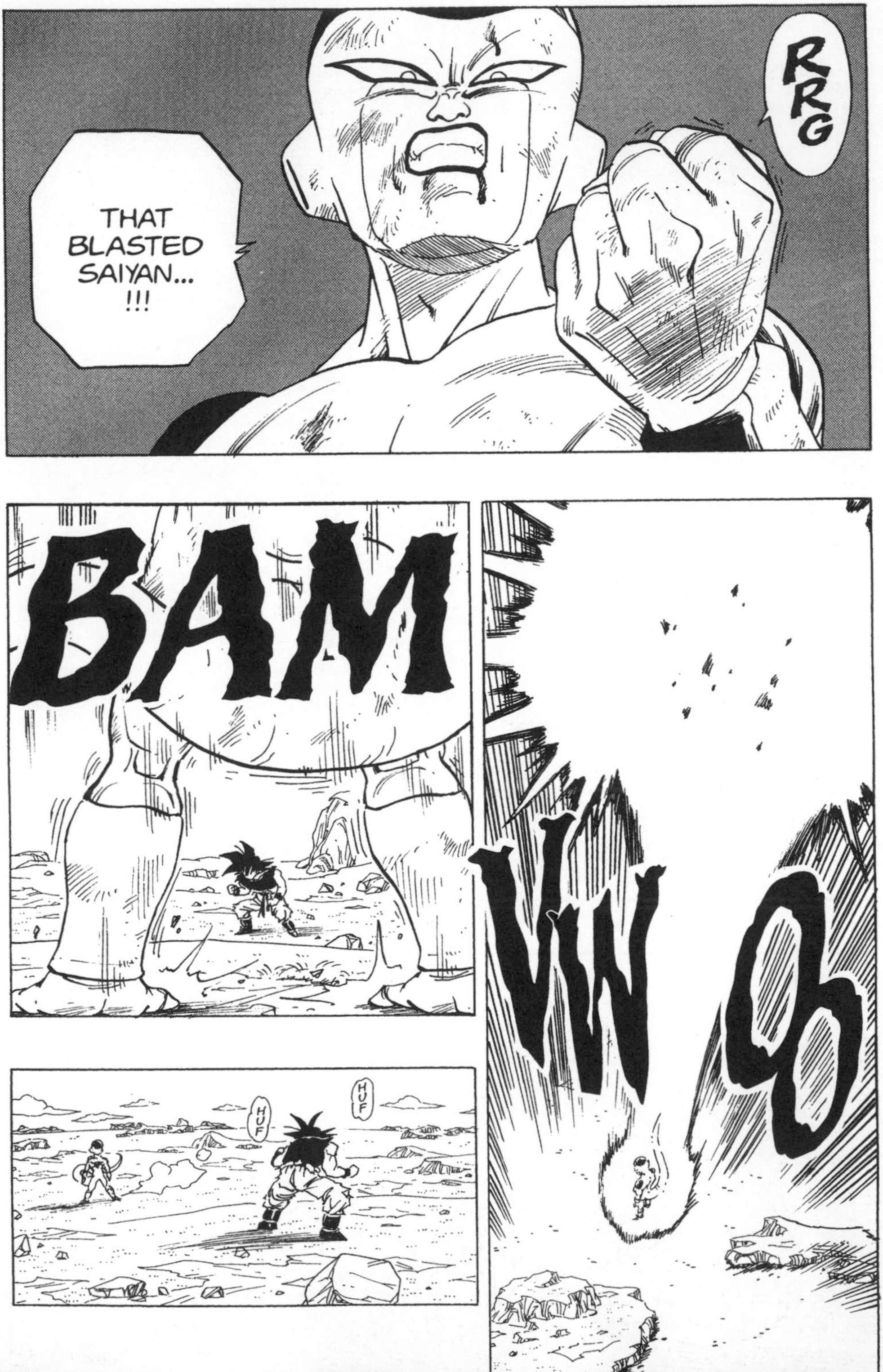
THAT BLASTED SAIYAN... !!!
RRG
BAM
HUF
HUF

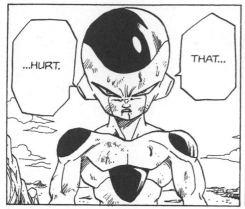

...HURT. THAT...

HUF HUF

IT HURT !!!!!

GYOWWW

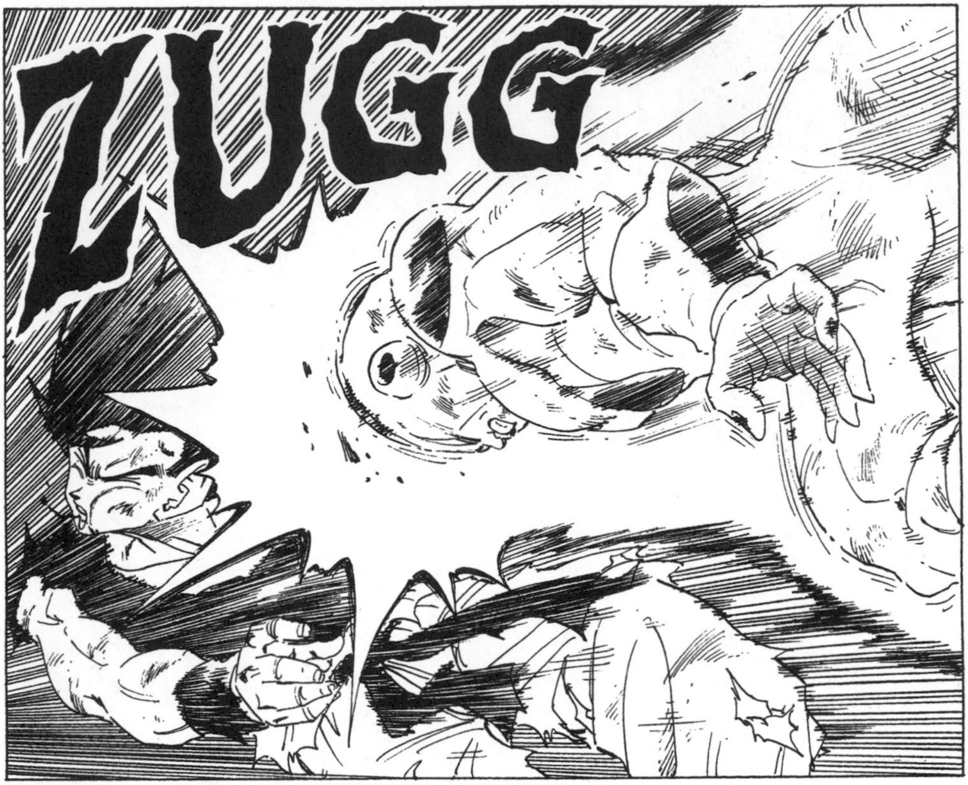
ZUGG

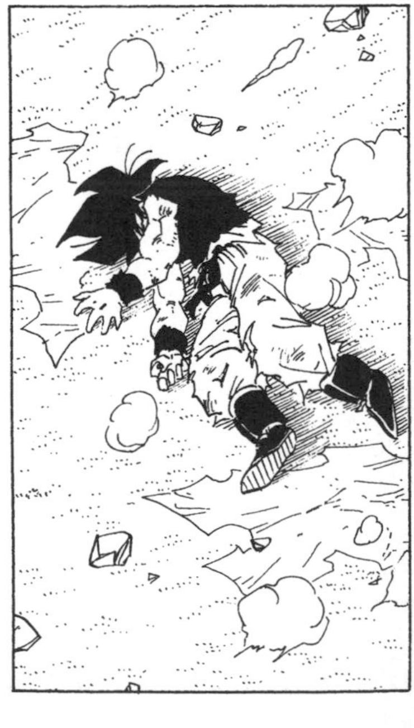

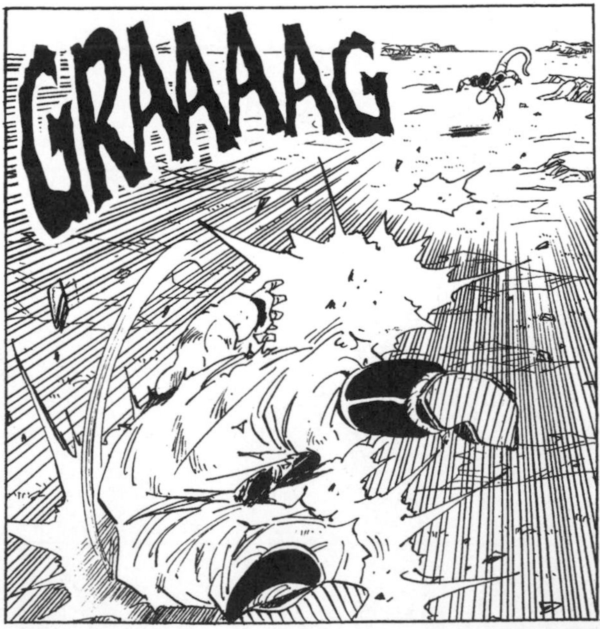
GRAAAAG

TM TM

NNH...

NNN...

VMM

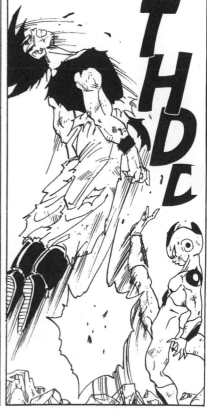

THDD

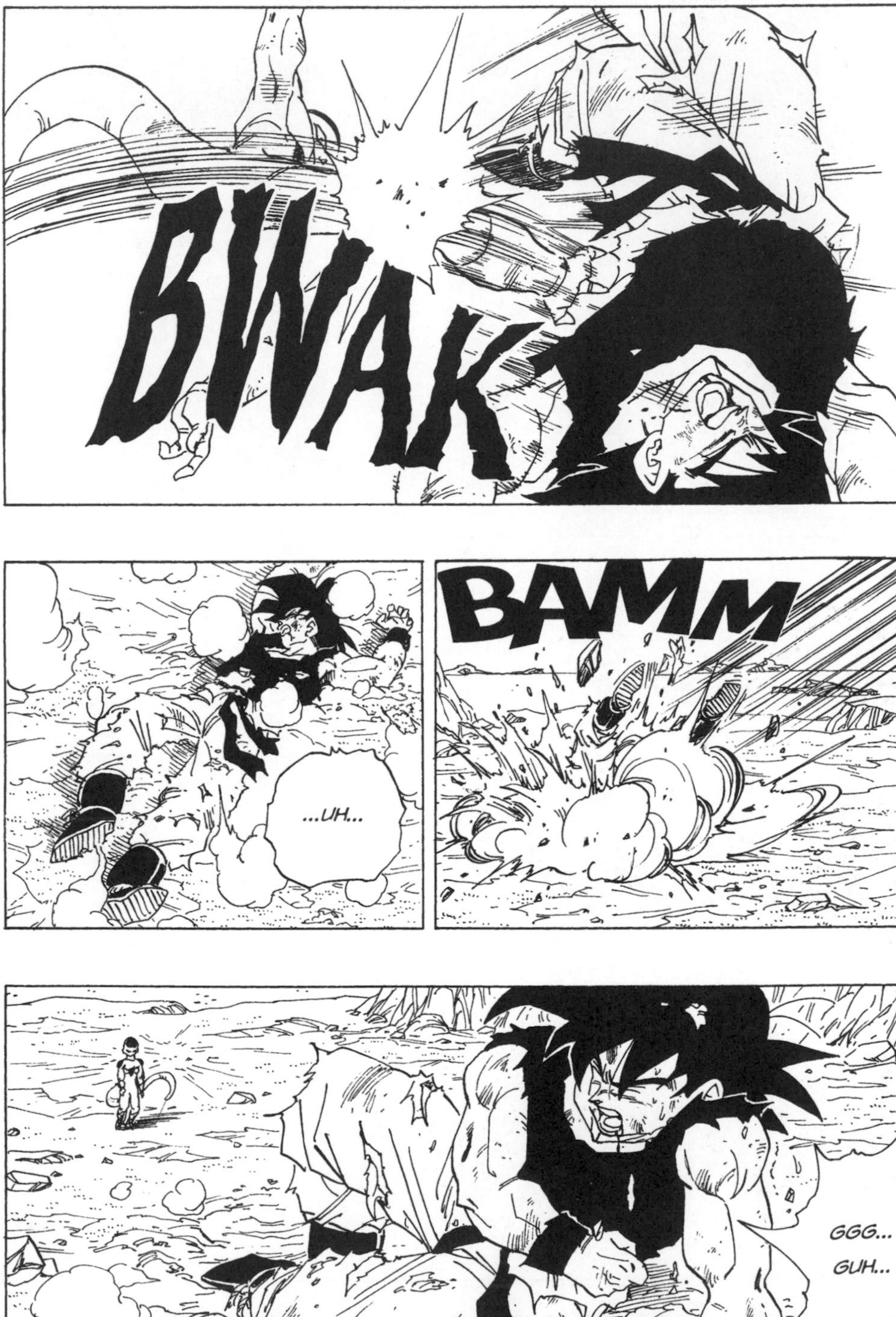
BWAK
BAMM
...UH...
GGG...
GUH...

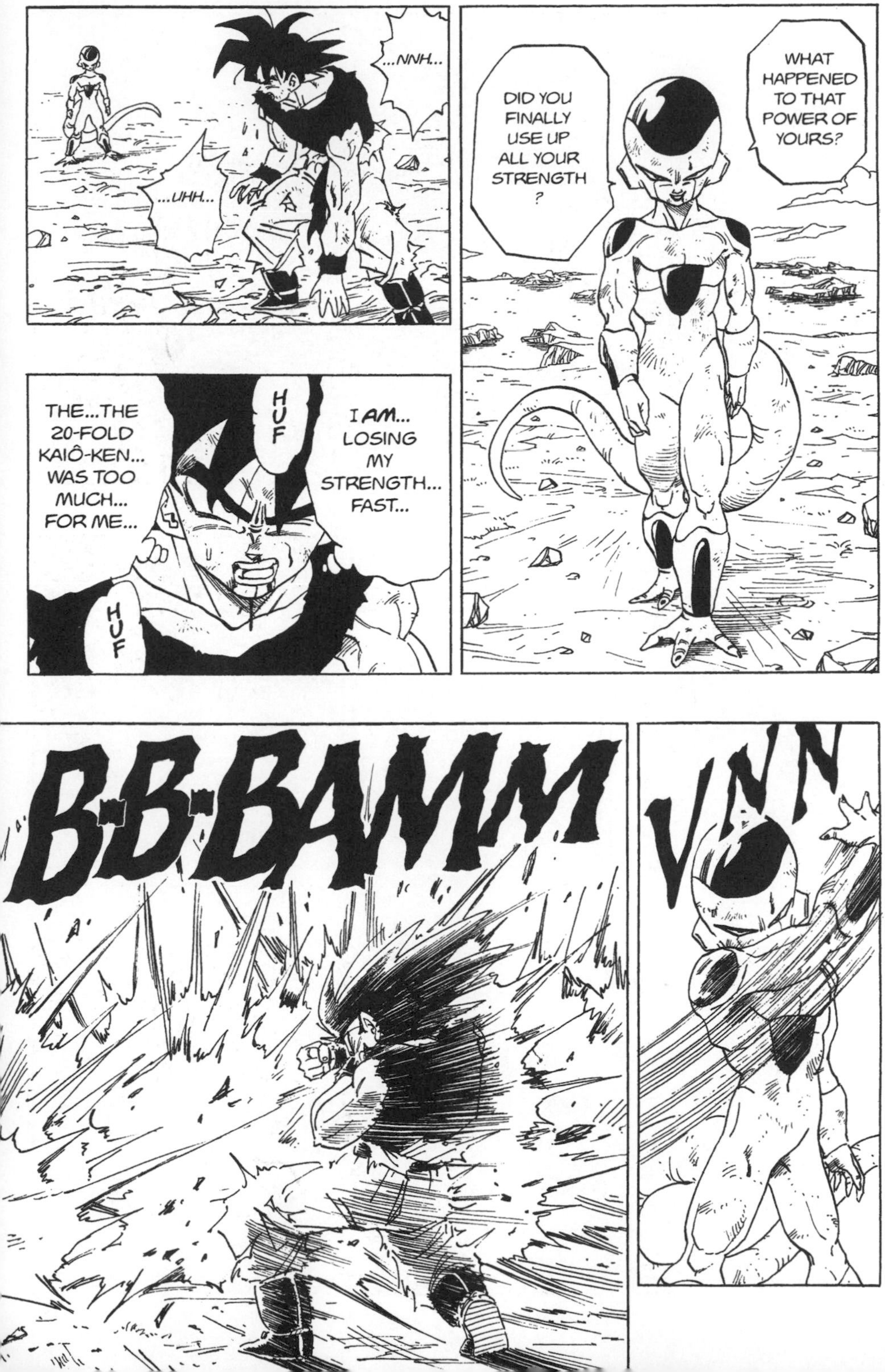
...NNH...
...UHH...
DID YOU FINALLY USE UP ALL YOUR STRENGTH?
WHAT HAPPENED TO THAT POWER OF YOURS?
THE...THE 20-FOLD KAIÔ-KEN... WAS TOO MUCH... FOR ME...
HUF
I *AM*... LOSING MY STRENGTH... FAST...
HUF
B-B-BAMM
VNN

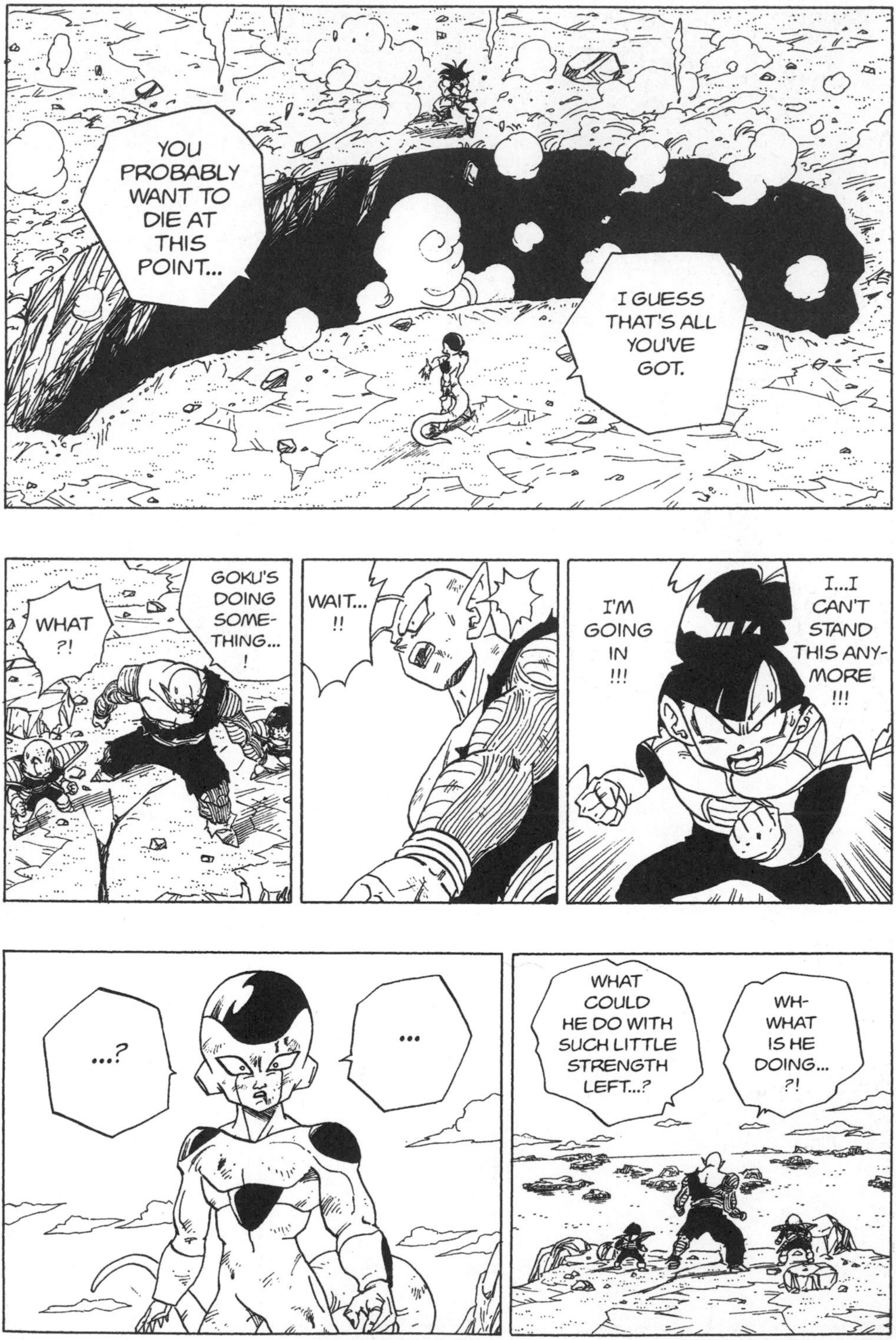
I GUESS THAT'S ALL YOU'VE GOT.
YOU PROBABLY WANT TO DIE AT THIS POINT...
I...I CAN'T STAND THIS ANYMORE !!!
I'M GOING IN !!!
WAIT... !!
GOKU'S DOING SOMETHING... !
WHAT ?!
WH-WHAT IS HE DOING... ?!
WHAT COULD HE DO WITH SUCH LITTLE STRENGTH LEFT...?
...
...?

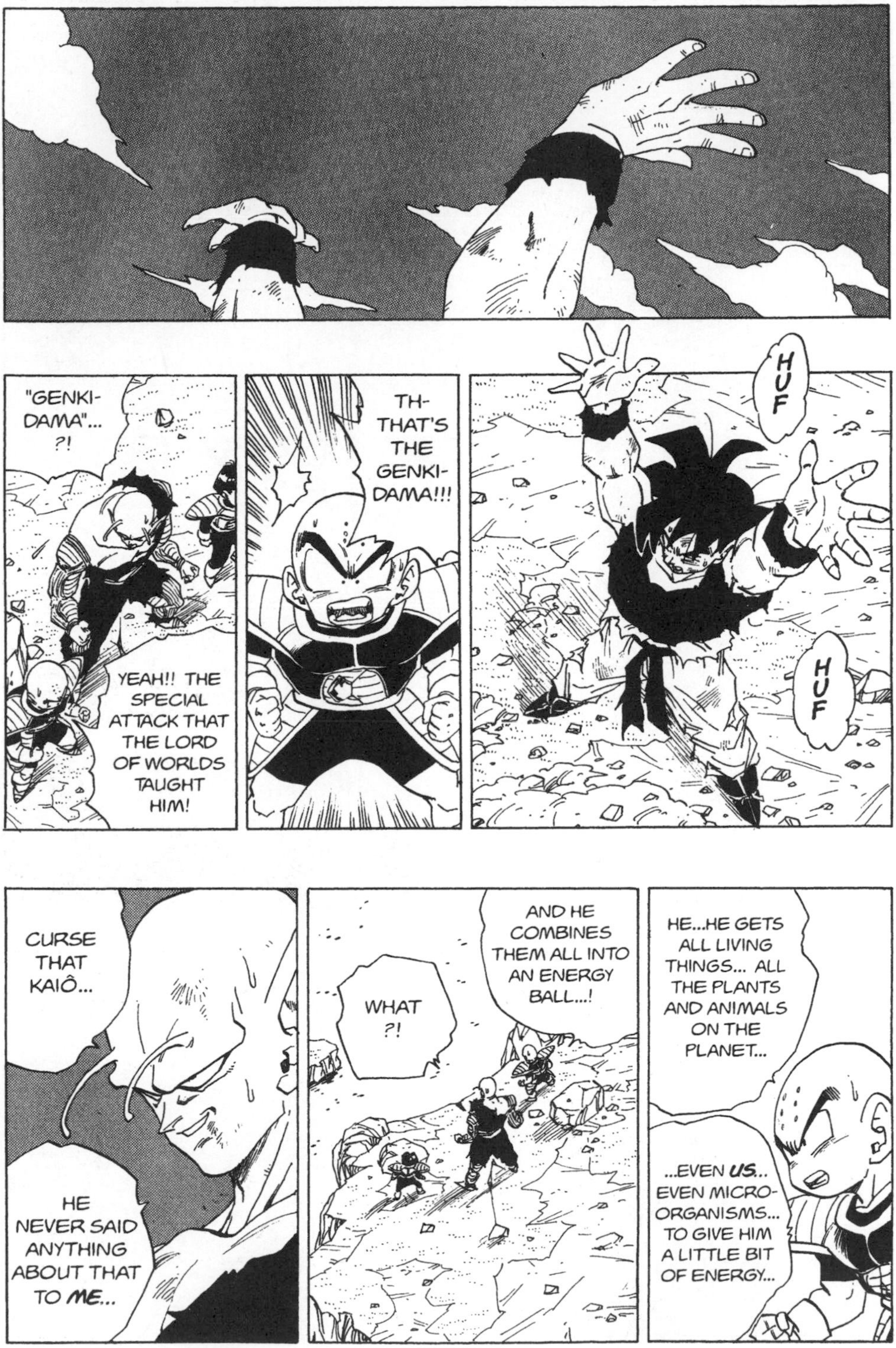
HUF
HUF
TH-THAT'S THE GENKI-DAMA!!!
"GENKI-DAMA"... ?!
YEAH!! THE SPECIAL ATTACK THAT THE LORD OF WORLDS TAUGHT HIM!
HE...HE GETS ALL LIVING THINGS... ALL THE PLANTS AND ANIMALS ON THE PLANET...
...EVEN *US*... EVEN MICRO-ORGANISMS... TO GIVE HIM A LITTLE BIT OF ENERGY...
AND HE COMBINES THEM ALL INTO AN ENERGY BALL...!
WHAT ?!
CURSE THAT KAIÔ...
HE NEVER SAID ANYTHING ABOUT THAT TO *ME*...

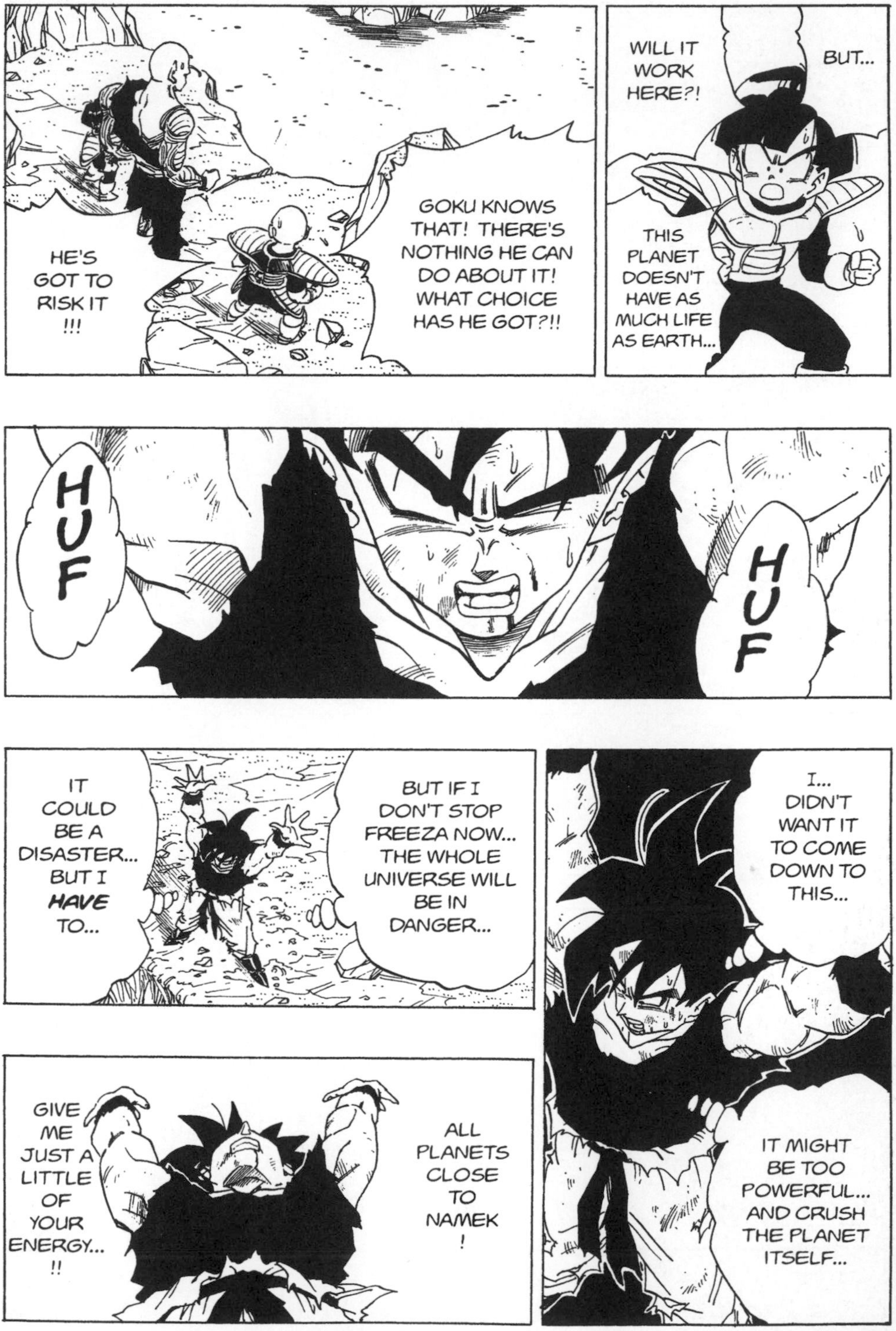

BUT...
WILL IT WORK HERE?!
THIS PLANET DOESN'T HAVE AS MUCH LIFE AS EARTH...
GOKU KNOWS THAT! THERE'S NOTHING HE CAN DO ABOUT IT! WHAT CHOICE HAS HE GOT?!!
HE'S GOT TO RISK IT !!!
HUF
HUF
IT COULD BE A DISASTER... BUT I *HAVE* TO...
BUT IF I DON'T STOP FREEZA NOW... THE WHOLE UNIVERSE WILL BE IN DANGER...
I... DIDN'T WANT IT TO COME DOWN TO THIS...
IT MIGHT BE TOO POWERFUL... AND CRUSH THE PLANET ITSELF...
ALL PLANETS CLOSE TO NAMEK !
GIVE ME JUST A LITTLE OF YOUR ENERGY... !!

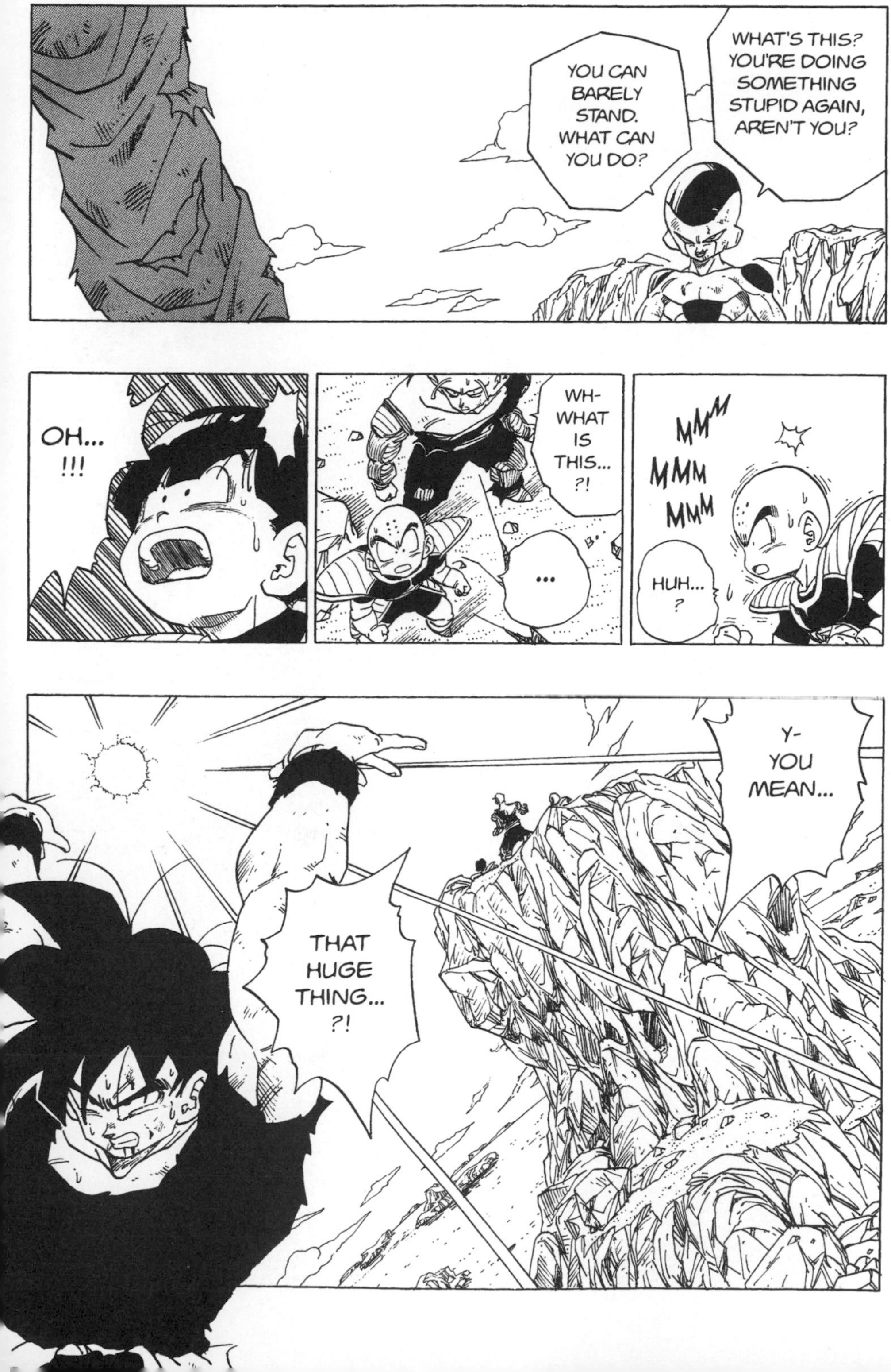
WHAT'S THIS? YOU'RE DOING SOMETHING STUPID AGAIN, AREN'T YOU?
YOU CAN BARELY STAND. WHAT CAN YOU DO?
MMMM MMM MMM
HUH...?
WH-WHAT IS THIS...?!
...
OH...!!!
Y-YOU MEAN...
THAT HUGE THING...?!

DBZ:121 • The Last Chance

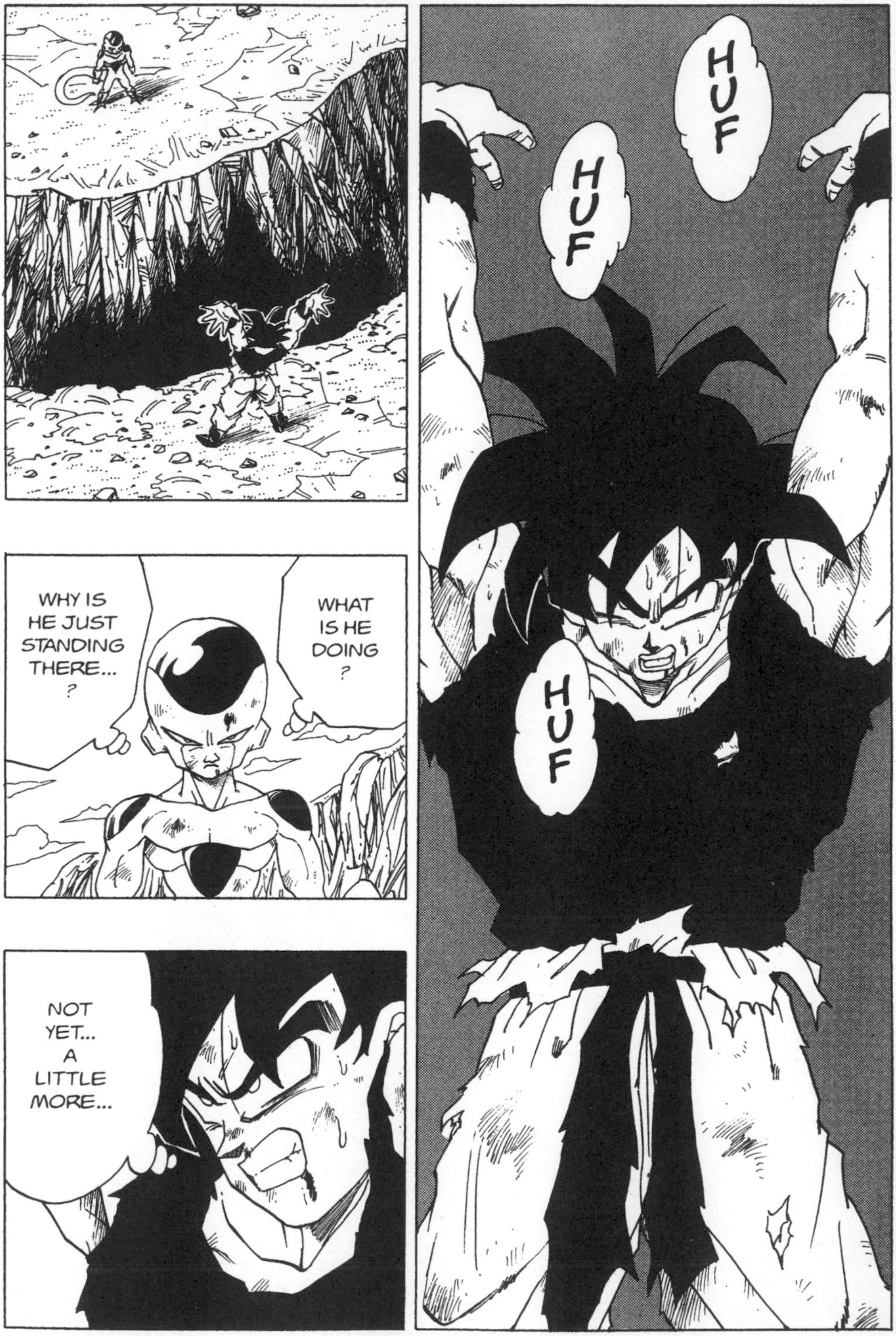
HUF HUF
HUF HUF
WHY IS HE JUST STANDING THERE...?
WHAT IS HE DOING?
NOT YET... A LITTLE MORE...
HUF HUF

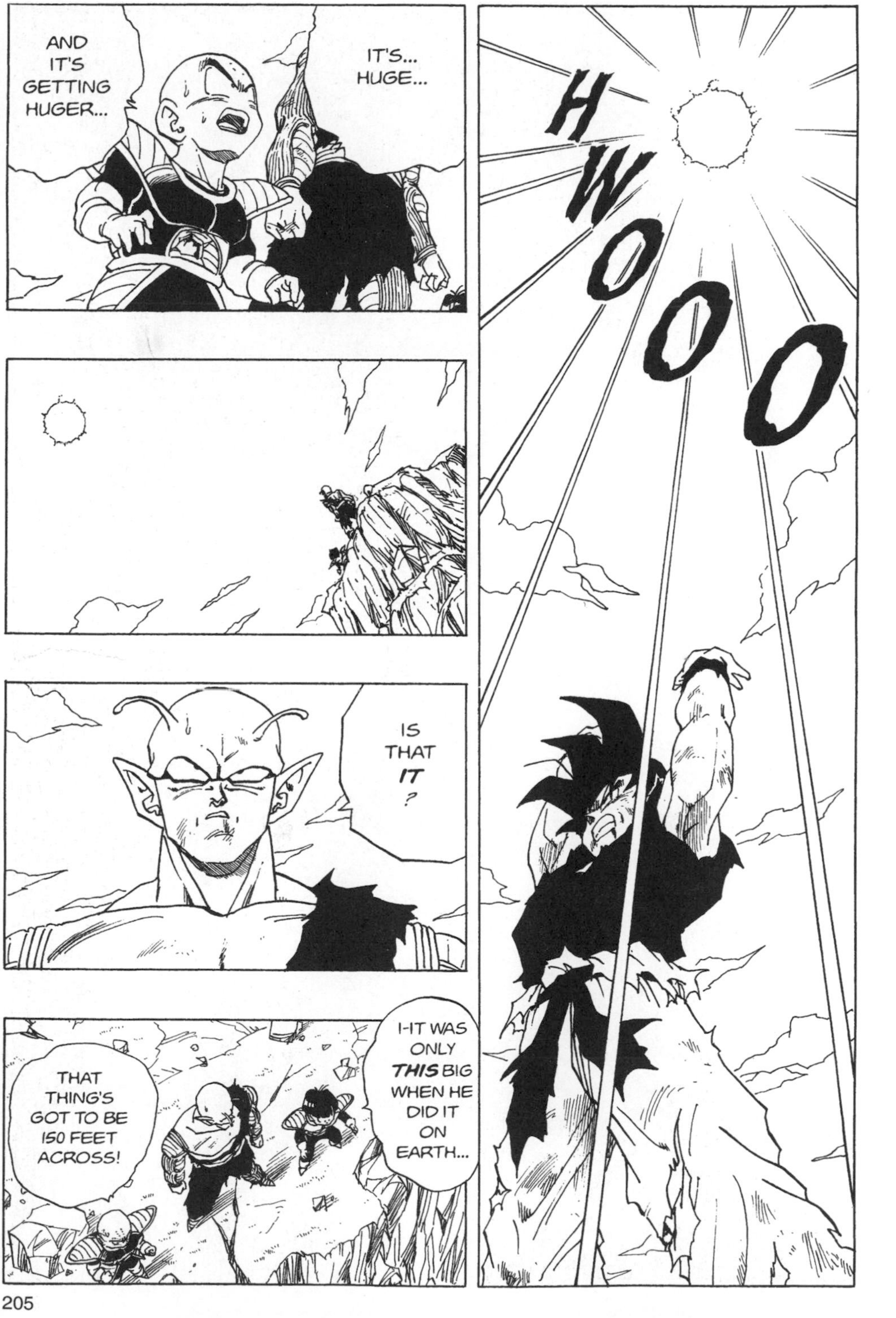
AND IT'S GETTING HUGER...
IT'S... HUGE...
HWOOOO
IS THAT *IT* ?
THAT THING'S GOT TO BE 150 FEET ACROSS!
I-IT WAS ONLY *THIS* BIG WHEN HE DID IT ON EARTH...

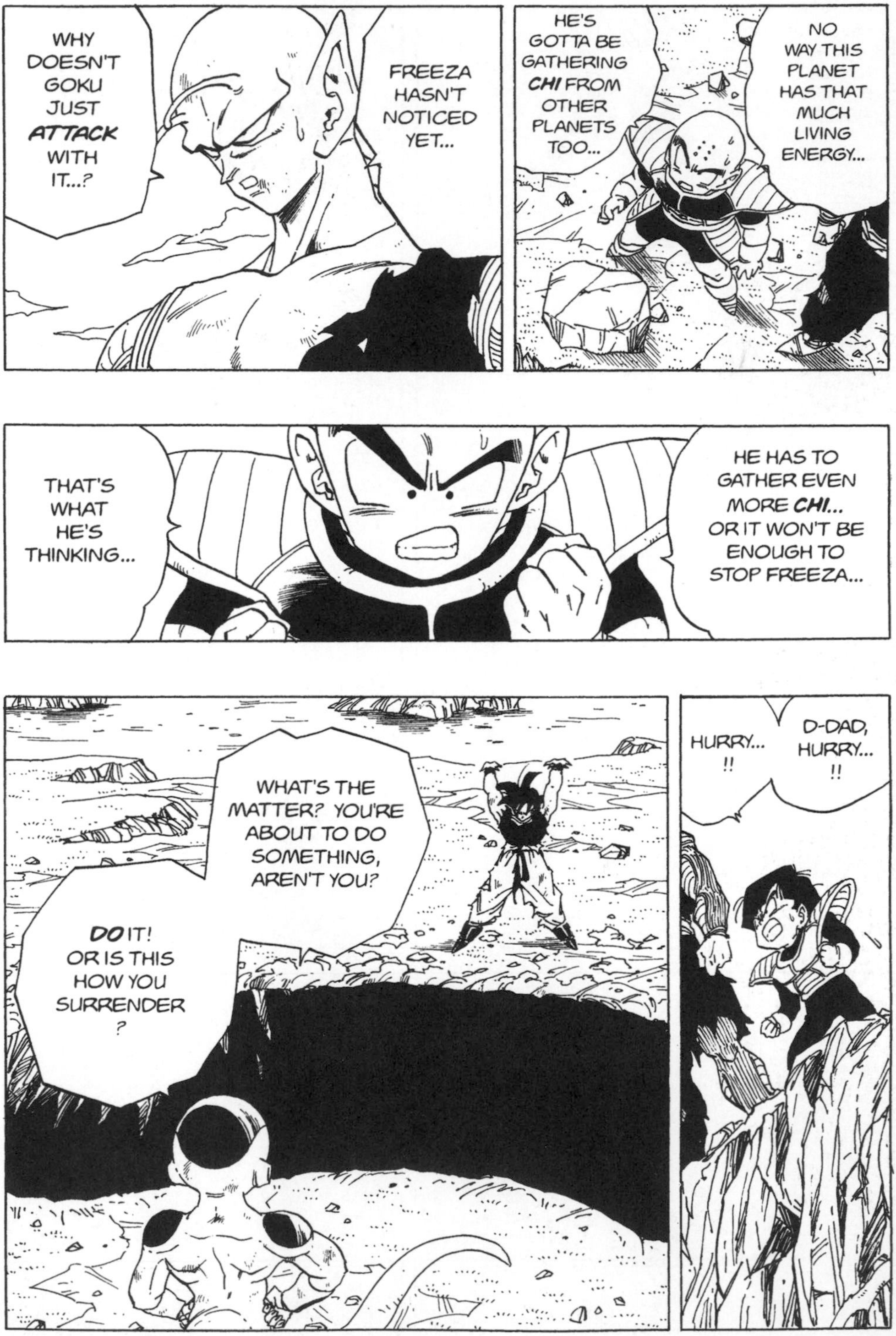
WHY DOESN'T GOKU JUST ATTACK WITH IT...?
FREEZA HASN'T NOTICED YET...
HE'S GOTTA BE GATHERING CHI FROM OTHER PLANETS TOO...
NO WAY THIS PLANET HAS THAT MUCH LIVING ENERGY...
THAT'S WHAT HE'S THINKING...
HE HAS TO GATHER EVEN MORE CHI... OR IT WON'T BE ENOUGH TO STOP FREEZA...
WHAT'S THE MATTER? YOU'RE ABOUT TO DO SOMETHING, AREN'T YOU?
DO IT! OR IS THIS HOW YOU SURRENDER?
D-DAD, HURRY... !!
HURRY... !!

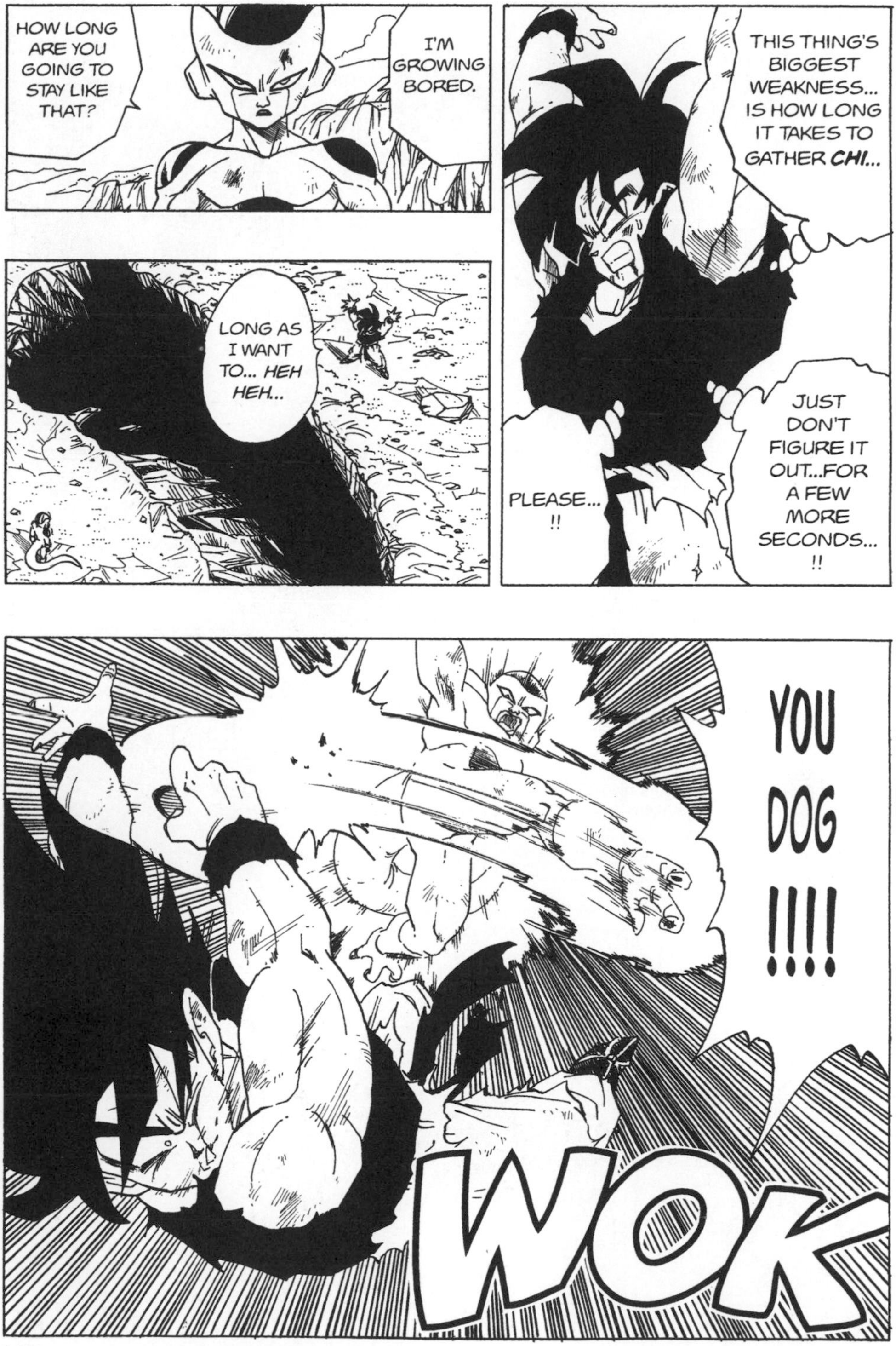

HOW LONG ARE YOU GOING TO STAY LIKE THAT?
I'M GROWING BORED.
LONG AS I WANT TO... HEH HEH...
THIS THING'S BIGGEST WEAKNESS... IS HOW LONG IT TAKES TO GATHER **CHI**...
JUST DON'T FIGURE IT OUT...FOR A FEW MORE SECONDS... !!
PLEASE... !!
YOU DOG !!!!
WOK

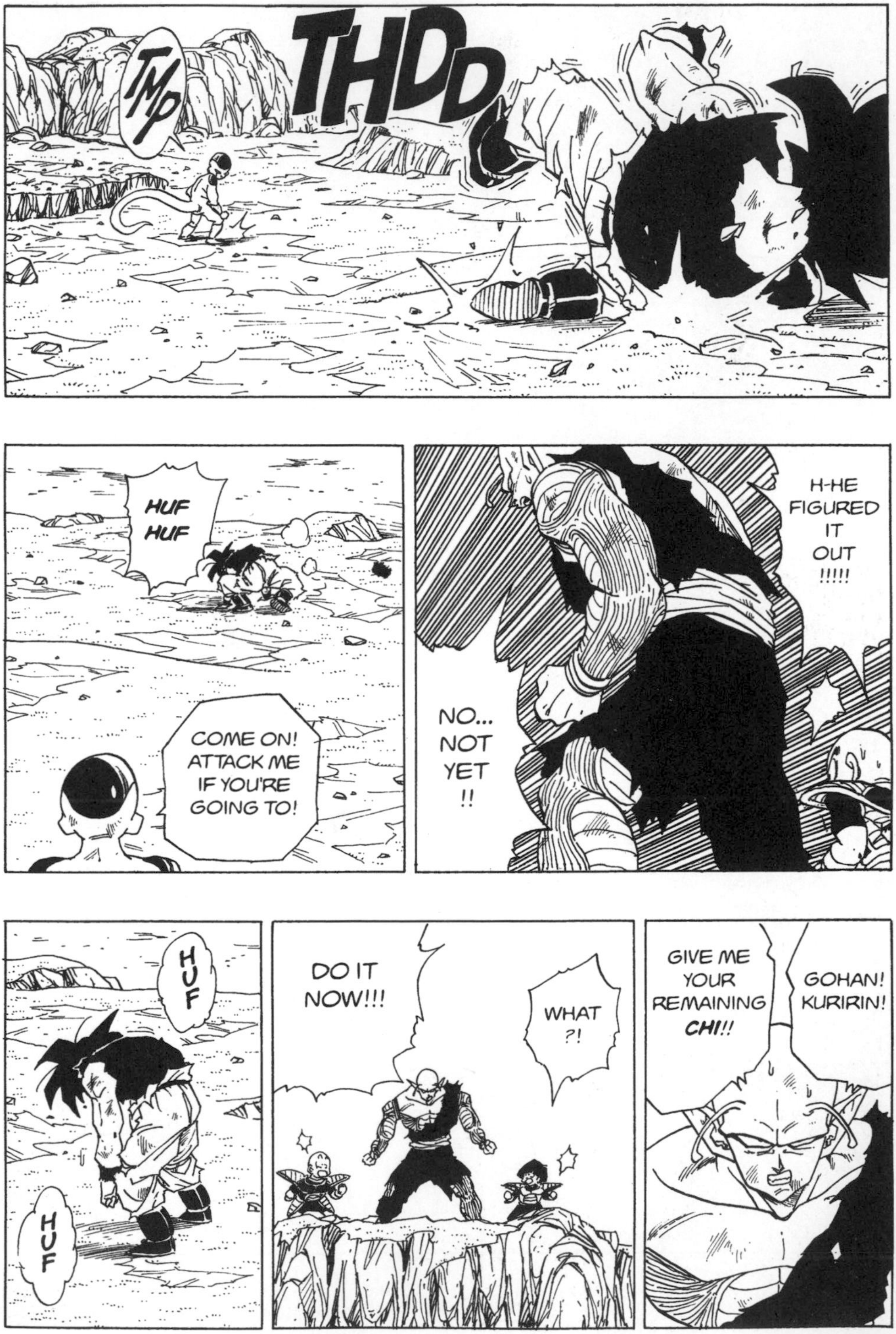
TMP
THDD
HUF HUF
COME ON! ATTACK ME IF YOU'RE GOING TO!
H-HE FIGURED IT OUT!!!!!
NO... NOT YET!!
HUF
HUF
DO IT NOW!!!
WHAT?!
GOHAN! KURIRIN!
GIVE ME YOUR REMAINING CHI!!

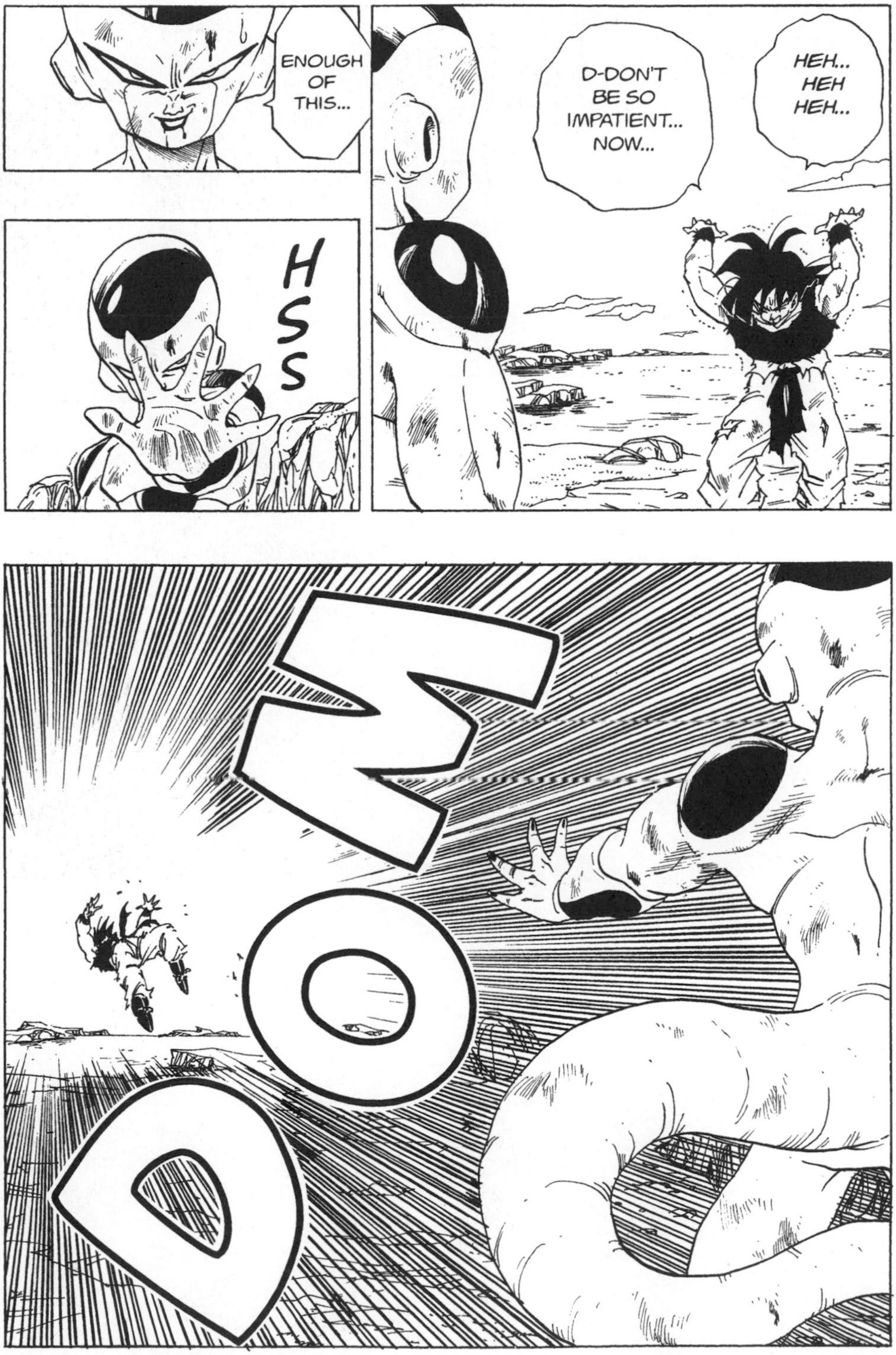
ENOUGH OF THIS...
HSS
D-DON'T BE SO IMPATIENT... NOW...
HEH... HEH HEH...
DOOM

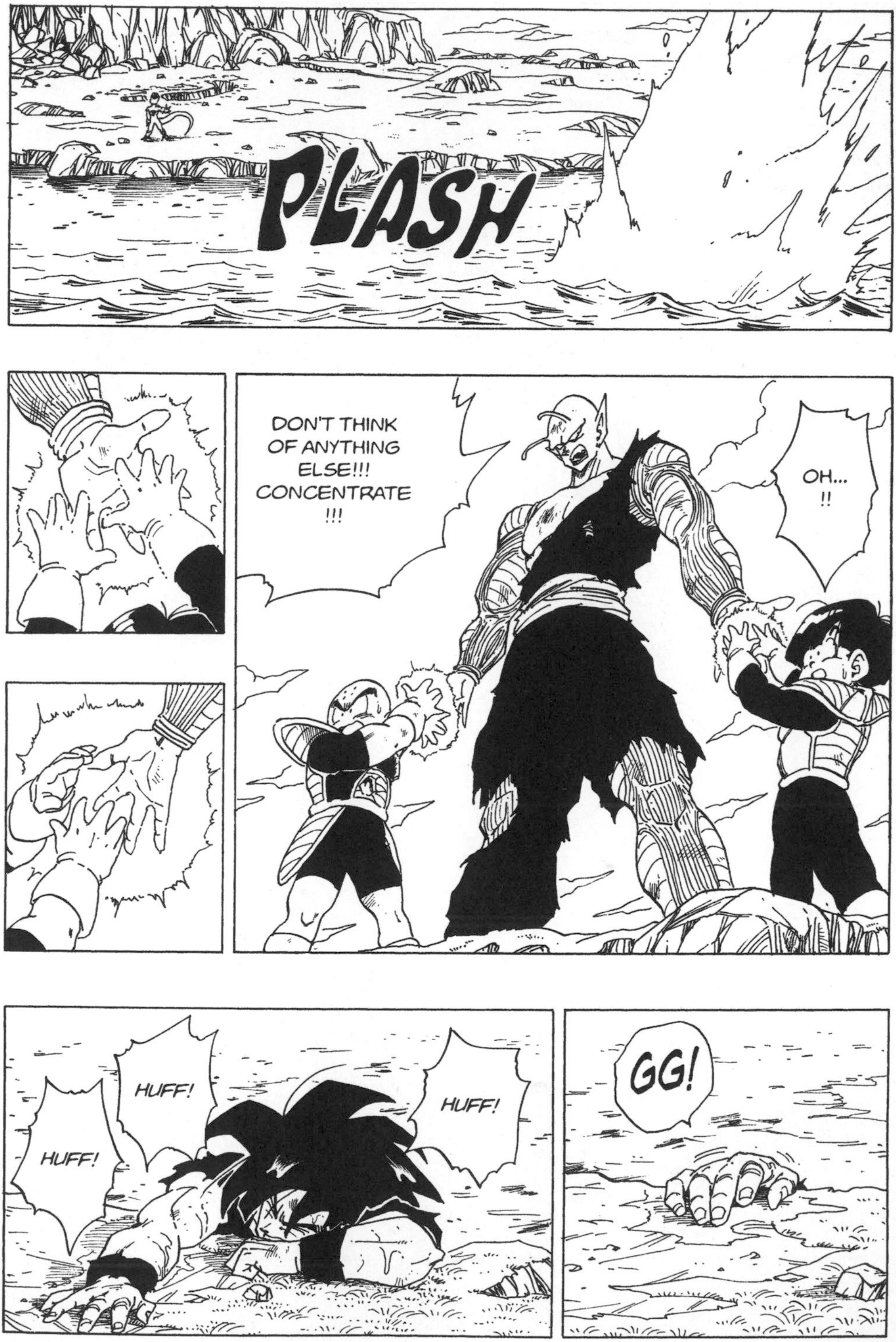
PLASH
DON'T THINK OF ANYTHING ELSE!!! CONCENTRATE !!!
OH... !!
HUFF!
HUFF!
HUFF!
GG!

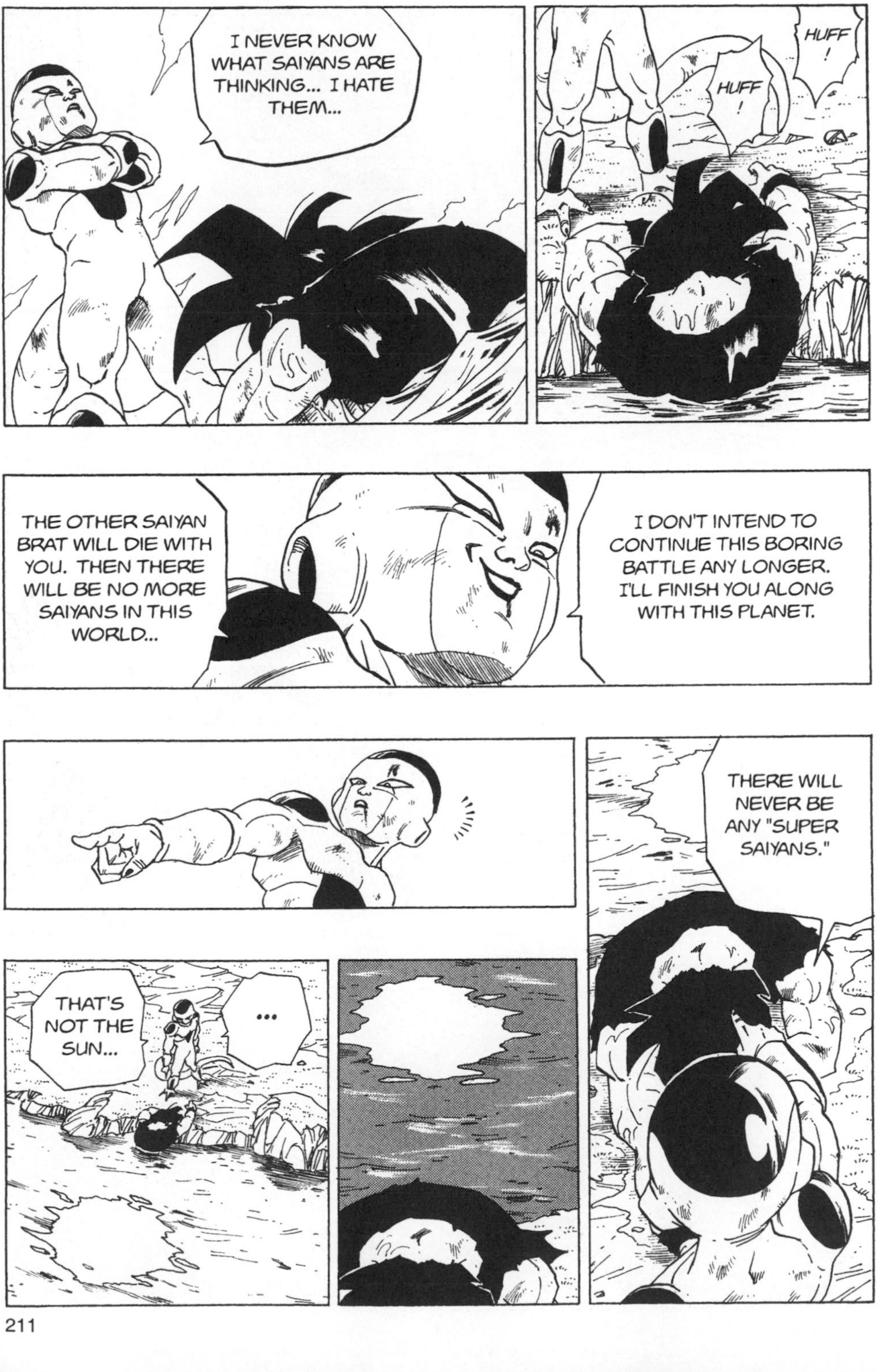
I NEVER KNOW WHAT SAIYANS ARE THINKING... I HATE THEM...
HUFF!
HUFF!
I DON'T INTEND TO CONTINUE THIS BORING BATTLE ANY LONGER. I'LL FINISH YOU ALONG WITH THIS PLANET.
THE OTHER SAIYAN BRAT WILL DIE WITH YOU. THEN THERE WILL BE NO MORE SAIYANS IN THIS WORLD...
THERE WILL NEVER BE ANY "SUPER SAIYANS."
THAT'S NOT THE SUN...
...

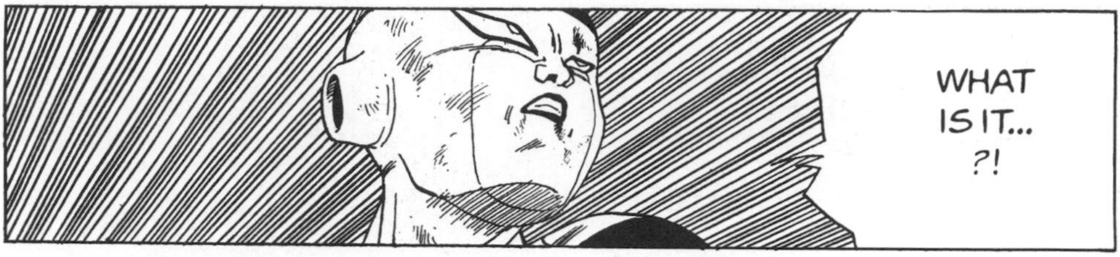
WHAT IS IT... ?!

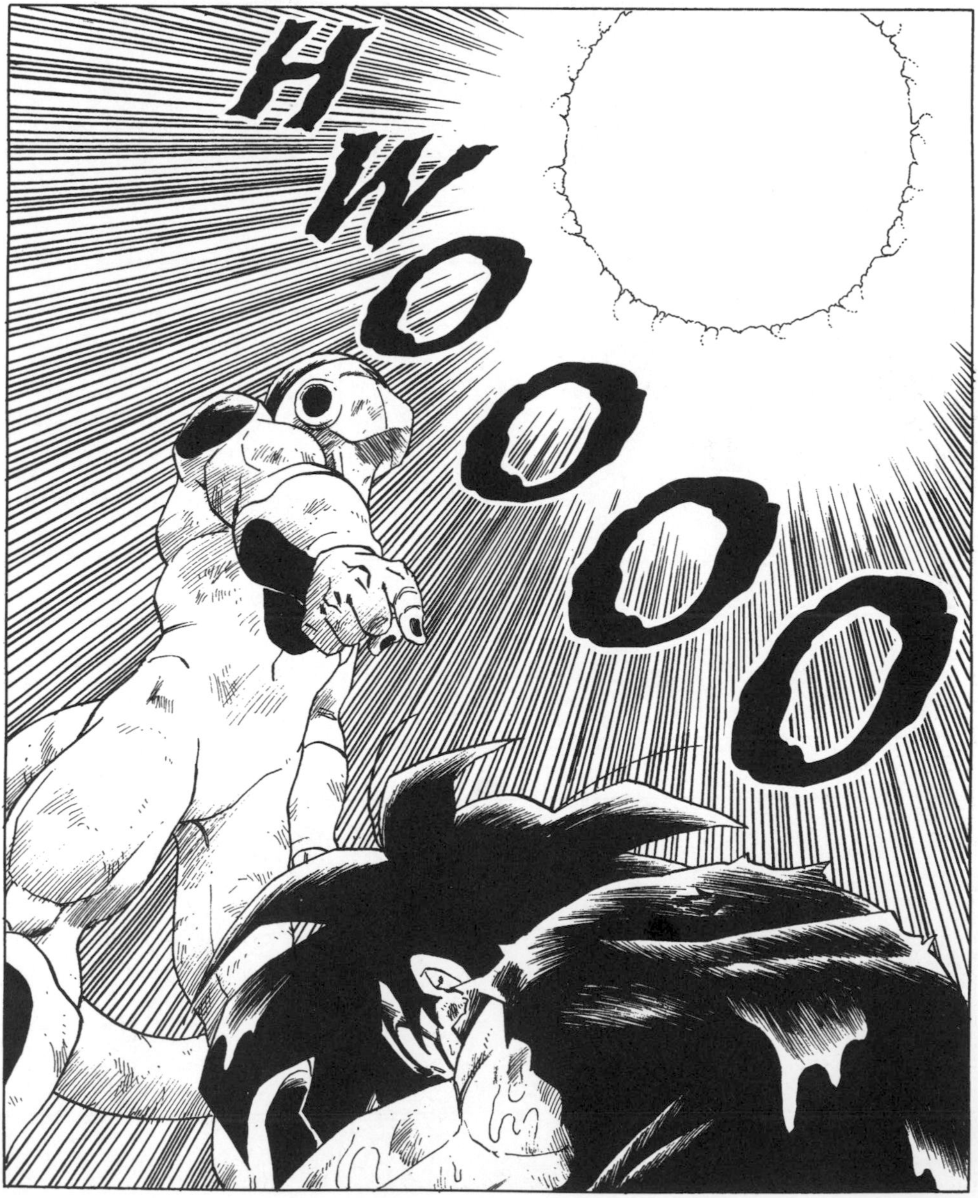
HWOOOOO

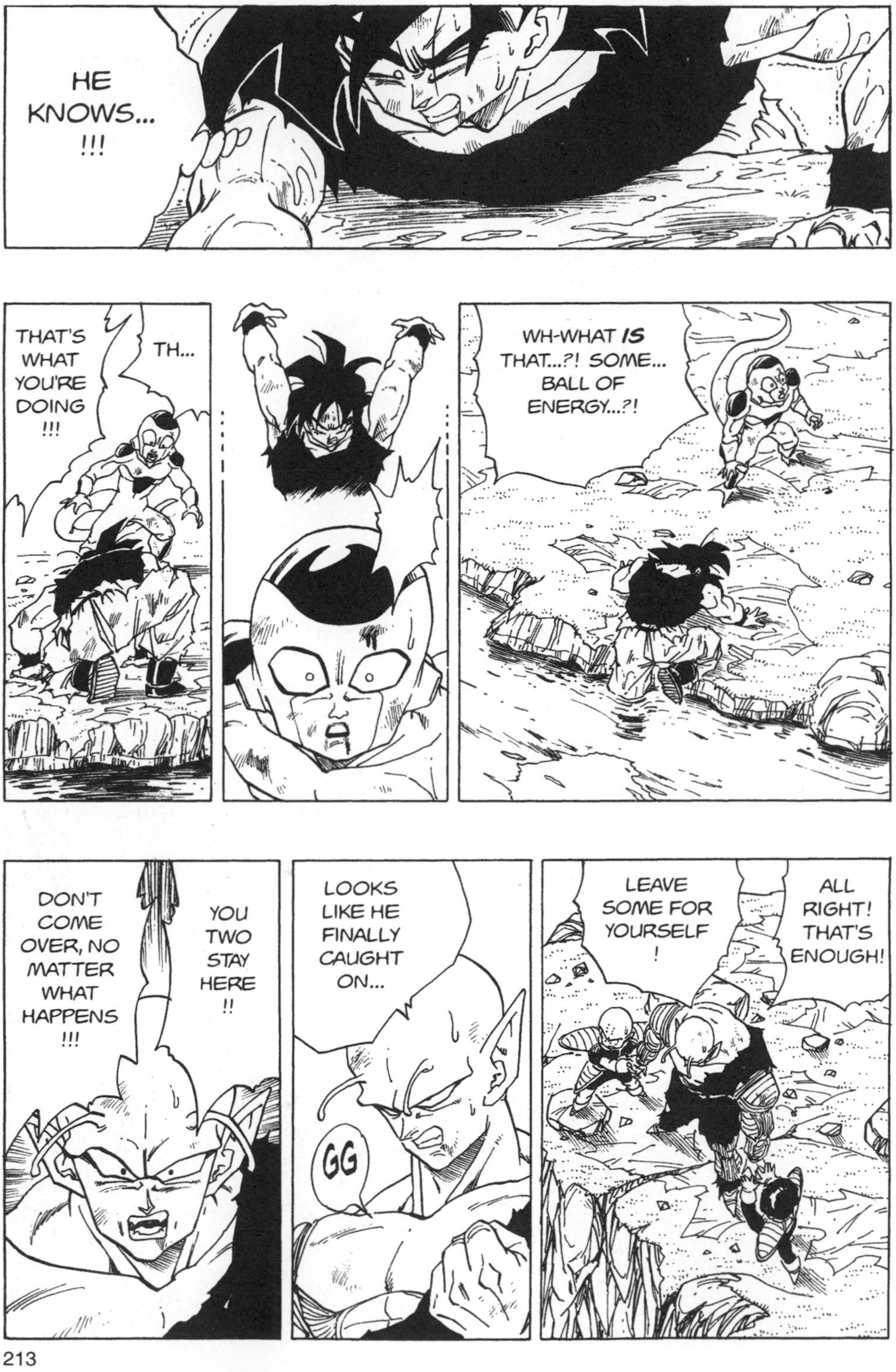

HE KNOWS... !!!
WH-WHAT *IS* THAT...?! SOME... BALL OF ENERGY...?!
TH...
THAT'S WHAT YOU'RE DOING !!!
ALL RIGHT! THAT'S ENOUGH!
LEAVE SOME FOR YOURSELF !
LOOKS LIKE HE FINALLY CAUGHT ON...
GG
YOU TWO STAY HERE !!
DON'T COME OVER, NO MATTER WHAT HAPPENS !!!

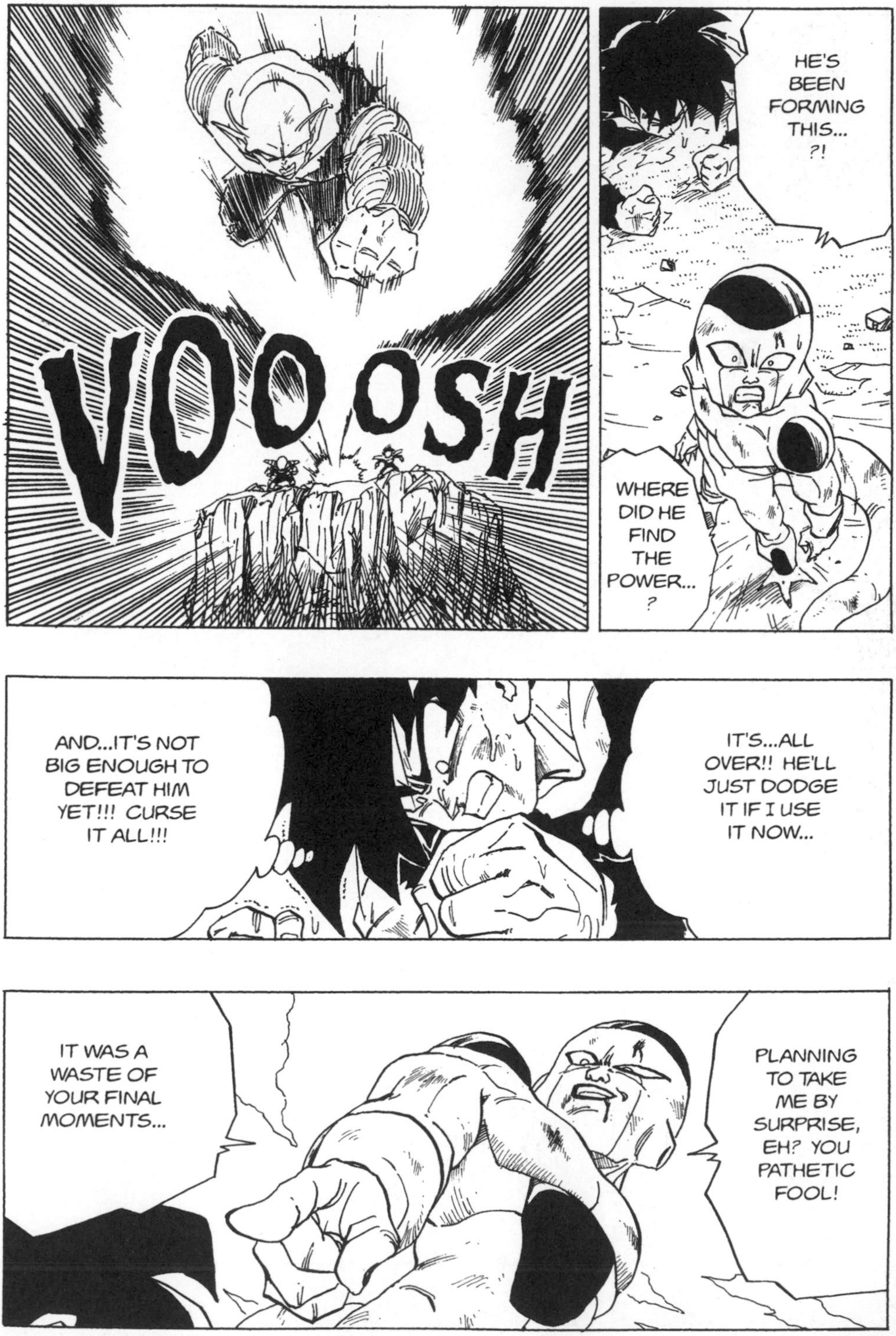
VOOSH
HE'S BEEN FORMING THIS...?!
WHERE DID HE FIND THE POWER...?
IT'S...ALL OVER!! HE'LL JUST DODGE IT IF I USE IT NOW...
AND...IT'S NOT BIG ENOUGH TO DEFEAT HIM YET!!! CURSE IT ALL!!!
PLANNING TO TAKE ME BY SURPRISE, EH? YOU PATHETIC FOOL!
IT WAS A WASTE OF YOUR FINAL MOMENTS...

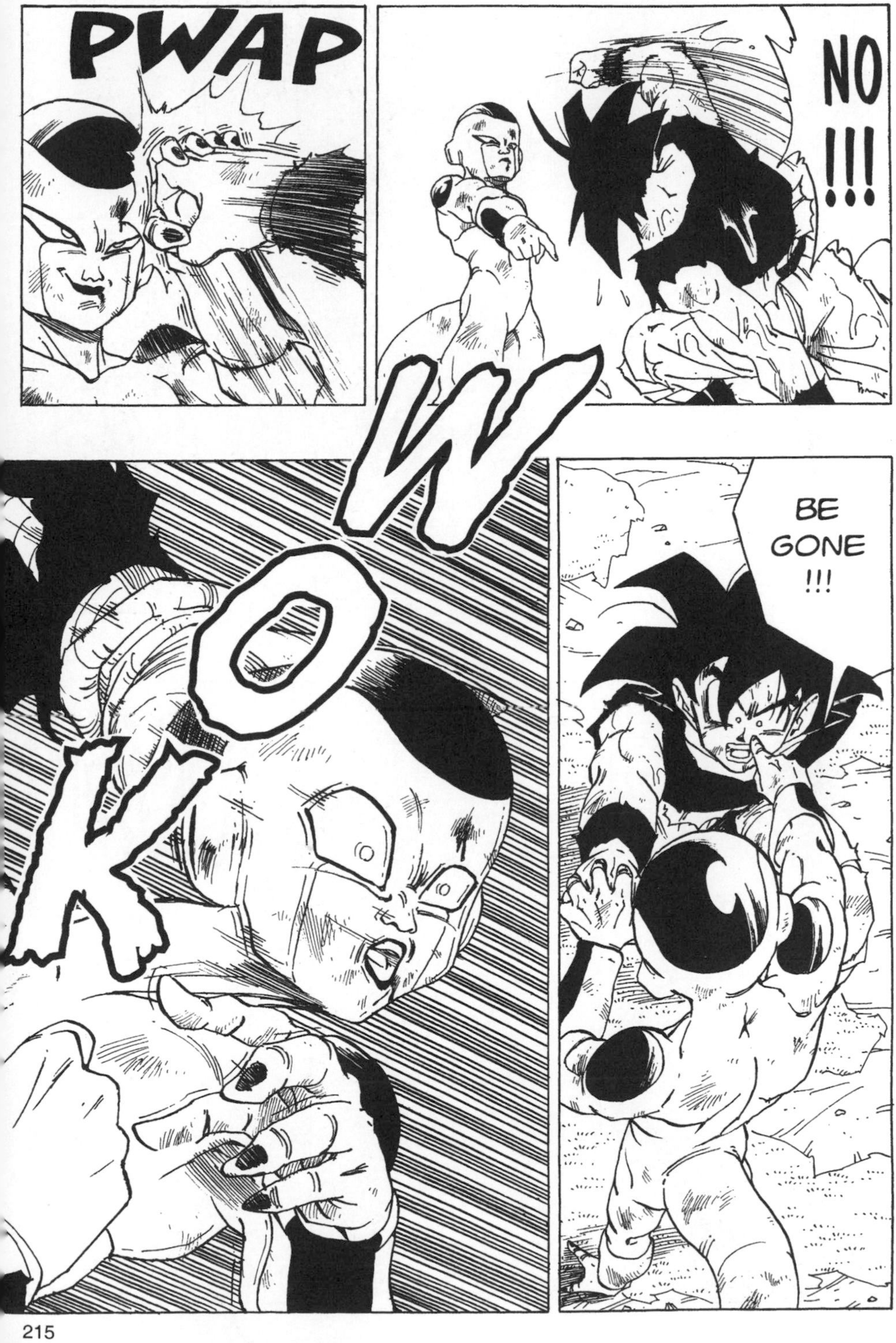
NO !!!
PWAP
BE GONE !!!
KOW

PICCOLO...
!!!

JUST
FINISH
THAT
THING
!!!

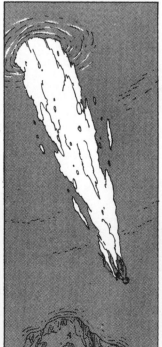

SPLASSSH

216

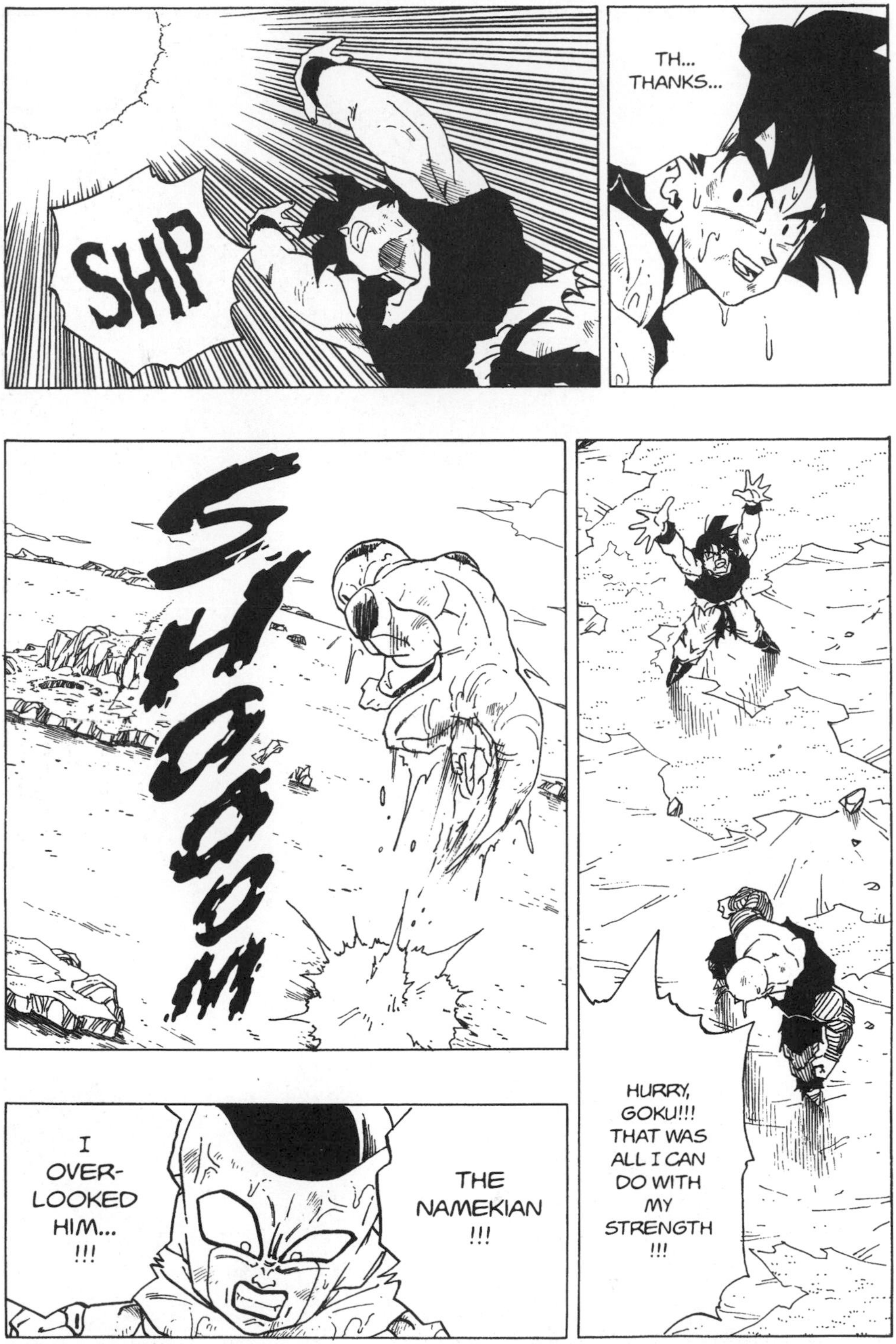
SHP
TH... THANKS...
SHOOOM
I OVER-LOOKED HIM... !!!
THE NAMEKIAN !!!
HURRY, GOKU!!! THAT WAS ALL I CAN DO WITH MY STRENGTH !!!

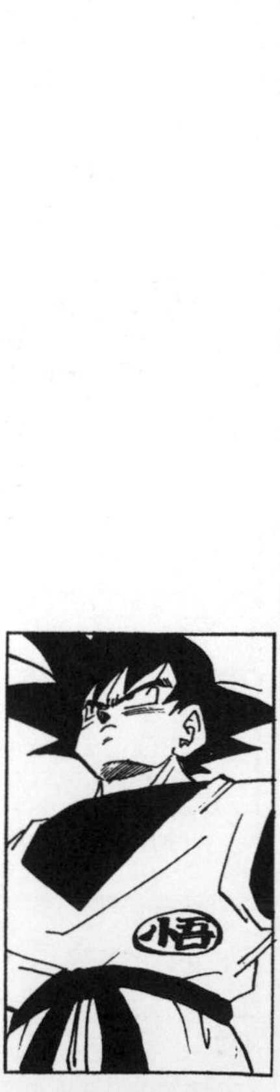
悟

DBZ:122 • The Galaxy Strikes Back!

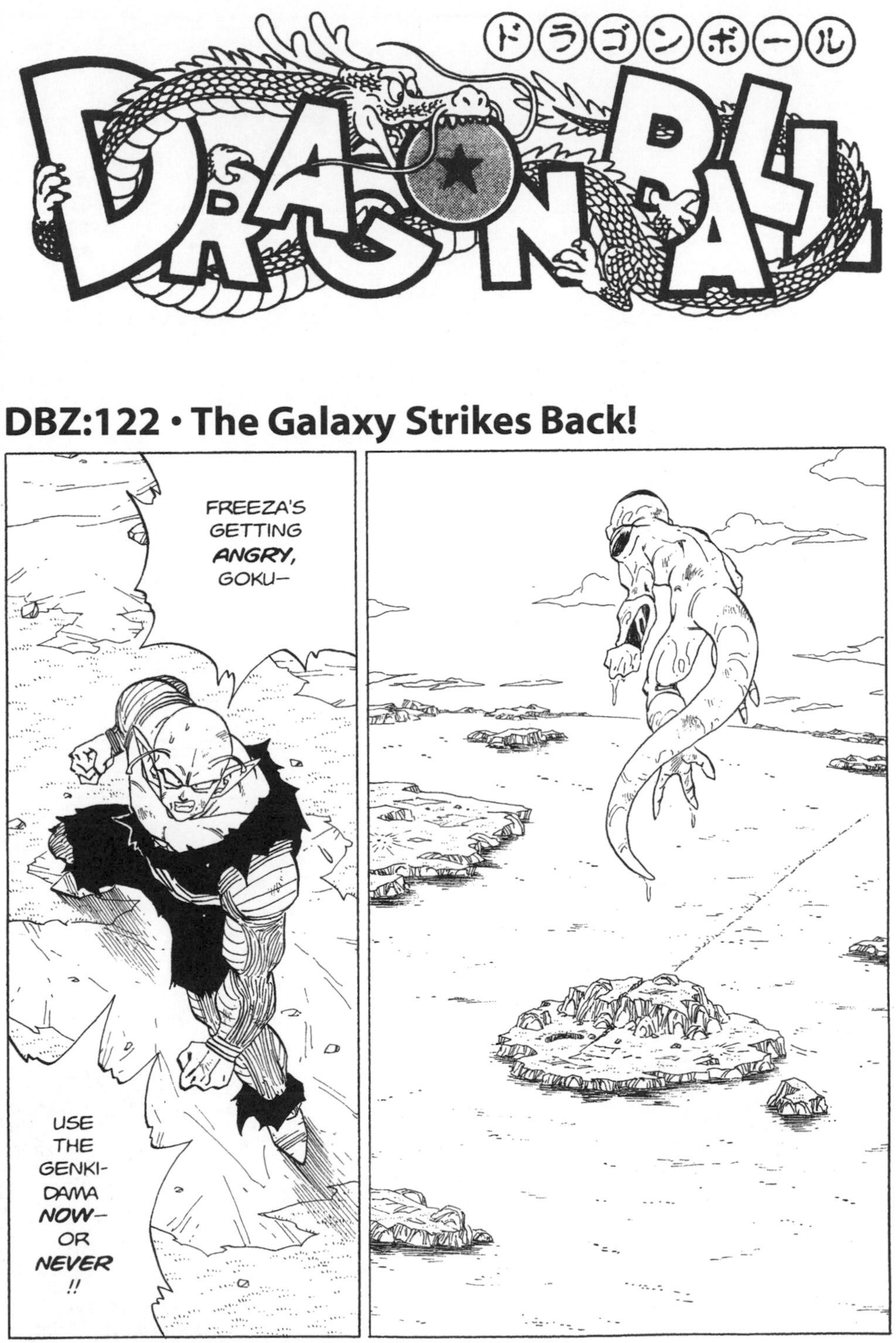
FREEZA'S GETTING ANGRY, GOKU—
USE THE GENKI-DAMA NOW—OR NEVER!!

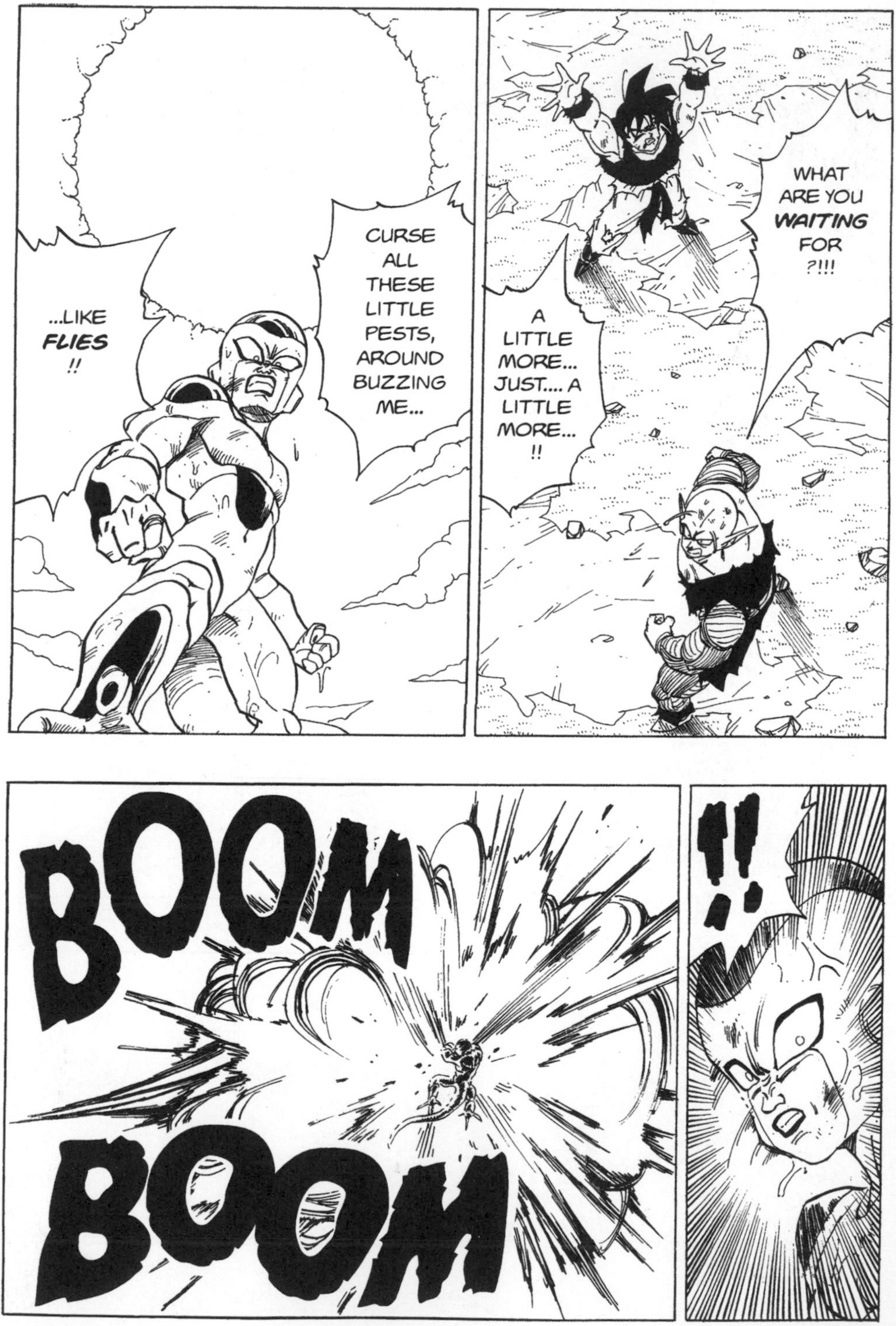
CURSE ALL THESE LITTLE PESTS, AROUND BUZZING ME...
...LIKE **FLIES** !!
WHAT ARE YOU **WAITING** FOR ?!!!
A LITTLE MORE... JUST.... A LITTLE MORE... !!
BOOM
BOOM
!!

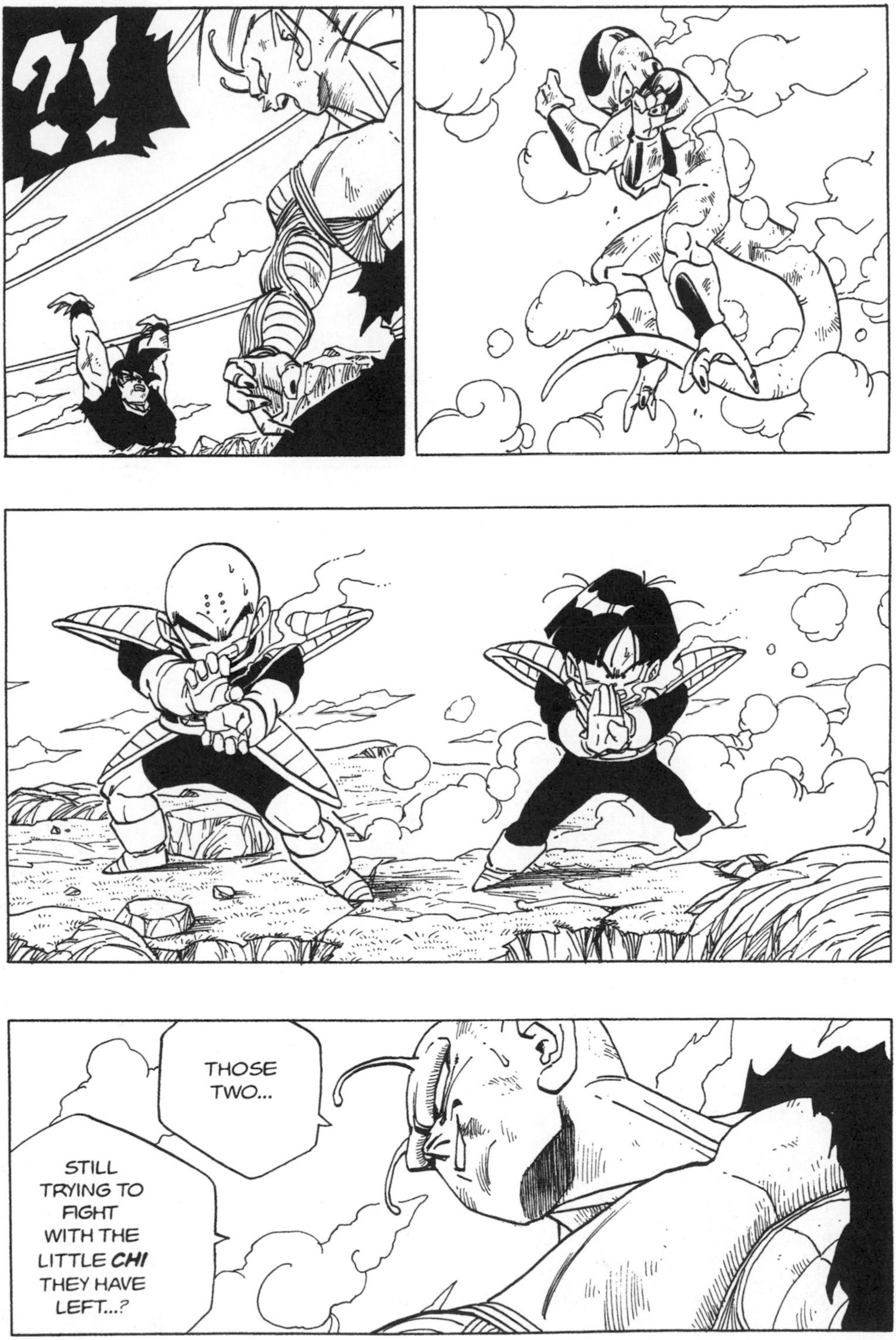
?!
THOSE TWO...
STILL TRYING TO FIGHT WITH THE LITTLE ***CHI*** THEY HAVE LEFT...?

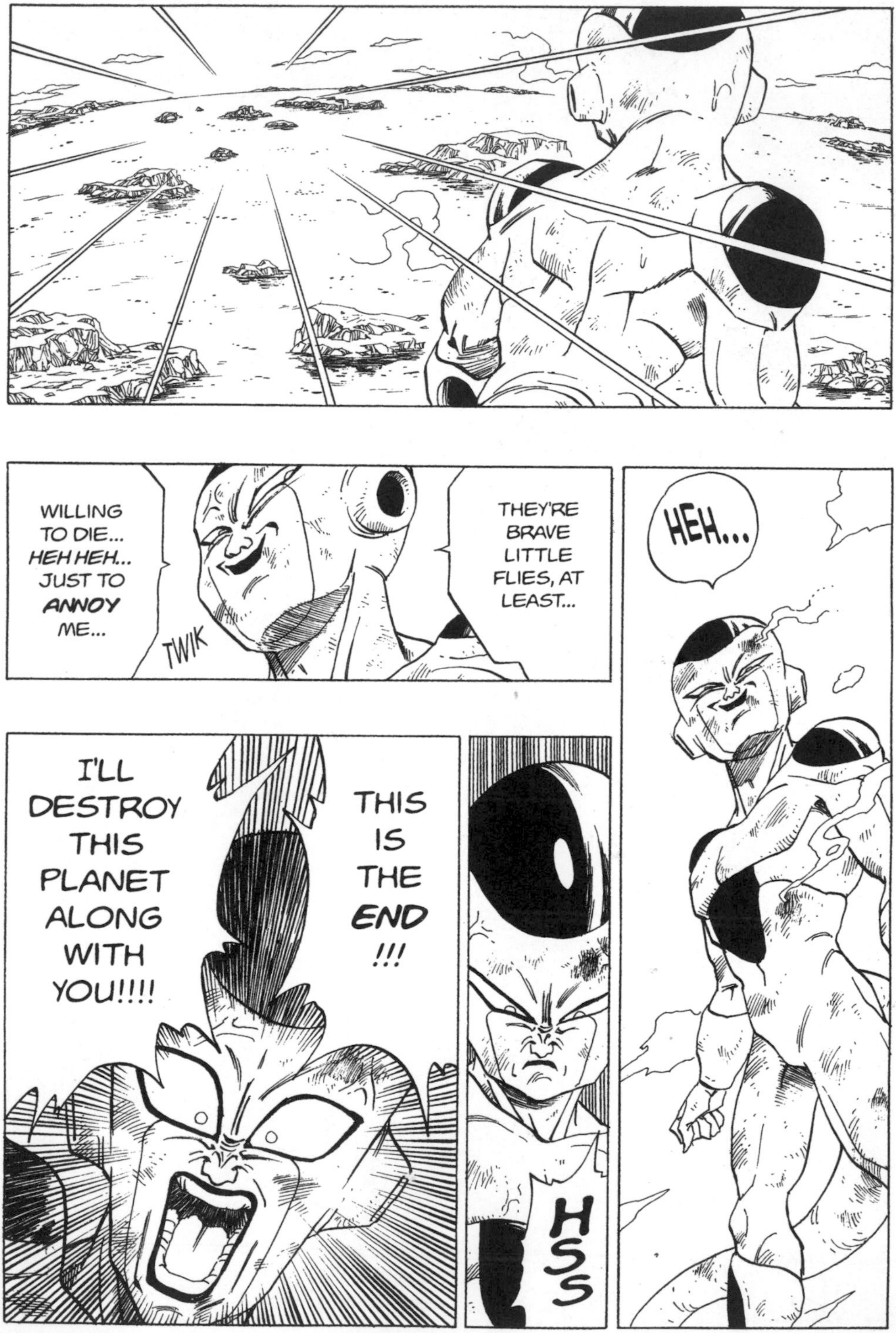
HEH...
THEY'RE BRAVE LITTLE FLIES, AT LEAST...
WILLING TO DIE... HEH HEH... JUST TO ANNOY ME...
TWIK
HSS
THIS IS THE END!!!
I'LL DESTROY THIS PLANET ALONG WITH YOU!!!!!

IT'S DONE!!!! ALL RIGHT!!!

DO IT!!!!

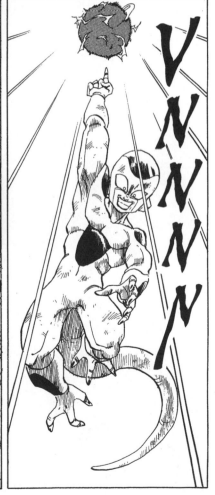

VNNNNN

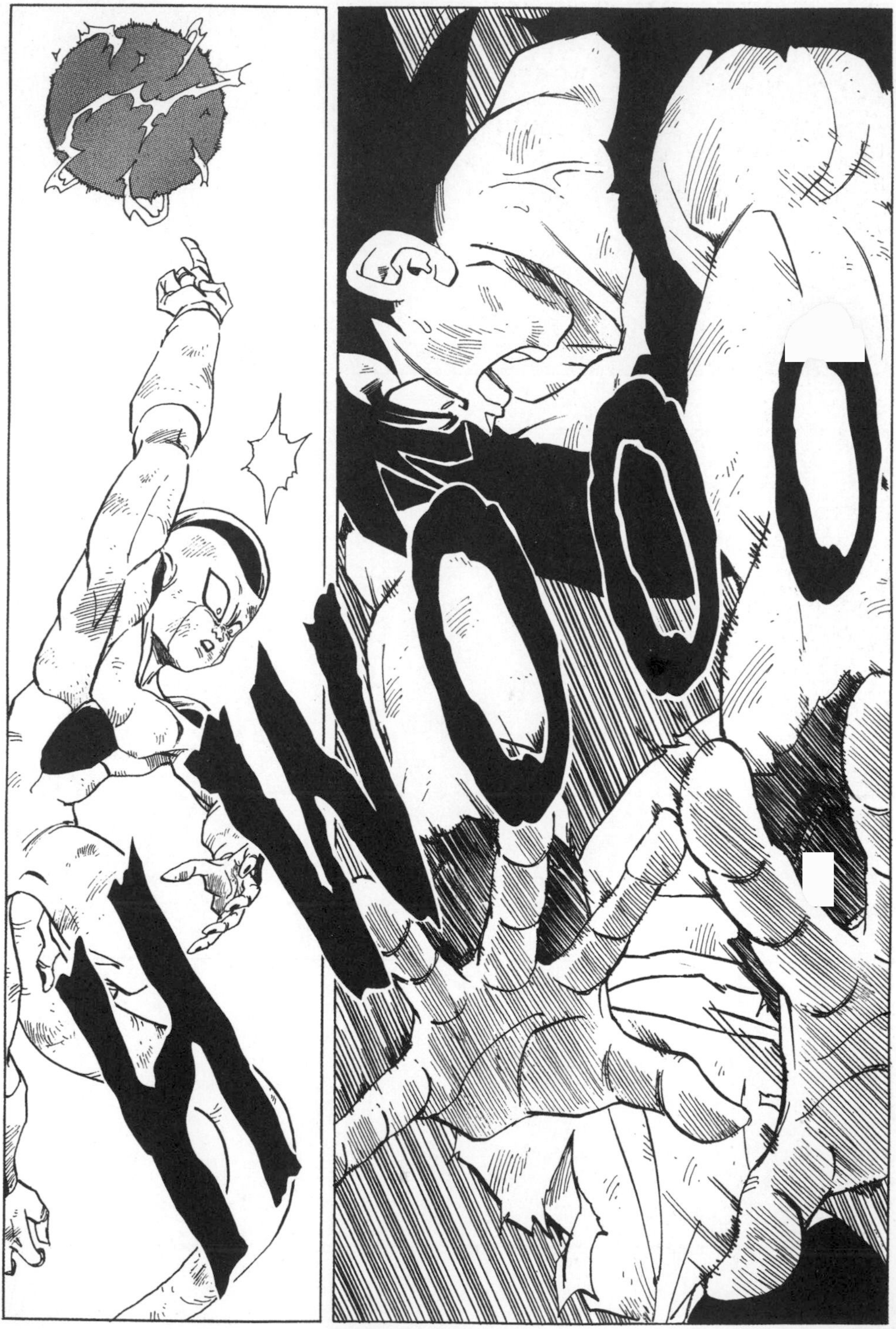

NOOOOO!!

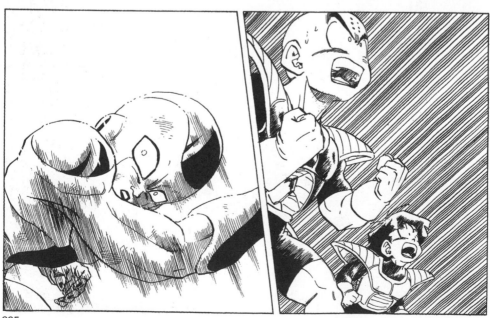

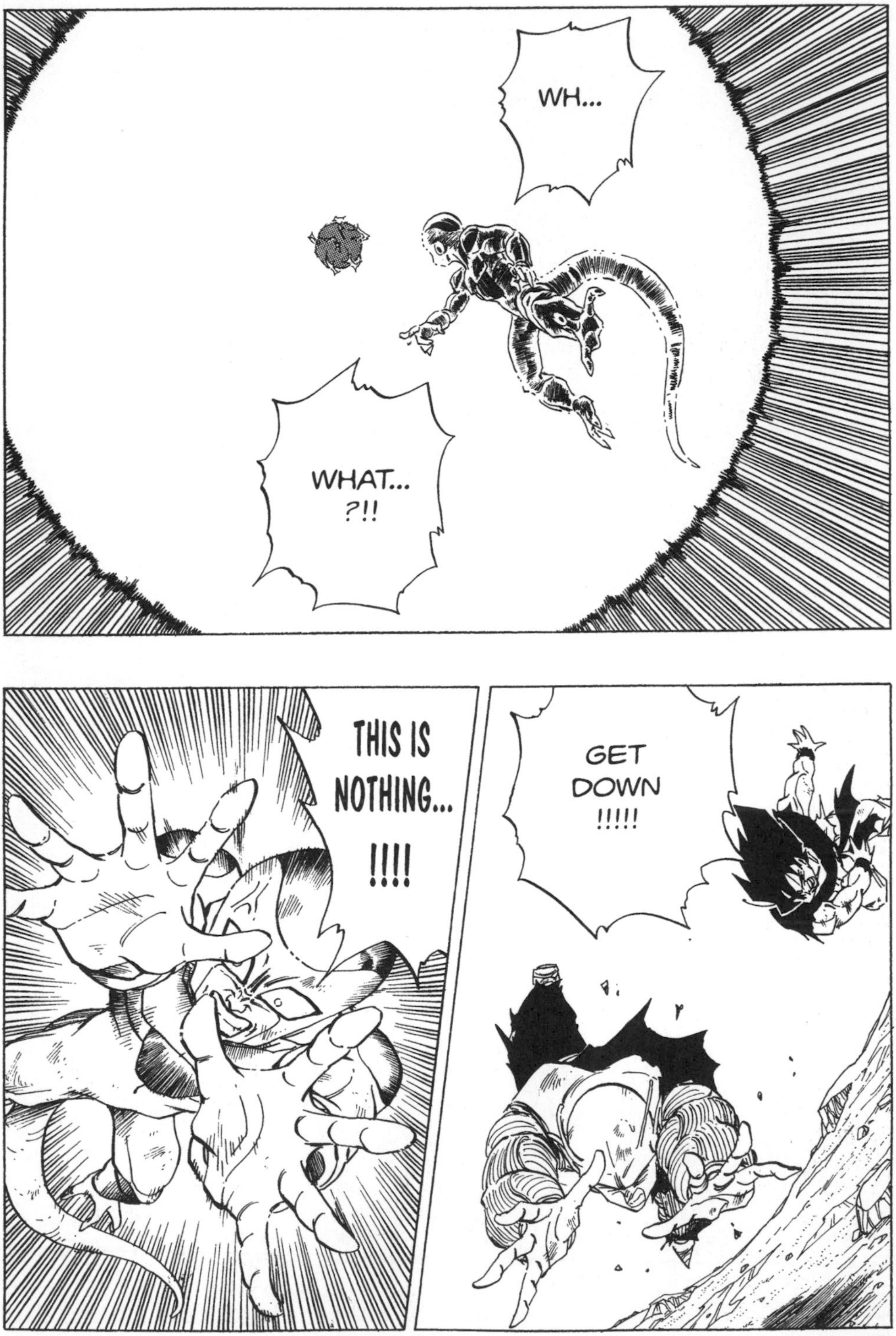
WH...
WHAT... ?!!
GET DOWN !!!!!
THIS IS NOTHING... !!!!

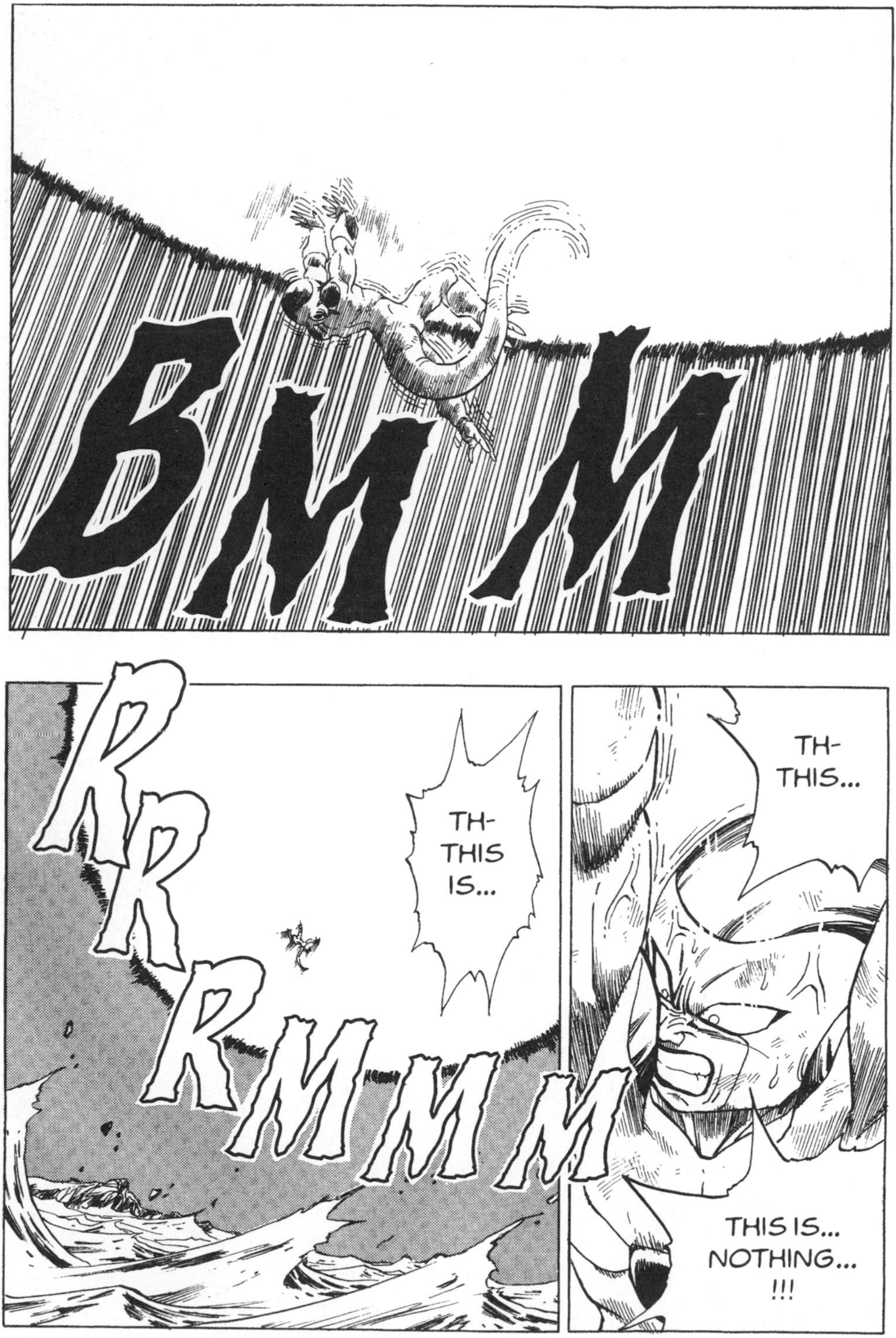
BMM
RRRMMMM
TH-
THIS
IS...
TH-
THIS...
THIS IS...
NOTHING...
!!!

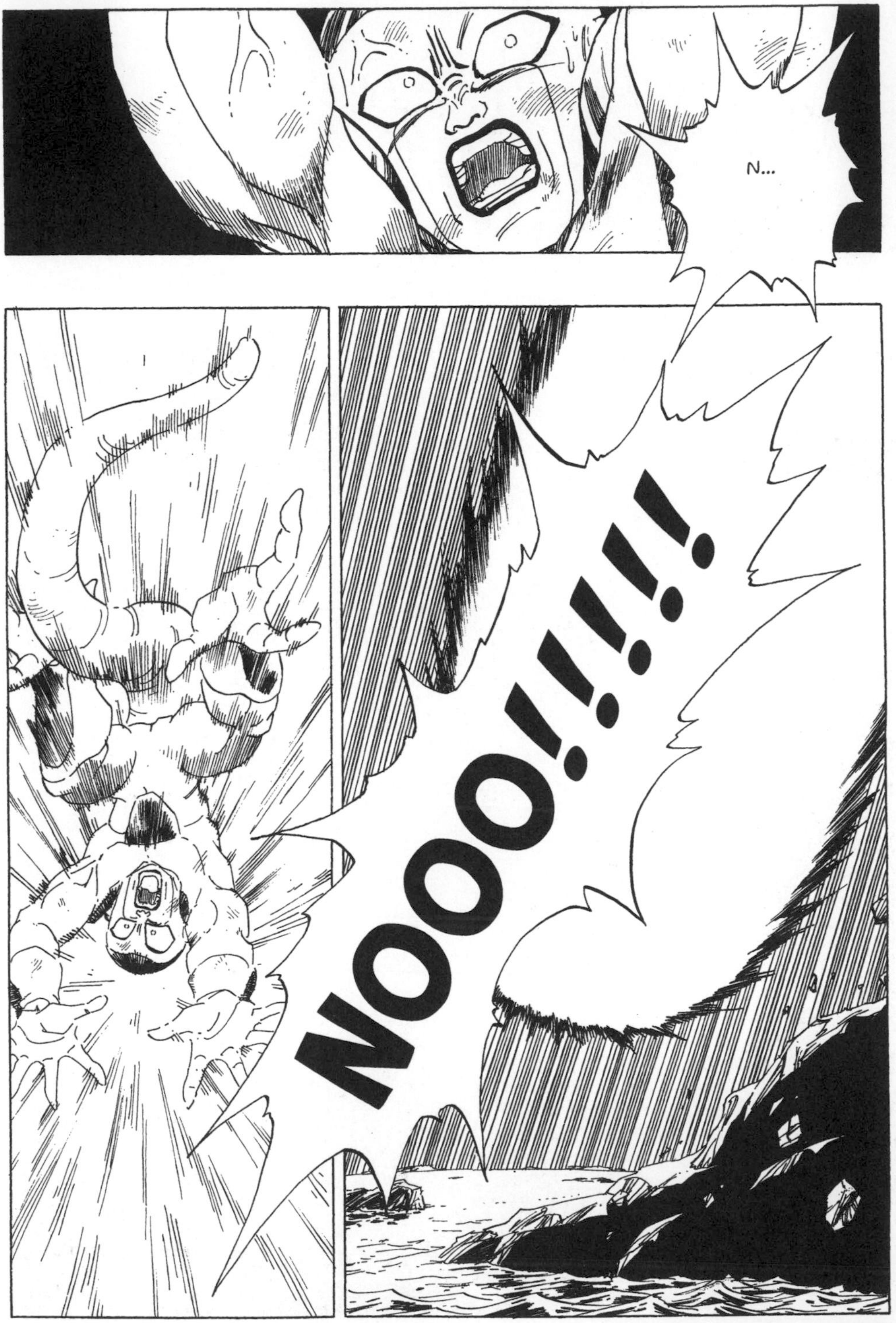
N...
NOOO!!!!!!

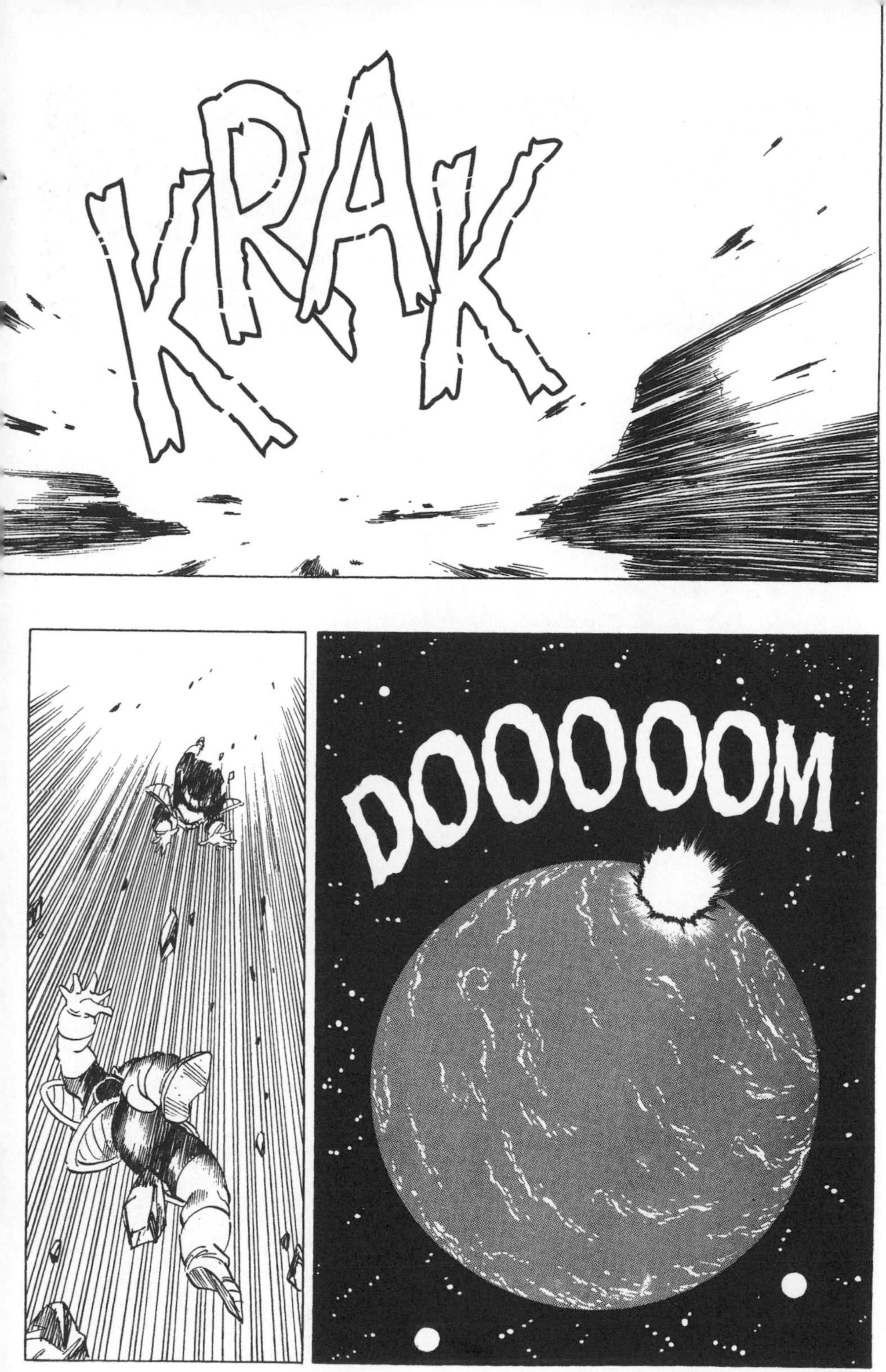
KRAK
DOOOOOM

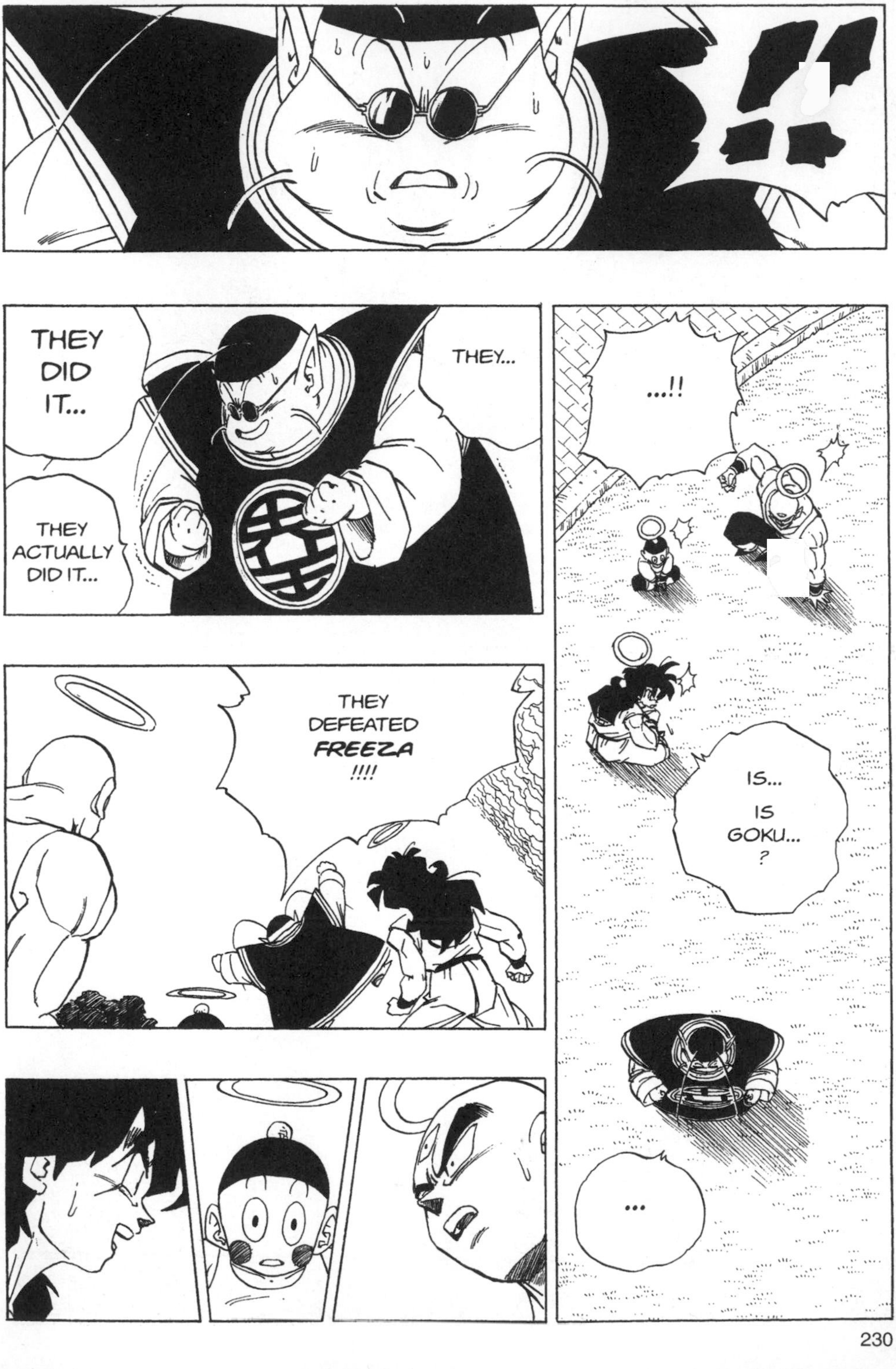
THEY...
THEY DID IT...
THEY ACTUALLY DID IT...
...!!
THEY DEFEATED FREEZA !!!!
IS... IS GOKU... ?
...

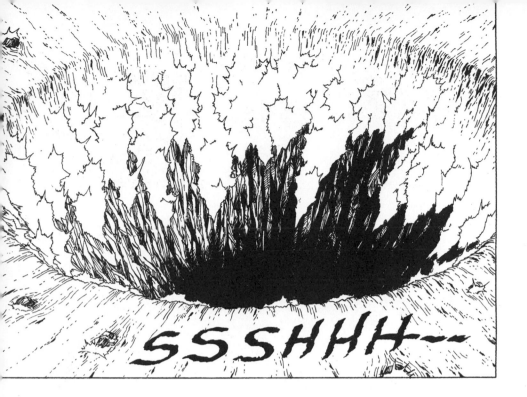

SSSHHH~~

K-KURIRIN...

HUFF

HUFF

...

RRRRR...

B-BUT WHERE'S DAD AND...

YEAH...

Y... YOU'RE ALIVE...

DBZ:123 • Life or Death

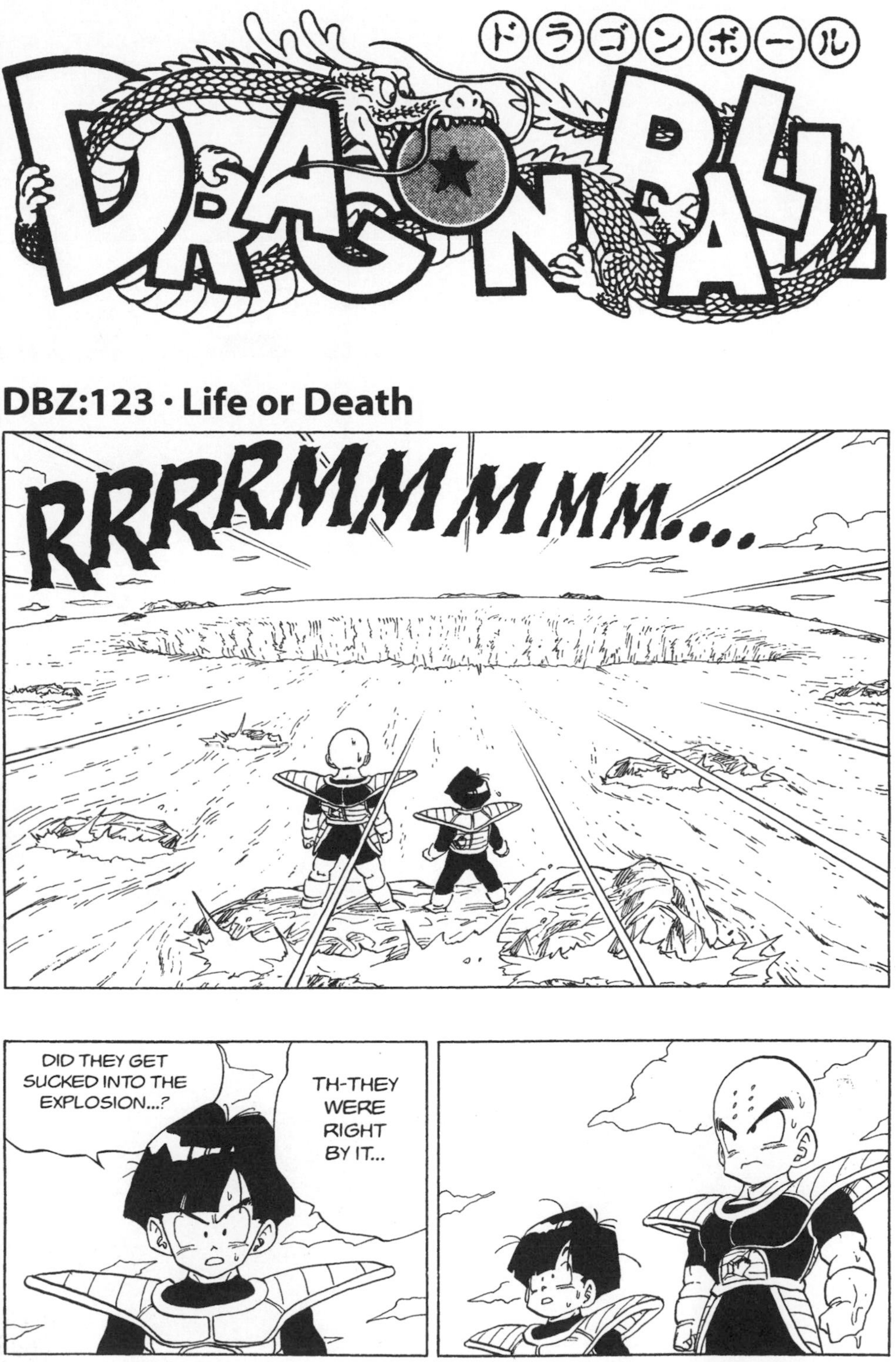

RRRRMMMMM....
DID THEY GET SUCKED INTO THE EXPLOSION...?
TH-THEY WERE RIGHT BY IT...

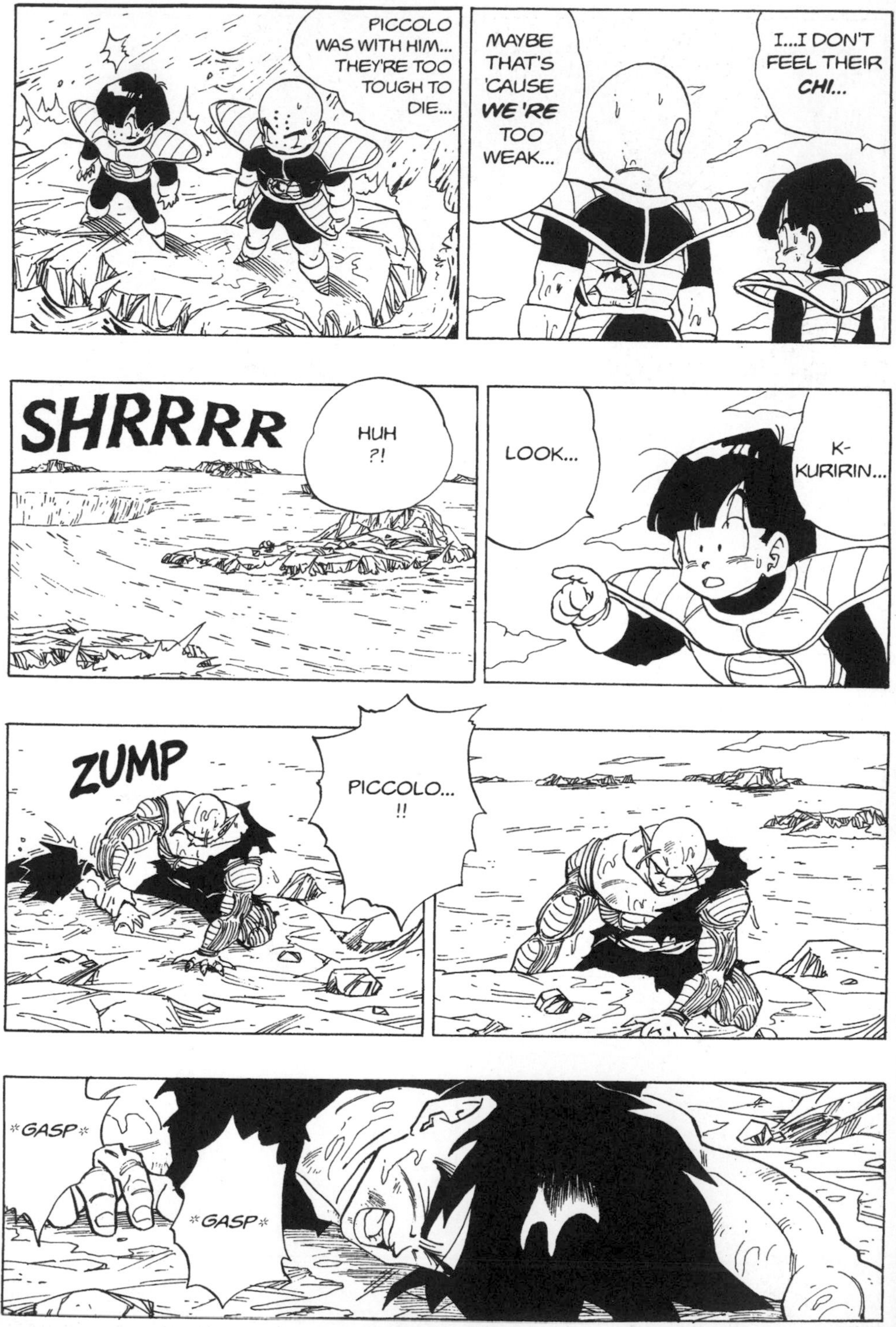
PICCOLO WAS WITH HIM... THEY'RE TOO TOUGH TO DIE...
I...I DON'T FEEL THEIR CHI...
MAYBE THAT'S 'CAUSE WE'RE TOO WEAK...
HUH ?!
SHRRRR
K-KURIRIN...
LOOK...
PICCOLO... !!
ZUMP
GASP
GASP

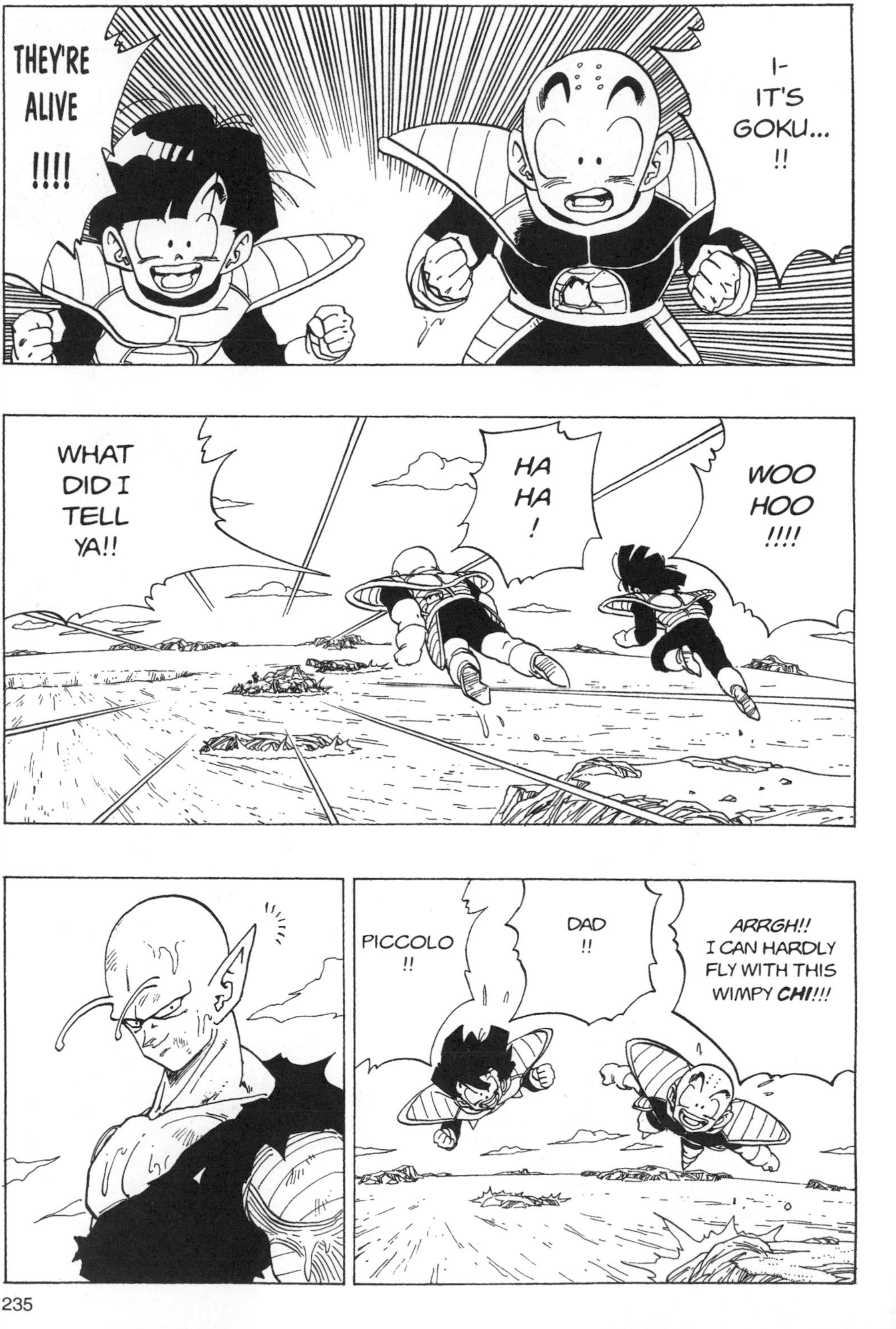
THEY'RE ALIVE !!!!
I- IT'S GOKU... !!
WHAT DID I TELL YA!!
HA HA !
WOO HOO !!!!
PICCOLO !!
DAD !!
ARRGH!! I CAN HARDLY FLY WITH THIS WIMPY CHI!!!

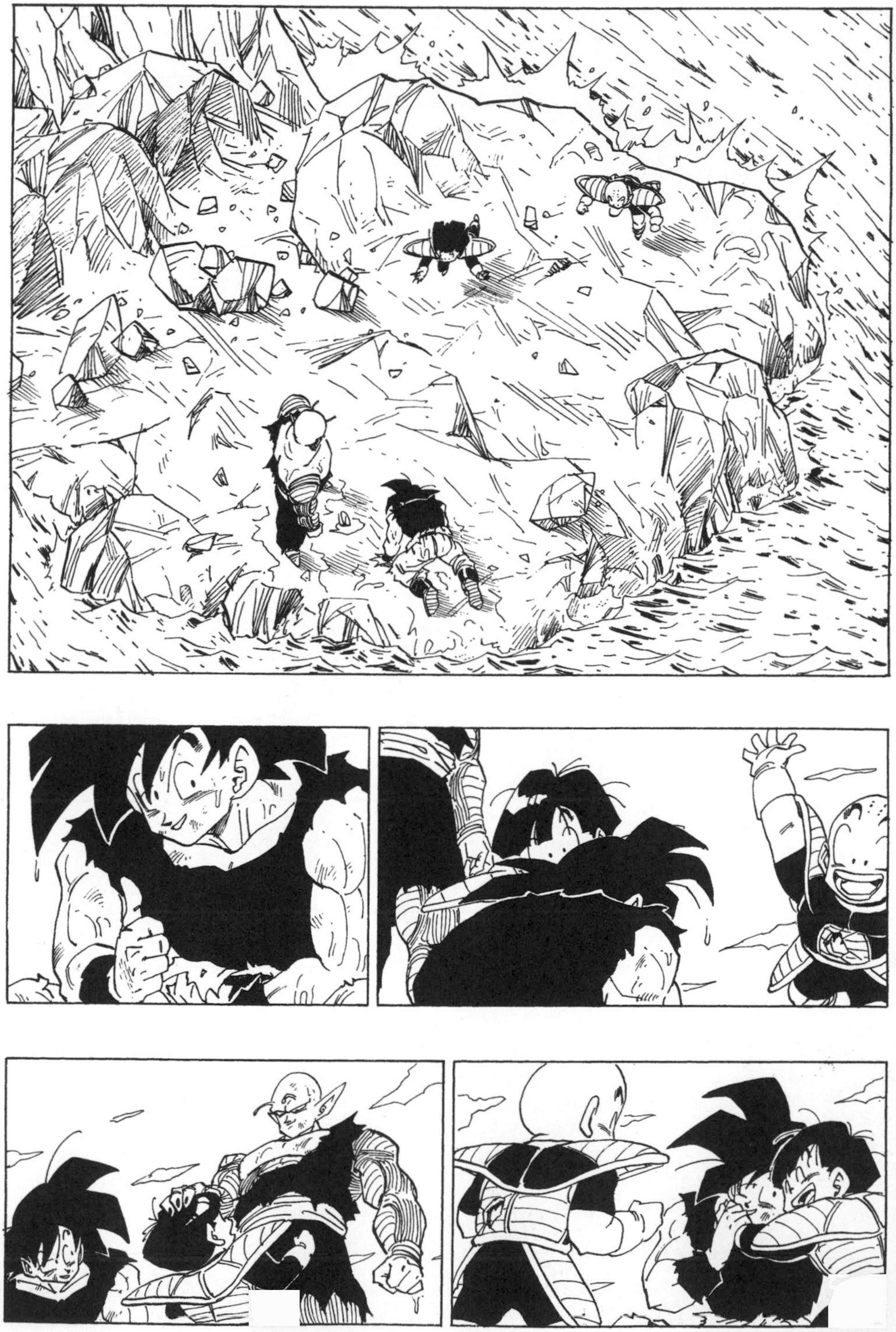

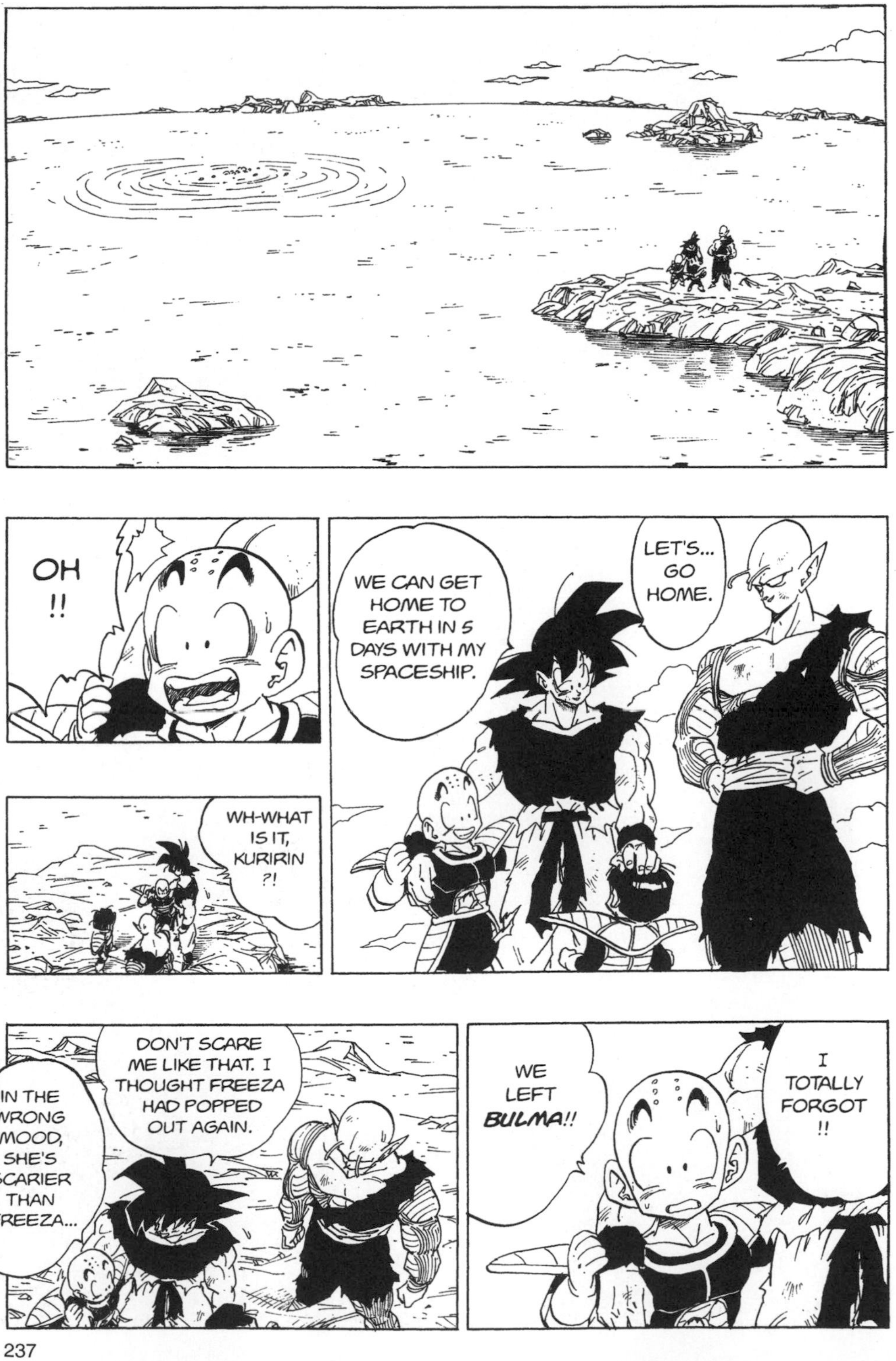
LET'S... GO HOME.
WE CAN GET HOME TO EARTH IN 5 DAYS WITH MY SPACESHIP.
OH !!
WH-WHAT IS IT, KURIRIN ?!
I TOTALLY FORGOT !!
WE LEFT BULMA!!
DON'T SCARE ME LIKE THAT. I THOUGHT FREEZA HAD POPPED OUT AGAIN.
IN THE WRONG MOOD, SHE'S SCARIER THAN FREEZA...

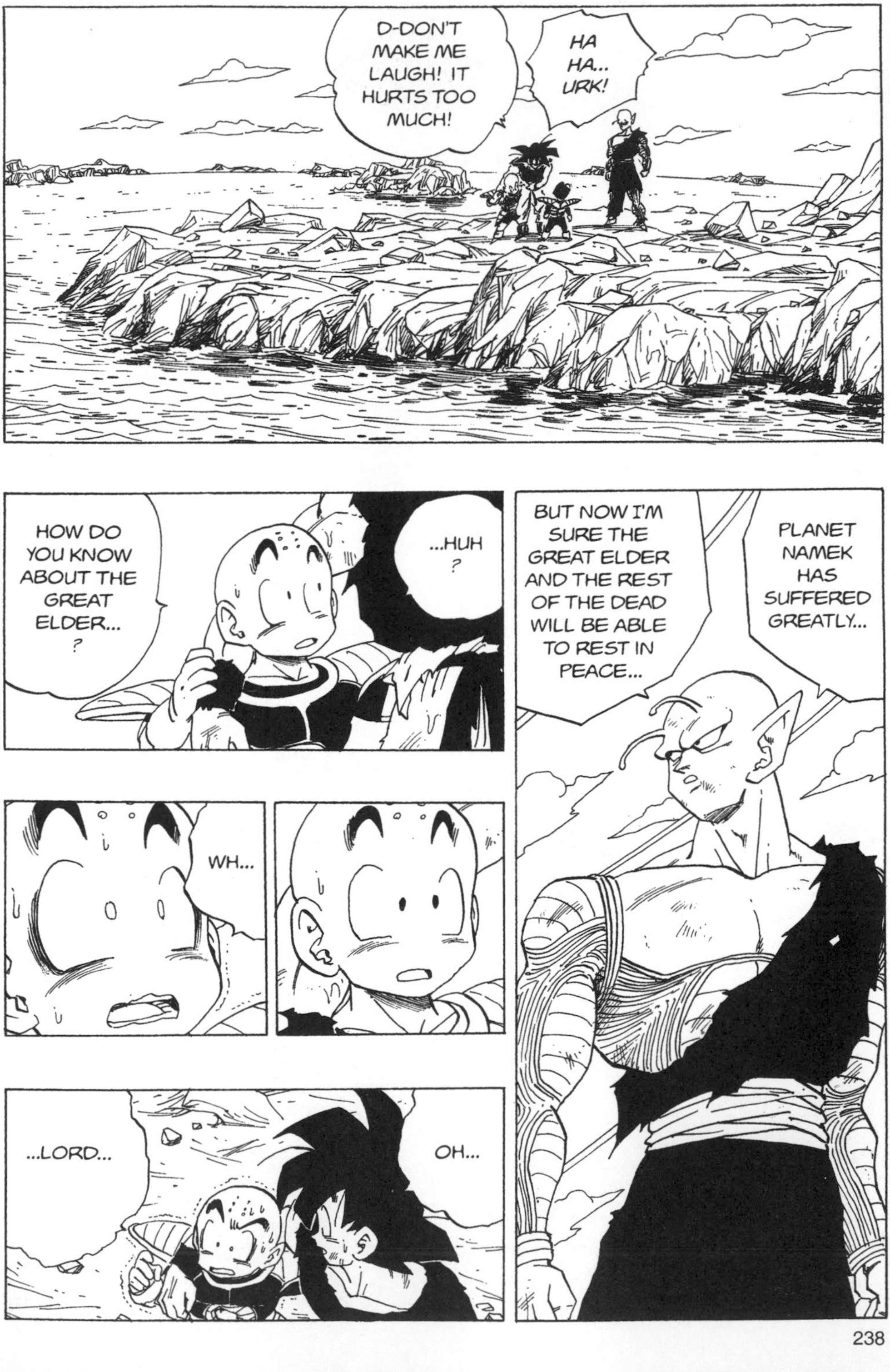
HA HA... URK!
D-DON'T MAKE ME LAUGH! IT HURTS TOO MUCH!
PLANET NAMEK HAS SUFFERED GREATLY...
BUT NOW I'M SURE THE GREAT ELDER AND THE REST OF THE DEAD WILL BE ABLE TO REST IN PEACE...
...HUH ?
HOW DO YOU KNOW ABOUT THE GREAT ELDER... ?
WH...
OH...
...LORD...

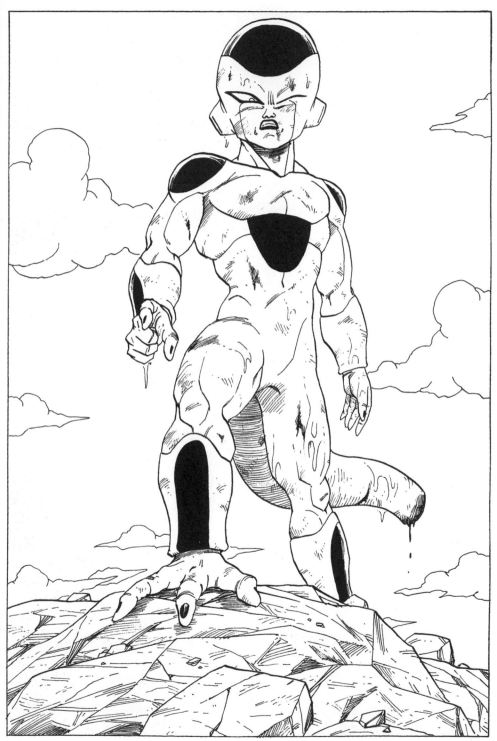

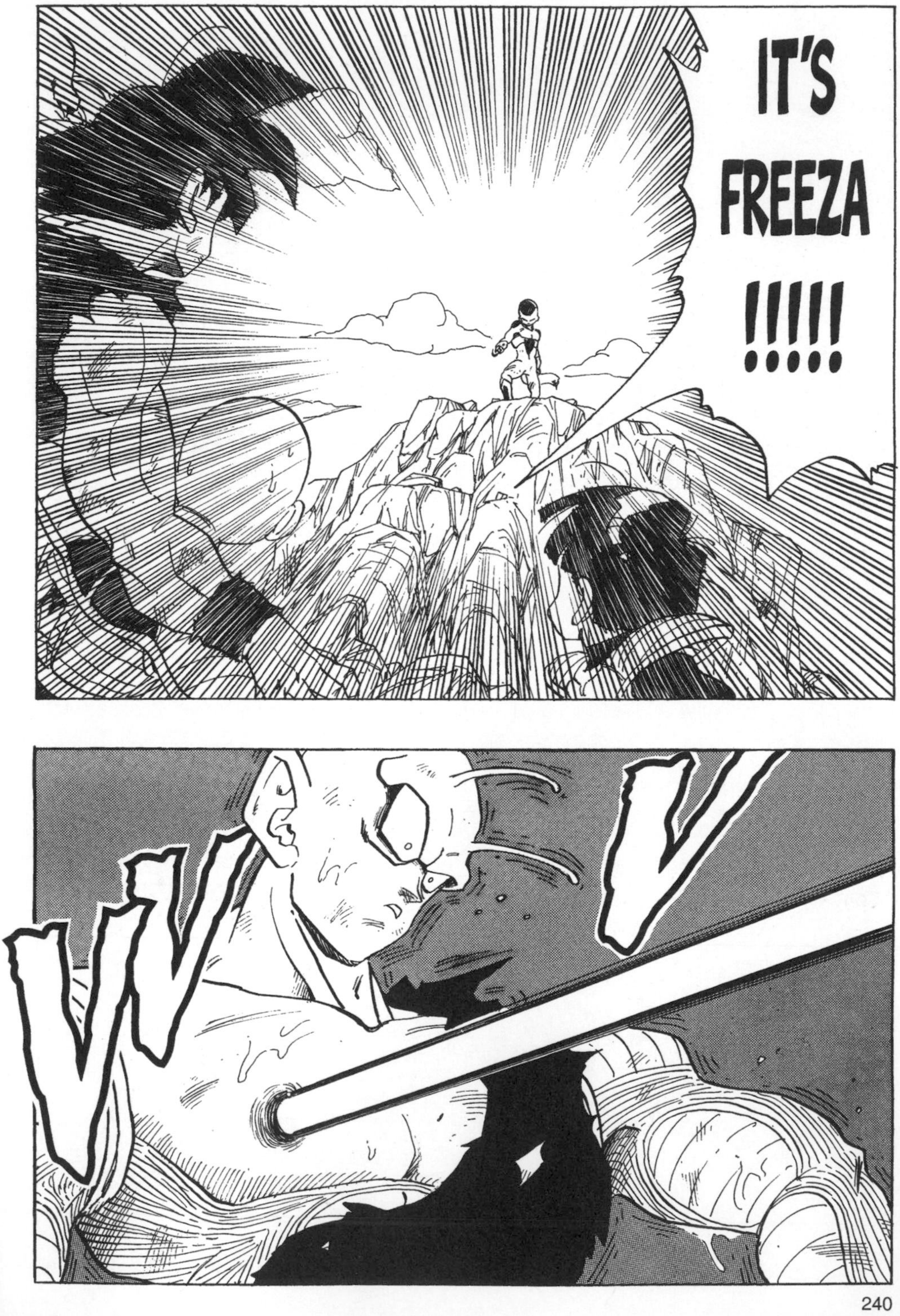
IT'S FREEZA !!!!!

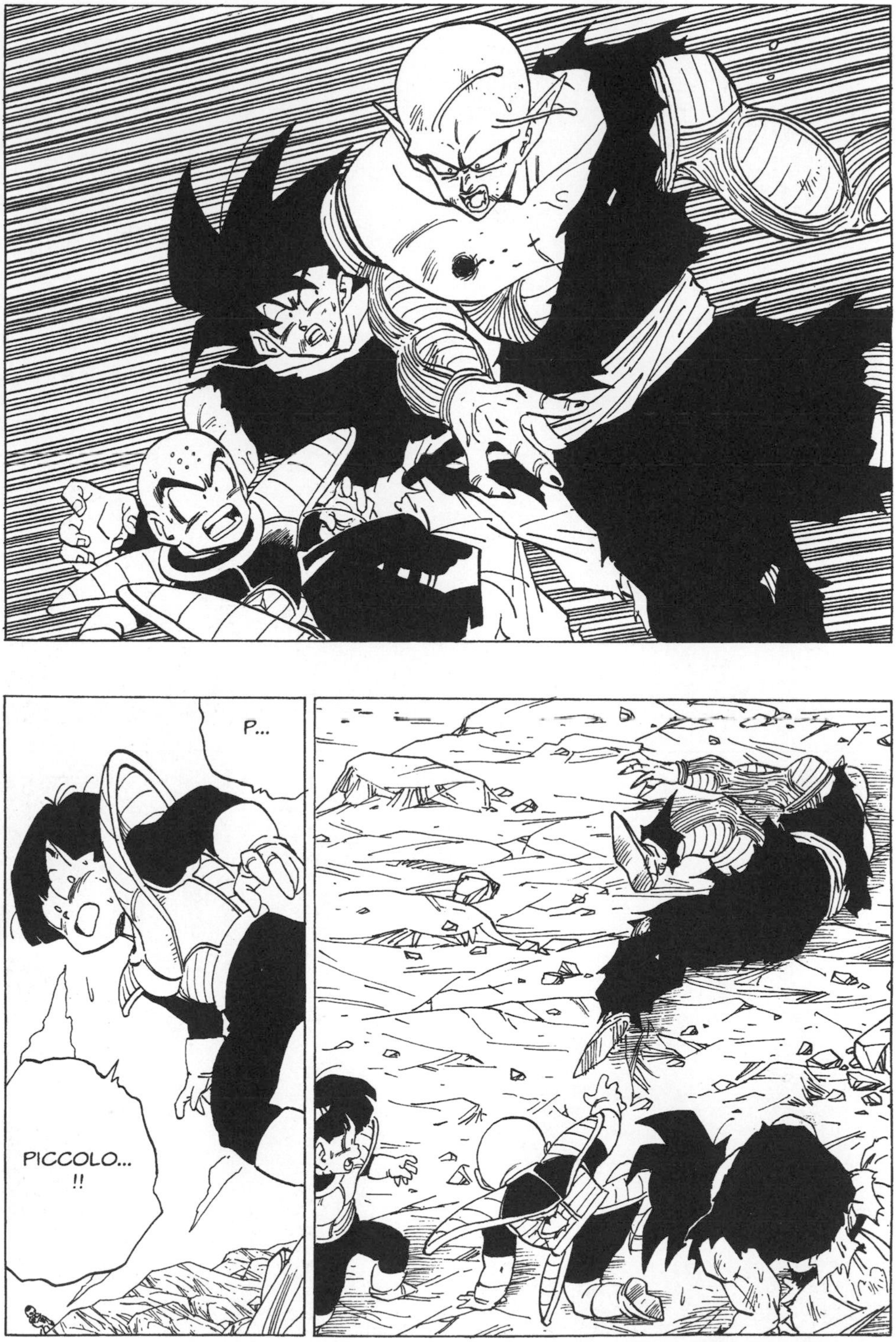
P...
PICCOLO... !!

PICCOLO !!!
EVEN I THOUGHT I WAS DEAD...
I NEARLY WAS...

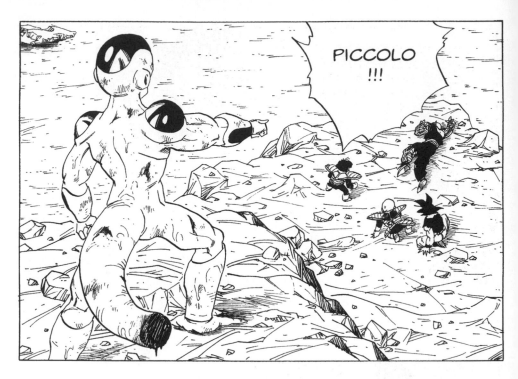

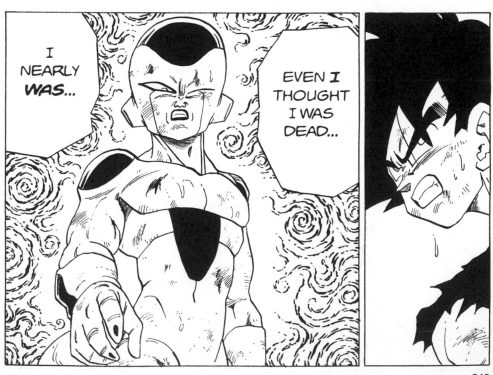

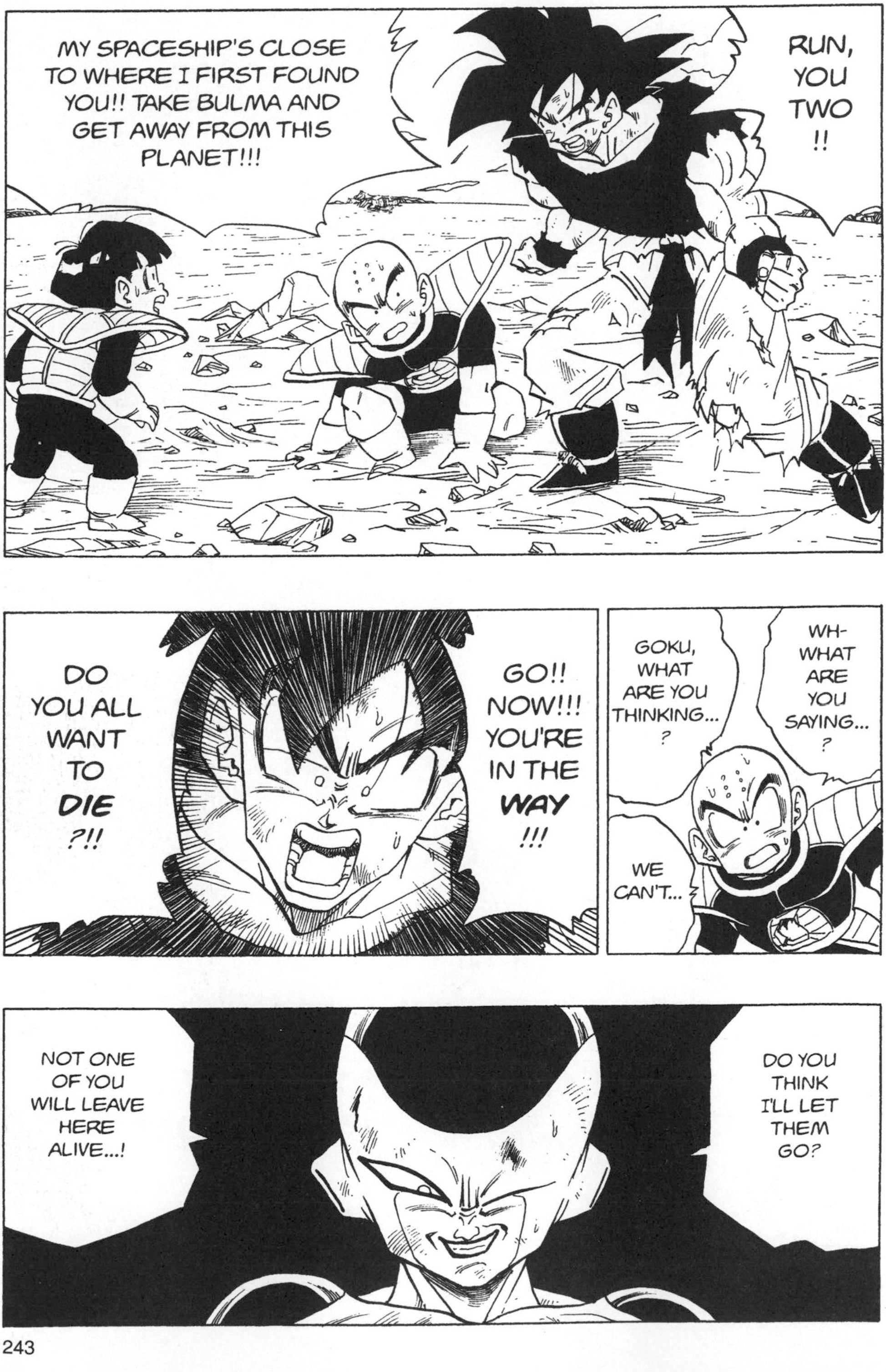
MY SPACESHIP'S CLOSE TO WHERE I FIRST FOUND YOU!! TAKE BULMA AND GET AWAY FROM THIS PLANET!!!
RUN, YOU TWO !!
DO YOU ALL WANT TO DIE ?!!
GO!! NOW!!! YOU'RE IN THE WAY !!!
GOKU, WHAT ARE YOU THINKING... ?
WH- WHAT ARE YOU SAYING... ?
WE CAN'T...
NOT ONE OF YOU WILL LEAVE HERE ALIVE...!
DO YOU THINK I'LL LET THEM GO?

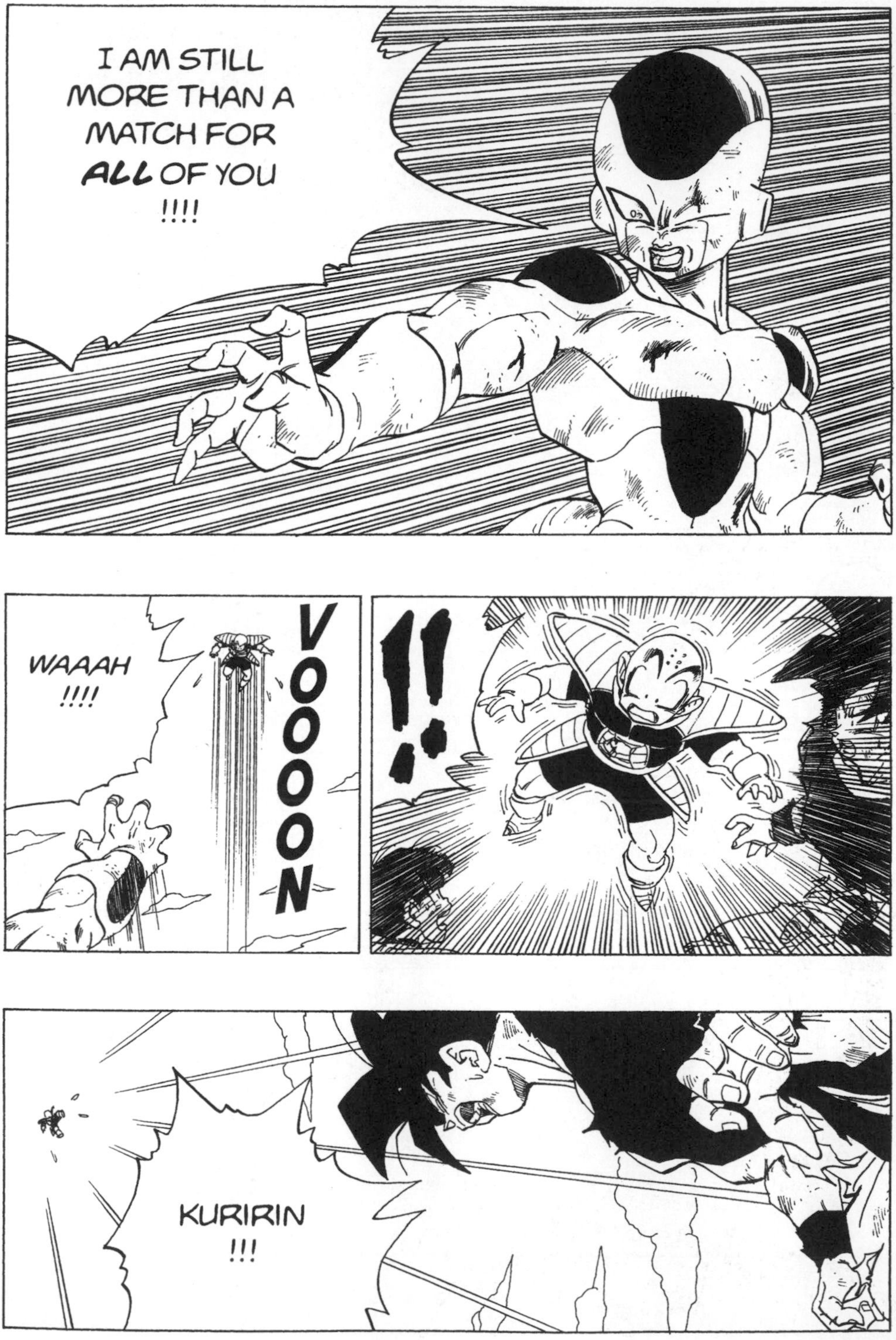
I AM STILL MORE THAN A MATCH FOR ALL OF YOU !!!!
!!
VOOOOON
WAAAH !!!!
KURIRIN !!!

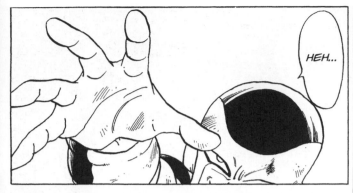

HEH...

GOKU
!!!!!

S-STOP
IT,
FREEZA
!!!!!

DOOM

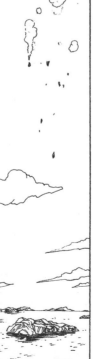

HEH HEH HEH...

WHO'S NEXT— THE BRAT?

Y-YOU'RE NOT... GONNA GET AWAY WITH THIS...
I JUST... WON'T.... LET YOU...
NNN NNNN
PW ICH
?!
BRRR
EH ?!

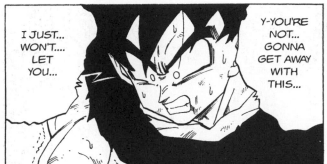

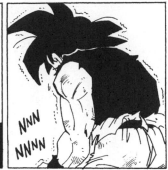

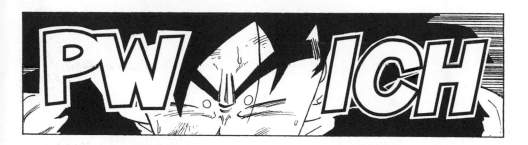

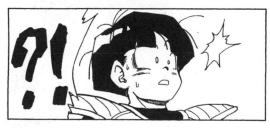

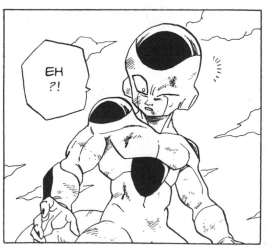

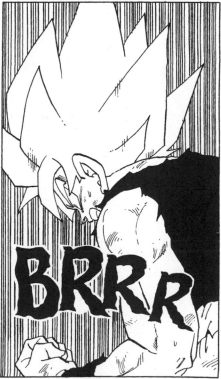

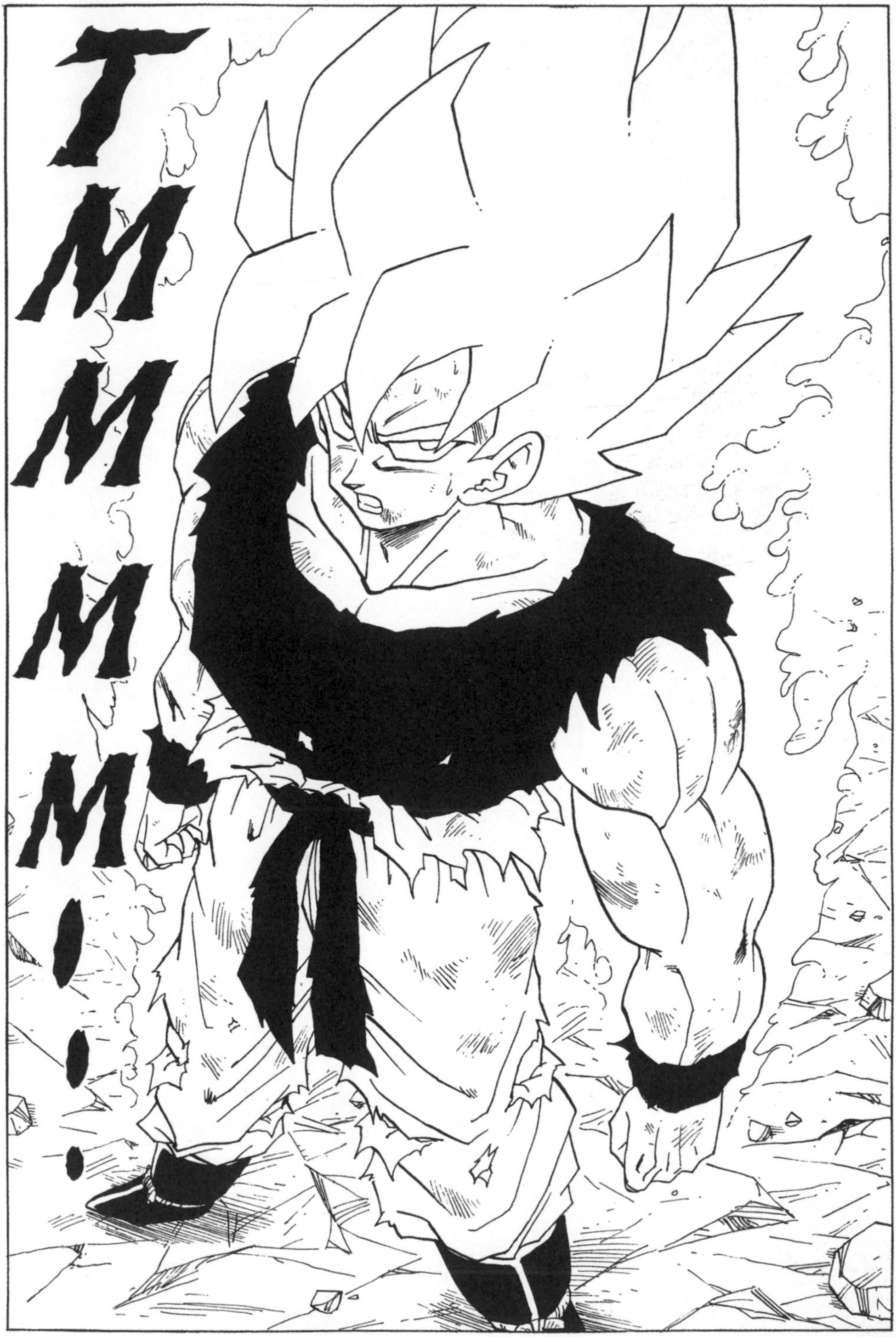
TMMMM......

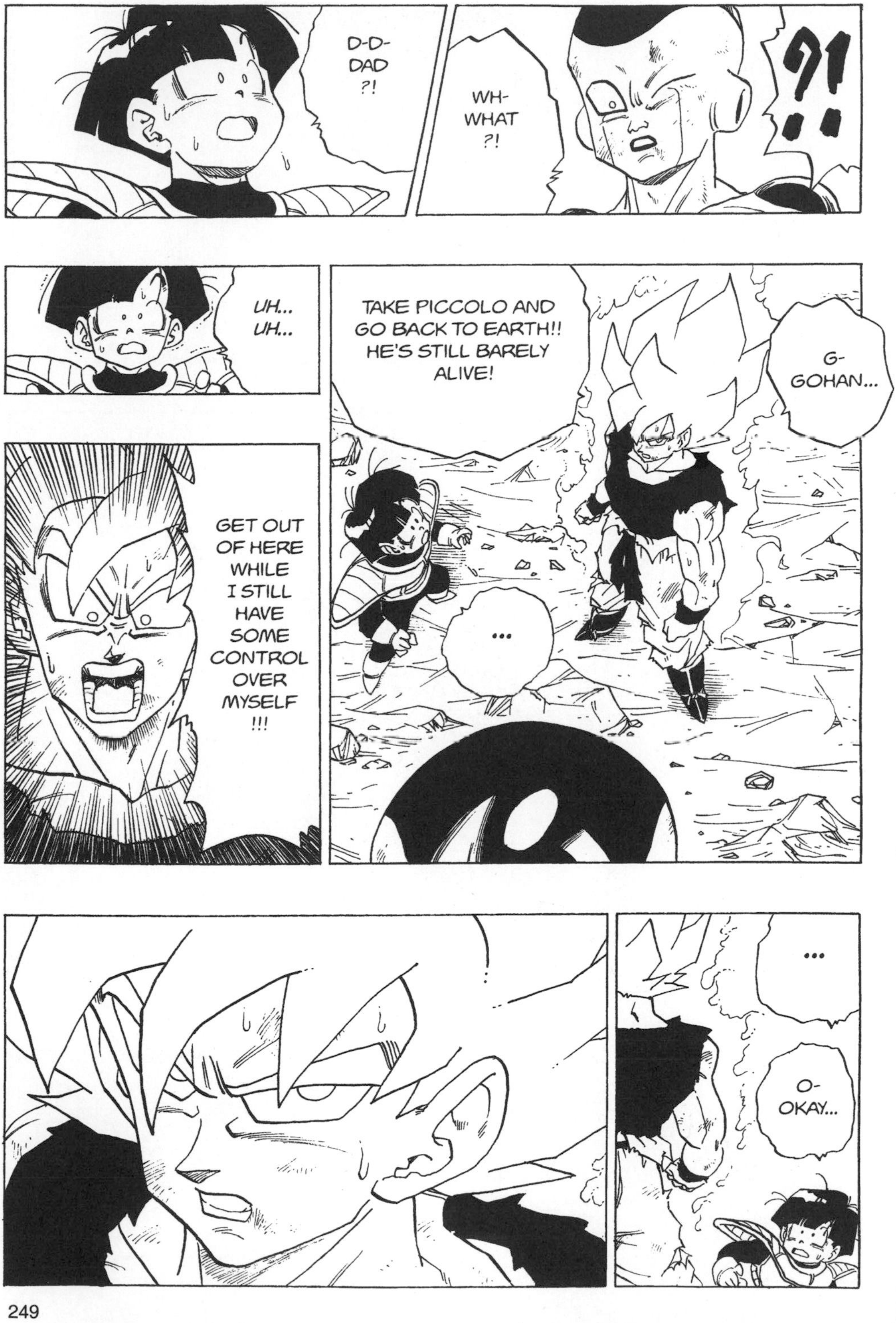
D-D-DAD ?!
WH-WHAT ?!
?!
UH... UH...
TAKE PICCOLO AND GO BACK TO EARTH!! HE'S STILL BARELY ALIVE!
G-GOHAN...
...
GET OUT OF HERE WHILE I STILL HAVE SOME CONTROL OVER MYSELF !!!
...
O-OKAY...

DBZ:124 • The Super Saiyan

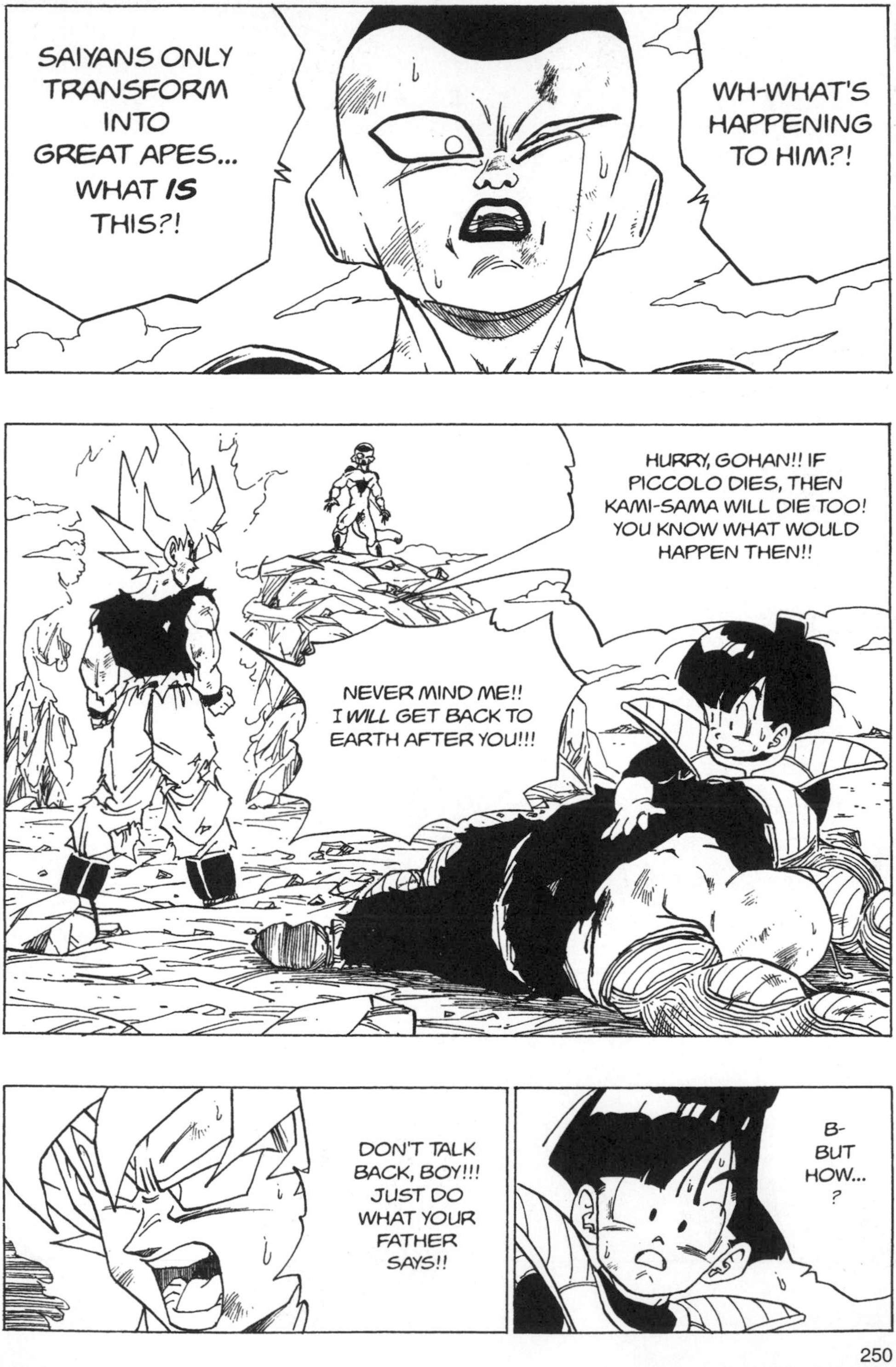
WH-WHAT'S HAPPENING TO HIM?!
SAIYANS ONLY TRANSFORM INTO GREAT APES... WHAT *IS* THIS?!
HURRY, GOHAN!! IF PICCOLO DIES, THEN KAMI-SAMA WILL DIE TOO! YOU KNOW WHAT WOULD HAPPEN THEN!!
NEVER MIND ME!! I *WILL* GET BACK TO EARTH AFTER YOU!!!
B-BUT HOW...?
DON'T TALK BACK, BOY!!! JUST DO WHAT YOUR FATHER SAYS!!

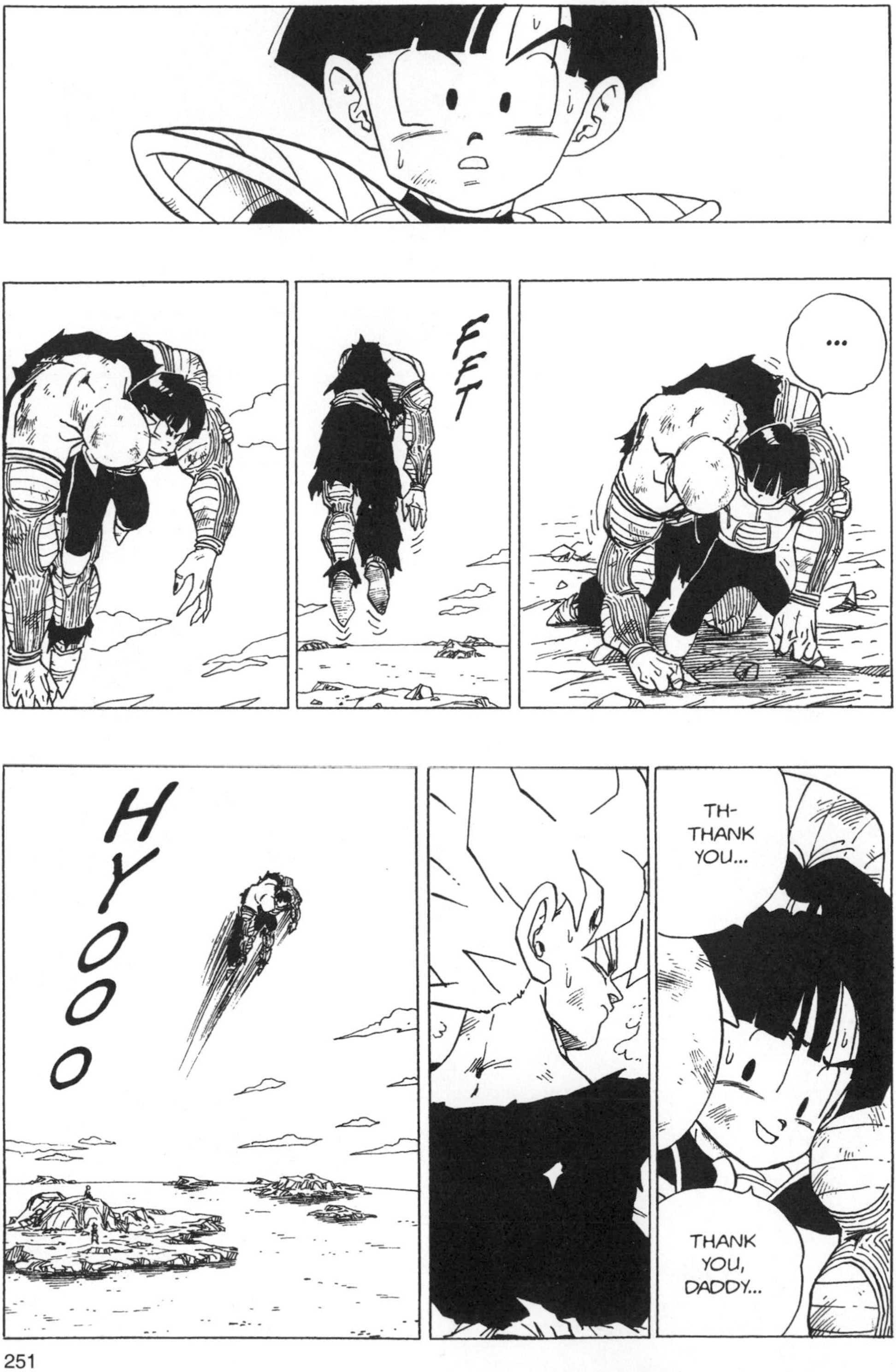
FFT
...
HYOOO
TH-
THANK
YOU...
THANK
YOU,
DADDY...

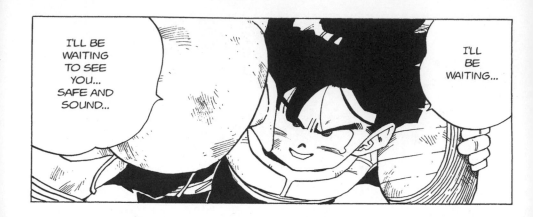

I'LL BE WAITING TO SEE YOU... SAFE AND SOUND...

I'LL BE WAITING...

VOON

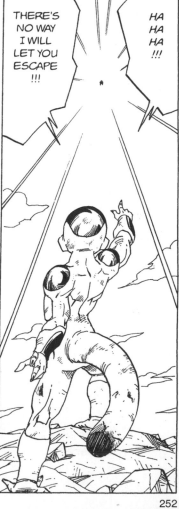

THERE'S NO WAY I WILL LET YOU ESCAPE !!!

HA HA HA !!!

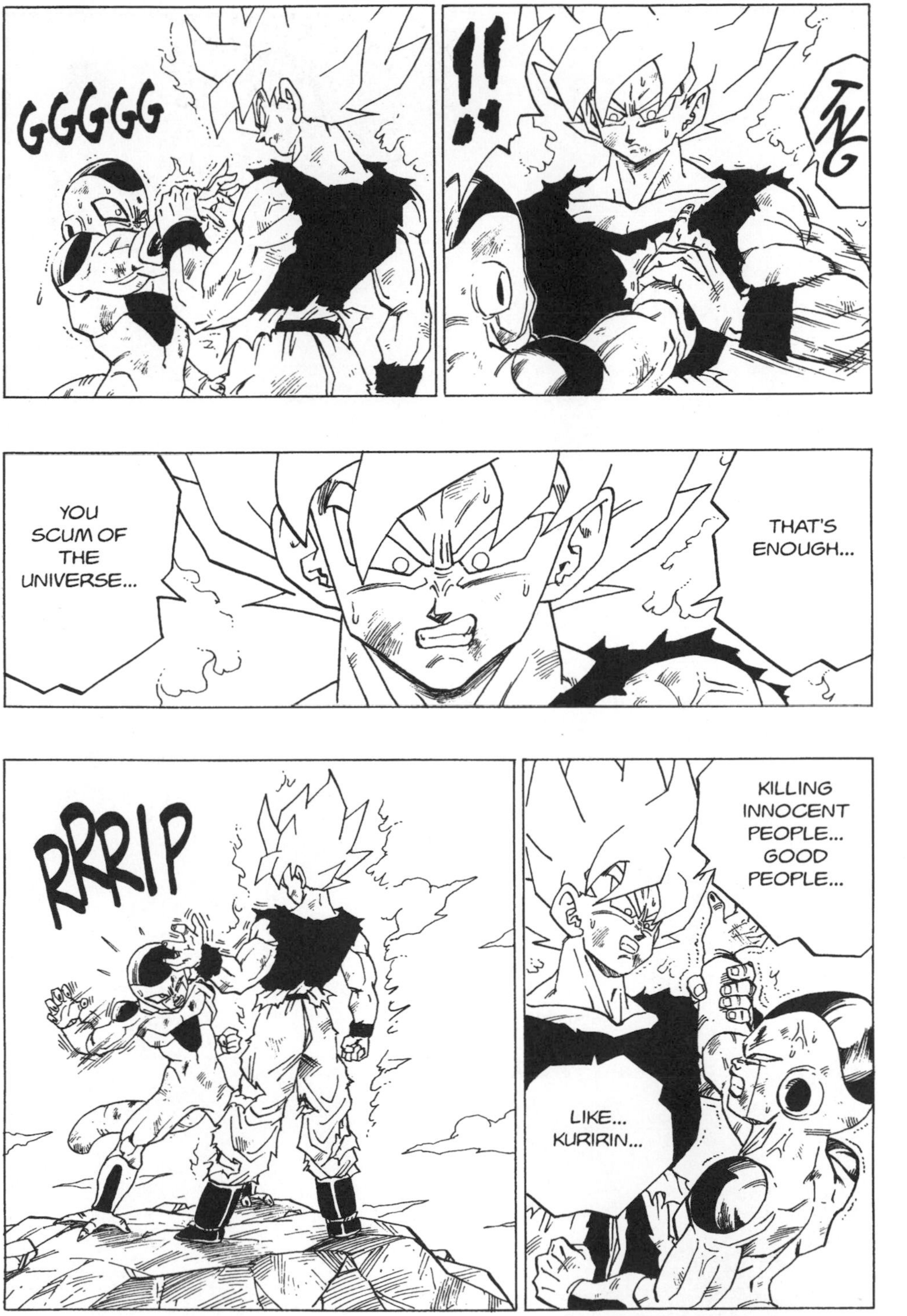

TNG
!!
GGGGG
THAT'S ENOUGH...
YOU SCUM OF THE UNIVERSE...
KILLING INNOCENT PEOPLE... GOOD PEOPLE...
LIKE... KURIRIN...
RRRIP

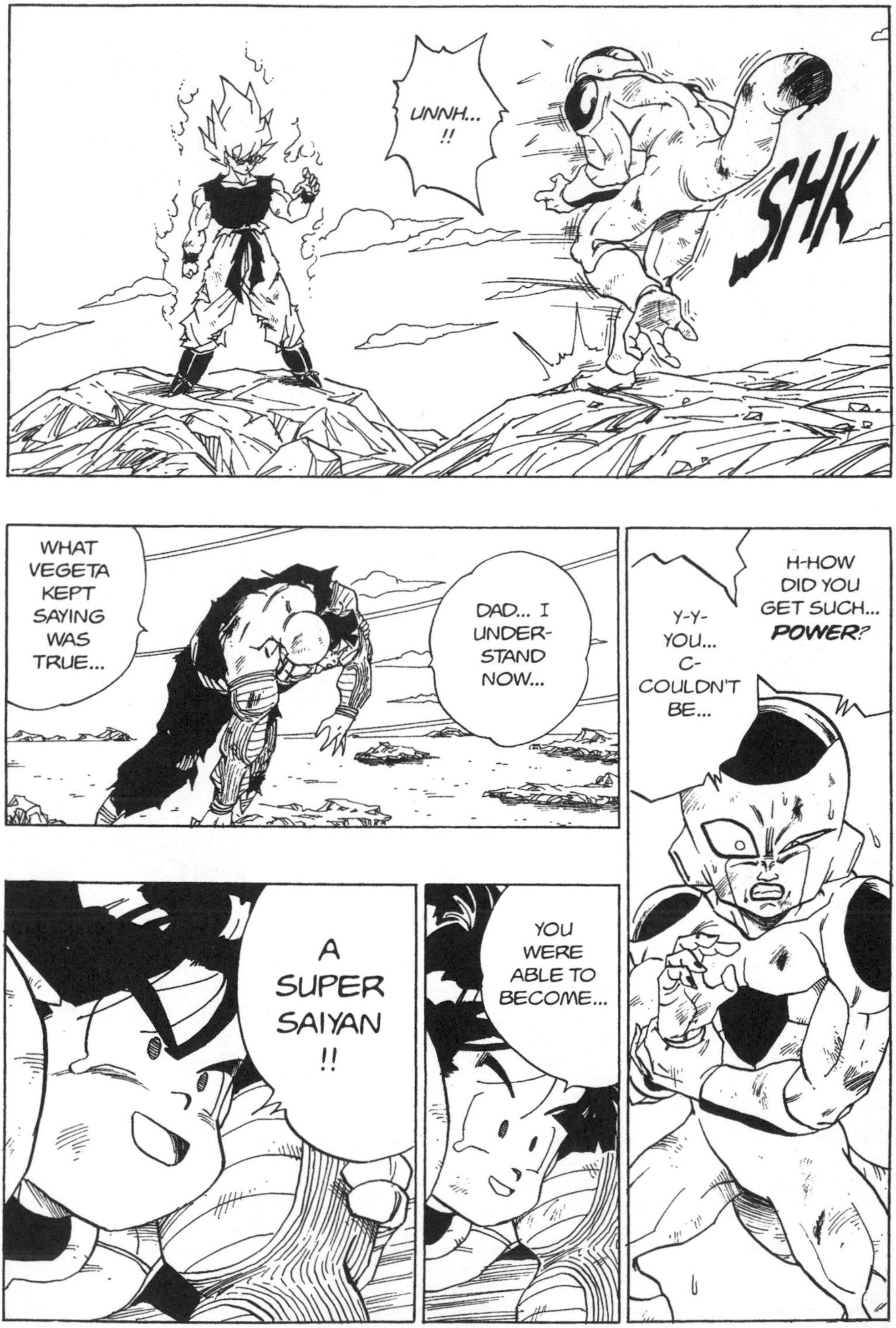
UNNH...!!
SHK
H-HOW DID YOU GET SUCH... POWER?
Y-Y-YOU... C-COULDN'T BE...
DAD... I UNDERSTAND NOW...
WHAT VEGETA KEPT SAYING WAS TRUE...
YOU WERE ABLE TO BECOME...
A SUPER SAIYAN!!

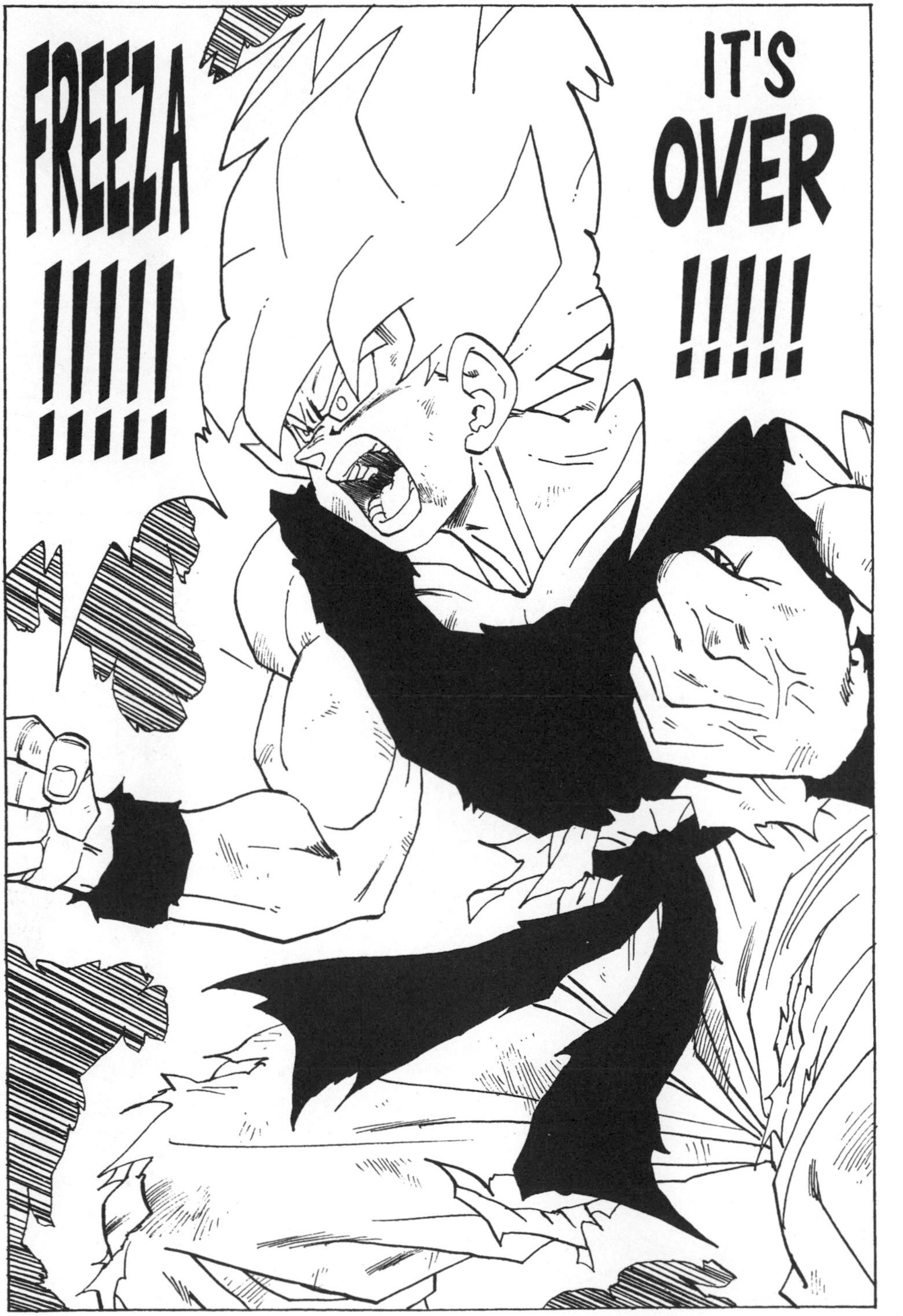
IT'S OVER !!!!!
FREEZA !!!!!

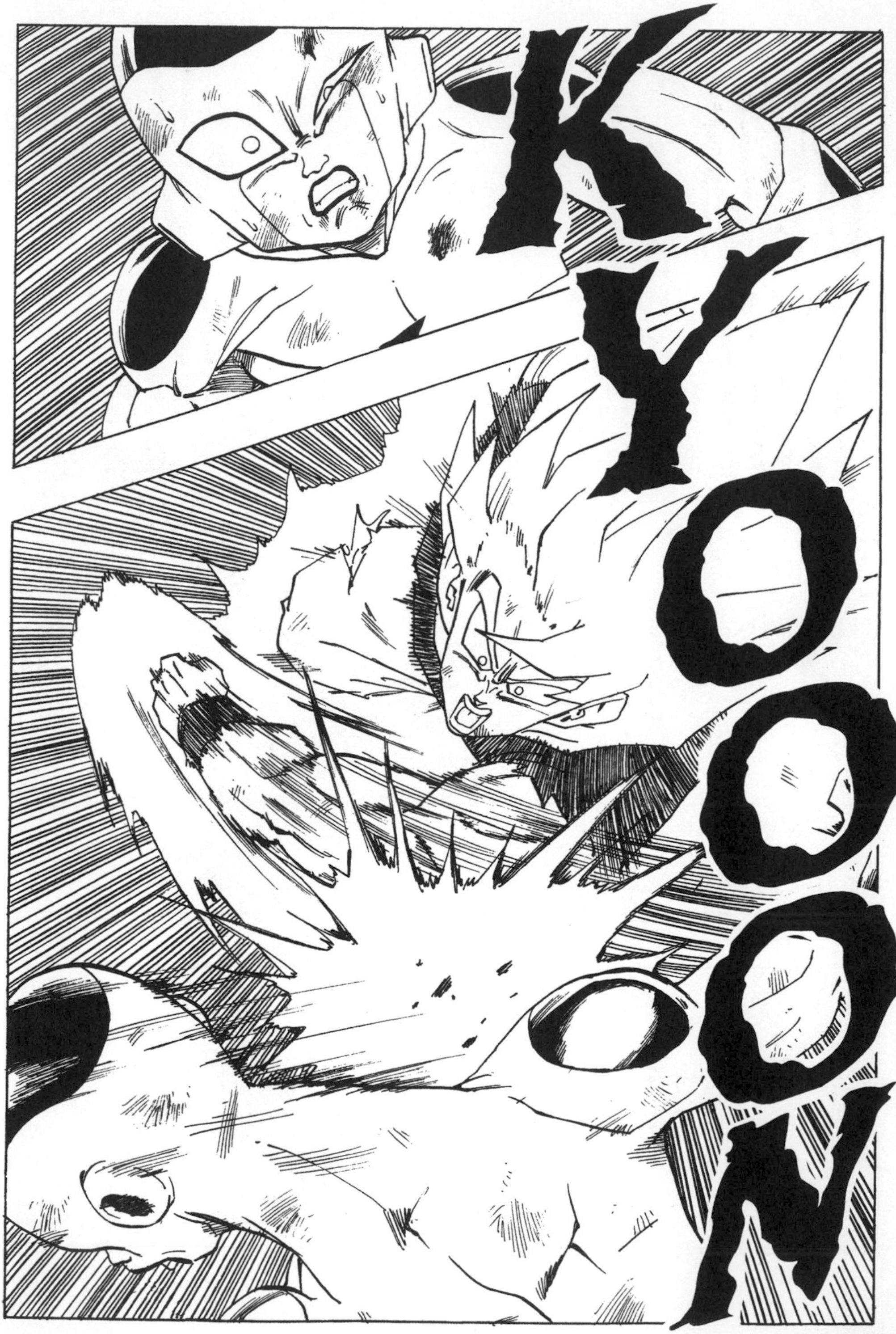
KYOOON

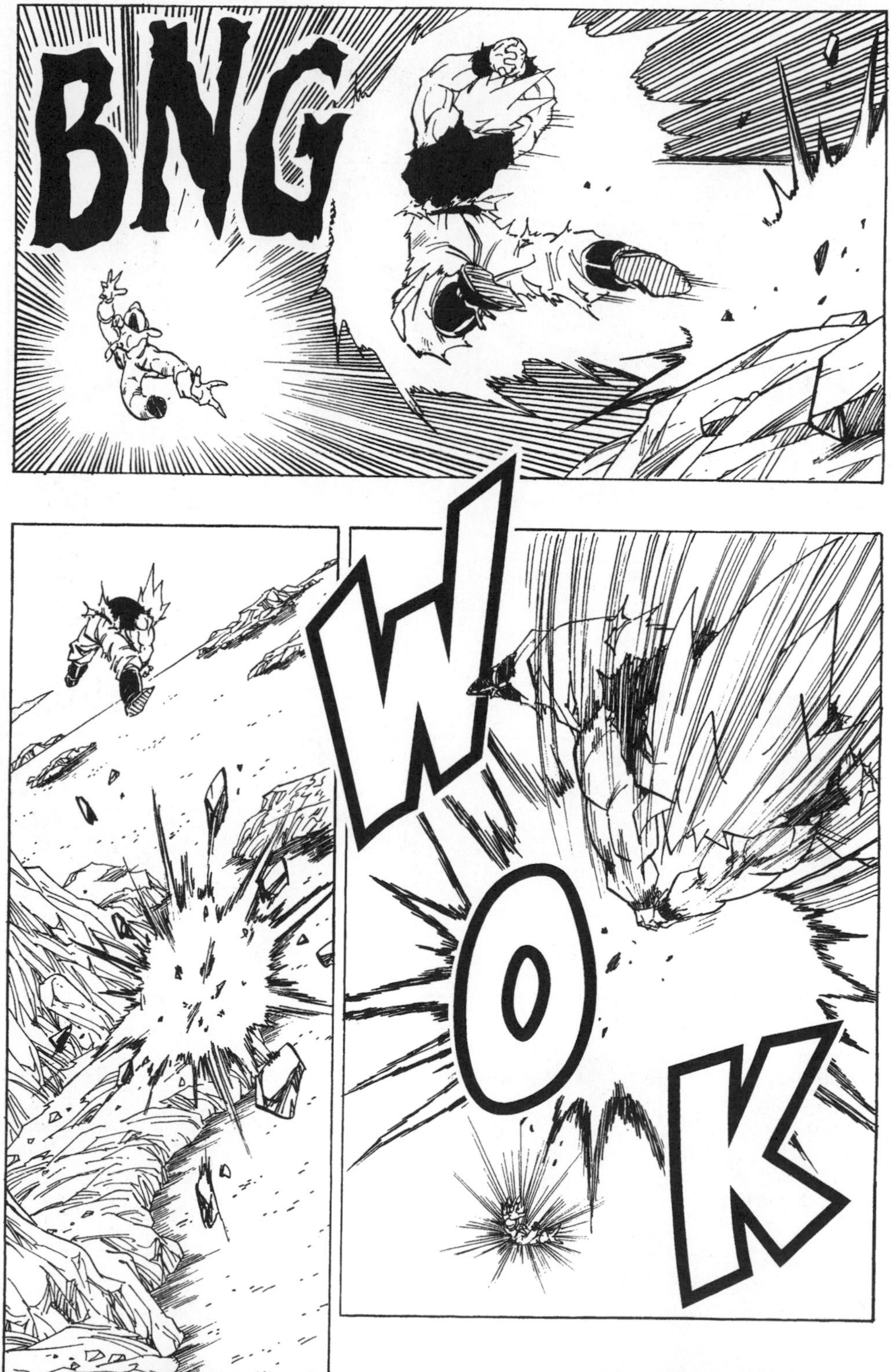
BNG
WOK

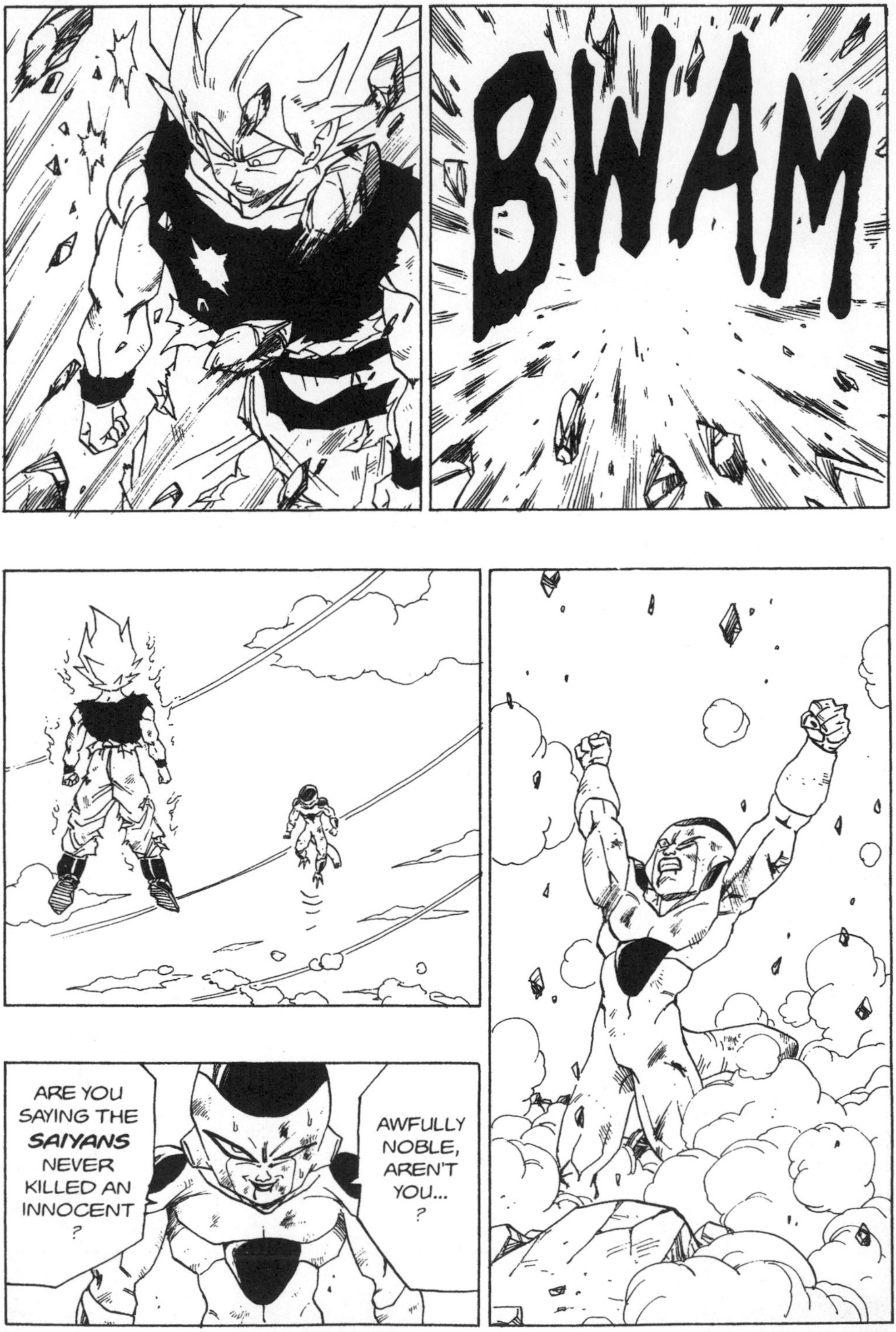
BWAM
AWFULLY NOBLE, AREN'T YOU...?
ARE YOU SAYING THE SAIYANS NEVER KILLED AN INNOCENT?

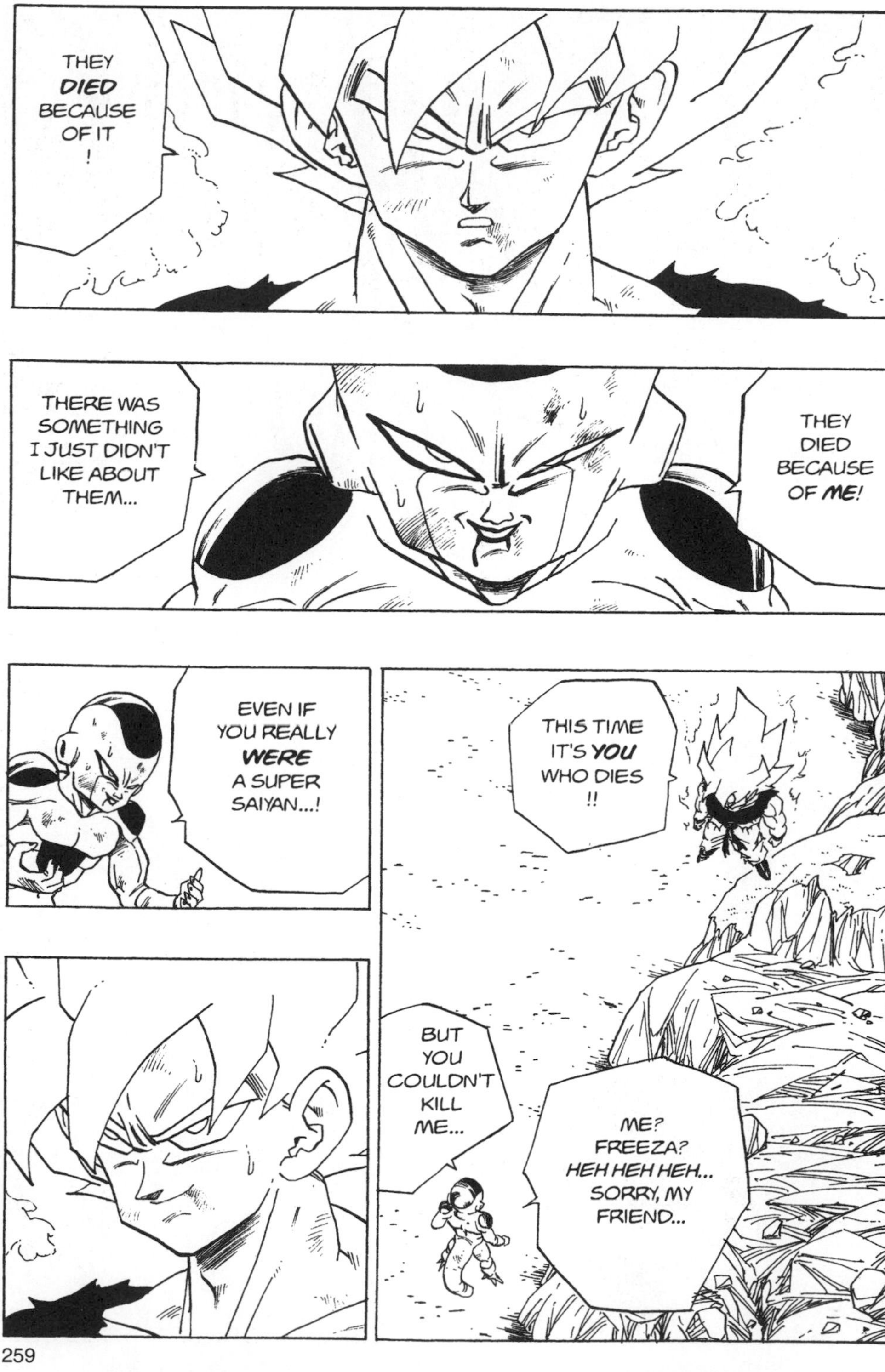
THEY DIED BECAUSE OF IT !
THERE WAS SOMETHING I JUST DIDN'T LIKE ABOUT THEM...
THEY DIED BECAUSE OF ME!
EVEN IF YOU REALLY WERE A SUPER SAIYAN...!
THIS TIME IT'S YOU WHO DIES !!
ME? FREEZA? HEH HEH HEH... SORRY, MY FRIEND...
BUT YOU COULDN'T KILL ME...

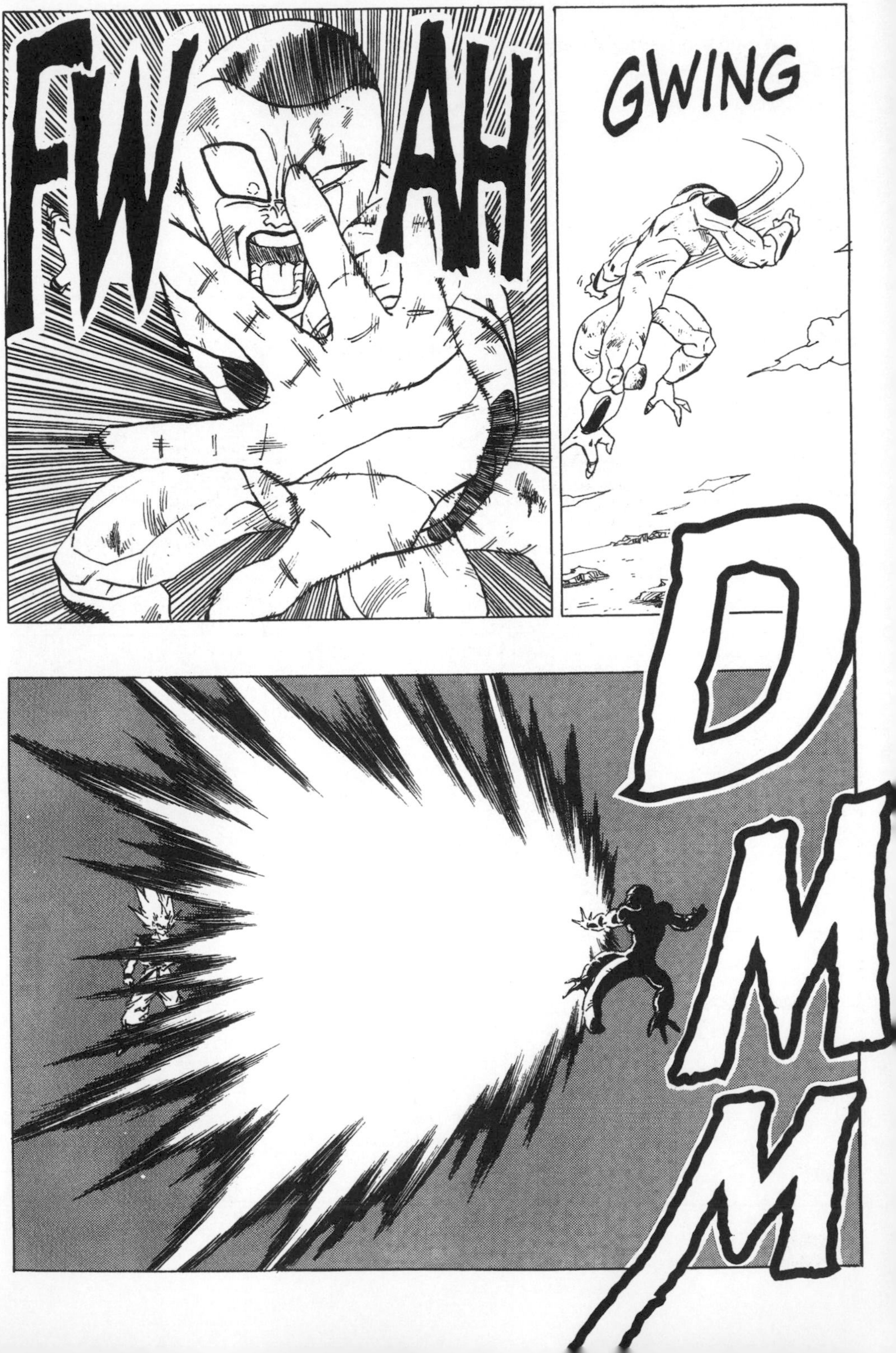

GWING
FWAAH
DMMM

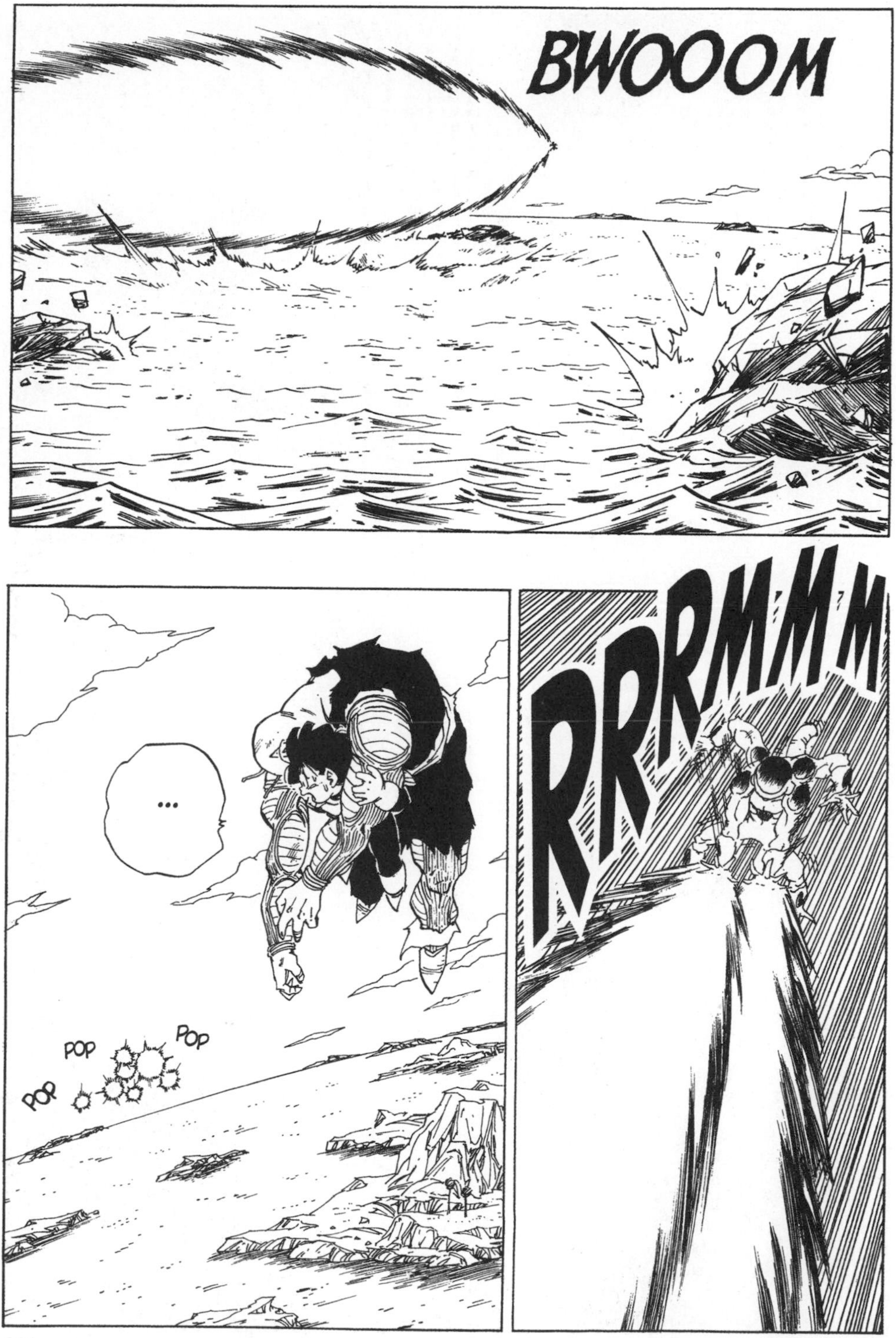
BWOOOM
RRRMMMM
...
POP
POP
POP

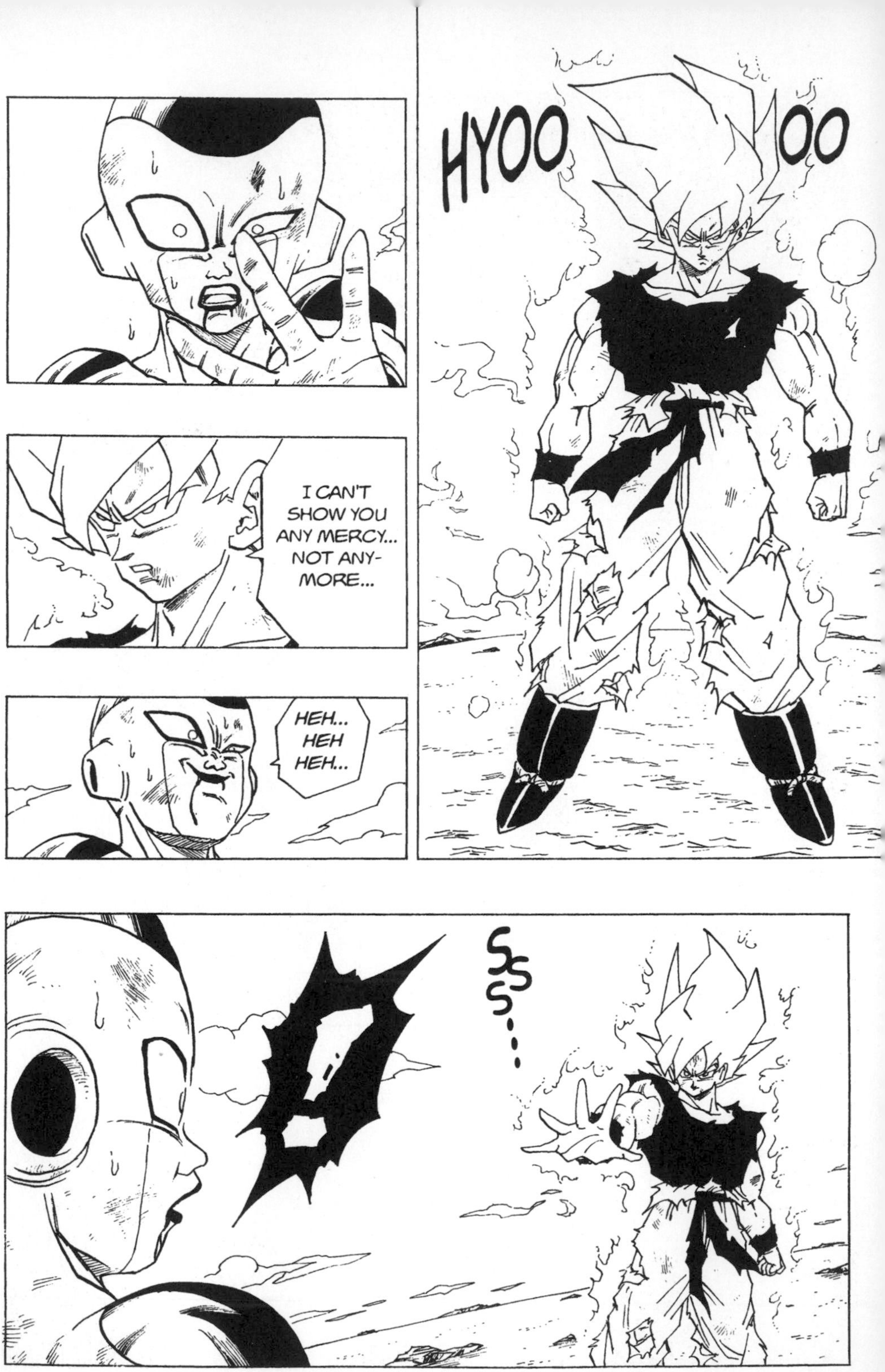
HYOO
OO
I CAN'T SHOW YOU ANY MERCY... NOT ANY-MORE...
HEH... HEH HEH...
SSS...

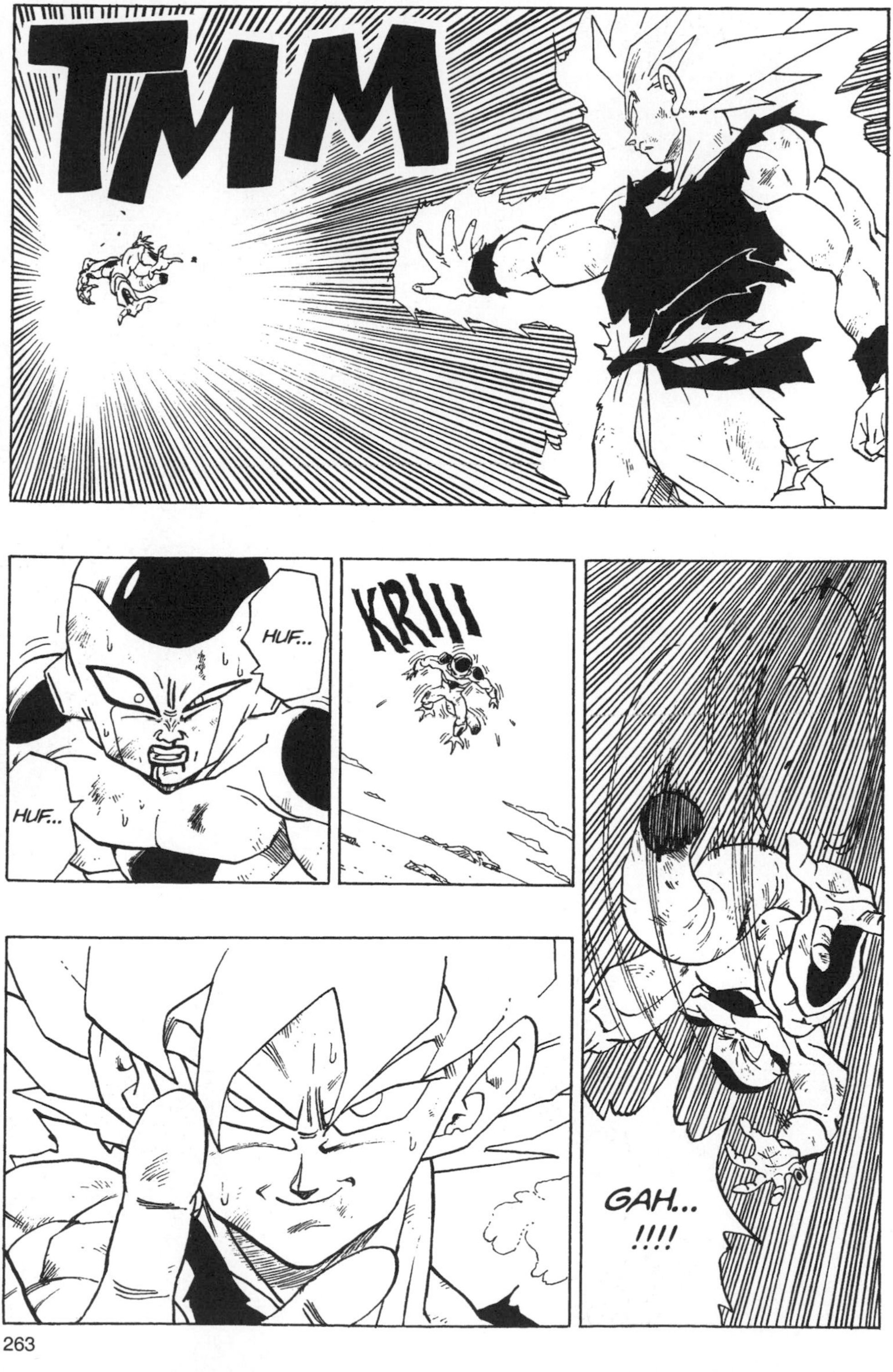
TMM
HUF...
HUF...
KRIII
GAH... !!!!

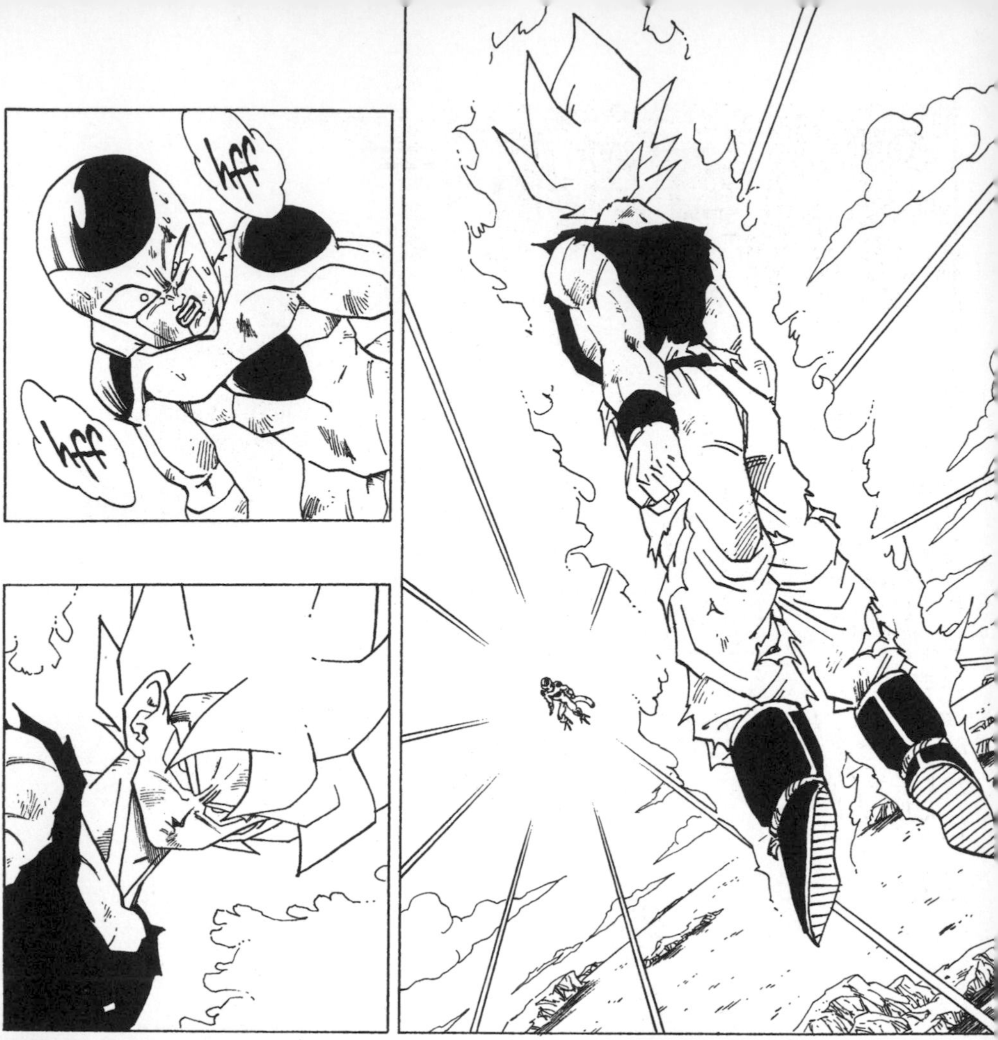
hff
hff

DBZ:125 • The Tables Turn

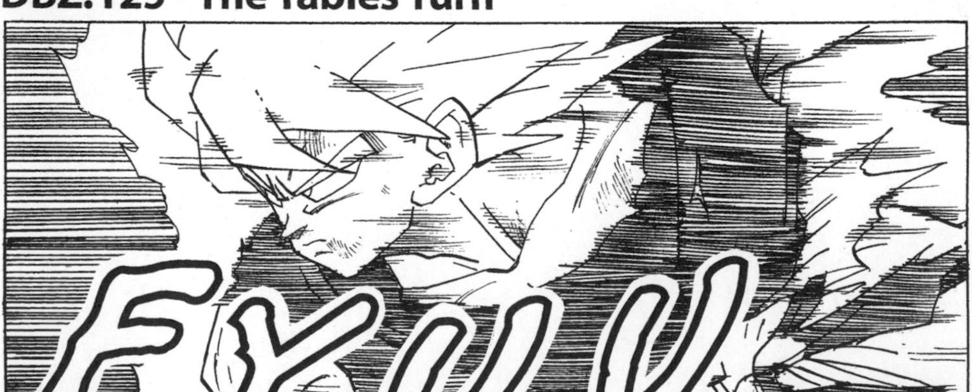
FYUU

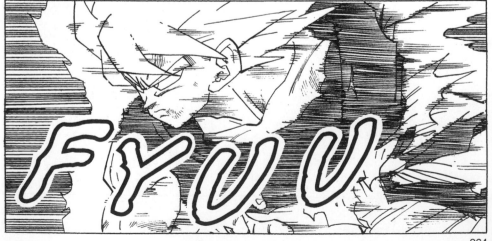

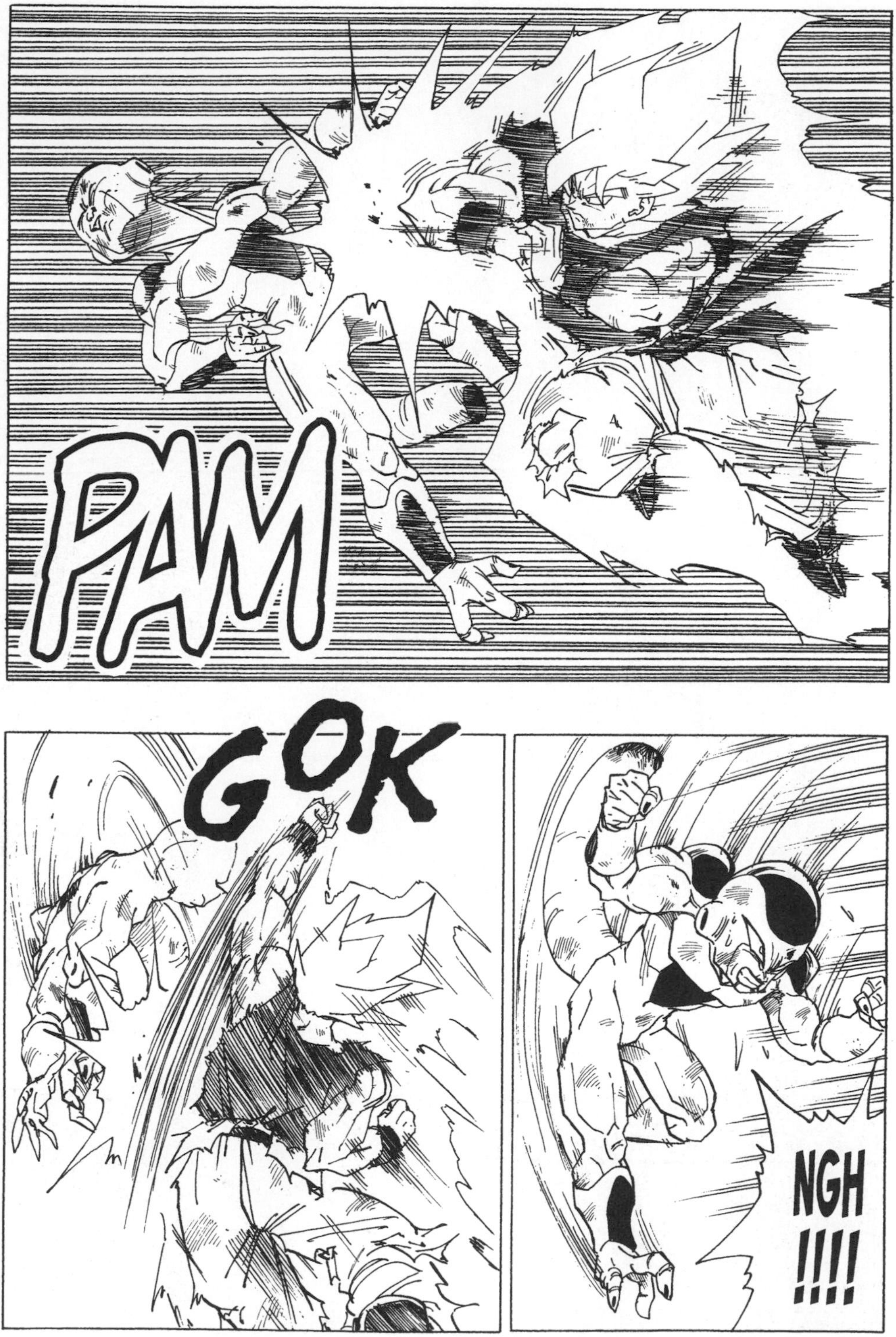
PAM
NGH !!!!
GOK

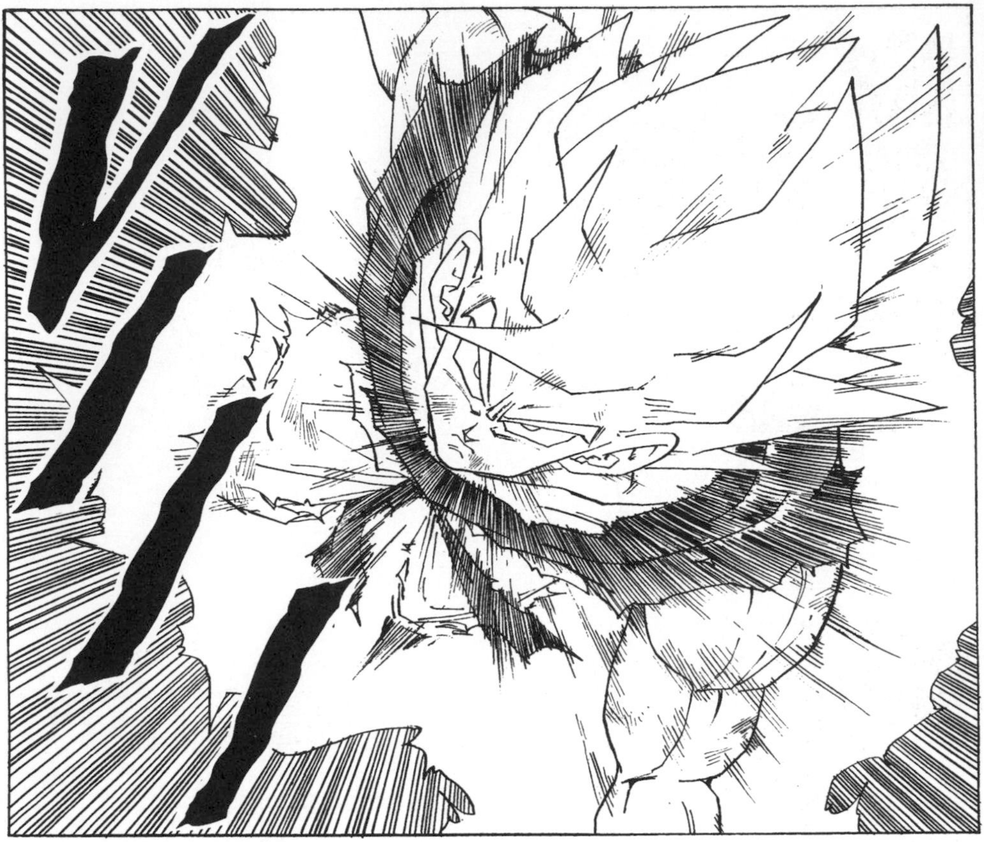

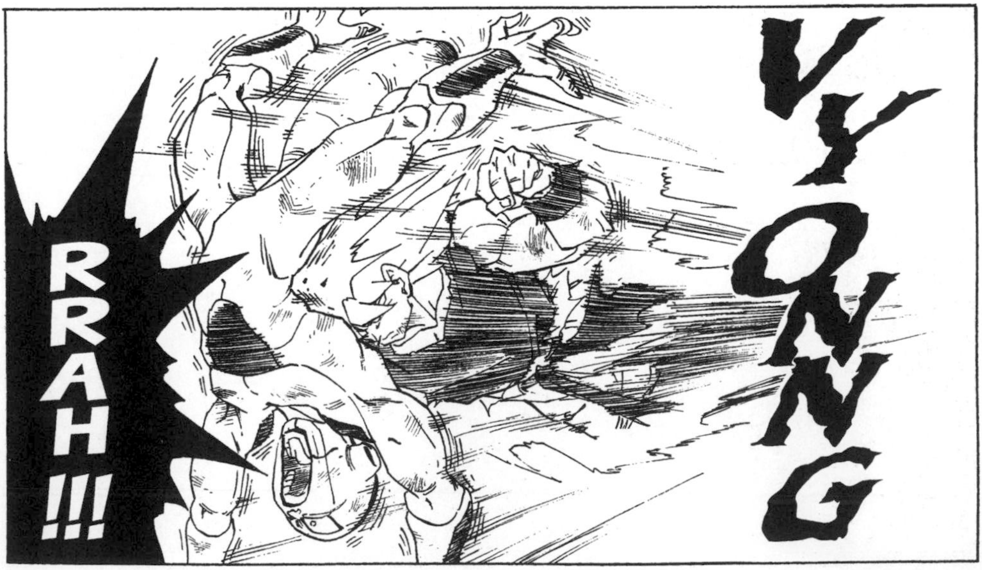
VYONNG
RRAH!!!

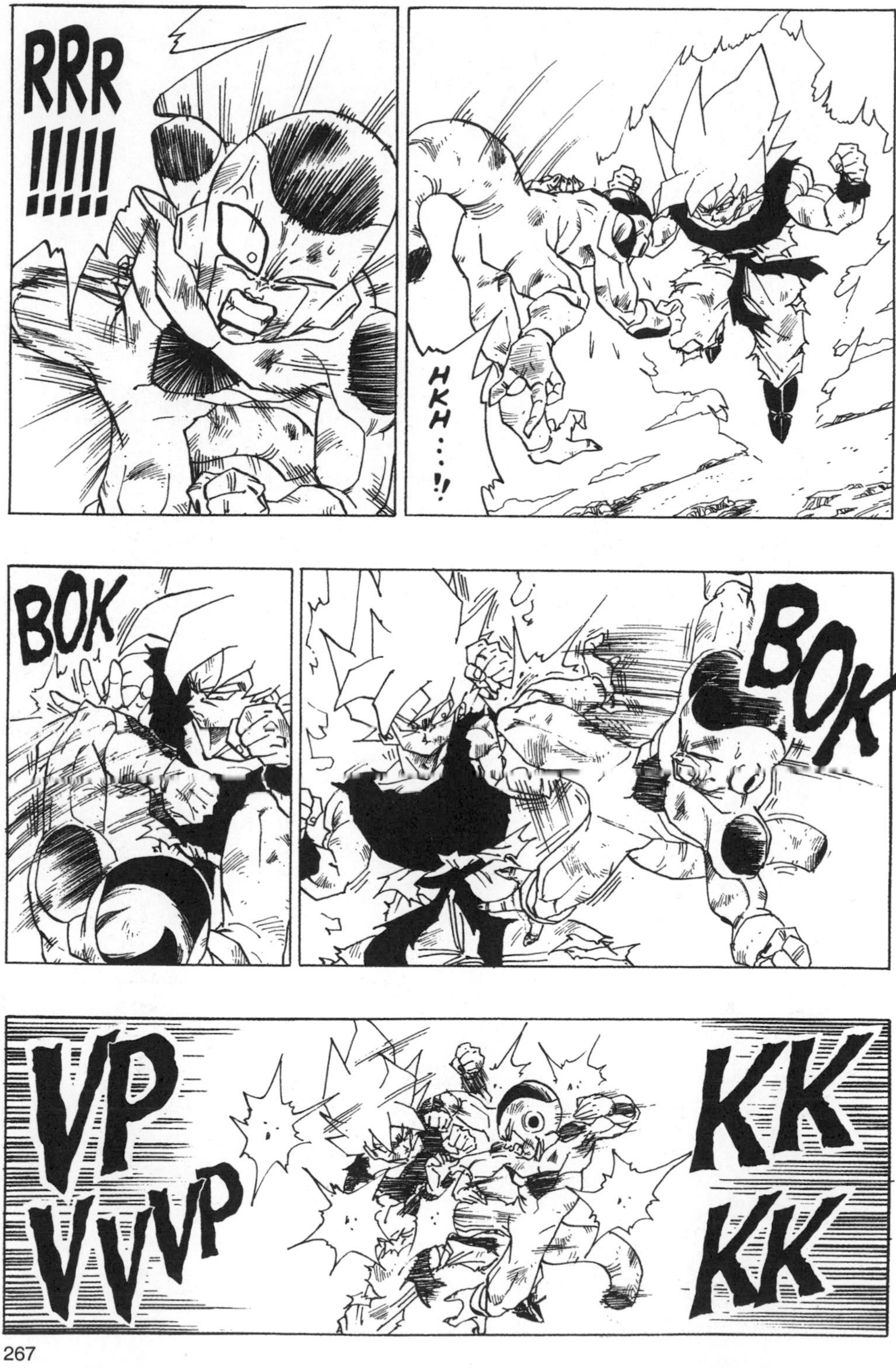
RRR
!!!!!
HKH...!!
BOK
BOK
VP
VVVP
KK
KK

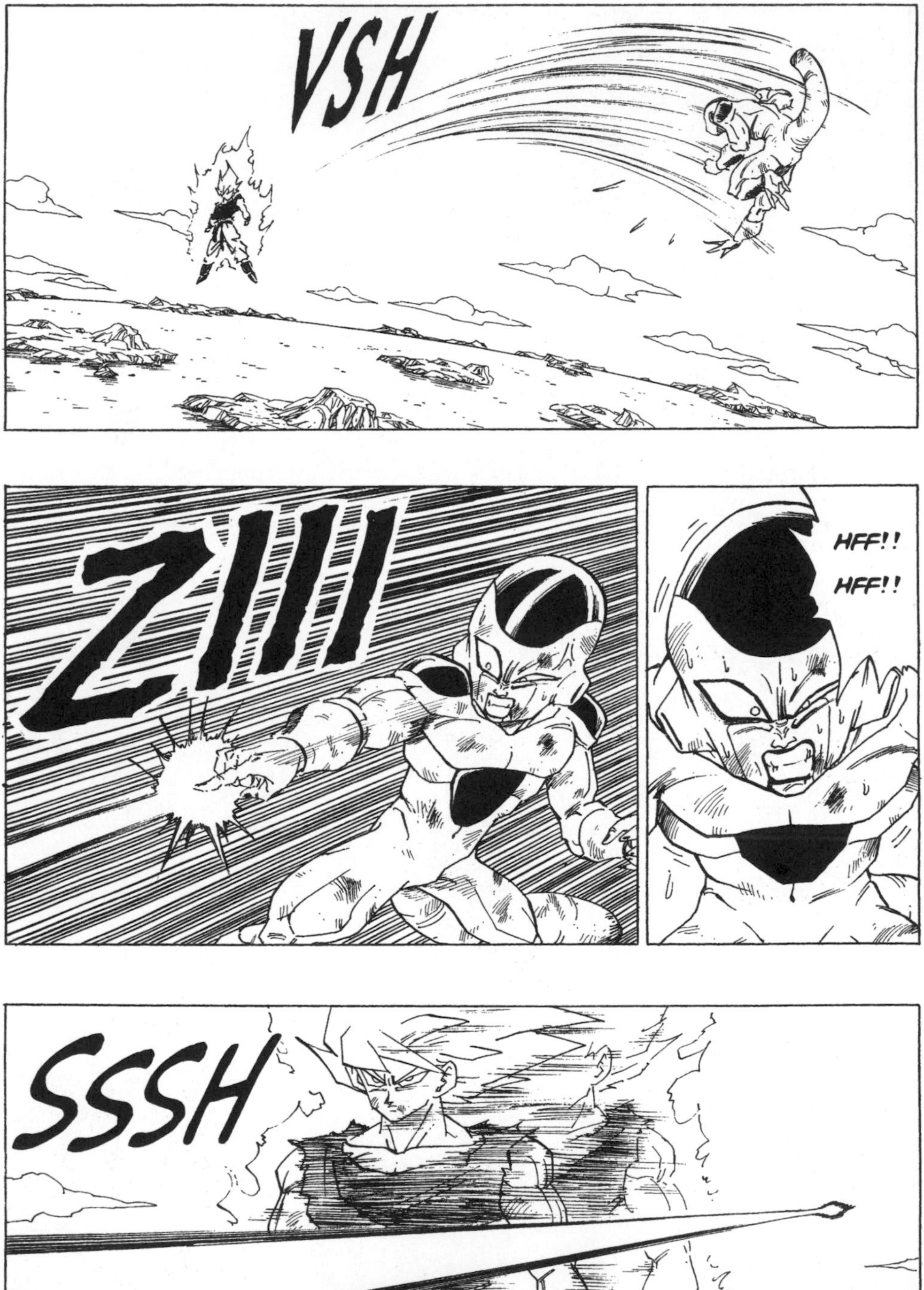
VSH
ZIIII
HFF!!
HFF!!
SSSH

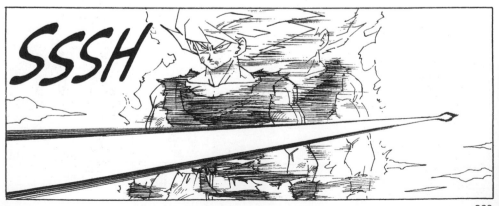

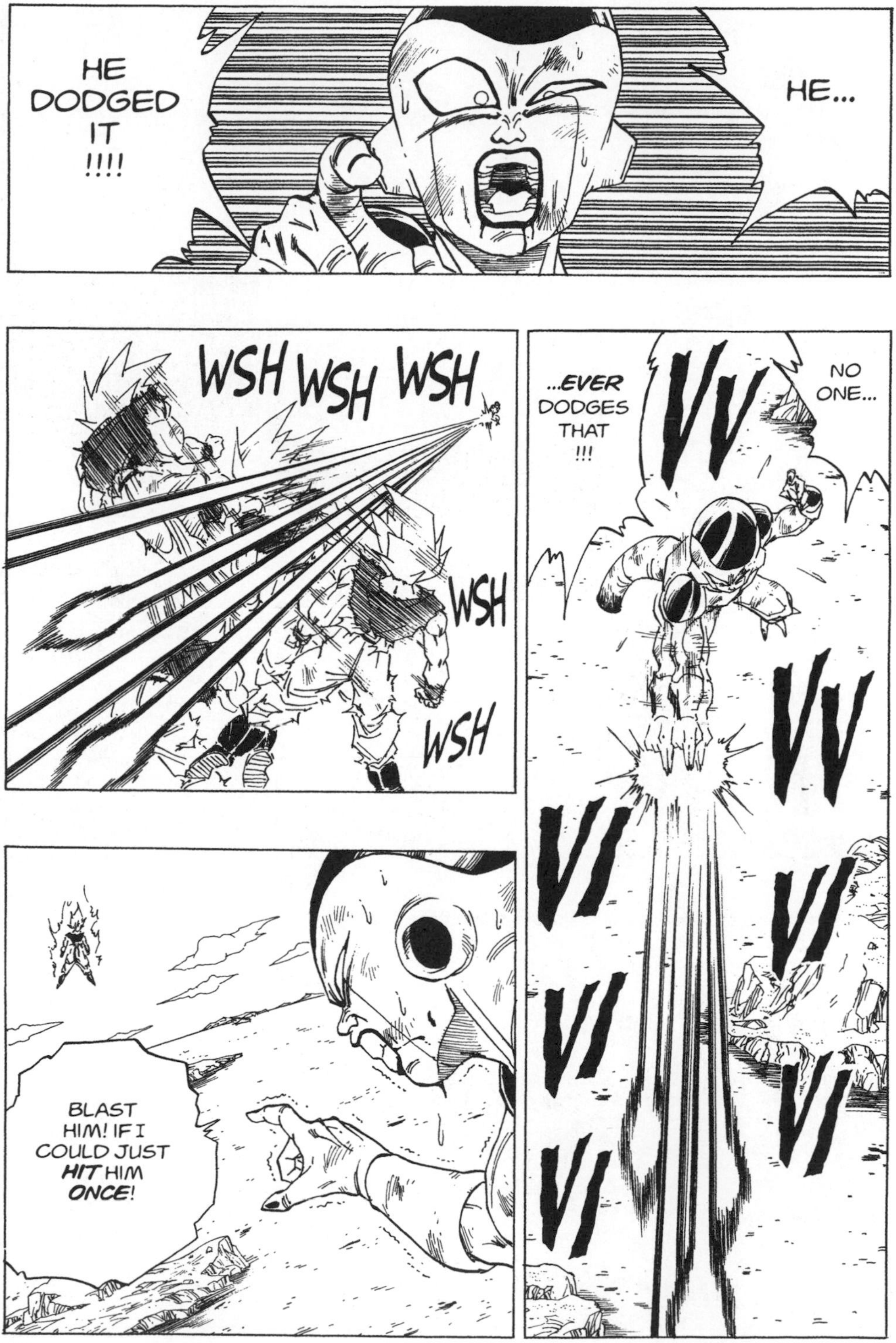

HE...
HE DODGED IT !!!!
NO ONE...
...*EVER* DODGES THAT !!!
WSH WSH WSH
WSH
WSH
BLAST HIM! IF I COULD JUST *HIT* HIM *ONCE*!

WHAT
DID
YOU...
?!

W...

HIT
ME.

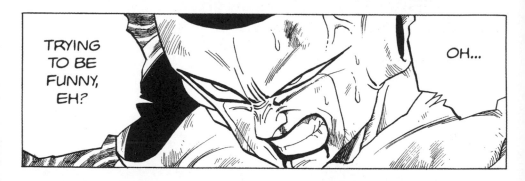

TRYING
TO BE
FUNNY,
EH?

OH...

LAUGH
AT
THIS
!!!!
....

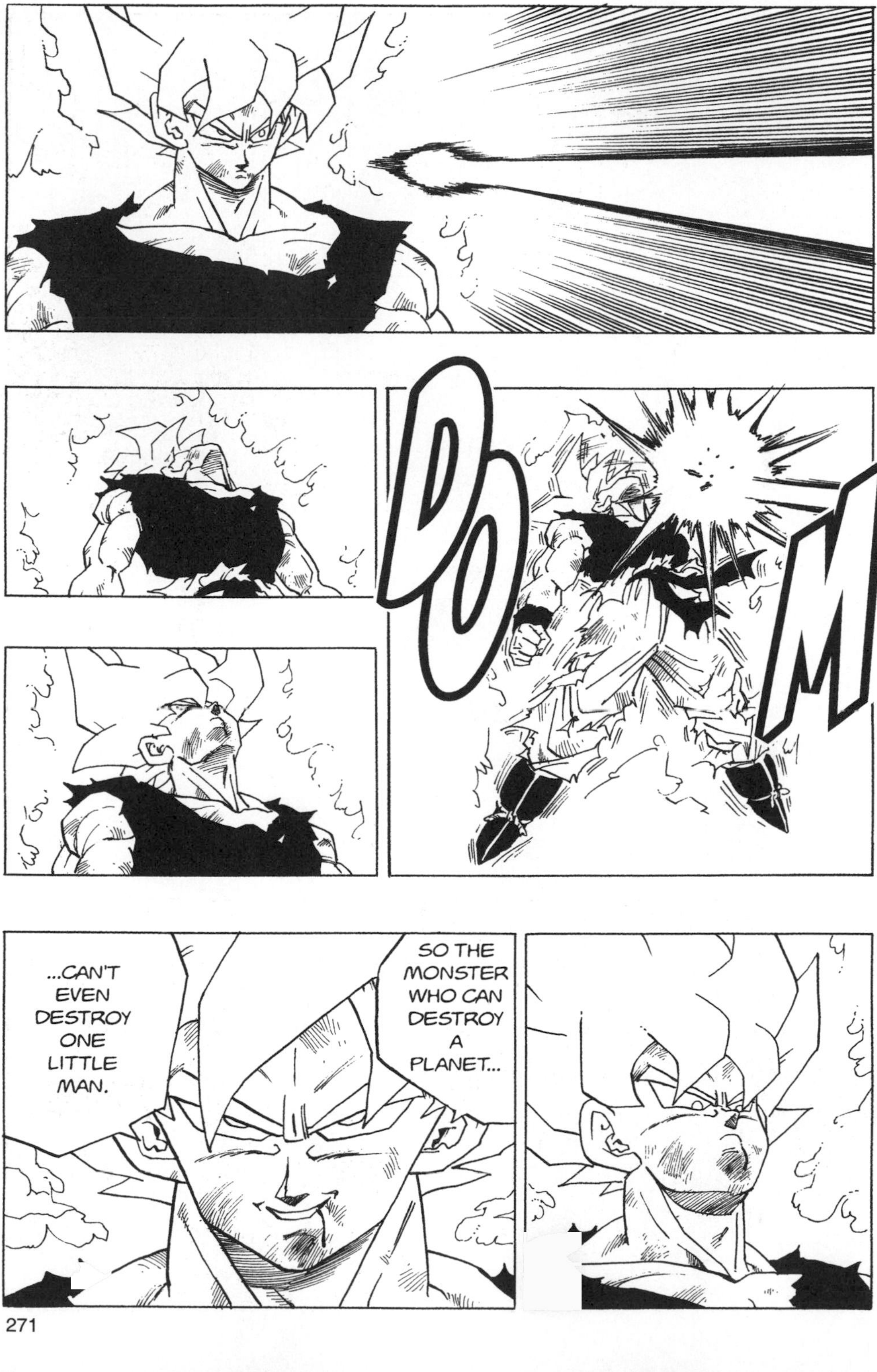
DOOM
SO THE MONSTER WHO CAN DESTROY A PLANET...
...CAN'T EVEN DESTROY ONE LITTLE MAN.

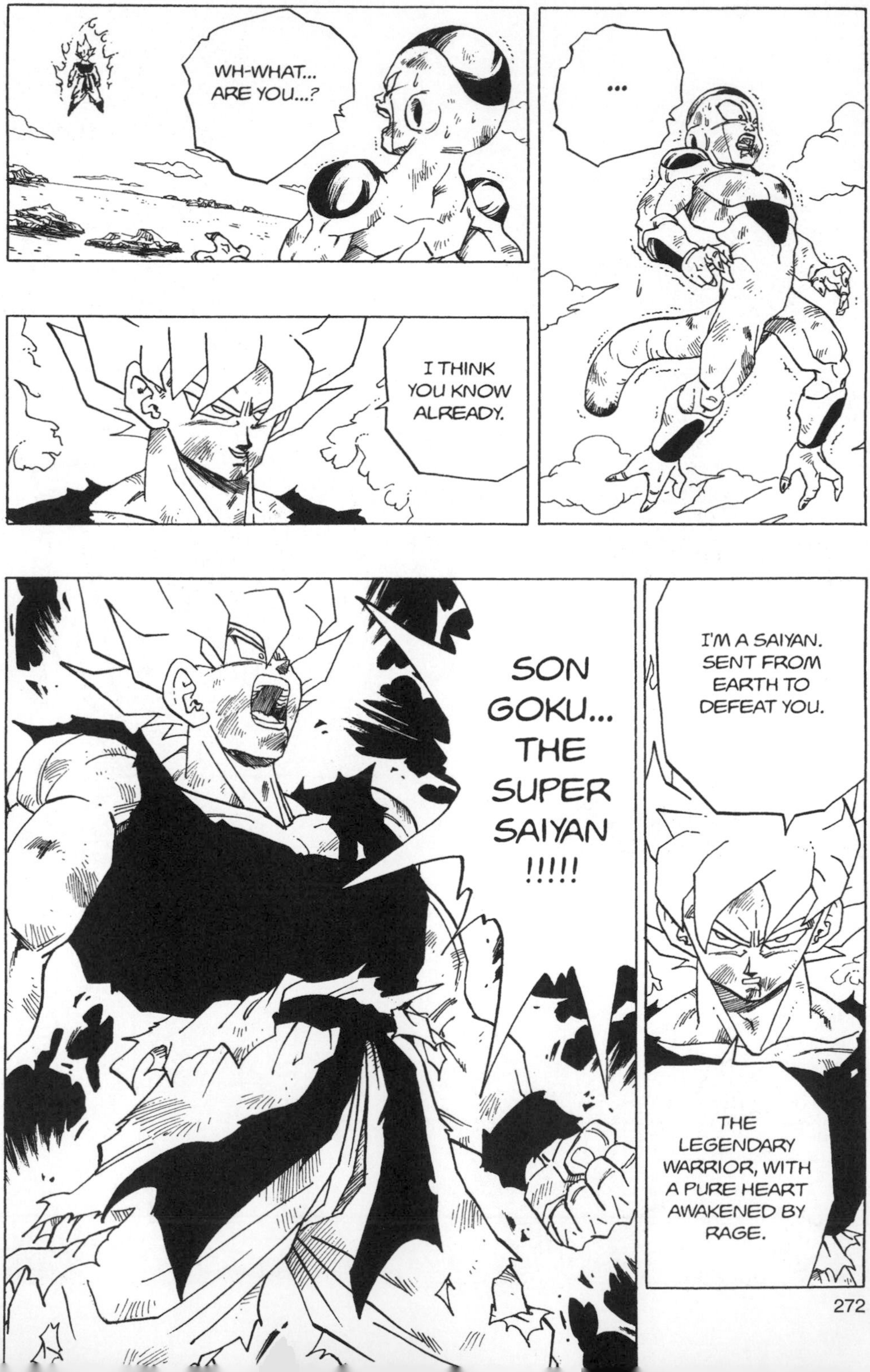
...
WH-WHAT... ARE YOU...?
I THINK YOU KNOW ALREADY.
I'M A SAIYAN. SENT FROM EARTH TO DEFEAT YOU.
THE LEGENDARY WARRIOR, WITH A PURE HEART AWAKENED BY RAGE.
SON GOKU... THE SUPER SAIYAN !!!!!

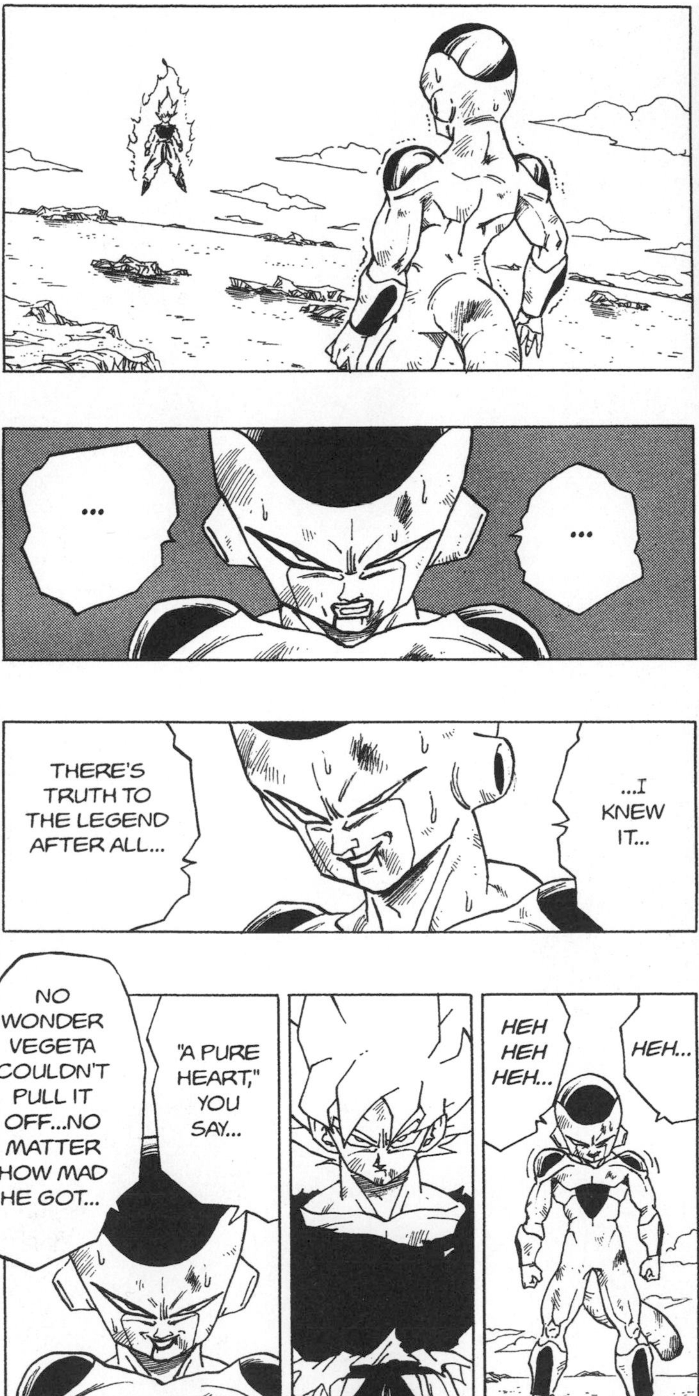
...
...
...I KNEW IT...
THERE'S TRUTH TO THE LEGEND AFTER ALL...
HEH...
HEH HEH HEH...
"A PURE HEART," YOU SAY...
NO WONDER VEGETA COULDN'T PULL IT OFF...NO MATTER HOW MAD HE GOT...

THE HUMILIATION!!
I, FREEZA!! BEATEN
BY A LOWLY...HALF-
EVOLVED...*SAIYAN...!!*

THIS IS A NIGHTMARE...
THAT'S WHAT IT IS!! I'M
GOING TO WAKE UP...AND
I'LL BE VICTORIOUS!!
I'LL BE *FREEZA!!*

B...

BLAST
HIM...
!!!

BLAST
HIM
TO
INFINITY
!!!!!

IT'S
OVER...

FREEZA.

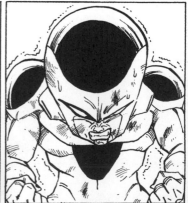

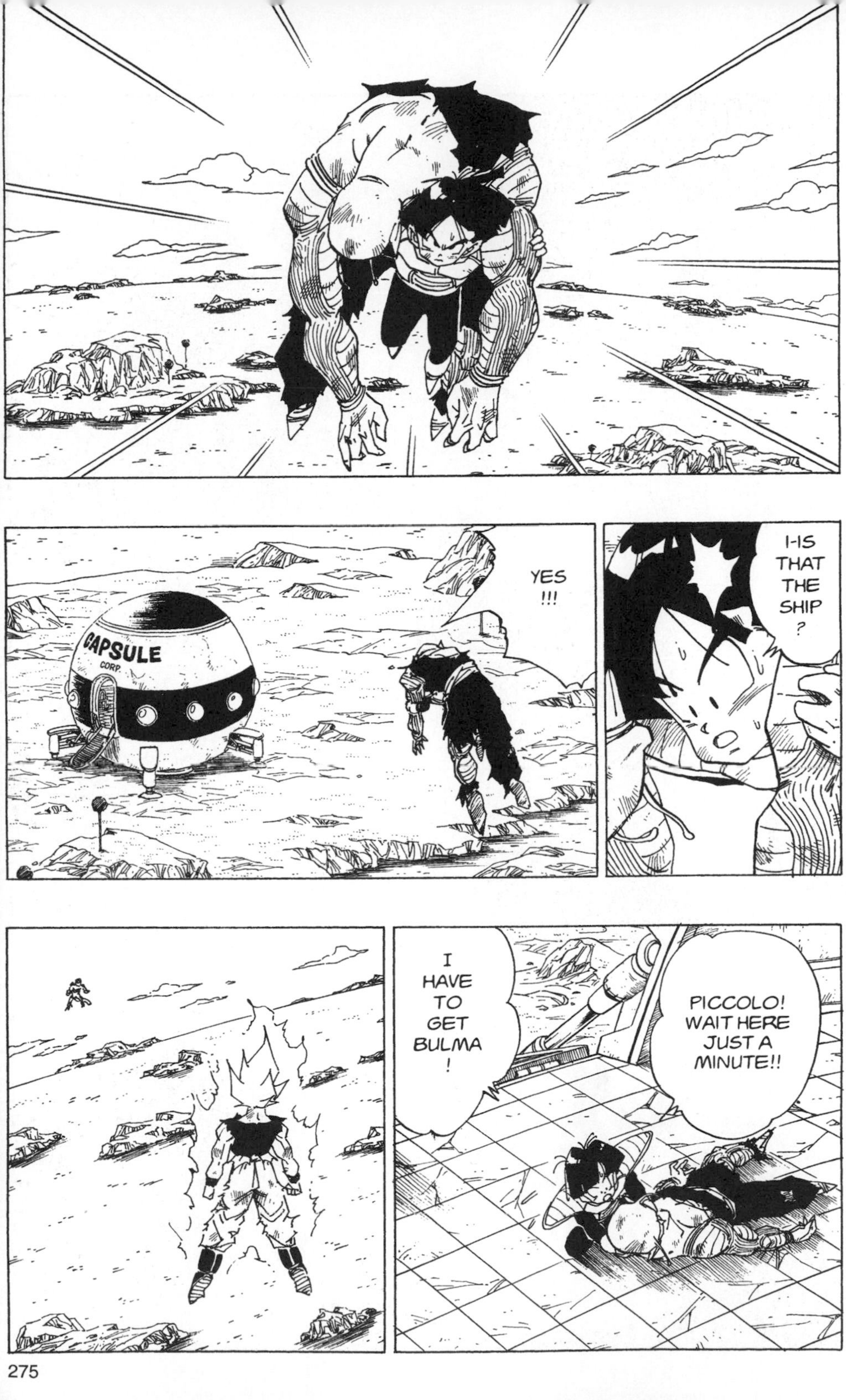
I-IS THAT THE SHIP?
YES!!!
PICCOLO! WAIT HERE JUST A MINUTE!!
I HAVE TO GET BULMA!

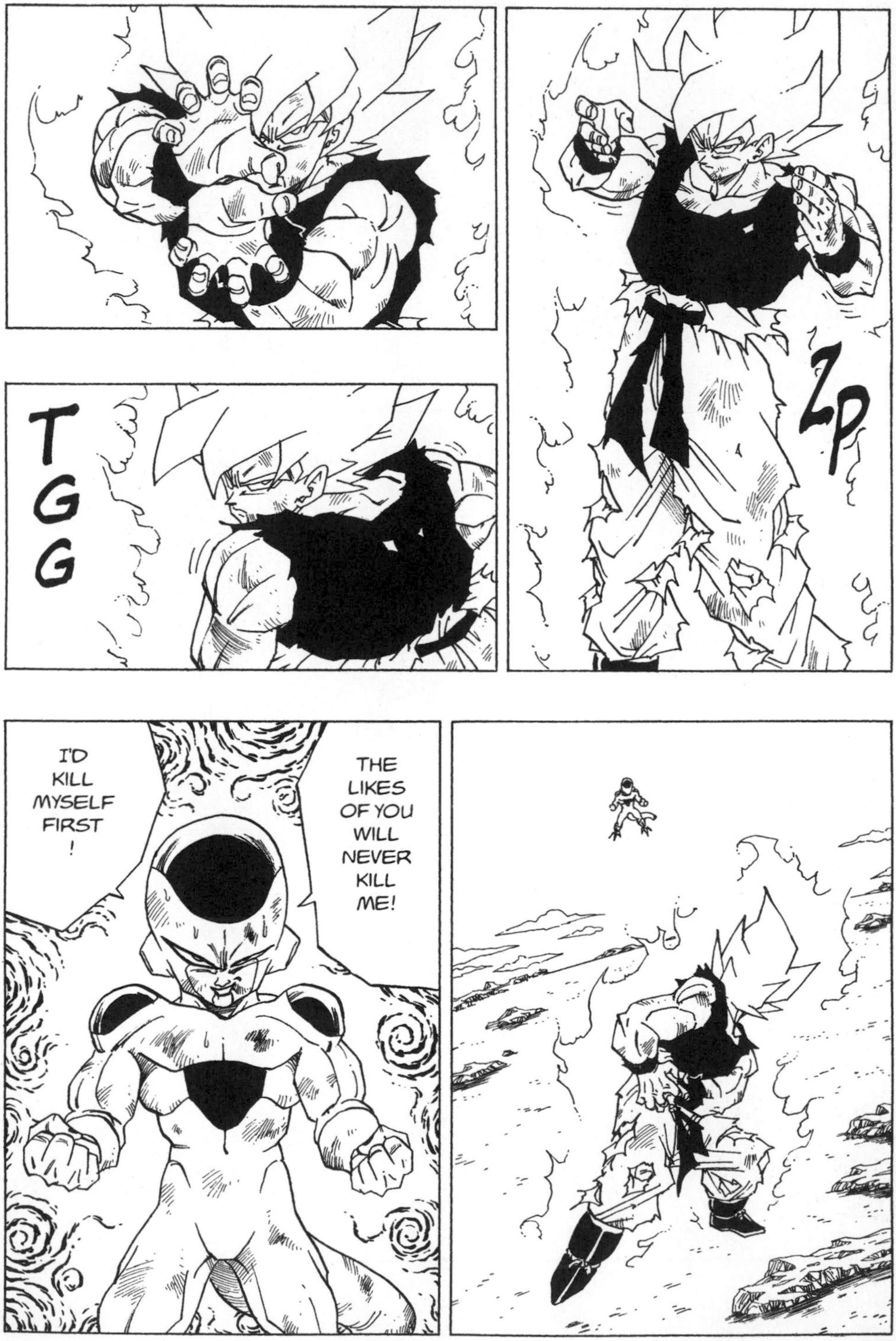
ZP
TGG
THE LIKES OF YOU WILL NEVER KILL ME!
I'D KILL MYSELF FIRST!

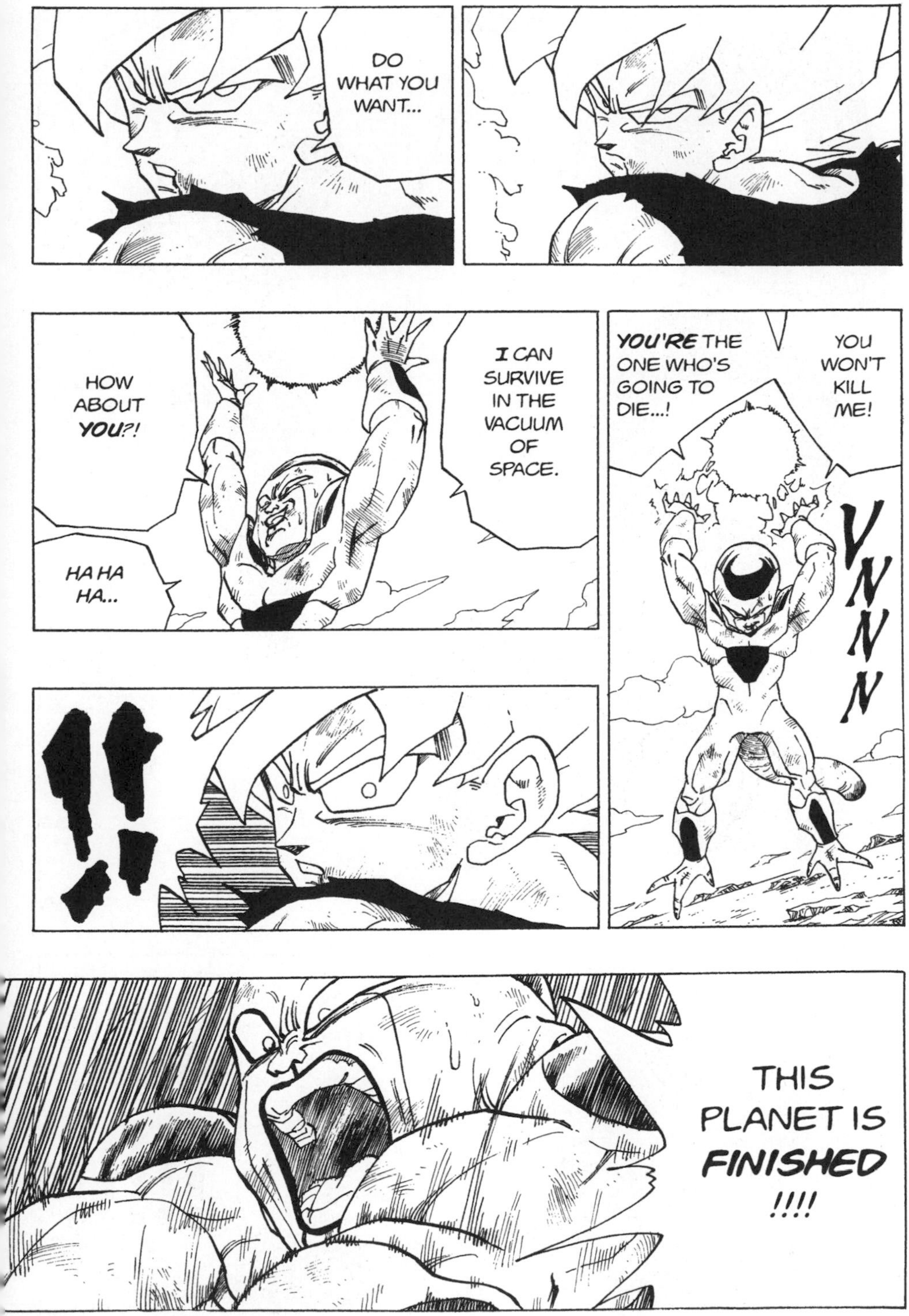
DO WHAT YOU WANT...
YOU WON'T KILL ME!
YOU'RE THE ONE WHO'S GOING TO DIE...!
VNNN
I CAN SURVIVE IN THE VACUUM OF SPACE.
HOW ABOUT *YOU*?!
HA HA HA...
!!
THIS PLANET IS **FINISHED** !!!!

DBZ:126 • The End of Namek?

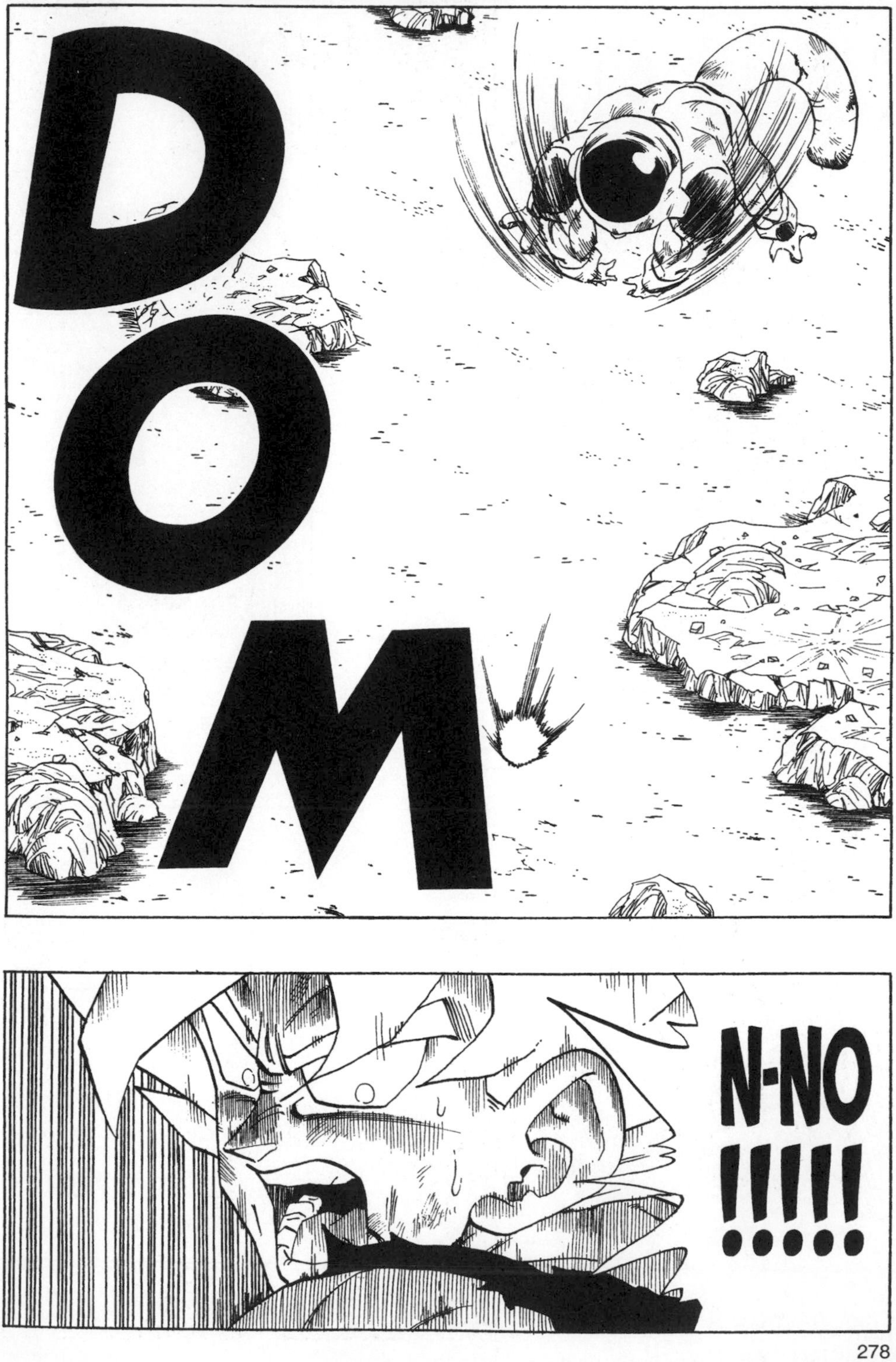
DOM
N-NO!!!!!

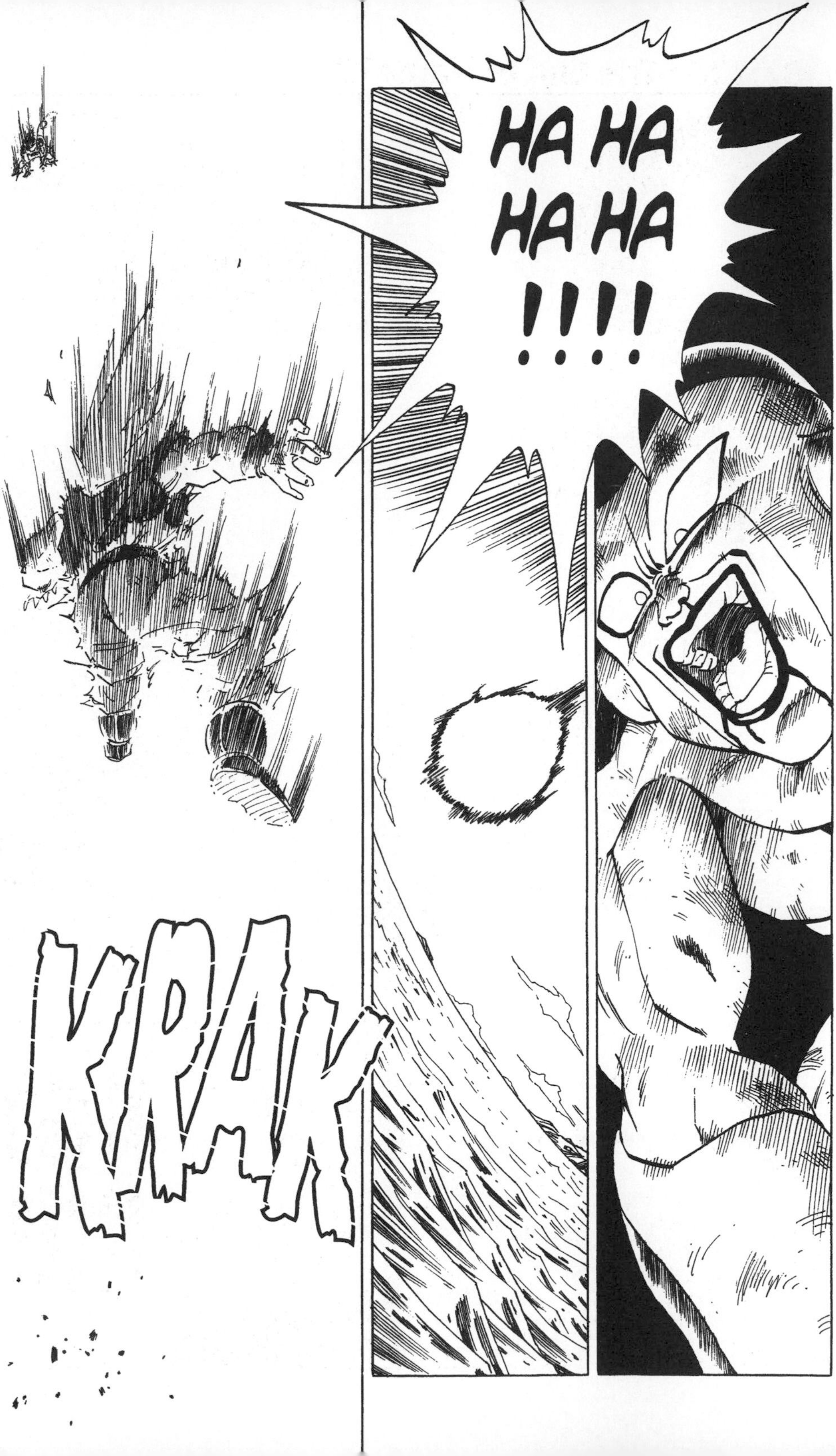
HA HA
HA HA
!!!!
KRAK

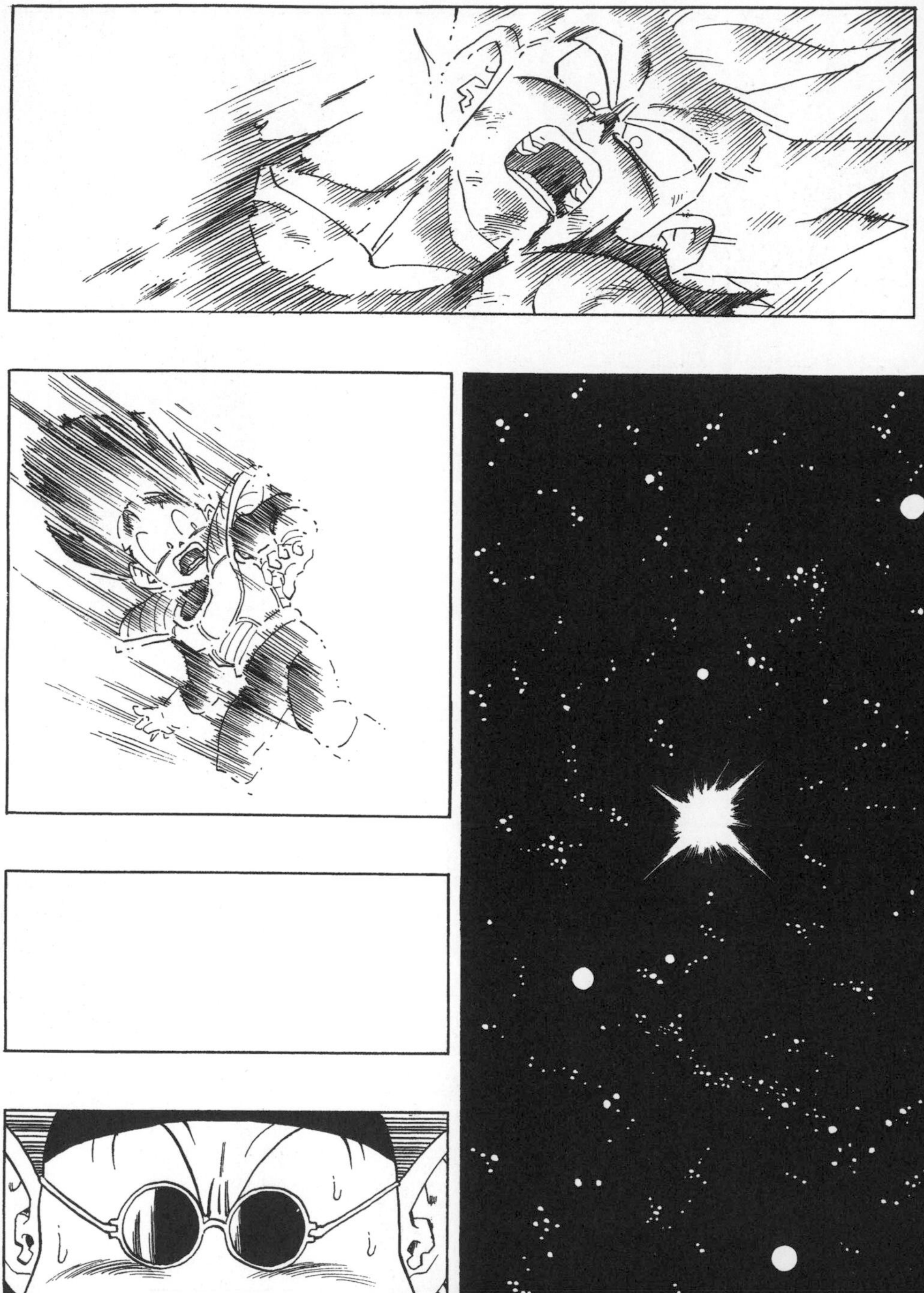

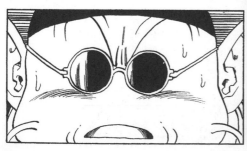

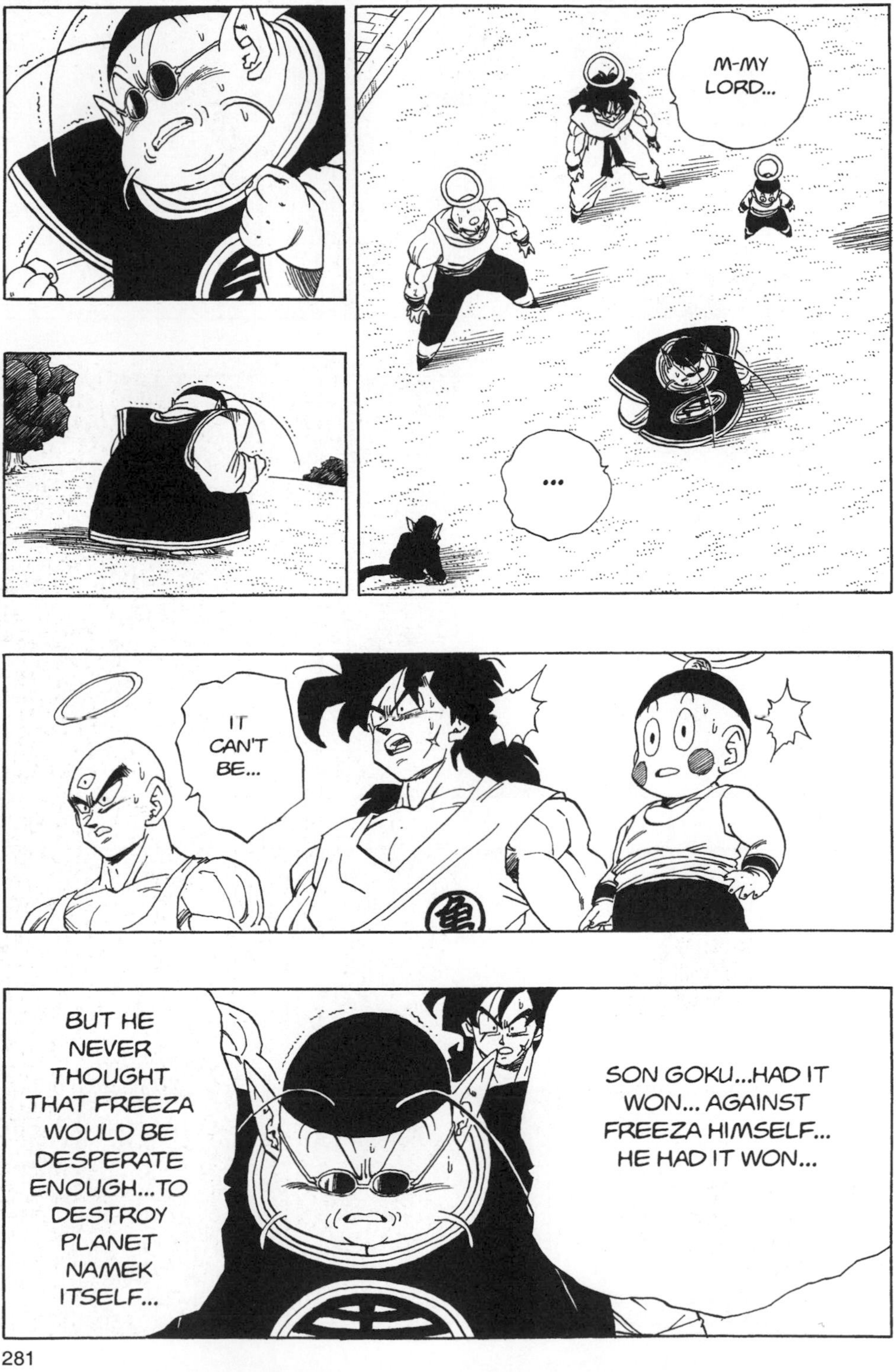
M-MY LORD...
...
IT CAN'T BE...
SON GOKU...HAD IT WON... AGAINST FREEZA HIMSELF... HE HAD IT WON...
BUT HE NEVER THOUGHT THAT FREEZA WOULD BE DESPERATE ENOUGH...TO DESTROY PLANET NAMEK ITSELF...

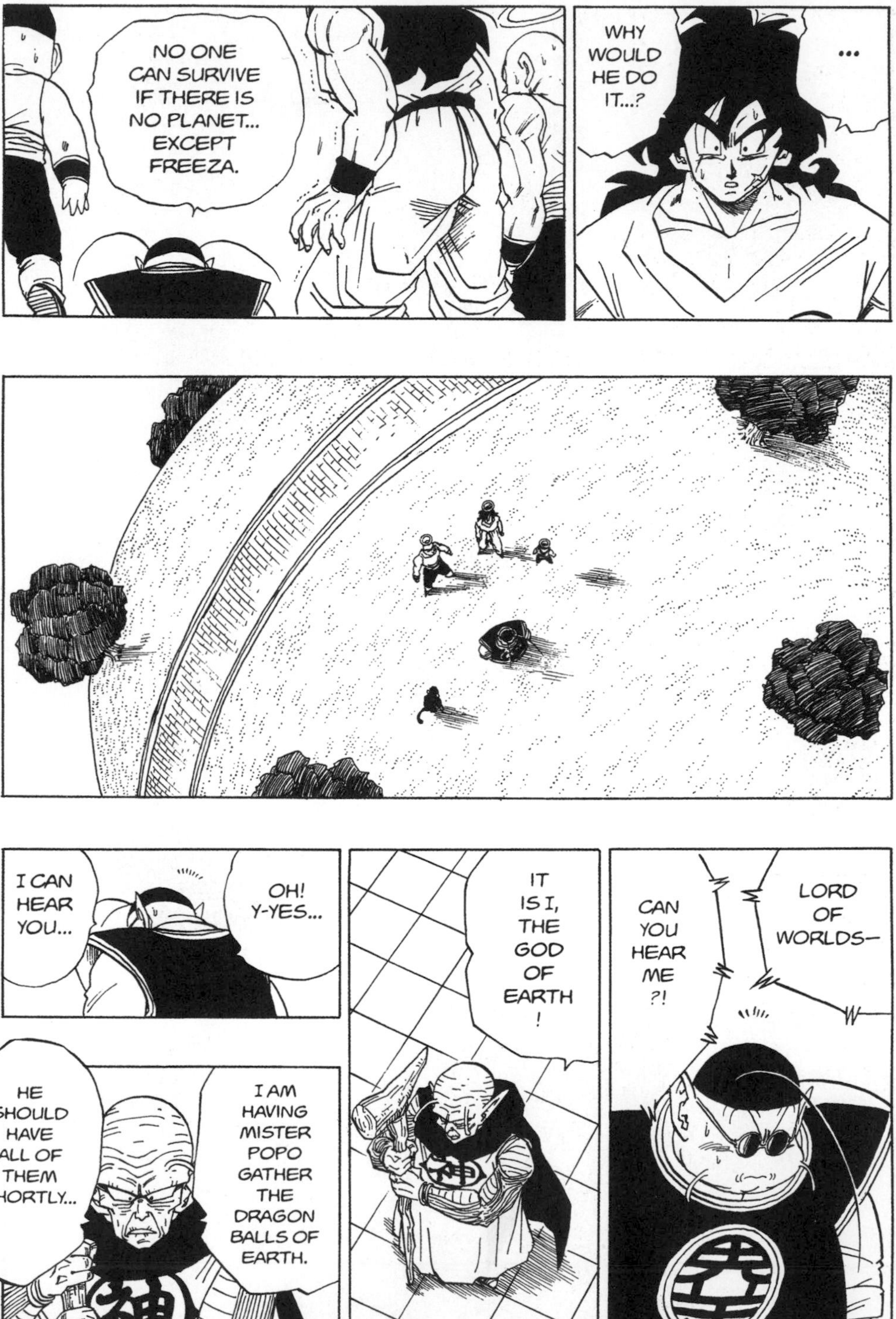
...
WHY WOULD HE DO IT...?
NO ONE CAN SURVIVE IF THERE IS NO PLANET... EXCEPT FREEZA.
LORD OF WORLDS—
CAN YOU HEAR ME?!
IT IS I, THE GOD OF EARTH!
OH! Y-YES...
I CAN HEAR YOU...
I AM HAVING MISTER POPO GATHER THE DRAGON BALLS OF EARTH.
HE SHOULD HAVE ALL OF THEM SHORTLY...

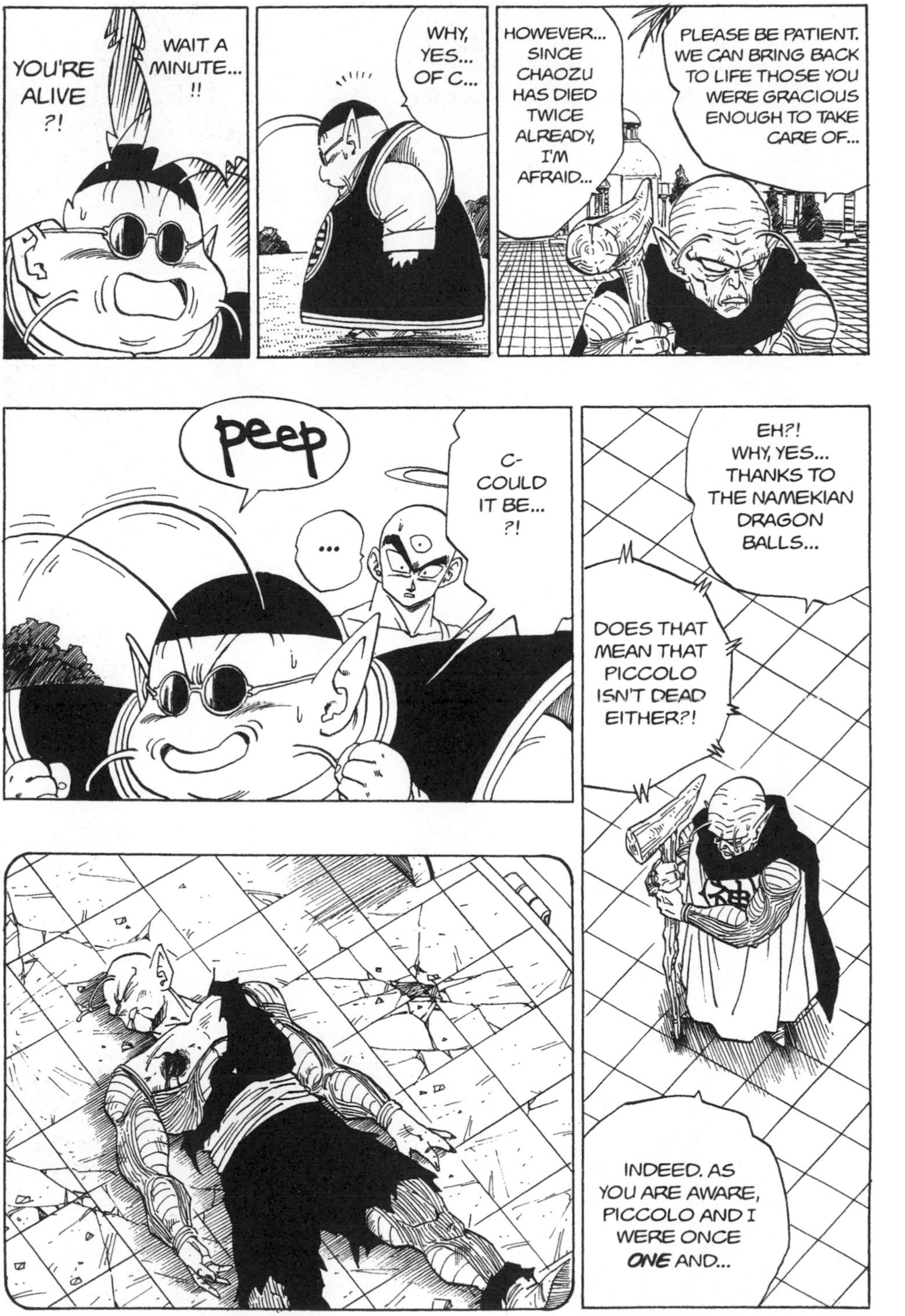
PLEASE BE PATIENT. WE CAN BRING BACK TO LIFE THOSE YOU WERE GRACIOUS ENOUGH TO TAKE CARE OF...
HOWEVER... SINCE CHAOZU HAS DIED TWICE ALREADY, I'M AFRAID...
WHY, YES... OF C...
WAIT A MINUTE... !!
YOU'RE ALIVE ?!
EH?! WHY, YES... THANKS TO THE NAMEKIAN DRAGON BALLS...
DOES THAT MEAN THAT PICCOLO ISN'T DEAD EITHER?!
INDEED. AS YOU ARE AWARE, PICCOLO AND I WERE ONCE *ONE* AND...
C-COULD IT BE... ?!
...
peep

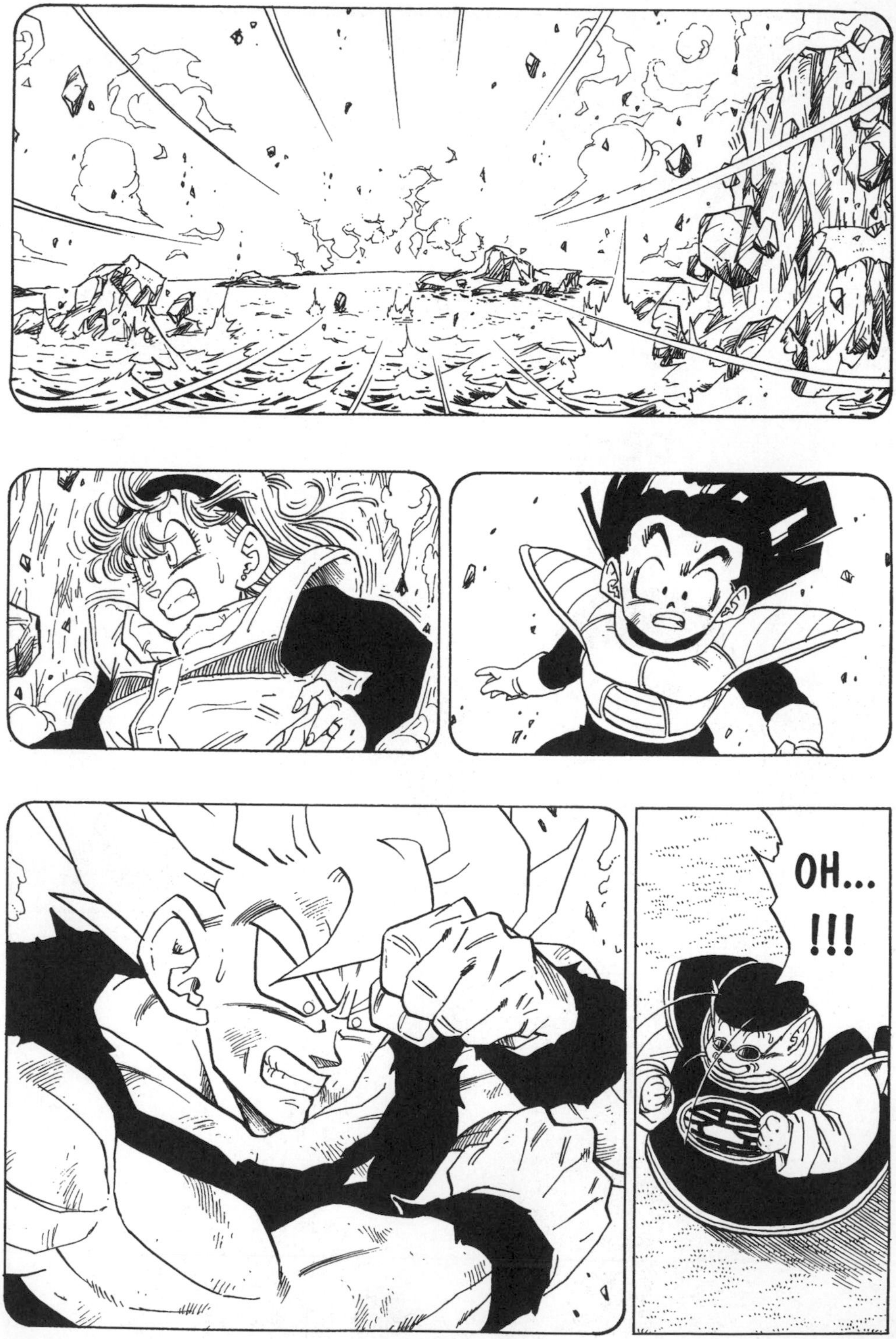
OH...
!!!

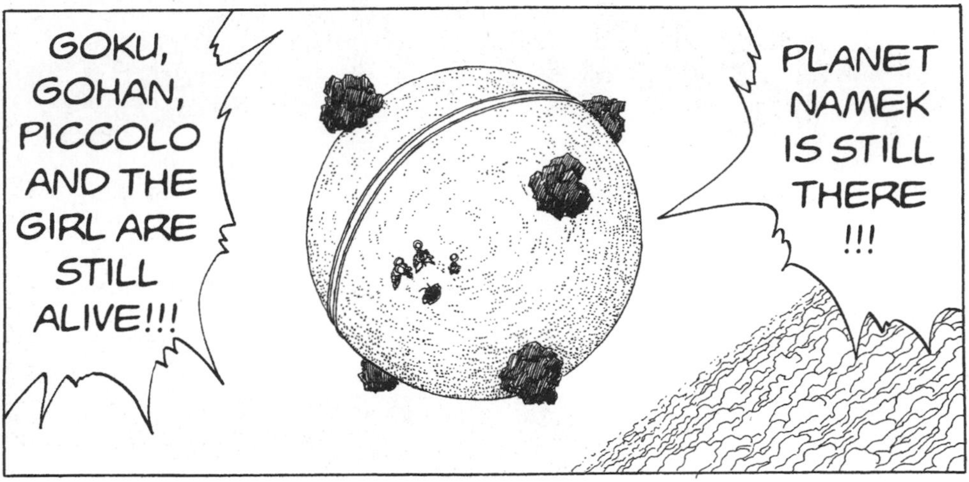
GOKU, GOHAN, PICCOLO AND THE GIRL ARE STILL ALIVE!!!
PLANET NAMEK IS STILL THERE !!!

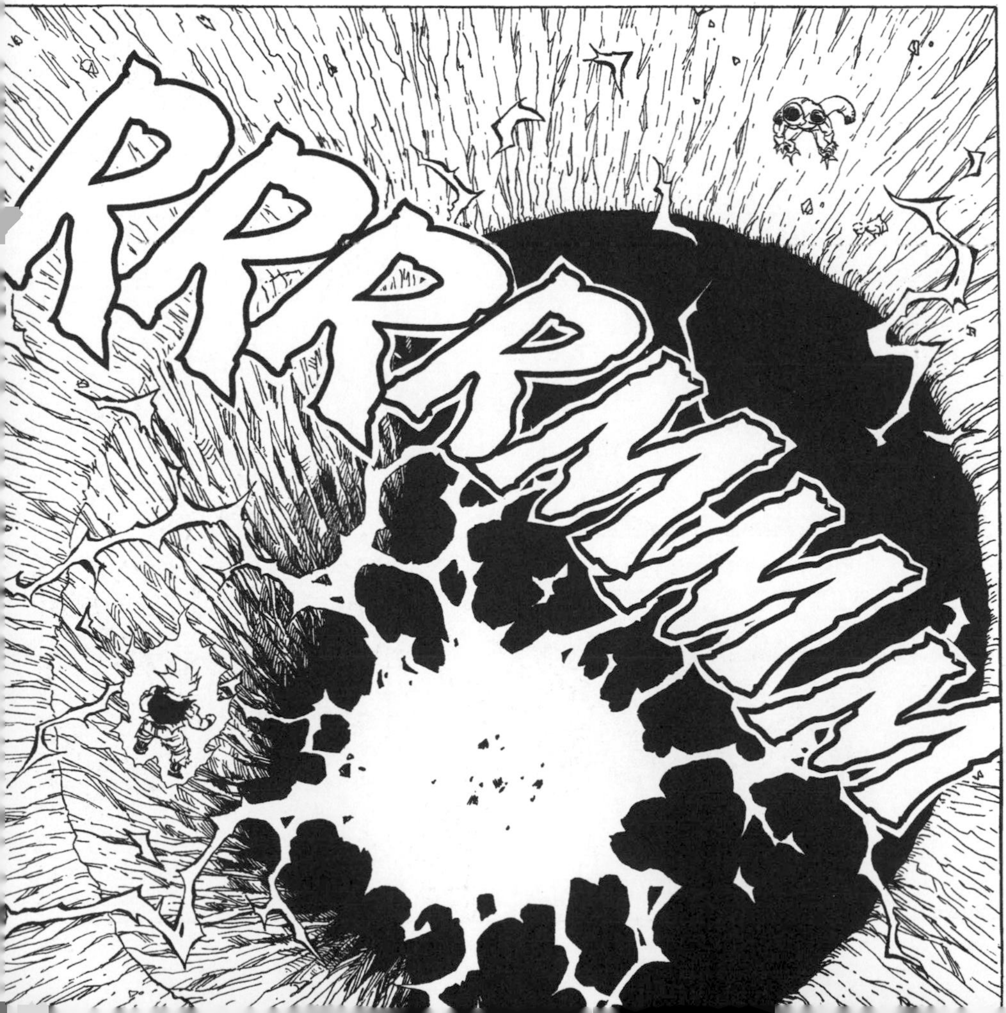

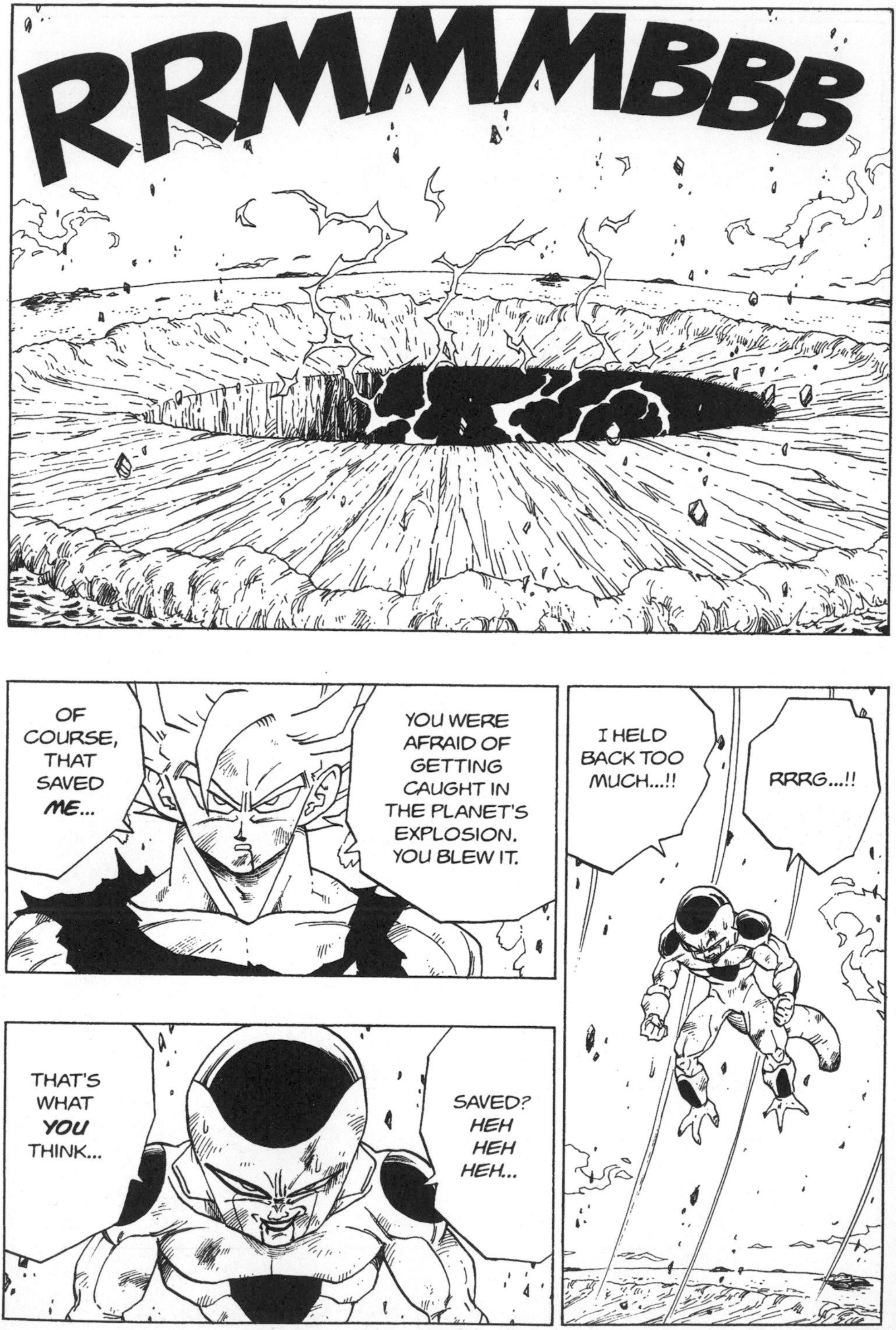
RRMMMBBB
RRRG...!!
I HELD BACK TOO MUCH...!!
YOU WERE AFRAID OF GETTING CAUGHT IN THE PLANET'S EXPLOSION. YOU BLEW IT.
OF COURSE, THAT SAVED *ME*...
SAVED? *HEH HEH HEH...*
THAT'S WHAT *YOU* THINK...

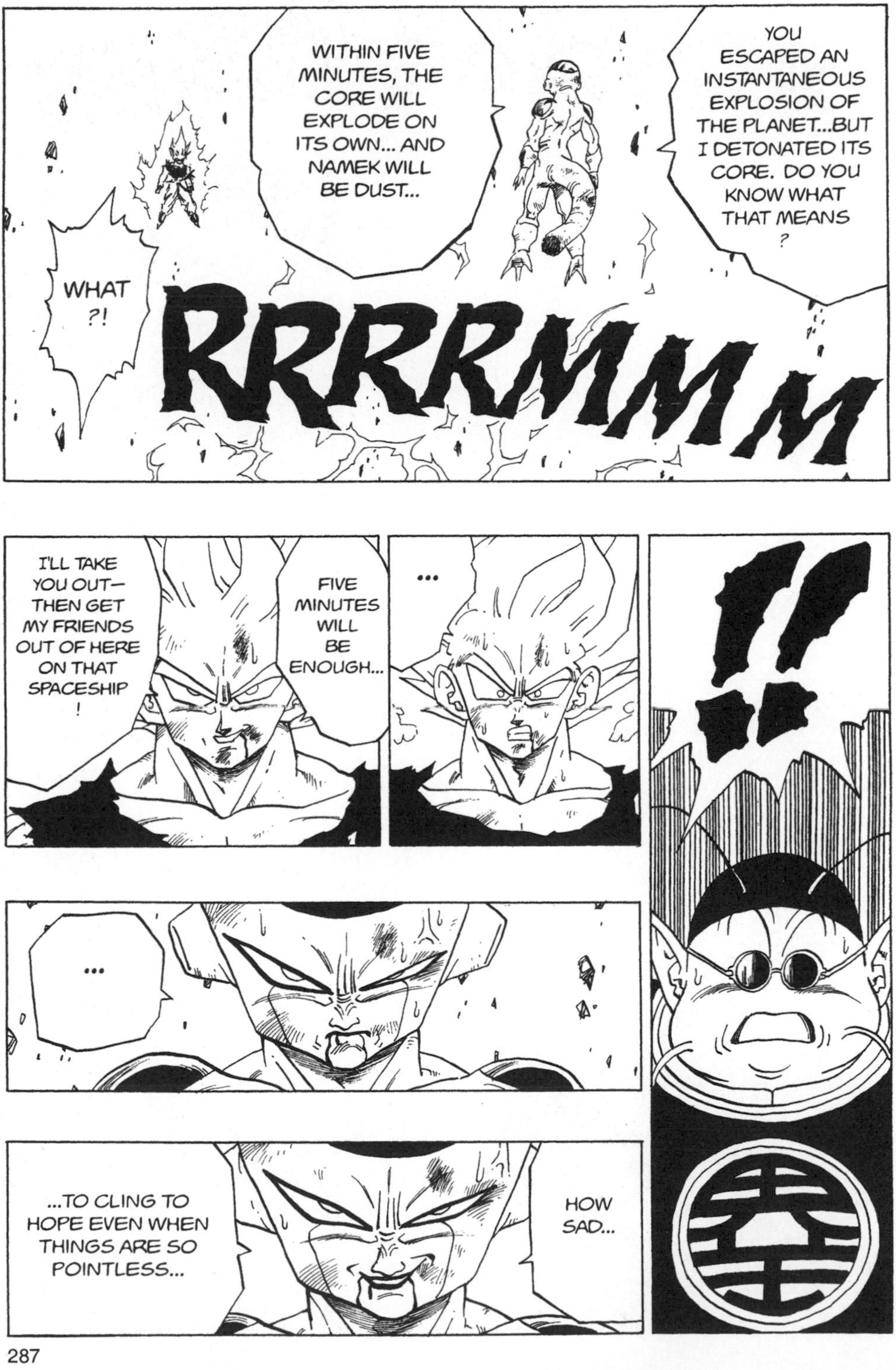
YOU ESCAPED AN INSTANTANEOUS EXPLOSION OF THE PLANET...BUT I DETONATED ITS CORE. DO YOU KNOW WHAT THAT MEANS?
WITHIN FIVE MINUTES, THE CORE WILL EXPLODE ON ITS OWN... AND NAMEK WILL BE DUST...
WHAT?!
RRRRMMMM
!!
...
FIVE MINUTES WILL BE ENOUGH...
I'LL TAKE YOU OUT—THEN GET MY FRIENDS OUT OF HERE ON THAT SPACESHIP!
...
HOW SAD...
...TO CLING TO HOPE EVEN WHEN THINGS ARE SO POINTLESS...

THEN TELL ME HOW YOU'LL "TAKE ME OUT" !!!!

IT'S TIME FOR YOU TO SEE MY FULL POWER REVEALED !!!!

WHY GO TO YOUR FULL POWER NOW...? MAYBE... BECAUSE YOUR BODY CAN'T WITHSTAND IT FOR LONG ANYMORE?!

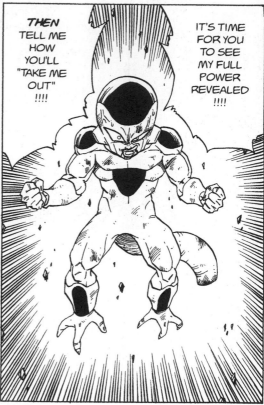

I'LL PUT AN END TO THIS ONCE AND FOR ALL !!!!!

I WON'T LET YOU BUY TIME FOR YOURSELF!!!

...

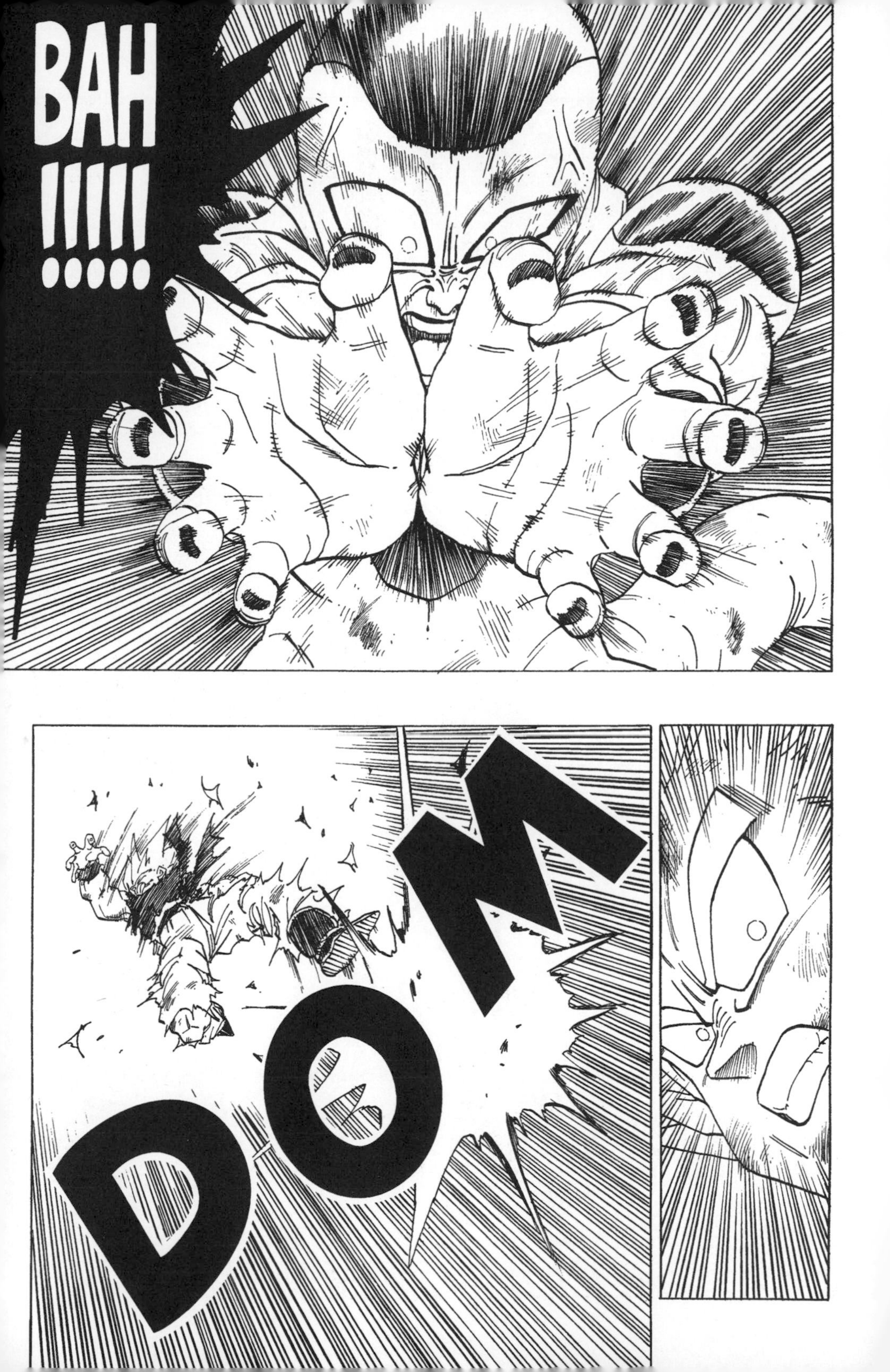

BAH!!!!!!
DOM

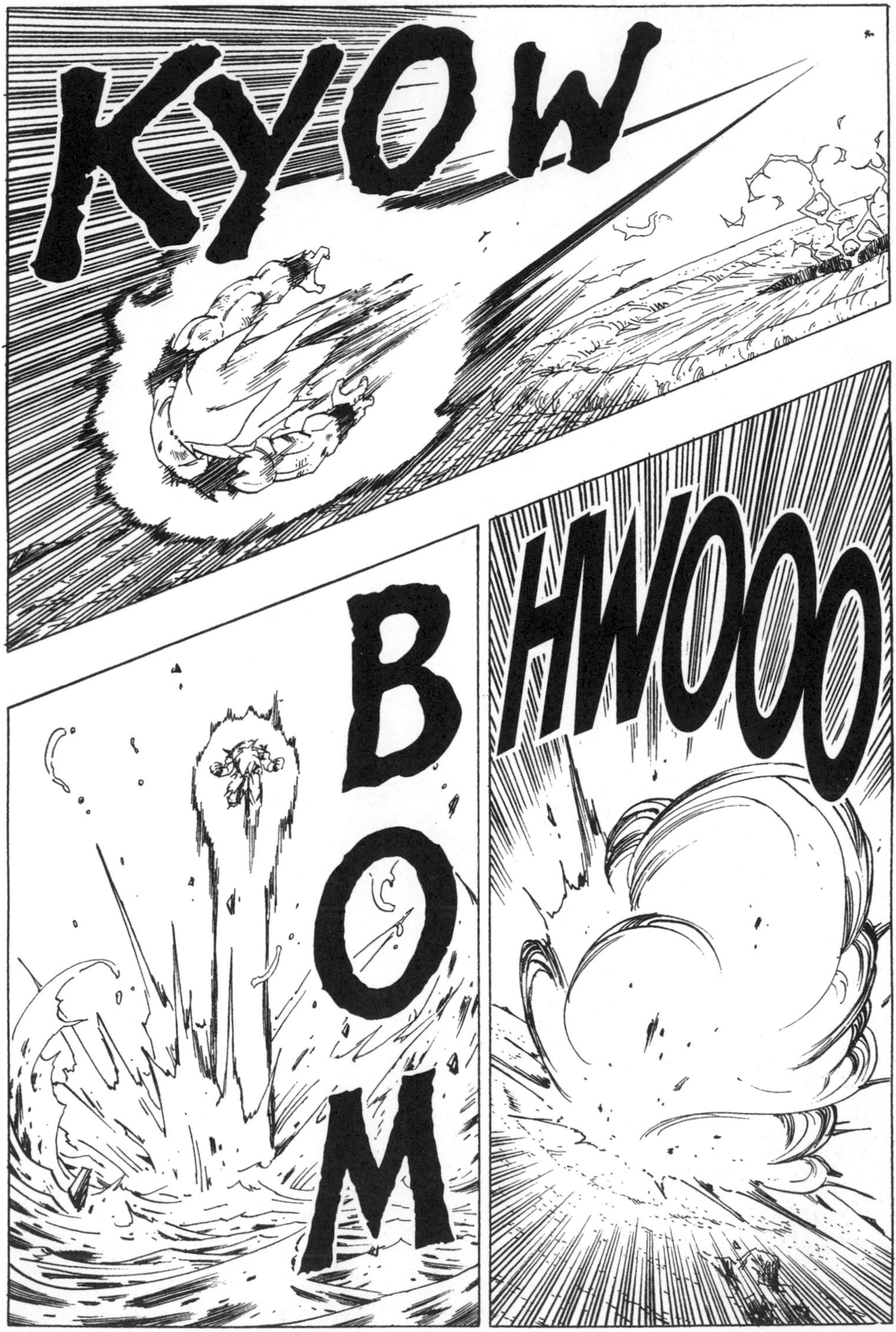
KYOW
HWOOO
BOOM

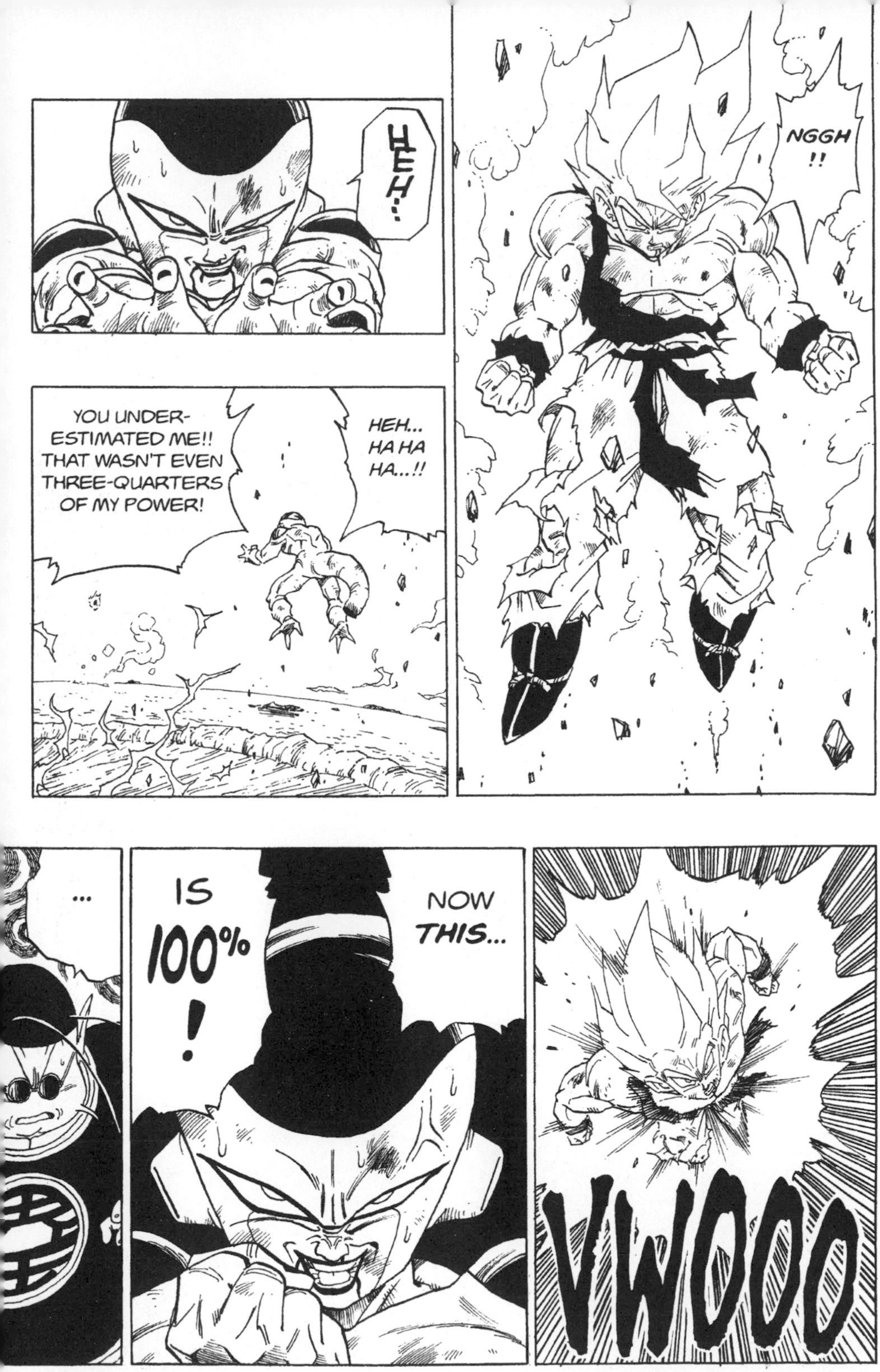
NGGH!!
HEH!!
HEH... HA HA HA...!!
YOU UNDER-ESTIMATED ME!! THAT WASN'T EVEN THREE-QUARTERS OF MY POWER!
VWOOO
NOW THIS...
IS 100%!
...

DBZ:127 · Maximum Desperation

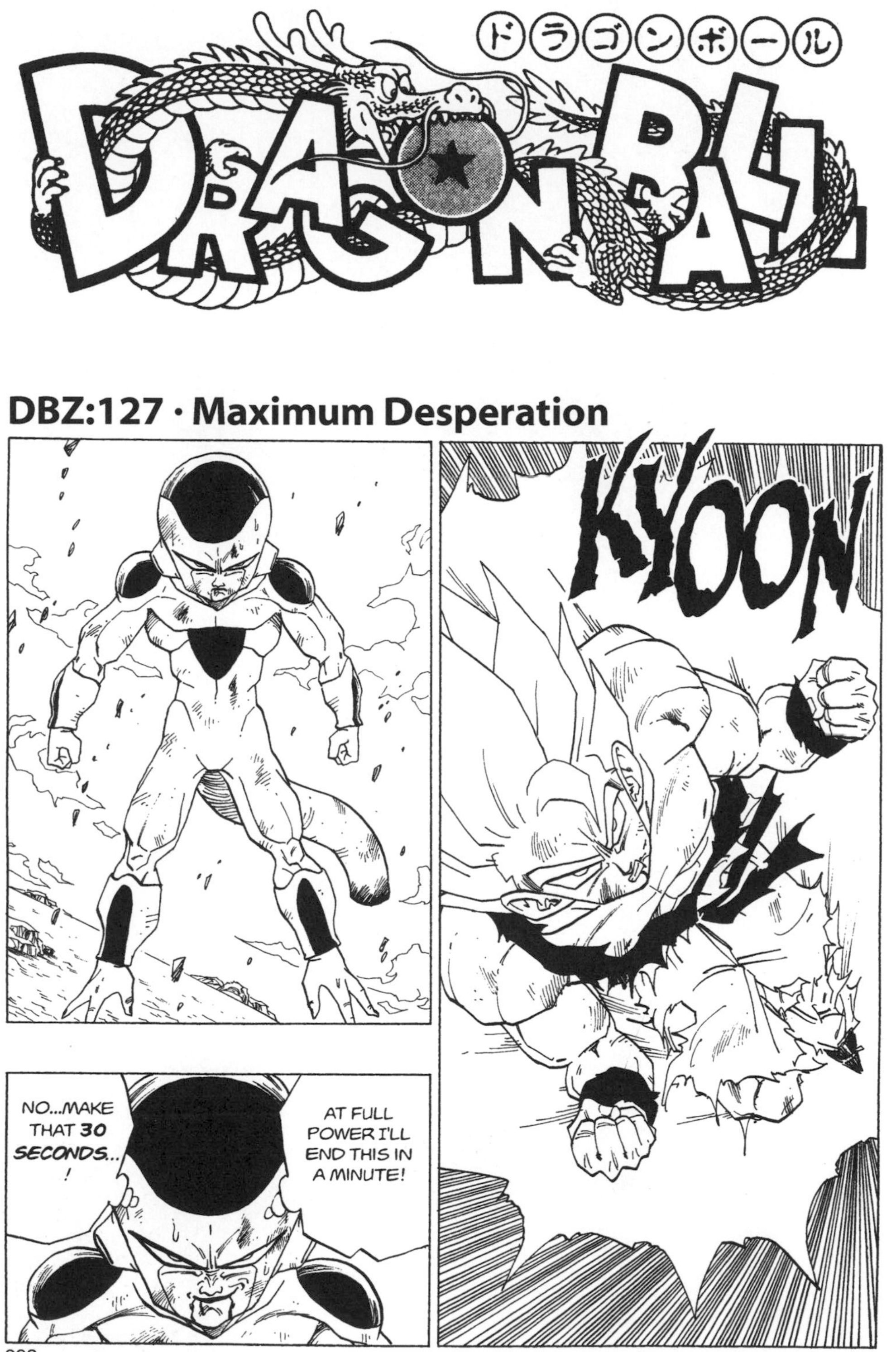
KYOON
AT FULL POWER I'LL END THIS IN A MINUTE!
NO...MAKE THAT 30 SECONDS...!

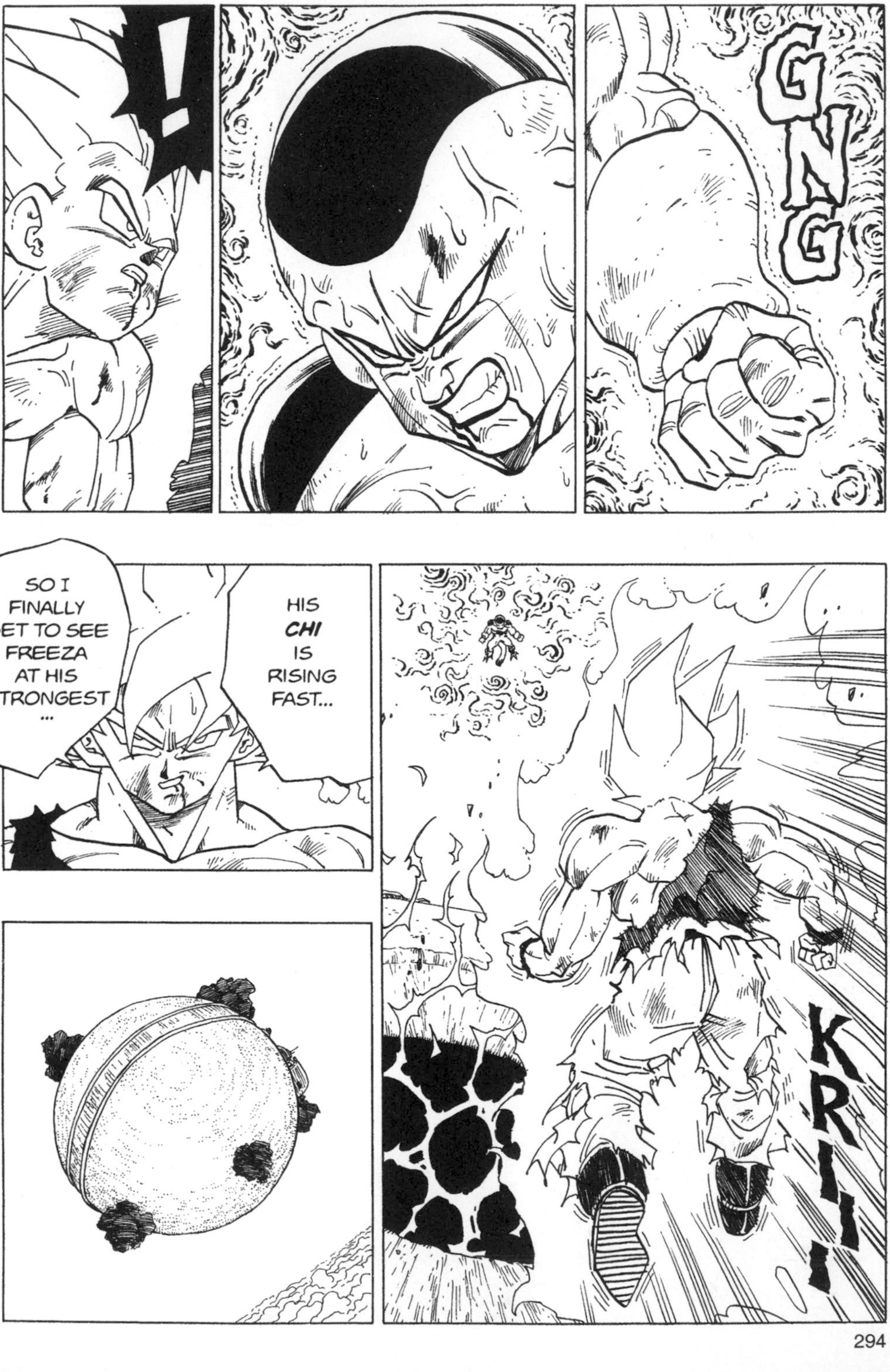
GNG
!
HIS CHI IS RISING FAST...
SO I FINALLY GET TO SEE FREEZA AT HIS STRONGEST ...
KRII

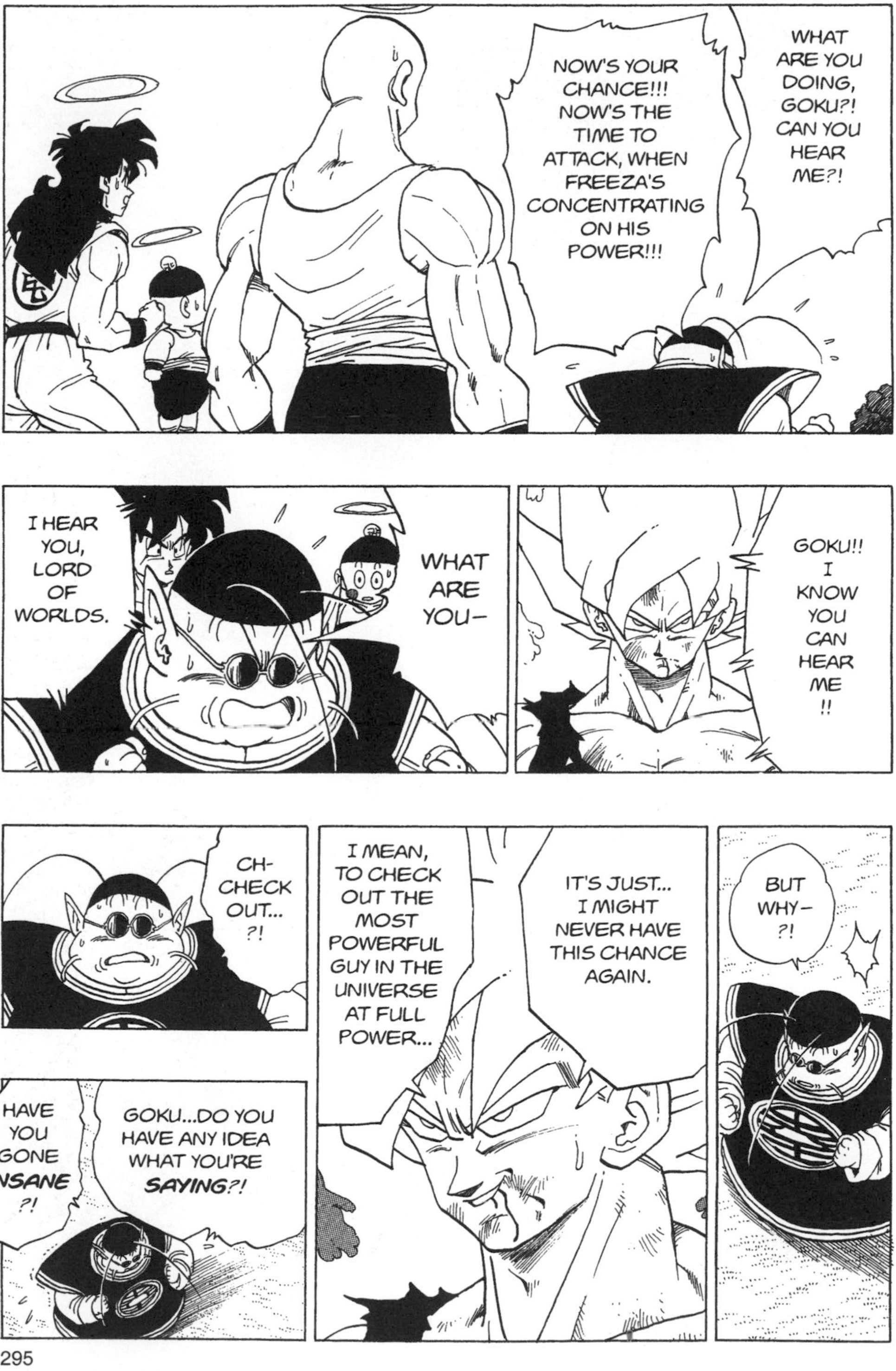

NOW'S YOUR CHANCE!!! NOW'S THE TIME TO ATTACK, WHEN FREEZA'S CONCENTRATING ON HIS POWER!!!
WHAT ARE YOU DOING, GOKU?! CAN YOU HEAR ME?!
I HEAR YOU, LORD OF WORLDS.
WHAT ARE YOU–
GOKU!! I KNOW YOU CAN HEAR ME!!
CH-CHECK OUT... ?!
I MEAN, TO CHECK OUT THE MOST POWERFUL GUY IN THE UNIVERSE AT FULL POWER...
IT'S JUST... I MIGHT NEVER HAVE THIS CHANCE AGAIN.
BUT WHY– ?!
HAVE YOU GONE *INSANE* ?!
GOKU...DO YOU HAVE ANY IDEA WHAT YOU'RE *SAYING*?!

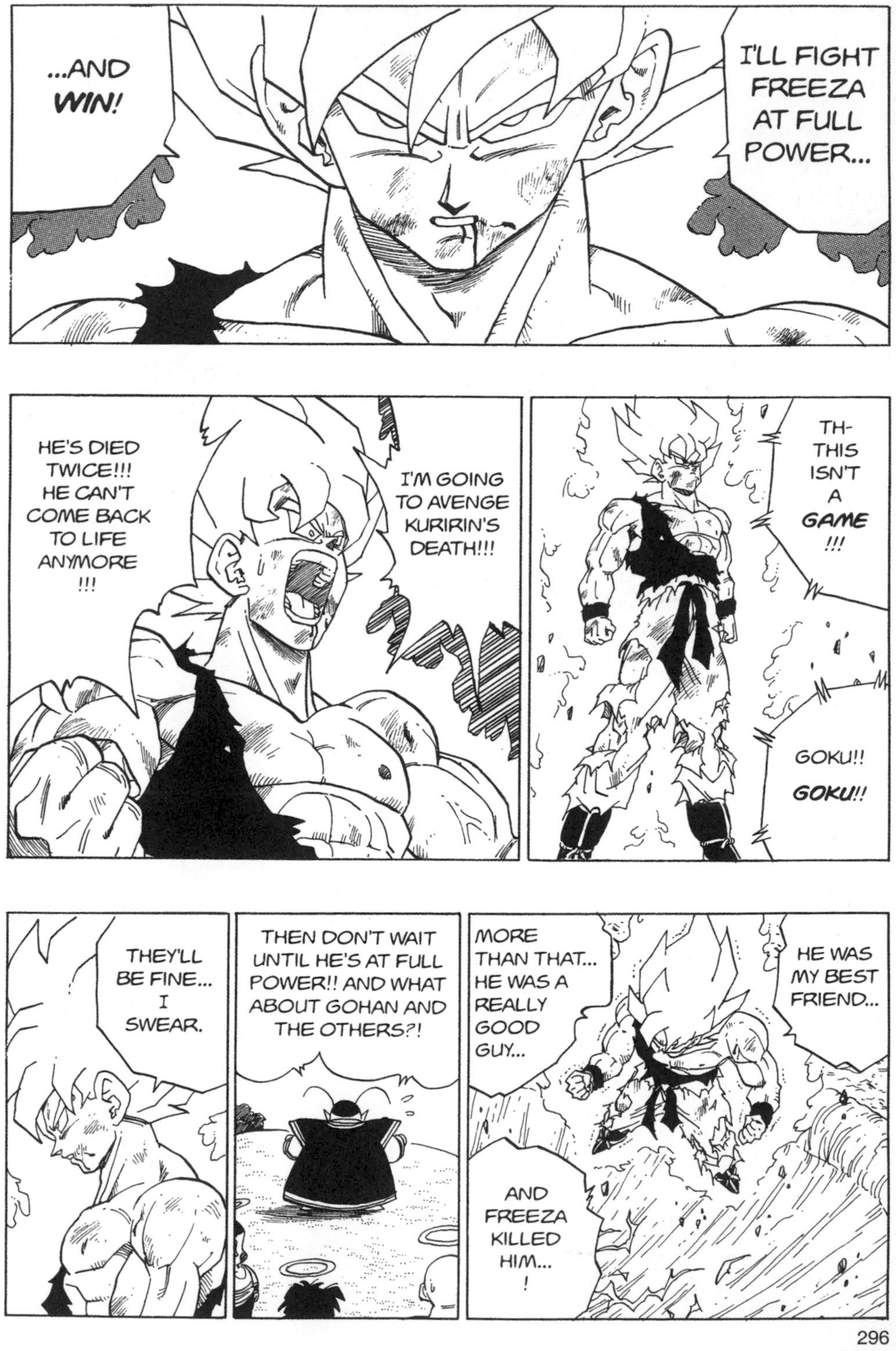

I'LL FIGHT FREEZA AT FULL POWER...
...AND WIN!
GOKU!! GOKU!!
TH- THIS ISN'T A GAME!!!
I'M GOING TO AVENGE KURIRIN'S DEATH!!!
HE'S DIED TWICE!!! HE CAN'T COME BACK TO LIFE ANYMORE!!!
HE WAS MY BEST FRIEND...
MORE THAN THAT... HE WAS A REALLY GOOD GUY...
AND FREEZA KILLED HIM...!
THEN DON'T WAIT UNTIL HE'S AT FULL POWER!! AND WHAT ABOUT GOHAN AND THE OTHERS?!
THEY'LL BE FINE... I SWEAR.

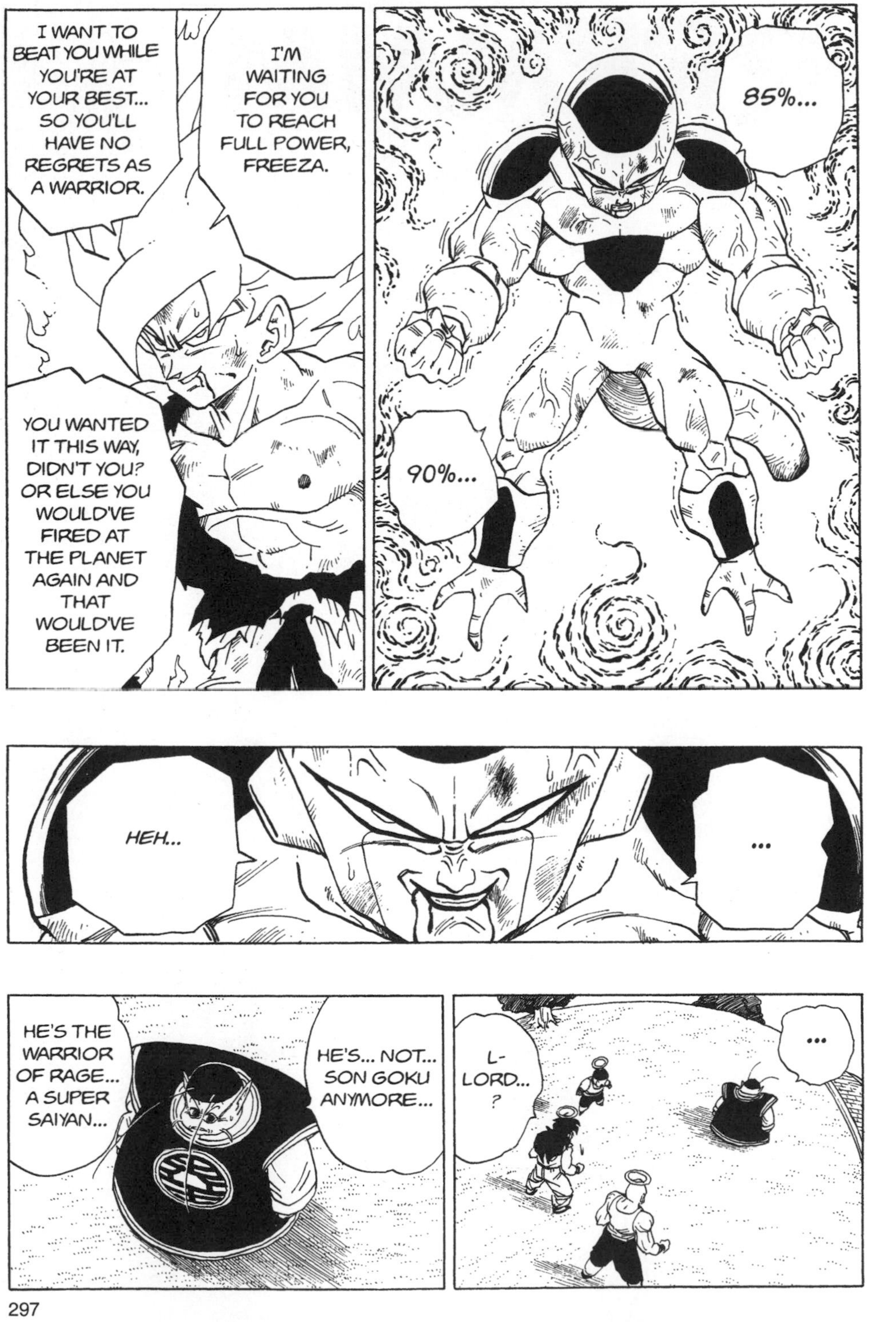
I'M WAITING FOR YOU TO REACH FULL POWER, FREEZA.
I WANT TO BEAT YOU WHILE YOU'RE AT YOUR BEST... SO YOU'LL HAVE NO REGRETS AS A WARRIOR.
YOU WANTED IT THIS WAY, DIDN'T YOU? OR ELSE YOU WOULD'VE FIRED AT THE PLANET AGAIN AND THAT WOULD'VE BEEN IT.
85%...
90%...
HEH...
...
HE'S... NOT... SON GOKU ANYMORE...
HE'S THE WARRIOR OF RAGE... A SUPER SAIYAN...
L-LORD...?
...

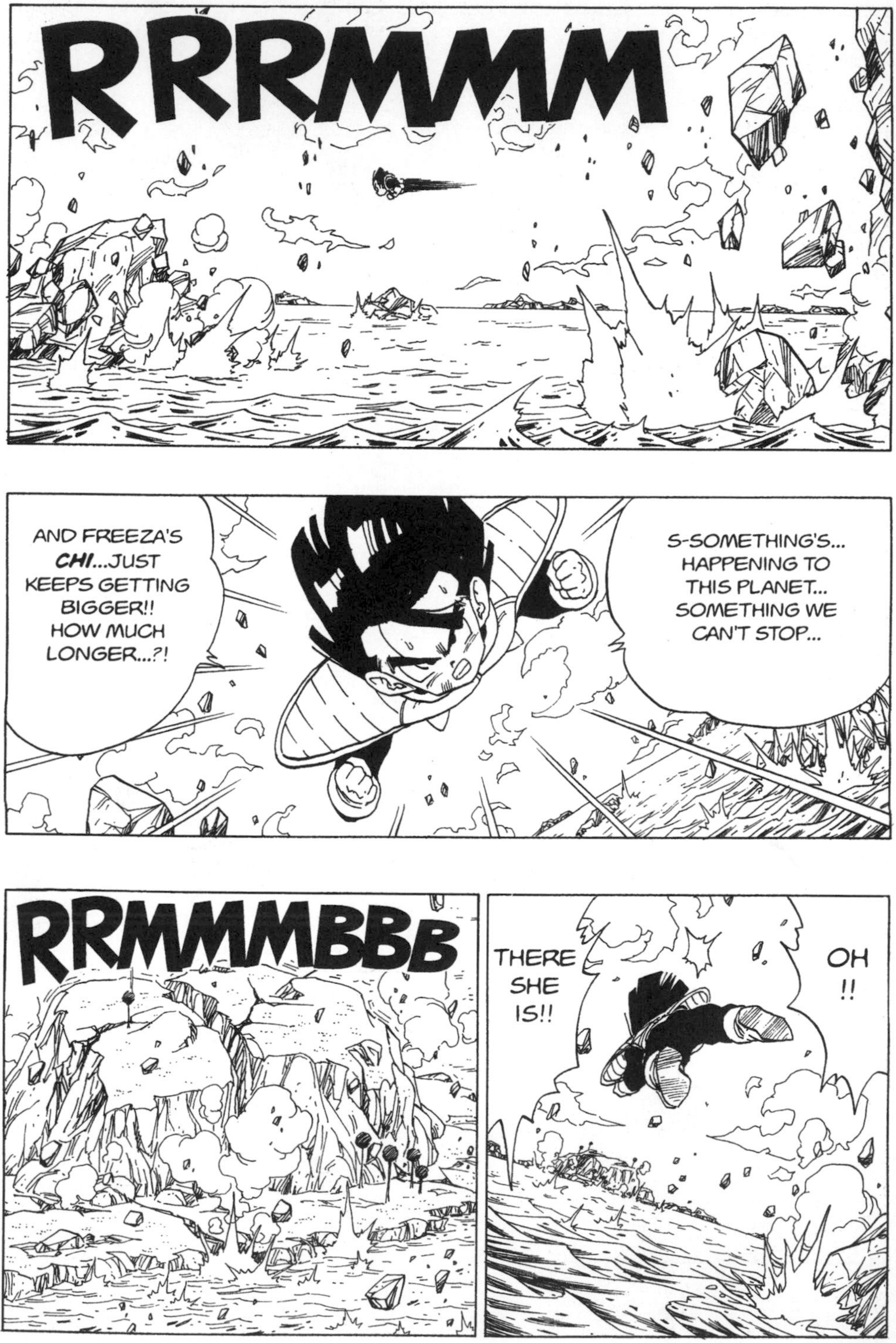
RRRMMM
AND FREEZA'S *CHI*...JUST KEEPS GETTING BIGGER!! HOW MUCH LONGER...?!
S-SOMETHING'S... HAPPENING TO THIS PLANET... SOMETHING WE CAN'T STOP...
RRMMMBBB
THERE SHE IS!!
OH !!

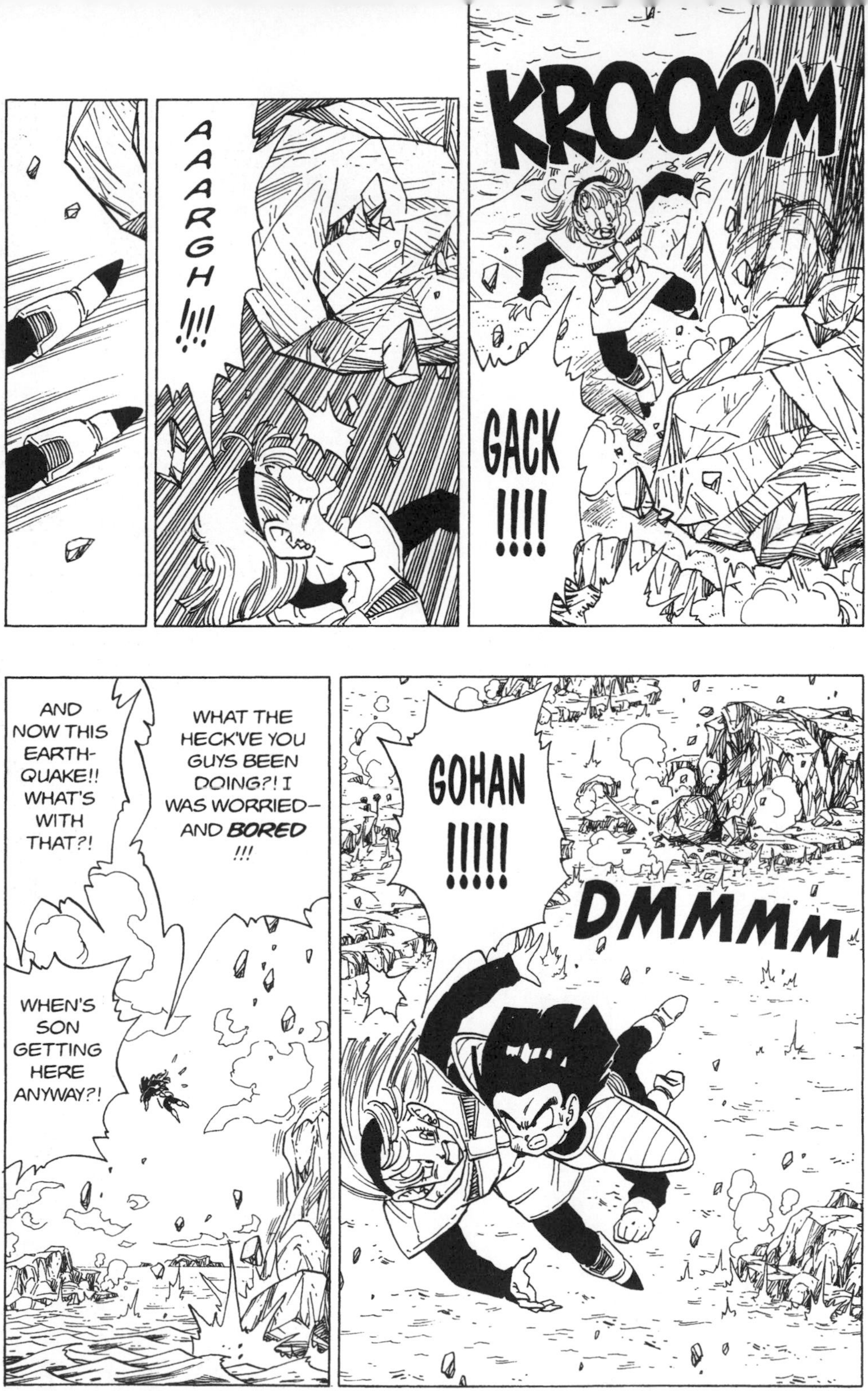
AAAARGH!!!!
KROOOM
GACK!!!!
GOHAN!!!!!
DMMMM
WHAT THE HECK'VE YOU GUYS BEEN DOING?! I WAS WORRIED— AND ***BORED*** !!!
AND NOW THIS EARTH-QUAKE!! WHAT'S WITH THAT?!
WHEN'S SON GETTING HERE ANYWAY?!

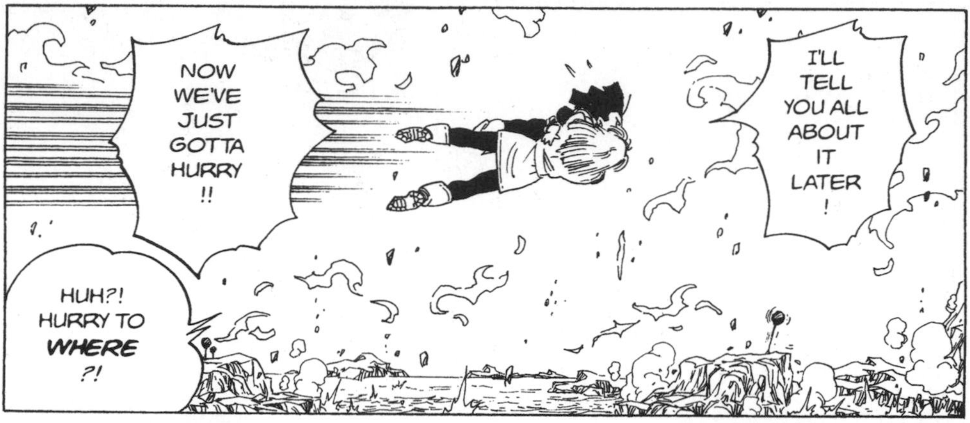
I'LL TELL YOU ALL ABOUT IT LATER !
NOW WE'VE JUST GOTTA HURRY !!
HUH?! HURRY TO *WHERE* ?!

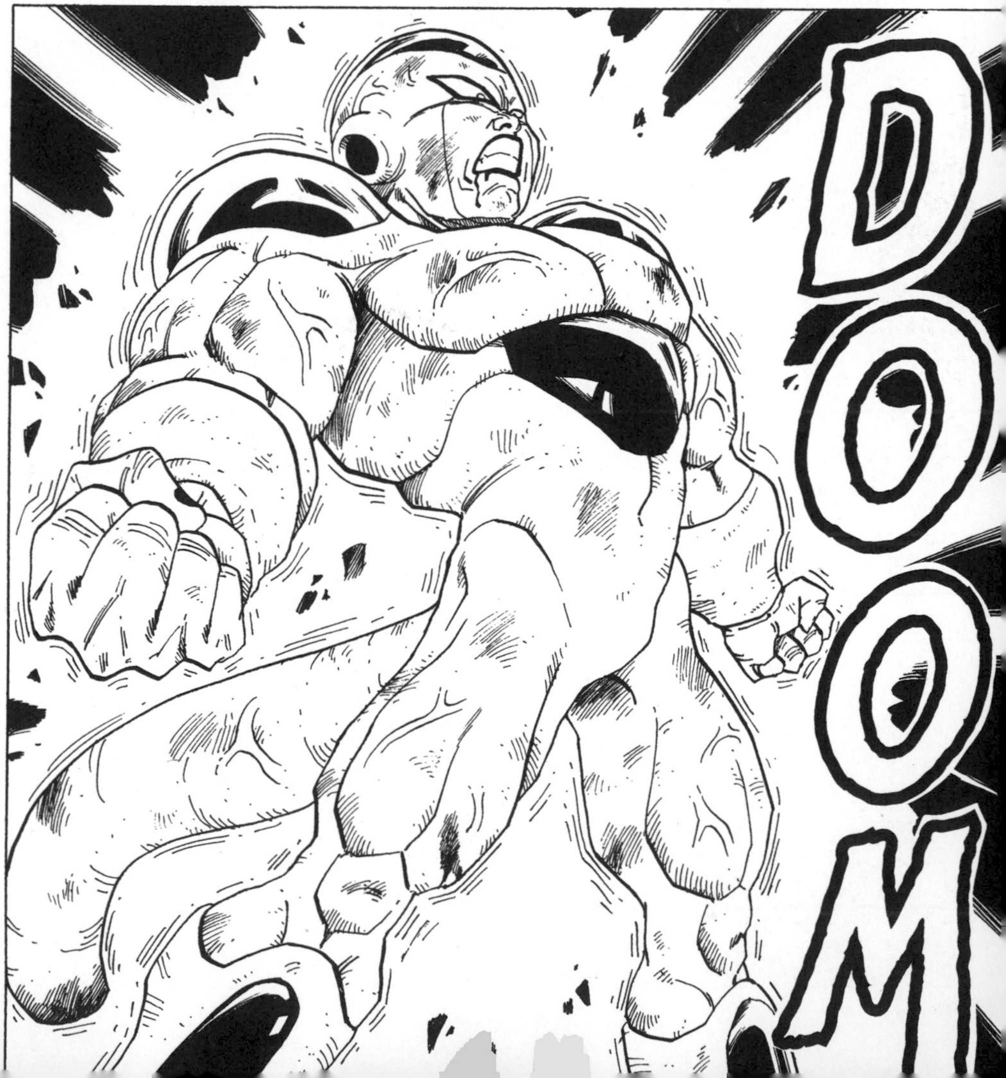
DOOOM

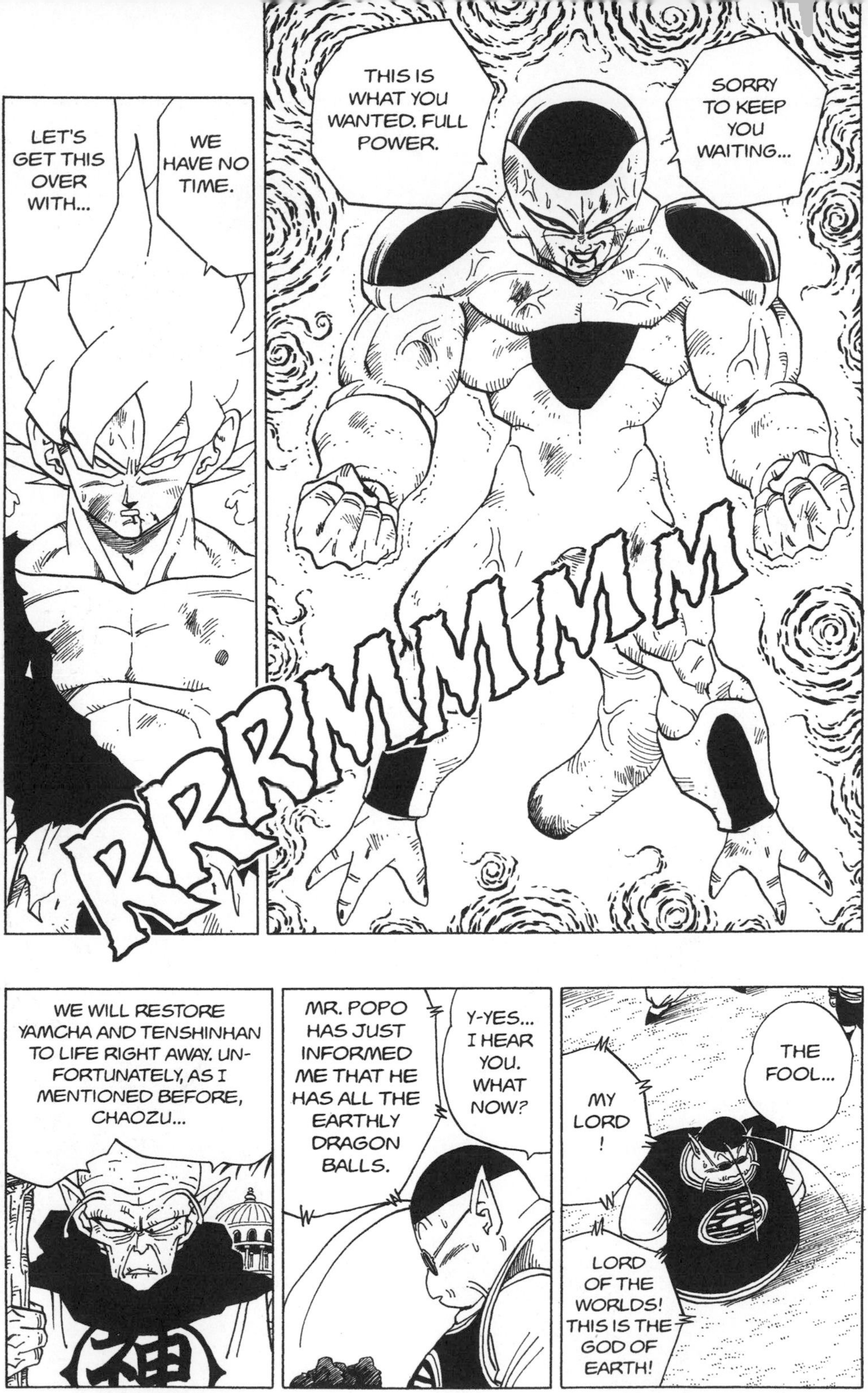
SORRY TO KEEP YOU WAITING...
THIS IS WHAT YOU WANTED. FULL POWER.
WE HAVE NO TIME.
LET'S GET THIS OVER WITH...
RRRMMMMMM
THE FOOL...
MY LORD!
LORD OF THE WORLDS! THIS IS THE GOD OF EARTH!
Y-YES... I HEAR YOU. WHAT NOW?
MR. POPO HAS JUST INFORMED ME THAT HE HAS ALL THE EARTHLY DRAGON BALLS.
WE WILL RESTORE YAMCHA AND TENSHINHAN TO LIFE RIGHT AWAY. UNFORTUNATELY, AS I MENTIONED BEFORE, CHAOZU...

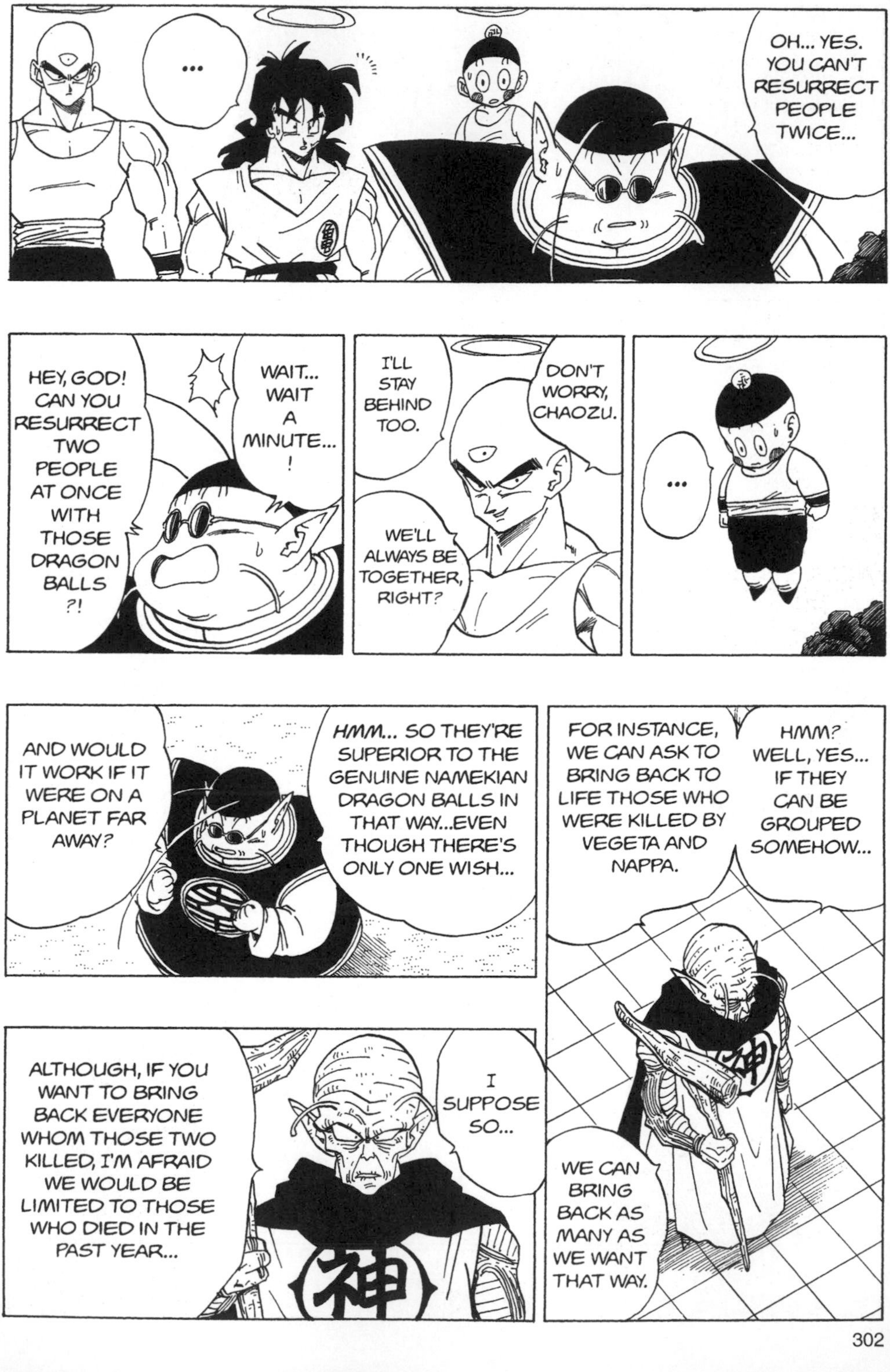
OH... YES. YOU CAN'T RESURRECT PEOPLE TWICE...
...
...
DON'T WORRY, CHAOZU.
I'LL STAY BEHIND TOO.
WE'LL ALWAYS BE TOGETHER, RIGHT?
WAIT... WAIT A MINUTE... !
HEY, GOD! CAN YOU RESURRECT TWO PEOPLE AT ONCE WITH THOSE DRAGON BALLS ?!
HMM? WELL, YES... IF THEY CAN BE GROUPED SOMEHOW...
FOR INSTANCE, WE CAN ASK TO BRING BACK TO LIFE THOSE WHO WERE KILLED BY VEGETA AND NAPPA.
WE CAN BRING BACK AS MANY AS WE WANT THAT WAY.
HMM... SO THEY'RE SUPERIOR TO THE GENUINE NAMEKIAN DRAGON BALLS IN THAT WAY...EVEN THOUGH THERE'S ONLY ONE WISH...
AND WOULD IT WORK IF IT WERE ON A PLANET FAR AWAY?
I SUPPOSE SO...
ALTHOUGH, IF YOU WANT TO BRING BACK EVERYONE WHOM THOSE TWO KILLED, I'M AFRAID WE WOULD BE LIMITED TO THOSE WHO DIED IN THE PAST YEAR...

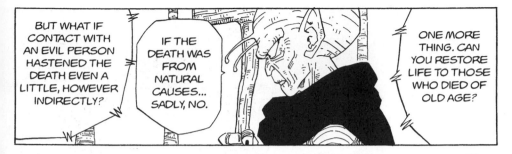

ONE MORE THING. CAN YOU RESTORE LIFE TO THOSE WHO DIED OF OLD AGE?
IF THE DEATH WAS FROM NATURAL CAUSES... SADLY, NO.
BUT WHAT IF CONTACT WITH AN EVIL PERSON HASTENED THE DEATH EVEN A LITTLE, HOWEVER INDIRECTLY?
HMM... I DON'T KNOW... WE'VE NEVER TESTED A CASE LIKE THAT...
HE MIGHT BE ABLE TO RETURN TO LIFE FOR THE AMOUNT OF TIME HIS LIFE WAS SHORTENED BY...
...BUT I CAN'T PROMISE...
...HMM...
LORD... WHAT ARE YOU...?
ALL RIGHT !!
I'VE DECIDED !!
KAMI! CHANGE THE WISH!
MAKE IT, "RESTORE LIFE TO THOSE WHO WERE KILLED BY FREEZA AND HIS MEN!"
WHAT ?!
LISTEN CLOSELY, BECAUSE WE ONLY HAVE A MOMENT! WE USE THESE EARTHLY DRAGON BALLS TO BRING BACK THOSE WHO WERE KILLED BY FREEZA...
THAT MEANS THE OTHER NAMEKIANS... AND POSSIBLY, FOR A SHORT WHILE, THE GREAT ELDER HIMSELF!

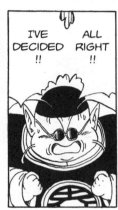

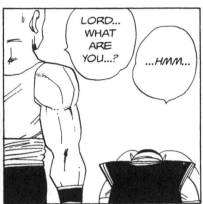

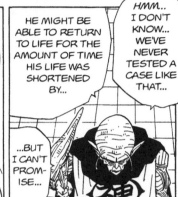

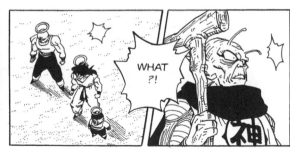

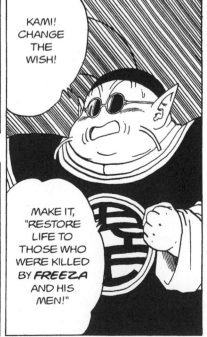

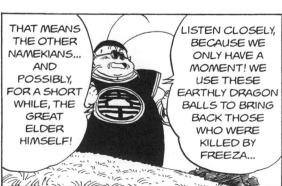

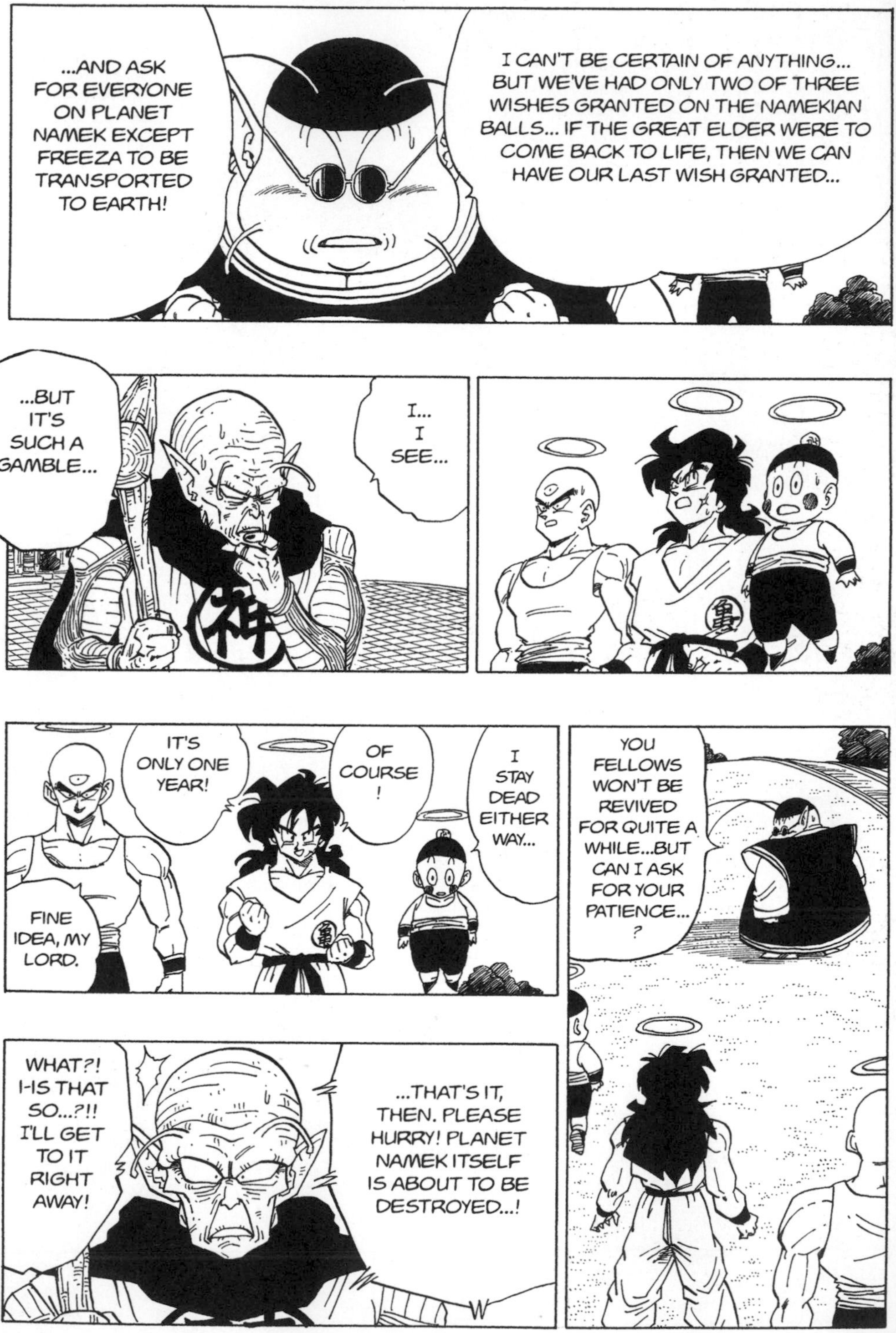

I CAN'T BE CERTAIN OF ANYTHING... BUT WE'VE HAD ONLY TWO OF THREE WISHES GRANTED ON THE NAMEKIAN BALLS... IF THE GREAT ELDER WERE TO COME BACK TO LIFE, THEN WE CAN HAVE OUR LAST WISH GRANTED...
...AND ASK FOR EVERYONE ON PLANET NAMEK EXCEPT FREEZA TO BE TRANSPORTED TO EARTH!
I... I SEE...
...BUT IT'S SUCH A GAMBLE...
YOU FELLOWS WON'T BE REVIVED FOR QUITE A WHILE...BUT CAN I ASK FOR YOUR PATIENCE...?
I STAY DEAD EITHER WAY...
OF COURSE!
IT'S ONLY ONE YEAR!
FINE IDEA, MY LORD.
...THAT'S IT, THEN. PLEASE HURRY! PLANET NAMEK ITSELF IS ABOUT TO BE DESTROYED...!
WHAT?! I-IS THAT SO...?!! I'LL GET TO IT RIGHT AWAY!

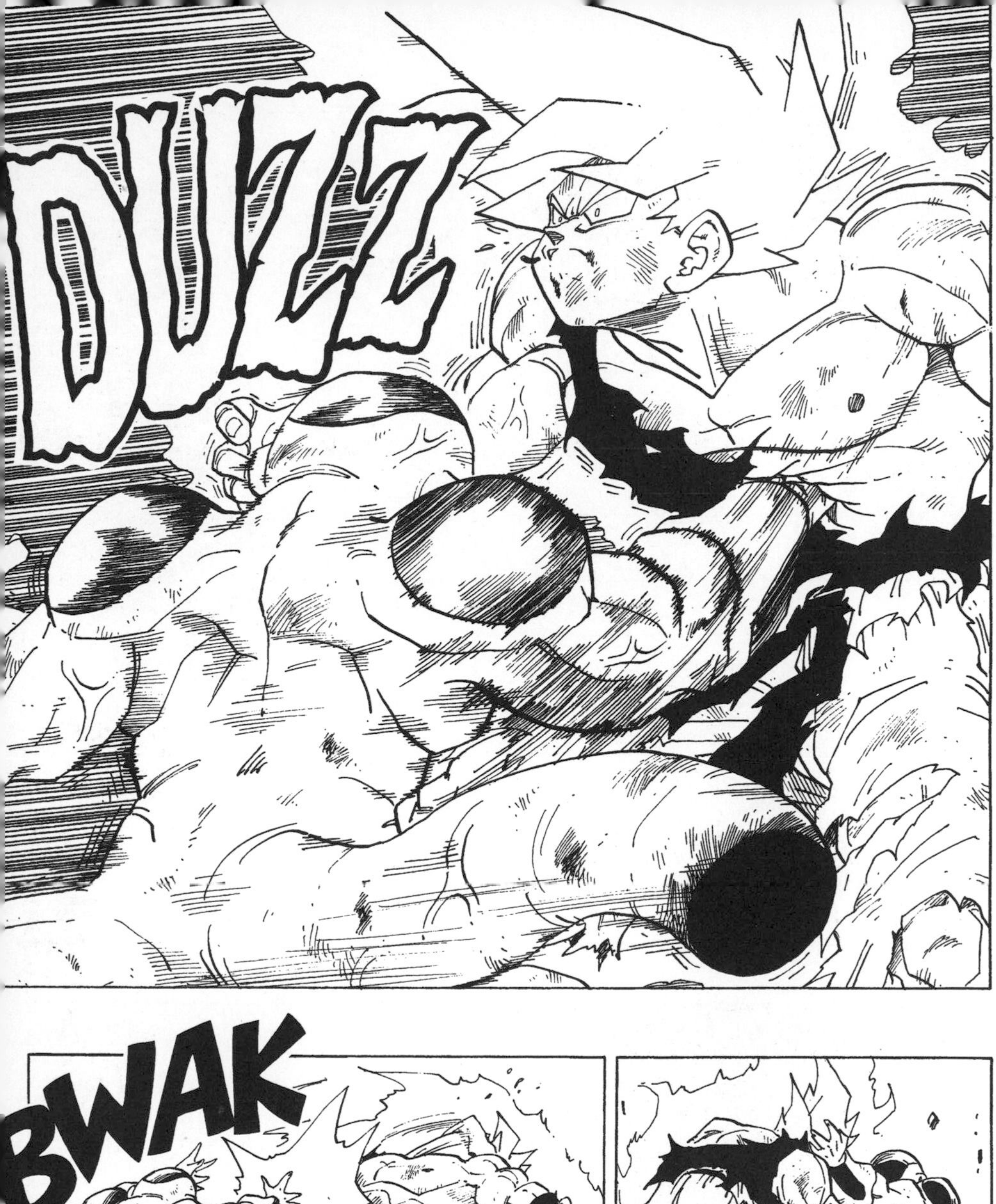
DUZZ

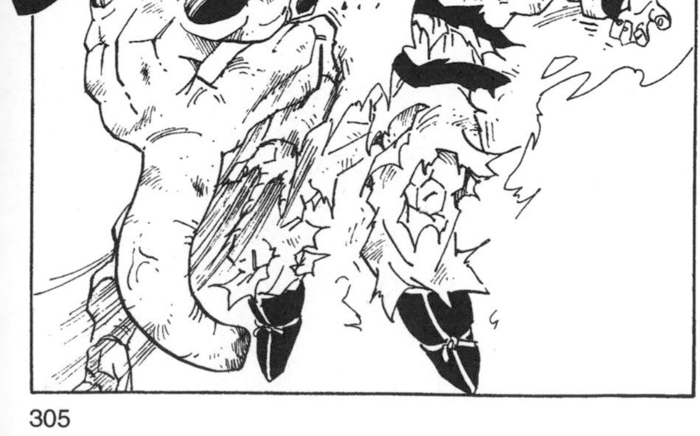
BWAK

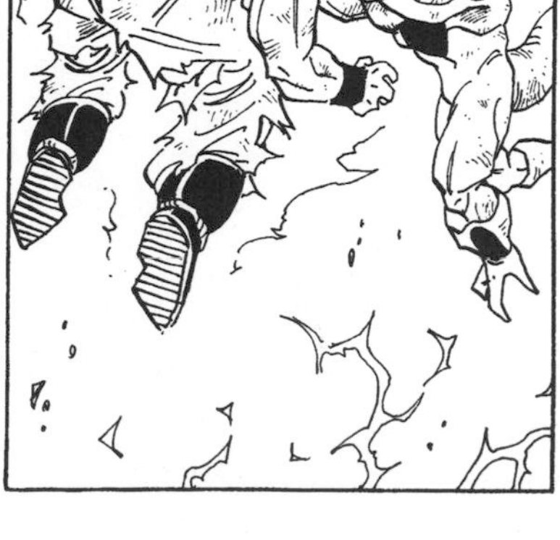

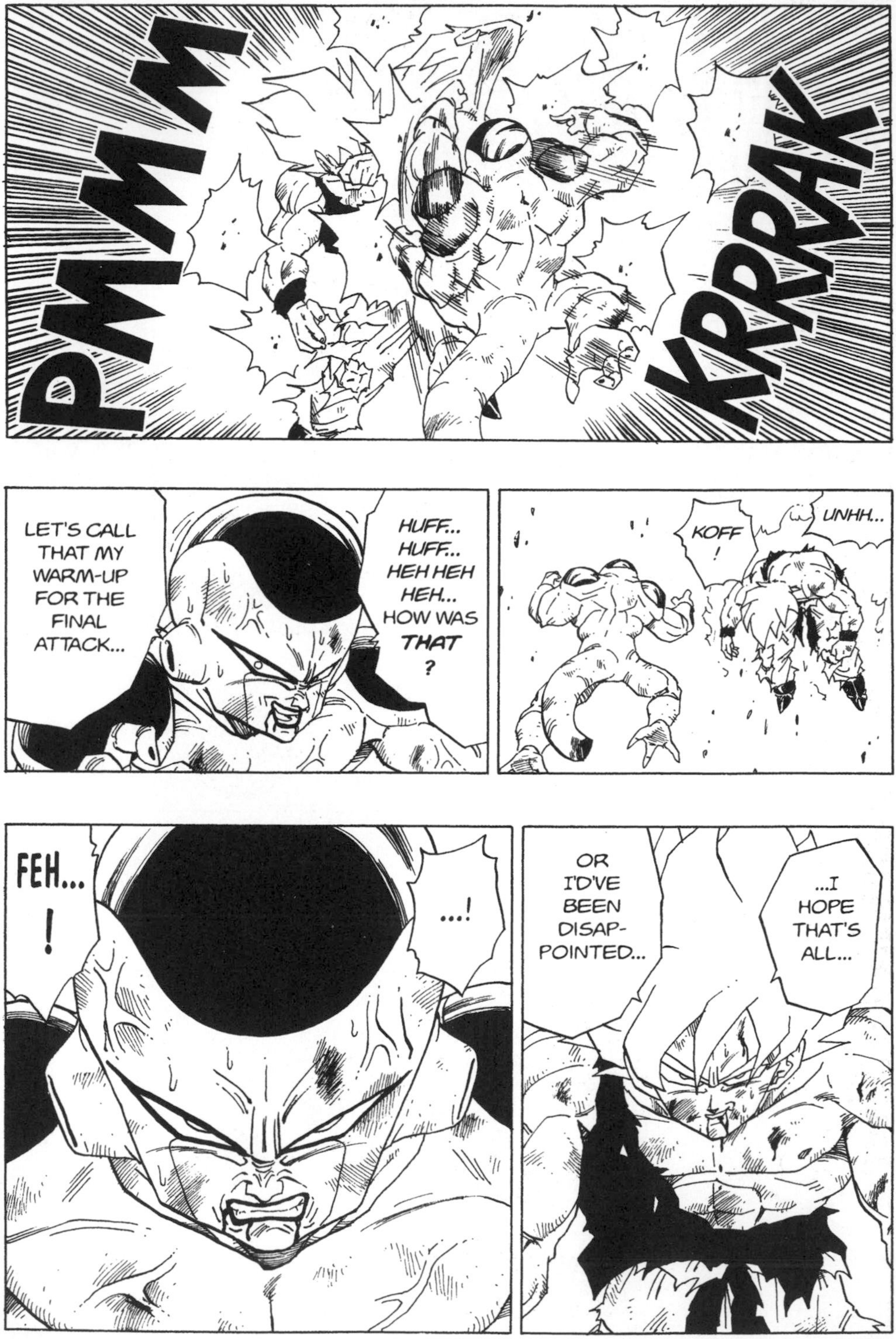
KRRAK
PMMM
UNHH...
KOFF!
HUFF... HUFF... HEH HEH HEH... HOW WAS THAT?
LET'S CALL THAT MY WARM-UP FOR THE FINAL ATTACK...
...I HOPE THAT'S ALL...
OR I'D'VE BEEN DISAPPOINTED...
...!
FEH...!

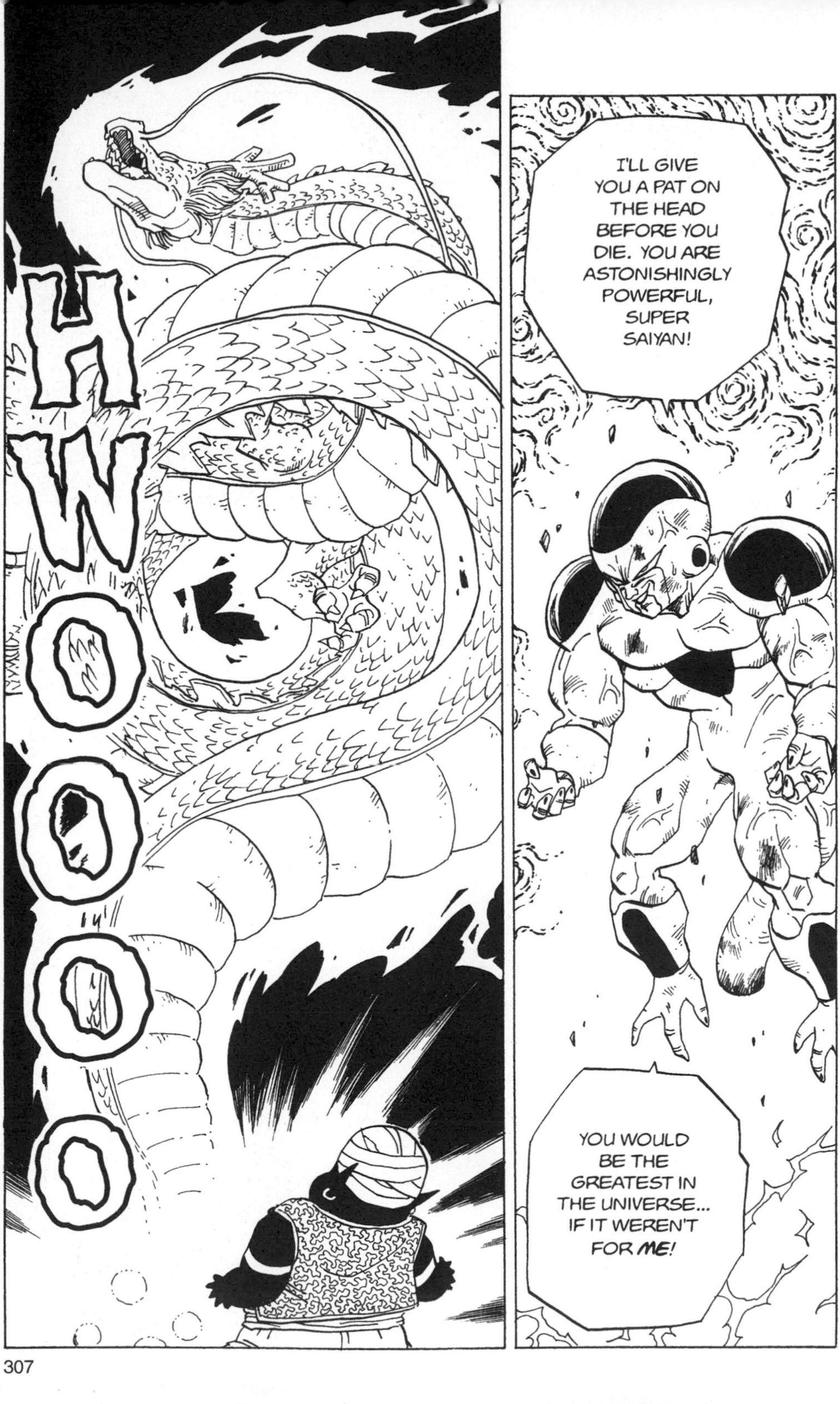

HWOOOO
I'LL GIVE YOU A PAT ON THE HEAD BEFORE YOU DIE. YOU ARE ASTONISHINGLY POWERFUL, SUPER SAIYAN!
YOU WOULD BE THE GREATEST IN THE UNIVERSE... IF IT WEREN'T FOR *ME*!

DRAGON BALL ドラゴンボール

DBZ:128 • Two Warriors, One Finish

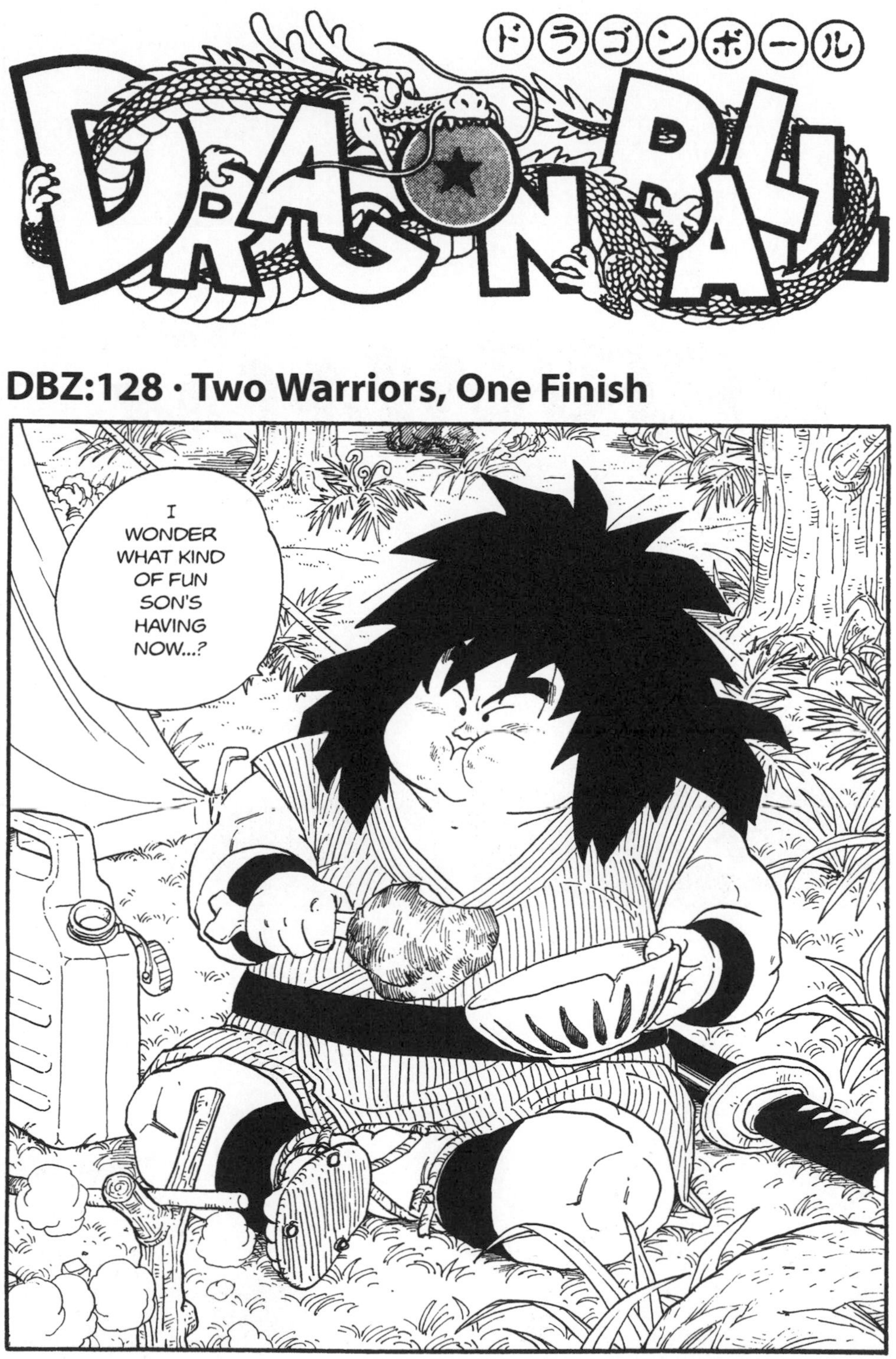
I WONDER WHAT KIND OF FUN SON'S HAVING NOW...?

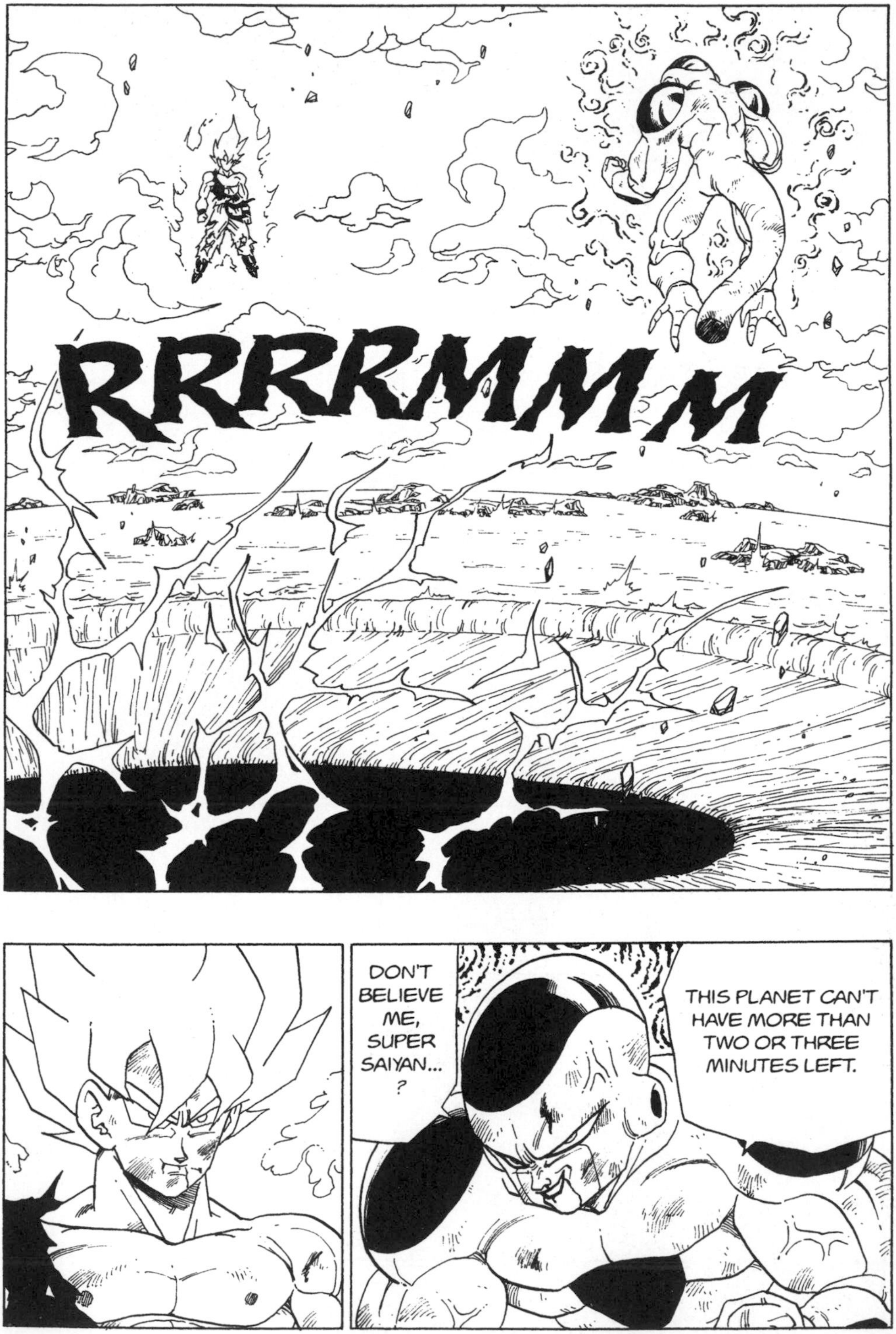
RRRRMMM
THIS PLANET CAN'T HAVE MORE THAN TWO OR THREE MINUTES LEFT.
DON'T BELIEVE ME, SUPER SAIYAN... ?

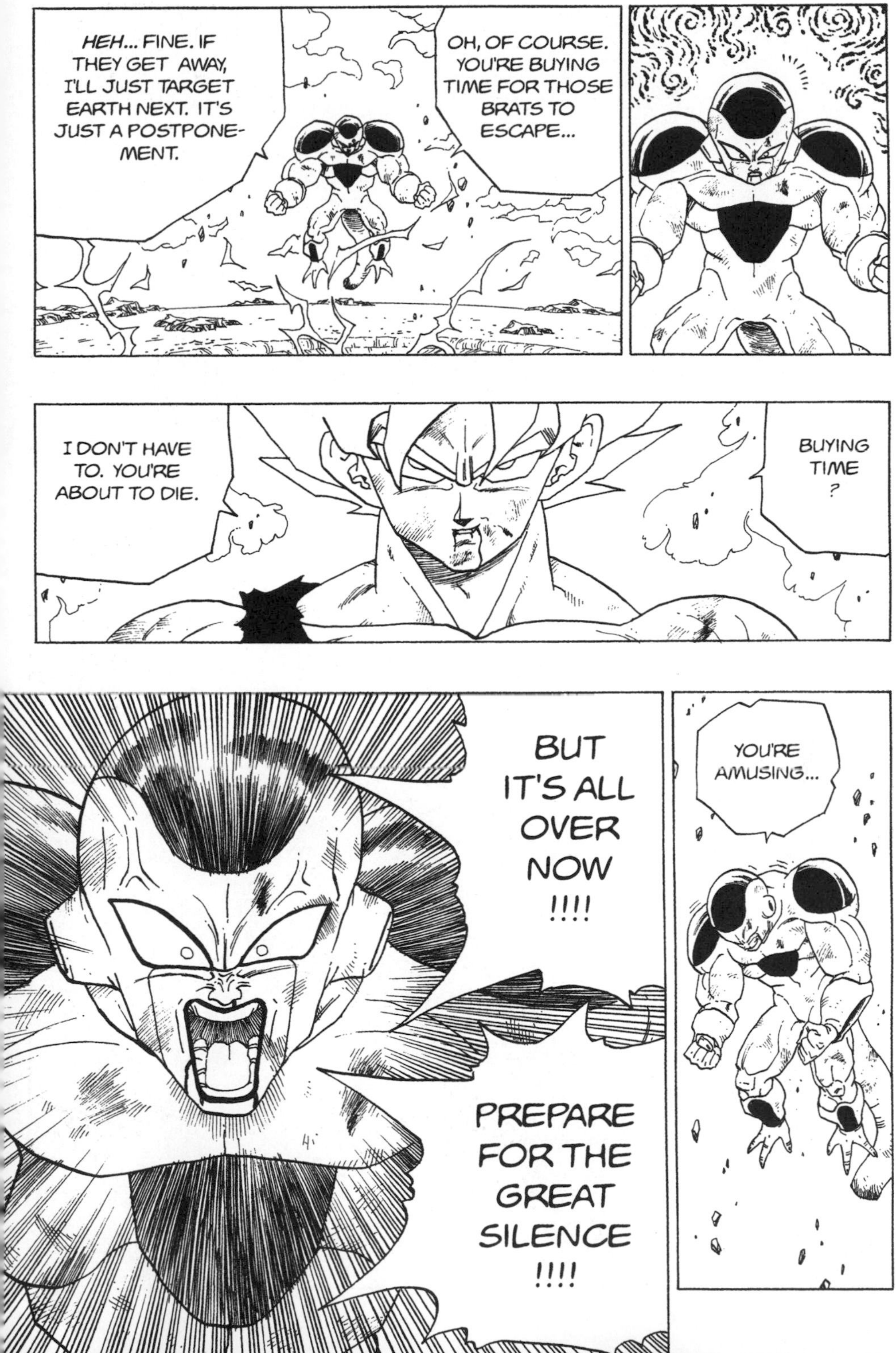
OH, OF COURSE. YOU'RE BUYING TIME FOR THOSE BRATS TO ESCAPE...
HEH... FINE. IF THEY GET AWAY, I'LL JUST TARGET EARTH NEXT. IT'S JUST A POSTPONEMENT.
BUYING TIME ?
I DON'T HAVE TO. YOU'RE ABOUT TO DIE.
YOU'RE AMUSING...
BUT IT'S ALL OVER NOW !!!!
PREPARE FOR THE GREAT SILENCE !!!!

HURRY UP!!

WHAT'S TAKING GOHAN AND THE REST SO LONG...?

SHP

HYAH!!!!

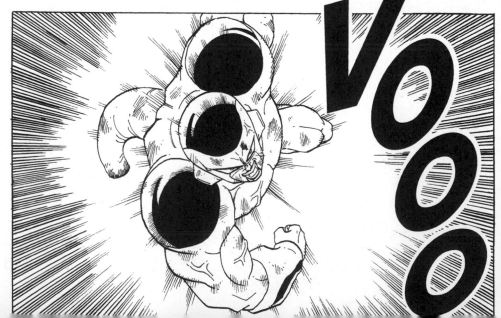

VOOO

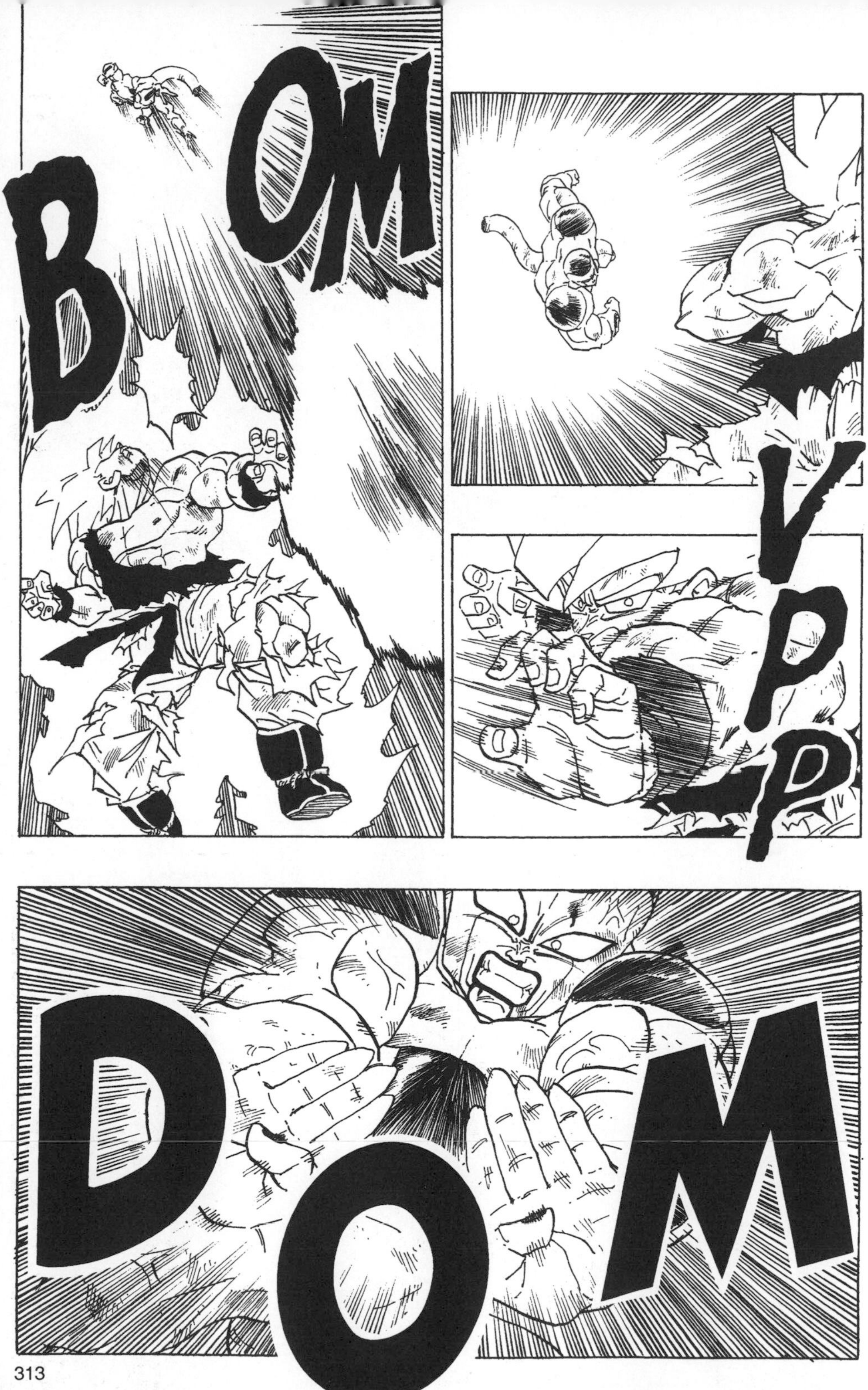
BOOM
VPPP
DOM

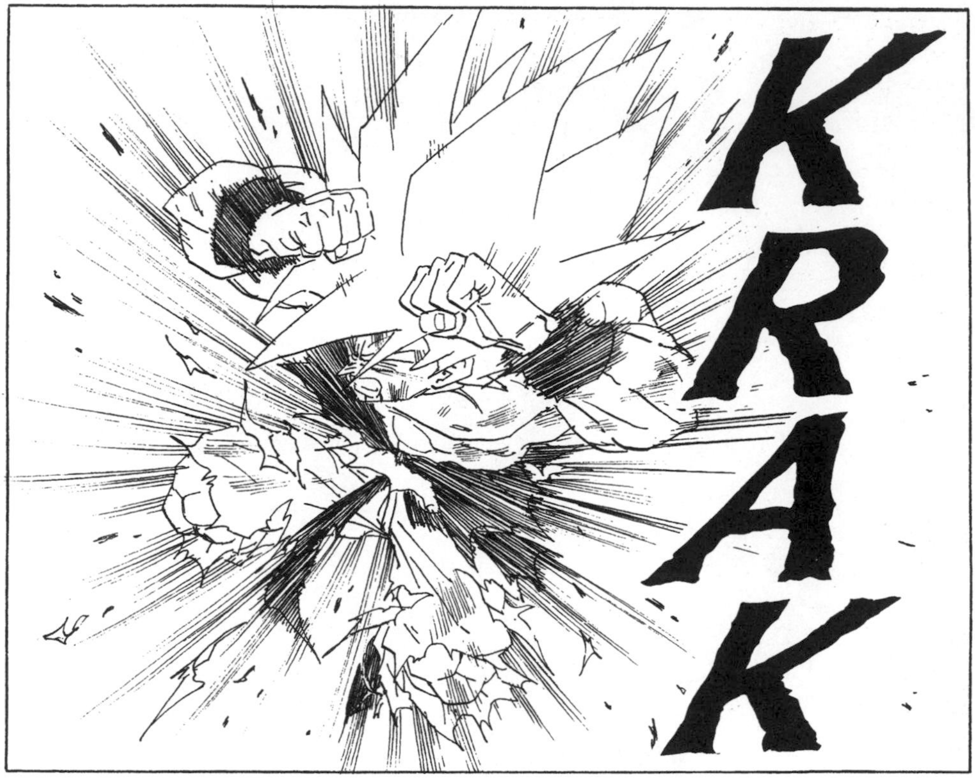
KRAK

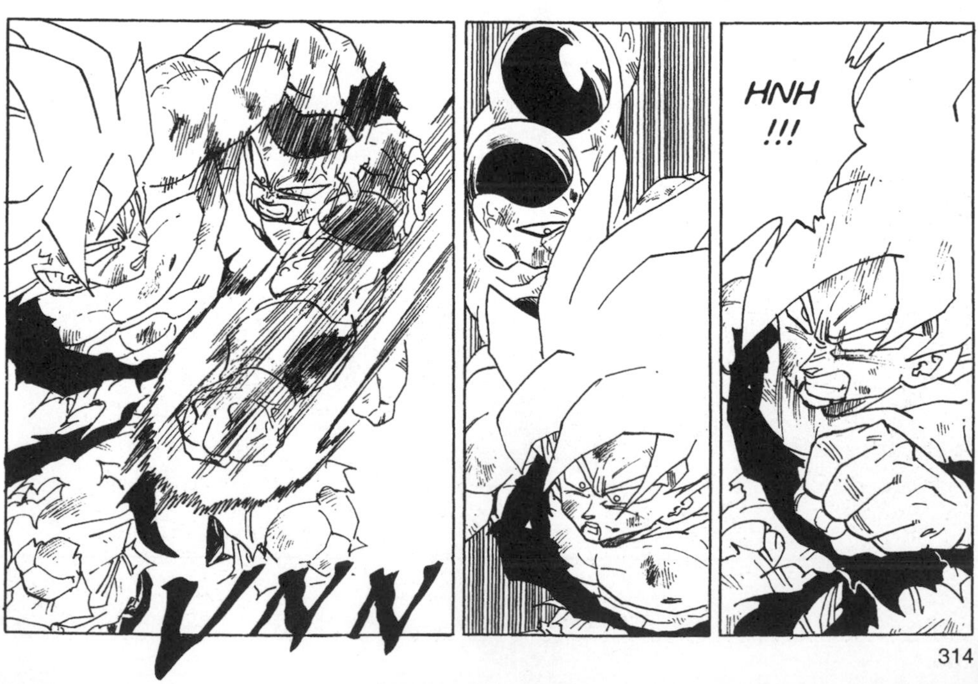
HNH !!!
VNN

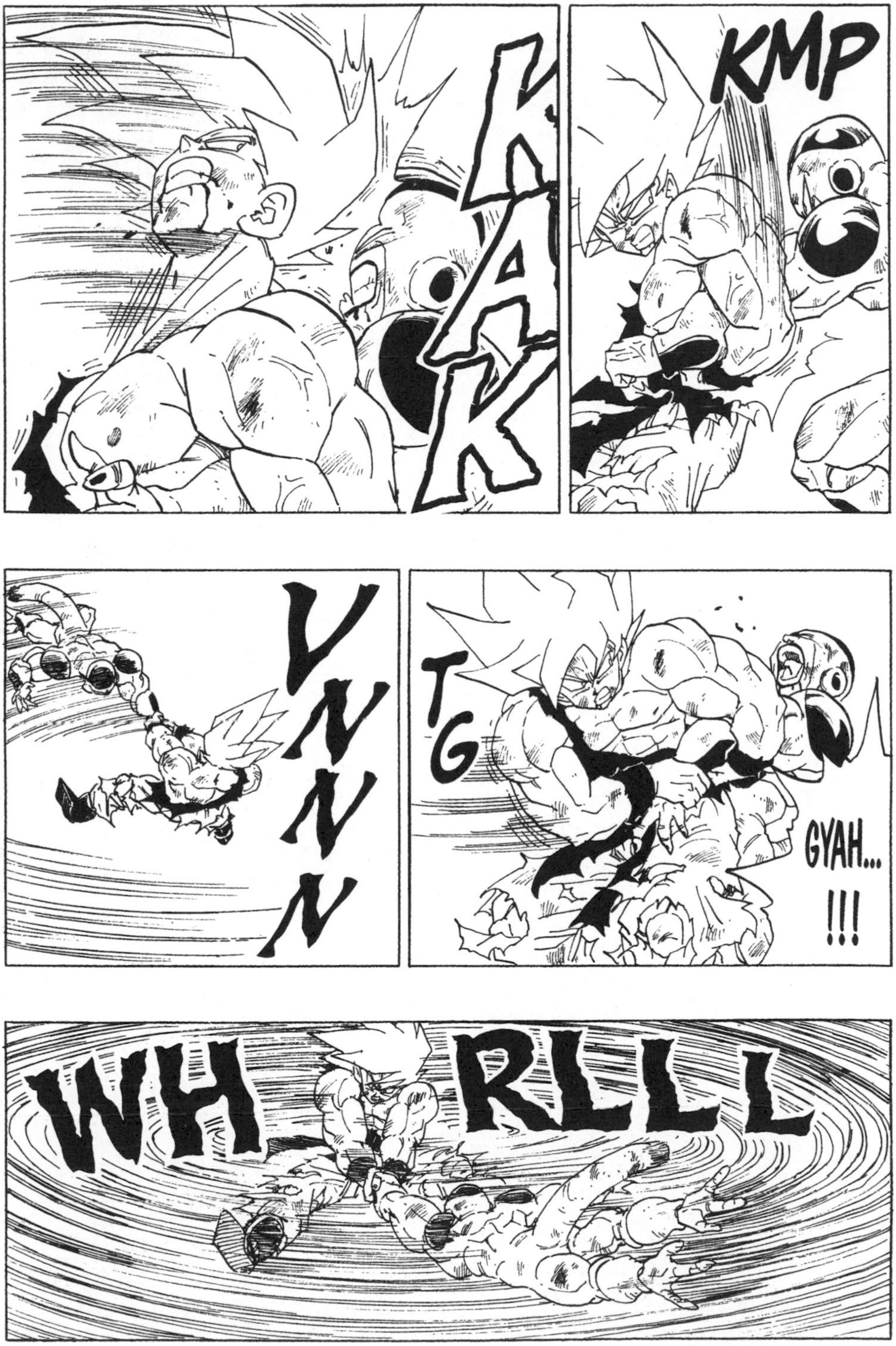
KAK
KMP
VNNN
TG
GYAH...
!!!
WH RLLL

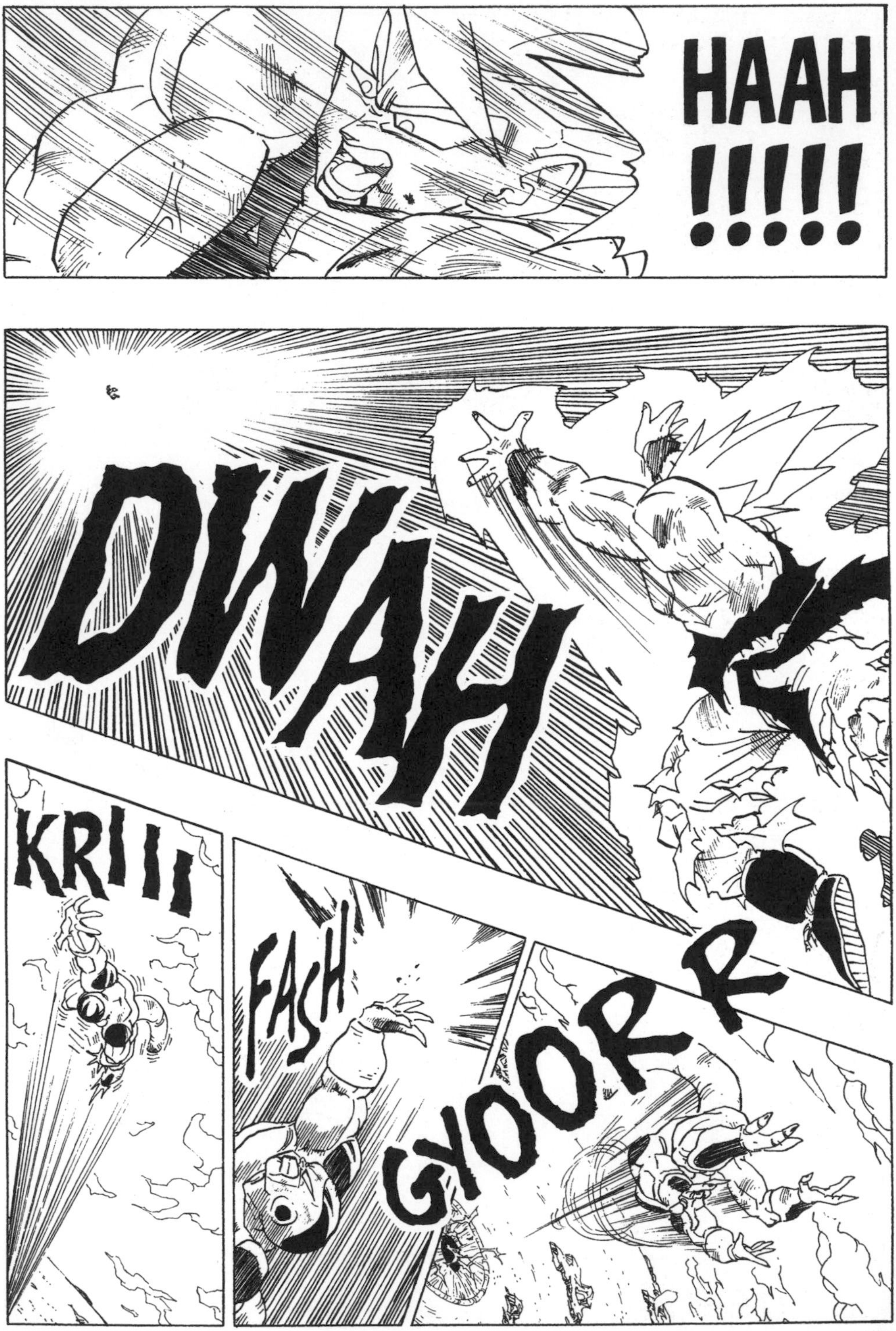
HAAH
!!!!!!
DWAH
GYOOR R
FASH
KRIII

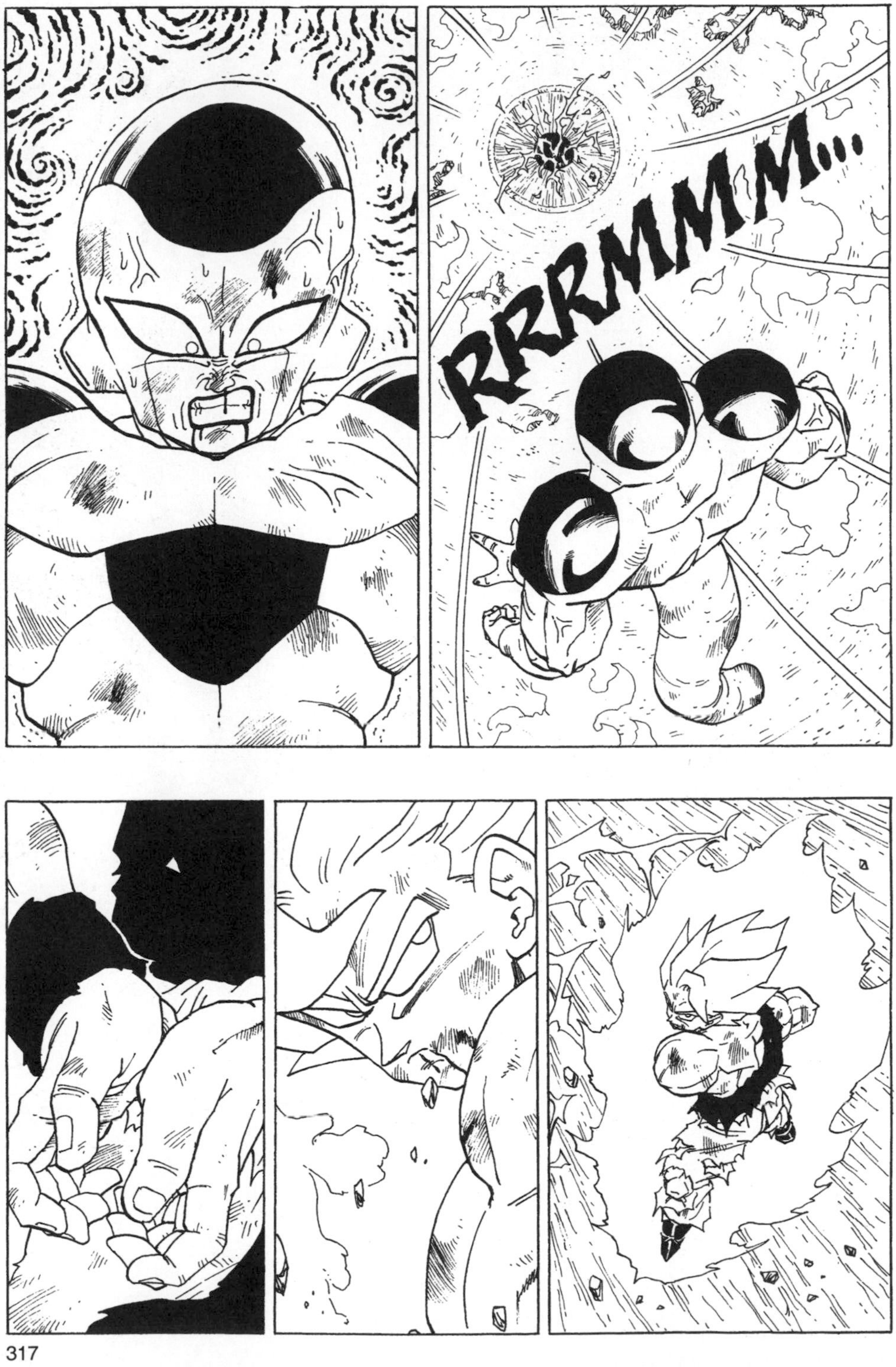
RRRMMMM...

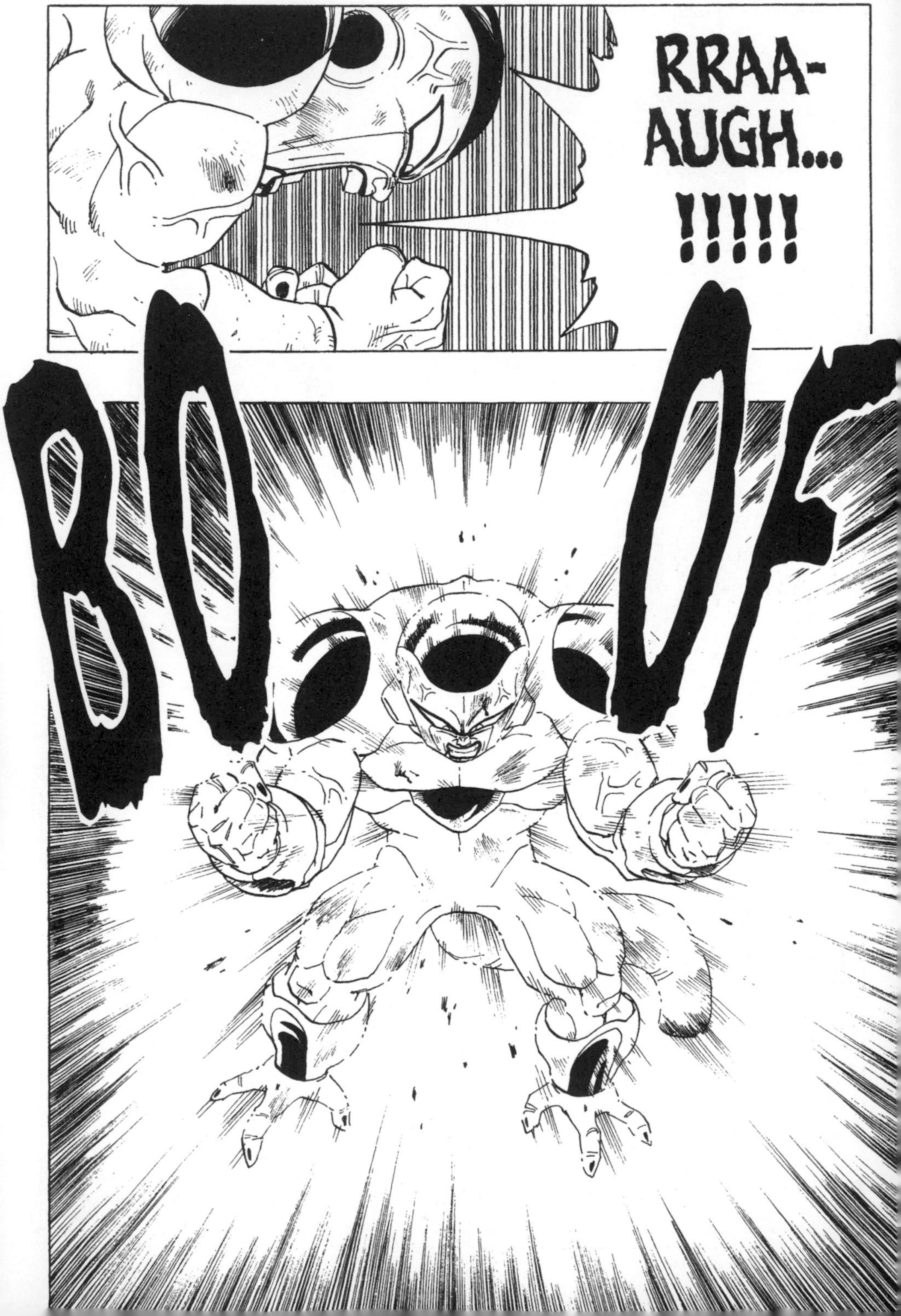
RRAA-
AUGH...
!!!!!
BOOF

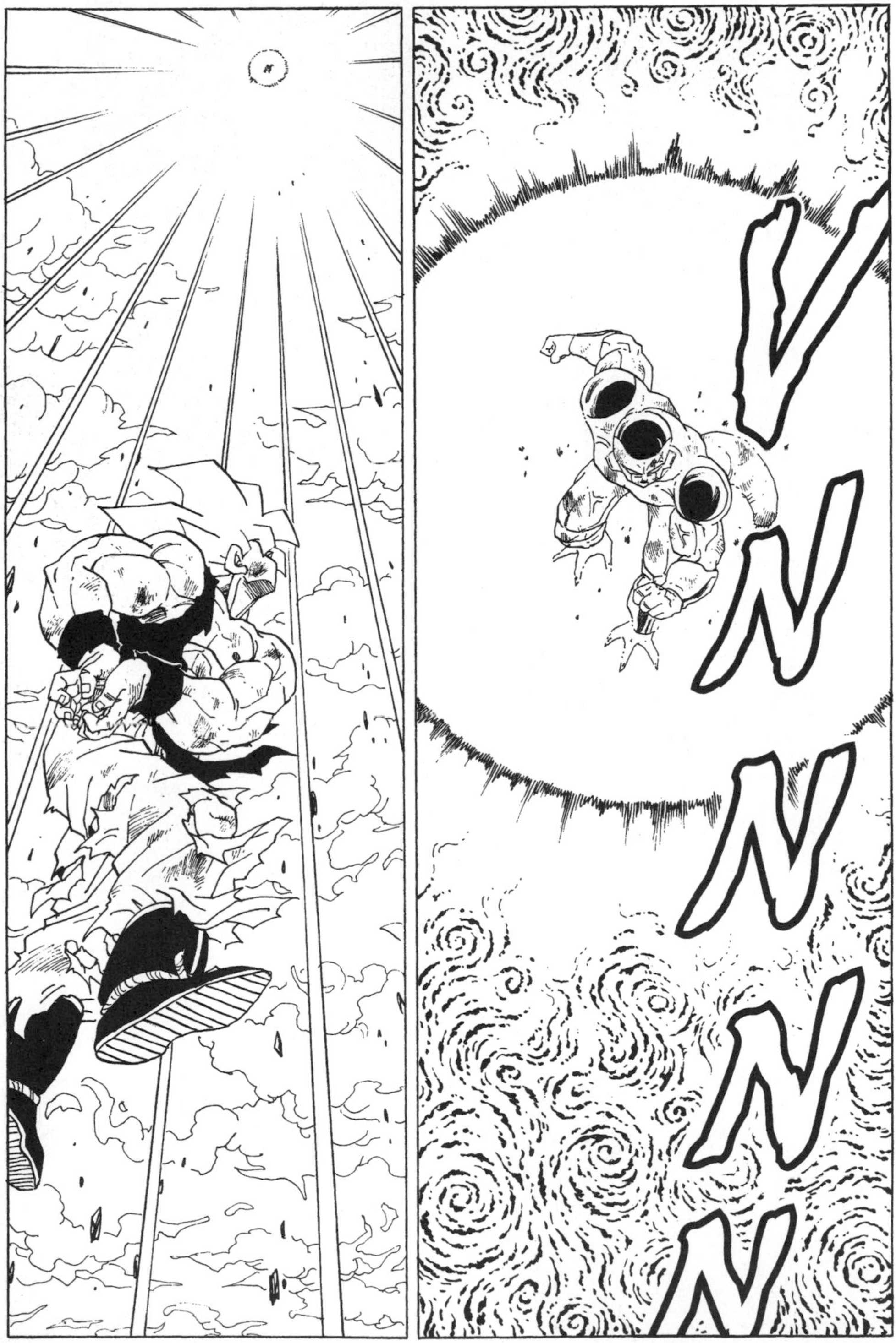
VNNNN

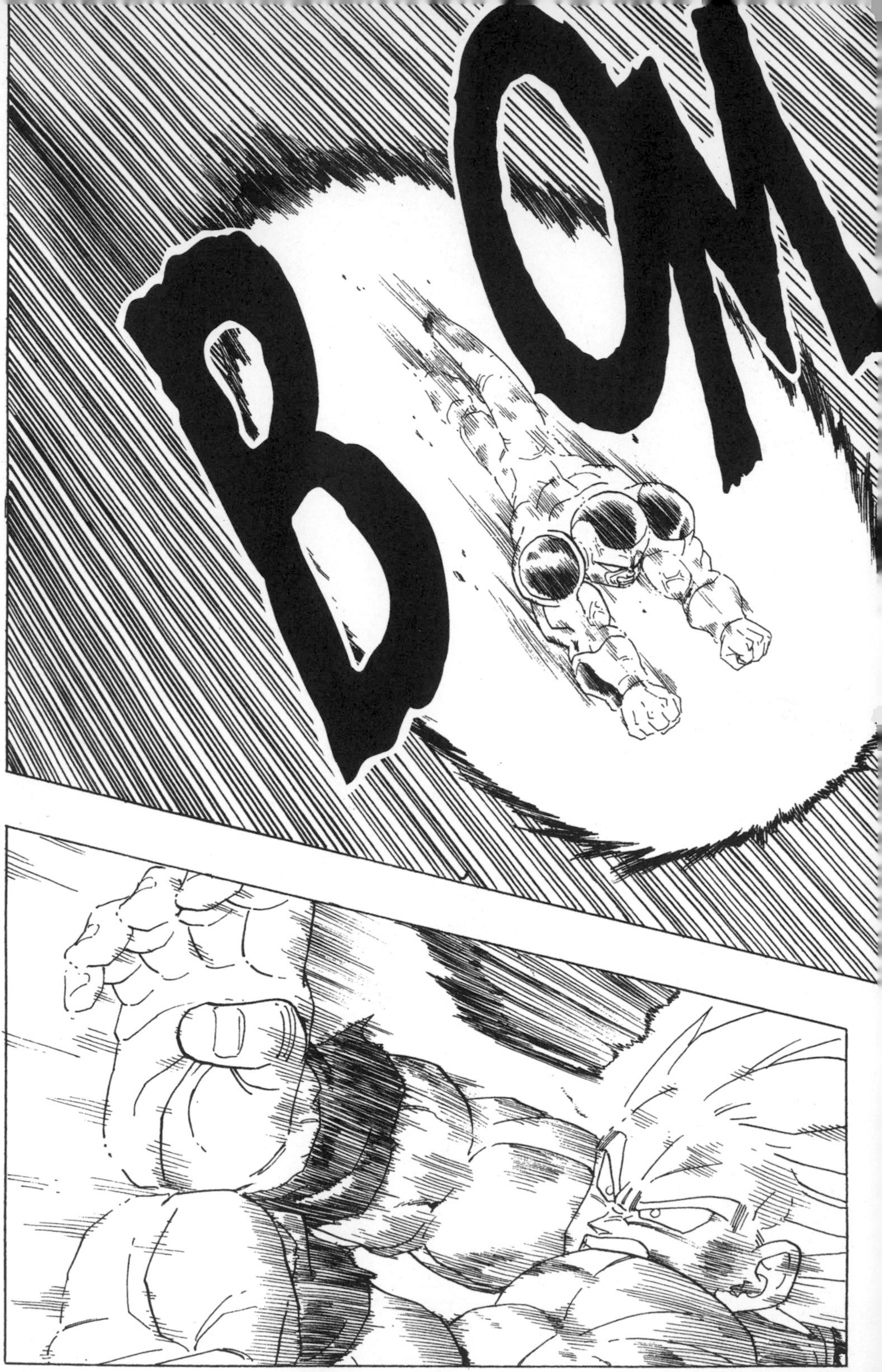
BOM

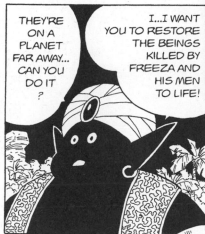

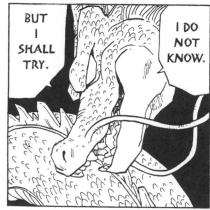

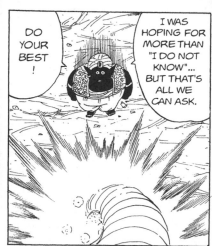

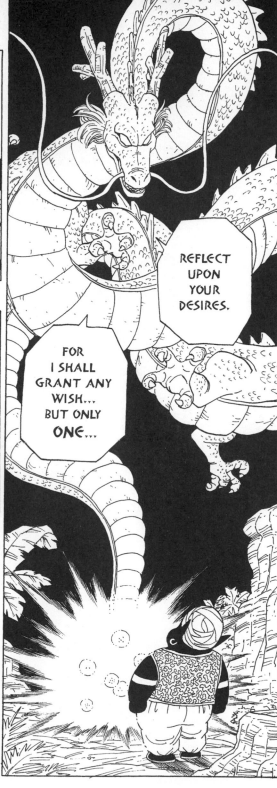

REFLECT UPON YOUR DESIRES.
FOR I SHALL GRANT ANY WISH... BUT ONLY ONE...
I...I WANT YOU TO RESTORE THE BEINGS KILLED BY FREEZA AND HIS MEN TO LIFE!
THEY'RE ON A PLANET FAR AWAY... CAN YOU DO IT ?
I DO NOT KNOW.
BUT I SHALL TRY.
I WAS HOPING FOR MORE THAN "I DO NOT KNOW"... BUT THAT'S ALL WE CAN ASK.
DO YOUR BEST !

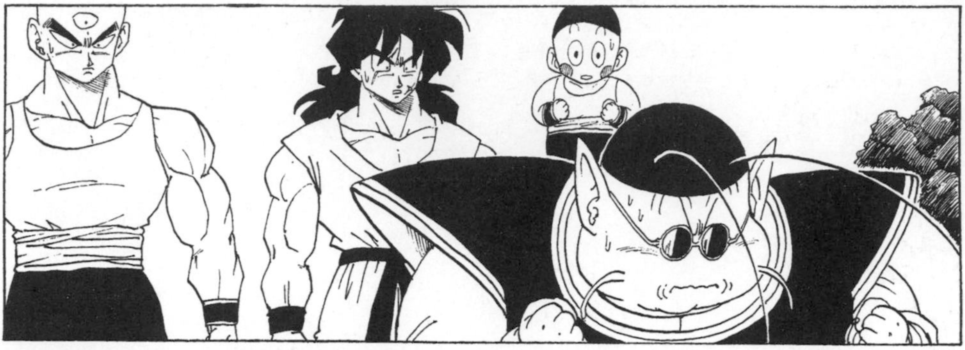

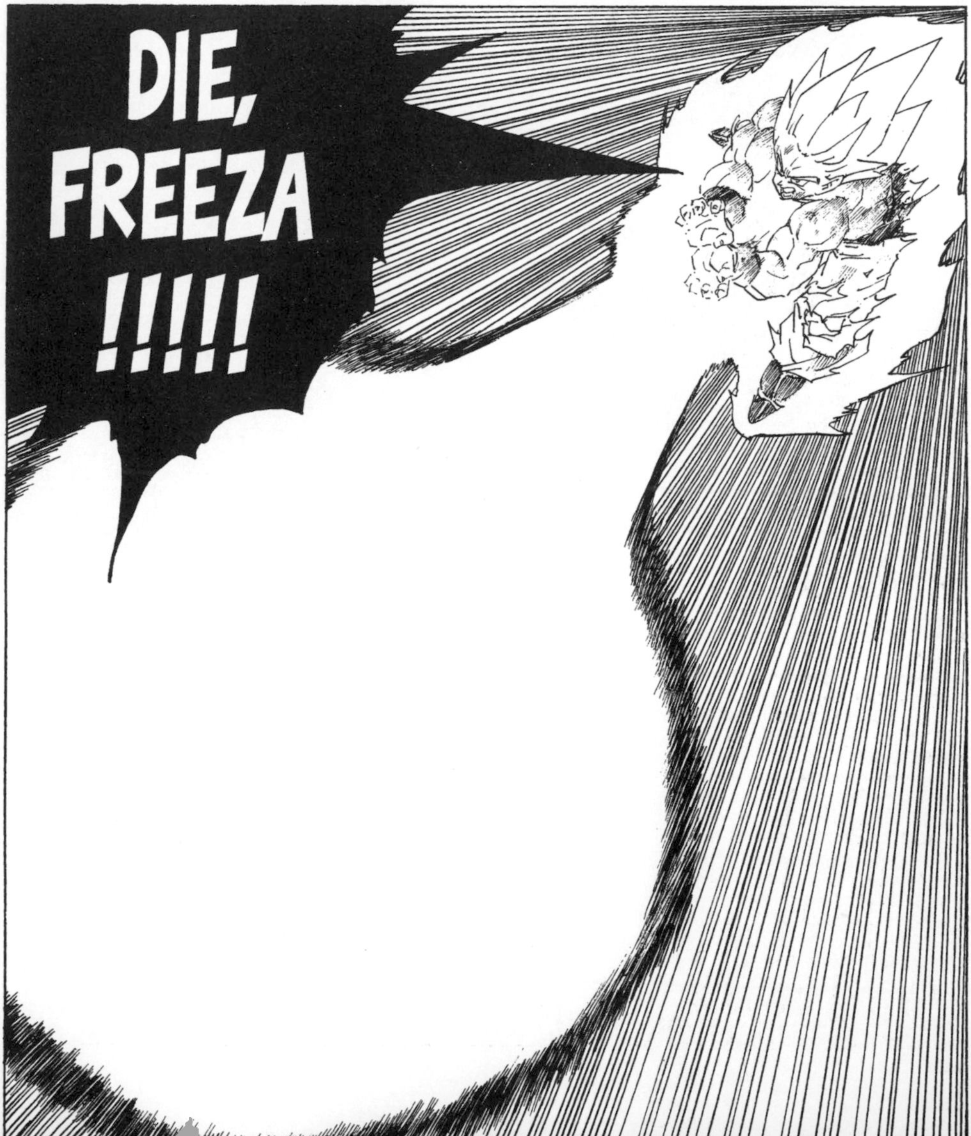
DIE, FREEZA !!!!!

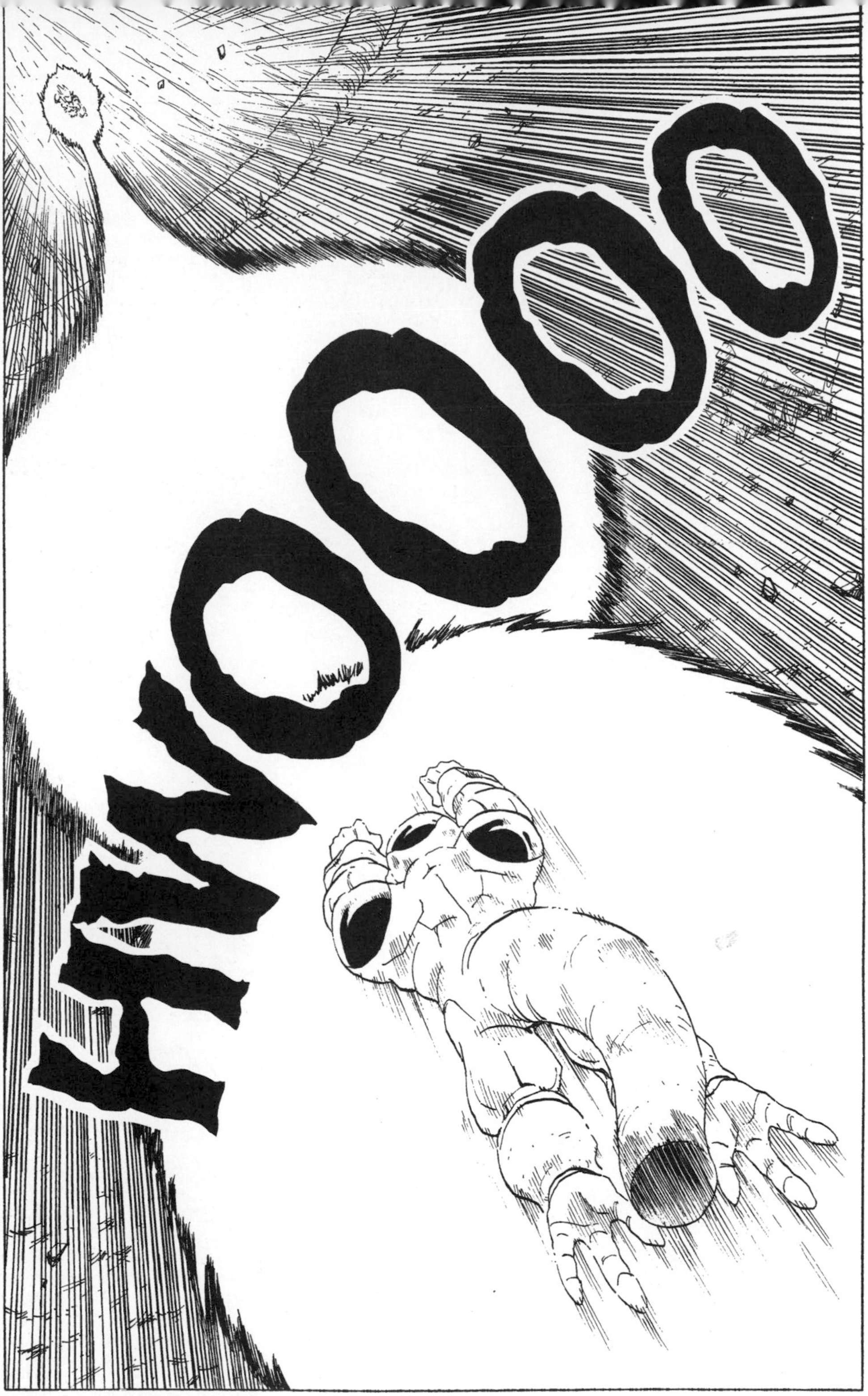
HWOOOO

DBZ:129 • The Two Wishes

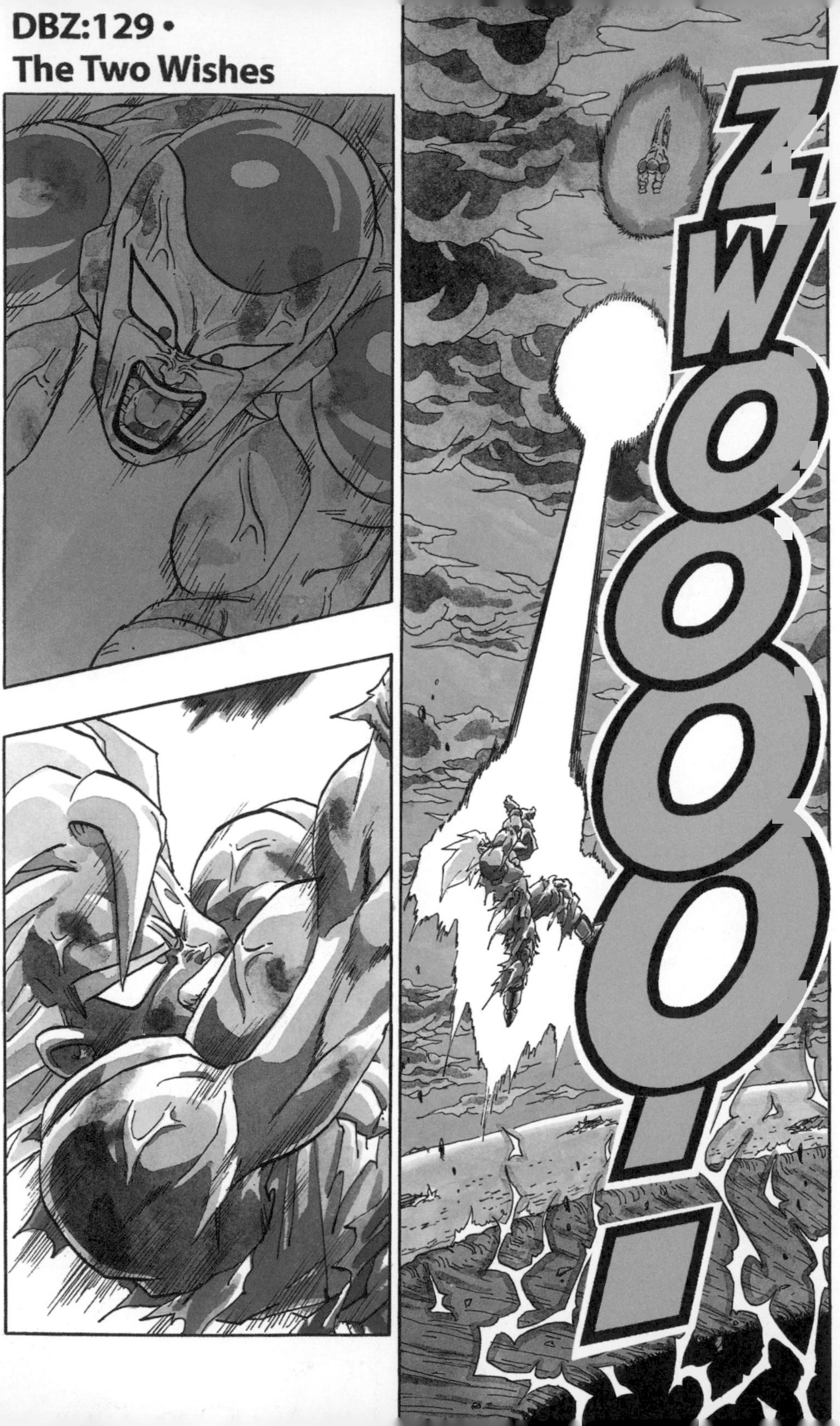
ZWOOOO!

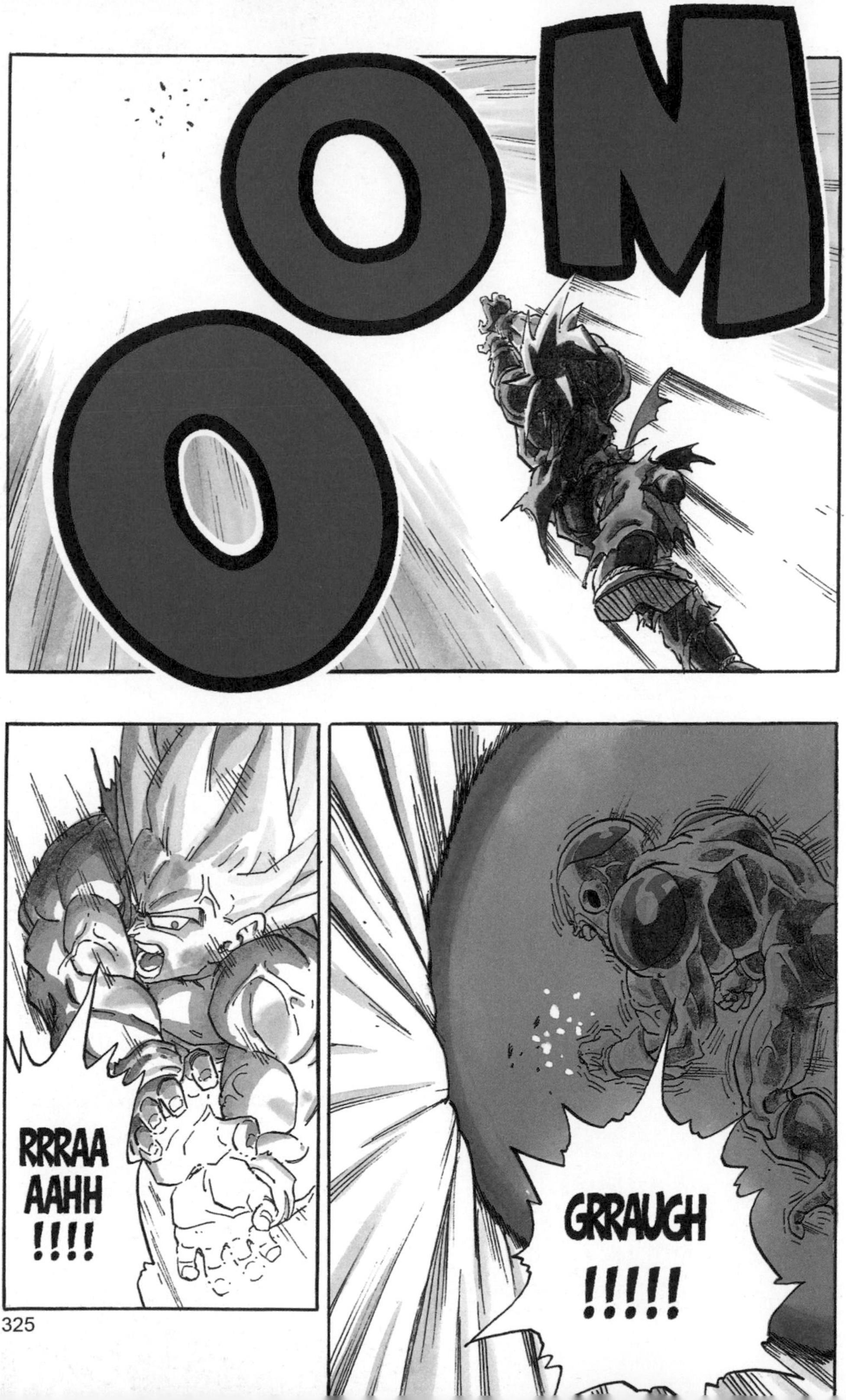
OOM
GRRAUGH !!!!!
RRRAA AAHH !!!!

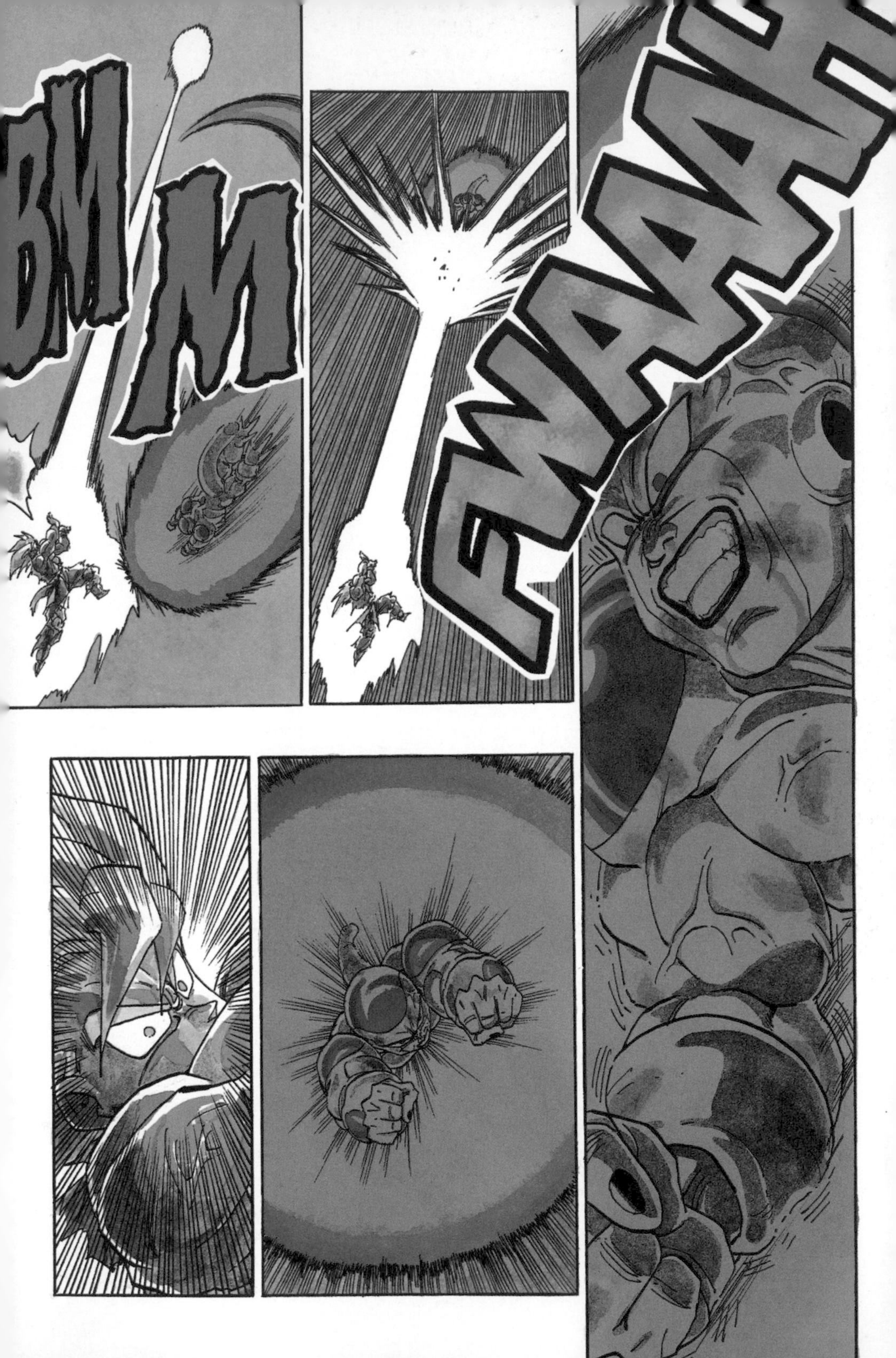
BMM
FWAAH

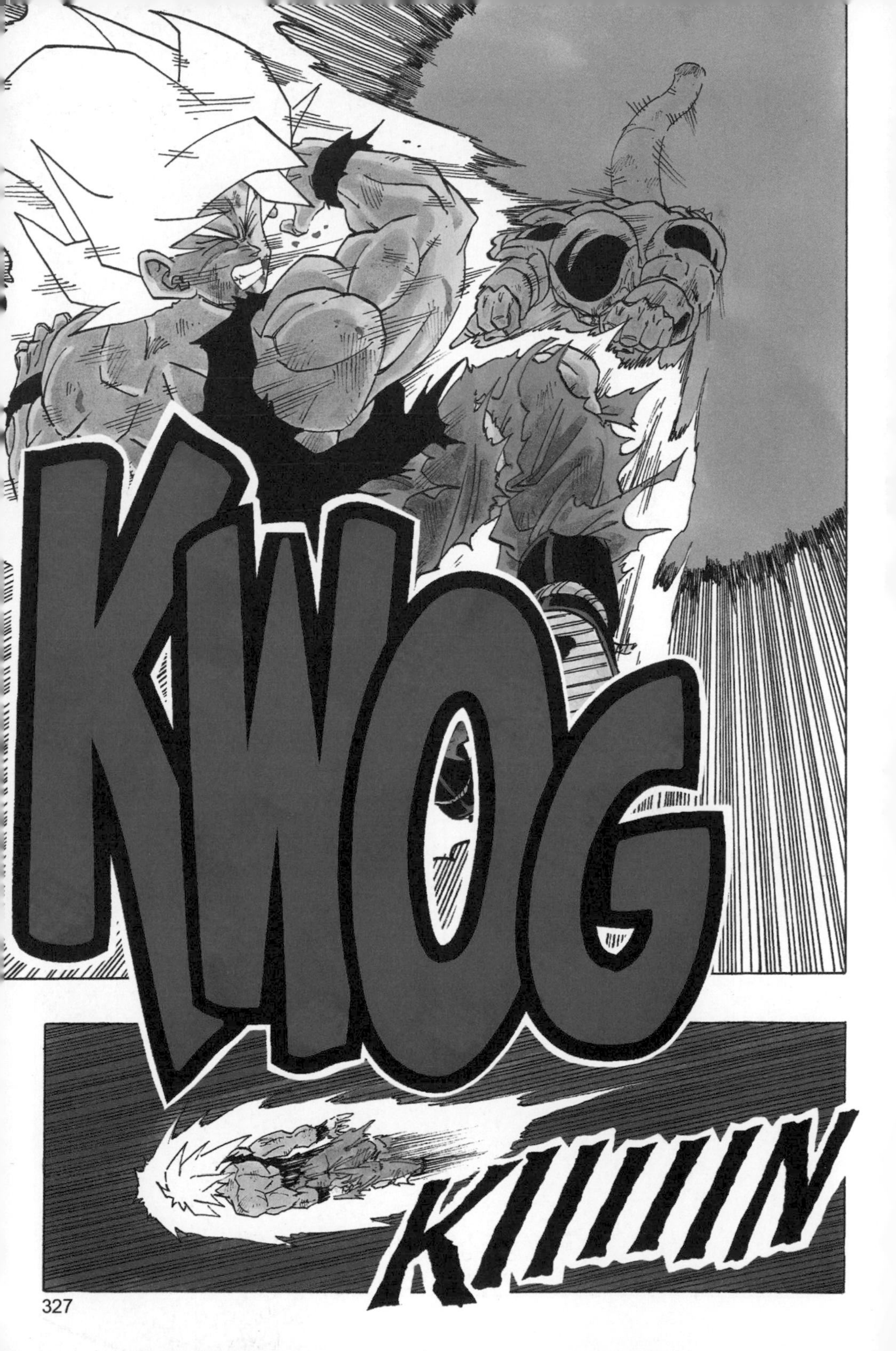
KWOG
KIIIIN

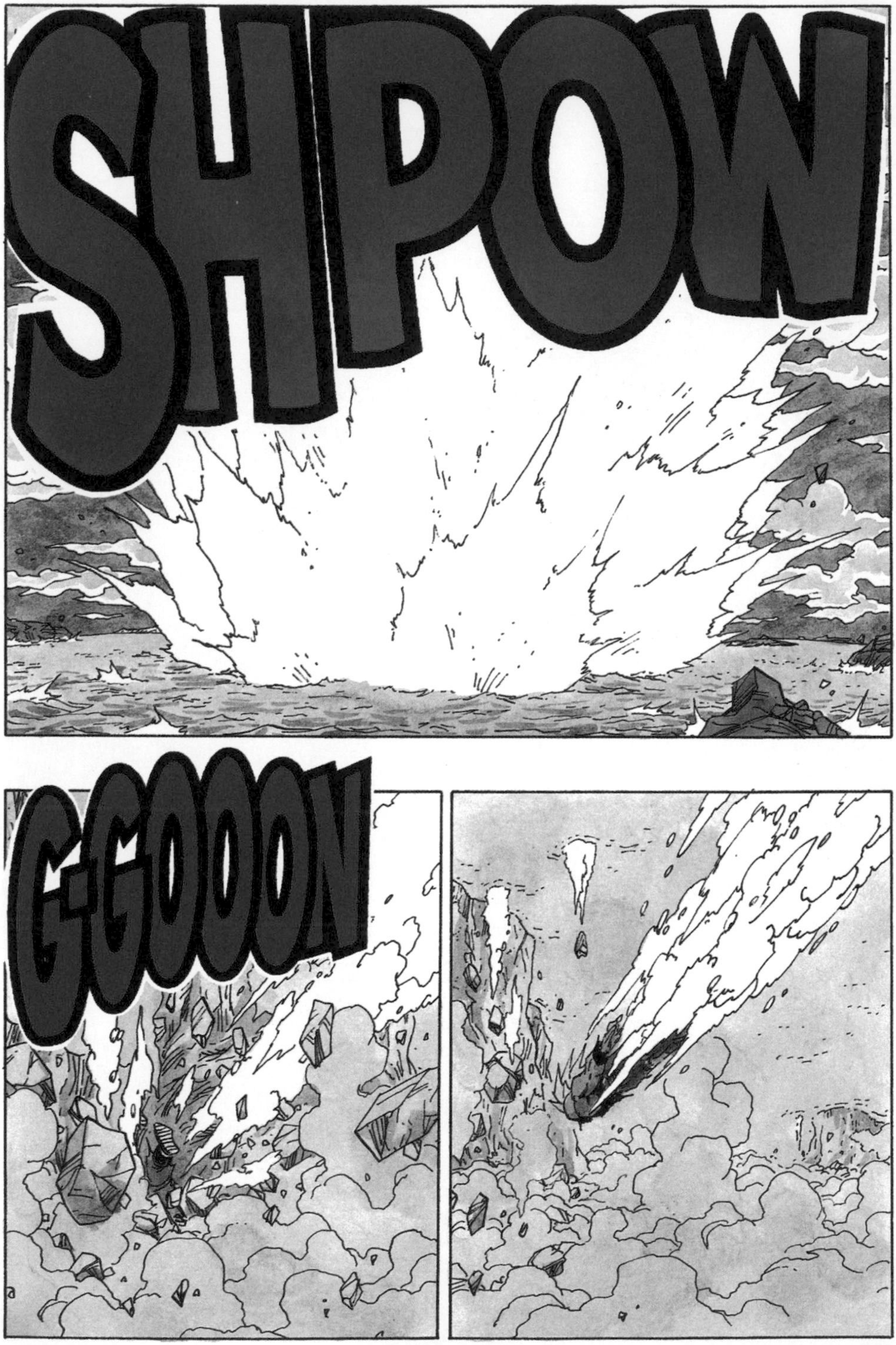
SHPOW
G-GOOON

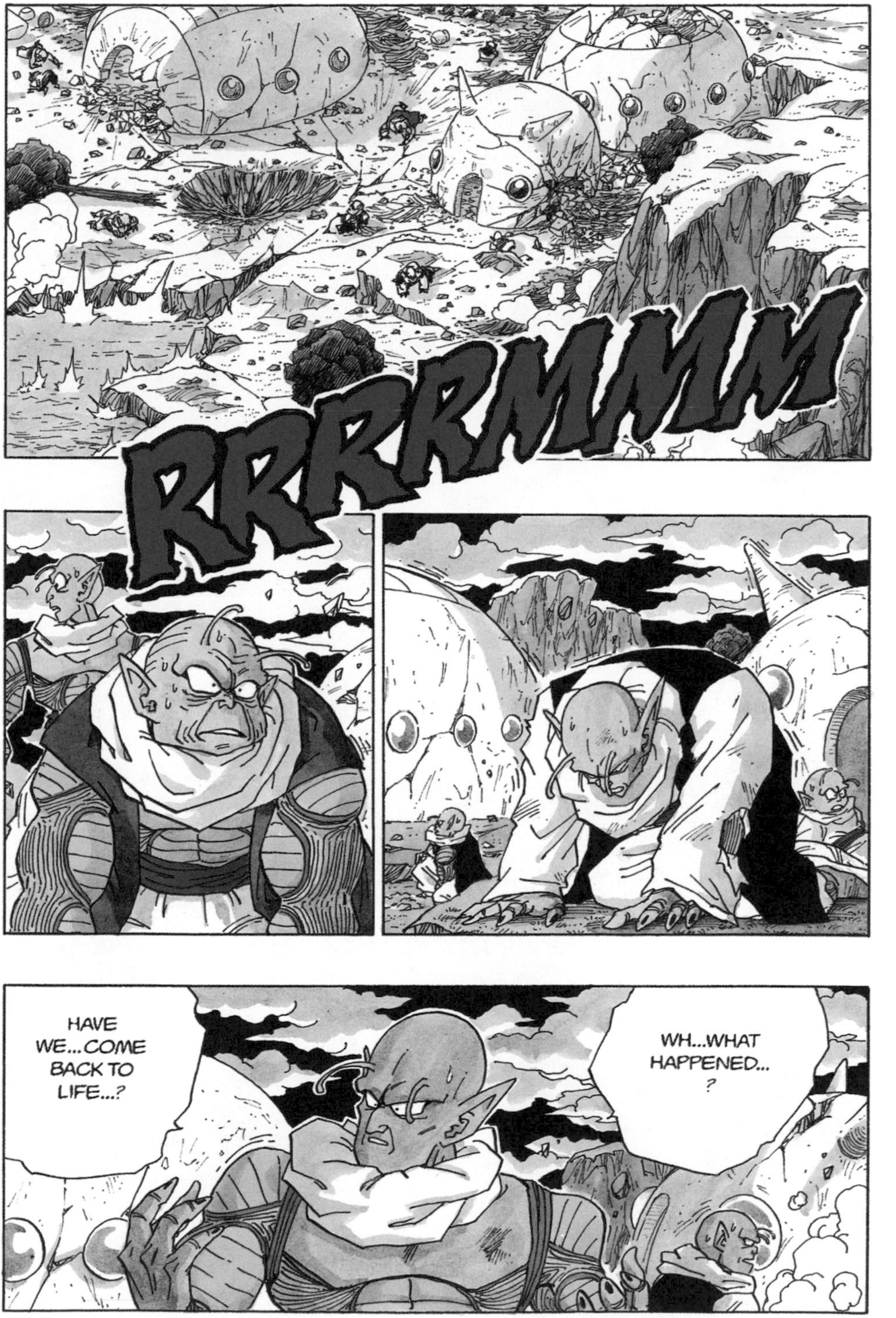
RRRRMMMM
WH...WHAT HAPPENED...?
HAVE WE...COME BACK TO LIFE...?

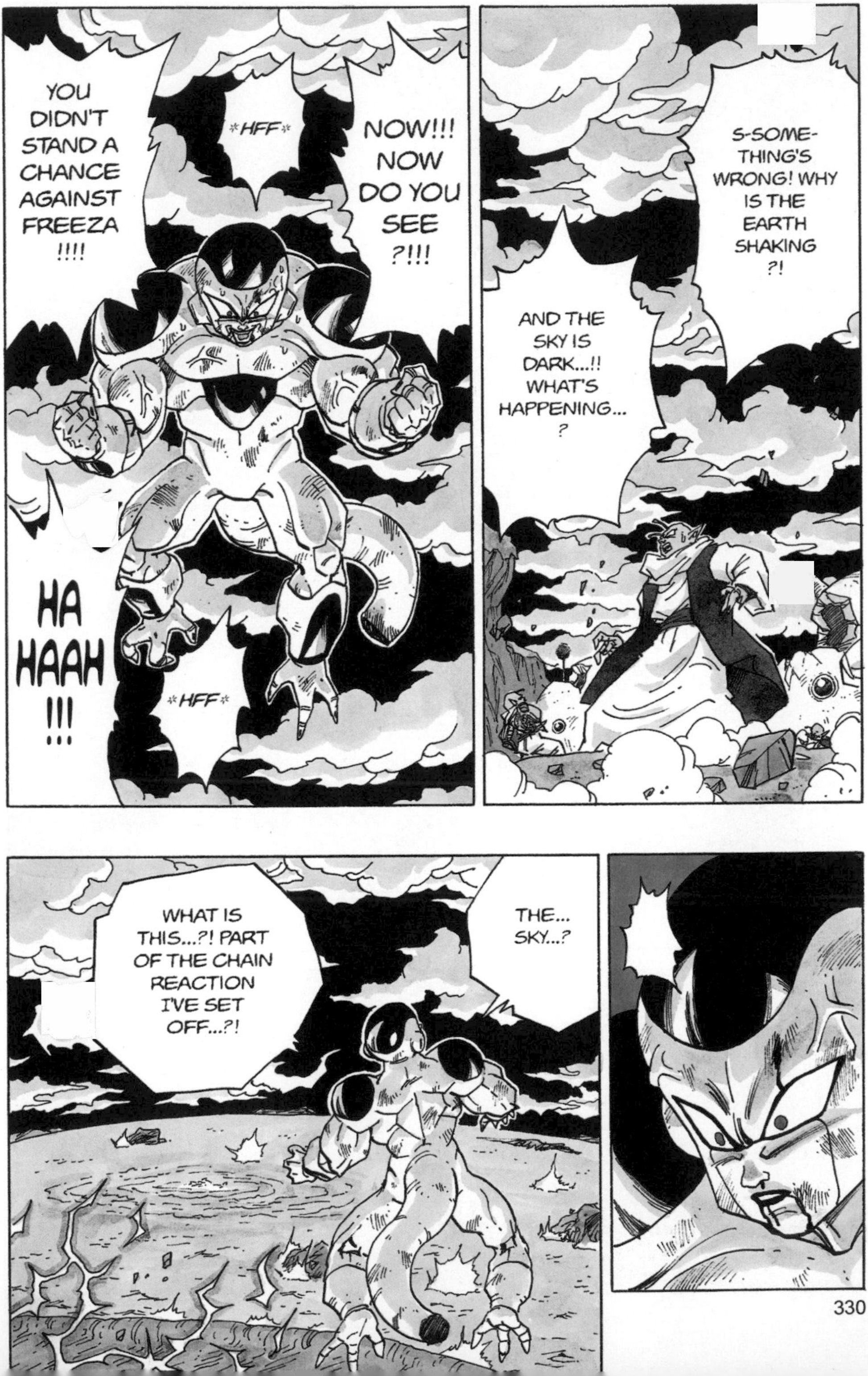
YOU DIDN'T STAND A CHANCE AGAINST FREEZA !!!!
HFF
NOW!!! NOW DO YOU SEE ?!!!
HA HAAH !!!
HFF
S-SOME-THING'S WRONG! WHY IS THE EARTH SHAKING ?!
AND THE SKY IS DARK...!! WHAT'S HAPPENING... ?
WHAT IS THIS...?! PART OF THE CHAIN REACTION I'VE SET OFF...?!
THE... SKY...?

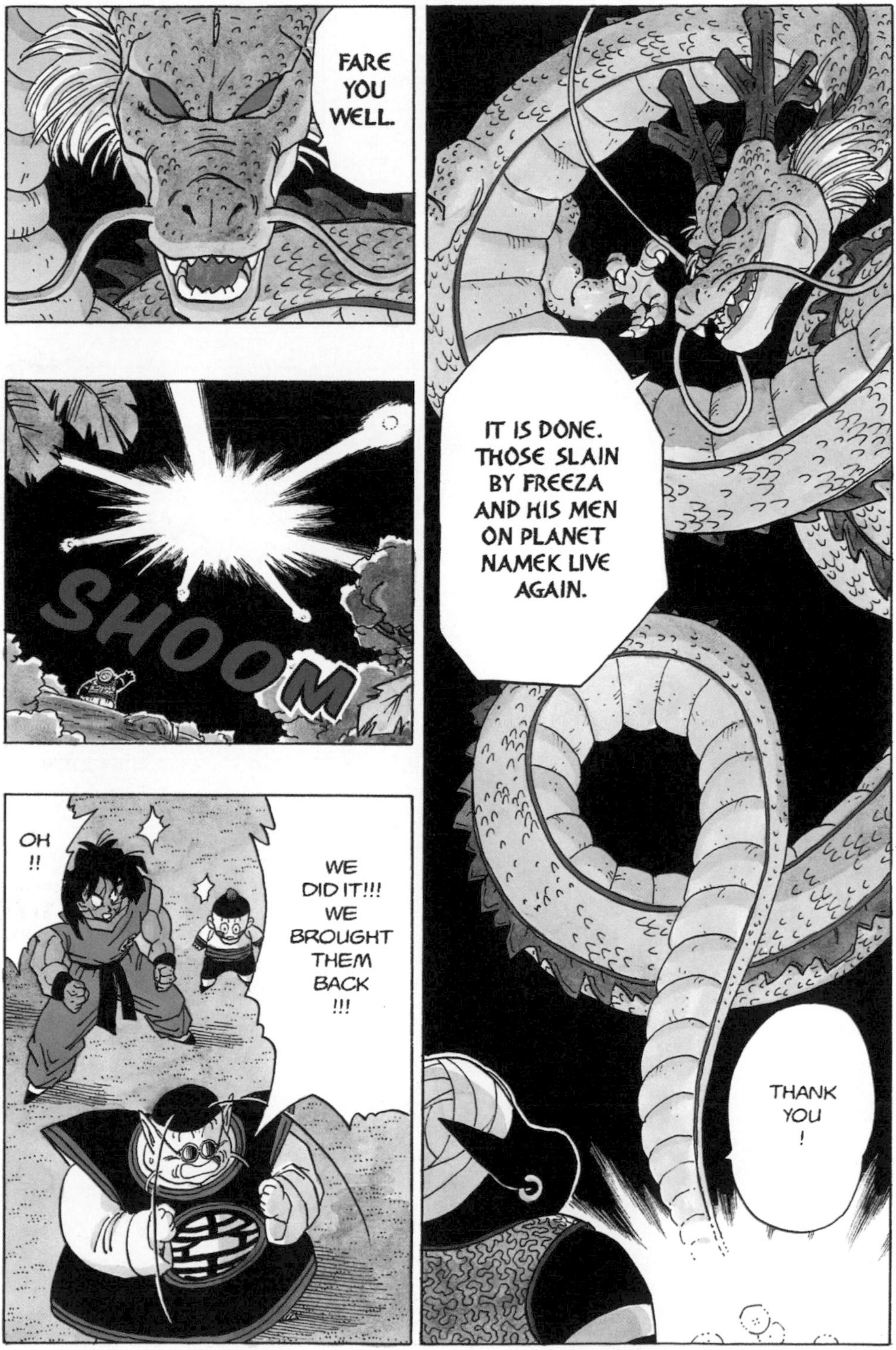

IT IS DONE. THOSE SLAIN BY FREEZA AND HIS MEN ON PLANET NAMEK LIVE AGAIN.
THANK YOU !
FARE YOU WELL.
SHOOM
OH !!
WE DID IT!!! WE BROUGHT THEM BACK !!!

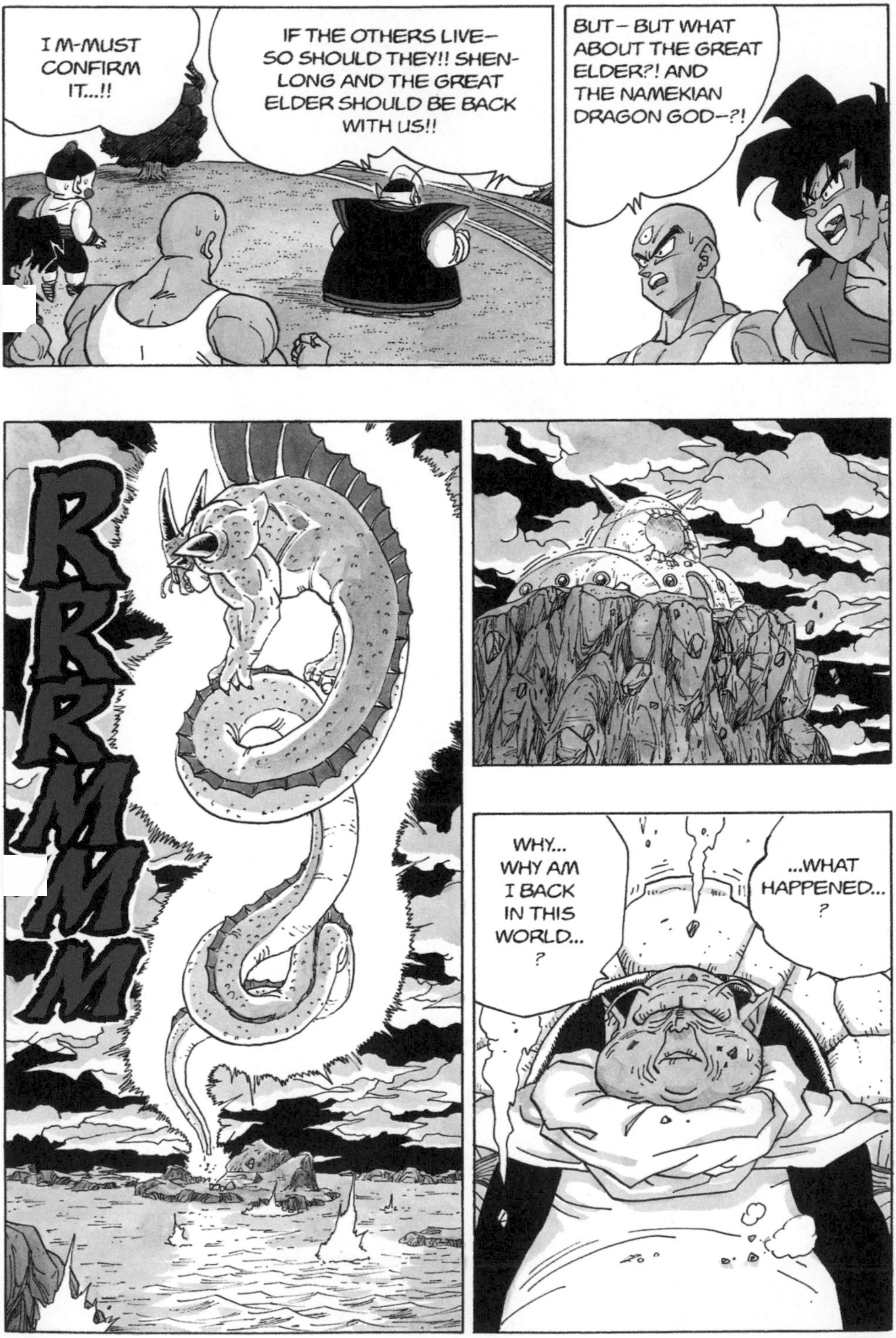
IF THE OTHERS LIVE— SO SHOULD THEY!! SHENLONG AND THE GREAT ELDER SHOULD BE BACK WITH US!!
I M-MUST CONFIRM IT...!!
BUT— BUT WHAT ABOUT THE GREAT ELDER?! AND THE NAMEKIAN DRAGON GOD—?!
RRRMMM
...WHAT HAPPENED...?
WHY... WHY AM I BACK IN THIS WORLD...?

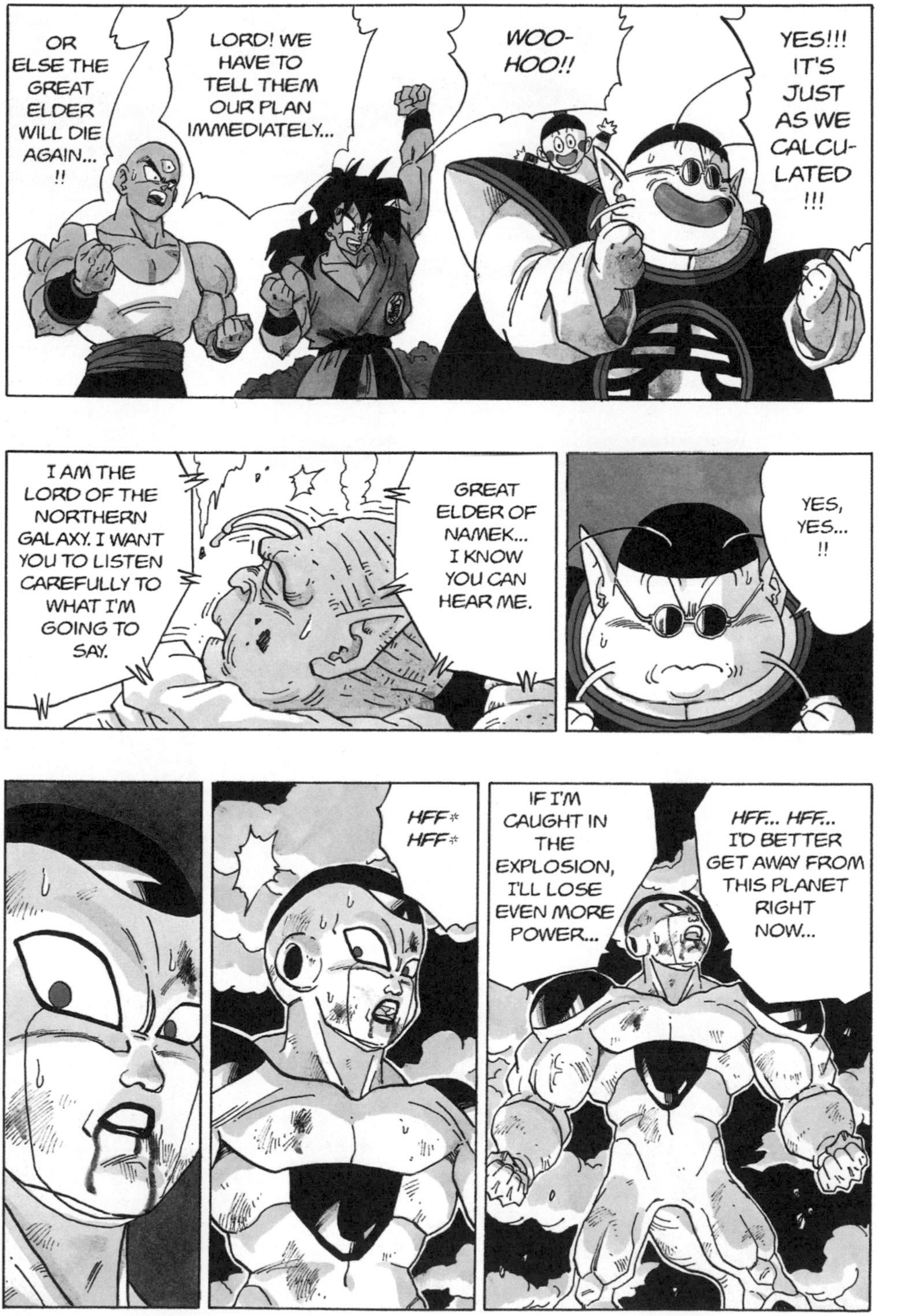
OR ELSE THE GREAT ELDER WILL DIE AGAIN... !!
LORD! WE HAVE TO TELL THEM OUR PLAN IMMEDIATELY...
WOO-HOO!!
YES!!! IT'S JUST AS WE CALCULATED !!!
I AM THE LORD OF THE NORTHERN GALAXY. I WANT YOU TO LISTEN CAREFULLY TO WHAT I'M GOING TO SAY.
GREAT ELDER OF NAMEK... I KNOW YOU CAN HEAR ME.
YES, YES... !!
HFF HFF
IF I'M CAUGHT IN THE EXPLOSION, I'LL LOSE EVEN MORE POWER...
HFF... HFF... I'D BETTER GET AWAY FROM THIS PLANET RIGHT NOW...

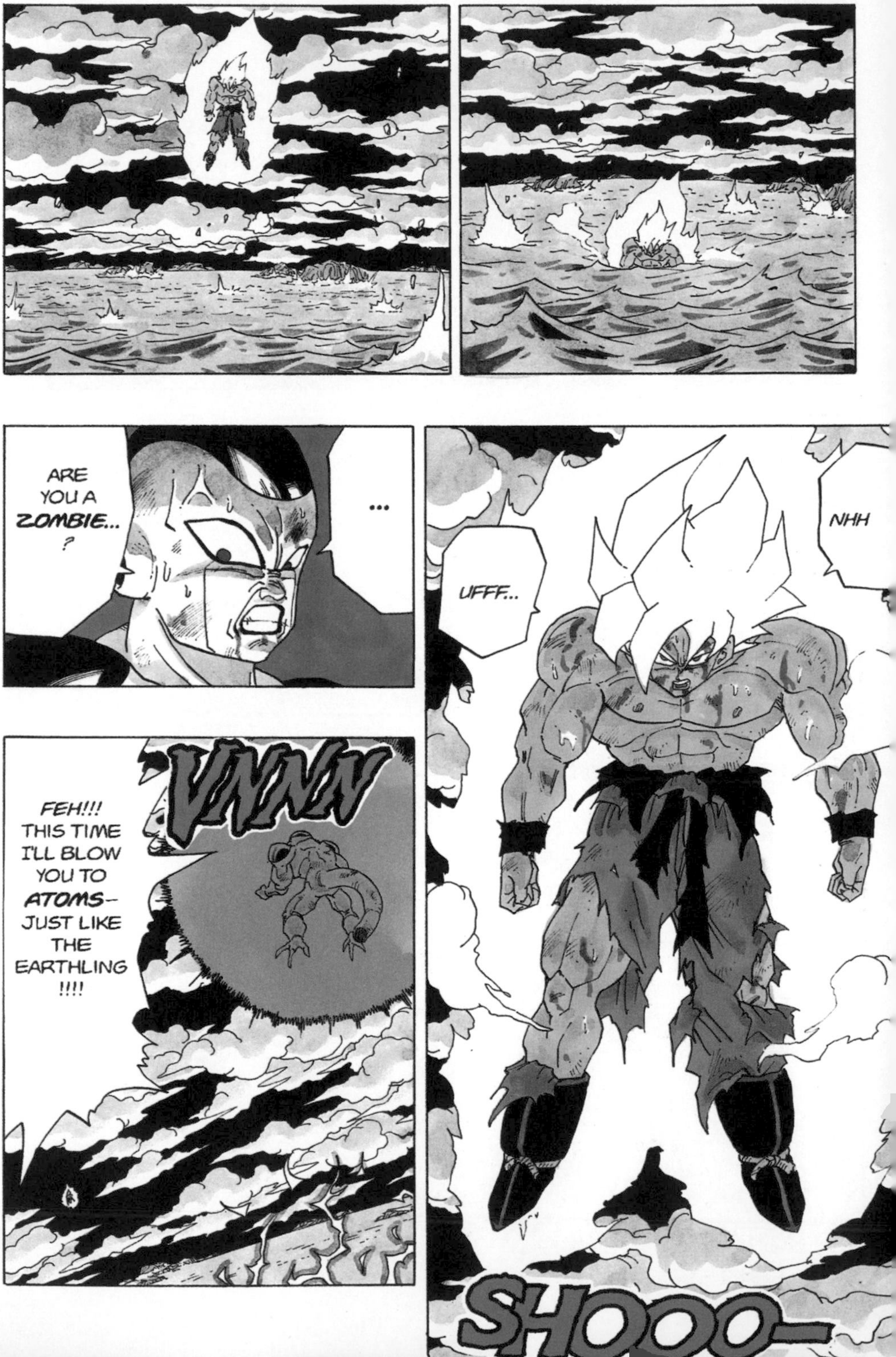
ARE YOU A ZOMBIE...?
...
UFFF...
NHH
SHOOO-
VNNN
FEH!!! THIS TIME I'LL BLOW YOU TO ATOMS- JUST LIKE THE EARTHLING!!!!

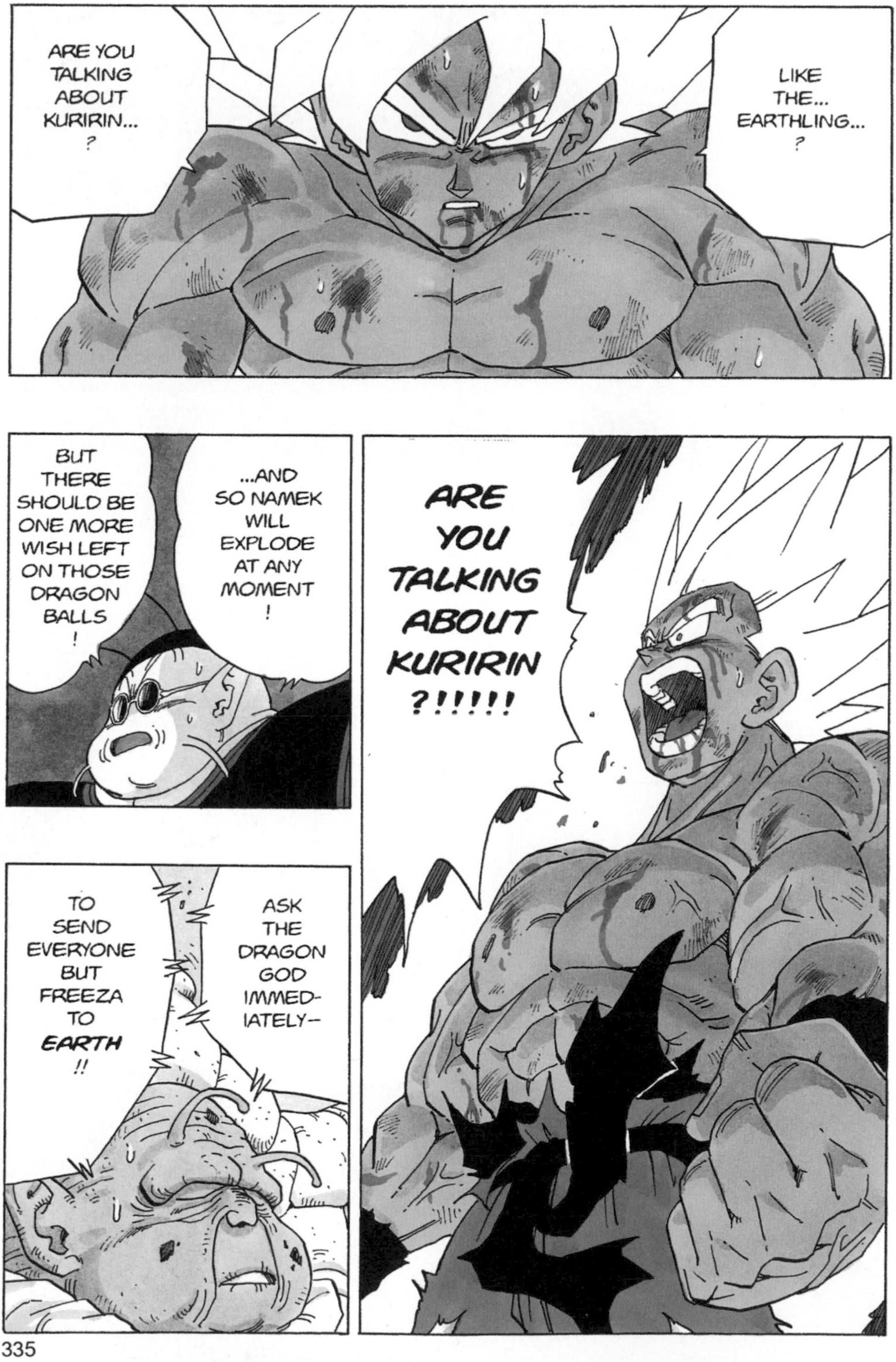
LIKE THE... EARTHLING... ?
ARE YOU TALKING ABOUT KURIRIN... ?
ARE YOU TALKING ABOUT KURIRIN ?!!!!!
...AND SO NAMEK WILL EXPLODE AT ANY MOMENT !
BUT THERE SHOULD BE ONE MORE WISH LEFT ON THOSE DRAGON BALLS !
ASK THE DRAGON GOD IMMEDIATELY—
TO SEND EVERYONE BUT FREEZA TO EARTH !!

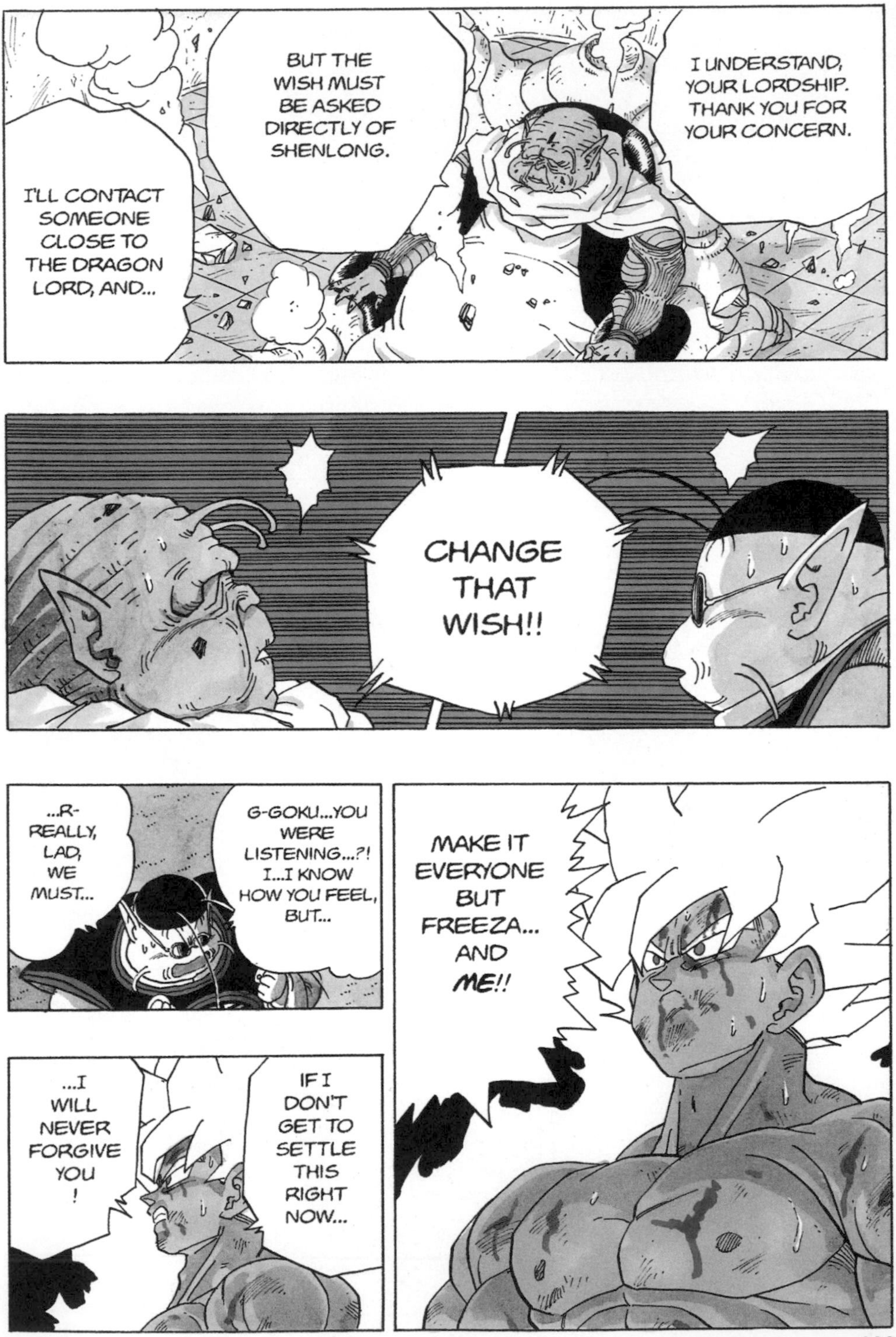
I'LL CONTACT SOMEONE CLOSE TO THE DRAGON LORD, AND...
BUT THE WISH MUST BE ASKED DIRECTLY OF SHENLONG.
I UNDERSTAND, YOUR LORDSHIP. THANK YOU FOR YOUR CONCERN.
CHANGE THAT WISH!!
G-GOKU...YOU WERE LISTENING...?! I...I KNOW HOW YOU FEEL, BUT...
...R-REALLY, LAD, WE MUST...
MAKE IT EVERYONE BUT FREEZA... AND *ME!!*
IF I DON'T GET TO SETTLE THIS RIGHT NOW...
...I WILL NEVER FORGIVE YOU!

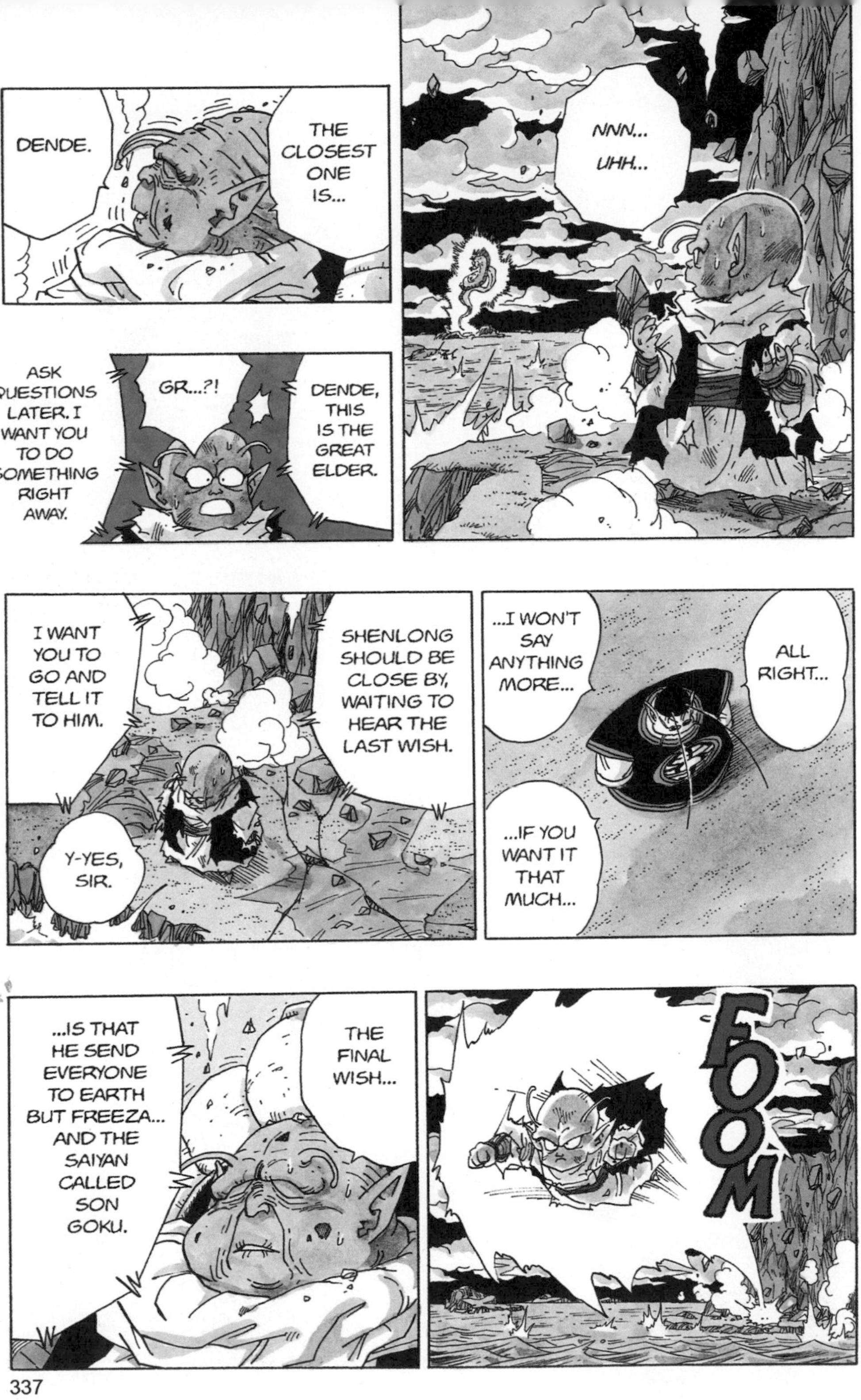

THE CLOSEST ONE IS...
DENDE.
DENDE, THIS IS THE GREAT ELDER.
GR...?!
ASK QUESTIONS LATER. I WANT YOU TO DO SOMETHING RIGHT AWAY.
NNN... UHH...
SHENLONG SHOULD BE CLOSE BY, WAITING TO HEAR THE LAST WISH.
I WANT YOU TO GO AND TELL IT TO HIM.
Y-YES, SIR.
ALL RIGHT...
...I WON'T SAY ANYTHING MORE...
...IF YOU WANT IT THAT MUCH...
THE FINAL WISH...
...IS THAT HE SEND EVERYONE TO EARTH BUT FREEZA... AND THE SAIYAN CALLED SON GOKU.
FOOM

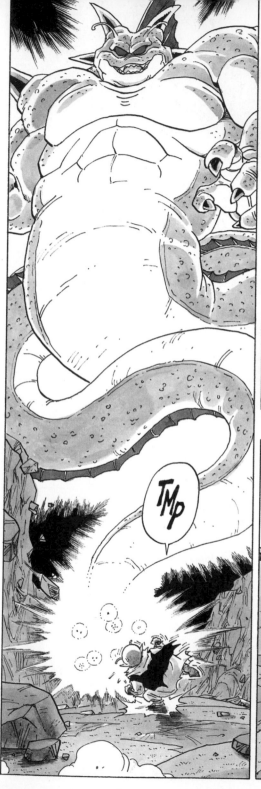

WH-WHAT'S HAPPENING TO THE SKY...?

H-HOW SHOULD I KNOW...?!

TMP

...AM I... ALIVE AGAIN?!

WH-WHY...

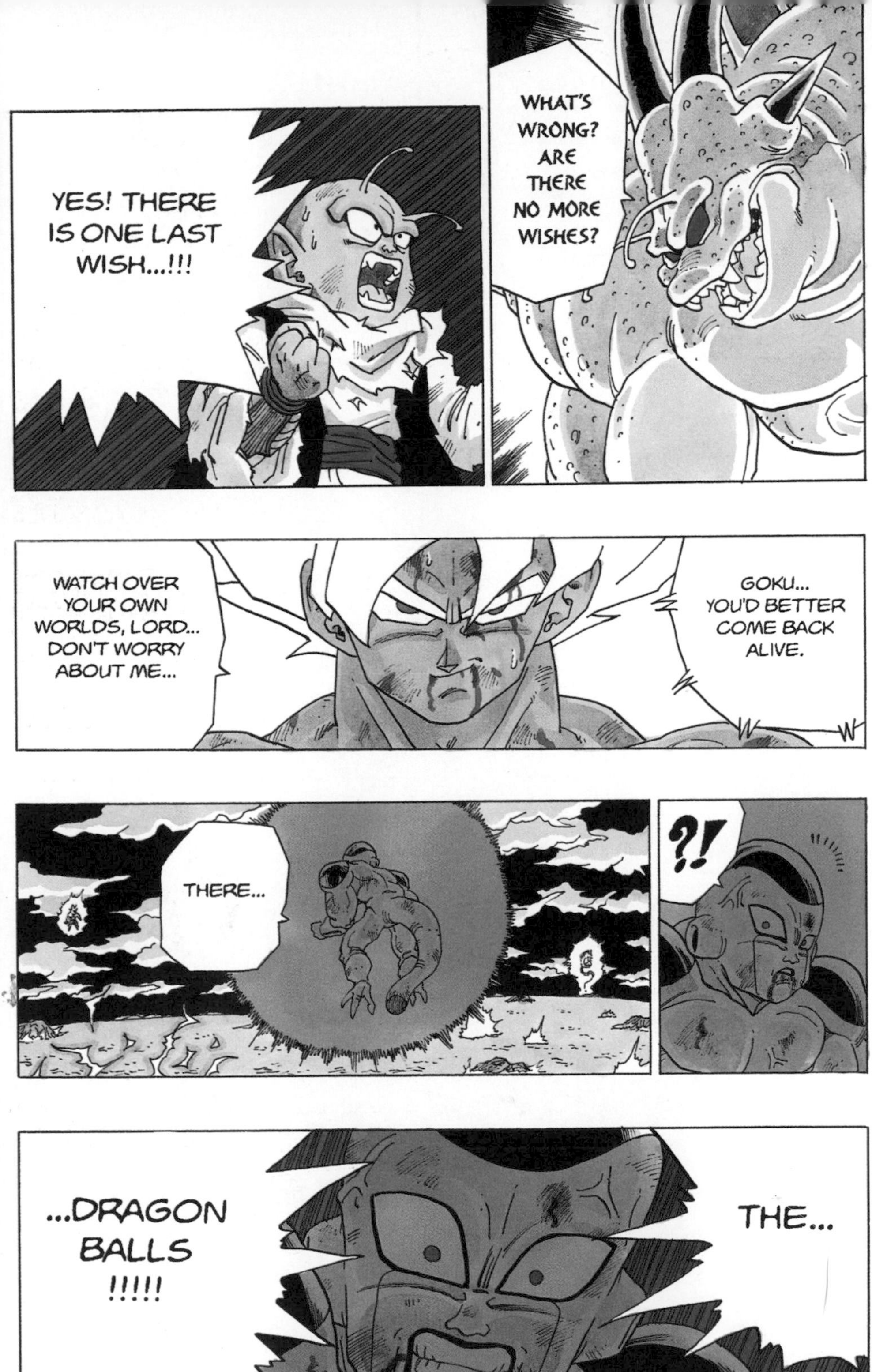
WHAT'S WRONG? ARE THERE NO MORE WISHES?
YES! THERE IS ONE LAST WISH...!!!
GOKU... YOU'D BETTER COME BACK ALIVE.
WATCH OVER YOUR OWN WORLDS, LORD... DON'T WORRY ABOUT ME...
?!
THERE...
THE...
...DRAGON BALLS !!!!!

DBZ:130 • The Quiet, Fierce Battle

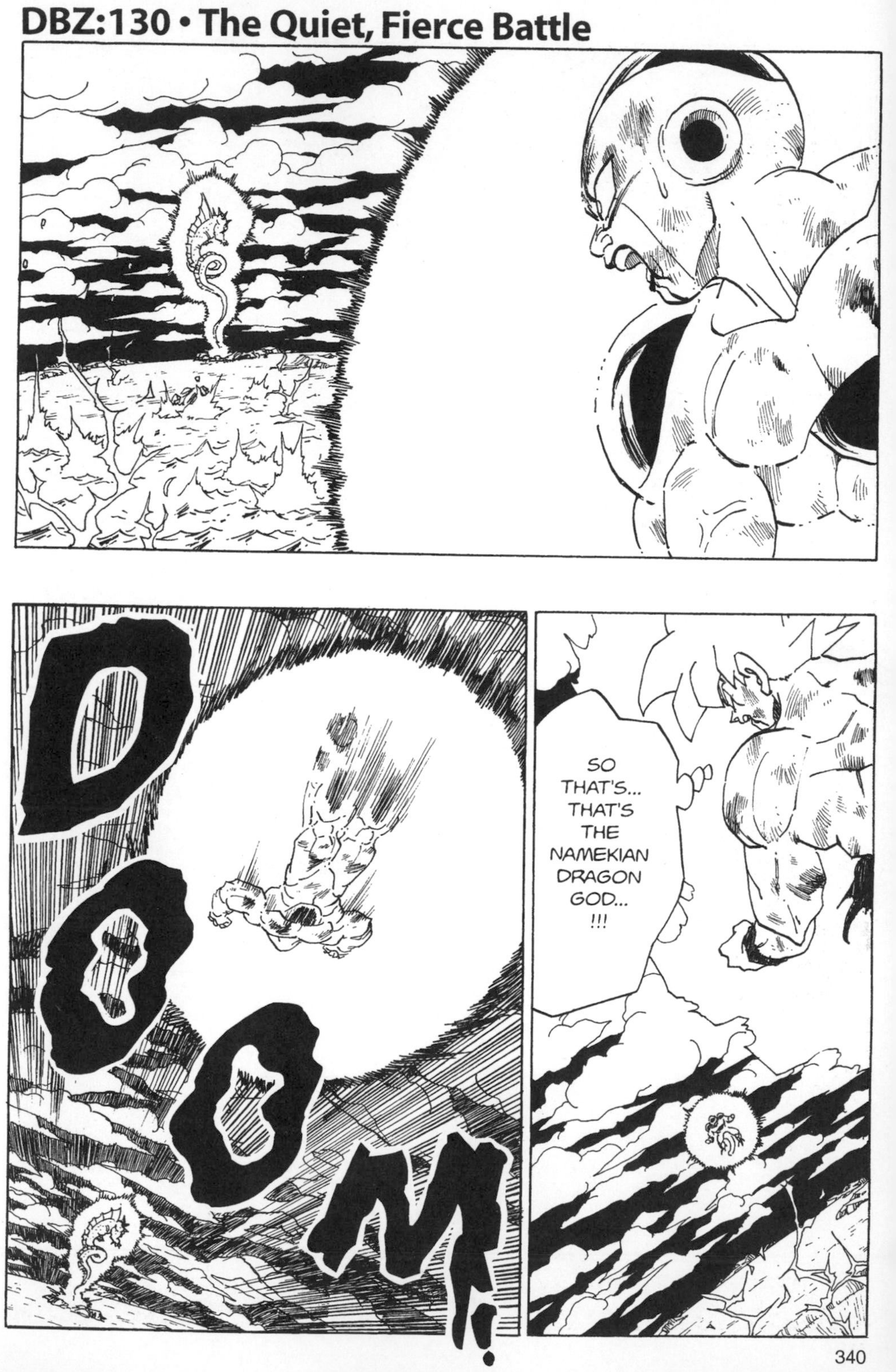
DOOM!
SO THAT'S... THAT'S THE NAMEKIAN DRAGON GOD... !!!

NGH!!!!!

SHEN-LONG! MAKE ME...

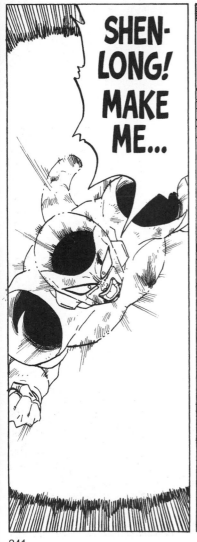

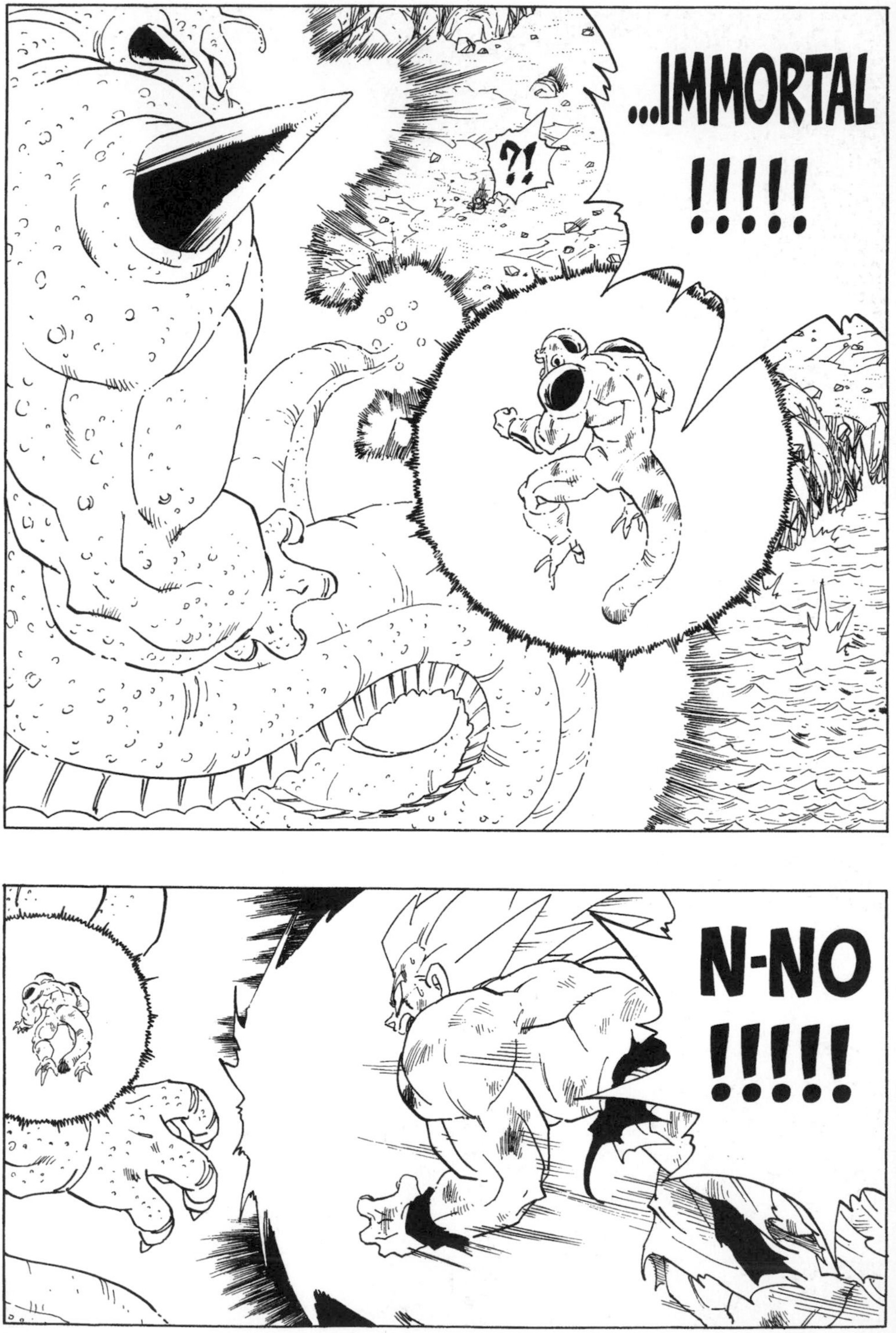
...IMMORTAL
!!!!!
?!
N-NO
!!!!!

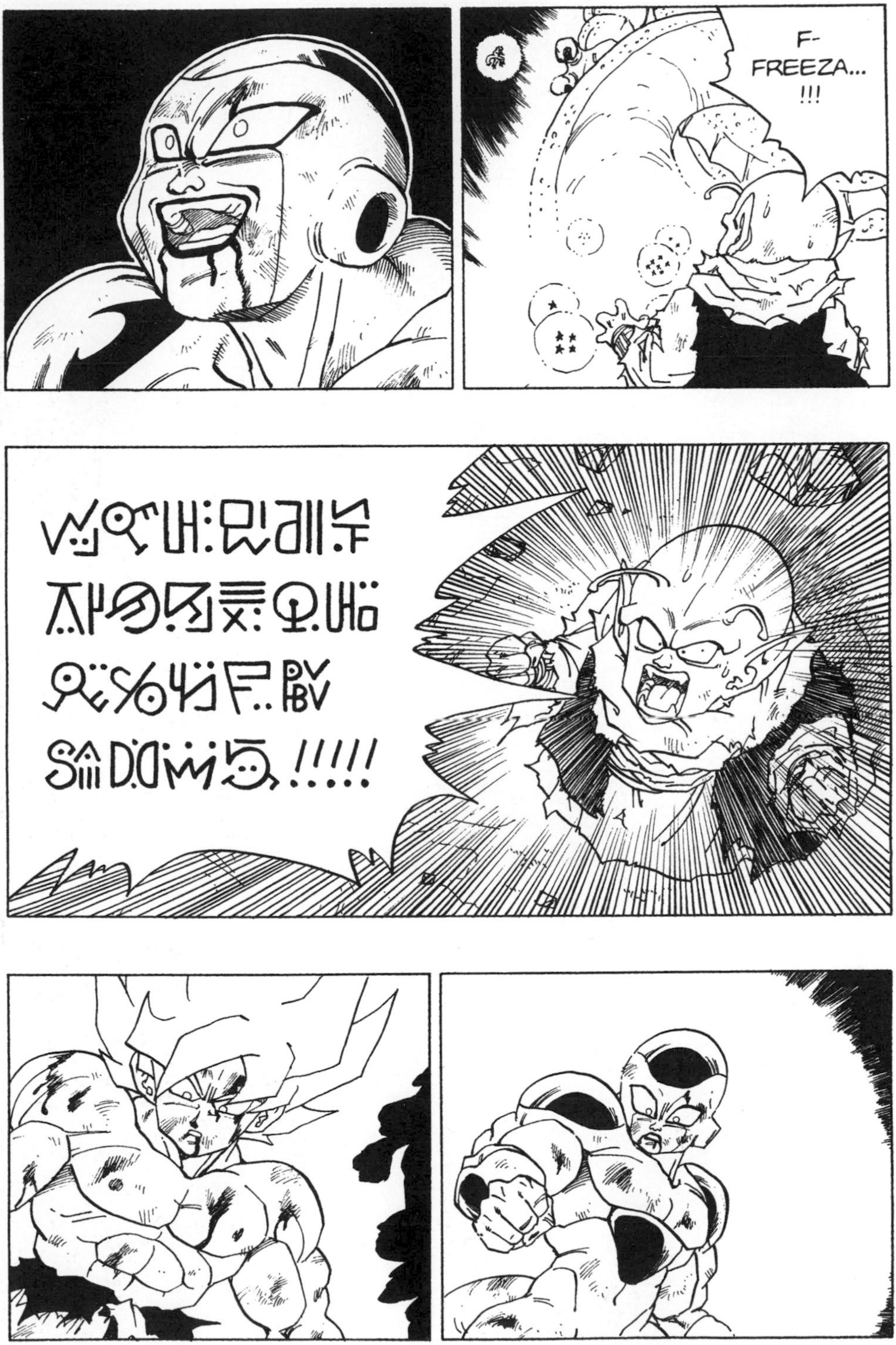
F-
FREEZA...
!!!

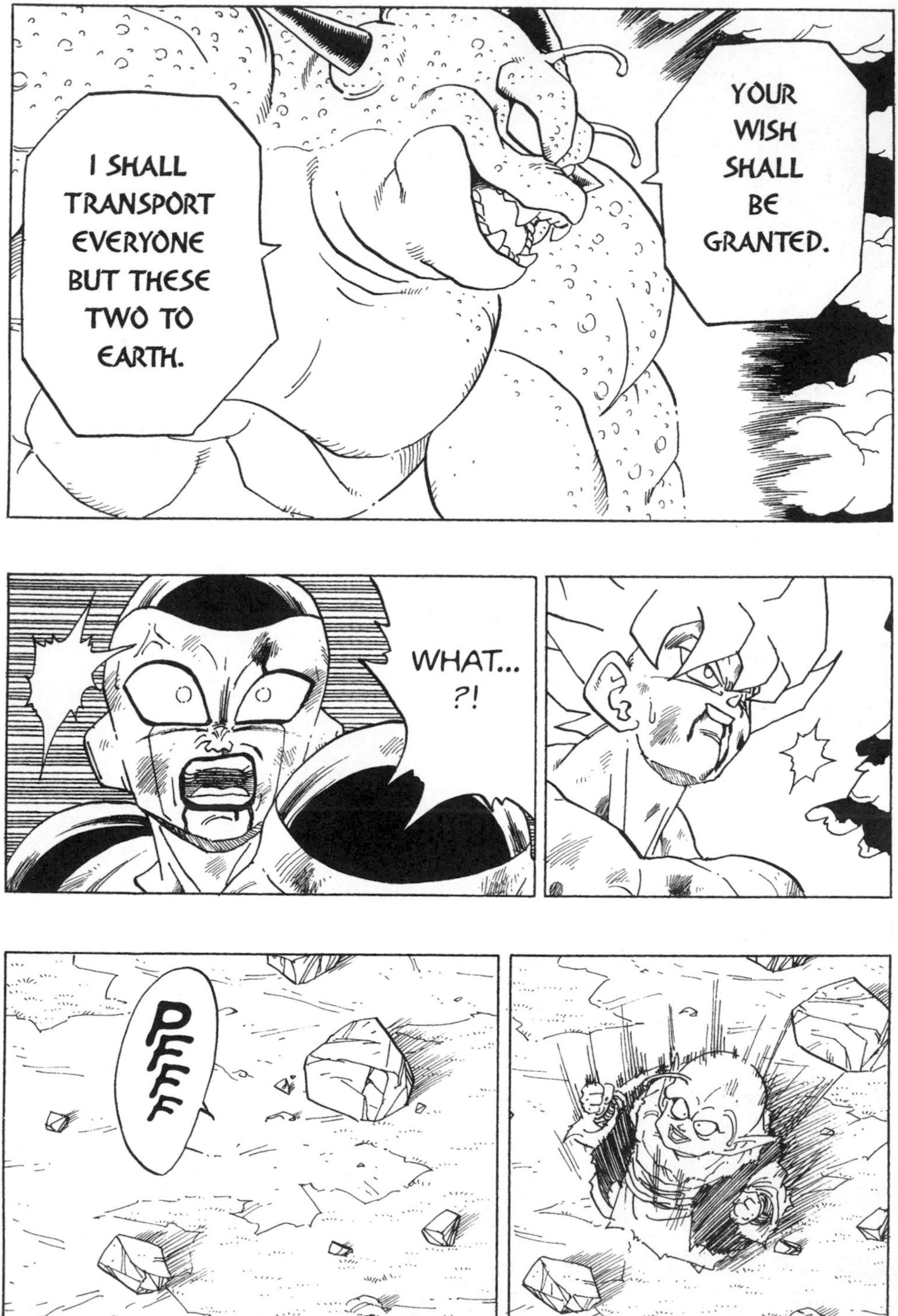
YOUR WISH SHALL BE GRANTED.
I SHALL TRANSPORT EVERYONE BUT THESE TWO TO EARTH.
WHAT... ?!
PFFF

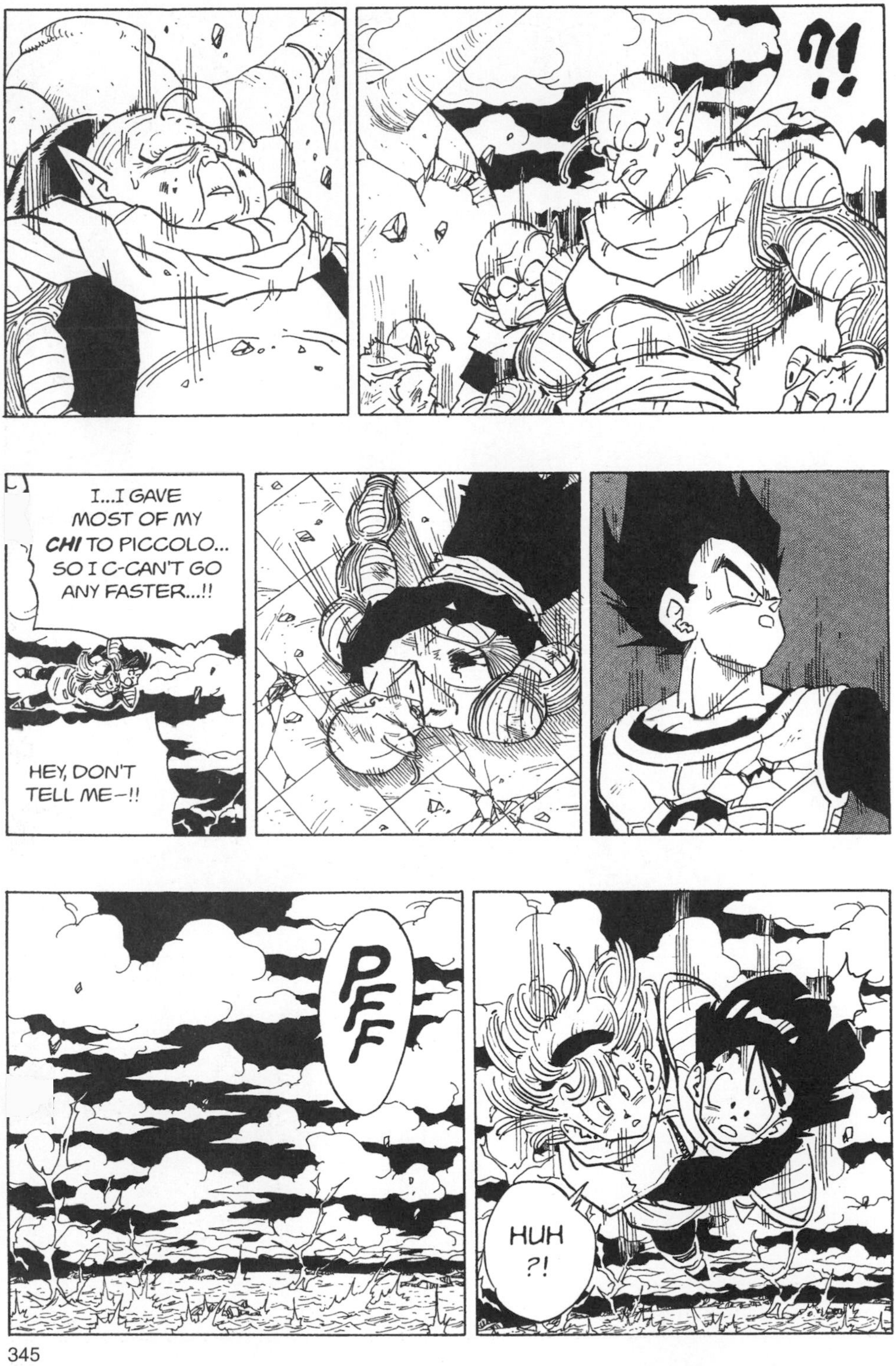
?!!
I...I GAVE MOST OF MY CHI TO PICCOLO... SO I C-CAN'T GO ANY FASTER...!!
HEY, DON'T TELL ME—!!
PFF
HUH ?!

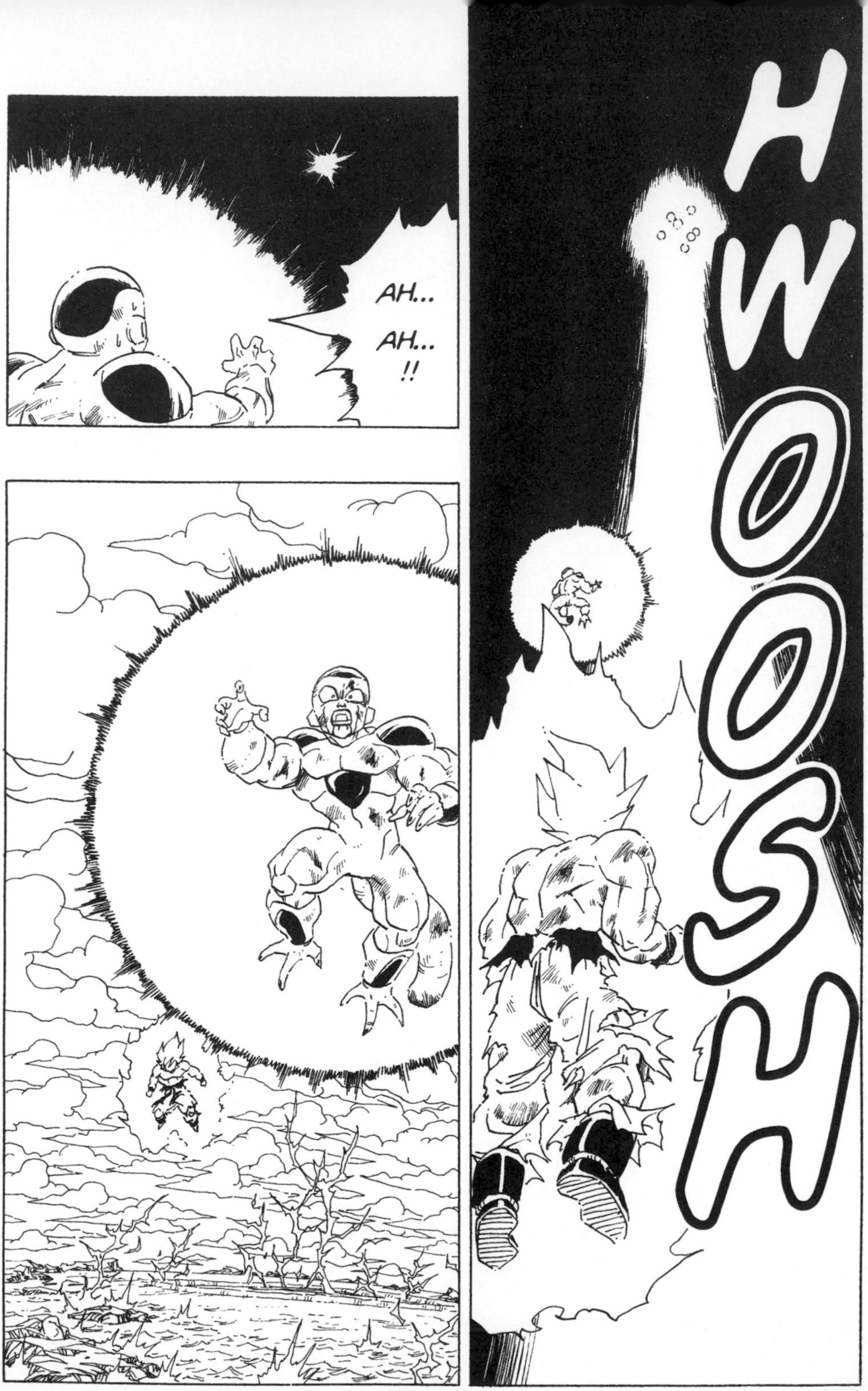
HWOOOSH
AH...
AH...
!!

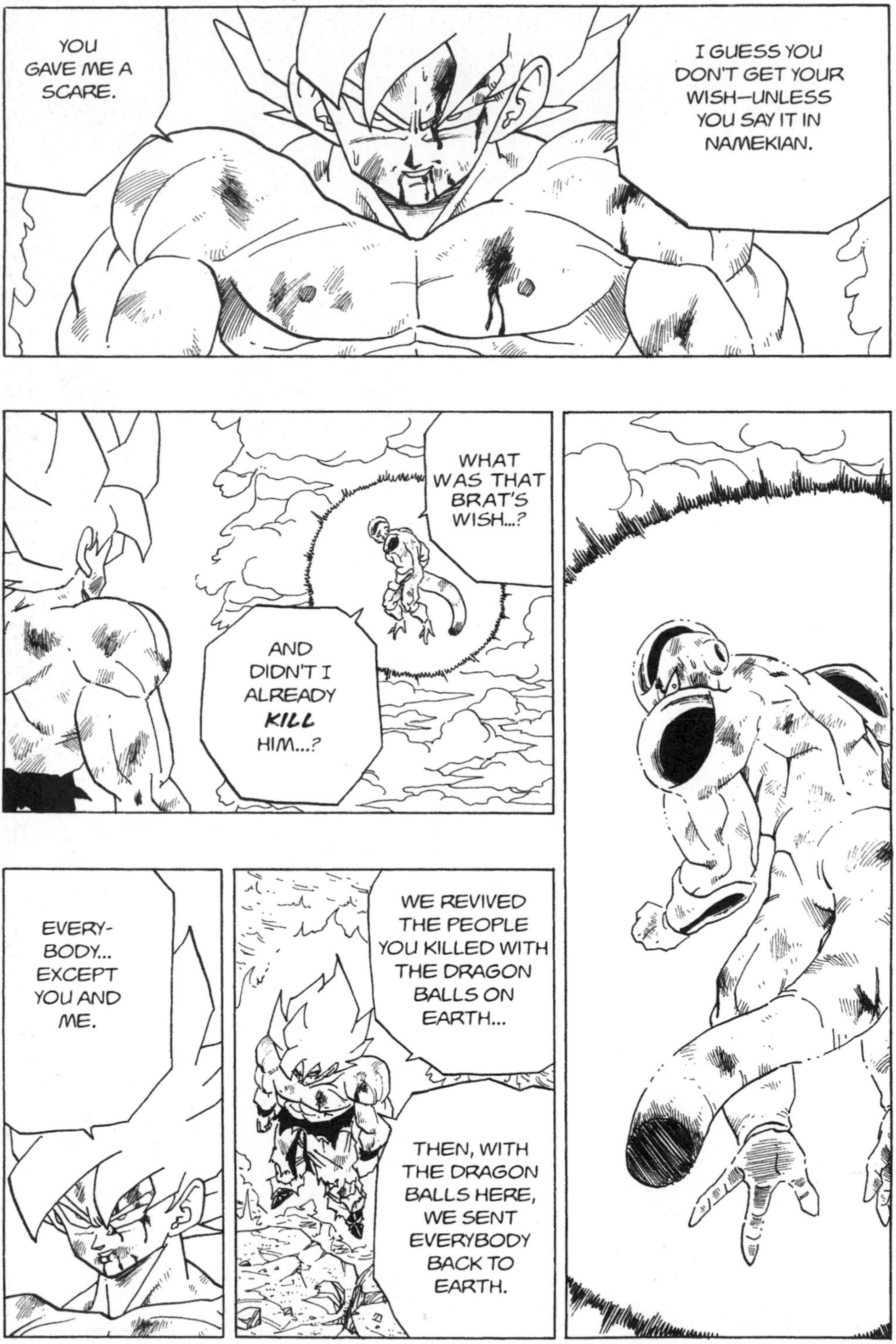
YOU GAVE ME A SCARE.
I GUESS YOU DON'T GET YOUR WISH—UNLESS YOU SAY IT IN NAMEKIAN.
WHAT WAS THAT BRAT'S WISH...?
AND DIDN'T I ALREADY **KILL** HIM...?
WE REVIVED THE PEOPLE YOU KILLED WITH THE DRAGON BALLS ON EARTH...
THEN, WITH THE DRAGON BALLS HERE, WE SENT EVERYBODY BACK TO EARTH.
EVERY-BODY... EXCEPT YOU AND ME.

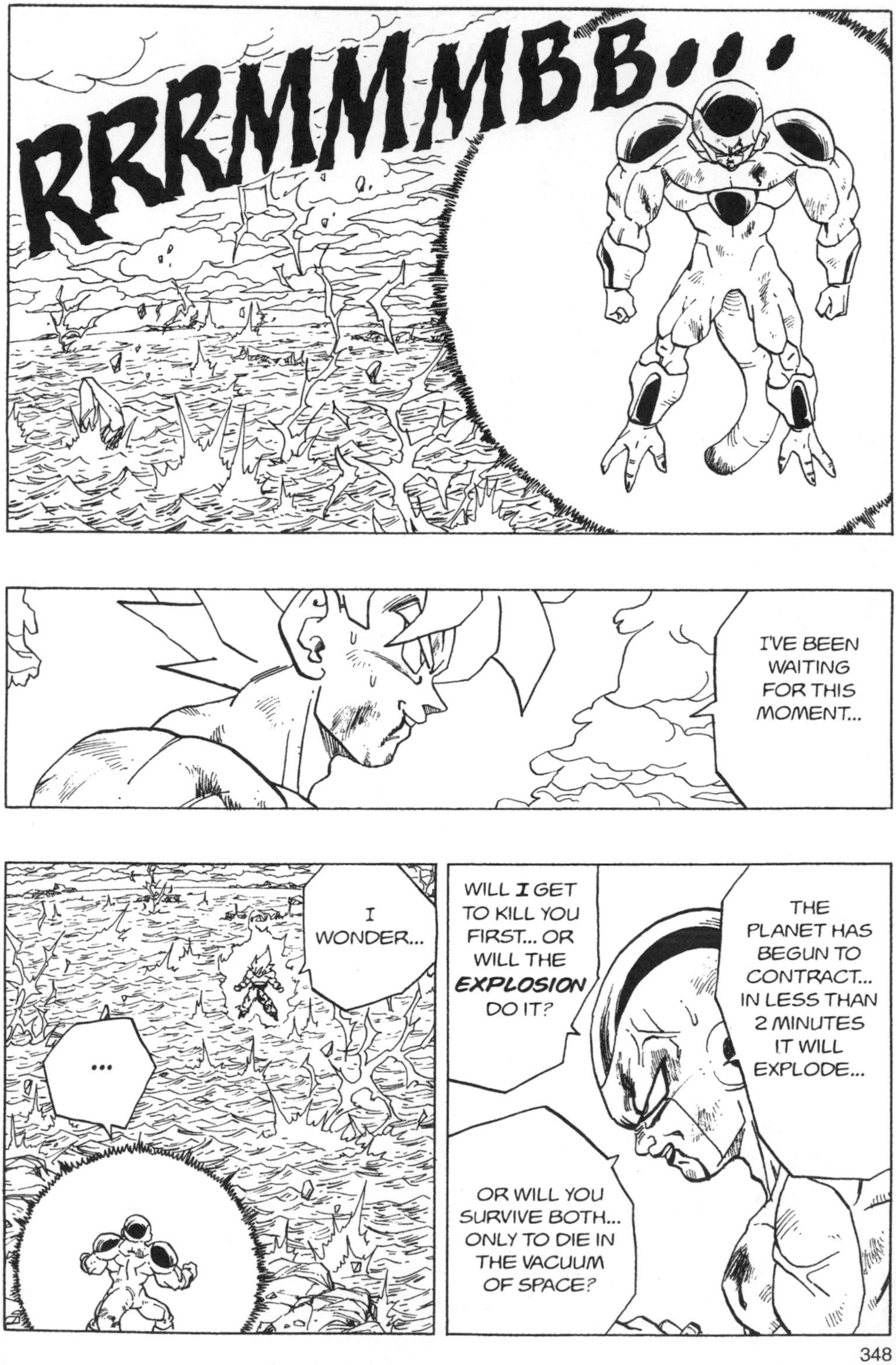

RRRMMMBB...
I'VE BEEN WAITING FOR THIS MOMENT...
I WONDER...
...
THE PLANET HAS BEGUN TO CONTRACT... IN LESS THAN 2 MINUTES IT WILL EXPLODE...
WILL *I* GET TO KILL YOU FIRST... OR WILL THE ***EXPLOSION*** DO IT?
OR WILL YOU SURVIVE BOTH... ONLY TO DIE IN THE VACUUM OF SPACE?

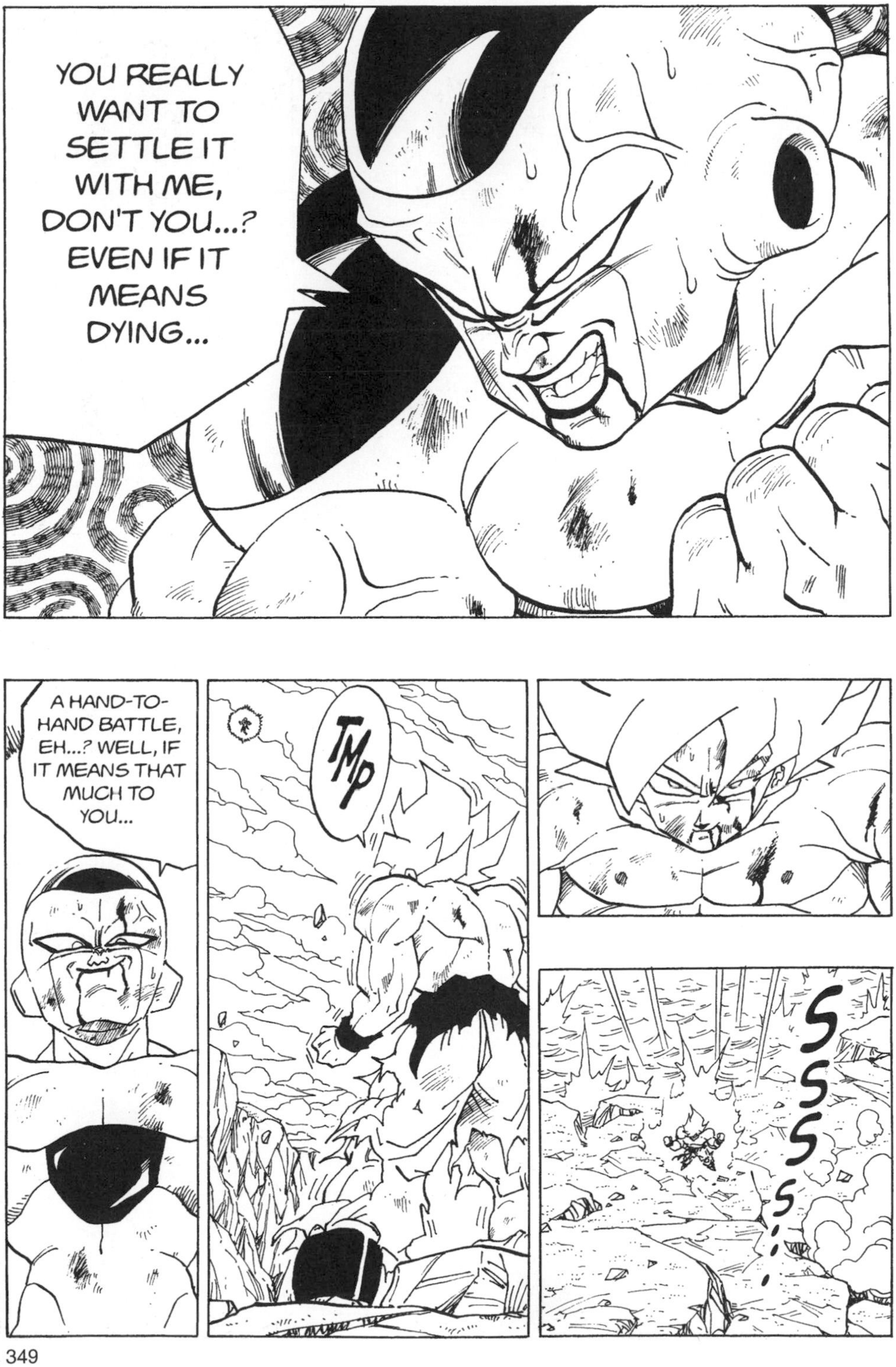
YOU REALLY WANT TO SETTLE IT WITH ME, DON'T YOU...? EVEN IF IT MEANS DYING...
A HAND-TO-HAND BATTLE, EH...? WELL, IF IT MEANS THAT MUCH TO YOU...
TMP
SSSSS...

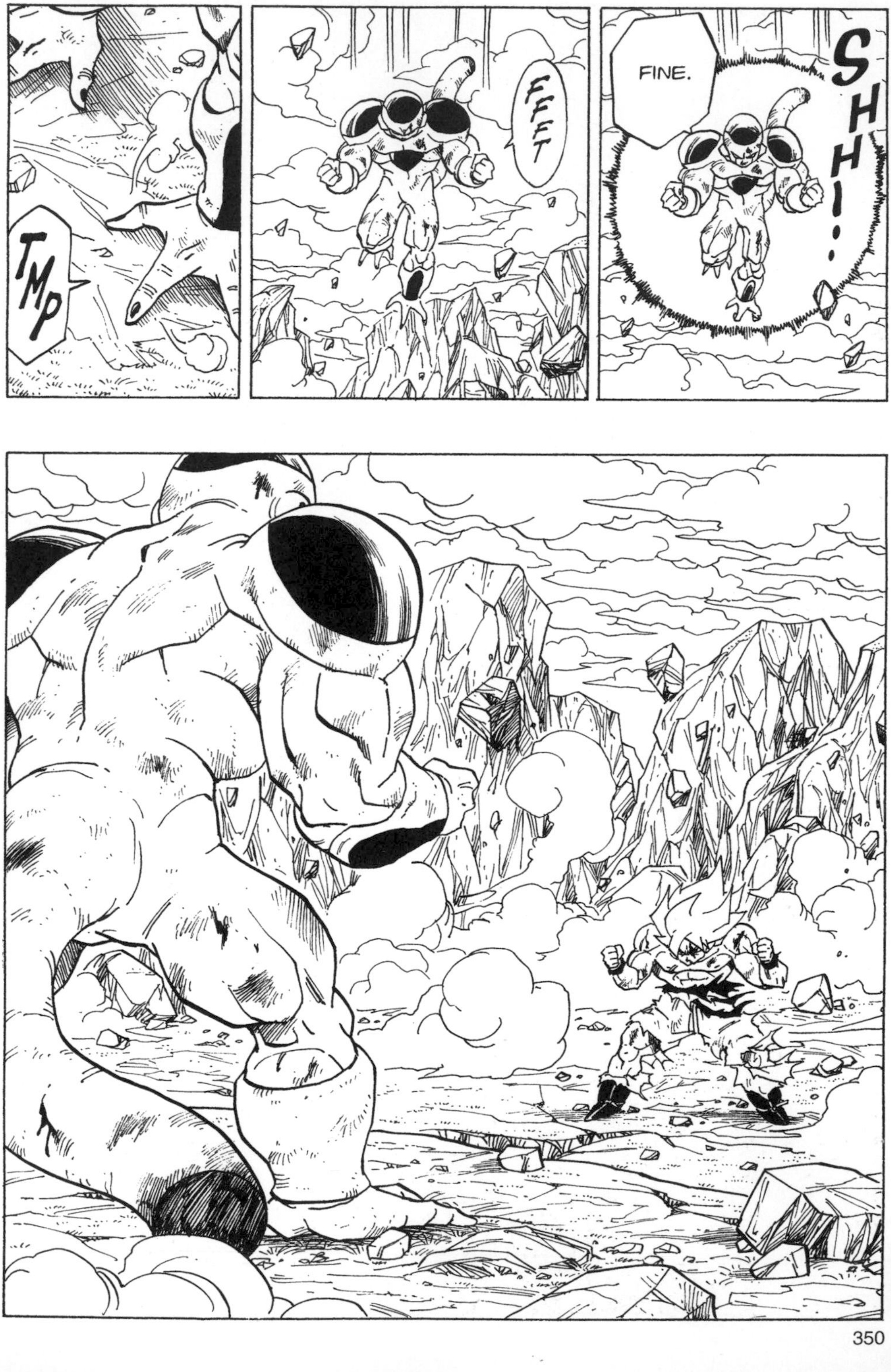
TMP
FFFT
FINE.
SHH!..

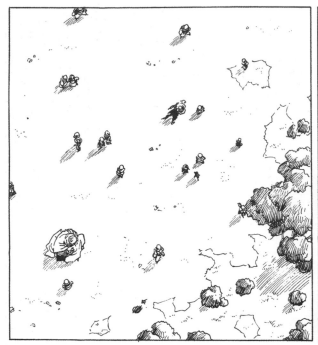

WH-WHERE ARE WE...?

HUH?! HUH?! WH-WHAT HAPPENED...?

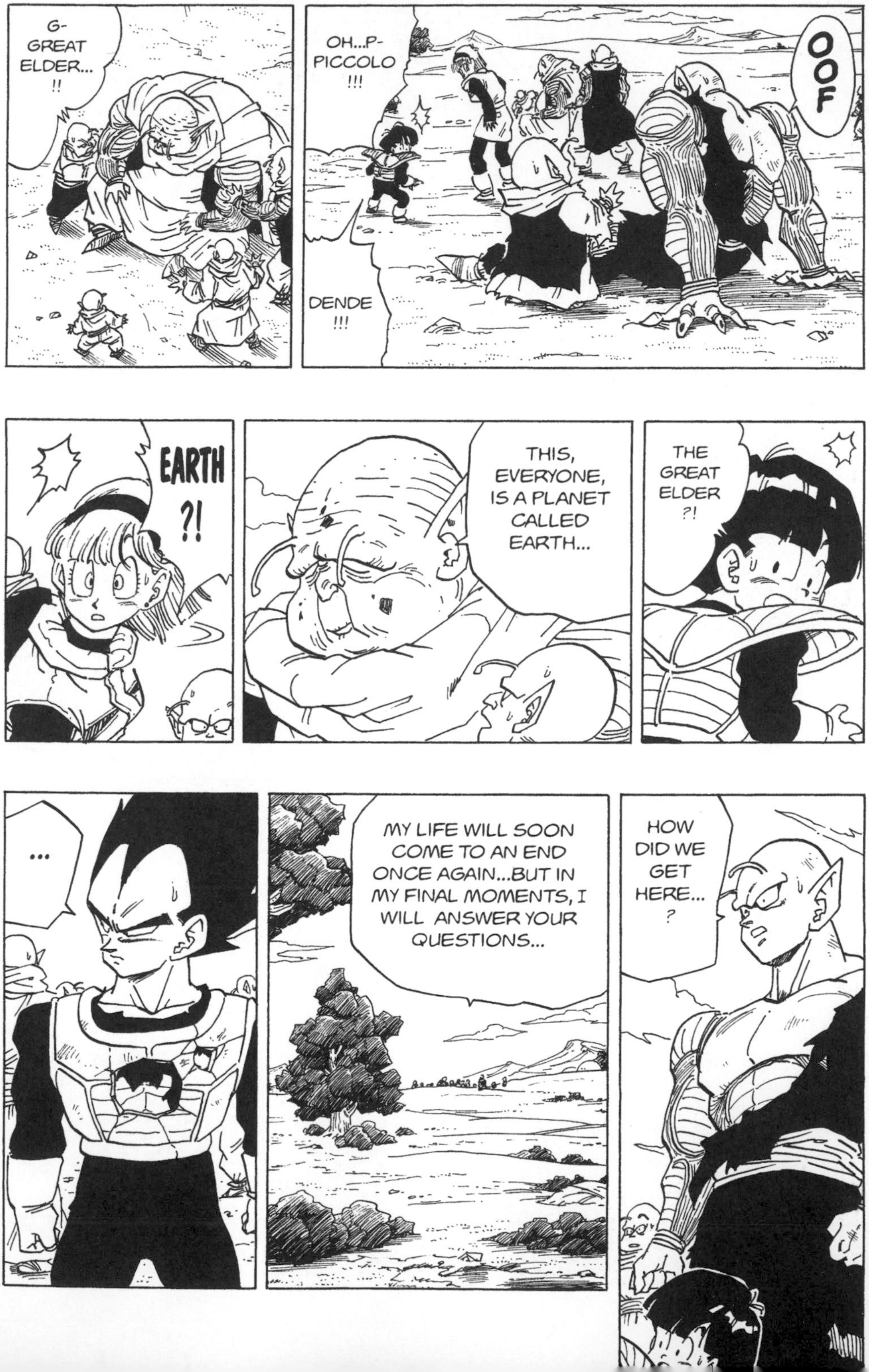
OOF
OH...P-PICCOLO!!!
DENDE!!!
G-GREAT ELDER...!!
THE GREAT ELDER?!
THIS, EVERYONE, IS A PLANET CALLED EARTH...
EARTH?!
HOW DID WE GET HERE...?
MY LIFE WILL SOON COME TO AN END ONCE AGAIN...BUT IN MY FINAL MOMENTS, I WILL ANSWER YOUR QUESTIONS...
...

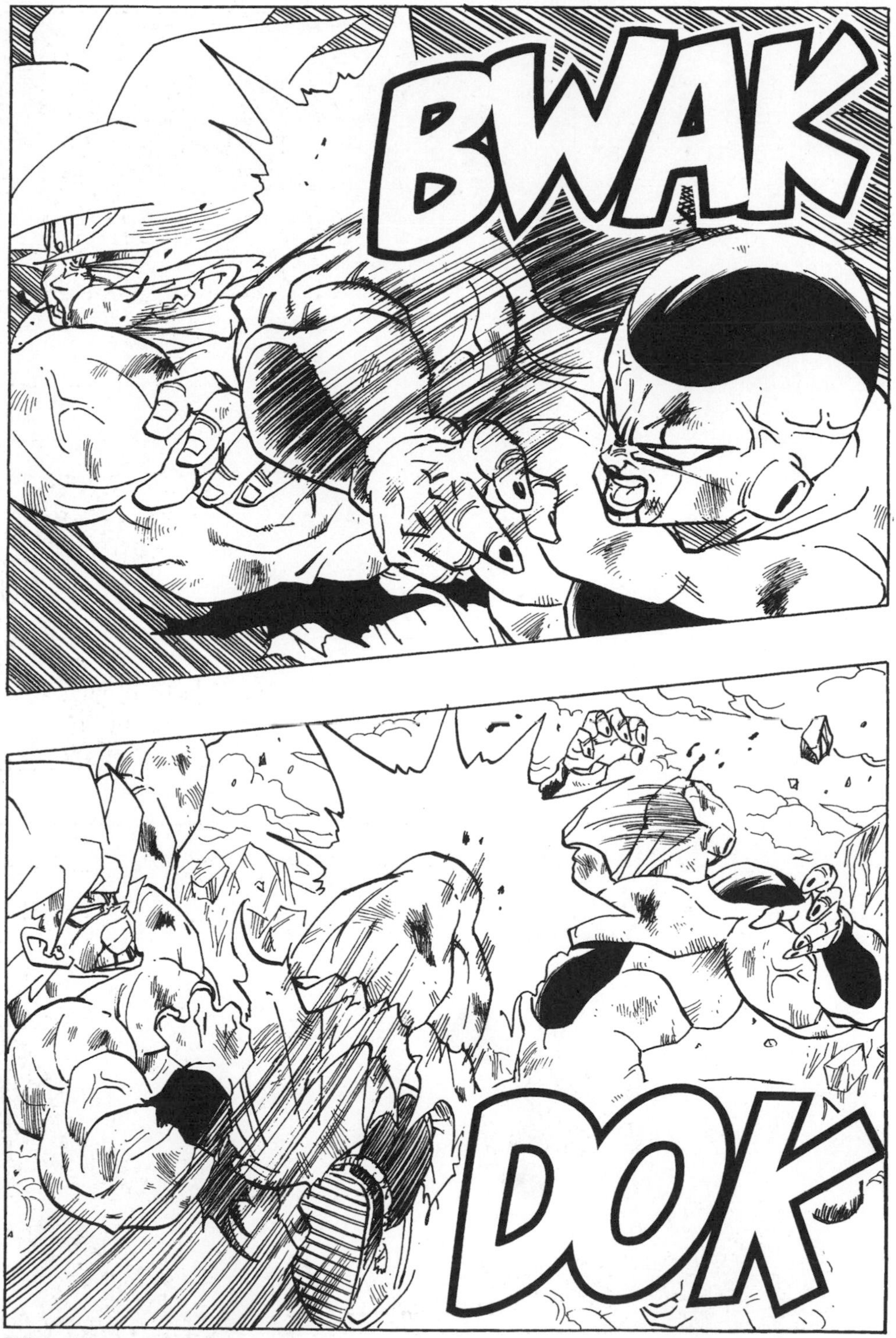
BWAK
DOK

DBZ:131 · Son Goku Quits

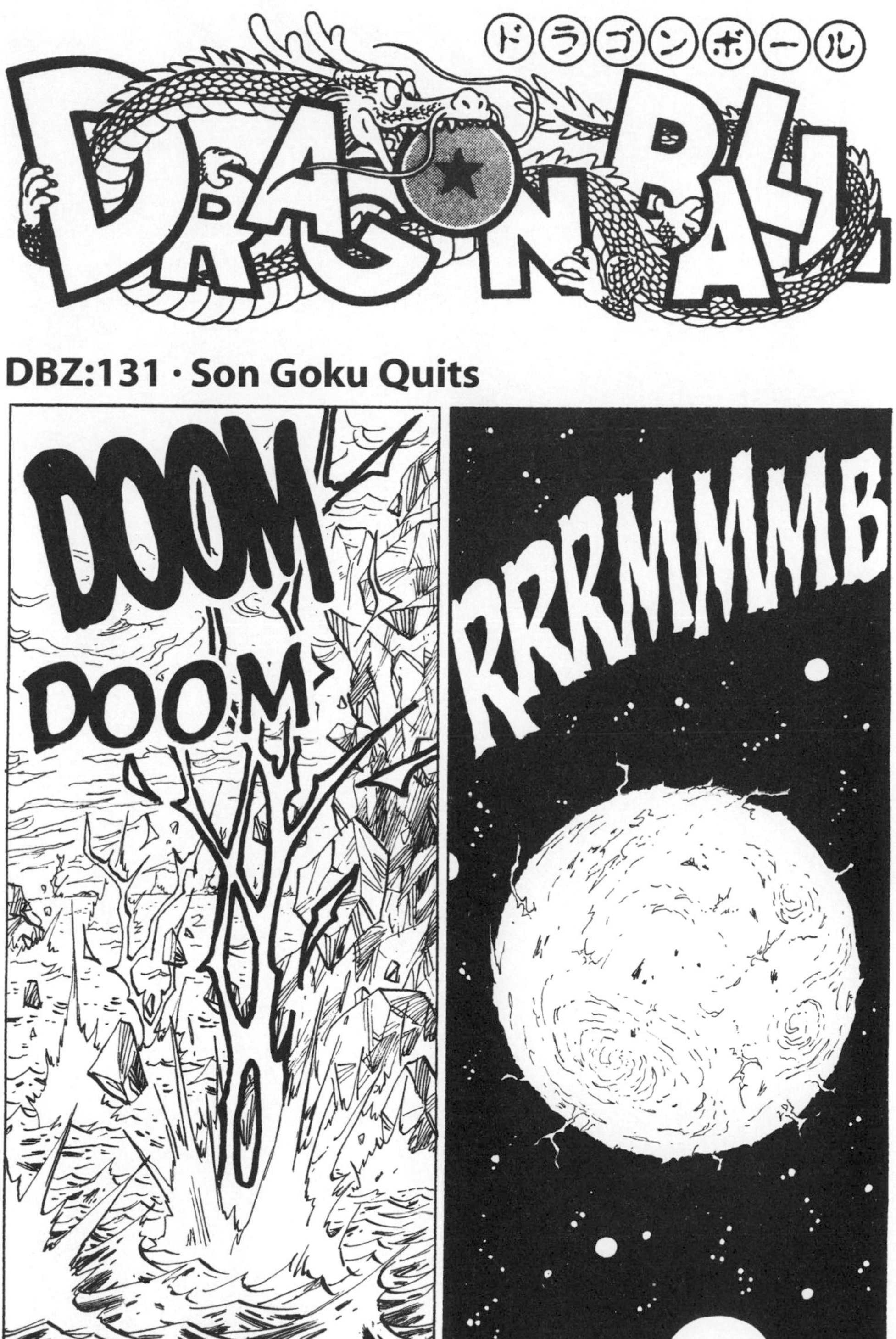
RRRMMMMB
DOOM
DOOM

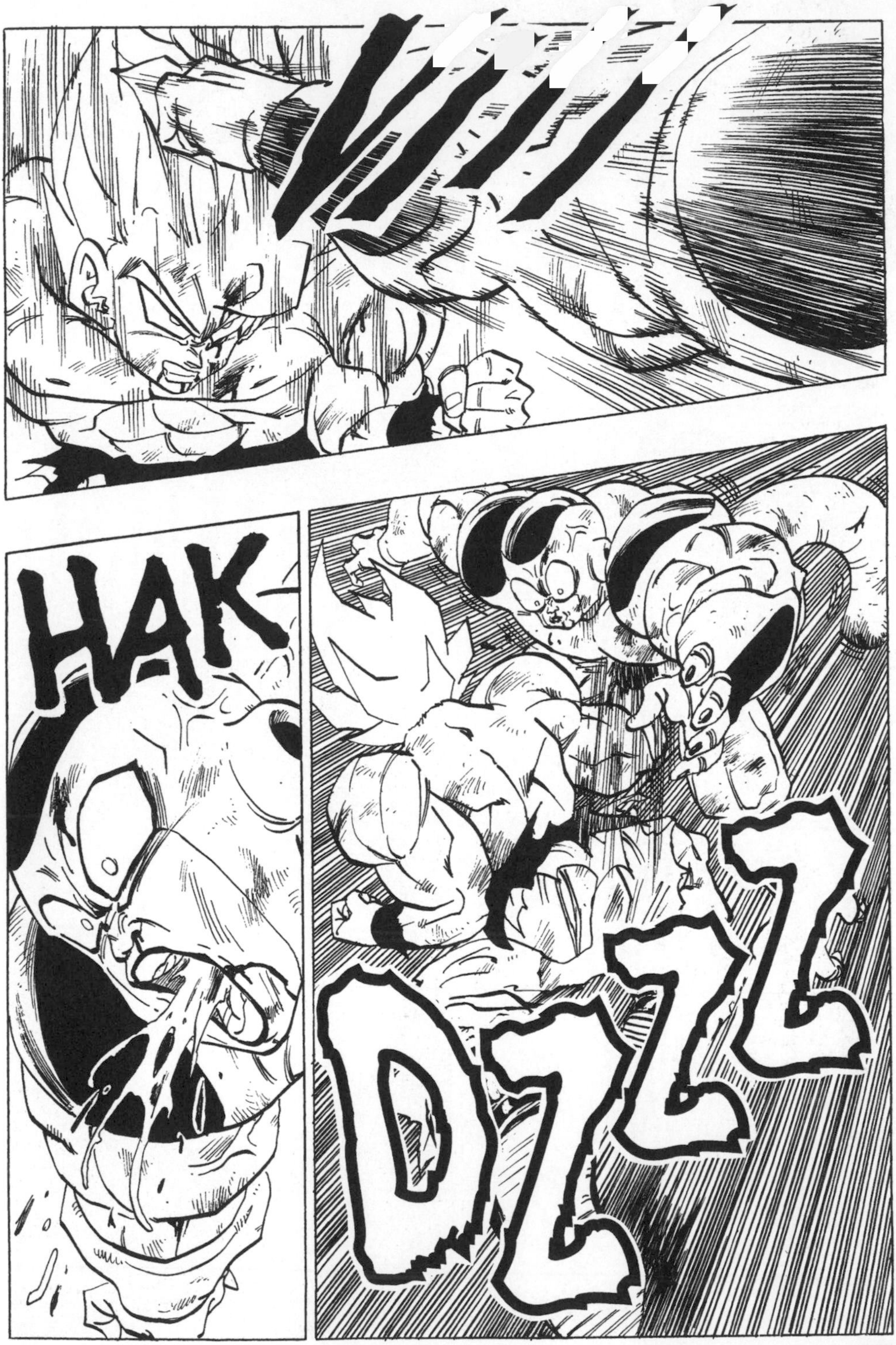
HAK
DZZ

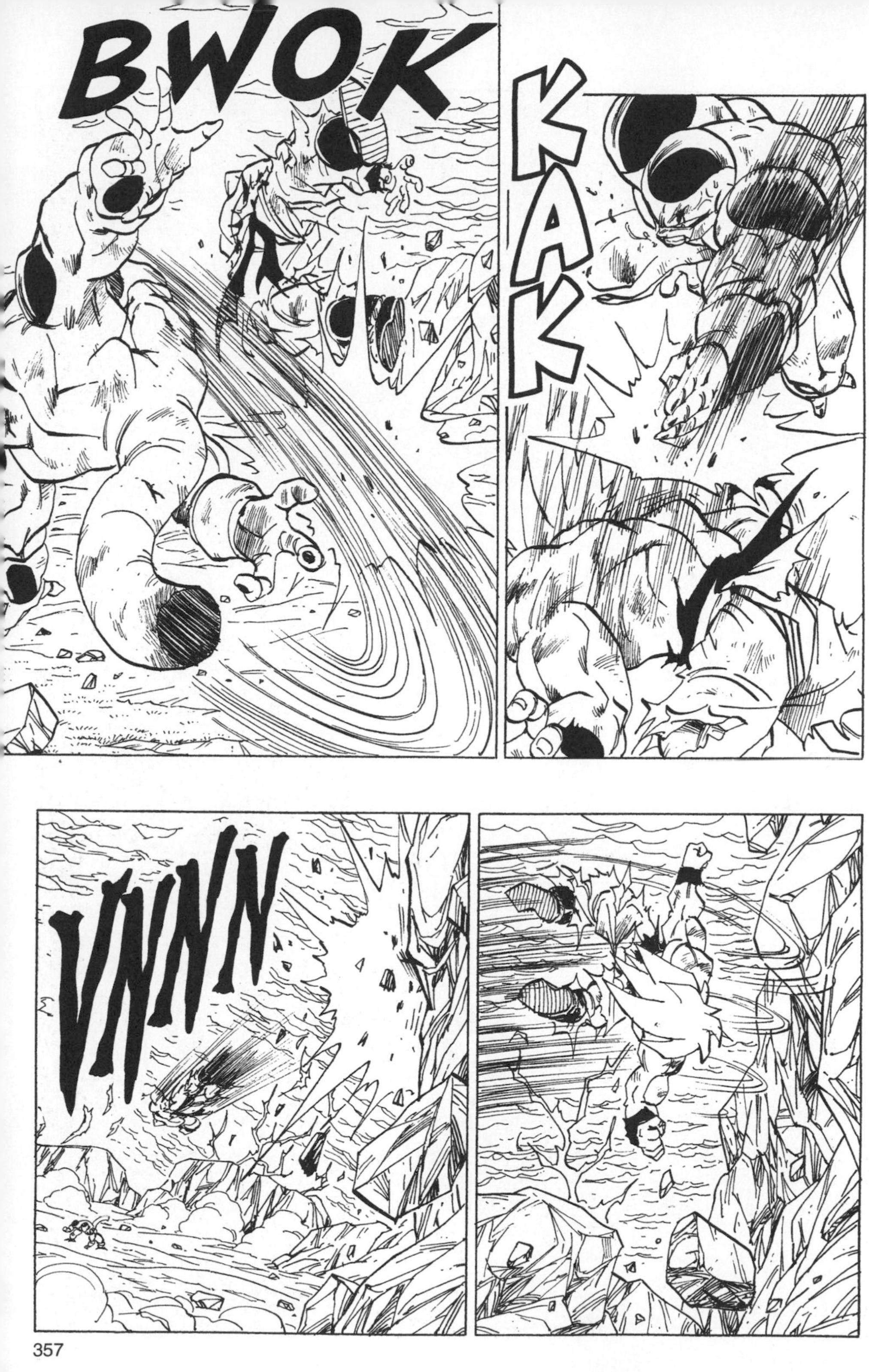
KAK
BWOK
VNNN

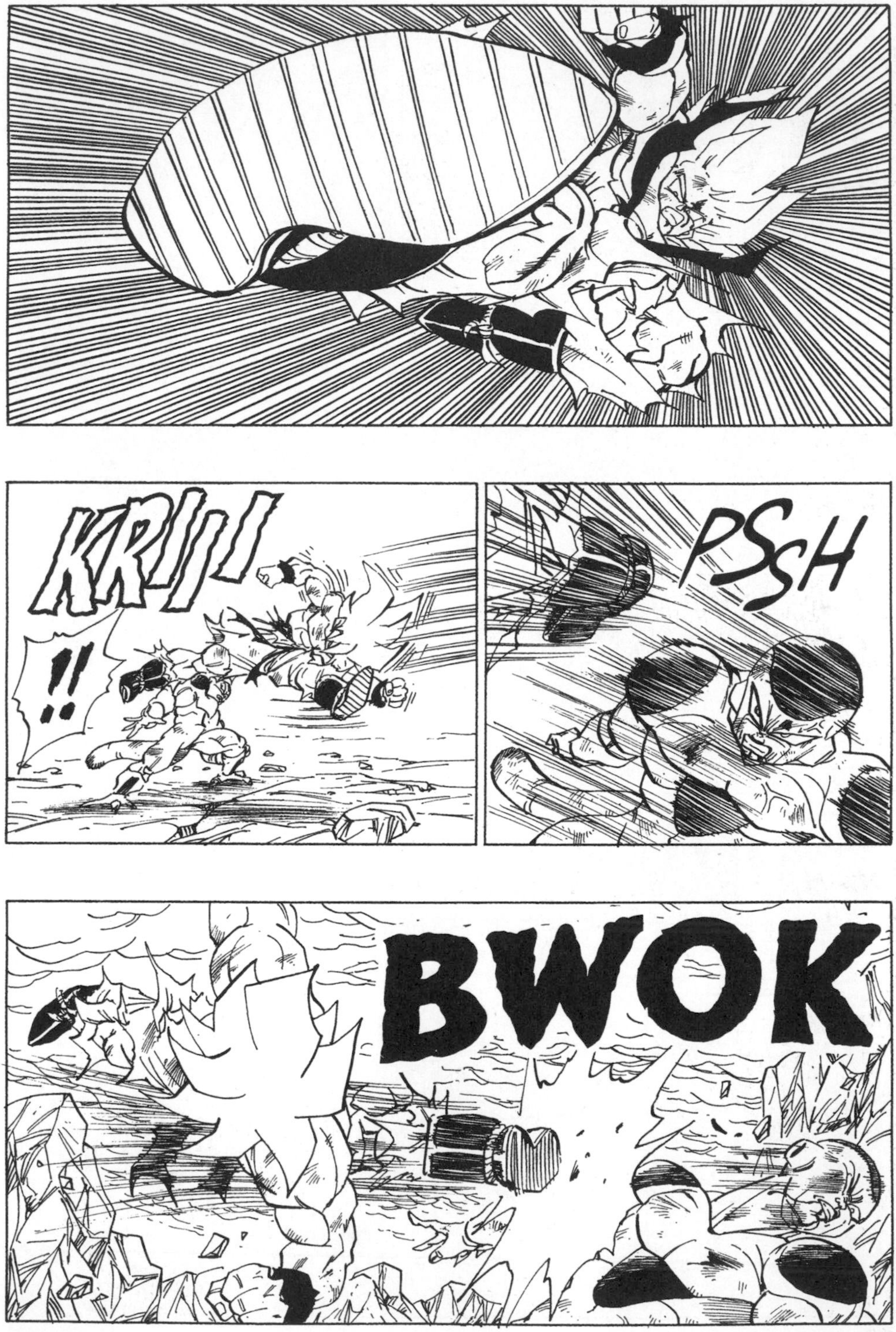
PSSH
KRUI
!!
BWOK

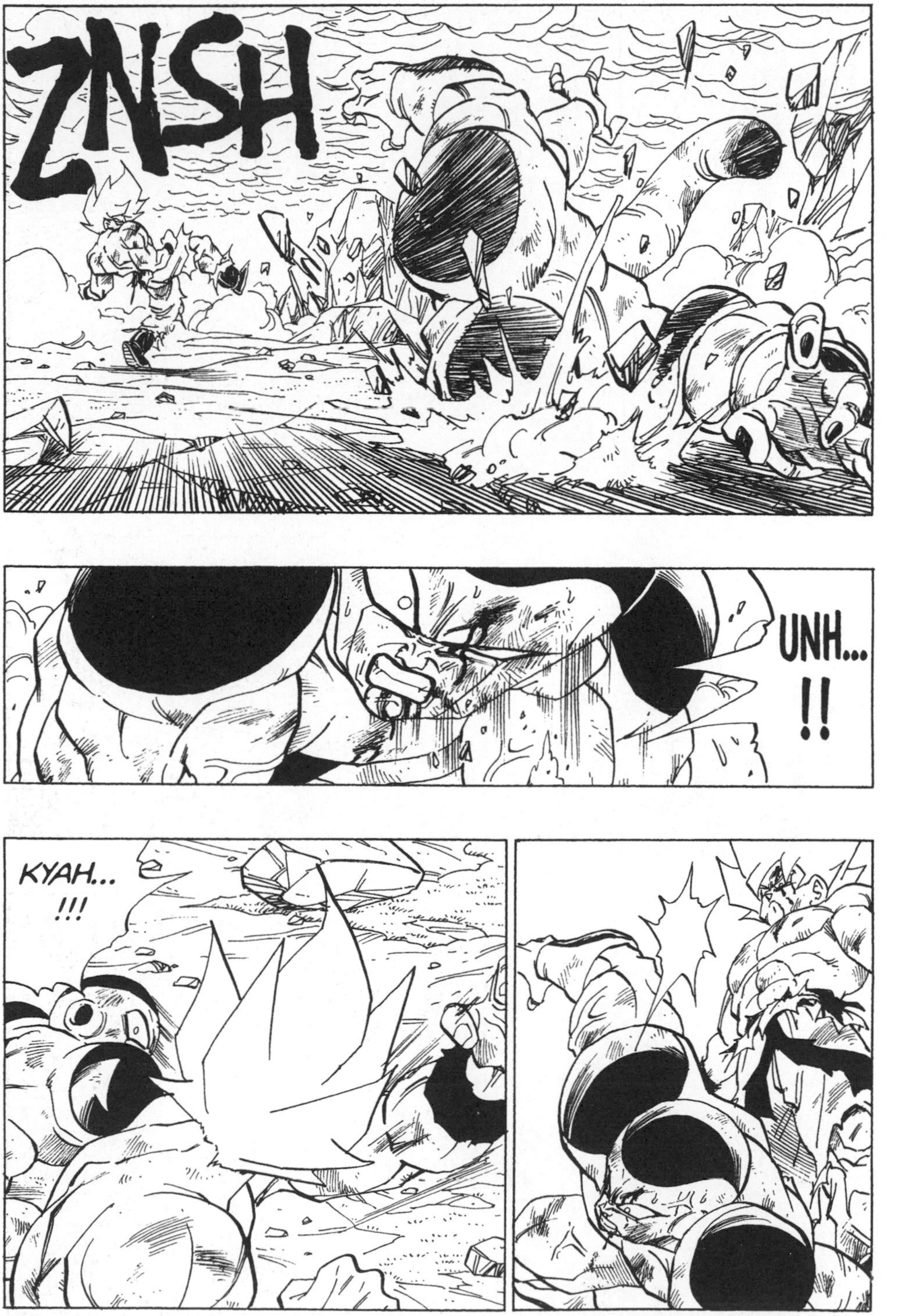
ZNSH
UNH...
!!
KYAH...
!!!

HAH
!!!!

KRAAAK

GNN

WAFT

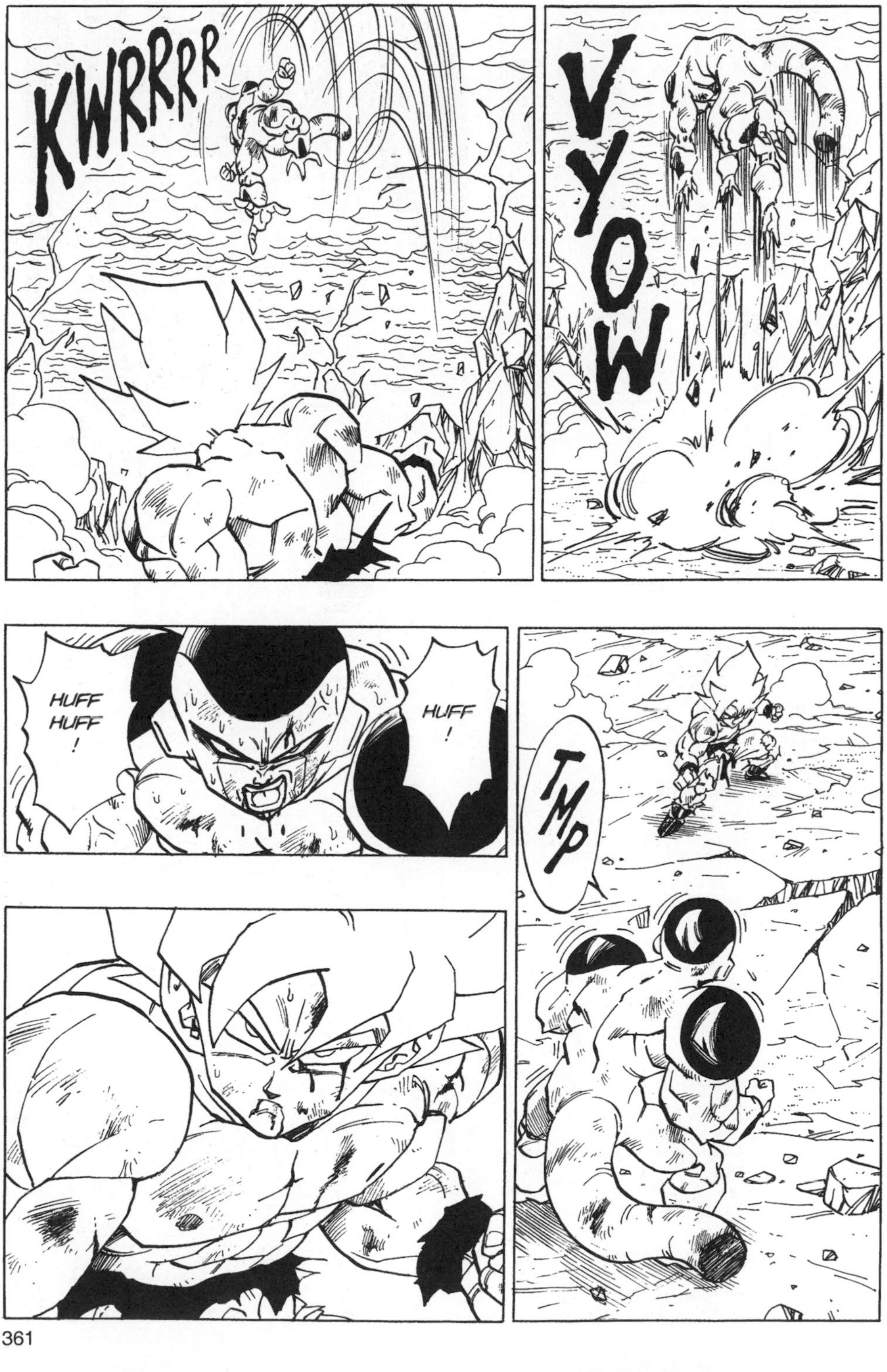
KWRRRR
VYOW
HUFF HUFF !
HUFF !
TMP

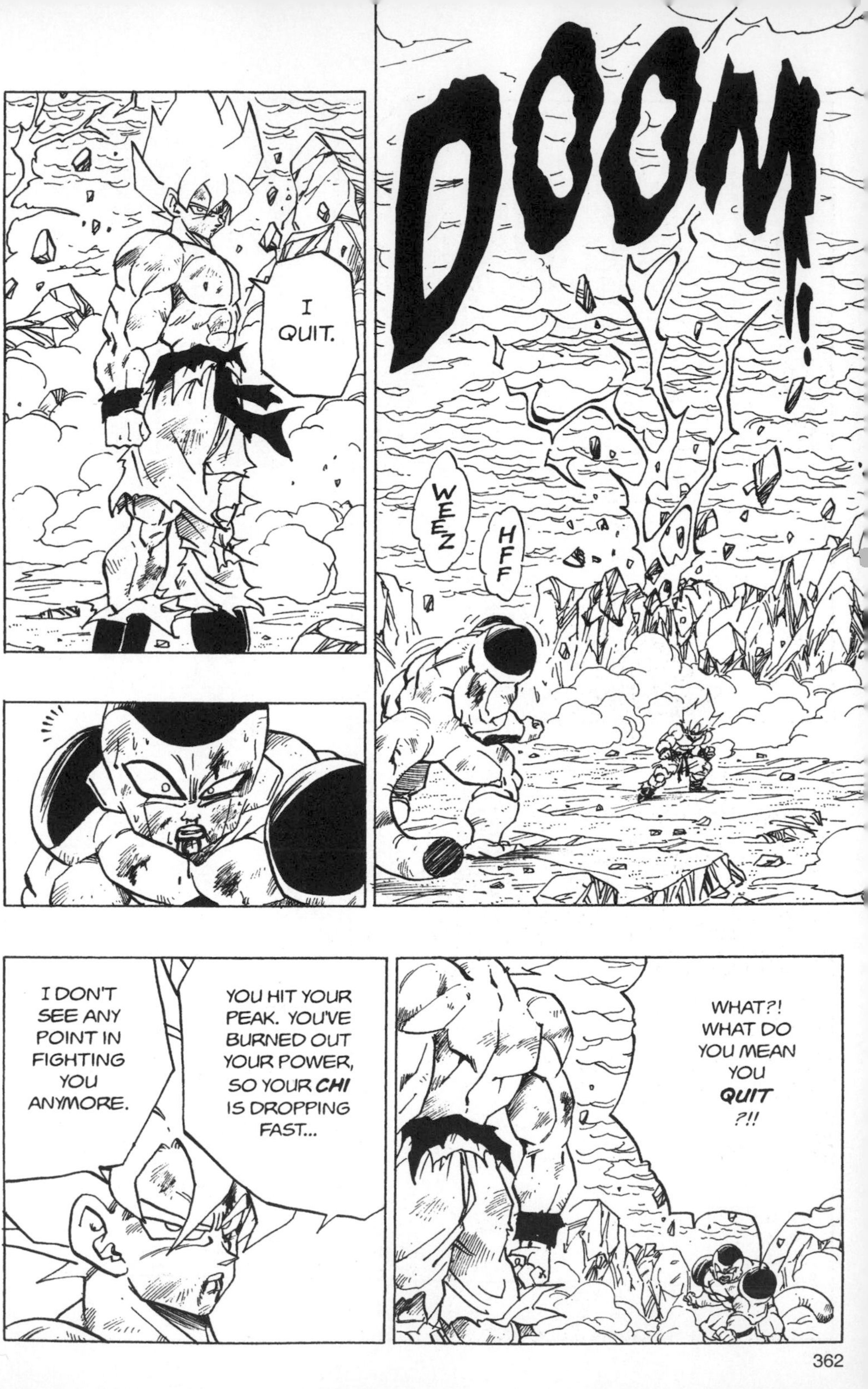
DOOM!!
WEEZ
HFF
I QUIT.
WHAT?! WHAT DO YOU MEAN YOU **QUIT** ?!!
YOU HIT YOUR PEAK. YOU'VE BURNED OUT YOUR POWER, SO YOUR ***CHI*** IS DROPPING FAST...
I DON'T SEE ANY POINT IN FIGHTING YOU ANYMORE.

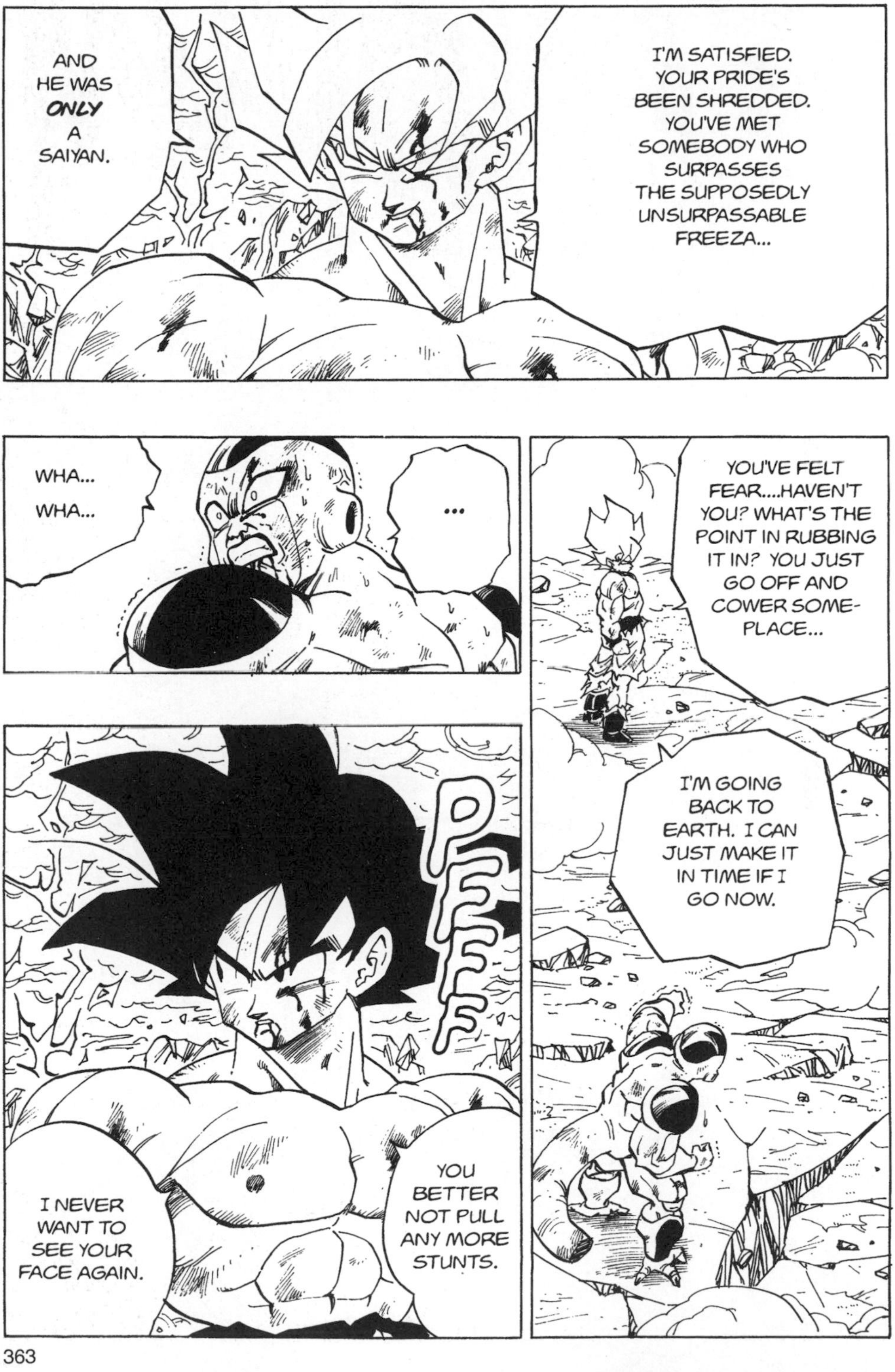

AND HE WAS *ONLY* A SAIYAN.
I'M SATISFIED. YOUR PRIDE'S BEEN SHREDDED. YOU'VE MET SOMEBODY WHO SURPASSES THE SUPPOSEDLY UNSURPASSABLE FREEZA...
WHA... WHA...
...
PFFF
I NEVER WANT TO SEE YOUR FACE AGAIN.
YOU BETTER NOT PULL ANY MORE STUNTS.
YOU'VE FELT FEAR....HAVEN'T YOU? WHAT'S THE POINT IN RUBBING IT IN? YOU JUST GO OFF AND COWER SOME-PLACE...
I'M GOING BACK TO EARTH. I CAN JUST MAKE IT IN TIME IF I GO NOW.

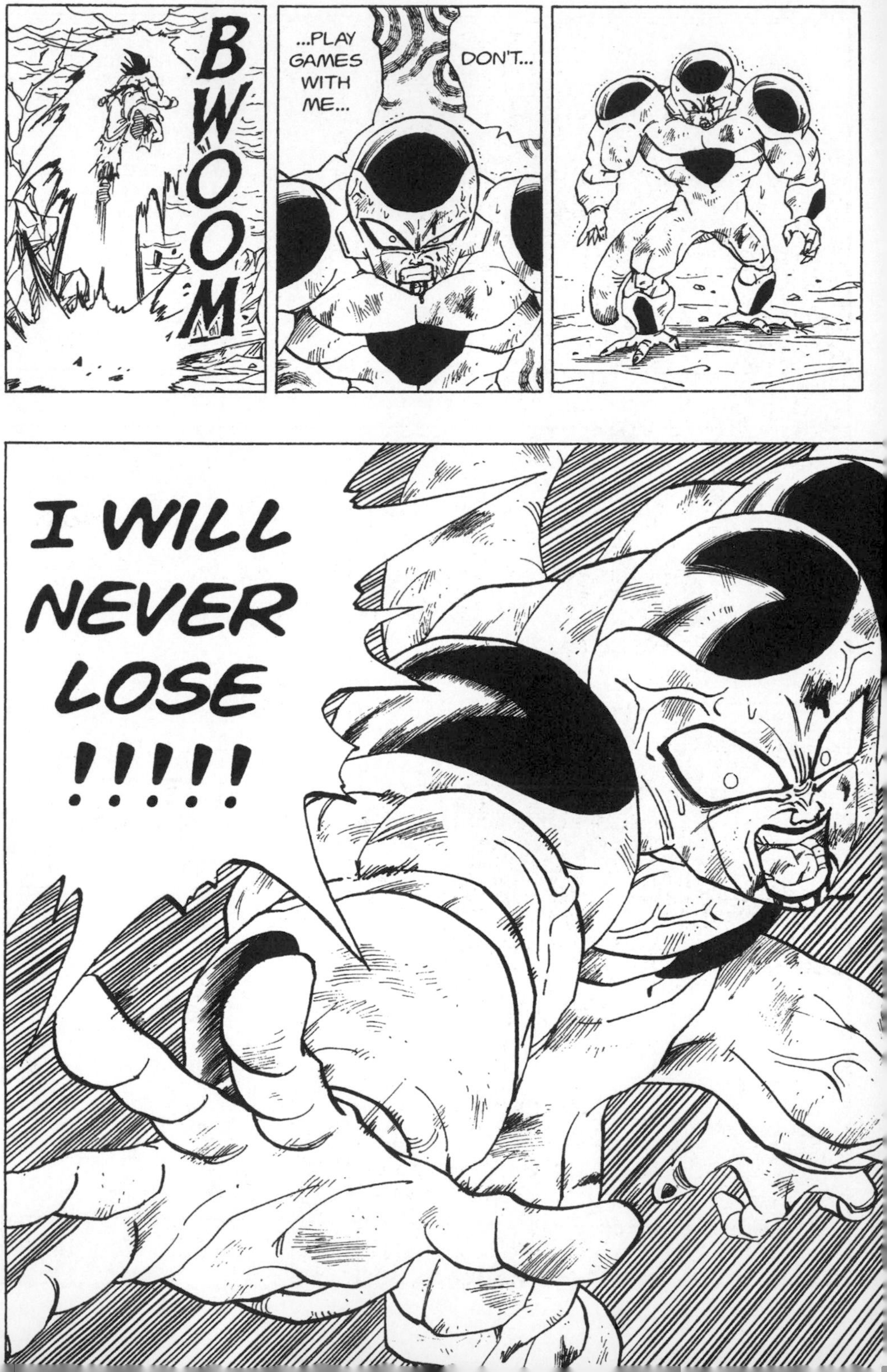
BWOOM
DON'T...
...PLAY GAMES WITH ME...
I WILL NEVER LOSE !!!!!

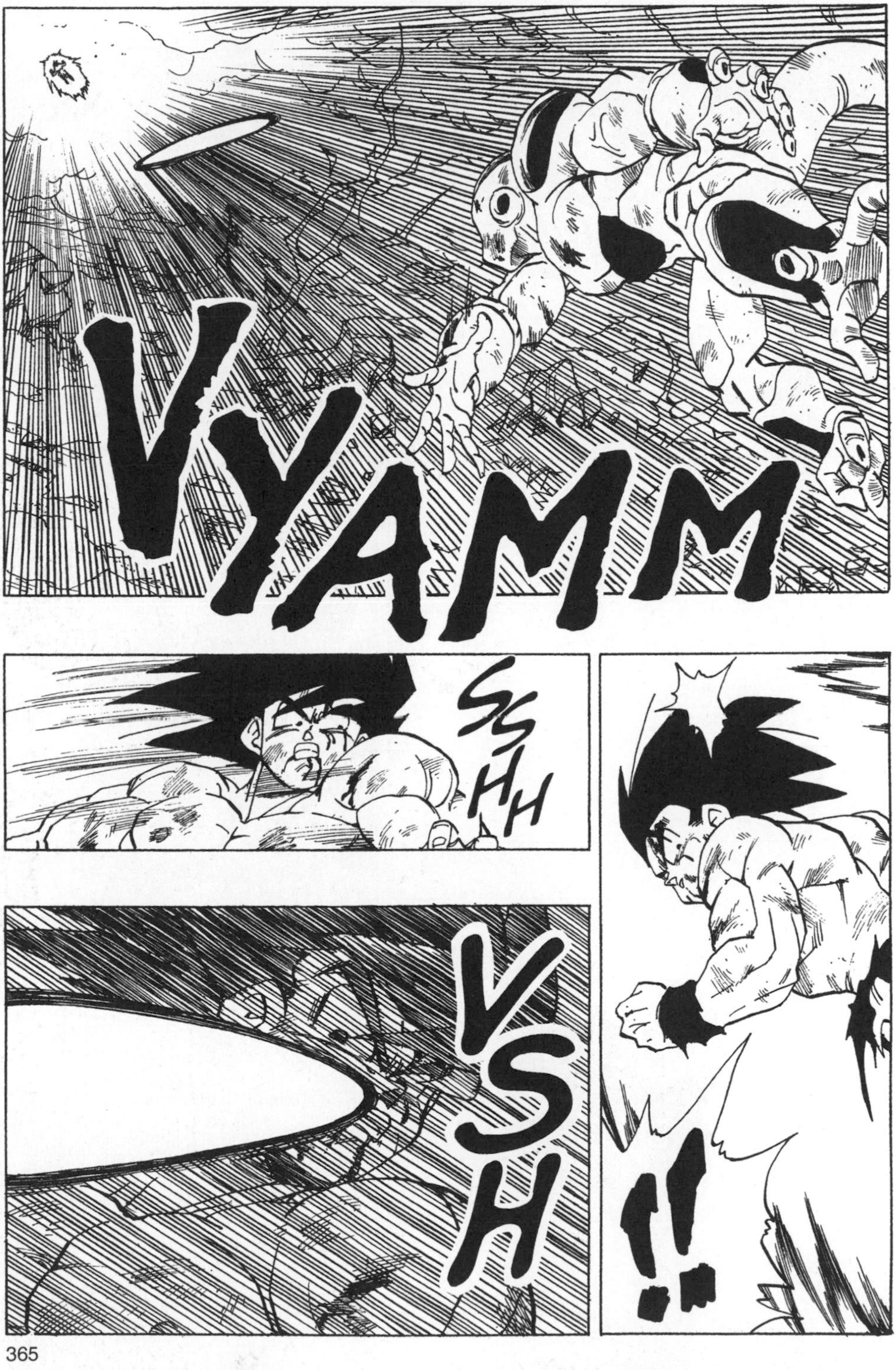
VYAMM
SSHH
VSSH
!!

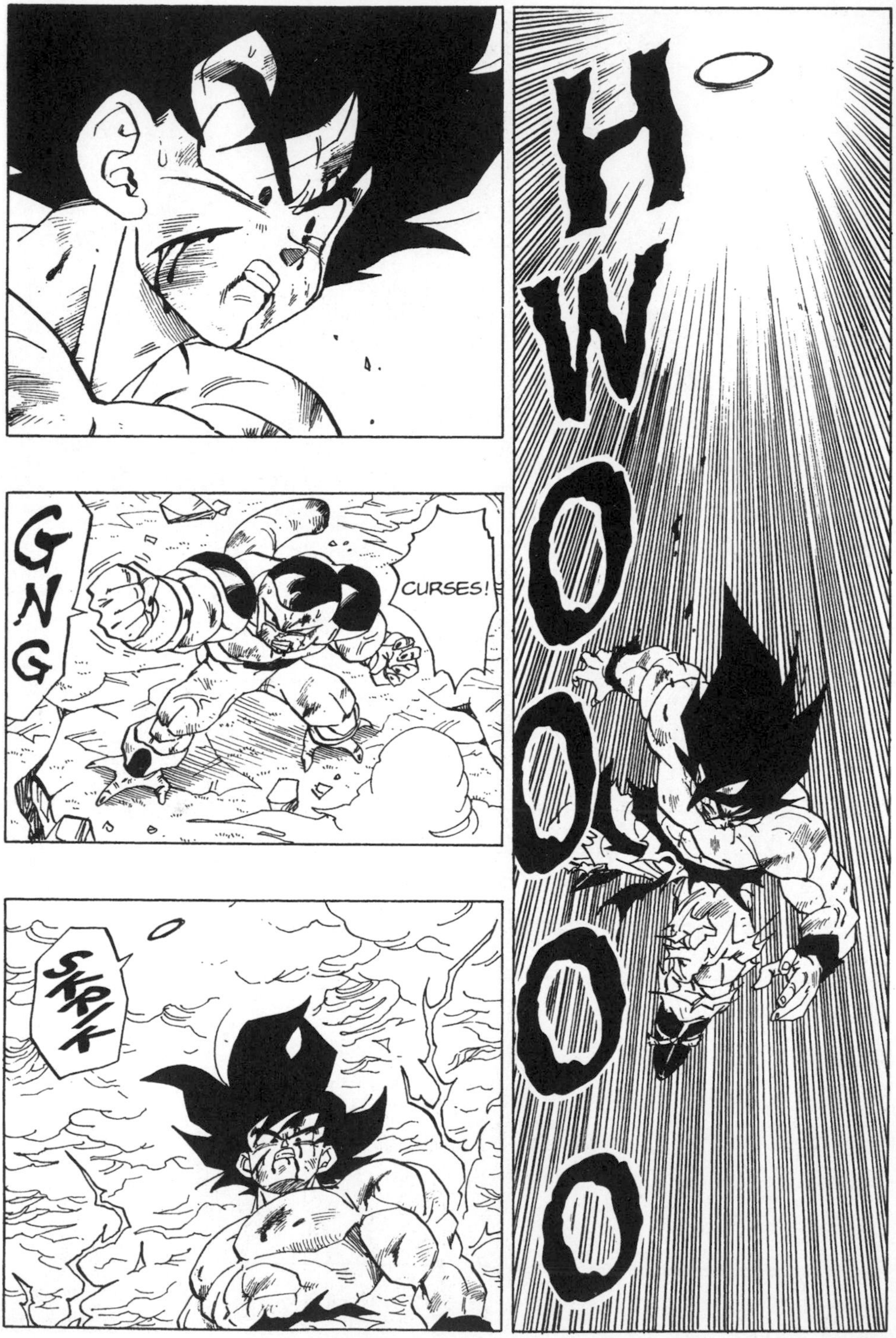
HWOOOOO
GNG
CURSES!
SKRIK

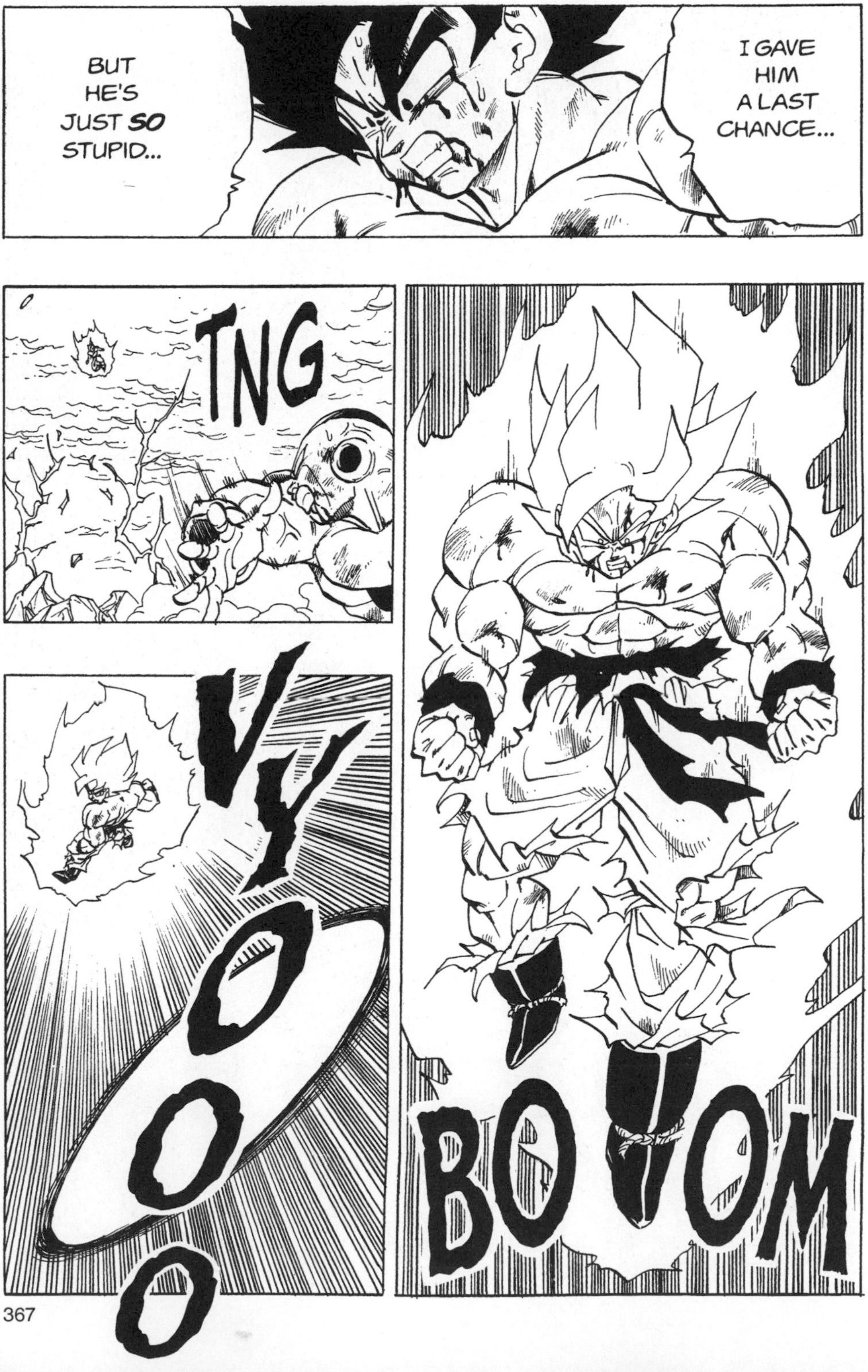
I GAVE HIM A LAST CHANCE...
BUT HE'S JUST SO STUPID...
TNG
BOOOM
VOOOO

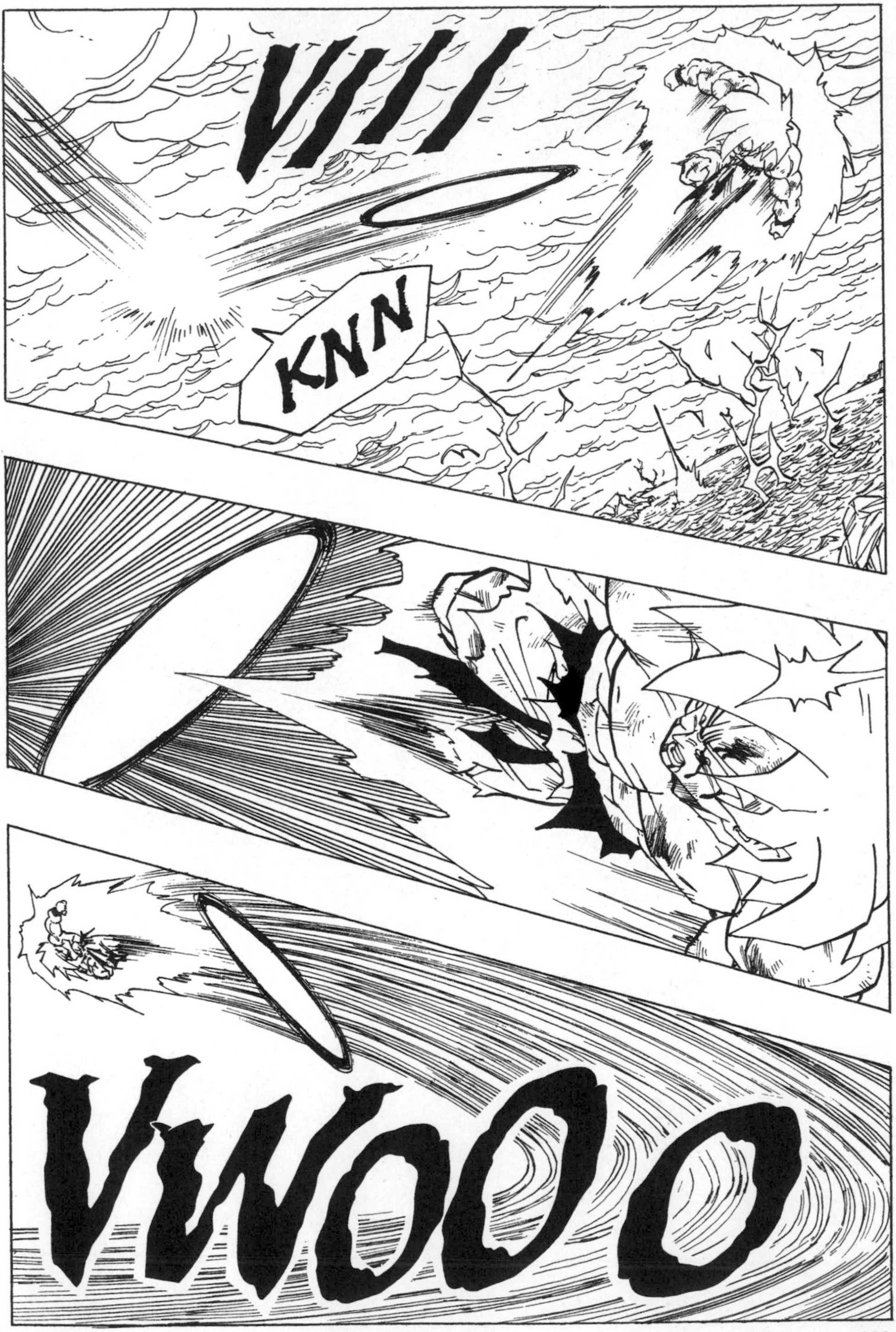
VIII
KNN
VWOOO

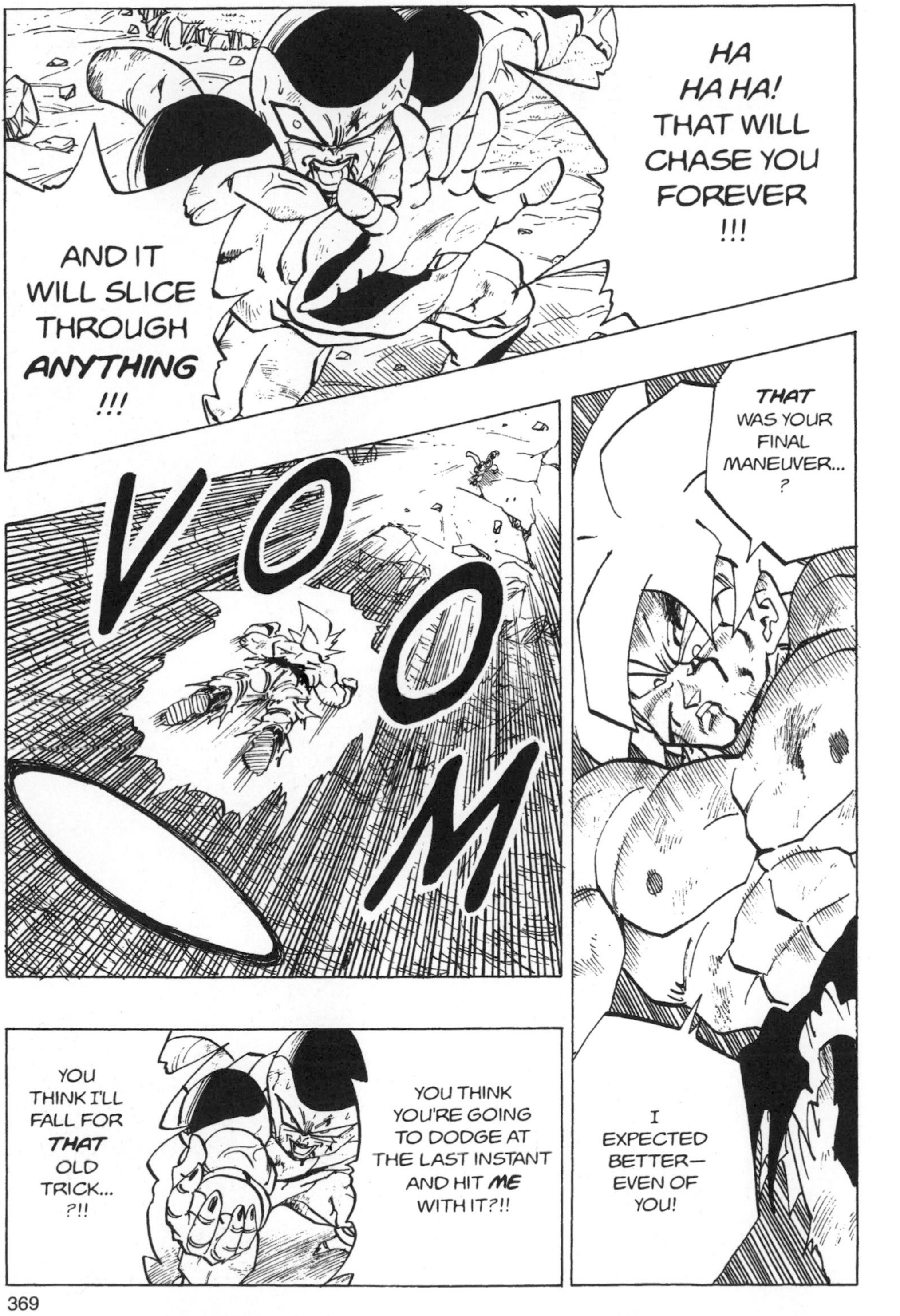
HA HA HA! THAT WILL CHASE YOU FOREVER !!!
AND IT WILL SLICE THROUGH ANYTHING !!!
THAT WAS YOUR FINAL MANEUVER... ?
I EXPECTED BETTER— EVEN OF YOU!
VOOM
YOU THINK YOU'RE GOING TO DODGE AT THE LAST INSTANT AND HIT ME WITH IT?!!
YOU THINK I'LL FALL FOR THAT OLD TRICK... ?!!

DragonBallZ

VOLUME 12

ENTER TRUNKS

DBZ : 132 • Son Goku's Choice

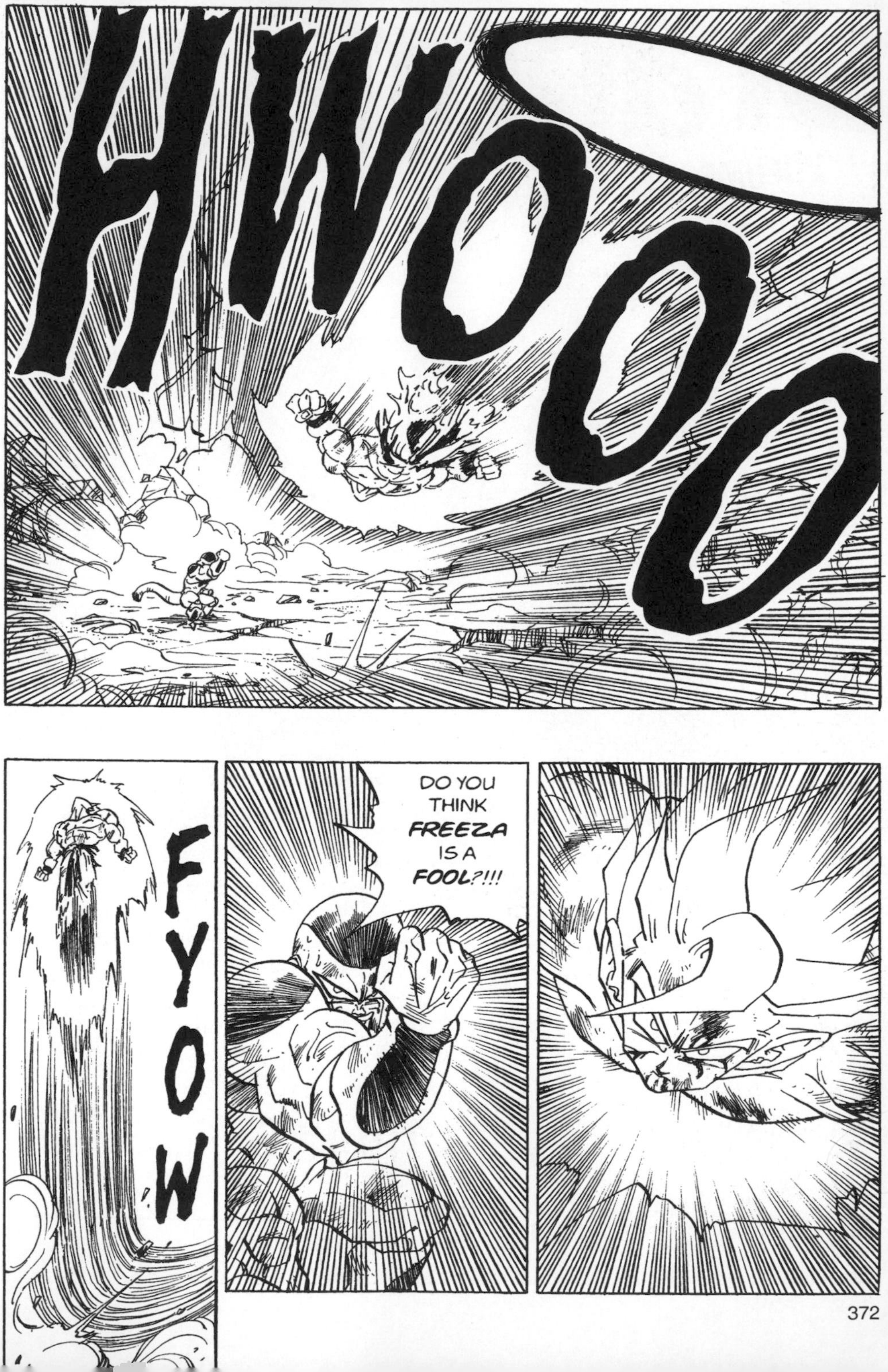
HWOOOO
FYOW
DO YOU THINK FREEZA IS A FOOL?!!!

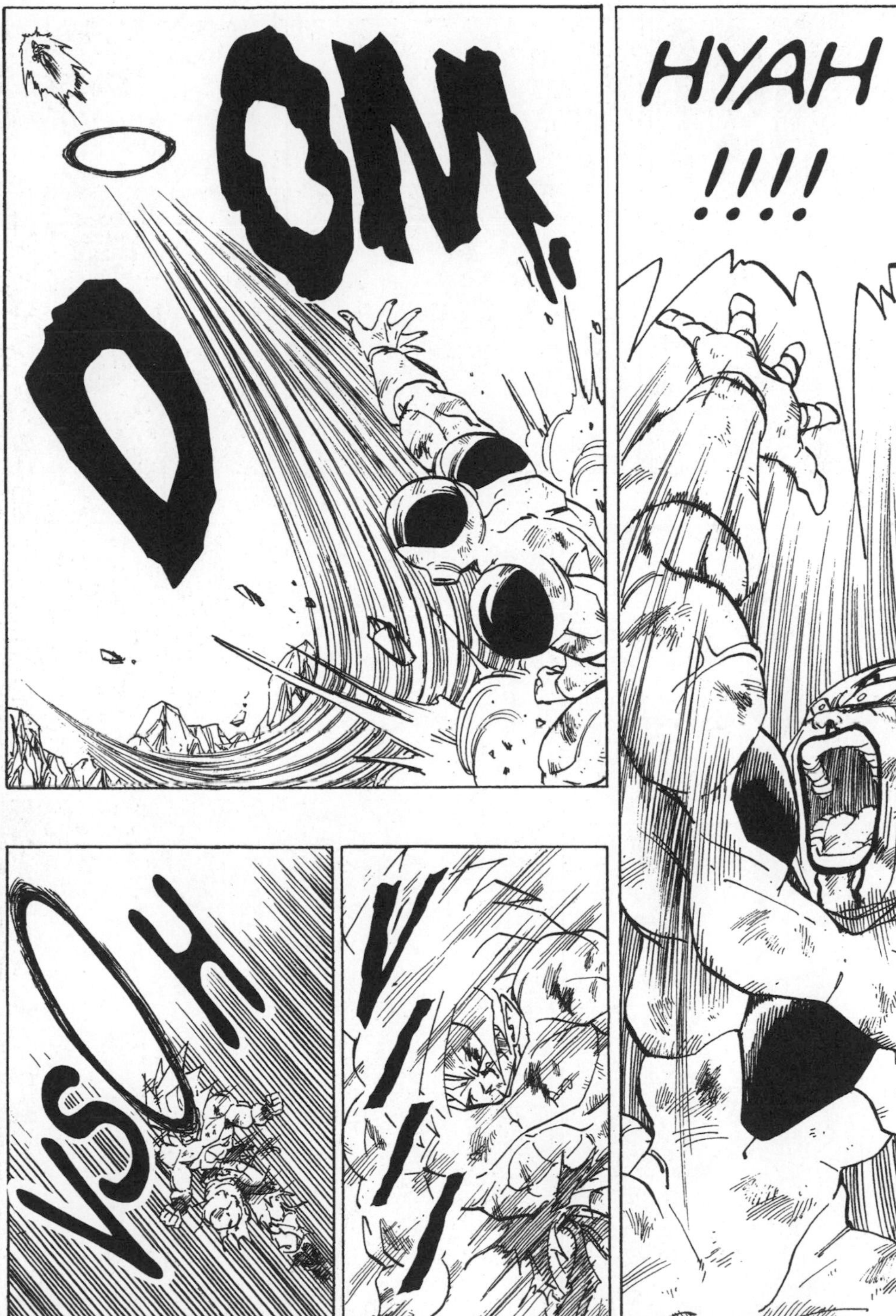
DOM!!
HYAH
!!!!
VSOH

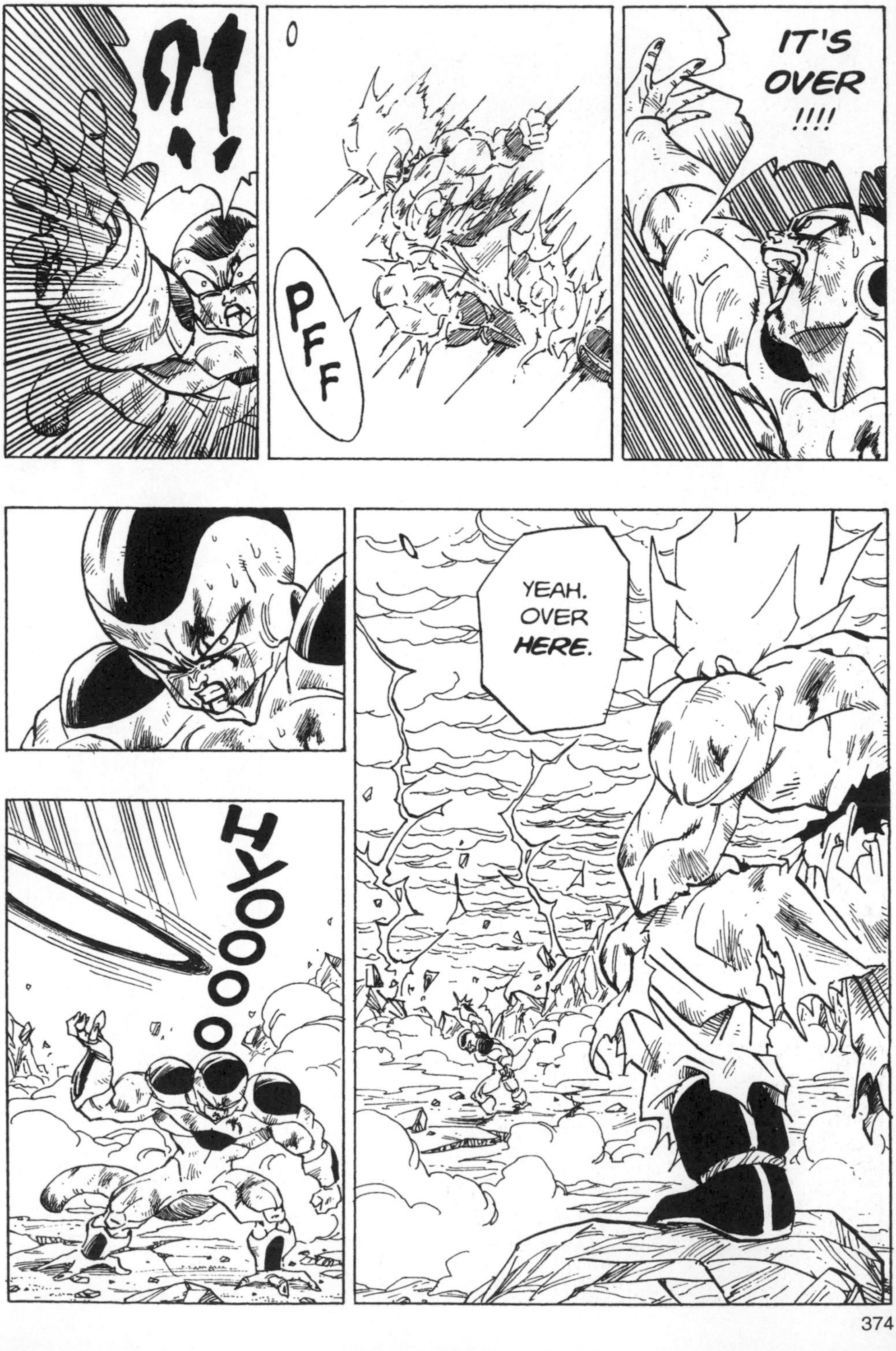
?!
PFF
IT'S OVER !!!!
YEAH. OVER HERE.
HYOOOOO

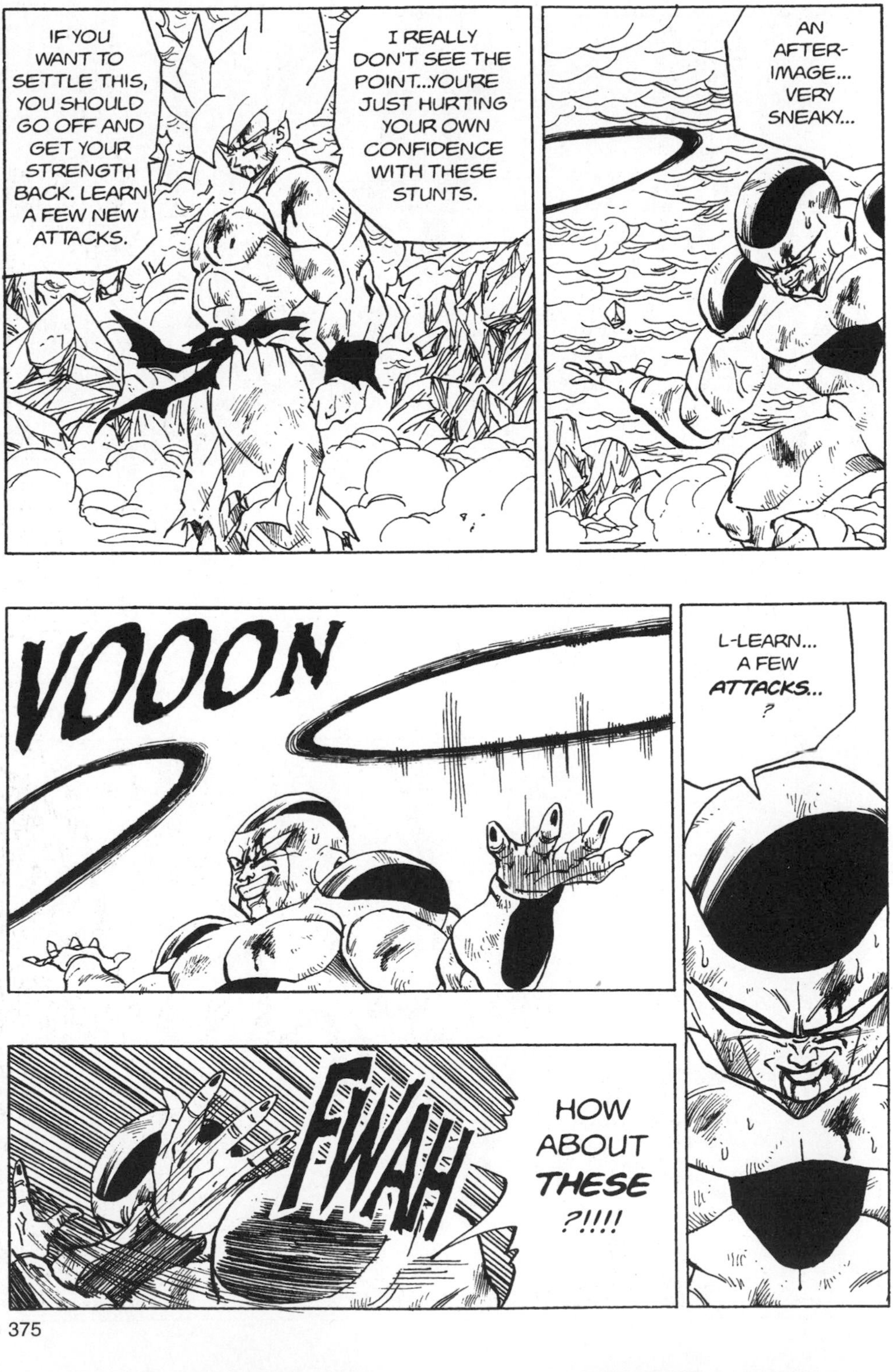
IF YOU WANT TO SETTLE THIS, YOU SHOULD GO OFF AND GET YOUR STRENGTH BACK. LEARN A FEW NEW ATTACKS.
I REALLY DON'T SEE THE POINT...YOU'RE JUST HURTING YOUR OWN CONFIDENCE WITH THESE STUNTS.
AN AFTER-IMAGE... VERY SNEAKY...
VOOON
L-LEARN... A FEW ATTACKS... ?
FWAH
HOW ABOUT THESE ?!!!!

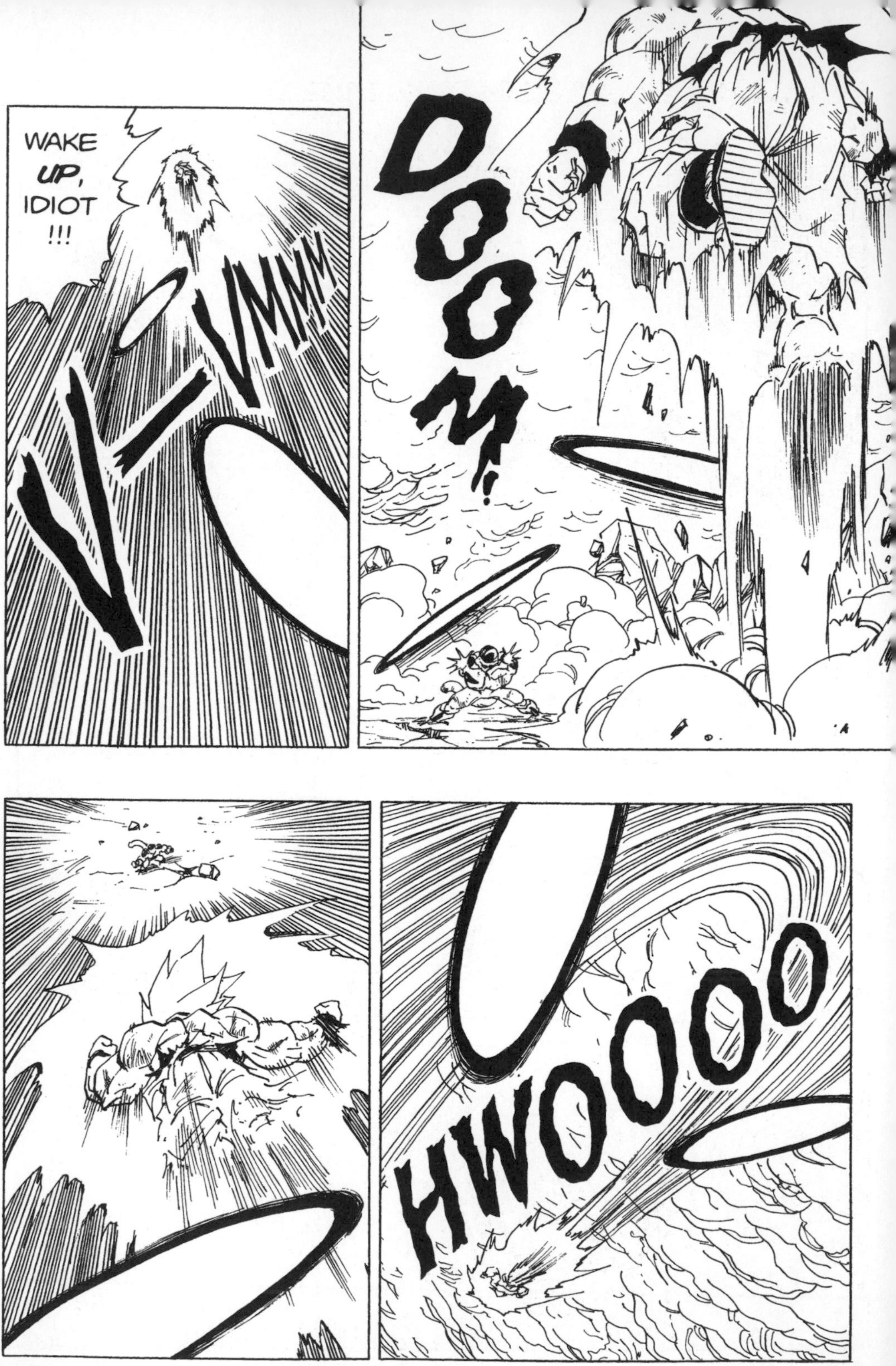
DOOOM!
WAKE UP, IDIOT!!!
HWOOOOO

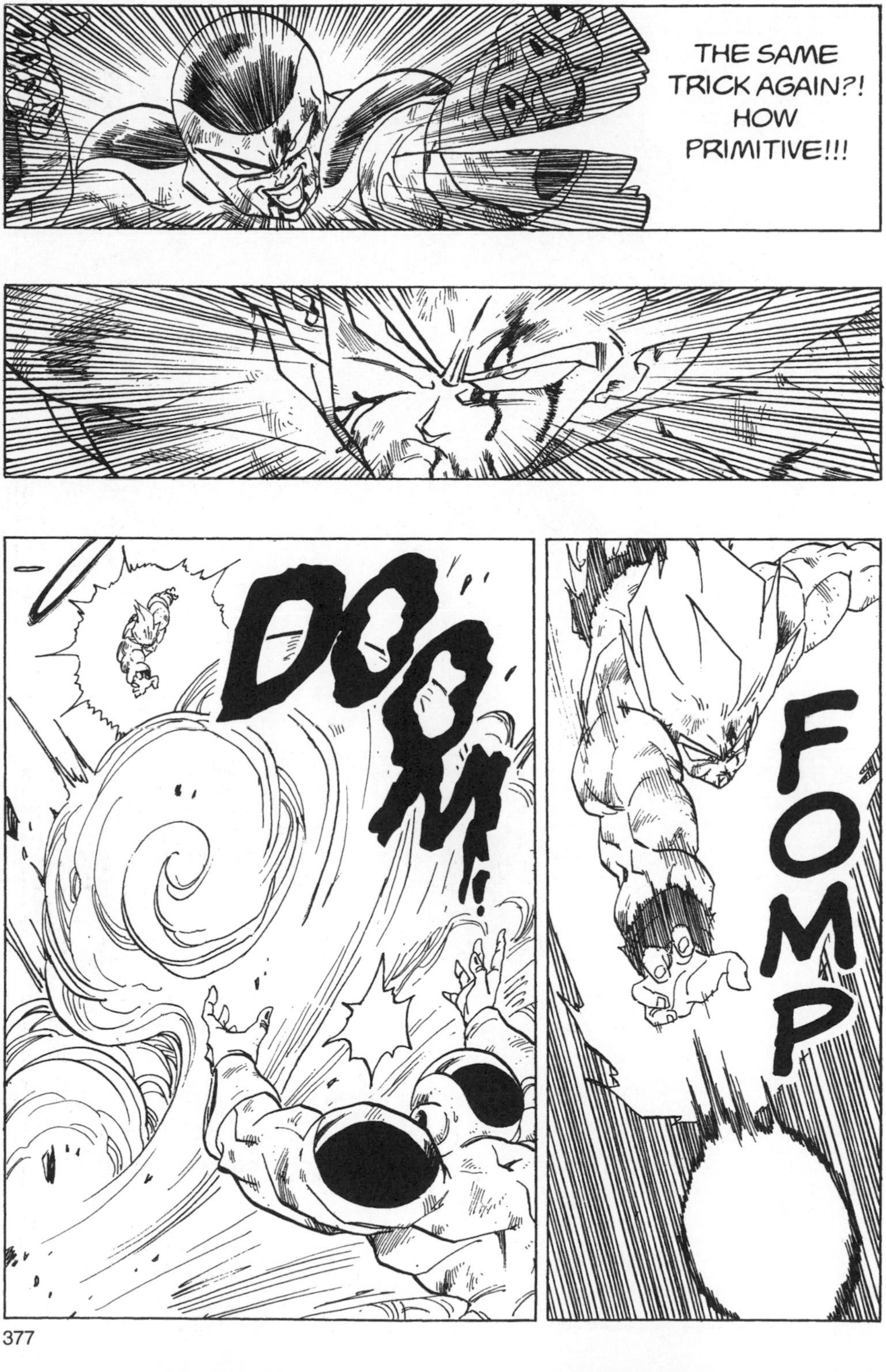
THE SAME TRICK AGAIN?! HOW PRIMITIVE!!!
DOOM!!
FOMP

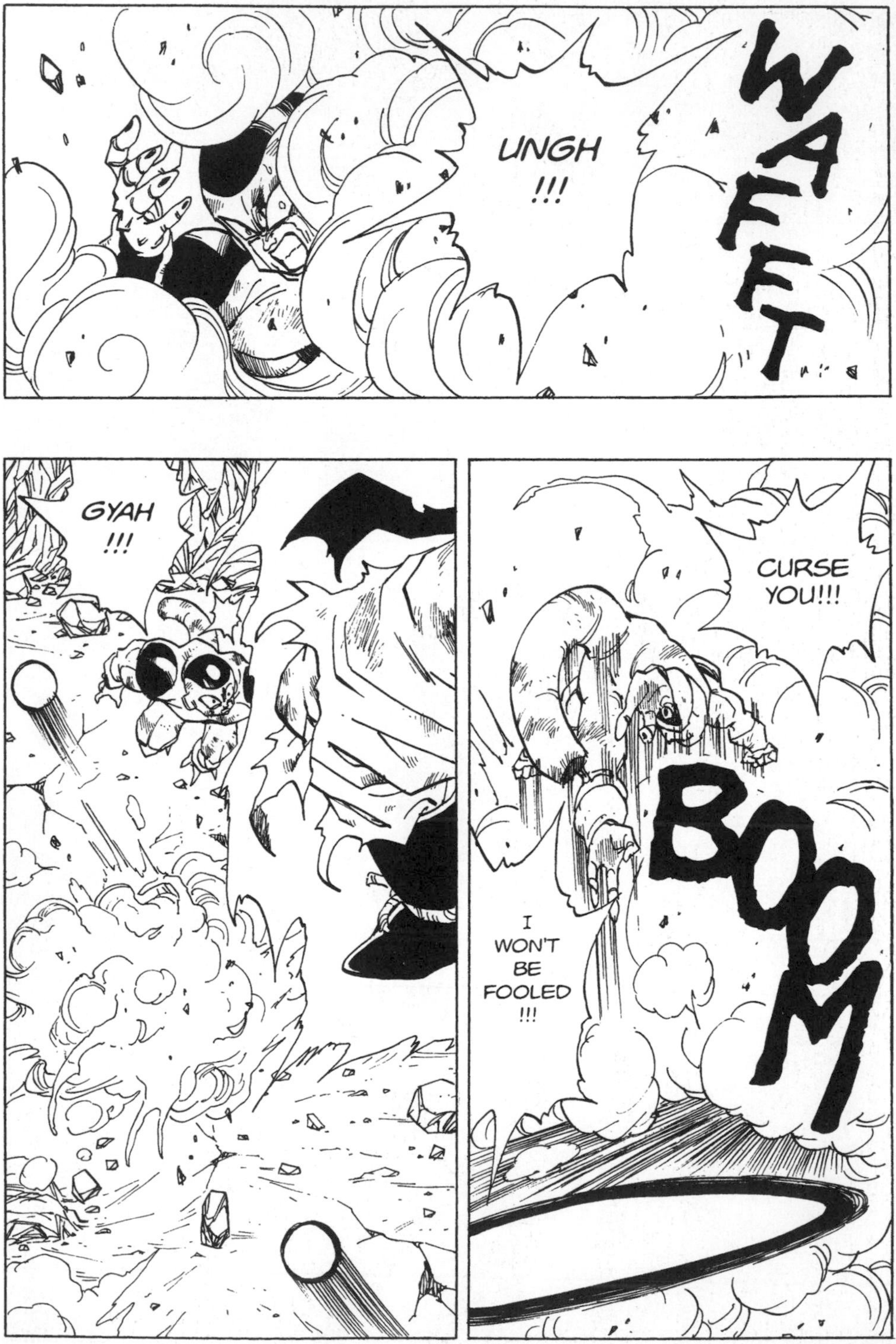
WAFFT
UNGH !!!
CURSE YOU!!!
BOOM
I WON'T BE FOOLED !!!
GYAH !!!

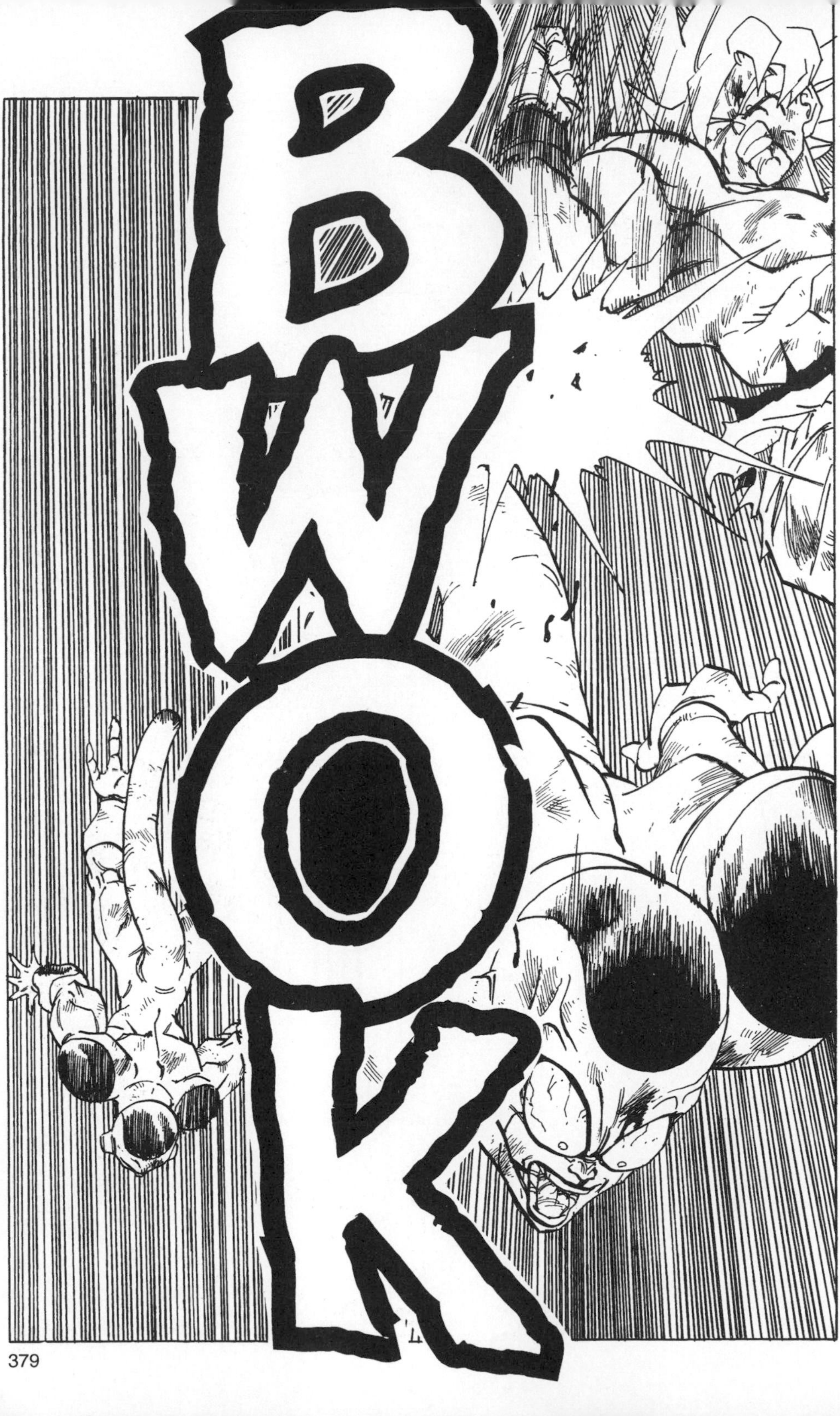
BWOK

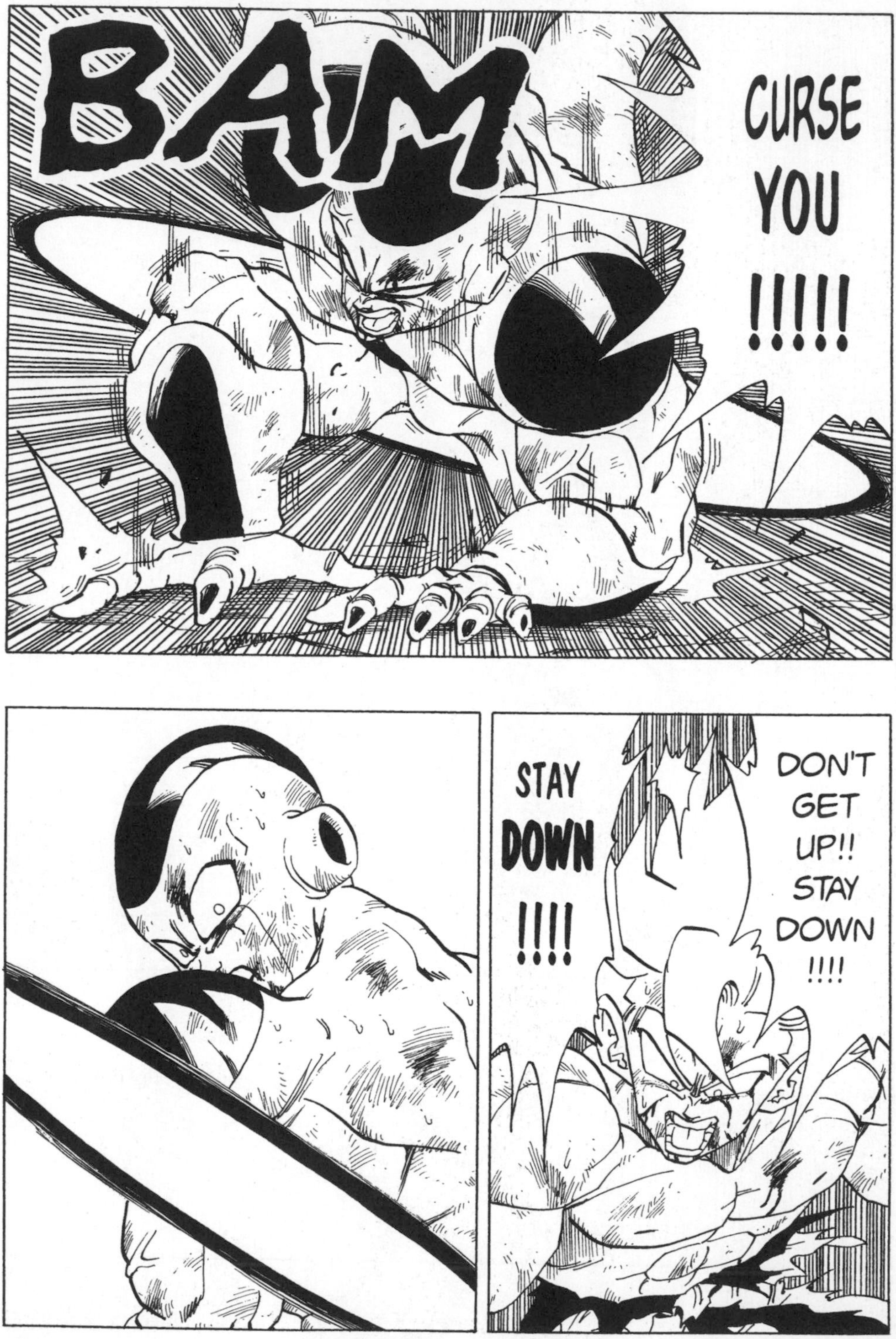
BAM
CURSE YOU !!!!!
DON'T GET UP!! STAY DOWN !!!!
STAY DOWN !!!!

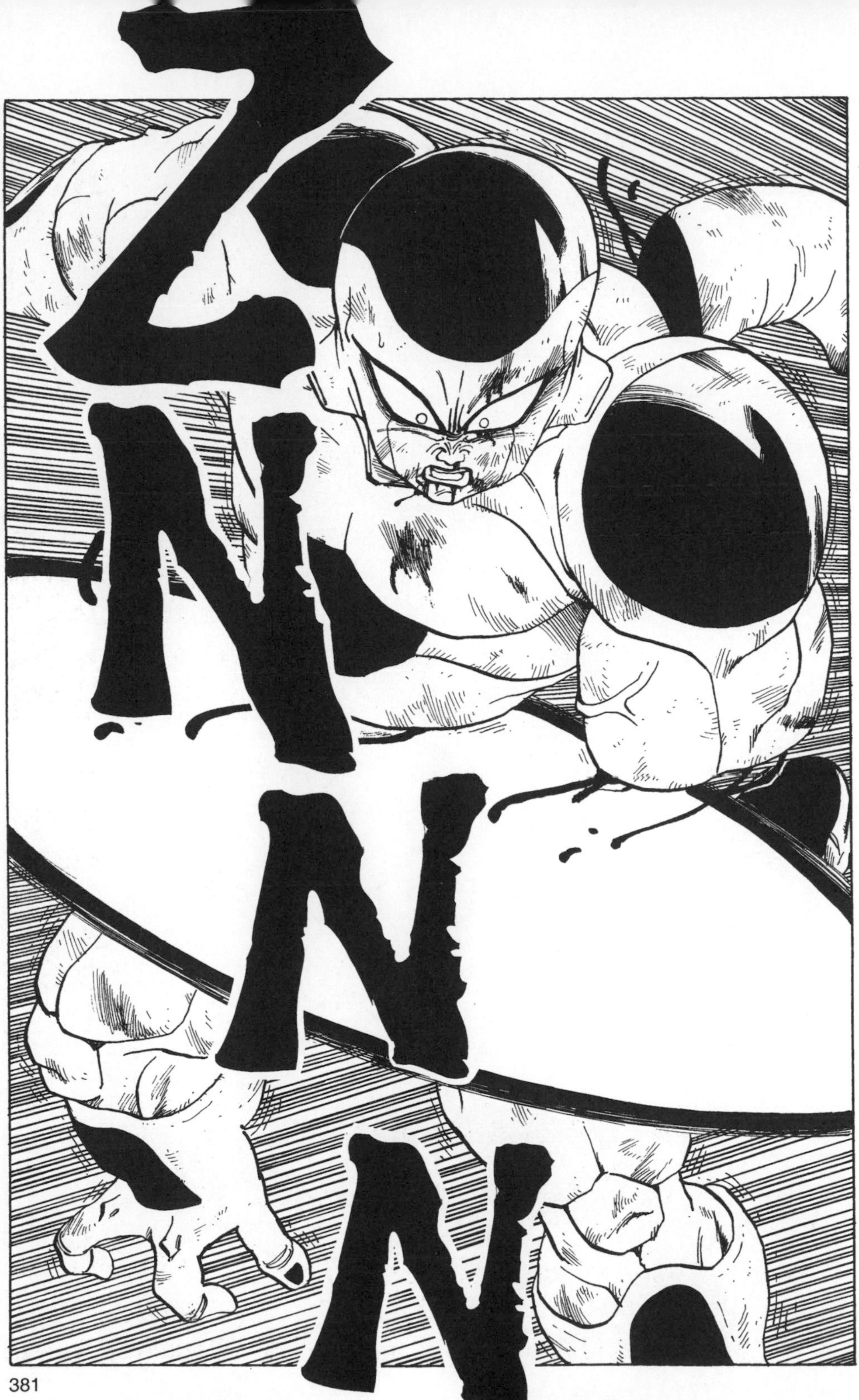
ZNNN

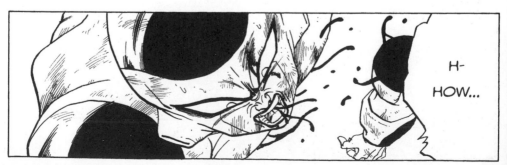

H-
HOW...

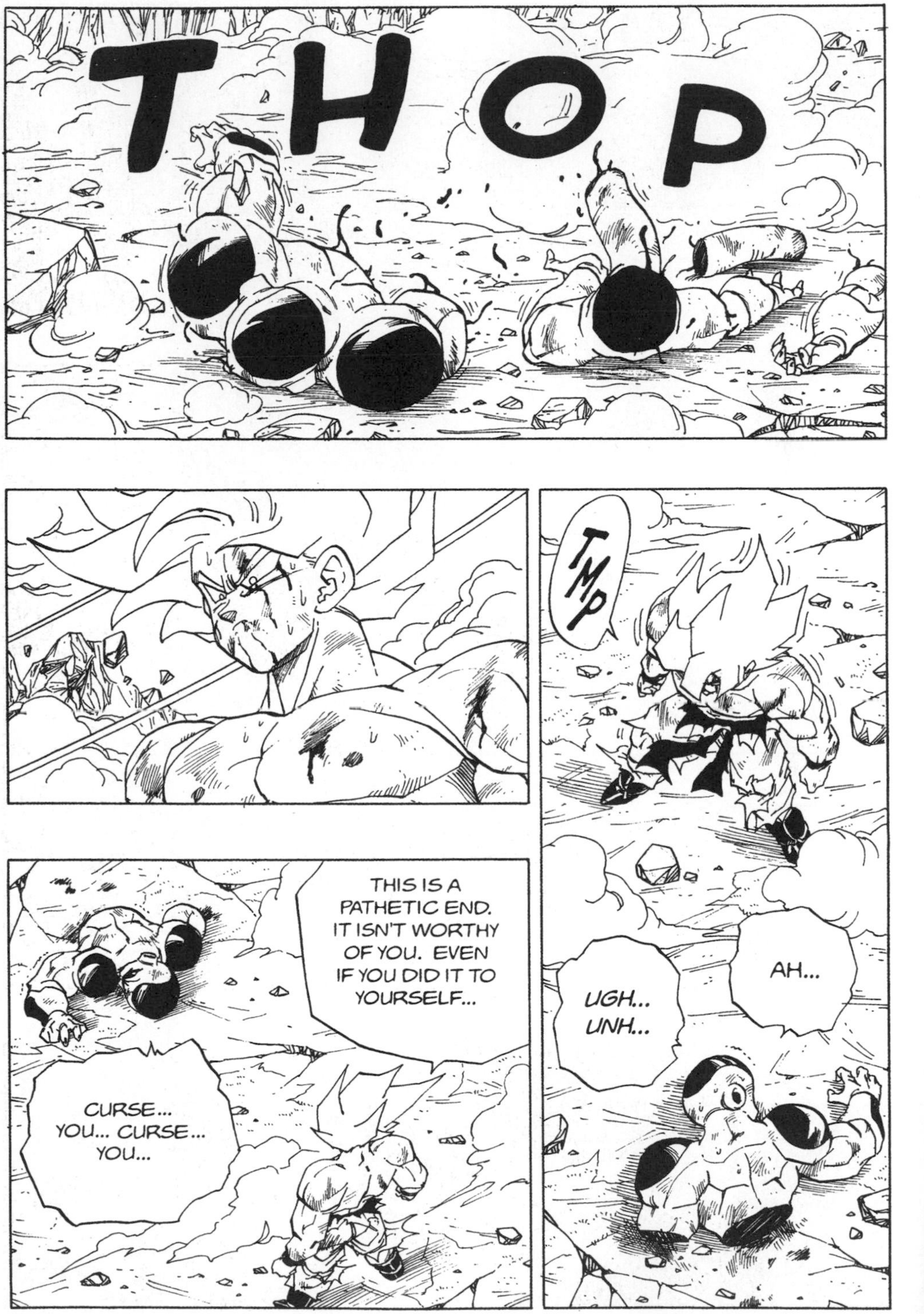
THOP
TMP
UGH... UNH...
AH...
THIS IS A PATHETIC END. IT ISN'T WORTHY OF YOU. EVEN IF YOU DID IT TO YOURSELF...
CURSE... YOU... CURSE... YOU...

NNN... NNNO...

YOU CAN SHARE THE FATE OF THE PLANET YOU'VE DESTROYED...

I HAVE TO GO BACK TO EARTH.

KOF! HUK!

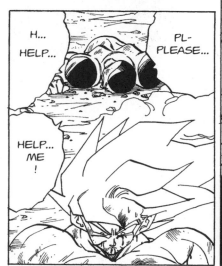

H... HELP...

PL- PLEASE...

HELP... ME !

HELP MEEE... !

WH-WHAT ARE YOU WAITING FOR?! ESCAPE NOW!!

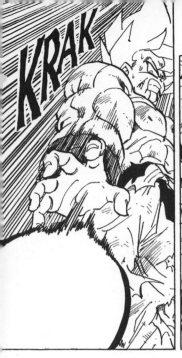

KRAK
P-
PLEASE...
!
HELP YOU?! THE WAY YOU HELPED EVERYBODY WHO BEGGED YOU FOR THEIR LIVES?!
BOOF
I'VE GIVEN YOU A LITTLE OF MY CHI... ENOUGH FOR YOU TO FLY A LITTLE...EVEN IN YOUR CONDITION...
NOW... YOU'RE ON YOUR OWN!

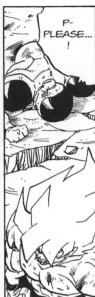

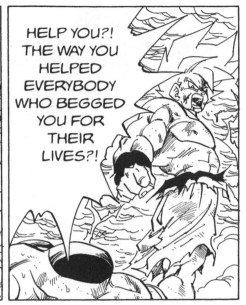

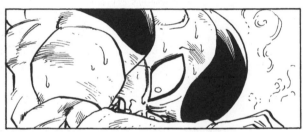

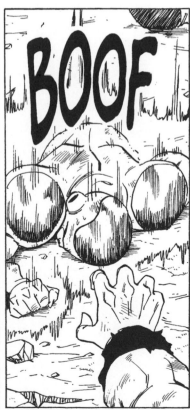

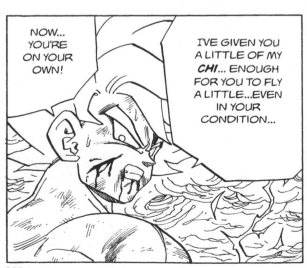

DBZ:133 • The End of Everything

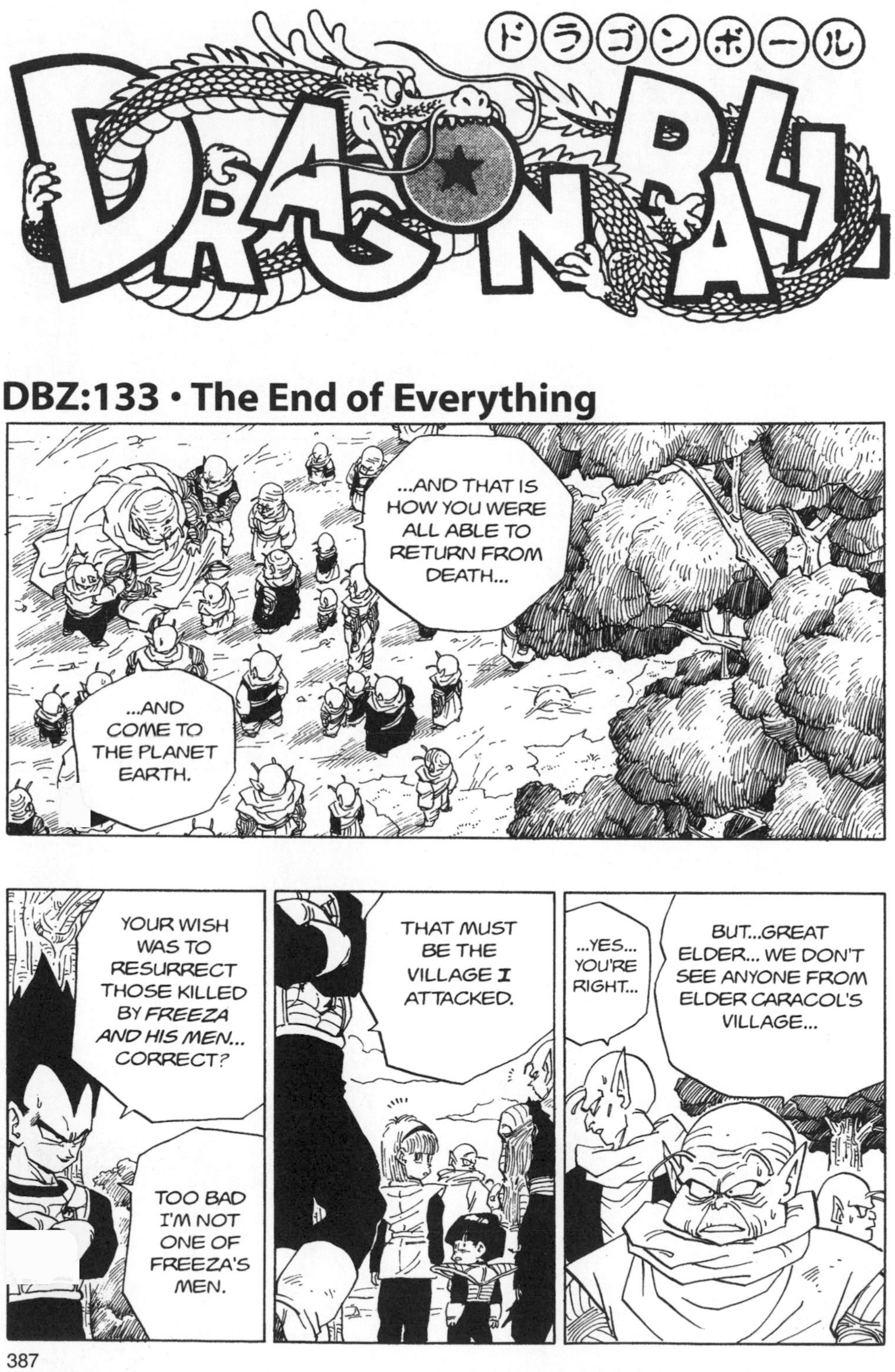
...AND THAT IS HOW YOU WERE ALL ABLE TO RETURN FROM DEATH...
...AND COME TO THE PLANET EARTH.
YOUR WISH WAS TO RESURRECT THOSE KILLED BY FREEZA AND HIS MEN... CORRECT?
TOO BAD I'M NOT ONE OF FREEZA'S MEN.
THAT MUST BE THE VILLAGE I ATTACKED.
BUT...GREAT ELDER... WE DON'T SEE ANYONE FROM ELDER CARACOL'S VILLAGE...
...YES... YOU'RE RIGHT...

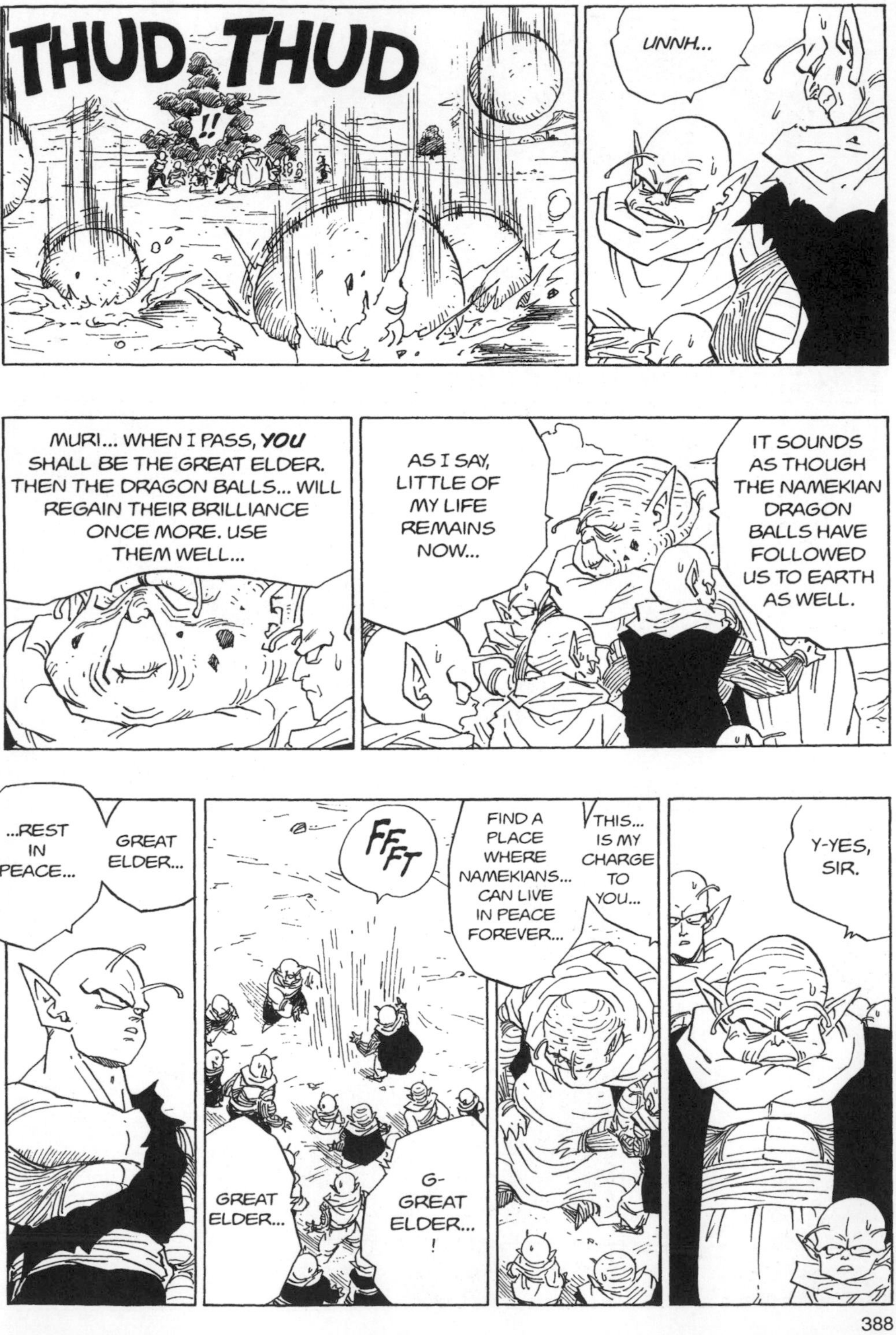
THUD THUD
!!
UNNH...
MURI... WHEN I PASS, *YOU* SHALL BE THE GREAT ELDER. THEN THE DRAGON BALLS... WILL REGAIN THEIR BRILLIANCE ONCE MORE. USE THEM WELL...
AS I SAY, LITTLE OF MY LIFE REMAINS NOW...
IT SOUNDS AS THOUGH THE NAMEKIAN DRAGON BALLS HAVE FOLLOWED US TO EARTH AS WELL.
...REST IN PEACE...
GREAT ELDER...
FFFT
GREAT ELDER...
G-GREAT ELDER...!
FIND A PLACE WHERE NAMEKIANS... CAN LIVE IN PEACE FOREVER...
THIS... IS MY CHARGE TO YOU...
Y-YES, SIR.

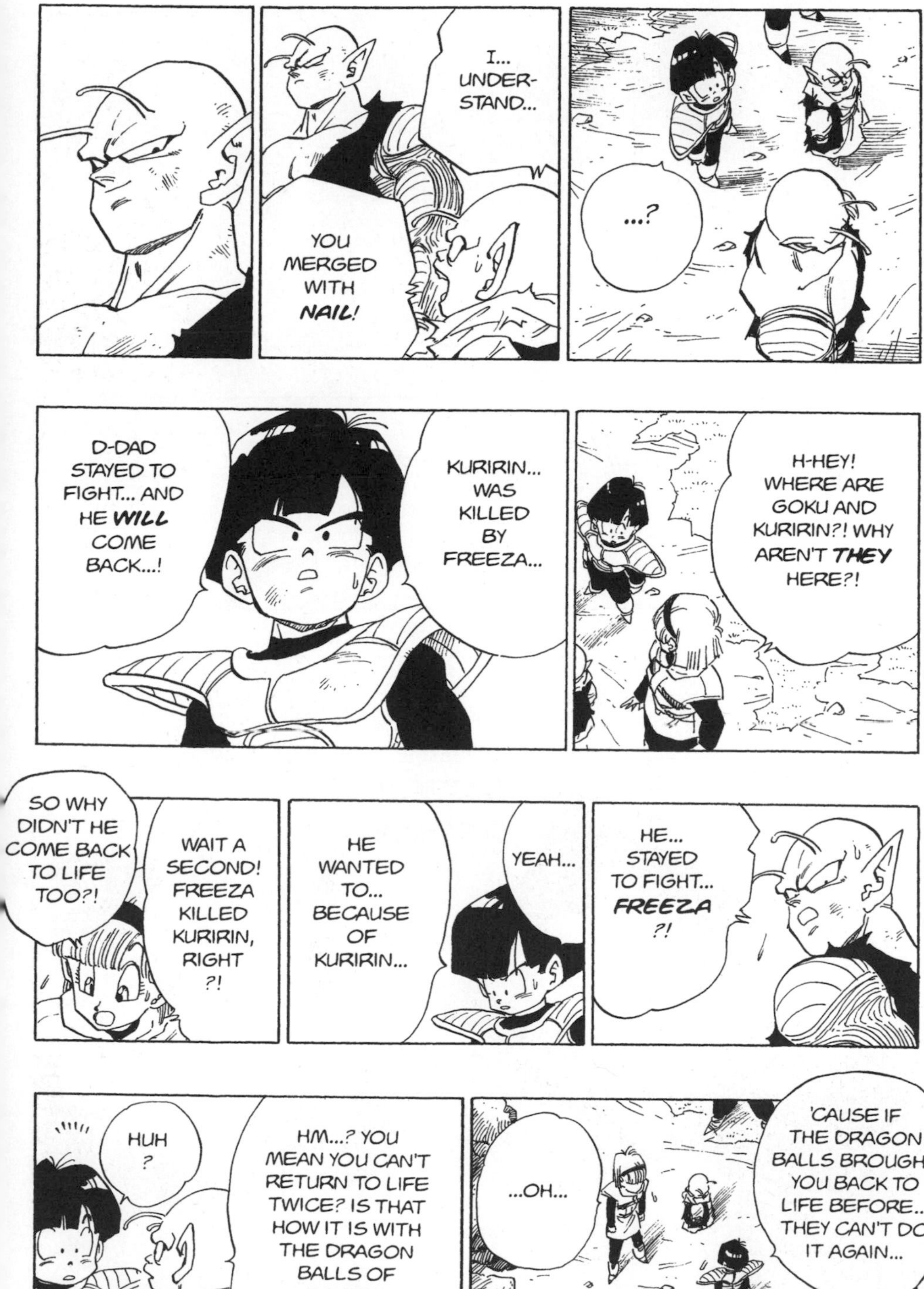
...?
I... UNDERSTAND...
YOU MERGED WITH NAIL!
H-HEY! WHERE ARE GOKU AND KURIRIN?! WHY AREN'T THEY HERE?!
KURIRIN... WAS KILLED BY FREEZA...
D-DAD STAYED TO FIGHT... AND HE WILL COME BACK...!
HE... STAYED TO FIGHT... FREEZA?!
YEAH...
HE WANTED TO... BECAUSE OF KURIRIN...
WAIT A SECOND! FREEZA KILLED KURIRIN, RIGHT?!
SO WHY DIDN'T HE COME BACK TO LIFE TOO?!
'CAUSE IF THE DRAGON BALLS BROUGHT YOU BACK TO LIFE BEFORE... THEY CAN'T DO IT AGAIN...
...OH...
HM...? YOU MEAN YOU CAN'T RETURN TO LIFE TWICE? IS THAT HOW IT IS WITH THE DRAGON BALLS OF EARTH?
HUH?

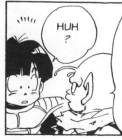

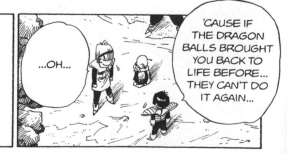

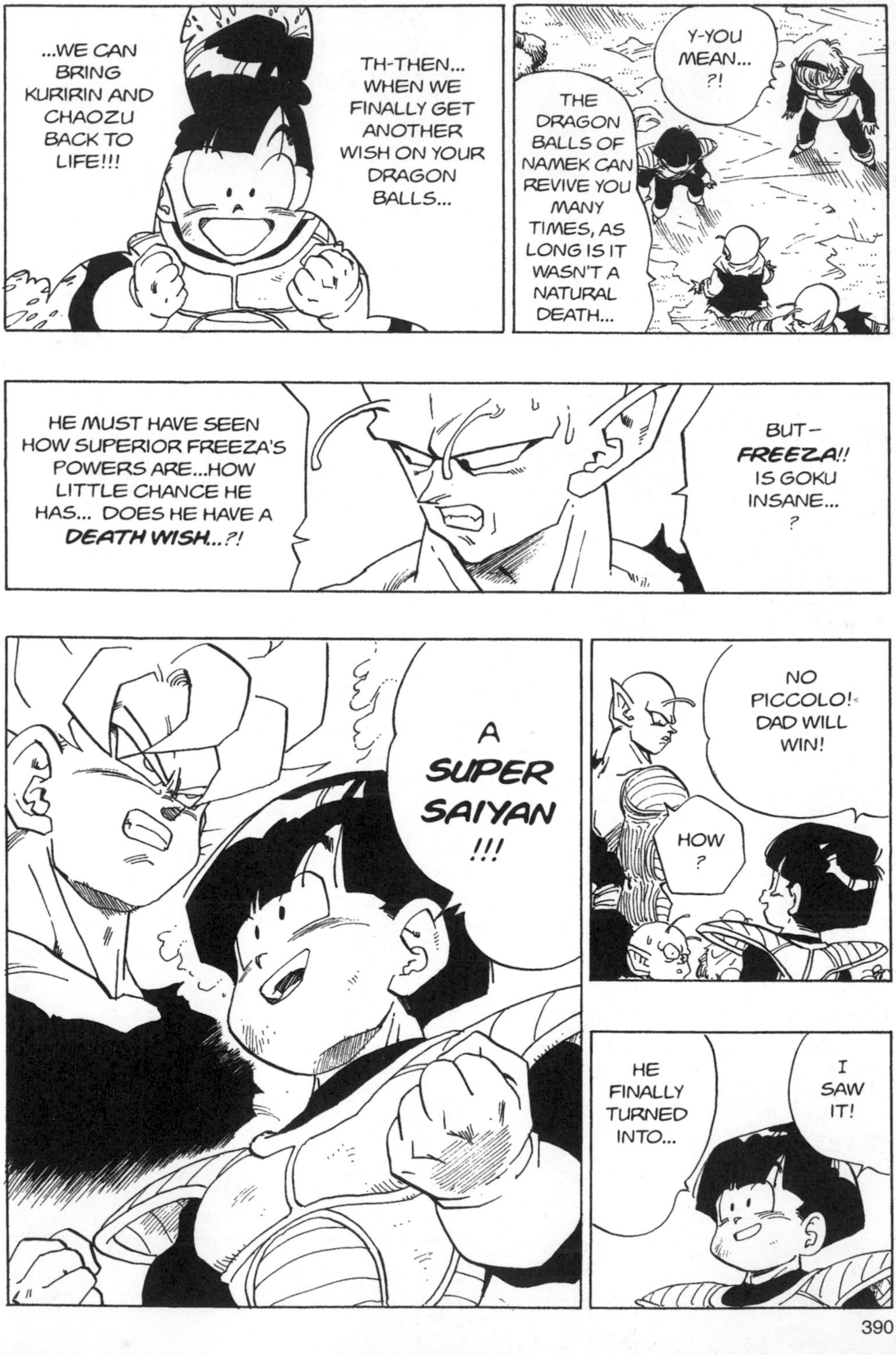

TH-THEN... WHEN WE FINALLY GET ANOTHER WISH ON YOUR DRAGON BALLS...
...WE CAN BRING KURIRIN AND CHAOZU BACK TO LIFE!!!
THE DRAGON BALLS OF NAMEK CAN REVIVE YOU MANY TIMES, AS LONG IS IT WASN'T A NATURAL DEATH...
Y-YOU MEAN...?!
HE MUST HAVE SEEN HOW SUPERIOR FREEZA'S POWERS ARE...HOW LITTLE CHANCE HE HAS... DOES HE HAVE A ***DEATH WISH***...?!
BUT— ***FREEZA***!! IS GOKU INSANE...?
NO PICCOLO! DAD WILL WIN!
HOW?
I SAW IT!
HE FINALLY TURNED INTO...
A ***SUPER SAIYAN*** !!!

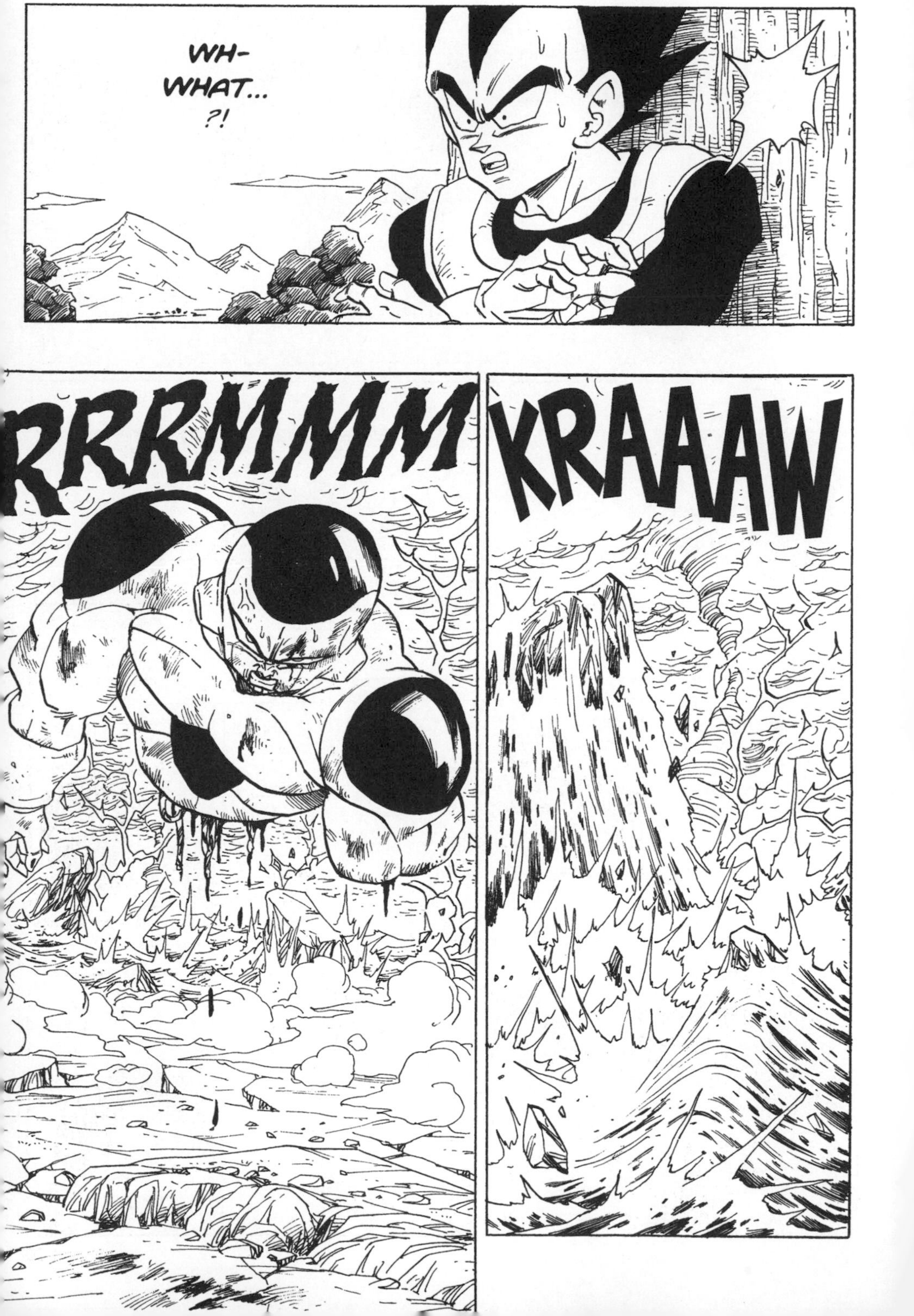

WH-
WHAT...
?!
RRRMMMM
KRAAAW

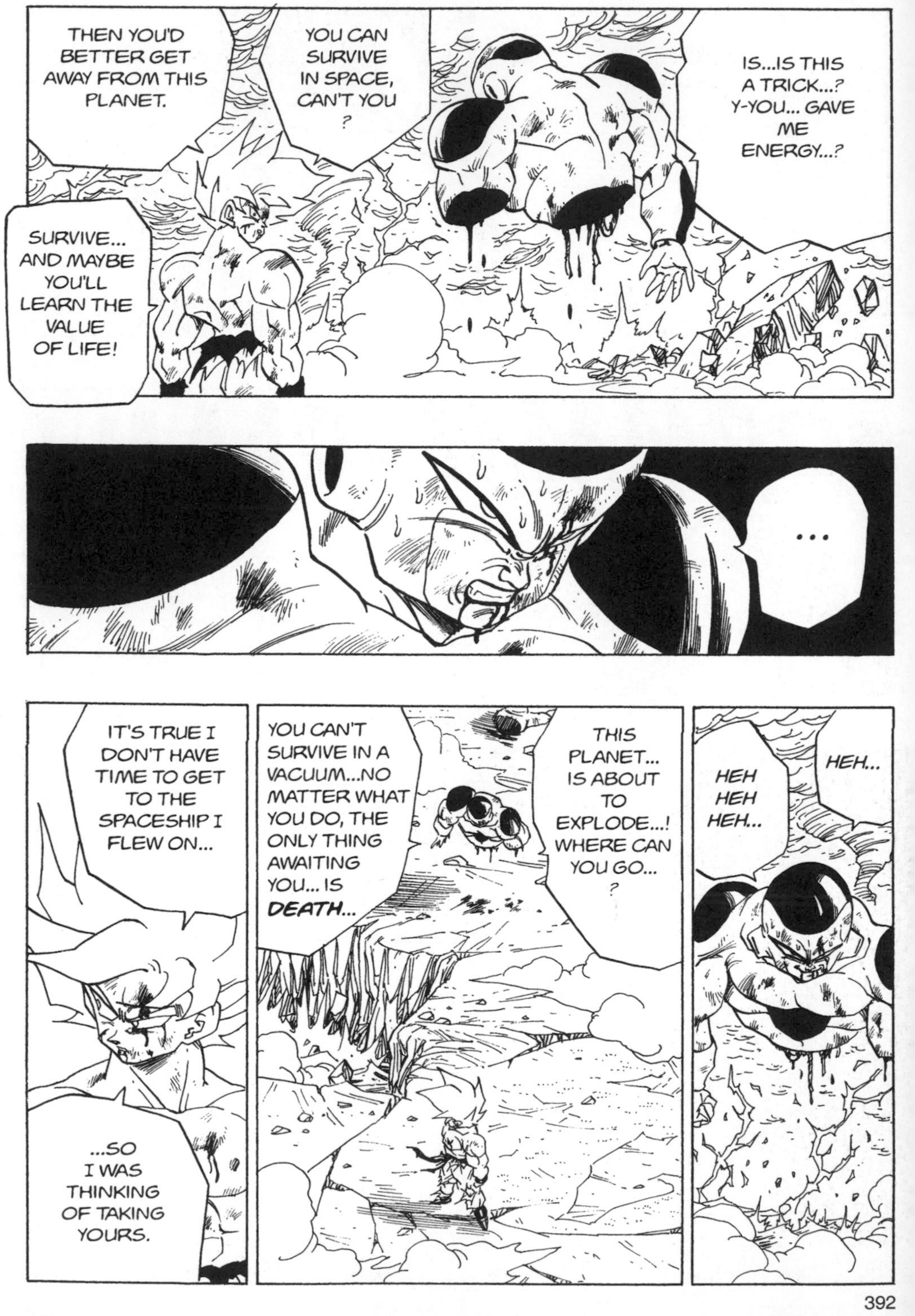
THEN YOU'D BETTER GET AWAY FROM THIS PLANET.
YOU CAN SURVIVE IN SPACE, CAN'T YOU ?
IS...IS THIS A TRICK...? Y-YOU... GAVE ME ENERGY...?
SURVIVE... AND MAYBE YOU'LL LEARN THE VALUE OF LIFE!
...
IT'S TRUE I DON'T HAVE TIME TO GET TO THE SPACESHIP I FLEW ON...
...SO I WAS THINKING OF TAKING YOURS.
YOU CAN'T SURVIVE IN A VACUUM...NO MATTER WHAT YOU DO, THE ONLY THING AWAITING YOU... IS DEATH...
THIS PLANET... IS ABOUT TO EXPLODE...! WHERE CAN YOU GO... ?
HEH HEH HEH...
HEH...

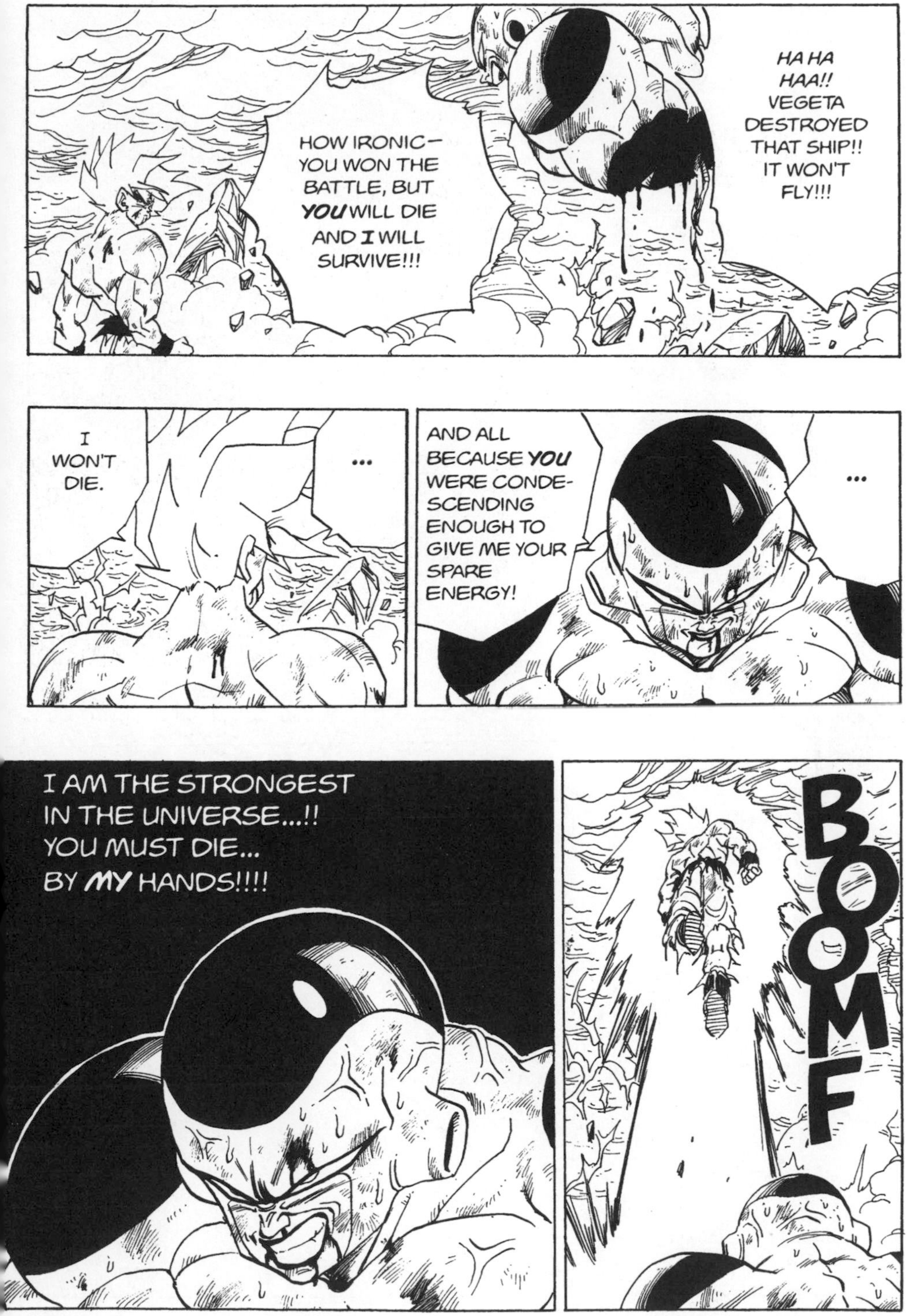
HA HA HAA!! VEGETA DESTROYED THAT SHIP!! IT WON'T FLY!!!
HOW IRONIC— YOU WON THE BATTLE, BUT YOU WILL DIE AND I WILL SURVIVE!!!
I WON'T DIE.
...
AND ALL BECAUSE YOU WERE CONDE-SCENDING ENOUGH TO GIVE ME YOUR SPARE ENERGY!
...
I AM THE STRONGEST IN THE UNIVERSE...!! YOU MUST DIE... BY MY HANDS!!!!
BOOMF

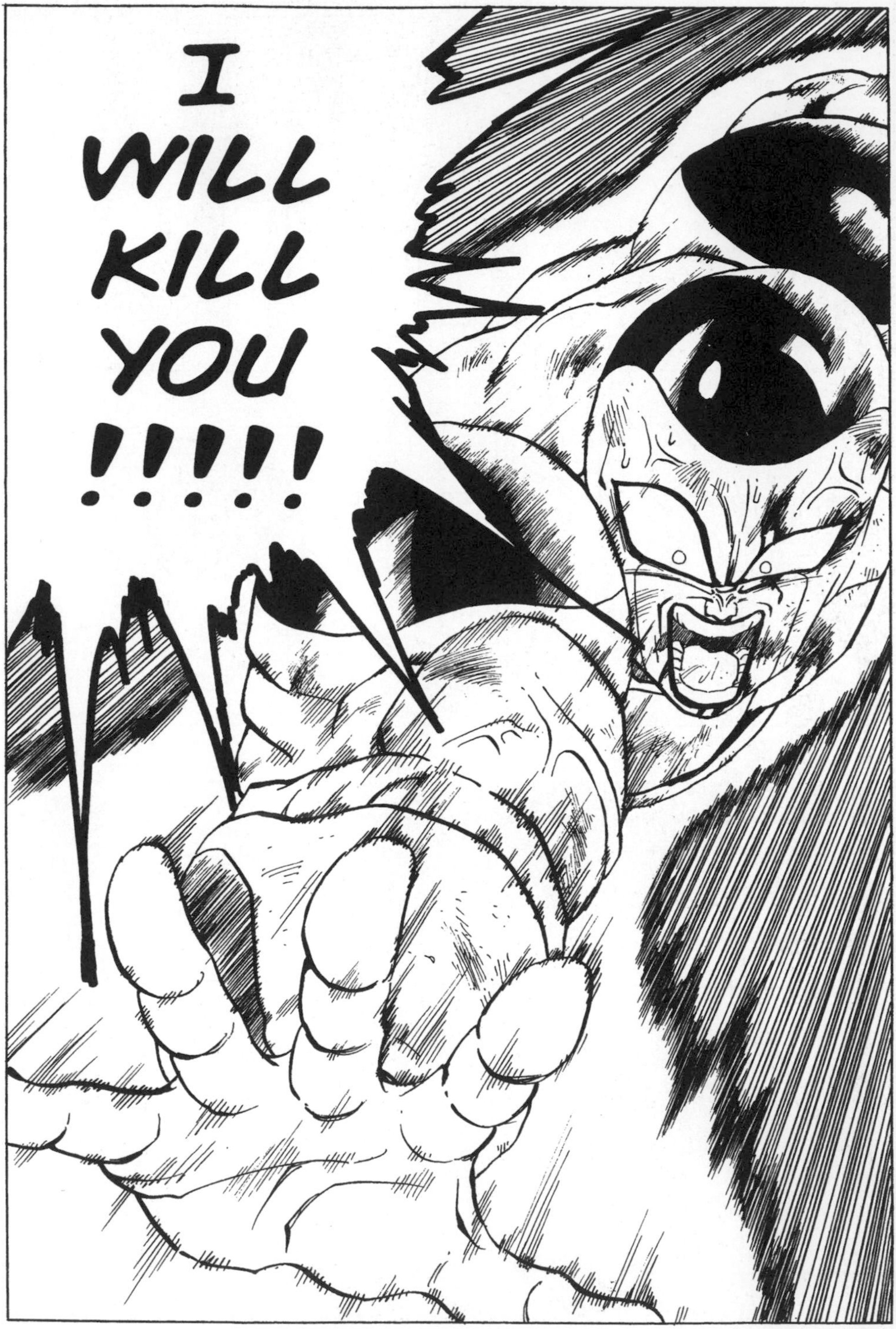
I WILL KILL YOU !!!!!

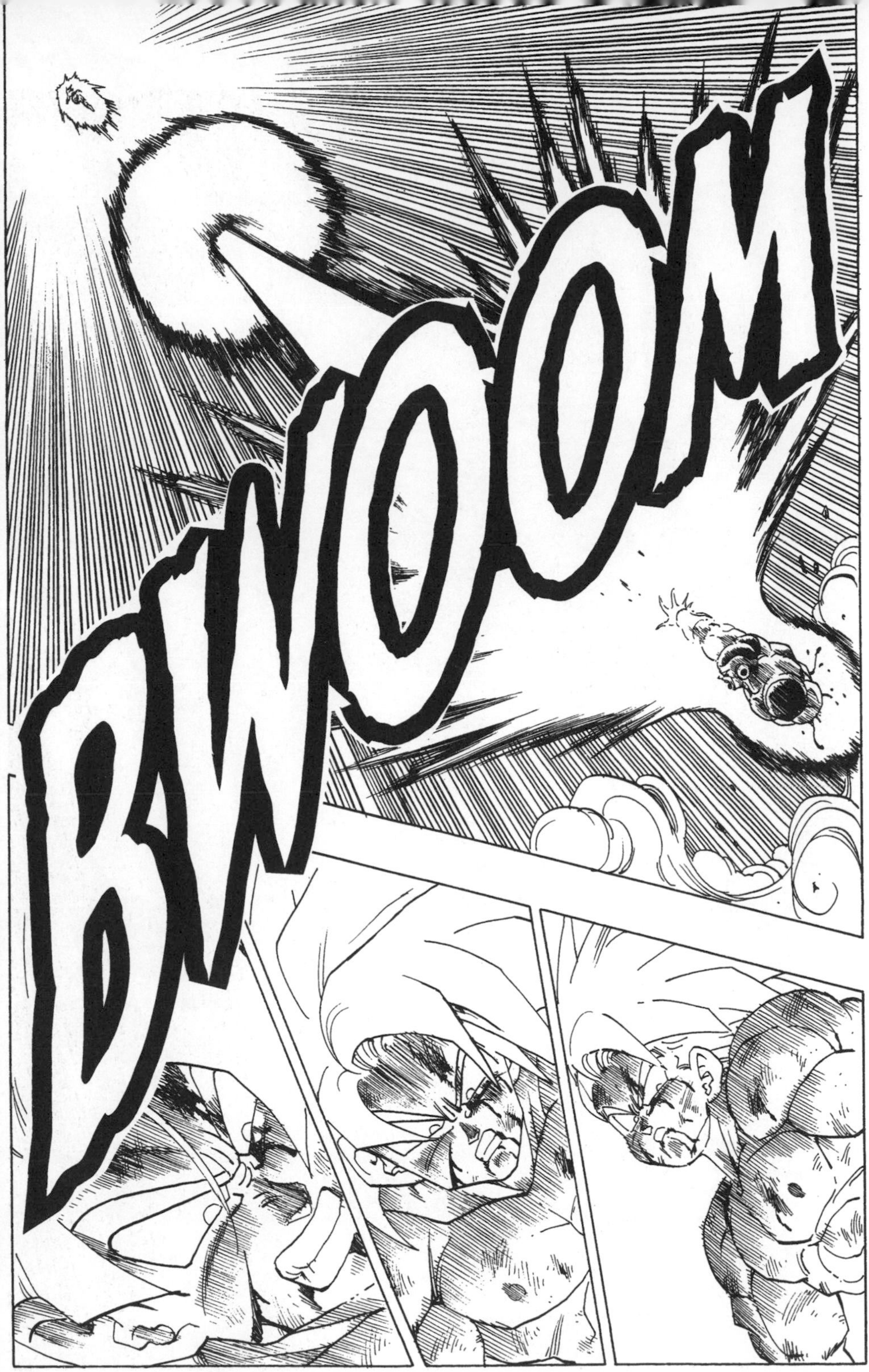
BWOOM

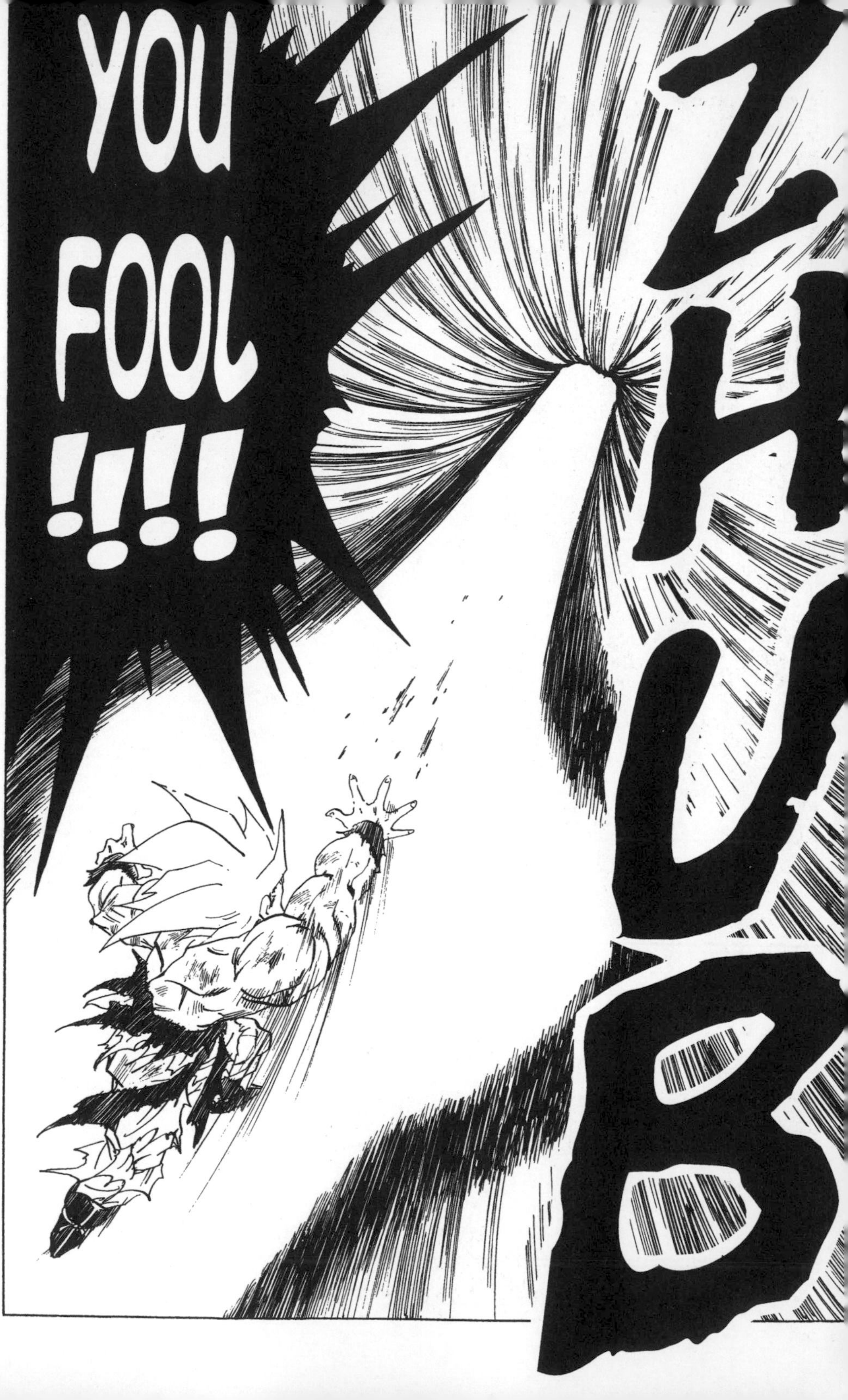
YOU FOOL!!!!

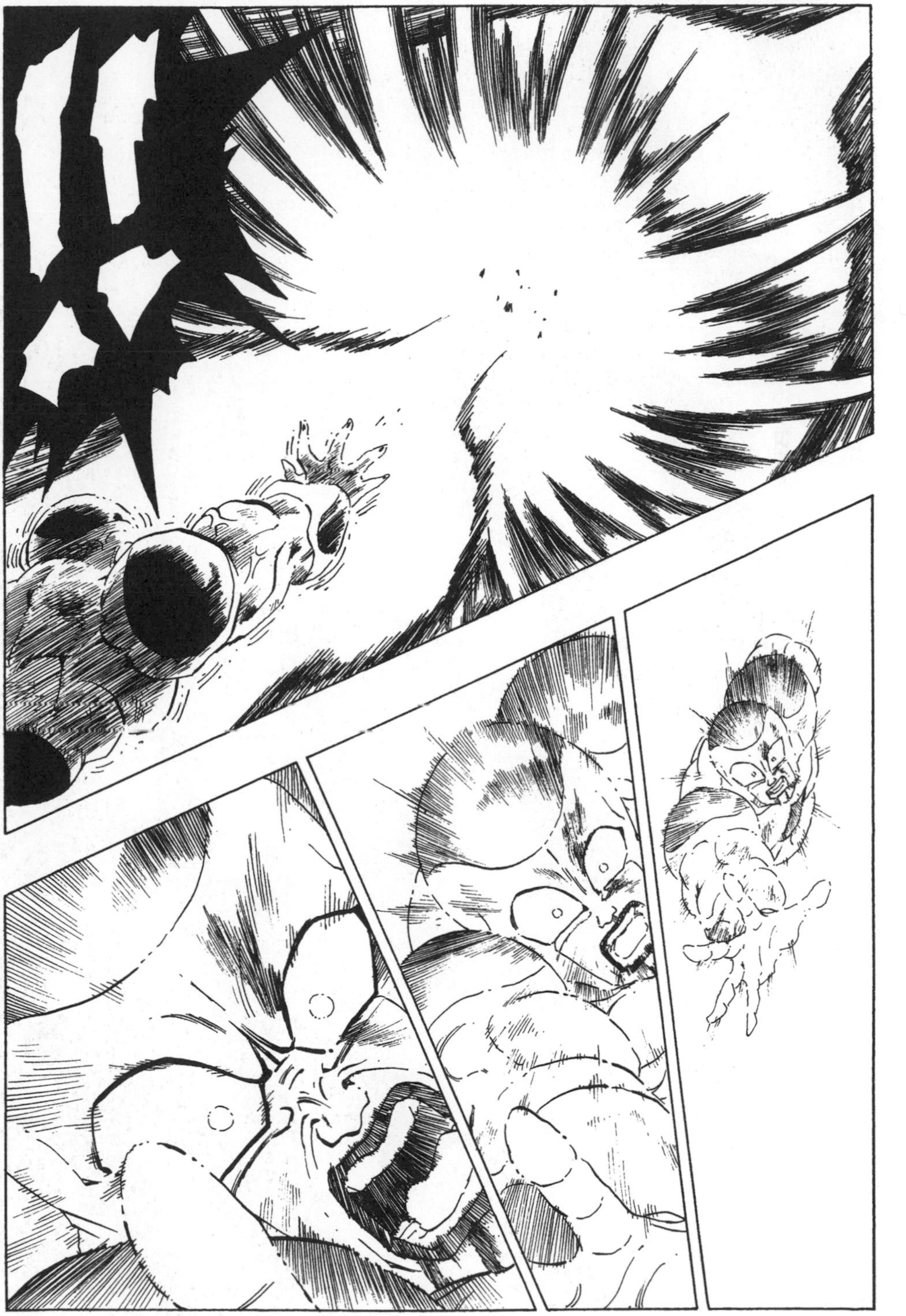

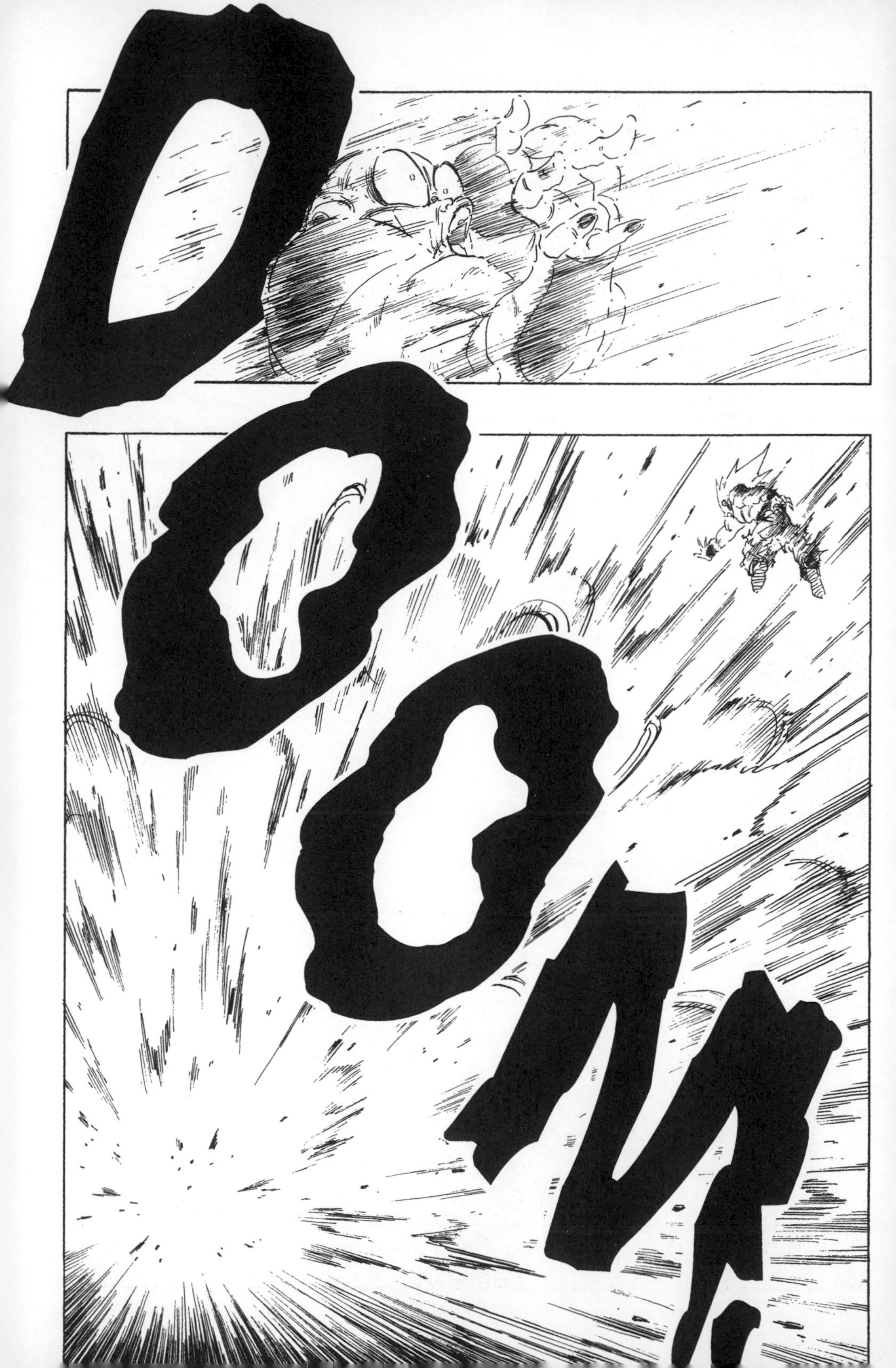
DOOM!

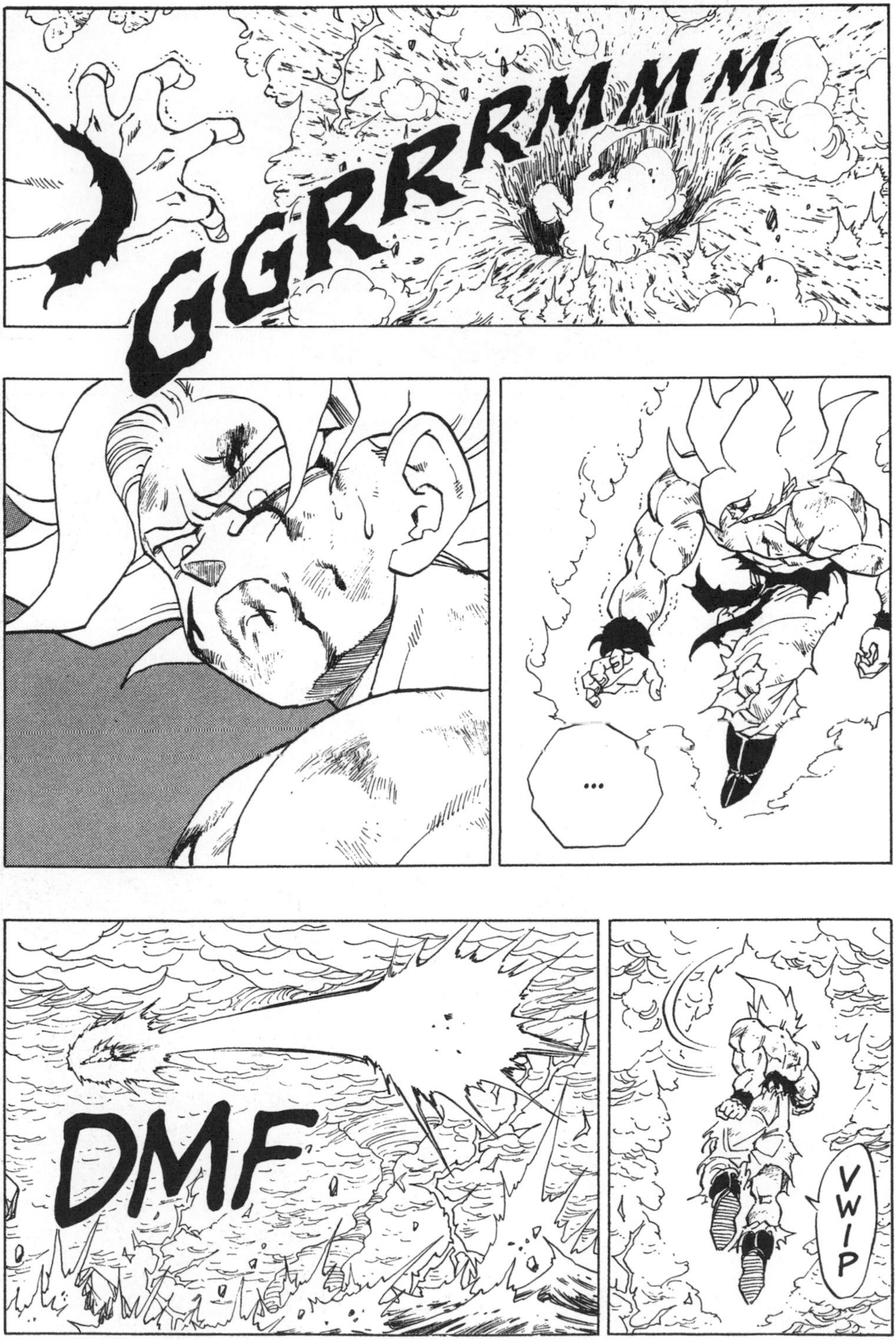
GGRRRMMM
...
DMF
VWIP

DBZ:134 • Namek's End

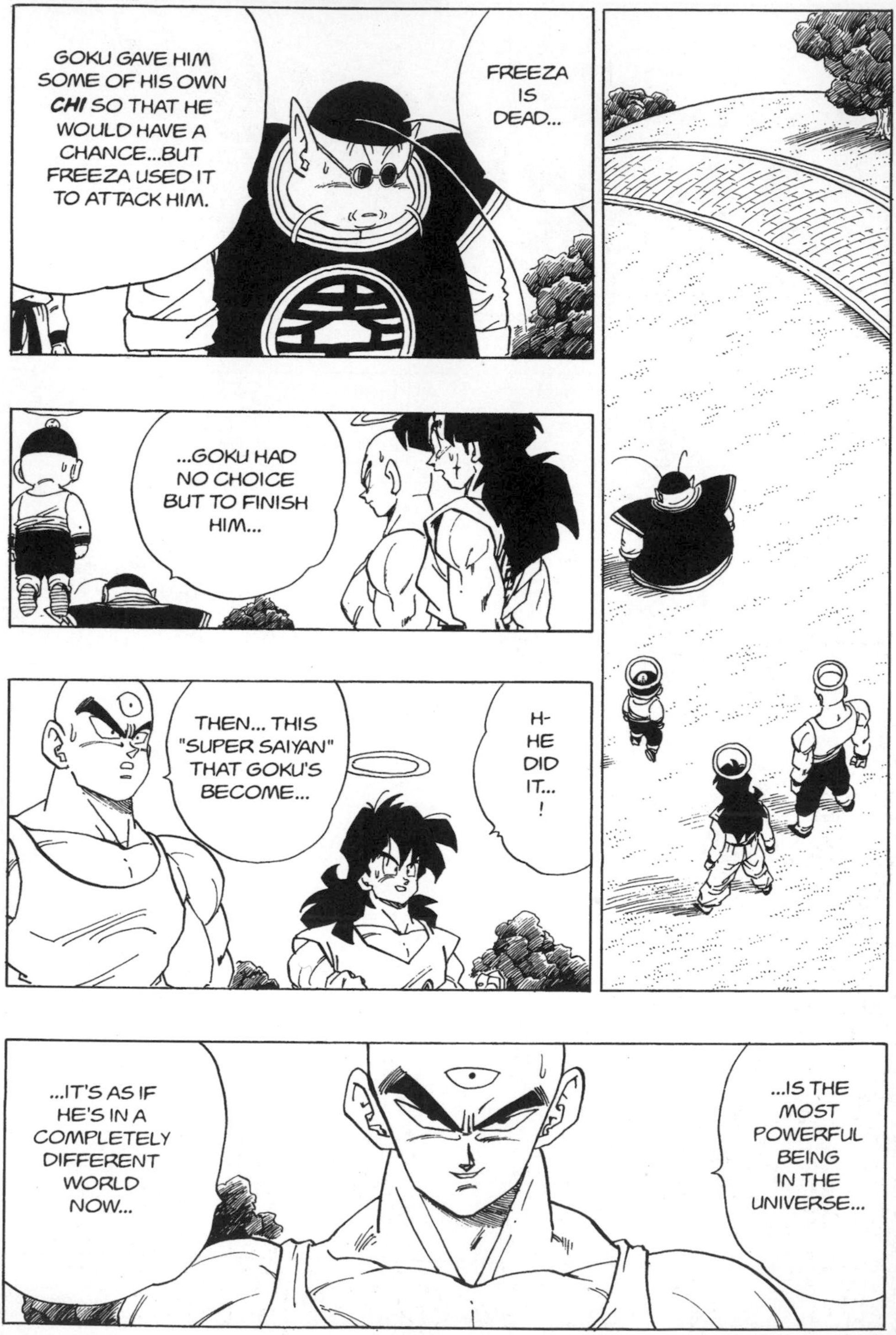
FREEZA IS DEAD...
GOKU GAVE HIM SOME OF HIS OWN *CHI* SO THAT HE WOULD HAVE A CHANCE...BUT FREEZA USED IT TO ATTACK HIM.
...GOKU HAD NO CHOICE BUT TO FINISH HIM...
H-HE DID IT...!
THEN... THIS "SUPER SAIYAN" THAT GOKU'S BECOME...
...IS THE MOST POWERFUL BEING IN THE UNIVERSE...
...IT'S AS IF HE'S IN A COMPLETELY DIFFERENT WORLD NOW...

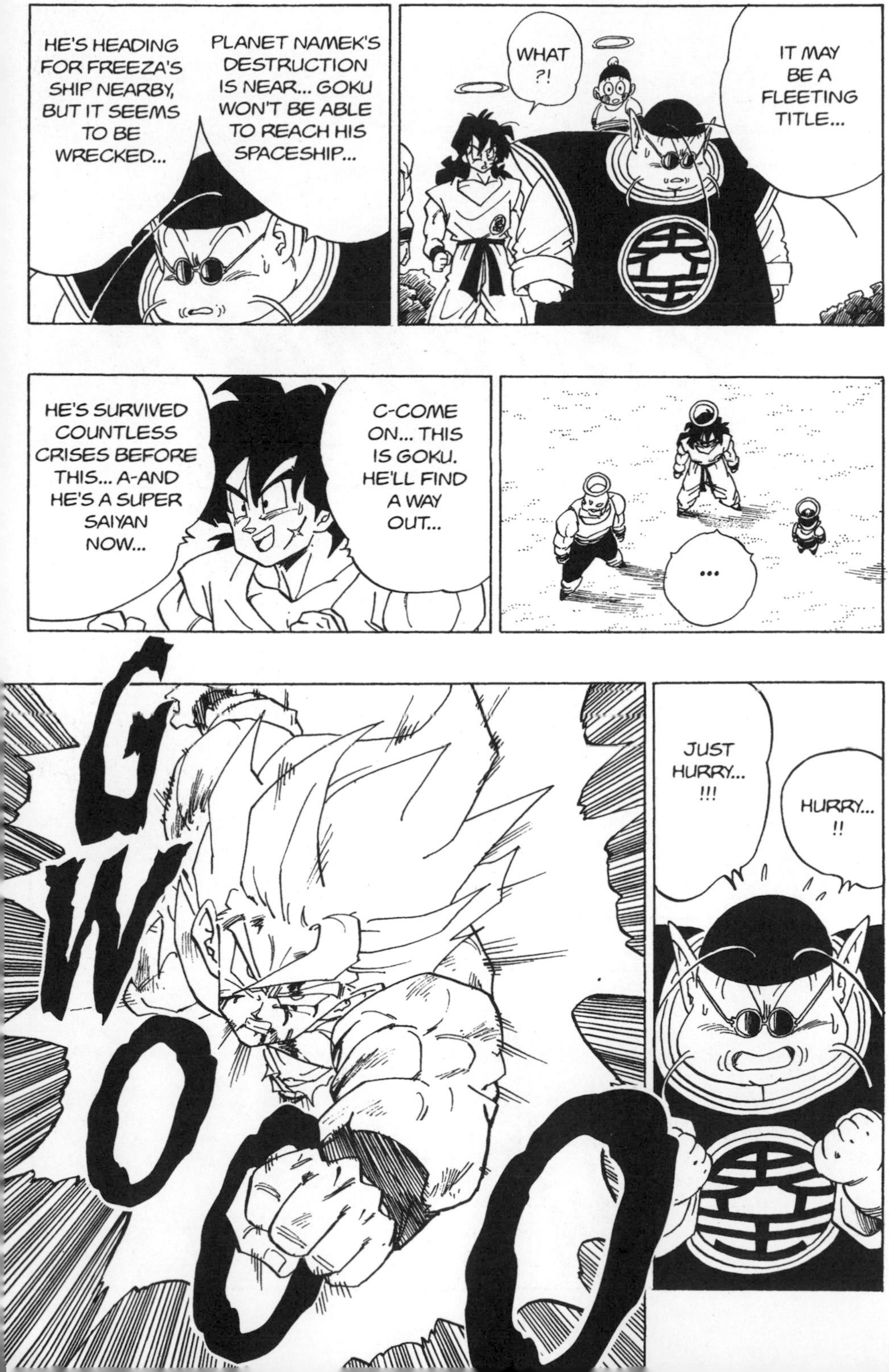
HE'S HEADING FOR FREEZA'S SHIP NEARBY, BUT IT SEEMS TO BE WRECKED...
PLANET NAMEK'S DESTRUCTION IS NEAR... GOKU WON'T BE ABLE TO REACH HIS SPACESHIP...
WHAT ?!
IT MAY BE A FLEETING TITLE...
HE'S SURVIVED COUNTLESS CRISES BEFORE THIS... A-AND HE'S A SUPER SAIYAN NOW...
C-COME ON... THIS IS GOKU. HE'LL FIND A WAY OUT...
...
GWOOOO
JUST HURRY... !!!
HURRY... !!

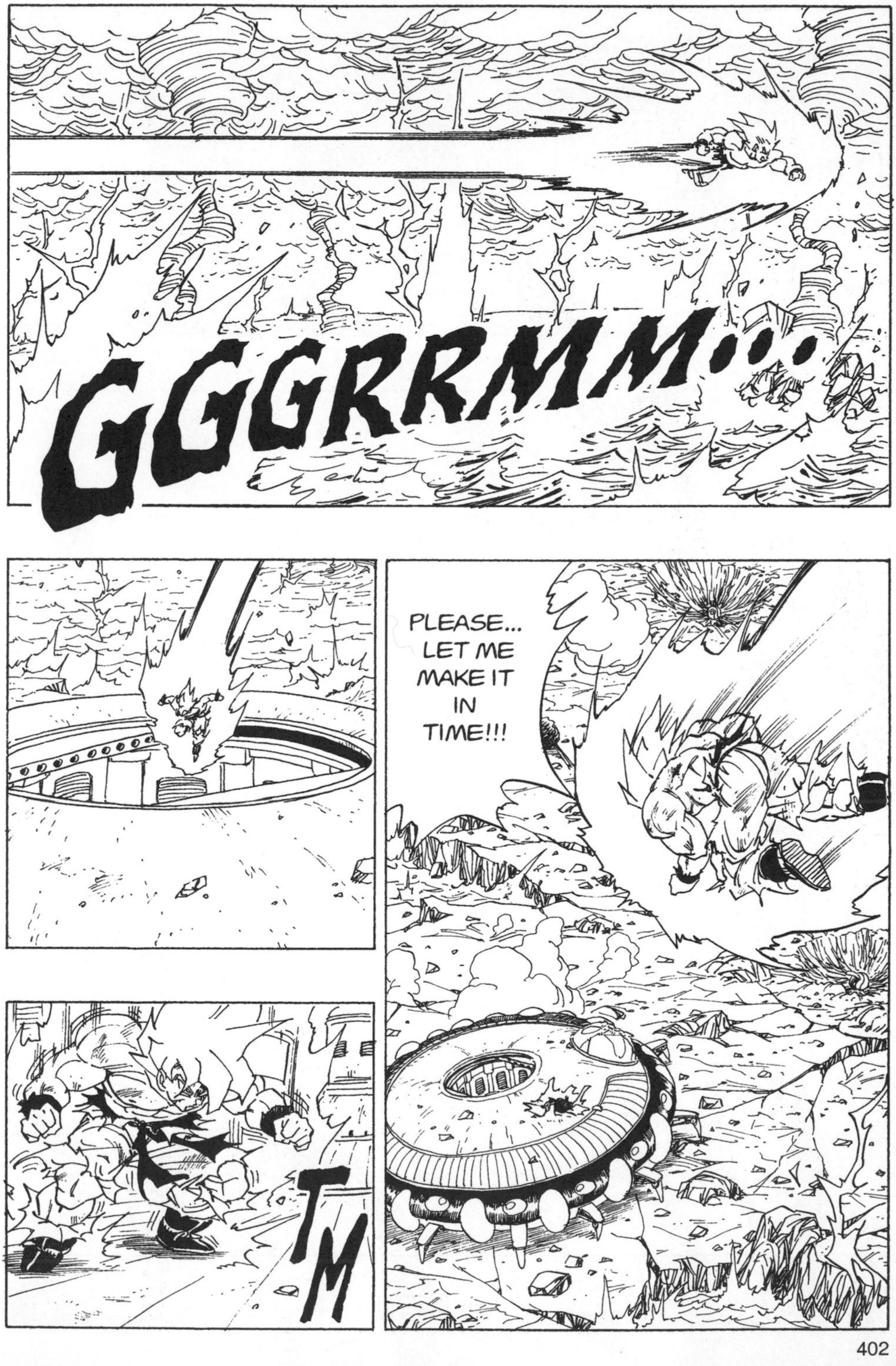
GGGRMM...
PLEASE... LET ME MAKE IT IN TIME!!!
TM

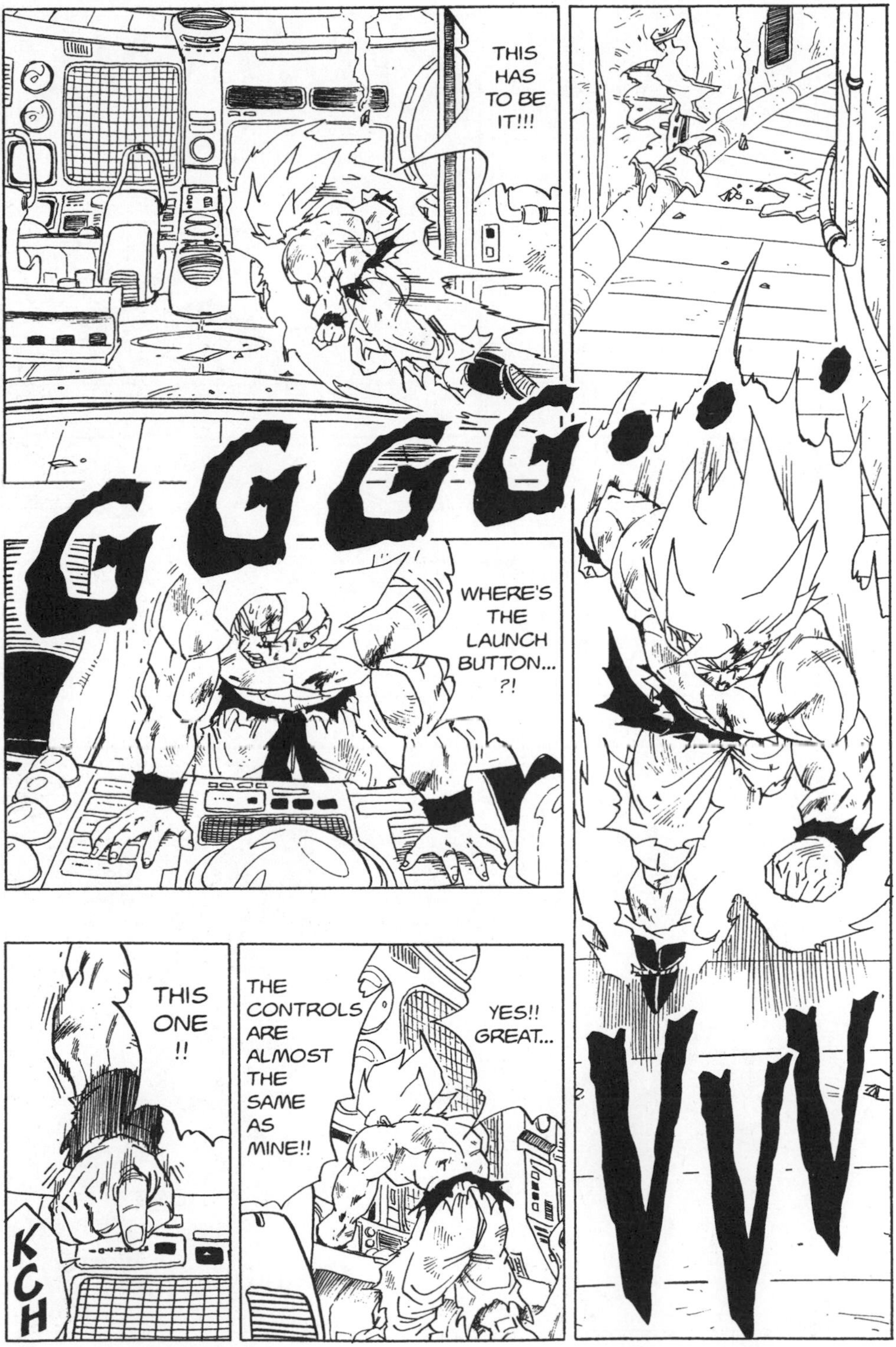
THIS HAS TO BE IT!!!
GGGG...
WHERE'S THE LAUNCH BUTTON...?!
VVV
THIS ONE !!
KCH
THE CONTROLS ARE ALMOST THE SAME AS MINE!!
YES!! GREAT...

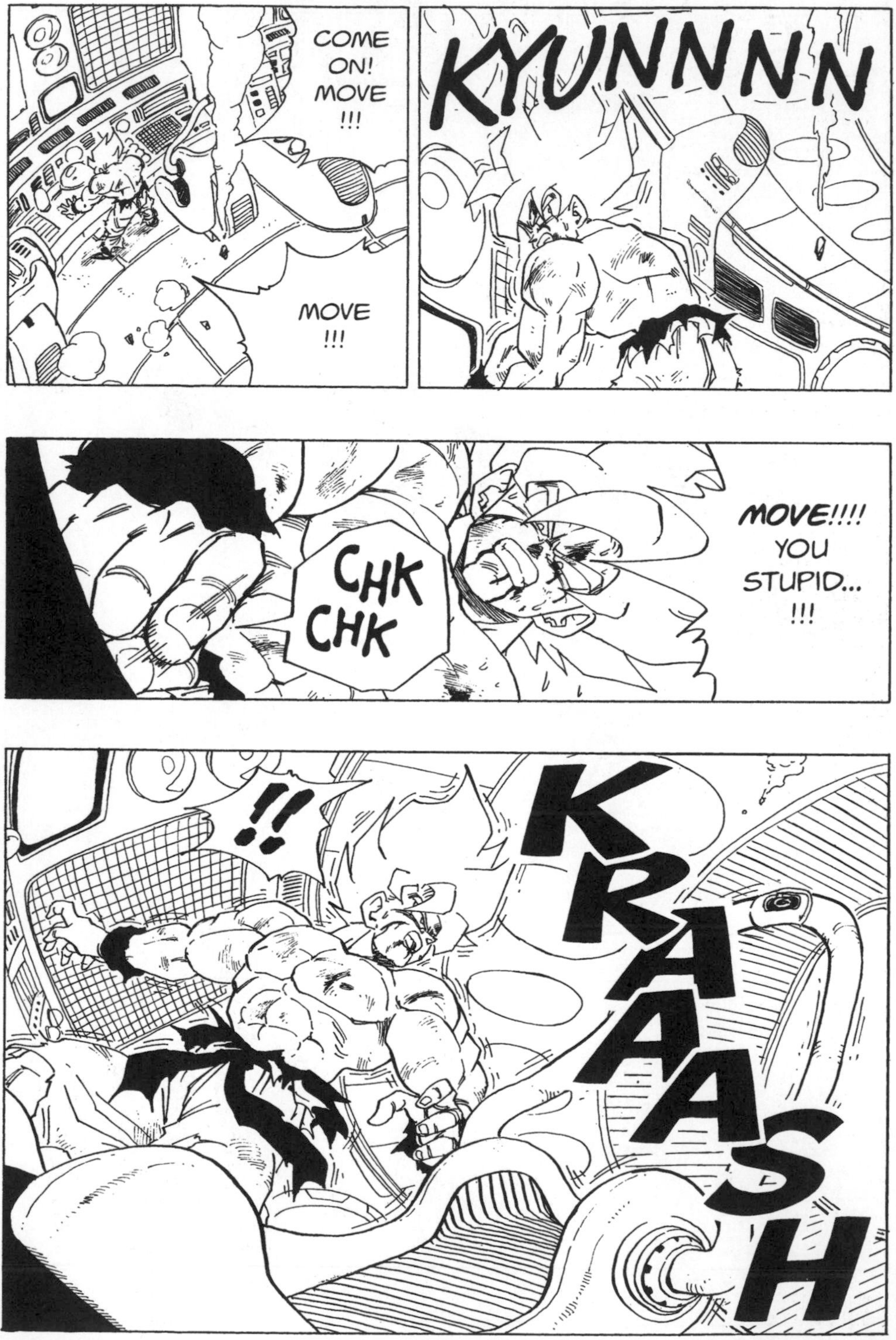
COME ON! MOVE !!!
MOVE !!!
KYUNNNN
MOVE!!!! YOU STUPID... !!!
CHK CHK
!!
KRAAASH

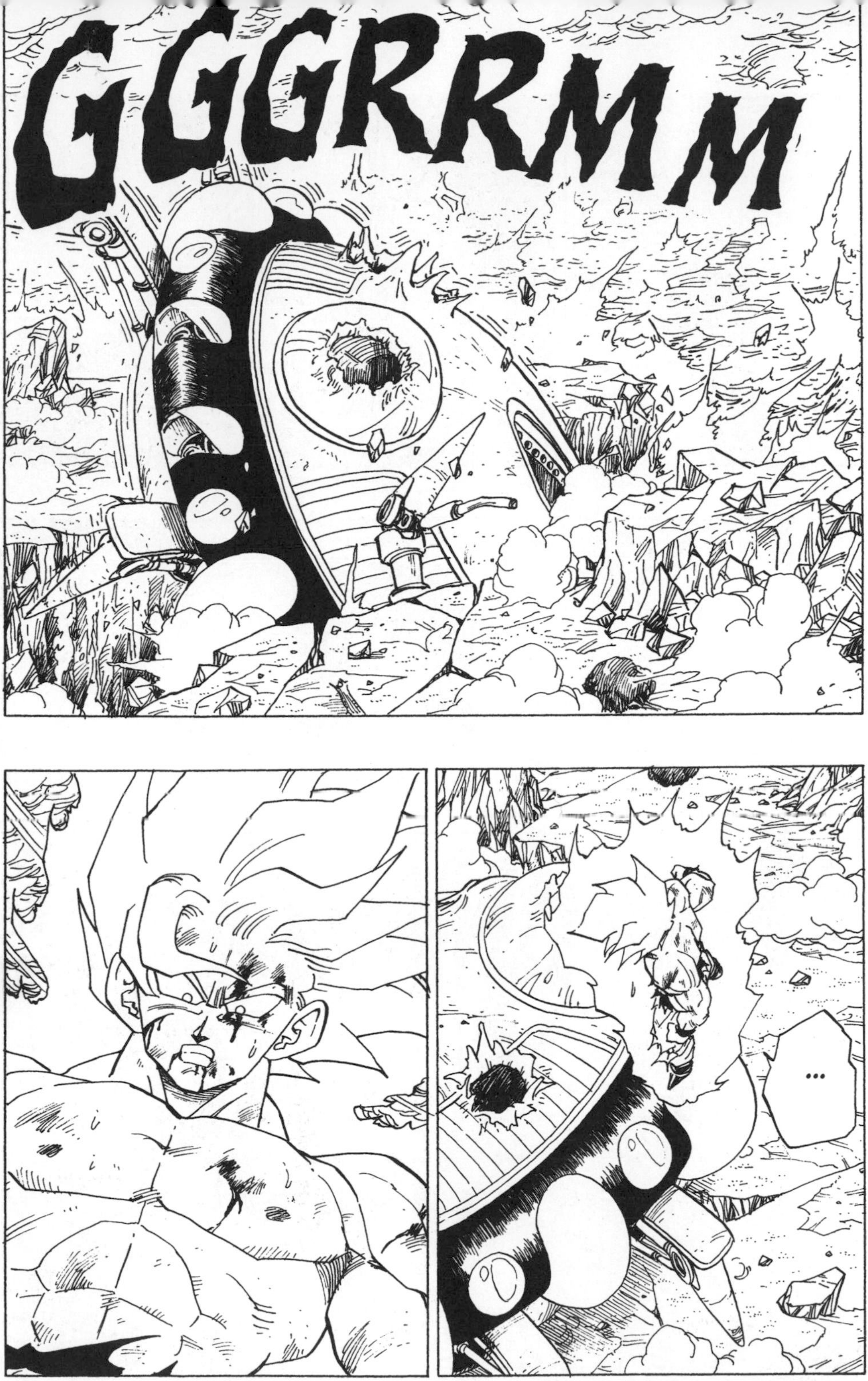
GGGRRMM
...

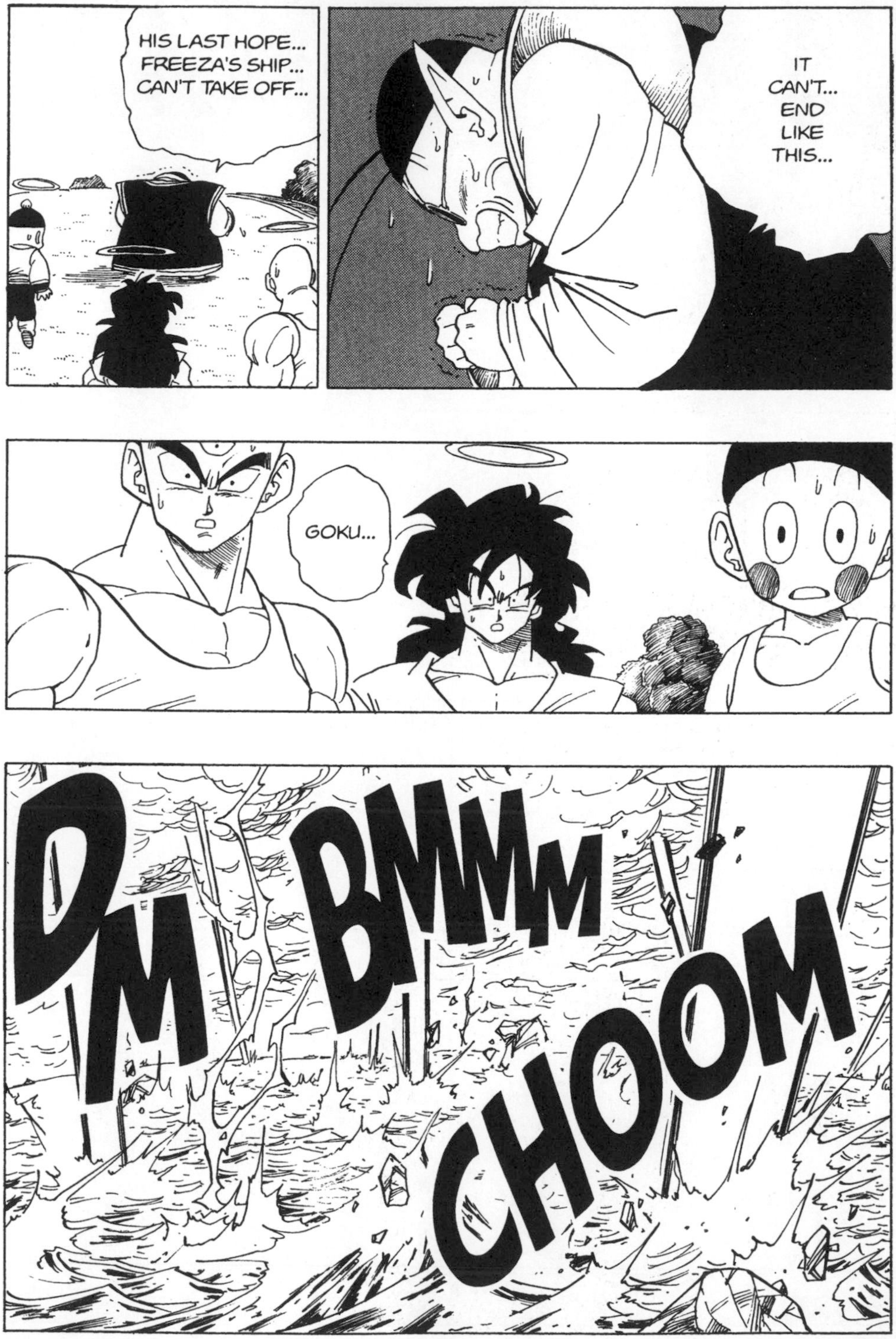
HIS LAST HOPE... FREEZA'S SHIP... CAN'T TAKE OFF...
IT CAN'T... END LIKE THIS...
GOKU...
DM BMMMM CHOOM

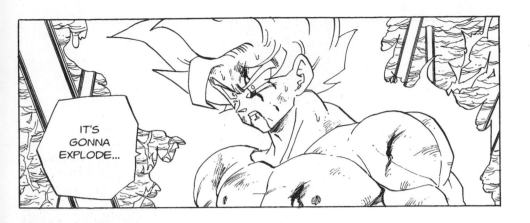

IT'S GONNA EXPLODE...

I CAN'T WATCH...!!

I...

...DON'T DIE...

G-GOKU...

I CAN'T **STOP** IT !!!!

DON'T DIE !!!!!

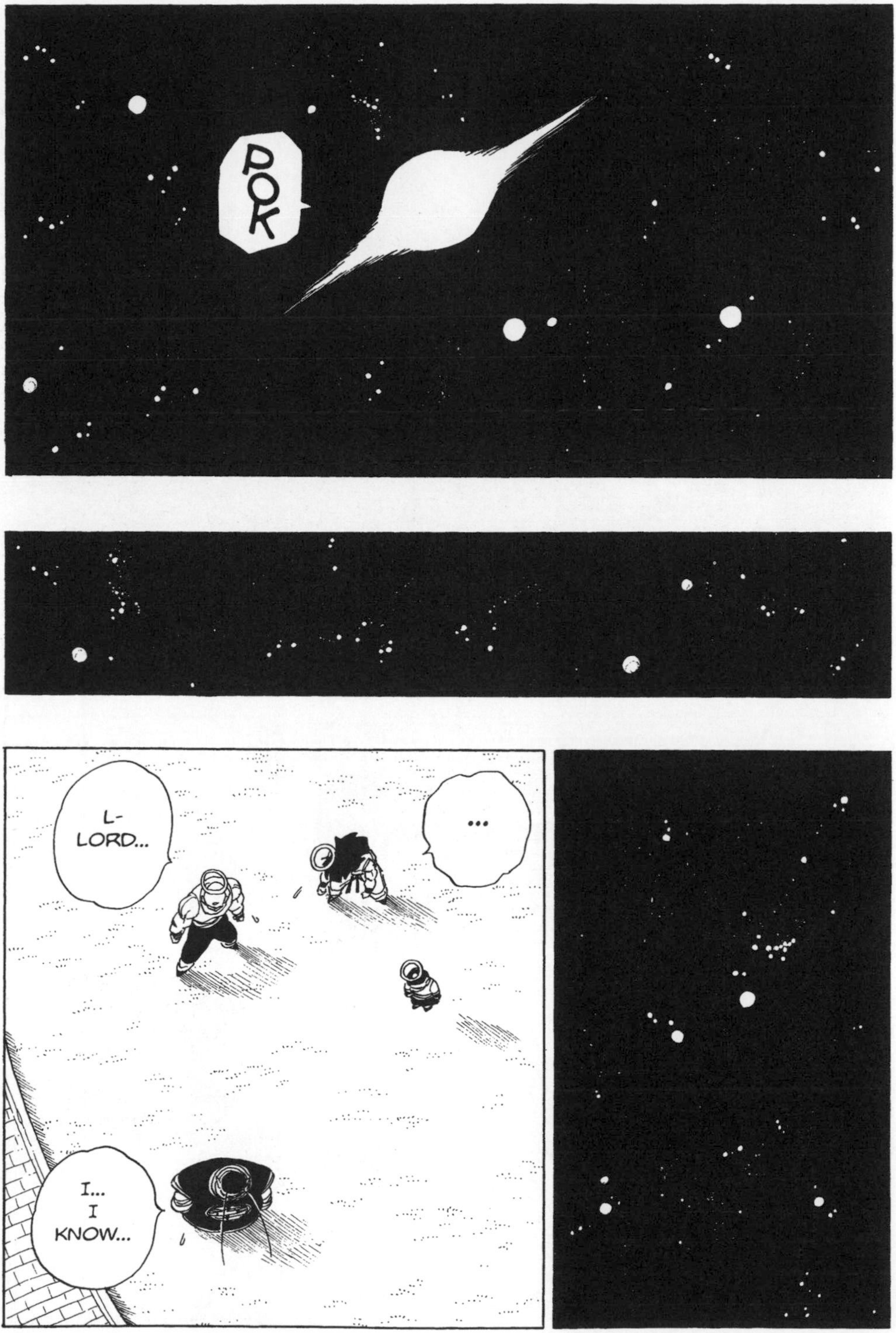
POK
L-LORD...
...
I... I KNOW...

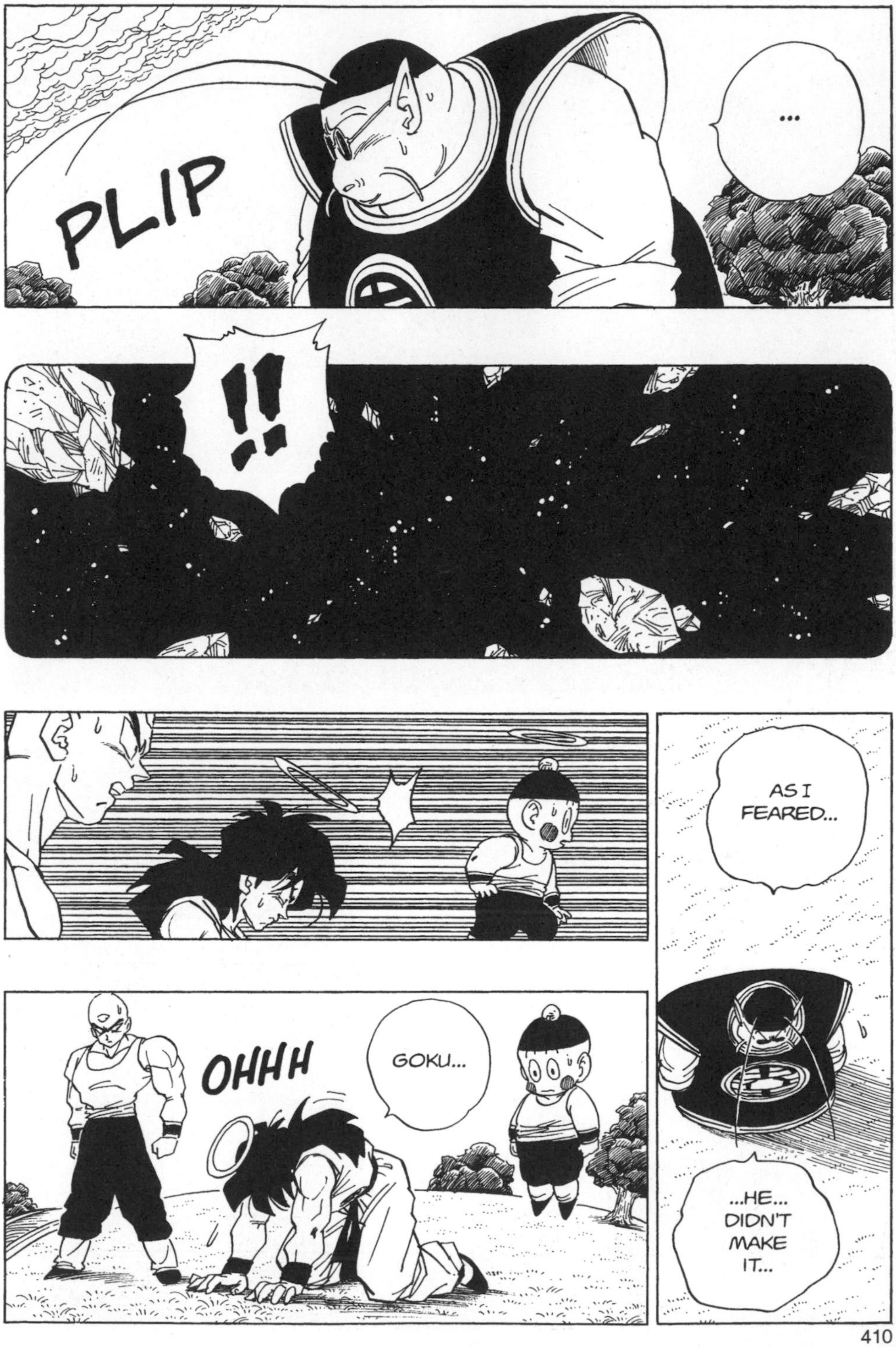
PLIP
...
!!
AS I FEARED...
OHHH
GOKU...
...HE... DIDN'T MAKE IT...

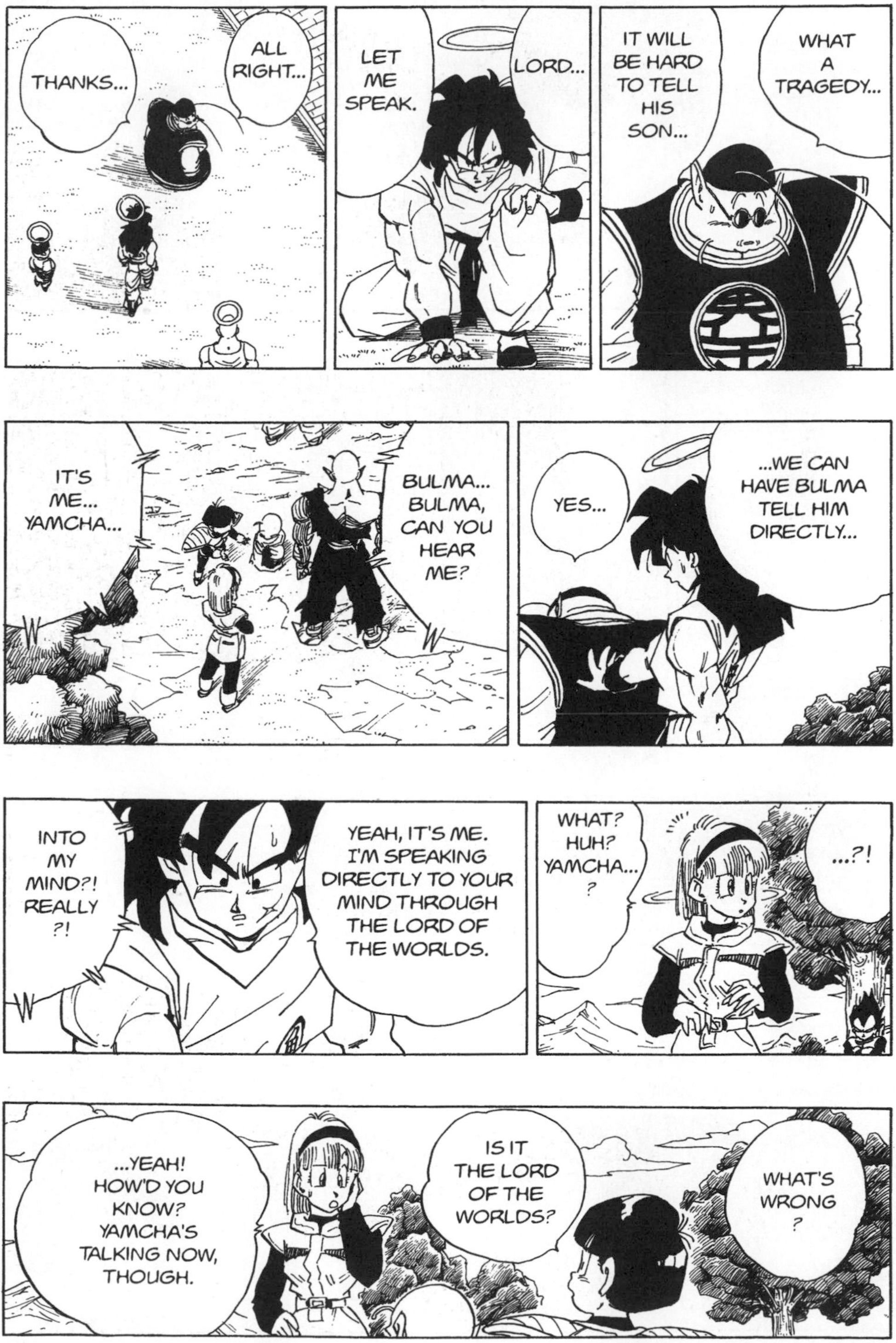
WHAT A TRAGEDY...
IT WILL BE HARD TO TELL HIS SON...
LORD...
LET ME SPEAK.
ALL RIGHT...
THANKS...
...WE CAN HAVE BULMA TELL HIM DIRECTLY...
YES...
BULMA... BULMA, CAN YOU HEAR ME?
IT'S ME... YAMCHA...
...?!
WHAT? HUH? YAMCHA...?
YEAH, IT'S ME. I'M SPEAKING DIRECTLY TO YOUR MIND THROUGH THE LORD OF THE WORLDS.
INTO MY MIND?! REALLY?!
WHAT'S WRONG?
IS IT THE LORD OF THE WORLDS?
...YEAH! HOW'D YOU KNOW? YAMCHA'S TALKING NOW, THOUGH.

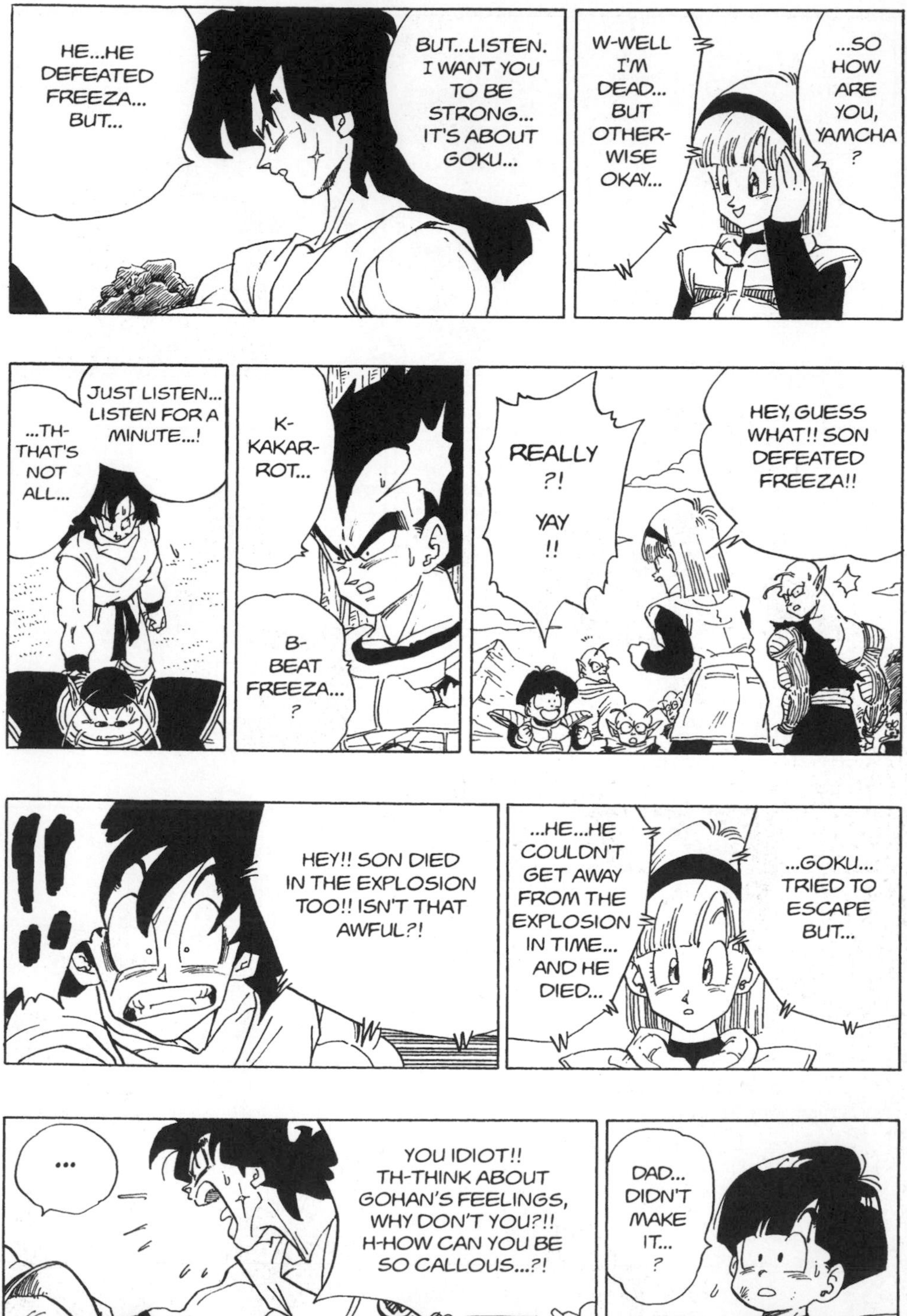
...SO HOW ARE YOU, YAMCHA?
W-WELL I'M DEAD... BUT OTHERWISE OKAY...
BUT...LISTEN. I WANT YOU TO BE STRONG... IT'S ABOUT GOKU...
HE...HE DEFEATED FREEZA... BUT...
HEY, GUESS WHAT!! SON DEFEATED FREEZA!!
REALLY?! YAY!!
K-KAKARROT...
B-BEAT FREEZA...?
JUST LISTEN... LISTEN FOR A MINUTE...!
...TH-THAT'S NOT ALL...
...GOKU... TRIED TO ESCAPE BUT...
...HE...HE COULDN'T GET AWAY FROM THE EXPLOSION IN TIME... AND HE DIED...
HEY!! SON DIED IN THE EXPLOSION TOO!! ISN'T THAT AWFUL?!
!!
DAD... DIDN'T MAKE IT...?
YOU IDIOT!! TH-THINK ABOUT GOHAN'S FEELINGS, WHY DON'T YOU?!! H-HOW CAN YOU BE SO CALLOUS...?!
...

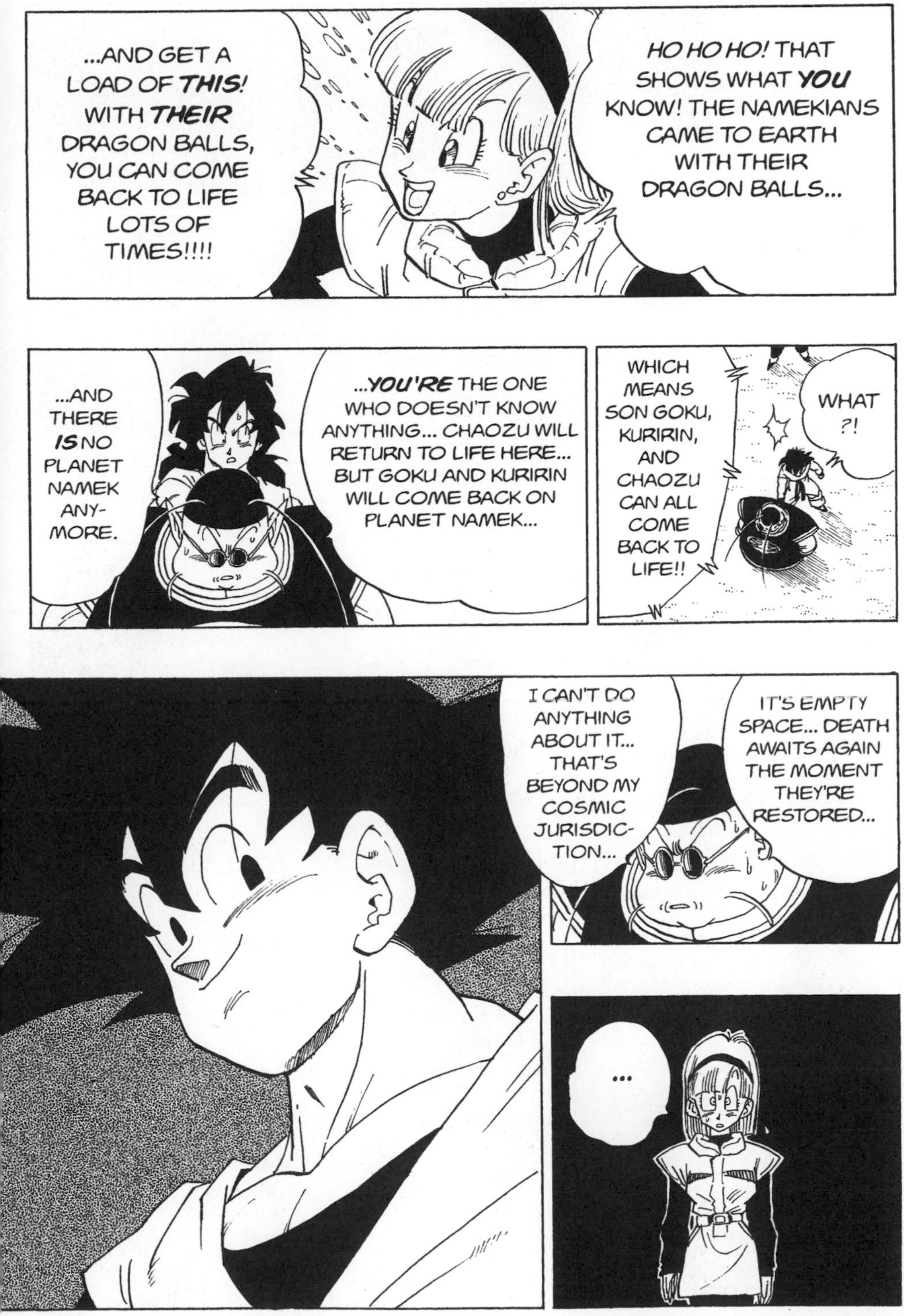

HO HO HO! THAT SHOWS WHAT YOU KNOW! THE NAMEKIANS CAME TO EARTH WITH THEIR DRAGON BALLS...
...AND GET A LOAD OF THIS! WITH THEIR DRAGON BALLS, YOU CAN COME BACK TO LIFE LOTS OF TIMES!!!!
WHICH MEANS SON GOKU, KURIRIN, AND CHAOZU CAN ALL COME BACK TO LIFE!!
WHAT ?!
...YOU'RE THE ONE WHO DOESN'T KNOW ANYTHING... CHAOZU WILL RETURN TO LIFE HERE... BUT GOKU AND KURIRIN WILL COME BACK ON PLANET NAMEK...
...AND THERE IS NO PLANET NAMEK ANY-MORE.
IT'S EMPTY SPACE... DEATH AWAITS AGAIN THE MOMENT THEY'RE RESTORED...
I CAN'T DO ANYTHING ABOUT IT... THAT'S BEYOND MY COSMIC JURISDIC-TION...
...

DBZ:135 • Where is Goku?

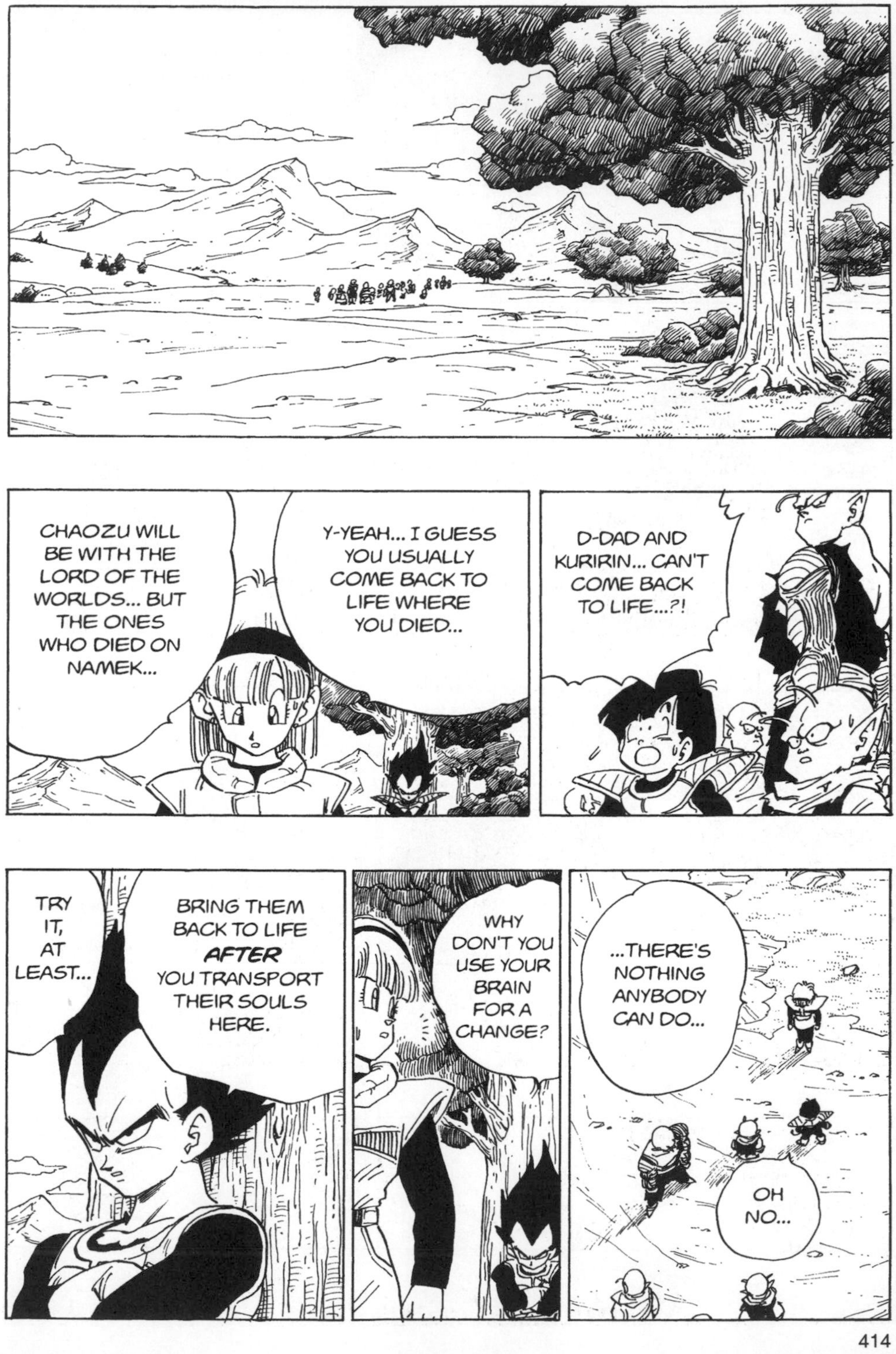

CHAOZU WILL BE WITH THE LORD OF THE WORLDS... BUT THE ONES WHO DIED ON NAMEK...
Y-YEAH... I GUESS YOU USUALLY COME BACK TO LIFE WHERE YOU DIED...
D-DAD AND KURIRIN... CAN'T COME BACK TO LIFE...?!
TRY IT, AT LEAST...
BRING THEM BACK TO LIFE AFTER YOU TRANSPORT THEIR SOULS HERE.
WHY DON'T YOU USE YOUR BRAIN FOR A CHANGE?
...THERE'S NOTHING ANYBODY CAN DO...
OH NO...

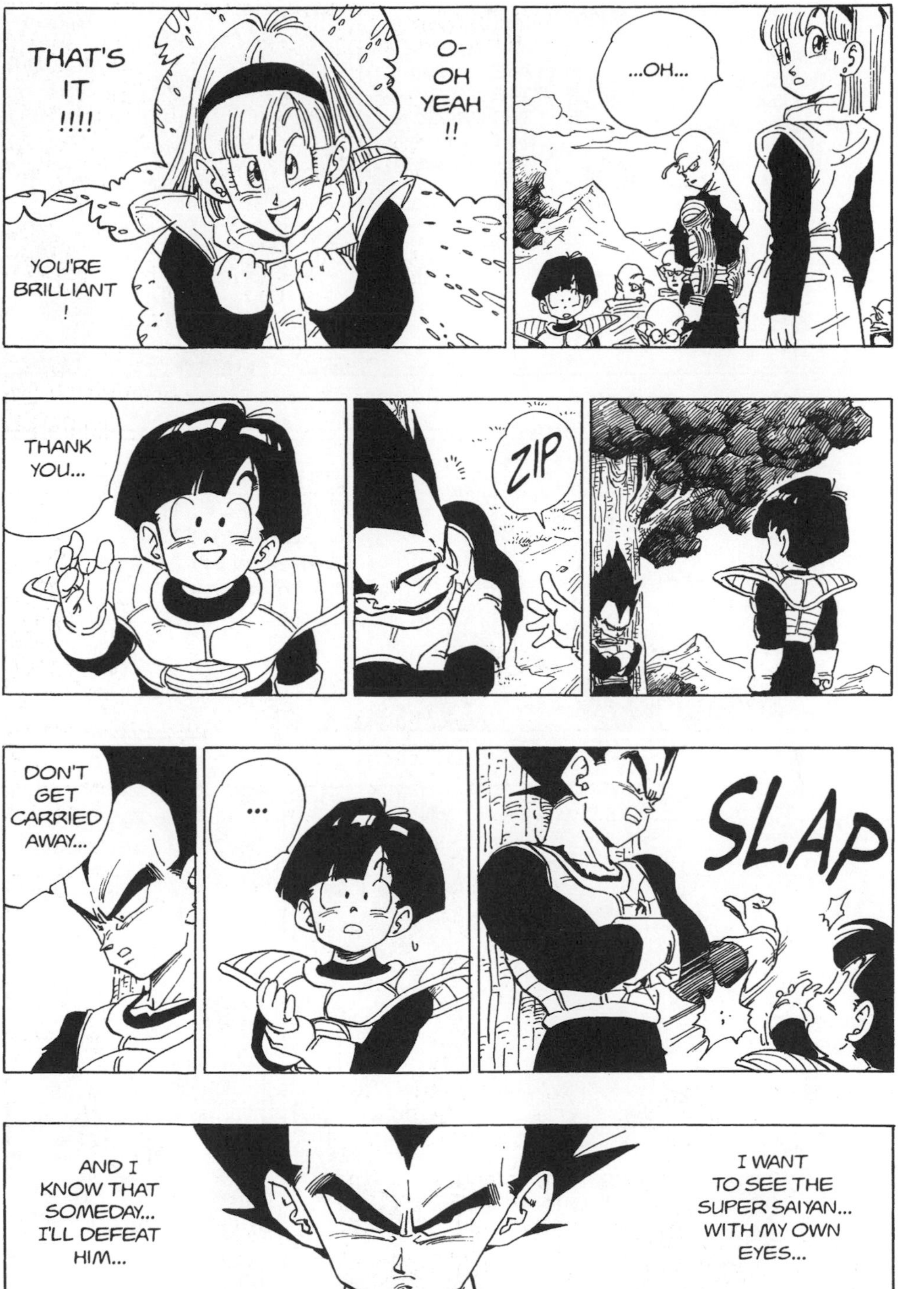
THAT'S IT !!!!
YOU'RE BRILLIANT !
O-OH YEAH !!
...OH...
THANK YOU...
ZIP
DON'T GET CARRIED AWAY...
...
SLAP
AND I KNOW THAT SOMEDAY... I'LL DEFEAT HIM...
I WANT TO SEE THE SUPER SAIYAN... WITH MY OWN EYES...

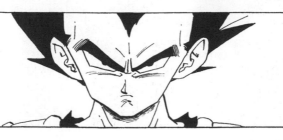

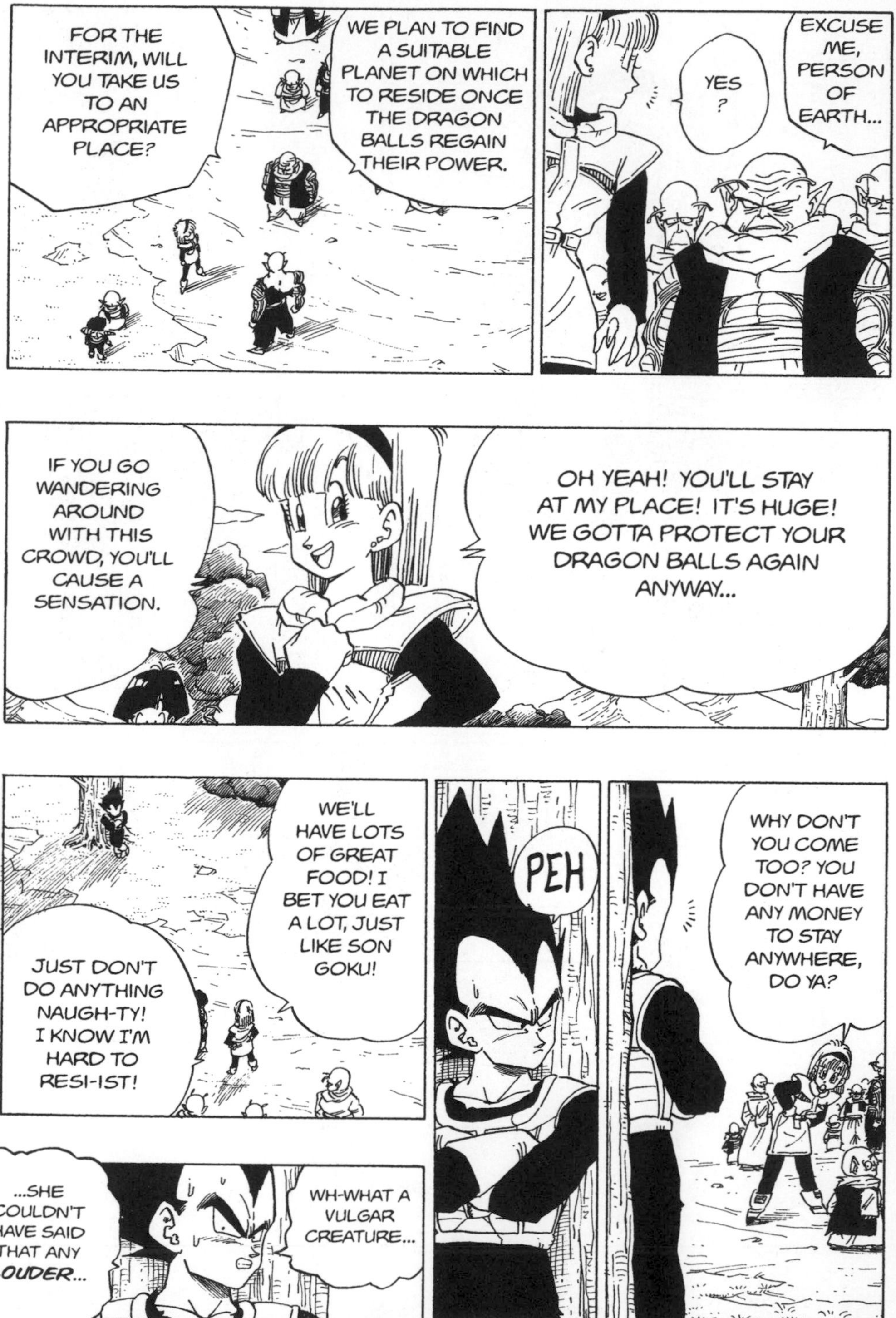
EXCUSE ME, PERSON OF EARTH...
YES?
WE PLAN TO FIND A SUITABLE PLANET ON WHICH TO RESIDE ONCE THE DRAGON BALLS REGAIN THEIR POWER.
FOR THE INTERIM, WILL YOU TAKE US TO AN APPROPRIATE PLACE?
OH YEAH! YOU'LL STAY AT MY PLACE! IT'S HUGE! WE GOTTA PROTECT YOUR DRAGON BALLS AGAIN ANYWAY...
IF YOU GO WANDERING AROUND WITH THIS CROWD, YOU'LL CAUSE A SENSATION.
WHY DON'T YOU COME TOO? YOU DON'T HAVE ANY MONEY TO STAY ANYWHERE, DO YA?
PEH
WE'LL HAVE LOTS OF GREAT FOOD! I BET YOU EAT A LOT, JUST LIKE SON GOKU!
JUST DON'T DO ANYTHING NAUGH-TY! I KNOW I'M HARD TO RESI-IST!
WH-WHAT A VULGAR CREATURE...
...SHE COULDN'T HAVE SAID THAT ANY LOUDER...

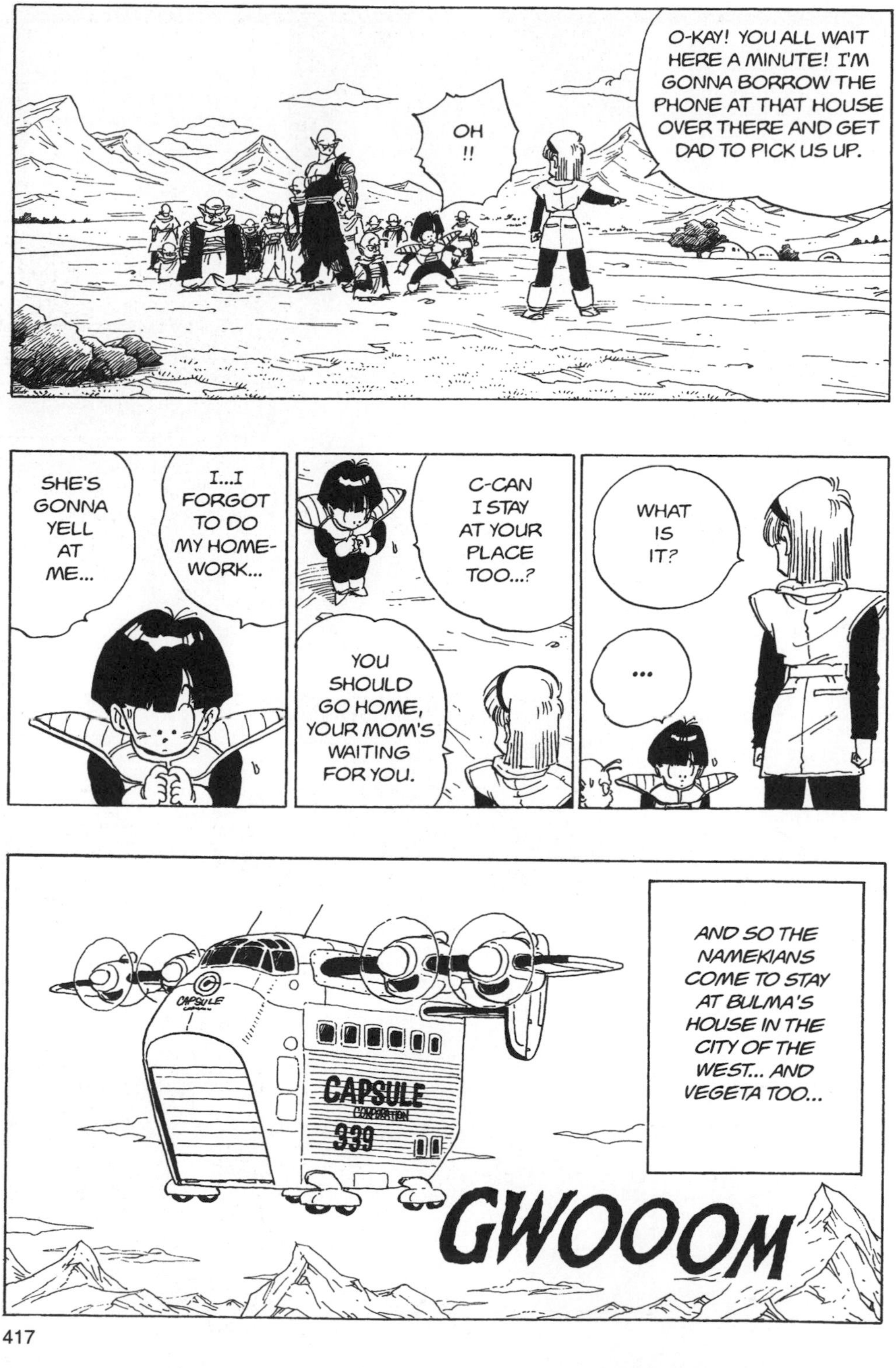
O-KAY! YOU ALL WAIT HERE A MINUTE! I'M GONNA BORROW THE PHONE AT THAT HOUSE OVER THERE AND GET DAD TO PICK US UP.
OH !!
WHAT IS IT?
...
C-CAN I STAY AT YOUR PLACE TOO...?
YOU SHOULD GO HOME, YOUR MOM'S WAITING FOR YOU.
I...I FORGOT TO DO MY HOME-WORK...
SHE'S GONNA YELL AT ME...
AND SO THE NAMEKIANS COME TO STAY AT BULMA'S HOUSE IN THE CITY OF THE WEST... AND VEGETA TOO...
CAPSULE
CAPSULE CORPORATION 339
GWOOOM

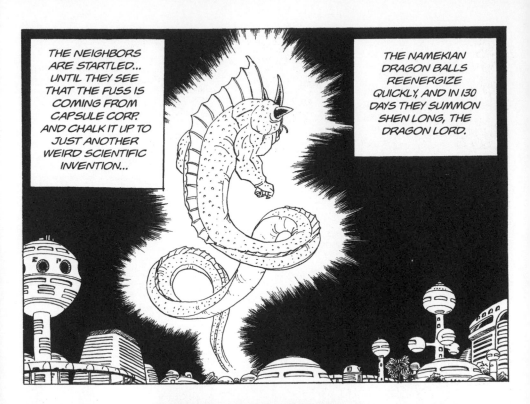

THE NEIGHBORS ARE STARTLED... UNTIL THEY SEE THAT THE FUSS IS COMING FROM CAPSULE CORP. AND CHALK IT UP TO JUST ANOTHER WEIRD SCIENTIFIC INVENTION...

THE NAMEKIAN DRAGON BALLS REENERGIZE QUICKLY, AND IN 130 DAYS THEY SUMMON SHEN LONG, THE DRAGON LORD.

STATE YOUR FIRST WISH.

NOW.

THE *REAL* SHENLONG IS HUGE...

HOO-EE!

I...I CAN'T BELIEVE IT'S TRUE....

BULMA

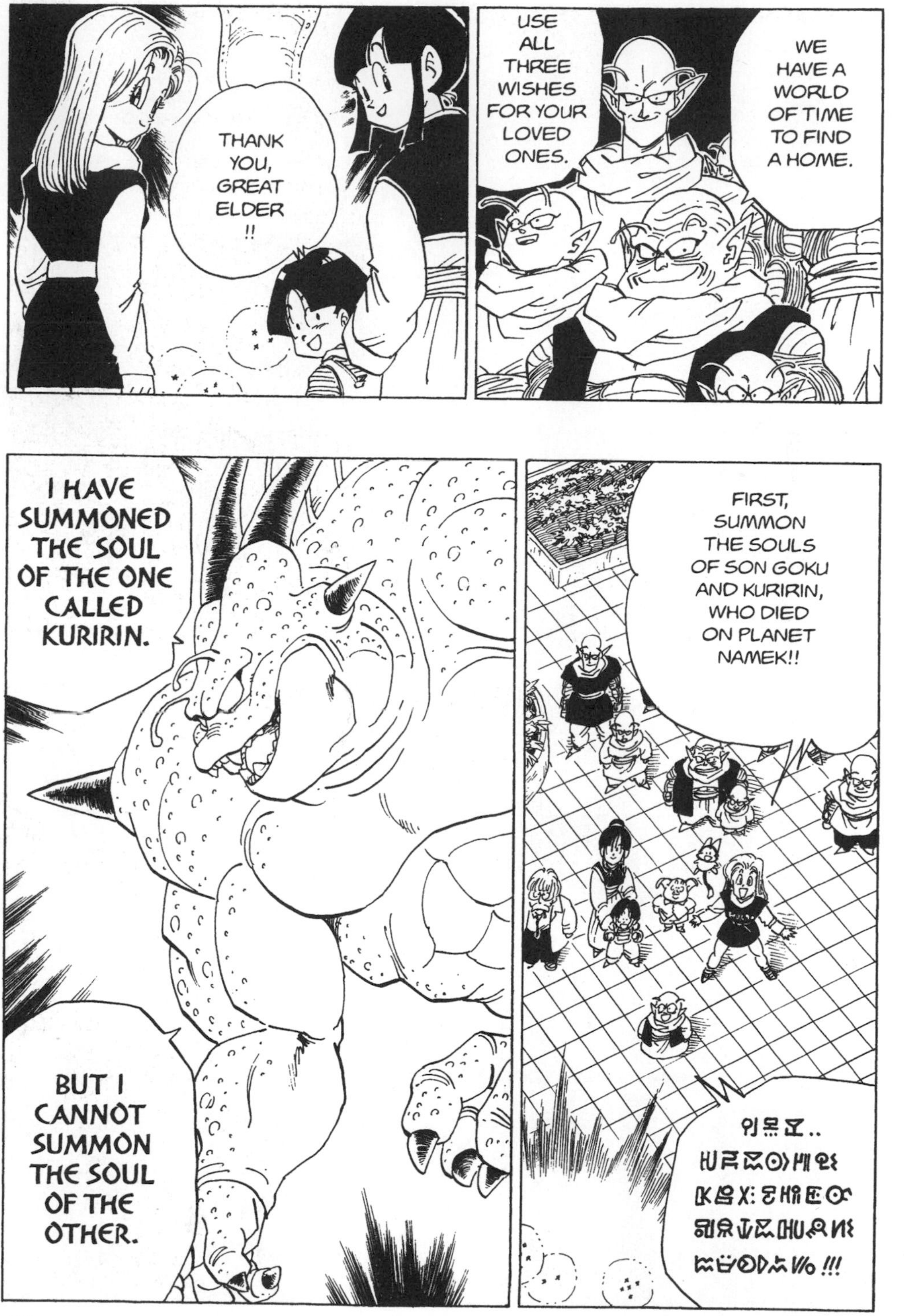
WE HAVE A WORLD OF TIME TO FIND A HOME.
USE ALL THREE WISHES FOR YOUR LOVED ONES.
THANK YOU, GREAT ELDER!!
FIRST, SUMMON THE SOULS OF SON GOKU AND KURIRIN, WHO DIED ON PLANET NAMEK!!
I HAVE SUMMONED THE SOUL OF THE ONE CALLED KURIRIN.
BUT I CANNOT SUMMON THE SOUL OF THE OTHER.

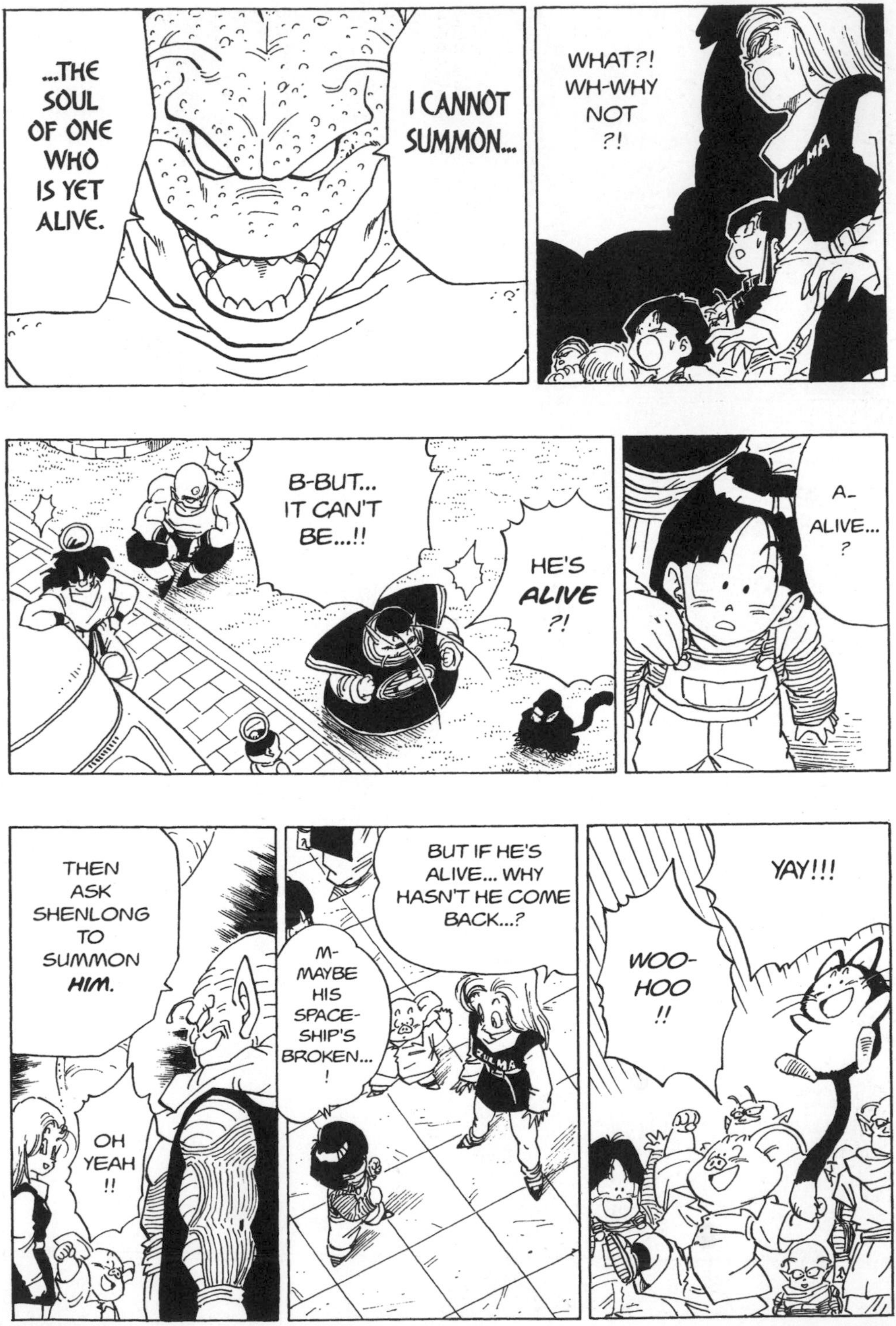
WHAT?! WH-WHY NOT ?!
I CANNOT SUMMON...
...THE SOUL OF ONE WHO IS YET ALIVE.
A- ALIVE... ?
HE'S ALIVE ?!
B-BUT... IT CAN'T BE...!!
YAY!!!
WOO- HOO !!
BUT IF HE'S ALIVE... WHY HASN'T HE COME BACK...?
M- MAYBE HIS SPACE- SHIP'S BROKEN... !
THEN ASK SHENLONG TO SUMMON HIM.
OH YEAH !!

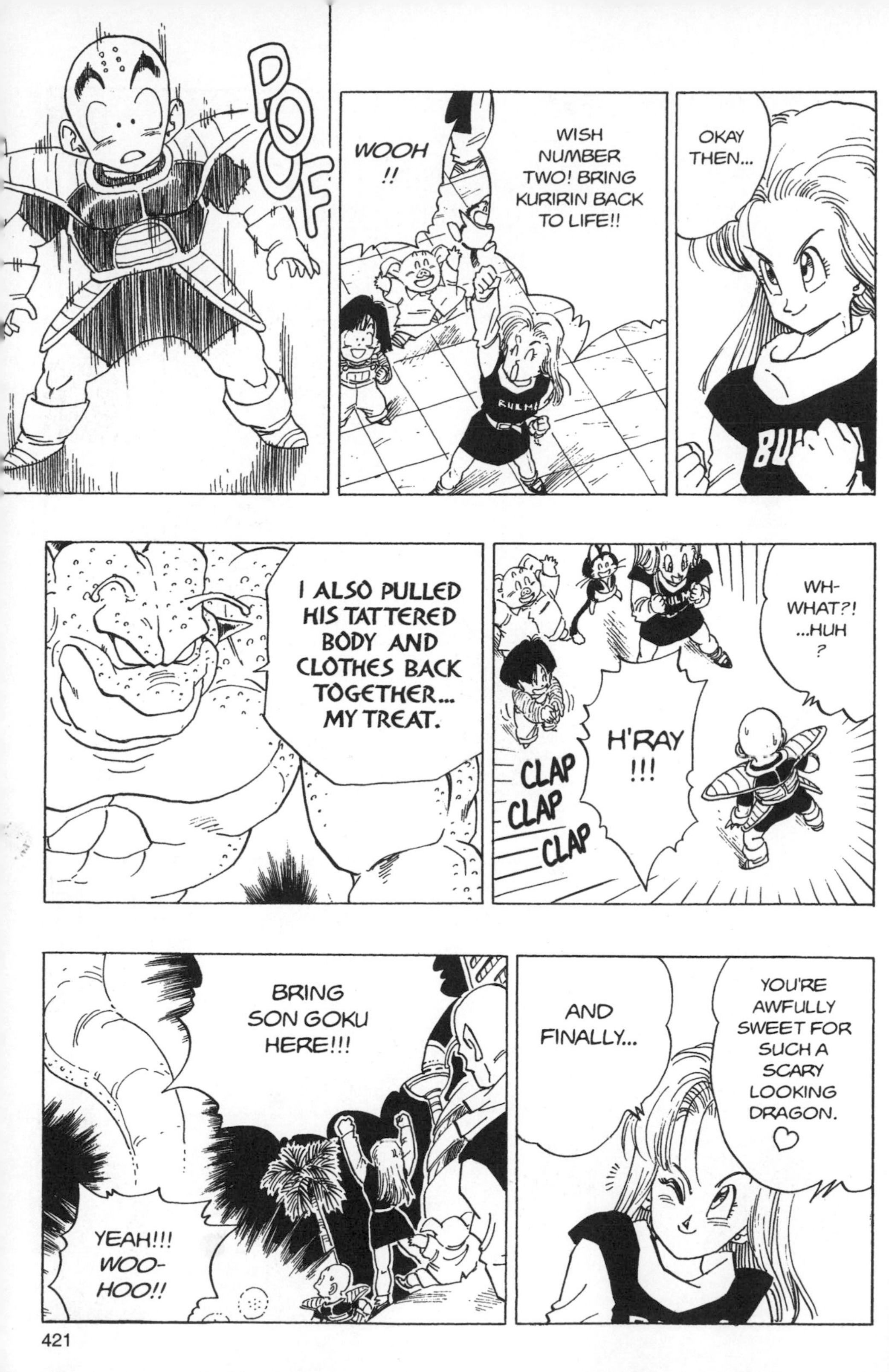
OKAY THEN...
WISH NUMBER TWO! BRING KURIRIN BACK TO LIFE!!
WOOH !!
POOF
WH- WHAT?! ...HUH ?
H'RAY !!!
CLAP CLAP CLAP
I ALSO PULLED HIS TATTERED BODY AND CLOTHES BACK TOGETHER... MY TREAT.
YOU'RE AWFULLY SWEET FOR SUCH A SCARY LOOKING DRAGON. ♡
AND FINALLY...
BRING SON GOKU HERE!!!
YEAH!!! WOO-HOO!!

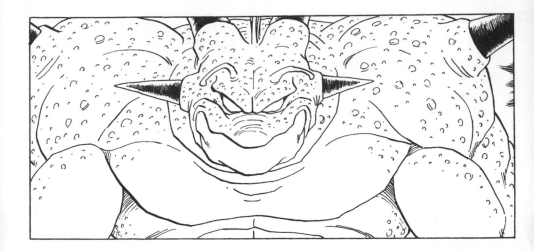

CH-CHOOSES?! WHY?!

HUH?!

HE SAYS HE WILL RETURN ON HIS OWN.

HE REFUSES.

WE MIGHT AS WELL BRING SOMEONE AT KAIÔ'S BACK TO LIFE.

IF HE SAYS HE'LL COME BACK ON HIS OWN, LET HIM BE.

HEH... JUST A JOKE...

HE DOESN'T WANT TO GO HOME!! HE'S AFRAID OF HIS WIFE!!

I KNOW!!!

NOW WE KNOW WHO THE *REAL* STRONGEST IN THE UNIVERSE IS!!!

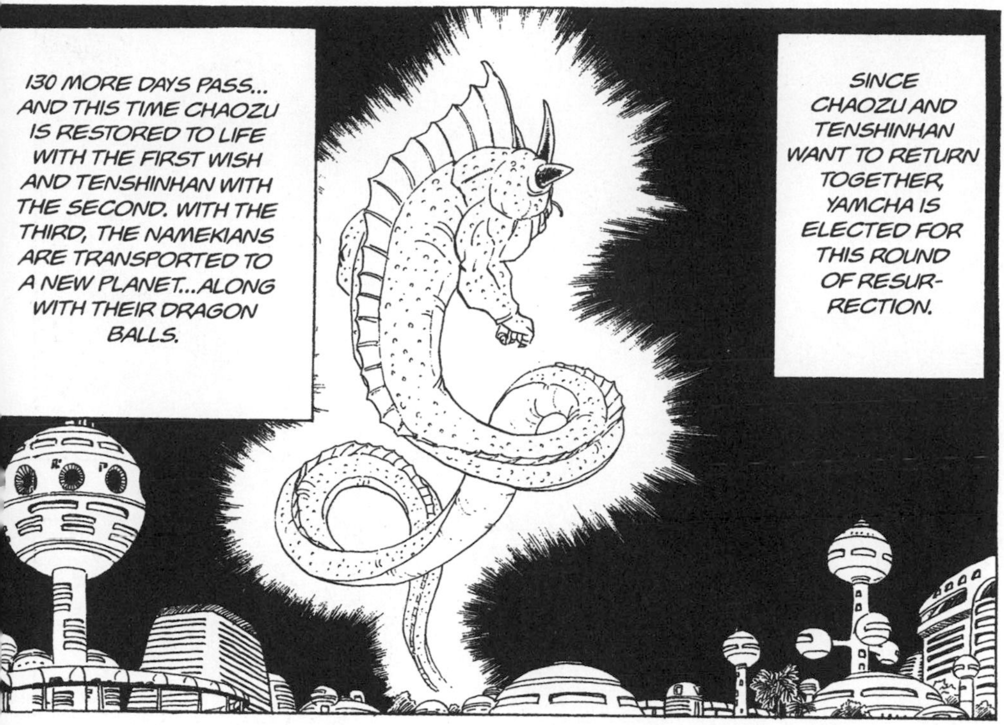
SINCE CHAOZU AND TENSHINHAN WANT TO RETURN TOGETHER, YAMCHA IS ELECTED FOR THIS ROUND OF RESUR-RECTION.
130 MORE DAYS PASS... AND THIS TIME CHAOZU IS RESTORED TO LIFE WITH THE FIRST WISH AND TENSHINHAN WITH THE SECOND. WITH THE THIRD, THE NAMEKIANS ARE TRANSPORTED TO A NEW PLANET...ALONG WITH THEIR DRAGON BALLS.

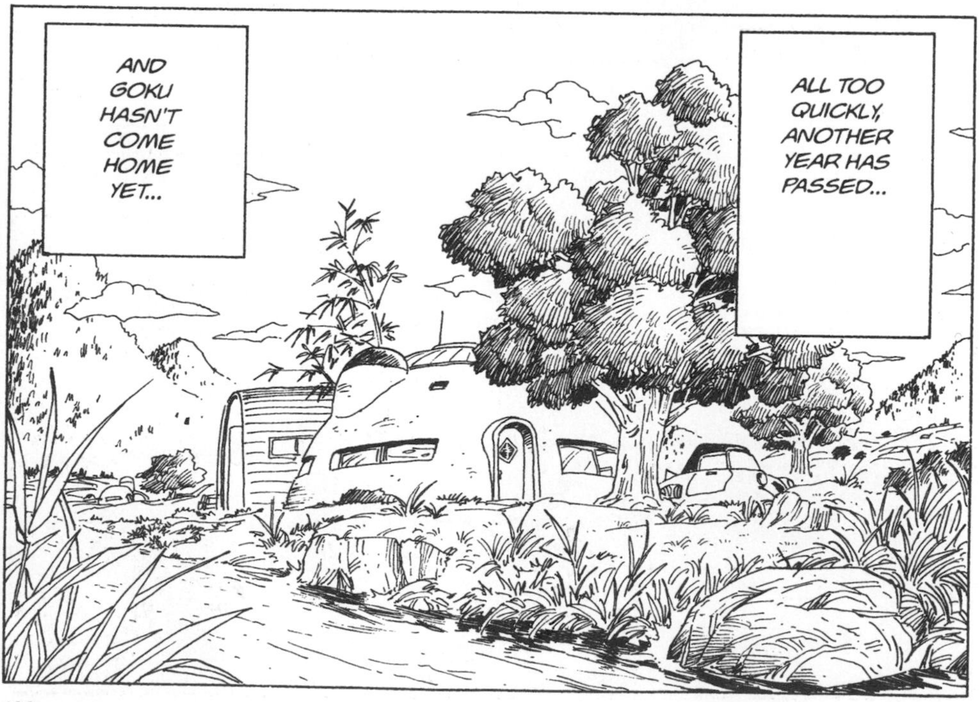
ALL TOO QUICKLY, ANOTHER YEAR HAS PASSED...
AND GOKU HASN'T COME HOME YET...

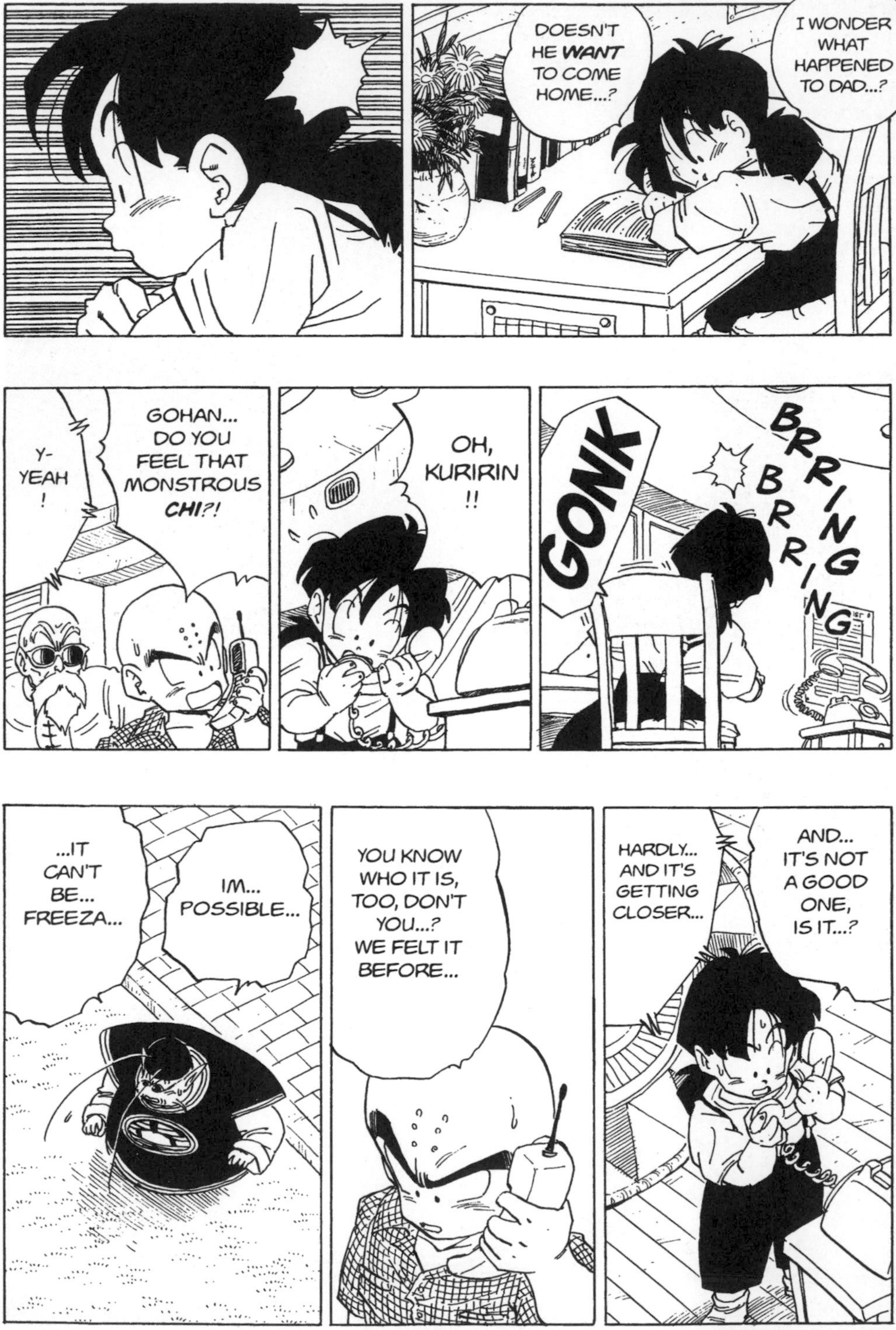
I WONDER WHAT HAPPENED TO DAD...?
DOESN'T HE *WANT* TO COME HOME...?
BRRING BRRING
GONK
OH, KURIRIN!!
GOHAN... DO YOU FEEL THAT MONSTROUS *CHI*?!
Y-YEAH!
AND... IT'S NOT A GOOD ONE, IS IT...?
HARDLY... AND IT'S GETTING CLOSER...
YOU KNOW WHO IT IS, TOO, DON'T YOU...? WE FELT IT BEFORE...
...IT CAN'T BE... FREEZA...
IM... POSSIBLE...

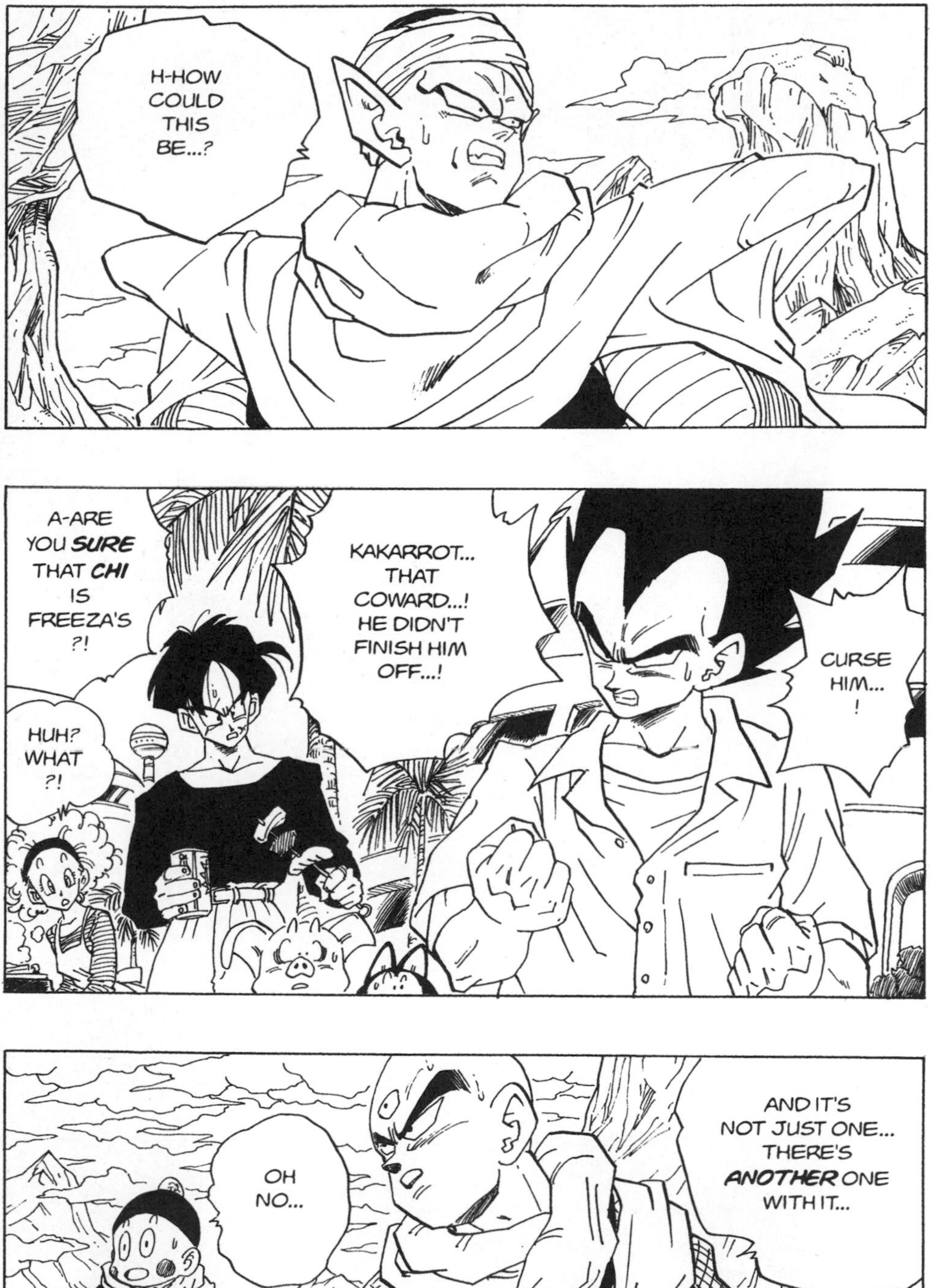
H-HOW COULD THIS BE...?
A-ARE YOU **SURE** THAT **CHI** IS FREEZA'S ?!
KAKARROT... THAT COWARD...! HE DIDN'T FINISH HIM OFF...!
CURSE HIM... !
HUH? WHAT ?!
OH NO...
AND IT'S NOT JUST ONE... THERE'S **ANOTHER** ONE WITH IT...

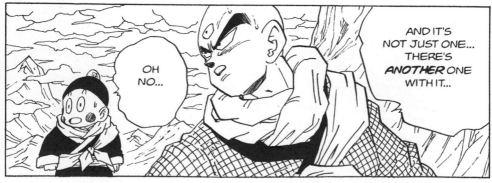

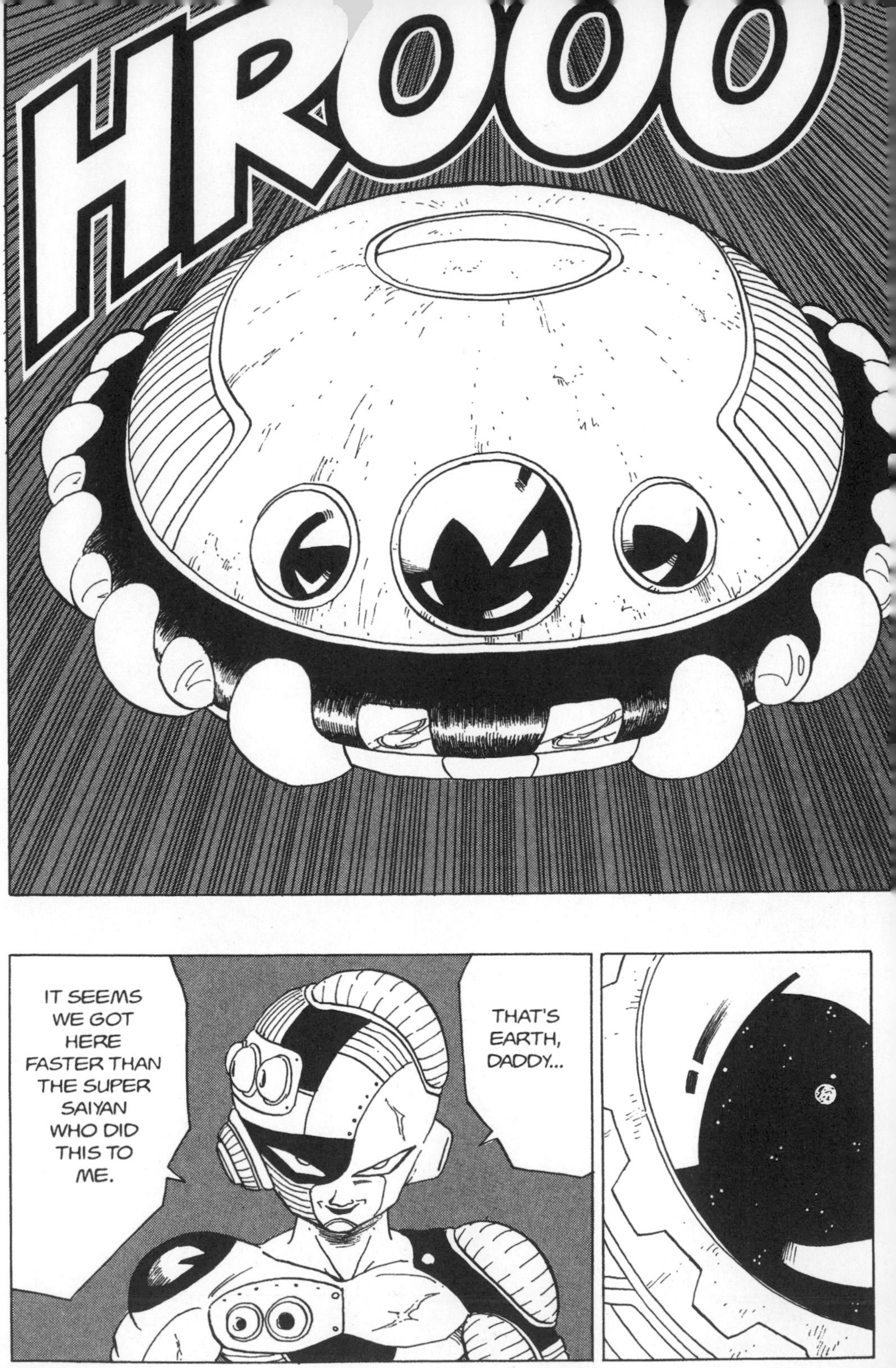
HROOO
THAT'S EARTH, DADDY...
IT SEEMS WE GOT HERE FASTER THAN THE SUPER SAIYAN WHO DID THIS TO ME.

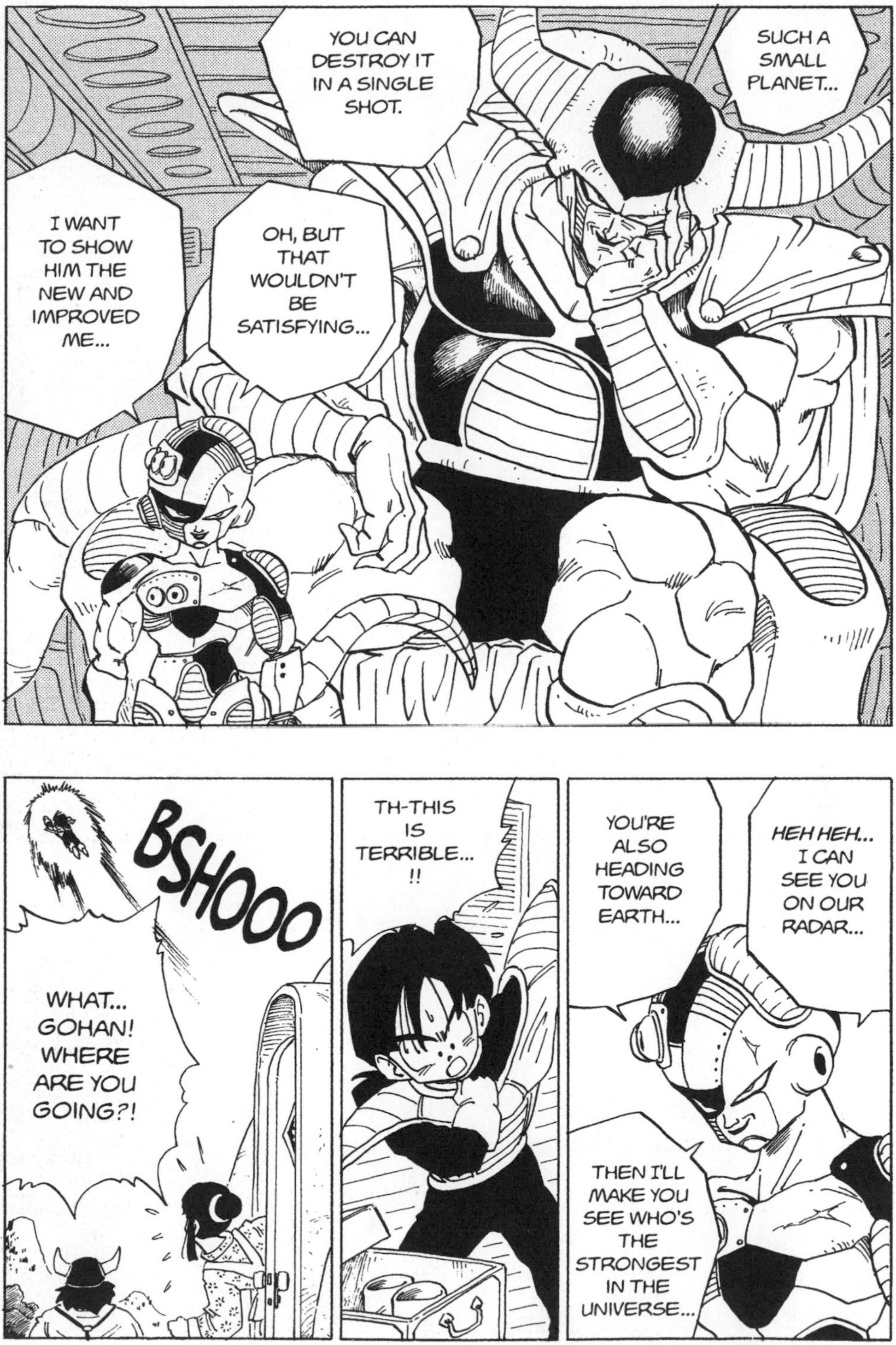
SUCH A SMALL PLANET...
YOU CAN DESTROY IT IN A SINGLE SHOT.
OH, BUT THAT WOULDN'T BE SATISFYING...
I WANT TO SHOW HIM THE NEW AND IMPROVED ME...
HEH HEH... I CAN SEE YOU ON OUR RADAR...
YOU'RE ALSO HEADING TOWARD EARTH...
THEN I'LL MAKE YOU SEE WHO'S THE STRONGEST IN THE UNIVERSE...
TH-THIS IS TERRIBLE... !!
BSHOOO
WHAT... GOHAN! WHERE ARE YOU GOING?!

DBZ:136 • The Coming of King Cold

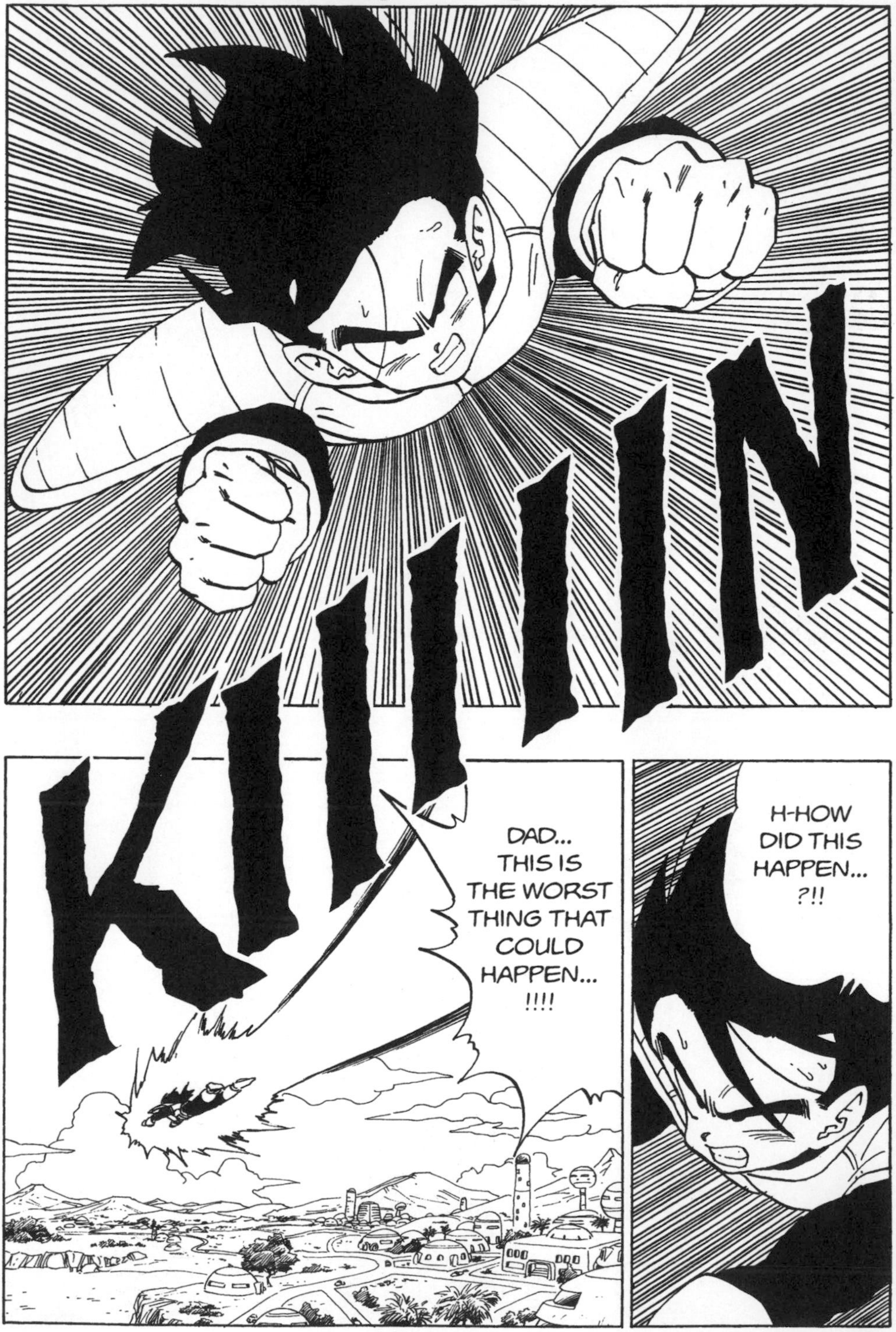
H-HOW DID THIS HAPPEN... ?!!
DAD... THIS IS THE WORST THING THAT COULD HAPPEN... !!!!

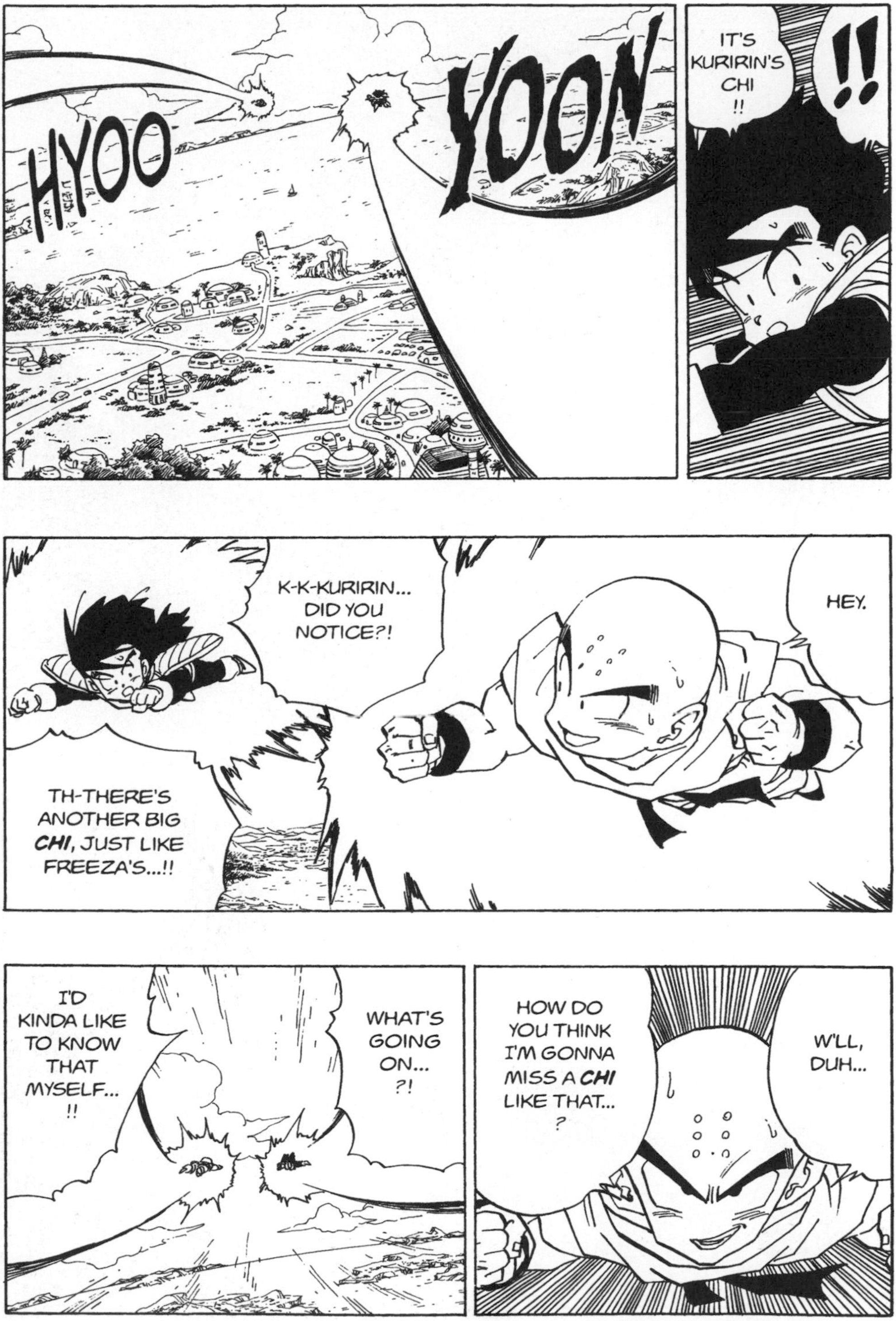
HYOO
YOON
IT'S KURIRIN'S CHI !!
!!
K-K-KURIRIN... DID YOU NOTICE?!
TH-THERE'S ANOTHER BIG CHI, JUST LIKE FREEZA'S...!!
HEY.
I'D KINDA LIKE TO KNOW THAT MYSELF... !!
WHAT'S GOING ON... ?!
HOW DO YOU THINK I'M GONNA MISS A CHI LIKE THAT... ?
W'LL, DUH...

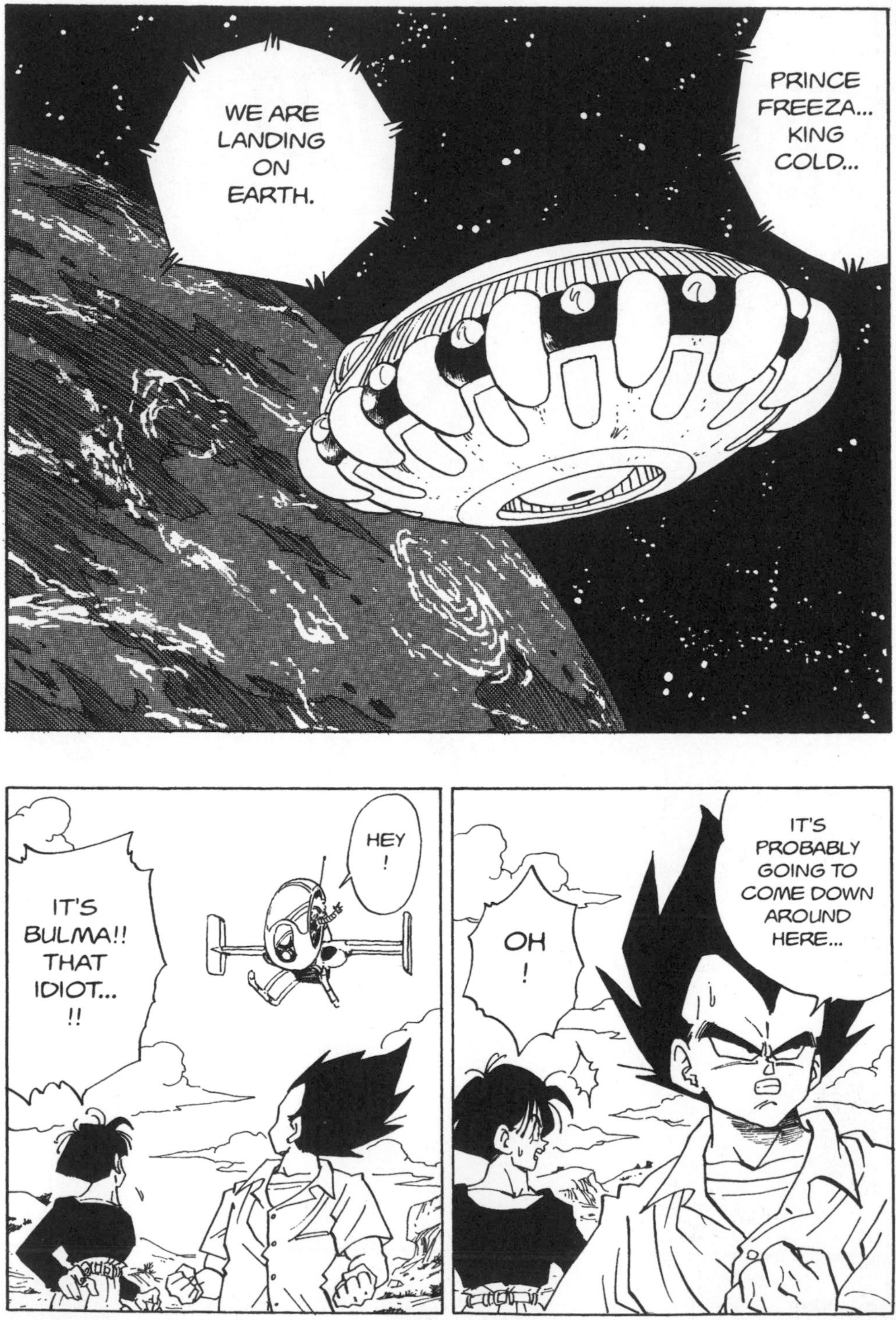
PRINCE FREEZA... KING COLD...
WE ARE LANDING ON EARTH.
HEY !
IT'S BULMA!! THAT IDIOT... !!
IT'S PROBABLY GOING TO COME DOWN AROUND HERE...
OH !

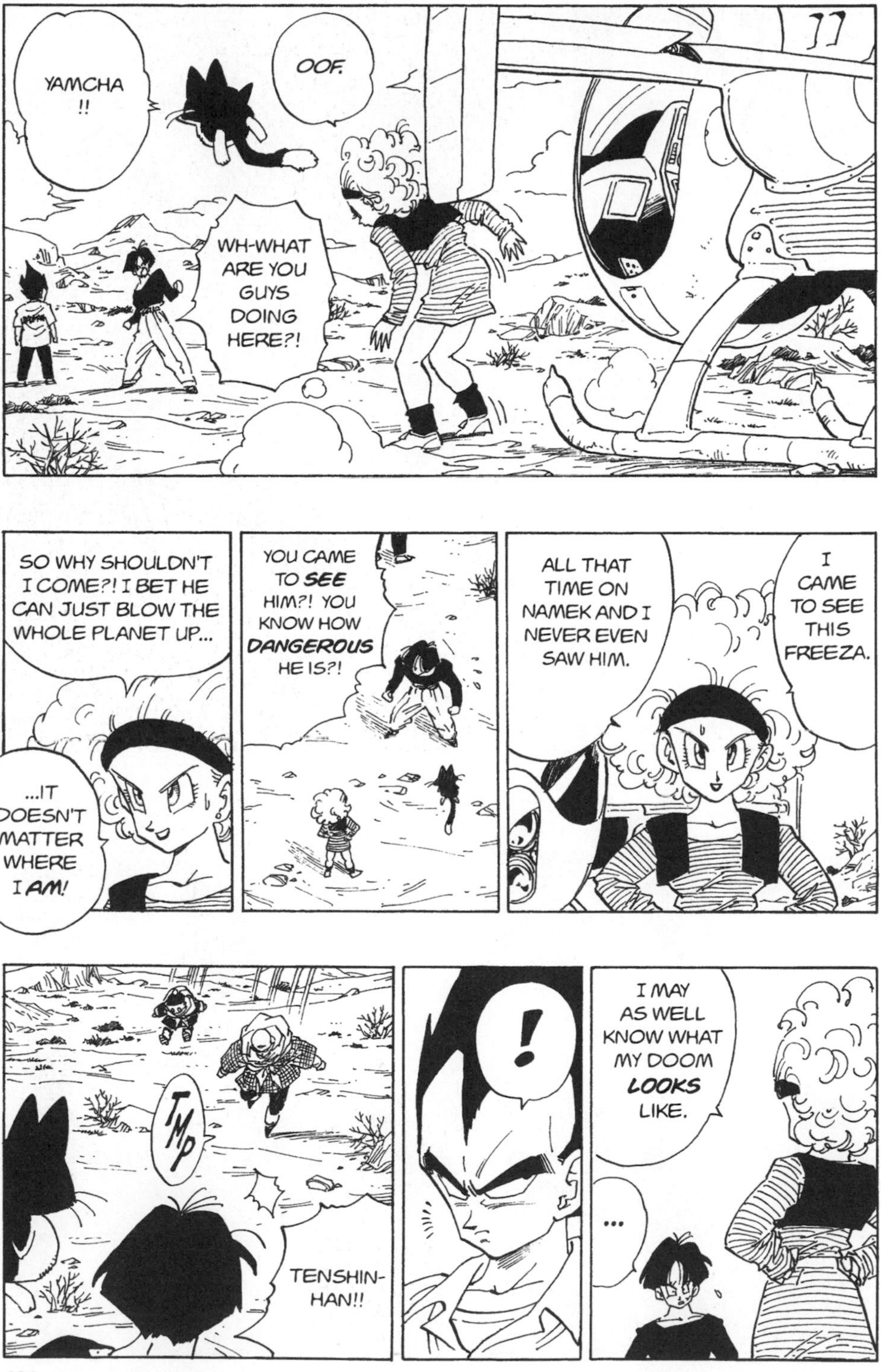

OOF.
YAMCHA !!
WH-WHAT ARE YOU GUYS DOING HERE?!
I CAME TO SEE THIS FREEZA.
ALL THAT TIME ON NAMEK AND I NEVER EVEN SAW HIM.
YOU CAME TO SEE HIM?! YOU KNOW HOW DANGEROUS HE IS?!
SO WHY SHOULDN'T I COME?! I BET HE CAN JUST BLOW THE WHOLE PLANET UP...
...IT DOESN'T MATTER WHERE I AM!
I MAY AS WELL KNOW WHAT MY DOOM LOOKS LIKE.
...
!
TMP
TENSHIN-HAN!!

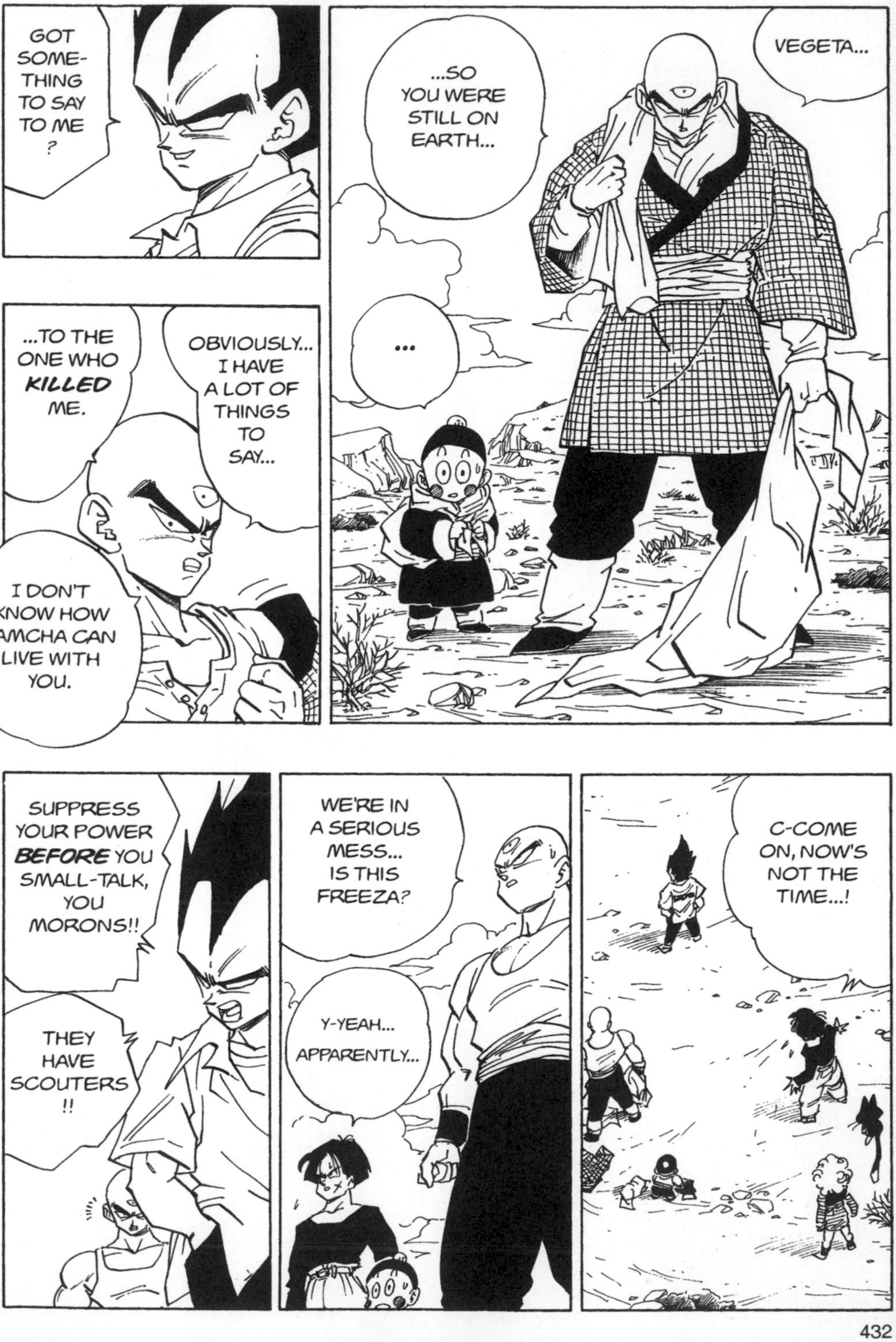
GOT SOMETHING TO SAY TO ME ?
VEGETA...
...SO YOU WERE STILL ON EARTH...
...
OBVIOUSLY... I HAVE A LOT OF THINGS TO SAY...
...TO THE ONE WHO KILLED ME.
I DON'T KNOW HOW YAMCHA CAN LIVE WITH YOU.
C-COME ON, NOW'S NOT THE TIME...!
WE'RE IN A SERIOUS MESS... IS THIS FREEZA?
Y-YEAH... APPARENTLY...
SUPPRESS YOUR POWER BEFORE YOU SMALL-TALK, YOU MORONS!!
THEY HAVE SCOUTERS !!

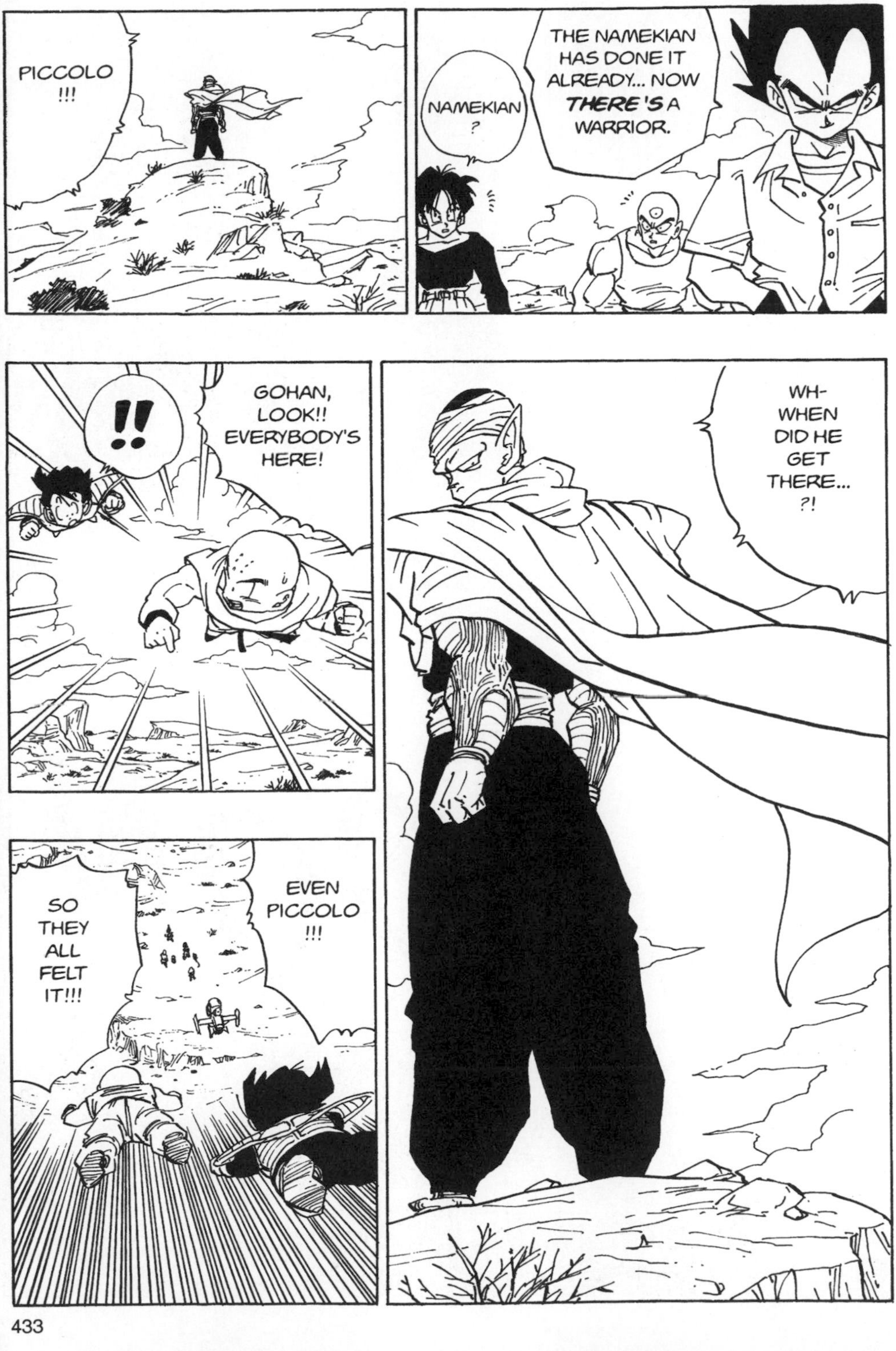
PICCOLO !!!
THE NAMEKIAN HAS DONE IT ALREADY... NOW THERE'S A WARRIOR.
NAMEKIAN ?
!!
GOHAN, LOOK!! EVERYBODY'S HERE!
SO THEY ALL FELT IT!!!
EVEN PICCOLO !!!
WH- WHEN DID HE GET THERE... ?!

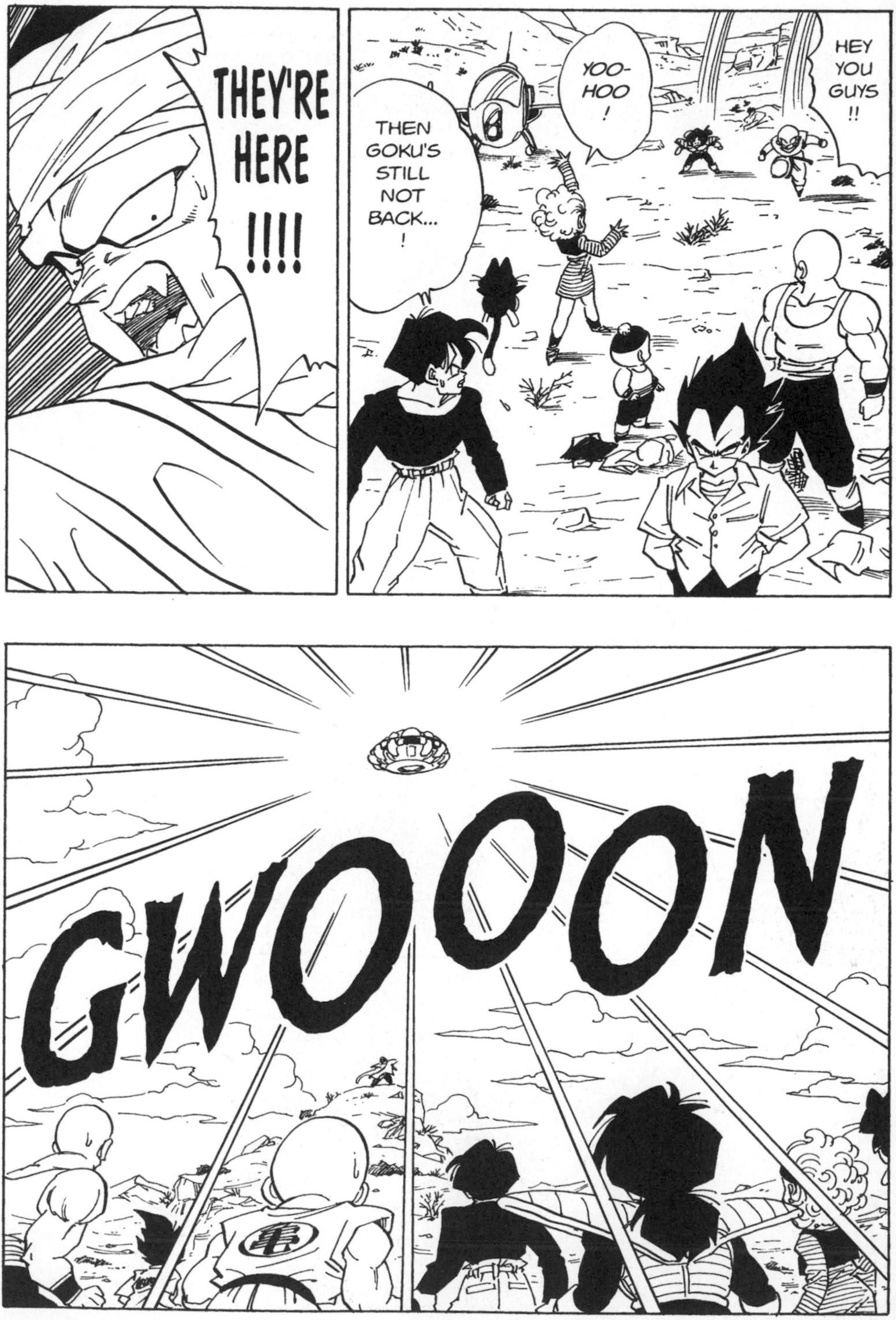
THEY'RE HERE !!!!
THEN GOKU'S STILL NOT BACK...!
YOO-HOO!
HEY YOU GUYS !!
GWOOON

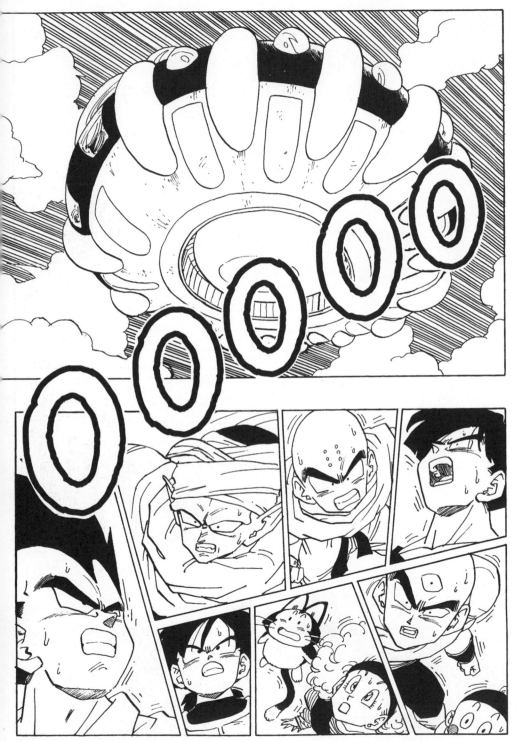

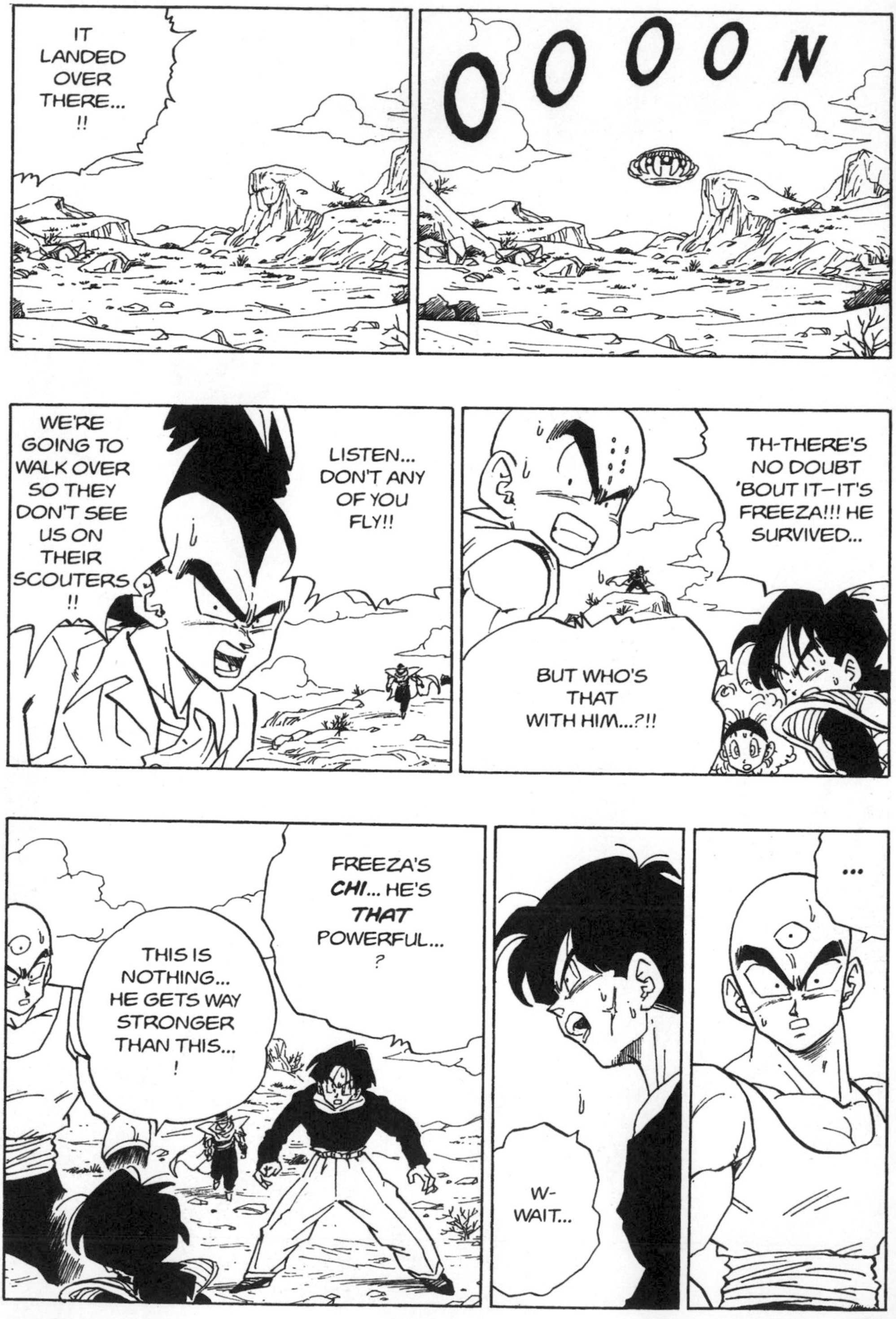
IT LANDED OVER THERE... !!
OOOON
WE'RE GOING TO WALK OVER SO THEY DON'T SEE US ON THEIR SCOUTERS !!
LISTEN... DON'T ANY OF YOU FLY!!
TH-THERE'S NO DOUBT 'BOUT IT—IT'S FREEZA!!! HE SURVIVED...
BUT WHO'S THAT WITH HIM...?!!
FREEZA'S CHI... HE'S THAT POWERFUL... ?
THIS IS NOTHING... HE GETS WAY STRONGER THAN THIS... !
W-WAIT...
...

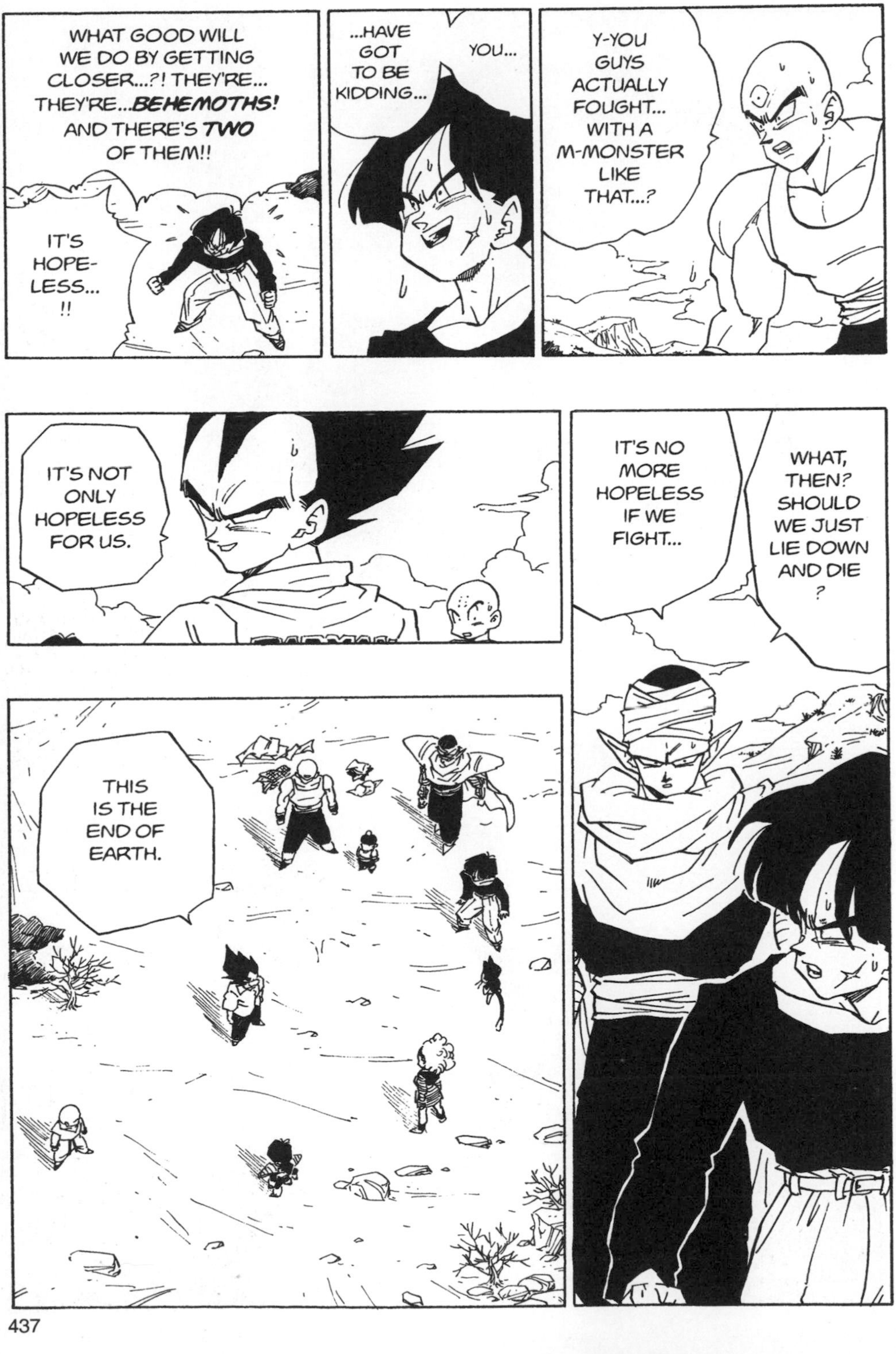
WHAT GOOD WILL WE DO BY GETTING CLOSER...?! THEY'RE... THEY'RE...**BEHEMOTHS!** AND THERE'S ***TWO*** OF THEM!!
IT'S HOPE-LESS... !!
...HAVE GOT TO BE KIDDING...
YOU...
Y-YOU GUYS ACTUALLY FOUGHT... WITH A M-MONSTER LIKE THAT...?
IT'S NOT ONLY HOPELESS FOR US.
THIS IS THE END OF EARTH.
IT'S NO MORE HOPELESS IF WE FIGHT...
WHAT, THEN? SHOULD WE JUST LIE DOWN AND DIE ?

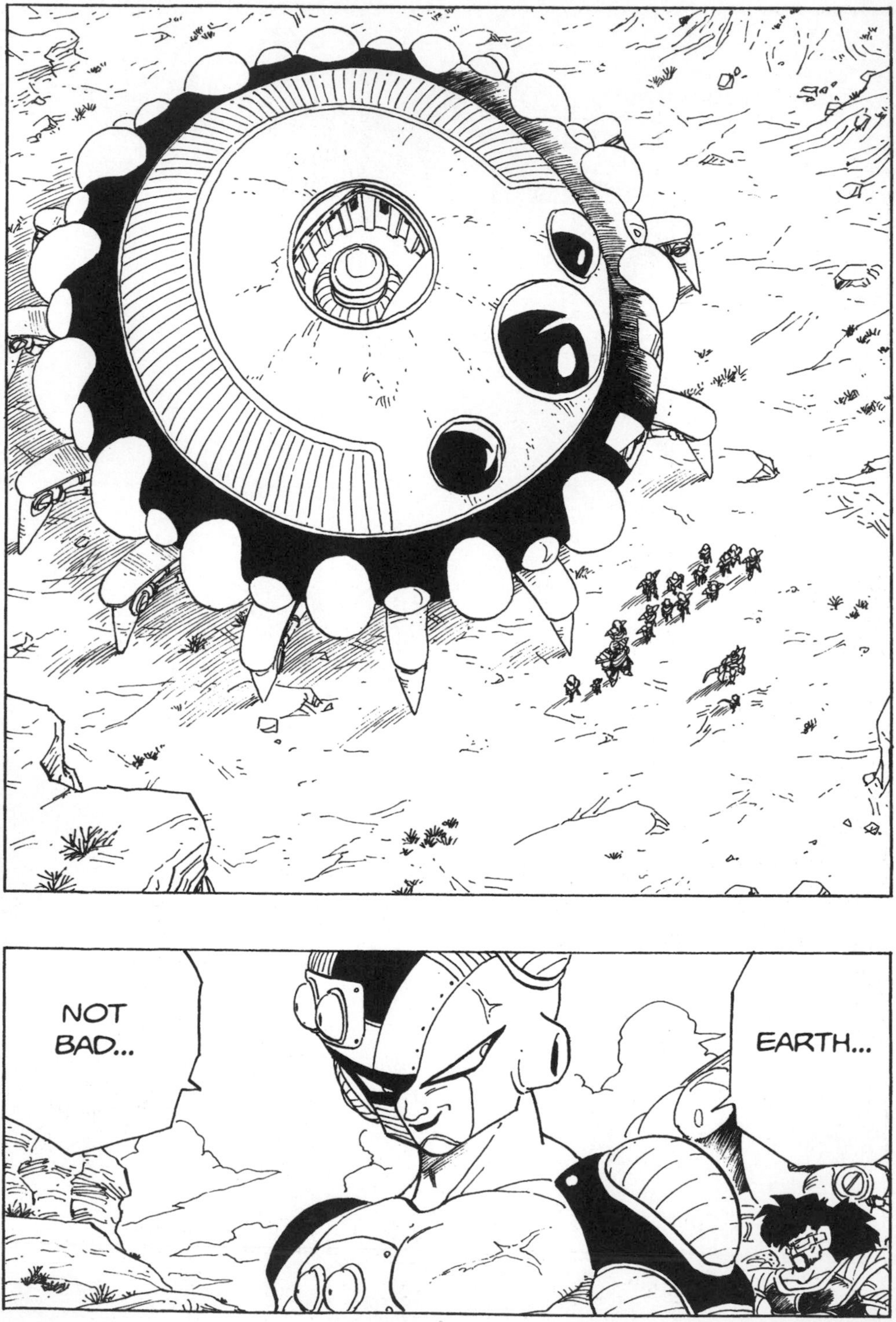
EARTH...
NOT BAD...

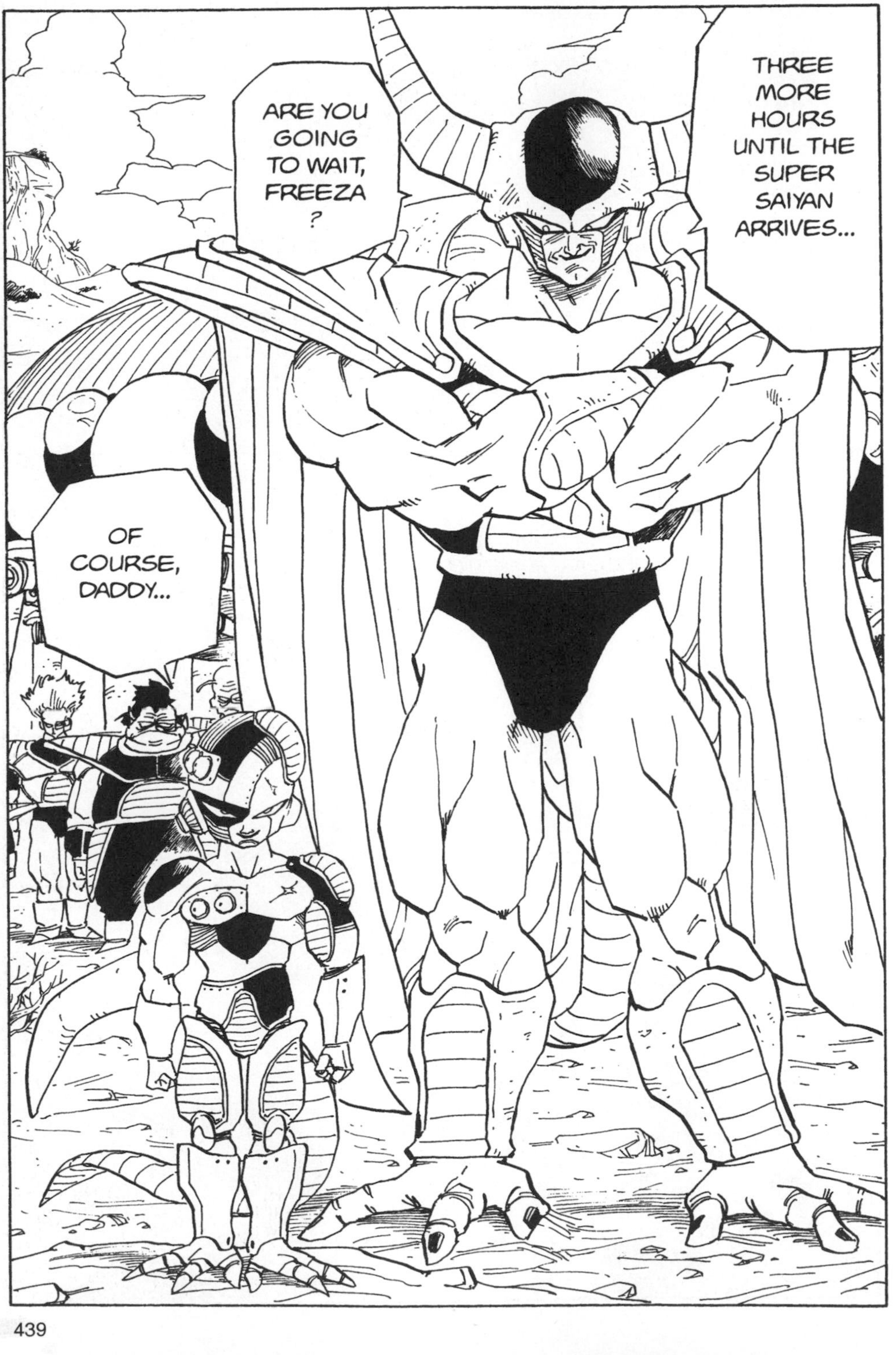
THREE MORE HOURS UNTIL THE SUPER SAIYAN ARRIVES...
ARE YOU GOING TO WAIT, FREEZA?
OF COURSE, DADDY...

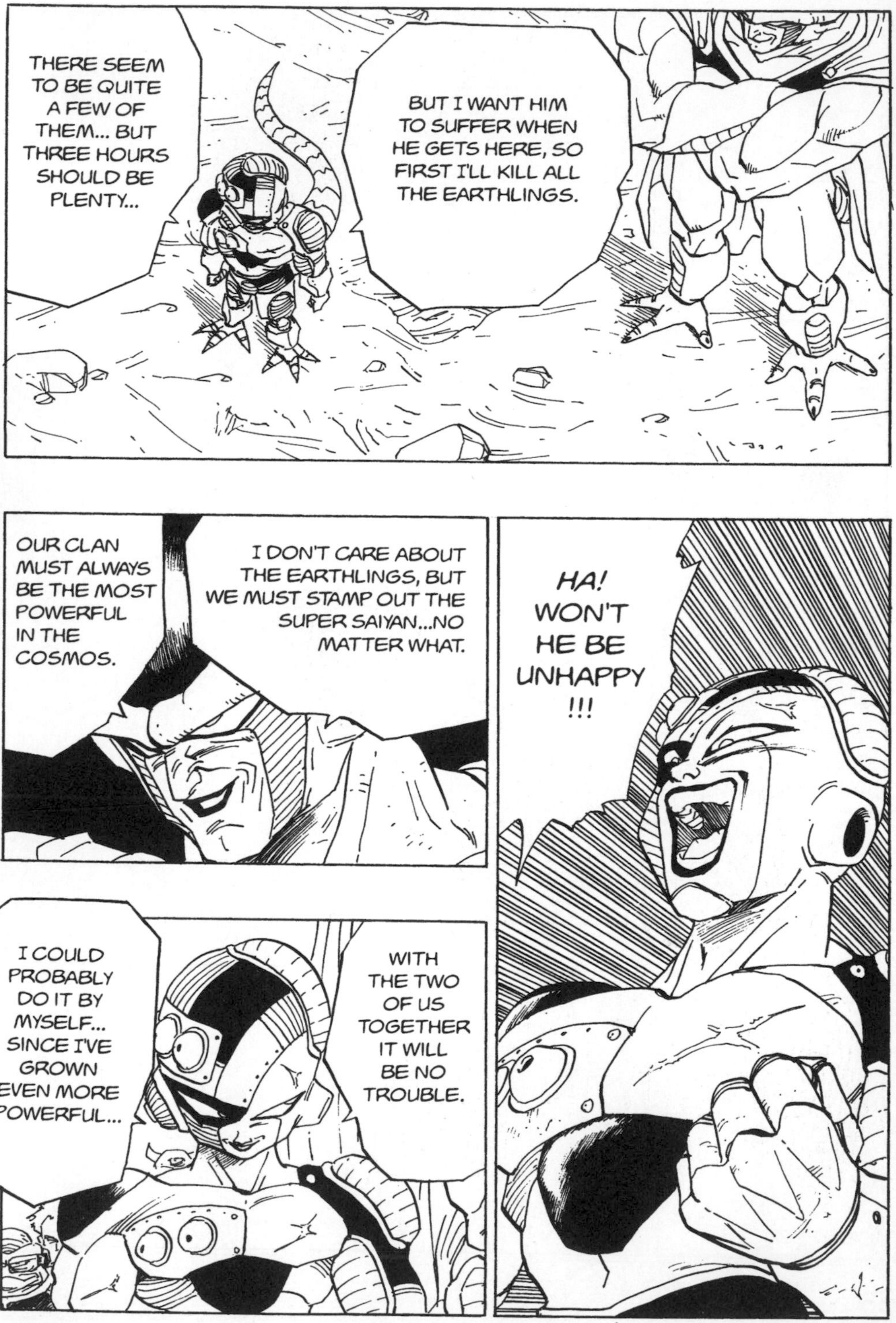

BUT I WANT HIM TO SUFFER WHEN HE GETS HERE, SO FIRST I'LL KILL ALL THE EARTHLINGS.
THERE SEEM TO BE QUITE A FEW OF THEM... BUT THREE HOURS SHOULD BE PLENTY...
HA! WON'T HE BE UNHAPPY!!!
I DON'T CARE ABOUT THE EARTHLINGS, BUT WE MUST STAMP OUT THE SUPER SAIYAN...NO MATTER WHAT.
OUR CLAN MUST ALWAYS BE THE MOST POWERFUL IN THE COSMOS.
WITH THE TWO OF US TOGETHER IT WILL BE NO TROUBLE.
I COULD PROBABLY DO IT BY MYSELF... SINCE I'VE GROWN EVEN MORE POWERFUL...

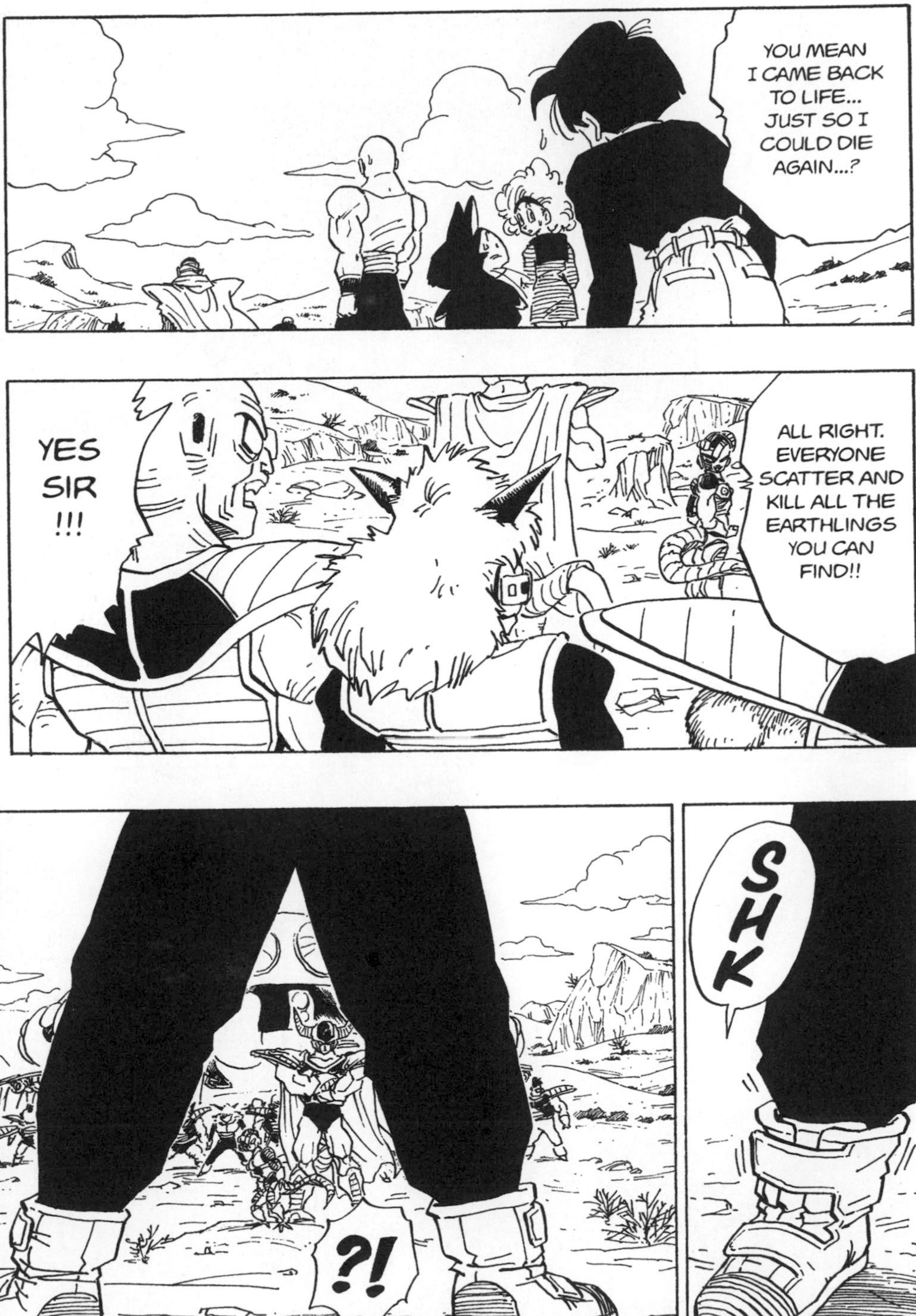
YOU MEAN I CAME BACK TO LIFE... JUST SO I COULD DIE AGAIN...?
ALL RIGHT. EVERYONE SCATTER AND KILL ALL THE EARTHLINGS YOU CAN FIND!!
YES SIR !!!
SHK
?!

DBZ: 137 • The Young Man of Mystery

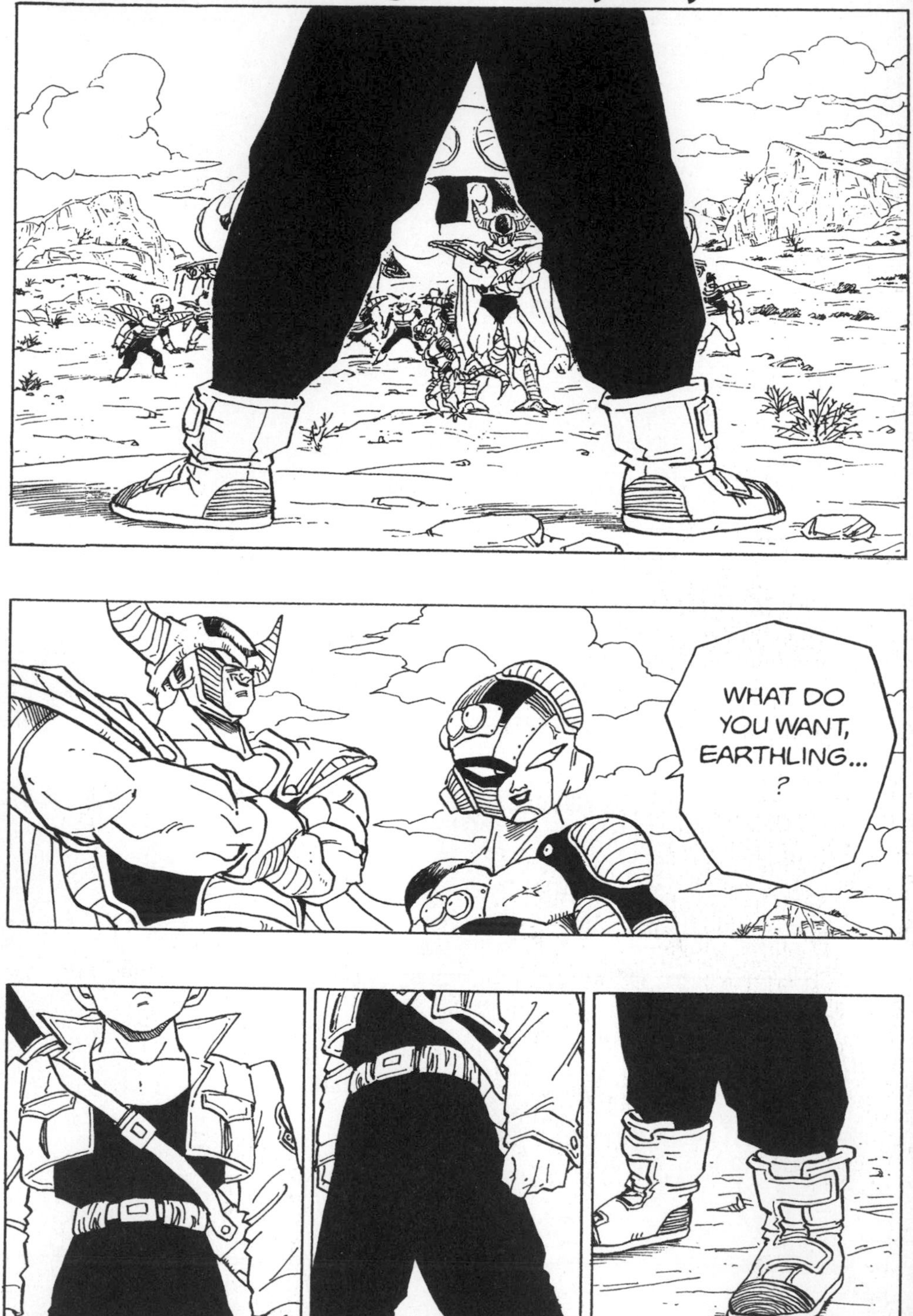
WHAT DO YOU WANT, EARTHLING... ?

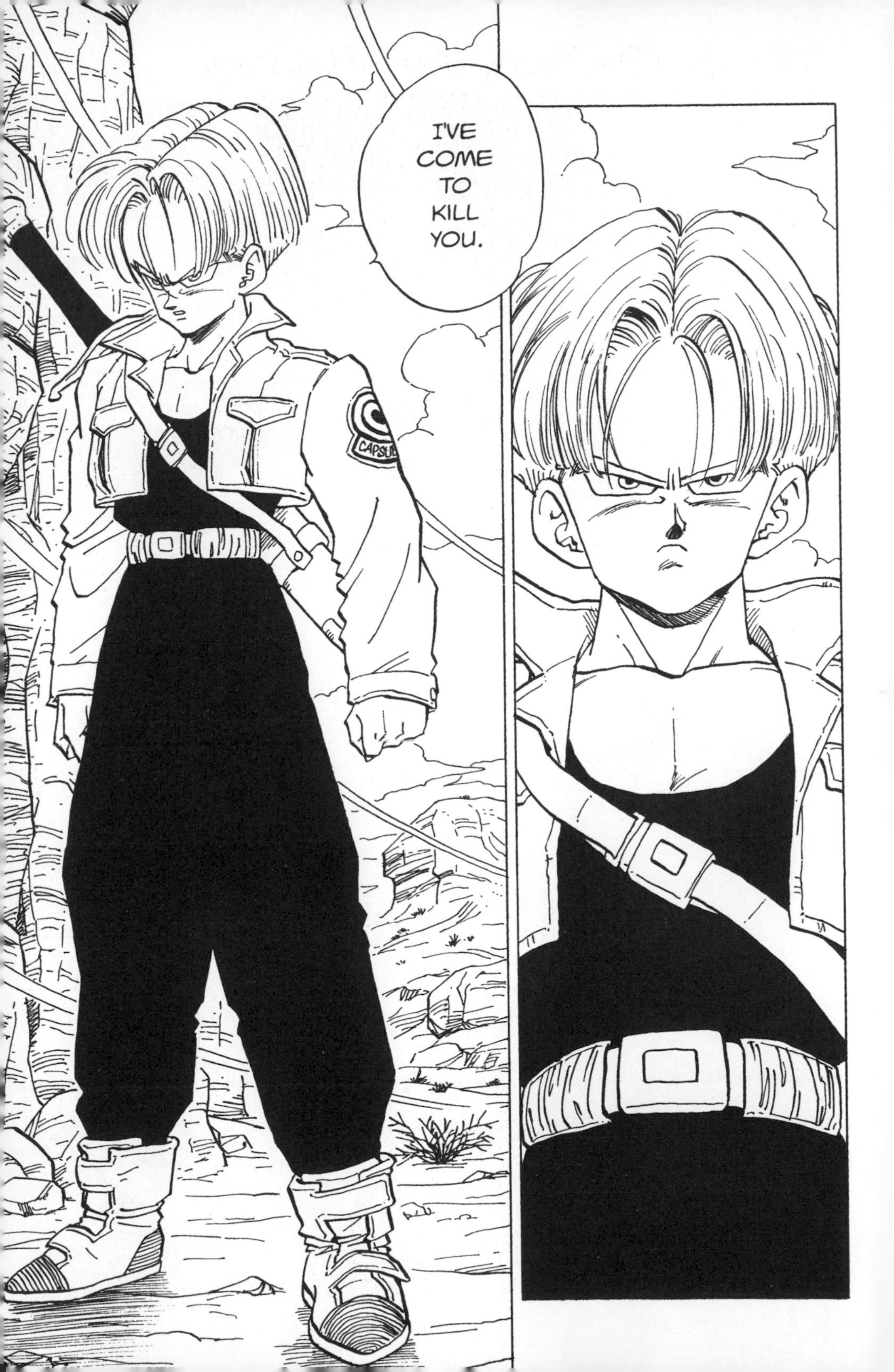
I'VE COME TO KILL YOU.
CAPSULE

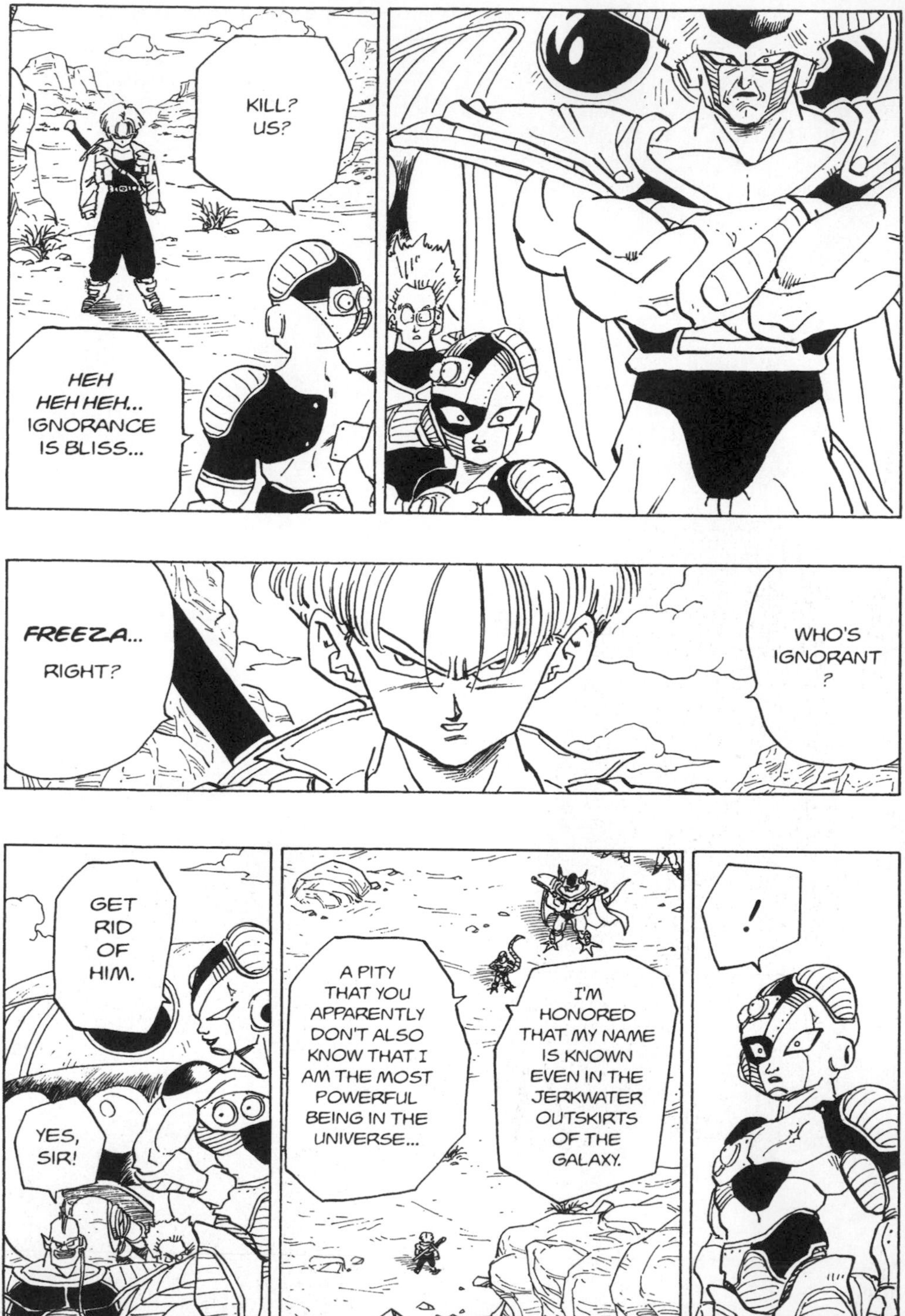
KILL? US?
HEH HEH HEH... IGNORANCE IS BLISS...
WHO'S IGNORANT ?
FREEZA... RIGHT?
!
I'M HONORED THAT MY NAME IS KNOWN EVEN IN THE JERKWATER OUTSKIRTS OF THE GALAXY.
A PITY THAT YOU APPARENTLY DON'T ALSO KNOW THAT I AM THE MOST POWERFUL BEING IN THE UNIVERSE...
GET RID OF HIM.
YES, SIR!

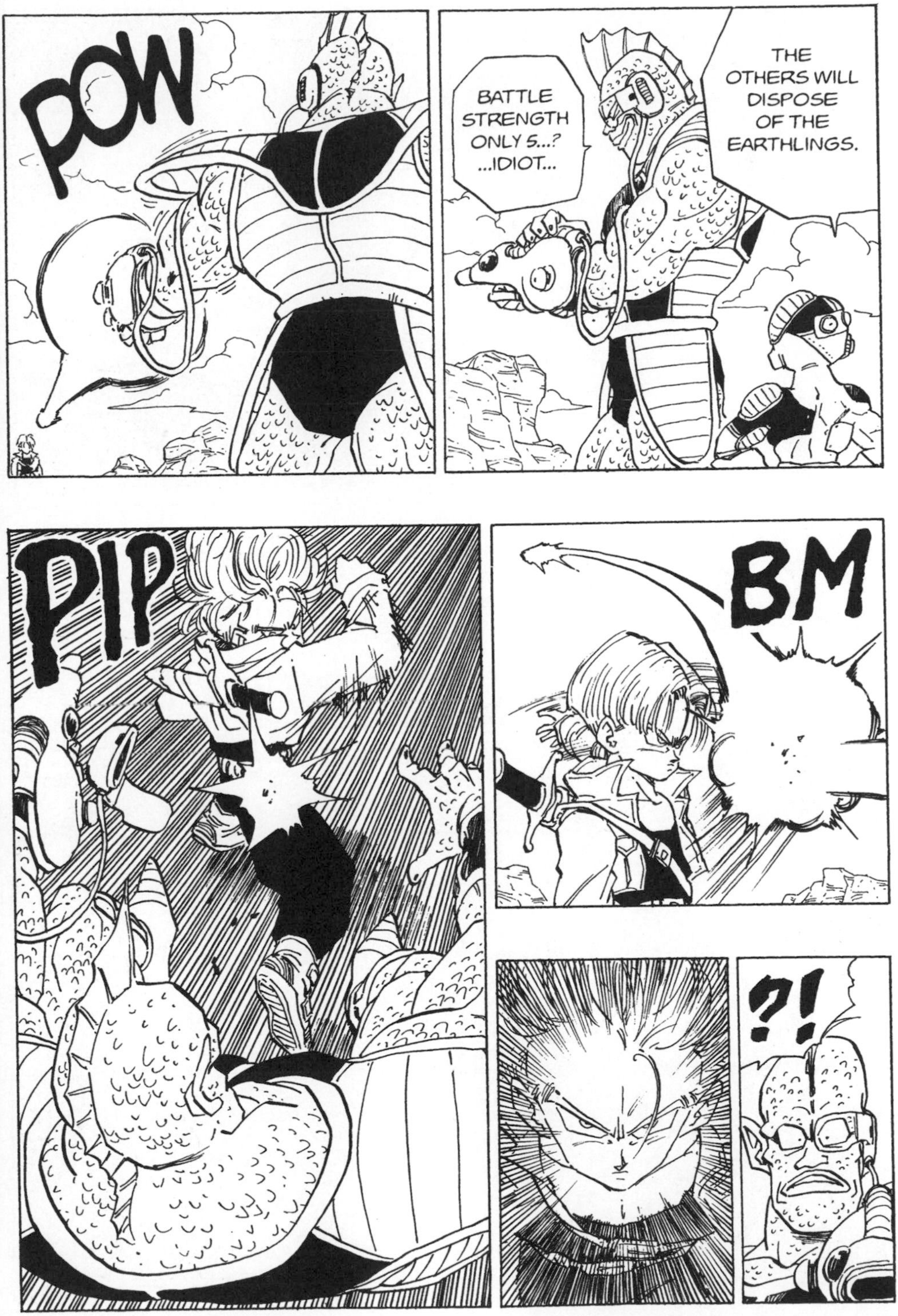
POW
BATTLE STRENGTH ONLY 5...? ...IDIOT...
THE OTHERS WILL DISPOSE OF THE EARTHLINGS.
PIP
BM
?!

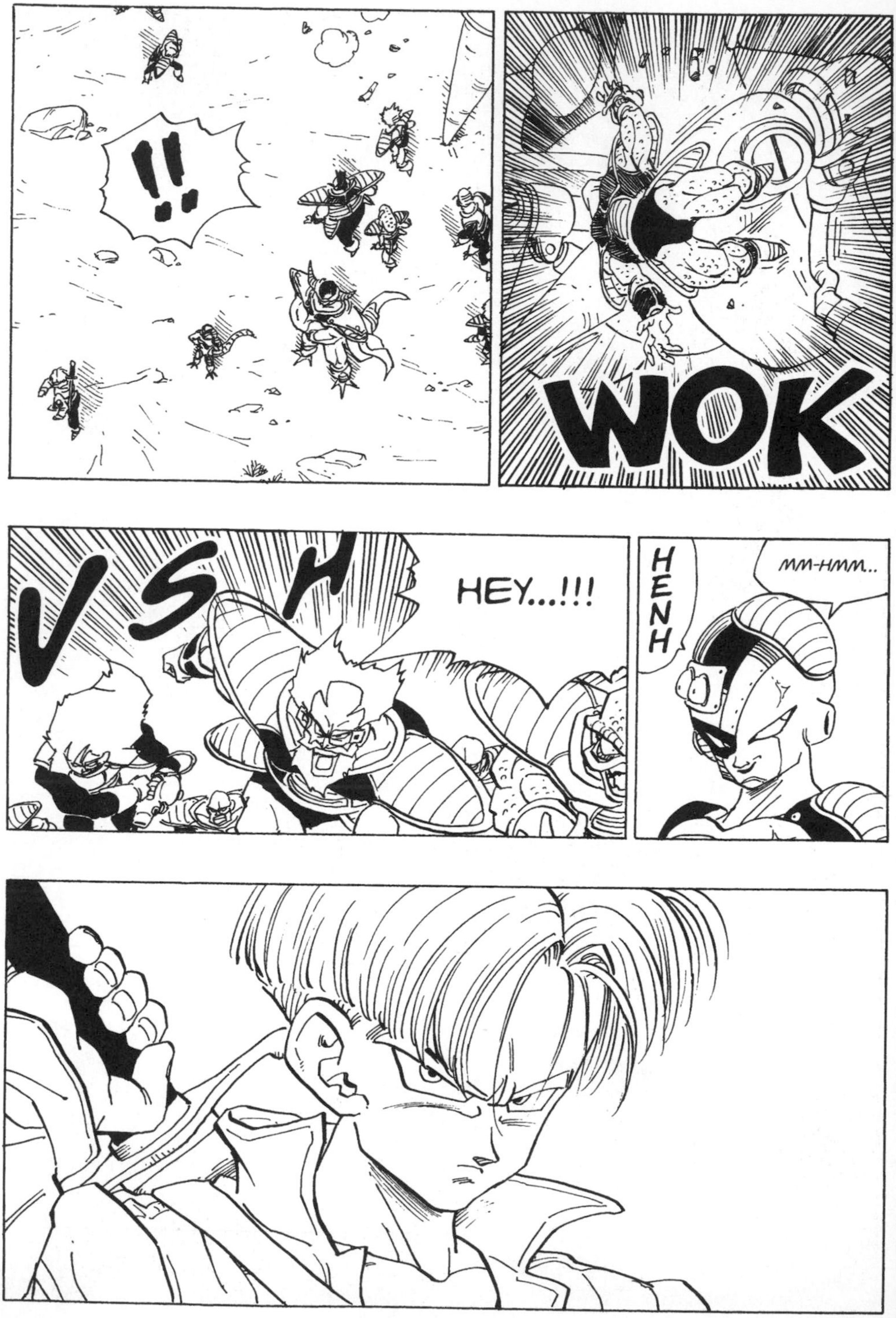
WOK
!!
MM-HMM..
HENH
HEY...!!!
VSH

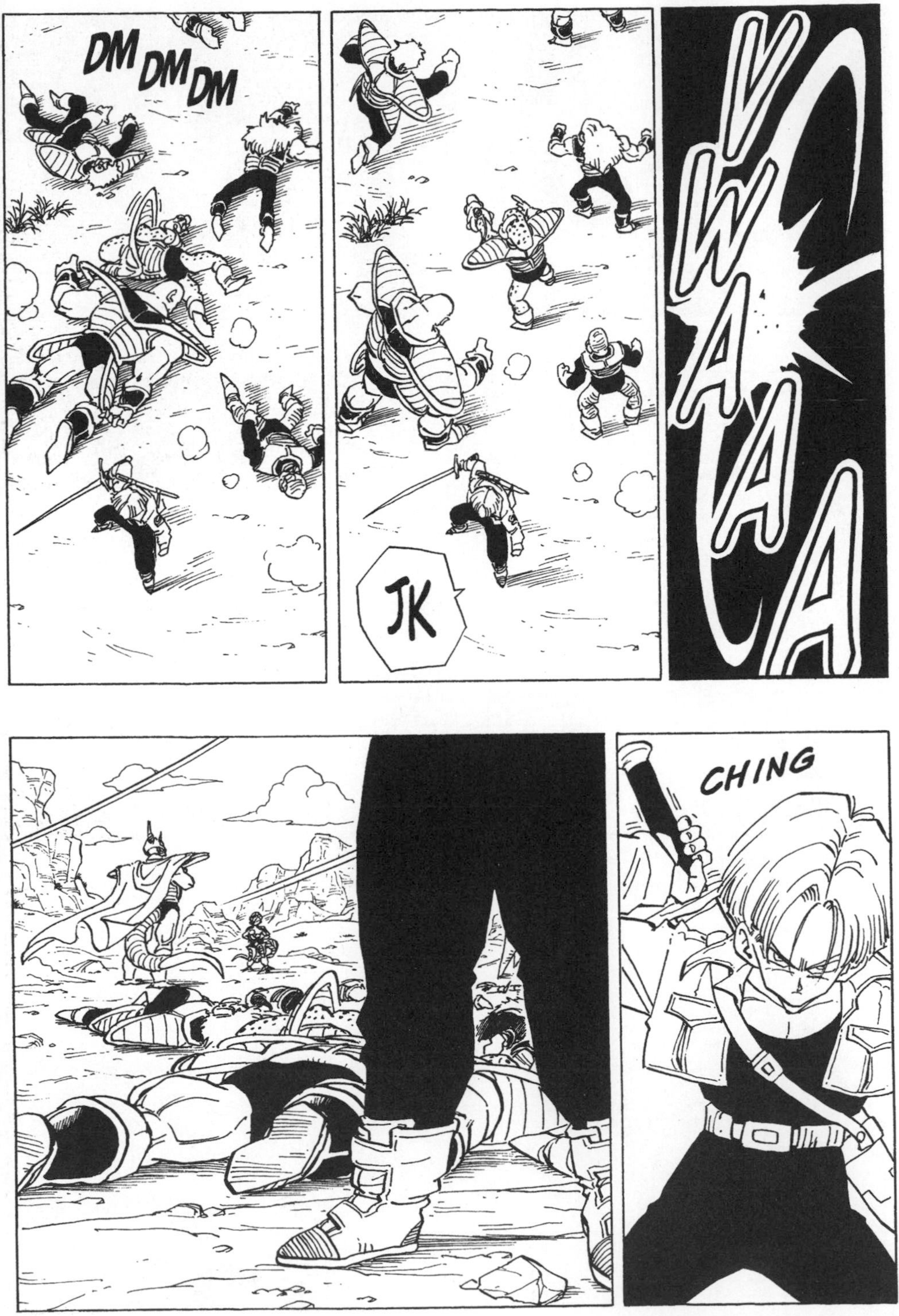
DM DM DM
JK
WAAAAA
CHING

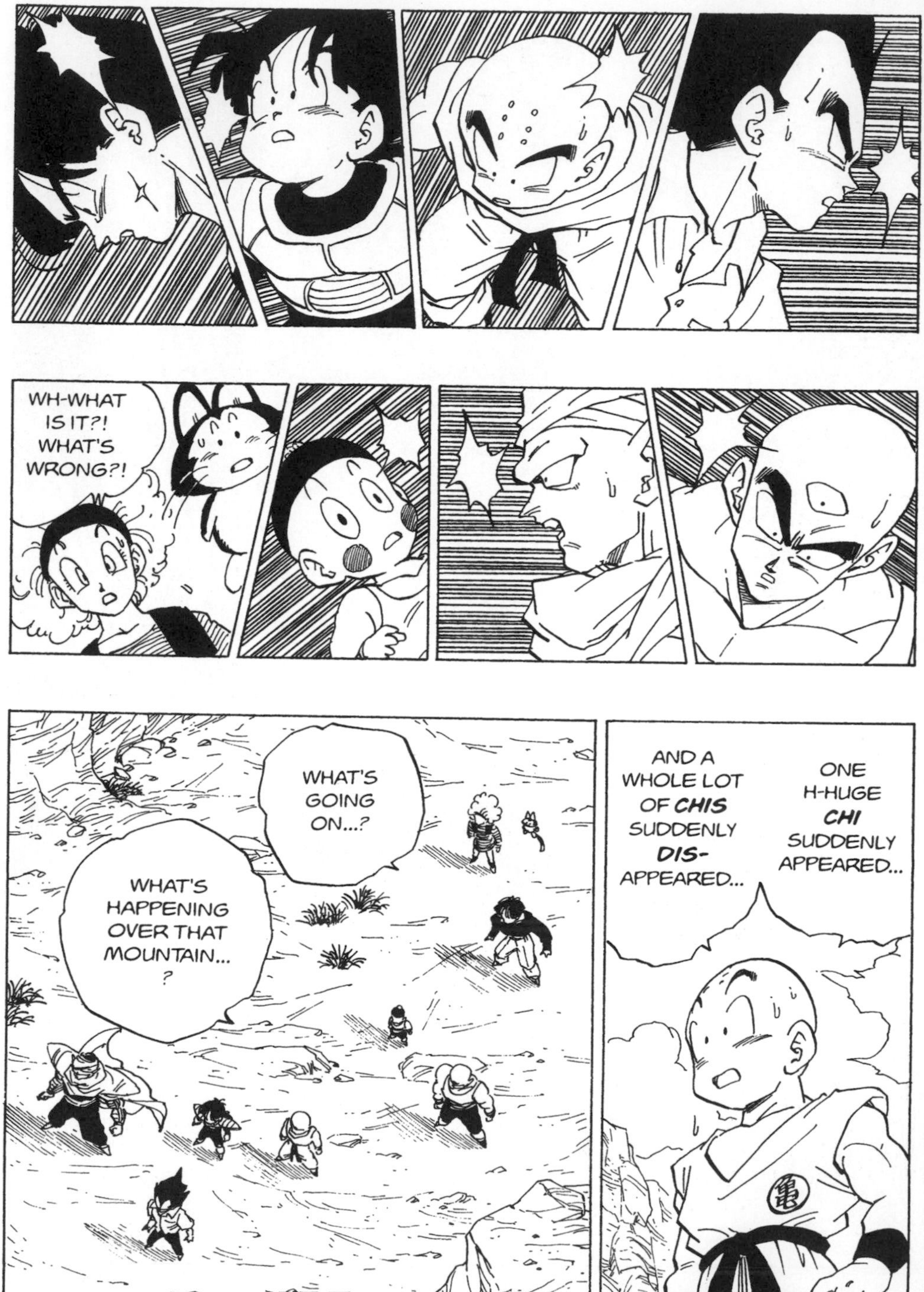
WH-WHAT IS IT?! WHAT'S WRONG?!
WHAT'S GOING ON...?
WHAT'S HAPPENING OVER THAT MOUNTAIN... ?
ONE H-HUGE CHI SUDDENLY APPEARED...
AND A WHOLE LOT OF CHIS SUDDENLY DIS-APPEARED...

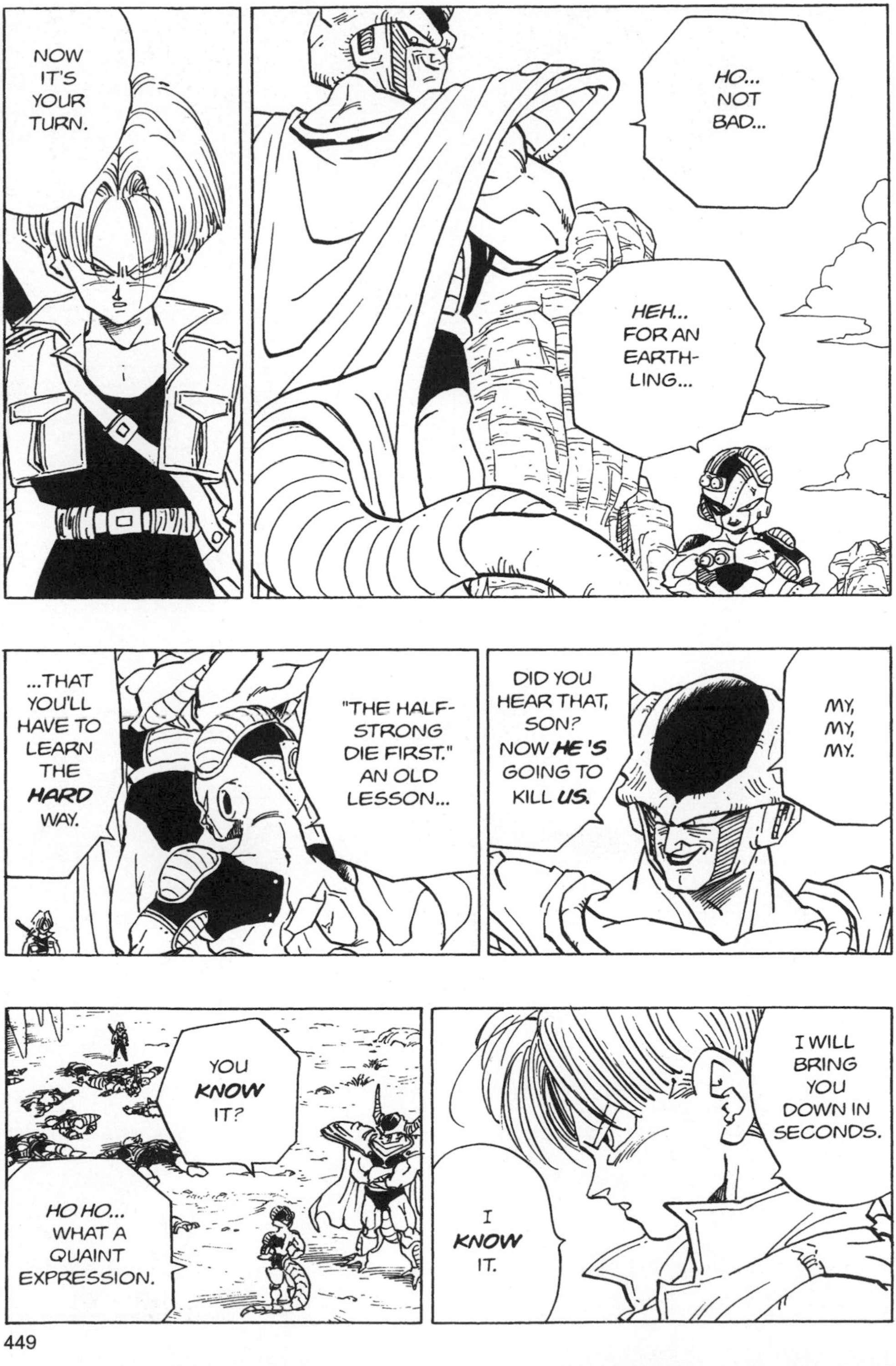
HO... NOT BAD...
HEH... FOR AN EARTHLING...
NOW IT'S YOUR TURN.
MY, MY, MY.
DID YOU HEAR THAT, SON? NOW **HE'S** GOING TO KILL **US.**
"THE HALF-STRONG DIE FIRST." AN OLD LESSON...
...THAT YOU'LL HAVE TO LEARN THE **HARD** WAY.
I WILL BRING YOU DOWN IN SECONDS.
I **KNOW** IT.
YOU **KNOW** IT?
HO HO... WHAT A QUAINT EXPRESSION.

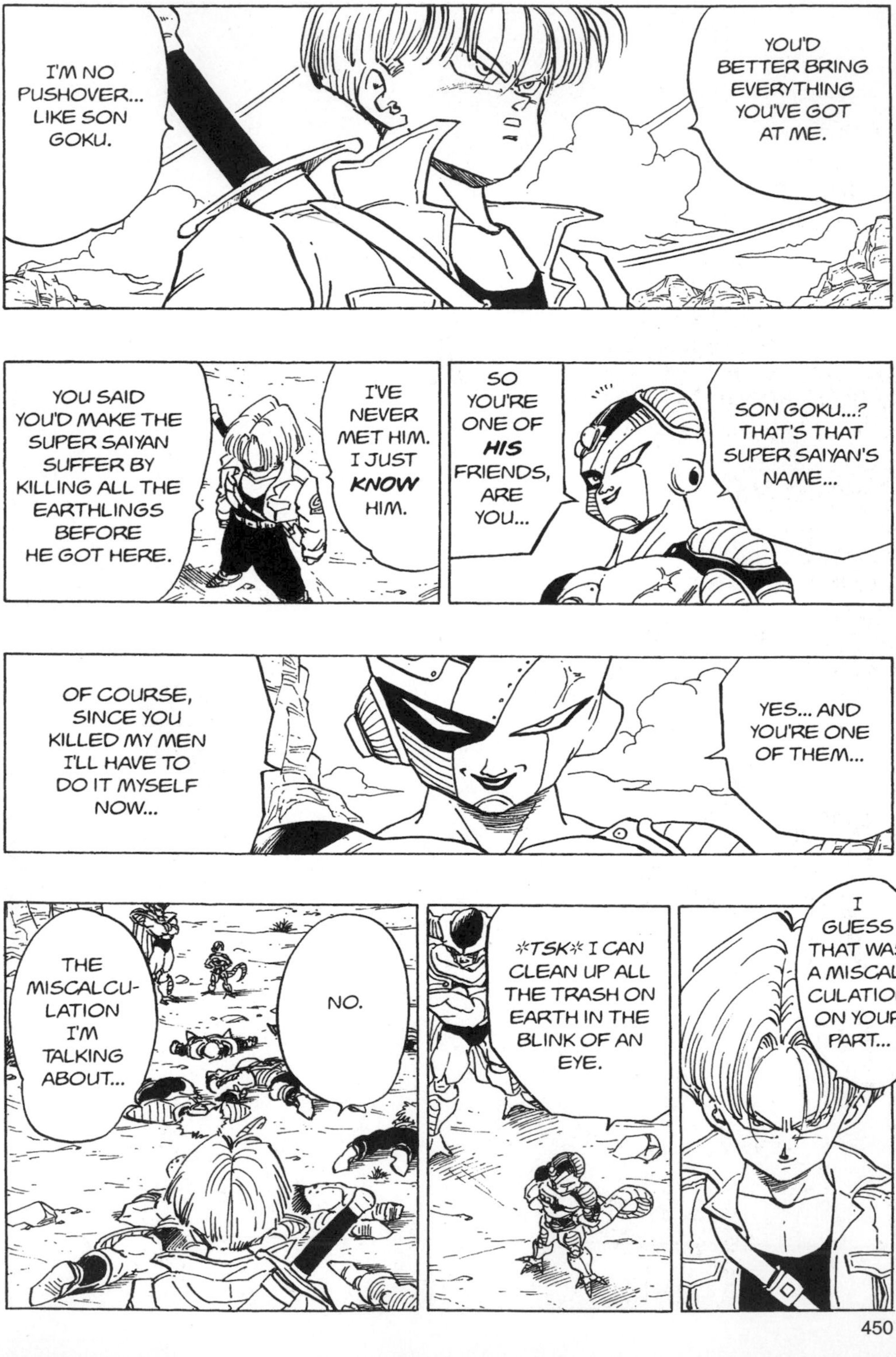
YOU'D BETTER BRING EVERYTHING YOU'VE GOT AT ME.
I'M NO PUSHOVER... LIKE SON GOKU.
SON GOKU...? THAT'S THAT SUPER SAIYAN'S NAME...
SO YOU'RE ONE OF **HIS** FRIENDS, ARE YOU...
I'VE NEVER MET HIM. I JUST ***KNOW*** HIM.
YOU SAID YOU'D MAKE THE SUPER SAIYAN SUFFER BY KILLING ALL THE EARTHLINGS BEFORE HE GOT HERE.
YES... AND YOU'RE ONE OF THEM...
OF COURSE, SINCE YOU KILLED MY MEN I'LL HAVE TO DO IT MYSELF NOW...
I GUESS THAT WAS A MISCAL-CULATION ON YOUR PART...
TSK I CAN CLEAN UP ALL THE TRASH ON EARTH IN THE BLINK OF AN EYE.
NO.
THE MISCALCU-LATION I'M TALKING ABOUT...

...WAS THINKING THAT SON GOKU IS THE ONLY SUPER SAIYAN...

...WHEN THERE'S ANOTHER ONE RIGHT HERE !!

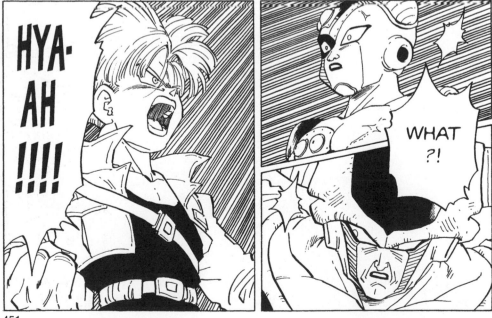

HYA-AH !!!!

WHAT ?!

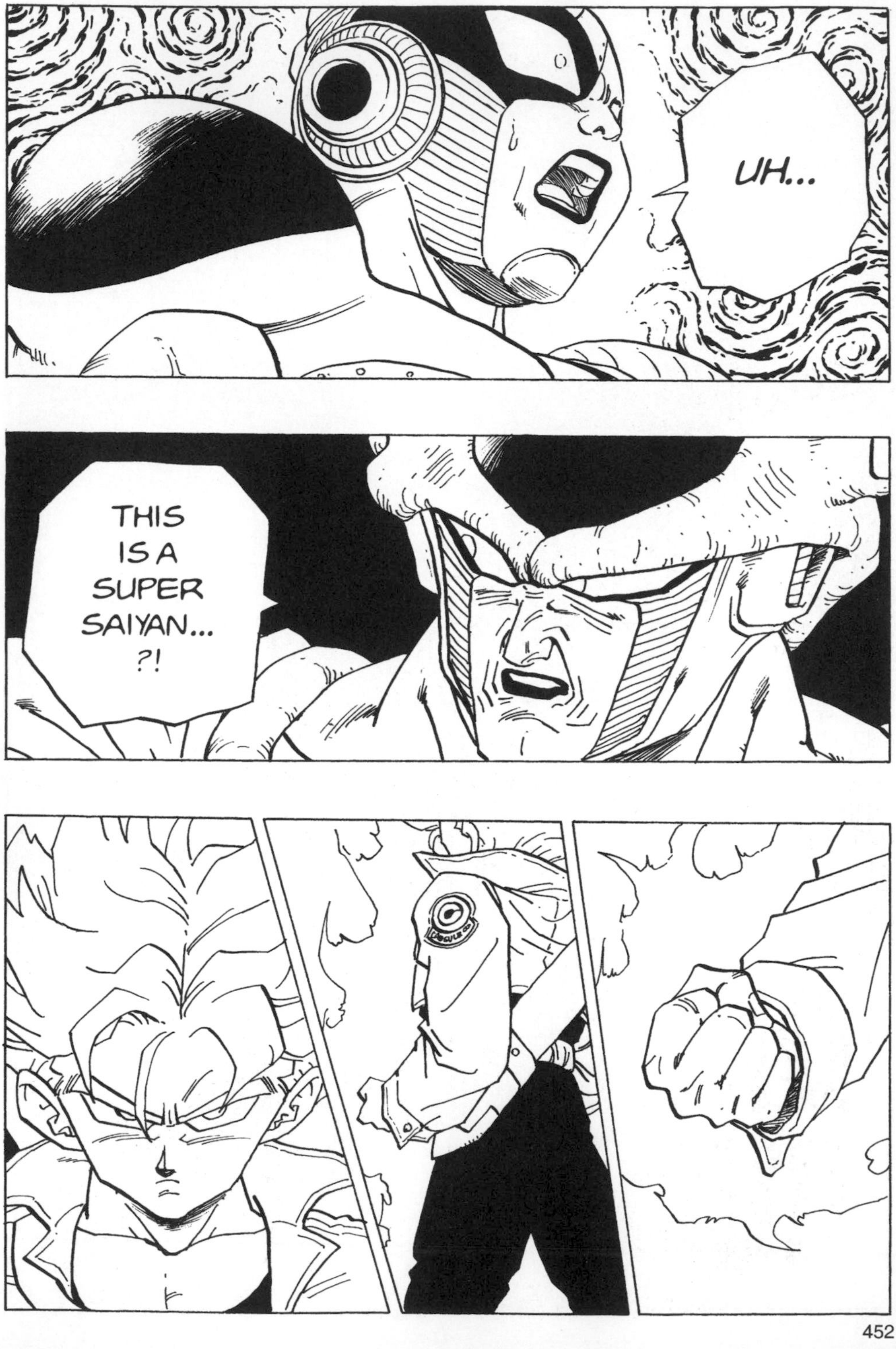
UH...
THIS IS A SUPER SAIYAN... ?!

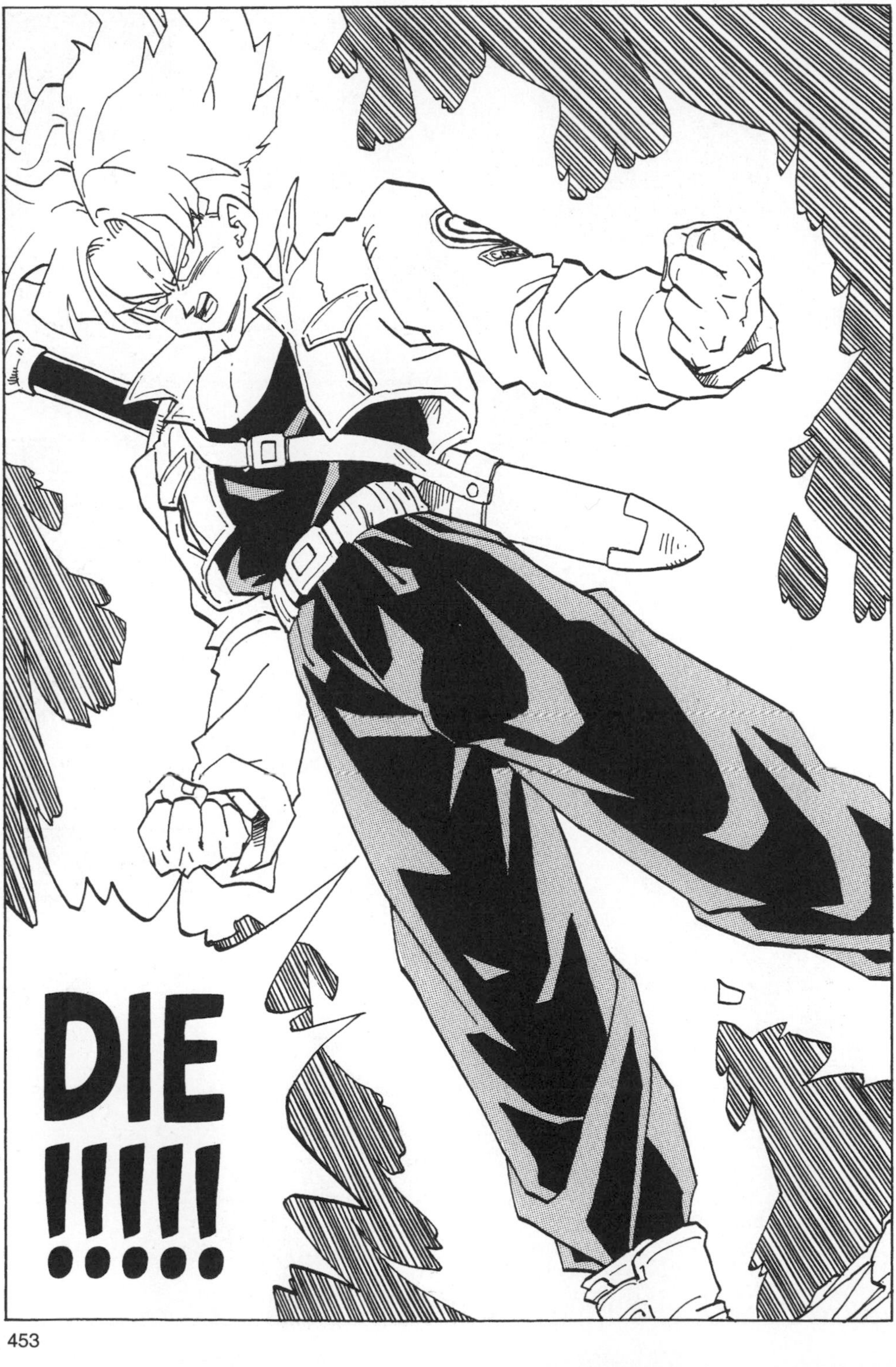
DIE
!!!!!

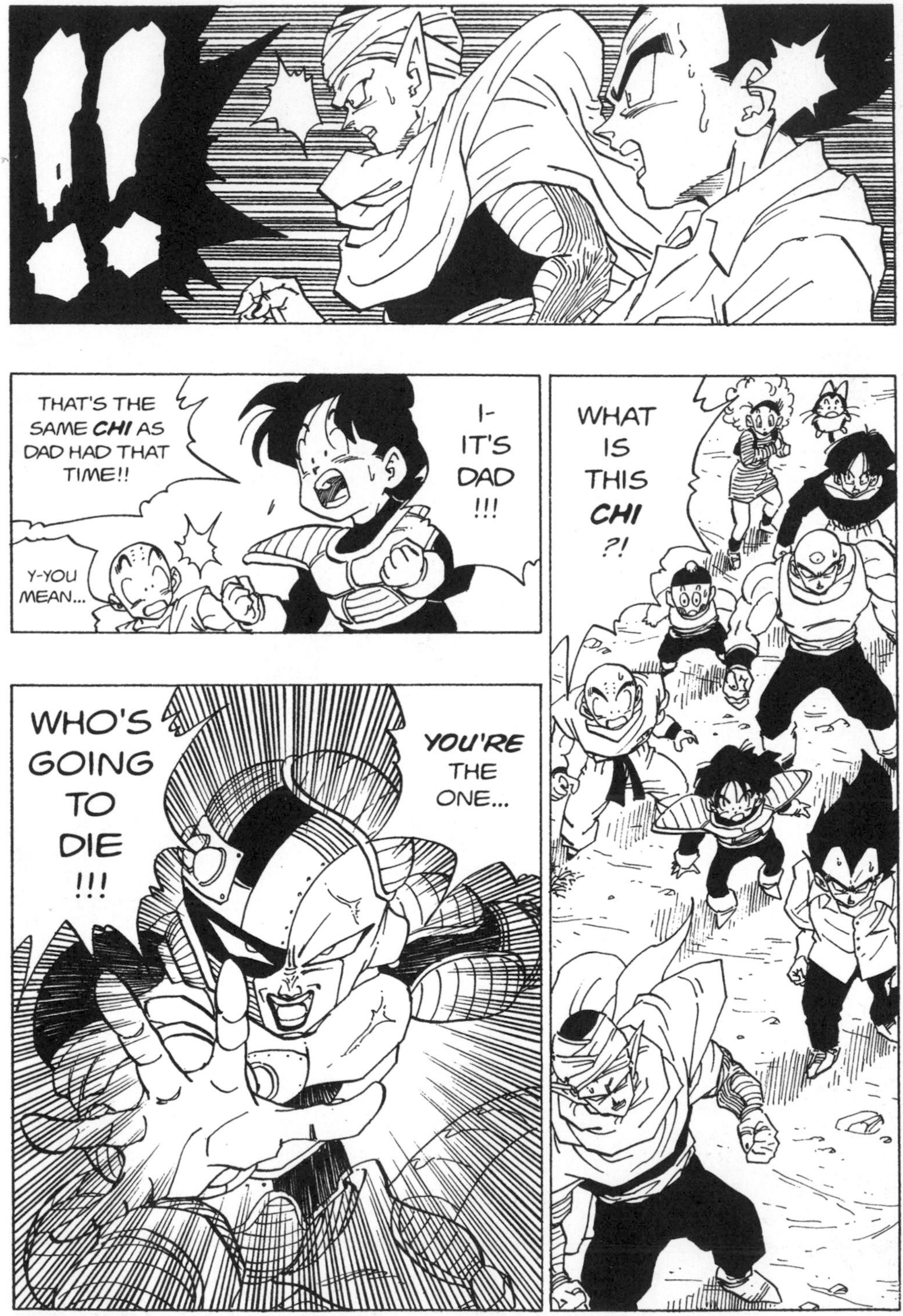
WHAT IS THIS **CHI** ?!
I- IT'S DAD !!!
THAT'S THE SAME **CHI** AS DAD HAD THAT TIME!!
Y-YOU MEAN...
WHO'S GOING TO DIE !!!
YOU'RE THE ONE...

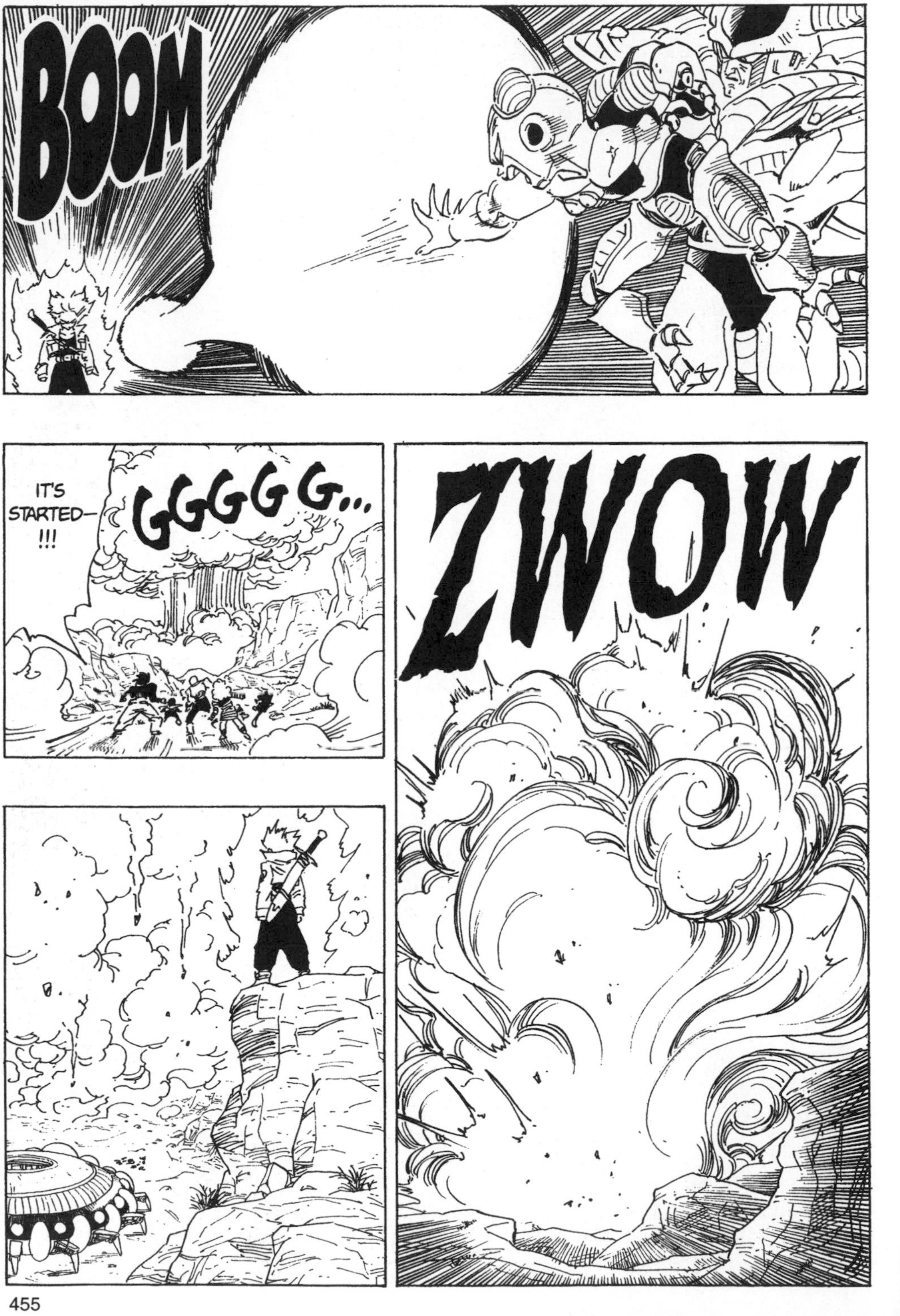
BOOM
IT'S STARTED—!!!
GGGGG...
ZWOW

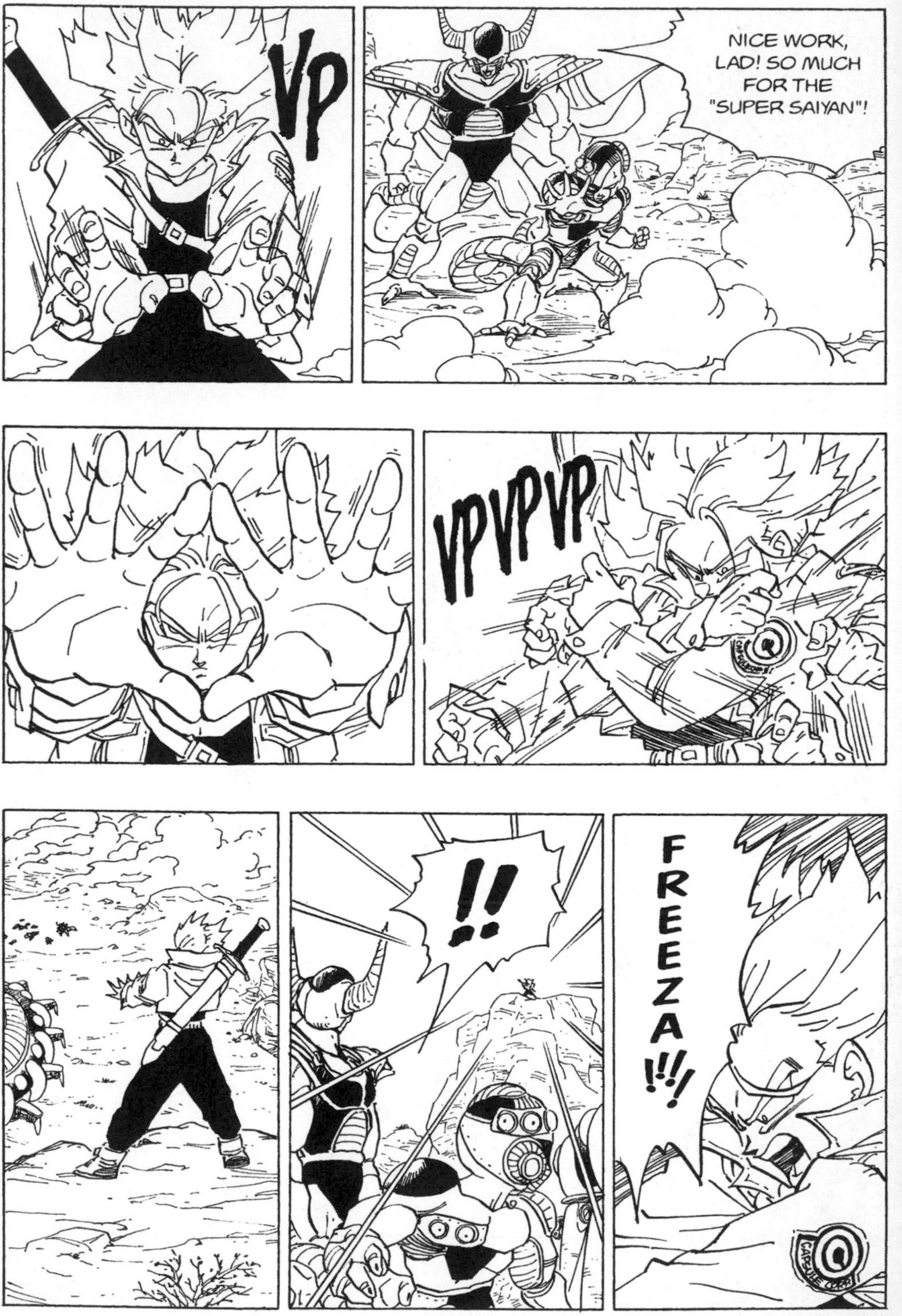
VP
NICE WORK, LAD! SO MUCH FOR THE "SUPER SAIYAN"!
VPVPVP
!!
FREEZA!!!

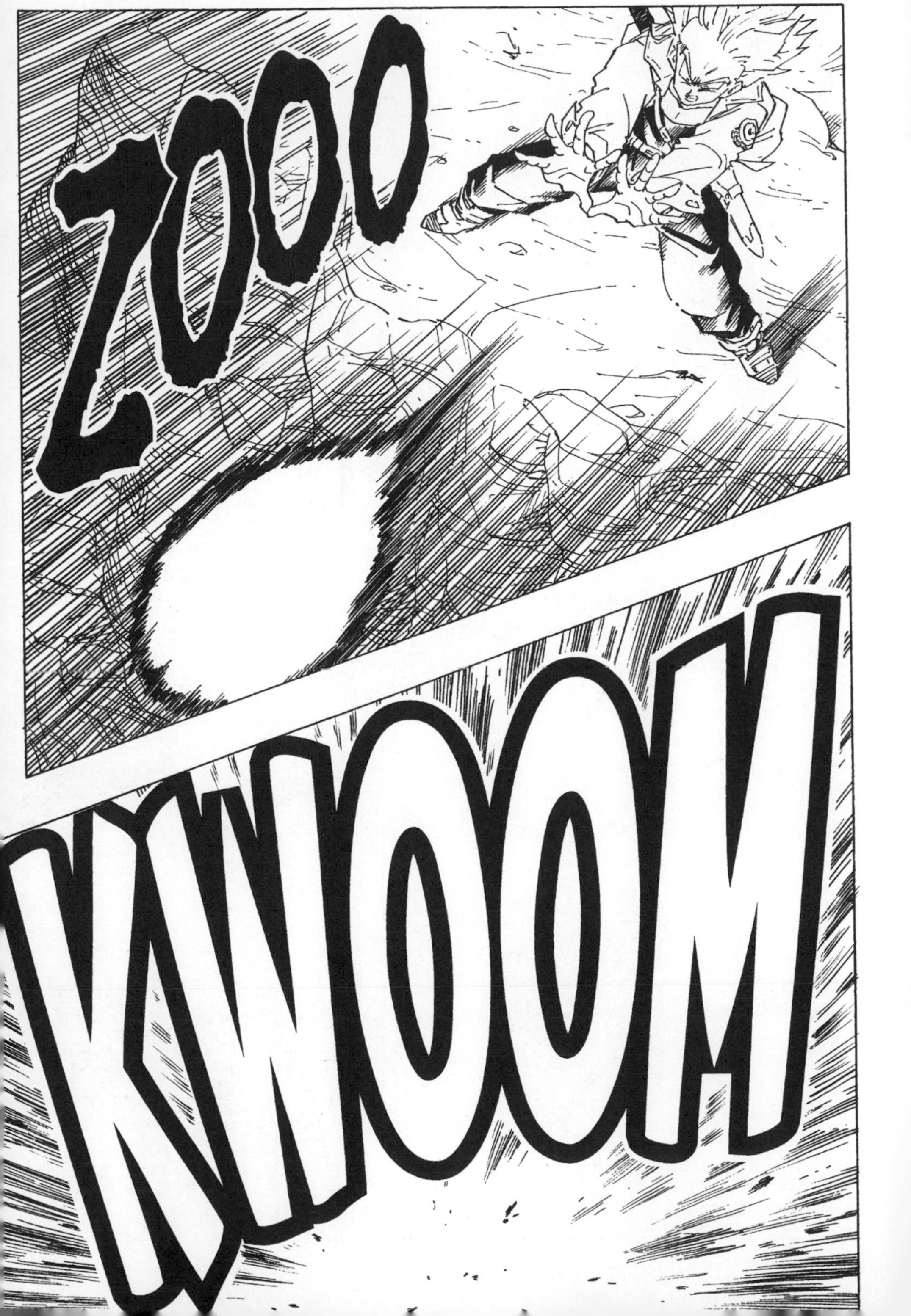
ZOOO
KWOOM

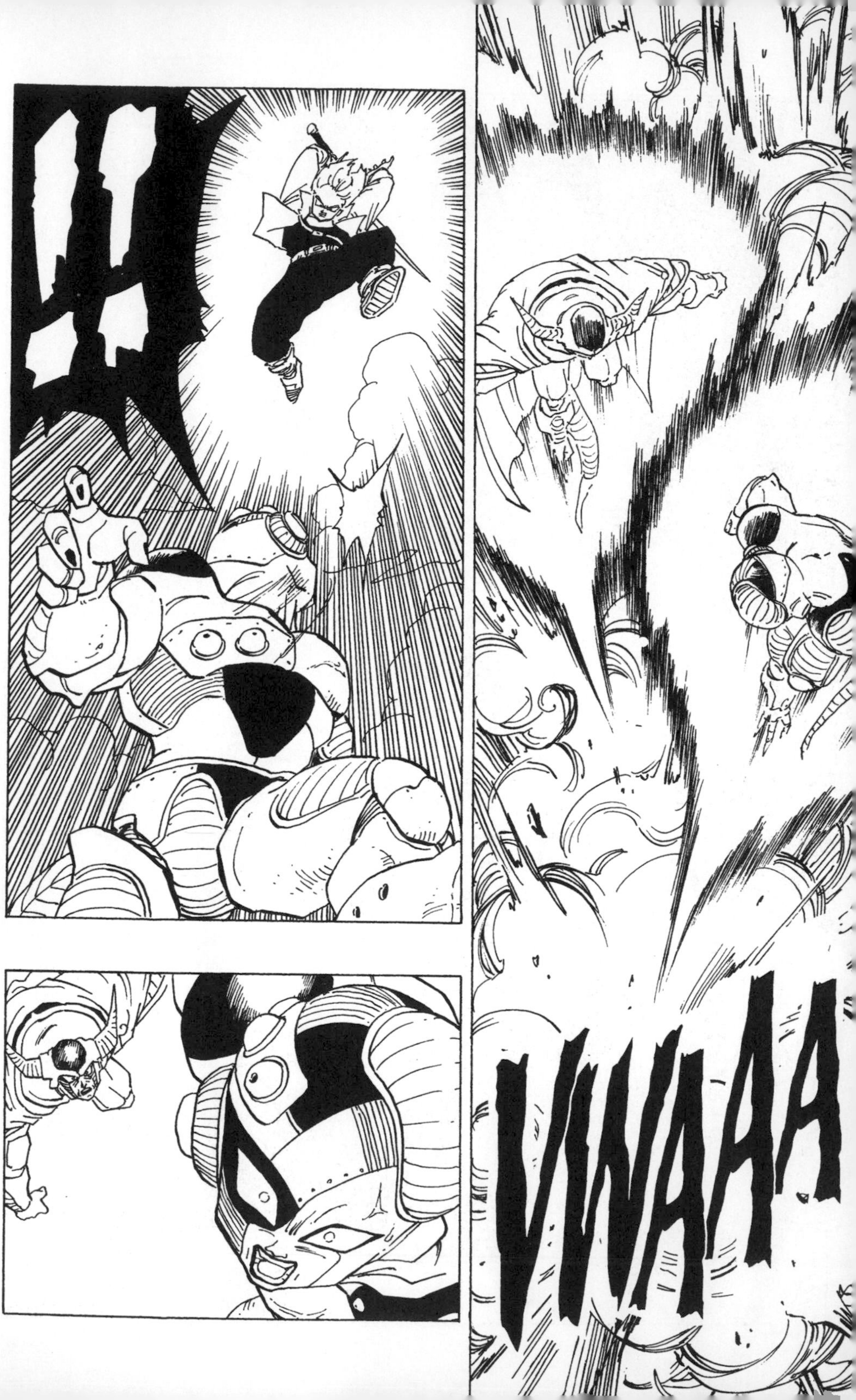
!!
VWAAA

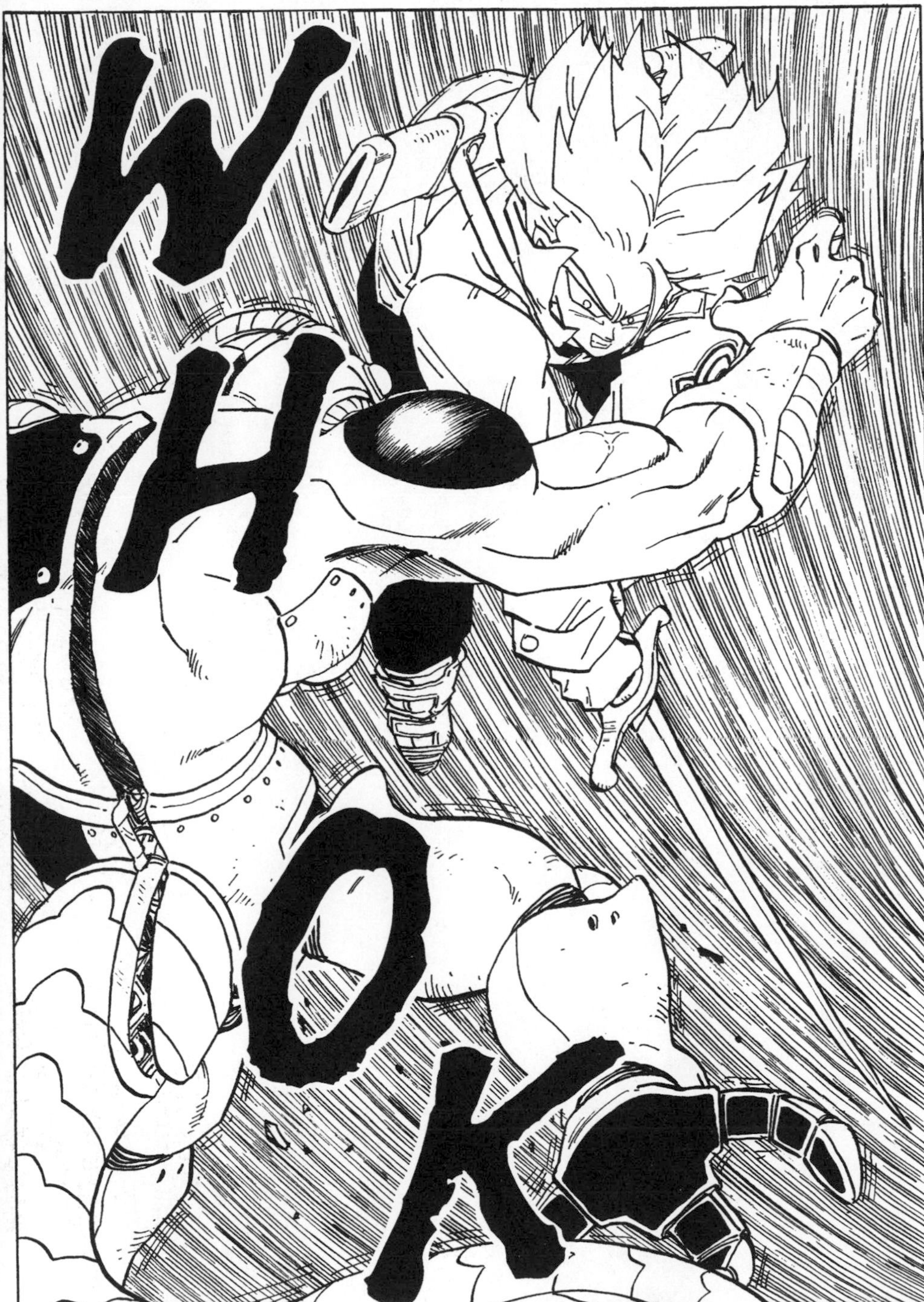
WHOK

DBZ:138 • The Second Super Saiyan

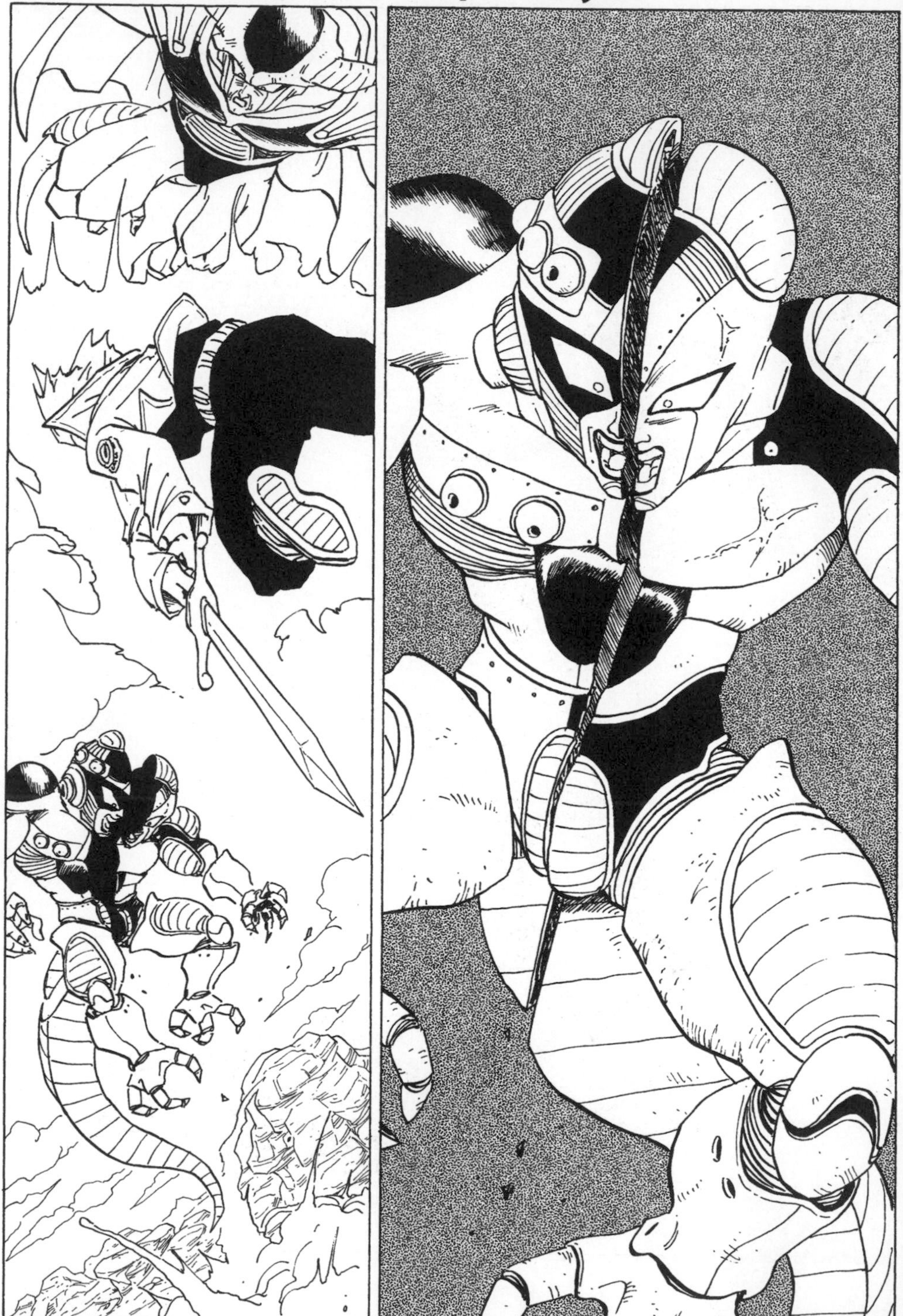

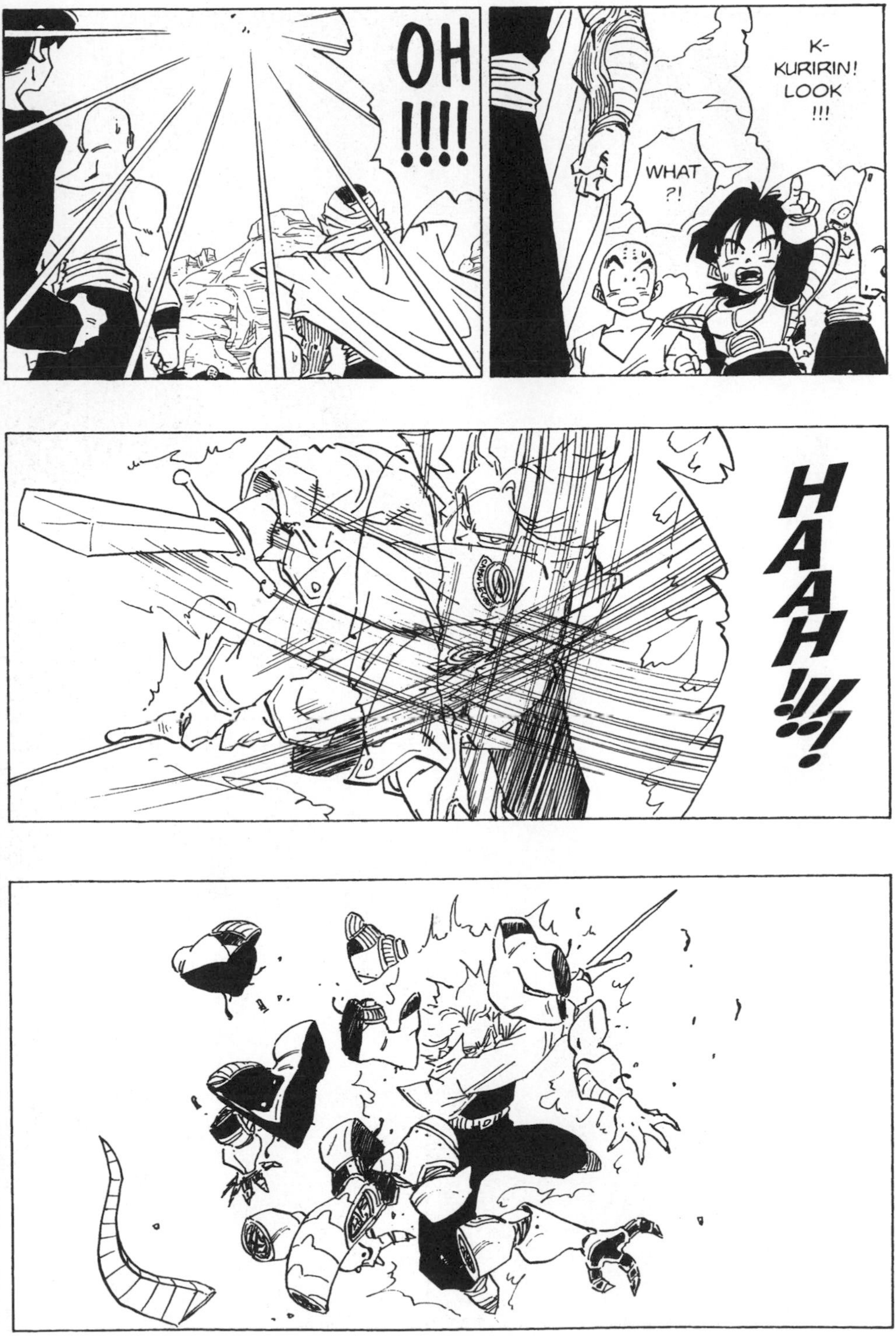
K-KURIRIN! LOOK!!!
WHAT?!
OH!!!!
HAAH!!!!

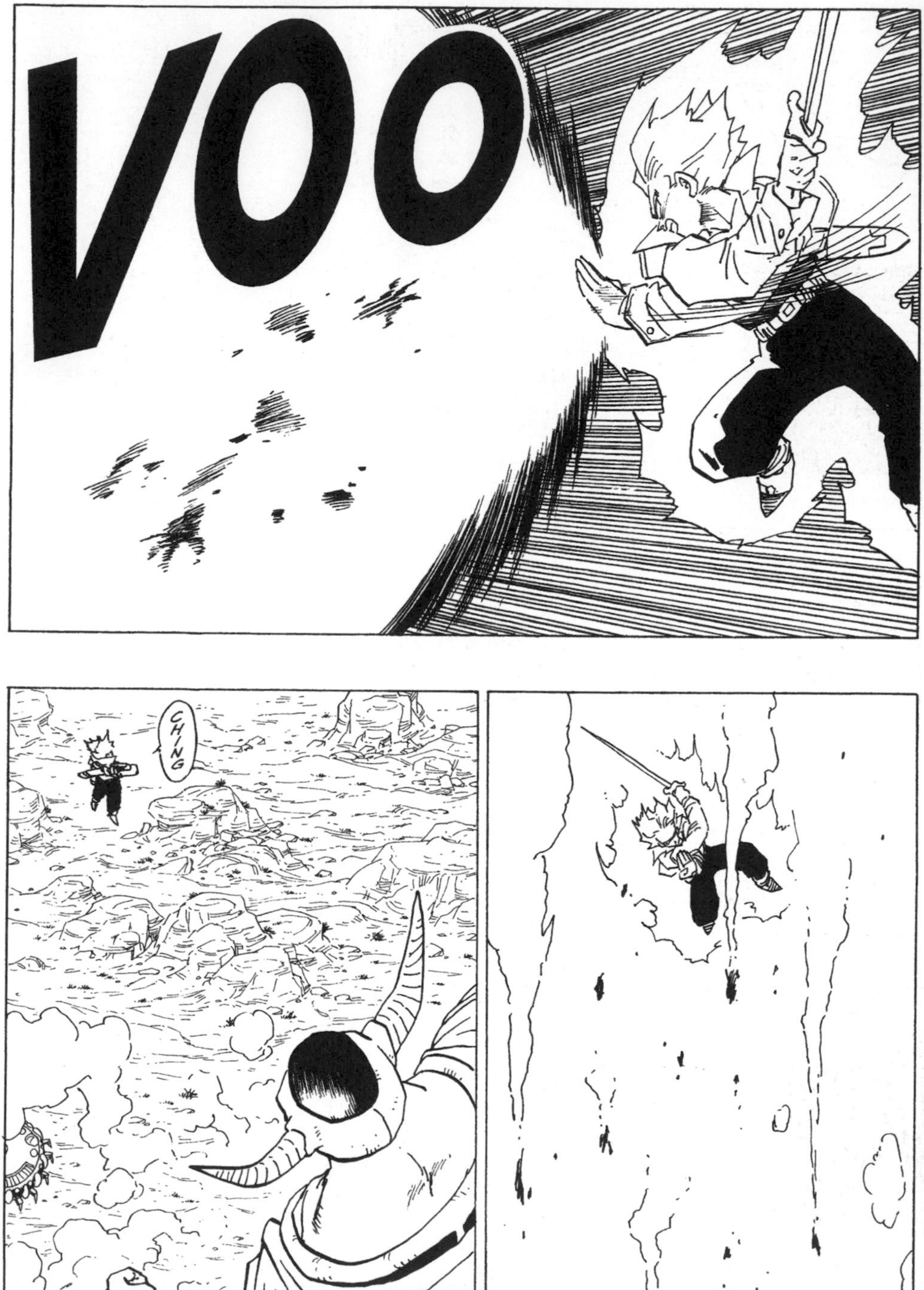
VOO
CHING

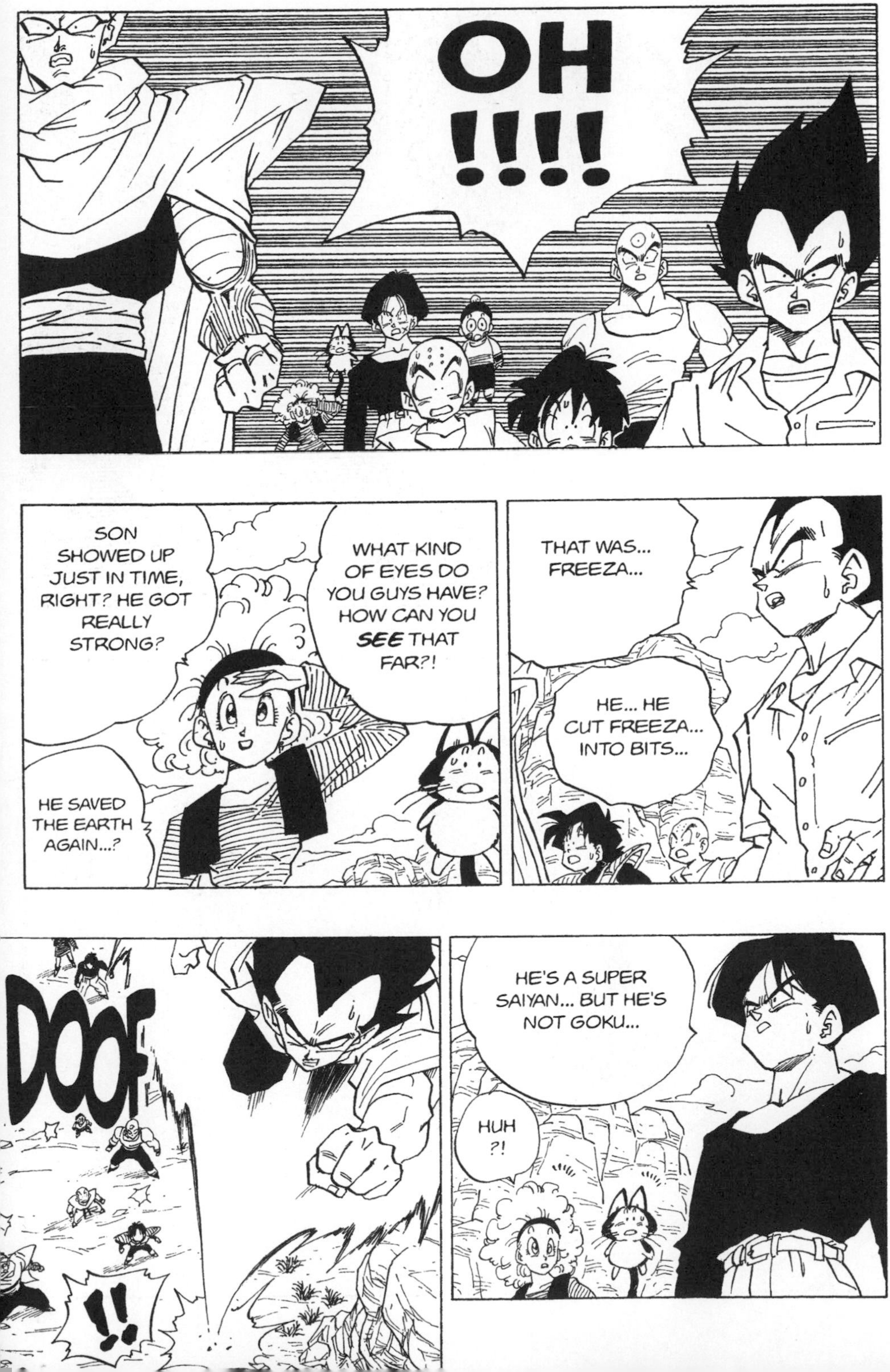
OH !!!!
SON SHOWED UP JUST IN TIME, RIGHT? HE GOT REALLY STRONG?
WHAT KIND OF EYES DO YOU GUYS HAVE? HOW CAN YOU *SEE* THAT FAR?!
HE SAVED THE EARTH AGAIN...?
THAT WAS... FREEZA...
HE... HE CUT FREEZA... INTO BITS...
DOOF
!!
HE'S A SUPER SAIYAN... BUT HE'S NOT GOKU...
HUH ?!

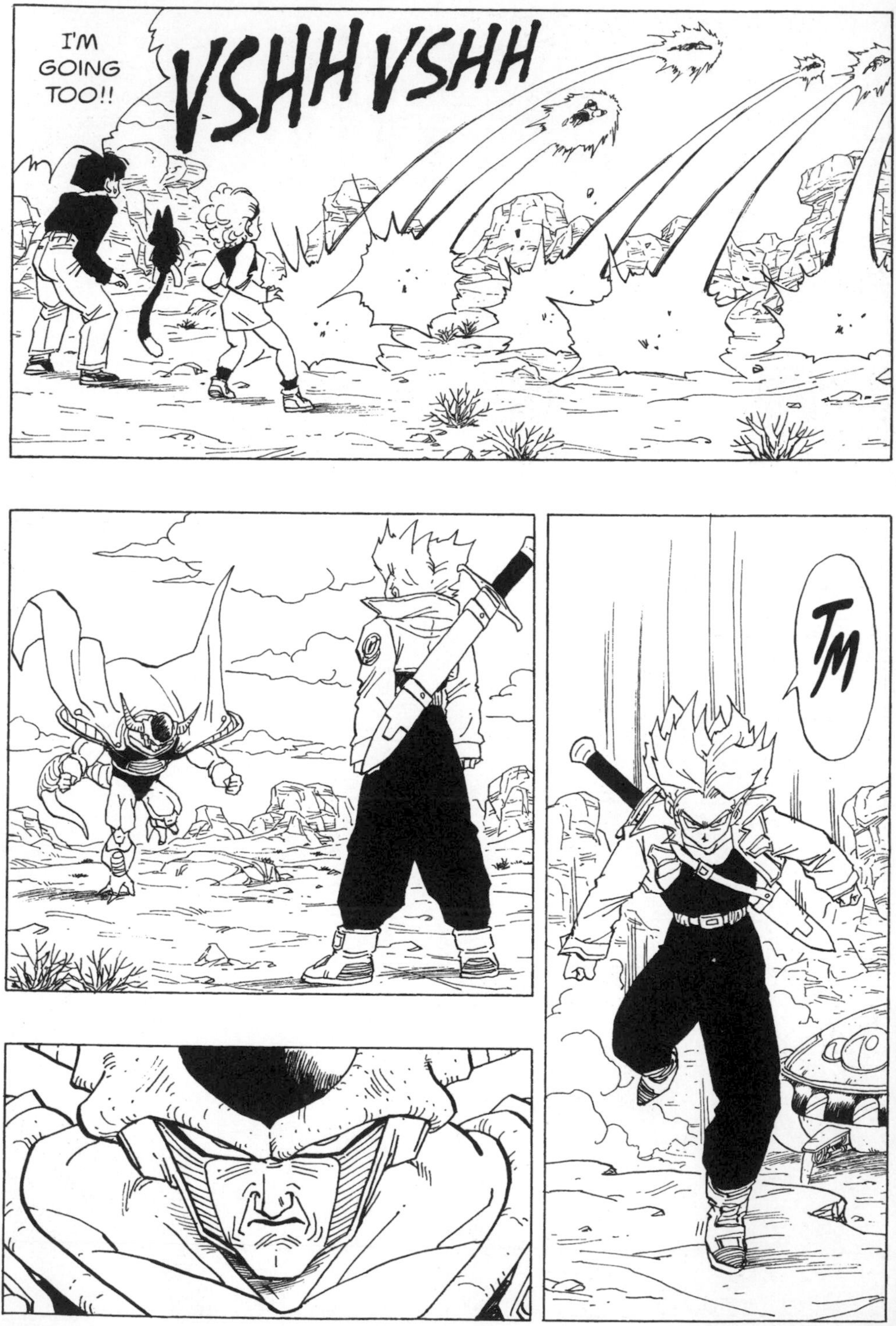

I'M GOING TOO!!
VSHH VSHH
TM

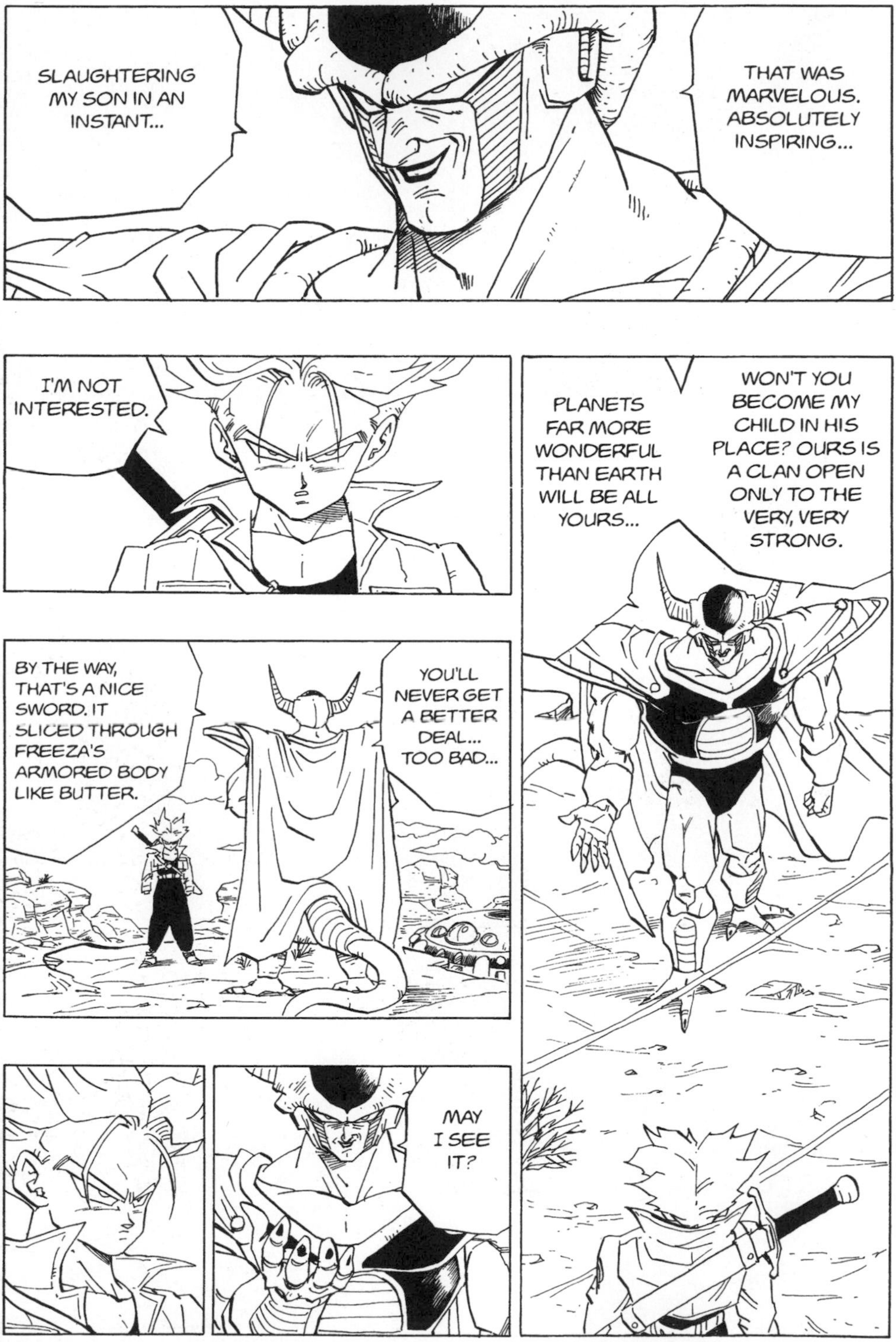
SLAUGHTERING MY SON IN AN INSTANT...
THAT WAS MARVELOUS. ABSOLUTELY INSPIRING...
WON'T YOU BECOME MY CHILD IN HIS PLACE? OURS IS A CLAN OPEN ONLY TO THE VERY, VERY STRONG.
PLANETS FAR MORE WONDERFUL THAN EARTH WILL BE ALL YOURS...
I'M NOT INTERESTED.
YOU'LL NEVER GET A BETTER DEAL... TOO BAD...
BY THE WAY, THAT'S A NICE SWORD. IT SLICED THROUGH FREEZA'S ARMORED BODY LIKE BUTTER.
MAY I SEE IT?

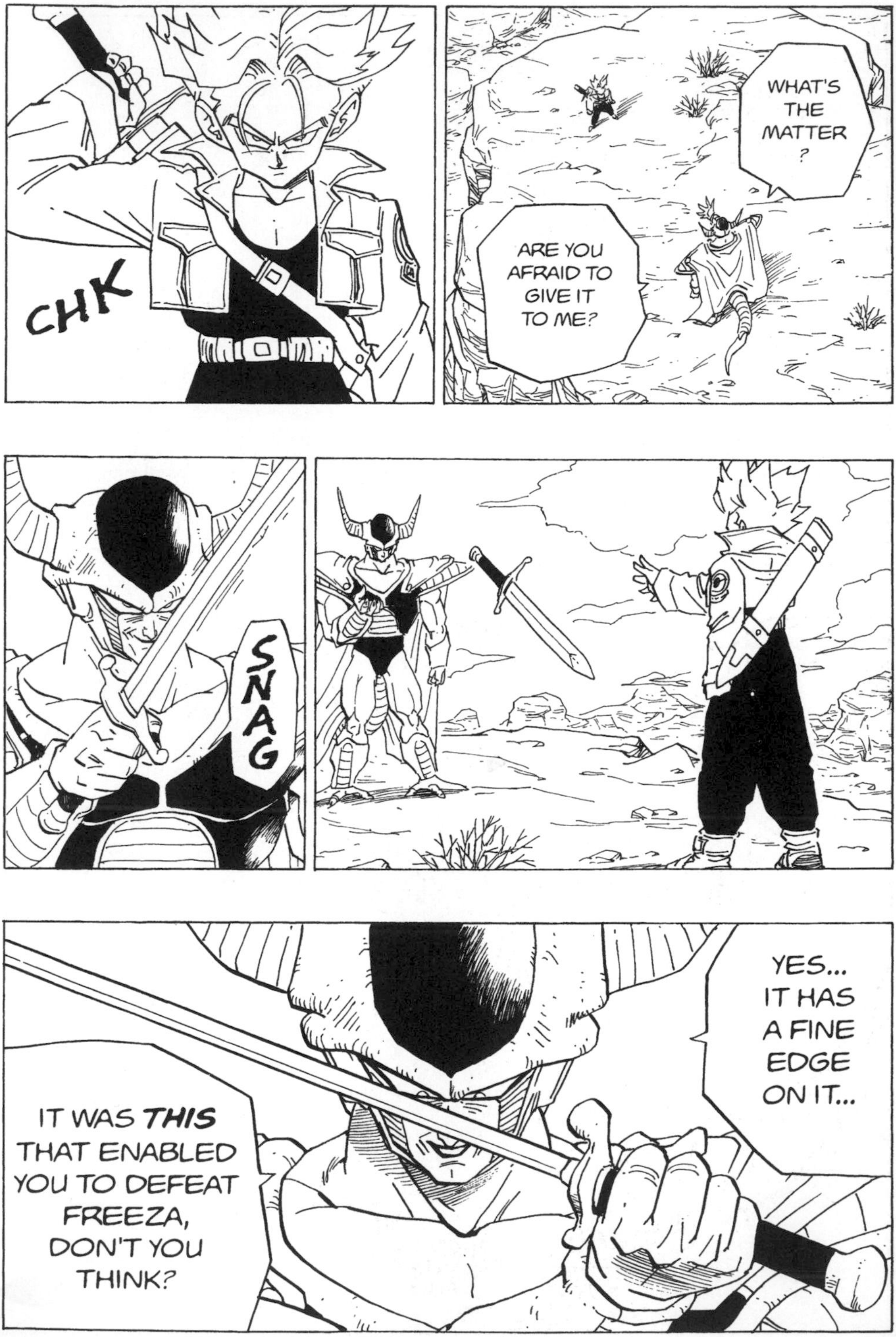
CHK
WHAT'S THE MATTER?
ARE YOU AFRAID TO GIVE IT TO ME?
SNAG
YES... IT HAS A FINE EDGE ON IT...
IT WAS **THIS** THAT ENABLED YOU TO DEFEAT FREEZA, DON'T YOU THINK?

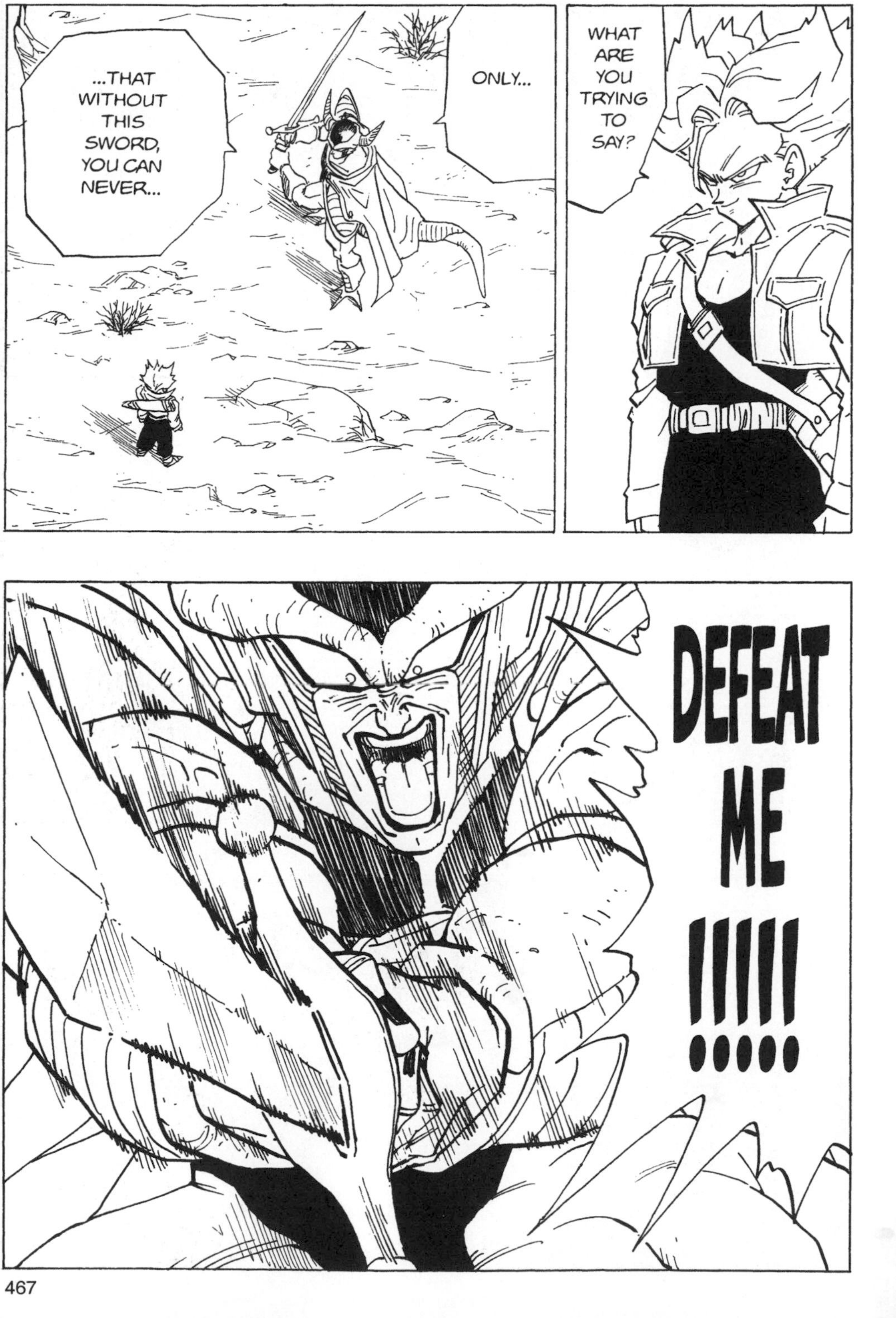
WHAT ARE YOU TRYING TO SAY?
ONLY...
...THAT WITHOUT THIS SWORD, YOU CAN NEVER...
DEFEAT ME !!!!!!

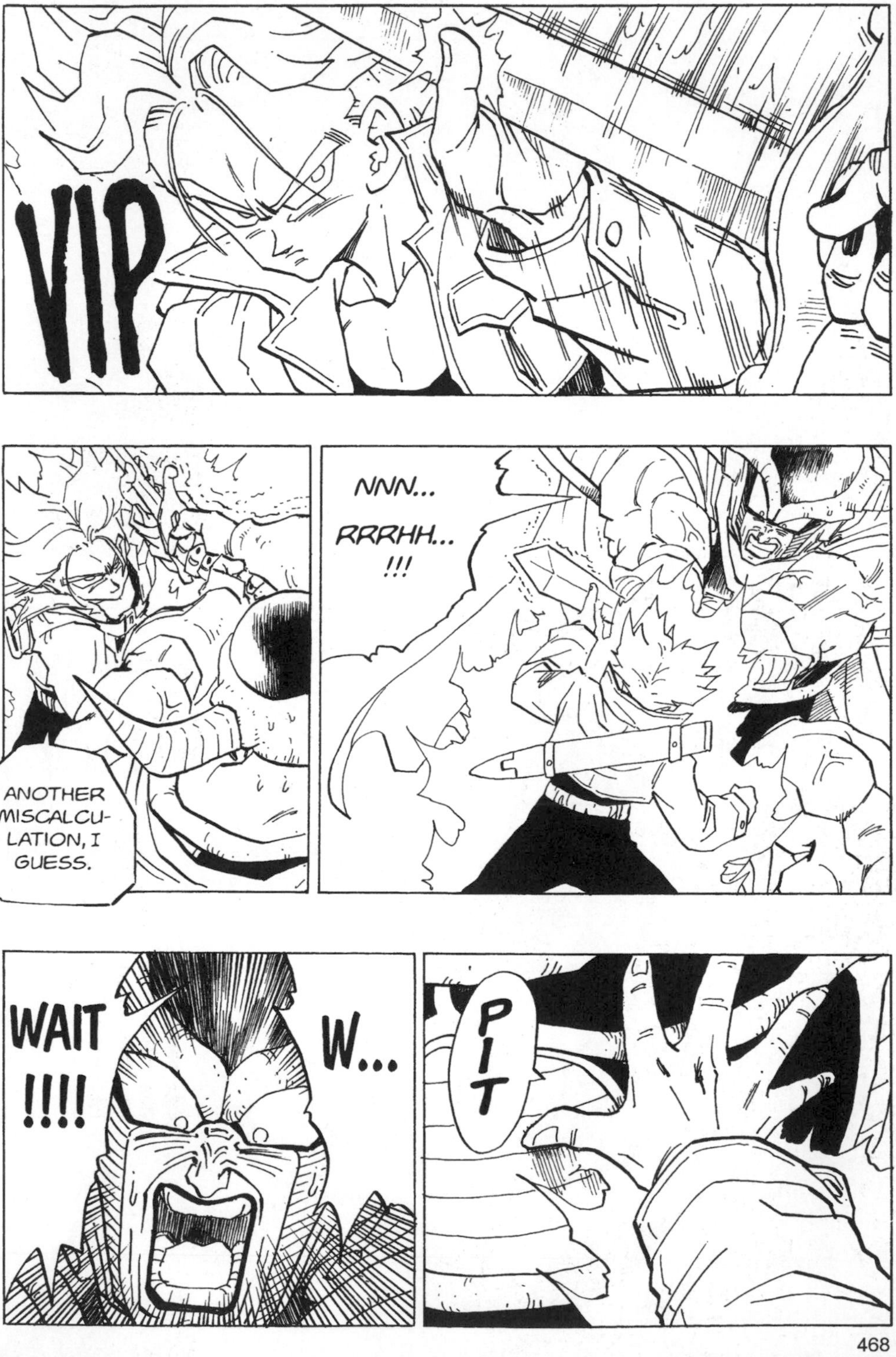
VIP
NNN... RRRHH... !!!
ANOTHER MISCALCULATION, I GUESS.
PIT
W...
WAIT !!!!

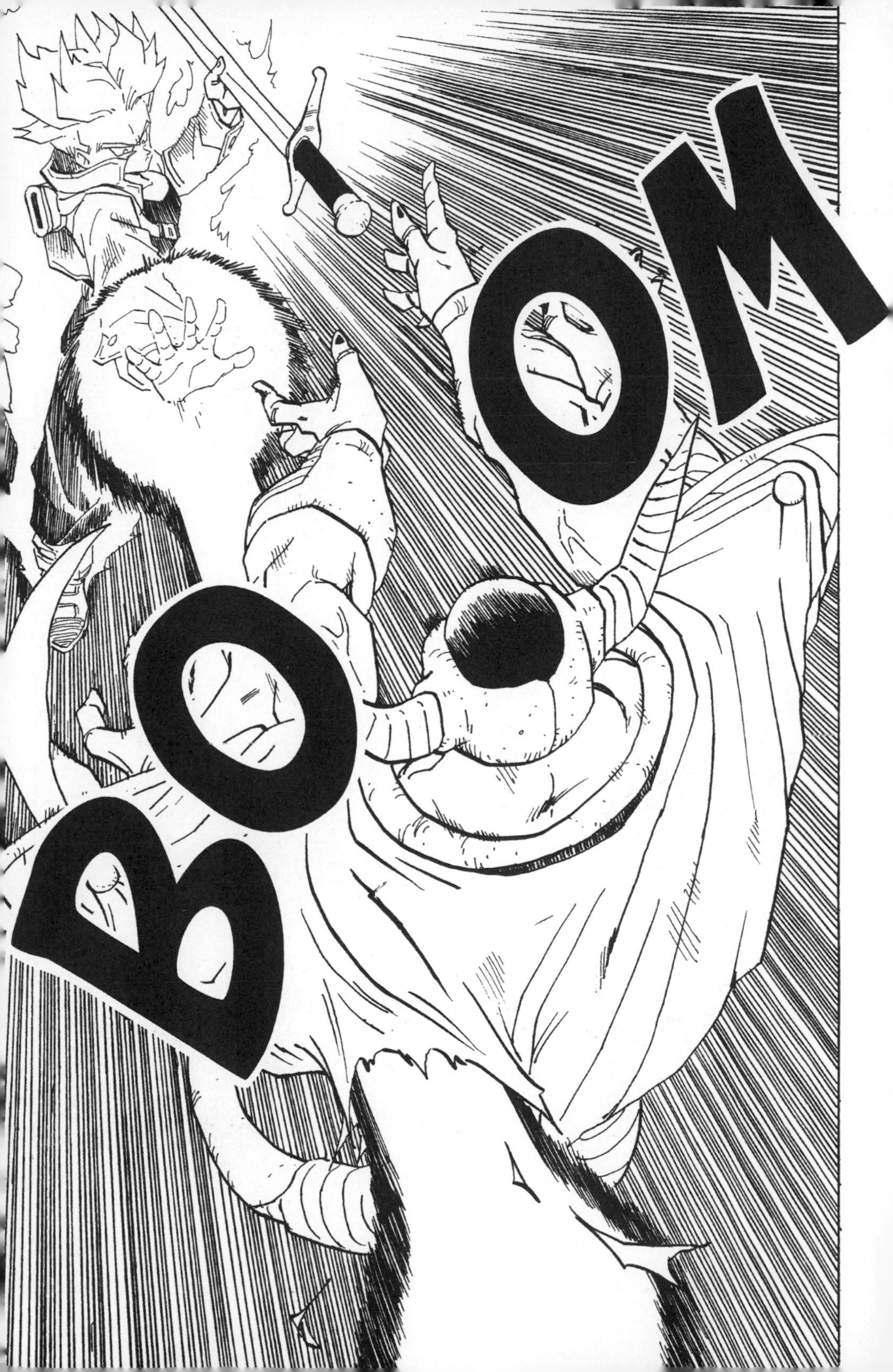
BOOOM

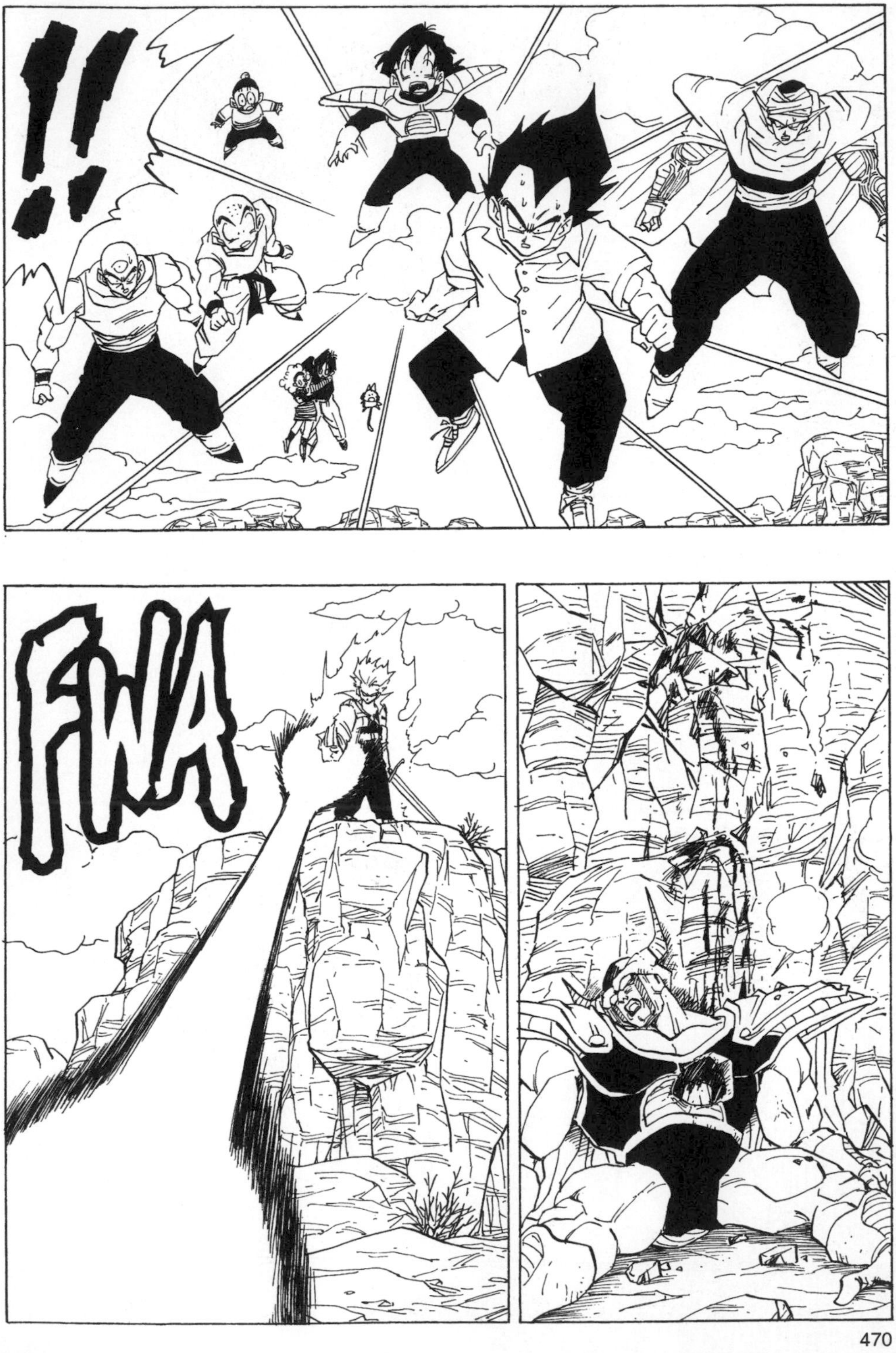
!!
FWA

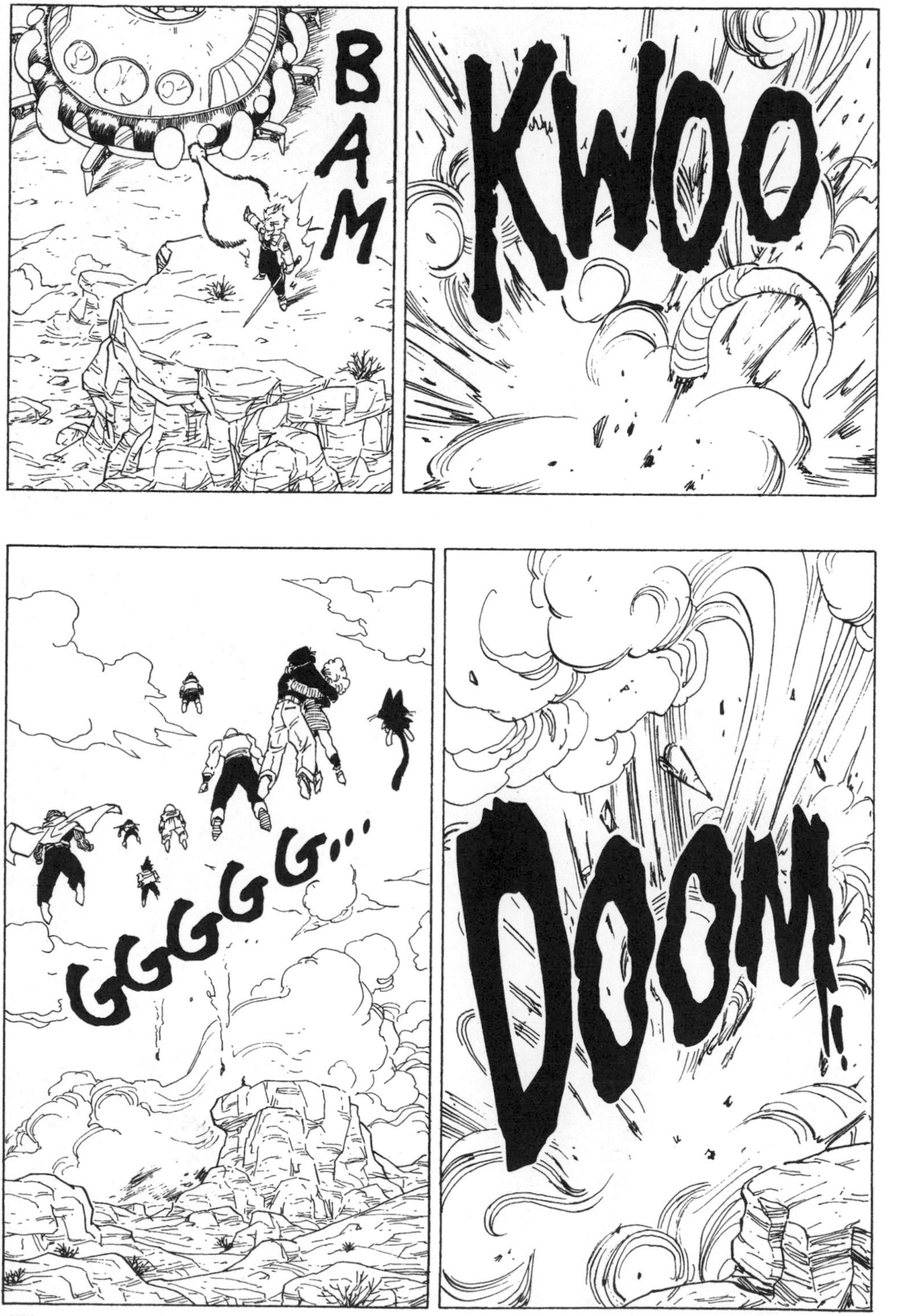
BAM
KWOO
GGGGG...
DOOM!!

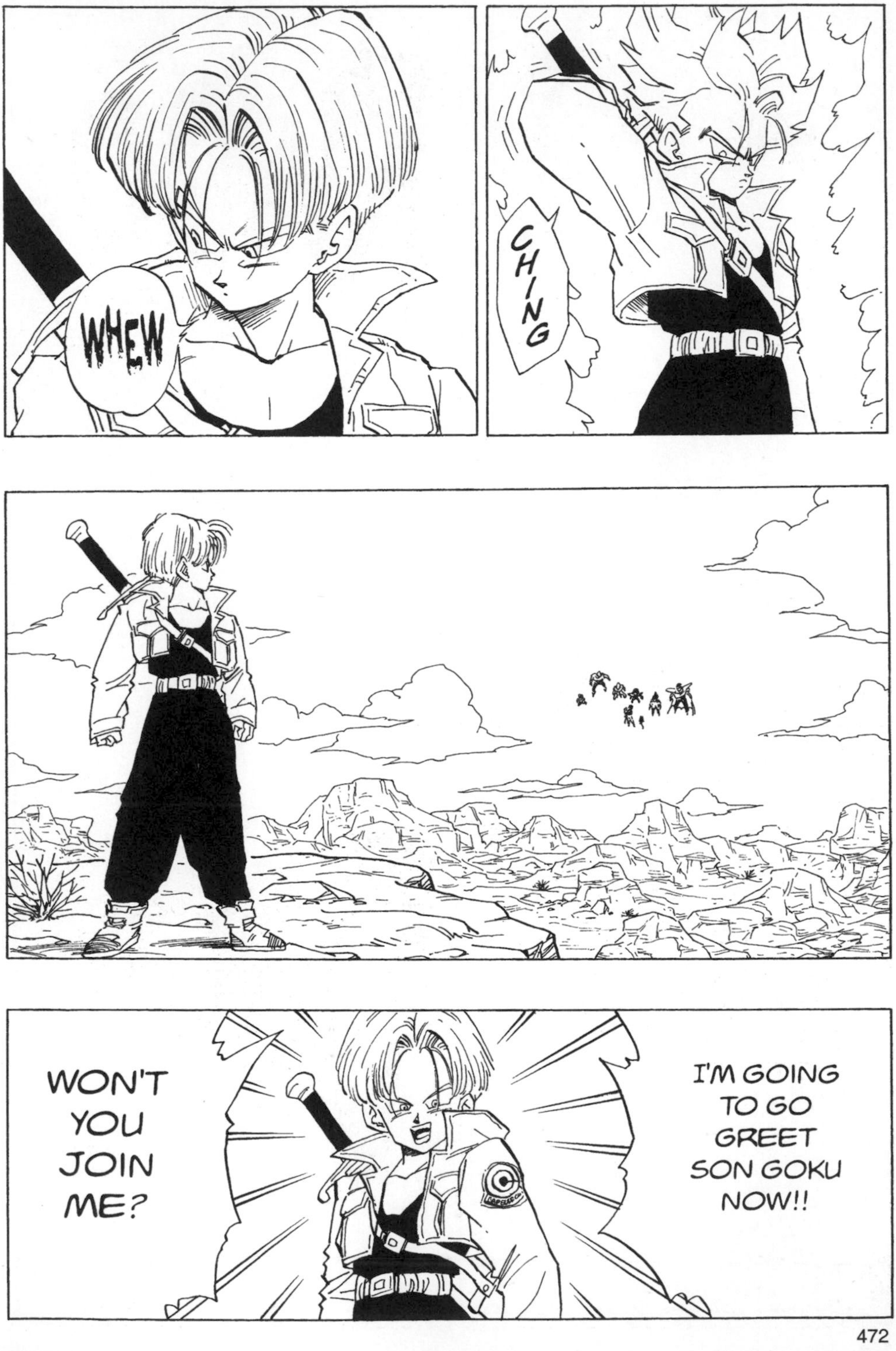
WHEW
CHING
I'M GOING TO GO GREET SON GOKU NOW!!
WON'T YOU JOIN ME?

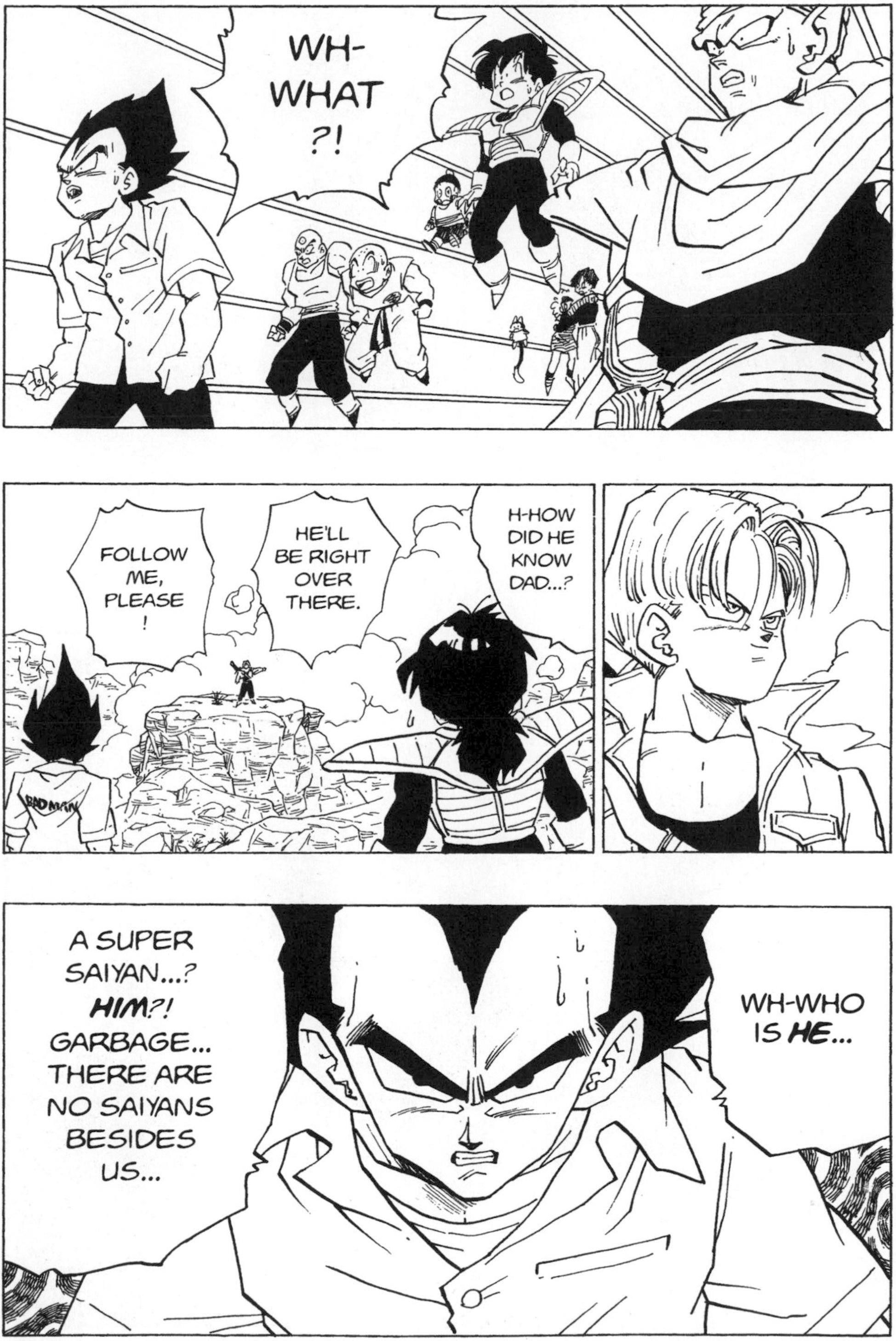
WH-WHAT ?!
H-HOW DID HE KNOW DAD...?
HE'LL BE RIGHT OVER THERE.
FOLLOW ME, PLEASE !
WH-WHO IS **HE**...
A SUPER SAIYAN...? ***HIM***?! GARBAGE... THERE ARE NO SAIYANS BESIDES US...

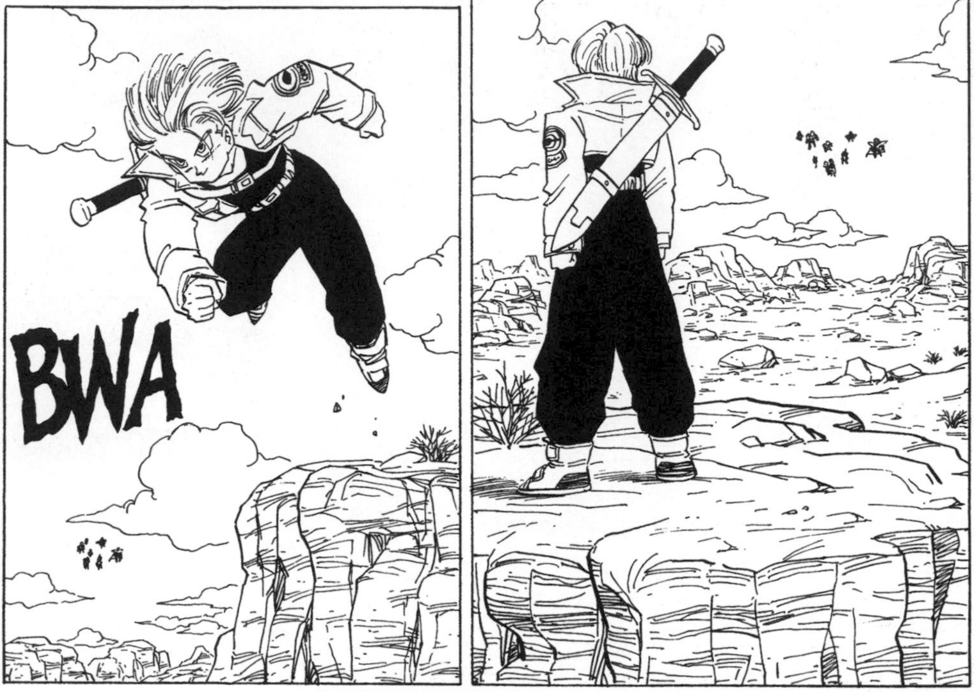
BWA

DBZ:139 • Son Goku Comes Home

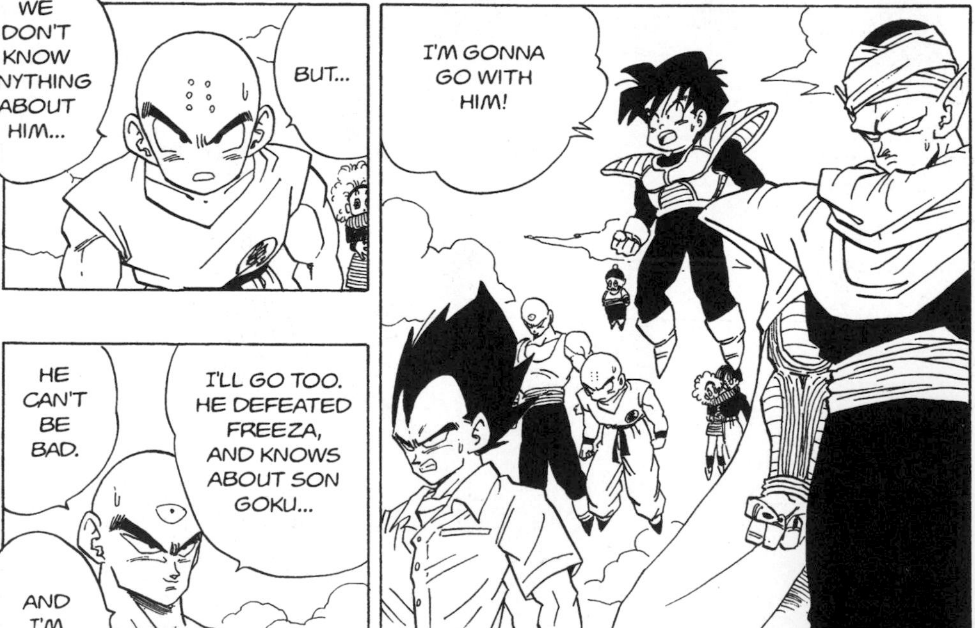
WE DON'T KNOW ANYTHING ABOUT HIM...
BUT...
I'M GONNA GO WITH HIM!
HE CAN'T BE BAD.
I'LL GO TOO. HE DEFEATED FREEZA, AND KNOWS ABOUT SON GOKU...
AND I'M CURIOUS...

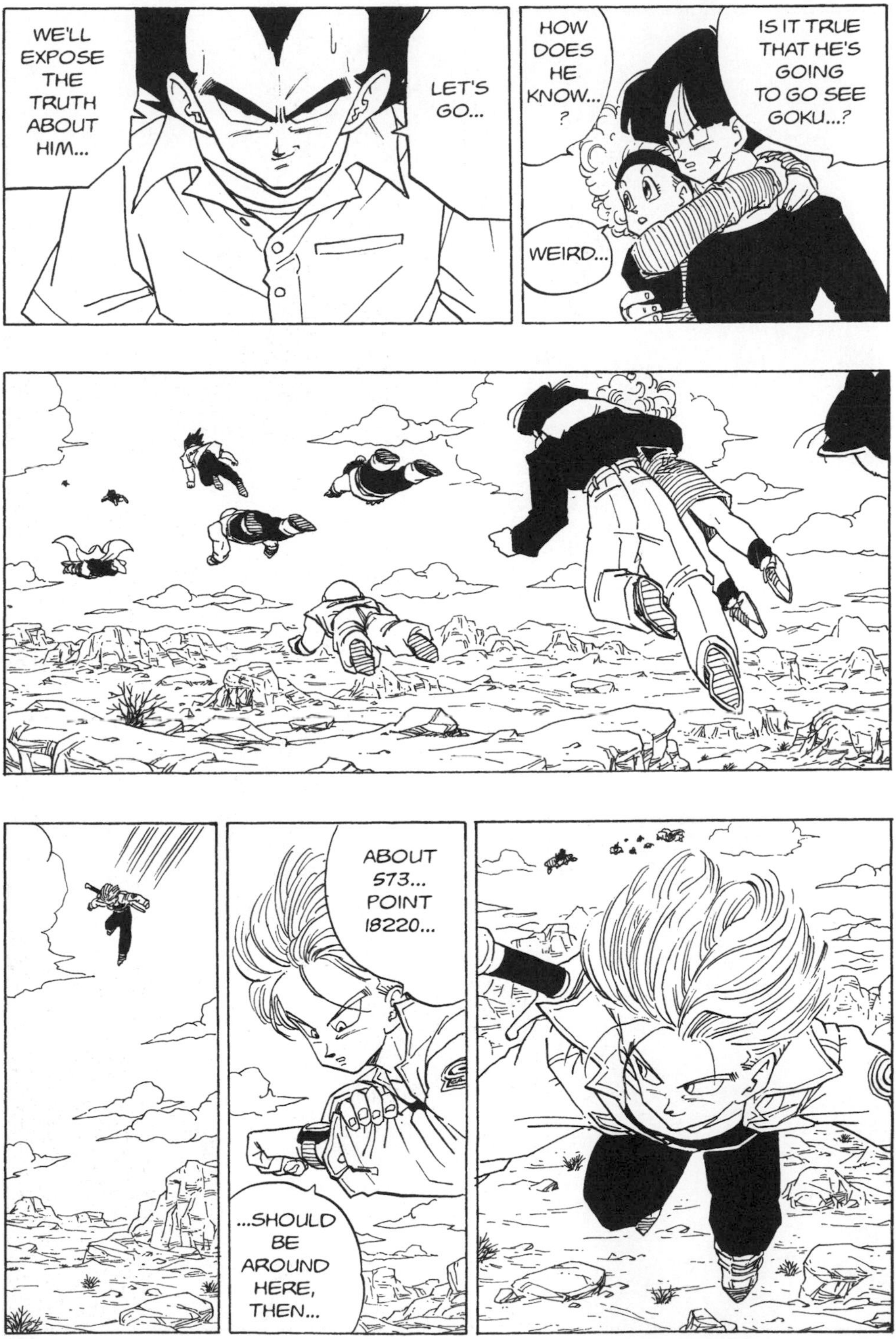
WE'LL EXPOSE THE TRUTH ABOUT HIM...
LET'S GO...
IS IT TRUE THAT HE'S GOING TO GO SEE GOKU...?
HOW DOES HE KNOW...?
WEIRD...
ABOUT 573... POINT 18220...
...SHOULD BE AROUND HERE, THEN...

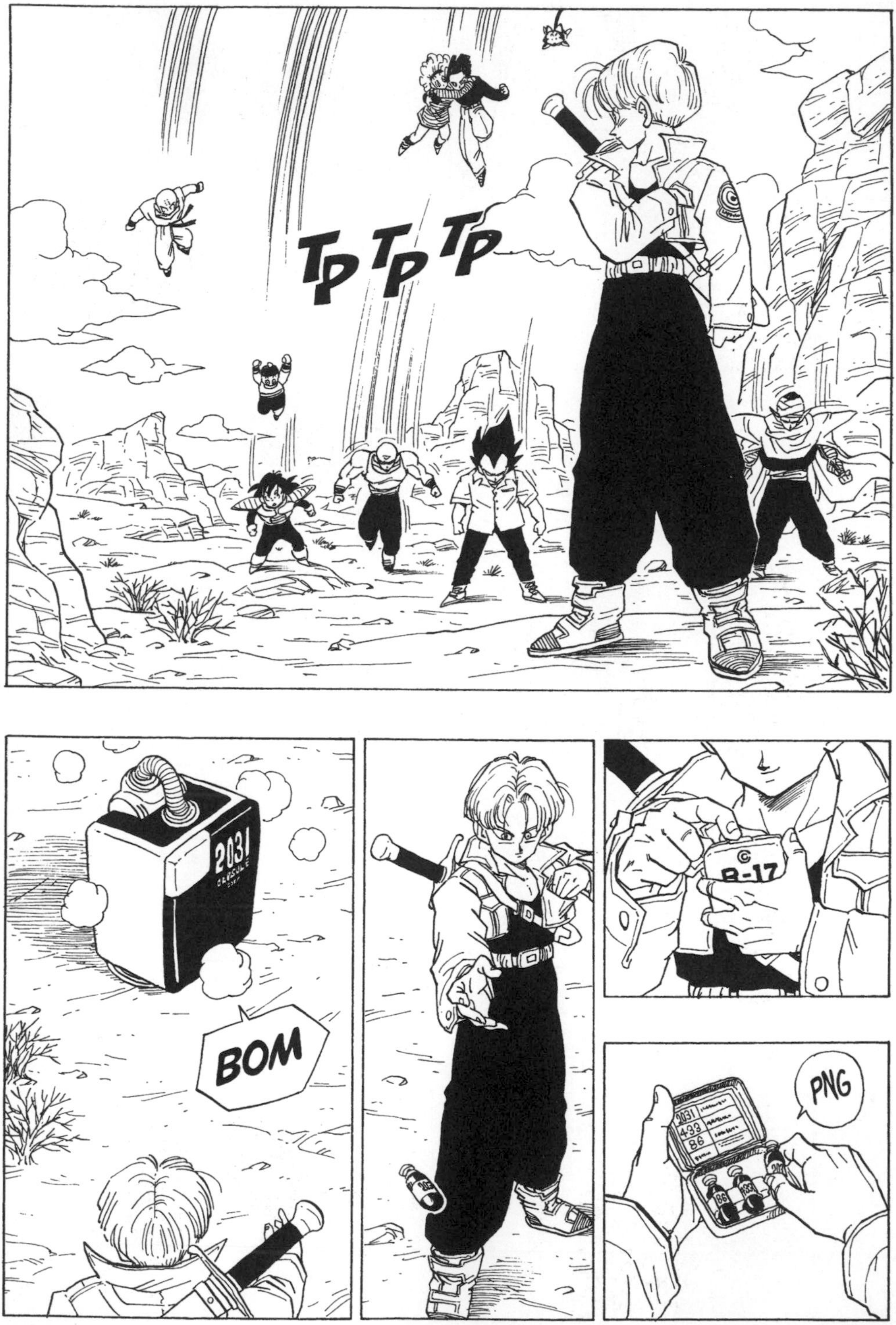
TP TP TP
BOM
2031
B-17
PNG

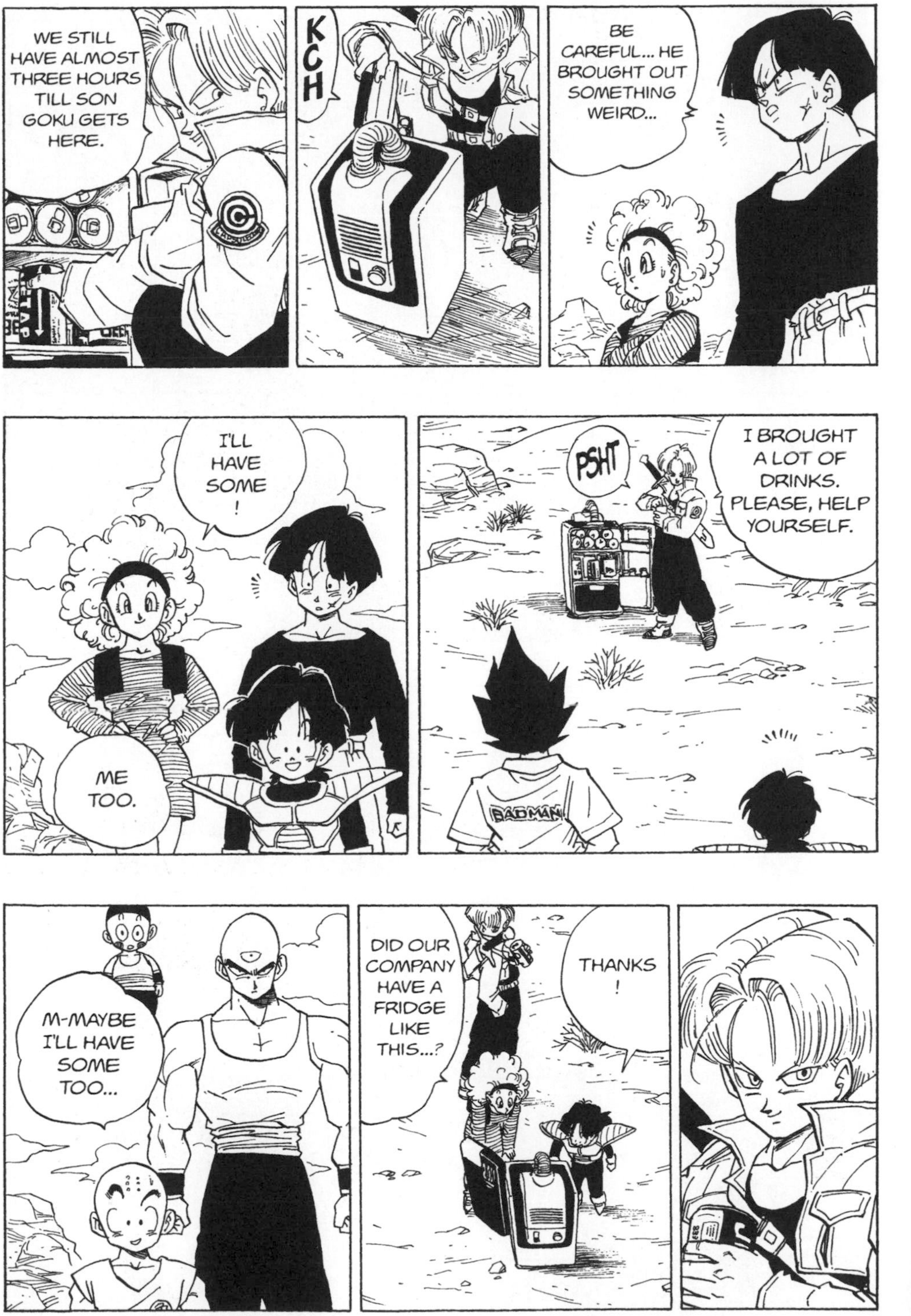
WE STILL HAVE ALMOST THREE HOURS TILL SON GOKU GETS HERE.
KCH
BE CAREFUL... HE BROUGHT OUT SOMETHING WEIRD...
PSHT
I BROUGHT A LOT OF DRINKS. PLEASE, HELP YOURSELF.
BADMAN
I'LL HAVE SOME!
ME TOO.
M-MAYBE I'LL HAVE SOME TOO...
DID OUR COMPANY HAVE A FRIDGE LIKE THIS...?
THANKS!

HOW DO YOU KNOW MY DAD?

HUH? ...ERRR... NO...

...HAVE WE MET BEFORE?

...WELL...

...THEN... HOW DO YOU KNOW THAT HE'S GOING TO GET HERE IN THREE HOURS?

NEVER BEEN PRIVILEGED TO MEET HIM.

I'VE ONLY HEARD ABOUT HIM.

I CAN'T TELL YOU...

I'M SORRY...

UM... WHEN YOU DEFEATED FREEZA...YOU WERE A SUPER SAIYAN... WEREN'T YOU?

WELL... YES, I WAS...

I'M SORRY... I CAN'T TELL YOU THAT EITHER...

WHO *ARE* YOU?

HOW DID YOU GET SO MUCH POWER?

WHAT DO YOU MEAN, YOU CAN'T TELL US?

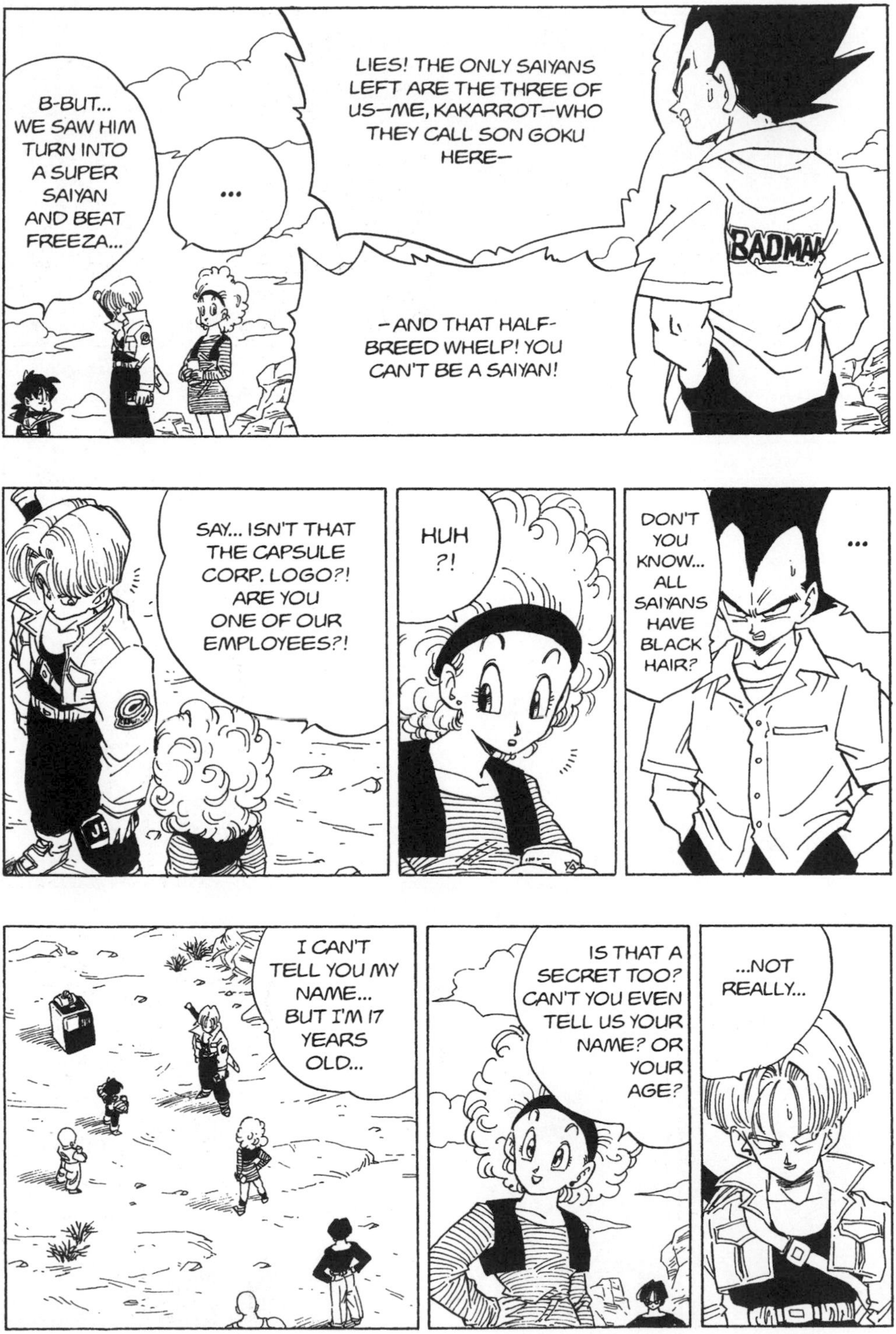
B-BUT... WE SAW HIM TURN INTO A SUPER SAIYAN AND BEAT FREEZA...
...
LIES! THE ONLY SAIYANS LEFT ARE THE THREE OF US—ME, KAKARROT—WHO THEY CALL SON GOKU HERE—
—AND THAT HALF-BREED WHELP! YOU CAN'T BE A SAIYAN!
SAY... ISN'T THAT THE CAPSULE CORP. LOGO?! ARE YOU ONE OF OUR EMPLOYEES?!
HUH ?!
DON'T YOU KNOW... ALL SAIYANS HAVE BLACK HAIR?
...
I CAN'T TELL YOU MY NAME... BUT I'M 17 YEARS OLD...
IS THAT A SECRET TOO? CAN'T YOU EVEN TELL US YOUR NAME? OR YOUR AGE?
...NOT REALLY...

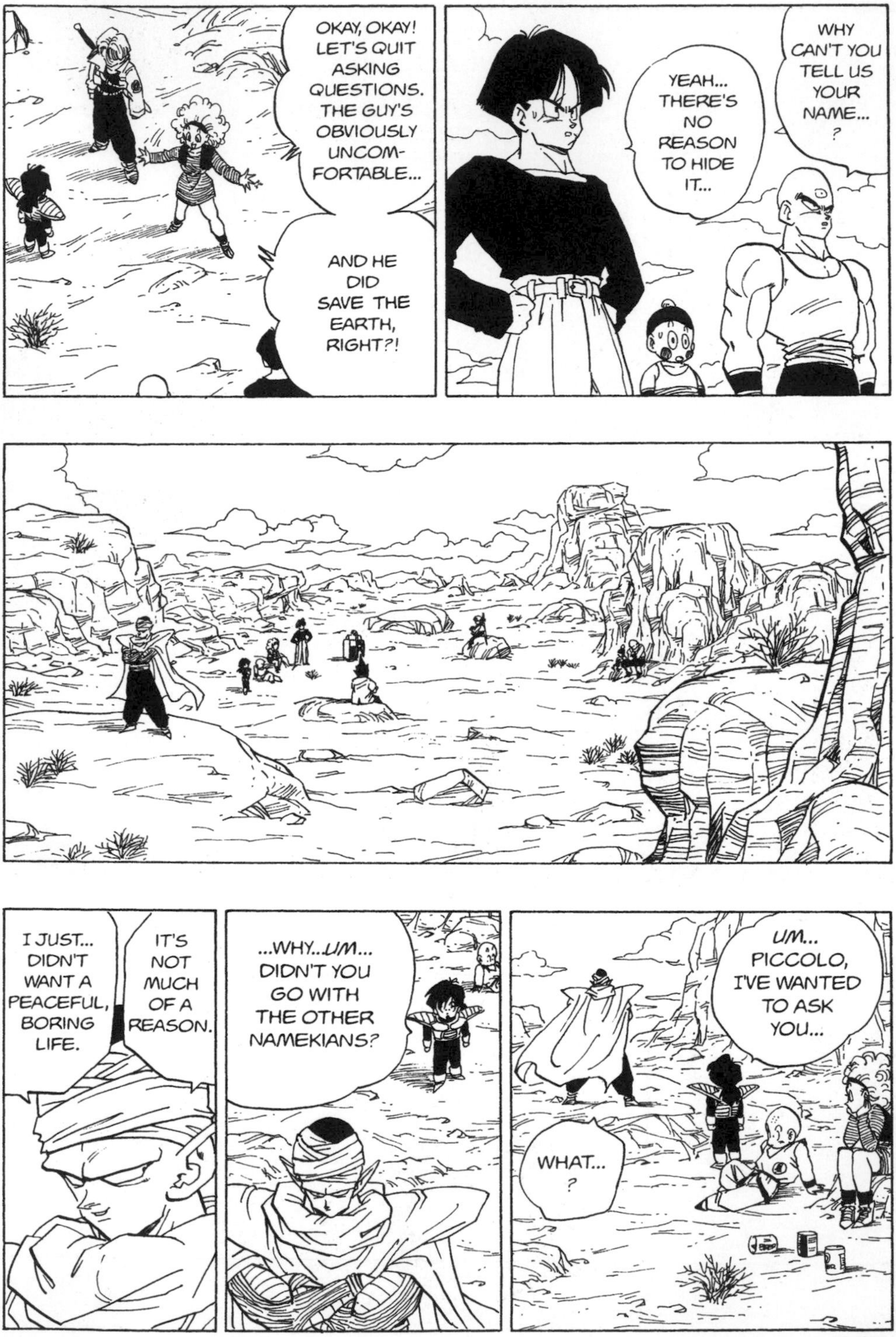
OKAY, OKAY! LET'S QUIT ASKING QUESTIONS. THE GUY'S OBVIOUSLY UNCOMFORTABLE...
AND HE DID SAVE THE EARTH, RIGHT?!
WHY CAN'T YOU TELL US YOUR NAME...?
YEAH... THERE'S NO REASON TO HIDE IT...
UM... PICCOLO, I'VE WANTED TO ASK YOU...
WHAT...?
...WHY...UM... DIDN'T YOU GO WITH THE OTHER NAMEKIANS?
IT'S NOT MUCH OF A REASON.
I JUST... DIDN'T WANT A PEACEFUL, BORING LIFE.

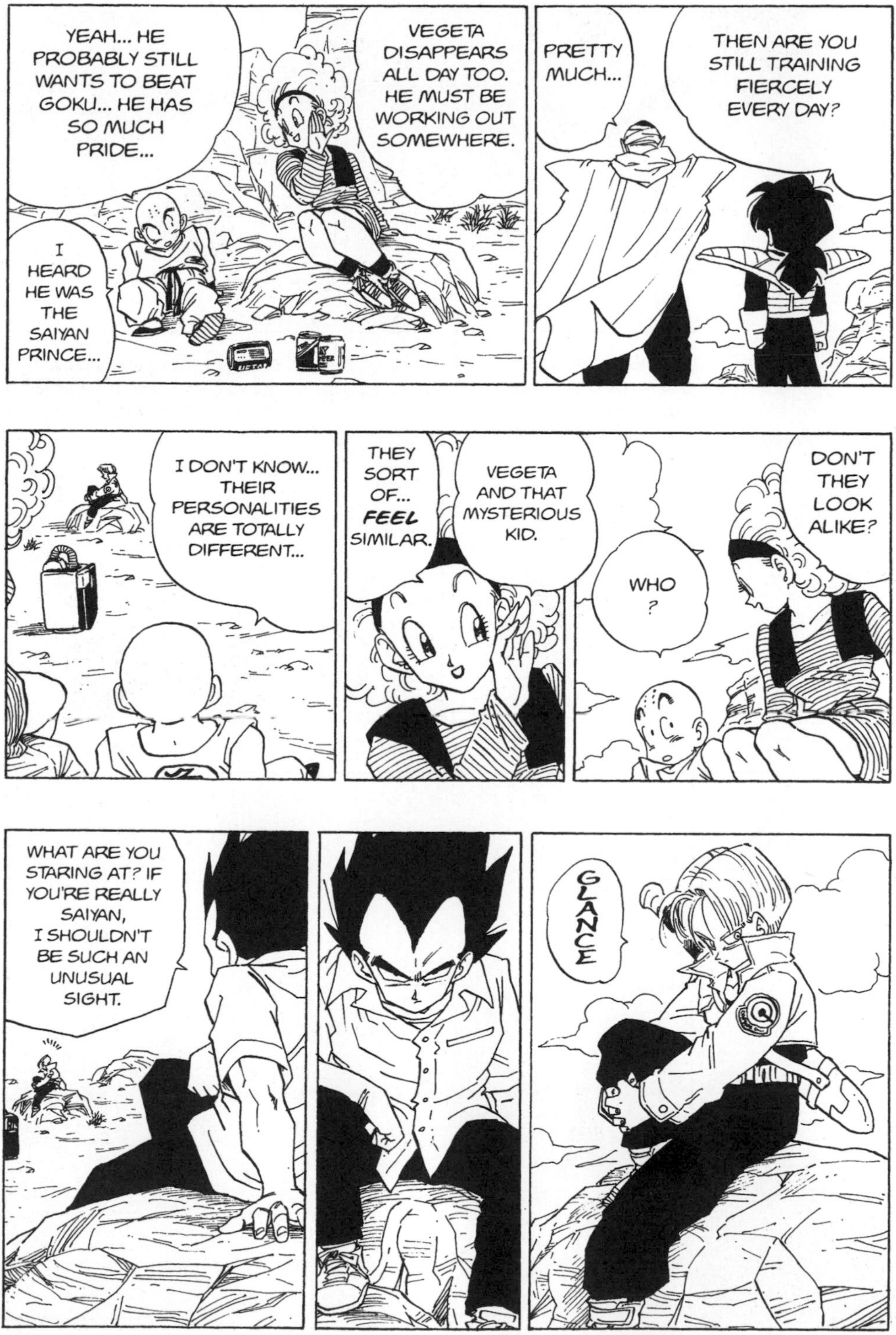
VEGETA DISAPPEARS ALL DAY TOO. HE MUST BE WORKING OUT SOMEWHERE.
YEAH... HE PROBABLY STILL WANTS TO BEAT GOKU... HE HAS SO MUCH PRIDE...
I HEARD HE WAS THE SAIYAN PRINCE...
THEN ARE YOU STILL TRAINING FIERCELY EVERY DAY?
PRETTY MUCH...
DON'T THEY LOOK ALIKE?
WHO?
VEGETA AND THAT MYSTERIOUS KID.
THEY SORT OF... FEEL SIMILAR.
I DON'T KNOW... THEIR PERSONALITIES ARE TOTALLY DIFFERENT...
GLANCE
WHAT ARE YOU STARING AT? IF YOU'RE REALLY SAIYAN, I SHOULDN'T BE SUCH AN UNUSUAL SIGHT.

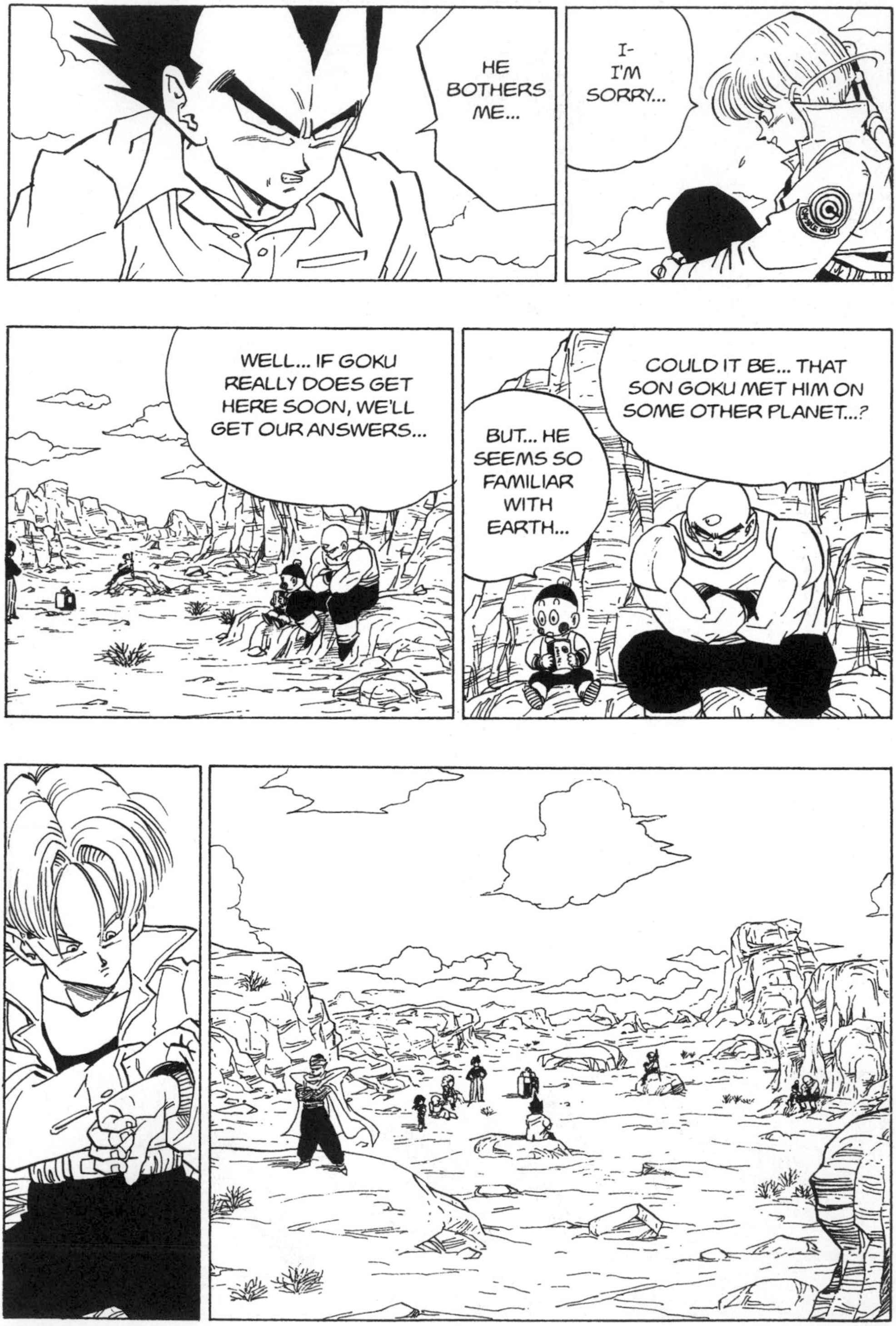
HE BOTHERS ME...
I- I'M SORRY...
WELL... IF GOKU REALLY DOES GET HERE SOON, WE'LL GET OUR ANSWERS...
COULD IT BE... THAT SON GOKU MET HIM ON SOME OTHER PLANET...?
BUT... HE SEEMS SO FAMILIAR WITH EARTH...

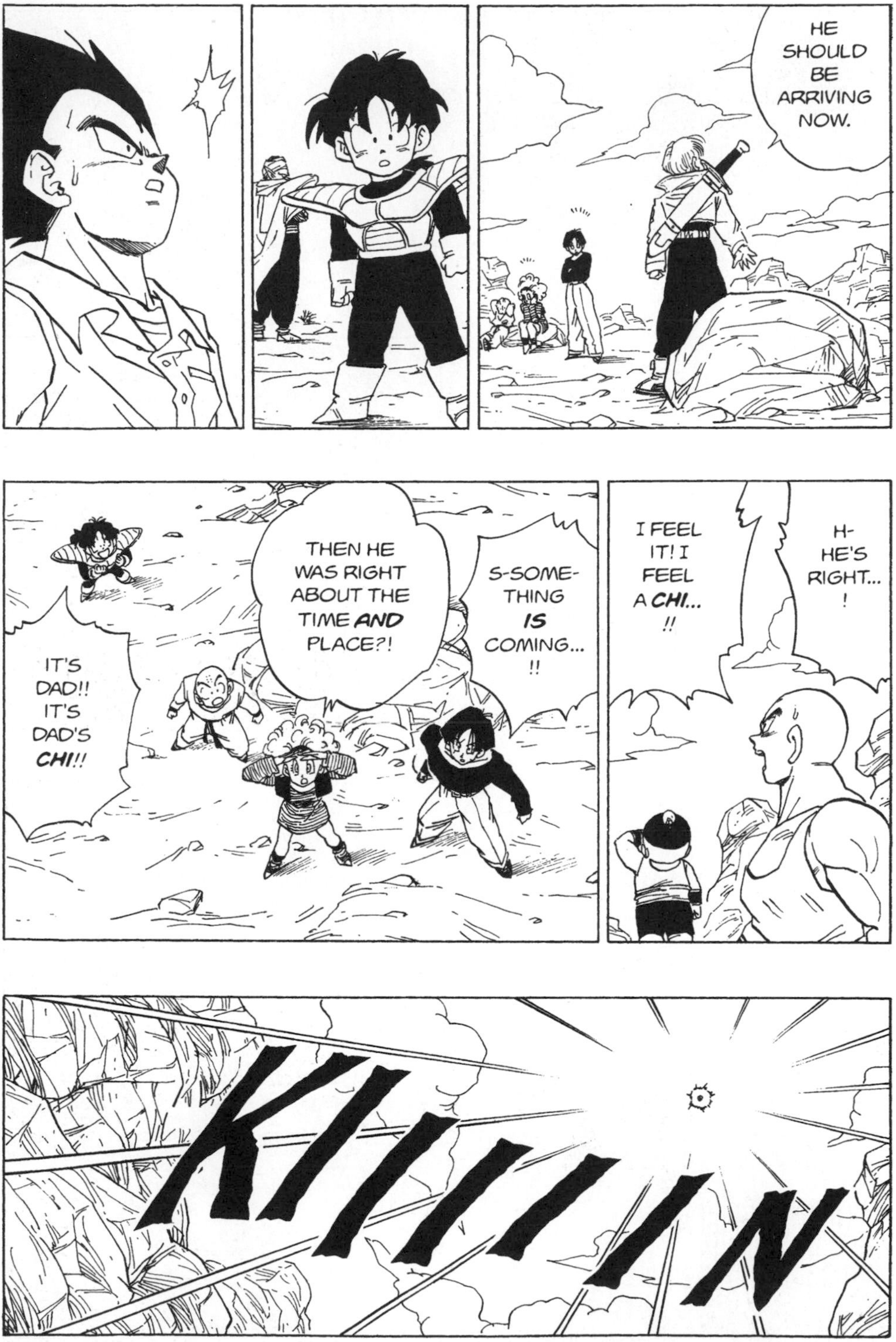
HE SHOULD BE ARRIVING NOW.
H-HE'S RIGHT...!
I FEEL IT! I FEEL A CHI...!!
S-SOMETHING IS COMING...!!
THEN HE WAS RIGHT ABOUT THE TIME AND PLACE?!
IT'S DAD!! IT'S DAD'S CHI!!
KIIIIIN

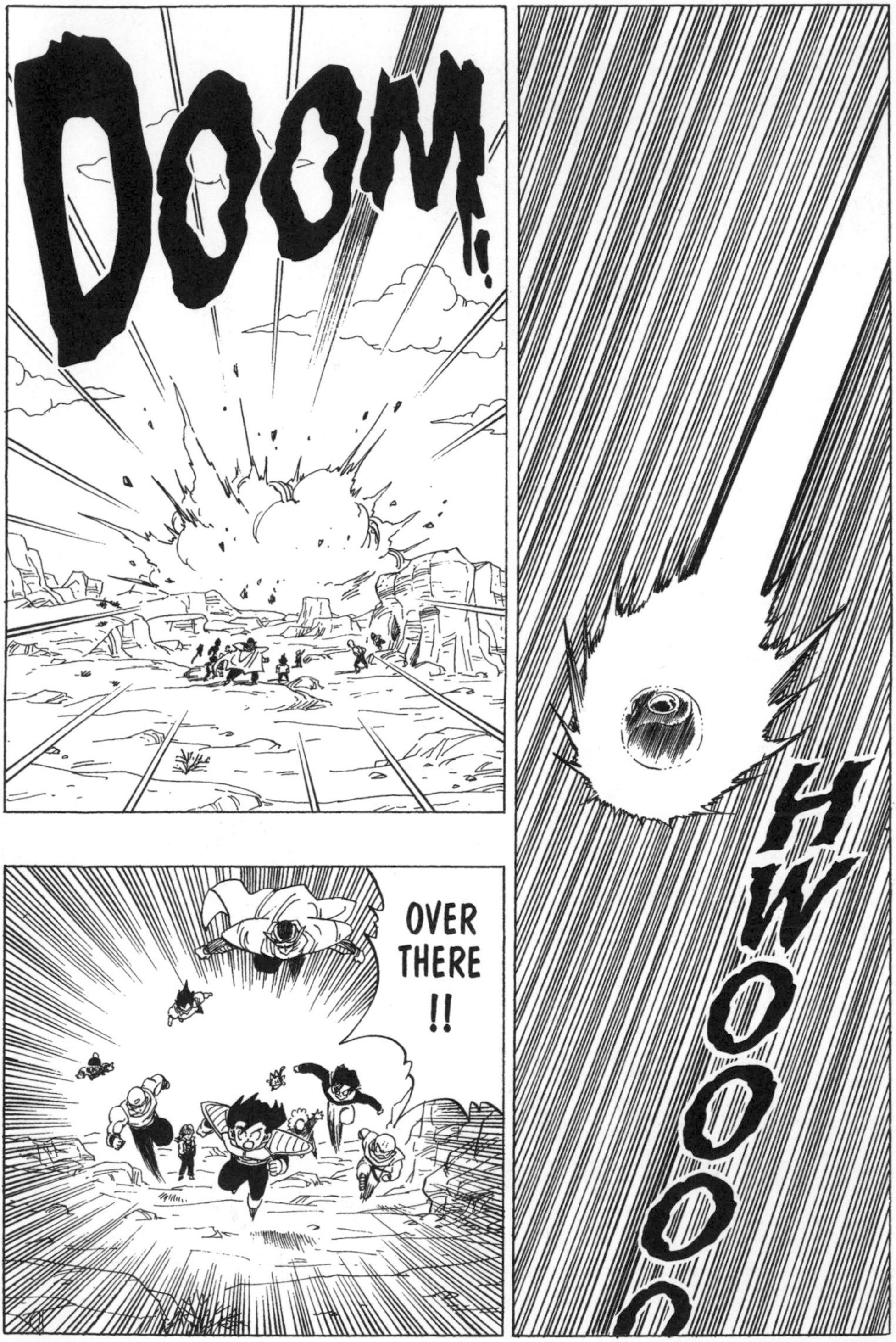
HWOOOOO
DOOM!!
OVER THERE !!

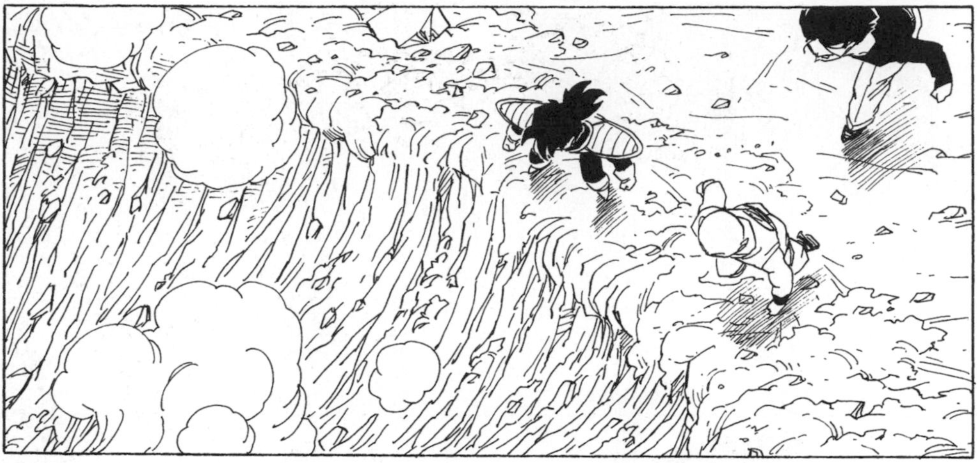

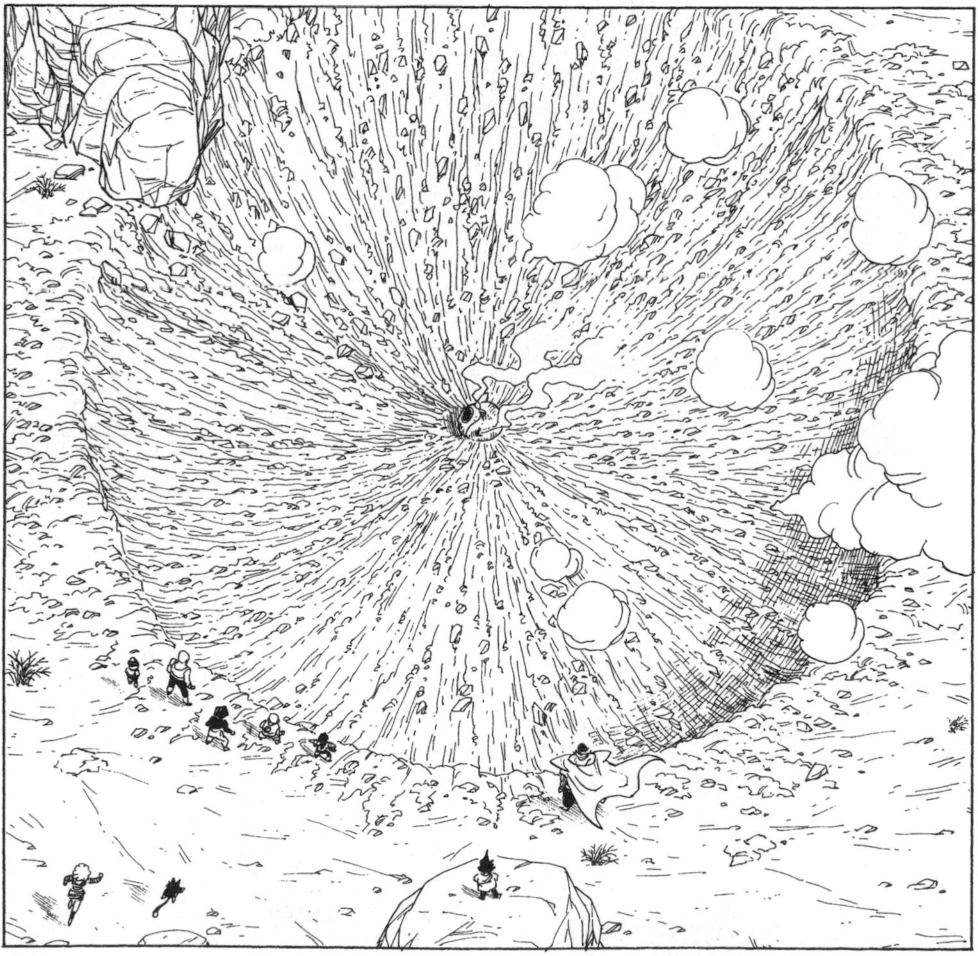

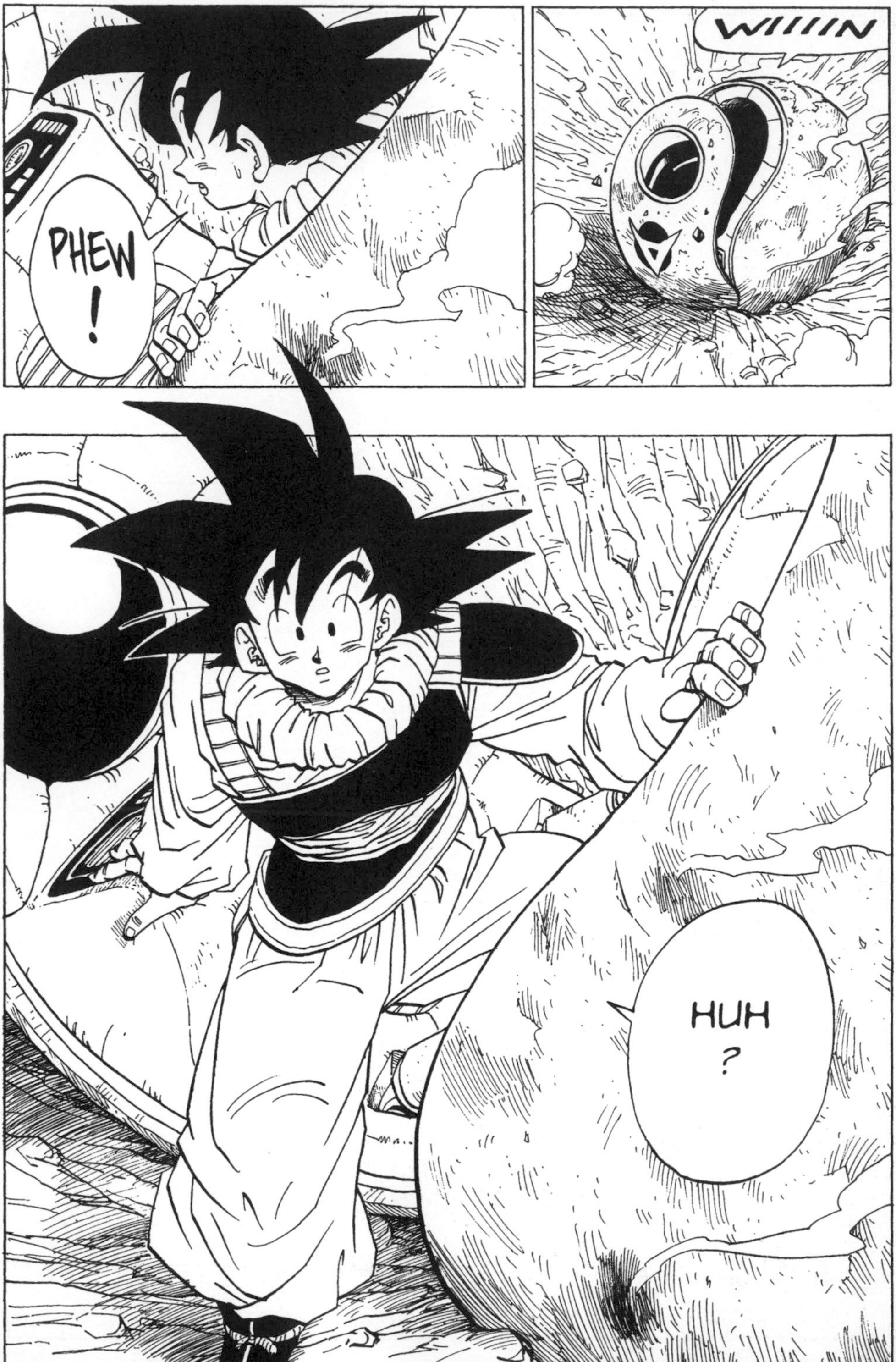
PHEW!
WIIIN
HUH?

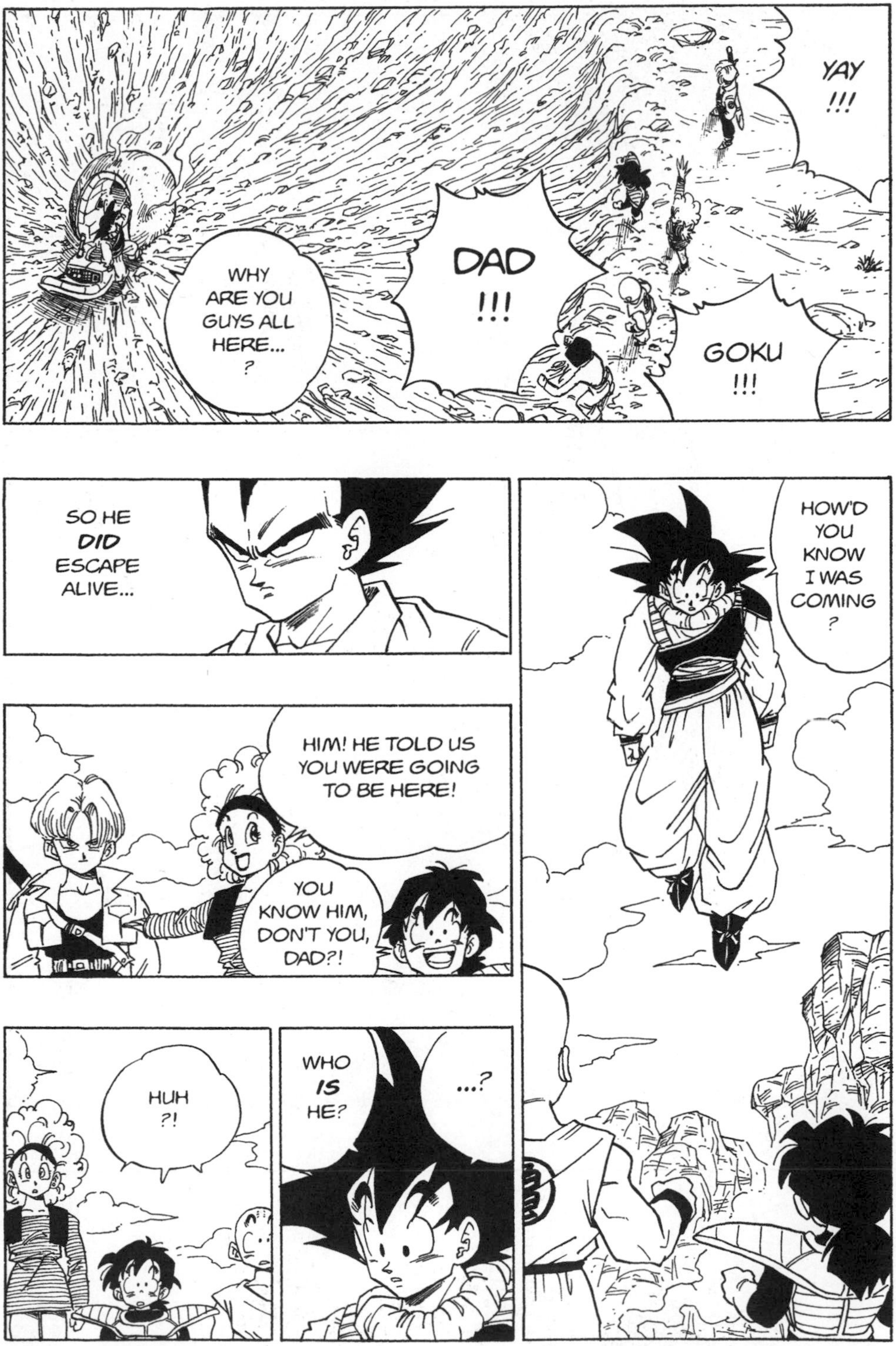
YAY !!!
DAD !!!
GOKU !!!
WHY ARE YOU GUYS ALL HERE... ?
SO HE DID ESCAPE ALIVE...
HOW'D YOU KNOW I WAS COMING ?
HIM! HE TOLD US YOU WERE GOING TO BE HERE!
YOU KNOW HIM, DON'T YOU, DAD?!
HUH ?!
WHO IS HE?
...?

DBZ:140 • The Boy from the Future

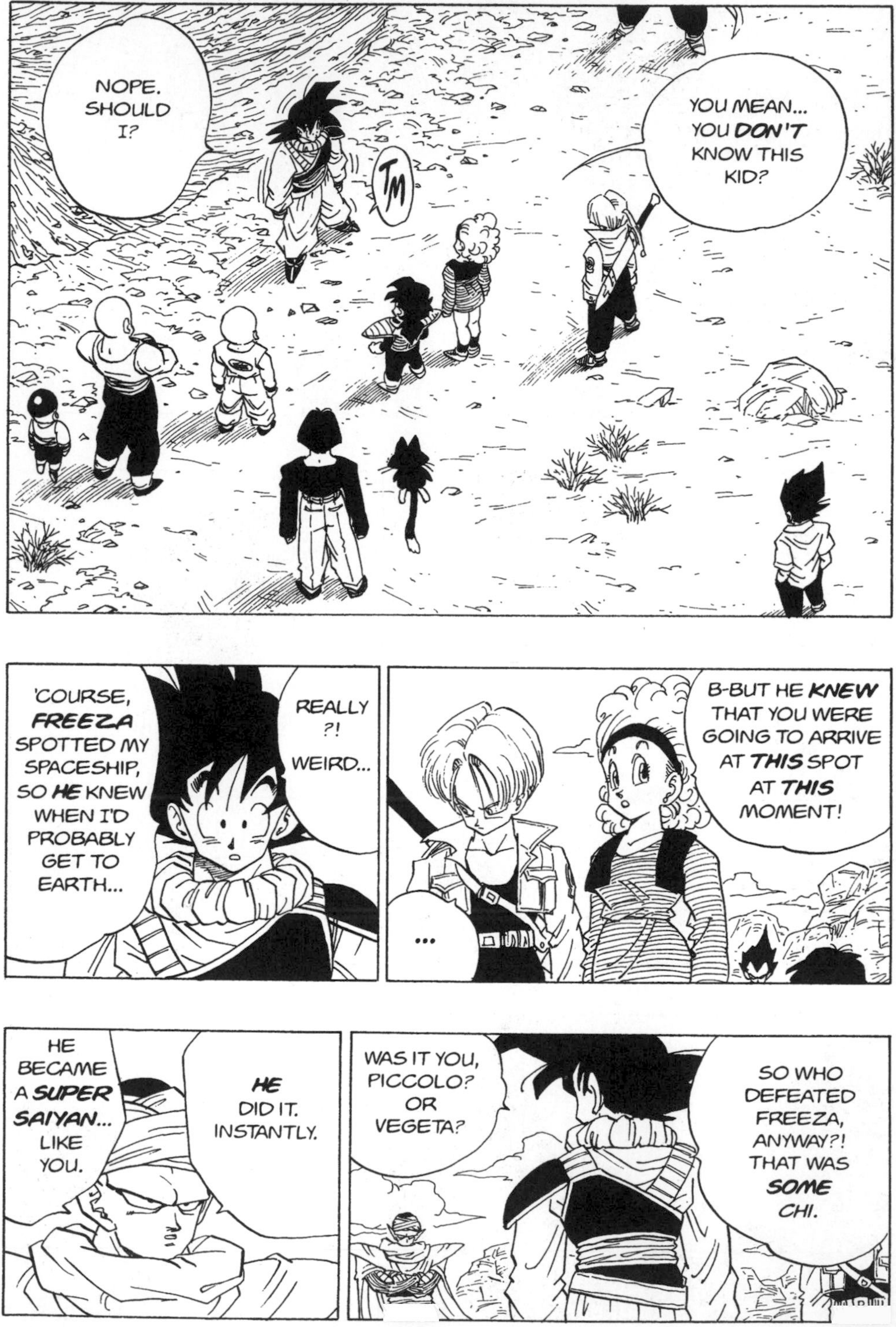
YOU MEAN... YOU DON'T KNOW THIS KID?
TM
NOPE. SHOULD I?
B-BUT HE KNEW THAT YOU WERE GOING TO ARRIVE AT THIS SPOT AT THIS MOMENT!
...
REALLY?! WEIRD...
'COURSE, FREEZA SPOTTED MY SPACESHIP, SO HE KNEW WHEN I'D PROBABLY GET TO EARTH...
SO WHO DEFEATED FREEZA, ANYWAY?! THAT WAS SOME CHI.
WAS IT YOU, PICCOLO? OR VEGETA?
HE DID IT. INSTANTLY.
HE BECAME A SUPER SAIYAN... LIKE YOU.

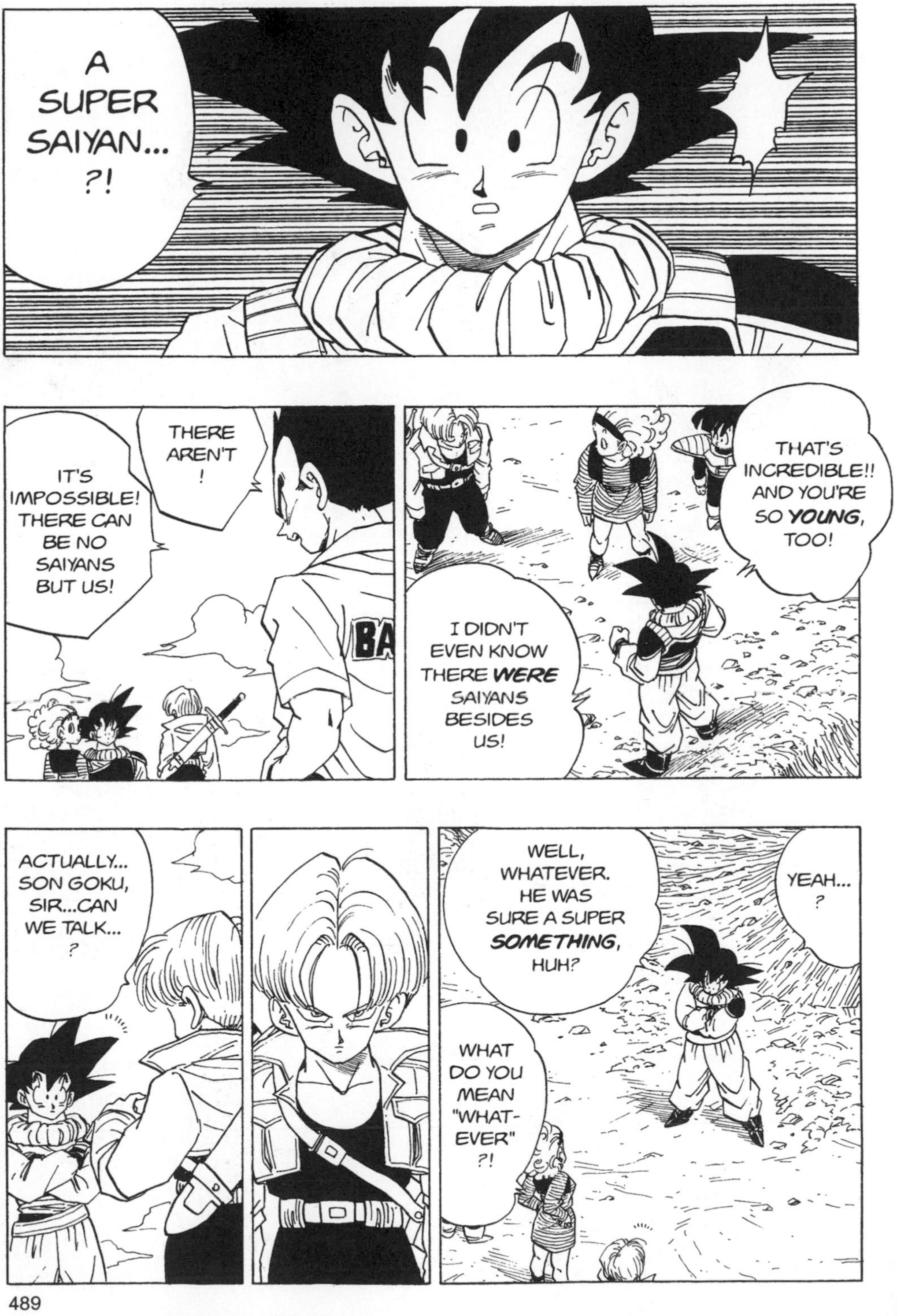
A SUPER SAIYAN... ?!
THAT'S INCREDIBLE!! AND YOU'RE SO YOUNG, TOO!
I DIDN'T EVEN KNOW THERE WERE SAIYANS BESIDES US!
THERE AREN'T!
IT'S IMPOSSIBLE! THERE CAN BE NO SAIYANS BUT US!
WELL, WHATEVER. HE WAS SURE A SUPER SOMETHING, HUH?
YEAH... ?
WHAT DO YOU MEAN "WHAT-EVER" ?!
ACTUALLY... SON GOKU, SIR...CAN WE TALK... ?

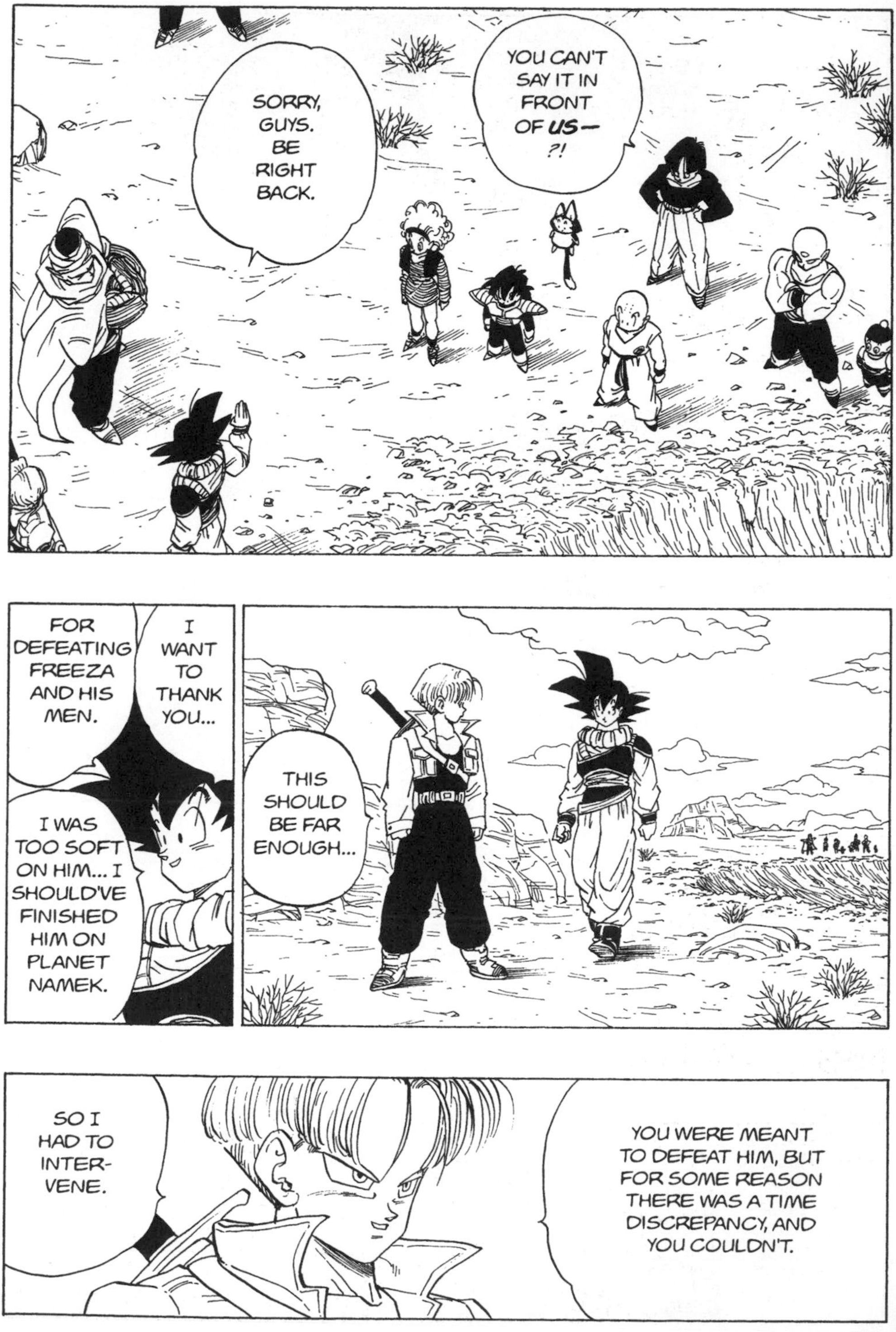

YOU CAN'T SAY IT IN FRONT OF US—?!
SORRY, GUYS. BE RIGHT BACK.
THIS SHOULD BE FAR ENOUGH...
I WANT TO THANK YOU...
FOR DEFEATING FREEZA AND HIS MEN.
I WAS TOO SOFT ON HIM... I SHOULD'VE FINISHED HIM ON PLANET NAMEK.
YOU WERE MEANT TO DEFEAT HIM, BUT FOR SOME REASON THERE WAS A TIME DISCREPANCY, AND YOU COULDN'T.
SO I HAD TO INTERVENE.

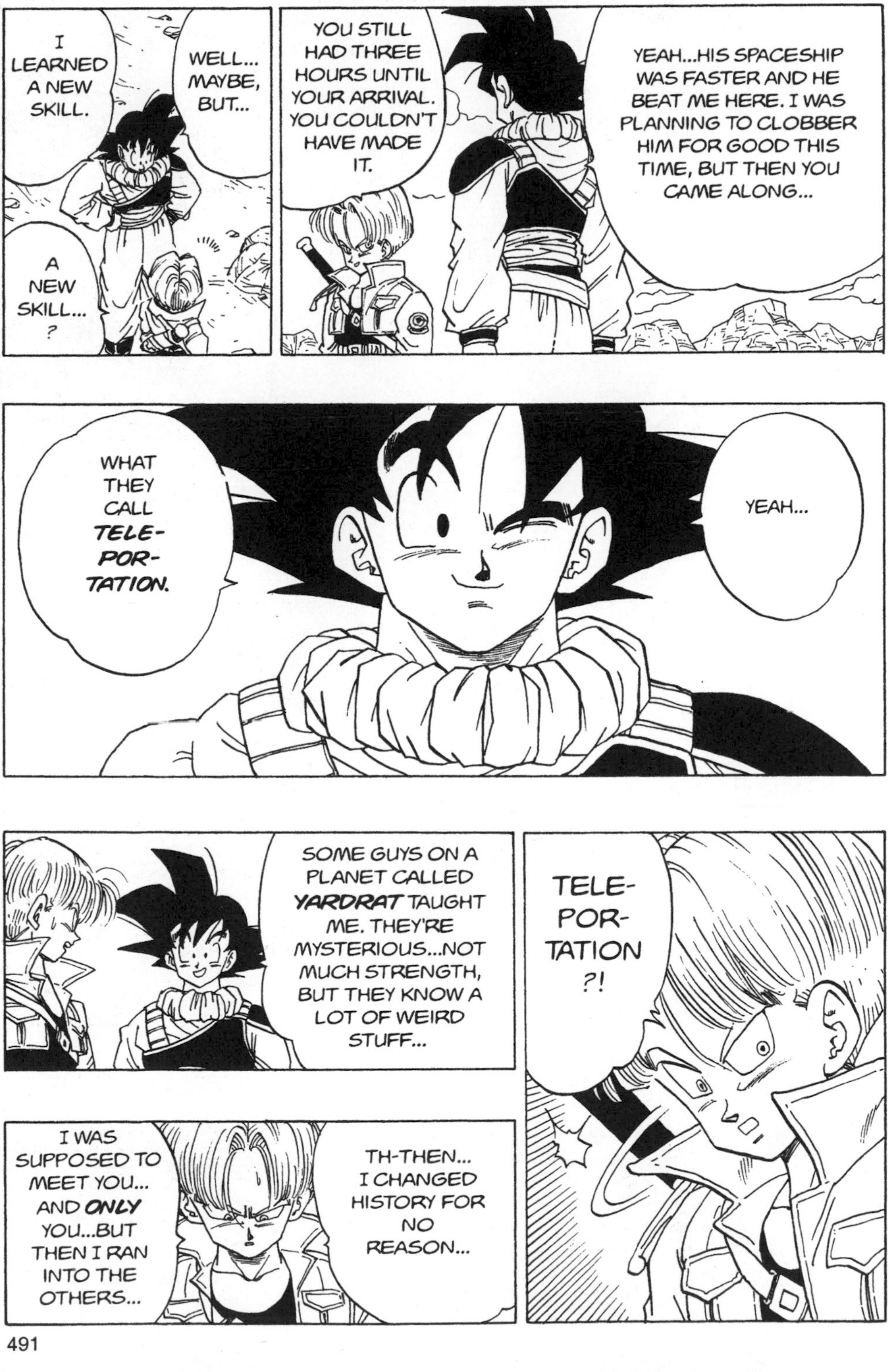
I LEARNED A NEW SKILL.
WELL... MAYBE, BUT...
A NEW SKILL... ?
YOU STILL HAD THREE HOURS UNTIL YOUR ARRIVAL. YOU COULDN'T HAVE MADE IT.
YEAH...HIS SPACESHIP WAS FASTER AND HE BEAT ME HERE. I WAS PLANNING TO CLOBBER HIM FOR GOOD THIS TIME, BUT THEN YOU CAME ALONG...
YEAH...
WHAT THEY CALL ***TELE-PORTATION.***
SOME GUYS ON A PLANET CALLED ***YARDRAT*** TAUGHT ME. THEY'RE MYSTERIOUS...NOT MUCH STRENGTH, BUT THEY KNOW A LOT OF WEIRD STUFF...
TELE-PORTATION ?!
TH-THEN... I CHANGED HISTORY FOR NO REASON...
I WAS SUPPOSED TO MEET YOU... AND ***ONLY*** YOU...BUT THEN I RAN INTO THE OTHERS...

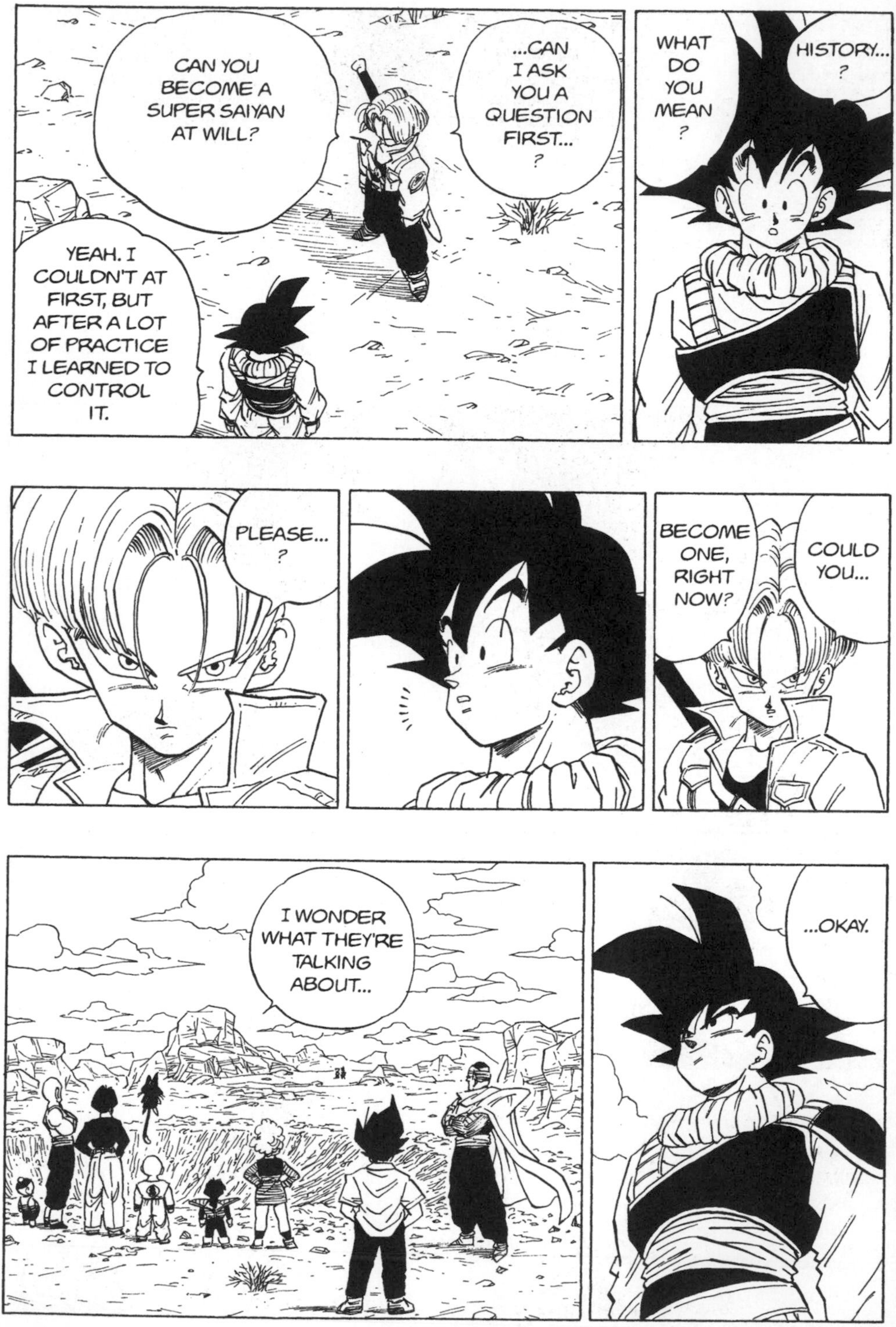
HISTORY...?
WHAT DO YOU MEAN?
...CAN I ASK YOU A QUESTION FIRST...?
CAN YOU BECOME A SUPER SAIYAN AT WILL?
YEAH. I COULDN'T AT FIRST, BUT AFTER A LOT OF PRACTICE I LEARNED TO CONTROL IT.
COULD YOU...
BECOME ONE, RIGHT NOW?
PLEASE...?
...OKAY.
I WONDER WHAT THEY'RE TALKING ABOUT...

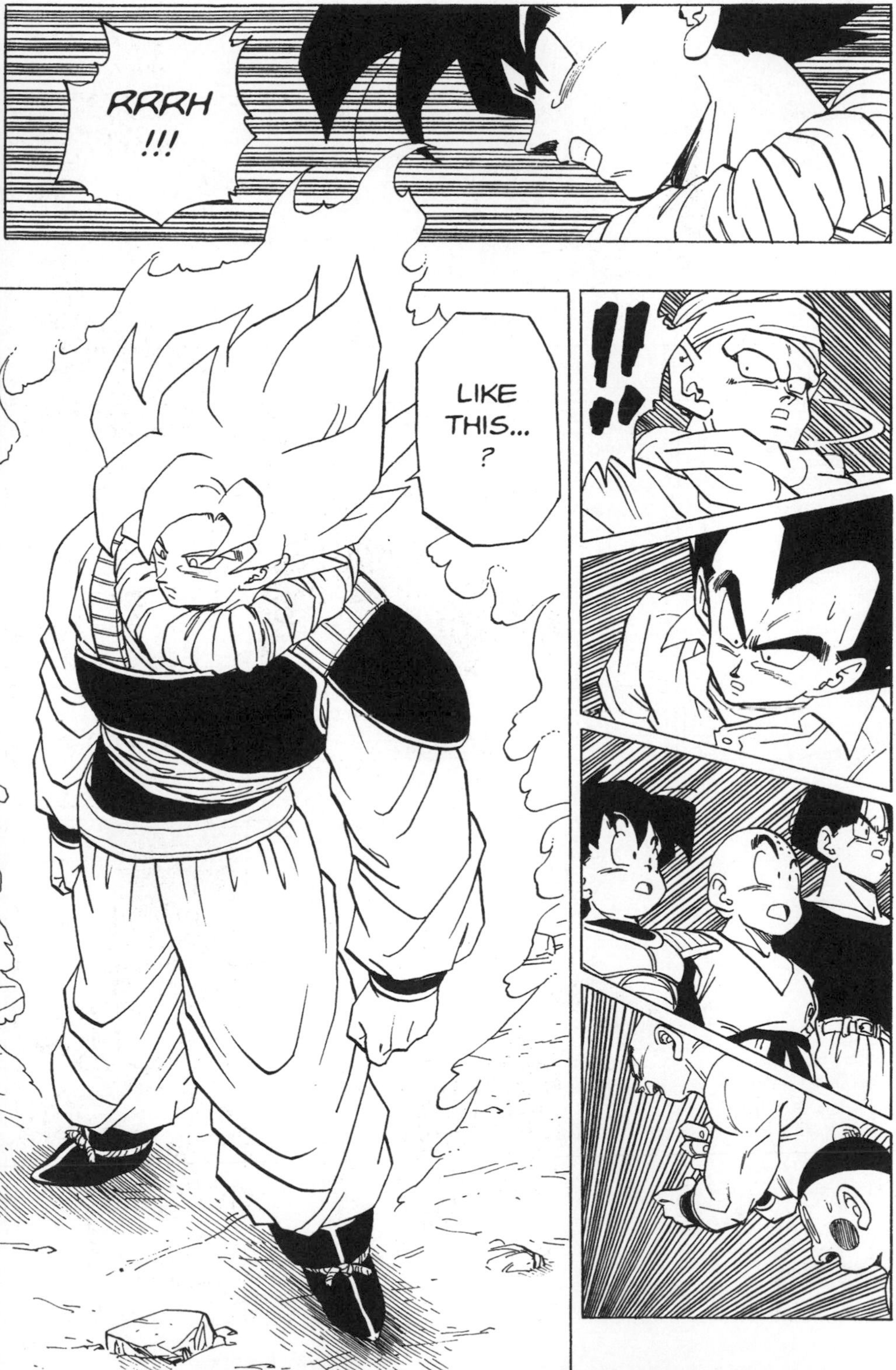
RRRH !!!
LIKE THIS... ?
!!

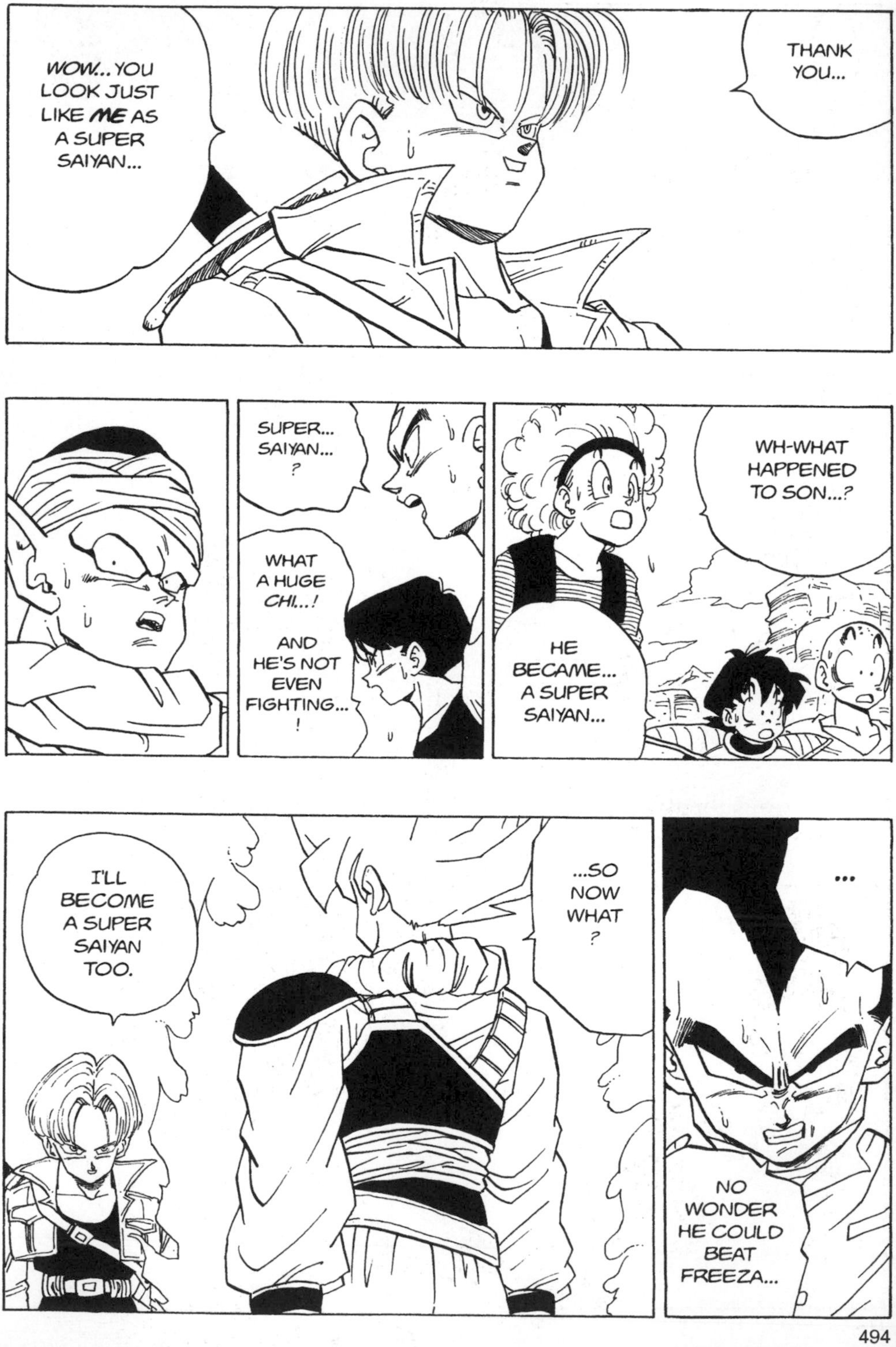
WOW... YOU LOOK JUST LIKE ME AS A SUPER SAIYAN...
THANK YOU...
SUPER... SAIYAN... ?
WHAT A HUGE CHI...! AND HE'S NOT EVEN FIGHTING... !
WH-WHAT HAPPENED TO SON...?
HE BECAME... A SUPER SAIYAN...
I'LL BECOME A SUPER SAIYAN TOO.
...SO NOW WHAT ?
...
NO WONDER HE COULD BEAT FREEZA...

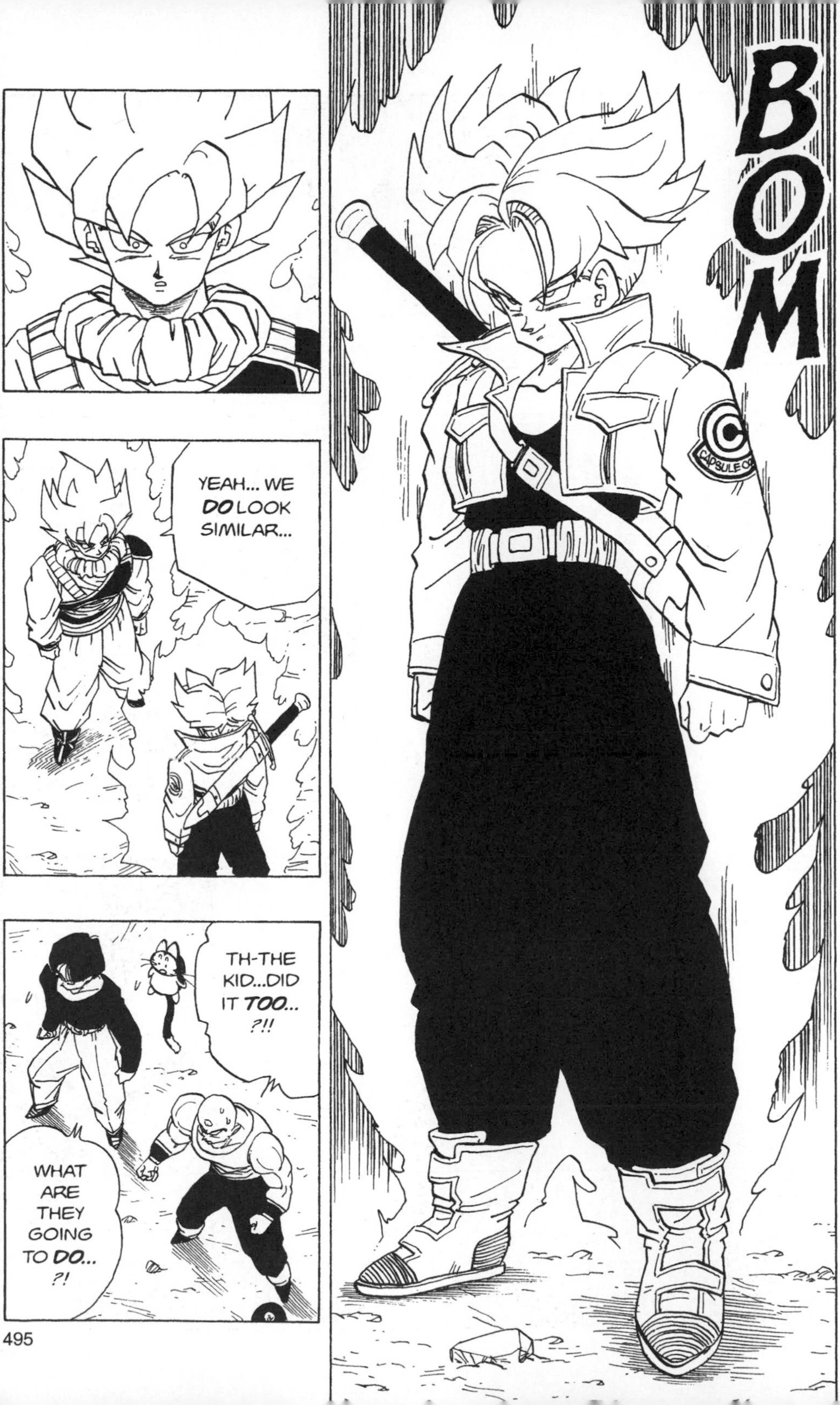
BOM
YEAH... WE DO LOOK SIMILAR...
TH-THE KID...DID IT TOO... ?!!
WHAT ARE THEY GOING TO DO... ?!

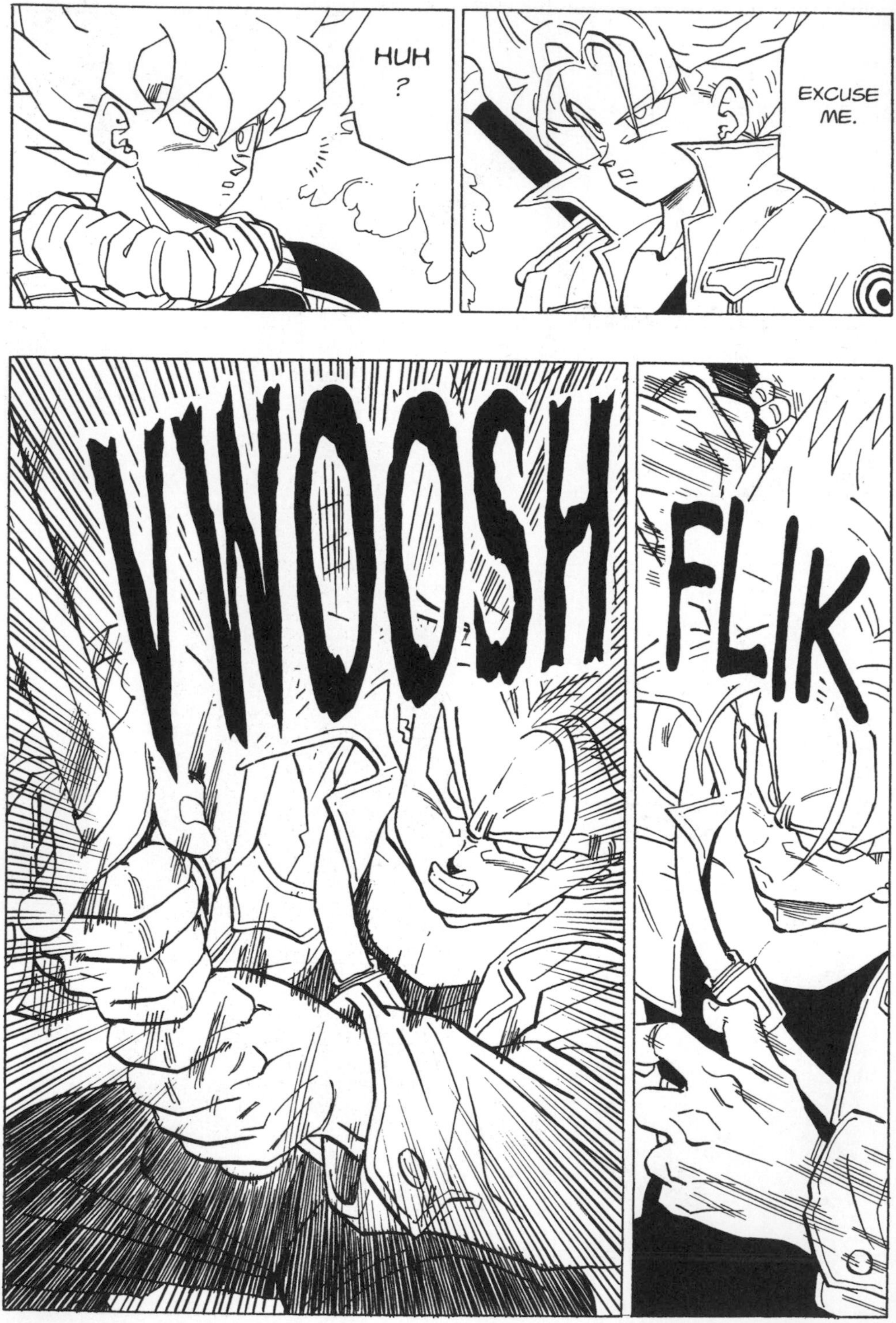
EXCUSE ME.
HUH ?
VWOOSH
FLIK

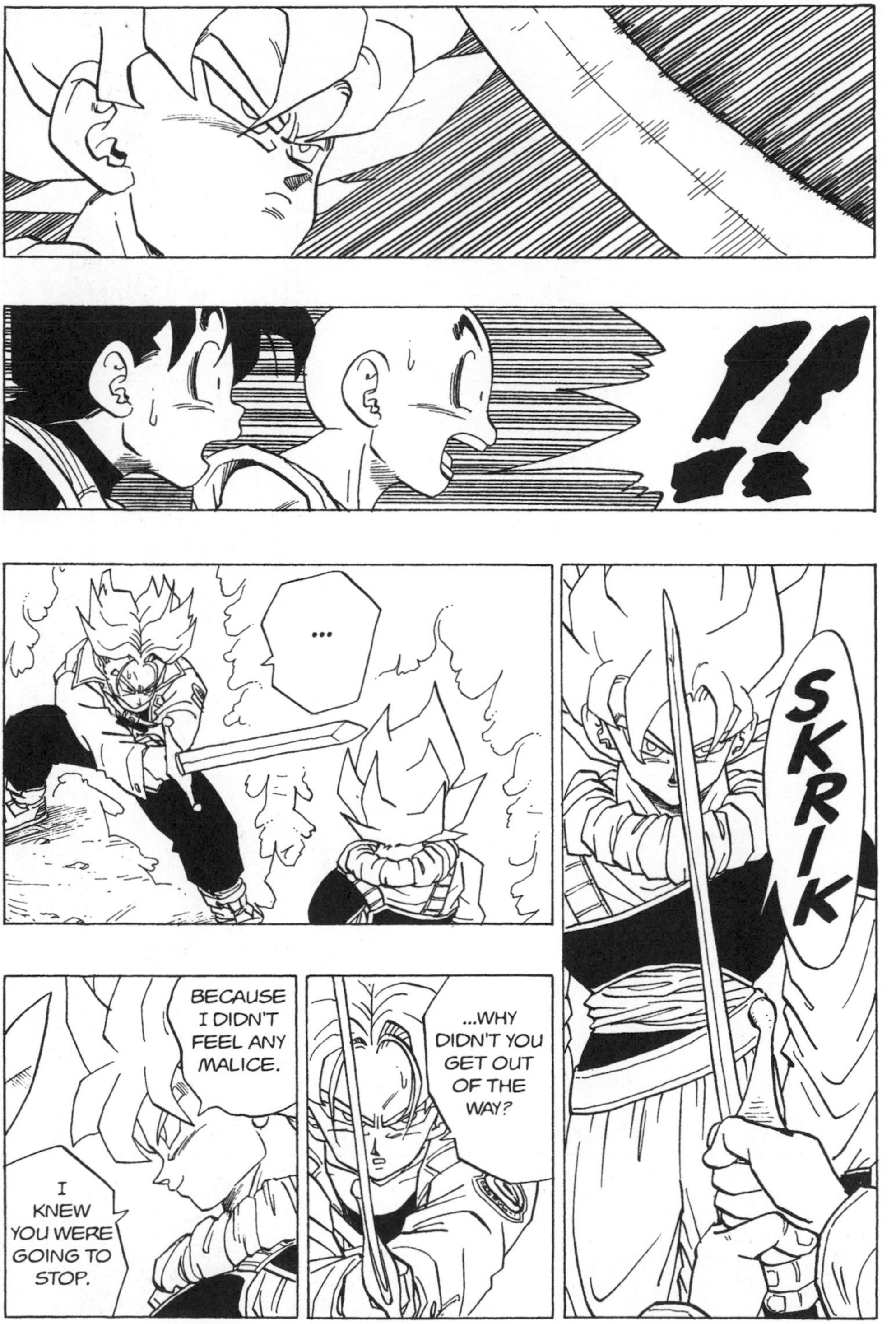
!!
...
SKRIK
...WHY DIDN'T YOU GET OUT OF THE WAY?
BECAUSE I DIDN'T FEEL ANY MALICE.
I KNEW YOU WERE GOING TO STOP.

OKAY.

...WELL... I WON'T STOP THIS TIME, ALL RIGHT?

...I SEE...

VNN

SS...

HWOO

498

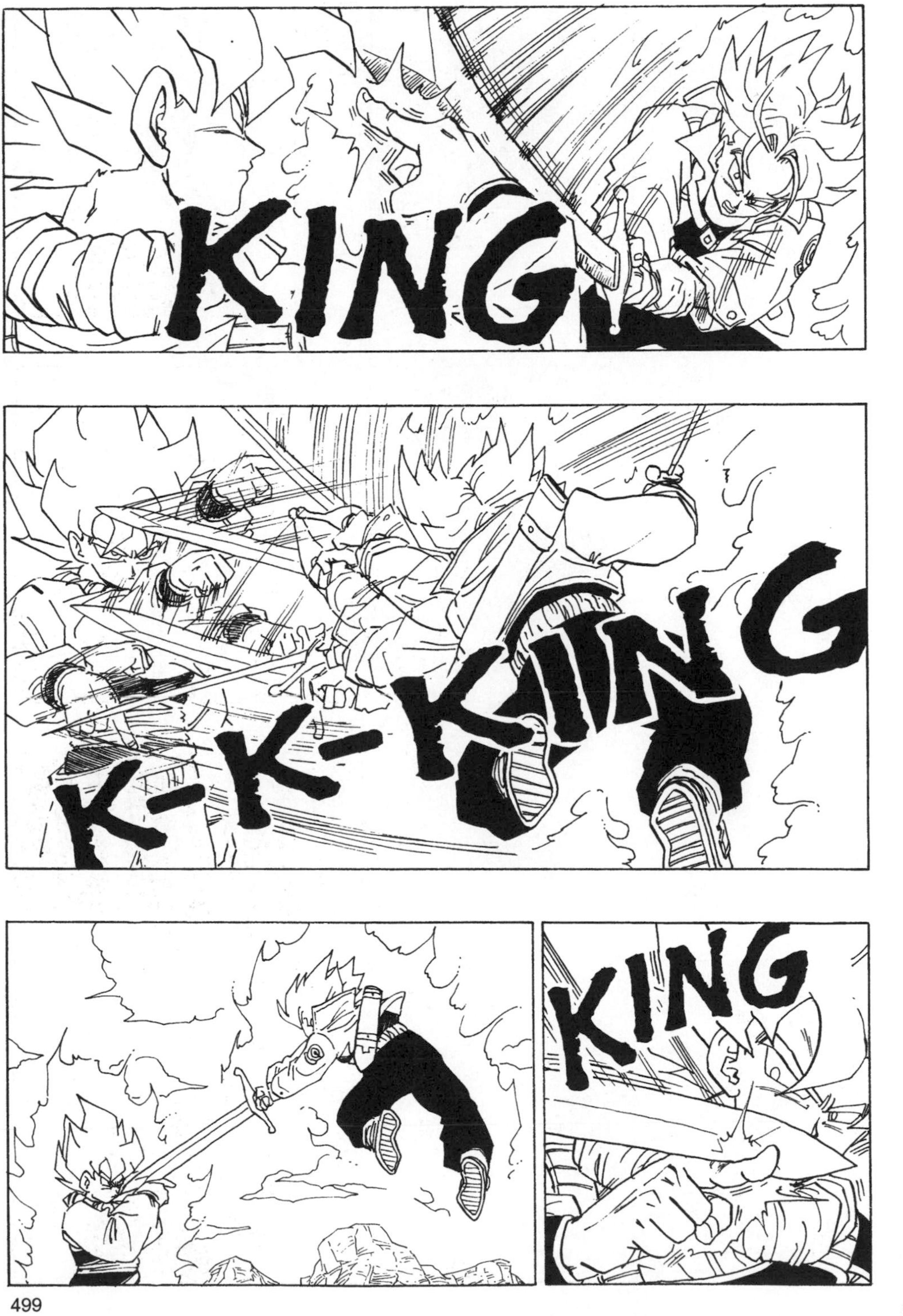
KING
K-K-KIING
KING

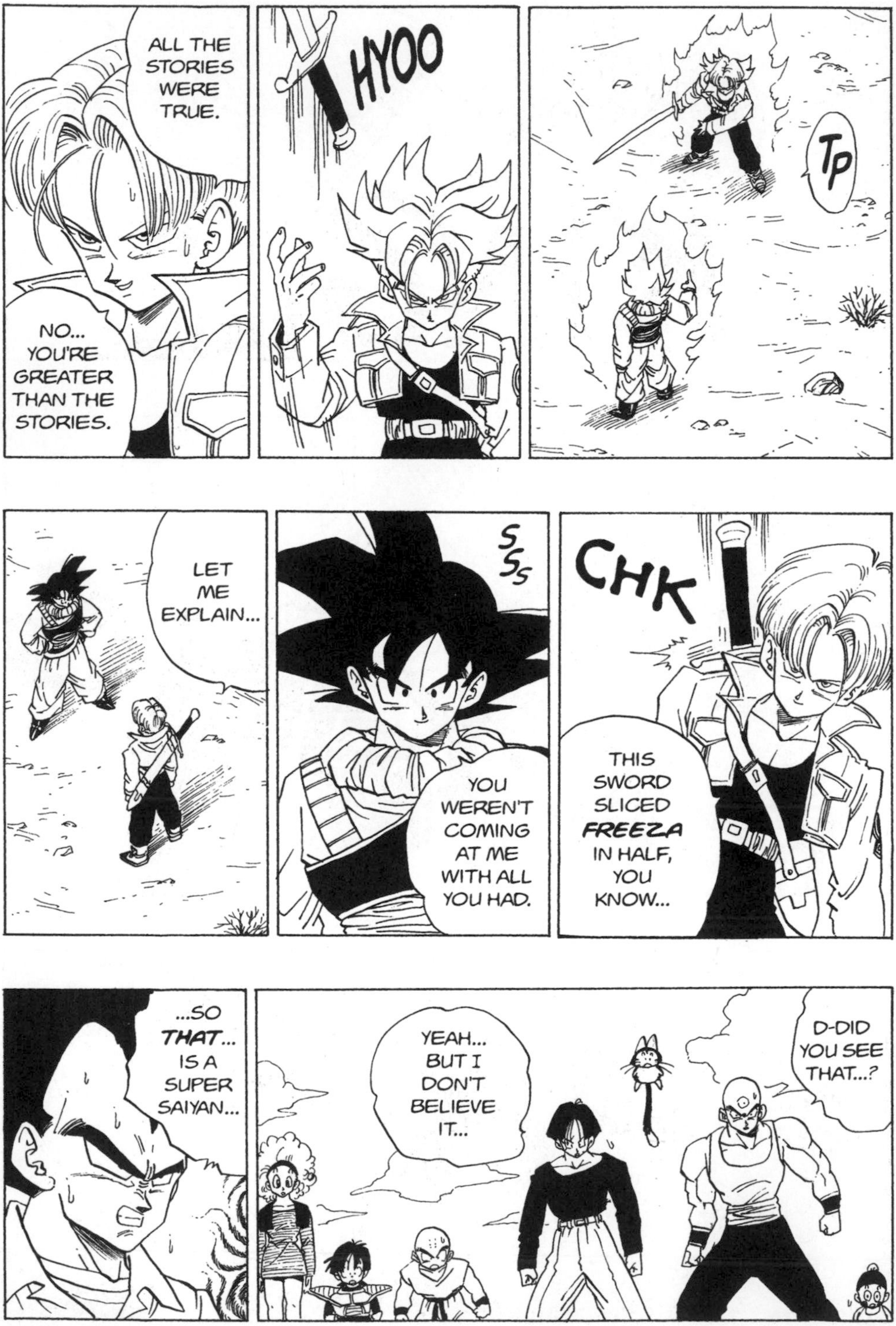
ALL THE STORIES WERE TRUE.
NO... YOU'RE GREATER THAN THE STORIES.
HYOO
TP
LET ME EXPLAIN...
SSS
YOU WEREN'T COMING AT ME WITH ALL YOU HAD.
CHK
THIS SWORD SLICED FREEZA IN HALF, YOU KNOW...
...SO THAT... IS A SUPER SAIYAN...
YEAH... BUT I DON'T BELIEVE IT...
D-DID YOU SEE THAT...?

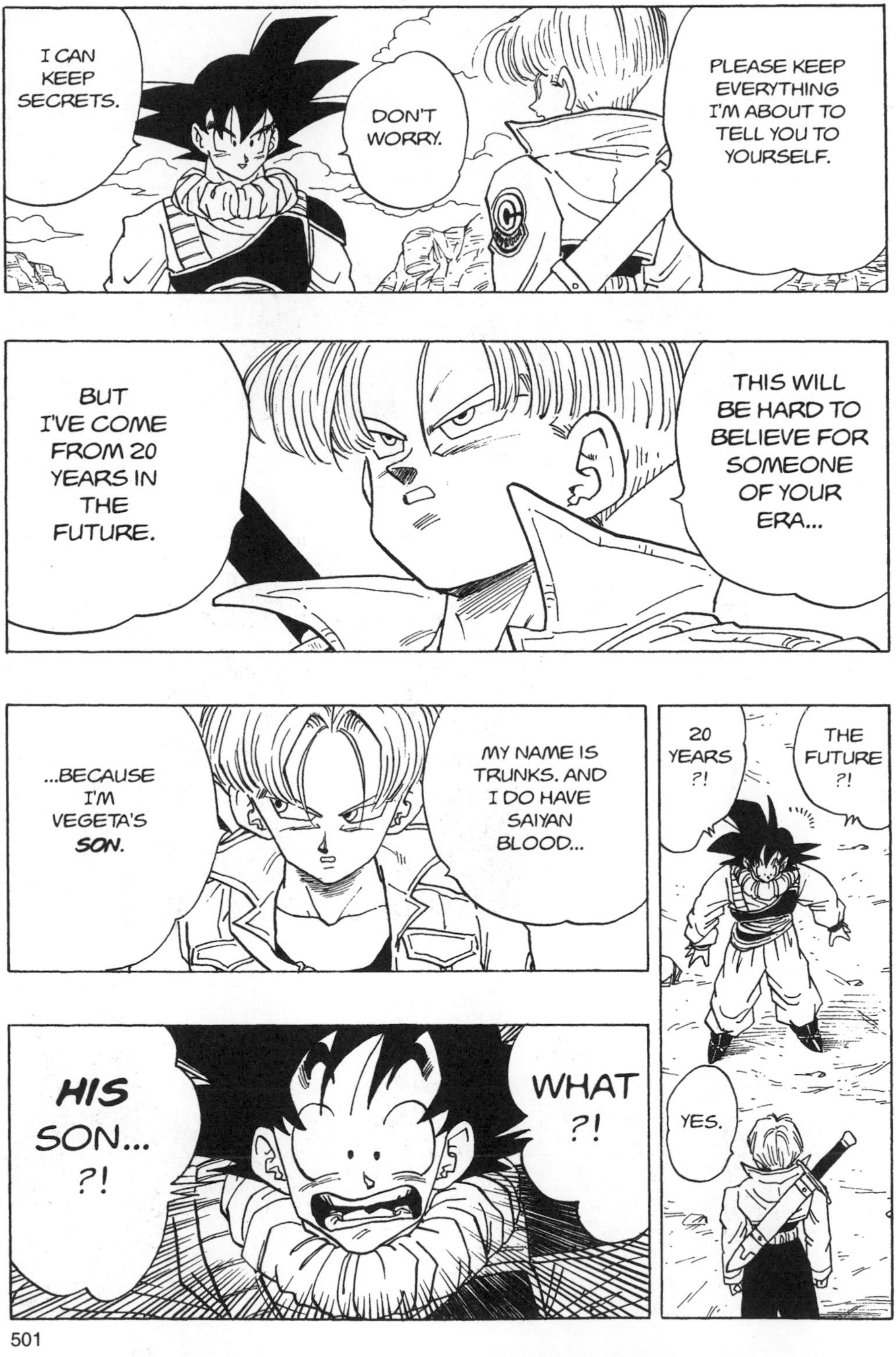
PLEASE KEEP EVERYTHING I'M ABOUT TO TELL YOU TO YOURSELF.
DON'T WORRY.
I CAN KEEP SECRETS.
THIS WILL BE HARD TO BELIEVE FOR SOMEONE OF YOUR ERA...
BUT I'VE COME FROM 20 YEARS IN THE FUTURE.
THE FUTURE ?!
20 YEARS ?!
YES.
MY NAME IS TRUNKS. AND I DO HAVE SAIYAN BLOOD...
...BECAUSE I'M VEGETA'S SON.
WHAT ?!
HIS SON... ?!

DBZ:141• The Terrifying Message

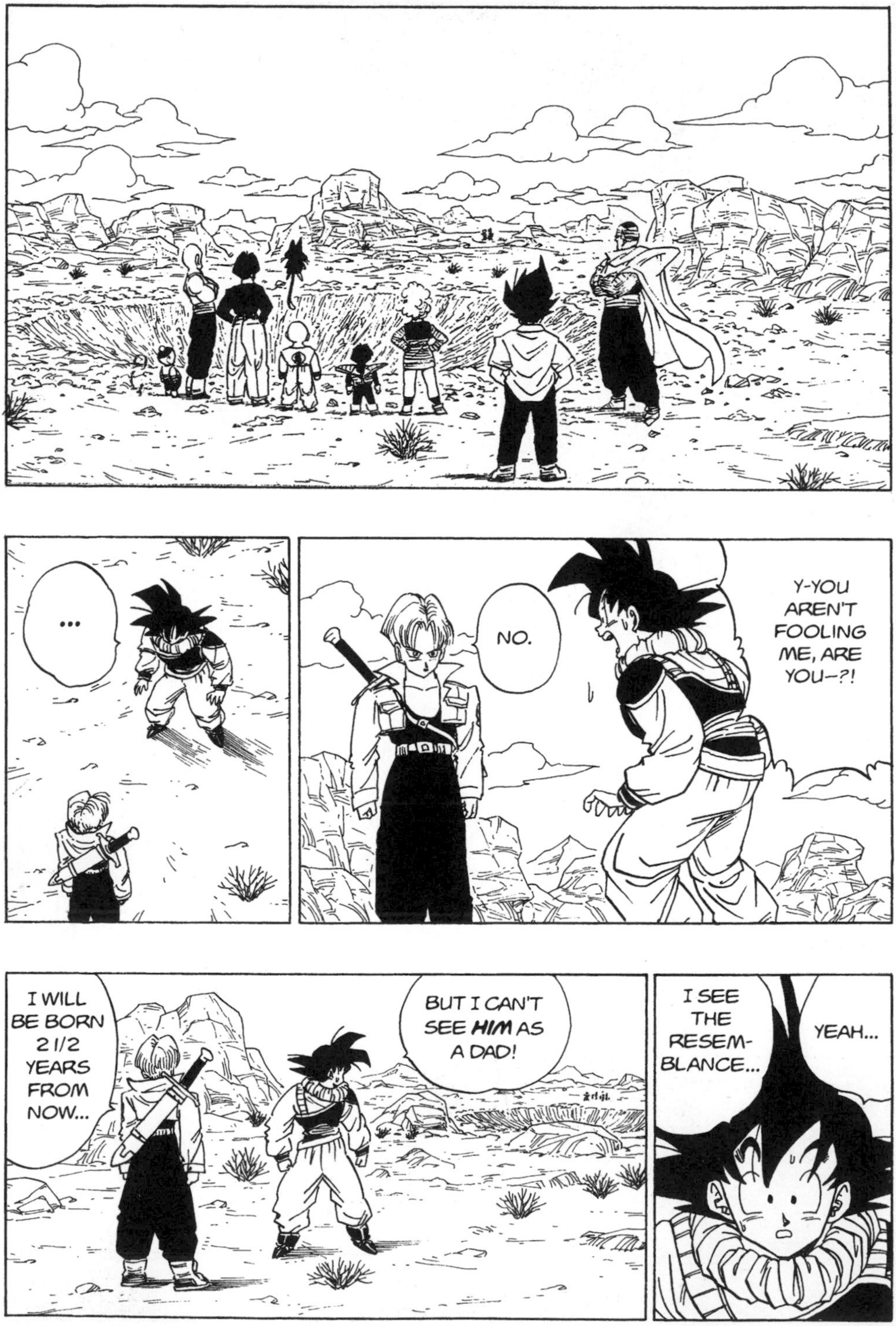
...
Y-YOU AREN'T FOOLING ME, ARE YOU–?!
NO.
I WILL BE BORN 2 1/2 YEARS FROM NOW...
BUT I CAN'T SEE HIM AS A DAD!
I SEE THE RESEM-BLANCE...
YEAH...

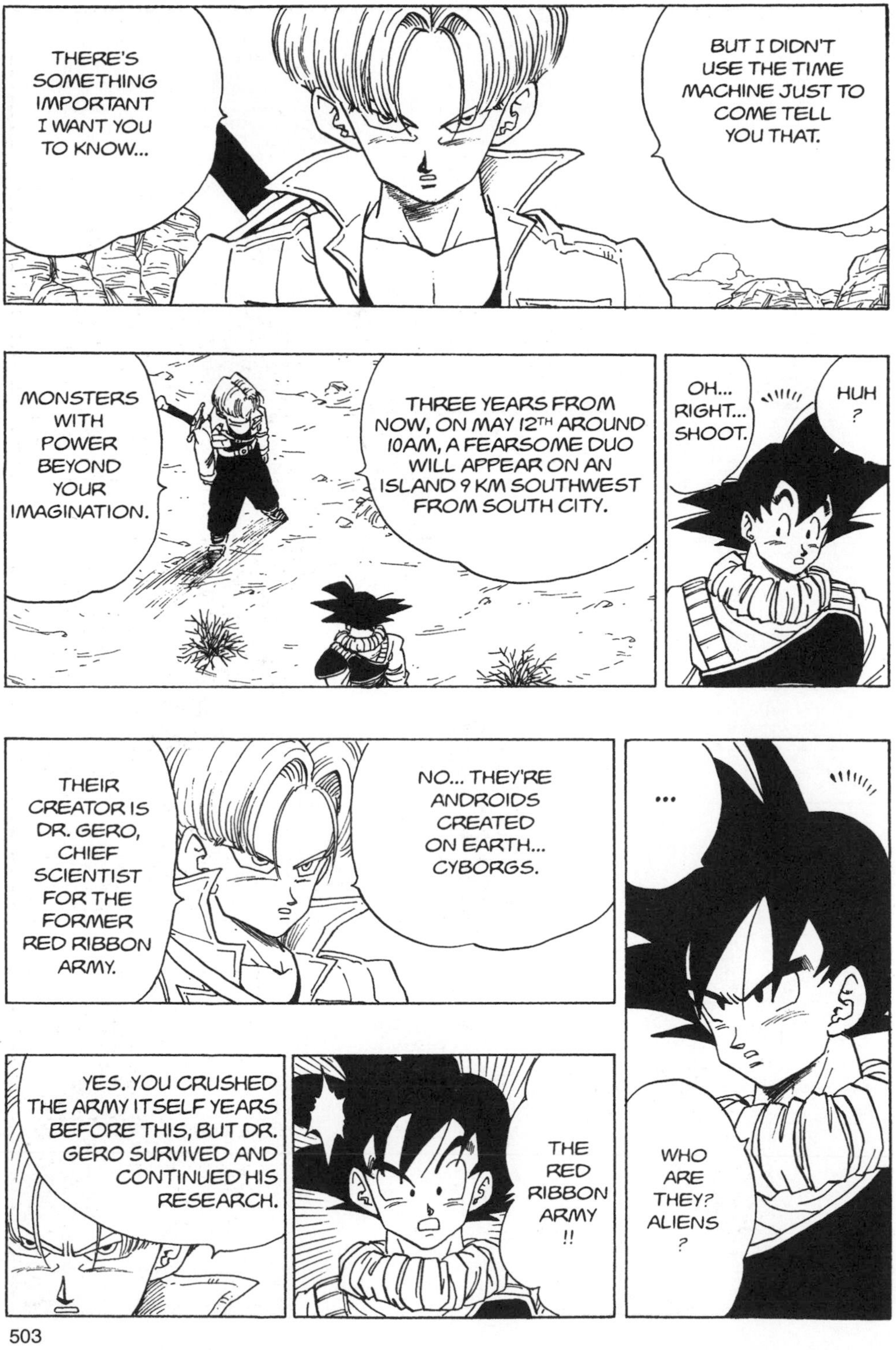
THERE'S SOMETHING IMPORTANT I WANT YOU TO KNOW...
BUT I DIDN'T USE THE TIME MACHINE JUST TO COME TELL YOU THAT.
THREE YEARS FROM NOW, ON MAY 12TH AROUND 10AM, A FEARSOME DUO WILL APPEAR ON AN ISLAND 9 KM SOUTHWEST FROM SOUTH CITY.
MONSTERS WITH POWER BEYOND YOUR IMAGINATION.
HUH?
OH... RIGHT... SHOOT.
WHO ARE THEY? ALIENS?
...
NO... THEY'RE ANDROIDS CREATED ON EARTH... CYBORGS.
THEIR CREATOR IS DR. GERO, CHIEF SCIENTIST FOR THE FORMER RED RIBBON ARMY.
THE RED RIBBON ARMY!!
YES. YOU CRUSHED THE ARMY ITSELF YEARS BEFORE THIS, BUT DR. GERO SURVIVED AND CONTINUED HIS RESEARCH.

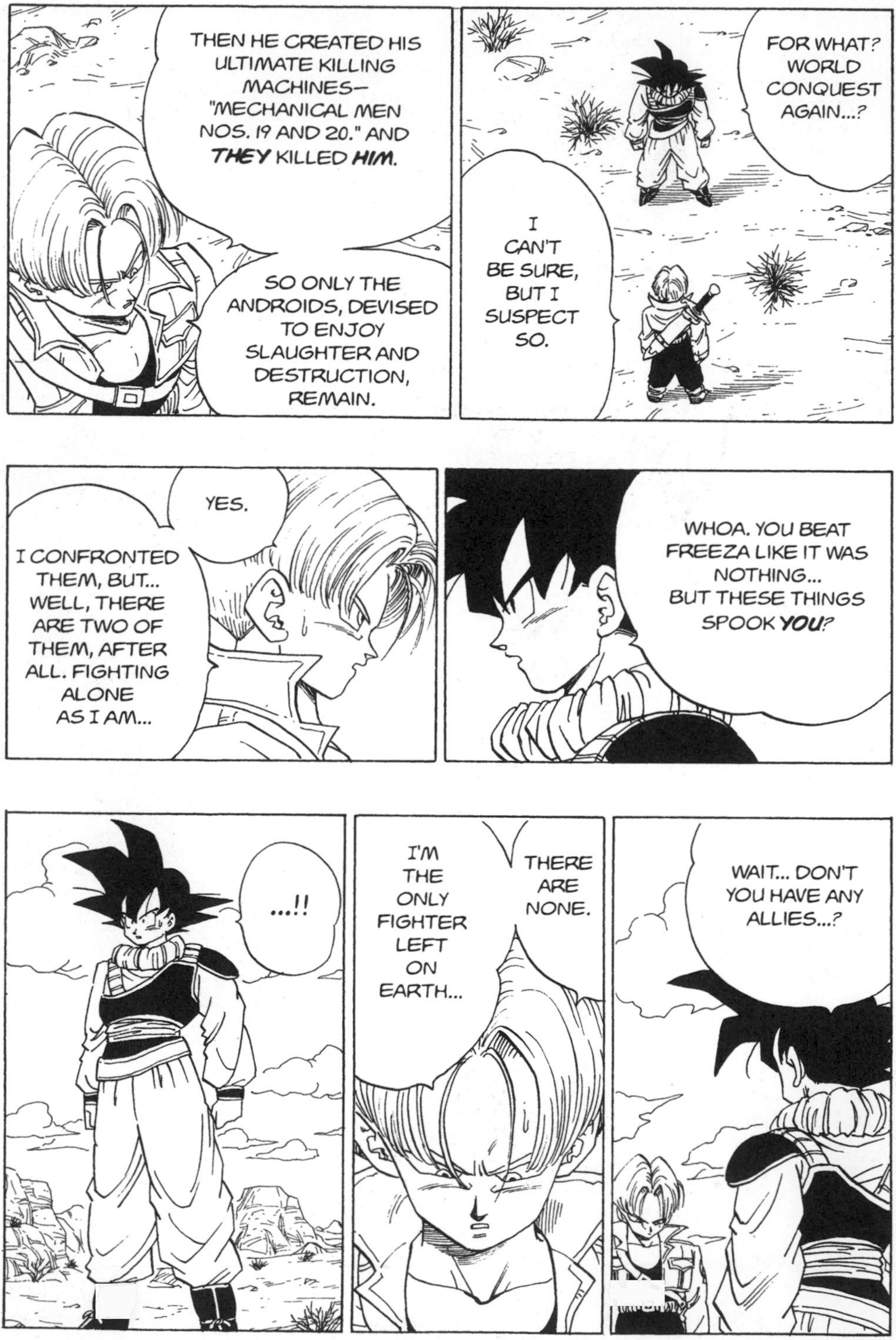
FOR WHAT? WORLD CONQUEST AGAIN...?
I CAN'T BE SURE, BUT I SUSPECT SO.
THEN HE CREATED HIS ULTIMATE KILLING MACHINES— "MECHANICAL MEN NOS. 19 AND 20." AND ***THEY*** KILLED ***HIM***.
SO ONLY THE ANDROIDS, DEVISED TO ENJOY SLAUGHTER AND DESTRUCTION, REMAIN.
WHOA. YOU BEAT FREEZA LIKE IT WAS NOTHING... BUT THESE THINGS SPOOK ***YOU***?
YES.
I CONFRONTED THEM, BUT... WELL, THERE ARE TWO OF THEM, AFTER ALL. FIGHTING ALONE AS I AM...
WAIT... DON'T YOU HAVE ANY ALLIES...?
THERE ARE NONE.
I'M THE ONLY FIGHTER LEFT ON EARTH...
...!!

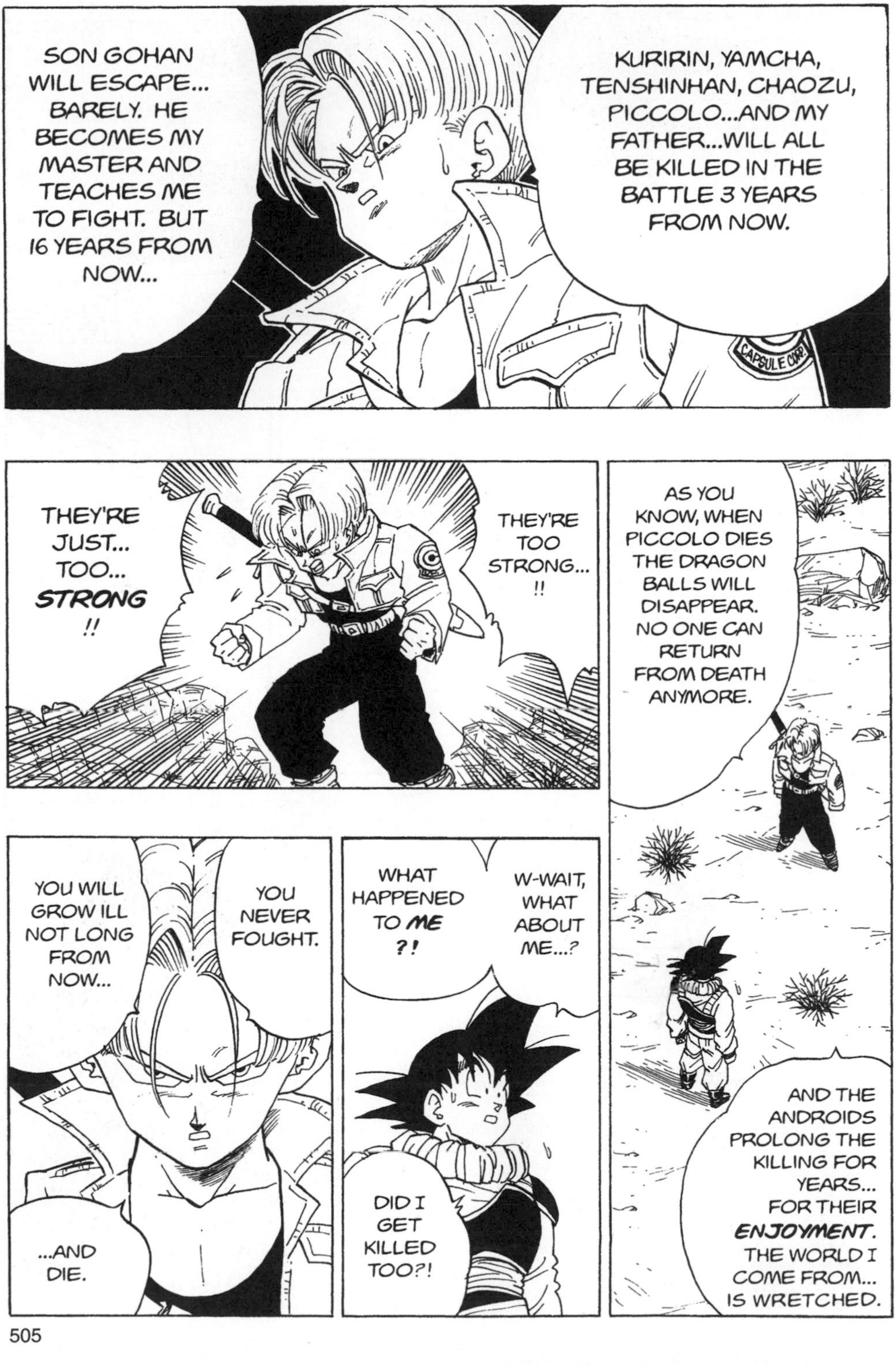
SON GOHAN WILL ESCAPE... BARELY. HE BECOMES MY MASTER AND TEACHES ME TO FIGHT. BUT 16 YEARS FROM NOW...
KURIRIN, YAMCHA, TENSHINHAN, CHAOZU, PICCOLO...AND MY FATHER...WILL ALL BE KILLED IN THE BATTLE 3 YEARS FROM NOW.
CAPSULE CORP.
AS YOU KNOW, WHEN PICCOLO DIES THE DRAGON BALLS WILL DISAPPEAR. NO ONE CAN RETURN FROM DEATH ANYMORE.
THEY'RE TOO STRONG... !!
THEY'RE JUST... TOO... STRONG !!
AND THE ANDROIDS PROLONG THE KILLING FOR YEARS... FOR THEIR ENJOYMENT. THE WORLD I COME FROM... IS WRETCHED.
W-WAIT, WHAT ABOUT ME...?
WHAT HAPPENED TO ME ?!
DID I GET KILLED TOO?!
YOU NEVER FOUGHT.
YOU WILL GROW ILL NOT LONG FROM NOW...
...AND DIE.

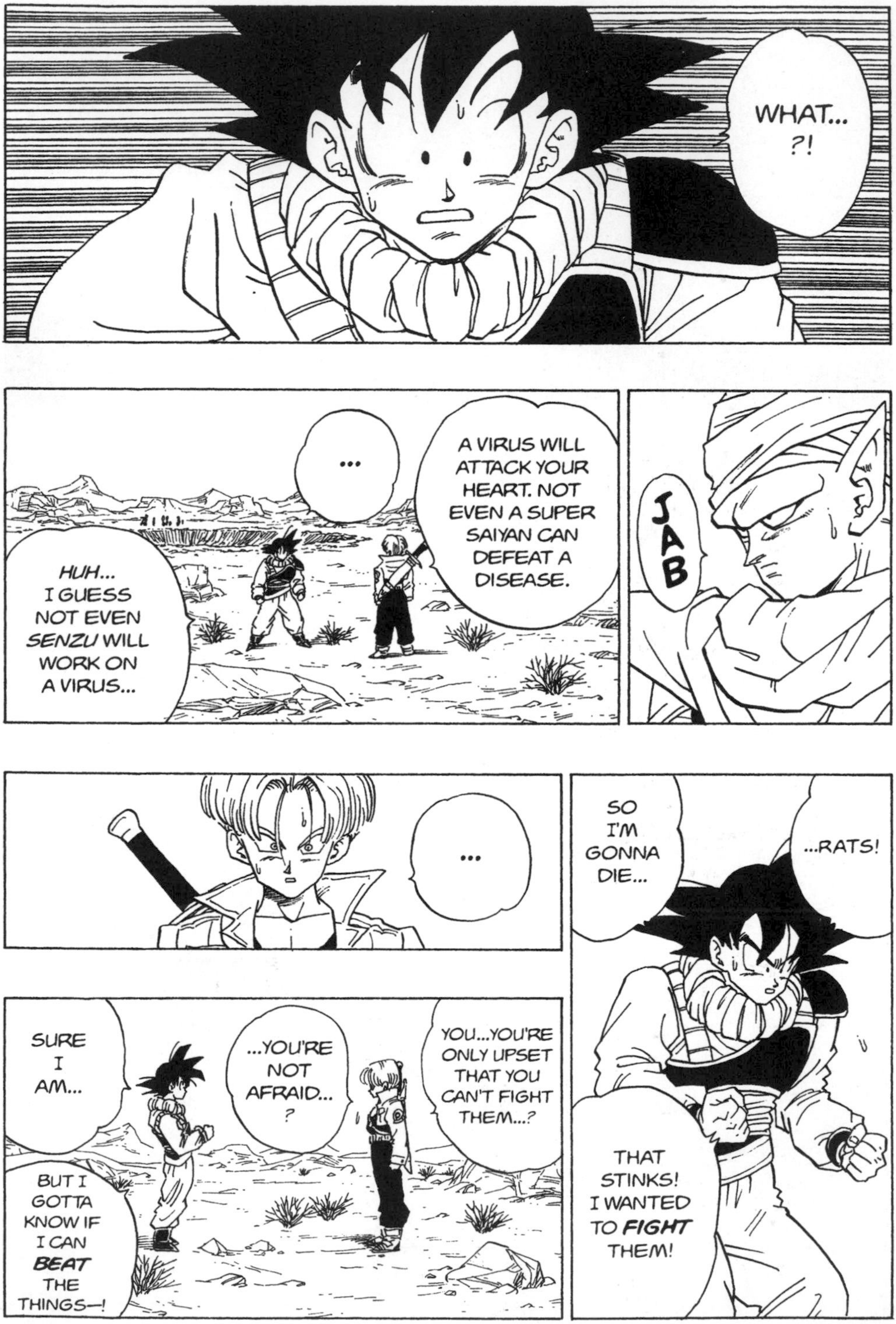
WHAT... ?!
A VIRUS WILL ATTACK YOUR HEART. NOT EVEN A SUPER SAIYAN CAN DEFEAT A DISEASE.
...
HUH... I GUESS NOT EVEN *SENZU* WILL WORK ON A VIRUS...
JAB
...
SO I'M GONNA DIE...
...RATS!
THAT STINKS! I WANTED TO ***FIGHT*** THEM!
YOU...YOU'RE ONLY UPSET THAT YOU CAN'T FIGHT THEM...?
...YOU'RE NOT AFRAID... ?
SURE I AM...
BUT I GOTTA KNOW IF I CAN ***BEAT*** THE THINGS—!

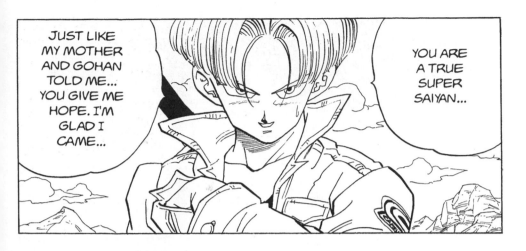

YOU ARE A TRUE SUPER SAIYAN...
JUST LIKE MY MOTHER AND GOHAN TOLD ME... YOU GIVE ME HOPE. I'M GLAD I CAME...
WHEN THE SYMPTOMS APPEAR, TAKE THIS.
WHAT'S THAT... ?
THIS IS YOUR MEDICINE. IT WAS AN INCURABLE DISEASE IN ***THIS*** TIME. BUT 20 YEARS FROM NOW THERE'LL BE A DRUG FOR IT.
WITH THIS... YOU WON'T HAVE TO DIE.
REALLY?! GREAT!! THANKS !!
GEEZ, WHY DIDN'T YOU SAY SO IN THE FIRST PLACE ?!
I REALLY SHOULDN'T BE DOING THIS... IT CHANGES THE FUTURE... BUT WITH A FUTURE LIKE OURS...

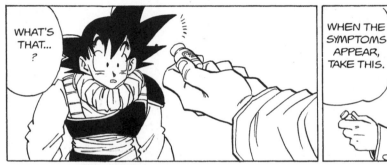

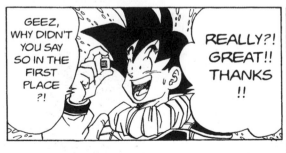

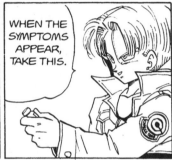

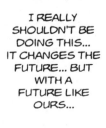

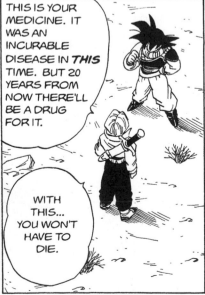

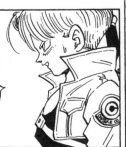

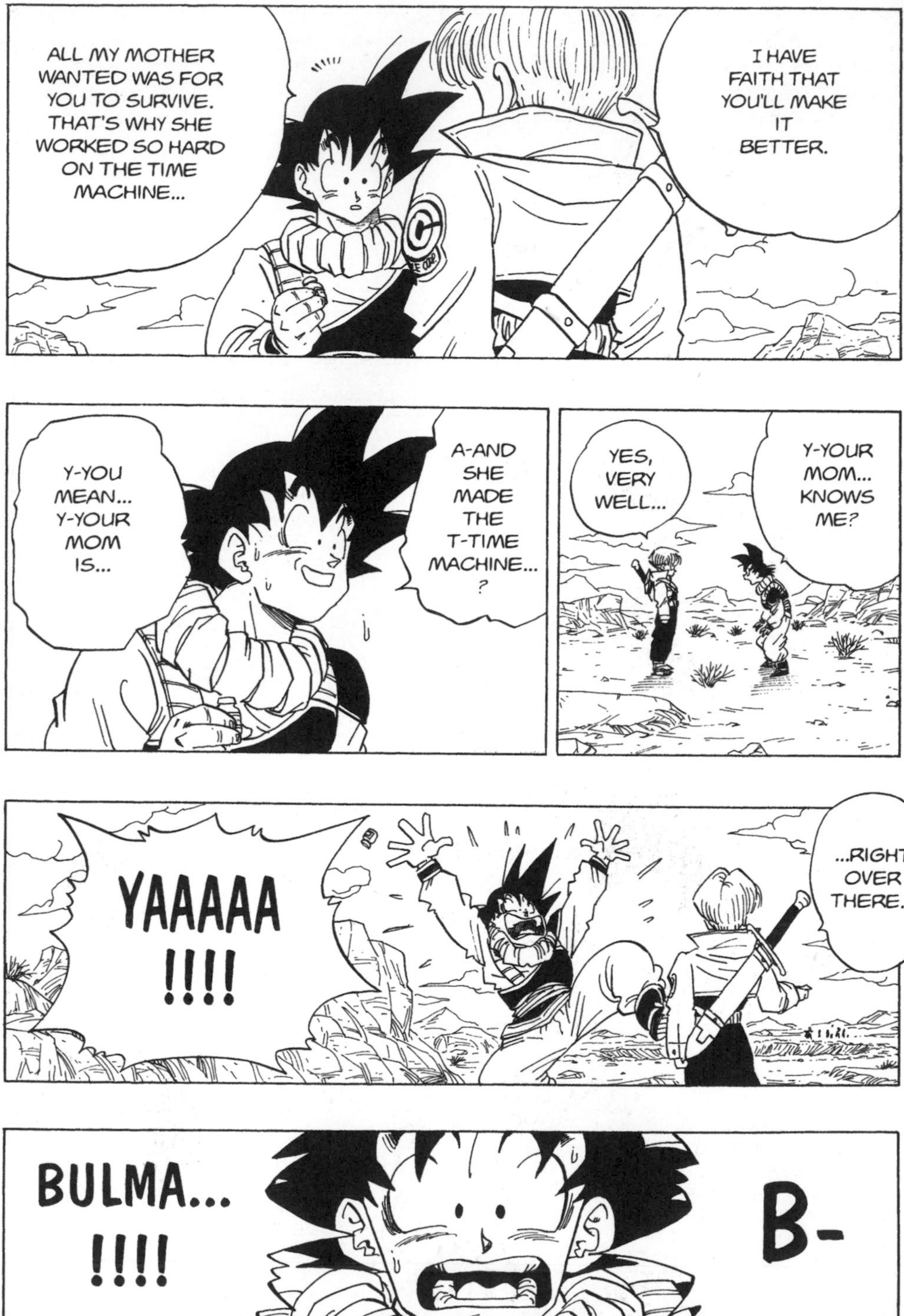
ALL MY MOTHER WANTED WAS FOR YOU TO SURVIVE. THAT'S WHY SHE WORKED SO HARD ON THE TIME MACHINE...
I HAVE FAITH THAT YOU'LL MAKE IT BETTER.
Y-YOU MEAN... Y-YOUR MOM IS...
A-AND SHE MADE THE T-TIME MACHINE...?
YES, VERY WELL...
Y-YOUR MOM... KNOWS ME?
YAAAAA !!!!
...RIGHT OVER THERE...
BULMA... !!!!
B-

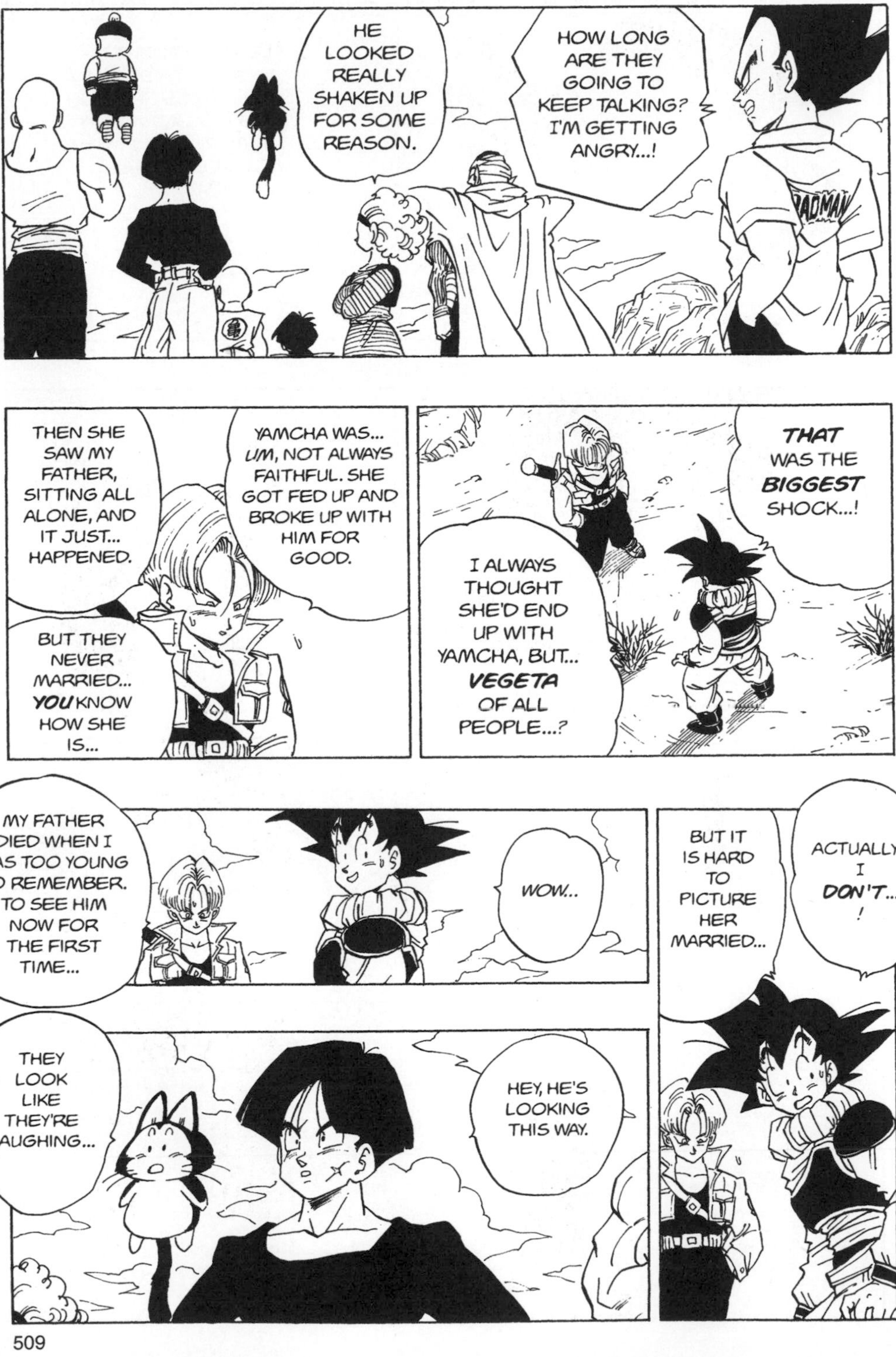
HOW LONG ARE THEY GOING TO KEEP TALKING? I'M GETTING ANGRY...!
HE LOOKED REALLY SHAKEN UP FOR SOME REASON.
THAT WAS THE BIGGEST SHOCK...!
I ALWAYS THOUGHT SHE'D END UP WITH YAMCHA, BUT... VEGETA OF ALL PEOPLE...?
YAMCHA WAS... UM, NOT ALWAYS FAITHFUL. SHE GOT FED UP AND BROKE UP WITH HIM FOR GOOD.
THEN SHE SAW MY FATHER, SITTING ALL ALONE, AND IT JUST... HAPPENED.
BUT THEY NEVER MARRIED... YOU KNOW HOW SHE IS...
ACTUALLY... I DON'T... !
BUT IT IS HARD TO PICTURE HER MARRIED...
WOW...
MY FATHER DIED WHEN I WAS TOO YOUNG TO REMEMBER. TO SEE HIM NOW FOR THE FIRST TIME...
HEY, HE'S LOOKING THIS WAY.
THEY LOOK LIKE THEY'RE LAUGHING...

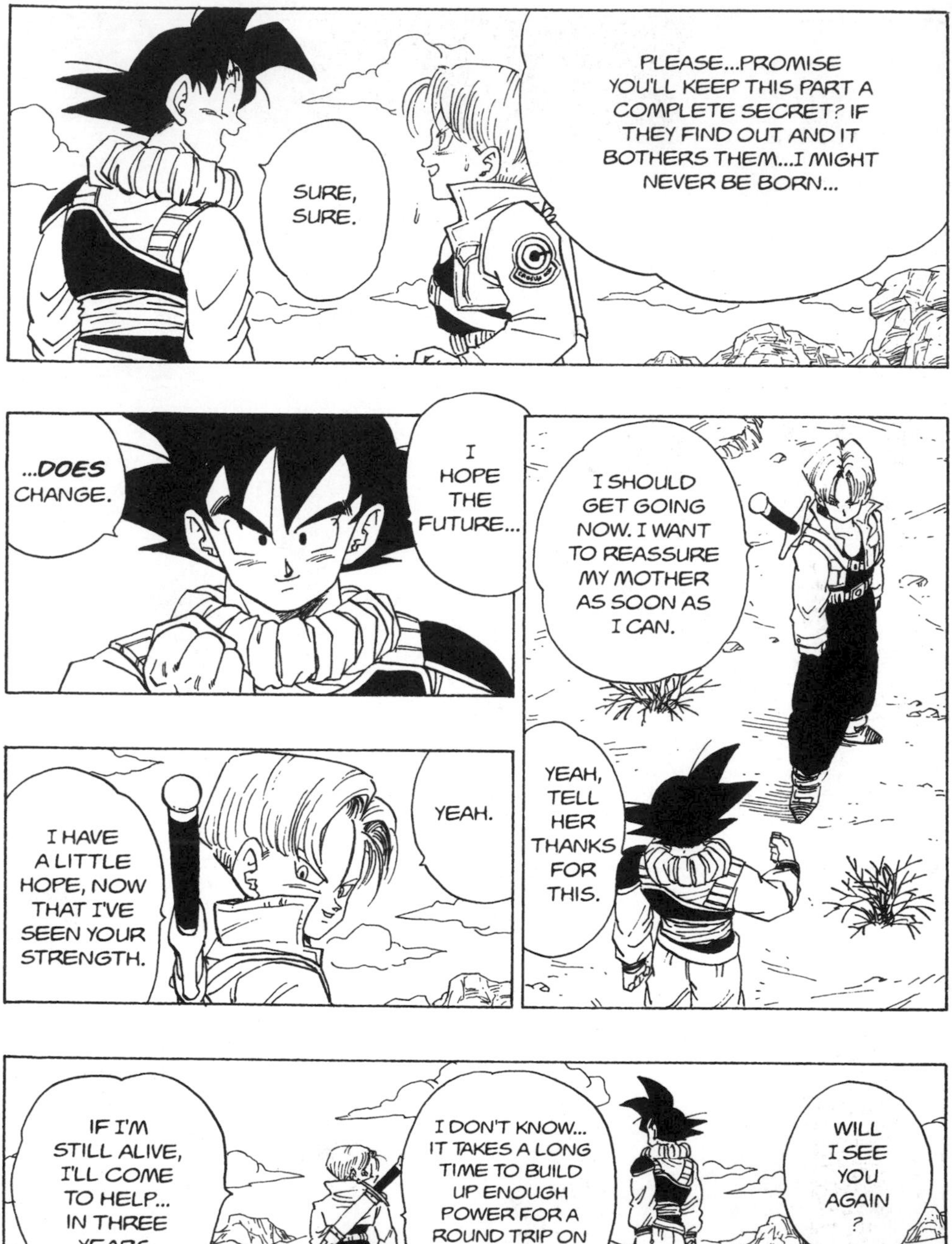
PLEASE...PROMISE YOU'LL KEEP THIS PART A COMPLETE SECRET? IF THEY FIND OUT AND IT BOTHERS THEM...I MIGHT NEVER BE BORN...
SURE, SURE.
I SHOULD GET GOING NOW. I WANT TO REASSURE MY MOTHER AS SOON AS I CAN.
YEAH, TELL HER THANKS FOR THIS.
I HOPE THE FUTURE...
...**DOES** CHANGE.
YEAH.
I HAVE A LITTLE HOPE, NOW THAT I'VE SEEN YOUR STRENGTH.
WILL I SEE YOU AGAIN ?
I DON'T KNOW... IT TAKES A LONG TIME TO BUILD UP ENOUGH POWER FOR A ROUND TRIP ON THE TIME MACHINE...
IF I'M STILL ALIVE, I'LL COME TO HELP... IN THREE YEARS.

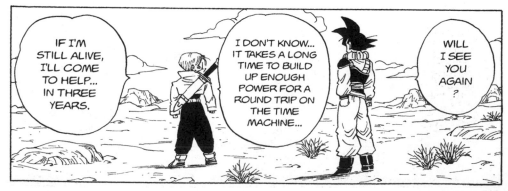

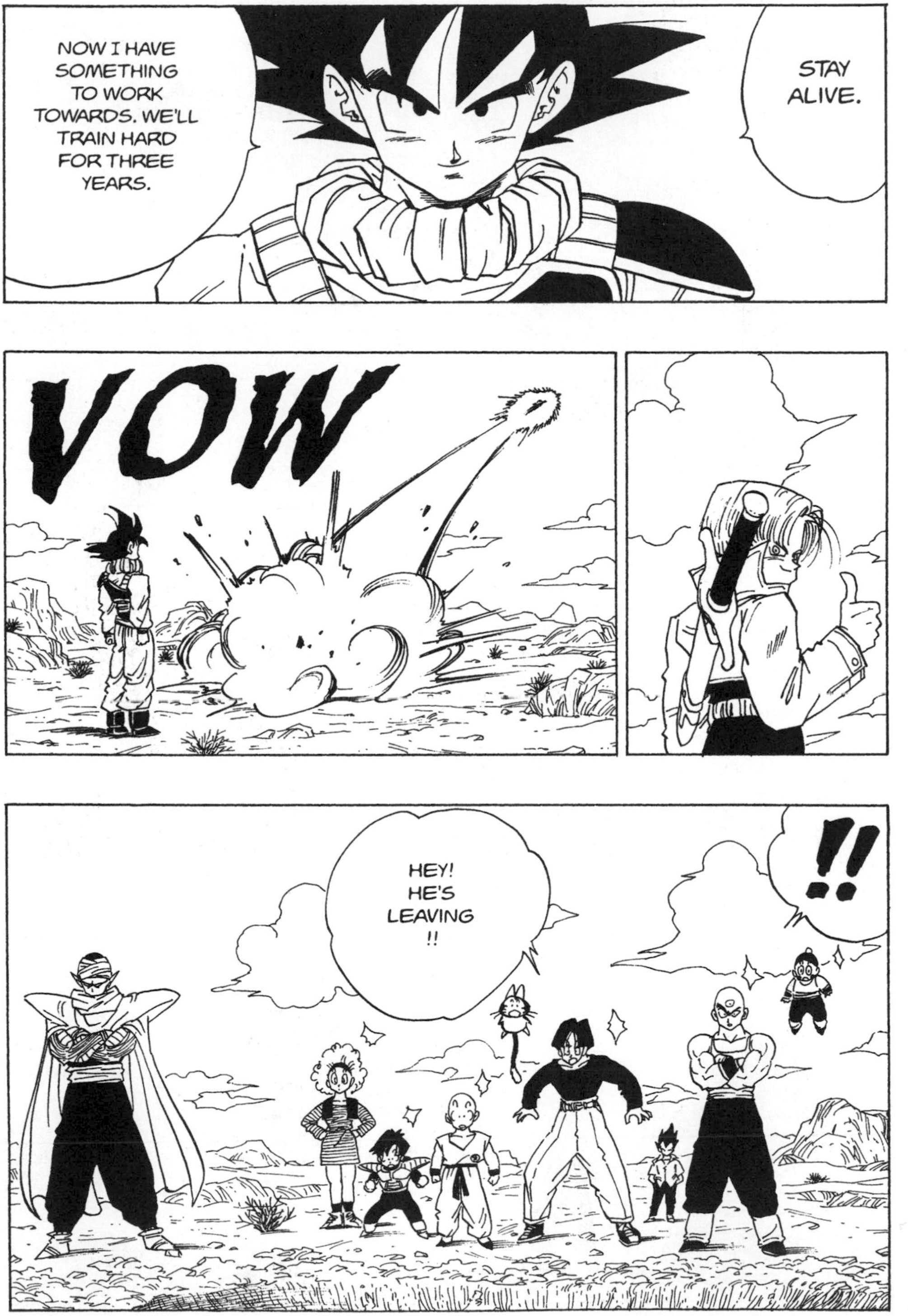

NOW I HAVE SOMETHING TO WORK TOWARDS. WE'LL TRAIN HARD FOR THREE YEARS.
STAY ALIVE.
VOW
HEY! HE'S LEAVING !!
!!

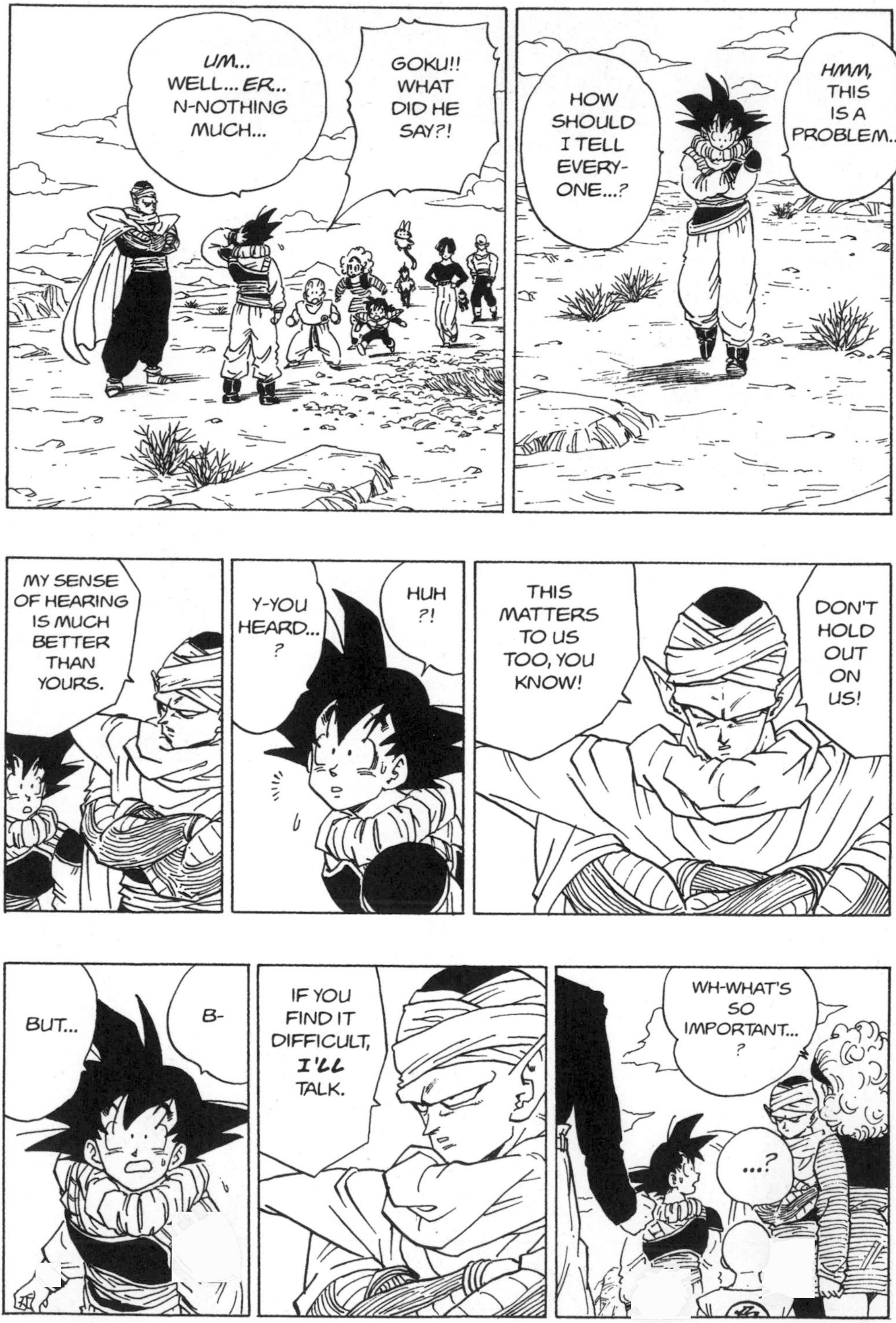
UM... WELL... ER... N-NOTHING MUCH...
GOKU!! WHAT DID HE SAY?!
HOW SHOULD I TELL EVERY-ONE...?
HMM, THIS IS A PROBLEM...
MY SENSE OF HEARING IS MUCH BETTER THAN YOURS.
Y-YOU HEARD...?
HUH?!
THIS MATTERS TO US TOO, YOU KNOW!
DON'T HOLD OUT ON US!
BUT...
B-
IF YOU FIND IT DIFFICULT, I'LL TALK.
WH-WHAT'S SO IMPORTANT...?
...?

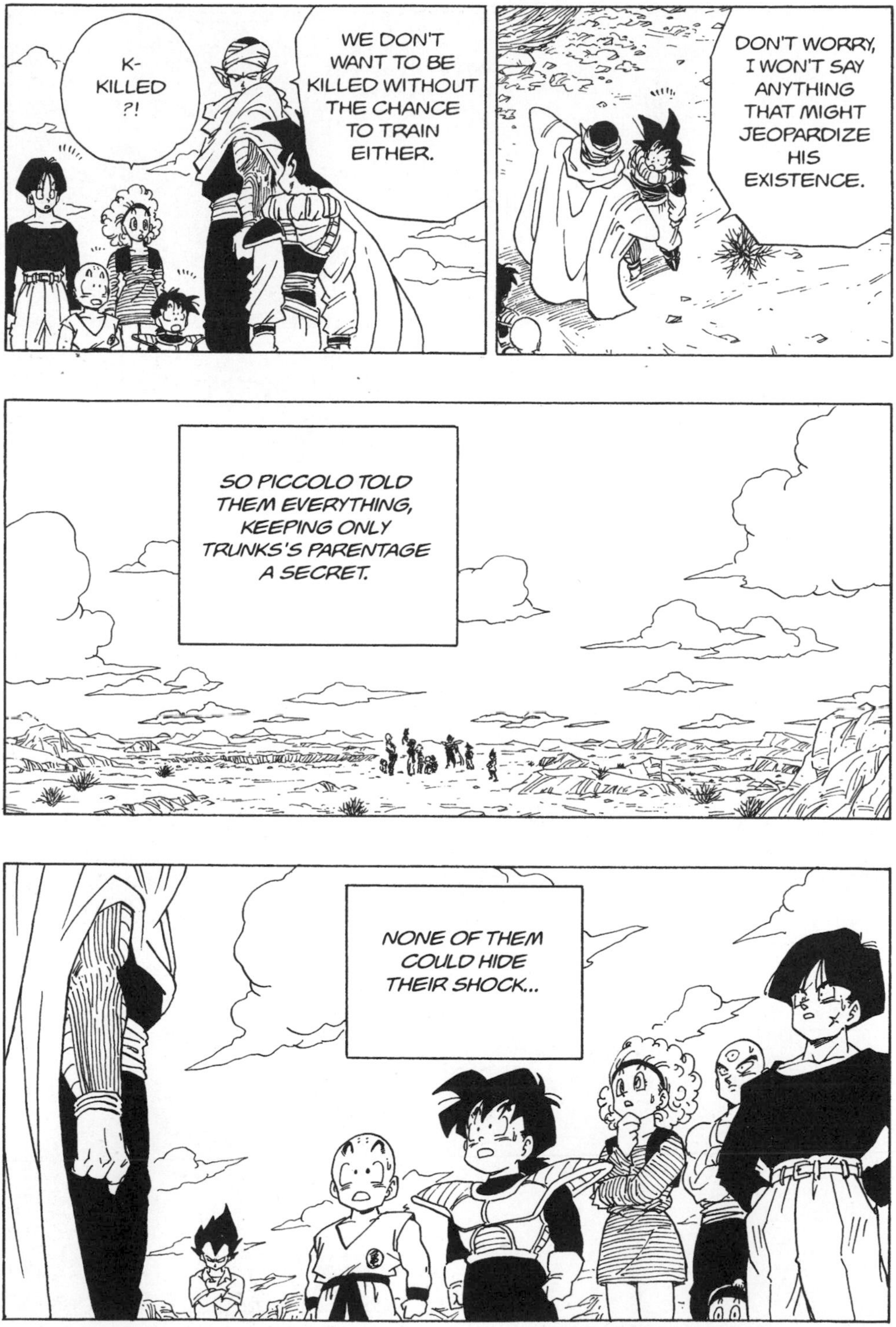
K-KILLED?!
WE DON'T WANT TO BE KILLED WITHOUT THE CHANCE TO TRAIN EITHER.
DON'T WORRY, I WON'T SAY ANYTHING THAT MIGHT JEOPARDIZE HIS EXISTENCE.
SO PICCOLO TOLD THEM EVERYTHING, KEEPING ONLY TRUNKS'S PARENTAGE A SECRET.
NONE OF THEM COULD HIDE THEIR SHOCK...

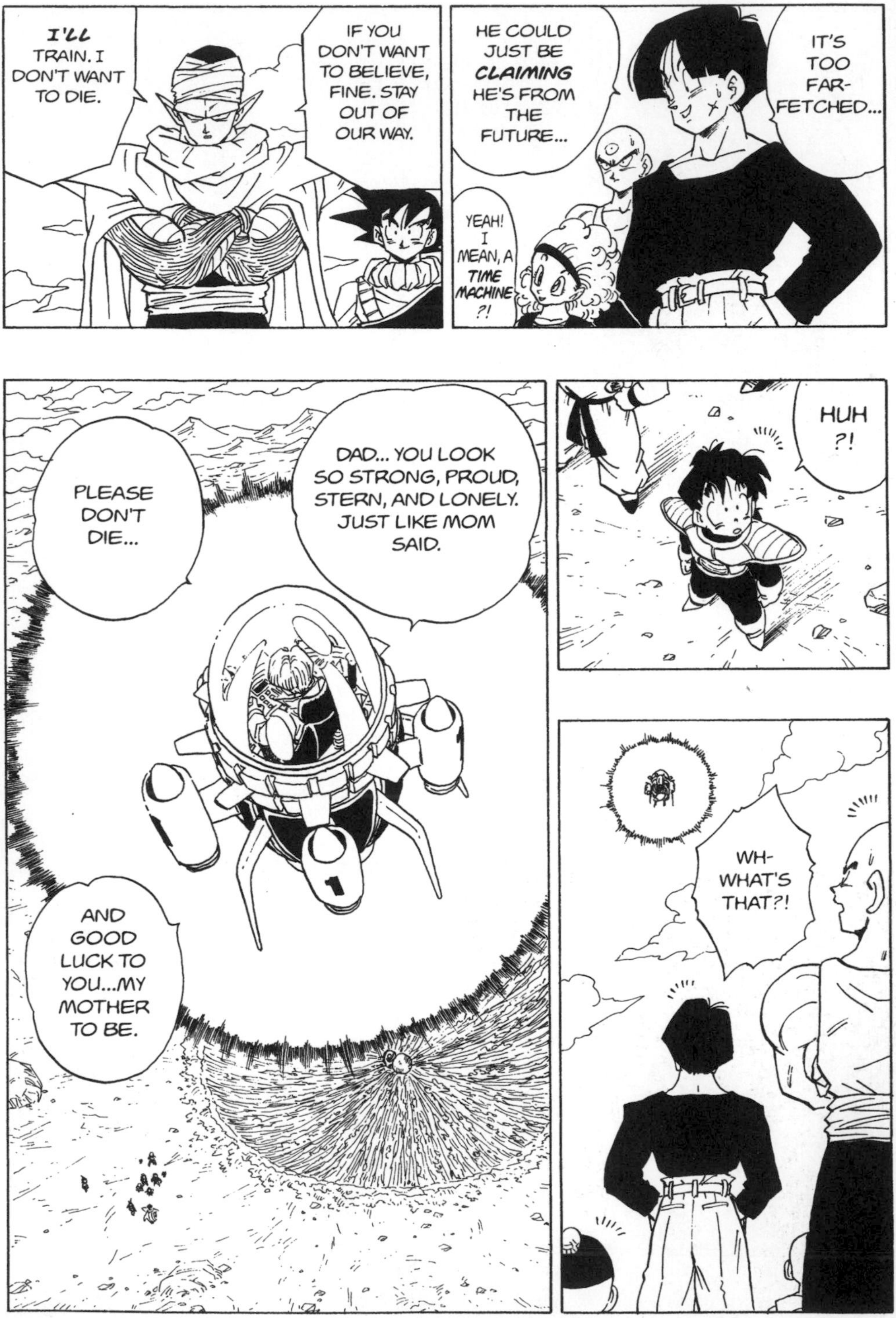
IT'S TOO FAR-FETCHED...
HE COULD JUST BE CLAIMING HE'S FROM THE FUTURE...
YEAH! I MEAN, A TIME MACHINE ?!
IF YOU DON'T WANT TO BELIEVE, FINE. STAY OUT OF OUR WAY.
I'LL TRAIN. I DON'T WANT TO DIE.
HUH ?!
DAD... YOU LOOK SO STRONG, PROUD, STERN, AND LONELY. JUST LIKE MOM SAID.
PLEASE DON'T DIE...
AND GOOD LUCK TO YOU...MY MOTHER TO BE.
WH- WHAT'S THAT?!

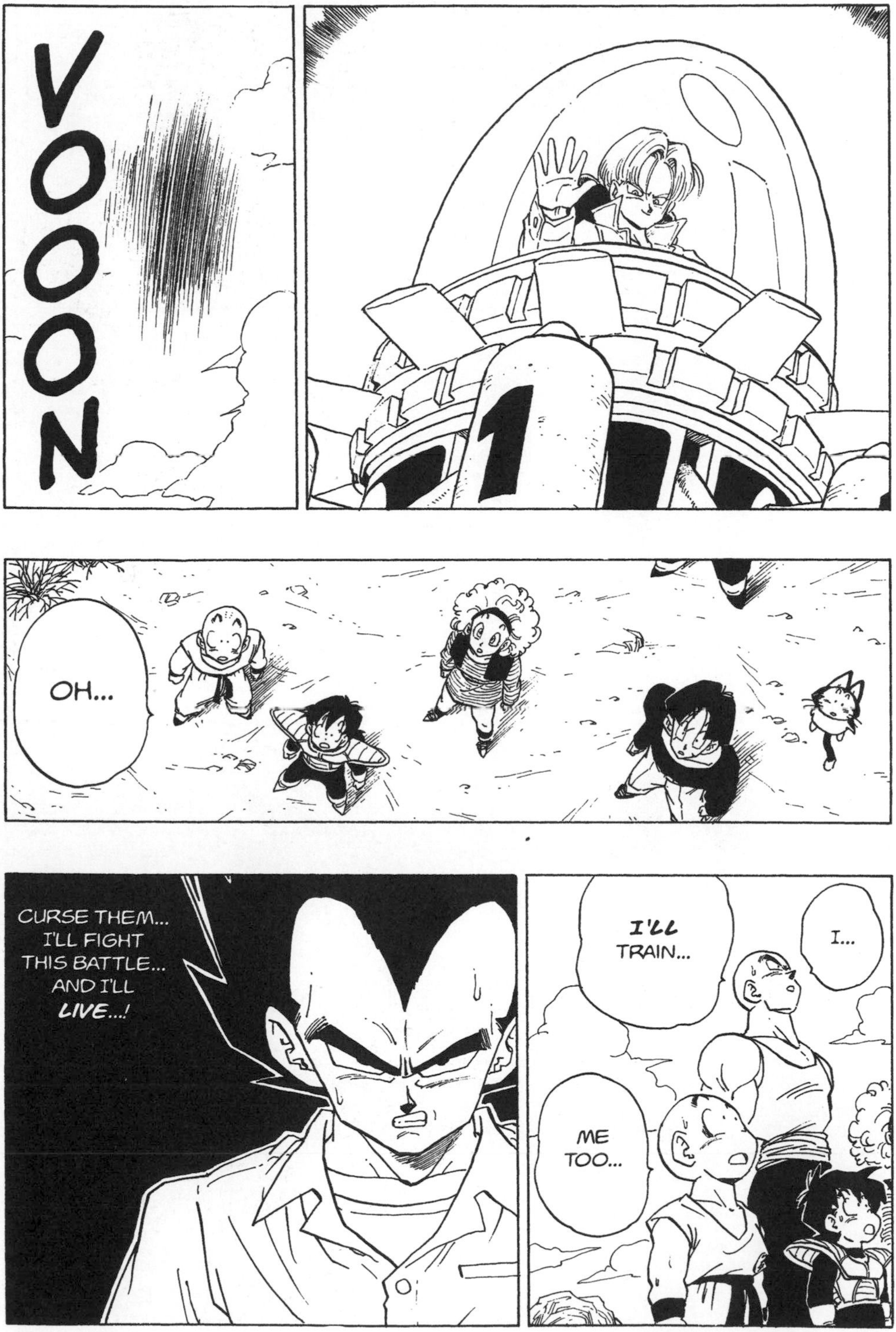
VOOON
OH...
CURSE THEM... I'LL FIGHT THIS BATTLE... AND I'LL *LIVE*...!
I...
I'LL TRAIN...
ME TOO...

DBZ:142 • The Risky Decision

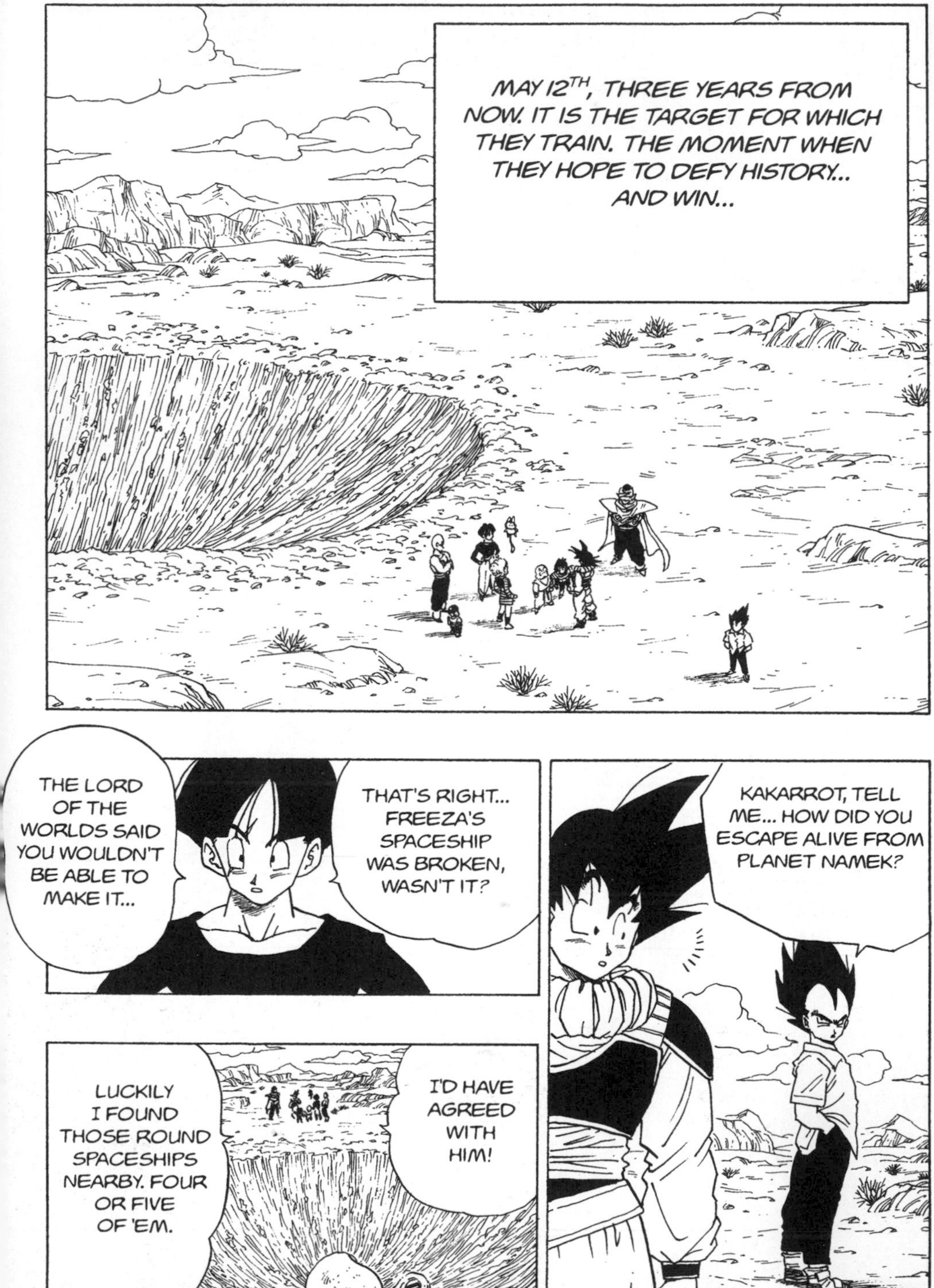
MAY 12TH, THREE YEARS FROM NOW. IT IS THE TARGET FOR WHICH THEY TRAIN. THE MOMENT WHEN THEY HOPE TO DEFY HISTORY... AND WIN...
THE LORD OF THE WORLDS SAID YOU WOULDN'T BE ABLE TO MAKE IT...
THAT'S RIGHT... FREEZA'S SPACESHIP WAS BROKEN, WASN'T IT?
KAKARROT, TELL ME... HOW DID YOU ESCAPE ALIVE FROM PLANET NAMEK?
LUCKILY I FOUND THOSE ROUND SPACESHIPS NEARBY. FOUR OR FIVE OF 'EM.
I'D HAVE AGREED WITH HIM!

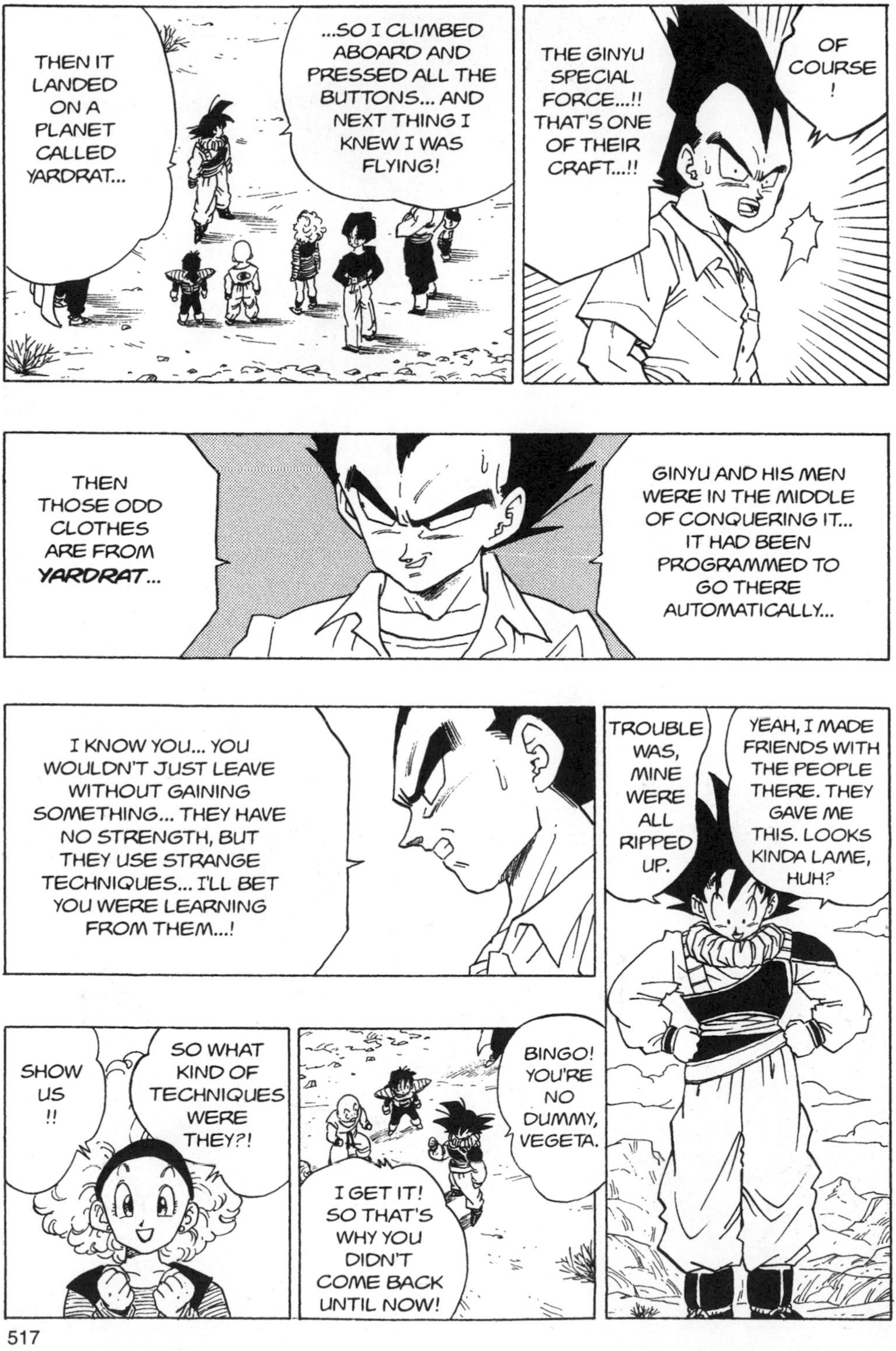

...SO I CLIMBED ABOARD AND PRESSED ALL THE BUTTONS... AND NEXT THING I KNEW I WAS FLYING!
THEN IT LANDED ON A PLANET CALLED YARDRAT...
THE GINYU SPECIAL FORCE...!! THAT'S ONE OF THEIR CRAFT...!!
OF COURSE !
THEN THOSE ODD CLOTHES ARE FROM YARDRAT...
GINYU AND HIS MEN WERE IN THE MIDDLE OF CONQUERING IT... IT HAD BEEN PROGRAMMED TO GO THERE AUTOMATICALLY...
I KNOW YOU... YOU WOULDN'T JUST LEAVE WITHOUT GAINING SOMETHING... THEY HAVE NO STRENGTH, BUT THEY USE STRANGE TECHNIQUES... I'LL BET YOU WERE LEARNING FROM THEM...!
YEAH, I MADE FRIENDS WITH THE PEOPLE THERE. THEY GAVE ME THIS. LOOKS KINDA LAME, HUH?
TROUBLE WAS, MINE WERE ALL RIPPED UP.
BINGO! YOU'RE NO DUMMY, VEGETA.
I GET IT! SO THAT'S WHY YOU DIDN'T COME BACK UNTIL NOW!
SO WHAT KIND OF TECHNIQUES WERE THEY?!
SHOW US !!

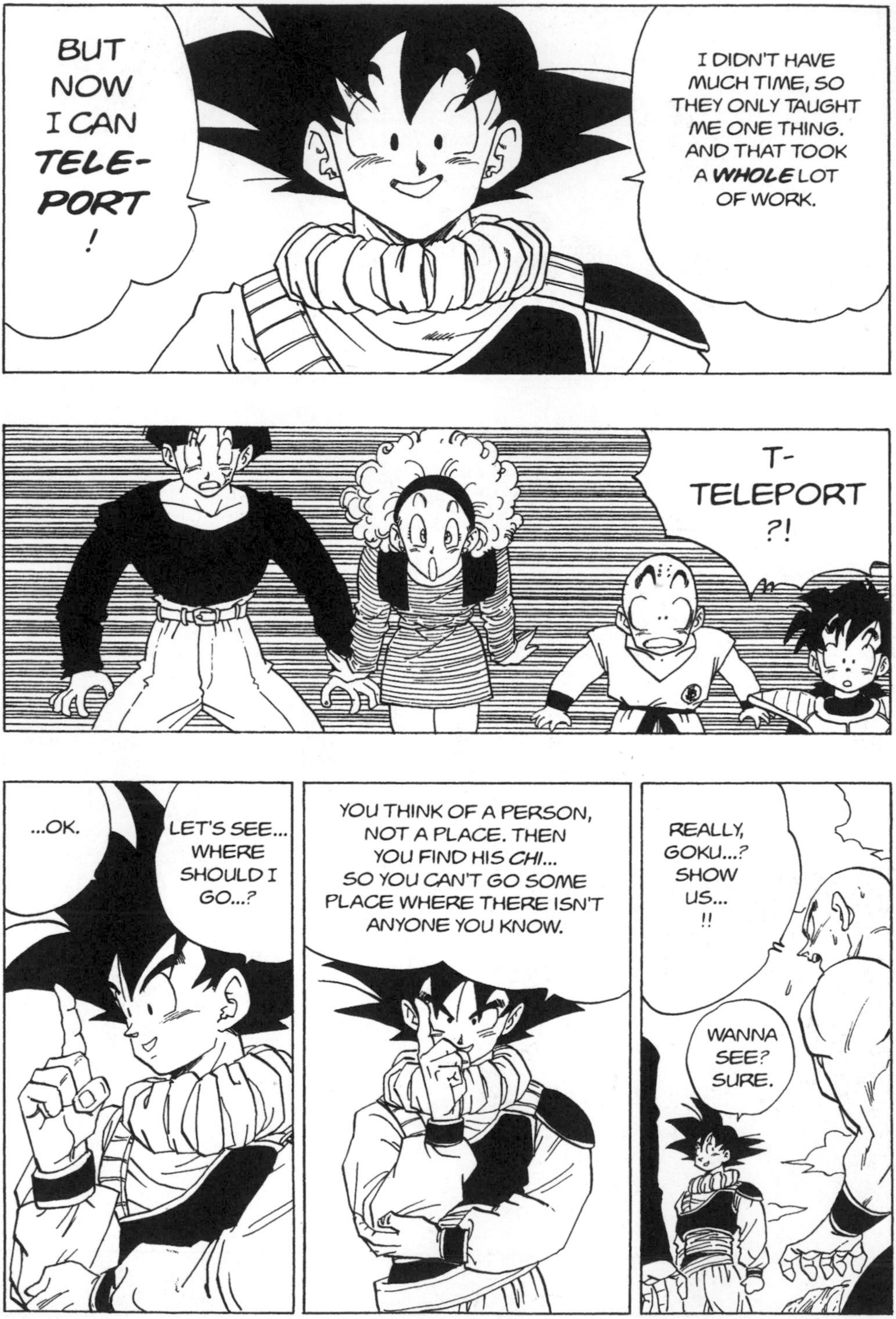
I DIDN'T HAVE MUCH TIME, SO THEY ONLY TAUGHT ME ONE THING. AND THAT TOOK A WHOLE LOT OF WORK.
BUT NOW I CAN TELE-PORT!
T-TELEPORT?!
REALLY, GOKU...? SHOW US...!!
WANNA SEE? SURE.
YOU THINK OF A PERSON, NOT A PLACE. THEN YOU FIND HIS CHI... SO YOU CAN'T GO SOME PLACE WHERE THERE ISN'T ANYONE YOU KNOW.
LET'S SEE... WHERE SHOULD I GO...?
...OK.

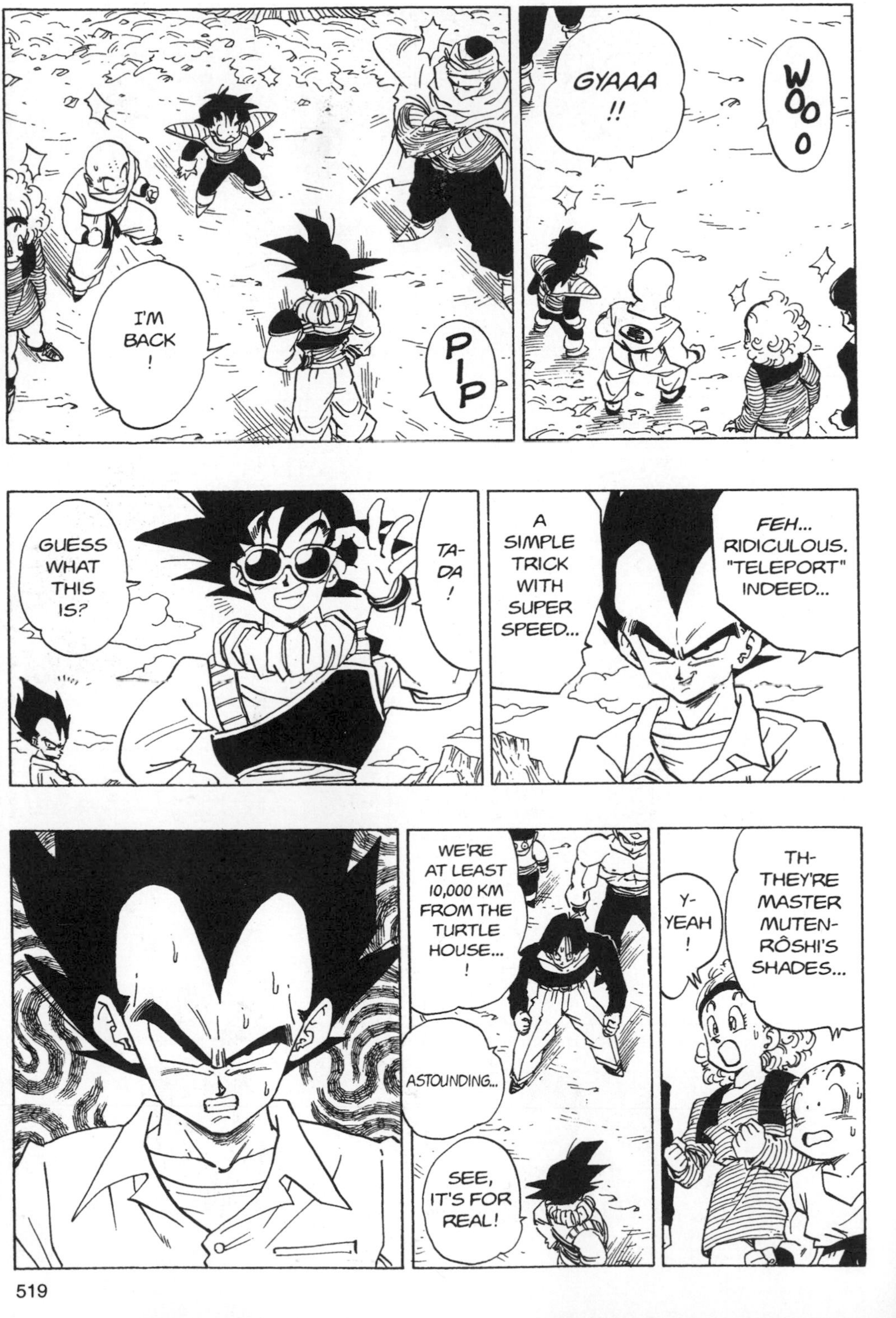
WOOO
GYAAA!!
PIP
I'M BACK!
FEH... RIDICULOUS. "TELEPORT" INDEED...
A SIMPLE TRICK WITH SUPER SPEED...
TA-DA!
GUESS WHAT THIS IS?
TH-THEY'RE MASTER MUTEN-RÔSHI'S SHADES...
Y-YEAH!
WE'RE AT LEAST 10,000 KM FROM THE TURTLE HOUSE...!
ASTOUNDING...
SEE, IT'S FOR REAL!

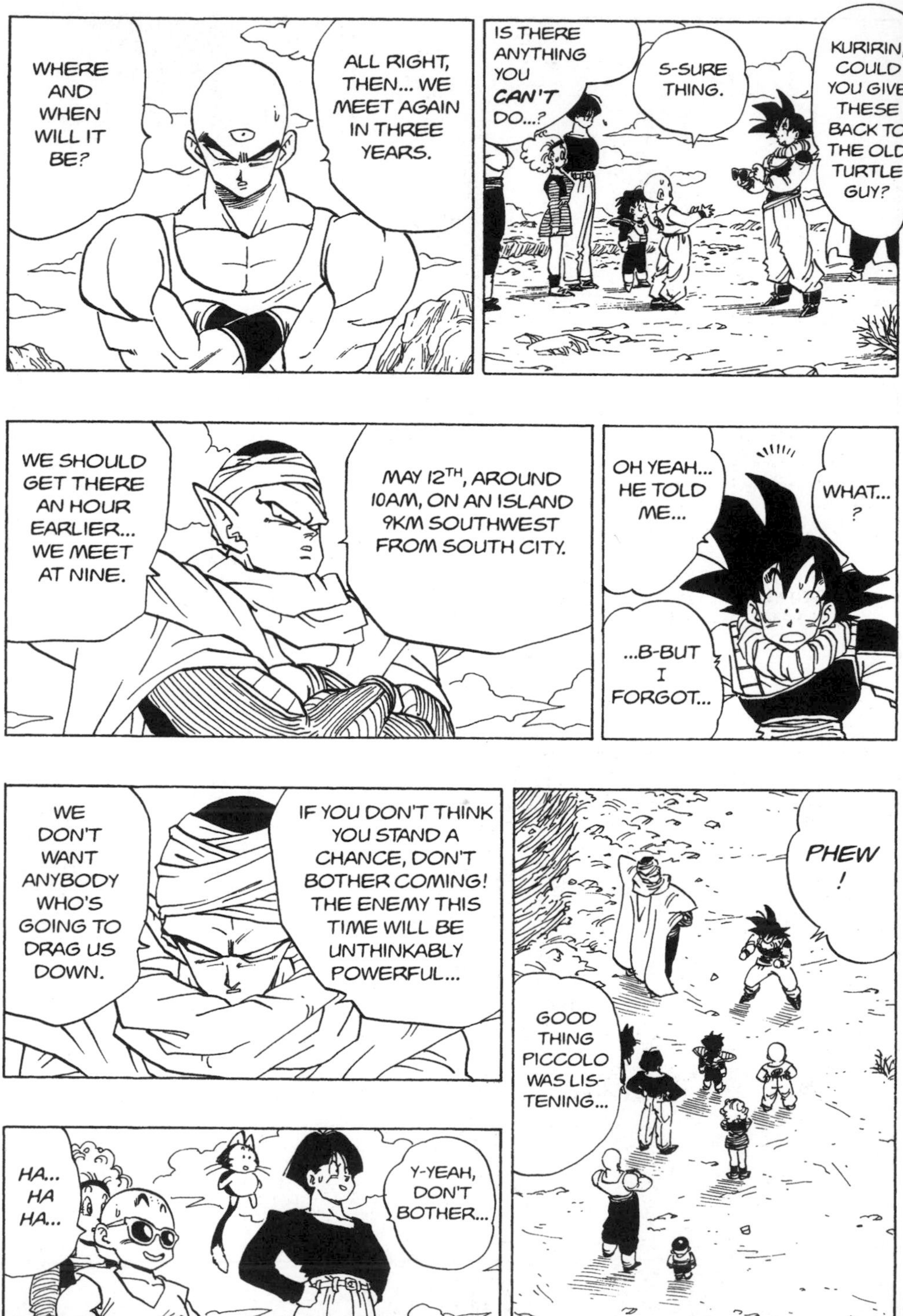
KURIRIN, COULD YOU GIVE THESE BACK TO THE OLD TURTLE GUY?
S-SURE THING.
IS THERE ANYTHING YOU CAN'T DO...?
ALL RIGHT, THEN... WE MEET AGAIN IN THREE YEARS.
WHERE AND WHEN WILL IT BE?
WHAT... ?
OH YEAH... HE TOLD ME...
...B-BUT I FORGOT...
MAY 12TH, AROUND 10AM, ON AN ISLAND 9KM SOUTHWEST FROM SOUTH CITY.
WE SHOULD GET THERE AN HOUR EARLIER... WE MEET AT NINE.
PHEW!
GOOD THING PICCOLO WAS LISTENING...
IF YOU DON'T THINK YOU STAND A CHANCE, DON'T BOTHER COMING! THE ENEMY THIS TIME WILL BE UNTHINKABLY POWERFUL...
WE DON'T WANT ANYBODY WHO'S GOING TO DRAG US DOWN.
Y-YEAH, DON'T BOTHER...
HA... HA HA...

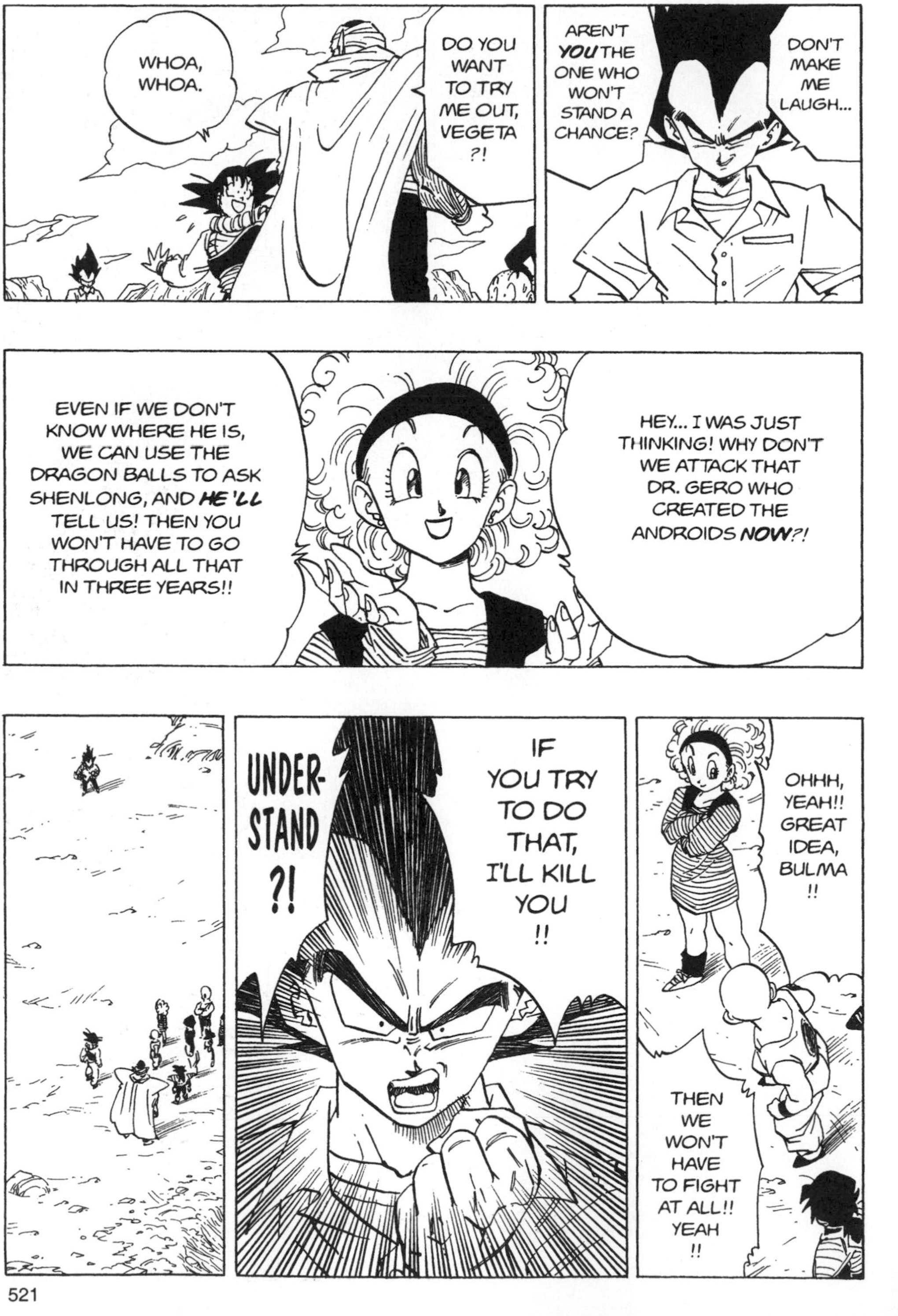
DON'T MAKE ME LAUGH...
AREN'T YOU THE ONE WHO WON'T STAND A CHANCE?
DO YOU WANT TO TRY ME OUT, VEGETA?!
WHOA, WHOA.
HEY... I WAS JUST THINKING! WHY DON'T WE ATTACK THAT DR. GERO WHO CREATED THE ANDROIDS NOW?!
EVEN IF WE DON'T KNOW WHERE HE IS, WE CAN USE THE DRAGON BALLS TO ASK SHENLONG, AND HE'LL TELL US! THEN YOU WON'T HAVE TO GO THROUGH ALL THAT IN THREE YEARS!!
OHHH, YEAH!! GREAT IDEA, BULMA!!
THEN WE WON'T HAVE TO FIGHT AT ALL!! YEAH!!
IF YOU TRY TO DO THAT, I'LL KILL YOU!!
UNDERSTAND?!

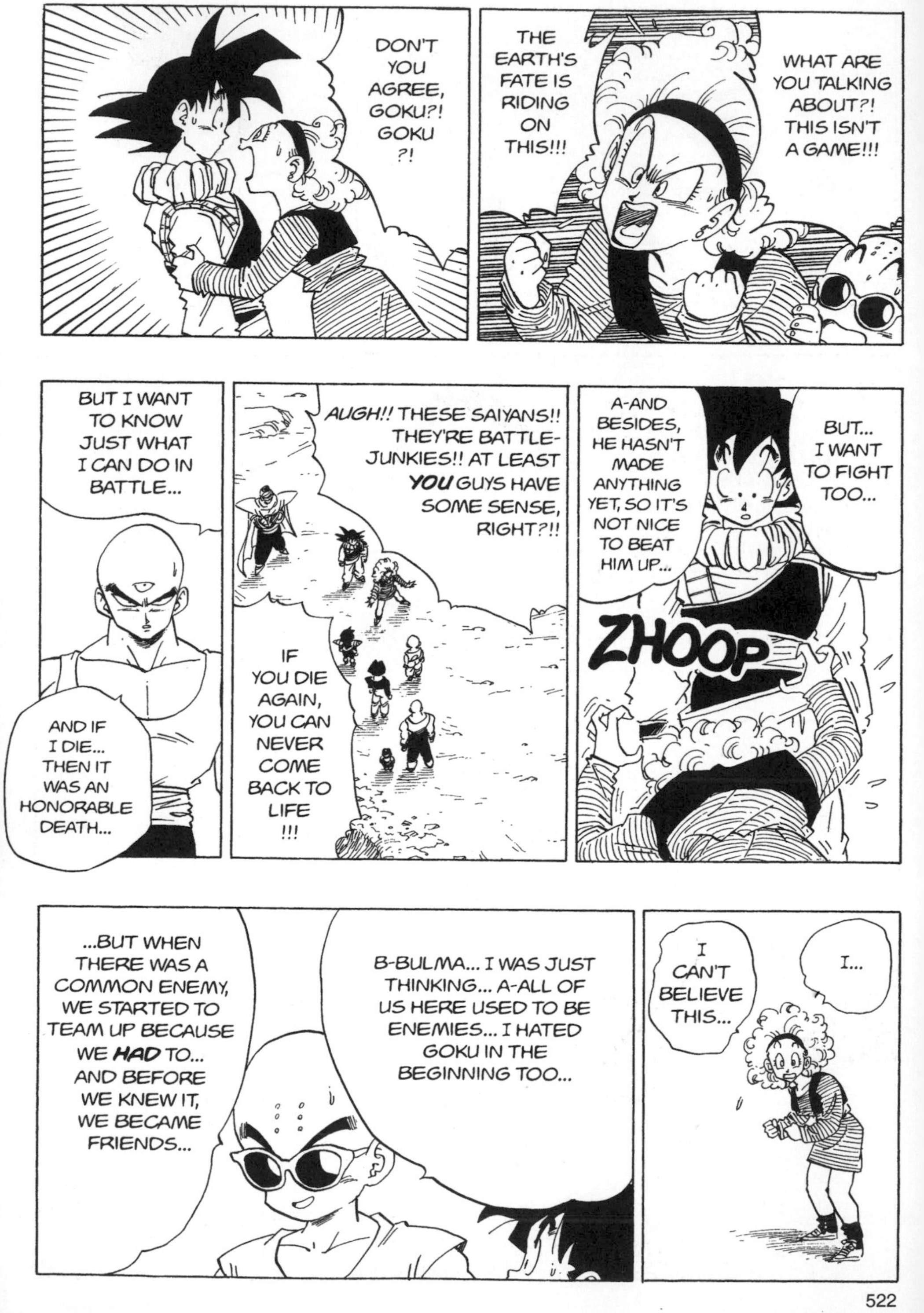
DON'T YOU AGREE, GOKU?! GOKU ?!
THE EARTH'S FATE IS RIDING ON THIS!!!
WHAT ARE YOU TALKING ABOUT?! THIS ISN'T A GAME!!!
BUT I WANT TO KNOW JUST WHAT I CAN DO IN BATTLE...
AND IF I DIE... THEN IT WAS AN HONORABLE DEATH...
AUGH!! THESE SAIYANS!! THEY'RE BATTLE-JUNKIES!! AT LEAST YOU GUYS HAVE SOME SENSE, RIGHT?!!
IF YOU DIE AGAIN, YOU CAN NEVER COME BACK TO LIFE !!!
A-AND BESIDES, HE HASN'T MADE ANYTHING YET, SO IT'S NOT NICE TO BEAT HIM UP...
BUT... I WANT TO FIGHT TOO...
ZHOOP
...BUT WHEN THERE WAS A COMMON ENEMY, WE STARTED TO TEAM UP BECAUSE WE HAD TO... AND BEFORE WE KNEW IT, WE BECAME FRIENDS...
B-BULMA... I WAS JUST THINKING... A-ALL OF US HERE USED TO BE ENEMIES... I HATED GOKU IN THE BEGINNING TOO...
I CAN'T BELIEVE THIS...
I...

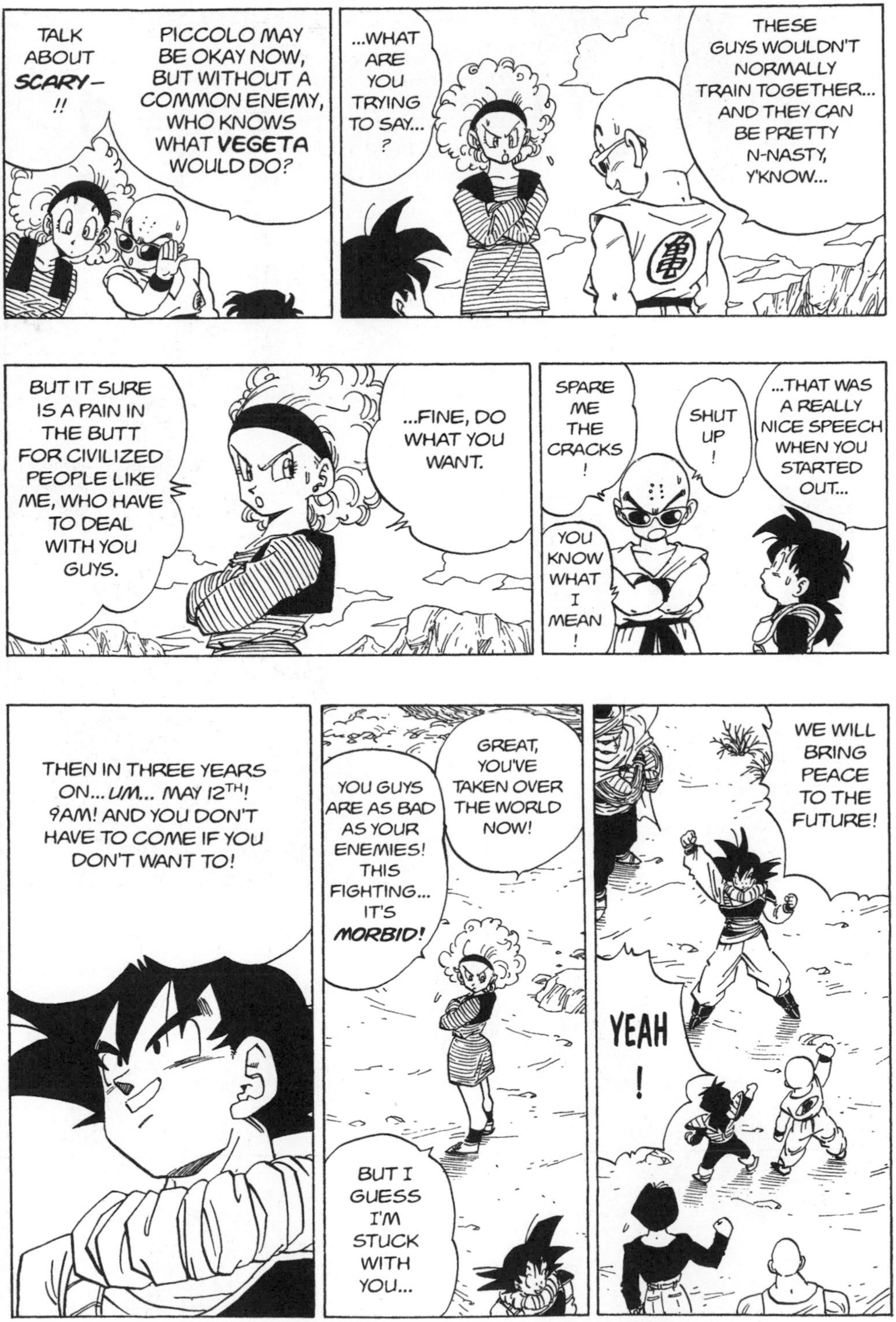
TALK ABOUT SCARY—!!
PICCOLO MAY BE OKAY NOW, BUT WITHOUT A COMMON ENEMY, WHO KNOWS WHAT VEGETA WOULD DO?
...WHAT ARE YOU TRYING TO SAY...?
THESE GUYS WOULDN'T NORMALLY TRAIN TOGETHER... AND THEY CAN BE PRETTY N-NASTY, Y'KNOW...
BUT IT SURE IS A PAIN IN THE BUTT FOR CIVILIZED PEOPLE LIKE ME, WHO HAVE TO DEAL WITH YOU GUYS.
...FINE, DO WHAT YOU WANT.
...THAT WAS A REALLY NICE SPEECH WHEN YOU STARTED OUT...
SHUT UP!
SPARE ME THE CRACKS!
YOU KNOW WHAT I MEAN!
THEN IN THREE YEARS ON... UM... MAY 12TH! 9AM! AND YOU DON'T HAVE TO COME IF YOU DON'T WANT TO!
YOU GUYS ARE AS BAD AS YOUR ENEMIES! THIS FIGHTING... IT'S MORBID!
GREAT, YOU'VE TAKEN OVER THE WORLD NOW!
BUT I GUESS I'M STUCK WITH YOU...
WE WILL BRING PEACE TO THE FUTURE!
YEAH!

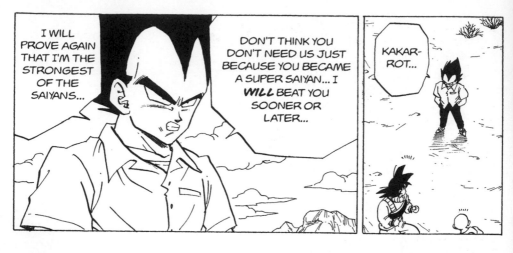

I WILL PROVE AGAIN THAT I'M THE STRONGEST OF THE SAIYANS...

DON'T THINK YOU DON'T NEED US JUST BECAUSE YOU BECAME A SUPER SAIYAN... I *WILL* BEAT YOU SOONER OR LATER...

KAKAR-ROT...

TOOO

WHAT-EVER...

VOO VOO

WE BETTER GET GOING TOO. SEE YOU IN THREE YEARS...

BYE BYE!

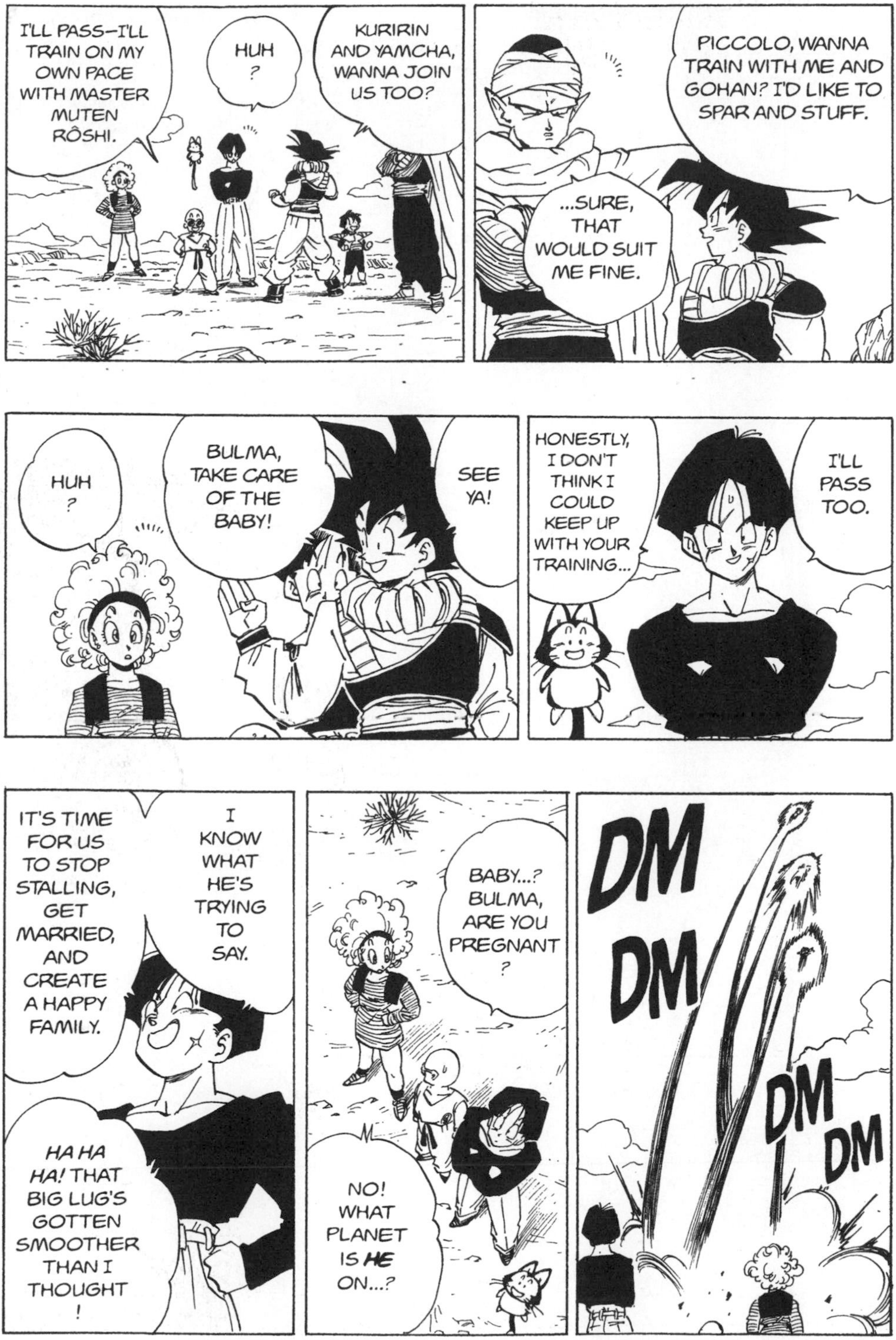
PICCOLO, WANNA TRAIN WITH ME AND GOHAN? I'D LIKE TO SPAR AND STUFF.
...SURE, THAT WOULD SUIT ME FINE.
KURIRIN AND YAMCHA, WANNA JOIN US TOO?
HUH ?
I'LL PASS—I'LL TRAIN ON MY OWN PACE WITH MASTER MUTEN RÔSHI.
I'LL PASS TOO.
HONESTLY, I DON'T THINK I COULD KEEP UP WITH YOUR TRAINING...
SEE YA!
BULMA, TAKE CARE OF THE BABY!
HUH ?
DM
DM
DM
DM
BABY...? BULMA, ARE YOU PREGNANT ?
NO! WHAT PLANET IS *HE* ON...?
I KNOW WHAT HE'S TRYING TO SAY.
IT'S TIME FOR US TO STOP STALLING, GET MARRIED, AND CREATE A HAPPY FAMILY.
HA HA HA! THAT BIG LUG'S GOTTEN SMOOTHER THAN I THOUGHT !

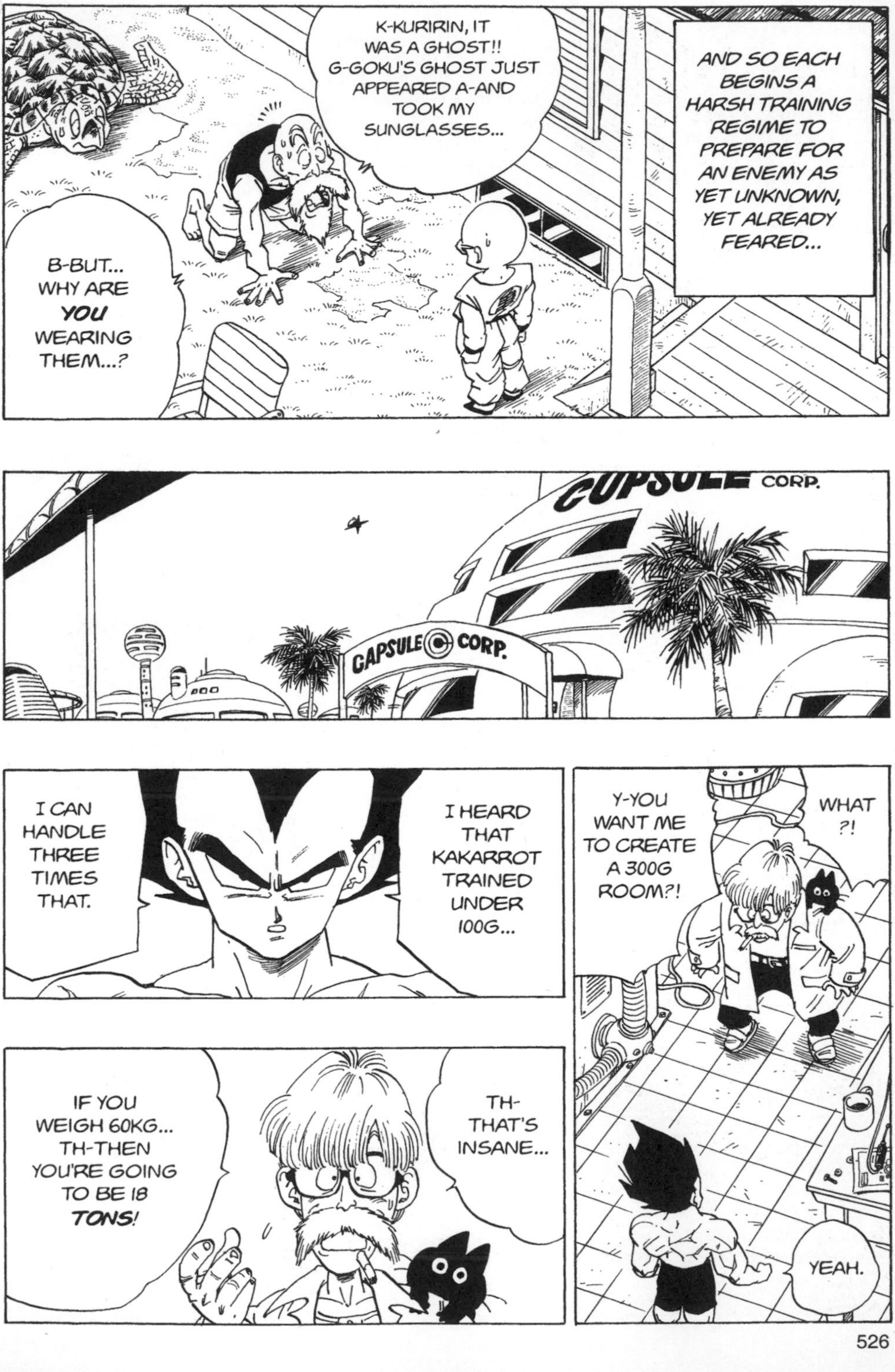
K-KURIRIN, IT WAS A GHOST!! G-GOKU'S GHOST JUST APPEARED A-AND TOOK MY SUNGLASSES...
B-BUT... WHY ARE ***YOU*** WEARING THEM...?
AND SO EACH BEGINS A HARSH TRAINING REGIME TO PREPARE FOR AN ENEMY AS YET UNKNOWN, YET ALREADY FEARED...
CAPSULE CORP.
CAPSULE CORP.
I HEARD THAT KAKARROT TRAINED UNDER 100G...
I CAN HANDLE THREE TIMES THAT.
WHAT ?!
Y-YOU WANT ME TO CREATE A 300G ROOM?!
YEAH.
TH- THAT'S INSANE...
IF YOU WEIGH 60KG... TH-THEN YOU'RE GOING TO BE 18 ***TONS***!

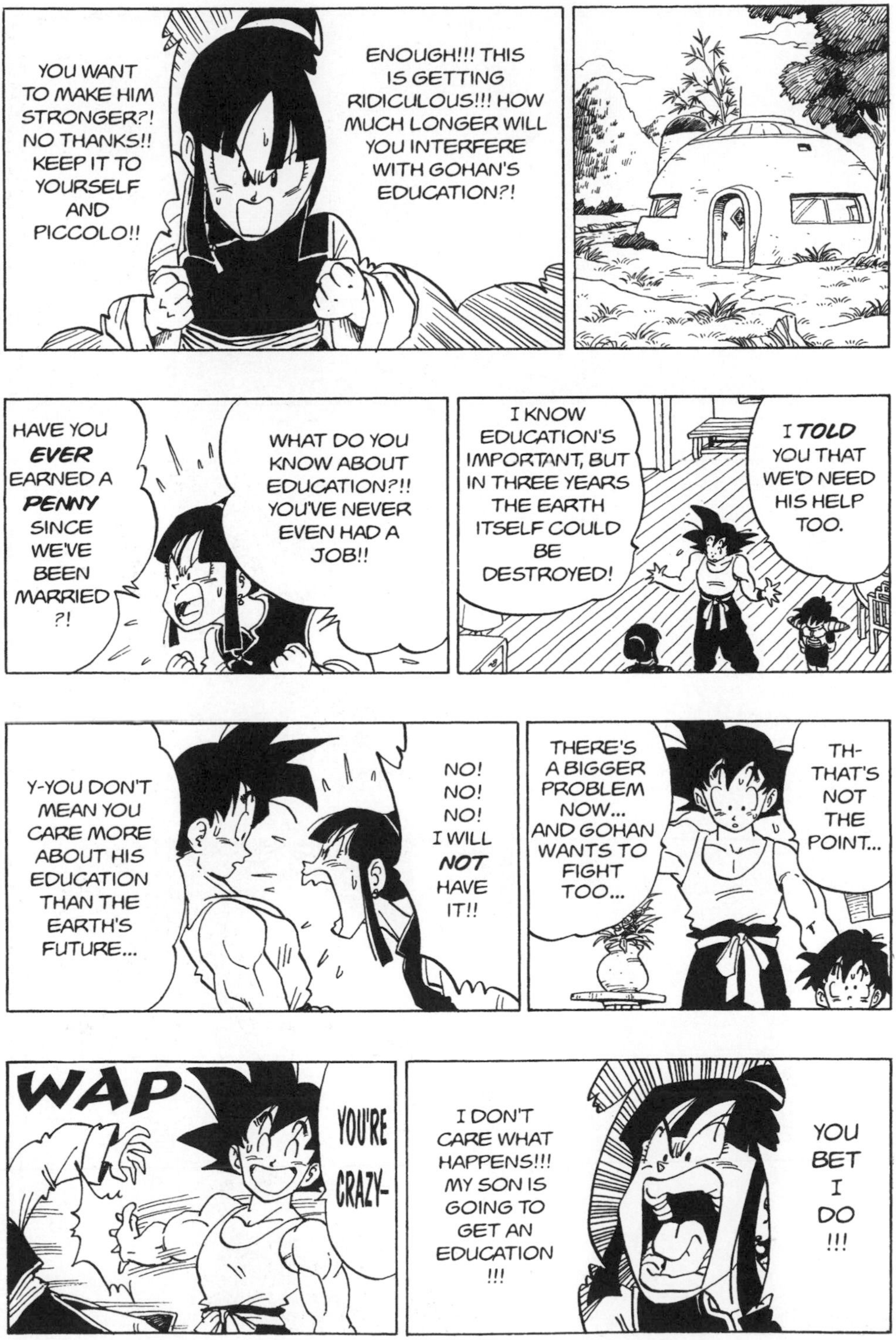
ENOUGH!!! THIS IS GETTING RIDICULOUS!!! HOW MUCH LONGER WILL YOU INTERFERE WITH GOHAN'S EDUCATION?!
YOU WANT TO MAKE HIM STRONGER?! NO THANKS!! KEEP IT TO YOURSELF AND PICCOLO!!
WHAT DO YOU KNOW ABOUT EDUCATION?!! YOU'VE NEVER EVEN HAD A JOB!!
HAVE YOU EVER EARNED A PENNY SINCE WE'VE BEEN MARRIED ?!
I TOLD YOU THAT WE'D NEED HIS HELP TOO.
I KNOW EDUCATION'S IMPORTANT, BUT IN THREE YEARS THE EARTH ITSELF COULD BE DESTROYED!
NO! NO! NO! I WILL NOT HAVE IT!!
Y-YOU DON'T MEAN YOU CARE MORE ABOUT HIS EDUCATION THAN THE EARTH'S FUTURE...
TH-THAT'S NOT THE POINT...
THERE'S A BIGGER PROBLEM NOW... AND GOHAN WANTS TO FIGHT TOO...
YOU BET I DO !!!
I DON'T CARE WHAT HAPPENS!!! MY SON IS GOING TO GET AN EDUCATION !!!
WAP
YOU'RE CRAZY-

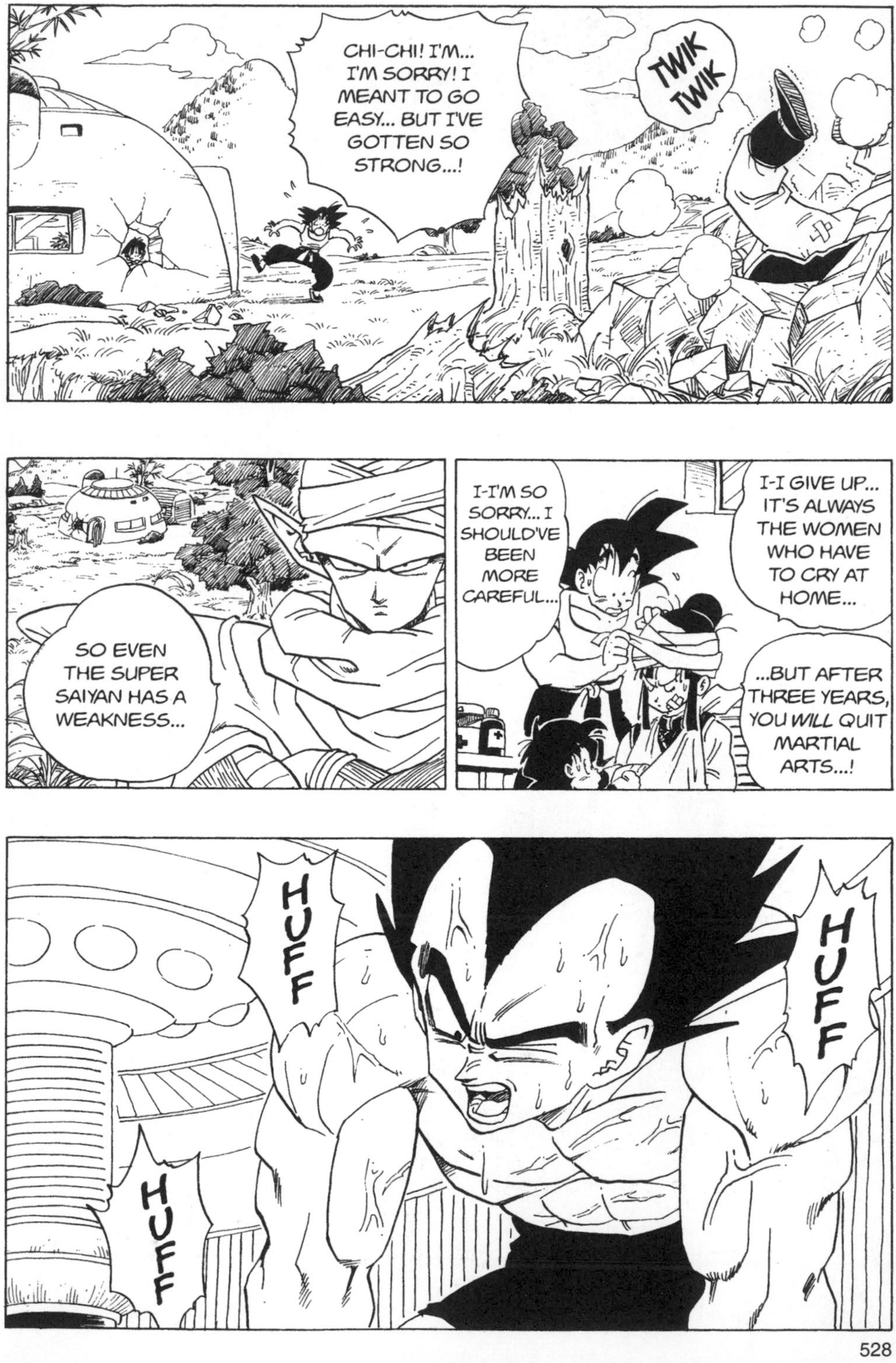

CHI-CHI! I'M... I'M SORRY! I MEANT TO GO EASY... BUT I'VE GOTTEN SO STRONG...!
TWIK TWIK
SO EVEN THE SUPER SAIYAN HAS A WEAKNESS...
I-I'M SO SORRY... I SHOULD'VE BEEN MORE CAREFUL...
I-I GIVE UP... IT'S ALWAYS THE WOMEN WHO HAVE TO CRY AT HOME...
...BUT AFTER THREE YEARS, YOU *WILL* QUIT MARTIAL ARTS...!
HUFF
HUFF
HUFF

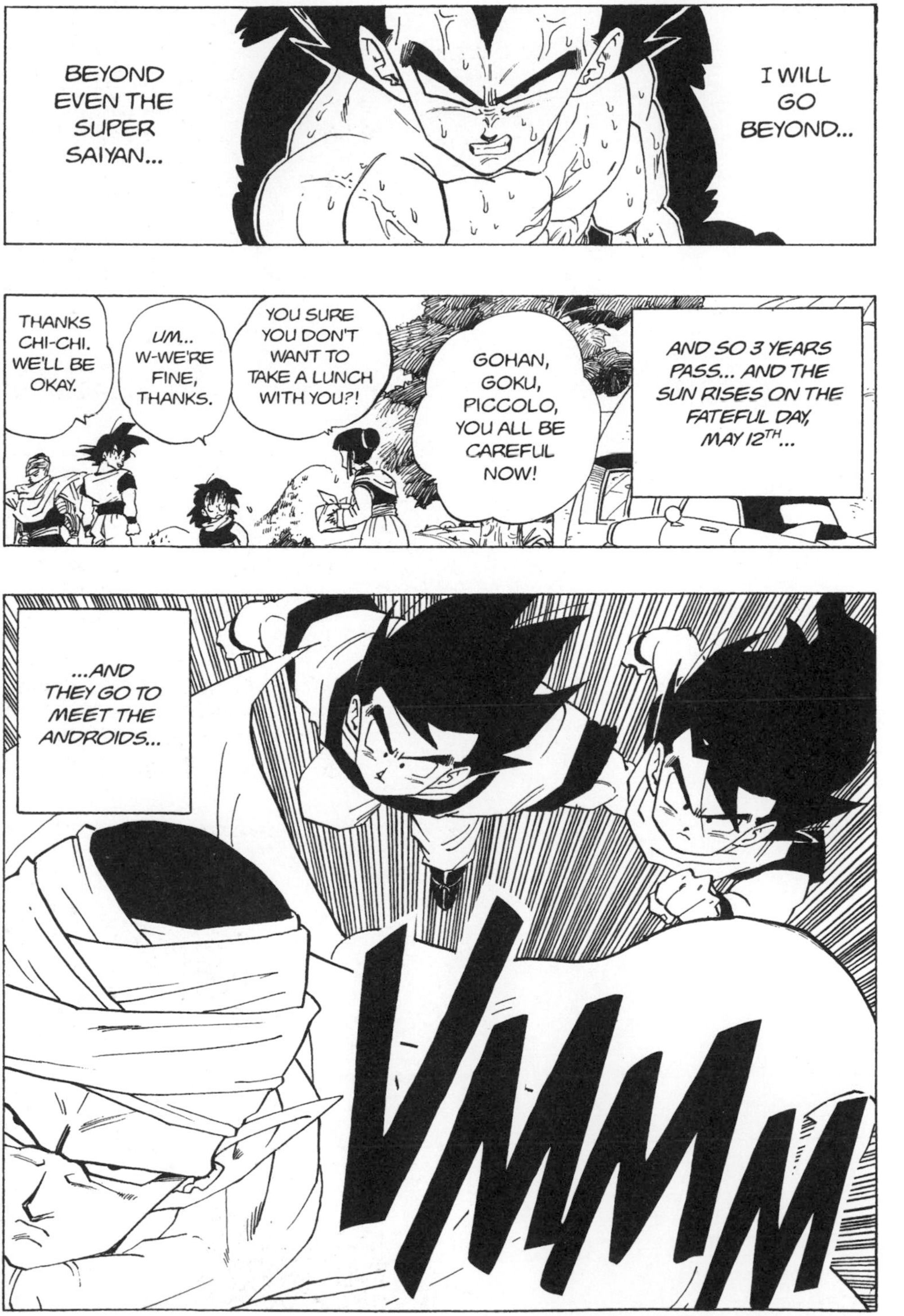
I WILL GO BEYOND...
BEYOND EVEN THE SUPER SAIYAN...
AND SO 3 YEARS PASS... AND THE SUN RISES ON THE FATEFUL DAY, MAY 12TH...
GOHAN, GOKU, PICCOLO, YOU ALL BE CAREFUL NOW!
YOU SURE YOU DON'T WANT TO TAKE A LUNCH WITH YOU?!
UM... W-WE'RE FINE, THANKS.
THANKS CHI-CHI. WE'LL BE OKAY.
...AND THEY GO TO MEET THE ANDROIDS...
VMMM

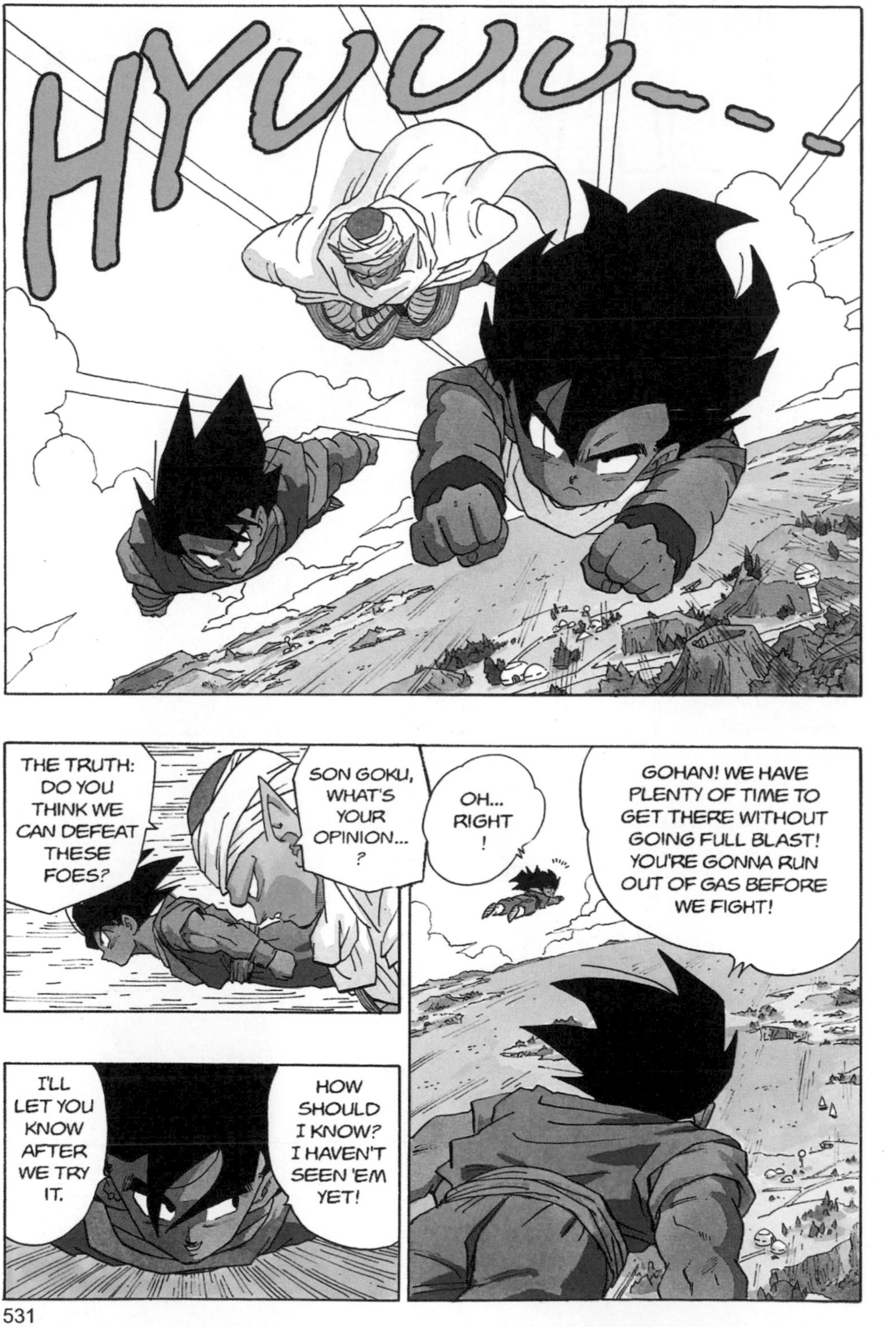
HYUUU---
GOHAN! WE HAVE PLENTY OF TIME TO GET THERE WITHOUT GOING FULL BLAST! YOU'RE GONNA RUN OUT OF GAS BEFORE WE FIGHT!
OH... RIGHT!
SON GOKU, WHAT'S YOUR OPINION...?
THE TRUTH: DO YOU THINK WE CAN DEFEAT THESE FOES?
HOW SHOULD I KNOW? I HAVEN'T SEEN 'EM YET!
I'LL LET YOU KNOW AFTER WE TRY IT.

BALL

ドラゴンボール

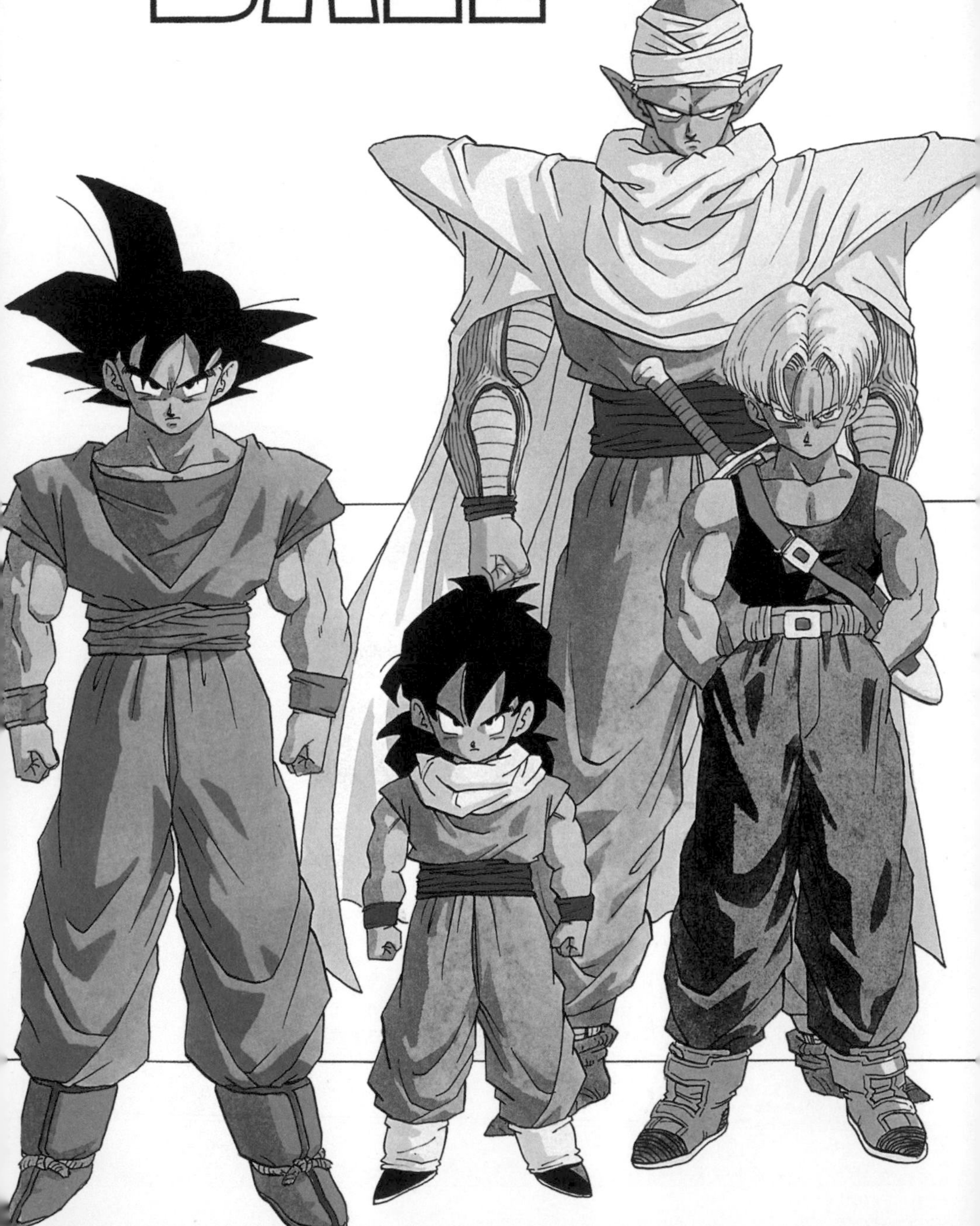

DRAGON

DBZ:143 • The Gathering of the Warriors

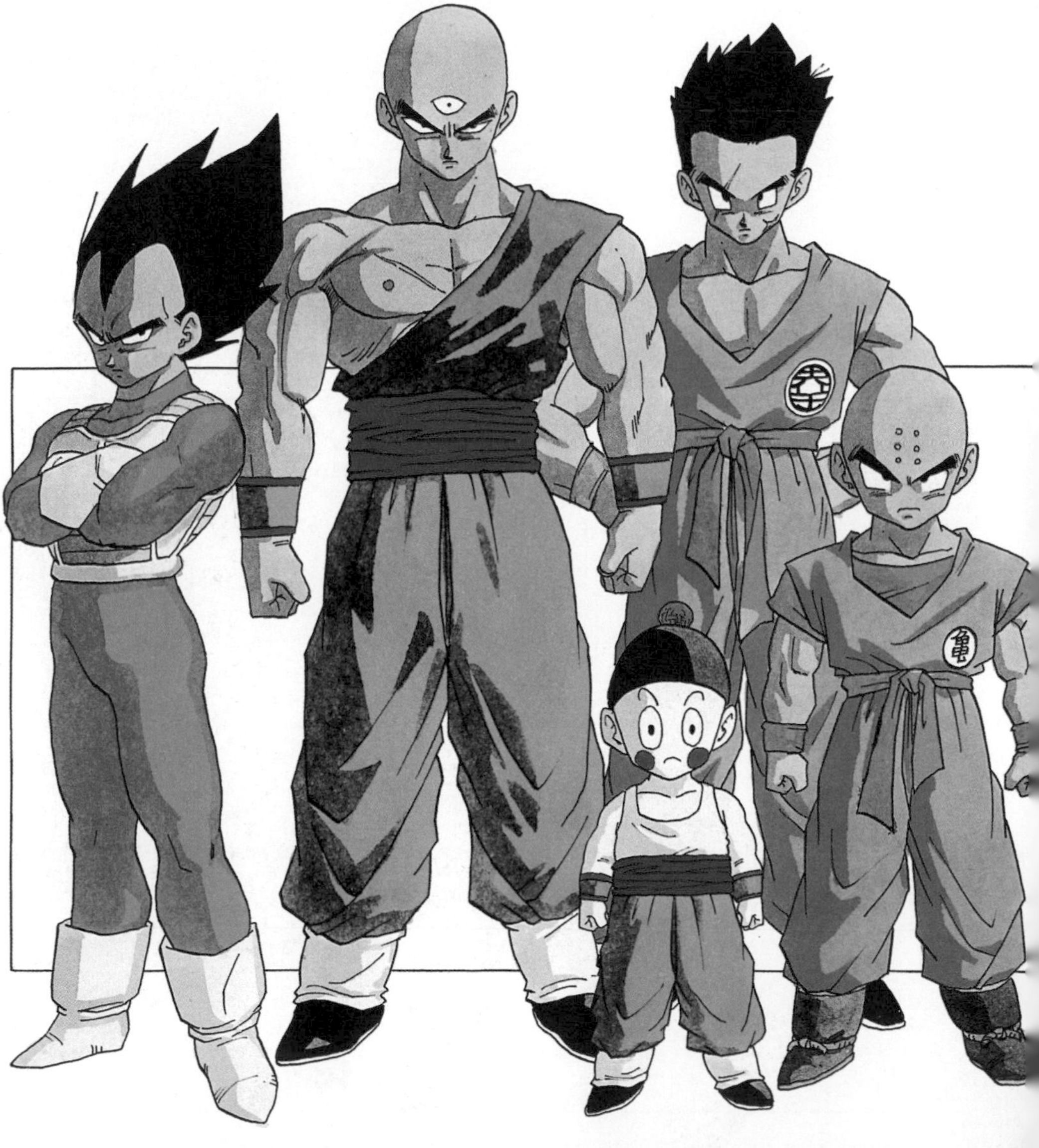

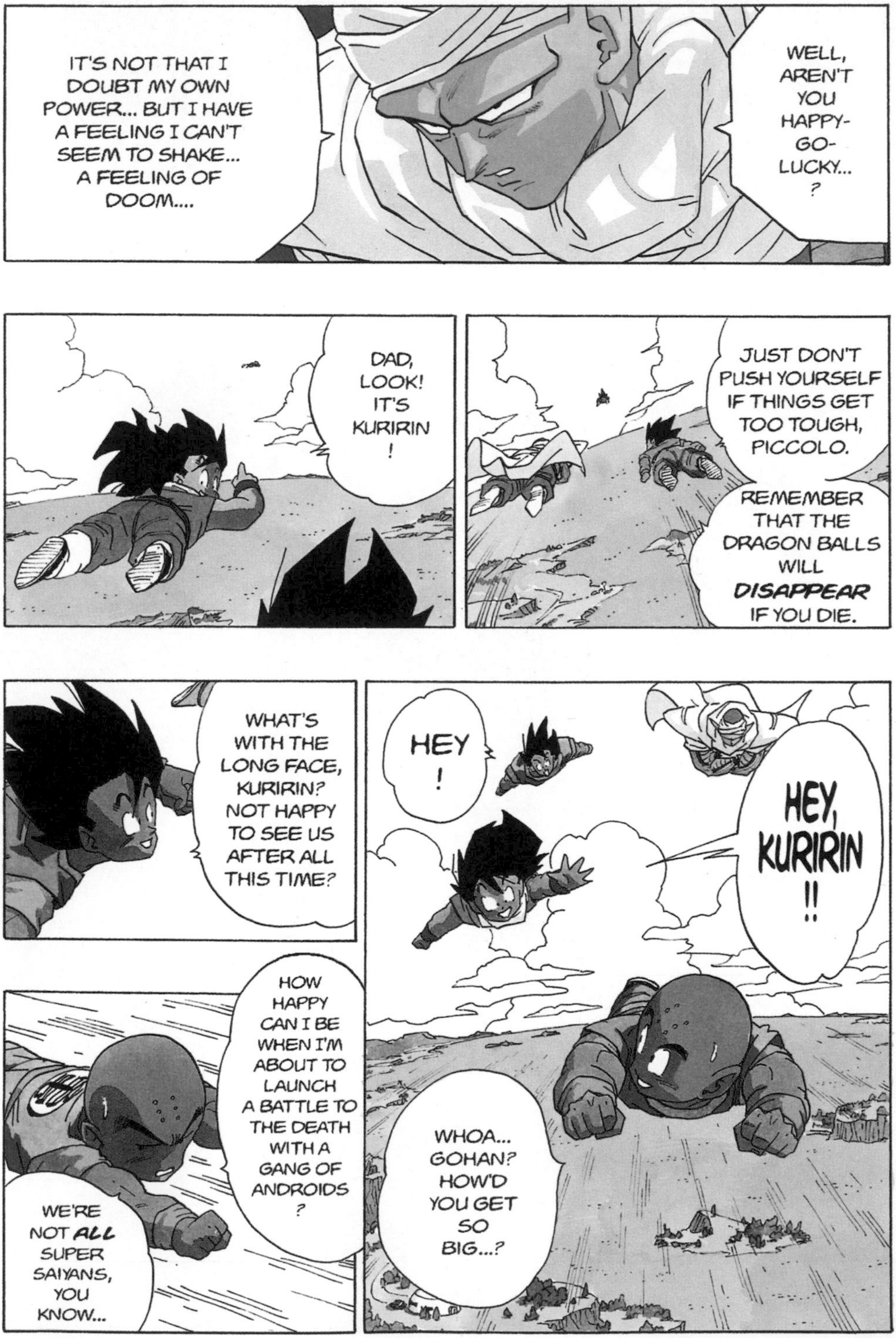
IT'S NOT THAT I DOUBT MY OWN POWER... BUT I HAVE A FEELING I CAN'T SEEM TO SHAKE... A FEELING OF DOOM....
WELL, AREN'T YOU HAPPY-GO-LUCKY...?
DAD, LOOK! IT'S KURIRIN!
JUST DON'T PUSH YOURSELF IF THINGS GET TOO TOUGH, PICCOLO.
REMEMBER THAT THE DRAGON BALLS WILL **DISAPPEAR** IF YOU DIE.
HEY!
HEY, KURIRIN!!
WHOA... GOHAN? HOW'D YOU GET SO BIG...?
WHAT'S WITH THE LONG FACE, KURIRIN? NOT HAPPY TO SEE US AFTER ALL THIS TIME?
HOW HAPPY CAN I BE WHEN I'M ABOUT TO LAUNCH A BATTLE TO THE DEATH WITH A GANG OF ANDROIDS?
WE'RE NOT **ALL** SUPER SAIYANS, YOU KNOW...

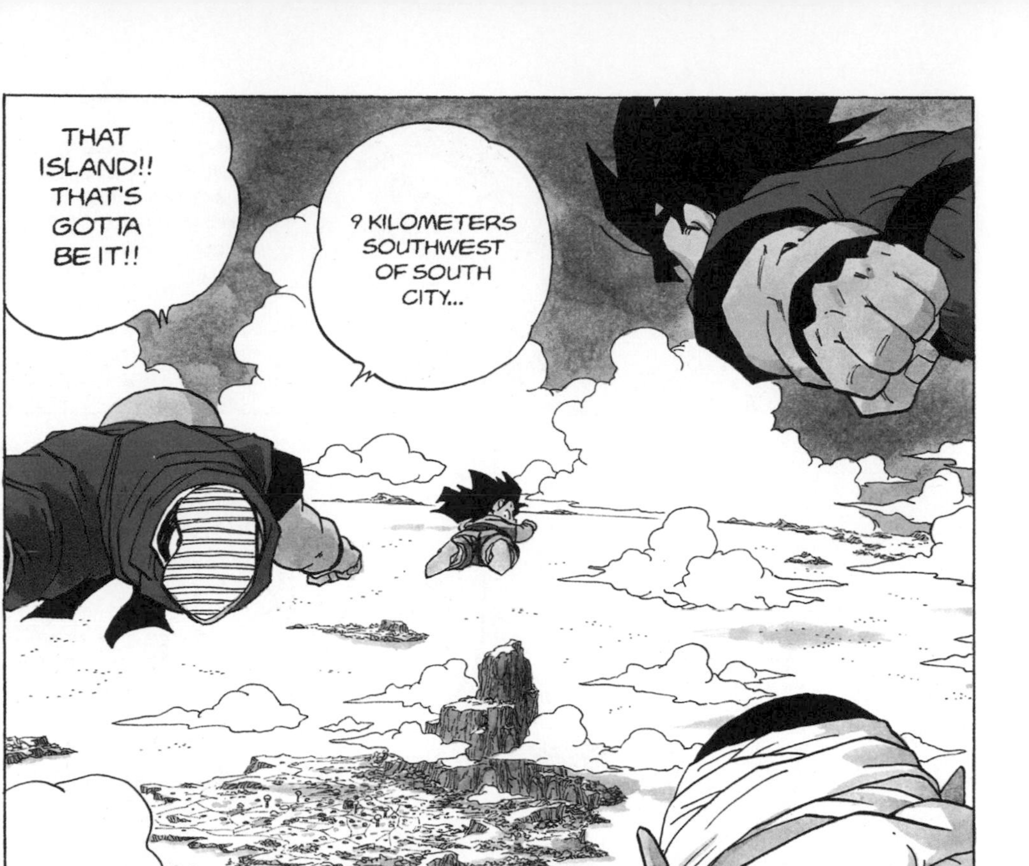
9 KILOMETERS SOUTHWEST OF SOUTH CITY...
THAT ISLAND!! THAT'S GOTTA BE IT!!

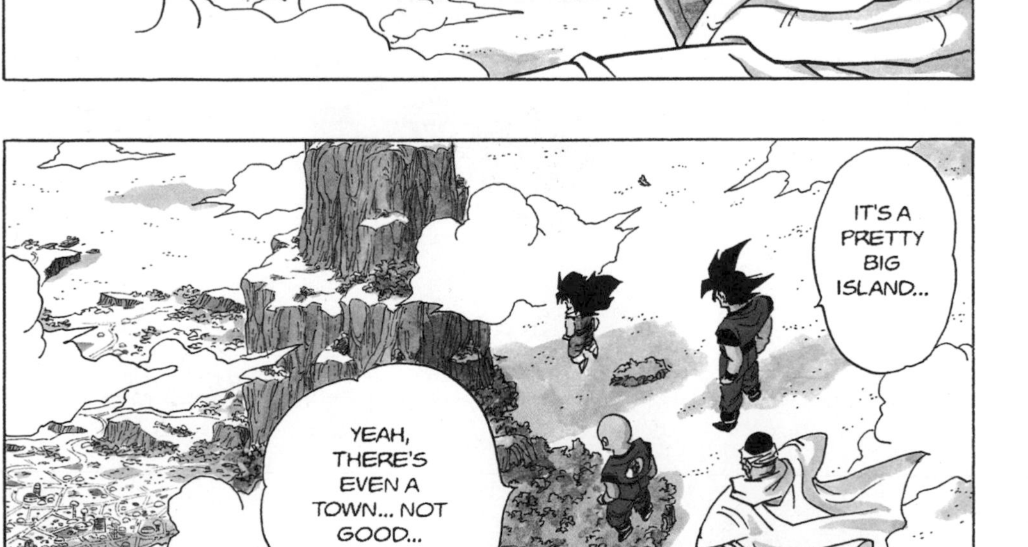
IT'S A PRETTY BIG ISLAND...
YEAH, THERE'S EVEN A TOWN... NOT GOOD...

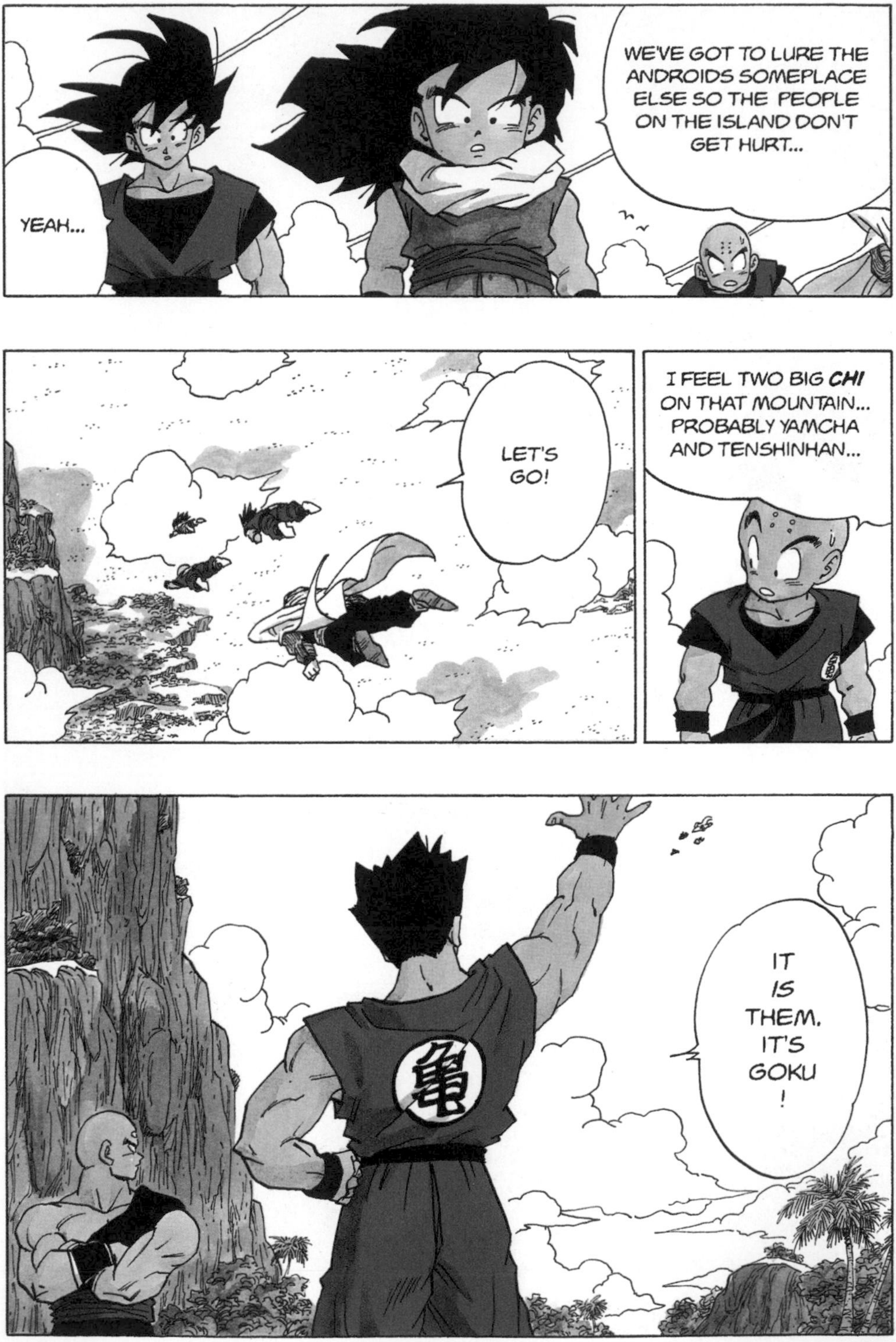
WE'VE GOT TO LURE THE ANDROIDS SOMEPLACE ELSE SO THE PEOPLE ON THE ISLAND DON'T GET HURT...
YEAH...
I FEEL TWO BIG *CHI* ON THAT MOUNTAIN... PROBABLY YAMCHA AND TENSHINHAN...
LET'S GO!
IT *IS* THEM. IT'S GOKU!

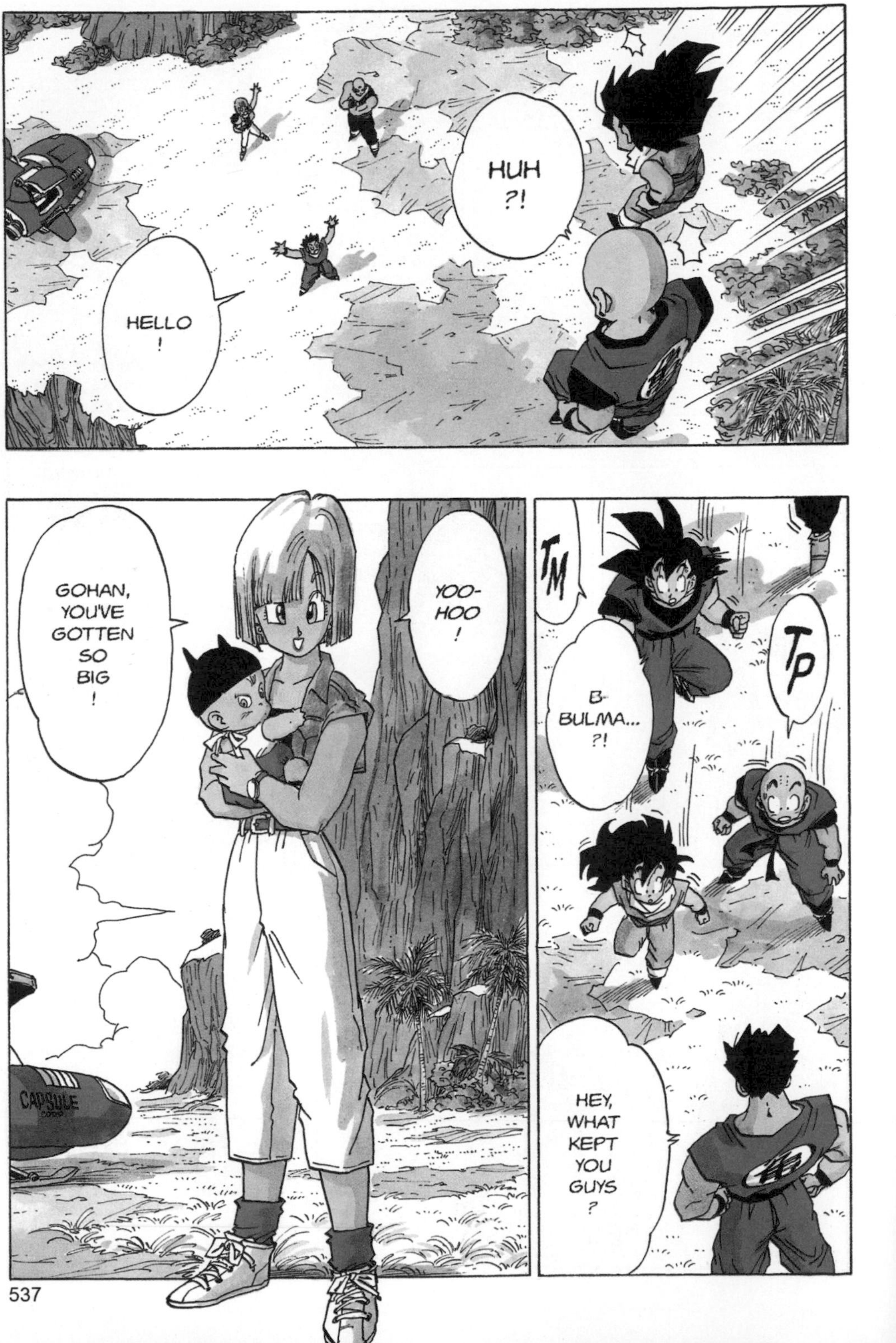
HELLO!
HUH?!
GOHAN, YOU'VE GOTTEN SO BIG!
YOO-HOO!
TM
B-BULMA...?!
TP
HEY, WHAT KEPT YOU GUYS?

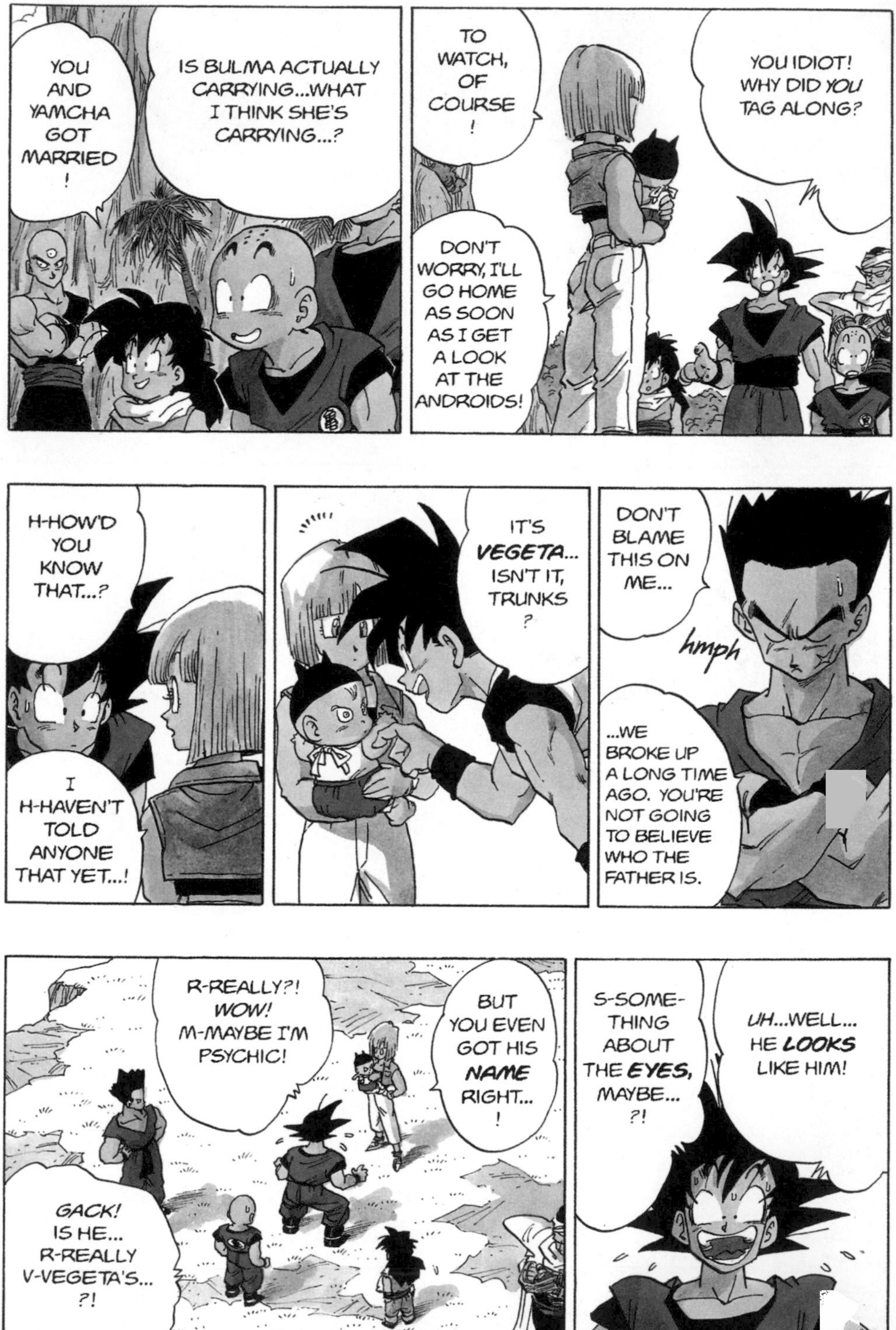

YOU AND YAMCHA GOT MARRIED!
IS BULMA ACTUALLY CARRYING...WHAT I THINK SHE'S CARRYING...?
TO WATCH, OF COURSE!
YOU IDIOT! WHY DID *YOU* TAG ALONG?
DON'T WORRY, I'LL GO HOME AS SOON AS I GET A LOOK AT THE ANDROIDS!
H-HOW'D YOU KNOW THAT...?
I H-HAVEN'T TOLD ANYONE THAT YET...!
IT'S ***VEGETA***... ISN'T IT, TRUNKS?
DON'T BLAME THIS ON ME...
hmph
...WE BROKE UP A LONG TIME AGO. YOU'RE NOT GOING TO BELIEVE WHO THE FATHER IS.
R-REALLY?! *WOW!* M-MAYBE I'M PSYCHIC!
BUT YOU EVEN GOT HIS ***NAME*** RIGHT...!
GACK! IS HE... R-REALLY V-VEGETA'S...?!
S-SOME-THING ABOUT THE ***EYES,*** MAYBE...?!
UH...WELL... HE ***LOOKS*** LIKE HIM!

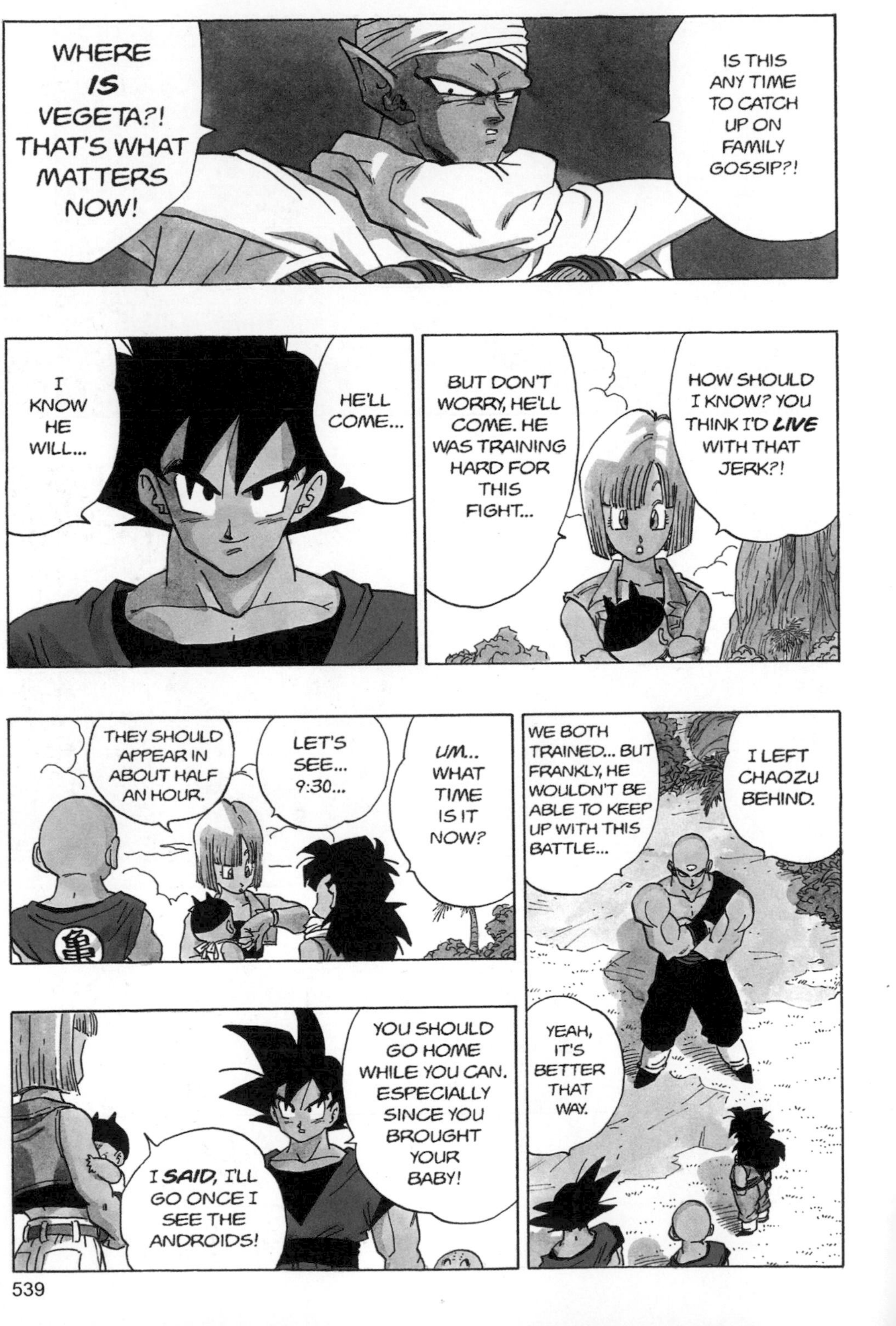

IS THIS ANY TIME TO CATCH UP ON FAMILY GOSSIP?!
WHERE *IS* VEGETA?! THAT'S WHAT MATTERS NOW!
HOW SHOULD I KNOW? YOU THINK I'D *LIVE* WITH THAT JERK?!
BUT DON'T WORRY, HE'LL COME. HE WAS TRAINING HARD FOR THIS FIGHT...
HE'LL COME...
I KNOW HE WILL...
I LEFT CHAOZU BEHIND.
WE BOTH TRAINED... BUT FRANKLY, HE WOULDN'T BE ABLE TO KEEP UP WITH THIS BATTLE...
YEAH, IT'S BETTER THAT WAY.
UM... WHAT TIME IS IT NOW?
LET'S SEE... 9:30...
THEY SHOULD APPEAR IN ABOUT HALF AN HOUR.
YOU SHOULD GO HOME WHILE YOU CAN. ESPECIALLY SINCE YOU BROUGHT YOUR BABY!
I *SAID*, I'LL GO ONCE I SEE THE ANDROIDS!

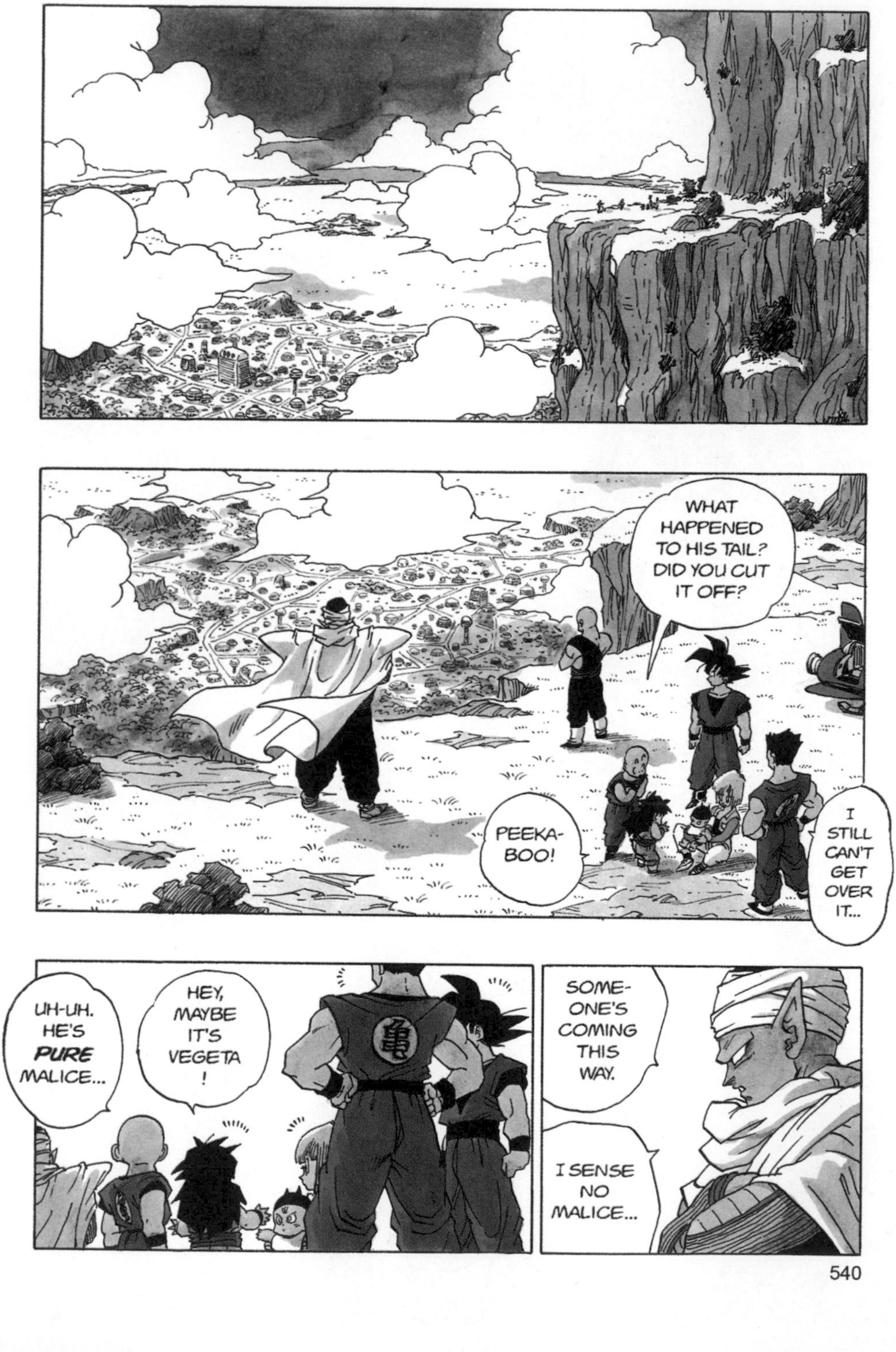
WHAT HAPPENED TO HIS TAIL? DID YOU CUT IT OFF?
PEEKA-BOO!
I STILL CAN'T GET OVER IT...
SOME-ONE'S COMING THIS WAY.
I SENSE NO MALICE...
HEY, MAYBE IT'S VEGETA!
UH-UH. HE'S **PURE** MALICE...

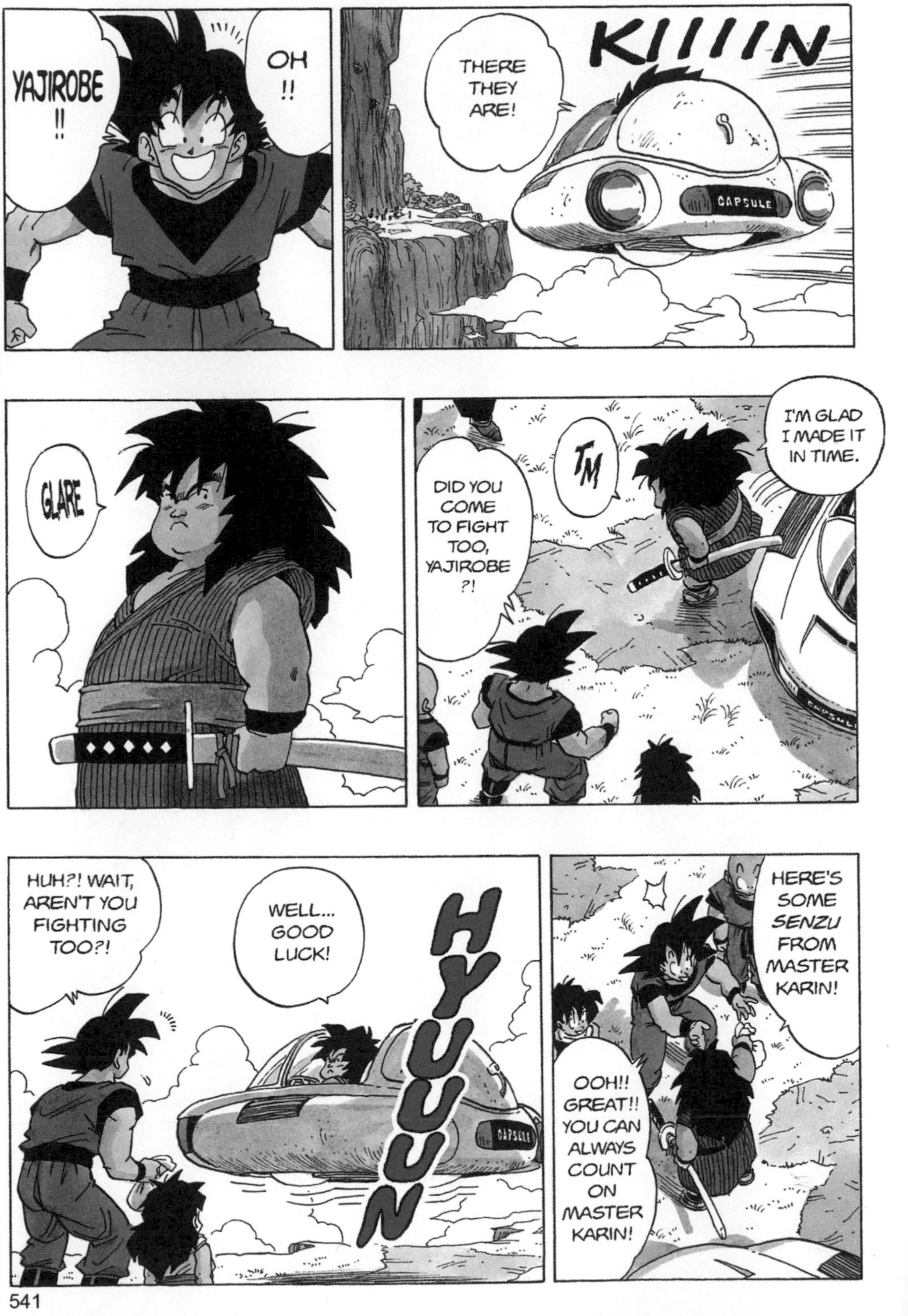
KIIIIN
THERE THEY ARE!
OH !!
YAJIROBE !!
I'M GLAD I MADE IT IN TIME.
TM
DID YOU COME TO FIGHT TOO, YAJIROBE ?!
GLARE
HERE'S SOME SENZU FROM MASTER KARIN!
OOH!! GREAT!! YOU CAN ALWAYS COUNT ON MASTER KARIN!
WELL... GOOD LUCK!
HYUUUN
HUH?! WAIT, AREN'T YOU FIGHTING TOO?!
CAPSULE

PYOOO

...

THERE'S TIMES EVEN **I** WON'T JOIN YOU!

UNLIKE YOU IDIOTS, I DON'T WANT TO DIE.

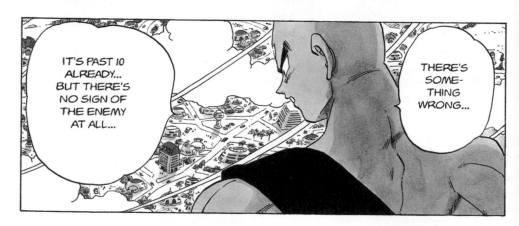

IT'S PAST 10 ALREADY... BUT THERE'S NO SIGN OF THE ENEMY AT ALL...

THERE'S SOME-THING WRONG...

HE SAID **AROUND** 10. IT'S ONLY 10:17. WHICH I WOULD CONSIDER "AROUND."

I TOLD YOU FROM THE START IT WAS SOME KIND OF TRICK!

HUH ?

BUT I CAN'T FEEL A SINGLE STRONG CHI. IF THEY'RE **THAT** POWERFUL, WE SHOULD BE ABLE TO FEEL THEM NO MATTER WHERE ON EARTH THEY ARE!

YOU'RE RIGHT...

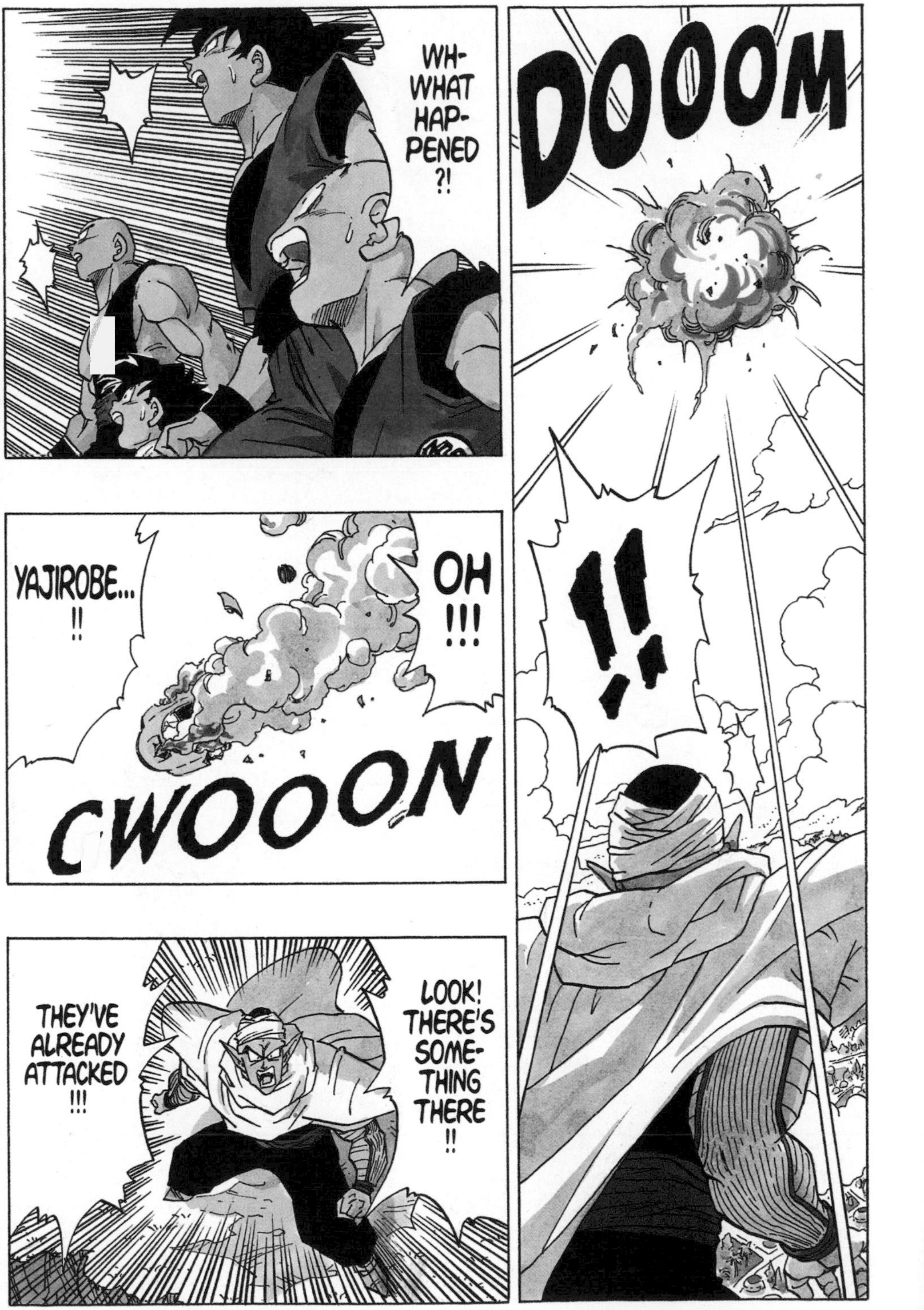
DOOOM
!!
WH-WHAT HAP-PENED ?!
OH !!!
YAJIROBE... !!
CWOOON
LOOK! THERE'S SOME-THING THERE !!
THEY'VE ALREADY ATTACKED !!!

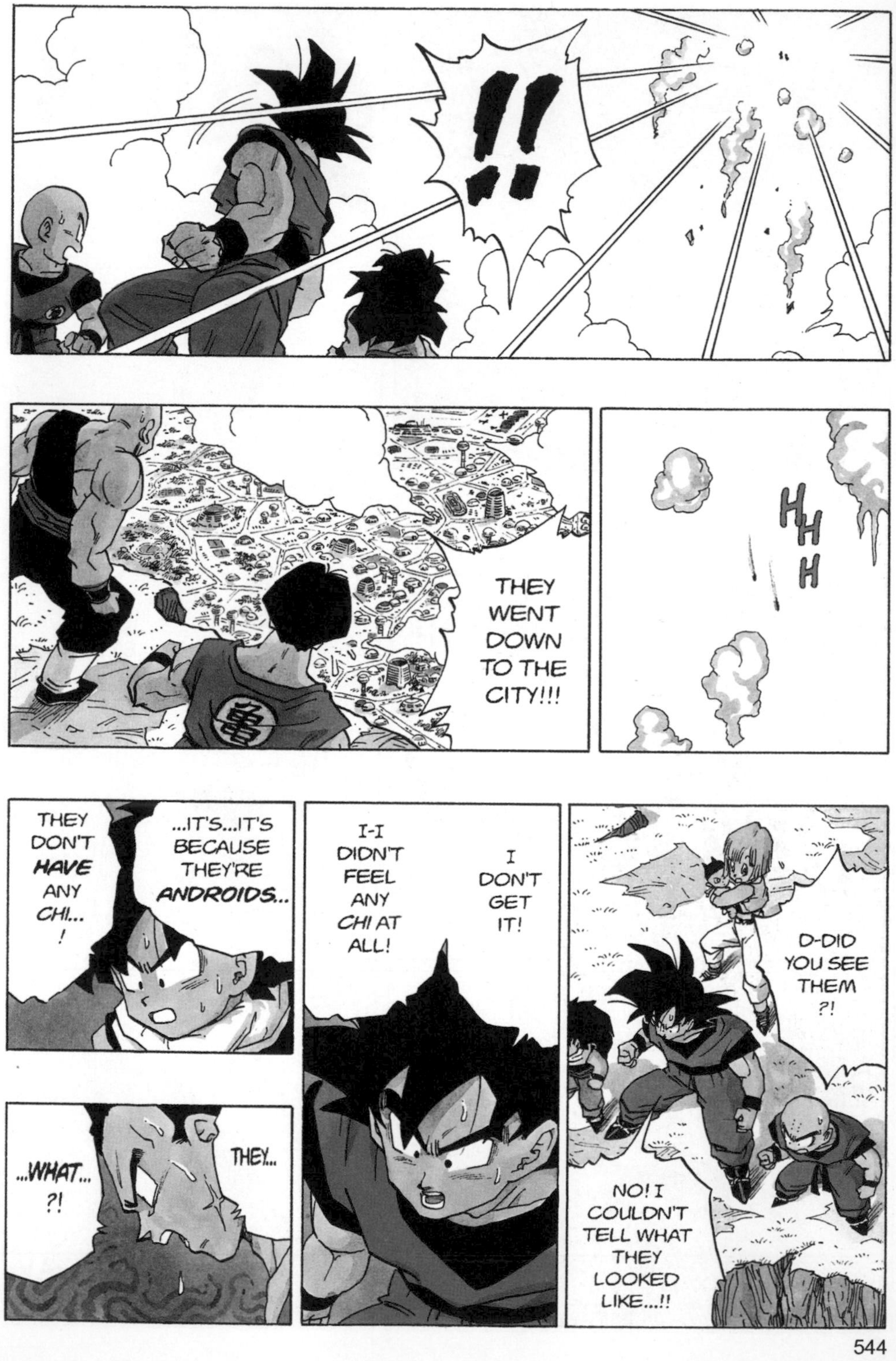
!!
HHH
THEY WENT DOWN TO THE CITY!!!
D-DID YOU SEE THEM?!
NO! I COULDN'T TELL WHAT THEY LOOKED LIKE...!!
I DON'T GET IT!
I-I DIDN'T FEEL ANY CHI AT ALL!
THEY...
...WHAT...?!
...IT'S...IT'S BECAUSE THEY'RE ANDROIDS...
THEY DON'T HAVE ANY CHI...!

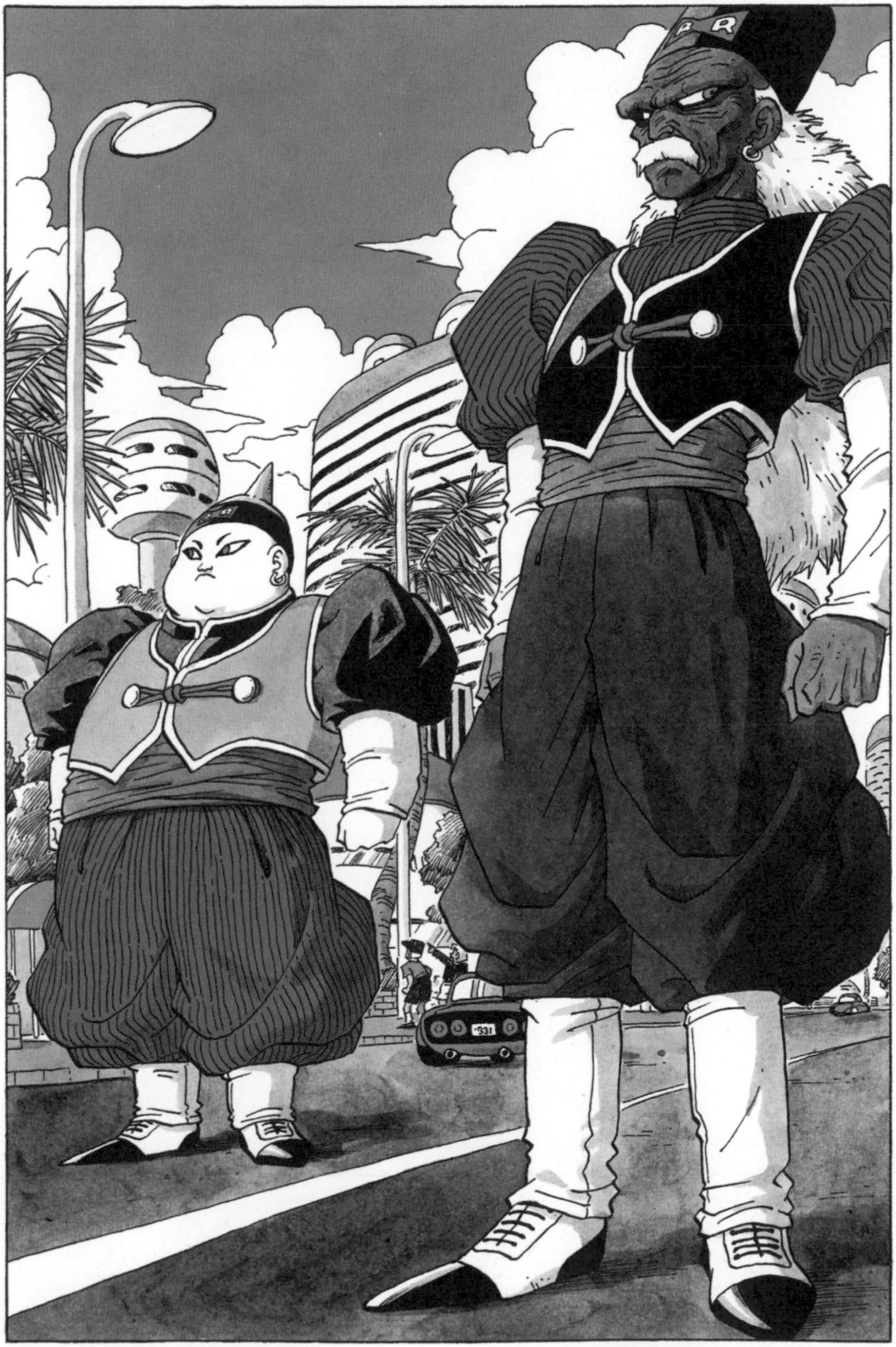

TITLE PAGE GALLERY

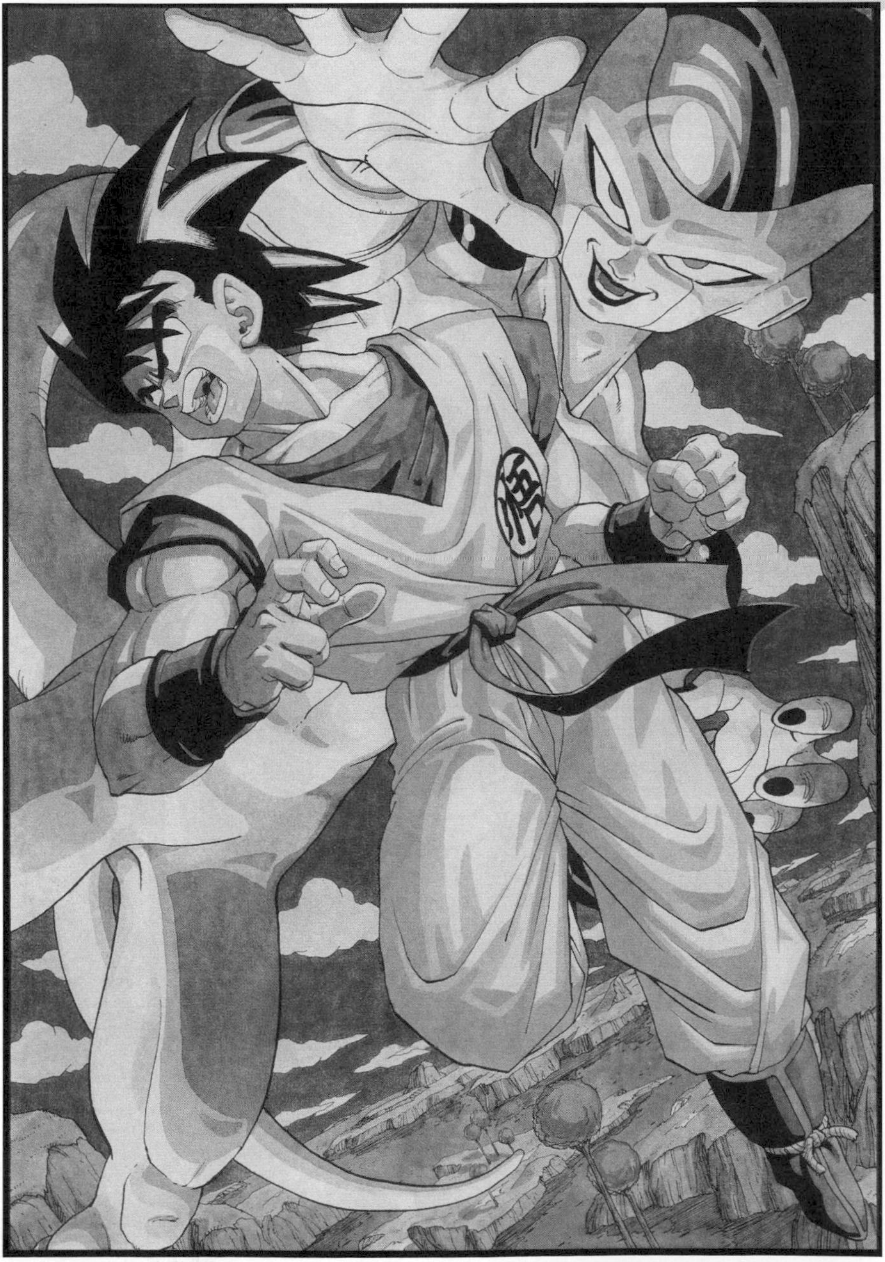

DRAGON BALL

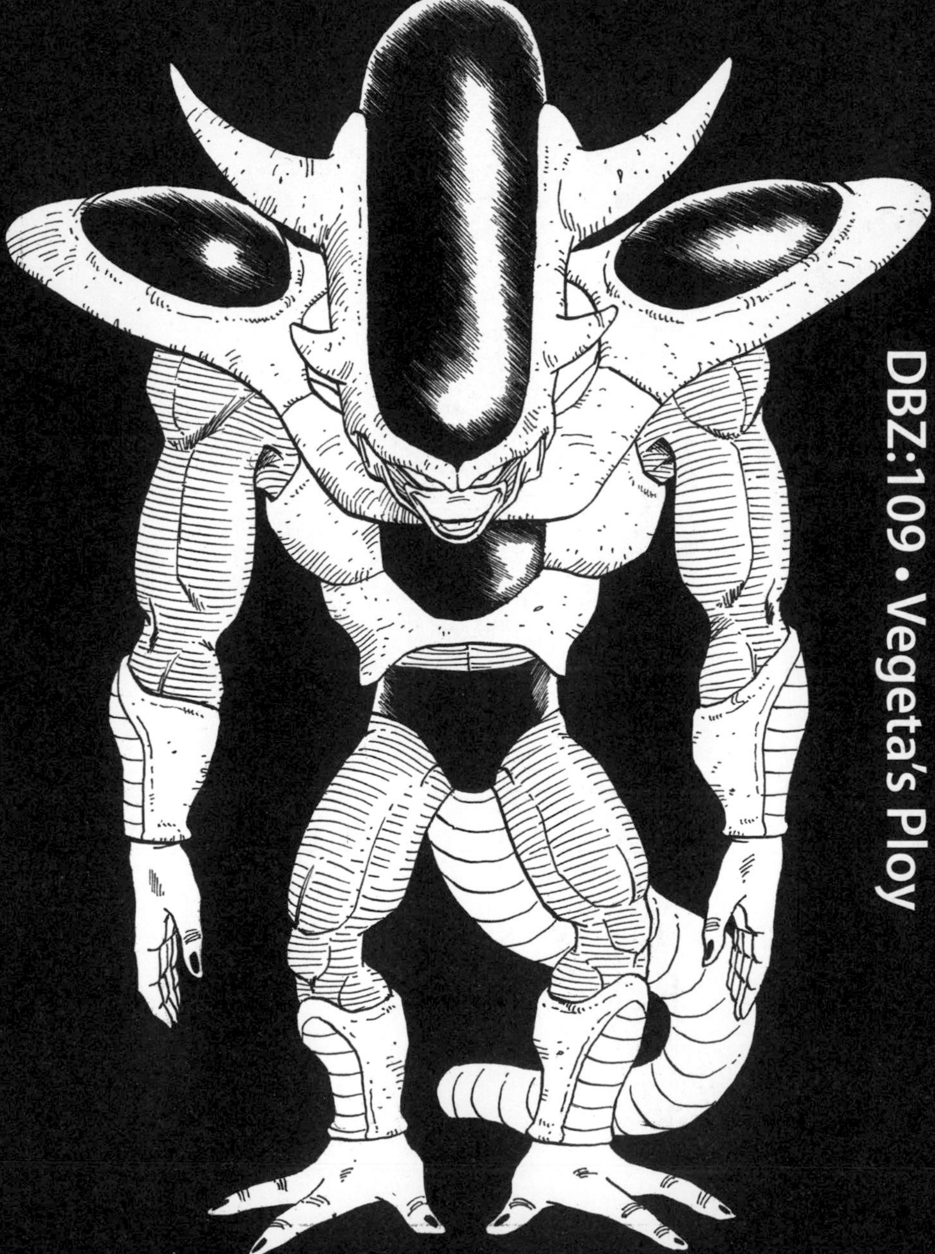

DBZ:109 • Vegeta's Ploy

DRAGON BALL

DBZ:112 • Son Goku...Resurrected!!

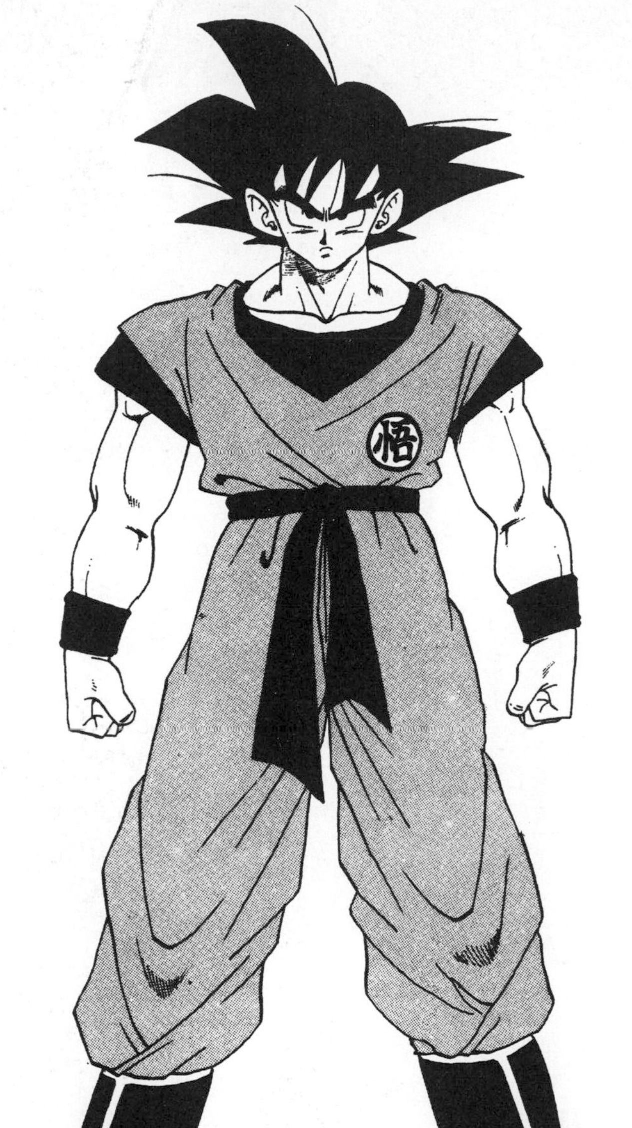

DRAGON BALL

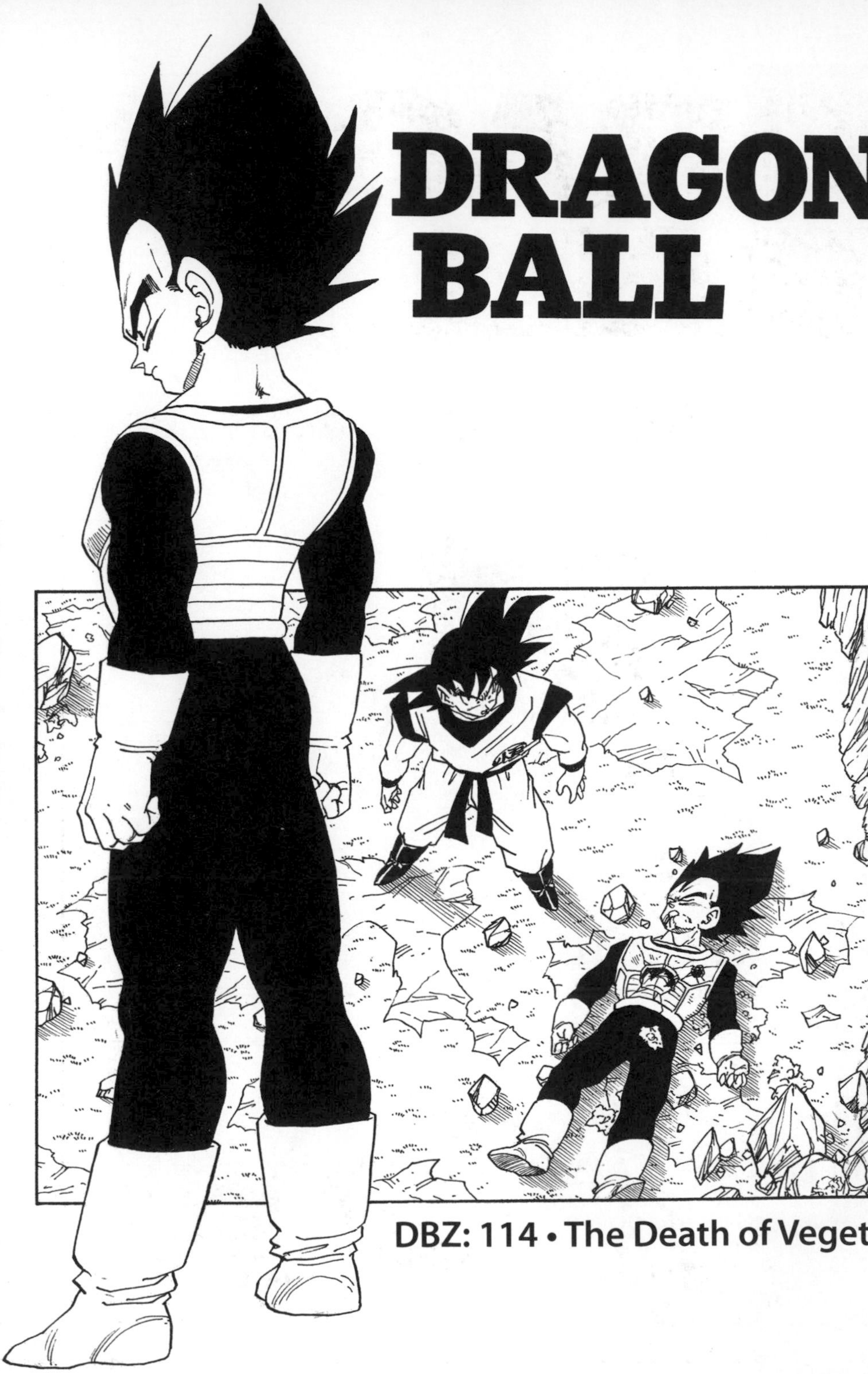

DBZ: 114 • The Death of Vegeta

DRAGON BALL

DBZ: 115 • Underwater Battle

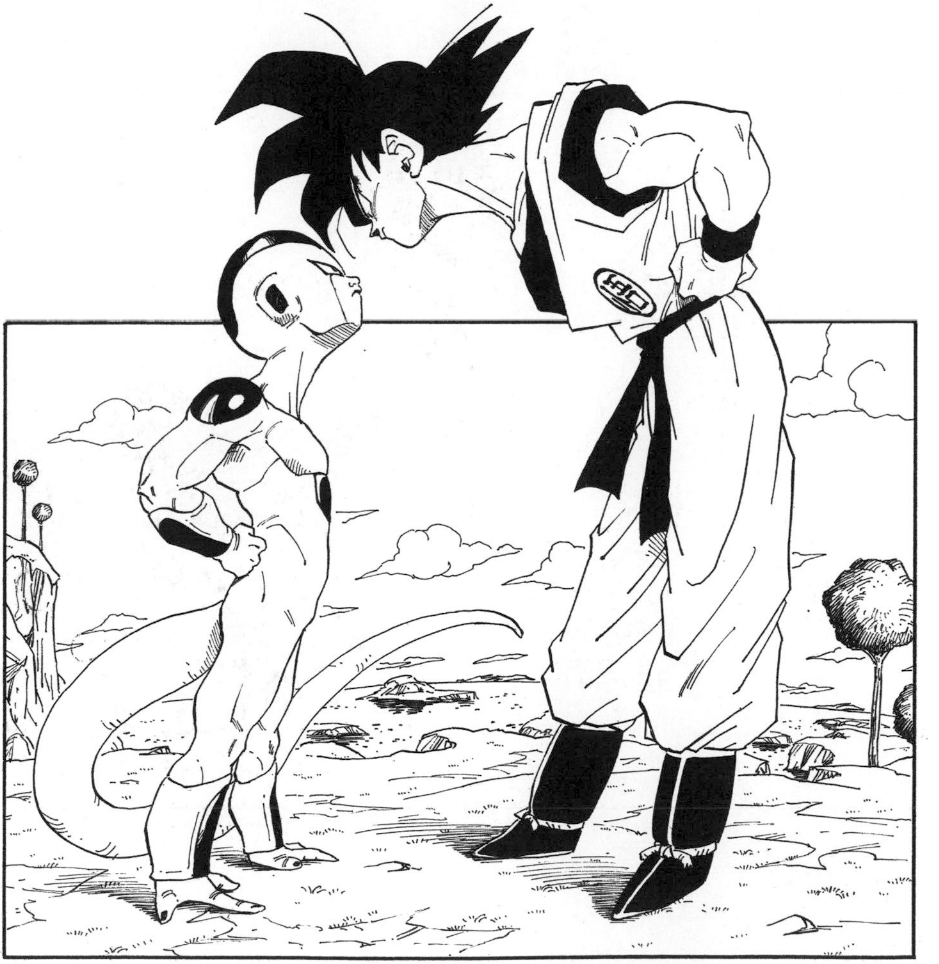

DRAGON BALL

DBZ:117 • Hand to Foot

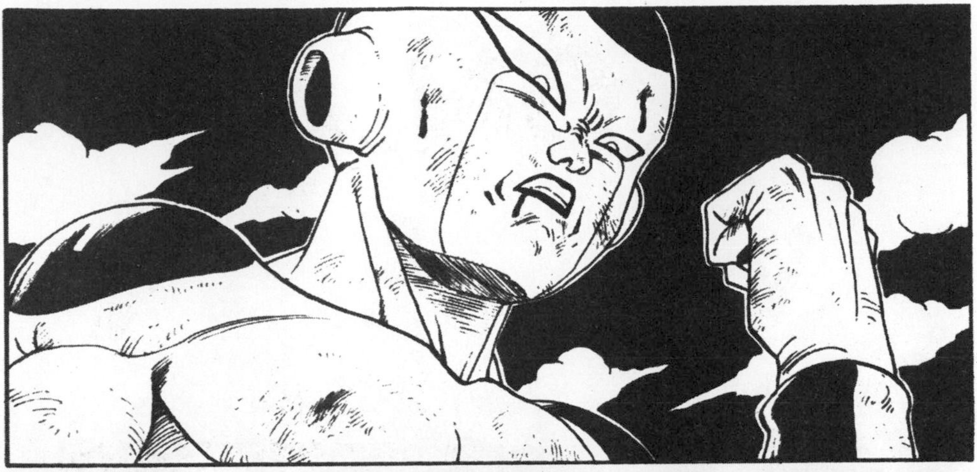

DRAGON BALL

DBZ:120 • The Great Genki-Dama

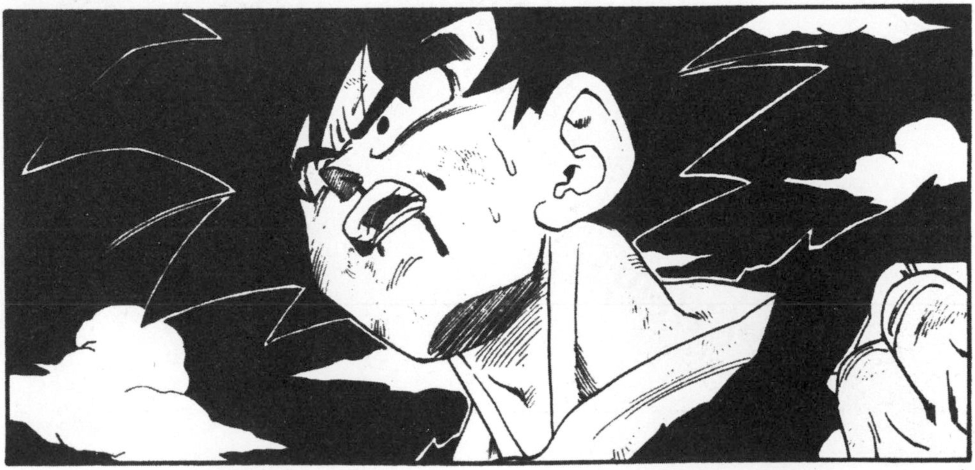

DBZ:121
The Last Chance

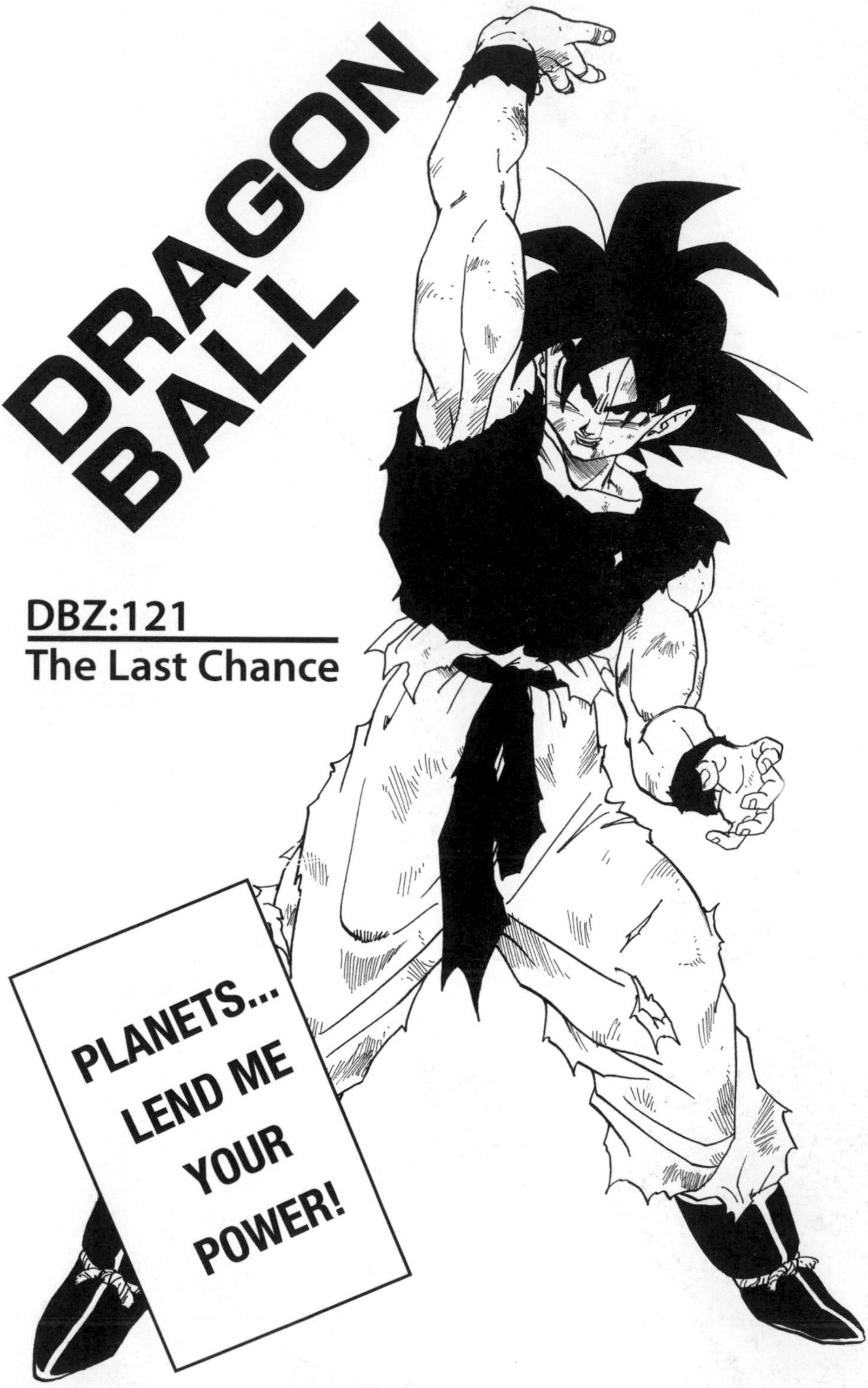
DRAGON BALL
PLANETS... LEND ME YOUR POWER!

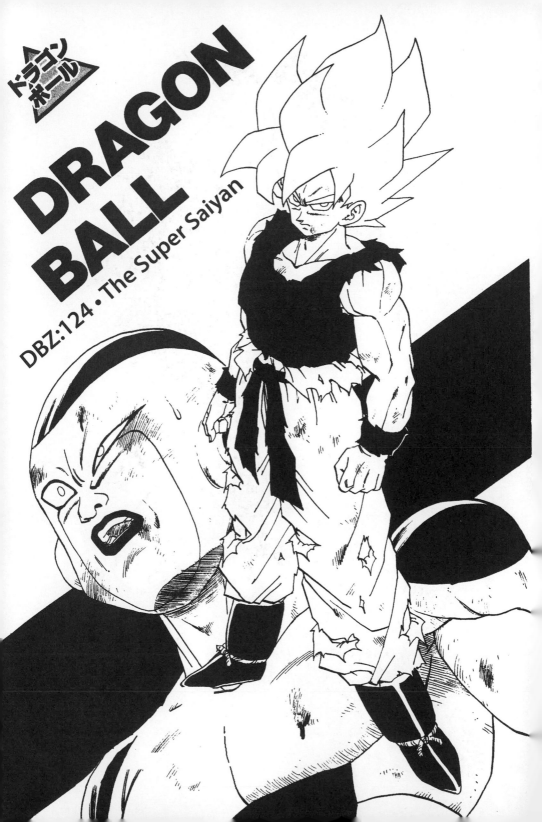

DRAGON BALL

DBZ:124 • The Super Saiyan

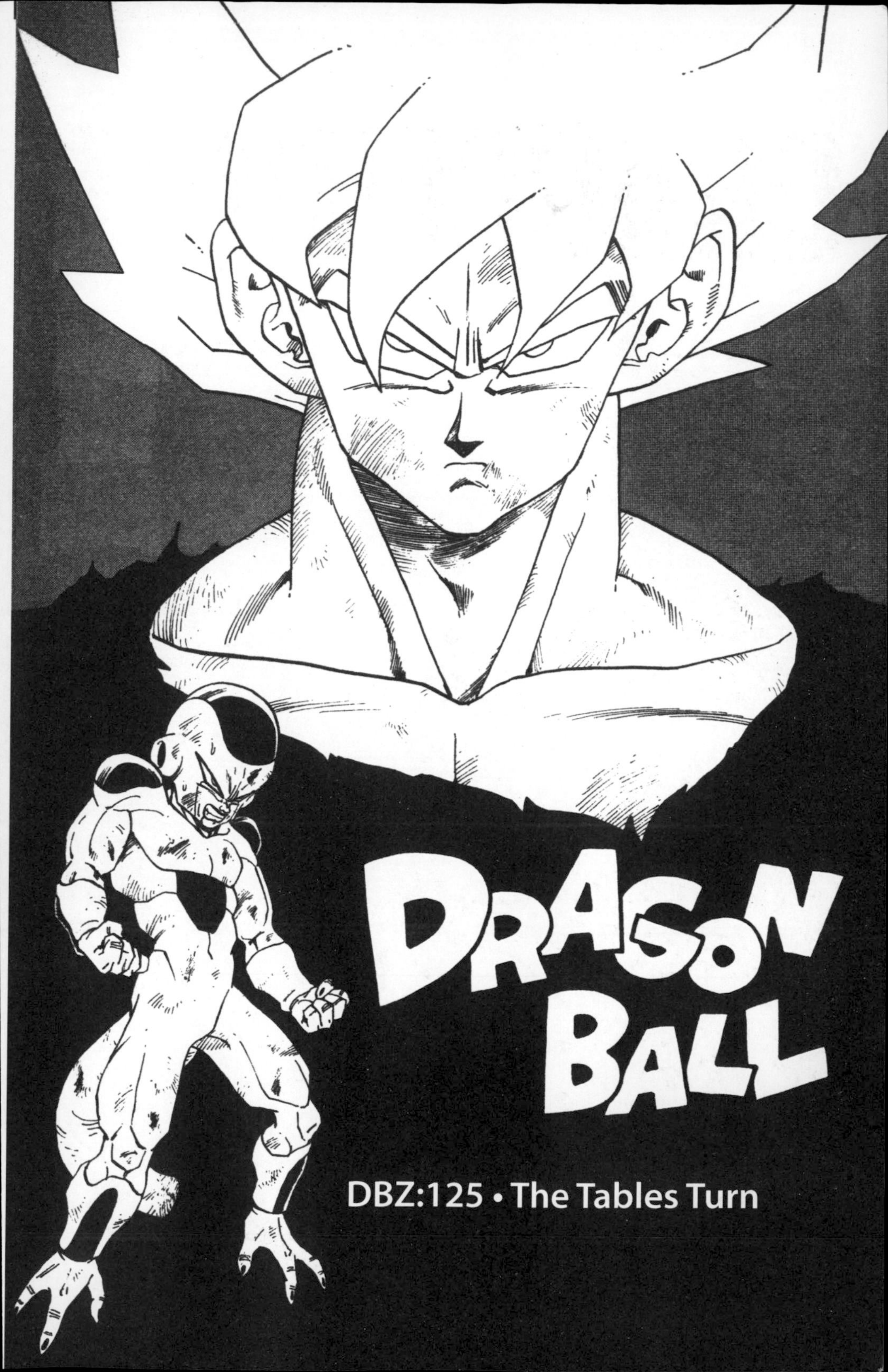
DRAGON BALL
DBZ:125 • The Tables Turn

DRAGON BALL

DBZ:132 • Son Goku's Choice

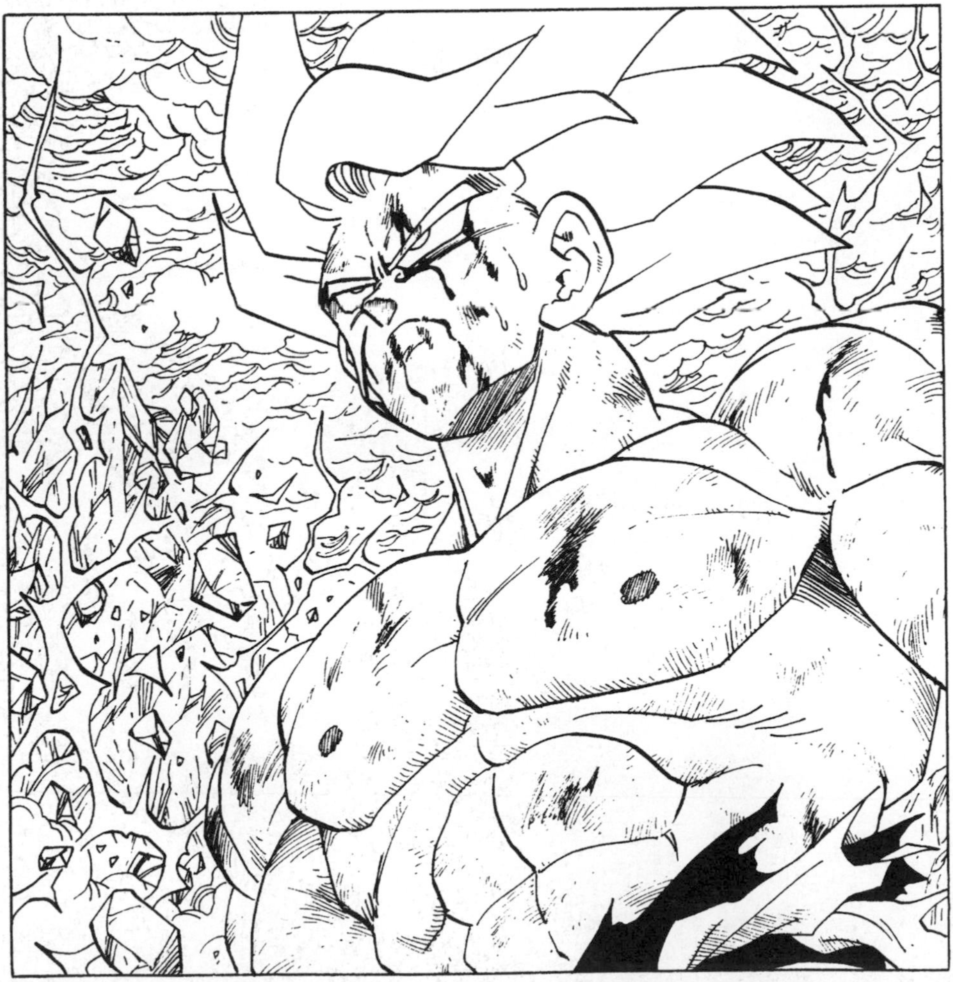

DRAGON BALL

DBZ:134 • Namek's End

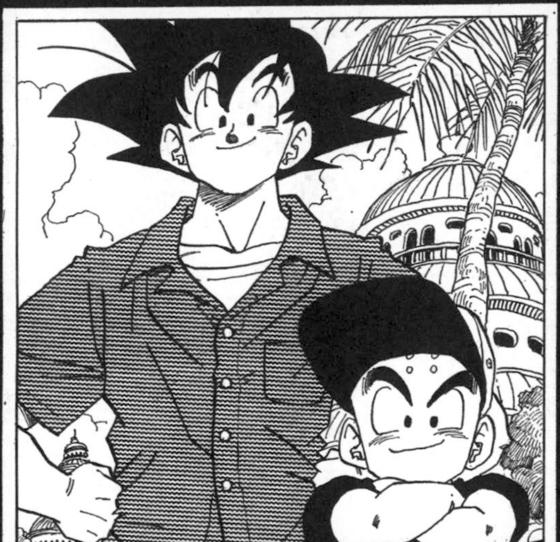
KRILLIN

DRAGON BALL

DBZ:135 • Where Is Goku?

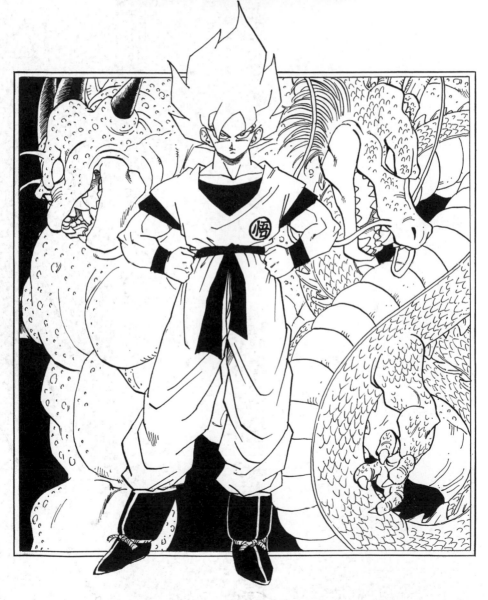

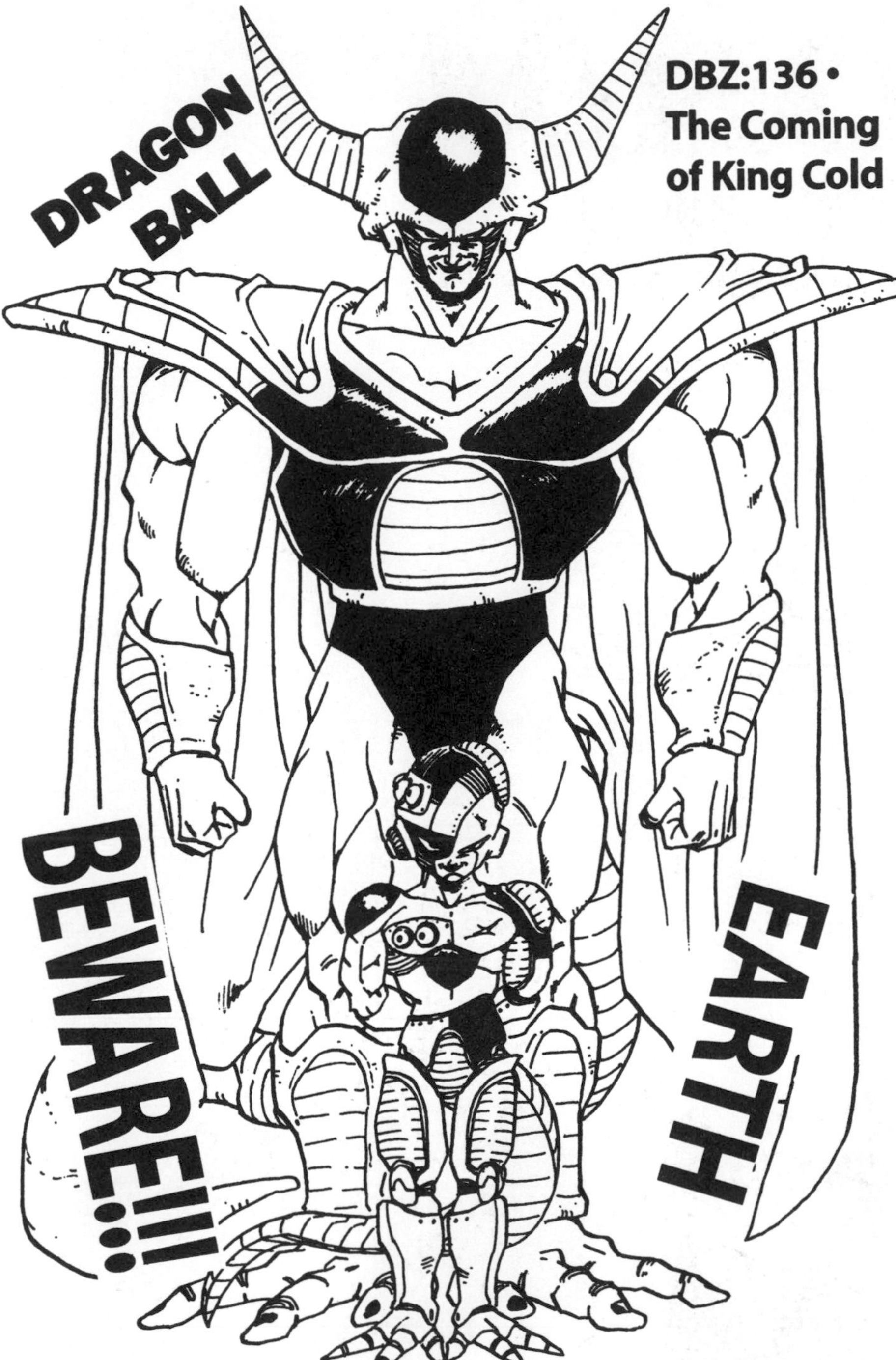
DRAGON BALL
DBZ:136 • The Coming of King Cold
BEWARE!!!
EARTH

DRAGON BALL

DBZ:137 • The Young Man of Mystery

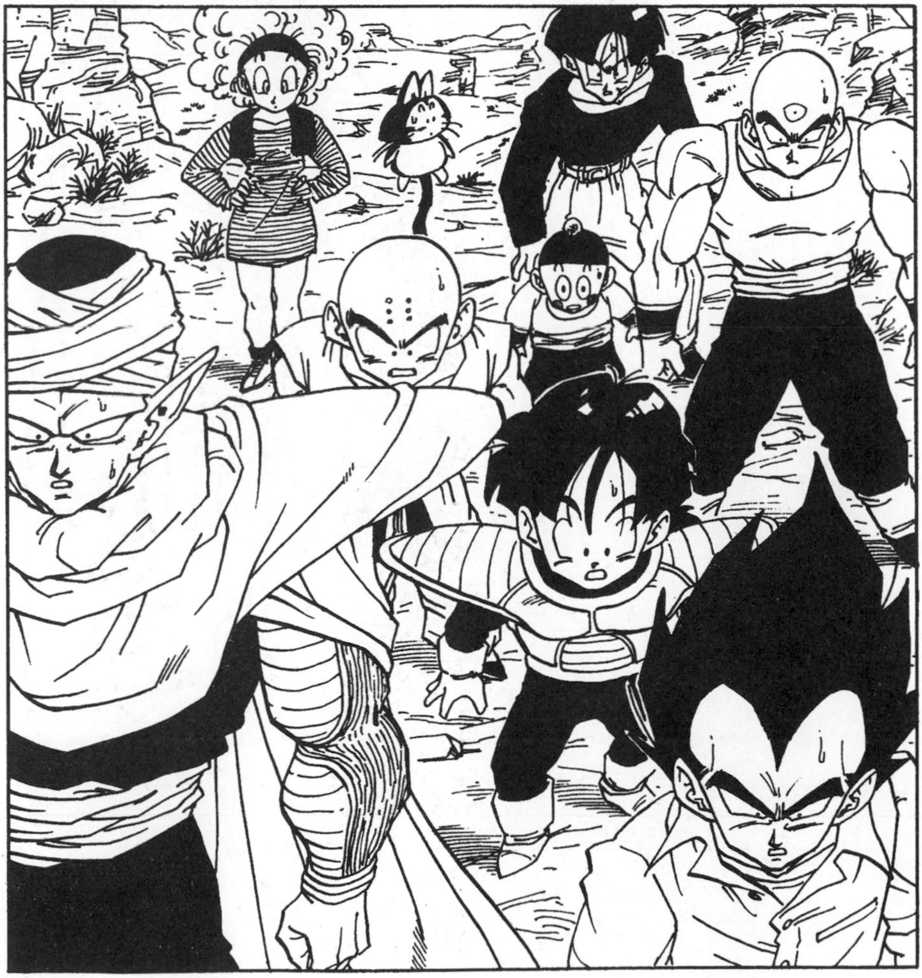

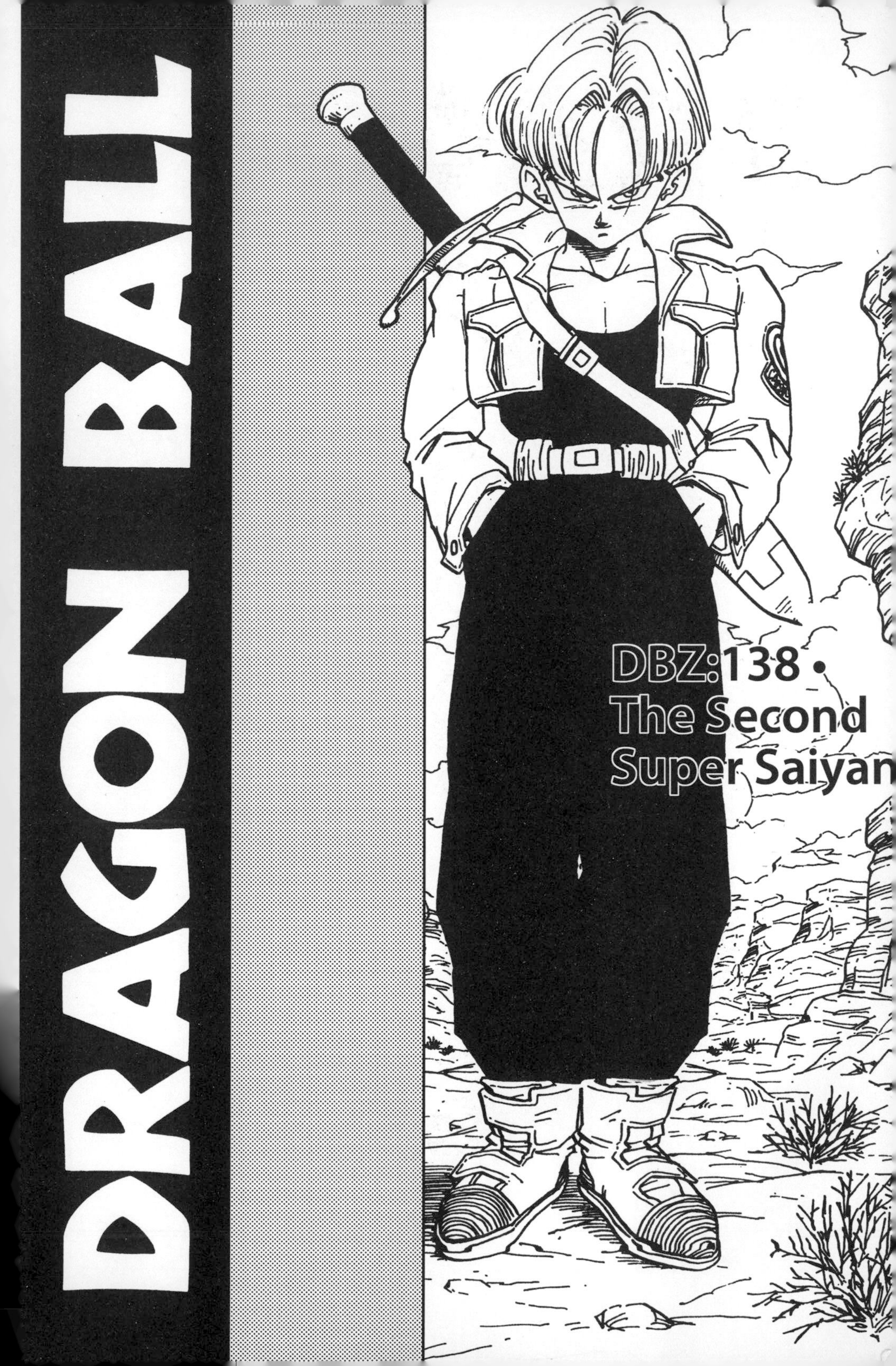
DRAGON BALL
DBZ:138 •
The Second
Super Saiyan

DRAGON BALL

DBZ:139 • Son Goku Comes Home

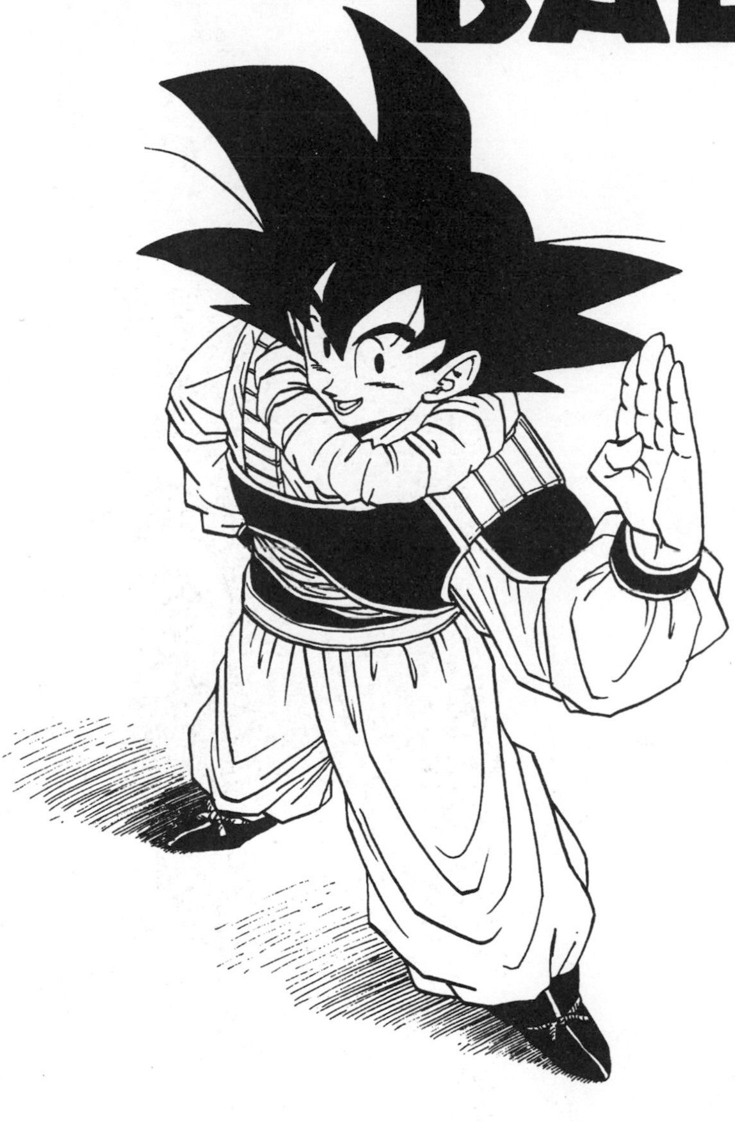

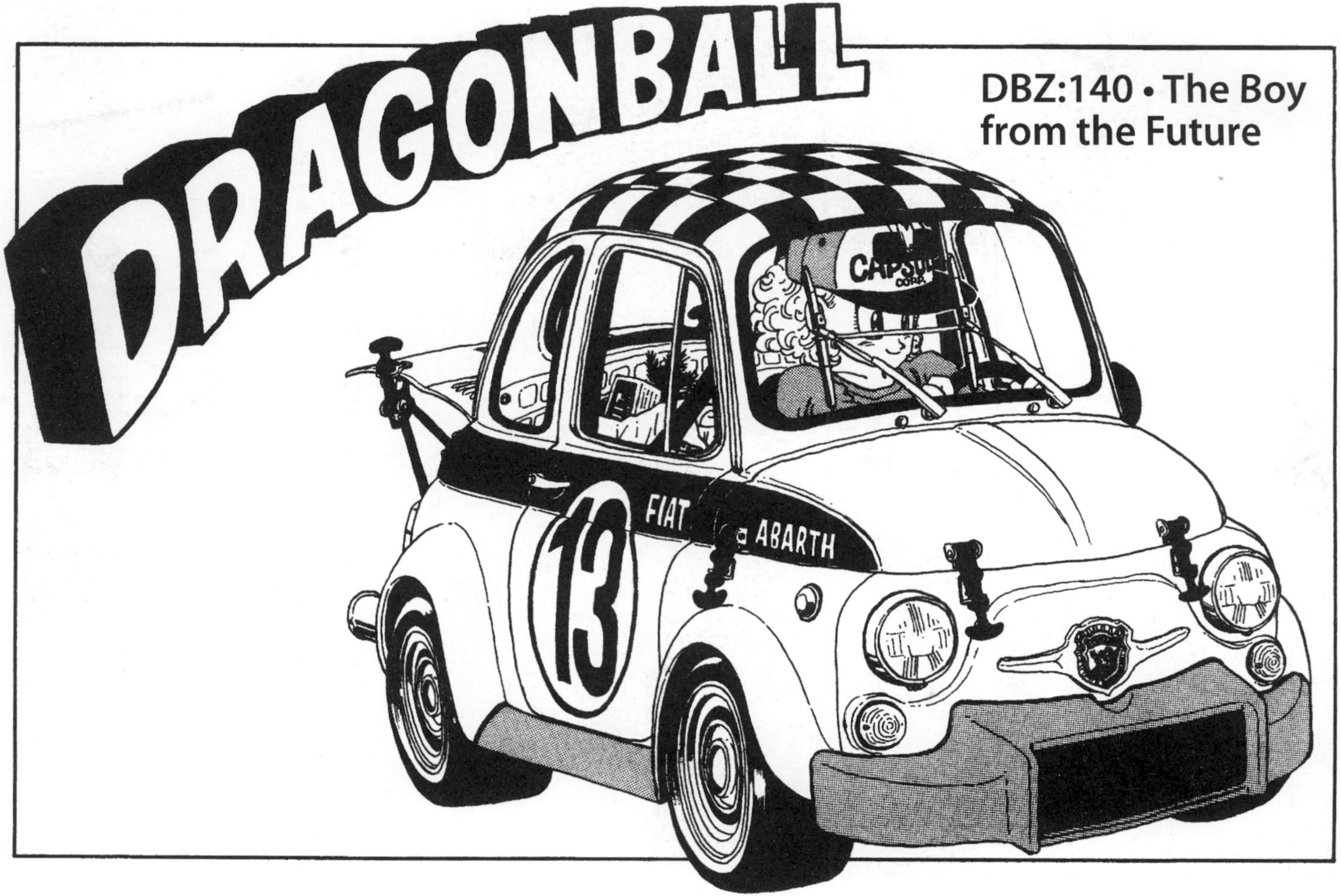
DRAGONBALL
DBZ:140 • The Boy from the Future
13
FIAT
ABARTH
CAPSULE CORP.

DRAGON BALL

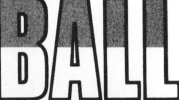

DBZ:141 • The Terrifying Message

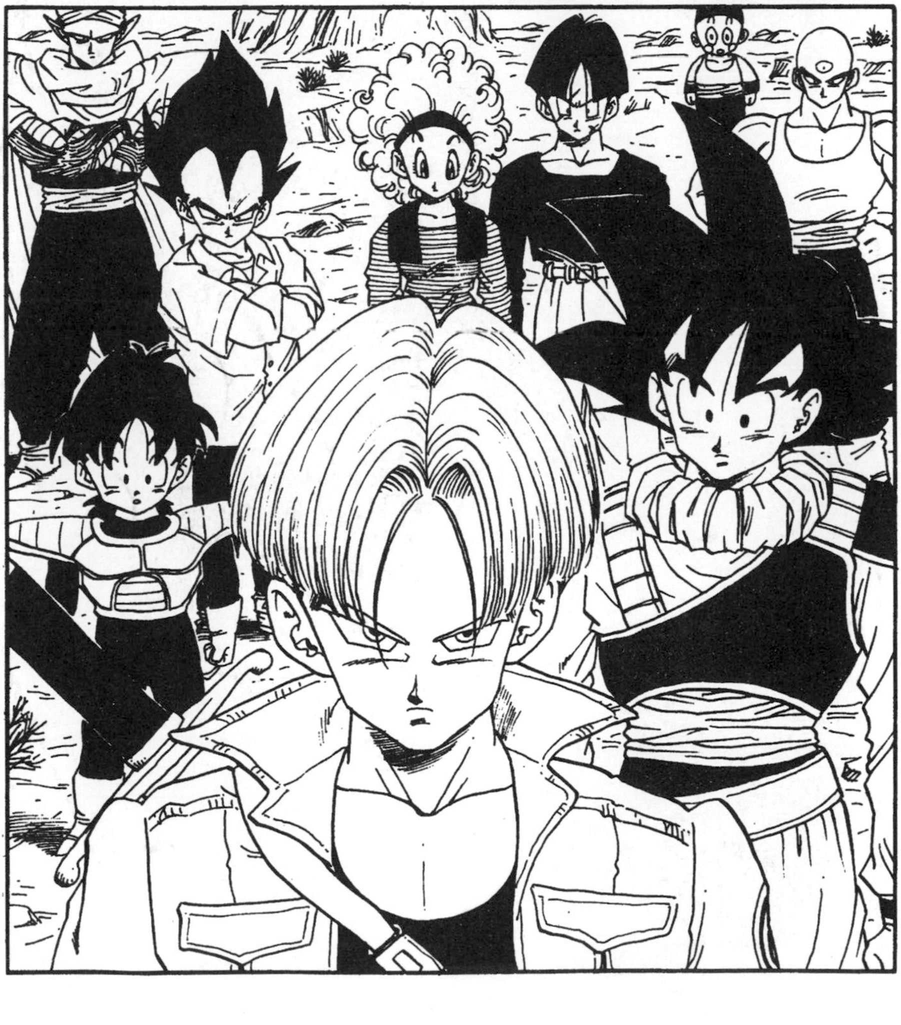

DRAGON BALL

DBZ:142 • The Risky Decision

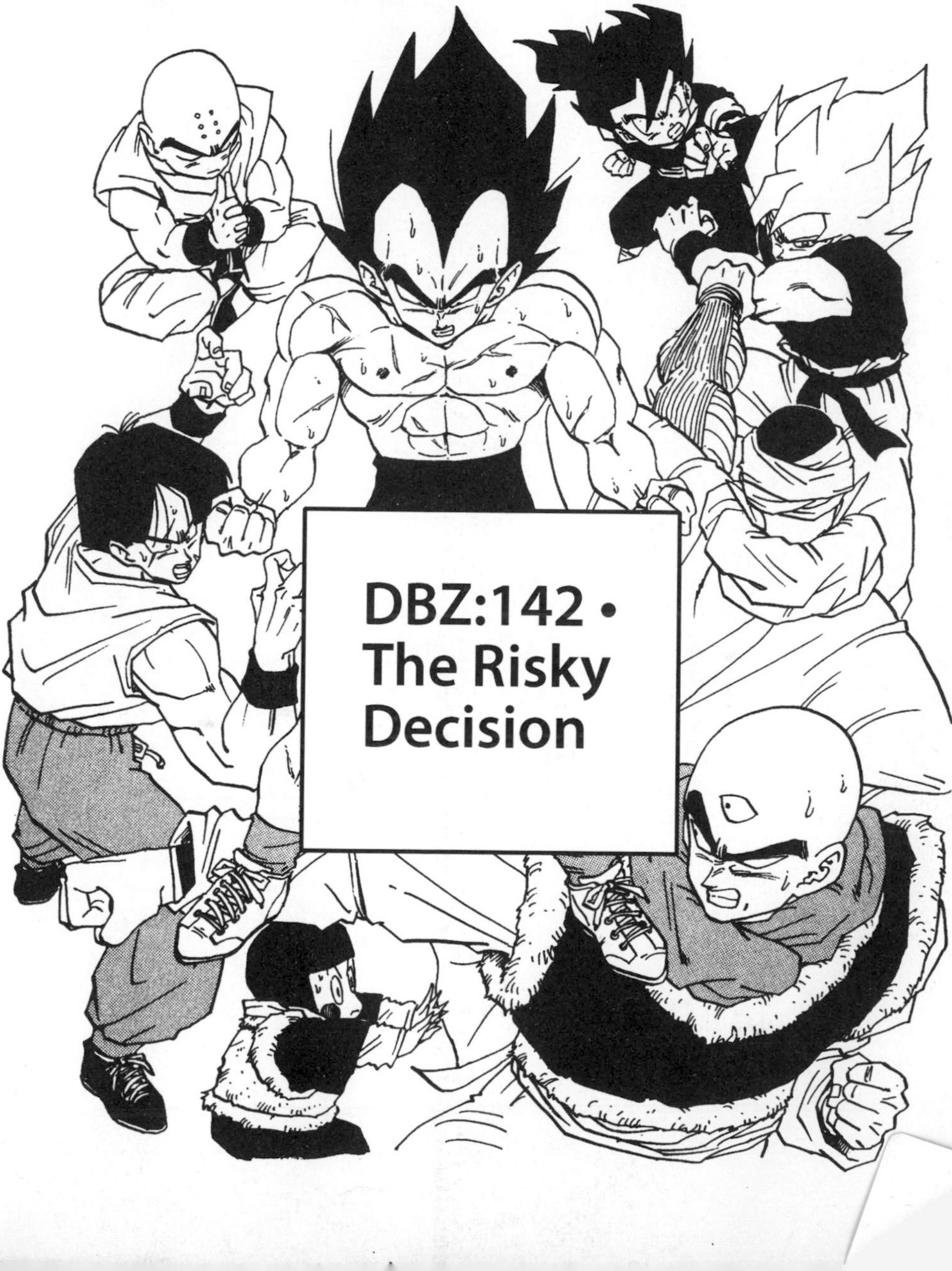

AUTHOR NOTES

1991

VOLUME 10

Our dog had puppies! She gave birth to three in all, but unfortunately one puppy died at birth, so now we have two puppies. When our cat gave birth, she didn't do so well on her own, and we had to assist with the labor and do things like cut the kittens' umbilical cords. We got ready several days in advance to help our dog with her labor, but she managed to do it all on her own. We really don't want to give the puppies away, so we are going to keep the both of them...

VOLUME 11

To be honest, I'm always struggling to come up with something to write about here. If you're busy working on a weekly serial, then there shouldn't be anything all that special happening in your life to write about. What's even more painful is coming up with the "What's happening in this issue" promo text for the table of contents in *Weekly Shonen Jump* magazine. This is a secret, but more than half of the comments made on that page are actually written by my editor, Mr. Kondo. He always asks me, "Did anything interesting happen this week?" Nothing really did...

1991

1991

VOLUME 12

I can't sit around doing nothing. I don't feel relaxed unless I'm totally involved in something. Kinda like how sharks have to keep swimming or die. I need to be immersed in something no matter how pointless it may be. But because of this, when I don't have anything to do, I get really restless and pace around in my room. It would really be nice if "work" was one of those things I could really get involved in...

IN THE NEXT VOLUME

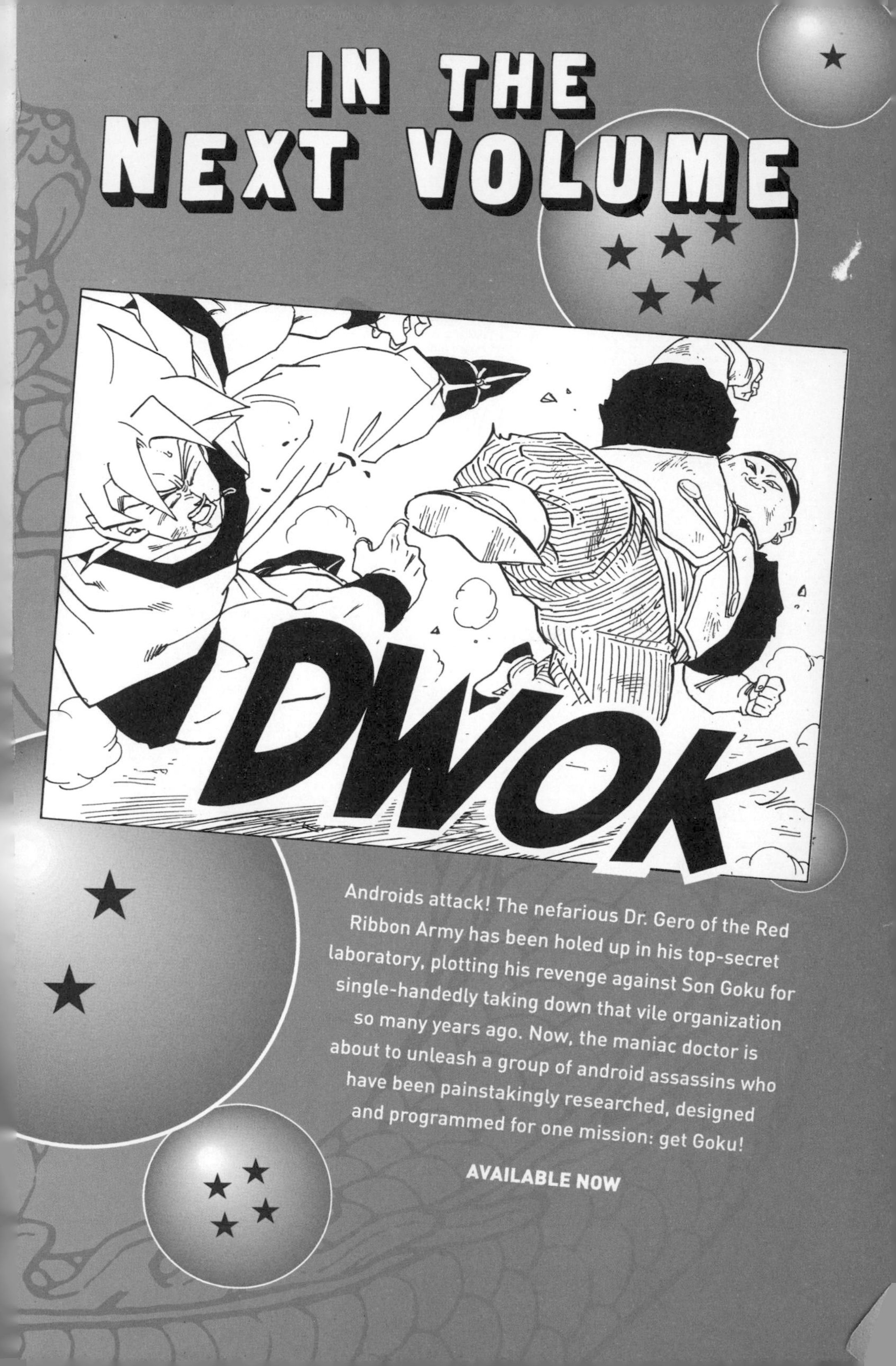
DWOK

Androids attack! The nefarious Dr. Gero of the Red Ribbon Army has been holed up in his top-secret laboratory, plotting his revenge against Son Goku for single-handedly taking down that vile organization so many years ago. Now, the maniac doctor is about to unleash a group of android assassins who have been painstakingly researched, designed and programmed for one mission: get Goku!

AVAILABLE NOW